The **Incredibly Wealthy**

Great Lives from History

The Incredibly Wealthy

Volume 1
Aaron of Lincoln – Bill Gates

Editor
Howard Bromberg
University of Michigan

SALEM PRESS
Pasadena, California   Hackensack, New Jersey

Editor in Chief: Dawn P. Dawson

Editorial Director: Christina J. Moose	*Research Supervisor:* Jeffry Jensen
Manuscript Editor: Rebecca Kuzins	*Research Assistant:* Keli Trousdale
Acquisitions Editor: Mark Rehn	*Production Editor:* Joyce I. Buchea
Editorial Assistant: Brett Weisberg	*Graphics and Design:* James Hutson
Photo Editor: Cynthia Breslin Beres	*Layout:* William Zimmerman

Cover photos (pictured left to right, from top left): King Louis XIV of France (The Granger Collection, New York); Queen Elizabeth II (Lichfield/Getty Images); Warren Buffett (AP/Wide World Photos); Oprah Winfrey (Getty Images); Kublai Khan (The Granger Collection, New York); Andrew Carnegie (The Granger Collection, New York); Pablo Picasso, self-portrait (The Granger Collection, New York); Donald Trump (Getty Images); Barbara Hutton (Archive Photos/Getty Images)

Library of Congress Cataloging-in-Publication Data

Great lives from history. The incredibly wealthy / editor, Howard Bromberg.
    p. cm. — (Great lives from history)
Includes bibliographical references and index.
    ISBN 978-1-58765-664-4 (set : alk. paper) — ISBN 978-1-58765-665-1 (vol. 1 : alk. paper) —
ISBN 978-1-58765-666-8 (vol. 2 : alk. paper) — ISBN 978-1-58765-667-5 (vol. 3 : alk. paper) —
    1. Wealth—History.   2. Rich people—Biography.   I. Bromberg, Howard.   II. Title: Incredibly wealthy.
HC79.W4G74 2011
305.5'2340922—dc22
                                                                                    2010042962

Contents

Publisher's Note

Great Lives from History: The Incredibly Wealthy (3 vols.) joins the *Great Lives* series, which provides in-depth critical essays on important men and women in all areas of achievement, from around the world and throughout history. The series was initiated in 2004 with *The Ancient World, Prehistory-476 C.E.* (2 vols.) and was followed in 2005 by *The Middle Ages, 477-1453* (2 vols.) and *The Renaissance, 1454-1600* (2 vols.); in 2006 by *The 17th Century, 1601-1700* (2 vols.) and *The 18th Century, 1701-1800* (2 vols.); in 2007 by *The 19th Century, 1801-1900* (4 vols.) and *Notorious Lives* (3 vols.); in 2008 by *The 20th Century* (10 vols.); and in 2010 by *Inventors & Inventions* (4 vols.). With this new installment, the entire series extends to 34 volumes, covering more than 5,300 lives.

Online Access

Salem provides access to its award-winning content both in traditional, printed form and online. Any school or library that purchases this three-volume set is entitled to free, complimentary access to Salem's online version of the content through our SALEM HISTORY DATABASE. Access is available through a code printed on the inside cover of this first volume, and that access is unlimited and immediate. Our online customer service representatives, at (800) 221-1592, are happy to help with any questions.

The advantages are clear:

- Complimentary with print purchase
- Fully supported
- Unlimited users at your library
- Full access from home or dorm rooms
- Immediate access via online registration
- A simple, intuitive interface
- User profile areas for students and patrons
- Sophisticated search functionality
- Complete content, including appendixes
- Integrated searches with any other Salem Press product you already have on the Salem History platform.

E-books are also available.

Scope of Coverage

Great Lives from History: The Incredibly Wealthy features 445 essays covering 446 people (including 43 women) from all time, worldwide. The vast majority of the individuals included in this set have never been covered in this series before, and all of them have never been covered from the perspective of how they generated and used their wealth, impacting society as a whole. Many of these individuals—major "players" but often persons behind the scenes—are not covered in other biographical reference works of this magnitude.

Each one of these essays has been specially written for this set. The subjects of these essays are wealthy people who earned their fortunes in a wide range of endeavors from ancient times into the twenty-first century—coverage that is essential in any liberal arts curriculum. The editor's criteria for including these individuals in this publication took into account the amount of their wealth; their historical significance; their representation from a wide range of countries and historical periods; the sources of their wealth from a vast range of endeavors; their relevance to class curricula; and their interest to high school, undergraduate, and general readers.

For purposes of this publication, the term "incredibly wealthy" is defined to include men and women who were or are among the wealthiest people at the time in which they lived. Many of these individuals were members of the wealthiest families of their times; profiles of numerous members of the Vanderbilt, Rothschild, and Rockefeller families, for example, are included here.

By category, the contents include persons whose sources of wealth fall into one or more of the following areas: acting (2), agricultural products (13), artwork (1), banking (65), church (4), computer industry (12), conquest (21), construction business (5), embezzlement (2), entertainment industry (9), financial services (9), gambling (1), golfing (1), government (37), horse breeding (5), inheritance (142), insurance (3), investments (97), law practice (3), liquor importation (1), lumber (2), manufacturing (68), marriage (17), media (27), metals refining (5), mining (22), moneylending (4), narcotics trafficking (4), oil (21), patents (21), privateering (4), product endorsements (1), railroads (26), ranching (2), real estate (135), retailing (14), sale of products (70), shipbuilding (1), shipping (14), slave trade (7), slave-holding (6), sports franchise (6), steel (10), telecommunications (4), telegraph (4), tourism (9), trade (85), transportation systems (8), tutoring (1), utilities (4), and writing (4).

The wealthy individuals covered in these volumes are also identified with one or more of the following countries or regions: Afghanistan (1), Argentina (1), Australia (3), Austria (4), Azerbaijan (1), Belgium (2), Bolivia (2), Brazil (4), Brunei (1), Cambodia (1), Canada (7), Chile (2), China (12), Colombia (1), Cuba (6), Cyprus (1), Czech Republic (1), Ecuador (1), Egypt (5), England (75), Ethiopia (1), France (22), Germany (19), Ghana (1), Greece (7), Hungary (3), India (14), Iran (5), Iraq (4), Ireland (6), Israel (1), Italy (23), Japan (9), Lithuania (1), Malaysia (1), Mali (2), Mauritania (1), Mexico (4), Mozambique (1), Netherlands (2), Nigeria (1), Northern Ireland (2), Peru (1), Philippines (1), Poland (2), Portugal (2), Russia (8), Saudi Arabia (3), Scotland (7), Senegal (1), South Africa (3), South Korea (1), Spain (10), Sri Lanka (1), Sweden (2), Switzerland (1), Thailand (3), Turkey (7), United Kingdom (81), United States (227), Wales (1), Yemen (1), and Zimbabwe (1).

ESSAY LENGTH AND FORMAT

Each essay is from 750 to 2,000 words in length (approximately 2 to 4 pages) and displays standard ready-reference top matter offering easy access to the following biographical information:

- The **name** of the individual, as best known.

- The individual's **nationality** and **occupation** (e.g., Japanese physicist).

- A **synopsis** highlighting the individual's historical importance in relation to his or her wealth and indicating why the person is studied today.

- ***Born*** and ***Died*** lines that list the most complete dates of birth and death available, followed by the most precise locations available, as well as an indication of when these data are unknown, only probable, or only approximate. Both contemporary and modern place names (where different) are listed; a question mark (?) is appended to a date or place if the information is considered likely to be the precise date or place but remains in question; a "c." denotes circa and indicates that historians have only enough information to place the date of birth or death near the year listed; and when a range of dates is provided for birth or death, historians are relatively certain that the birth or death year could not have occurred outside the date range.

- ***Also known as***, a listing of other versions of the individual's name, including full names, birth names, alternative spellings, pseudonyms, and nicknames.

- ***Sources of wealth***, a listing of the industries, occupations, business ventures, and other ways in which the subjects earned their fortunes, from acting through writing.

- ***Bequeathal of wealth***, a listing of how the subjects disseminated their wealth, including charitable endeavors, artistic patronage, or bequests to family members or other individuals.

The body of each essay, which also includes a byline for the contributing writer-scholar, is divided into the following four parts:

- ***Early Life*** provides facts about the individual's upbringing and the environment in which he or she was reared, as well as the pronunciation of his or her name (if unfamiliar to English speakers). This section describes the individual's early life, particularly as it laid the groundwork for his or her later wealth. Where little is known about the person's early life, historical context is provided.

- ***First Ventures*** describes the individual's early career, endeavors, enterprises, and other efforts and risks that led to success (and failures), or other circumstances of the subject's life that laid the groundwork for mature wealth.

- ***Mature Wealth***, the heart of the essay, consists of a straightforward, generally chronological, account of how the individuals earned their fortunes, emphasizing the most significant achievements in their lives and careers. This section emphasizes not only the creation of their wealth but also how the individuals managed (or mismanaged) their fortunes during their lifetimes.

- ***Legacy*** provides an overview of the long-range significance of the individual's wealth, emphasizing its impact on history, business, charity, architecture, culture, and other areas of endeavor. This section explains why it is important to study this individual.

The end matter of each essay includes the following resources:

- ***Further Reading***, a bibliography, is a starting point for further research.

- *See also* lists cross-references to essays in the set covering other individuals of interest.

SPECIAL FEATURES

Several features distinguish this set:

- *Complete List of Contents*: This alphabetical list of contents appears in all three volumes.

- *Key to Pronunciation*: A key to in-text pronunciation of unfamiliar names appears in all volumes. Pronunciation guidelines for difficult-to-pronounce names are provided in the first paragraph of the essay's "Early Life" section.

- **Sidebars**: A key feature of many of the essays in this publication is a sidebar on an aspect of the individual's wealth, the lives of wealthy people, or the specific businesses and endeavors in which some individuals generated and spent their fortunes. With topics such as charitable foundations, patronage of the arts, and "Great Wealth and Oil," these sidebars also present a thematic look at economic history.

- **Photographs**: 253 photographs illustrate the essays.

The back matter to Volume 3 includes several appendixes:

- *More Wealthy Persons from History*, a directory of other wealthy people throughout history, with brief descriptions of their significance and the sources of their wealth

- *Chronological List of Entries*, a listing of the 446 wealthy persons covered, arranged by birth year, useful as a "time line" of coverage

- *Electronic Resources*, a guide to Web sites and electronic databases providing additional information about wealthy persons

- *Bibliography*, a comprehensive listing of books about wealth in history, arranged by geographic locale, as well as some of the key industries and businesses (e.g., oil) that generate great wealth

Finally, Volume 3 ends with three useful indexes:

- **Category Index**: entries by area of achievement, from acting to writing.

- **Geographical Index**: entries by country or region.

- **Subject Index**: comprehensive index including personages, corporations, business ventures, philanthropic endeavors, fields of endeavor, concepts, technologies, terms, and other topics of discussion, with full cross-references for alternative spellings and to the category and geographical indexes.

USAGE NOTES

The worldwide scope of *Great Lives from History* resulted in the inclusion of names and words transliterated from languages that do not use the Roman alphabet. In some cases, there is more than one transliterated form in use. In many cases, transliterated words in this set follow the American Library Association and Library of Congress (ALA-LC) transliteration format for that language. However, if another form of a name or word has been judged to be more familiar to general readers, it is used instead. The variants for names of essay subjects are listed in ready-reference top matter and are cross-referenced in the subject and personages indexes. The Pinyin transliteration was used for Chinese topics, with Wade-Giles variants provided for major names. In a few cases, a common name that is not Pinyin has been used. Sanskrit and other South Asian names generally follow the ALA-LC transliteration rules, although again, the more familiar form of a word is used when deemed appropriate for general readers.

Titles of books and other literature appear, upon first mention in the essay, with their full publication and translation data as known: an indication of the first date of publication or appearance, followed by the English title in translation and its first date of appearance in English.

Throughout the set, readers will find a limited number of abbreviations used in both top matter and text, including "r." (reigned), "b." (born), "d." (died), and "fl." (flourished).

CONTRIBUTORS

Salem Press would like to extend its appreciation to all involved in the development and production of this work. The essays have been written and signed by scholars of history, humanities, the sciences, and other disciplines related to the essays' topics. Without these expert contributions, a project of this nature would not be possible. A full list of the contributors' names and affiliations appears in the front matter of this volume.

Special thanks go to Howard Bromberg, the set's editor, without whose guidance and creative vision this publication would not have been possible. Clinical Assistant

Professor of Law at the University of Michigan Law School, Dr. Bromberg developed the contents list and sidebar topics, as well as contributing significantly to this work. He has practiced law as Legislative Counsel to Congressman Thomas Petri of Wisconsin and as a prosecutor in the Appeals Bureau of the New York County District Attorney's Office; has taught at Chicago and Stanford Law Schools and at the Peking University School of Transnational Law; was Associate Professor and Assistant Dean of Clinical and Professional Skills Programs at Ave Maria Law School; and, as Associate Director at Harvard Law School, helped establish Harvard's First-Year Lawyering Program. Professor Bromberg serves on the Advisory Committee of the State of Michigan Moot Court Competition. In 2005-2006, he chaired that committee and was also Director of the annual competition. He has published more than 100 articles and essays in legal history and biography. His B.A and J.D. degrees are from Harvard Law School and his J.S.M. degree is from Stanford Law School.

Editor's Introduction

If history is made by great men and women, it is gilded by the incredibly wealthy. Riches give individuals the ability to influence human affairs, shape economies, provoke war, purchase peace, build monuments, dominate others, or relieve distress. Wealth can be used for either good or bad ends, but it is rare that great wealth passes through history without leaving a trace.

Great Lives from History: The Incredibly Wealthy chronicles the lives of men and women of great wealth. Every attempt has been made to include figures from various nations and historical periods. The essays represent a range of ways in which wealth was derived, used, and disseminated. The subjects of the essays were culled, and their lives were written, based on the widest range of sources—biographies, economic histories, general histories, and records of businesses and foundations. (Sources can be found in the bibliographies at the end of each essay and in the appendix.) The chief criterion for inclusion was not sheer wealth but the impact of that wealth upon history.

Varieties of Wealth

The varieties of wealth are manifold. In ancient times, wealth was possessed in chattel—livestock, produce, vineyards, and ornaments. With the growth of commerce, more liquid means of wealth were required in the form of gold coins, silver plate, jewels, jade, tapestries, ointments, and porcelains. Until modern times, holdings in land were the badge of riches. Sadly, wealth has also been marked by ownership of persons—slaves, indentured servants, and serfs. With the Industrial Revolution and the rise of market economies and capitalism, wealth has taken one dominant form: the accumulation of money, denominated in the various currencies of the world.

History—the written record of human activity—in a sense began with wealth, as the ancient Sumerians invented writing by chiseling their business accounts on clay tablets. The earliest business family represented in *Great Lives from History: The Incredibly Wealthy* are the Egibis, who built a trading empire in ancient Babylon. Other persons chronicled from the ancient world include Biblical figures, Greek legends, Roman actors and charioteers, Mesoamerican emperors, Chinese imperial bureaucrats, Muslim caliphs, and a slave who became the wealthiest banker of golden age Athens. Plunder was an accepted means of acquiring wealth in early societies. Conquerors who seized wealth are included in these volumes, as well as those who, often under the impulses of the nascent world religions, gave wealth away.

The medieval period saw the emergence of feudalism in Europe and elsewhere. Feudal lords—British peers (dukes, marquesses, earls, viscounts, and barons), Russian boyars, Mexican ranchers, Argentine hacienda *patróns*, Prussian Junkers, and the like—acquired vast holdings in land. With their property, these landed lords obtained equally valuable feudal incidents, rents, tithes, crops, and services, as well as peasants to work the land. The Middle Ages and the Renaissance were also a time of world wide exploration and commerce. Great wealth took new forms. Banking families in the Italian city-states funded English kings, Renaissance artists, and Spanish explorers. The Hanseatic League of merchants controlled the Baltic and North Sea trade. Merchant princes in the Mughal Empire traded diamonds, indigo, and textiles. The world craved sugar from plantations in Cyprus, Brazil, and Jamaica. Timbuktu merchants measured their wealth in the acquisition of Islamic manuscripts; the Mali Empire traded gold, salt, and slaves. In the Age of Exploration, European ships expanded the slave trade across the Atlantic and brought home vast quantities of silver from the mines of Potosi in Peru and Zacatecas and La Valenciana in Mexico. Much of this silver found its way to Asia in the Spanish galleon trade and the commercial armadas of the Dutch and English East India Companies. The European ships returned laden with exquisite fabrics, teak furniture, and costly spices. Cotton and opium from India were traded for silk from China. The Chinese Cohong merchants of Canton reaped fortunes from tea; the Chinese merchants of Yangzhou confined themselves to the domestic trade, but benefiting from a government monopoly in salt, they gained fortunes rivaling the Cohongs.

With the Industrial Revolution, the ranks of the wealthy became dominated by a new phenomenon: the modern businessman, whether industrialist, entrepreneur, merchandiser, or investor. The nineteenth century saw the greatest private fortunes in human history as new business organizations—corporations, trusts, and conglomerates—enabled capitalists to amass hitherto uncontemplated riches. The rising economic strength of the United States created great fortunes for Southern tobacco planters, Northwest fur traders, New York financiers, New England whalers, Midwest industrialists, Michigan cereal sellers, Pennsylvania steel and coal tycoons, Nevada silver mine owners, Chicago salesmen and retailers, Newport society matrons, Detroit automakers, St. Louis brewers, California canners, Florida real estate agents, Washington lumbermen, Texas oil barons and ranchers, operators of steamships in trans-Appalachian canals and the Atlantic and Pacific Oceans, and railroad entrepreneurs knitting the nation together with steel tracks.

By the turn of the twentieth century, industrial production had replaced land as the chief source of wealth in the world. Just as with cuisine, clothing, music, and other artifacts of civilization, wealth takes on the trappings of the culture which engendered it. Personal fortunes are alike in their economic capabilities and privileges; they are distinctive in their national character, correlating with the resources and mores of the community. The ranks of the incredibly wealthy were made up of Austrian bankers; German and Swedish industrialists; British generals; Cuban sugar magnates; South African Randlords; French vintners, cosmeticians, and designers; Greek shippers; Latin American tin, cocoa, and banana kings; Russian commodities "oligarchs"; Canadian distillers and media barons; Japanese *zaibatsu*; Iranian peddlers; Arabian sheiks; Swiss chocolatiers; Hong Kong property developers; Hollywood film producers; and Silicon Valley semiconductor, microprocessor, and computer manufacturers and software developers. Although restricted in ownership of property, women were the backbone of numerous familial fortunes. Minority populations faced huge obstacles to economic success, but *Great Lives from History: The Incredibly Wealthy* recounts successful African American, Hispanic, and Native American entrepreneurs from the United States; Lebanese businessmen in Latin America; Armenian traders in Asia; Jewish bankers in Europe; Coptic merchants in Egypt; Parsi industrialists in India; and other wealthy members of minority groups.

PRIVATE WEALTH

Great Lives from History: The Incredibly Wealthy is about private wealth. The people who are profiled claimed incredible riches as their own, riches that were privately possessed and freely alienable, secure, and unencumbered, without the prior claim of states or governments. The largest number of subjects are drawn from late nineteenth and early twentieth century Great Britain and the United States. This is not merely because this is an English-language book; rather, these two countries

saw the greatest accumulation of wealth in private hands during this period. Earlier wealth was rarely produced without the backing of the sovereign. Even in England, wealth was produced at the behest of the monarch or as the fruit of aristocratic titles and privileges. At the disfavor of the king or queen, a British duke could be attainted, his fortune confiscated. In the United States, wealth was separated from direct state control. Titles of aristocracy were forbidden; bills of attainder were expressly prohibited. The U.S. Constitution enshrined freedom of contract, limited taxation, liberty of work, and the right to property. For the first time in history, an elite class arose with no connection to royalty or aristocracy but only to the raw mechanics of enterprise and industry. If subsidies and illicit favors were squeezed from the legislature by American monopolists of the Gilded Age, that fact was disguised, not brandished.

Obviously royalty possessed enormous wealth. The Pharaohs could command the workforce of Egypt to build their monuments and pyramids. When William the Conqueror claimed the English throne in 1066, he also claimed ownership to the land of all England and promulgated the *Domesday Book* to enforce his claim. However in the truest sense, the wealth of the sovereign belonged to the state, not the ruler. The monarch was endowed with power; his or her wealth was a mere by-product of that power. If deposed, the monarch's wealth was transferred to the succeeding ruler. In Rome, the emperor passed his personal treasury, the *fiscus*, to the next emperor, not to his heirs. The resplendent crown jewels of England and Persia were passed from dynasty to dynasty, the individual property of no person. Indeed, the sovereign was usually expected to provide for state expenses out of his or her own pocket, and the seemingly richest monarchs, such as Philip II of Spain, Henry VIII of England, and Charles V of the Holy Roman Empire, were perennially in debt, due to the expenses of the state that they bore. The few royals included in *Great Lives from History: The Incredibly Wealthy* used their wealth to build great monuments, such as Angkor Wat temple, the Süleymaniye mosque, the Taj Mahal, and the Palace of Versailles. This book also includes modern constitutional monarchs, who, with the disappearance of their power, have acquired full possession over their estates.

Until the era of the modern nation-state, members of the nobility were minor royalty, ruling over cities, fiefdoms, and principalities. Again, their wealth pertained more to their offices and ranks than to themselves. The aristocrats included in *Great Lives from History: The Incredibly Wealthy* tend to more recent vintage, as the princely classes have likewise lost their jurisdiction of power but gained personal riches.

The requirement that wealth be private, unencumbered, and secure has led to the exclusion of the most infamous outlaws, regardless of the extent of their transient wealth. Criminals such as Pablo Escobar and Charles Ponzi are included because of their unique places in social history.

Finally, the emphasis on private wealth excludes the so-called kleptocrats—heads of state who helped themselves to great riches from their nations' treasuries. Nicolae Ceauşescu of Romania, Mobutu Sese Seko of Zaire (Democratic Republic of the Congo), the Duvaliers of Haiti, Ferdinand Marcos of the Philippines, Suharto of Indonesia, Sani Abacha of Nigeria, Bakili Muluzi of Malawi, Jean-Bédel Bokassa of the Central African Republic, Kim Jong Il of North Korea, and Slobodan Milošević of Serbia are alleged to have secreted billions of dollars for their own pleasures. If so, the extent of their gains will have to be explored in other venues.

SIDEBARS: FOUNDATIONS OF WEALTH

The lives of the incredibly wealthy are a microcosm of the world's economic activity. The lengthier essays in *Great Lives from History: The Incredibly Wealthy* include a sidebar that is meant to illustrate an aspect of the subject's fortune that transcends his or her lifespan and makes a permanent impact on world history. These sidebars treat businesses, castles, palaces, cathedrals, skyscrapers, schools, colleges and universities, hospitals, museums, libraries, gardens, and mansions.

Two special uses of the word "foundation" are worth noting in the sidebars. First are the treatments of the foundations, or the derivations, of great wealth in the world economy. These sidebars treat such topics as the intersection of wealth with religion, gold, oil, salt, railroads, conglomerates, art, literature, publishing, sport, slavery, cuisine, and automobiles, among other subjects.

The second use of the word "foundation" in the sidebars is literal—the philanthropic foundations that are the mainstay of modern fortunes. In the twentieth century there was hardly a multimillionaire who did not endow a nonprofit foundation for philanthropic purposes. These foundations were created for a variety of reasons, some of which were certainly noble, but they were also established to generate good will, arrange familial affairs, and achieve favorable legal and tax statuses. The Ford, Rockefeller, and Carnegie Foundations were probably the most influential over the course of the century. Among the largest and most significant of the thousands

of other foundations are the Stichting INGKA Foundation, Li Ka Shing Foundation, Bill and Melinda Gates Foundation, Robert Wood Johnson Foundation, W. K. Kellogg Foundation, the Kamehameha Schools supported by the Bernice Pauahi Bishop Estate, Muḥammad bin Rāshid Āl Maktūm Foundation, David and Lucile Packard Foundation, William and Flora Hewlett Foundation, and Annenberg Foundation.

MORE WEALTHY PEOPLE FROM HISTORY

In the back matter of Volume 3, *Great Lives from History: The Incredibly Wealthy* includes a directory of about two hundred additional wealthy people from history, with brief descriptions of their significance. These persons, also of historical importance, are included in abbreviated fashion for various reasons. For some, the record of their lives is sparse. Unlike talent or achievement, wealth is easily passed on to the next generation, even if dispersed; this section includes family members whose combined wealth propels them into the ranks of the incredibly wealthy. Finally, this section completes the list of contemporary persons whose fortune exceeds $10 billion; their long-term significance, however, remains to be determined.

COMPARING WEALTH

Calculating and comparing the extent of wealth are important features of *Great Lives from History: The Incredibly Wealthy*, both as a tool of selection and as a mainstay of the essays. However, it must be remembered that comparative wealth is incapable of exact measurement. In ancient times, wealth consisted largely of land and livestock and could not be quantified. Even when wealth took the form of money, obstacles to calculation remain. For one, the changing value of money over the centuries makes comparison difficult. Likewise, historical epochs differ in their rates of taxation, costs of labor and goods, and interest rates, all of which complicate comparisons. In addition, any transnational comparison will be complicated by the varying exchange rates of the world's currencies.

Nevertheless, a rough estimate of wealth, even from the most primitive times, is possible and employed in most of the essays. The most valuable tools for gleaning wealth are probate records, but information can also be found in memoirs, travelogues, tax records, court assessments, wills, and other records. To correlate historic wealth in modern terms, economic historians use various methods, such as the change in the consumer price index, comparative percentages of gross national product, gross domestic product per capita, and comparative daily wages of workers. Although these methods yield different results, all allow for an approximation of historic wealth in modern dollars. Due to the perennial effects of inflation, nominal wealth (the actual dollar value of a person's fortune at the time) must be converted to real wealth (a person's comparative fortune in modern dollars). Using the U.S. dollar as an example, nominal wealth of $500,000 in 1800 may be roughly akin to $3 million in 1850, $18 million in 1900, $125 million in 1950, and $6.5 billion in 2000. In other words, John D. Rockefeller, whose nominal wealth was estimated as high as $1.4 billion in an age of low taxation and inexpensive labor, must be counted as richer than Bill Gates, whose fortune was estimated at $53 billion in 2010.

Differences in the rates of exchange between countries must also be accounted. To give a useful example from Europe, the economic historian Niall Ferguson has estimated the exchange rate of the British pound in the middle of the nineteenth century to be at about 25 francs (whether French, Belgian, or Swiss), 500 Spanish reals, 6 Russian rubles, 6 Neapolitan ducats, and 7 Prussian thalers. (In 1850, 1 British pound was worth about 5 U.S. dollars.) Ferguson estimates the exchange rate in 1913 of 1 British pound to be about 20 German marks, 25 French francs, 25 Italian lire, 24 Austrian crowns, 9.5 Russian rubles, and 5 U.S. dollars. In 1950, the exchange rate for 1 U.S. dollar was about one-third of a British pound, 4 German Deutsche marks, 360 Japanese yen, and about 5 Indian rupees.

With these tools in hand, several historians have ranked Marcus Licinius Crassus as the richest person of the classical world. Alanus Rufus has been ranked as the richest person of medieval England, with his real wealth approximated at £82 billion or $122 billion in modern money. By most accounts John D. Rockefeller possessed the greatest real fortune in history, with his nominal wealth of $1.4 billion in the early twentieth century estimated to be worth as much as $200 billion in modern dollars.

In 2000, *The Wall Street Journal* published a time line of the fifty richest people of the second millennium (http://interactive.wsj.com/public/resources/documents/mill-1-timeline.htm). Cynthia Crossen, the newspaper's senior editor, selected the ten most distinctive and representative people from this list in *The Rich and How They Got That Way: How the Wealthiest People of All Times from Genghis Khan to Bill Gates Made Their Fortunes* (2000). In addition to Gates, Crossen included Mansa Mūsā, Maḥmūd of Ghazna, Genghis Khan, Pope Alex-

ander VI, Jakob Fugger, John Law, Sir Richard Arkwright, Wu Bingjian, and Hetty Green.

Comparisons of modern wealth have been made more accessible by the American business magazines *Fortune* and *Forbes*, which consistently calculate and publish lists of the wealthiest people in the United States and the world. (Since 1989, *The Sunday Times* has published an annual list of the one thousand richest people in the United Kingdom.) These lists are compiled carefully by expert staffs and are reliable. In addition, the annual *Forbes* list of the world's richest people is measured in terms of U.S. dollars. *Forbes* first published a list of the thirty wealthiest Americans on March 2, 1918. John D. Rockefeller topped this list, with a fortune of $1.2 billion, followed by Henry Clay Frick ($225 million), Andrew Carnegie ($200 million), George F. Baker ($150 million), William Rockefeller ($150 million), and Edward Harkness ($125 million). *Fortune* published a list of the seventy-six wealthiest Americans in November, 1957. J. Paul Getty topped this list, with a fortune in the range of $700 million to $1 billion. In the second highest range of $400 million to $700 million were John D. Rockefeller, Jr., H. L. Hunt, Arthur Vining Davis, and four members of the Mellon family.

Forbes began publishing its annual list of the world's wealthiest people in 1996. That year, Bill Gates topped the list with $18.5 billion, followed by Warren Buffet with $15 billion. In the *Forbes* list published on March 9, 2010, Gates's wealth had grown to $53 billion and Buffet's to $47 billion, well illustrating the time value of money. Nevertheless, Gates and Buffet had been displaced as the world's wealthiest persons by Mexican businessman Carlos Slim, with a fortune of $53.5 billion. Occupying positions four through six in 2010 were Mukesh Ambani ($29 billion), Lakshmi Mittal ($28.7 billion), and Larry Ellison ($28 billion).

THE INCREDIBLY WEALTHY

The incredibly wealthy have been viewed with admiration and disdain. The largest private fortunes were probably those compiled by American industrialists of the last half of the nineteenth century, such men as John D. Rockefeller, Andrew Carnegie, Cornelius Vanderbilt, Frederick Weyerhaeuser, and J. P. Morgan. The muckraking journalists called these men "robber barons," while their apologists called them "captains of industry." Their dominance and innovations in the oil, steel, coal, lumber, railroad, and banking businesses accelerated the American standard of living. However, they were also accused of brutal exploitation of workers and consumers.

Carnegie pleaded with his peers to be generous with their fortunes, and he founded the Carnegie Foundation, the Carnegie Endowment for World Peace, Carnegie Hall in New York City, the Carnegie Institution in Washington, D.C., and Carnegie museums and libraries throughout the nation. Carnegie, however, also received blame for the violent suppression of the Homestead Strike of 1892. Were these industrialists primarily plutocrats, absorbing an unfair portion of the nation's wealth, or were they philanthropists, both in the goods they produced and the foundations they endowed?

In the end, it seems that the wealthy, like others, faced individual choices about the accumulation of their wealth and its uses for ignoble ends or for the betterment of humankind. Thus, there may be no better way to assess the role of the incredibly wealthy in human affairs than by reading a collective biography of their lives, one gilded life at a time.

—Howard Bromberg
Clinical Assistant Professor of Law
University of Michigan Law School

CONTRIBUTORS

Emily Alward
Las Vegas, Nevada

Carolyn Anderson
*University of Massachusetts,
Amherst*

Andy Argyrakis
Tribune Media Services

James A. Arieti
Hampden-Sydney College

Amanda J. Bahr-Evola
*Southern Illinois University,
Edwardsville*

Renzo Baldasso
The Newberry Library

Chloe M. Ball
Spelman College

Jane L. Ball
Yellow Springs, Ohio

Janet M. Ball
Apache County Library District

David Barratt
Montreat College

Melissa A. Barton
Westminster, Colorado

Albert A. Bell, Jr.
Hope College

Alvin K. Benson
Utah Valley University

Milton Berman
University of Rochester

R. Matthew Beverlin
Rockhurst University

Cynthia A. Bily
Macomb Community College

Kevin Birch
Salisbury University

Howard Bromberg
University of Michigan

Kendall W. Brown
Brigham Young University

Thomas W. Buchanan
Ancilla Domini College

Jeffrey L. Buller
Florida Atlantic University

Michael H. Burchett
Limestone College

William E. Burns
George Washington University

Susan Butterworth
Salem State College

Joseph P. Byrne
Belmont University

Jennifer L. Campbell
Lycoming College

Avelina Carrera
Universidad de Valladolid

Bernard A. Cook
Loyola University

Tyler T. Crogg
*Southern Illinois University,
Carbondale*

Robert L. Cullers
Kansas State University

Anita Price Davis
Converse College

Bruce J. DeHart
*University of North Carolina at
Pembroke*

James I. Deutsch
Smithsonian Institution

Joseph Dewey
*University of Pittsburgh,
Johnstown*

Jonathan E. Dinneen
Bridgewater, Massachusetts

Marcia B. Dinneen
Bridgewater State College

Steven L. Driever
*University of Missouri at
Kansas City*

Thomas Drucker
*University of Wisconsin,
Whitewater*

Thomas Du Bose
*Louisiana State University,
Shreveport*

Victoria Erhart
Strayer University

Jack Ewing
Boise, Idaho

Thomas R. Feller
Nashville, Tennessee

Alan S. Frazier
University of North Dakota

Hans G. Graetzer
South Dakota State University

Johnpeter Horst Grill
Mississippi State University

Scot M. Guenter
San Jose State University

Irwin Halfond
McKendree University

Jan Hall
Columbus, Ohio

Michael R. Hall
*Armstrong Atlantic State
University*

Randall Hannum
*New York City College of
Technology, CUNY*

Wells S. Hansen
Milton Academy

C. Alton Hassell
Baylor University

A. W. R. Hawkins
West Texas A&M University

Bernadette Zbicki Heiney
*Lock Haven University of
Pennsylvania*

James J. Heiney
*Lock Haven University of
Pennsylvania*

Mark C. Herman
Edison State College

Mary Hurd
East Tennessee State University

Raymond Pierre Hylton
Virginia Union University

Robert Jacobs
Central Washington University

Carolyn Janik
Eckerd College

Bruce E. Johansen
University of Nebraska at Omaha

Susan Jones
Palm Beach Atlantic University

Mark S. Joy
Jamestown College

Karen N. Kähler
Pasadena, California

Marylane Wade Koch
*University of Memphis,
Loewenberg School of Nursing*

Grove Koger
Boise State University

Kathryn Kulpa
University of Rhode Island

Timothy Lane
Louisville, Kentucky

Eugene Larson
Los Angeles Pierce College

Norma Lewis
Byron Center, Michigan

Roy Liebman
*California State University,
Los Angeles*

Ralph W. Lindeman
*Kent State University, Geauga
Campus*

Victor Lindsey
East Central University

Roger D. Long
Eastern Michigan University

Bernadette Flynn Low
*Community College of Baltimore
County, Dundalk*

R. C. Lutz
CII Group

Roxanne McDonald
Wilmot, New Hampshire

Thomas McGeary
Champaign, Illinois

Paul Madden
Hardin-Simmons University

Martin J. Manning
United States Department of State

Laurence W. Mazzeno
Alvernia College

Scott A. Merriman
Troy University

Julia M. Meyers
Duquesne University

Alice Myers
Bard College at Simon's Rock

Byron J. Nakamura
*Southern Connecticut State
University*

Leslie Neilan
*Virginia Polytechnic Institute and
State University*

Caryn E. Neumann
Miami University of Ohio

William A. Paquette
Tidewater Community College

Barbara Bennett Peterson
University of Hawaii

Allene Phy-Olsen
Austin Peay State University

Michael Polley
Columbia College of Missouri

Steven Pressman
Monmouth University

Victoria Price
Lamar University

Betty Richardson
Southern Illinois University at Edwardsville

Edward A. Riedinger
Ohio State University

Carl Rollyson
Baruch College, CUNY

Richard Sax
Lake Erie College

Jean Owens Schaefer
University of Wyoming

Elizabeth D. Schafer
Loachapoka, Alabama

Beverly Schneller
Millersville University

Sara Schulte
Rockhurst University

Eric Schuster
Harry S. Truman Chicago Community College

Martha A. Sherwood
Kent Anderson Law Office

R. Baird Shuman
University of Illinois at Urbana-Champaign

Narasingha P. Sil
Western Oregon University

María Silva
Universidad Finis Terrae, Chile

Paul P. Sipiera
William Rainey Harper College

Shumet Sishagne
Christopher Newport University

Amy Sisson
Houston Community College

Douglas D. Skinner
Texas State University, San Marcos

Richard L. Smith
Ferrum College

Sonia Sorrell
Pepperdine University

Brian Stableford
Reading, United Kingdom

Polly D. Steenhagen
Delaware State University

Theresa Stowell
Adrian College

Cynthia J. W. Svoboda
Bridgewater State College

Nicholas C. Thomas
Auburn University at Montgomery

John E. Thorburn
Baylor University

Anh Tran
Wichita State University

Paul B. Trescott
Southern Illinois University

Larry W. Usilton
University of North Carolina at Wilmington

Hongjie Wang
Armstrong Atlantic State University

Shawncey Webb
Taylor University

Robert Whaples
Wake Forest University

Winifred Whelan
St. Bonaventure University

Carlis White
Slippery Rock University of Pennsylvania

Scott Wright
University of St. Thomas

Lisa A. Wroble
Edison State College

KEY TO PRONUNCIATION

    Many of the names of personages covered in *Great Lives from History: The Incredibly Wealthy* may be unfamiliar to students and general readers. For these unfamiliar names, guides to pronunciation have been provided upon first mention of the names in the text. These guidelines do not purport to achieve the subtleties of the languages in question but will offer readers a rough equivalent of how English speakers may approximate the proper pronunciation.

Vowel Sounds

Symbol	Spelled (Pronounced)
a	answer (AN-suhr), laugh (laf), sample (SAM-puhl), that (that)
ah	father (FAH-thur), hospital (HAHS-pih-tuhl)
aw	awful (AW-fuhl), caught (kawt)
ay	blaze (blayz), fade (fayd), waiter (WAYT-ur), weigh (way)
eh	bed (behd), head (hehd), said (sehd)
ee	believe (bee-LEEV), cedar (SEE-dur), leader (LEED-ur), liter (LEE-tur)
ew	boot (bewt), lose (lewz)
i	buy (bi), height (hit), lie (li), surprise (sur-PRIZ)
ih	bitter (BIH-tur), pill (pihl)
o	cotton (KO-tuhn), hot (hot)
oh	below (bee-LOH), coat (koht), note (noht), wholesome (HOHL-suhm)
oo	good (good), look (look)
ow	couch (kowch), how (how)
oy	boy (boy), coin (koyn)
uh	about (uh-BOWT), butter (BUH-tuhr), enough (ee-NUHF), other (UH-thur)

Consonant Sounds

Symbol	Spelled (Pronounced)
ch	beach (beech), chimp (chihmp)
g	beg (behg), disguise (dihs-GIZ), get (geht)
j	digit (DIH-juht), edge (ehj), jet (jeht)
k	cat (kat), kitten (KIH-tuhn), hex (hehks)
s	cellar (SEHL-ur), save (sayv), scent (sehnt)
sh	champagne (sham-PAYN), issue (IH-shew), shop (shop)
ur	birth (burth), disturb (dihs-TURB), earth (urth), letter (LEH-tur)
y	useful (YEWS-fuhl), young (yuhng)
z	business (BIHZ-nehs), zest (zehst)
zh	vision (VIH-zhuhn)

COMPLETE LIST OF CONTENTS

VOLUME 1

VOLUME 2

VOLUME 3

Appendixes

Indexes

The Incredibly Wealthy

AARON OF LINCOLN
English banker and financier

Aaron of Lincoln founded an international network of finance that allowed him to lend money and collect returns efficiently. His financial dealings contributed to the building and maintaining of major Cistercian monasteries and other Christian foundations, including the Cathedral and Abbey Church of St. Alban's and Lincoln Minster.

Born: c. 1125; probably Lincoln, England
Died: 1186; probably Lincoln, England
Sources of wealth: Banking; moneylending
Bequeathal of wealth: Government

EARLY LIFE
Virtually nothing is known of the early years of Aaron of Lincoln. Since there was little documentation of births in the twelfth century, his age can be surmised only by estimate and his place of birth or dwelling from the designation at the end of his name.

FIRST VENTURES
Aaron of Lincoln first appears in approximately 1166 C.E., when documentary evidence mentions his name in regard to money being paid to him by King Henry II through a transaction with the sheriff of Lincoln, almost certainly as the result of a loan. Most scholars believe that Aaron was well under way with his business ventures by this time, loaning money at interest to various individuals and entities. The source of his wealth at this point in his career is uncertain. Materials providing information for his biography are mostly business records, and few, if any, personal records remain.

MATURE WEALTH
The twelfth century saw the organization of the Jewish community throughout England in a vast structure mobilized to offer credit and collect on indebtedness with great efficiency. Although it is unknown whether this was the invention of Aaron of Lincoln or another great financier, Isaac, fil Joce, Aaron certainly developed this network to its fullest and most efficient extent. Laws forbidding Christians to loan money at interest were at the heart of this opportunity, and due to legal and religious restrictions on professions among the Jews, providing capital for Christian ventures of various types offered an opportunity for Aaron to create great wealth.

Aaron's investments included not only money for capital projects, such as abbeys and cathedrals, but also investments in farming operations and loans to small lenders. The interest rates that he and other lenders of the period charged were often very high, as much as 60 percent, but he is also known to have loaned a small amount to a female debtor named Truue at no interest at all. His business interests were comprehensive and successful.

Although he used a network of assistants, he was not in partnership with other Jewish lenders of the period, as the king generally forbade such partnerships. According to law, the estates of Jewish moneylenders reverted to the Crown upon their deaths. Partnership would have delayed the acquisition of their wealth by the Crown, although often, in practice, the monarch took only a percentage of the estate, allowing heirs to continue the business of lending, which profited the state greatly, given the various fees and taxes on the business's activities.

At Aaron's death in 1186, his total wealth was so great that the king chose to take the whole of his property, including Aaron's own treasury and material wealth at his house, as well as administration of his loans to others. Because of the extent of this wealth, a special government branch, the exchequer of Aaron, was set up to administer the loans. Concluding this business would take at least twenty years. The actual treasure of Aaron was shipped to France by King Henry and was lost when the ship sank in the English Channel. Aaron's wealth has been approximated at 2.5 percent of the national income of the period, the equivalent of almost £28 billion in 2010.

LEGACY
Aaron's acquisition of wealth demonstrates that a financier could employ a network of agents spread over a large area to conduct almost limitless financial activities effectively and efficiently, without having to attend to every transaction personally. The immense structure that Aaron created to carry on his financial activities, the most successful early example of this type, makes him worthy of study and remembrance.

—*Susan Jones*

FURTHER READING
Beresford, Philip, and William D. Rubinstein. *The Richest of the Rich: The Wealthiest 250 People in Britain*

Since 1066. Petersfield, Hampshire, England: Harriman House, 2007.

Dobson, R. B. *The Jews of Medieval York and the Massacre of March, 1190*. York, England: Borthwick Papers, 1974.

Hyamson, A. M. *A History of the Jews in England*. London: Chatto & Windus, 1908.

Jacobs, Joseph. "Aaron of Lincoln." *Jewish Quarterly Review* 10, no. 4 (July, 1898): 629-648.

_____. *The Jews of Angevin England*. New York: G. P. Putnam's Sons, 1893.

See also: Eleanor of Aquitaine; Godric of Finchale.

'ABBĀS THE GREAT
Persian monarch and military leader

Under Shah 'Abbās the Great, Ṣafavid Persia reached its height of political unity, economic prosperity, and cultural advancement. A homogenous state was created, with the Shī'ite faction of Islam as the official religion and Farsi as the national language. 'Abbās's new capital, Isfahan, became one of the world's most beautiful cities.

Born: January 27, 1571; Persia (now Iran)
Died: January 19, 1629; Ashraf, Mazandaran, Persia (now in Iran)
Also known as: Shah 'Abbās I; Shah 'Abbās the Great; 'Abbās I of Persia
Sources of wealth: Conquest; trade
Bequeathal of wealth: Children; artistic patronage

EARLY LIFE
'Abbās (AH-bas) the Great was born into a royal Persian family surrounded by palace intrigues. At age five, his life nearly ended when his uncle, Shah Ismā'īl II (r. 1576-1577), ordered the execution of 'Abbās and all of his brothers. Ismā'īl's own untimely death prevented the murders. At the age of sixteen, 'Abbās gained support from several leading nobles to seize the throne from his inept and nearly blind father, Shah Muḥammad Khudabanda (r. 1578-1587).

FIRST VENTURES
To unify a disintegrating Ṣafavid empire, 'Abbās moved to quash the rebellious Turkmen and Uzbek people. By 1598, after ten years of costly military campaigns, Persia's eastern borders were secured. It was now time to confront the Ṣafavids' major adversary, the Ottoman Turks.

To prepare to fight the Turks, 'Abbās created the *ghulam* system. *Ghulams* were personal slaves of the shah who would be trained either to be administrators, if they were bright, or to be professional soldiers of a new, standing army. Most of the *ghulams* were non-Persians and came from the Armenian, Circassian, and Georgian populations that had come under Ṣafavid rule. They were converted to Shī'ite Islam and were totally immune from Persian tribal politics. Other foreigners helped Persia forge an army capable of battling the Turks and helped construct the administrative apparatus needed to govern a re-created Persia more efficiently.

'Abbās the Great. (Hulton Archive/Getty Images)

MATURE WEALTH

In preparation for war, in 1598 ʿAbbās moved the capital from Qazwin to the more defensible central Persian city of Isfahan. From Isfahan, ʿAbbās had more central communication links with the entire country and with trading outlets on the Persian Gulf. ʿAbbās invested heavily in Isfahan, making it one of the most beautiful cities in the world. The magnificence of his capital and court and the lavish patronage given to philosophers, scientists, and artists were intended to symbolize the dawning of a new, glorious age for the Ṣafavids. A new central government administration, which ran relatively smoothly, was also constructed in Isfahan. New provinces were created and put under the administration of royal governors, many of whom were *ghulams*. All was designed to concentrate power into ʿAbbās's hands. National unity was further attempted by completing forced conversion to Shīʿism and by establishing Farsi as the national language.

The war against Turkey began in 1603, and an initial success was the retaking of Tabriz, given to the Ottomans by ʿAbbās at the start of his reign. In 1605, a major victory was achieved at Bossora, and ʿAbbās gained control of Shivran and Kurdistan. Finally in 1623, after a year-long siege, Baghdad was seized from Ottoman rule. The holy Shīʿite cities of Karbala and Najaf also came under Ṣafavid control. Not resting on his accomplishments, ʿAbbās was able to obtain naval aid from the British East India Company, and he used this assistance in 1622 to end Portuguese control of the strategically located island of Hormuz. Thus, ʿAbbās became master of the Persian Gulf.

LEGACY

Control of Hormuz produced close economic ties with Great Britain and the Netherlands, and a lucrative trade was created of Persian silks for English cloth. The sale of silk was made a royal monopoly. Under ʿAbbās, carpet weaving also became a major industry. It soon became fashionable for wealthy European homes to have fine Persian rugs. Porcelain, detailed metalwork, and miniatures also became manufactures in demand. To stimulate economic activity, ʿAbbās invested in building highways, bridges. and even merchant lodges along trading routes. He granted immunities and special privileges to attract European merchants. He also ordered many Armenian merchants to settle in Isfahan in order to help build up the silk trade with India. ʿAbbās's economic policies integrated Persia into world trade and led to a general period of prosperity.

—Irwin Halfond

FURTHER READING

Melville, Charles, ed. *Safavid Persia: The History and Politics of an Islamic Society.* New York: St. Martin's Press, 1996.

Monshi, Eskandar. *History of Shah Abbas the Great.* Boulder, Colo.: Westview Press, 1978.

Savory, Roger. *Iran Under the Safavids.* New York: Cambridge University Press, 1980.

See also: Aga Khan I; Yaḥyā ibn Khālid al-Barmakī; Hārūn al-Rashīd; Marduk-nāsir-apli.

SHELDON ADELSON
American investor, property developer, and hotel and casino owner

Adelson managed to accumulate one of the largest American fortunes of the early twenty-first century through shrewd investing and vision. He gave much of his wealth to further Jewish education in the Las Vegas area and to advance medical research. He also supported Republican political causes and worked to extend the influence of Israel in the United States and the Middle East.

Born: August 1 or 4, 1933; Boston, Massachusetts
Also known as: Sheldon Gary Adelson
Sources of wealth: Real estate; tourism; investments
Bequeathal of wealth: Educational institution; political organization

EARLY LIFE

Sheldon Gary Adelson (A-dehl-suhn) is the son of Jewish parents whose families came from Lithuania and the Ukraine. He was born in a lower-class area of Dorchester, a neighborhood in Boston, where his mother owned a knitting shop and his father drove a taxicab and sold advertisements. Adelson sold newspapers as a boy. He moved to New York in the early 1950's to attend City College, where he majored in real estate and finance, but he left college without obtaining the required credits to graduate. He served a tour of duty in the army and then went to work as a stenographer on Wall Street. He became a millionaire by the early 1960's by consulting with companies on how to sell their shares in the stock market.

He thereafter returned to Boston and began speculating in businesses and increasing his wealth.

FIRST VENTURES

In Boston, Adelson began investing, eventually acquiring more than seventy different companies, the most profitable being a tour and travel business, American International Travel Service, which he bought with two friends in the 1960's. The tour service subsequently generated millions of dollars. However, he lost his fortune when the stock market declined in the late 1960's. He soon recouped his losses in the real estate brokerage business, but he lost another fortune when the condominium market crashed in the early 1970's.

In 1971, he bought a majority share of a company that published computer magazines. He then began producing shows about computers, the first one held in Dallas, Texas, in 1973. By 1984, his Interface Group had produced more than forty shows, and his Computer Dealers Exposition (COMDEX) company, designed to bring computer manufacturers and retailers together, became the largest trade show in Las Vegas. By the 1980's, Interface Company's net income exceeded $250 million, and Adelson was producing trade shows in many cities in the United States, Europe, and Japan.

MATURE WEALTH

Looking for more opportunities, in 1988 Adelson and his partners from Interface bought the Sands Hotel and Casino in Las Vegas, which in the public mind was forever associated with Frank Sinatra and the Rat Pack. The new owners renovated the Sands, adding a $60 million convention center. Because of a declining economy, however, the convention center did not open until 1995. In that year, Adelson and his partners sold their interest in the trade show industry to Japanese investors for $862 million. Adelson's profits in the transaction amounted to more than $500 million.

In 1996, Adelson razed the aging Sands in a nationally televised implosion to make way for his new project, a Venetian-themed hotel, for which he had gotten the idea while honeymooning with his second wife in Venice in 1991. The Venetian, a casino and hotel, in which all of the rooms were suites, opened in 1999. Constructed at a cost of $1.5 billion, the new hotel was a huge financial success. In 2003, Adelson added the Venezia Tower to the hotel, enlarging the facility to more than four thousand suites, eighteen first-class restaurants, and a shopping mall complete with canals, gondolas to transport the patrons, and singing gondoliers to pole them throughout the mall.

Adelson then turned his attention to the Far East, where he was among the first American investors to recognize a huge gambling and resort potential. He built the first Las Vegas-style casino in the People's Republic of China, the Sands Macau, in a former Portuguese colony off the Chinese coast at a cost of $265 million. He planned to build seven more casinos in the same area, including the

Sheldon Adelson visits the Marina Bay Sands construction site in Singapore. (AP/Wide World Photos)

THE DR. MIRIAM AND SHELDON G. ADELSON EDUCATIONAL CAMPUS

The Las Vegas campus that bears the names of property developer Sheldon Adelson and his wife, Dr. Miriam Ochsorn Adelson, was initially founded in 1980. Back then, it was known as the Hebrew Academy, with fifty-seven Jewish students in kindergarten through second grade. Ten years later, the school moved to another location and became the Milton I. Schwartz Hebrew Academy, with enrollment expanded to include a preschool and kindergarten through eighth-grade students. A $25 million gift from the Adelsons in 2005 enabled the school to break ground for a new campus, to expand to include high school students, and to separate into three institutions: the Milton I. Schwartz Hebrew Academy for students in kindergarten through fourth grade, the Adelson Middle School for grades five through eight, and the Adelson Upper School for ninth- through twelfth-graders.

By 2009, the school was located in a $65 million ultramodern campus in the planned community of Summerlin, home to a dozen private schools, most of which are affiliated with religious institutions. The campus featured a research library and technology center; eighteen high school classrooms with three science laboratories; sixteen middle school classrooms with three science labs; twenty-four elementary school classrooms; a 350-seat performing arts theater; art studios; and a sports and fitness center with two indoor swimming pools, two basketball courts, an indoor running track, a volleyball court, tennis courts, a fencing area, and a soccer field. Enrollment in 2008 had increased to more than four hundred students enrolled in preschool through eleventh grade, and in 2009 the first twelve-grade class was in attendance. The curriculum includes instruction in the Hebrew language, Jewish religious texts, and other aspects of Judaic studies in addition to the students' other course work.

The campus is coeducational, and about 2 percent of its enrollees are students of color. It employs sixty-eight classroom teachers, 75 percent of whom have advanced degrees. Average class size is eighteen, and the teacher-student ratio is one teacher for five students. The dress code is formal. Yearly tuition for grades one through eight was $14,345 in 2009, with preschool, kindergarten, and high school students paying a slightly higher amount.

On the Adelson Educational Campus Web page, the School Notes state that "our comprehensive approach emphasizes educating each student to be academically stimulated, emotionally secure and physically healthy in a drug-free environment. It is our vision that our students will become the moral and ethical leaders of tomorrow. We are committed to providing students with an education that prepares them for life."

$2.4 billion Venetian Macau, which opened in August, 2007. Adelson also invested $12 billion to construct approximately twenty thousand hotel rooms in Macau's Cotai Strip, with the intention of modeling this area after the Las Vegas Strip. He became the first American to acquire a casino license in Singapore, where he planned to build the $5.4 billion Marina Bay Sands resort.

To raise the capital for these ambitious enterprises, Adelson took his company, Las Vegas Sands Corporation, public in December, 2004. The success of the company's initial stock offering resulted in *Forbes* magazine ranking Adelson as the world's third-richest man, with a net worth of more than $20 billion. Because of the economic downturn, however, Adelson's rank among the world's richest declined to 178th by 2008.

Adelson has devoted a considerable portion of his wealth to Jewish philanthropic enterprises, such as the Birthright Israel organization. Birthright Israel provides financial assistance to enable young Jews between the ages of eighteen and twenty-six to travel to Israel. He contributed $25 million to the Yad Vashem Holocaust Martyrs' and Heroes' Remembrance Authority in Israel. He and his wife, Dr. Miriam Ochsorn Adelson, have donated more than $25 million to the Milton I. Schwartz Hebrew Academy in Las Vegas in order to build a high school.

The Adelsons have also given considerable financial support to medical research, founding the Dr. Miriam and Sheldon G. Adelson Medical Research Foundation in 2007. The foundation is especially concerned with neural repair and rehabilitation. Adelson has suffered with peripheral neuropathy and has walked with the aid of a cane since 2001. Miriam Adelson, a native of Israel, operates drug rehabilitation clinics in Las Vegas and Tel Aviv. Adelson's adopted son Mitchell died of a drug overdose in 2005; his other adopted son, Gary, also suffers from drug dependency. The couple has plans to open more drug clinics in Israel and the United States. In early 2007, Adelson established the Adelson Family Charitable Foundation, which will eventually donate $200 million or more each year to Jewish and Israeli causes. The foundation's first gift was a pledge of $25 million to

Birthright Israel, which allowed the organization to double its capacity and bring twenty thousand participants to Israel during the summer of 2007.

Adelson has also been heavily involved in politics since accumulating his wealth. Although both he and his wife came from traditionally liberal families, he has contributed primarily to conservative political causes. In 2006, for example, he gave $1 million to former congressman Newt Gingrich's conservative political organization, Solutions for Winning the Future. In 2007, Adelson founded Freedom's Watch, a lobbying group that supports the involvement of the United States in Iraq, a militant stance toward Iran, and Republican candidates for Congress. Freedom's Watch began an advertising campaign in 2007 urging members of Congress, whose support for the Iraq War was wavering, to continue to back the conflict. In 2007, Adelson also began publishing a newspaper, *Israel HaYom* (Israel today), which strongly opposes a two-state solution for the Israel-Palestine dispute and supports Israeli Prime Minister Benjamin Netanyahu.

Since 2000, Adelson's detractors have accused him of corrupt business practices and attempting to influence public policy by buying political influence, although Adelson has been acquitted of several infractions in lawsuits brought against him.

LEGACY

Sheldon Adelson accumulated an enormous fortune because of his business acumen, his ruthlessness (some would say unscrupulousness), his vision, and his willingness to take chances. He realized the potential for trade shows on a massive scale and the advantages of Las Vegas as a venue for these shows. He recognized the future of the gaming industry was in the upscale, family-oriented luxury hotels, and he built one of the first and most profitable of these hotels in Las Vegas. He was among the first to see the potential of the Far Eastern gaming industry and invested heavily in that area of the world.

However, perhaps his most far-reaching legacy is his influence on American policy in the Middle East. His lobbying efforts on behalf of Israel and the policies of Prime Minister Netanyahu will continue to affect the United States' position in that volatile area of the world for generations to come. His generosity has also had a beneficial effect on Jewish education in the United States and on medical research and drug rehabilitation efforts in Israel and America.

—Paul Madden

FURTHER READING

Binkley, Christina. *Winner Takes All: Steve Wynn, Kirk Kerkorian, Gary Loveman, and the Race to Own Las Vegas*. New York: Hyperion, 2008. Focuses on the role of three entrepreneurs instrumental in the transformation of Las Vegas. Devotes relatively little space to Adelson, other than to denigrate his contributions to the building of the "new" Las Vegas.

Fallows, James. *Postcards from Tomorrow Square: Reports from China*. New York: Vintage, 2008. Thirteen articles, most reprinted from the *Atlantic Monthly*. One of the articles, "Macau's Big Gamble," deals with the gambling complex off China's coast, with which Adelson is heavily involved

Gilder, George. *The Israel Test*. New York: Richard Vigilante Books, 2009. A strong endorsement of the beneficial role of the state of Israel in world society and of its prime minister, Benjamin Netanyahu. Expounds virtually the same interpretation of Israel's influence on world history and Netanyahu's policies as Adelson's newspaper. Includes bibliography and endnotes.

Mearsheimer, John J., and Stephen M. Walt. *The Israel Lobby and U.S. Foreign Policy*. New York: Farrar, Straus and Giroux, 2008. A well-documented denunciation of the malign influence of pro-Israel lobbying groups (including Adelson's Freedom's Watch) on American policy in the Middle East. Blames the "Israel lobby" for the Iraq War. Includes bibliographical references.

Smith, John L. *Sharks in the Desert*. New York: Barricade Books, 2005. A history of the Las Vegas casinos expressed through biographies of many of the men who built the gaming industry. Follows the story from the earliest mob-related casinos through the Howard Hughes era to the twenty-first century's corporate giants, including Adelson.

See also: Donald Bren; Leona Helmsley; Kirk Kerkorian; J. Willard Marriott; Jay A. Pritzker; Donald Trump; Steve Wynn.

CLAUDIUS AESOPUS
Roman actor

As the leading tragic actor of his time, Aesopus was able to acquire a vast fortune. He was, however, considered a spendthrift and was seen by later writers as an example of the decadent lifestyle of the rich during the Late Republic.

Born: fl. first century B.C.E.; place unknown
Died: After 55 B.C.E.; place unknown
Also known as: Clodius Aesopus
Sources of wealth: Acting; tutoring
Bequeathal of wealth: Children

EARLY LIFE

Nothing is known of the childhood or early life of Claudius Aesopus (KLOH-dee-uhs ay-SOH-puhs). Ancient writers were concerned with his skill as an actor and his great wealth. His cognomen, Aesopus, has led some scholars to suggest that he had once been a slave. However, it is just as likely that he was born a free Greek and later attained Roman citizenship. The latter is supported in that Cicero, the Roman statesman, would hardly have spoken of Aesopus in such endearing terms had he been of servile origin.

FIRST VENTURES

Much of the information about Aesopus comes from brief accounts in the surviving writings of ancient authors, particularly those of Cicero. According to Cicero, Aesopus was an established tragic actor by 91 B.C.E. and had performed at many state-sponsored theatrical shows. Valerius Maximus states that Aesopus would observe the manners of orators in the forum in order to hone his craft. He was known not only for his strong voice but also for his use of gestures, an important element of any form of public speaking in ancient Rome. Plutarch writes that Aesopus was so passionate an actor that on one occasion he struck and killed an attendant who crossed the stage.

MATURE WEALTH

Aesopus attained his great wealth by performing in plays and as a hired tutor to the up-and-coming statesmen of his day. His acting career reached a high point in 57 B.C.E., when he performed in two separate plays; he modified the lines to garner praise and support for the exiled Cicero. Indeed, Cicero was one of the statesmen who hired Aesopus as a tutor in order to improve his public speaking. The latest mention of Aesopus is contained in a letter to Cicero from his friend Atticus. Atticus states that Aesopus was among the retired actors who performed at the games celebrating the opening of the Theater of Pompey in 55 B.C.E. According to the fifth century C.E. writer Macrobius, Aesopus's estate was worth 20 million sesterces at his death. While such factors as inflation and differences in standards of living make modern dollar equivalents of ancient money untenable, it can be said that Aesopus was certainly among the wealthiest individuals of his time. To put Aesopus's wealth in its proper context, it should be considered that in his time the property qualification for a Roman senator was 800,000 sesterces, and that a day laborer earned approximately 1,000 sesterces a year.

While admired by many for his skill as an actor and tutor, Aesopus was criticized for mismanaging his wealth. Pliny states that he showed no respect for his lavish fortune, serving up dinners worth 100,000 sesterces that featured cooked songbirds costing 6,000 sesterces each. His son, Marcus Clodius Aesopus, continued to squander the family fortune. He was said to have concocted a favorite drink by dissolving an expensive pearl in vinegar.

LEGACY

While actors were generally looked down upon in Roman society, the case of Aesopus demonstrates that the very best not only were in high demand but also were able to attain great wealth, reflecting the popularity of the theater in the Late Republic. They were also sought out as tutors by those, like Cicero, who wished to become important statesmen, thus demonstrating the important reciprocal nature of acting and public speaking in Roman society. The mismanagement of his wealth, however, caused Aesopus to be criticized by his contemporaries as an example of the excesses and decadent lifestyle of the rich.

—*Kevin Birch*

FURTHER READING

Cicero. *Pro Sestio*. Translated by Robert A. Kaster. New York: Oxford University Press, 2006.
Easterling, Pat, and Edith Hall. *Greek and Roman Actors: Aspects of an Ancient Profession*. Cambridge,

England: Cambridge University Press, 2002.

Macrobius. *The Saturnalia*. Translated by Percival Vaughan Davies. New York: Columbia University Press, 1969.

Slater, William J., ed. *Roman Theater and Society:*

E. Togo Salmon Papers I. Ann Arbor: University of Michigan Press, 1996.

See also: Marcus Licinius Crassus; Gaius Maecenas; Roscius.

AGA KHAN I
Ismāʿīlī political and spiritual leader

Aga Khan I, spiritual and political leader of the Ismāʿīlī Shīʿite community of Islam, acquired his wealth from the tithing of his followers, as well as from horseracing and other investments. He used his wealth in a variety of civic and philanthropic ventures to improve the quality of life for his followers in South Asia, the Middle East, and Africa.

Born: 1800; Kahak, Persia (now in Iran)
Died: April, 1881; Bombay (now Mumbai), India
Also known as: Ḥasanʿalī Shāh (birth name);
  Muḥammad Ḥasan
Sources of wealth: Inheritance; church; investments
Bequeathal of wealth: Children

EARLY LIFE
Aga Khan (AH-gah kahn) I was born Ḥasan ʿalī Shāh in Kahak, Persia (now Iran), the son of the forty-fifth Ismāʿīlī imam, Shah Khalil Allah, and Bibi Sarkara, the daughter of a Persian poet. The untimely murder of Khalil Allah in 1817 elevated Aga Khan to the position of forty-sixth imam of the Nizārī Ismāʿīlī Muslims but left the new imam destitute. Aga Khan's mother moved the family to the Persian holy city of Qom and later to Tehran, seeking redress for Shah Khalil's murder by businessmen in Yazd.

Fatḥ ʿAlī Shāh , the shah of Persia, punished the murderers of Khalil Allah, gave Aga Khan's family land in the Mahallat and Kerman regions of Persia, and married Aga Khan to his daughter, Sarv-i Jahān Khānum. Fatḥ ʿAlī Shāh's generosity was based on his fears that the Ismāʿīlīs might seek revenge against him for their imam's murder.

FIRST VENTURES
Ismāʿīlīs are Shīʿite Muslims who believe that the rightful successor to the Prophet Muḥammad must be a blood descendant of the Prophet's daughter, Fāṭimah, whose husband Ali was both the Prophet's cousin and his son-in-law. In 1094, the Ismāʿīlīs split into two branches, the Mustalis and the more numerousNizārīs, as the result of a disagreement over which son of the eleventh imam of the Shīʿite sect should be recognized as the twelfth imam. The Nizārīs accepted blind obedience to their spiritual leader, sanctioning the imams' ruthless murders of political opponents. The Nizārīs came to be called Hashishi (hashish eaters), who consumed the plant before committing political assassinations throughout the Muslim world; the word "assassin" is derived from the word "Hashishi." Their history of violence relegated them to the mountain regions of Syria, Persia, and Afghanistan. In 1256, the Mongols destroyed most of the Nizārīs' Persian followers. The Nizārīs sought converts in Egypt, Africa, and China. Ismāʿīlī converts, called Khojas, settled in western India around Bombay and would eventually become the base of Aga Khan I's followers.

The title Aga Khan I was conferred on Ḥʿalī Shāh by his father-in-law, Fatḥ ʿAlī Shāh. Aga Khan means "lord chief." Aga Khan I governed Mahallat province and was known for his lust for both battles and beautiful women. He was reputed to have fathered more than three thousand children, but only three of his sons were considered legitimate. Light-skinned with a striking appearance, Aga Khan I displayed a gallant manner that masked his ambition.

Aga Khan's refusal to permit the marriage of his daughter to the prime minister of Persia in 1837 caused a rift with the Persian government under the new shah, Aga Khan's brother-in-law. Aga Khan considered the marriage proposal an insult because the prime minister's family was from a lower class. His refusal led to a battle between the Ismāʿīlī and Persian forces in 1838-1840, resulting in a defeat for Aga Khan's troops and his flight to the Sind region (now in Pakistan). While in the Sind, Aga Khan aided the British in the Punjab region of India in their war against the Afghans, fought in 1841-1842. By helping Charles James Napier conquer the Sind in 1843-

1844, Aga Khan was awarded a British pension of 1,000 rupees, or about $500.

Between 1845 and 1848, Aga Khan immigrated to Bombay (now Mumbai), where many Ismāʿīlīs resided, and in 1846 he was declared a political prisoner and re-moved to Calcutta by the British under pressure from the shah of Persia, who feared Aga Khan. Aga Khan returned to Bombay in 1848 after the death of his Persian brother-in-law, Muḥammad Shah Qajar. In Bombay, the Aga Khan established his religious headquarters, or *durkhana*, a place of pilgrimage where his associates and supporters could visit. Aga Khan paid the expenses of more than one thousand dependents, family members, retainers, and a troop of two hundred cavalry.

MATURE WEALTH

The Bombay High Court on November 12, 1866, confirmed the title and rights of Aga Khan I. Under the British raj, Aga Khan was granted princely status with the right to use the initials H. H. (for His Highness) before his name. He resided in the Bombay palaces of Poona and Aga Hall. Aga Khan agreed to take no active part in Indian politics, but he did accept a seat on the Bombay legislative council.

Aga Khan I was widely recognized for his participation in the sports of hawking and breeding hounds, and he maintained a lavish stable of Persian, Arabian, English, and Turkomen racehorses. He successfully took legal action against a rival, more liberal branch of the Ismāʿīlīs, who criticized his morals. Aga Khan reorganized his sect's finances around the practice of tithing (donating 10 percent of income), providing gifts for special occasions, and the ritual of Kahada-Khuaraki, at which large meals for families were auctioned off and the revenue donated to Aga Khan. All of the funds he collected were invested in horses and real estate. Aga Khan died in 1881 and was buried at a shrine in Bombay.

LEGACY

Aga Khan I redefined the image and purpose of Ismāʿīlī Muslims. The expulsion of Aga Khan from Persia, his elevation to princely status by the British, and his shrewd investments led to a complete image makeover for this branch of Shīʿite Muslims. Investments and tithing formed

---

THE AGA KHAN DEVELOPMENT NETWORK AND THE ISMĀʿĪLĪ IMAMAT

The Aga Khan Development Network is a nonprofit organization funded by Aga Khan IV and by donations. The network seeks to improve living conditions and opportunities for poor people in Asia and Africa, regardless of faith, origin, or gender. The organization works in more than twenty-six countries and employs sixty thousand people. Among its projects, the network has brought water to dry regions; funded business enterprises; built medical facilities and nursing schools; and promoted education for Ismāʿīlī Muslims. In the twenty-first century, the network's projects have included financing centers for the study of Islam in Western nations.

The network consists of several agencies, including organizations focusing on microfinance, education services, economic development, health services, planning and building, and culture, as well as Aga Khan University and the University of Central Asia. Each agency is chartered with a specific mandate but is designed to work with the other organizations in order to achieve common goals. The network's budget for 2008 was $450 million; these funds were provided by the Aga Khan Fund for Economic Development, which generates annual revenues of $1.5 billion and reinvests surplus revenue in development projects.

The network was founded by Aga Khan IV, the forty-ninth imam and spiritual leader of the Ismāʿīlīs. Aga Khan IV has led the network for more than fifty years, and he has been instrumental in obtaining funding from national governments, multinational institutions, and private sector organizations. The Ismāʿīlī community contributes volunteer time, professional services, and financial contributions. Although the network initially was established to benefit the Ismāʿīlī Islam community in South Asia and East Africa, the organization has expanded its reach to Egypt, India, Kyrgyzstan, and Mali.

Ismāʿīlī Muslims believe that revelation ceased with the death of the Prophet Muḥammad, but the need for spiritual and moral guidance continues under the leadership of a direct descendant of the Prophet. The Ismāʿīlīs are the second-largest Shīʿite Muslim community, with the largest residing in Iran. Aga Khan IV has emphasized the role of intellect in the realm of faith, maintaining that intellect is revealed through the Prophet Muḥammad and through man's own virtue in remembering that the mind is God's creation. The projects of the Aga Khan Development Network emphasize that God's creation is not static but continues through scientific projects and other endeavors. Aga Khan IV has stated that confronting the challenges of science and ethics is a requirement of the Islamic faith. His guidance provides a liberating framework with which to enable an individual's quest for meaning and to find solutions to problems experienced by Ismāʿīlī Shīʿites in a global age.

the basis of Aga Khan I's wealth, and his fortune was supplemented by silver, gold, and diamond celebrations in which Ismāʿīlīs brought these commodities to match his weight. The funds raised from these celebrations were invested and contributed to Aga Khan's charitable contributions, which were designed to benefit Ismāʿīlīs. In the process, the Ismāʿīlīs under Aga Khan I became an international organization with followers residing in twenty-five countries. With a strengthened religious and political organization, Aga Khan I engaged in humanitarian, educational, and philanthropic endeavors benefiting Ismāʿīlīs on a global stage.

—*William A. Paquette*

FURTHER READING

Aga Khan III. *The Memoirs of Aga Khan*. New York: Simon & Schuster, 1954. A fascinating autobiography written by His Highness Aga Khan III about his life, spiritual leadership of the Ismāʿīlī Muslims, wives, sons, and grandsons.

Ali, Mumtaz Ali Taiddin Sadik. *Genealogy of the Aga Khan*. Karachi, Pakistan: Islamic Book, 1990. The history of the descent of the Aga Khans from the Prophet Muḥammad and the Prophet's son-in-law and cousin, Ali.

Anderson, Stephen E., ed. *Improving Schools Through Teacher Development*. Exton, Pa.: Swets and Zeitlinger, 2002. A series of case studies about the Aga Khan Foundation's projects in East Africa under Aga Khan IV.

Daftary, Farhad. *A Short History of the Ismailis*. Princeton, N.J.: Markus Weiner, 1998. A detailed history about the evolution of the Ismāʿīlī sect of the Muslim faith from the founding of Islam to the present leadership under the Aga Khans.

Dumasia, Naoroji M. *The Aga Khan and His Ancestors*. New Delhi, India: Readworthy, 2008. Provides a biographical and historical sketch of Aga Khan IV and his predecessors, who came from Persia and placed their Ismāʿīlī imam in Bombay, India.

Edwards, Anne. *Throne of Gold: The Lives of the Aga Khans*. New York: William Morrow, 1995. The first major study written by a Westerner about the Aga Khans, their descent from the Prophet Muḥammad, and their wanderings from Egypt to Syria, Persia, and ultimately India.

See also: ʿAbbās the Great; Yaḥyā ibn Khālid al-Barmakī; Hārūn al-Rashīd.

AGAMEMNON
Greek king and military leader

Agamemnon, the king of Mycenae, is a well-known figure in Greek mythology and literature. His fortune, though considerable in its own right for a Homeric king in the Greek epic tradition, has come to symbolize the wealth and power of Mycenaean civilization of the late Bronze Age (c. 1580-1150 B.C.E.).

Born: fl. thirteenth-twelfth century B.C.E.; Greece
Died: fl. thirteenth-twelfth century B.C.E.; Greece
Sources of wealth: Inheritance; conquest
Bequeathal of wealth: Spouse

EARLY LIFE
According to Homeric and Greek mythological traditions, Agamemnon (ag-uh-MEHM-non) belonged to the royal line of Atreus. Hittite records from the fourteenth century B.C.E. attest to a certain Attarssiyas of Ahhiyawa, which may refer to Atreus, Agamemnon's father. Any connection, however, between Agamemnon, or his family, and specific historical figures in the Greek Bronze Age must remain speculative.

FIRST VENTURES
Agamemnon's early wealth would have come from inheritance, as he was the eldest son and heir of Atreus, the king of Mycenae. The historian Thucydides mentioned that Agamemnon's grandfather Pelops had acquired a great fortune in Asia Minor and had settled in Mycenae in the Peloponnese. Unfortunately, the house of Atreus was sullied by a troubled past filled with political intrigue, murder, rape, incest, and religious sacrilege. As a result, Agamemnon and his brother Menelaus found themselves deposed from their home city of Mycenae after the death of their father. Both Agamemnon and Menelaus took refuge in the city of Sparta, where they married the daughters of King Tyndareus. Menelaus married the beautiful Helen, while Agamemnon took the hand of the notorious Clytemnestra. Later, Agamemnon,

with his brother's aid, returned to Mycenae, where he restored his immediate family to power and became king. As ruler of Mycenae, Agamemnon had access to the wealth and resources of one of the richest cities mentioned in Homer's *Iliad* (c. 750 B.C.E.; English translation, 1611).

MATURE WEALTH

Agamemnon was at the height of his wealth and power during the Trojan War, when he was the leader of the Greek expedition sent to retrieve Helen. Throughout Homer's *Iliad*, Agamemnon's epithet is the "Son of Atreus, wide-ruling," from "Mycenae, rich in gold." The epic tradition states that he was able to muster an armada of 1,186 ships from twenty-eight different areas in Greece. Agamemnon himself commanded one hundred of these ships, the largest of any single contingent of Greek heroes. Homer's famous catalog of ships provides evidence that Agamemnon had expanded his control over large areas of the Peloponnese and enjoyed the riches that his increased power provided.

The campaign against the Trojans was long and difficult, lasting for a good part of a decade. During the war's tenth year, a disagreement over the distribution of war booty between Agamemnon and the Greeks' best warrior, Achilles, jeopardized the entire conflict. In an attempt to mollify Achilles' hurt feelings, Agamemnon made the great warrior a substantial gift offering that included seven bronze tripods, twenty shining cauldrons, twelve horses, seven skilled women from the island of Lesbos, and an amount of gold equivalent to the value of five pairs of oxen. These gifts were of enormous value in a premonetary, gift-exchange economy. Eventually, the city of Troy fell, and the Greek heroes left for home. Upon his return to Mycenae, Agamemnon was struck down by his wife, Clytemnestra, and her lover Aegisthus.

LEGACY

For centuries, Agamemnon and Mycenae were relegated to the realm of legend and mythology until the excavations of archaeologist Heinrich Schliemann brought to light the existence of a Bronze Age Greek civilization, which closely resembled in some aspects the civilization described in Homer's epic poems. In 1876, Schliemann, while excavating the city of Mycenae, discovered a group of grave circles containing magnificent objects, including a golden mask of such quality that it prompted Schliemann to exclaim that he had found the tomb of Agamemnon himself. Although modern analysis of Schliemann's finds date the mask and the circle graves to a time earlier than when Agamemnon supposedly lived, the golden artifacts and wealth found at Mycenae have become synonymous with its legendary king.

—*Byron J. Nakamura*

FURTHER READING

Aeschylus. *The Oresteia Trilogy.* Translated by E. D. A. Morshead. Mineola, N.Y.: Dover, 1996.

Gere, Cathy. *The Tomb of Agamemnon.* Cambridge, Mass.: Harvard University Press, 2006.

Homer. *The Iliad.* Translated by Robert Fitzgerald. New York: Oxford University Press, 2008.

McDonald, William A., and Carol G. Thomas. *Progress into the Past: The Rediscovery of Mycenaean Civilization.* 2d ed. Bloomington: University of Indiana Press, 1990.

Schofield, Louise. *The Mycenaeans.* Oxford, England: British Museum Press, 2007.

Wood, Michael. *In Search of the Trojan War.* Rev. ed. Berkeley: University of California Press, 1998.

See also: Hipponicus II; Nicias; Pasion.

GIOVANNI AGNELLI
Italian automobile manufacturer

Agnelli ruled the automaker Fiat, one of Italy's largest companies. As head of the family-run firm for more than forty years, he became a great Italian industrialist, as well as a power broker. He oversaw Fiat's purchase of the Lancia, Maserati, Alfa Romeo, and Ferrari car companies.

Born: March 12, 1921; Turin, Italy
Died: January 24, 2003; Turin, Italy
Also known as: Gianni Agnelli
Sources of wealth: Inheritance; manufacturing; sale of products
Bequeathal of wealth: Spouse; relatives; charity

Giovanni Agnelli with the cars produced by his Fiat factory. (Time & Life Pictures/Getty Images)

EARLY LIFE

Giovanni "Gianni" Agnelli (joh-VAHN-nee jee-AH-nee ag-NEL-lee) was the grandson and namesake of Giovanni Agnelli, the founder of the Italian car company Fiat S.p.A., and the son of industrialist Edoardo Agnelli and Virginia Bourbon del Monte, daughter of an Italian aristocrat. Agnelli attended the Pinerolo Cavalry Academy and studied law at the University of Turin, though he never practiced as an attorney. When Italy entered World War II, Agnelli joined a tank regiment and saw service at the Russian front. Wounded twice in Russia, Agnelli recovered to serve in North Africa. A German officer in North Africa shot Agnelli in the arm during a bar fight over a woman. After Italy surrendered in 1943, Agnelli became a liaison officer with the occupying American forces because of his fluency with English.

FIRST VENTURES

Upon the death of his grandfather in 1945, Agnelli became the head of the family. He began learning the family business under the guidance of Vittorio Valleta, who headed Fiat until an Agnelli could take over the company. Like many Italian industrialists, who combine money with status by marrying into the nobility, Agnelli married Princess Marella Caracciolo of Castagneto, a socialite, in 1953. With a reputation as one of Italy's greatest playboys, Agnelli continued to be involved with other women throughout his marriage, including film star Anita Ekberg and fashion designer Jackie Rogers. He undoubtedly spent a good deal of money in his pursuit of women, while also developing a reputation as a man of exquisite fashion taste.

MATURE WEALTH

In 1963, Agnelli became managing director of Fiat; three years later, he became chairman. One of the major events of his professional life took place in 1966, when he orchestrated a joint venture between Fiat and Soviet automaker AutoVAZ, in which Russia built an automobile plant capable of producing 660,000 cars per year. Much of Agnelli's professional life, however, involved dealing with Italy's powerful trade unions. By appealing directly to Italians, Agnelli broke the power of the unions in the 1980's.

Agnelli spent his money on art, especially paintings, and on fashionable clothes. He could often be found in a custom-made suit designed by the Caraceni fashion house with an expensive wristwatch worn over the cuff. Typical of an automobile magnate, he also loved fast cars, as well as sailing, skiing, and horses. A famous soccer fan, he briefly owned the Italian club Juventus. Agnelli also spent money and time to promote Italy. The city of Turin won the honor of hosting the 2006 Winter Olympics largely because of Agnelli's promotional efforts. In 1991, Agnelli became a senator for life, with the honor serving as tribute to his long service to Italy.

Agnelli succumbed to prostate cancer and died in 2003. As he lay in state in an art gallery that he had recently donated to Turin, more than 100,000 people paid their respects. Agnelli's funeral, broadcast on television, brought thousands of mourners to Turin's cathedral. Agnelli bequeathed his famed collection of paintings to the city of Turin. Fiat remained in Agnelli family hands, though General Motors purchased 20 percent of the company in 2000.

LEGACY

Agnelli provided jobs for Italians in the years after World War II, protecting them from poverty and earning the undying love of many people. To Italians, Agnelli was far more than an industrialist. With his love of fashion, appreciation for beauty, and financial influence, he became symbolic of Italy itself. Italians watched his every move and reacted to his death with tears. His demise was like the death of an Italian king.

For most of Agnelli's lifetime, Fiat held a major share of the Italian car business. In 1990, 75 percent of Italians bought a Fiat. By the time of Agnelli's death, however, only about 33 percent of Italians purchased a Fiat. The company reported a $1.3 billion loss for 2002, and many Italians doubted that Fiat would survive for much longer.

—*Caryn E. Neumann*

FURTHER READING

Fabbrin, Sergio, and Vincent Della Sala, eds. *Italian Politics: Italy Between Europeanization and Domestic Politics*. New York: Berghahn, 2004.

Friedman, Alan. *Agnelli and the Network of Italian Power*. London: Harrap, 1989.

See also: Walter P. Chrysler; Chung Ju Yung; John F. Dodge; Henry Ford; Soichiro Honda; Alfred P. Sloan.

MOHAMMED HUSSEIN ALI AL AMOUDI
Saudi Arabian investor

Born in a small provincial town in Ethiopia, Al Amoudi was ranked by Forbes *magazine in 2010 as the world's sixty-fourth-richest person, with a net worth of $1 billion. Although he is involved in diverse ventures all over the world, his investments constitute a sizable portion of the Ethiopian economy.*

Born: 1946; Dessie, Ethiopia
Also known as: Mohammed Hussein Ali Al Amoudi
Sources of wealth: Construction business; investments; real estate; oil; mining; tourism
Bequeathal of wealth: Relatives; charity

EARLY LIFE

Mohammed Hussein Ali Al Amoudi (moh-HAH-mehd hoo-SAYN ah-LEE ahl ah-MOO-dee) was born in Dessie, Ethiopia, in 1946, the son of a Yemeni father and an Ethiopian mother. He grew up in Weldeya, a small ru-

ral town in Ethiopia, before he moved in 1965 to Saudi Arabia, where he became a citizen.

FIRST VENTURES

In Saudi Arabia, Al Amoudi embarked upon his first business venture. Although the details of his early business remain scanty, it is known that his initial wealth was acquired after he left his job as a cement dealer to become a construction material supplier to a Swedish-operated project for the Saudi defense ministry. Al Amoudi was said to have been a front man for Sultan bin Abdul Aziz al-Saud, the Saudi minister of defense and aviation.

MATURE WEALTH

After his first investments in construction-related businesses in Saudi Arabia, Al Amoudi rapidly branched out into real estate development, the oil and gas industries, mining, agriculture, hotels, and finance. His investments were organized under four conglomerate companies—Corral Group, MIDROC Europe, MIDROC Ethiopia, and ABV Rock Group—and were scattered across the globe, with significant concentration in Sweden, North Africa, the Middle East, and Ethiopia. Preem Petroleum, part of the Corral Group, is the largest integrated petroleum company in Sweden. Svenska Petroleum, Al Amoudi's other Swedish holding, has been engaged in explorations off the West African coast. Corral Morocco Gas and Oil and Corral Oil Company are major players in the gas and oil industries in Morocco and Lebanon, respectively.

However, nowhere do Al Amoudi's investments have as much impact as in Ethiopia, where his MIDROC Ethiopia conglomerate consists of thirty enterprises and business interests and is the largest privately held business in the country. In addition to his extensive control over gold mines and construction-related businesses, Al Amoudi has moved to expand his investments in Ethiopian farms. The Al Amoudi-owned Saudi Star Agricultural Development Company has been negotiating with the Ethiopian government to acquire about 500,000 hectares of agricultural land that would be used to grow food in Ethiopia for Saudi Arabia.

LEGACY

Al Amoudi is a truly self-made billionaire who rose from an impoverished boyhood in a remote district in Ethiopia to become one of the richest men in the world. His far-flung business empire employs more than forty thousand people. He has made generous donations to several charity organizations, including the William J. Clinton Foundation. Al Amoudi sponsors the St. George Football Club, one of the best-known soccer teams in Ethiopia. He has paid the medical expenses of a number of individuals in Ethiopia who needed treatment abroad. The Ethiopian government has awarded him the First Special Millennium Golden Medal for his "exemplary deeds for the de-

velopment of Ethiopia and its people." He has also been honored by King Carl XVI Gustaf of Sweden with the Swedish Royal Order of the Polar Star, and he has been recognized by the World Bank and the U.S. State Department for his support of African development through his investments.

There are persistent reports that Al Amoudi's holdings are partially a front for the Saudi royal family. Al Amoudi has also been accused of using his enormous wealth and close association with the Ethiopian government to force out business competitors and create a virtual monopoly on several lucrative sectors in the Ethiopian economy. In addition, there are allegations that Al Amoudi has been using his considerable wealth and influence to evade regulations and proper scrutiny of his business performance in Ethiopia. His open support for the government in power during the fiercely contested 2005 Ethiopian election has earned him widespread condemnation from opponents of the regime. The few private newspapers in Ethiopia including *The Reporter*, have run a series of articles alleging corruption and inefficient practices in Al Amoudi's business enterprises in that country.

—*Shumet Sishagne*

FURTHER READING

APS Review Gas Market Trends. "Saudi Arabia: The Private Placements." (October 20, 2003).

Kroll, Luisa, and Matthew Miller, eds. "The World's Billionaires." *Forbes* 185 (March 10, 2010).

Rice, Andrew. "A Global Land Grab for Food: Fear of Hunger Drives a Land Grab, Nations Scramble to Buy African Farm Tracts to Secure Food Supplies." *International Herald Tribune*, November 21, 2009, p. 10.

See also: Al-Waleed bin Talal; Mohammed bin Laden; Aliko Dangote.

AL-WALEED BIN TALAL
Saudi Arabian investor

Al-Waleed bin Talal may have been the leading global investor of the last decade of the twentieth and the first decade of the twenty-first century, with substantial holdings in 120 countries. He also was the largest single foreign investor in the United States.

Born: March 7, 1955; Riyadh, Saudi Arabia
Also known as: Al-Waleed bin Talal bin Abdul Aziz Al Saud; Al-Walid bin Talal; Walīd ibn Talāl; Alwaleed
Sources of wealth: Inheritance; investments
Bequeathal of wealth: Relatives; charity; educational institution

EARLY LIFE
Al-Waleed bin Talal (ahl-WAH-leed bihn tah-LAHL) bin Abdul Aziz Al Saud is the son of Prince Talal bin Abdulaziz Al Saud and Princess Mona El-Sohl. Al-Waleed's father was the twenty-first son of King Abdulaziz bin Saud, the founder of modern Saudi Arabia, and Al-Waleed is a royal prince of the Saudi kingdom. (According to Arabic custom, the son takes the name of his father as part of his surname with the prefix "bin" or "ibn.") Princess El-Sohl is the daughter of Riad El-Sohl, the first prime minister of modern Lebanon. Al-Waleed was the oldest of three children born to his parents before they divorced in 1968.

As a result of the divorce, Al-Waleed was raised in both Lebanon and Saudi Arabia, and he has remained attached to both nations, as well as to the United States, where he attended college. He went to the Pinewood and Choueifat Schools in Lebanon, but he was a lackluster student. During this time, however, he did grow more attached to his Islamic faith. At nineteen, he enrolled in Menlo College in Atherton, California, near Stanford University. He also married his cousin, Princess Dalal Al Saud. They had two children, a son Khaled, born on April 12, 1978, and a daughter Reem, born on June 20, 1982.

FIRST VENTURES
In 1979, Al-Waleed returned to Saudi Arabia. For most of human history, the Arabian Peninsula has known little material prosperity. However, in the 1930's American geologists discovered the world's largest oil reserve beneath the area's desert sands. By the 1970's, the oil wealth of the Saudi royal family and its five thousand princes had become legendary. The Saudi economy was booming, and with $30,000 from his father, Al-Waleed set up his first company, the Kingdom Establishment for Trading and Contracting. Al-Waleed also accumulated a steady stream of income from the 5 percent commission that every foreign venture had to pay an Arabian representative in order to do business in the kingdom, a reliable source of revenue for Saudi princes and other well-connected Saudi businessmen. Al-Waleed received commissions from real estate and construction projects.

After earning a master's degree from Syracuse University, Al-Waleed borrowed 1 million riyals (equivalent at this time to about $300,000 in U.S. currency), and he expanded his business ventures by entering the banking sector. In 1986, he acquired control of the unprofitable United Saudi Commercial Bank. He revamped its operations by dismissing some employees and providing incentives to others, and the bank turned a profit within two

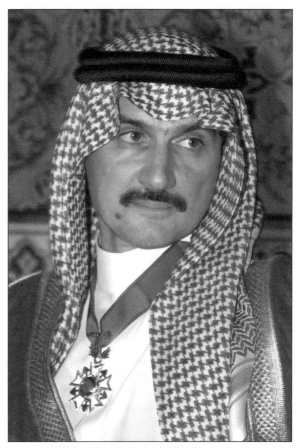

Al-Waleed bin Talal. (AP/Wide World Photos)

15

STOCK MARKETS

In the modern world, there is no greater generator of wealth than the stock market. According to *Forbes* magazine's 2010 list of the world's billionaires, the three richest men accumulated their fortunes through spectacular increases in the value of their core stock holdings: Carlos Slim, with his shares of the Telmex telephone company; Bill Gates, with shares in Microsoft Corporation; and Warren Buffett, with shares in Berkshire Hathaway, Inc. The importance of the stock market reflects the dominance of the corporate model in the modern economy. It also demonstrates the movement of wealth from tangible assets, such as land, cattle, and gold, into financial instruments that can be denominated in stock shares and financial derivatives.

A stock market exchange is a medium that enables investors to buy and sell shares of companies. The rise of the joint-stock company—the first corporation—and the first modern stock exchange occurred simultaneously. The Dutch East India Company was chartered in 1602 in order to sell shares in the company's trade. Stock markets emerged to enable shares or stocks in this company to be exchanged for an agreed upon price. By 1607, one-third of the stock of the Dutch East India Company had been sold to secondary purchasers. In 1609, the Amsterdam Stock Exchange was founded in order to create an orderly secondary market for these shares. With the formation of similar joint-stock companies throughout the world, stock exchanges were created in the world's major financial markets.

Stock markets have been a critical means of raising money for corporations and of capitalizing major industries. Countless fortunes have been made—and lost—in the stock market. Stock markets have seen bubbles, panics, crashes, fraud, and every other spectacle of the modern fluctuating economy. By 2008, the size of the world's stock markets was estimated at more than $37 trillion, with the derivatives market—financial instruments that derive their prices from the price of underlying securities—at more than twenty times that amount, or a staggering $791 trillion. In separating ownership of the company from its management and liability, stock markets have allowed millions of average investors to participate in corporate ownership.

However, dispersing ownership among millions of uncoordinated, "part-time" shareholders can create difficulties. Accountability for the conditions and wages of workers can become attenuated. In addition, in the late twentieth and early twenty-first centuries corporate scandals arose when chief executive officers received hundreds of millions of dollars in compensation from corporate boards of directors and when lawyers collected billions of dollars from companies in which share prices declined or mergers were completed, to the detriment of shareholders.

Al-Waleed bin Talal is one of the most important stock market investors of modern times. As of 2009, he had significant holdings in 120 countries and was the single largest foreign investor in the United States. He has formulated some cardinal rules of investing. He maintains that one should always be patient and should not chase the stock market but should wait until stock prices decline before making investments. He also advises individuals to invest in "liquid" companies—or companies in which stock can be bought and sold easily and rapidly—so an investment can be sold quickly. Each investment should be equal to at least 1 percent of an individual's net worth, even if that net worth is in the billions of dollars, in order to make a significant impact on one's overall investment portfolio.

---

years. He then acquired the Saudi Cairo and Saudi American Banks, as well as the Savola and Al-Azizia Panda food operations. Al-Waleed then turned his attention to the United States, buying $250 million worth of shares in Citibank and Chase Manhattan, Manufacturers Hanover, and Chemical Banks.

MATURE WEALTH

By 1990, Al-Waleed had become a billionaire and the largest investor in the Middle East. That year, he made the most important investment of his career by obtaining 207 million shares of the undercapitalized Citibank at $2.50 a share. In 1991, he invested another $590 million in Citibank, making him its single largest shareholder. He then bought shares of other large American companies, including technology pioneer Apple Computer, Inc. Al-Waleed made a $345 million investment in Euro Disney, giving him a 24 percent stake in this amusement park. He has purchased world-famous hotels, such as the Plaza in New York City, the George V in Paris, and the Fairmont, Four Seasons, and Movenpick hotel chains. He has also invested in the Canary Wharf commercial real estate project in London, the Saks Incorporated retail chain, and Planet Hollywood restaurant and resort chain.

In Saudi Arabia, Al-Waleed's Kingdom Establishment holding company has played a dominant role in the economy. In 1985, he built the Kingdom Tower in Riyadh, a 994-foot-tall building that was the largest skyscraper in the Middle East. This real estate development, valued at 1.7 billion riyals ($453 million), includes the Kingdom Centre, with a shopping mall, a hotel, and an expansive apartment complex. Al-Waleed also constructed the modern Kingdom Hospital at a cost of 400 million riyals ($107 million), the Kingdom School for 330 million riyals ($88 million), and the Kingdom City residential complex for 400 million riyals ($107 million).

In 2005, *Forbes* magazine ranked Al-Waleed the fifth-richest person in the world, with assets of $21.5 billion. His Kingdom Holdings investment portfolio included $11.4 billion in the banking sector, primarily in Citibank. His stake in real estate, hotels, and Saudi Arabian construction projects totaled $4.6 billion. He also had invested $3.1 billion in Euro Disney and other entertainment ventures, including the Arabic recording label Rotana. His stake in the technology and Internet companies Apple Computer, Inc., Hewlett-Packard, Kodak, Motorola, Amazon.com, eBay, and Priceline was more than $1 billion. Al-Waleed was the largest single foreign investor in the United States. His Savola group of food-related investments in Saudi Arabia was worth almost $500 million. In addition, his personal trove of cash, palaces, planes, and boats was worth more than $5 billion. Al-Waleed had slipped to number nineteen in *Forbes* 2010 list of world billionaires, and his estimated net worth had declined to $19.4 billion.

Al-Waleed's wealth raises questions about the source of his fortune. His critics charge that he has made his money through his royal connections. Dan Briody, author of *The Iron Triangle: Inside the Secret World of the Carlyle Group* (2003), improbably suggests that Al-Waleed was a front man for secret government money supplied to him by Saudi defense minister Sultan bin Abdul Aziz. Al-Waleed, however, has insisted that he is essentially a self-made man, providing documentation to support his argument. Although he has conceded the benefits of the start-up money provided by his father and the prestige of his royal name, he has claimed that he earned his billions of dollars through his own investments.

He is certainly a disciplined investor, who has devoted his time and resources to economic research. One of his heroes is the world chess champion Garry Kasparov, whom Al-Waleed admires for his strategic and long-term thinking, qualities which Al-Waleed aimed to duplicate in his investment strategy.

Al-Waleed's status as the world's largest Middle Eastern investor has also generated controversy. After the terrorist attack on of the World Trade Center in New York City on September 11, 2001, he offered a $10 million donation to the Twin Tower Fund, which was rejected by Mayor Rudy Giuliani because of political statements that Al-Waleed had made regarding Middle Eastern politics.

In December, 1994, Al-Waleed divorced Princess Dalal. Two years later, he married Princess Iman Sudairi, but they divorced within a year. Since then, he has been married to two other women. With an annual income of more than $500 million a year, Al-Waleed has been able to live a princely lifestyle. His palace in Riyadh cost hundreds of millions of dollars to build and maintain, with a staff of more than two hundred servants and groundskeepers. The palace measures 460,000 square feet, with 420 rooms, 1,500 tons of Italian marble, exquisite silk carpets, 520 televisions, a forty-five-seat film theater, eight elevators, three swimming pools, a bowling alley, and tennis courts. His 120-acre desert compound outside Riyadh boasts a zoo, a farm, horse stables, and five artificial lakes. He has vacationed in a 283-foot yacht, the *5KR*, off the coast of Cannes, France, tended to by hundreds of employees in power boats. His fleet of personal planes includes a luxurious Boeing 747 jumbo jet; his fleet of cars numbers more than one hundred. In his palace, he stores fifty boxes of jewelry, worth $700 million.

LEGACY

Al-Waleed spends about $100 million a year on charity, which includes building Islamic mosques throughout the world; donating to the needy in Saudi Arabia, Lebanon, and Palestine; and providing disaster relief. He has funded centers in universities in Cairo, Egypt; Beirut, Lebanon; Syracuse, New York; and Exeter, England. In 2005, he donated $20 million each to Georgetown University and Harvard University to establish Islamic study centers.

—Howard Bromberg

FURTHER READING

Appleby, Joyce. *The Relentless Revolution: A History of Capitalism.* New York: Norton, 2010. Surveys the role of corporations, stocks, and stock exchanges in the development of capitalist economies.

Briody, Dan. *The Iron Triangle: Inside the Secret World of the Carlyle Group.* Hoboken, N.J.: John Wiley, 2003. Exposé of the Carlyle private equity investment group. Calls Al-Waleed clownish and an inept investor.

Ferguson, Niall. *The Ascent of Money: A Financial History of the World.* New York: Penguin, 2008. A history of human economies, with a chapter on the rise and role of world stock markets.

Khan, Riz. *Al-Waleed: Businessman, Billionaire, Prince.* New York: William Morrow, 2005. Favorable, authorized biography, with a complete list of Al-Waleed's investments in 2005. Includes an introduction by for-mer president Jimmy Carter and a documentary digital videodisc about Al-Waleed, his lifestyle, and his investments.

See also: Mohammed Hussein Ali Al Amoudi; Moham-med bin Laden; Sultan Hassanal Bolkiah.

EIGHTEENTH DUCHESS OF ALBA
Spanish aristocrat and socialite

The eighteenth duchess of Alba holds more titles than anyone in the world, with more than fifty titles of nobility. The sole heir to her family's fortune, landholdings, palaces, and private collections of art and artifacts, her net wealth is conservatively estimated at $500 million.

Born: March 28, 1926; Madrid, Spain
Also known as: María del Rosario Cayetana Alfonsa Victoria Eugenia Francisca Fitz-James Stuart y Silva (birth name); Cayetana Fitz-James Stuart; Duchess of Alba de Tormes
Sources of wealth: Inheritance; real estate; agricultural products
Bequeathal of wealth: Children

Eighteenth Duchess of Alba. (AFP/Getty Images)

EARLY LIFE
The eighteenth duchess of Alba (AHL-bah) is related by birth to Mary, Queen of Scots; Christopher Columbus; Empress Eugénie of France; and British prime minister Winston Churchill. Her ancestor, María del Pilar de Silva, thirteenth duchess of Alba, was the subject of *The White Duchess* (1795), a noted painting by Spanish artist Francisco de Goya.

Her name at birth was María del Rosario Cayetana Alfonsa Victoria Eugenia Francisca Fitz-James Stuart y Silva. An only child, the duchess's father was the seven-teenth duke of Alba, Don Jacobo Fitz-James Stuart y Falcó, who served as Spain's ambassador to Great Brit-ain during World War II; her mother was María del Rosario de Silva y Gurtubay, the fifteenth duchess of Aliaga and the ninth marchioness of San Vicente del Barco. Known by her nickname Tana, she grew up in an atmosphere of wealth and luxury. She was born in 1926 and lived in the eighteenth century Li-ria Palace in Madrid, which was destroyed during the Spanish Civil War (1936-1939) but subsequently rebuilt.

FIRST VENTURES
In one of the most expensive wed-dings ever, the duchess was mar-ried in 1947 to the duke of Soto-mayor's son, Pedro Luis Martínez de Iroju y Artácoz. The couple had six children, all of whom were titled and made grandees after she became the eighteenth duchess of Alba upon the death of her father in 1953. The duchess's children are all surnamed Fitz-James Stu-art y Martínez de Irujo and include

Carlos, eighteenth duke of Huéscar, born in 1948; Alfonso, duke of Aliaga, born in 1950; Jacobo, count of Siruela, born in 1954; Fernando, marquis of San Vicente del Barco, born in 1959; Cayetano, count of Salvatierra, born in 1963; and María Eugenia, eleventh duchess of Montoro, born in 1968.

Despite marriage and motherhood, the attractive and vivacious duchess was rumored to have engaged in numerous affairs with toreadors and flamenco dancers at her more secluded palaces in Cordoba and Seville. Her husband died of cancer in 1972, and six years later she married a former Jesuit priest and scholar, Jesús Aguirre y Ortiz de Zárate, who was temporarily given the title "duke of Alba." Her second husband and eldest son coadministered the extensive family properties until Zárate's death in 2001.

MATURE WEALTH

A well-known socialite and celebrity, the duchess of Alba has been an intimate of Spain's royalty and nobility. Although troubled late in life with physical problems, she continued to perform extensive charity work and has been a member, officer, and benefactor of many cultural organizations. She owns two agribusinesses, Euro Explotaciones Agrarias and Eurotéchnica Agraria, which have received millions of dollars in government subsidies. She also owns eighty-five thousand acres of land.

The duchess's residence, Liria Palace, features regular public tours of selected family treasures, from which she derives income. The items on display include paintings by Goya, Titian, Rembrandt, Peter Paul Rubens, Fra Angelico, Bartolomé Esteban Murillo, and El Greco. Display cases feature such unique items as the first Bible translated into Spanish, known as the Alba Bible (1430);

King Ferdinand II and Queen Isabella I's marriage certificate; a document freeing Columbus from jail; and crown jewels. Tourists can also view masterpieces of tapestry that drape the walls, priceless porcelain figurines, suits of armor, and the duchess's own collection of perfume bottles.

LEGACY

The duchess planned to marry for a third time when she was eighty years old. Her intended was antiques dealer Alfonso Díez Carabantes, twenty-four years her junior. Her desire became a point of contention among her six children. Three believed she should be allowed to marry; the others, including her eldest son Carlos, the future duke of Alba, opposed the wedding. Although the dukes and duchesses of Alba are exempt from kneeling before the pope and allowed other singular privileges, they are also subject to the Spanish monarchy. Therefore, the duchess must gain permission to marry from King Juan Carlos I. As of June, 2010, the king was against the wedding, but Queen Sofia was in favor of the proposed union, and the issue remained unresolved.

—Jack Ewing

FURTHER READING

Ham, Anthony. *Madrid*. Footscray, Vic.: Lonely Planet, 2008.

Junquera y Matos, José. *Spanish Splendor*. New York: Rizzoli International, 2004.

Rogers, Eamon. *Encyclopedia of Contemporary Spanish Culture*. New York: Routledge, 2001.

See also: Brooke Astor; Doris Duke; Barbara Hutton; Gloria Vanderbilt.

MIGUEL DE ALDAMA
Cuban sugar magnate and investor

The wealthiest Cuban of the nineteenth century, Aldama supported Cuban independence, and for this reason his plantations and mansions were confiscated by the Spanish government.

Born: May 9, 1820; Havana, Cuba
Died: March 15, 1888; Havana, Cuba
Also known as: Miguel de Aldama Alfonso
Sources of wealth: Inheritance; agricultural products; slave trade; investments
Bequeathal of wealth: Children; confiscated

EARLY LIFE
Miguel de Aldama (mee-GEHL day ahl-DAH-muh) Alfonso was the oldest son of Domingo de Aldama, the wealthiest planter in Cuba, and Maria Rosa Alfonso, who came from a wealthy planter family. Cuban sugar was a much desired commodity, and Cuban sugar magnates were among the wealthiest in the Spanish empire. The Aldama family traveled in elaborate stage coaches with uniformed servants and outriders.

As was typical of wealthy Spaniards, the young Aldama received a cosmopolitan education. After instruction at the San Cristobel de Carruguao preparatory school, at age fifteen he was sent to Europe, where he studied in Hamburg, Berlin, Paris, and England. He returned to Cuba at the age of twenty-three. Aldama inherited his parents' estates and was considered to be the wealthiest man in Cuba.

FIRST VENTURES
Aldama owned five large sugar plantations in the Matanzas sugar zone. His Santa Rosa and La Concepcion sugar mills were the most productive in Cuba, encompassing three thousand acres worked by more than two thousand slaves. His Santa Rosa mansion contained more than twenty-five bedrooms and a dining table that seated fifty people. Aldama's revenue from his sugar plantations was estimated at $3 million a year. Aldama used his wealth to initiate enterprising banking ventures. He invested $4.5 million in banks that loaned money against the value of plantations and other properties. He similarly established banks to promote mercantile trade and agricultural production. His loan in 1857 of $3 million financed construction of a 150-mile railroad from Havana to Matanzas to Cardenas, and he became the chief shareholder in the Cuban rail industry.

MATURE WEALTH
Aldama and his father built a splendid mansion, Palacio Aldama, in Havana. Construction started in 1840, and the residence was designed by the Dominican architect Manuel José Carrera. Palacio Aldama featured two adjacent grand stone houses, marble floors, balconies and balustrades made of cast-iron and bronze, and hand-painted tiles. The banquet hall sat one hundred. The great hall featured two magnificent paintings, one of the Pilgrims landing on Plymouth Rock, the other of conquistador Hernán Cortés landing in Mexico. Aldama was an ardent Cuban patriot, who favored Cuba's independence from Spain and supported the ill-fated rebellion of Narciso López in 1851. The magnificence and symbolism of Palacio Aldama might indicate Aldama's hope that the residence would become the executive mansion of a Cuban republic. Aldama was also a patron of Cuban artists and writers.

Aldama's plantations produced about forty-eight thousand 425-pound boxes of white sugar annually. At the peak of his fortune, Aldama was worth about $12 million when the price of Cuban sugar doubled during the Civil War in the United States. Another Cuban rebellion broke out in 1867, prompting brutal repression by Spanish troops, including the pillaging of the Aldama residences. In 1869, Aldama was compelled to go into exile in Europe and New York. He spent the next two decades rallying for Cuban independence, spending about $2 million for this cause. On December 9, 1872, he wrote a letter from Paris in which he declared that all of his slaves in Cuba should be set free.

Settling in New York in 1877, Aldama became the president of the Cuban Revolutionary Committee. In the 1870's, the Spanish government confiscated his property in Cuba, valued at $5 million. Aldama returned to Cuba in 1885 but was unable to regain his property. He died of a liver ailment three years later. The estate he left to his daughters, Rosa and Lola del Monte, was worth only a fraction of his former fortune.

LEGACY
Like George Washington and Simón Bolívar, Aldama was a wealthy man who risked his fortune for independence. It was said that Aldama built Palacio Aldama in the hope that it would become the executive mansion of an independent Cuban republic. However, he was forced to flee Cuba, his wealth was confiscated, and he died in

relative poverty. On January 17, 1956, Cuba issued a postage stamp in his honor. The Palacio Aldama, which since 1987 has housed the Instituto de Historia de Cuba (institute of Cuban history), is considered the most important neoclassical building in Cuba and remains one of Havana's cultural treasures.

—*Howard Bromberg*

FURTHER READING

Chaffin, Tom. *Fatal Glory: Narciso López and the First Clandestine U.S. War Against Cuba.* Baton Rouge: Louisiana State University Press, 2003.

Pedroso, Antonio. *Miguel Aldama.* Havana, Cuba: A. Muniz, 1948.

Williams, Eric. *From Columbus to Castro: The History of the Caribbean, 1492-1969.* New York: Vintage, 1984.

Zanetti, Oscar, and Alejandro Garcia. *Sugar and Railroads: A Cuban History, 1837-1959.* Chapel Hill: University of North Carolina Press, 1998.

See also: Emilio Bacardi; Manuel Calvo; Antonio López y López; José Xifré.

VAGIT ALEKPEROV
Azerbaijani oil magnate

Alekperov began his involvement in the Russian oil business in his teens. He used imagination, aggressiveness, and savvy to move steadily upward in the industry hierarchy before founding one of the world's largest oil companies, becoming enormously rich in the process.

Born: September 1, 1950; Baku, Azerbaijan, Soviet Union
Source of wealth: Oil
Bequeathal of wealth: Unknown

EARLY LIFE

Vagit Alekperov (vah-JEET ah-lehk-PEH-rawf) was the youngest of five children born to an oil worker who died when Alekperov was a child. Alekperov began working at age eighteen at Kaspmorneft, a Caspian Sea oil production facility. While employed as an oil-drilling operator on a platform rig, he attended the Azerbaijan Oil and Chemistry Institute, earning a doctoral degree in 1974.

FIRST VENTURES

Alekperov worked for Kaspmorneft until 1979, moving up from engineer to production director. He then went to work at Surgutneftegaz, a large oil and gas concern in western Siberia, where he rose to a high executive position while earning a reputation as a hydrocarbon energy expert. In 1985, he accepted a job at Bashneft, a Russian oil refining company, where he directed a production facility in Siberia.

Two years later, Alekperov became chief executive at Kogalymneftegaz, an oil and gas facility with enormous reserves but poor production figures. Employing the best business tactics of both capitalism and communism—a capitalistic focus on the bottom line, combined with socialistic concerns for workers' comfort and safety—he quickly increased production of crude oil from 2 million barrels to 240 million barrels. Alekperov's efforts caught the notice of Soviet president Mikhail Gorbachev, who in 1990 appointed Alekperov the nation's deputy minister of oil and gas. In his new position, Alekperov became an outspoken advocate of vertical integration of state-owned industries.

MATURE WEALTH

In 1991, following the Soviet Union's dissolution and the ascent of Boris Yeltsin to the presidency of the new Russian Federation, state industries began to be privatized. Alekperov became president of a huge new oil concern formed from three of Russia's largest energy production associations: Langepasneftegaz, Uraineftegaz, and Kogalymneftegaz. By 1993, when Alekperov resigned his post as deputy minister of oil and gas, the unwieldy company name had been condensed to Lukoil, and the operation had become a private concern.

By 2009, thanks to Alekperov's administration, Lukoil was Russia's largest oil company—and the world's second largest behind Exxon—with more than twenty billion barrels of proven reserves. The fully integrated company, Russia's largest taxpayer, employed more than 100,000 workers who explored, drilled, refined, distributed, and retailed diesel fuel, gasoline, and kerosene. With Alekperov at its helm, Lukoil was the

Vagit Alekperov. (AP/Wide World Photos)

first Russian company to be listed on the London Stock Exchange, and it was later listed on the New York Stock Exchange. Lukoil was also the first Russian firm to acquire an American company, obtaining Getty Petroleum Marketing, Inc., and its thirteen hundred U.S. gas stations in 2000.

Alekperov, who continued to serve as president of Lukoil and was named chairman of the board of directors in 2001, grew extremely wealthy, earning an annual salary of $1.5 million, supplemented by generous bonuses and ownership of a 10 percent block of Lukoil stock. He also owns a $20 million private jet, and according to *Forbes* magazine was the world's fifty-eighth-richest individual, with a net worth $10.6 billion in 2010.

LEGACY

Alekperov and Lukoil became major political and economic forces in Russia, but their success has not always been smooth or without controversy. Alekperov has been accused of using his relationships with local political officials to create difficulties for foreign investors in order to gain shares in oil exploration projects for his company. Both he and his company have suffered setbacks. For ex-

ample, as a result of the Iraq War, Lukoil lost a $2 billion investment in exploration rights in the West Qurna oil fields.

However, Alekperov has managed to survive these allegations and setbacks and continues to build his empire. In the early twenty-first century he diversified his business ventures, moving into banking and media, and Lukoil explored new markets in China and South America.

—*Jack Ewing*

FURTHER READING

Grace, John D. *Russian Oil Supply: Performance and Prospects.* Oxford, England: Oxford University Press, 2005.

Hoffman, David. *The Oligarchs: Wealth and Power in the New Russia.* New York: PublicAffairs Books, 2003.

LeVine, Steve. *The Oil and the Glory: The Pursuit of Empire and Fortune on the Caspian Sea.* New York: Random House, 2007.

See also: George B. Kaiser; David H. Koch; T. Boone Pickens.

ALEXANDER VI
Italian pope

Living in the style of a secular Renaissance prince, Alexander VI disgraced his church by using the Papacy to amass great wealth.

Born: January 1, 1432; Jàtiva, Valencia, Aragon (now in Spain)

Died: August 18, 1503; Rome, Papal States (now in Italy)

Also known as: Rodrigo de Borja y Doms (birth name); Rodrigo Borgia

Sources of wealth: Inheritance; church

Bequeathal of wealth: Relatives; church

EARLY LIFE
Alexander VI was born Rodrigo Borja y Doms (rod-REE-goh BOR-jah ee doms), the favorite nephew of Pope Calixtus III. Borja's uncle adopted him, appointed him to numerous church positions, and sent him to the University of Bologna to study law.

FIRST VENTURES
When Borgia was twenty-five, Calixtus named his nephew a cardinal-deacon, and the next year Borgia was appointed vice chancellor of the church. Borgia held this lucrative position until his own elevation to the position of pope in 1492. In 1476, he was appointed bishop of Porto, and he was made dean of the Sacred College of Rome.

Despite his ordination to the priesthood, Borgia remained preoccupied with the accumulation of wealth, as well as the welfare of his family. A handsome man, known for his charm and love of frivolity, he fathered several children with several mistresses. He lived in a magnificent style, indulging his love of cardplaying and revelry.

MATURE WEALTH
Borgia was elected pope by a two-thirds majority on August 11, 1492, amid allegations, never substantiated, that he had bribed several cardinals to vote in his favor. He took the name Alexander to honor the pagan conqueror Alexander the Great, as well as the five previous popes with the same name. Intelligent and eloquent, he restored order to the city of Rome, which had been the scene of considerable violence and more than two hundred assassinations before he as-

sumed the papacy. He ruled skillfully, constructing a plan to reform church administration. Deeply superstitious, in the manner of his time, he consulted astrologers and feared evil omens. However, his theology was orthodox Catholicism, and it was rumored that he prayed all day and caroused all night. His interests remained family, wealth, women, and the Church—in that order.

Alexander used the Papacy to advance the interests of his children, not only to help them but also to strengthen his own political power. His son Cesare Borgia, though only eighteen at the time, was consecrated bishop of several wealthy sees, and at nineteen was appointed a cardinal. Cesare's political intrigues would inspire Niccolò Machiavelli's political treatise, *Il principe* (wr. 1513, pb. 1532; *The Prince*, 1640).

Alexander also arranged three lucrative and politically influential marriages for his daughter Lucrezia Borgia, a celebrated beauty. He betrothed Lucrezia to

Alexander VI.

Giovanni Sforza, a member of the powerful family who ruled Milan, hoping that this union would connect the Sforzas and the Borgias. When Alexander no longer had political use for this marriage, he annulled it and arranged for Lucrezia to marry the son of the king of Naples, who was killed in 1501. Alexander then married his daughter to Duke Alfonso I of Ferrera, hoping that this union would further his political power in the Romagna region of Italy. To this end, Alexander encouraged his son Cesare to establish a powerful principality in the Romagna, the most politically contentious area of the Papal States.

Alexander declared a jubilee year in 1500, sending pilgrims and their gold flocking to Rome. The Church's sale of indulgences financed building projects, in addition to Cesare Borgia's military exploits. After crushing powerful Roman families, the Borgias seized their estates. Fortunes were further augmented by strategic assassinations and simony, the selling of church offices. Although the Borgias were rumored to be Marranos— Sephardic Jews who had converted to Christianity— Alexander freely confiscated possessions from Jews who had settled in Rome after their expulsion from Spain.

The pope found ways to increase his wealth at every turn, even stockpiling wheat and selling contracts to work alum mines. For a price, he issued dispensations to princes wishing to annul inconvenient marriages. He created new positions for cardinals, sometimes charging the recipients as much as 25,000 gold ducats. Although his lavish banquets, tournaments, and spectacles—not to mention the exploits of his children—were costly, the pope indulged himself fully. Because it was impossible to separate Borgia personal wealth from that of the Church, nobody has ever fully calculated his total fortune.

Alexander's abuses did not escape notice. Johann Burckard, a papal official, kept a detailed diary of the activities that transpired during Alexander's term as pope, and the document was useful for later biographers and historians. A more contemporary threat was the Florentine friar Girolamo Savonarola, who denounced the licentiousness and criminality of the pope, calling for a council to depose him. Although Savonarola was executed in 1498, the decadence of the papal court under the Borgias would prove a powerful weapon for the leaders of the Reformation that would soon divide Western Christendom.

Alongside his moral laxness and financial abuses, Alexander was one of his era's most significant art patrons, using some of the Papacy's money to hire artists who beautified the Vatican. He employed painters and architects to rehabilitate the Borgo Nuovo, the region around the Vatican. Alexander commissioned Michelangelo to design the rebuilding of St. Peter's Cathedral and employed architect Donato Bramante to build the Tempietto, a commemorative martyrium in the courtyard of the church of San Pietro in Montorio. The painter Pinturichhio decorated many of the Vatican's new and rebuilt apartments, creating a famous portrait of Alexander kneeling in adoration of the miracle of the Resurrection. Alexander's patronage also enabled Michelangelo to complete the *Pietà*, his sculptural depiction of Mary holding Jesus after the Crucifixion.

Alexander became seriously ill during a banquet he attended in 1503 and died shortly thereafter on August 18. Although it was rumored that he had been poisoned, modern scholars generally believe that he succumbed to a plague.

LEGACY

Most Catholic historians designate the reign of Alexander VI as the lowest point in papal history, pointing to his financial corruption, immoral behavior, and political machinations. Still, Alexander's career was not without achievements. He reformed monasteries and encouraged Christian missions to the New World.

Of even greater significance was his patronage of painting and architecture. He restored Castel Sant'Angelo, which remains one of the architectural treasures of Rome. He hired prominent architects to design buildings in the Vatican and financed the work of Michelangelo and the painter Pinturicchio, among other artists. There have been more saintly popes than Alexander, but few popes have left so large an imprint upon the world's great art.

—*Allene Phy-Olsen*

FURTHER READING

Cloulas, Ivan. *The Borgias*. Translated by Gilda Roberts. New York: Franklin Watts, 1989.

Hibbert, Christopher. *The Borgias and their Enemies: 1431-1419*. New York: Houghton Mifflin Harcourt, 2008.

Johnson, Marion. *The Borgias*. New York: Penguin, 2002.

See also: Scipione Borghese; Agostino Chigi; Giovanni de' Medici; Lorenzo de' Medici; Jacopo de' Pazzi; Filippo Strozzi.

PAUL ALLEN
American computer engineer, investor, and philanthropist

Allen left college to pursue his dream of technology and computers with his school friend Bill Gates. Together they changed how individuals communicate by founding Microsoft Corporation, a company that developed software for personal computers. Allen later became a multibillionaire well known for his business ventures and philanthropic support of diverse groups.

Born: January 21, 1953; Seattle, Washington
Also known as: Paul Gardner Allen
Sources of wealth: Computer industry; sale of products; investments; sports franchise
Bequeathal of wealth: Charity; educational institution; medical research

EARLY LIFE
Paul Gardner Allen was born in 1953 to Kenneth S. and Faye Gardner Allen, hardworking people from humble backgrounds. Kenneth worked as an assistant director in the University of Washington library, while Faye taught elementary school. By the time Allen was born, they had achieved a comfortable middle-class status. Allen and his father enjoyed watching sports. Allen also loved to build model airplanes and perform science experiments; he wanted to know how things worked. His appreciation of music, especially of rocker Jimi Hendrix, would grow stronger over time. Allen attended Lakeside, a prestigious private preparatory school, where he shared an interest in computer programming with another student, Bill Gates. Allen was two years older and tall, while Gates was younger, shorter, and came from a privileged family background. With several other young men, they established the Lakeside Programmers Group.

FIRST VENTURES
Allen had a vision of linking people in what he termed a "wired world." After graduating from high school in 1971, he attended Washington State University for two years before dropping out to pursue his dream with Gates. Allen and Gates wanted to develop computer software for the new personal computers. They pooled their funds of about $360 to purchase an Intel 8008 chip in order to build a computer that provided traffic volume count analysis, a method of tracking the number of vehicles crossing a given location. Soon the young entrepreneurs started a computer company called Traf-O-Data to sell computers to users employed in traffic departments.

They decided to close this company but would later use their technology in another way.

Allen worked for Honeywell International, Inc., as a computer programmer when Gates became a student at Harvard University. Allen read a cover story in *Popular Electronics* about the Altair 8800, one of the earliest successful personal computers that was developed by Micro Instrumentation and Telemetry Systems (MITS). Allen saw the potential in this microcomputer. He and Gates cowrote a Beginner's All-Purpose Symbolic Instruction Code (BASIC) software program for personal computers and started a new company, Micro Soft, in 1975, later changed to Microsoft. MITS started selling their software program.

Microsoft was incorporated in 1981. Allen led the technology side, while Gates negotiated contracts with business prospects. Microsoft was soon serving well-

Paul Allen. (AP/Wide World Photos)

known clients, such as Radio Shack, Texas Instruments, and Apple Computer, Inc., and the firm had sales of more than $1 million.

MATURE WEALTH

In 1980, Allen and Gates were contacted by International Business Machines (IBM) about programming for IBM's personal computers. About the same time, Microsoft purchased a computer operating system called Q-DOS for $59,000. Gates and Allen would further develop this system as MS-DOS, a universal personal computer operating system that became the primary product of choice at IBM. Around this time, Allen headed Microsoft's research and development efforts, helping to create the company's Microsoft Word software and Microsoft Windows operating system.

In 1982, Allen was diagnosed with Hodgkin's disease, a form of cancer that develops in the lymphatic system. Although he still worked in a limited way, he decided to retire from Microsoft in 1983. He spent time with his family and did the activities he loved, such as traveling and yachting. Allen continued to serve on Microsoft's board of directors and held a 13 percent interest in the company's stock. In 1985, his wealth was reported at $150 million, and before long his interest in Microsoft made him a billionaire. He resigned from Microsoft's board in 2000.

A knowledgeable investor, Allen bought stock in high-tech companies and other corporations, including America Online, CNET, USA Networks, Priceline.com, and Ticketmaster, and continued to hold stock in Microsoft. Some of his investments and business ventures paid off, while others did not. For example, Allen invested about $170 million in the Ticketmaster company and later sold it in 2002 for $586 million. In 1994, Allen spent $500 million to obtain a 24 percent interest in DreamWorks SKG, an American film and television studio cofounded by director Steven Spielberg. Allen's investment in the company soared to about $675 million within ten years, and some estimate that his share in DreamWorks may be worth as much as $900 million.

THE ALLEN INSTITUTE FOR BRAIN SCIENCE

The Allen Institute for Brain Science is a nonprofit medical research organization located in Seattle, Washington. Paul Allen, the cofounder of Microsoft Corporation, established the institute in 2003. The organization seeks to discover the workings of the brain and the brain's relationship to genes and to disease. Some of the institute's research focuses on understanding the brain's function in respect to cognition, language, emotion, and memory. In 2009, the institute was conducting research on genetic diversity in mice, transgenic mice, the human cortex, and sleep.

Allen's donation of $100 million to this research organization demonstrates his tendency to invest in what he terms "venture philanthropy," or major nonprofit efforts that reflect his passions and interests. Allen recognized that the government probably would not finance research connecting computer science with neuroscience and genomics, so he provided the seed money for the effort. The institute has since obtained additional contributions and solicits private and public donations and collaborations in order to fulfill its mission.

The Allen Institute for Brain Science provides free information for scientists, research hospitals, universities, and pharmaceutical and biotechnology companies. The organization's initial project was the development of the Allen Brain Atlas, an electronic database of gene expression in the mouse brain. In 2006, *Time* magazine listed the atlas as one of the top ten medical breakthroughs for the year. The atlas's Web site at http://www.brain-map.org enables users to assess the Allen Mouse Brain Atlas; Allen Developing Brain Atlas; and Allen Spinal Cord Atlas, a map of gene expression in the spinal cords of juvenile and adult mice. To create the atlas, researchers and scientists studied scans of ultrathin slices of brain tissue from mice and mapped every gene in a mouse's brain. These scans track the cellular level of more than twenty thousand genes in order to help scientists discover how the genes are turned on in various areas of the brain. Teachers can use the resources on the atlas's Web site to teach students about brain anatomy. Resources include a three-dimensional model to investigate the mouse brain and to view genome expression data in a virtual laboratory.

In 1993, Allen founded Starwave, a software and Web site company. Five years later, he sold this company to the Walt Disney Company for around $200 million. Allen owns Vulcan, Inc., which he founded with Jo Allen Patton in 1986. This multifaceted company seeks to change the world by improving people's quality of life through creativity. Vulcan has produced independent films, advocated the need for a sustainable environment, created interactive museums, and helped the community through the Paul G. Allen Family Foundation. In addition, Allen built the Experience Music Project and Science Fiction Museum and Hall of Fame in Seattle at a cost of around $240 million. Among other features, the museum contains exhibits about Jimi Hendrix and Michael Jackson.

Allen enjoys his passions and pays for them. In 2003, he spent about $2 million for *Octopus*, a 416-foot yacht complete with its own permanent crew. *Octopus* is the fourth largest yacht in the world and contains two helicopters, a submarine, a music recording studio, and an ocean floor crawling vehicle. Allen also collects aircraft, such as his two Boeing 757's, and he spent $20 million to construct SpaceShipOne, the first privately owned rocket. His love of sports can be seen in his purchase of two franchises—the National Basketball Association's Portland Trail Blazers and the National Football League's Seattle Seahawks. His financial return on the Trail Blazers has been less than desired. After the team lost about $100 million in a single season, Allen revamped its management and sold players to create a better team.

In 2005, Allen's fortune was recorded at $20 billion, although by some estimates he has been worth as much as $30 billion. He suffered losses in the 2008 recession, and, according to *Forbes* magazine, his net worth was $13.5 billion in 2010, making him the thirty-seventh-richest person in the world and the tenth-wealthiest person in the United States.

In 2009, Allen was single and lived with his mother and sister in a forty-thousand-square-foot home on an almost eight-acre private retreat on Mercer Island, his hometown; his home is valued at $121 million. He is a guitarist and plays in a local band. Allen is known as a private man who rarely interacts with the media. In November, 2009, Vulcan, Inc., announced that Allen had been diagnosed with non-Hodgkin's lymphoma and had begun chemotherapy. Like Hodgkin's lymphoma, for which Allen was treated in the 1980's, non-Hodgkin's lymphoma is a cancer of the lymphatic system.

LEGACY

Paul Allen was one of the pioneers of the personal computer industry, creating software and operating systems that would eventually be used by millions of people worldwide. He is also a generous philanthropist. For example, in 2003, he gave $100 million to the Allen Institute for Brain Science. The following year, Allen consolidated six charitable organizations into the Paul G. Allen Family Foundation, which has made donations of around $1 billion. According to some estimates, the foundation makes annual contributions of around $30 million. Allen also provided $5 million to the New Mexico Museum of Natural History and Science in Albuquerque in order to establish a microcomputer exhibit.

—*Marylane Wade Koch*

FURTHER READING

Armstrong, David, and Peter Newcomb, eds. "The Four Hundred Richest Americans." *Forbes*, September 24, 2004. Details the year's wealthiest Americans, with Microsoft cofounders Bill Gates at number one and Allen at number three.

Forbes. "The World's Billionaires, 2010," March 10, 2010. Provides basic information about Allen, estimating his wealth at $13.5 billion.

Greene, Jay, and Ron Grover. "The $12 Billion Education of Paul Allen." *BusinessWeek*, no. 3881 (May 3, 2004): 96-100. Explains Allen's many losses and bad investments, with insights into how he changed to a more conservative investment approach.

Heim, Kristi. "Passion for Arts and Science Drives Paul Allen's Eclectic Approach." *Seattle Times*, July 29, 2007. Discusses Allen's philanthropic passions for the arts and sciences and the diversity of his donations. Allen often provides donations in the Pacific Northwest area.

Linn, Allison. "Paul Allen's Ventures Often Start with the Question, 'What Do I Love?'" *Deseret News*, January 16, 2005. Gives specific examples of how Allen's diverse choices of business ventures reflect his answer to the one question, "What do I love?"

Rich, Laura. *The Accidental Zillionaire: Demystifying Paul Allen*. Hoboken, N.J.: John Wiley & Sons, 2002. Provides details about Allen's early and adult lives that give the reader insights into this quiet, media-shy billionaire. Depicts Allen as integral to Microsoft's success.

See also: Steven Ballmer; Jeff Bezos; Sergey Brin; Mark Cuban; Michael Dell; Larry Ellison; Bill Gates; Steve Jobs; Gordon E. Moore; David Packard; H. Ross Perot.

NUNO ÁLVARES PEREIRA
Portuguese military leader, aristocrat, and saint

A member of Galician nobility and a national hero of Portugal, Álvares Pereira was richly rewarded for outstanding military exploits that helped secure his country's independence from Spain. He was also the progenitor of the house of Bragança, which later ruled Portugal and Brazil.

Born: July 24, 1360; Bomjardim, Portugal
Died: April 1, 1431; Lisbon, Portugal
Also known as: Holy Constable; Brother Nuno of St. Mary; Saint Friar Nuno de Santa Maria Álvares Pereira
Source of wealth: Government
Bequeathal of wealth: Charity; dissipated

EARLY LIFE
Nuno Álvares Pereira (NOO-noh AL-var-ehz peh-RAY-ee-ruh) was the grandson of Gonçalo Pereira, the archbishop of Braga. Nuno was illegitimate, one of the many children of Álvaro Gonçalves Pereira, the grand prior of Crato. As an infant, Nuno was legitimized by royal fiat to enable him to receive an education appropriate for nobility.

At the age of thirteen, Álvares Pereira joined the army and quickly proved to be a brilliant, fearless tactician during running battles with invading Castilian forces. He was shortly thereafter made a knight of the realm, and he became a model of knightly virtue. At age sixteen, Álvares Pereira married a widow, Leonor de Alvim, daughter of João Pires de Alvim. The couple had two sons, who died when they were young, and a daughter, Beatriz, who survived to adulthood.

FIRST VENTURES
Upon the death of King Ferdinand I in 1383, Portugal was plunged into civil war. The population was divided between two possible successors: Fernando's daughter Beatrice, wife of King John I of Castile, and Fernando's brother John of Aviz, grand master of the Knights of Aviz. Álvares Pereira, who supported John of Aviz, was appointed a constable (commander) of Portuguese forces, and in this position he succeeded in fending off incursions by Castilians who disputed John of Aviz's succession. Greatly outnumbered, Álvares Pereira decisively defeated Castilian troops in several confrontations that culminated in an overwhelming victory in 1385 at the Battle of Aljubarrota, which secured Portuguese independence.

After ascending to the throne, John of Aviz (now King John I) named Álvares Pereira the third count of Ourém, second count of Arraiolos, and seventh count of Barcelos. Each hereditary title came with lands, castles and palaces, and their contents—prizes of great value.

MATURE WEALTH
Álvares Pereira continued to serve John I as military commander until 1411, when the Treaty of Ayton-Segovia ended the war between Portugal and Castile and Castile recognized John as Portugal's undisputed monarch. A devout Catholic often witnessed praying on the battlefield, Álvares Pereira was known for his religious devotion and exemplary lifestyle. He used much of his wealth to construct churches in Souzel, Monsaraz, Carmante, and other places. He erected a massive monastery in Lisbon, and he began construction of the magnificent Gothic-style Batalha Monastery.

After his wife died in 1387, Álvares Pereira did not remarry. In 1401, he gave the hand of his daughter, Beatriz, in marriage to Afonso, the son of John I and the duke of Bragança. After peace was restored to Portugal in 1411, Álvares Pereira began to give away his possessions to the needy, military veterans, and friends. In 1423, he renounced his titles and divested his remaining wealth to take vows as a monk, Brother Nuno of St. Mary, at the Carmelite monastery he founded in Lisbon. He died and was buried there eight years later, at the age of seventy.

LEGACY
Nuno Álvares Pereira's immense treasure was willingly scattered by his own hand. The monastery he built in Lisbon was destroyed in the great earthquake of 1755, though other churches he constructed remained standing into the twenty-first century. His influence was of incalculable value to Portuguese history. Through his daughter Beatriz and her husband Duke Afonso, the house of Bragança was established. Bragança descendants would reign in Portugal from 1640 to 1910 and in Brazil from 1815 to 1889, and the house would be well represented in other European royal dynasties.

From his time to the early twenty-first century, Álvares Pereira has been honored as a hero in Portugal. The faithful attested to miracles associated with him, and a movement to have him declared a saint arose after his death. In 1918, Pope Benedict XV beatified Álvares

Pereira, and in 2008, Pope Benedict XVI proclaimed him Saint Friar Nuno de Santa Maria Álvares Pereira. His feast day is November 6.

—*Jack Ewing*

FURTHER READING
Camões, Luís de. *The Lusiads*. Translated with an introduction and note by Landeg White. Reprint. Oxford, England: Oxford University Press, 2008.

Disney, A. R. *A History of Portugal and the Portuguese Empire: From Beginnings to 1807*. Vol. 1. Cambridge, England: Cambridge University Press, 2009.
Gomez, Rita Costa. *The Making of a Court Society: Kings and Nobles in Late Medieval Portugal*. Cambridge, England: Cambridge University Press, 2003.

See also: Diego Hurtado de Mendoza; Seventh Duke of Medina Sidonia; Juan Antonio Corzo Vicentelo.

MUKESH AMBANI
Indian entrepreneur and industrialist

As the chairman and largest shareholder of Reliance Industries, Limited, Ambani greatly expanded this company founded by his father. He became the wealthiest man in the world in 2007, the first Indian to claim that title.

Born: April 19, 1957; Aden, Yemen
Also known as: Mukesh Dhirubhai Ambani
Sources of wealth: Inheritance; oil; manufacturing
Bequeathal of wealth: Unknown

EARLY LIFE
Mukesh Dhirubhai Ambani (mew-KESH dihr-OB-hi ahm-BAH-nee) was born in Aden, Yemen, in 1957, to Gujarati-speaking Hindu parents who soon moved to Mumbai, India. The next year, his father, Dhirubhai Ambani, established a small spice-trading company that eventually became a yarn manufacturer and then Reliance Industries. The family lived in a modest tenement apartment, and Ambani learned frugal habits that would stay with him into adulthood.

By the late 1960's, the business was thriving and the family moved to a wealthy neighborhood, but Ambani and his siblings were never pampered. Their father, who had not completed high school, insisted that they be educated and that they use public transportation and learn the everyday skills that working-class people need for survival. Ambani attended the Abaay Morischa School in Mumbai, and he then completed a bachelor's degree in chemical engineering at Mumbia's University Institute of Chemical Technology. The family spoke Gujarati at home—a habit Ambani never abandoned.

FIRST VENTURES
As the oldest son in a traditional patriarchal culture, Ambani was always heir apparent and was groomed to succeed his father. He was named a member of the board of directors of the ever-diversifying and expanding Reliance Industries while still in his late teens. In 1979, Ambani began a master of business administration program at Stanford University in California. When he was only halfway through the program, his father, who believed that business education was best obtained through working in business, called him home to set up a yarn factory in a small village. This was no small venture: Ambani, Sr., gave his son the equivalent of $100 million to start the project, sure that he could make a success of it. Ambani showed a talent for management and a willingness to involve himself in the gritty details that helped build loyalty among his workers. Under his guidance, the yarn business led to the manufacture of polyester fibers, which led to the development of a petrochemical business.

MATURE WEALTH
Dhirubhai Ambani was a legend, widely admired and beloved because he was seen to have succeeded through hard work and honorable dealings. When he died in 2002, Reliance Industries was a huge, publicly owned multinational corporation, dealing in industrial manufacturing, petrochemicals, electrical power, banking, biotechnology, and communications technology. After the founder's death, Ambani and his brother Anil fought for control of the company until their mother, a major stockholder, stepped in and divided the company into two independent entities. Ambani became chairman, managing director, and the largest shareholder of Reliance Industries, the largest business in India.

More reform-minded than his father or his brother, Ambani undertook enormous projects to help meet the energy demands of India's growing middle class and to

Mukesh Ambani. (AP/Wide World Photos)

help combat the enduring poverty of the lower classes. He engaged in deep-water offshore exploration for oil and natural gas to reduce the amount of energy India needs to import, and he built the world's largest oil refinery, part of a $6 billion complex at Jamnagar, in the state of Gujarat. He established a network of grocery stores and other retail stores to help poor farmers find markets for their goods and create jobs for middle-class merchants. These projects had significant social effects on the developing nation, while making handsome profits for Reliance. Ambani also owned the Mumbai Indians cricket team.

LEGACY

Ambani is often said to be the face of an emerging Indian capitalism. His derives his wealth from such modern industries as petrochemicals, telecommunications industries, and online gambling—and from success in the stock market. By reaching the top of the list of the world's wealthiest people, and by being ranked among the most respected business leaders in the world, he has inspired other Indians to believe that they—and their country—can succeed in the twenty-first century.

—*Cynthia A. Bily*

FURTHER READING

Forbes, Nausaud, and David Wield. *From Followers to Leaders: Managing Technology and Innovation in Newly Industrializing Countries.* New York: Routledge, 2002.

Hiscock, Geoff. *India's Global Wealth Club: The Stunning Rise of Its Billionaires and Their Secrets of Success.* Hoboken, N.J.: Wiley, 2007.

Khanna, Tarun. *Billions of Entrepreneurs: How China and India Are Reshaping Their Futures—and Yours.* Cambridge, Mass.: Harvard Business Press, 2007.

See also: Ghanshyam Das Birla; Jamsetji Tata.

AMENHOTEP III
Egyptian royalty

Amenhotep III's wealth reflects ancient Egypt at the apex of its power and prestige throughout the ancient Near East.

Born: c. 1403 B.C.E.; Thebes, Egypt
Died: c. 1349 B.C.E.; Thebes, Egypt
Also known as: Amenhophis III; Amenhotep the Magnificient; Nubmaatre
Sources of wealth: Inheritance; trade
Bequeathal of wealth: Children

EARLY LIFE

Amenhotep (ah-mehn-HOH-tehp) III inherited the throne of ancient Egypt from his father, Thutmose IV, whose reign had continued the successful policies of conquest and diplomacy that typified the vibrant Eighteenth Dynasty. At the time of Amenhotep's accession, Egypt stood at the head of an empire that included Egyptian outposts, tributary states, and closely aligned kingdoms directly bordering Egypt in Africa and extending into a significant portion of southwestern Asia. The extent of Egypt's domination can be attributed mostly to Amenhotep's great-grandfather, Thutmose III, whose conquests progressed up the Levantine coastline and concluded on the upper reaches of the Euphrates River in northern Mesopotamia. Following Thutmose III's successes, Amenhotep II and Thutmose IV (Amenhotep's grandfather and father, respectively) maintained Egypt's hold on these territories militarily and opened successful diplomacy with outlying regions that included the powerful Mesopotamian kingdom of Mitanni.

FIRST VENTURES

It is generally understood that Amenhotep was young when he began his reign, possibly as young as two and as old as twelve years of age. The stability of Egypt's empire at the time allowed him to enjoy a rule that lasted more than three decades and to live a luxurious life with little regard to military activity, concentrating his attentions on pleasurable activities. His marriage to a commoner, Queen Tiy, most certainly provided him the support of her family, which included several powerful figures in the Egyptian military. His wealth was based primarily on the religious understanding that the Pharaoh was the physical embodiment of the god Horus and therefore the master of all of Egypt and its resources. However, his wealth was augmented by the flood of goods that entered Egypt as a result of its extraterritorial holdings and network of allied states whose kings were referred to as "brothers."

MATURE WEALTH

While it is impossible to calculate precisely how wealthy Amenhotep III was, there are numerous indications of his estimable wealth from various sources. The breadth of his building program throughout Egypt attests to the extensive available resources of both materials and man-

A mural depicting Amenhotep III. (De Agostini/Getty Images)

power that enabled him to leave his mark on the land—only hints of which still survive. However, those that survive include the monumental twin statues (commonly known as the Colossi of Memnon), which served as guardian figures to his memorial temple (now completely dismantled), which was said to have had "floors adorned with silver and all its doors with fine gold." He made extensive additions to the Temple of Amun at Karnak, which still stands as a testament to the grandeur of the age. In addition, the numerous discarded artifacts at Malkata, his palace complex near Thebes, indicate that the property covered no less than eighty acres. Commemorative scarabs found throughout the ancient Near East detail the killing of 102 "fierce lions" in just one of the several hunting expeditions that he enjoyed as a young man. Diplomatic marriages filled his harem with the sisters and daughters of the kings of Mitanni, Babylon (both in Mesopotamia), and Arzawa (in Anatolia). More explicit testimony regarding his wealth was provided by Tushratta, king of Mitanni, who noted that "in my brother's land gold is as plentiful as dust." The truth of such a statement is suggested by the staggering wealth of grave goods retrieved in 1922 from the tomb of Tutankhamen, the boy-king who ascended to the throne less than twenty years following Amenhotep's death.

LEGACY

Amenhotep III's reign marked the high point of ancient Egypt's power. The wealth he enjoyed provided the eco-nomic basis for the reign of his son, Amenhotep IV, better known as Akhenaton, who famously attempted to impose the singular worship of the Aten (the disc of the Sun). As reflected in the diplomatic correspondence recovered from his capital at Amarna, Akhenaton's preoccupation with establishing his religious reforms kept him from responding to various challenges to Egypt's domination in the Levant. Nevertheless, Akhenaton's activities were well supported by his father's accumulated wealth, despite the troubles Egypt experienced in its larger empire. The richness of Amenhotep III's reign, though diminished by Akhenaton's inattention and Tutankhamen's minority, bridged the gap until Ramesses II of the Nineteenth Dynasty restored the basis for Egypt's international prominence.

—Carlis White

FURTHER READING

Fletcher, Joann. *Chronicle of a Pharaoh: The Intimate Life of Amenhotep III*. New York: Oxford University Press, 2000.

Giles, Frederick John. *The Amarna Age: Egypt*. Warminster, England: Aris and Phillips, 2001.

Shaw, Ian, ed. *The Oxford History of Ancient Egypt*. New York: Oxford University Press, 2000.

Watterson, Barbara. *Amarna: Ancient Egypt's Age of Revolution*. Charleston, S.C.: Tempus, 1999.

See also: Cleopatra VII.

WALTER ANNENBERG
American publisher and diplomat

Annenberg, son of disgraced publisher Moses Annenberg, redeemed the family name and transformed his father's failure into a $6 billion fortune. Before his death, Annenberg, through the Annenberg Foundation, gave $2 billion to learning institutions, and his philanthropy continues into the twenty-first century.

Born: March 13, 1908; Milwaukee, Wisconsin
Died: October 1, 2002; Wynnewood, Pennsylvania
Also known as: Walter Hubert Annenberg; Walter H. Annenberg
Sources of wealth: Inheritance; media
Bequeathal of wealth: Spouse; children; educational institution; museum; charity

EARLY LIFE

Walter Hubert Annenberg was the eighth child and only son of Moses and Sadie Annenberg, Jewish refugees from East Prussia, Germany, who immigrated to the United States in 1882, settling in Chicago. In 1906, Moses, Sadie, and their children moved to Milwaukee, where Moses (better known as Moe) distributed newspapers for publisher William Randolph Hearst. Walter was born with a withered right ear, causing partial deafness; he also stuttered and was extremely shy and sensitive. Moe attempted to help Walter become tougher by bringing home a boxing bag and encouraging athletic activities. Walter attended the German-English Academy in Milwaukee, a tough school for minds and bodies, from age six to twelve. In 1920, amid the World War I paranoia about anything German in Milwaukee, Moe accepted a huge promotion from Hearst and moved his family to New York.

FIRST VENTURES

The life that greeted Walter at the Great Neck, Long Island, estate that his father purchased from noted musician George S. Cohan was a clear indication of the Annenbergs' rising status. Walter enrolled at the Peddie School, a preparatory school in New Jersey. A mediocre student, between classes he placed orders with his father's stock brokerage firm. His teachers, believing he was a financial wizard, felt compelled to seek his advice. At the end of his senior year, Walter had made enough money to donate $17,000 to Peddie for an athletic running track.

Walter entered the Wharton School of Finance and Commerce at the University of Pennsylvania, which he found even more boring than Peddie. He avoided classes, spending time near a brokerage office and playing the stock market with relish. He obtained his father's permission to drop out of school and spend more time trading stocks. In eighteen months, Walter amassed a $3 million portfolio ($28.3 million at 2010 value). In the crash of 1929, Walter's $3 million vanished, and he was $350,000 in debt. Moe absorbed Walter's losses and forced him to swear he would never again trade recklessly.

MATURE WEALTH

Upon the death of his father in 1942, Walter Annenberg assumed total control of the Annenberg estate, which at that point was practically bankrupt. In 1940, Moe had been sentenced to three years in federal prison for tax evasion, but he did not serve out his entire sentence and

Walter Annenberg. (AP/Wide World Photos)

THE ANNENBERG FOUNDATION

Walter Annenberg established the M. L. Annenberg Foundation in memory of his father, Moses Annenberg, in July, 1989, with a grant of $1 billion, one-third of the revenue from the sale of Triangle Publications. The foundation was the successor to the Annenberg School at Radnor, Pennsylvania, which Annenberg founded in 1958. The Annenberg Foundation aims to advance public well-being through improved communication. Toward that end, the organization has encouraged the development of effective ways to share ideas and knowledge.

The primary program areas of the foundation are education and youth development; civic, community, and environmental issues; and health and human services. The organization contributes funds to institutions, not individuals, and has made grants to public elementary and secondary school systems. Annenberg Media, a part of the Annenberg Foundation, promotes excellence in teaching by supplying free multimedia resources, video collections, and related interactive activities to schools, colleges, and communities. Annenberg Media programs are frequently viewed on Public Broadcasting System (PBS) stations and are designed for high school and university students.

Annenberg's gifts to educational institutions have become legendary. Between 1960 and 1998, he gave $177 million to the University of Southern California to establish and support the school's Annenberg Center for Communication. His generous gifts to the University of Pennsylvania from 1960 through 1998 amounted to $239 million and were used to finance the Annenberg School of Communica-

tion. His grants to his alma mater, Peddie School, between 1927 and 1998 totaled an astounding $131.6 million. He also gave $55.2 million to Northwestern University, $50 million to the United Negro College Fund, $25 million to Harvard University, and $10 million to the University of Notre Dame. Other universities received smaller amounts, ranging from several hundred thousand dollars to $5 million.

In 1993, Annenberg issued a $500 million challenge to initiate reform in some of the nation's largest and most troubled schools, both urban and rural. He proffered the $500 million for matching grants of two-to-one in some instances, and five years after his announcement of the gift, $500 million was donated by businesses, foundations, universities, and individuals.

Annenberg's interest in art inspired gifts to the Metropolitan Museum of Art for $165 million and an art collection valued at $1 billion in 1991, as well as grants to other art institutions in the United States and abroad. In addition to the arts grants, Annenberg gave $11.3 million to the Eisenhower Medical Center in California, $15 million to the United Jewish Appeal, and enormous amounts for presidential libraries.

Following Annenberg's death, the Annenberg Foundation was under the sole directorship of his widow, Leonore Annenberg, until her death in 2009. At that time, the foundation announced its move to California, leaving only a small presence at Radnor, Pennsylvania. A new director, Annenberg's daughter Wallis Annenberg Weingarten, assumed control of the organization.

---

was released in 1942. He died several weeks later. Having been groomed to take over the business since his birth, Annenberg had spent years enjoying the family's wealth and observing his father's methods, but suddenly he inherited very little money and also a debt of $5 million of the $9.5 million fine that the U.S. government had levied against his father. Annenberg was left his father's shares of stock in Triangle Publications, Inc., and control of the *Philadelphia Inquirer*, *Daily Racing Form*, the Massillon (Ohio) *Independent* newspaper, *Screen Guide*, *Radio and Movie Guide*, *Click* (a photo publication), and a small group of pulp detective magazines.

In 1944, Annenberg replaced *Click* with *Seventeen*, a "wholesome" magazine for teens. Pursuing a conservative policy, he ruled out advertisements for liquor, beer, cigarettes, bridal gowns, honeymoon suites, or hair coloring. Annenberg wanted *Seventeen* to encourage respect between teens and their parents. This popular mag-

azine offered advice on fashion, beauty, etiquette and behavior, and it flourished under the editorship of Enid Annenberg, Walter Annenberg's sister, whose skills helped promote circulation to nearly two million. Within six years, advertising revenues climbed to $18 million.

Annenberg had two children with his first wife, Canadian Veronica Dunkelman, before their marriage ended in 1950. His second wife was Leonore (Lee) Rosenstiel, whom he married in 1951. At this time, he also began expanding his business. Since his father's death, Annenberg had managed to get his business affairs on solid financial footing, and he paid off the government fine. He and Lee began to build an art collection and turn their home, Inwood, in Wynnewood, Pennsylvania, into a place filled with fine art and furnishings.

By 1953, Annenberg had begun making plans for a television publication that would provide complete program listings and feature stories about people in the television industry. He bought *TV Digest* in Philadelphia, *TV Forecast* in Chicago, and *TV Guide* in New York, and to prevent anyone else from copying his idea, he persuaded other television magazine publishers to become franchisees of his publication, *TV Guide*. All his advisers had vetoed the idea of starting the television publication, but Annenberg, who operated largely by instinct, pursued the project, which turned out to be the best business move he ever made. The first issue, released for the week April 3-9, 1953, appeared in ten cities and sold 1,560,000 copies. Despite the fact that the number of circulation copies declined the following week and on through the summer, circulation expanded in the fall, and by late 1955, *TV Guide* was producing thirty-nine editions and boasting a circulation of three million copies weekly.

Passionately interested in converting the "vast wasteland" of television into high-quality programming, Annenberg began his experimental program, *University of the Air*, on his own television station, WFIL. At very little cost, he began broadcasting college courses throughout eastern Pennsylvania, Delaware, and southern New Jersey, with the cooperation of twenty-two colleges in the area that were pleased to put their best professors on the air. Annenberg's educational program eventually aired on five other television stations owned by Triangle Publications and garnered prestigious awards, including the George Foster Peabody Award, broadcast journalism's highest honor.

The following year, WFIL, an American Broadcasting Company (ABC) affiliate, transferred a popular local radio program, *Bandstand*, which consisted of a disc jockey playing popular music, to television, with instant success. Six years later, Annenberg moved Dick Clark, radio emcee of *Bandstand*, to a ninety-minute network television production of *American Bandstand*. The show began airing in 1957 and by its fourth week had become television's number one daytime program.

President Richard Nixon nominated Annenberg for the post of ambassador to the Court of St. James, and following a contentious hearing, Annenberg was confirmed in 1969. During his five-and-a-half-year stay in London, Annenberg was made an honorary member of the British Empire by Queen Elizabeth II. When he and Lee returned home, he began to consolidate his wealth. Having sold the Philadelphia *Inquirer* and the Philadelphia *Daily News* in 1969 to Knight Ridder for $55 million, Annenberg next divested himself of Triangle Publications, selling *Seventeen*, *TV Guide*, and other publications to Australian media magnate Rupert Murdoch for $3 billion. Devoting his efforts to his famed art collection

and to running the Annenberg Foundation, Annenberg divided his time between Pennsylvania and his four-hundred-acre estate, Sunnylands, at Rancho Mirage, California. Annenberg died of complications from pneumonia October 1, 2002, at Wynnewood, Pennsylvania, at the age of ninety-four. His net worth was estimated at $6 billion.

LEGACY

Annenberg's impulse for giving—a trait inherited from his mother—was apparent in his early career, when he helped some of his employees during lean times. As his wealth increased, he turned toward his two favorite interests, young people and education. Insisting that young people shape the character of the United States, he saw education as the key to the quality of their leadership as adults.

Although some of Annenberg's gifts were noteworthy for their "leverage"—meaning recipients were required to double or triple his contribution and, with the help of partners, raise more money—a great many others were outright gifts. Annenberg's generosity assisted schools for white and black students, sent much of his art collections to museums around the world, and provided donations for medical research and new hospitals, as well as bestowing money for community charities and presidential libraries.

—Mary Hurd

FURTHER READING

Cooney, John. *The Annenbergs*. New York: Simon & Schuster, 1982. Well-researched biography of Walter Annenberg that follows his lifelong effort to escape the taint on the family name because of his father's conviction for tax fraud.

Dobrin, Peter. "Annenberg Foundation Shifts Its Base." Philadelphia *Inquirer*, March 13, 2009. Public announcement of the Annenberg Foundation's move from Radnor, Pennsylvania, to California, following the death of Annenberg's widow. Article contains information relating to the foundation's contributions to Pennsylvania.

Domanico, Raymond, Alexander Russo, and Carol Innerst. *Can Philanthropy Fix Our Schools? Appraising Walter Annenberg's $500 Million Gift to Public Schools*. Darby, Pa.: Diane, 2000. Study indicates that Annenberg's huge donations have resulted in very little progress in urban school systems.

Fonzi, Gaeton. *Annenberg: A Biography of Power*. New York: Weymouth and Talley, 1969. Very critical account of Annenberg's rise to fame and wealth, specifically his use of the Philadelphia *Inquirer* as a weapon against those he disliked.

Glueck, Grace. "Walter Annenberg, 94, Dies; Philanthropist and Publisher." *The New York Times*, October 2, 2002. Excellent source of information concerning Annenberg's life events and achievements.

See also: Barbara Cox Anthony; Lord Beaverbrook; Silvio Berlusconi; Michael Bloomberg; Anne Cox Chambers; Katharine Graham; William Randolph Hearst; John H. Johnson; Robert L. Johnson; John Kluge; Rupert Murdoch; Samuel I. Newhouse; Kerry Packer; Ted Turner; Oprah Winfrey.

BARBARA COX ANTHONY
American investor and philanthropist

As a director of the media empire Cox Enterprises, Anthony oversaw and inspired its expansion from a newspaper chain into the new arena of cable television and related communications ventures, without abandoning its original interests. The heir to a $12.4 billion fortune, she gave away up to half her annual income, sometimes anonymously, and often to causes for which she herself worked, such as education and animal health.

Born: December 8, 1922; Dayton, Ohio
Died: May 28, 2007; Honolulu, Hawaii
Also known as: Barbara Cox (birth name); Barbara Anthony Cox
Sources of wealth: Inheritance; media
Bequeathal of wealth: Children; relatives; educational institution

EARLY LIFE

Barbara Cox Anthony was born in Dayton, Ohio, in 1922, the second daughter of James M. Cox and his second wife, Margaretta Parker Blair. In addition to owning the *Dayton Daily News*, Cox had a notable political career, serving four years in the House of Representatives and three terms as governor of Ohio before running for president on the Democratic Party ticket in the election of 1920. After losing this race, however, Cox withdrew from electoral politics at the age of fifty and devoted himself to building a business empire.

Anthony grew up in a hilltop manor called Trailsend, located just outside Dayton. Her early years were privileged and apparently happy. Trails for walking and riding surrounded her home, and she loved competitive sports, such as tennis and the rodeo. The family accompanied her father when he traveled to Europe on appointive missions. President Franklin D. Roosevelt, who had been her father's running mate in 1920, visited Trailsend in 1940, and she remembered sitting in on their political discussions. There is no record of Anthony having attended college after high school graduation, but her experiences traveling and meeting important people of her time were unique for a midwestern teenager.

FIRST VENTURES

Anthony was the daughter of a self-made and determinedly pragmatic man who wanted to run everything he touched. It is not surprising that, already in possession of enough wealth to make her way in the world, she set out for Miami, Florida, in the early 1940's. There she met and married a young naval aviator, Bradford Ripley. Like many brides of this time, she lost her new husband in World War II. Still living in Miami, she then met and married Stanley C. Kennedy II, a member of the United States Navy demolition team (now the United States Navy SEALs) and the son of the founder of Inter-Island Airways (later Hawaiian Airlines). The couple moved to Hawaii in the late 1940's. Anthony, intrigued by the islands' natural beauty, never moved away. Her marriage to Kennedy produced two children, James and Blair. Although she traveled back and forth to Dayton in the late 1940's and 1950's to visit her parents, and presumably sat in on family business councils, her main focus during this time was on family members' needs and Hawaiian institutions.

In both arenas she continued to widen her activities as time passed. After she and Kennedy divorced, she married contractor Jimmy Glover; upon his death, she stayed actively involved in raising two stepchildren, Glover's son and daughter, as well as her own children. She maintained an interest in the Dayton Arboretum and served on various boards in Hawaii, but she kept a low profile in order to maintain her privacy.

MATURE WEALTH

Meanwhile, the Cox newspaper chain had expanded by buying two Atlanta, Georgia, newspapers, the *Atlanta Journal* and the *Constitution*, and several radio stations. The elder Cox died in 1957, leaving his son by his first marriage, James M. Cox, Jr., as head of Cox Enterprises. Under his leadership the company diversified into such ventures as business publishing, motion-picture production (it purchased Bing Crosby Productions in 1967), and automobile auction management, although the first two ventures were dissolved within a decade. The company's first tentative steps into cable television systems

---

LA PIETRA

Of all the states, Hawaii has the largest percentage of its elementary and secondary students in private schools. One of the most creative is La Pietra, with which Barbara Cox Anthony was associated almost since its inception. La Pietra is the only nondenominational all-girls' school in the state. The school is located in Honolulu, at the base of Diamond Head and on the grounds of the old Dillingham estate.

La Pietra opened in 1964 as Hawaii School for Girls, with Anthony and Lorraine Cooke as its original founders. Classes were held in Honolulu's Central Union Church for the first five years. The Dillingham villa, named "La Pietra" (meaning stone or gem in Italian), was left to the older, prestigious Punahou School by its owners, the Walter F. Dillinghams. However, Punahou did not want the estate and put it on the market, where it languished for a while. Eventually Cooke and Anthony raised the money needed to buy the house and grounds, and they engaged an architectural firm to draw up plans for converting the mansion into a workable school. A freestanding six-classroom building was added to the campus in 1976. The site itself was on or near an ancient temple site, where events crucial to Hawaiian history took place in the early 1800's.

Anthony served as chairwoman of the school's board of trustees for more than two decades. She was also the school's "angel," providing financial aid for approximately half of its enrollees, as well as funding for more general school needs. Her own daughter Blair attended La Pietra.

The school is small, and in 2009 it had a total enrollment of fewer than four hundred students attending grades six through twelve. It is primarily a college preparatory school, and in the early twenty-first century its curriculum placed increasing emphasis on technology. A laptop computer was issued to every sixth-grade student. Like many private schools, it keeps the teacher-student ratio low and takes pride in innovative courses. For example, classes are offered in computer animation, marine biology, and modern Asian history, subjects not even available at many colleges.

In early 2008, several La Pietra students attended the presidential inauguration along with their teacher, Maya Soetoro-Ng, the sister of incoming President Barack Obama. La Pietra's benefactor might be gratified at this latter-day connection of her favorite school with the White House.

---

began in 1962 in Lewistown, Pennsylvania. Both Anthony and her sister Anne Cox Chambers of Atlanta served as active directors, as Cox Enterprises was determined to remain a family business. Virtually all its new enterprises were hugely profitable. When James M. Cox, Jr., died in 1974, he left 95 percent of his holdings to his two sisters.

By this time, Anthony had remarried again. Her husband, Garner Anthony II, a real estate and financial investor in Hawaii, became chairman of the Cox Enterprises, while she became chairwoman of Dayton Newspapers. As dual directors of the larger company, the Anthonys led it through a spectacular growth period, building it into one of the largest cable television providers in the United States and combining the separate newspaper and broadcasting companies under the Cox Enterprises' umbrella.

Other than chairing Dayton Newspapers, which of necessity was exercised largely on a long-distance basis, Anthony never served in an executive capacity of any profit-making company. However, because of her ownership position and dynamic personality, she was an effective and active director, keeping in touch with all major issues and generally having the right instincts about the companies' directions and futures. She preferred to hire good people to manage her companies and to trust them with the day-to-day operations. This being said, both Anthony and her enterprises were fortunate in having family members who were able to carry out the executive functions effectively. For example, in 1988, James Cox Kennedy, her son, became chairman and chief executive officer of the much expanded Cox Enterprises. One of his major ventures was the purchase of Trader Publications, a publisher of magazines and Web listings of cars, boats, and other items for sale nationwide.

Cox Enterprises doubled in value between 1992 and 1997, operating some three hundred separate businesses. Anthony herself regularly appeared on the *Forbes* magazine lists of the four hundred wealthiest individuals, with an estimated worth of approximately $12.6 billion in her later years. She was the only resident of Hawaii who was a billionaire.

In addition to her strictly business interests, Anthony invested in several ventures which, while profitable, also tied into her particular enthusiasms. In girlhood she had competed in rodeos, and her continued love of animals and nature led to ownership of a 7,500-acre ranch on the slopes of Mount Hualalai, Hawaii, devoted to the breeding of Gertrudis cattle and the production of kona coffee and cut flowers. Another large ranch operation, the Winderadeen Corporation, with cattle, quarter horse, and sheep production, was established in Australia after her daughter Blair Parry-Okeden moved there.

Anthony loved sports and was physically active through her later years, snow skiing and playing tennis even after joint replacement surgery. She died in 2007, a month after suffering a stroke.

LEGACY

Anthony was more known in Hawaii for her philanthropy and work on charitable boards than for her business success. Although she preferred to make many gifts of her money anonymously, her work with such institutions as the La Pietra school, a children's hospital in Honolulu, and many other educational and health care institutions was substantial and public. She did not confine her philanthropies to Hawaii. She endowed two faculty chairs, in oncology and equine orthopedics, at Colorado State University, and another chair at the University of Sydney. Her ties with Dayton, Ohio, led to support of numerous college scholarships for Miami Valley high school graduates and to a children's medical center in Dayton, which later bore her name.

Unlike her sister Anne Cox Chambers, Anthony stayed largely out of her family's traditional involvement in electoral politics. However, she did serve as a member of the Democratic Senatorial Campaign Committee and of Senator Bill Bradley's presidential campaign in the 1999-2000 preprimary season.

Anthony's life exemplified many of the qualities prized by those who extol the American ideal of free enterprise: responsible stewardship of inherited wealth; growth of a family fortune through careful management and investments in related industries; and diverse philan-

thropic efforts with personal involvement, as well as the giving of money. Her fortune, which passed to her heirs, seemed poised to remain intact, if not grow further, under the management of the family's younger generations. Perhaps the most noticeable impact of her work was the importance of Cox Communications and Cox Broadband in the lives of many Americans, who relied on these companies as their links to the communications media.

—Emily Alward

FURTHER READING

Cook, Lynn J. "America's Private Giants: Survival Instincts" *Forbes* 170, no. 11 (November 25, 2002): 182. Describes the business strategy of James Kennedy, Cox's chief executive, which made the company profitable, even in bad times, and enabled it to keep abreast of new technologies.

Cox, James M. *Journey Through My Years*. New York: Simon and Schuster, 1946. Reprint. Macon, Ga.: Mercer University Press, 2004. The autobiography of Anthony's hard-driving father. Heavily focused on political events but gives insight into the daughter's early life.

Glover, Charles. *Journey Through Our Years: The Story of Cox Enterprises, Inc*. Marietta, Ga.: Longstreet Press, 1998. Company history, written by the man who was Cox Newspapers' first editor in chief.

Morris, Charles E. *The Progressive Democracy of James M. Cox*. Indianapolis, Ind.: Bobbs-Merrill, 1920. Reprint. Whitefish, Mont.: Kessinger, 2004. Reissue of Cox's "campaign biography," providing the candidate's views on issues of the day.

Smolan, Rick, and David Elliot Cohen. *Hawai'i 24/7*. New York: D. K., 2004. Spectacular photo-essay collection showing the natural beauty that captivated Anthony. Includes views of Kapi'olani Park, adjacent to the La Pietra school, whose teams practice there.

See also: Walter Annenberg; David and Frederick Barclay; Silvio Berlusconi; Michael Bloomberg; Anne Cox Chambers; Katharine Graham; John H. Johnson; Robert L. Johnson; Rupert Murdoch; Samuel I. Newhouse; Kerry Packer; Ted Turner; Oprah Winfrey.

ELIZABETH ARDEN
American cosmetics magnate

Arden used her early wealth to grow her line of cosmetics and open an ever-increasing number of salons and spas, thus making her brand one of the first highly successful, woman-owned businesses. This foresight ultimately made her one of the world's richest entrepreneurs.

Born: December 31, 1884; Woodbridge, Ontario, Canada
Died: October 19, 1966; New York, New York
Also known as: Florence Nightingale Graham (birth name); Elizabeth N. Graham
Sources of wealth: Manufacturing; sale of products
Bequeathal of wealth: Relatives; employees

EARLY LIFE

Elizabeth Arden was born Florence Nightingale Graham in Woodbridge, Ontario, Canada, on December 31, 1884, the fourth of five children born to tenant farmers who had emigrated from Great Britain. Lacking the financial resources for college, she dropped out of high school but later enrolled in nursing school in Toronto. Despite the name "Florence Nightingale" (a famous nurse during the Crimean War), she soon realized that nursing was not the career for her.

Arden left Canada for good in 1908, living first with her brother, William, and getting her first taste of the cosmetics business. She married Thomas J. Lewis in 1915 and became an American citizen. Lewis acted as her business manager. After nearly twenty years of marriage, the couple divorced. She followed that with a two-year marriage to a Michael Evlonoff, a Russian prince.

FIRST VENTURES

Arden became convinced that women would be willing to spend large sums of money to enhance their looks, and she began developing creams in her spare time. She opened a salon with Elizabeth Hubbard but soon became the sole proprietor. Believing the name "Florence Nightingale" evoked the wrong image for a salon, she changed it to Elizabeth Arden. Some say she used her former partner's first name; others believe she borrowed the name from Elizabeth I, queen of England. The surname "Arden" came from the poem *Enoch Arden* by Alfred, Lord Tennyson.

Arden traveled to France to study beauty and massage techniques used in the upscale Paris salons so she could offer her clientele the best services. She introduced eye makeup to the United States, and hers were the first salons to offer cosmetic makeovers, a marketing ploy still practiced in the beauty industry. From the start she understood the importance of spending money to make money and had the fortitude to make moves others would have deemed too risky.

MATURE WEALTH

By the 1930's, Arden's meteoric growth included salons in Europe and South America, as well as the United States and Canada. She concluded, correctly, that even in the most difficult of times, women who were able would continue buying beauty enhancement products. Her European ventures put her under suspicion of the Federal Bureau of Investigation (FBI) and the agency's director, J. Edgar Hoover, during World War II amid false rumors that the salons were used as fronts for Nazi Party operations.

Elizabeth Arden. (Hulton Archive/Getty Images)

ELIZABETH ARDEN, INC.

Elizabeth Arden, Inc., could have died with its founder. Elizabeth Arden remained sole owner until her death in 1966 at age eighty-one, and because she considered herself to be the company, she never made concrete plans for it to outlive her.

To a large extent she *was* the company. Her attention to the tiniest of details, such as calling her establishments "salons" instead of "parlors," conjured an image of upper-class wealth guaranteed to reach her target market. She changed her name, intuitively knowing the name she attached to her business should reflect the type of clientele she expected to attract. In her mind her birth name, Florence Nightingale, sounded like the name of a health clinic. Her instincts were proven correct when her early patrons included a veritable who's who of money and influence.

She made sure all of her employees were trained in cosmetic application techniques that enhanced a woman's natural beauty, so her clients never appeared to have "clown faces" or wore makeup that in any way looked artificial. She might be accused of micromanaging, but her hands-on approach made the company so well known that a late 1930's reporter wrote, "only three company names are known everywhere in the world: Coca-Cola, Elizabeth Arden and Singer [sewing machines]."

Following Arden's death the company went through a succession of owners, the first being pharmaceutical giant Eli Lilly and Company. The business changed hands twice more before its acquisition by Unilever PLC in 1990, where it became part of the conglomerate's Prestige Personal Products Group, which also included Calvin Klein's fashion and beauty products. The company was sold again in 2001, this time to FFI (formerly known as French Fragrances, Incorporated) for about $190 million in cash, plus company stock that allowed Unilever 18 percent ownership. By then annual sales were approximately $890 million. In 2010, Elizabeth Arden, Inc., was a publicly owned, independent company.

Over the years the company has capitalized on the public's obsession with celebrities, adding brands, such as actor Elizabeth Taylor's fragrances, and using movie stars to advertise its products. Hollywood beauty Catherine Zeta-Jones, who in 2009 was the "face" of Elizabeth Arden, epitomized the company's concept of the modern woman: beautiful, talented, and successful in her own right. While these actors can by no means be considered average, it is to the company's credit that it chose to be represented by mature women, not girls still in the fresh bloom of youth. The company has become more community-minded over the years and contributes heavily to causes, including AIDS (acquired immunodeficiency syndrome) research and child welfare. Elizabeth Arden, Inc., is, and has always been, opposed to testing its products on animals.

Ever alert to new marketing possibilities, Arden developed a lipstick she named Montezuma Red to match the red trim on the uniforms of women in the armed forces, thus subtly planting the seed that wearing makeup to work was both acceptable and desirable.

The phenomenal success of Arden paved the way for other women to succeed in the beauty business, notably her first competitor, Helena Rubinstein. Their legendary rivalry lasted for decades, fueled in part when Arden's former husband, Thomas J. Lewis, went to work for Rubinstein following their divorce. Rubinstein had acted in retaliation after Arden recruited her sales manager. That both women courted the same customers, and both succeeded, shows the scope of the industry Arden began. In the years that followed, Estée Lauder and others joined the industry that seemingly had no bounds.

From the earliest days of her career, Arden knew the socially privileged were her target market. By consistently developing exceptional products for that segment, she created a client list that included First Ladies Mamie Eisenhower and Jacqueline Kennedy, Queen Elizabeth II, the Queen Mother, and the almost royal Wallis Simpson, along with the elite of mid-1900's Hollywood and Broadway. In the 1940's, her annual sales reached $60 million.

Diversification became the key to her company's growth, and, by association, the growth of her own substantial wealth. She began adding millinery and fashion to her mix of products and services. Oscar de la Renta was one of her first designers. Not content with salons alone, Arden turned her limitless energy to developing resort spas where women could be pampered for several weeks or longer. Her first spas were in New York and Arizona. She was ahead of the curve in other ways as well: She was the first, for example, to produce fragrances for men and to open a men's boutique.

Arden indulged in another love, horses, and bred thoroughbreds, leading some to say she built her wealth on fast horses and rich women. Her horses included Jet Pilot, the 1947 Kentucky Derby winner. She used the name

Elizabeth N. Graham in racing circles and owned close to 150 horses. In 1945, her Maine Chance Farm took in more prize money than any other American stable. After her death, Arden was inducted into the Canadian Horse Racing Hall of Fame. She approached racing as she approached everything else—with total commitment—a living testament to one of her advertising slogans: "Hold fast to youth and beauty." She named her first (and America's first) fragrance "Blue Grass" after the Kentucky horse country surrounding her farm near Lexington.

Arden was above all a hard-driven businesswoman, with her hand in virtually every slice of her empire's pie. Even so, she strove for an illusion of softness, probably to appear less intimidating. Whether it was due to the nature of her company, or just something she deemed a good business strategy, she retained a public persona of femininity. One way she accomplished this was by making pink her signature color, even to the extent of using it as one of her stable's racing colors.

Arden died on October 19, 1966, in New York City, still the grande dame of the cosmetics industry. She is buried in Sleepy Hollow, New York, under the name Elizabeth N. Graham, a combination of her birth and professional names and the name she used in horse racing.

LEGACY

One of Elizabeth Arden's legacies is bringing the use of cosmetics into the mainstream. Formerly, such products were used primarily by actresses, prostitutes, and other women commonly looked down upon. Arden and others following in her footsteps, including rivals Helena Rubinstein and Estée Lauder, made it acceptable for a woman to enhance her appearance, and in so doing enhance her self-esteem. Her Red Door Salons, each with a uniformed doorman, serve a worldwide, upscale clientele, but less privileged women can buy lower-cost alternatives at their neighborhood drugstores. Once cosmetics gained acceptability, they paved the way for companies like Revlon, Max Factor, and the door-to-door marketer Avon Products, Inc.

As one of the first women entrepreneurs to achieve great wealth in a business climate dominated by men,

Arden opened the door, if only a crack, for women who entered business, irrespective of their chosen industry. She proved conclusively that with a marketable idea, good business instincts, and dogged determination, there are no limits to what one can achieve.

—Norma Lewis

FURTHER READING

Kearney, Mark, and Randy Ray. *I Know That Name! The People Behind Canada's Best Known Names from Elizabeth Arden to Walter Zeller*. Toronto: Dundurn Press, 2002. A fun and fact-filled account of more than one hundred Canadian-born individuals who achieved great success and how the companies they founded turned them into household names. Arden is the one to beat when it comes to international name recognition.

Peiss, Kathy. *Hope in a Jar: The Making of America's Beauty Culture*. New York: Henry Holt, 1999. Explains in detail "how women created the cosmetics industry and cosmetics created the modern woman." Arden and Helena Rubinstein are key figures in the book, along with Avon Products, Inc., and other companies that cater to those with modest incomes.

International Directory of Company Histories. 117 vols. Chicago: St. James Press, 1988-2010. Volumes 8 and 40 contain information about Elizabeth Arden.

Woodhead, Lindy. *War Paint: Madame Helena Rubinstein and Miss Elizabeth Arden, Their Lives, Their Times, Their Rivalry*. New York: John Wiley and Sons, 2004. Fascinating, well-researched work describing the premier grandes dames of cosmetics, including their storied five-decade feud. The book is particularly interesting because their lives play out against London, Paris, and New York society—the source from which they drew their clientele. It also touches on such diverse subjects as the two world wars and the birth of modern advertising.

See also: John H. Johnson; Anita Roddick; Helena Rubinstein; Jay Van Andel; Madam C. J. Walker.

SIR RICHARD ARKWRIGHT
British industrialist and inventor

Arkwright was an archetypal self-made man who acquired great wealth by exploiting an invention of his own making in his own factories, thus becoming a key contributor to the Industrial Revolution of the eighteenth century. He also won considerable fame by virtue of the ostentatious deployment of his wealth in buying land and building a castle fit for one of the new kings of industry.

Born: December 23, 1732; Preston, Lancashire, England
Died: August 3, 1792; Cromford, Derbyshire, England
Sources of wealth: Manufacturing; patents; real estate
Bequeathal of wealth: Children

EARLY LIFE

Sir Richard Arkwright was the sixth of seven surviving children of Thomas Arkwright and Ellen Arkwright (née Hodgkinson). The family was poor and Arkwright received little formal education, although two of his elder sisters attended a blue coat (charity) school and passed on what they learned to their siblings. In his early teens he was apprenticed to a barber in the town of Kirkham, but he moved to Bolton-le-Moors in 1750 to work for the wig maker Edward Pollit. He continued to work for Pollit's widow for a short time, but by 1755 he had set up a barber's stall in a passage leading to an inn, shaving chins for a penny. On March 31 of that year he married Patience Holt, the daughter of a schoolmaster, and borrowed £60 from her father in order to expand his business. The couple's only child, also named Richard, was born on December 19, 1755. The marriage does not appear to have been happy; when Patience died on October 6 in the following year, she was buried with her mother under her maiden name.

On March 21, 1761, Arkwright married Margaret Biggins of Pennington, and he repaid the debt he owed his first wife's father with the bulk of an inheritance that she had received; he invested the rest in an inn, the Black Boy, whose publican he

became. The business failed, and he returned to wig making, also dabbling, as most eighteenth century barbers did, in bleeding (a surgical practice) and tooth extraction. He began buying hair on a large scale, ostensibly making use of a secret dyeing technique in making his wigs. Margaret bore three children, one of whom—Susanna, born on December 20, 1761—survived into adulthood.

FIRST VENTURES

The device that made Arkwright's fortune mechanized one of the oldest traditional crafts, spinning yarn. Arkwright's spinning machine, subsequently known as a water-frame once it was adapted for use in association with a water mill, was not the only such device invented at the time; James Hargreaves's spinning jenny was virtually contemporary. Arkwright, however, was a deter-

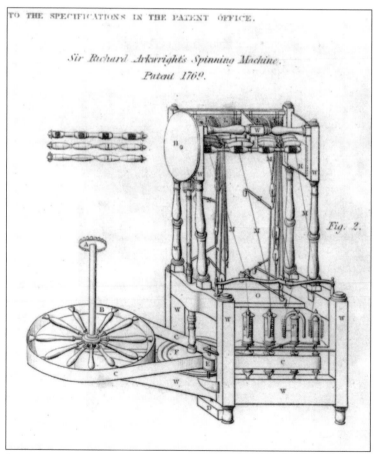

Sir Richard Arkwright's yarn spinning machine helped mechanize textile production. (Library of Congress)

mined opportunist who carried his machine all the way through the developmental process to full-scale industrial production. Arkwright's invention was understandably shrouded in secrecy and was embroiled in controversy from the start.

The search for such a process had been urgent for some time, but an earlier machine patented by Lewis Paul and John Wyatt in 1738 had proved impracticable. Thomas Highs of Leigh subsequently claimed to have devised the innovations that he carelessly confided to Arkwright in conversation. However, what is certain is that in 1767, Arkwright formed an association with a clockmaker named John Kay (sometimes mistakenly confused with another John Kay, who invented the fly-shuttle), who made him a model of a spinning machine, for which they began to seek financing.

After failing to find backers in Manchester and Preston, Arkwright and Kay took two of their relatives, the former publican John Smalley and the merchant David Thornley, into partnership in order to build and exploit a full-scale machine in Nottingham. They petitioned for a patent on June 8, 1878, but it was not granted until July 3, 1769, perhaps because they had trouble scraping together the money to pay the fee. Thornley had to sell part of his share to Smalley when his own capital ran out, and a new fifth share in the association was taken by Samuel Need and Jedediah Strutt, who provided the financing necessary to construct a horse-drawn mill, to be managed by Arkwright and Thornley.

The Nottingham mill did not start production until Christmas, 1772, by which time the partners had already commissioned the construction of a new mill on the River Derwent at Cromford in Derbyshire, driven by water power. The original intention had been to spin yarn for stockings (Strutt was already involved in that trade), but the yarn produced by Arkwright's machine was thin enough and strong enough to serve as the warp on a loom, so the Cromford mill began to produce calico, with an efficiency that astonished its owners and their rivals. Arkwright set up his headquarters there and began to expand his operation relentlessly. Strutt joined forces with other entrepreneurs to lobby Parliament to reduce excise duties on British cotton goods. When they were successful, the profits made by Arkwright's Cromford mills increased rapidly, and the company set out to dominate the trade, applying for further patents that would have established a virtual monopoly. The result of these moves was an intense competition, which was also reflected within the partnership as Arkwright attempted to squeeze out his associates.

MATURE WEALTH

Arkwright's legal wrangles came to a head in July, 1781, when he sued nine other manufacturers for breaching his patents. It was during this period that Highs came forward to lay charges of theft against Arkwright—charges that were never substantiated, but probably contributed to the eventual result of the conflict, which was the cancellation of Arkwright's patents in 1785. By that time, however, most of Arkwright's original partners were dead and he had become exceedingly rich, thanks to the huge profits he had made during the previous decade from his Cromford mills. The cancellation of the patents initiated a free-for-all that brought about a boom in the cotton industry throughout the north of England, but Arkwright never lost the crucial commercial advantage he had gained before his patents were canceled, and he remained the largest manufacturer in the country.

Arkwright was just as desperate to make social progress as economic progress, although he labored under the handicap of a personality that did not allow him to make friends easily and often alienated those he had. He was deeply resented by the landed gentry of Derbyshire, who mocked him relentlessly as an upstart when he bought Willersley Manor, near Cromford, in 1782, but if he cared he did not show it. When his daughter Susanna married the lead merchant and iron manufacturer Francis Hurt, he was able to give her a dowry of £15,000. His increasing political influence within the country reached a climax when he was knighted in 1786 and subsequently became high sheriff of Derbyshire.

In 1788, Arkwright involved himself in a project to construct a Cromford canal, but it soon ran into difficulties, allegedly because of his attempts to monopolize the project and its anticipated profits. His reputation for avarice and ostentation reached its zenith soon thereafter. Arkwright bought the manor of Cromford itself in 1789, and he promptly commissioned the construction of a grandiose stately home, which he named Willersley Castle. The traditional gentry were horrified by the prospect, and abusive comments were made about the priorities of its design; its library was said to be exceedingly small and ill-lit, and the whole enterprise was sometimes called a folly. However, it actually turned out to be a fine house, by no means tasteless in its architecture or furnishing. Arkwright bought a town house in London in the same year, although he actually lived for the greater part of his later life in Rock House, situated on a hill overlooking his Cromford mills.

In 1790, Arkwright introduced the first steam engine into his works at Nottingham, thus completing the foundations of the revolution in textile production that changed the face of England in the early nineteenth century. The *Gentleman's Magazine* estimated his fortune at the time of his death to be "not far short" of £500,000, but that was a guess; his family kept the details of his inheritance to themselves, and the sum did not include his various properties.

LEGACY

Although he suffered all through his life from asthma, Arkwright insisted on working from 5:00 A.M. to 9:00 P.M. every day, and his industry became legendary. He became a heroic role model to the industrialists who followed him, but he also became a villain in the eyes of subscribers to the "rage against the machine" carried forward by active Luddites and the Romantic writers, who tended to equate industrialization with spoliation. One of his mills was said to have been demolished by rioters while police and military forces looked on sympathetically, although the reports might have been exaggerated. He was in any case unmoved by opposition of any sort. He was in essence a man who successfully reinvented the wheel—spinning being for most of its history at least as significant an application of the wheel as wheeled transport, whose utility was limited until roads improved sufficiently to accommodate such vehicles.

—*Brian Stableford*

WILLERSLEY CASTLE

As he approached the age of sixty, Sir Richard Arkwright commissioned the architect William Thomas to design for him a stately home on a sixty-acre site overlooking the valley of the River Derwent at Cromford, where his chief mills were situated. Construction began in 1790. The residence is a two-and-a-half-story edifice constructed in sandstone, with seven principal bays and two wings jutting out toward the edge of the cliff, equipped with fake battlements and a series of mock-turrets. The principal internal feature of note is the glass-domed Well Gallery in the center of the building, approached via an archway designed and supplied by the prestigious firm of Robert and James Adam. The fireplaces in the principal ground floor rooms were also supplied by the Adam brothers, who also sold Arkwright his London town house. The furniture for Willersley Castle was ordered from Edward Wilson of The Strand in London, and the luxury plate glass was imported from France.

Work on the "castle" was almost completed when a fire on August 8, 1791, destroyed the interior, and the shell of the building had to be completely restored—work undertaken by Thomas Gardner and Edward Blore. They had not finished when Arkwright died in 1792, and it was his eldest son, also named Richard, who eventually took up residence in the house in 1796. It was subsequently handed on to Arkwright's third son, Peter, whose descendants lived there until 1925. In 1927, the house was refashioned by the Wesley Guild, a group of wealthy Methodist businessmen, for use as a holiday center. It was used as a maternity hospital during World War II and then reverted to its use as a hotel, operated by an organization subsequently known as the Christian Guild.

FURTHER READING

Ashton, T. S. *The Industrial Revolution, 1760-1830.* New ed. Oxford, England: Oxford University Press, 1998. A comprehensive general history, which places Arkwright's contribution to the Industrial Revolution in its broader context and explains its historical importance.

Bell, David. *Derbyshire Heroes.* Newbury, Berkshire, England: Countryside Books, 2004. Arkwright is here considered in the company of other highly influential figures in the history of his adopted county. The text is part of a notable series of local interest books.

Craven, Maxwell, and Michael Stanley. *The Derbyshire Country House.* Derby, Derbyshire, England: Breedon Books, 1991. A guide to the stately homes of Derbyshire, which includes an account of the history and architecture of Willersley Castle. Although primarily aimed at tourists, it is a conscientiously detailed work.

Fitton, R. S. *The Arkwrights: Spinners of Fortune.* Manchester, England: Manchester University Press, 1990. By far the most significant book on its subject, offering a scrupulous account of the contribution made by the first Richard Arkwright and his descendants to the textile revolution, focusing primarily on the economic aspects of their enterprise and its abundant rewards.

Witzel, Morgan. *Fifty Key Figures in Management.* New York: Taylor and Francis, 2003. A collection of exemplary accounts of ingenious entrepreneurialism, which juxtaposes Arkwright and other makers of the Industrial Revolution with modern businesspersons, making an interesting study in comparison and contrast.

See also: Moses Brown; Francis Cabot Lowell; James Morrison; John Rylands; Samuel Slater.

GIORGIO ARMANI
Italian entrepreneur and fashion designer

Armani founded a fashion empire and is the most successful Italian designer in history. A very private person, he devotes his time to running his business and charity.

Born: July 11, 1934; Piacenza, Italy
Source of wealth: Sale of products
Bequeathal of wealth: Charity

EARLY LIFE
Giorgio Armani (JOR-jee-oh ahr-MAHN-ee) was born in rural Piacenza, Italy, to a hardworking family. His way to escape World War II, which claimed the lives of several friends and caused him and his sister to be strafed, was going to the cinema, where he developed his love of fashion, particularly from the 1930's. After the war the family moved to Milan and Armani began studying medicine, which he hated. In 1957, he returned to Milan after completing military service. An interest in photography led to a job at La Rinascente, Milan's largest department store. On the basis of his photographs of his sister, Armani was hired as a window dresser, his first job in fashion.

FIRST VENTURES
In 1961, Armani began working for Nino Cerruti, designing menswear for the Hitman line. In 1970, Armani left Cerruti to open a new business with Sergio Galeotti, his business partner until Galeotti's untimely death in 1985, freelancing and marketing his own designs. His first major collection, shown in Florence in 1973, included leather as an everyday fabric. This success led to the 1974 creation of his own label, Giorgio Armani S.p.A. menswear, followed in 1975 by his women's wear line. Armani's designs are characterized by his love of sophistication and comfort. Basing women's wear on menswear, he revolutionized the structure of suits and was instrumental in introducing menswear fabrics into women's wear lines. He is credited with the creation of the unstructured suit and the power suit. In 1980, Armani became world famous after designing the clothes for the film *American Gigolo*, starring Richard Gere.

MATURE WEALTH
Capitalizing on *American Gigolo*, Armani opened his first store in 1982, Emporio Armani Milan. He encouraged film stars to wear Armani clothes at the Academy Awards, ushering in the trend of designer-dressed actors on the red carpet. In 1982, Armani graced the cover of *Time*, the second fashion designer ever so honored. The 1980's began a decades-long period of continuing growth for Giorgio Armani S.p.A. and his personal fortune. Although Galeotti's death devastated Armani, he threw himself into work, diversifying and designing eyewear, blue jeans, prêt-à-porter, haute couture, accessories, perfume, underwear, and foodstuffs, while maintaining his original men's and women's wear lines. Armani took over many Italian fashion businesses, such as the knitwear firm Deanna S.p.A, Simint manufacturing company, and Guardi shoemakers. Armani loves cinema, and

Giorgio Armani. (AFP/Getty Images)

he has designed wardrobes for more than two hundred films.

The 2000's saw a move from purely clothing- and accessory-based designs to a greater interest in large-scale fashion. Having helped to design worldwide Armani retail sites, he developed the Armani Home collection of household furnishings. In 2005, he contracted to build and design a group of resort hotels, beginning in Dubai. Throughout his career Armani has retained total financial and creative control of his empire, making it one of the only fashion houses to be owned by a single person. Armani is a self-professed workaholic whose personal wealth was reported in 2010 at $5.3 billion, making him number 144 on *Forbes* magazine's list of the world's billionaires. His company grosses $1.69 billion annually.

LEGACY
Armani contributes to many charities, focusing on the arts, children, refugees, science, and the environment. He cofounded the Martin Scorsese Cinema Foundation to save old films. His work supporting international refugees led to an ambassadorship with the United Nations High Commissioner for Refugees (UNHCR). He has do-

nated money to build and restore theaters, museums, research facilities, and medical centers. Since the 1990's he has worked for many environmental charities, including musician Bono's Project Red and Don't Bungle the Jungle. He has raised millions of dollars through the sales of T-shirts and other products specifically designed for charities, such as the UNICEF (United Nations International Children's Emergency Fund) Armani doll. He built a breeding facility in Seoul in order to help save the Korean tiger. One of the most honored fashion designers, Armani spends his time continuing to design and to help the less fortunate around the globe.

—Leslie Neilan

FURTHER READING
Celent, Germano, and Harold Koda. *Giorgio Armani.* New York: Harry N. Abrams, 2000.
Martin, Richard, and Harold Koda. *Giorgio Armani: Images of Man.* New York: Rizzoli, 1990.
Molho, Renata. *Being Armani: A Biography.* Milan: Baldini Castoldi Dalai Editore, 2008.

See also: Jan Antonín Bat'a; Ralph Lauren; Kokichi Mikimoto; Gloria Vanderbilt.

PHILIP DANFORTH ARMOUR
American industrialist and philanthropist

Armour, cofounder and chairman of Armour & Co., introduced modern and innovative technology and production methods to large meatpacking operations. Armour & Co. was among the largest employers in Chicago's historic stockyards and meatpacking industry. He used his wealth for philanthropic and educational ventures, founding the Armour Institute of Technology, later renamed the Illinois Institute of Technology.

Born: May 16, 1832; Stockbridge, New York
Died: January 6, 1901; Chicago, Illinois
Source of wealth: Sale of products
Bequeathal of wealth: Children; charity; educational institution

EARLY LIFE
Philip Danforth Armour was born in 1832 in Stockbridge, New York, the fourth of eight children of Danforth Armour and Juliana Brooks Armour. Danforth

left Connecticut to run a rural New York family farm, where his children learned to slaughter cattle and produce soap from the fats. Armour attended the local Methodist church with his family and went to school in the nearby towns of Valley Mills and Cazenovia. He worked as a farm laborer for his family and neighbors, clerked in a store, and was employed as a driver on the Chenango Canal in New York, which connected the Susquehanna River to the Erie Canal. In 1852, he borrowed a wagon from the family and headed to California, lured there by the gold rush.

FIRST VENTURES
Armour was a determined entrepreneur. In the Sacramento Valley of California, Armour developed and leased aqueduct systems (sluiceways), bringing water to gold diggers and washers, which proved more profitable than mining. Returning east, he worked briefly in Milwaukee, Wisconsin, operating a soap business, then in St. Paul, Minnesota, where he partnered with James J.

Hill, selling hides, then returned to Milwaukee and founded a grocer provisions firm with Frederick B. Miles. In 1862, he visited Cincinnati, Ohio, and observed the booming Civil War demand for salt pork.

It was in Cincinnati that Armour met and married Malvina Belle Ogden (1842-1927). They would have two sons, J. Ogden Armour (1863-1927) and Philip Danforth Armour, Jr. (1869-1900).

In 1862, Armour took a half interest in the Milwaukee slaughterhouse founded by John Plankinton (1820-1891). By then, Armour's brother Herman Ossian Armour (1837-1901) was already the operator of a successful Milwaukee grocer provision firm, and another brother, Joseph Francis Armour (1842-1881), was a Chicago grain dealer. Before war's end Philip Armour sold short on pork, making Plankinton and Armour wealthy, while the fall in pork prices drove many of their Cincinnati competitors out of business. Armour would henceforth become an influential speculator in agricultural commodities. Railways, cattle, and pigs would make Chicago a center for agricultural industries in post-Civil War America, and Armour and his brothers set their sights there.

Philip Danforth Armour. (Archive Photos/Getty Images)

MATURE WEALTH

Armour and his brothers acted aggressively to build their businesses. Plankinton and Armour expanded to Kansas City, Missouri; Henry Armour opened Armour, Plankinton, and Co. in New York (later H. O Armour and Co.); brother Simeon Armour (1828-1899) established Armour Packing Co. in Kansas City (the two merged into a single firm in the 1890's); and Andrew Watson Armour (1829-1893) founded the Armour Brothers bank in Kansas City. The Armour yards and packinghouses in Chicago became the biggest in the city. Philip Armour led these enterprises with aggressive and astute business acumen, epitomizing the hard-nosed business culture of his era.

Armour was a great believer in trade and thrift (rather than in religion), as well as in the sciences that enabled their application in production. Thus he sought to employ the enormous amounts of waste, including heads, feet, tankage, and other matter, that packinghouses produced. Armour was among the first to fully incorporate and profit from the side businesses of manufacturing glue, oil, tallow, fertilizer, oleomargarine, sausage casings, pharmaceuticals, and other products from the

nonmeat portions of farm animals. Eventually lower-quality meat was canned and sold as inexpensive new food products, such as pork and beans. Armour hired chemists and built a laboratory at his Chicago facilities to make possible the most efficient and profitable reuse of all parts of farm animals. He purchased competitors' businesses or founded his own, including fertilizer and soap firms, and had designs on tanneries and related businesses until the antitrust legislation of the early 1900's and the Packers and Stockyards Act of 1921 slowed the company's growth. It was these businesses related to meatpacking that made Armour & Co. the largest of its kind in Chicago and a global innovator in industrial agriculture processing.

Armour, who built and directed the collection of companies that he and his brothers commanded, shared a large, nonpartitioned office with three hundred employees at the Home Insurance Building on Chicago's LaSalle Street. Tall, weighing 250 pounds, he was known as a plain speaker whom few dared to cross. He became one of the wealthiest men of Chicago's Gilded Age, along with Marshall Field, George Mortimer Pullman, and Armour's chief rival, Gustavus Franklin Swift, who pio-

ILLINOIS INSTITUTE OF TECHNOLOGY

The origins of the Illinois Institute of Technology go back to 1886, when Philip Danforth Armour established the Armour Mission in Chicago to offer classes to young people of all races and ethnicities. It was operated by the Plymouth Congregational Church, led by the influential Reverend Frank Wakely Gunsaulus (1856-1921), who would help direct Armour's charitable efforts.

Armour sought to enlarge the missions founded in 1874 in Chicago by his late brother Joseph Francis Armour. The mission facility had been designed by the noted architects John Wellborn Root and Daniel Hudson Burnham. A row of apartments were built adjacent to the mission, and Armour encouraged company mangers and officials to live there so their rent might help enrich the mission's programs, which included an administrative and teaching staff, more than two thousand pupils, and a library. Librarian Julia A. Beveridge began offering technical classes in woodworking, mechanical drawing, and designing, and she is credited with providing the inspiration for the school's curriculum.

Opened in 1893, the Armour Institute of Technology was led by Gunsaulus. A technical school open to all young men who could pass the stiff entrance exams, regardless of race or ethnicity, the institute charged a maximum $60 annual tuition and was free for poorer students. A high-school-level academy was also built to serve young women. The institute's opening coincided with the 1893 World's Columbian Exposition held in Chicago, and some of the exposition's mechanical and electrical equipment was purchased for school use. Armour donated $3 million to the institute before his death. His wife Malvina and his son J. Ogden Armour donated another $1 million.

First courses included mechanical, electrical, and mining engineering, taught by a select faculty. The institute soon expanded its curriculum in civil engineering, chemistry, and library science, and became a premier institution in engineering education. In 1901, it graduated the first African American to receive a degree in chemical engineering, Charles Warner Pierce (1867-1947). In 1938, noted architect Ludwig Mies van der Rohe (1886-1969) assumed leadership of the institute's architecture program, which was operated jointly with the Art Institute of Chicago and named the Chicago School of Architecture.

In 1940, the Armour Institute of Technology merged with the Lewis Institute, a small Chicago liberal arts college, and changed its name to the Illinois Institute of Technology (IIT). By 2009, IIT was a distinguished university, providing degrees in engineering, science, psychology, architecture, business, design, and law.

---

neered the refrigerated railway car for beef transportation. Armour relentlessly applied practical business methods to lower costs and inefficiencies, and he employed professional mangers to oversee a diverse empire. He kept a vigorous schedule, arriving at his offices by six o'clock in the morning and holding first meetings soon thereafter.

Confronting the problem of transportation and distribution, Armour partnered with railroad magnates; became an owner in the Chicago, Milwaukee, and St. Paul Railroad Company and in the Baltimore and Ohio Railroad; and established distribution centers for beef, pork, and grain throughout the country and in Europe. Armour overcame considerable public opposition to fresh beef, as it challenged commonly held notions of food safety and competed (many claimed unfairly) with local butchers. The Armour brand became widely known, and Armour had the motto "We Feed the World" painted on his company's railway cars.

Chicago's South Side, where the Back of the Yards neighborhood and the stockyards and slaughterhouses were located, was known for its unsafe and poor living and working conditions. Upton Sinclair's best-selling book *The Jungle* (1906) depicted the stark life of packinghouse workers, and Jane Addams's Hull House settlement programs were established nearby to provide educational and other services to these residents. Staunchly antiunion, Armour defeated major strike waves in 1879, 1886, and 1894, and the company required workers to sign agreements not to join a union. The industry remained nonunion during Armour's lifetime.

Armour's supporters pointed to his undeniable generosity, his scorn for wealthy "society," his genuine love of children, and his ease with working men. He established the Armour Mission in Chicago in 1886, and in 1893 he founded the Armour Institute. These institutions became the passions of his life.

Armour died pf pneumonia in January, 1901, after a series of illnesses.

LEGACY

Armour was one of the most innovative industrialists of late nineteenth century America. He represented the ideal of the self-made man of his era, and his Armour &

Co. businesses embodied the great maturation of the United States into a sophisticated industrial agricultural provider to the world.

His personal fortune was estimated at more than $30 million. He was survived by his wife and older son, J. Ogden Armour, who took on the Armour business with great composure, having served as a partner since 1884. His son took the company to new heights, at one point grossing $1 billion in a single year, but the company barely survived the post-World War I economic slump.

—Eric Schuster

FURTHER READING

Geisst, Charles R. *Wheels of Fourtune: A History of Speculation from Scandal to Respectability.* Hoboken, N.J.: Wiley, 2007. Exposition of Armour's speculative business ventures.

Hakutani, Yoshinobu, ed. *Selected Magazine Articles of Theodore Dreiser.* Madison, N.J.: Fairleigh Dickinson University Press, 1985. Includes Dreiser's essential interview with Armour.

Hubbard, Elbert. *Philip D. Armour.* Reprint. Whitefish, Mont.: Kessinger, 2005. Hubbard, a contemporary of Armour, wrote this essay in a triumphal form that celebrated American enterprise, and it serves as the best example of hagiography of the subject.

Leech, Harper, and John Charles Carroll. *Armour and His Times.* New York: D. Appleton-Century, 1938. A detailed, sympathetic overview of Armour, his business dealings, competitors, associates, and the industry. Includes reproductions and quotations of Armour's writings, as well as photographs of his family and business partners.

Miller, Donald L. *City of the Century: The Epic of Chicago and the Making of America.* New York: Simon & Schuster, 1996. A social history of the growth of nineteenth century Chicago, including a large section on the development of the meatpacking industry.

United States Office of Education. *Art and Industry: Education in the Industrial and Fine Arts in the United States.* Washington, D.C.: U.S. Government Printing Office, 1898. An official and very detailed account of the establishment of the Armour Mission and the Armour Institute of Technology.

See also: Marshall Field; James J. Hill; George Mortimer Pullman; Julius Rosenwald; Louis F. Swift.

WILLIAM HENRY ASPINWALL
American merchant and steamship and railroad owner

Aspinwall established himself as one of New York's most successful merchants in the 1830's and 1840's. His Pacific Mail Steamship Line was launched just before the beginning of California's gold rush and became immensely profitable, as did the railroad his firm constructed across Panama in the 1850's.

Born: December 16, 1807; New York, New York
Died: January 18, 1875; New York, New York
Sources of wealth: Trade; railroads; shipping
Bequeathal of wealth: Spouse; children

EARLY LIFE
William Henry Aspinwall (AS-pihn-wawl) was born into a respected New York merchant family. His father, John, and uncle were importers and wholesalers of dry goods. G. G. & S. Howland, a merchant partnership run by the brothers of Aspinwall's mother, was one of the city's most successful businesses. Aspinwall attended Bancel's Boarding College in New York City and became so adept at French and Spanish that he tutored in these languages after graduation.

FIRST VENTURES
In 1832, Aspinwall and his cousin William Howland were brought into G. G. & S. Howland to learn the business, and the firm was renamed Howland & Aspinwall in 1834. Three years later, Aspinwall's two uncles ceased active management of the firm, and Aspinwall began receiving a one-quarter share of its profits as a partner. Aspinwall was increasingly recognized as the dominant partner, known for his quiet, pious character, careful attention to detail, and conservative business decisions. The firm's ships carried goods to and from Europe, the West Indies, China, and South America. They secured a monopoly on trade with Venezuela, due to ties with President José Antonio Páez. By the mid-1840's. Aspinwall also became director or trustee of several banks and in-

surance companies and served as vice consul for Tuscany.

MATURE WEALTH

Aspinwall began to take greater risks in the mid-1840's, when he ordered shipbuilders Smith and Dimon to construct the world's first clipper ship, following naval architect John Willis Griffiths's radical new design. Aspinwall had second thoughts in the face of great public skepticism, which delayed construction, making the *Rainbow* the second clipper ship to be launched. Aspinwall's next clipper, the *Sea Witch*, astounded the shipping world by sailing from Canton, China, to New York in only seventy-four days. The speed and profitability of Aspinwall's vessels led to a flood of orders for the new clipper ships.

In late 1847, Aspinwall made another daring move, establishing the Pacific Mail Steamship Company after purchasing a contract to run a government-subsidized shipping line from Panama to Oregon. At the conclusion of the Mexican War in 1848, there were only about twenty thousand inhabitants scattered along the two thousand miles of the United States' newly acquired West Coast, and most observers believed the $199,000 annual government subsidy would not cover the costs of running three steamers along routes that had no coal stations or repair yards, inadequate port facilities, and very little freight or passenger potential. The construction of three wooden-hulled, paddle-wheel steamers began at once, and the first, the *California*, left New York on October 6, 1848. It carried only seven passengers from New York, its captain became ill, and it ran into a string of difficulties on its voyage around South America, but its voyage became the stuff of legend. When the beleaguered ship reached the Pacific coast of Panama, it found a mob of fifteen hundred men clamoring to reach California's gold fields. Because of the gold rush, Aspinwall's line expanded rapidly and became immensely profitable.

With even greater foresight, Aspinwall had already sent a surveying team to Panama and quickly negotiated for the rights to build a railroad across the isthmus. Panama's geography, climate, and disease-carrying mosquitoes made construction difficult, expensive, and slow. In late 1851, the partially built railroad was on the verge of running out of capital, as construction costs far out-

stripped estimates, and stock in Aspinwall's Panama Railroad Company fell to pennies per share. At this point, Aspinwall pledged his personal fortune to continue the project, saving the railroad, which was completed in 1855 at a cost of $8 million (about $200 million at 2010 prices) and about six thousand lives.

In 1856, Aspinwall began to withdraw from active management of his businesses and to turn the reins of the merchant house over to his younger brother and son. During the Civil War, Howland & Aspinwall acted as a government purchasing agent in Europe, but Aspinwall surprised Secretary of War Edwin M. Stanton by remitting his commissions from these purchases back to the government. Aspinwall also served on a secret mission to England to impede Confederate efforts to buy and outfit ships that would raid Union commerce.

LEGACY

In his retirement, Aspinwall became a philanthropist and amassed a sizable art collection, with paintings by Thomas Gainsborough, Rembrandt, Peter Paul Rubens, Titian, Diego Velázquez, and others. He was a founder of the Metropolitan Museum of Art and a founding trustee of the Society for the Prevention of Cruelty to Animals.

Although he was one of the world's wealthiest men at his death in 1875, with net assets valued around $4 million ($80 million in 2010), time quickly obscured Aspinwall's fame and contributions. Howland & Aspinwall evolved into an investment, commission, and banking firm before ceasing operations in the mid-1890's. The Pacific Mail underwent numerous changes of leadership and ownership, while the Panama Railroad eventually became the property of the Panama Canal in the early twentieth century, and the port town of Aspinwall, Panama, was renamed Colón.

—Robert Whaples

FURTHER READING

Kemble, John H. *The Panama Route, 1848-1869*. Berkeley: University of California Press, 1943.
Somerville, Duncan S. *The Aspinwall Empire*. Mystic, Conn.: Mystic Seaport Museum, 1983.

See also: Anthony N. Brady; Daniel Drew; William Thaw; Cornelius Vanderbilt; Peter A. B. Widener.

BROOKE ASTOR
American philanthropist and socialite

Astor inherited one of America's great fortunes and became one of America's best known philanthropists, developing a personal involvement and style rare in American philanthropy. She continued her work until age ninety-five, when she closed the Vincent Astor Foundation.

Born: March 30, 1902; Portsmouth, New Hampshire
Died: August 13, 2007; Briarcliff Manor, New York
Also known as: Roberta Brooke Russell Kuser Marshall Astor; Roberta Brooke Russell (birth name)
Source of wealth: Inheritance
Bequeathal of wealth: Children; charity

EARLY LIFE

Brooke Astor was the only child of Marine officer John Henry Russell, Jr., and Mabel Howard Astor. Mother and child joined Russell at stations in Hawaii, Panama, and China. In Brooke's memoirs (*Patchwork Child*, 1962, rev. 1993; *Footprints*, 1980), she recalled learning from Chinese Buddhist priests to respect all living beings, an attitude that governed her philanthropic work. The family returned to the United States in 1914. In 1919, she married wealthy John Dryden Kuser. Her only child, Anthony Kuser, was born in 1924. The abusive marriage ended in 1930. In 1932, she married stockbroker Charles "Buddie" Marshall; her son changed his name to Anthony Marshall. After Marshall's 1952 death, she became an editor of *House and Garden* magazine. In 1953, she married Vincent Astor (1891-1959).

FIRST VENTURES

At Vincent Astor's death, his estate was worth $127 million. Brooke Astor received $2 million in cash, valuable real estate, and a $60 million trust fund. Much of this fortune had been amassed by John Jacob Astor (1763-1848), a fur trader who invested profits in increasingly valuable New York real estate. He leased land rather than sold it, allowing developers to build for maximum profit and disclaiming responsibility for the squalid tenements that resulted. Trusts kept money in the family. When John Jacob Astor IV died in the 1912 sinking of the RMS *Titanic*, his son Vincent inherited $87 million. He received his wealth outright, not in trust, and was free to rid the estate of slum properties, selling some to the city of New York for less than appraised value. In 1948, he es-

tablished the Vincent Astor Foundation, to which he bequeathed $60.5 million. His widow was to head the foundation.

MATURE WEALTH

Under Vincent Astor, the foundation routinely donated about $175,000 each year to established charities, such as the American Red Cross and the Astor Home for Children, which he helped found. Brooke Astor redefined the foundation's mission, insisting that New York, the source of the family's wealth, should receive most of the money. She began personal on-site tours to potential recipients to ensure that money would be well used. In her first year, grants totaled more than $3 million.

Her interests included educational and cultural institutions, such as the New York Public Library and the

Brooke Astor. (AP/Wide World Photos)

Metropolitan Museum of Art; her support was crucial during New York's fiscal crisis in the 1970's. Animal welfare grantees ranged from the Bronx Zoo to the Seniors' Animal Veterinary Endowment to provide treatment for the aging pets of the elderly. The foundation also donated heavily to redevelopment of the Bedford-Stuyvesant neighborhood in Brooklyn, one of the most impoverished in the city. She closed the foundation in 1997. Final grant recipients included Partnership for the Homeless, the Animal Medical Center, and the Women's Housing and Economic Development Center.

Her mind gradually failed. Her son, Anthony Marshall, took charge of her until 2006, when a guardianship petition by his son Philip Marshall resulted in Astor's friend Annette de la Renta becoming guardian and Chase Bank taking charge of Astor's financial affairs. Investigation of Anthony Marshall's handling of Astor's funds began in 2006; the validity of 2004 codicils to Astor's will was questioned. In 2007, Marshall was charged with sixteen counts, including grand larceny and fraud, for defrauding his mother and stealing tens of millions of dollars from her. He was tried in 2009, and on October 8 was convicted of fourteen of the sixteen counts against him. On December 21, 2009, he was sentenced to serve one to three years in prison, the minimum sentence allowed.

LEGACY

Astor was a woman of enormous personal wealth, leaving an estate of $198 million. She also possessed great social intelligence and vitality, making an outstanding contribution to her adopted city. The discipline provided by her international childhood, magazine editorship, and continual writing (memoirs, novels, essays, and poetry) gave her exceptional administrative skills. She recalled her husband telling her she would have fun administering the foundation, and she did. Her efforts gained her many honors, including a Medal of Freedom awarded by President Bill Clinton in 1998, her ninety-sixth year.

—*Betty Richardson*

FURTHER READING

Gordon, Meryl. *Mrs. Astor Regrets: The Hidden Betrayals of a Family Beyond Reproach.* Boston: Houghton Mifflin Harcourt, 2008.

Kavaler, Lucy. *The Astors: A Family Chronicle of Pomp and Power.* New York: Dodd, Mead, 1966.

Kiernan, Frances. *The Last Mrs. Astor: A New York Story.* New York: W. W. Norton, 2007.

See also: Eighteenth Duchess of Alba; Caroline Schermerhorn Astor; John Jacob Astor; Vincent Astor; William Backhouse Astor, Jr.; John Bouvier; Doris Duke; Barbara Hutton; Gloria Vanderbilt.

CAROLINE SCHERMERHORN ASTOR
American heiress and socialite

Astor stood at the forefront of Gilded Age society. Born into a respected old New York colonial family, she married into America's richest dynasty and used its wealth and position to become the uncontested leader of high society in New York.

Born: September 22, 1830; New York, New York
Died: October 30, 1908; New York, New York
Also known as: Caroline Webster Schermerhorn (birth name)
Sources of wealth: Inheritance; marriage
Bequeathal of wealth: Children; charity

EARLY LIFE

Caroline Schermerhorn Astor (KEHR-uh-lin SKAYR-murn AS-tuhr) was born Caroline Webster Schermerhorn in New York City in 1830. The daughter of Helen White and Abraham Schermerhorn, she was the youngest of eight children. Her father, a wealthy banker, merchant, and landowner, was worth about $500,000 when she was born. Her father was descended from the city's original Dutch settlers, and her mother could trace her lineage back to King James I of Great Britain. Caroline attended a school run by a Frenchwoman and completed her studies in Europe.

FIRST VENTURES

In 1853, she married William Backhouse Astor, Jr., grandson of the first John Jacob Astor, whose work in the fur trade and subsequent investments in land had made his family the wealthiest in America. Over the next decade, bearing and raising children occupied Caroline's time. She had four daughters, Emily, Helen, Charlotte Augusta, and Caroline, before giving birth to a male heir, John Jacob IV.

In 1872, when her mother-in-law Margaret Astor

died, Caroline claimed for herself the title of *the* Mrs. Astor. The wife of the eldest Astor son, John Jacob Astor III, should have assumed Margaret's role as the family's social matriarch, but she lacked her sister-in-law's social ambitions. Caroline's hunger for status may have sprung from concern for her children. She had four daughters for whom she needed to secure the best possible marriages. Caroline's husband William shunned society gatherings. However, he seemed willing enough to pay for his wife's elaborate entertainments, jewels, dresses, springs in London and Paris, and summers in Newport, Rhode Island.

MATURE WEALTH

With the help of distant cousin Ward McAllister, who became her majordomo and publicist, Caroline Astor assumed the role of high society's leader. McAllister popularized the concept of the Four Hundred—the notion that only about four hundred people, the approximate number that Astor's ballroom could accommodate, constituted the cream of New York society. He contributed to the formal and somewhat stout Astor's mystique, naming her the "Mystic Rose" after a paradisiacal vision in the literary works of Dante. Society's inner circle, and those hoping to enter it, vied for Astor's invitations.

Astor's grand parties were initially held in the four-story family home at 350 Fifth Avenue, where an unprepossessing brownstone exterior belied a sumptuous interior. In 1881, Astor's husband purchased her a sixty-two-room summer home in Newport, Rhode Island, that became another high-society hub. After William died in 1892, Caroline had a double home constructed for herself and her son's family at 840 Fifth Avenue. This imposing château, completed in 1896, included a massive shared ballroom.

William's death was followed in 1893 by that of their daughter Helen. By the time Astor emerged from two years of mourning, she had slipped from the pinnacle of society. She continued in a diminished fashion for the next decade, throwing her last ball in 1905 and her last dinner party in 1907. She spent her final year in declining health, dying of a heart ailment in 1908. She bequeathed most of her estate, valued at about $1.8 million, to her two surviving daughters, the family jewelry to her son, and $5,000 each to her butler and a charity for the blind.

LEGACY

Astor embodied the intermingling of New York's old, traditional colonial families with its newer wealth. Unlike her conservative ancestors, she used her money to emulate the opulent lifestyle of the European aristocracy.

Caroline Schermerhorn Astor. (©Bettmann/CORBIS)

However, she erected societal barriers to exclude the nouveau riche, who had not had enough time in high society to learn its niceties. She and McAllister determined that it took three generations of wealth to produce a gentleman, a rule under which her third-generation husband was acceptable and the second-generation Vanderbilts were not. In a chaotic, post-Civil War New York where respected old families suddenly found themselves rubbing elbows with robber barons, Astor represented order and taste.

—*Karen N. Kähler*

FURTHER READING

Cowles, Virginia. *The Astors*. New York: Knopf, 1979.

Homberger, Eric. *Mrs. Astor's New York*. New Haven, Conn.: Yale University Press, 2002.

King, Greg. *A Season of Splendor: The Court of Mrs. Astor in Gilded Age New York*. Hoboken, N.J.: Wiley & Sons, 2009.

Patterson, Jerry E. *The First Four Hundred*. New York: Rizzoli, 2000.

See also: Brooke Astor; John Jacob Astor; Vincent Astor; William Backhouse Astor, Jr.; Cornelia Martin; Consuelo Vanderbilt.

JOHN JACOB ASTOR
American merchant and entrepreneur

Astor became the first American multimillionaire. A German immigrant who came to the United States immediately after the Revolutionary War, he sold everything from musical instruments to tea but made most of his money in the fur trade. Astor's wealth set up his family as one of America's richest and most influential dynasties.

Born: July 17, 1763; Walldorf, Baden (now in Germany)
Died: March 29, 1848; New York, New York
Also known as: Johann Jakob Astor (birth name)
Sources of wealth: Trade; real estate
Bequeathal of wealth: Children; charity

EARLY LIFE
John Jacob Astor was the youngest of six children of Jacob Astor, a butcher, and Maria Magdalena Vorfelder. Astor's mother died three years after he was born; his father remarried and had six more children. Astor was born in Walldorf, Baden, which had an excellent school system, giving him a better education than most boys of his time and background. He followed the traditional pattern of leaving school at thirteen after being confirmed in the Lutheran Church. He then apprenticed as a butcher in his father's shop but did not like the trade.

Astor's older brother George made musical instruments in London, and Astor joined him in 1779. When the American Revolution ended in 1783, Astor set sail to join another brother, Henry, in New York. He sold musical instruments and sheet music in New York City for several months as a way to raise money to enter the fur trade. In 1784, he began to sell furs to the London market. A year later, in September, 1785, he married Sarah Todd. The couple would have eight children.

FIRST VENTURES
Astor continued to sell musical instruments but became increasingly involved in the fur trade. Meanwhile, he used his wife's connections to the old Dutch families of New York to increase his social prominence and business opportunities. He developed friendships with most of the leading politicians and businessmen in New York City. He later befriended politicians James Monroe, Henry Clay, and John C. Calhoun, among others, and would occasionally provide loans for friends.

While Astor's wife ran the musical instruments store, he made multiple buying trips to Albany, New York, a regional fur-trading outlet. In 1787, Astor rented a warehouse in Montreal, Canada, the fur-trading center in North America, and began making deals with traders. Many of the pelts that Astor purchased were beaver, which were used to make fashionable hats for Europeans. Since British law prohibited direct trade between Canada and the United States, Astor shipped his pelts to

John Jacob Astor. (Library of Congress)

London and then to New York or smuggled them overland.

MATURE WEALTH

By the early 1790's, Astor had become the leading American fur trader. He wasted no opportunity to make money. On the return voyage to the United States, he would ship teas and silk, which he would then sell for a handsome profit. In 1803, Astor purchased eight ships and created his own fleet. In addition to furs, his ships carried ginseng to China, which paid six times the American price for the herb.

By 1807, Astor had become the first American millionaire and the leading American fur trader. However, he had no particular allegiance to any country. Never a nationalist, Astor traded with anyone. In his dealings with Canada and Great Britain during President Thomas Jefferson's 1808 embargo on trade, Astor broke the law. He would engage in war profiteering during the War of 1812.

In 1808, Astor created the American Fur Company in order to establish a West Coast trading base. The American Fur Company also did business in the Great Lakes region and in the St. Louis-Missouri River area. Except for a break during the War of 1812, Astor's ships moved between China, Europe, Latin America, Hawaii, and the Pacific coast of North America. In 1827, Astor sold his ships and ended regular trade with China because of increased costs.

Astor used much of the profits from his fur trading to invest in real estate. From 1800 until his death in 1848, Astor is estimated to have spent more than $2 million in land deals for both urban and agricultural tracts in the vicinity of New York City. As Manhattan and the rest of the city grew, the value of Astor's real estate leaped. By the 1820's, he was collecting more than $100,000 in rental payments. The rental money would continue to benefit Astor's descendants long after his death.

One of Astor's major real estate projects was the Park Hotel, later named the Astor House. Begun in 1834 in New York City, it cost more than $400,000 to build. Upon its opening in 1836, it was the most famous hotel in the United States. However, Astor had less success with his developments west of New York City. A settlement he established in 1835 did not succeed. In 1838, the

---

ASTOR LIBRARY

John Jacob Astor left very little of his fortune to charitable causes, with the exception of $460,000 that he contributed to the Astor Library. The millionaire may have been influenced by criticism from educator Horace Mann, who publicly condemned him for not giving back more to the society that enriched him. Mann, the founder of the American public school system, called Astor "insane." In the 1820's, as Astor contemplated retirement and put an eye toward his legacy, he began to consider making a substantial charitable contribution. Writer Joseph Green Cogswell suggested that Astor fund a library to enhance the Astor name and give New Yorkers access to the cultural heritage of the world. In 1837, Astor agreed to fund a library. As befits such a founder, the Astor Library would be the greatest in the United States.

Unsure where to place the building, Astor finally decided upon some less valuable lots in Lafayette Place. This decision shows that he still had some trouble giving away money. Astor also repeatedly changed his mind about the library's architecture, personnel, and book purchasing. Cogswell managed to persuade the old millionaire to give him permission to buy a private European library that came on the market.

When the Astor Library finally opened in 1849, Cogswell had stocked it with 100,000 volumes at a time when the Library of Congress housed only 50,000 books and Harvard University's library held 72,000 volumes. The books were not loaned out and the hours of operation were limited, but the library quickly became established as a major source of reference and research. Astor's son, William Backhouse Astor, subsequently supplemented his father's endowment to keep the library strong.

The Astor Library's holdings merged into the New York Public Library in 1895. The former site of the Astor Library now houses the New York Shakespeare Festival's Joseph Papp Public Theater.

---

township of Astor joined with another town to form Green Bay, Wisconsin.

It would be far-fetched to categorize Astor as a humanitarian. He paid little attention to civic duties. He gave $5,000 of the $20,000 needed to build a home for poor old women and made donations to New York City's fire department. However, he made no other significant charitable bequests during his lifetime, except for financing the Astor Library.

Astor focused on his family. In the aftermath of the 1818 drowning death of a grandson, Astor left for Europe in 1819 with his two surviving sons and daughter Eliza (he and his wife would eventually survive all but two of their eight children). The group included Astor's oldest son, the mentally ill John Jacob Astor, Jr. The family traveled through Europe for the next fifteen years, with Astor purchasing a home on the shores of Lake Geneva, Switzerland, in 1824. Astor received regular reports from his business partners and remained actively involved in all of his business interests. In 1834, Astor returned permanently to the United States.

As Astor saw death approaching, he wound down his business affairs. Furs were no longer as profitable as they once had been because the mechanization of cloth manufacturing allowed manufacturers to make clothes for less money than producing them from furs. Additionally, western expansion had brought considerable competition in the fur business, with an accompanying increase in costs.

In 1834, Astor divided the first business monopoly in American history when he sold the northern and southern segments of the American Fur Company. His son, William Backhouse Astor, put the value of the empire at $1 million. Astor kept his real estate. At the time of his death, Astor's estate was valued by executors at $8 million, but this does not include property. Most biographers put the total value of the estate at between $20 and $30 million.

Legacy

Astor helped establish the young United States as a major trading nation. He did not transform business in any way but instead proved to be a master in the art of trading. He was a shrewd businessman rather than an innovator.

America's first millionaire and likely the richest man in the United States at the time of his death, Astor saw his only duty as making money for his family. He spent too much energy on amassing wealth to be able to easily give it away to strangers. He found it far easier to be generous with his family. The bulk of Astor's estate went to his son William, with the other half left in trust for grandson John Jacob Astor III. Astor left $50,000 to his hometown of Walldorf in order to care for the elderly and to provide education for poor children. He also left $30,000 to the German Society of New York to be used to help immigrants, as well as $30,000 to the Home for Aged Ladies. New York City's Blind Asylum, Half-Orphan Asylum, and German Reformed Church received minor gifts. As a result of the vast amount of wealth, the dynasty founded

by Astor became one of America's most famous families and a foundation of the *Social Register.*

—*Caryn E. Neumann*

Further Reading

Cowles, Virginia. *The Astors.* New York: Alfred A. Knopf, 1979. A good history of Astor and his many descendants.

Gates, John D. *The Astor Family.* Garden City, N.Y.: Doubleday, 1981. Shows the effects of enormous wealth upon Astor and his descendants.

Haeger, John Denis. *John Jacob Astor: Business and Finance in the Early Republic.* Detroit: Wayne State University Press, 1991. Sets Astor's business in historical context.

Irving, Washington. *Astoria: Or, Anecdotes of an Enterprise Beyond the Rocky Mountains.* Reprint. New York: KPI, 1987. Astor commissioned this book from Irving, a personal friend. This account of Astor's fur business first appeared in 1836.

Madsen, Axel. *John Jacob Astor: America's First Multimillionaire.* New York: John Wiley, 2001. This is the standard biography of Astor, with equal coverage of his professional and personal lives.

Porter, Kenneth W. *John Jacob Astor: Business Man.* Cambridge, Mass.: Harvard University Press, 1931. Reprints nearly four hundred pages of documents, including Astor's will.

Smith, Arthur D. Howden. *John Jacob Astor: Landlord of New York.* New York: Blue Ribbon Books, 1929. Astor bought a considerable amount of land, including Astoria in Queens, New York, and then made a fortune by leasing it. Despite its age, this book is readily available and appeared in 2005 in a Cosimo Classics edition.

Terrell, John Upton. *Furs by Astor: The Full Story of the Founding of a Great American Fortune.* New York: William Morrow, 1963. This solid biography of Astor focuses on the business side of his life.

See also: Brooke Astor; Caroline Schermerhorn Astor; Vincent Astor; William Backhouse Astor, Jr.; Donald Smith.

VINCENT ASTOR
American heir, investor, and philanthropist

Astor was the first member of his immensely wealthy family to gain a reputation for philanthropy. He had no heirs and left much of his vast fortune to the Vincent Astor Foundation, which continued to support charitable causes for almost four decades after his death.

Born: November 15, 1891; New York, New York
Died: February 3, 1959; New York, New York
Also known as: William Vincent Astor
Sources of wealth: Inheritance; real estate; investments
Bequeathal of wealth: Spouse; charity

EARLY LIFE
William Vincent Astor was born in New York City in 1891. The son of Ava Willing and John Jacob Astor IV and the grandson of Caroline Schermerhorn Astor and William Backhouse Astor, Jr., Vincent was born into one of America's wealthiest families. During his teens he attended Westminster School in Simsbury, Connecticut, and St. George's School in Newport, Rhode Island. His strict and emotionally distant father gave the schoolboy an allowance of only fifty cents a month, which would be reduced by fifteen cents if Vincent's grades were poor or if he behaved badly. The young man fared better at Harvard University, where he received a $2,000 annual allowance, from which he had to pay for his tuition and board. In April, 1912, his life changed abruptly when his father died aboard the RMS *Titanic*, making twenty-year-old Vincent the youngest Astor to inherit. He left college and immersed himself in learning how to manage the family estate.

FIRST VENTURES
Astor's father, who was worth $87 million at his death, bequeathed $70 million to his son, about $63 million of which was in real estate. Vincent's inheritance included the Hudson Valley retreat Ferncliff, the yachts *Noma* and *Nourmahal*, and a garage of thirty automobiles. Vincent officially took control of the

Astor estate upon his twenty-first birthday. Shortly thereafter, he broke from his forebears' tradition of merely owning land and ventured into developing it. He also strayed from expected Astor behavior by establishing a playground in Harlem and making other recreational provisions for slum children.

In 1914, he married longtime acquaintance Helen Dinsmore Huntington. During World War I, Astor served in the navy, ultimately rising to the rank of captain. He also contributed to war loans, gave the navy his yacht *Noma*, and offered Ferncliff for use as a hospital.

In 1919, Vincent and Helen moved into the palatial Astor residence at 840 Fifth Avenue, an imposing château that Vincent's father and grandmother Caroline had

Vincent Astor walks his dog while visiting Marblehead, Massachusetts. (©Bettmann/CORBIS)

THE VINCENT ASTOR FOUNDATION

Vincent Astor established the charitable trust that bore his name in 1948 with the intention of using the trust for "the alleviation of human misery." The foundation initially provided grants to hospitals, children's homes, and other institutions. Astor's will left half of his estate, or $65 million, to the foundation.

Upon his death in 1959, Astor's widow Brooke became the foundation's president. During her tenure, which spanned four decades, foundation funds were allocated to a variety of charities, including the Metropolitan Opera Association, the New York Botanical Garden, the Natural History Museum, the Bronx Zoo, the Pierpont Morgan Library, the East Harlem Tutorial Program, the Navy Yard Boys' Club, and the Greater New York Ice Hockey League. Many of the gifts granted during Brooke Astor's tenure reflected her own background and interests: her childhood in China, her passion for learning and the written word, and her love for her dachshunds.

New York's Metropolitan Museum of Art received $10 million from the foundation in order to add a Chinese courtyard to its Asian galleries. Astor Court, which features a covered walkway, a small reception area, a half pavilion, a koi pond, a skylight, and Ming Dynasty furniture, was modeled on a scholar's courtyard in the Garden of the Master of the Fishing Nets in Suzhou, a city inland from Shanghai, China, known for its fine garden architecture. The courtyard's components were crafted in Suzhou and installed by a team of Chinese engineers and craftsmen. Astor Court opened to the public in 1981.

In the early 1980's, Brooke focused the foundation's philanthropy on the ailing New York Public Library. Her efforts and contributions helped popularize the library as a cause. The foundation's $10 million gift to the library in 1985 ignited a fund-raising campaign that generated $300 million. The foundation's gift designated $7 million for the library's unrestricted endowment and $3 million for annual operations of the research libraries. Brooke and Vincent Astor are memorialized through several library fellowships, awards, and facilities that bear their names, including the Vincent Astor Gallery, an exhibition space at the New York Public Library for the Performing Arts at Lincoln Center Plaza. Other notable foundation activities included the 1982 establishment of the Astor Chair of Comparative Medicine at New York's Animal Medical Center (AMC) and the 1995 funding of AMC's Senior Assistance Veterinary Effort, which supplies medical care for the pets of elderly indigent persons.

With no direct Astor heirs to whom she could pass the foundation, Brooke decided it should not continue after she retired from management. In 1997, at the age of ninety-five, she dissolved the foundation and gave away its remaining assets. At the time of her death, on August 13, 2007, she was renowned as one of New York's greatest philanthropists, having given $25 million to the New York Public Library alone.

---

shared. (John Jacob, who divorced Vincent's mother in 1910, left the Fifth Avenue house, a sixty-two-room summer house in Newport, Rhode Island, and a $5 million trust to his second wife Madeleine; when she remarried in 1919, she forfeited these benefits, which reverted to Vincent.) While the Astors held an annual January ball in remembrance of Vincent's grandmother Caroline, famed for her elaborate high-society entertainments, they also hosted charitable banquets.

MATURE WEALTH

In the years after World War I, Astor began selling off many family properties, including the Schermerhorn Building on Broadway for $1.5 million and the Longacre Building on Times Square for $2.5 million. Sale of the Waldorf-Astoria Hotel, jointly owned by Astor and the British branch of the family, brought each party $7.56 million; the hotel was demolished and the Empire State Building erected in its place. Other Astor-owned hotels, the St. Regis and the Knickerbocker, were also liquidated. Even Astor's Fifth Avenue home went on the market, fetching $3.5 million in 1925. Vincent and Helen moved to a smaller, $250,000 Georgian-style town home at 130 East 80th Street.

Over the course of roughly a decade, this real estate liquidation yielded more than $40 million, which Astor profitably reinvested in stocks. He also acquired shares in the first motion picture adaptation of Lew Wallace's novel *Ben Hur: A Tale of the Christ* (1880). He used his $371,000 from the 1925 blockbuster film to purchase a new and better yacht, christened *Nourmahal* in honor of the yacht his father and grandfather had owned. The $1.75 million *Nourmahal*, built in 1928, had a forty-two-man crew and an annual operating cost of $125,000. For years, Astor made annual South Pacific and Caribbean cruises aboard *Nourmahal*. On a 1930 trip to the Galápagos Islands, he brought along a team of naturalists from the New York Aquarium, the American Museum of

Natural History, and the Brooklyn Botanic Garden to collect biological specimens for their institutions.

Astor was an early supporter of Franklin D. Roosevelt, a distant relative and Hudson Valley neighbor. He placed *Nourmahal* at Roosevelt's disposal, and it was aboard Astor's yacht that the rattled president-elect collected himself after surviving a 1933 assassination attempt in Miami, Florida. Astor later conducted espionage for President Roosevelt under the entirely credible cover of a wealthy man enjoying a pleasure cruise.

Astor disliked his family's history as slumlords, and he strove to divest himself of his inherited tenement holdings. In the early 1930's, after some lower East Side tenements caught fire, Astor worked with the city housing authority to sell off his holdings for $189,000, much less than their actual value. Astor provided assistance to the tenants, helping them move out and find alternate housing. The tenements were razed and the city's first low-cost public housing constructed.

In 1933, Astor became owner of the weekly magazine *Today* with an initial investment of $250,000. Four years later, the magazine was merged into *Newsweek*, and Astor became the majority stockholder. It took roughly ten years and $5 million of Astor's money for *Newsweek* to break even. *Newsweek* was one of Astor's passions, along with the St. Regis Hotel. Built by and inherited from his father, the luxury hotel was among the properties he had sold off during the 1920's. However, he reacquired the St. Regis in 1934 and spent $500,000 to improve it. Under Astor's watch, the hotel once again became a popular Manhattan destination.

In 1940, Astor's wife divorced him, and shortly after he married Mary Benedict "Minnie" Cushing. During World War II he transferred his beloved *Nourmahal* to the Navy. After the war he went through another period of liquidating his real estate holdings, investing the profits in the stock market. The resulting returns would nearly double the inheritance he received from his father.

Astor and his second wife divorced in 1953. That same year he married the recently widowed Mary Brooke Russell Marshall, better known as Brooke, the editor of *House and Garden*. Infamous for his moodiness, Astor nonetheless warmed to Brooke's young grandsons, roughhousing with them and taking them for rides on the narrow-gauge railroad he had built at Ferncliff.

In 1955, he unveiled plans for Astor Plaza, a forty-six-floor luxury office building at Park Avenue and Fifty-third Street. After investing $75 million in this ambitious project, Astor found himself unable to raise financing for its development. Three years later he sold his interest to First National City Bank, losing $3 million in the process.

Astor fell ill during a trip abroad in 1958. The next year, after a period of poor health, he died of a heart attack at the age of sixty-seven. He left his widow Brooke $2 million outright and a trust fund of more than $60 million. Half of his estate, $65 million, went to the Vincent Astor Foundation. Astor's estranged half brother John Jacob Astor VI, the son of John Jacob Astor IV and his second wife Madeleine, contested the will. He challenged Vincent's mental competence at the time the will was drafted and claimed undue influence by the executors. After several months, when it became clear his efforts would be fruitless, he settled for $250,000 offered by Brooke.

Legacy

The Astor family traditionally had a reputation for keeping their wealth largely to themselves. Their charitable donations were generally viewed as meager in comparison to what they were capable of contributing. Vincent, by contrast, was "the Astor who gave it away." His philanthropy set him apart from his ancestors, as did the social conscience that prompted him to reject the role of slumlord. While he enjoyed private yachts, airplanes, multiple homes, and other amusements of the rich, he also worked hard at managing and expanding his estate. After his death in 1959, the foundation that he established—and the woman in whose hands it was left—continued to improve life for New Yorkers for the rest of the century.

—Karen N. Kähler

Further Reading

Astor, Brooke. *Footprints*. Garden City, N.Y.: Doubleday, 1980. Astor's third wife devotes part 3 of this autobiography to life with Vincent. Part 4 focuses on her work as head of the Vincent Astor Foundation.

Cowles, Virginia. *The Astors*. New York: Knopf, 1979. Presents Astor's life in the context of his family's rise, importance, and influence. Includes a select bibliography, an index, a family tree, and copious illustrations.

Gates, John D. *The Astor Family*. Garden City, N.Y.: Doubleday, 1981. Chapter 15 is an overview of Astor's life, while chapter 16 discusses the Vincent Astor Foundation's philanthropy after his death. Includes a bibliography, an index, and an Astor genealogical chart.

Gordon, Meryl. *Mrs. Astor Regrets: The Hidden Betrayals of a Family Beyond Reproach.* Boston: Houghton Mifflin Harcourt, 2008. While Gordon's book focuses on the later years of Astor's widow Brooke, chapter 5 succinctly portrays Vincent Astor's youth, career, personality, marriages, and death. Includes notes, a bibliography, and photographs.

Kiernan, Frances. *The Last Mrs. Astor: A New York Story.* New York: W. W. Norton, 2007. Chapter 5 of this biography of Astor's widow describes Vincent's background and their marriage. Subsequent chapters look at the Vincent Astor Foundation's work. Includes photographs, a bibliography, and an index.

Sinclair, David. *Dynasty: The Astors and Their Time.* New York: Beaufort Books, 1984. Chapter 6 provides a detailed account of Astor's early years, while chapter 10 chronicles his later life. Includes illustrations, a genealogical chart, a bibliography and sources, and an index.

See also: Brooke Astor; Caroline Schermerhorn Astor; John Jacob Astor; William Backhouse Astor, Jr.

WILLIAM BACKHOUSE ASTOR, JR.
American heir and landowner

Astor was the grandson of self-made millionaire John Jacob Astor. He inherited the family's wealth and spent much of his life letting others manage it, becoming better known for spending his fortune on diversions than increasing or sharing it.

Born: July 12, 1830; New York, New York
Died: April 25, 1892; Paris, France
Sources of wealth: Inheritance; real estate
Bequeathal of wealth: Spouse; children

EARLY LIFE
William Backhouse Astor, Jr., the second son of Margaret Armstrong and William Backhouse Astor, Sr., was born in New York City in 1830. He graduated from Columbia University in 1849 and then spent the next year abroad. In 1853, he married Caroline Webster Schermerhorn, a wealthy and pedigreed descendant of one of New York's earliest Dutch settlers. Over the next decade, the couple had five children: Emily, Helen, Charlotte Augusta, Caroline, and John Jacob IV.

FIRST VENTURES
Astor's grandfather, John Jacob Astor, had been a poor German immigrant who made a fortune in the fur trade and increased it through real estate investments, becoming the wealthiest American of his day. When he died in 1848, his estate was worth more than $20 million. During the life of William Backhouse Astor, Sr., this fortune grew to $45 million. Much of the Astor wealth was in New York City real estate, from fashionable Manhattan properties to overcrowded lower East Side tenements.

As a second son, William Backhouse Astor, Jr., found that elder brother John Jacob Astor III left him little or no role in managing the Astor estate. Lacking direction, the younger Astor pursued his passion for country life and travel.

After the birth of their son, Astor's wife Caroline focused on becoming the uncontested leader of New York

William Backhouse Astor, Jr. (The Granger Collection, New York)

society. Their four-story brownstone at 350 Fifth Avenue was the site of countless high-society occasions. While content to fund his wife's social ambitions, Astor took no interest or pleasure in entertaining. He spent much of his time in Europe, at sea, or at Ferncliff, a country retreat he constructed in New York's Hudson River Valley.

MATURE WEALTH

While his father and brother managed the family estate, Astor led a life of leisure. At Ferncliff, he established stables for horse breeding, one of his favorite pastimes. An enthusiastic yachtsman, he had *Ambassadress* built in 1867, at the time the largest private sailing yacht ever constructed. Two decades later, he commissioned *Nourmahal*, a 250-foot-long steam yacht.

An extended yacht trip along Florida's coast during the 1870's interested Astor in the state's development potential. He constructed a railroad from Palatka to St. Augustine, a block of houses in Jacksonville, and a twelve-thousand-acre town on the St. Johns River. Originally called Manhattan, the town was later renamed Astor in his honor.

In 1875, the elder William died, leaving an estate of at least $100 million. After the payment of various bequests, equal shares of the fortune, an estimated $20 million each, went to sons John Jacob and William. (John Jacob is believed to have received more of the estate, presumably through gifts made during their father's life.)

In 1892, during a visit to Paris, William Astor, Jr., died from lung congestion. He left an estate valued at between $30 and $40 million, most of which he bequeathed to his son. He set up a trust for his wife, providing her $50,000 annually. No more than $5 million was divided among his daughters and their children. Of the $145,000 left to public institutions, $50,000 went to the Astor Library.

LEGACY

By the third generation, the Astor dynasty had gained a reputation for making staggering amounts of money (much of it from rents paid by poor tenants living in Astor-owned slums) without contributing significantly to the general community. William Astor, Jr., did little to improve public opinion of his family. An ill-tempered, heavy drinker, womanizer, and absentee husband and father, he would become known as the first of the "decadent Astors." Friends asserted that he contributed extensively to charities; if so, he gave in too discreet and secretive a manner to have won recognition for his generosity. Overshadowed in business by his father and brother and in society by his wife, he chose to live the life of pleasure that his inherited fortune could furnish him.

—*Karen N. Kähler*

FURTHER READING

Cowles, Virginia. *The Astors*. New York: Knopf, 1979.

Homberger, Eric. *Mrs. Astor's New York*. New Haven, Conn.: Yale University Press, 2002.

King, Greg. *A Season of Splendor: The Court of Mrs. Astor in Gilded Age New York*. Hoboken, N.J.: Wiley & Sons, 2009.

Patterson, Jerry E. *The First Four Hundred*. New York: Rizzoli, 2000.

See also: Brooke Astor; Caroline Schermerhorn Astor; John Jacob Astor; Vincent Astor.

ATAHUALPA
Incan royalty

To Atahualpa and his subjects, gold (called "sweat of the sun"), silver ("tears of the moon"), and other precious minerals were prized primarily for symbolic, religious, or decorative value. However, it was their intrinsic worth that was sought by the Spanish conquistadors, and in relentless pursuit of treasure, they trampled Atahualpa and the Inca Empire into the dust.

Born: c. 1502; Cuzco, Inca Empire (now in Peru)
Died: August 29, 1533; Cajamarca, Inca Empire (now in Peru)
Also known as: Atahuallpa; Atabalipa; Sapa Inca
Sources of wealth: Inheritance; conquest
Bequeathal of wealth: Confiscated

EARLY LIFE
Atahualpa (ah-tah-WAHL-pah) was born into a dynamic family in a turbulent era, when the Old and the New Worlds clashed. His mother was a royal concubine and Atahualpa was one of more than fifty children sired by Huayna Capac, eleventh Sapa Inca ("only Inca," or "supreme leader," called "the son of the Sun"). Although Ninan Cuyochi (born c. 1490) was eldest son and first in line to succeed his father as Sapa Inca, Atahualpa was his father's favorite. He enjoyed every privilege of the ultrawealthy, often accompanying Huayna Capac on military campaigns. Huayna Capac was so impressed with Atahualpa's courage that he vowed to divide the Inca Empire between Atahualpa and Ninan Cuyochi.

FIRST VENTURES
Atahualpa grew up surrounded by every imaginable luxury among numerous half brothers and half sisters in Cuzco, the richest city in the Western Hemisphere, where tribute poured in from every corner of the empire. In the mid-1520's, the empire was ravaged by a smallpox epidemic. Huayna Capac died of the disease; his heir Ninan

Atahualpa, after his capture by the Spanish conquistadors, kneels before Francisco Pizarro. (Hulton Archive/Getty Images)

Coyochi also perished. Into the vacuum swept Atahualpa's brother Huáscar, lord of Cuzco, who became Sapa Inca in 1527. Atahualpa, meanwhile, took control of Quito in the north. After several years of coexistence, the brothers collided in civil war. Initially, Huáscar prevailed, and his army defeated Atahualpa at Chillopampa and captured him. Atahualpa escaped, regrouped his army, and routed Huáscar's army at Chimborazo. Huáscar was later executed, and Atahualpa also put to death many members of the royal family to eliminate rivals.

MATURE WEALTH

Atahualpa became Sapa Inca in 1532—just months before the Spanish landed on the west coast of South America. Thus he did not long enjoy the perquisites of his position. As supreme leader, anything within his vast realm was his, and he had the power of life and death over his millions of subjects. Atahualpa had access to an unlimited number of concubines. By law, all gold and silver in the empire belonged to him, and he used gold in great abundance to decorate his palace, gild temples, adorn his person, and surround himself with gleaming objects of great beauty but of only aesthetic value to him. He was carried aloft on a golden throne, and he wore a necklace of emeralds and golden ornaments in his hair.

In late 1532, the Spanish under Francisco Pizarro encountered Atahualpa and his entourage in Cajamarca. In an act of treachery that would often be repeated, the Spanish ambushed Atahualpa's unarmed Indian courtiers and slaughtered thousands. Atahualpa was held hostage. To ransom himself, he offered to fill a large room with the treasures the Spanish wanted. The room was eventually stuffed with gold and silver artifacts. However, the Spanish accused Atahualpa of various acts of sacrilege and strangled him to death. As a result of the murder, additional tons of gold destined for Spanish coffers were allegedly diverted to unknown caches and remain hidden to this day.

LEGACY

Material riches meant little to Atahualpa and the Incas, even though they were fabulously wealthy by contemporary standards, because they had no monetary system. Gold, silver, and jewels were merely attractive baubles. Power and control were all that really mattered to the supreme leader, who commanded the ultimate fate of all food, animals, humans, and objets d'art within the empire.

While wonderfully crafted golden objects of Incan handiwork still exist in museums, most treasures obtained from Atahualpa's ransom were melted down to form ingots. Even as the once-powerful Inca Empire quickly fell apart, the empire's gold helped fund the expansion of the Spanish Empire. Ironically, the gold—alloyed with iron, copper, or other metals to increase strength or malleability—was deemed inferior to the gold obtained during the conquest of the Aztecs in the 1520's.

—*Jack Ewing*

FURTHER READING

Levin, Mark R. *The Last Inca: Atahualpa*. El Cajon, Calif.: Unarius, 1993.

Miller, Leo Edward. *The Hidden People: The Story of a Search for Incan Treasure*. New York: Charles Scribner's Sons, 1920. Reprint. Whitefish, Mont.: Kessinger, 2008.

Prescott, William Hickling. Reprint. *The History of the Conquest of Peru*. New York: Modern Library, 1998.

See also: Montezuma II.

JORGE WOLNEY ATALLA
Brazilian sugarcane and biofuels magnate

Atalla, who owned sugar mills and plantations in Brazil, realized that sugarcane could be converted to alcohol and used as a source of power, supplementing the nation's lack of fossil fuels. He became an international representative of Brazil, exporting Brazilian goods around the world and sponsoring a Brazilian Formula One racing team.

Born: 1929; Jaú, Brazil
Died: July 31, 2009; São Paulo, Brazil
Sources of wealth: Manufacturing; agricultural products
Bequeathal of wealth: Relatives; charity; sporting event

EARLY LIFE
Jorge Wolney Atalla (ZHORE-jay VOHL-nay ah-TAHL-yah) was descended from Lebanese immigrants who came to Brazil and settled in the booming state of São Paulo, becoming prosperous landholders. His father was a physician and his mother inherited a considerable number of cattle and coffee landholdings. Atalla's family sent him to study in the United States, where he graduated with a degree in petroleum engineering from the University of Tulsa in Oklahoma. However, when his father decided to return to his medical practice, the young Atalla was ordered to return home to manage the family enterprises.

FIRST VENTURES
Atalla used his advanced technical education to modernize the family's business operations through technological and managerial improvements. He expanded the family holdings, selecting properties and businesses that were available at bargain prices. His purchases included sugar plantations and mills because a glut of sugar on world markets had reduced their price. Atalla examined alternative uses for sugar, particularly its use in producing alcohol as a combustible fuel.

Brazil's economy was becoming more industrialized, but this growth was hampered by a shortage of fossil fuels. Industrial managers, particularly motor vehicle manufacturers, quickly saw the benefit of using ethanol and other alcohol-based fuels as alternative sources of power. The development of alcohol and alternative biofuels became major national priorities and was subsidized by the government. Atalla led the proalcohol movement and sponsored sugar research institutes. His work helped create ate fuel for Brazilian motor vehicles, industry, and agriculture. As the need for sugar-derived fuel increased, sugar production, which had traditionally been centered in the northeastern part of Brazil, shifted to São Paulo and other places in the south. Extensive rural areas that were used to grow food were converted to biofuel production.

MATURE WEALTH
The sugar business was only one of the industries that were part of the Atalla Group. Atalla's conglomerate exported sugar, coffee, iron ore, wood products, and other raw materials. In the mid-1970's, as the price of coffee rose on world markets, Atalla bought Hills Brothers Coffee, an American company based in San Francisco. At this time, it was unprecedented for a Brazilian company to acquire a foreign industrial enterprise. The acquisition projected the image of Brazil as an expanding economic power and earned Atalla the acclaim of other Brazilian businesspeople.

More important, Atalla's international business operations allowed him to expand his export business. Like other twentieth century Brazilian conglomerates, such as the Votorantim Group and Camargo Corrêio, the Atalla Group's international business was dependent on minimized domestic competition. Such conglomerates enjoyed government promotion, sponsorship, subsidies, and regulatory advantages.

Atalla's increasing wealth enabled him to represent Brazil throughout the world. He promoted Brazilian Formula One racing, sponsored by his sugar cooperative, Copersucar (*açucar* is the Portuguese word for sugar). Copersucar race drivers won numerous championships in worldwide competitions.

By the end of the twentieth century, Atalla's accumulating wealth placed him on the *Forbes* magazine list of billionaires, with family holdings valued at approximately $1.3 billion. At the end of his career, however, his sugar enterprise had declined in production and profitability. Despite the attention given to his multinational feats, he was not someone who welcomed public interest in his business ventures. He led a subdued private life, on which there is scant public information. Hardly any obituaries appeared at the time of his death on July 31, 2009.

LEGACY
Jorge Wolney Atalla demonstrated that the Brazilian economy had developed to such a point that it could com-

pete in the world arena in the fields of business and sports. He was a leading figure in the Brazilian-Lebanese community and a longtime patron of the Brazilian Red Cross. Ironically, one of his sons, who bore his name, became a cinematographer whose most noted film was a documentary portraying the hardships and injustices suffered by sugarcane workers. The wealth accrued by Atalla and other Brazilian conglomerate leaders reflected the stark income chasm between rich and poor in the economically developing Brazil.

—*Edward A. Riedinger*

FURTHER READING

Agra Informa. *Sugar and Ethanol in Brazil: A Study of the Brazilian Sugarcane, Sugar, and Ethanol Industries*. Tunbridge Wells, England: Author, 2007.

Dean, Warren. *The Industrialization of São Paulo, 1880-1945*. Austen: University of Texas Press, 1969.

Fausto, Boris. *A Concise History of Brazil*. Cambridge, England: Cambridge University Press, 2006.

See also: Sebastião Camargo; Francisco Matarazzo; José de Moraes.

AURANGZEB
Mughal emperor

As emperor of Mughal India, Aurangzeb ruled over the richest and most fabled empire in the world. The wealth of India increasingly attracted the European powers to extend their trade, and ultimately their territory, in India.

Born: November 3, 1618; Dohad, Mālwa, India
Died: March 3, 1707; Ahmadnagar, Maharashtra, India
Also known as: Muhī-ud-Dīn Muḥammad Aurangzeb (birth name); ʿĀlamgīr I
Sources of wealth: Inheritance; conquest
Bequeathal of wealth: Children

EARLY LIFE

Aurangzeb (AW-rahng-zehb), the third eldest of four sons of the great Mughul emperor, Shah Jahan, was born in 1618. He was sent to live with his grandfather, Emperor Jahāngīr, where he was taught in Arabic and memorized the Qurʾān. In 1634, at the age of sixteen, he was given command of a force of ten thousand horses, and the following year he was sent to the south of India, the Deccan, to suppress a rebellion in Bundelkhand. He was then appointed the viceroy of the Deccan, a position he held for eight years.

FIRST VENTURES

In February, 1645, Aurangzeb was appointed governor of the rich province of Gujerat. He was an austere, puritanical leader who did not live ostentatiously or succumb to drink and drugs. He ran a strong and effective government, and he was rewarded by his father, who raised his salary to the vast sum of 6 million rupees a year. In 1646, Aurangzeb was sent to head the Central Asian campaign

Aurangzeb. (Library of Congress)

and was then appointed the governor of Multan before leading a campaign in Afghanistan. In July, 1652, he returned to the Deccan as the area's governor, and it was there that he kept the jewels from the sultan of Golconda, even though his father believed they were his property. By this time Aurangzeb was a powerful and wealthy regional leader with a strong and loyal following. Aurangzeb's father, Shah Jahan, fell ill in Āgra in 1657, and Aurangzeb moved north to seize the shah and his enormous treasury. Aurangzeb then waged a murderous civil war against his three brothers, imprisoned his father, and crowned himself emperor on July 31, 1658. Aurangzeb was now one of the richest men in the world.

MATURE WEALTH

Aurangzeb's reign can be divided into two twenty-five-year periods. The first was spent in the north of India, mostly at Delhi and Āgra, where he consolidated and expanded his power and wealth. In Bihar, he defeated the raja of Palamau in 1661 and annexed the raja's kingdom. Aurangzeb also acquired Assam in 1662, although he lost it five years later, and he incorporated Chittagong in 1666. His twenty-one separate provinces generated, on paper, a revenue of 334.5 million rupees. In addition, he collected taxes on the tithes paid by Muslims (*zakāt*), and in 1679 he reestablished the poll tax (*jizya*) on non-Muslims, which had been abolished in 1564. Comparatively small amounts of less than 3 million rupees, or 1 percent of total revenue per year, were also raised through import duties on foreign trade, which played only a small part in the Mughal economy.

The cost of India's imported silver, gold, copper, lead, high-quality woolen clothing, horses, spices, tobacco, glassware, wine, and slaves was offset by the export of cotton goods, pepper, indigo, and saltpeter. Aurangzeb ended the lavish building program conducted by his father, and he was renowned for his comparative miserliness. In 1679 he went to Ajmer to annex Marwar, which

led to a military offensive in the Deccan, where he spent the last twenty-five years of his life in a futile attempt to expand his territory.

LEGACY

The Mughal Empire began its rapid decline after the death in 1707 of Aurangzeb because he bankrupted his realm in his attempt to expand it. He was the last of the "great Mughals," as well as a pious and strict Muslim. His reimposition of the poll tax, his prohibition against the building of Hindu temples, and his sanctioning of the destruction of old Hindu temples alienated Hindus and Sikhs and led to rebellion, most famously by the Maratha Hindu ruler, Śivājī. After Śivājī's death in 1680, Aurangzeb was only able to capture Bijapur in 1686 and Golconda in 1687. To control these territories, Aurangzeb moved his capital to Aurangabad in the Deccan. He doubled the size of his military corps to more than fourteen thousand officers as he faced an increasing number of revolts, but his huge, cumbersome army remained vulnerable to guerrilla attack. When he died in 1707 while on military campaign, he was buried in a modest tomb by the side of the road near Aurangabad.

—*Roger D. Long*

FURTHER READING

Bhave, Y. G. *From the Death of Shivagi to the Death of Aurangzeb: The Critical Years*. New Delhi, India: Northern Book Centre, 2000.

Eraly, Abraham. *The Mughal Throne: The Saga of India's Great Emperors*. London: Weidenfeld & Nicolson, 2003.

Richards, John F. *The Mughal Empire*. Part 1, vol. 5 of *The New Cambridge History of India*. Cambridge, England: Cambridge University Press, 1993.

See also: Fateh Chand; Abdul Ghafur; Shah Jahan; Virji Vora; Shantidas Zaveri.

Emilio Bacardi
Cuban liquor company executive

Bacardi used his influence with Cuban insurgents and the Spanish colonial government to maintain and expand the fortunes of his family's rum-distilling business during long periods of rebellion in Cuba. He established the Emilio Bacardi Moreau Museum to house his extensive collections of art and artifacts.

Born: June 5, 1844; Santiago de Cuba, Cuba
Died: August 28, 1922; Santiago de Cuba, Cuba
Also known as: Emilio Bacardi Moreau
Sources of wealth: Manufacturing; sale of products
Bequeathal of wealth: Spouse; children; charity; museum

Early Life

Emilio Bacardi Moreau (eh-MEE-lehoh bah-KARD-ee MOH-roh) was born in 1844 in Santiago de Cuba, Cuba, the eldest of four children of Facunda Bacardi Massó (1813-1866). When Emilio was a child, his father Facundo, a successful retailer, entered the fledgling rum business by purchasing a distillery for 3,000 gold pesos (almost $6,000). At twenty-one, Emilio entered the family business, but he was divided between his duties to the family and his desire to be a leader in the Cuban independence effort.

First Ventures

The period between 1868 and 1878 was marked by internal strife in Cuba that adversely affected the nation's sugar plantations. Bacardi was active in Cuba's effort to gain independence from Spain at the same time he worked in the family business. In 1874, Facundo Bacardi bought out his partners and with his sons formed a new corporation, Bacardi y Compania. Soon the company's products gained international recognition by winning major prizes at world's fairs. Key to the products' successes were the oak barrels in which the rum was cured, the quality of the Cuban sugar and molasses used in the blends, and the secret family recipe that made Bacardi's taste uniquely desirable.

At thirty-three, Bacardi became president of the firm, and he used his connections as a patriot and prominent businessman to promote a product that was distinctly Cuban. In September, 1879, Bacardi was arrested for his involvement in the Cuban independence movement. He was tried and deported to penal institutions in Spain and North Africa. The year 1880 proved deadly for Bacardi's

business, and his company, which was nearly $40,000 in debt and lacked cash flow, declared bankruptcy. By 1883, however, Bacardi y Compania had returned to some of its former stability, posting a profit of nearly 23,000 pesos. During this period, Bacardi was torn between his Cuban independence efforts and his partnership within his family company, but he managed to balance both and earn a great deal of respect as a Cuban entrepreneur.

Mature Wealth

Despite the death of his wife in 1885 and his father in 1886, Bacardi began a corporate reorganization that would lead to his company's worldwide fame. Bacardi, as head of both the firm and family, hired Enrique Scheug as the company's financial manager and redistributed ownership of the remaining Cuban distillery to prevent the Spanish government from seizing its operations. In 1888, the Bacardi company's rums won international acclaim in spirits competitions. Profits trebled to nearly 65,000 pesos in 1891. As another period of political instability emerged in 1895, Bacardi kept positive working relations with Cuban sugar planters. However, in 1896, he was arrested and again sent to North Africa after he was found guilty of participating in political activities.

In 1898, Bacardi went to Jamaica, where his family had gone for safety, and in August, 1898, he returned to Santiago de Cuba to resume work. The Bacardi brothers and Scheug managed to survive the political uprisings, but the company earned only marginal profits between 1891 and 1893. However, Bacardi rums proved popular with the American soldiers who came to Cuba at the end of the nineteenth century to fight in the Spanish-American War. American efforts to annex Cuba were under way and General Leonard Wood set up operations there. Wood appointed Bacardi the mayor of Santiago de Cuba. Bacardi became active in rebuilding and restoring Cuba after many years of strife. He was elected mayor of Santiago de Cuba in 1901, and the following year Cuba gained independence from Spain. Bacardi was elected to the Cuban senate in 1905. Ten years later, exhausted from wrangling with the United States and disappointed by aspects of the new Cuban government, Bacardi resigned from politics and fully devoted himself to the family business.

Bacardi led the company into the twentieth century by

THE EMILIO BACARDI MOREAU MUSEUM

Emilio Bacardi Moreau, the Cuban rum executive, founded a museum to house his collection of artifacts in 1899. For many years his museum was a small-scale operation. By 1922, however, the museum's collection had grown large enough to be housed in a Palladian-style building in Bacardi's hometown, Santiago de Cuba. The museum opened in the fall of 1927 and continued to operate into the twenty-first century.

The museum displays a variety of artifacts in three dedicated exhibit areas: the Art Room, the History Room, and the Archaeology Room. Its collection includes an Egyptian mummy and two Peruvian mummies that Bacardi had collected, as well as artifacts highlighting the aesthetic development of Cuban arts, representative items from major world cultures, textiles, and items that once belonged to Cuban patriots, including Antonio Maceo and Carlos Manuel de Cespedes. Museum guides generally describe the holdings as "eclectic," since they appear to be items that Bacardi either liked or was able to obtain in world art markets. In 2006, eighty-four items were stolen from the collection, only to be recovered three days later.

The museum has played a significant role in promoting Cuban art. Before the country became independent, Cuban art either was religious in nature or consisted of decorative objects reflective of Spanish traditions. By collecting paintings by Cuban artists, Bacardi expanded the range of the nation's artwork. Although artistic patronage was a feature of Cuban society from the seventeenth century, the late nineteenth and early twentieth centuries marked a new era in private collecting, particularly of imported artworks from major dealers in Europe. By 1913, there were three public art museums in Cuba including the Emilio Bacardi Moreau Museum—the Museo Nacional in Havana and a museum in Cárdenas—and these institutions followed the Bacardi tradition of exhibiting Cuban regional art as well as international works.

make drinking his company's beverages appear both fun and patriotic. Bacardi moved easily in government circles and his company enjoyed sufficient growth to enable it to add new operations in New York, Puerto Rico, and Barcelona, Spain.

As the business expanded, Emilio's brother, Facundo, Jr., created more new tastes, such as sipping rums that are not mixed with other liquids, promoted more rum-based cocktails, and updated distillation techniques. When certain doctors in Cuba indicated that rum drinking was medicinal, the Bacardi company promoted the health benefits of its products. In 1913, company profits were estimated at more than 175,000 pesos, and they would quadruple by the end of World War I.

In 1919, the company reorganized and incorporated under the name Compania Rum Bacardi, S.A. The company's partners, the Bacardi brothers and Scheug, were all millionaires, and they managed operations valued at roughly $4 million. In the 1920's, Emilio, who was remarried to Elvira Cape, enjoyed world travel, and on his trips he began to collect items for his museum, including an Egyptian mummy. In February, 1922, the company opened another distillery. The firm remained strong because its ownership continued to be held by the Bacardi family, with Emilio and his descendants, as well as those of his brothers, holding $10,000 worth of company stock per person.

LEGACY

Emilio Bacardi died on August 28, 1922, and the city of Santiago de Cuba engaged in two days of public mourning for one of its patriots, philanthropists, and leading businessmen. Bacardi was also a journalist and an author of fiction, memoirs, and essays on Cuban politics. When his brother, Facundo Bacardi, Jr., died in 1926, *The New York Times* reported that the family's company was worth $50 million.

—*Beverly Schneller*

FURTHER READING

Calvo Ospina, Hernando. *Bacardi: The Hidden War.* London: Pluto Press, 2002. Translated by Stephen

introducing new rum drinks, ably marketed by Scheug, including a mixture of rum and Coca-Cola known as the Cuba Libré (free Cuba) and the daiquiri. The Cuba Libré was named after the slogan of the Cuban independence movement and was a particularly popular drink in the United States. The daiquiri initially was a drink popular with miners and was made from crushed ice, rum, and lime juice. At the 1904 World's Fair in St. Louis, Bacardi rums beat the competition and the company expanded into more global markets. During this time, Emilio Bacardi continued to lead the business from strength to strength with new rum blends and new methods of distilling.

With Bacardi as Santiago de Cuba's mayor and one of Cuba's leading businessmen, philanthropy and corporate growth occurred simultaneously. Bacardi used high-visibility public events, including sponsoring a baseball team, to position his rum brands with the public and to

Wilkinson and Alasdair Holden. Provides a short history of the Bacardi firm and is a source of financial information about Emilio Bacardi's period of management.

Coulombe, Charles. *Rum: The Epic Story of the Drink That Conquered the World.* New York: Kensington, 2004. A history of rum that includes information on Bacardi's involvement in the Cuban independence movement.

Gjelten, Todd. *Bacardi and the Long Fight for Cuba: The Biography of a Cause.* New York: Viking, 2008. A history of the Barcardi rum company and its involvement in Cuban politics. Depicts the distiller as a model corporate citizen and its family managers, including Emilio, as leaders in both the Cuban indepen-

dence movement and Fidel Castro's subsequent insurrection.

Haig, Matt. *Brand Loyalty: How the World's Top One Hundred Brands Thrive and Survive.* London: Kogan Page, 2004. A capsule examination of how the Bacardi family established their company and how the firm maintains its quality spirits and reputation.

Perez, Louis A., Jr. *Cuba Between Reform and Revolution.* New York: Oxford Univeristy Press, 1988. Offers detailed information on the independence movement and its impact on sugar production in Cuba.

See also: Miguel de Aldama; Adolphus Busch; Manuel Calvo; Edward Cecil Guinness; Antonio López y López; José Xifré.

RAÚL BAILLÈRES
Mexican banker and businessman

Baillères created a diverse business empire in Mexico during the twentieth century. Favoring free market capitalism over a state-run economy, he founded the Instituto Technológico Autónomo de México (ITAM) in order to train a new generation of Mexican political and economic leaders.

Born: 1895; Silao, Guanajuato, Mexico
Died: January 3, 1967; Mexico City, Mexico
Also known as: Raúl Baillères Chávez
Sources of wealth: Banking; investments
Bequeathal of wealth: Children; educational institution

EARLY LIFE
Raúl Baillères Chávez (rah-OOL bi-YAR-ehs CHAH-vehs) was born in 1895 in Silao, Guanajuato, Mexico, the son of Alberto Baillères. As a teenager, he worked with his father, a small businessman who sold seeds and groceries to the local population. With no money and virtually no formal education, Baillères left home in 1915 to seek his fortune in Mexico City. He obtained employment with a local investment firm, the Casa Lacaud. He was subsequently employed by the investment and trade department of the Chase Manhattan Bank in Mexico City. His talent as a silver trader laid the foundation of his future wealth.

FIRST VENTURES
During the early years of the Great Depression, Baillères left his job at Chase Manhattan. Taking advantage of the uncertain economic situation, he used his savings to purchase discounted stock in Mexican businesses and finan-

cial institutions from foreign investors eager to divest themselves of their Mexican holdings. In 1934, Baillères established Crédito Minero, S.A. (later the Banco Cremi), the first financial lending institution in Mexico primarily dedicated to mining activities. During the 1930's, Baillères, who supported free market capitalism, opposed the state-run corporatist economic strategies promulgated by Mexican president Lázaro Cárdenas. From 1941 to 1942, Baillères was the president of the Asociación de Banqueros de México, the nation's association of bankers. By this time, he had become a leading figure in Mexico's banking and business sectors.

MATURE WEALTH
During the 1940's, Baillères expanded his financial and business interests. In 1941, he led a group of Mexican investors that purchased the Cervecería Moctezuma, S.A., the largest brewery in Mexico. At the same time, he also acquired a controlling interest in El Palacio de Hierro, an upscale department store in Mexico City reminiscent of Harrods in London. In 1946, Baillères donated 2 million pesos to the presidential election campaign of Miguel Alemán. Alemán defeated opponent Ezequiel Padilla to become the first nonmilitary candidate to be elected president of Mexico since the Mexican Revolution.

On March 29, 1946, in an attempt to create an academically rigorous institution of higher education, Baillères, with the support of several like-minded industrialists and bankers, established the Instituto Tecnológico de México. In 1963, this university was granted autonomous status from the Mexican government and renamed the Instituto Tecnológico Autónomo de México (ITAM). Baillères argued that the national university, the Universidad Nacional Autónoma de México, was infested with leftist professors dedicated to the economic policies of Cárdenas. As such, it was Baillères's goal to create an institution of higher education, modeled on the Massachusetts Institute of Technology (MIT), dedicated to economic change in Mexico. Until his death, Baillères was the president of the Mexican Cultural Association, ITAM's founding entity, and he was an active financial supporter of the institution. In the early twenty-first century, ITAM was one of Mexico's preeminent institutions of higher education, and many people consider ITAM the best private university in the country.

Baillères's financial wealth dramatically increased during the 1950's and 1960's. Following his death in 1967, his vast financial empire was taken over by his son, Alberto. In 2009, Alberto Baillères was the second-wealthiest person in Mexico, with an estimated worth of $6 billion.

LEGACY
Although he lacked a formal university education, Baillères created a successful business empire and laid the foundation for a Mexican university that has trained several generations of Mexican businesspeople. Graduates of ITAM, including the majority of the Mexican team that negotiated the North Atlantic Free Trade Agreement (NAFTA) and President Felipe Calderón, who assumed office in 2006, have played a crucial role in the economic liberalization process initiated in Mexico in the 1980's.

—Michael R. Hall

FURTHER READING

Babb, Sarah. *Managing Mexico: Economists from Nationalism to Neoliberalism*. Princeton, N.J.: Princeton University Press, 2001.

Camp, Roderic A. *Entrepreneurs and Politics in Twentieth Century Mexico*. Oxford, England: Oxford University Press, 1989.

_____. *Mexico's Mandarins: Crafting a Power Elite for the Twenty-first Century*. Berkeley: University of California Press, 2002.

Reynolds, Clark W. *The Mexican Economy: Twentieth Century Structure and Growth*. New Haven, Conn.: Yale University Press, 1977.

See also: Enrique Creel; Carlos Slim.

GEORGE F. BAKER
American investment banker

Baker was one of the original directors of First National Bank of New York City, and he built a substantial fortune through his dominant role in banking and investment financing in the late nineteenth and early twentieth centuries. He made significant philanthropic gifts during his life, including donations to Harvard and Cornell Universities.

Born: March 27, 1840; Troy, New York
Died: May 2, 1931; New York, New York
Also known as: George Fisher Baker
Sources of wealth: Banking; investments
Bequeathal of wealth: Children; educational institution

EARLY LIFE
George Fisher Baker had little formal education, and no one in his family had any experience in business or finance. Baker worked briefly in a variety of retail businesses before becoming a clerk in New York State's Department of Banking in 1856. Here he became an expert in identifying the notes issued by banks throughout the country, and he grew familiar with the laws and standard practices of banking. Perhaps most important, he also became acquainted with some of the leading men in the state's banking industry, who came to appreciate Baker's expertise in banking matters.

FIRST VENTURES
Baker became an associate of John Thompson, one of the principal founders of First National Bank of New York City. This was the first federally chartered bank created under the National Banking Act of 1863. Thompson invited Baker to join this new bank, to invest in it, and to become one of its original directors. Thompson also offered to loan Baker money to buy stock in the bank, but Baker declined the loan because he did not want to assume its debt. Instead he used his own savings of $3,000 to buy his stock. His initial investment bought him thirty shares out of the original issue of two thousand. Later in

life, he said he regretted not taking advantage of Thompson's offer and buying more stock.

MATURE WEALTH

Throughout his career in investment banking, Baker weathered three of the American economy's worst storms—the Panics of 1873 and 1907 and the early years of the Great Depression. The Panic of 1873, caused by the bankruptcy of the Northern Pacific Railway, which in turn led to the failure of Jay Cooke's investment firm, marked a turning point in Baker's career and fortunes. Amid the financial crisis, Sam Thompson, president of First National Bank and the son of John Thompson, wished to liquidate the bank's assets and get out of the banking business. Sam's brother, Fred Thompson, sided with Baker, and the two men worked together to keep the bank open. Baker arranged to gradually buy out the interests of the Thompson family, and he became the principal owner of First National Bank, assuming its presidency in 1877. His fortune at this time was estimated at about $100,000.

In the remaining years of the nineteenth century, Baker became an associate and often a business ally of industrialist and investment banker J. P. Morgan, especially concerning investments in the railroad and steel industries. Morgan also became a director of First National Bank. In 1901, Morgan and Baker were two of the principal investors who created U.S. Steel, the first corporation in the United States to be capitalized with a value of more than $1 billion. Baker also worked closely with Morgan to calm the financial crisis during the Panic of 1907.

LEGACY

Having weathered previous financial crises, Baker was not overly concerned about the onset of the Great Depression in 1929. He later conceded he had been foolish to ignore the warnings of his son and other advisers. Baker's fortune may have been as high as $200 million at the beginning of the Depression. When he died in May, 1931, his estate was valued at $73 million. During his lifetime, Baker had made sizable gifts to numerous charities. His largest gifts were several donations to Cornell University, totaling $2 million, and $6 million to Harvard University in 1924 to enable the university to construct and furnish the buildings for the Harvard Business School. Baker also gave $1 million to endow the Baker Library at Dartmouth College, and he financed the Baker Athletic Field at Columbia University in New York City.

—*Mark S. Joy*

George F. Baker. (Library of Congress)

FURTHER READING

Cruikshank, Jeffrey L. *A Delicate Experiment: The Harvard Business School, 1908-1945*. Boston: Harvard Business School Press, 1987.

Khurana, Rakesh. "The Invention of the University-Based Business School." In *From Higher Aims to Hired Hands: The Social Transformation of American Business Schools and the Unfulfilled Promise of Management as a Profession*. Princeton, N.J.: Princeton University Press, 2007.

Logan, Sheridan A. *George F. Baker and His Bank: A Double Biography*. St. Joseph, Mo.: Sheridan A. Logan, 1981.

Strouse, Jean. *Morgan: American Financier.* New York: Random House, 1999.

See also: Jay Cooke; Clarence Dillon; Anthony Joseph Drexel; Otto Kahn; J. P. Morgan; Jacob Schiff.

STEVEN BALLMER
American entrepreneur and business executive

Ballmer has guided one of the computing industry's most influential companies, Microsoft Corporation, to a place of market dominance. His brilliant marketing strategies and salesmanship, combined with his aggressiveness in promoting his company, brought Microsoft from a small company to a multinational giant that has generated billions of dollars of revenue and revolutionized personal computing.

Born: March 24, 1956; Detroit, Michigan
Also known as: Steven Anthony Ballmer
Source of wealth: Sale of products
Bequeathal of wealth: Spouse; children

EARLY LIFE
Steven Anthony Ballmer was born in Detroit, Michigan, in 1956. His father was a middle manager at the Ford Motor Company. Ballmer attended a private high school with his sister, where he was known for the energy and motivation that would become his hallmark at Microsoft Corporation. He attended Harvard University, where he met Bill Gates, who would later be one of the founders of Microsoft. Ballmer graduated magna cum laude with a degree in applied mathematics and economics.

FIRST VENTURES
Ballmer started working at Proctor & Gamble in 1977 as an assistant product manager but left within two years. He enrolled at Stanford University's business school in 1979. He dropped out after Gates called with an offer to work at Microsoft and a chance to own 10 percent of the company's stock. Ballmer started as the senior vice president of system software, where he was the head recruiter. Ballmer himself could not program computers, but had an eye for talent. He later moved on to vice president of sales and support. Microsoft worked a deal with International Business Machines (IBM) to create an op-

Steven Ballmer. (AP/Wide World Photos)

erating system for their new line of personal computers, which would be known as MS-DOS. Gates and his Microsoft cofounder, Paul Allen, worked on technical issues, and Ballmer dealt with the business aspects of the company.

MATURE WEALTH

Gates received most of the media attention, especially after the departure of Allen in 1983. Ballmer was in charge of the core of the business—operating systems—in the 1980's. He recruited top students from first-rate universities to work at Microsoft. He pushed the marketing and sales efforts. Where Gates came up with ideas, Ballmer put those ideas into practical application.

Ballmer was the one who saw the importance of Apple Computer, Inc.'s graphical user interface and strove to make sure that Microsoft had a competing product, Windows. He forged deals with major players in the computer industry and helped drive software innovations. Between 1991 and 1995, Microsoft sales increased at the rate of a $1 billion per year; by 1995, company revenues were close to $6 billion.

Ballmer was key to the success of Windows 95 and designed everything from pricing to the distribution of Microsoft's products. His enthusiasm and salesmanship complemented the keen marketing strategies that he crafted for Microsoft's future. In 1995, Microsoft had more than twenty thousand people on its payroll. Because he brought Microsoft to a prominent position in the computer industry, Ballmer did very well financially and was ranked the twenty-ninth-richest man in America. As of 1999, he was worth an estimated $23 billion. In 2000, he became the chief executive officer and president of Microsoft.

Ballmer's aggressive marketing tactics caused some controversy. Two lawsuits in 2001 and 2003 cost Microsoft more than $2 billion. Regardless of these missteps, Microsoft had revenues of more than $26 billion for 2004, and Ballmer's net worth of $12.4 billion placed him nineteenth on the *Forbes* magazine list of the world's wealthiest people.

LEGACY

Ballmer is generally hailed as the architect of Microsoft's success. His passion for Microsoft's success led it to the forefront of the computing industry. The mark that he has left on the face of computing is undeniable, as shown by the fact that a commanding majority of personal computers run some kind of Microsoft product. He helped to bring personal computing to a mass audience. The average person can use a computer with more ease because of the innovations that he helped develop and bring to the public. Ballmer uses some of his wealth to donate to political causes.

—James J. Heiney

FURTHER READING

Foley, Mary Jo. *Microsoft 2.0: How Microsoft Plans to Stay Relevant in the Post-Gates Era.* Indianapolis, Ind.: John Wiley & Sons, 2008.

Maxwell, Frederic Alan. *Bad Boy Ballmer.* New York: HarperCollins, 2003.

Slater, Robert. *Microsoft Rebooted: How Bill Gates and Steve Ballmer Reinvented Their Company.* New York: Portfolio, 2004.

See also: Paul Allen; Jeff Bezos; Sergey Brin; Mark Cuban; Michael Dell; Larry Ellison; Bill Gates; Steve Jobs; Gordon E. Moore; David Packard; H. Ross Perot.

SIR JOHN BANKS
British merchant, landowner, and banker

Banks is an important figure in the growth of government finance as a source of individual wealth, and his life demonstrates how private bankers played an increasing role in shaping Great Britain's government policy.

Born: 1627; near Maidstone, Kent, England
Died: 1699; Aylesford, Kent, England
Also known as: Sir John Bankes
Sources of wealth: Trade; banking; real estate
Bequeathal of wealth: Children

EARLY LIFE

Sir John Banks was born in Kent, southeast of London, on August 19, 1627. His father, Caleb Banks, was a prosperous woolen draper and substantial landowner, with an income of £800 a year in 1640. Caleb served for a time as the mayor of Maidstone. This town was a particularly fortuitous location for an individual pursuing commerce in the seventeenth century, as Maidstone was one of the principal hubs through which agricultural products passed to supply the city of London, the British fleet, and Great Britain's expanding colonial empire. In an era when water transport was the only practical means of moving heavy goods, proximity to major rivers connecting metropolitan areas was crucial.

Little is known of John Banks's early life. He attended Emmanuel College, Cambridge University, and most probably worked in his father's business until 1652, when he became a partner in a syndicate supplying food to the British navy. At that time, the navy was the most comprehensive and in some respects the largest industry in Britain.

FIRST VENTURES

The years encompassing Banks's early rise in fortune were ones of political upheaval. The struggles between King Charles I and Parliament ultimately resulted in Charles's deposition and execution and precipitated a civil war that lasted from 1642 to 1646. Banks began his independent business career during the administration of Oliver Cromwell and continued it through the Stu-

art restoration and the reigns of Charles II, James II, and William III and Mary II. The effects of these dramatic political changes on business and commerce in southern England were not profound and could be manipulated to great advantage by a person skilled in keeping a low political profile and meeting the needs of whichever entity had ascendancy. Banks was such a person. As a merchant, he had political sympathies with the parliamentarians; as a conventional Anglican, he had no philosophical attachment to Puritanism. The king and Parliament both depended on the services of well-capitalized merchants and were prepared to overlook past affiliation with political rivals.

Throughout his career, Banks maintained just enough involvement in politics to nurture the connections he

An ambassador for Queen Elizabeth I stands before India's emperor, seeking permission to charter the East India Company. (Hulton Archive/Getty Images)

needed to secure government contracts. He represented Kentish boroughs in the House of Commons under Cromwell, Charles II, and William III, but he was always a backbencher on the ministerial side of the Commons. Unlike his father, he avoided civil offices that entailed large financial and ceremonial obligations. In 1661, Charles II made him a baronet, a hereditary honor intermediate between knighthood and the peerage that was generally conferred on financially successful men who contributed to Great Britain's colonial expansion.

The naval supply business, lucrative in its own right, also led Banks to become a government creditor. Cromwell's government, embroiled in a series of wars with the Dutch, was slow to pay suppliers, and undercapitalized merchants were forced to sell promissory notes at a steep discount. Banks eventually realized a considerable profit from these notes and was also able to negotiate increasingly favorable terms on the loans he made directly to the British government. The law set a ceiling of 6 percent interest on loans, but premiums, bonuses, and actual dispensations, readily conferred by a cash-strapped government, could result in a much higher profit.

In 1655, Banks married Elizabeth Dethick, daughter of John Dethick, a wealthy London merchant and a former lord mayor of London. Dethick was a stockholder in the British East India Company and for a time was also a member of a rival syndicate engaged in the East India trade. Elizabeth brought substantial assets and connections to the marriage. The couple had three surviving children. Banks spared no expense preparing his son, Caleb, to take his place as a prominent member of society, at one time hiring the philosopher John Locke to be Caleb's private tutor. Caleb, however, proved a disappointment. He achieved no distinction in any field, never married, and left no heirs when he died at the age of twenty-six. Banks's daughter Mary married Heneage Finch, the second son of a prominent Nottingham businessman and jurist. Finch was later elevated to the peerage as the first earl of Aylesford, and he and Mary inherited most of Banks's estate.

THE BRITISH EAST INDIA COMPANY

The British East India Company (also known as the English East India Company or the East India Company), established under royal charter from Queen Elizabeth I on December 31, 1600, was a joint-stock company given a monopoly on sea trade between England and all regions between the Cape of Good Hope and the Strait of Magellan. In its first two decades of operation, this trade consisted mainly of spices from the East Indies and led to direct competition with the already established Dutch trade routes. In 1608, the company founded a transshipment station at Surat, in southern India, which evolved into a fort and trading post. Trade with India expanded rapidly in the seventeenth century, mainly through the establishment of enclaves as stipulated in treaties with the Mughal emperors of Bengal. By 1647, the company had twenty-three factories (trading posts) in India, each with its own factor, or governor, and a defense force under its control. The firm's main items of trade in the seventeenth century were cotton, silk, indigo, saltpeter, and tea.

The political and military control that the company came to exercise over the entire Indian subcontinent developed gradually. King James I, Oliver Cromwell, and King Charles II all granted additional privileges and powers to the company when renewing its charter. Acts of Parliament under Charles II authorized the company to acquire territories, wage war and negotiate peace, mint money, and exercise civil jurisdiction. Robert Clive's territorial acquisitions in the mid-eighteenth century made British India a nation governed by a corporation, while the East India Company Acts of 1773 and 1784 brought the civil and military aspects of the region's administration firmly under the control of Parliament. The company lost its monopoly on the India trade in 1813, and following the Sepoy Mutiny of 1857 the firm was nationalized by the Government of India Act (1858). The tremendous wealth generated by the East India Company made its members a major lobbying force in Parliament and helped shape British foreign and colonial policy for more than two centuries.

MATURE WEALTH

In the late 1650's, Banks became a partner in the Levant Company, which exported cloth, lead, and tin to the eastern Mediterranean and imported oil, silk, and dyes. In 1661, he became a stockholder in the British East India Company, for which he later intermittently served as director between 1669 and 1685. Direct involvement in these merchant ventures provided substantial income, though for most of the period after 1660 this revenue was overshadowed by the money Banks earned through government finance and rents on landed property.

The saltpeter trade illustrates the complex connections between trade and government policy in seventeenth century England. The government's need for saltpeter for gunpowder manufacture greatly exceeded domestic supplies. Imports from India, channeled through the British East India Company, supplied the deficit. To no small extent, the government needed the gunpowder to fight the Dutch over control of the India trade. Banks and the British East India Company profited at all stages. They enjoyed a virtual monopoly on import, could set their prices, were able to negotiate exemptions from import duties, and, most important, loaned the government the money to buy their product.

Banks also invested in the Royal African Company and served as its director from 1674 until 1676. The company's sole business was the African slave trade, and its activities in attempting to enforce its monopoly precipitated the second Anglo-Dutch War of 1665-1667.

In 1672, Banks negotiated a loan of £36,500 of his own funds and an additional £47,512 of East India Company funds to the government, to be repaid from the rents of "fee farms," or the agricultural land seized from monasteries under Henry VIII. In 1685, Banks had a total income of £7,580 a year, including £2,462 from the British East India Company and £4,163 from rents, including fee farms. His household expenditures were around £3,000 a year and included the maintenance of two large establishments, an impressive town house in Lincoln's Inn Fields in London, and The Friars, a former Carmelite priory in Aylesford that Banks purchased in 1657 and transformed into a fine Caroline mansion.

Increasingly, Banks invested profits from his business ventures in landed property, which was typical in England at the time. Although the landed property produced a smaller return than moneylending or commerce, it was a more secure means of income and brought Banks a measure of prestige that investments in stock did not. The Friars was Banks's country estate, with extensive agricultural lands and the rights to manage the civil life of Aylesford; these rights were originally granted to the priory by the king and remained attached to it when the land was sold to successive owners.

LEGACY

At the time of his death in 1699, Banks had an annual income of about £5,000 a year and total assets of £180,000, making him a multimillionaire by early twenty-first century standards and one of the richest men in England. Considering the magnitude of his wealth, he left remarkably little in the way of a direct legacy. He is possibly best remembered as the friend of the diarist Samuel Pepys, the secretary of the navy and a fellow member of the Royal Society, who enjoyed Banks's hospitality and mentions him frequently in his diary. Banks endowed no charities or institutions, and his heirs were distinguished neither by philanthropy nor by profligacy, content to be

wealthy country gentlemen with no taste for politics or adventure. The Friars, eventually leased to tenants, burned in 1930. It has since been restored as a historic site but as the original medieval Carmelite priory rather than the seventeenth century mansion.

The effects of the commercial activities that Banks oversaw in India and West Africa were profound, far-reaching, and extremely negative from the point of view of the native populations, but it is difficult to assess how much he was personally responsible for the economic and social conditions in these areas. Were his management of, and profiting by, the slave trade considered pivotal, he would perhaps deserve a place among the villains of history instead of being an obscure figure who did not even qualify for an entry in the encyclopedic *Dictionary of National Biography* until 2004.

—*Martha A. Sherwood*

FURTHER READING

Bowen, H. V. *The Business of Empire: The East India Company and Imperial Britain, 1756-1833.* Cambridge, England: Cambridge University Press, 2006. Provides good background material, although the emphasis is on a later period and on the military and political rather than commercial aspects of history.

Coleman, D. C. "Sir John Banks." In *Oxford Dictionary of National Biography: From the Earliest Times to the Year 2000*, edited by H. G. C. Matthew and Brian Harrison. Oxford, England: Oxford University Press, 2004. Authoritative source of biographical information on lesser-known British figures.

_____. *Sir John Banks, Baronet and Businessman: A Study of Business, Politics, and Society in Later Stuart England.* London: Greenwood Press, 1975. A scholarly and thorough work based on an analysis of Banks's surviving commercial records.

Coote, Stephen. *Samuel Pepys: A Life.* New York: Palgrave for St. Martin's Press, 2001. A readable account based on the diaries of a contemporary and friend of Banks; provides a good introduction to seventeenth century society and politics.

Glaisyer, Natasha. *The Culture of Commerce in England, 1660-1720.* Woodbridge, Suffolk, England: Boydell Press, 2006. Describes the process by which commerce became increasingly central to English national identity and exercised increasing influence in political life.

See also: James Craggs; Stephen Fox; Thomas Guy; First Duke of Marlborough.

DAVID AND FREDERICK BARCLAY
British businessmen

The Barclay brothers were listed among the twenty wealthiest people in the United Kingdom in The Sunday Times *Rich List. In 2007, their wealth was estimated at £1.8 billion ($3.2 billion), compared with £750 million ($1.3 billion) in 2004. In 2000, they were knighted for their donations of £40 million ($71 million) to medical research.*

DAVID BARCLAY

Born: October 27, 1934; London, England
Also known as: Sir David Barclay

FREDERICK BARCLAY

Born: October 27, 1934; London, England
Also known as: Sir Frederick Barclay
Sources of wealth: Media; retailing; real estate
Bequeathal of wealth: Relatives

EARLY LIVES

David Barclay was born ten minutes before his twin brother, Frederick Barclay. The brothers were two of ten children born to Scottish-Catholic parents. They grew up in Shepherd's Bush, a working-class area of London. Their father, a salesman, died when they were twelve. The Barclay brothers attended public school until the age of sixteen, when they went to work in the accounts department of General Electric. They later worked as painters and decorators. The brothers have worked as partners for the majority of their lives, although David is often the spokesman for the two.

FIRST VENTURES

By the time they were twenty-eight, the Barclays were buying boardinghouses, which they then renovated into hotels. They purchased the Howard Hotel, overlooking the Thames, in 1975. In 1983, they purchased the

David and Frederick Barclay. (AP/Wide World Photos)

Ellerman Group, a brewing and shipping company, for £45 million ($80 million). They began acquiring their wealth when they sold the brewing operations of the Ellerman Group for £240 million ($425 million) within ten years after purchasing the company. Their proceeds from the sale were used to buy the Ritz Hotel in Picadilly in 1995.

The brothers entered the media field by buying two newspapers, *The European* in 1992 and *The Scotsman* in 1995. *The European* later went out of business, and *The Scotsman* was sold at a profit in 2005. In 1998, they relaunched another newspaper, *Sunday Business*, and in 2004 they bought the Telegraph Group, which includes two newspapers and a magazine. The brothers typically buy a business, work with it for a time, and then sell it at a profit. In the newspaper business, this strategy has required them to reduce the number of journalists and to repeatedly replace editors.

MATURE WEALTH

In 1999, the Barclays partnered with Boots, a leading British pharmacy chain, to create handbag.com, a fashion, beauty, and celebrity Web site. The site was sold in 2006 at a profit of £22 million ($39 million). In 2002, the brothers' financial company, LW Investments, bought Littlewoods, a retail company that owns a chain of department stores and a mail-order catalog. They sold off the department store chain, kept the mail-order catalog, and began selling the company's merchandise on Shop Direct, their online retail business. In 2009, the brothers expanded Shop Direct by purchasing Woolworth's, a venerable but ailing retailer. The Barclays planned to sell Woolworth's merchandise, including its Ladybird line of children's clothing, online at Shop Direct, which maintains a majority of the home shopping market in the United Kingdom. In 2009, the brothers also bought Standard Life Bank to add to their existing retail banking business, Barclays Bank. In addition to the Ritz, the Howard, and other hotels, the Barclays own the Hotel Mirabeau in Monte Carlo, Monaco.

The brothers are tax exiles and list their addresses as Monaco. They own Brecqhou, an island in the English Channel, where they have built a castle for their families; the brothers have three sons and a daughter. The castle required the labor of a thousand employees working in shifts for one year. The island has its own electricity, water, landscaped parks, swimming pools, employee village, and helipad. The Barclays have clashed with the authorities in the neighboring island of Sark over Sark's jurisdiction over Brecqhou.

LEGACY

David and Frederick Barclay have had a major impact on the United Kingdom through their newspapers, hotels, online shopping business, and bank. By 2009, their multifaceted empire was controlled by David's oldest son, Aidan. In the twenty-first century, the billionaire brothers were two reclusive knights, living in their own castle on their own island.

—C. Alton Hassell

FURTHER READING

Boogan, Steve. "What Did the Barclay Brothers Say About Being Made Knights of Their Castle? Nothing, as Usual." *The Independent*, June 17, 2000, p. 5.

"Millionaire Barclay Brothers Invite Cardinal to Pray in Their Chapel." *British Church Newspaper*, January 23, 2004.

Morris, Derek, and P. J. Freeman. *March UK Ltd and the Home Shopping and Home Delivery Business of GUS PLC: A Report on the Merger Situation*. London: Stationery Office, 2004.

"Standard Life Confirms Barclays Deal." *Edinburgh Evening News*, October 26, 2009.

Tryhorn, Chris. "Who Are the Barclay Brothers?" *Media-Guardian*, June 23, 2004.

See also: Richard Branson; Deborah Cavendish; Elizabeth II; John Ellerman; Gerald Grosvenor; Anita Roddick; J. K. Rowling; David Sainsbury.

RIDOLFO DE' BARDI
Italian banker and merchant

Bardi greatly expanded his family's banking business and other commercial ventures, making the Bardi firm the leading merchant house in fourteenth century Florence. However, his financial involvement in the Hundred Years' War led to a decline in the business he had worked hard to build.

Born: c. 1300; Florence (now in Italy)
Died: c. 1360; place unknown
Also known as: Ridolfo di Bartolo Bardi; Ridolfo di Bardi
Sources of wealth: Inheritance; banking; trade
Bequeathal of wealth: Children

EARLY LIFE
Ridolfo de' Bardi (Ree-DAHL-foh dee BAHR-dee) was one of fourteen children of Bartolo di Iacopo Bardi and his wife, Tedalda Acciaiuoli. Bardi's father was a prominent member of Florence's political class and an active member of the cloth merchants guild (Calimala); his great-grandfather Ricco di Bardo (also known as Riccus Bardi) was the patriarch of the clan, siring seven sons. By 1342 the Bardi family claimed 142 adult males, making it one of the largest of Florentine *famiglie* (families). Ridolfo's uncle Iacopo directed the Bardi businesses until at least 1300, leaving Ridolfo's father, who died in 1310, to dabble in politics and administration.

An artist's depiction of fourteenth century Italian bankers. Ridolfo di' Bardi's bank and other commercial ventures made his family's firm the leading merchant house in fourteenth century Florence. (Hulton Archive/Getty Images)

FIRST VENTURES

Iacopo's successor was his son Lapo, who was joined as partners by nephews Ridolfo and Giovanni in the year of their father's death. The young men worked under Lapo's direction until his death in 1322. Ridolfo probably represented the firm in Naples during this period, as he was known to be the favorite commercial agent of the kingdom's ruler, Robert.

MATURE WEALTH

Banking, which included holding cash deposits, loaning cash, arranging transfers at a distance, and exchanging currencies, had been a small part of the Bardi family portfolio. Under Ridolfo's new leadership in 1322, banking played a much larger role, although it presented tremendous risks. From the mid-1320's to 1340, Florence underwent several blows that damaged its reputation and strained its resources, leaving the city-state in deep debt that was parceled out to leading families, including the Bardis.

In the late 1330's, the royal administration in Naples caused a run on the Bardis' bank after the family failed to support a Florentine bid to possess the city of Lucca. The return and fall of Walter de Brienne, Duke of Athens, who ruled Florence from 1342 to 1343, cost Florence 400,000 florins and stirred the lower class to sack the town houses of the wealthy, who had initially supported Brienne. Bardi's immediate family suffered much, sharing part of the 60,000-florin Bardi clan loss. Worse, Robert, the king of Naples, had died in January, 1343, owing 100,000 florins to the Bardi firm, a debt repudiated by his successor.

In 1337, the firm's international dominance began its decline as the first stages of the Hundred Years' War erupted. The French king, Philip VI, pressured Florentine bankers for loans by jailing their compatriots and seizing assets within the kingdom. The English king, Edward III, already deeply in debt to the Italians, sought more cash while letting current debt payments lapse, and royal debt grew. Between 1311 and 1326 the Bardi banks had lent his father, Edward II, some £68,000. Royal revenues, such as customs duties, were assigned to the Bardi

firm, which had to collect these funds. Meanwhile, the Bardi banking house continued to provide cash for royal expenses, while Edward III continued to pledge royal and church revenues. Edward granted the Bardi and the Peruzzi families, who, since 1337, had worked in partnership, a monopoly selling royal wool. By the early 1340's, royal claims and Bardi counterclaims led to legal action and a royal audit of the two families' business, during which Ridolfo was imprisoned as a hostage in London. Royal accounts in 1345 acknowledged that the king owed more than £50,000, but he made restitution of less than 1 percent. Panic and runs on the Bardi bank in Florence led to economic chaos. In 1357, Ridolfo lost control of the family business to his brother Filippo.

LEGACY

Born into a mercantile clan in an era of great risk taking and great fortunes, Ridolfo de' Bardi rose past his kin to control one of the age's great commercial ventures. Skillfully and patiently he expanded his firm's capitalization and spread its risk among prominent clients, including four kings and a pope. However, his dealings with King Edward III led to the eventual bankruptcy of the Bardi merchant house, which temporarily ruined Florence's economy. Although Bardi was a brilliant businessman, the mere disapproval of a monarch would cause his life's work to crash.

—Joseph P. Byrne

FURTHER READING

Becker, Marvin. *Florence in Transition*. Vol. 1. Baltimore: Johns Hopkins University Press, 1967.

Brucker, Gene. *Florentine Politics and Society, 1343-1378*. Princeton, N.J.: Princeton University Press, 1962.

Najemy, John. *A History of Florence, 1200-1575*. New York: Blackwell, 2006.

See also: Orlando Bonsignori; Agostino Chigi; Francesco Datini; Giovanni de' Medici; Lorenzo de' Medici; Jacopo de' Pazzi; Filippo di Peruzzi; Filippo Strozzi.

FRANCIS BARING
British banker, investor, and merchant

Baring was one of the first great British merchant bankers. He helped manage the British government's debt during the American Revolution and the Napoleonic Wars. His financial network extended throughout Western Europe and North America.

Born: April 18, 1740; Exeter, Devonshire, England
Died: September 11, 1810; Lee, Kent, England
Also known as: Sir Francis Baring, first baronet
Sources of wealth: Banking; trade
Bequeathal of wealth: Children

EARLY LIFE
Francis Baring was the third of four surviving sons of John and Elizabeth Baring. He was born partially deaf. One of his grandfathers had been a Lutheran pastor in Germany; his maternal grandfather was a prosperous grocer in Exeter in the county of Devon, England. His father was a leading textile merchant in Exeter, then the largest city west of London. His father died when Baring was only eight years old. He was largely brought up by his mother, who had a good business sense, under which his father's business continued to thrive. She extended the business to London. Baring moved to London for his education and then in 1755 was apprenticed to Samuel Touchet, a London merchant, for seven years.

FIRST VENTURES
On the completion of this apprenticeship in 1762, Baring joined his two older brothers in setting up two firms or "houses": John and Francis Baring & Co. of London and John and Charles Baring & Co. of Exeter. The Exeter branch needed a London base for many of its transactions. The two houses were interlinked in their finances. In 1767, he married Harriet Herring, the daughter of a merchant in Croydon. Around this time, he also injected some £20,000 into his business. He and his wife eventually had twelve children—six boys and six girls. Harriet Baring died in 1804.

Charles was not a good businessman and Francis frequently had to bail him out. John was also not much interested in the business, preferring to become a member of Parliament for Exeter in 1776. In the end, John became a sleeping partner only. Meanwhile, Francis was being recognized for his business acumen, and by 1771 he was a director of the Royal Exchange Assurance, a post he held until 1780.

The two firms did not do well at first, perhaps because of the brothers' inexperience. Francis's own capital had fallen from £10,000 after his marriage to only £2,500 in 1777. The two houses had to be restructured and separated. Thereafter, Baring prospered.

Gradually, the Barings' business was turning from trading to banking, particularly the financing of import-export trade in its many different facets. Baring acted as London agent for many Western European and North American firms, buying and selling consignments for them, collecting payments, arranging shipping and warehousing, making advances, and accepting bills of exchange.

Of the European houses, the Dutch bank of Hope & Co. was the most important. It had used the Barings for its British deals, and Baring tried to merge his business with Hope. One of the Dutch partners married one of Baring's daughters, and Baring later tried to get his son Alexander to work for Hope. During the Napoleonic Wars at the end of the eighteenth century, Hope was forced to relocate to London, and the firm worked closely with Baring's companies, eventually merging with them.

Before the American Revolution, Baring had seen the potential of trade with the United States. His first American client was a Philadelphia merchant in 1774. Through this contact he was introduced to one of America's richest men, William Bingham. Baring was consulted in the final negotiations over America's independence.

MATURE WEALTH
Beginning in 1777, the capital of Baring's business rose steadily, from £20,000 in 1777 to £400,000 in 1804. Baring's stake in this was a modest 12 percent in 1777, rising to 54 percent by 1804. Profits likewise rose steadily, from £40,000 during the 1790's to £200,000 by 1802. By then, Baring was taking the lion's share, so that his personal wealth grew from £5,000 when he started in 1763 to £64,000 in 1790 and to £500,000 by 1804. As a result of this expansion, in 1781 two additional partners were brought into the business, though only one, Charles Wall, stayed on, eventually marrying Baring's eldest daughter.

During the American Revolution, Baring had traded in supplies for the British army. He also marketed the British debt incurred by the war, probably making about

BARINGS BANK

Until its collapse in 1995, Barings Bank (1762-1995) was the oldest merchant bank in the city of London. It was founded in 1762 by three brothers—Francis, John, and Charles Baring—who originally established two family firms, one in London and the other in Exeter, with interlinking finances.

The bank's first major venture was its 1803 negotiation of the Louisiana Purchase on behalf of Napoleon I, even though he was at war with England at the time. Technically, the United States bought Louisiana from Barings and its Dutch partners, Hope & Co. Napoleon discounted the purchase price to 87.5 percent, which meant he received only $8.8 million. One of the bank's principals, Alexander Baring, traveled to Paris to confer with the French director of the public treasury before bringing the purchase documents to the United States. The company also helped finance much of the railroad development in North America in the ensuing century.

Barings Bank continued to prosper in the nineteenth century until it overextended itself in transactions with Argentina and Uruguay. In 1890, Argentina reneged on its debt to the bank, and the Bank of England set up a consortium to provide financial relief. Barings received £17 million, the first bail-out package in British banking history. The bank was restructured, its control returned to the Baring family, and it became somewhat more cautious. For example, it refused to get involved in financing the German recovery after World War I, and so was spared the collapse of the German economy ten years later. However, Barings was soon dwarfed by larger banks, as British banking continued to develop.

By the 1920's, the bank had established ties with the British royal family under King George V, and these connections remained until its ultimate demise. During World War II, Barings liquidated British assets in the United States in order to finance Great Britain's war efforts.

Sadly, the demise of the bank came through the illegal speculating of just one man, Nick Leeson, in 1995. Leeson had been operating in Barings's Singapore office for three years, speculating in futures. Lax oversight from London and the breech of some banking regulations enabled Leeson to mount massive debts, far more than the bank was worth. Leeson was jailed but the bank had to be sold.

The Dutch bank ING bought Barings Bank for the nominal sum of £1 and payment of its debts. ING sold off Barings's American business and merged its European business into its own. The name "Baring" only survives as a minor Swiss bank, Banque Baring Brothers Sturdza, S.A., under the direction of Eric Sturdza.

ment to help it negotiate with the Barbary States of North Africa, and he also negotiated the purchase of British armaments for the United States.

Baring had won the confidence of London and other European merchants through his good business methods, his sound judgment, and his pleasant manner. He now began to win the confidence of leading politicians in the British cabinet through contacts made by his brother John. His sister had married a member of Parliament. Politicians were impressed by Baring's forward-looking views on the economy and commerce. Prime Minister William Pitt, the Younger, appointed him a commissioner to investigate the payment of fees in 1784. That same year Baring became a member of Parliament for Devon. He served four sessions in Parliament, where he was noted for being a logical speaker, especially when discussing matters of commerce and expressing his belief in free trade. Although he opposed Pitt's war policy against France, seeing it as a waste of resources and a hindrance to trade, Pitt awarded him a baronetcy in 1793.

During the Napoleonic Wars, Baring again bought up government debt over a period of fifteen years, helping to finance a conflict he theoretically opposed. These transactions brought him some £190,000 in profit.

From 1779 he was a director of the British East India Company, a vastly profitable concern that ran all Indian trade. Baring made sure the company retained its monopoly, and he opposed government attempts to control it politically by making India a colony. Pitt commissioned Francis to renegotiate the company's charter.

In 1803, Baring began withdrawing from active management of his firm, and the next year he gave up his partnership. Charles Wall became the firm's manager, with three of Baring's sons assisting. In 1807, the name of the firm was changed from Sir Francis Baring & Co. to Baring Brothers. Baring had already begun to live like a gentleman, purchasing several country houses outside London; by 1803, these homes were worth £60,000. He then decided to settle at Stratton in Hampshire, some sixty miles southwest of London, which he furnished with old masters and luxury furniture and fittings.

£19,000 in profit. After the war, he speculated in American property and bought large chunks of what is now the state of Maine. Several of his daughters married American merchants. He became the London banker for the Bank of the United States. In 1795, he sold some $800,000 worth of stocks for the United States govern-

LEGACY

At his death in 1810, Baring was able to leave his children some £175,000. His capital at Baring Brothers was £70,000, his estates were worth £400,000, and his paintings were worth £30,000. His son Thomas succeeded to the baronetcy and estates. Another son, Francis, became a member of Parliament, eventually becoming Lord Northbrook.

Although fortunes like Baring's became more common during the Industrial Revolution of the nineteenth century, Baring's rise as a "prince of merchants" was unusual in his time. He can be said to be Great Britain's first merchant banker, instrumental in founding a long-lived firm. His sound financial judgment and honest dealings laid the foundation not only for Barings Bank but also for other merchant banks; this in turn laid the groundwork for London's centrality as the banking and financial capital of the world in the nineteenth century, taking away much of the importance of the Dutch and German financial centers. His ability to handle the national debt gave Great Britain a sound basis for its leadership in its fight against Napoleon I. Baring was truly an international figure, whose company represented Napoleon during negotiations for the Louisiana Purchase, conducted business with the newly created United States and with South American nations, and built railroads throughout North America.

—David Barratt

FURTHER READING

Hidy, Ralph W. *The House of Baring in American Trade and Finance: English Merchant Bankers at Work, 1763-1861.* Vol. 14 in *Harvard Studies in Business History.* Cambridge, Mass.: Harvard University Press, 1949. Provides the fullest account of Barings's American dealings.

Orbell, John. *Baring Brothers & Co. Limited: A History to 1939.* London: Baring Brothers, 1985. An in-house account of the rise of the bank and its history till the beginning of World War II.

Pears, Iaian. *Stone's Fall.* London: Jonathan Cape, 2009. A novel based on the Barings Bank collapse of 1890, examining what drove the bank to make such unwise investments.

Wechsberg, Joseph. *The Merchant Bankers.* London: Weidenfeld and Nicholson, 1967. Sets Baring Brothers in the wider context of merchant banking.

See also: Samuel Fludyer; Samuel Loyd; Moses Montefiore; Nathan Mayer Rothschild.

YAḤYĀ IBN KHĀLID AL-BARMAKĪ
Persian government official and landowner

Chief minister for the legendary Caliph Hārūn al-Rashīd, Yaḥyā ibn Khālid al-Barmakī accumulated vast wealth from government revenues, resulting in the downfall of his illustrious family.

Born: Date unknown; Balkh, Persia (now in Afghanistan)
Died: 805 C.E.; Baghdad (now in Iraq)
Sources of wealth: Inheritance; government
Bequeathal of wealth: Confiscated

EARLY LIFE

The Barmakīd family originated in the city of Balkh in the Oxus river valley. Located in what is now northern Afghanistan, Balkh was the capital of Greek Bactria and later incorporated into the Buddhist Kushan empire. The Barmakīds were a priestly Persian family, although different accounts state that their religion was either Zoroastrianism or Buddhism. After the Muslim conquest of the Near East, Khālid ibn Barmak converted to Islam and supported the 'Abbasīd uprising against the Damascus Umayyad caliphate. When the 'Abbasīds triumphed, establishing a new Islamic caliphate in Baghdad, Khālid became the chief financial administrator. Khālid's son, Yaḥyā ibn Khālid al-Barmakī (yah-YAH IH-bihn KAH-lihd al-bahr-MAK-ih), was raised in a family of exceeding influence and wealth.

FIRST VENTURES

The Arabic 'Abbasīds increasingly relied on Persians and other non-Arabs to administer their kingdom, and the brilliant Barmakīds proved to be especially able administrators. Yaḥyā served as the governor of Rayy, governor of Azerbaijan, and secretary and adjutant to the royal prince, Hārūn al-Rashīd. In an ominous foreboding, the Caliph Al-Mansūr in 775 demanded that Khālid and his son Yaḥyā pay the caliph the sum of 3 million dirhams. (A silver dirham is roughly equal to $4; about 10 dirhams equaled 1 golden dinar.) After Al-Mansūr's death, Yaḥyā carefully guided Hārūn to succeed to the caliphate in 786. Hārūn appointed Yaḥyā vizier, an office equivalent to prime minister, and also named him a royal emir and entrusted him with the royal seal.

MATURE WEALTH

In the golden age of the ʿAbbasīd Dynasty, the wealth and opulence of the Barmakīds rivaled that of the caliphate. Yaḥyā, along with his four sons, Jafar, Fadl, Mūsā, and Muḥammad, governed the great Islamic empire. As vizier, Yaḥyā distributed wheat throughout the kingdom, arranged for the swift delivery of mail, and built mosques, roads, and canals. He was granted a large share of government revenues, allowing him to acquire great treasures and vast tracts of land. The Barmakīd palaces lining the Tigris River were the most splendid in the kingdom. Yaḥyā's mansion was lined with gold tile; Jafar's cost 20 million dirhams.

To preserve his position, Yaḥyā distributed millions of dirhams to the leading ʿAbbasīd families and generals. He freely granted money to petitioners and supplicants. He was a patron of the arts and sciences, supporting poets and commissioning translations of Ptolemy's *Almagest* (c. 150 B.C.E.) and a scientific manual on the prism. He sent an expedition to India to gather information on medicinal plants and had two Sanskrit medical texts, including Ravigupta's *Siddhasāra* (ocean of attainments), translated into Arabic.

The great wealth of the Barmakīds, and their extravagance, proved their downfall. In 803, Hārūn ordered the sudden arrest of Yaḥyā and his sons. Jafar, who had been Hārūn's intimate friend, was cruelly executed; Yaḥyā, his three other sons, and his allies perished in prison. Although ʿAbbasīd historians record various motives for this catastrophic turn of events, one stands out: Hārūn had become envious of the power and wealth of the Barmakīds, reputed to exceed his own. Yaḥyā's estate, possessed of 30,672,000 in gold dinars alone, with ru-

mors of vast treasures secreted away, was confiscated. The Barmakīd family was heard from no more.

LEGACY

Few court favorites in history have had as dramatic a fall as Yaḥyā ibn Khālid al-Barmakī. Possessed of his family's ingenuity and resources, he administered the Islamic empire under the greatest of ʿAbbasīd caliphs. His patronage assisted the literary and scientific renaissance of Islam's golden age. However, his success and riches inflamed his master, the caliph Hārūn, who purged the Barmakīd family, neither the first nor the last ministers of state to fall prey to jealous monarchs.

The Barmakīd name is preserved in history. The wonderful Arabic folktales, *The Arabian Nights' Entertainments* (fifteenth century; also known as *The Thousand and One Nights*), recount the cleverness of Yaḥyā, Jafar's adventures with Hārūn, and the family's fall from grace, a story echoed in modern American films, such as *The Thief of Baghdad* (1940) and *Aladdin* (1994). A "Barmecidal" or "Barmedice" feast refers to a lavish but imaginary banquet, and these words derive from the family name Barmakī.

—Howard Bromberg

FURTHER READING

Axworthy, Michael. *A History of Iran: Empire of the Mind*. Philadelphia: Basic Books, 2008.

Kennedy, Hugh. *When Baghdad Ruled the Muslim World: The Rise and Fall of Islam's Greatest Dynasty*. Cambridge, Mass.: Da Capo Press, 2005.

Tabarī. *The History of al-Tabarī*. Vol. 30 in *The ʿAbbasīd Caliphate in Equilibrium*. Translated by C. E. Bosworth. Albany: State University of New York Press, 1989.

See also: ʿAbbās the Great; Aga Khan I; Hārūn al-Rashīd; Marduk-nāsir-apli.

BARNEY BARNATO
British diamond mining magnate

From his humble East London beginnings, Barnato, once a stage magician, made a fortune in the South African diamond fields and helped to make the diamond industry an economic powerhouse.

Born: February 21, 1851; London, England
Died: c. June 14, 1897; Atlantic Ocean, near the coast of Madeira
Also known as: Barnett Isaacs (birth name)
Source of wealth: Mining
Bequeathal of wealth: Relatives

EARLY LIFE
Barney Barnato (BAR-nee bar-NAH-toh) was the stage name of Barnett Isaacs, who was born in Whitechapel, one of poorest sections of London, in 1851. The son of a Jewish shopkeeper, he left school by age fourteen and took a series of jobs, including bouncer at a public house (tavern). Some of his relatives, including a brother, had moved to South Africa after diamonds were discovered there. In 1873, Barnato also immigrated and joined his brother, who had become a stage magician. According to legend, his stage name came from a part of their act where he would call out, "And Barnett, too," which audiences popularized as "Barnato." Eventually he made it his legal name.

FIRST VENTURES
Barnato possessed an excellent business sense. He began buying diamonds from miners and then purchased the mining claims themselves in the Kimberley diamond fields. He eventually formed the Barnato Diamond Mining Company. It is said that his genial, extroverted personality was of considerable help in his quest to secure claims. By 1885, he owned so many claims that he expanded his company by merging it with another, establishing the Kimberley Central Mining Company. Cecil Rhodes (after whom the country of Rhodesia was named) was also purchasing mining claims, and Barnato and Rhodes became rivals who fought to control the majority of the diamond claims. However, their goal was impeded by Compagnie Française de Diamant du Cap, a French company that also controlled numerous claims at the Kimberley diamond fields.

MATURE WEALTH
Both Barnato and Rhodes made overtures to the French company, and Rhodes was able to raise enough financing to purchase it. He then offered the company to Barnato for no cash but for shares in Barnato's Kimberley Central Mining Company. As a result, Rhodes owned a considerable stake in Barnato's company, which apparently had been Rhodes's real objective all along. The two men continued to battle for control of the diamond business, causing the price of stock in Barnato's firm to triple to almost £50 per share. Rhodes and his associates eventually emerged as the victors, owning three-fifths of the company, and in 1888, Barnato ceded control of the firm. However, some of his unhappy shareholders went to court to try to reverse the transaction. The judge ruled that Rhodes's De Beers Consolidated Mines, Ltd., could buy the assets of Barnato's company if Barnato agreed to place his firm in voluntary liquidation, which he then proceeded to do.

As part of the settlement, Barnato was made a life governor in Rhodes's company, and the influential Rhodes even arranged to have Barnato elected to the Cape Colony assembly. As their part of the £5.339 million transaction, the Barnato brothers retained some £4 million, at this time a fabulous sum. Rhodes's company, renamed De Beers Consolidated Mines Ltd. (which in the twenty-first century remained one of the world's leading diamond merchants), now controlled the vast majority of South Africa's diamond-producing wealth.

Barnato continued to serve as a member of the assembly until 1897, the year of his death. It is speculated that political events in South Africa involving the British and the Boers had greatly affected him personally and financially. It is also possible that he was still unhappy about losing the company he had so diligently built. On a sea voyage with his wife, he apparently committed suicide at the age of forty-six by jumping into the sea from the ship. His body was recovered and buried in a Jewish cemetery in England.

LEGACY
The entrepreneurial skills of Barney Barnato helped the African diamond industry to evolve from its somewhat chaotic "Wild West" beginnings, with its multitude of small, low-profit claim holdings, to an organized and extremely profitable business. The De Beers company, of which he was a director, became the world's leading diamond company.

—Roy Liebman

FURTHER READING

Jackson, Stanley. *The Great Barnato: Barney Barnato, 1852-1897*. London: Heinemann, 1970.

Leasor, James. *Rhodes and Barnato: Architects of Empire*. Philadelphia: Trans-Atlantic, 1997.

Lewisohn, Richard. *Barney Barnato: From Whitechapel Clown to Diamond King*. New York: Dutton, 1938.

See also: Alfred Beit; Cecil Rhodes.

P. T. BARNUM
American entertainer and entrepreneur

Barnum was one of the first people to "make it rich" in the entertainment business. He justified and made it somewhat more acceptable to profit from questionable entertainments, such as his exhibition of persons with physical oddities. Barnum also made money by operating a circus and making it a nationally known touring attraction.

Born: July 5, 1810; Bethel, Connecticut
Died: April 7, 1891; Bridgeport, Connecticut
Also known as: Phineas Taylor Barnum

P. T. Barnum. (Library of Congress)

Source of wealth: Entertainment industry
Bequeathal of wealth: Spouse; children; relatives; charity

EARLY LIFE

Phineas Taylor Barnum (FIHN-ee-uhs TAY-lor BAHR-nuhm) did not go to college but started working at a fairly young age. He ran a store, and he also learned the art of the lottery from his namesake, his grandfather Phineas Taylor. Barnum thought it was easier to earn money by running lotteries than by performing physical labor, and he operated a lottery out of his store, in addition to selling merchandise. From this experience in his store he gained skills of self-promotion, learning the dealing and scheming that would come in handy for his later careers as a showman and circus operator.

Barnum also was a frequent writer and became politically active. He spoke out against many reforms desired by church leaders, including the blue laws restricting work and amusements on Sundays. He wrote negative editorials about these reforms in a self-published newspaper. These editorials caused church leaders to sue him for libel, and Barnum spent time in jail. This experience and the ban on lotteries in Connecticut led Barnum to move to New York City. After gaining financial success, however, Barnum returned to Connecticut.

FIRST VENTURES

Barnum began his career as a showman soon after moving to New York City. He purchased Joyce Heth, a very aged African American slave, and presented her as George Washington's nurse. Barnum claimed that Heth was more than 160 years old and took her on a tour around the country. Barnum coached Heth about what to say and trained her to sing songs about Washington as an infant. Barnum greatly profited from this hoax. In response to questions about Heth's age and to appear that he had nothing to hide, Barnum offered to autopsy her body upon her death. Barnum conducted a public autopsy, with fifteen hundred people paying admission to get in. When the doctor concluded that Heth was really only eighty years old, Barnum then claimed that Heth was still alive and in Europe. The Heth autopsy was a template for the publicity stunts that Barnum would devise throughout his career.

With the profits from this venture, Barnum launched a touring troupe of what would later be called "circus freaks." He had mixed success, due in part to the economic recession from 1839 through 1843. Barnum survived the downturn and opened a museum in 1842.

MATURE WEALTH

The museum in many ways was a sort of carnival midway, minus the games, in a fixed building. Barnum continued to employ his trademark advertising with, among other things, balloon rides from the roof and posters in the windows advertising the exhibits. He also continued to plan his various hoaxes and attractions. His first major hoax after buying the building was to exhibit the Fiji Mermaid, which was a monkey's head sewed onto the tail of a fish. Even after most people had debunked the mermaid, Barnum continued to advertise it with the argument that no one knew for sure whether it was a hoax, so the public should come and see for itself.

Barnum never considered that he was cheating his customers if he gave them humbug along with entertainment. He also, it appears, considered his humbug different from the fortune tellers and other traditional carnival attractions. Barnum's exhibits included General Tom Thumb, the stage name of Charles Sherwood Stratton, who was only two-feet tall. Thumb was four years old when he started working for Barnum, even though Barnum presented him as being eleven. Thumb, with help from Barnum, imitated Napoleon I and other famous figures. Barnum and Thumb toured Europe, and Thumb continued to appear in Barnum's troupe for many years. Thumb took part in one of the most famous weddings of the 1860's, in which he married another short person, Mercy Lavinia Warren Bump. Barnum capitalized on every element of the wedding, even displaying Bump's

---

BARNUM AND BAILEY CIRCUS

The Barnum and Bailey Circus, which later became the Ringling Brothers and Barnum & Bailey Circus, was the first of the nationally known circus troupes. P. T. Barnum started his circus in 1871 as a traveling version of his curiosity show, and he labeled it as such. The word "circus" did not appear in his first advertisements. By 1872, Barnum was calling his attraction "the Greatest Show on Earth," the phrase that has become associated with his circus. Barnum advertised his collection of "freaks" and employed some of the same marketing ploys he had used for his museum. His was one of the first circuses to travel by train and to invent the circus train that eventually became a common feature of these shows. The train allowed his circus to travel more easily in order to perform in numerous venues, making the show a universal attraction.

Barnum relied on the expertise of managers whose circuses merged with his show, while he focused on the promotion of his attractions, including the creation of his "Greatest Show on Earth" slogan. One of these mergers was with the Cooper and Bailey Circus, founded by James Anthony Bailey. Among Barnum's most successful circus promotions was the publicity surrounding Jumbo, a huge elephant. He purchased this elephant from the London Zoo in 1882, buying him for the then-astronomical sum of $10,000 (many people at the time worked for a dollar a day or less). Barnum popularized the term "jumbo," helping to bring it into the American lexicon. In spite of his well-publicized connection with Barnum, Jumbo was with the circus for only three years, dying in a train accident in 1885. Jumbo and the other circus animals were moving across the tracks in a train yard when a locomotive hit the elephant. Most likely, the animal panicked and his handlers were unable to get him out of the way. Ever the promoter, Barnum told a story of how Jumbo charged into the fray, rescued a smaller elephant from the locomotive, and died as a hero. Not content with this promotion, Barnum also displayed the skeleton of Jumbo, along with his stuffed hide.

After Barnum's death, the circus was purchased by Bailey, who continued its operation. In 1907, the Barnum and Bailey Circus was purchased by the Ringling Brothers, creating the troupe that continues to perform into the twenty-first century.

---

wedding dress in his museum's windows for months after the ceremony.

Barnum followed up the Tom Thumb tour of Europe with perhaps his greatest coup—organizing a series of American concerts for Jenny Lind. Lind was a great Swedish singer and was loved in Europe. Without ever hearing her sing, Barnum offered her the unheard-of sum of $1,000 a night to perform in the United States. Lind accepted and the tour was a huge popular success. Nearly everywhere Barnum and Lind went, Lind sang to full houses. The tour also was a financial success for Barnum, repaying him more than his investment. Barnum continued to operate his museum and to conduct hoaxes

A poster from the mid-1890's advertises the "great ethological Congress of curious people from all parts of the world," one of the exhibits at the Barnum and Bailey Circus. (Library of Congress)

for the rest of his career, but Lind was one of his few high-culture attractions.

Barnum generally had success in his amusements, but he failed in other areas. He went nearly bankrupt several times and had repeated tragedies with fire, including having his mansion burn down, but he always recovered. Barnum opened up theaters and tried to make theatergoing a family activity. He also generally closed his museum on Sunday, in keeping with the moral ideas of the time. In his theaters, he tried to adapt the plays of William Shakespeare and similar attractions for the nineteenth century audience, striving to make these presentations interesting for families. Barnum also continued his self-promotion. He wrote his autobiography, which went through many revisions, and he did not oppose other companies' efforts to publish it, viewing this as excellent publicity.

Some of Barnum's other ventures did not succeed. His investment in a variety of companies in the 1850's led to his personal bankruptcy. However, he hooked up again with Tom Thumb, toured Europe, regained his wealth, and built himself another mansion after a fire destroyed his home. He continued to add oddities and attractions to his shows, exhibiting the first widely publicized conjoined twins, Chang and Eng Bunker. After two fires in the late 1860's, however, Barnum turned to the circus business.

Barnum's circus initially was a touring show of many oddities similar to what might have been seen in his museum. He purchased a rival circus and allowed the former owners to continue running it while he handled its publicity. Tom Thumb and his wife toured with the circus in the early 1880's. Throughout that decade and until his death in 1891, Barnum continued to devote his efforts to his circus business.

LEGACY

Barnum left several legacies, one of which he himself disputed. He was alleged to have said, "There's a sucker born every minute," but Barnum himself denied originating or using that phrase. He viewed himself as providing entertainment and argued that people were not suckers if they enjoyed his attractions, even if they never saw what they paid money to see. Thus, if someone paid to see the Fiji Mermaid but only saw a monkey sewed onto a fish, Barnum would argue that it was not a sham if one enjoyed the exhibit. Barnum also tried to revive the theater, and he created the modern traveling circus.

Barnum gave generously to colleges. Tufts University named a hall after him, and the school's mascot is Jumbo, named after the most famous elephant in Barnum's circus. Barnum is less well known for his one-year term as mayor of Bridgeport, Connecticut, and for his advocacy in support of moral censorship laws, including Connecticut's law banning the use of contraceptives.

—*Scott A. Merriman*

FURTHER READING

Barnum, P. T. *The Life of P. T. Barnum*. Champaign: University of Illinois Press, 2000. A reprint of the original 1855 edition of Barnum's autobiography.

Cook, James W., ed. *The Colossal P. T. Barnum Reader: Nothing Else Like It in the Universe*. Champaign: University of Illinois Press, 2005. Discusses many aspects of Barnum's life businesses, including his writings, his promotions, and the written material that survives related to his museums. Organized around various themes and includes notes and an index.

Harding, Les. *Elephant Story: Jumbo and P. T. Barnum Under the Big Top*. Jefferson, N.C.: McFarland, 2000.

Chronicles Jumbo's experiences in Barnum's circus and the elephant's life before then, including his capture in Africa.

Kunhardt, Philip B., Jr., Philip B. Kunhardt III, and Peter W. Kunhardt. *P. T. Barnum: America's Greatest Showman*. New York: Knopf, 1995. Biography of Barnum that includes a large number of photographs, some of which are quite rare.

Saxon, Arthur H. *P. T. Barnum: The Legend and the Man*. New York: Columbia University Press, 1995. Meticulously researched biography. Includes bibliography and an extensive index.

See also: Richard Branson; Mark Cuban; Walt Disney; David Geffen; Robert L. Johnson; Sumner Redstone; Steven Spielberg.

BASIL II

Byzantine monarch and military leader

Basil II labored almost obsessively and with great success to maximize the income and wealth of the Byzantine state, which he controlled and effectively owned as basileus *(emperor). He built up such a large treasury that he had to excavate additional storage rooms in the imperial palace.*

Born: 958; Constantinople, Byzantium (now Istanbul, Turkey)

Died: December 15, 1025; Constantinople

Also known as: Basil Porphyrogenitus (birth name); Bulgaroktonos (Bulgar Slayer)

Sources of wealth: Conquest; real estate; government

Bequeathal of wealth: Relatives

EARLY LIFE

Basil (BAZ-ihl) II, born Basil Porphyrogenitus, was the son of the Byzantine emperor Romanus II and his second wife, the tavern keeper Theophano. When their father died in 963, Basil and his brother Constantine jointly inherited the imperium as children but held no power. Instead, the monarchy ascended successively to two generals acting as coemperors: Nicephorus II Phocas, who married Basil's mother but was assassinated, with her assistance, several years later, and John I Tzimisces, who married Basil's aunt Theodora. Both generals dealt primarily with wars and diplomacy and were generally successful. Meanwhile, Basil and Constantine developed reputations as self-indulgent and frivolous, more interested in womanizing and other idle pursuits than in statecraft. Their father had the same reputation, and Constantine never changed.

FIRST VENTURES

With the death of John I Tzimisces in 976, Basil became sole emperor, and his brother never challenged him. His great-uncle, Basil Lecapenus, a eunuch, held power as chamberlain. Meanwhile, another general, Bardas Skle-

ros, sought to rule as Nicephoras and John Tzimisces had. He was ultimately defeated by rival general Bardas Phocas, who supported Basil II and his chamberlain. At some point, young Basil began to pay more attention to state affairs, and in 985 he finally assumed power himself. Basil Lecapenus was exiled and his vast wealth, much of it a product of corruption, was seized.

By now, Basil II had completely lost his youthful frivolity. He had no interest in scholarship, art, rhetoric, or regal display, and he showed no personal feelings. He never married or had any known royal favorite. He was pious and commissioned a calendar of saints' days, the *Menologion*, and other religious works.

After Basil's brief and unsuccessful campaign against the Bulgars, which Anatolian magnates saw as proof that they should run the state, the emperor faced further civil war. Basil arranged a then-unprecedented royal marriage of his sister Anna to Vladimir I, the crown prince of Kiev, in return for Vladimir's conversion to Orthodox Christianity and his mercenary force, which became Basil's Varangian Guard. The guards' help, the sudden death of Bardas Phocas, and the incipient blindness of the aged Bardas Skleros enabled Basil to unify the empire in 989. Normal tax receipts at that time are estimated at approximately 54,000 pounds of gold.

MATURE WEALTH

Basil's sole concern was the wealth and power of his empire. For the next thirty years, his primary activity and expense was a long war against the Bulgars, occasionally interrupted in the early years by difficulties in Armenia and Syria. He was finally able to concentrate enough attention in the west to defeat the Bulgars near Serrai. In a notoriously cruel act, Basil blinded most of his prisoners. Samuel, the Bulgarian czar, collapsed and died when the prisoners returned. Basil soon completed the conquest.

Basil annexed Bulgaria entirely, but he treated it leniently, with low taxes paid in kind rather than in gold. He then took care of unfinished business in the east, annexing most of Armenia but never recovering Edessa in Syria. He planned to recover Sicily from the Arabs, but he died first.

Bardas Skleros, whom Basil asked for advice in 989, recommended that Basil assess high taxes and other exactions upon the great magnates. Basil accepted this advice, and in 996 he confiscated the land that the magnates had acquired during the past sixty years. Much of this property was returned to small landholders, and much of it went to the emperor. Basil subsequently required that the magnates pay all of the taxes that the local peasants were unable to pay. One source reports that Basil remitted taxes for two years near the end of his life.

LEGACY
The Byzantine Empire reached its apogee under Basil II, and when he died in 1025, he left a treasury estimated at 200,000 pounds of gold. However, he failed to leave an heir, and his brother succeeded him as Emperor Constantine VIII. The decline of the Byzantine Empire began almost immediately after Basil's death, with much of the treasury spent on imperial frivolities. However, the imperial downfall was well cushioned for half a century thanks to the wealth that Basil left behind, and the empire temporarily expanded in the east and in Sicily.

—Timothy Lane

FURTHER READING

Holmes, Catherine. *Basil II and the Governance of Empire, 976-1025*. Oxford, England: Oxford University Press, 2006.

Norwich, John Julius. *Byzantium: The Apogee*. New York: A. A. Knopf, 1992.

Treadgold, Warren. *A Concise History of Byzantium*. New York: Palgrave, 2001.

See also: Süleyman the Magnificent.

ROBERT BASS
American investor

Bass was ranked as the 176th-richest person, with a net worth of $4.5 billion, in Forbes *magazine's 2010 list of the world's billionaires. He and the equity firm he founded have invested in a wide variety of businesses, including the media, publishing, oil, aircraft, and financial services.*

Born: 1948; Fort Worth, Texas
Also known as: Robert Muse Bass
Sources of wealth: Inheritance; oil; investments
Bequeathal of wealth: Relatives; charity; educational institution

EARLY LIFE
Robert Muse Bass was one of four sons born to Perry Richardson Bass and Nancy Lee Muse Bass. His uncle was Texas oil tycoon Sid W. Richardson, who was one of the wealthiest people in the United States when he died in 1959. Bass and each of his brothers inherited $2.8 million from their uncle. Part of Bass's education was received at two preparatory schools, Phillips Andover Academy and Governor Dummer Academy (now The Governor's Academy). He earned a B.A. from Yale in 1971 and an M.B.A. from Stanford University in 1974. Bass began his career at Wells Fargo Bank, and in 1974 he joined Bass Brothers Enterprises, the investment vehicle that Bass's father had organized for his sons.

FIRST VENTURES
Although Bass began to invest on his own in 1983, he continued to work with his brothers, controlling one of the largest private oil companies in the United States. Bass earned hundreds of millions of dollars in the late 1980's, buying up banking institutions that were in trouble, correcting the problems, and reselling the banks for a profit. One example of these ventures was the acquisition of American Savings Bank, which Bass eventually sold to Washington Mutual Bank in 1996.

MATURE WEALTH
Bass founded Oak Hill Capital Partners, a private equity firm, in 1999. He later established two associated companies, Oak Hill Capital Management Partners and Oak Hill Capital Partners II; the latter firm purchased companies, restructured them, and eventually resold them. Bass's firms have made several billion dollars worth of investments in numerous enterprises, including *The New York Times'* Broadcast Media Group, consisting of nine television stations; the Duane Reade drugstore chain; GE Capital International Services, an Indian outsourcing

company; The Container Store, Inc.; Alibris, an online book exchange; Jacobson Companies; Caribbean Restaurants, Burger King's exclusive franchisee in Puerto Rico; Southern Air Holdings, Inc.; Primus International, Inc.; and the Atlantic Broadband Group. One of Oak Hill's tactics is to invest in enough stock to force a company to restructure and to become more profitable—or risk being taken over by Oak Hill; either way, Bass's companies obtain a profit on their investments. Bass also founded Keystone, Inc., Oak Hill Venture Partners, and Oak Hill Securities Funds. As chairman of Aerion Corporation, he is a leader in the development of a supersonic business jet.

Although Bass's three brothers are all billionaires, he is the richest of the clan. Following his father's lead, he has donated a great deal of money to spur the growth of Fort Worth, Texas, especially in the city's downtown area, where many buildings have been remodeled.

LEGACY

Although some people are made uncomfortable by the changes required when Bass acquires a business, his takeover generally results in a more profitable enterprise that benefits everyone involved in the venture. Bass's reorganizations and investments have changed many businesses and, in the process, have changed the lives of millions of Americans. Bass is also a generous philanthropist. He has given $13 million to renovate the Yale University library, $25 million to Stanford University, and $10 million to Duke University. In addition, he has devoted his time to causes that are important to him. For example, he fought construction of a highway in Fort Worth that would have demolished part of the city's historic district. Bass has been a chairman of Stanford Management Company, the National Trust for Historic Preservation, and Cook Children's Hospital, and in 2009 he was a trustee of Rockefeller University, Groton School, Middlesex School, and the Amon Carter Museum.

—C. Alton Hassell

FURTHER READING

Cowan, Alison Leigh. "Robert Bass's Year of Major Deals." *The New York Times*, September 6, 1988, p. D5.

Cox, Bob. "Business Jet Poised to Take Off." *Fort Worth Star-Telegram*, October 19, 2009.

Fuquay, Jim. "Times Sells Media Group to Bass' Firm." *Fort Worth Star-Telegram*, January 5, 2007.

Giddens, David. "Bass' Oak Hill II Raises $1.3B." *Dallas Business Journal*, February 25, 2005.

Landy, Heather. "Bass, Two Others Invest in The Container Store Company." *Fort Worth Star-Telegram*, April 23, 2005.

See also: Warren Buffett; Carl Icahn; Kirk Kerkorian; T. Boone Pickens; George Soros.

JAN ANTONÍN BAT'A
Czech industrialist

Through his organizational genius, Bat'a presided over the growth of a moderately successful Czech shoe company that he turned into an international giant.

Born: March 7, 1898; Zlín, Moravia, Austro-Hungarian Empire (now in Czech Republic)
Died: August 23, 1965; São Paulo, Brazil
Also known as: Jan Bat'a; The King of Shoes
Sources of wealth: Trade; sale of products
Bequeathal of wealth: Relatives

EARLY LIFE

Jan Antonín Bat'a (yahn AHN-toh-neen BAH-tya) was born in 1898 in Zlín, Moravia, which was then part of the Austro-Hungarian Empire and is now in the Czech Republic. The Bat'a family had been cobblers for many generations when it established a small shoe-manufacturing company in 1894. The family first became rich when it supplied shoes to the military during World War I. Following the war, Czechoslovakia (what is now the Czech Republic and Slovakia) became an independent country, and the Bat'a firm was one of the first companies in the world to mass-produce shoes.

FIRST VENTURES

Upon the death of his half brother Tomas in an airplane crash in 1932, Bat'a assumed control of the family's company. By that time, the firm employed about 16,500 people and was internationally famous. Under his leadership the company began expanding from its base in Zlín throughout Europe, North America, India and other Asian countries, and North Africa.

MATURE WEALTH

Bat'a continued to grow his company, and by 1942 business had increased sixfold, with the firm employing almost 108,000 people worldwide, including at subsidiaries in the United States and Canada. He also diversified Bat'a products to include the manufacture of tires, chemicals, and textiles, established department stores, and even branched out into railroads, film studios, and airplane manufacturing. The company became the second largest in Czechoslovakia, after the Škoda Works, a munitions manufacturer. Many of the Bat'a factories were located next to small towns, dubbed Bat'a-villes, that were based on the "ideal city" concept and were built to house the firm's workers.

Following the German occupation of Czechoslovakia in 1939, Bat'a and his family left for the United States and remained there for more than a year. When he decided to leave he was placed on an international blacklist by the British government, who accused Bat'a of Nazi Party sympathies because his company had continued operating in Czechoslavakia during the German occupation. Bat'a sought refuge in Brazil, and while there he eventually founded several towns.

It is reported that Bat'a supplied aid to numerous Czechoslovakian Jewish families during World War II, helping them to escape the country, and that he also saved many other Czechs from being used as Nazi slave labor. He also reportedly sent financial assistance to the Czech government in exile in England. Following the war, the Czech government nationalized the Bat'a Shoe Company. Bat'a was accused, in absentia, of crimes against the state but was acquitted of some sixty-four charges.

When the Communists seized control of Czechoslovakia in 1948, Bat'a was again tried in absentia and sentenced to fifteen years. Once known as the King of Shoes, he was now portrayed as an exploitive capitalist, and his name was removed from the company, which was now to be called Svit. The company continued to be operated by the Bat'a family in other countries, however.

With Bat'a in exile in Brazil and his nephew Thomas J. Bata living in Canada, the company's operations were split in two. There began a struggle for control of the company, engendering many lawsuits, and young Thomas finally won complete control in 1949. In the early twenty-first century, the Bata Shoe Organization was headquartered in Lausanne, Switzerland, employed more than forty thousand people, operated thirty-three factories in twenty-two countries, and maintained a chain of five thousand retail stores in more than fifty countries. In late 2007, more than forty years after his death, Bat'a was finally cleared by the Czech judiciary.

LEGACY

Jan Antonín Bat'a took over an already prosperous company, and through his organizational skills made it into an international powerhouse, with an estimated fourteen billion pairs of shoes sold by 2009. His visionary establishment of the Bat'a-villes, with their modern facilities for his employees, helped maintain a generally content workforce. If reports are true, his aid to the legitimate Czech government and people during wartime was of material assistance to the welfare of his native country.

—Roy Liebman

FURTHER READING

Bata, Thomas J., and Sonja Sinclair. *Bata: Shoemaker to the World*. Toronto: Stoddart, 1990.

Bat'a, Tómas. *Knowledge in Action: The Bat'a System of Management*. Translated by Otilia M. Kabesova. Washington, D.C.: IOS Press, 1991.

Bat'a Shoe Company. *Why Was J. A. Bat'a Condemned? Collection of Documents About the Collaborating Activities of the Former Proprietor of the Bat'a Concern, Brazil Citizien—J. A. Bat'a*. Zíln, Czechoslovakia: Author, [194-].

See also: Giorgio Armani; Ralph Lauren.

LORD BEAVERBROOK
Canadian and British newspaper publisher, investor, and politician

Beaverbrook gained a fortune in Canada and later in England by selling bonds and investing in businesses with economic potential, notably in British newspapers. He created the Beaverbrook Foundation to continue his charitable interests after his death.

Born: May 25, 1879; Maple, Ontario, Canada
Died: June 9, 1964; Cherkley, Surrey, England
Also known as: Sir William Maxwell Aitken, first Baron Beaverbrook; William Maxwell Aitken (birth name)
Sources of wealth: Media; financial services; investments
Bequeathal of wealth: Children; charity

EARLY LIFE
Sir William Maxwell Aitken, first Baron Beaverbrook, was born in Maple, Ontario, on May 25, 1879. His family soon moved to Newcastle, New Brunswick, Canada, where his father, a Presbyterian minister, had accepted a new position. Aitken always identified Newcastle as his hometown. Described as a mischievous boy, his "puckish" character remained with him his entire life. Uninspired by school, he made pocket money by devising numerous stratagems, such as selling soap to obtain a bicycle. At the age of thirteen he founded a newspaper, a career he would pursue with greater success later in life. After failing the Latin examination for university he accepted a position as a law clerk, but he spent time selling life insurance and as a correspondent for a local newspaper. He bought a bowling alley, which he resold at a profit, and he lost money investing in frozen meat, which was ruined in a thaw.

FIRST VENTURES
In 1900, he abandoned selling insurance policies in favor of selling bonds. The Canadian economy was booming, but the stock exchange was limited in scope and most businessmen purchased bonds. Aitken was an excellent salesman, whose integrity was beyond dispute. With his commissions, he bought stagnant companies, made them profitable, and sold the now more valuable stock, and he then moved on to invest in other companies. His Royal Securities Corporation was the first company to sell bonds in eastern Canada.

MATURE WEALTH
By 1907, Aitken had become a millionaire in Canadian dollars. However, he was involved in disputes with his fellow investors in the Royal Securities Corporation; his partners wanted higher dividends, but Aitken preferred to retain profits for future investments. His success in part was due to his appreciation of the value of personal publicity, and in the early twentieth century publicity meant coverage in newspapers. The apex of Aitken's financial accomplishments occurred in 1909 and 1910, when he organized a number of successful mergers in such businesses as cast-iron manufacturing, railroad freight car construction, and the cement and steel industries. His appreciation of a unified Canadian market was in part a reaction to the growing economic power of the

Lord Beaverbrook. (Library of Congress)

United States. Aitken saw the British Empire as a potential economic unit, and for the rest of his life he championed the cause of "imperial preference" which would knit the empire into a single economic whole by encouraging free trade within the empire and establish tariffs against nonempire nations.

In 1908, Aitken made his first trip to London, where he acquired several new businesses, including London's Colonial Bank. He was introduced to Bonar Law, a Conservative Party politician and a fellow Canadian who shortly became Aitken's greatest hero. Aitken returned to England in 1910, and although he frequently said he would eventually make his permanent residence in Canada, he never did. Through his business connections in London—he briefly became a major shareholder in Rolls-Royce—he became involved in politics as a member of the Conservative Party. His tie with Law strengthened, and he developed connections with several of England's major publishers and journalists, notably Lord Northcliffe of the *Daily Mail*, an icon of "popular" journalism, and R. D. Blumenfeld, editor of the *Daily Express*. With Law's support, in 1910 Aitken was elected a member of Parliament from Ashton-under-Lyne, a textile center near Manchester. Aitken only rarely attended Parliament, preferring then and later to be a go-between among the major politicians of the day, working out compromises and obtaining solutions. When World War I came in 1914, he published a newspaper for Canadian troops in Great Britain and France, as well as creating the Canadian war records office.

In Britain, Aitken's most lasting economic endeavor was in the newspaper business. In 1911, he invested in the *Daily Express*, which had been failing financially. He acquired a controlling interest in the newspaper in 1916. At the same time he was deeply involved in the machinations that brought down Prime Minister H. H. Asquith, bringing to power David Lloyd George, who requested that King George V grant Aitken a peerage, in part because of the support the government was receiving from Aitken's newspapers. In February, 1917, Aitken took his seat in the House of Lords as Lord Beaverbrook, the name taken from a stream where he had fished as a

BEAVERBROOK ART GALLERY

In 1947, Lord Beaverbrook became chancellor of New Brunswick University at Fredericton, New Brunswick, Canada. He already had a long connection to the university, and through the years he had provided many scholarships, as well as funding the Lady Beaverbrook Gymnasium and the Lady Beaverbrook Residence for men.

An old friend of Beaverbrook, Sir James Dunn, was an art patron at Canada's Dalhousie University, and the always competitive Beaverbrook decided to emulate Dunn. Beaverbrook had little interest in art and limited tastes, which included English landscapes, such as those of J. M. W. Turner and John Constable, portraits by Sir Joshua Reynolds and Thomas Gainsborough, and the French painters François Boucher and Jean-Honoré Fragonard, with their voluptuous females. He also acquired paintings by his friends, including Winston Churchill, Walter Sickert, and Graham Vivian Sutherland, who had painted a portrait of Beaverbrook. Beaverbrook's collection, along with several works by Salvador Dalí from Beaverbrook's last wife, Christofor Dunn (Sir James Dunn's widow) was donated to the Beaverbrook Art Gallery when it opened in 1959. William Constable, a descendant of the early nineteenth century landscape painter John Constable, officiated at the opening.

One biographer suggests that Beaverbrook believed his own collection was sufficient for the gallery; thus the gallery was complete in 1959. In any event, he made little provision for additional purchases or further expansion of the gallery's facilities. The gallery did continue to add to its collections, focusing on paintings by Canadian artists. In 1994, the gallery was officially designated as New Brunswick's Provincial Art Gallery.

In 2003, a dispute occurred between the Beaverbrook Art Gallery and the Beaverbrook Foundations of the United Kingdom and Canada. The foundations demanded that the gallery return the numerous paintings that Beaverbrook had donated, intending to sell them at auction to raise funds for the foundations. In a legal decision rendered in 2007, it was decided that 85 of the 133 contested works would remain with the gallery. The United Kingdom foundation was unwilling to accept that award and appealed the decision, but in 2009 the appellate court ruled in favor of the gallery.

boy. In the new government, Beaverbrook became the chancellor of the duchy of Lancaster and was placed in charge of war propaganda. He resigned his position at the end of the war in 1918, vowing never to hold office again unless there was another war. Beaverbrook enjoyed politics, and although he remained a Conservative, he was never a reliable party politician. After World War I he disposed of Royal Securities Corporation and the Colonial Bank; newspapers became his central interest.

Beaverbrook used his newspapers to publicize himself and to advocate his long-standing commitment to imperial preference, but he was also sincerely interested in publishing the best possible newspapers. He invested heavily in the *Daily Express*, and he increased the newspaper's profits by expanding its advertising, an innovative practice that eventually was adopted by most other newspapers. However, he also was a strong believer in providing "news," and his publications had more foreign correspondents than any of the other British newspapers. In 1918, Beaverbrook started publishing a second newspaper, the *Sunday Express*, and in time this newspaper held an important position among elite newspapers, such as *The Sunday Times* and *The Observer*, and popular but at times salacious publications, such as *News of the World*. Although London was the center of English newspaper publishing, Beaverbrook also founded the *Scottish Daily Express*. In 1923, he acquired the *Evening Standard*. Beaverbrook allowed the editors of his newspapers to have considerable leeway in both content and policies, although he exerted his control in his advocacy of empire and in his opposition to socialism and any British involvement in European or continental affairs.

Beaverbrook remained a wealthy man during the Great Depression. In early 1929 he sold his stocks and put the money in bonds, thus insulating himself from the worldwide stock market crash. As a solution to the economic crisis, Beaverbrook, through his newspapers, launched an "Empire Crusade," which was a continuation of his long campaign for imperial preference. This campaign fared no better than his earlier attempts because there was widespread fear among voters that imperial preference would result in increased food prices. As the shadow of fascism spread across Europe, Beaverbrook favored a policy of "No More War" through British isolation from continental affairs. He opposed the League of Nations, believing the organization was more likely to lead to war than to peace. Through his newspapers, he continually predicted that there would be no war in Europe, or no war that would involve Great Britain. However, Britain declared war on September 3, 1939, after Nazi Germany invaded Poland. After the crushing German campaign in Western Europe, in May, 1940, Winston Churchill became prime minister. After the fall of France in June, the Nazis turned against Britain. One of Churchill's earliest acts was to appoint Beaverbrook the minister of aircraft production. In this position, Beaverbrook's energy and unorthodox methods enabled Britain to win the Battle of Britain, and this victory was perhaps "his finest hour."

After World War II, Beaverbrook withdrew from politics. He opposed the socialism of the Labour Party and deplored the developing Cold War between the former allies. In addition to his English residences, he acquired a home in southern France and two in the West Indies, and throughout the year he journeyed from one to another, always keeping in close contact with his newspapers by telephone. He wrote several well-regarded works on the events and people of the World War I years.

It is impossible to know the extent of Beaverbrook's fortune because he gave much of it away during his lifetime, but one biographer estimates it was in the range of $40 million. His benefactions were often in the form of investments that he made in the name of the recipient and were distributed to members of his family, friends from childhood, political friends and foes, educational institutions, and the Presbyterian Church. In 1906, he married Gladys Drury, who was from one of Canada's most distinguished families. It proved to be a satisfactory marriage, and the couple had three children. Beaverbrook had other female relationships, but he was devastated when Gladys died in 1927. For many years his closest female companion was Mrs. Jean Norton until her death in 1945. In 1963, the year before his death, he married Christofor Dunn, the widow of an old Canadian friend.

LEGACY

Beaverbrook's major economic legacy was his profitable British newspapers, particularly the *Daily Express* and *Sunday Express*, which provided England's middle classes with publications that were readable and interesting and presented accurate coverage of the major news stories of the day. In 1954, he established the Beaverbrook Foundation, which supports numerous charitable causes in Canada and the United Kingdom.

—*Eugene Larson*

FURTHER READING

Chisholm, Anne. *Lord Beaverbrook: A Life*. New York: Knopf, 1993. A major biography that distances itself from the subject, unlike Taylor's more intimate work on Beaverbrook.

Nowell, Iris. *Women Who Give Away Millions: Portraits of Canadian Philanthropists*. Toronto: Hounslow Press, 1996. Includes discussion of Christofor Dunn's role in Beaverbrook's philanthropy.

Poitras, Jacques. *Beaverbrook: A Shattered Legacy*. Fredericton, N.B.: Goose Lane, 2007. The author focuses on Beaverbrook's Canadian connections, including the bitter dispute between the Beaverbrook foundations and the Beaverbrook Art Gallery.

Richards, David Adams. *Lord Beaverbrook.* Toronto: Penguin, 2008. A well-written, brief biography of Beaverbrook, one of the volumes in Penguin's Extraordinary Canadians series.

Taylor, A. J. P. *Beaverbrook.* New York: Simon & Schuster, 1972. The definitive biography by an eminent English historian, who knew Beaverbrook personally.

Young, Kenneth. *Churchill and Beaverbrook.* London: Eyre and Spottiswoode, 1966. A well-written account of both the political and the personal relationship of these two larger-than-life figures.

See also: Walter Annenberg; Barbara Cox Anthony; Anne Cox Chambers; Katharine Graham; William Randolph Hearst; Samuel I. Newhouse.

NINTH DUKE OF BEDFORD
British aristocrat, agriculturalist, and politician

The dukes of Bedford are from an old, established, aristocratic family who own estates, London property, and stately homes. The family historically was involved in government and often served in the military, and the ninth duke of Bedford maintained both of these traditions.

Born: October 16, 1819; London, England
Died: January 14, 1891; London, England
Also known as: Francis Charles Hastings Russell (birth name)
Sources of wealth: Inheritance; real estate
Bequeathal of wealth: Children

EARLY LIFE
Francis Charles Hastings Russell, the ninth duke of Bedford, was the grandson of John Russell, sixth Duke of Bedford. His father, Major-General Lord George William Russell, was the duke's second son and a soldier, fighting in the Crimean War, and an aide-de-camp to King William IV and the young Queen Victoria. His mother was Elizabeth Anne Rawdon, also from an aristocratic family, a somewhat ambitious lady praised by Lord Byron. His parents married in 1817.

Bedford followed his father into the army, entering the Scots Fusilier Guards in 1838. He retired after his marriage to Lady Elizabeth Sackville West in 1844. The couple had four children, two boys, George and Herbrand, and two girls, Ella and Ermyntrude. Again following his father's footsteps and the family tradition, Bedford entered politics, becoming a Liberal Party member of Parliament for Bedfordshire from 1847 to 1872. In 1866, he broke with Prime Minister William Ewart Gladstone over the Irish Home Rule Bill, and thenceforth Bedford sat as member of Parliament from the Unionist Party.

FIRST VENTURES
It was Bedford's uncle, also named Francis Russell, who had inherited the family title on the death of the sixth duke. The Bedfords had a long history as aristocrats, dating back to the time of Henry VIII in the sixteenth century. Woburn Abbey, in Bedfordshire, had been given them by Henry's son, Edward VI, in 1547. The abbey, now one of England's grandest stately homes, had been a Cistercian abbey and became the main family residence in 1619.

Bedford's cousin, William, then became the eighth duke on the death of his father, but he died without an heir in 1872. As a result, Bedford became the ninth duke, and he was thus elevated to the House of Lords; his position as a member of Parliament ended, and he inherited Woburn Abbey, its estates in Bedfordshire, and many other estates throughout England, totaling some 90,000 acres. He also inherited large properties in fashionable areas of London near Woburn Square and Tavistock Square in Bloomsbury, later identified with the British Museum.

MATURE WEALTH
Woburn Abbey had been largely redeveloped by John Russell, the famous fourth duke of Bedford in the eighteenth century, and was then landscaped by noted landscape architect Humphry Repton in 1802. The ninth duke decided not to make additional improvements to the abbey but developed his estates around Tavistock in the West Country and in the fens of Cambridgeshire. He also turned his attention to the agricultural condition of his estates, becoming involved in experimental work, especially with fertilizers and stock breeding. In 1879, he succeeded the Prince of Wales as president of the Royal Agricultural Society, a public acknowledgment of his en-

deavors. He also improved his Bloomsbury estate, which increased its value by about £1 million.

Bedford channeled his political interests into being the lord lieutenant of the county of Huntingdon between 1884 and 1891, while his wife became the mistress of the robes for Queen Victoria from 1880 until 1883. In 1880, Bedford was made a Knight of the Garter, a select group of leading men of public affairs. However, at this time he also became increasingly hypochondriacal, and in 1891, after contracting pneumonia, he shot himself through the head while temporarily insane.

LEGACY

Bedford bequeathed the family estates to his older son, George. These properties had increased in value and quality, largely because of their agricultural improvements. It is perhaps no coincidence that in the twenty-first century Woburn Abbey survived as a leading British

stately home, and the house, furnishings, and art treasures are open to the public. In 1970, Safari Park, a menagerie of African animals, was opened to the public on the grounds of the estate.

—David Barratt

FURTHER READING

Bedford, John Robert Russell. *The History and Treasures of Woburn Abbey: Home of the Dukes of Bedford*. London: Pitkin Pictorials, 1962.

"The Death of the Duke of Bedford." *The Times*, January 15, 1891.

Sutton, Denys, ed. *Woburn Abbey and Its Collections*. London: Apollo, 1966.

See also: John Deere; Charles Henry de Soysa; Henry Francis du Pont; Hugh Grosvenor; Cyrus Hall McCormick; First Duke of Sutherland; Tan Kah Kee.

ALFRED BEIT
British mining magnate

Beit was one of the most important of the Randlords—the magnates who exploited the mineral wealth in Great Britain's Cape Colony (now in South Africa). He was also a generous philanthropist, creating the Beit Trust in order to benefit the people of southern Africa.

Born: February 15, 1853; Hamburg (now in Germany)
Died: July 16, 1906; Welwyn, England
Source of wealth: Mining
Bequeathal of wealth: Relatives; charity

EARLY LIFE

The family of Alfred Beit (bit) descended from Sephardic Jews who had converted to Lutheranism and lived in Hamburg. Alfred's father, Siegfried Beit, was a prosperous silk merchant. Siegfried and his wife, Laura Hahn Beit, had six children, of which Alfred was the second oldest. An uninspired student, Alfred seemed destined for a career in business. When he was eighteen, he went to work for a diamond merchants' firm in Amsterdam. In 1875, D. Lippert and Company, a diamond trading firm, sent him to the British colony in southern Africa, where diamonds had been discovered several years earlier.

For most of human history, southern Africa was a sparsely populated, rugged area that was of interest to traders only as a stopping point for ships rounding the

Cape of Good Hope on their voyages between Europe and Asia. However, the region acquired a new importance after gold and diamonds were discovered there in the late nineteenth century. Although there were enormous quantities of these commodities, they were buried deep in the ground, unlike the diamonds that had been found in India for millennia, which lie close to the surface, or the gold ore deposited in rivers and rock formations throughout the world. Obtaining these precious commodities would require innovative, enterprising, and efficient mining techniques. Of all the mining magnates in southern Africa, or Randlords, as they came to be called, Beit proved to be the most capable of devising new methods for extracting gold and diamonds.

FIRST VENTURES

Beit made his way to Kimberley, the center of diamond mining in Great Britain's Cape Colony. At this time, Kimberley was a wild town in which a large number of people had come to seek their fortunes. Beit was unprepossessing physically, with little social elegance. Nevertheless, he had two advantages over the other miners. Unlike many of the adventurers, he was studious and analytical. He had also been trained in the best diamond shops of Amsterdam. He realized that the diamonds from the Kimberley mines, which were held in low regard, were in fact high-quality gems, which were worth about

Miners at southern Africa's Kimberley diamond fields around the end of the nineteenth century. The discovery of diamonds and gold in the region resulted in massive profits for the Randlords. (The Granger Collection, New York)

ten times more money than diamond merchants had been receiving for them.

Beit borrowed £2,000 from his father and set up his own diamond firm, purchasing as much of the land around Kimberley as he could. As the diamond industry grew, he was able to rent his land at £1,800 a month, and he eventually sold his entire stake for £260,000. His firm set up several trading stations near the mines. He earned a reputation for trading diamonds fairly, quickly, and accurately. In the 1880's, he became associated with two other leading Randlords who were trading diamonds—Cecil Rhodes and Julius Charles Wernher. He and Wernher established the firm of Wernher, Beit. In addition, Beit helped Rhodes amalgamate the Kimberley mines into Rhodes's great diamond conglomerate, De Beers Consolidated Mines, Ltd., with Beit investing £250,000 in this new enterprise.

Gold was discovered in southern Africa in 1886, and

Beit immediately turned his attention to this new commodity. Because this gold was buried deep in the ground, many people were skeptical about the long-term success of the area's gold mines. However, Beit saw opportunities where others saw obstacles. He realized that with new and improved engineering techniques, gold could be extracted at an increasingly reduced cost, leading to increasingly greater profits. He acquired several gold mines and brought in the best engineers from the British Empire to devise extraction methods. As a result, his firm pioneered new mining techniques and earned substantial profits. The engineering methods used in his mines were copied by other Randlords.

MATURE WEALTH

Beit showed excellent judgment in assessing the value of South Africa's diamonds and gold. However, his political instincts were often less astute. He became interested in the northern frontier that eventually became the colony of Rhodesia, and he was frustrated by the Boers, the perennial enemy of the British colonists in southern Africa. He supported the Jameson Raid (1895-1896), in which the British sought to overthrow the Boer Republics. For his part in the ill-conceived raid, Beit was censured by the House of Commons. Nevertheless, he heavily financed the British military force stationed in southern Africa. In 1902, a strengthened British military overcame fierce Boer resistance in the Second Boer War (1899-1902). Beit also supported the projected development of railway lines in South Africa and Rhodesia.

Beit never married. He moved into the seven-thousand-acre Tewin Water estate in Welwyn, England. His home there was a Regency-style mansion with Victorian additions. In 1895, he had a mansion built for him in Park Lane, London, by the architect Eustace Balfour. Beit filled his London mansion with his impressive collection of paintings by English, Dutch, and Spanish masters and with bronze statues from the Italian Renaissance. He endowed several professorships at Oxford University, and he made donations to the school's Bodleian Library. He also used his fortune to support artistic and civic causes.

Beit had always suffered from poor health, and in 1903 he had a stroke. He died on July 16, 1906. His estate was probated twelve days later and assessed at close to £8 million, which would be about $6 billion in 2010 U.S. currency. The bulk of his estate went to his brother, Otto Beit, but he also bequeathed about £2 million to charity. Additional benefactions included £130,000 to the Lon-

RANDLORDS

For most of recorded history, southern Africa was little populated and little regarded. However, this part of the world began to attract attention in the nineteenth century with two discoveries: diamonds in 1866 and gold in 1886. Soon the mad rush was on for these commodities, resulting in a new class of incredibly wealthy magnates—the Randlords. Named for the Rand gold fields, this group of about fifty mining magnates is without parallel in history. During their heyday in the late nineteenth century, the Randlords became known for their rapid accumulation of wealth, their colorful exploits, and their domination of the fortunes of Great Britain's Cape Colony in what is now South Africa. The Randlords kept mansions in London and estates in the English countryside. They were the wealthiest subjects of the British Empire, both admired and hated, with their wealth and philanthropy earning them baronetcies from Great Britain. They competed with one another fiercely but also conspired in facing the formidable threats posed by the oppressed miners of African and mixed ancestry and the cantankerous Boer colonists.

Sir Joseph Robinson (1840-1929) is perhaps the first of the magnates properly called a Randlord. He owned shares in several of the earliest mines to be discovered, earning a great fortune from the West Rand mine. Alfred Beit (1853-1906) was perhaps the most farsighted of the Randlords in his development of South Africa's diamond and gold industries. Cecil Rhodes (1853-1902), Beit's friend and partner, also drew a great fortune from mining gold and diamonds. He established the De Beers Consolidated Mines, Ltd., in 1888, the most dominant diamond monopoly and conglomerate in history. Rhodes left much of his fortune to endow professorships and scholarships at Oxford University. Jul-

ius Charles Wernher (1850-1912), another partner of Beit, built his fortune largely on gold mining.

The colorful Barney Barnato (1851-1897) and his brother Harry (1850-1908) established Barnato Brothers, a company that made enormous profits by extracting diamonds from the Kimberley mines. Although Barney lost a good deal of his fortune in stock speculation, he still managed to leave more than £1 million upon his death; Harry left £5.8 million. Thomas Cullinan (1862-1936) controlled the Premier mine, which he bought in 1902 for £52,000. In 1905, the 3,106.75-carat Cullinan Diamond, the largest diamond ever found, was extracted from the Premier mine. This diamond was presented to King Edward VII as a gift, and it subsequently was incorporated into the British crown jewels. On February 26, 2010, a 507-carat diamond from the Cullinan mine was sold to the Chow Tai Fook Jewelry Company for $35.3 million, the largest amount ever paid for a rough diamond.

John Hays Hammond (1855-1936), an American, became the leading engineer of the Rand mines. When he returned to the United States, he was hired by Daniel Guggenheim, of the Guggenheim mining magnates, who through their Guggenex and ASARCO trusts controlled much of the world's mining and smelting operations. Hammond's total income was more than $1 million a year, propelling him into the ranks of the very wealthy.

Sir Ernest Oppenheimer (1880-1957) was the greatest mining magnate of the twentieth century. In 1917, he and American financier J. P. Morgan founded the Anglo American Corporation, a gold mining company which eventually became the majority stakeholder in De Beers.

don Imperial College of Technology, £200,000 for the general betterment of Rhodesia, £250,000 to construct a university and medical college in Johannesburg, and £20,000 each to King Edward VII Hospital and Guy's Hospital. He bequeathed his art collection to museums in London, Berlin, and Hamburg. His most important benefaction was £1.2 million to create the Beit Railway Trust in order to develop railway and telegraph operations in southern Africa. This trust would be administered by his brother Otto and other trustees. Beit's instructions for the Beit Railway Trust allowed for the future use of its funds for public charities and education.

LEGACY

Beit was one of the leading Randlords, and the one with perhaps the most impressive history. His diamond-trading firm and engineering techniques enabled diamonds and gold to be efficiently extracted from South African mines. In a period when the miners were heartlessly exploited, Beit's operations were known for their humane treatment of these workers.

Beit also was one of the world's leading philanthropists. The Beit Railway Trust constructed most of the bridges that were built in central and southern Africa in the first half of the twentieth century. In 1932, the trust made a large grant in order to initiate civil aviation in South Africa. In 1954, the trust was reconstituted by an act of Parliament into an incorporated charity and renamed the Beit Trust. In the twenty-first century, the Beit Trust provided scholarships and grants in support of health, education, welfare, and environmental projects in Malawi, Zambia, and Zimbabwe.

—Howard Bromberg

FURTHER READING

Beit, Alfred, and J. Lockhart. *The Will and the Way.* New York: Longmans, Green, 1958. A history of the first fifty years of the Beit Railway Trust, reincorporated as the Beit Trust. One of the authors is Beit's nephew, Sir Alfred Beit, the son of Otto Beit and a trustee of the Beit Trust.

Fort, George. *Alfred Beit: A Study of the Man and His Work.* London: Ivor Nicholson and Watson, 1932. An early biographical work. Outdated but remains the only full-length biography of Beit.

Kanfer, Stefan. *The Last Empire: De Beers, Diamonds, and the World.* New York: Farrar, Straus and Giroux, 1995. Lively account of the fortunes of the Randlords. Praises the unprepossessing Beit as the most advanced of the Randlords in terms of his skill and gentility.

Meredith, Martin. *Diamonds, Gold, and War: The British, the Boers, and the Making of South Africa.* New York, PublicAffairs, 2008. Account of South African gold, diamonds, and Randlords, and the roles they played in the British war with the Boers.

Pye-Smith, Charlie. *For the Benefit of the People.* Woking, England: Longmans, Green, 2007. The centenary history of the Beit Trust, with an emphasis on its current projects in Africa.

Wheatcroft, Geoffrey. *The Randlords.* New York: Athenaeum, 1986. A history of the colorful and profitable exploits of South Africa's gold and diamond mining magnates.

See also: Barney Barnato; Cecil Rhodes.

SAMUEL BELLAMY
British privateer

Bellamy was the captain of a band of pirates who plundered more than fifty ships in the early eighteenth century, amassing some of the great wealth then flowing through the Caribbean and along the Atlantic coast of British North America. He then lost all of his loot—and his life—in one terrible storm.

Born: baptized March 18, 1689; Hittisleigh, Devonshire, England
Died: April 26, 1717; off the coast of Wellfleet, Massachusetts
Also known as: Black Sam; Black Bellamy
Source of wealth: Privateering
Bequeathal of wealth: Dissipated

EARLY LIFE
After spending his childhood in the Devonshire countryside, Samuel Bellamy (BEHL-ah-mee) left the area to seek his fortune at sea. Not much is known for certain about where his early years as a sailor took him, though it is likely he spent some time in the Caribbean. In 1715, according to tradition, while working in the area of Cape Cod he fell in love with a local girl named Mary Hallett. To make a better life for her he determined to use his maritime skills to get a ship and seek out some of the recently wrecked Spanish galleons along the coast of Florida. He convinced Rhode Island native Paulsgrave Williams to join him and provide the capital needed for this project.

FIRST VENTURES
Although Bellamy and Williams did not secure any of the particular treasure that first drew them toward the Caribbean, they quickly discovered that they had the talent and strategy well suited to piracy. Beginning with two periaguas, or large canoes, they soon successfully stole the merchantman ship *St. Marie* from Captain Henry Jennings, and they then joined forces with a leading pirate in the area, Benjamin Hornisgold. Hornisgold, however, refused to rob British vessels, while Bellamy made no such distinction, making him popular with his men. On a democratic vote, Bellamy, at the age of twenty-seven, was elected leader of the gang of 170 pirates, and in one year he had already amassed booty worth thousands of British pounds.

MATURE WEALTH
A crowning achievement was Bellamy's capture and appropriation of the slave ship *Whydah*, which was well equipped with guns and with a three-hundred-ton hull then laden with ivory, indigo, spices, and other valuables, not to mention a separate stash of silver, gold, and gems valued between £20,000 and £30,000. Each member of the pirate crew who served with Bellamy, including the cabin boy and the pirates of African and Indian descent, was entitled to at least £100 of that loot, but the share for Bellamy was still considerable, and he proceeded to gather even more.

In the spring of 1717, Bellamy and Williams devised a plan to lead separate groups out of the Bahamas, pirating up the coast of North America, with Williams connecting in Rhode Island with friends and relatives to help market some of the plunder and Bellamy stopping by Cape Cod for provisions and most likely a visit to Hallett. Just off the coast of Cape Cod, very close to Bellamy's goal, the *Whydah,* holding accumulated wealth taken from fifty-three other vessels, got caught in a terrible and deadly night storm. Only two people aboard ship survived, and Bellamy went down with his vessel. It was the costliest pirate shipwreck ever recorded. One of the two survivors testified in court that among the many treasures lost that night were 180 bags of gold and silver, which the pirates had stored in chests kept between decks.

LEGACY
New England diver Barry Clifford devoted his life to undersea probing for the *Whydah*, and in 1984 he found the first verifiable evidence and remains of the ship, thanks to modern techniques of underwater sand bed monitoring. In 1988, a Massachusetts court awarded him finder's rights. Subsequent excavation attempts into the twenty-first century have led to the establishment of the Whydah Museum in Provincetown, Massachusetts, where visitors can see what treasures have been recovered so far—some gold, silver, jewelry, and pieces of eight—and learn more about Bellamy and the life of eighteenth century pirates.

—*Scot M. Guenter*

FURTHER READING
Clifford, Barry, and Paul Perry. *Expedition "Whydah": The Story of the World's First Excavation of a Pirate*

Treasure Ship and the Man Who Found Her. New York: Cliff Street, 1999.

Defoe, Daniel. *A General History of the Robberies and Murders of the Most Notorious Pirates.* Reprint. Guilford, Conn.: Lyons Press, 2002.

Woodard, Colin. *The Republic of Pirates.* Orlando, Fla.: Harcourt, 2007.

See also: Elias Hasket Derby; Francis Drake; John Hawkwood; Israel Thorndike.

AUGUST BELMONT
American banker, horse breeder, and diplomat

Belmont was a leading figure in New York banking circles, wielding the considerable influence that his wealth conferred. Among the recipients of his beneficence were the Democratic Party, when it was long out of power, and the Union during the Civil War, when Belmont used his influence with powerful foreign banking interests to deny European funding to the Confederacy. He also became a noted sportsman who helped to modernize horse racing.

Born: December 8, 1816; Alzei, Rhenish Prussia (now in Germany)
Died: November 24, 1890; New York, New York
Also known as: August Schoenberg (birth name)
Sources of wealth: Banking; horse breeding
Bequeathal of wealth: Relatives

EARLY LIFE
August Belmont was born in 1816 in Alzei, a small city in the Rhenish Palatinate, to Simon and Frederika Elsaas Schoenberg. There is some difference of opinion as to when the original family name of Schoenberg received its literal translation into the French-sounding Belmont, but it is most probable that young August adopted the name when he began his American career. His father was a fairly successful Jewish landowner, so young August could reasonably expect to choose his own career and look forward to a life of relative comfort.

Ending his schooling at about the age of fourteen, he became a low-level employee at the Frankfurt offices of the great house of Rothschild, Europe's leading banking concern. According to some reports, his mother had secured the position for him through a family connection. Starting out, according to legend, as an unpaid floor sweeper, Belmont's intelligence and ambition soon became apparent, and while still a teenager he was rapidly promoted within the company. He was transferred to the Rothschild branch in Naples, Italy, where one of his tasks was negotiating contracts with representatives of the pope. During this time, he may have begun to develop the

appreciation of art that in later life would bring him much renown as a collector.

FIRST VENTURES
It was a business trip to Havana, Cuba, for the Rothschilds in 1837 that gave Belmont the opportunity to branch out on his own. While still at sea he learned that the company that dealt with the Rothschild business interests in the United States had failed in the financial Panic of 1837. After completing his assignment in Havana, Belmont arrived in New York and established August Belmont and Company with little capital other than

August Belmont. (Archive Photos/Getty Images)

102

his connection to the legendary house of Rothschild. He was barely twenty-one years old.

At its inception, Belmont's Wall Street firm dealt primarily in foreign currency exchange, a lucrative enterprise but not one that engendered huge profits. It was the company's later move into the more expansive banking business that enabled Belmont to earn a vast fortune. In his private life, Belmont seemed to exhibit the swashbuckling qualities that he perhaps lacked in his early business dealings. In 1841, for example, he engaged in a duel in Indiana over a female acquaintance, and he carried the scars of that incident for the rest of his life. He was also a gambler who would lose large sums in an evening, and it was not long before his reputation for high living became well known in New York society.

MATURE WEALTH

Belmont became an American citizen and soon was a leading figure in the Democratic Party. In 1844, he was named the American consul general to the Austrian empire, a position he held until 1850, when he resigned to protest Austria's harsh treatment of those who sought Hungary's independence during the Hungarian Revolution of 1848. Belmont was a fun-loving man who possessed considerable personal charisma, and in 1849 he further solidified his place in society by marrying the well-connected Caroline Slidell Perry. She was the daughter of Matthew C. Perry, commodore of the U.S. Navy who within a few years was to help open Japan to foreign trade, and the niece of war hero Oliver Hazard Perry. Belmont and his wife built a large mansion on Manhattan's newly fashionable Fifth Avenue, and he further burnished his reputation as a bon vivant.

In 1853, President Franklin Pierce appointed Belmont to be the minister to the Netherlands, and Belmont lived in The Hague for four years. Although continuing to run his company, he seemed to be equally interested in his growing collection of paintings and his position within the Democratic Party leadership. Belmont be-

---

THE BELMONT STAKES

Following the Civil War, August Belmont became passionate about thoroughbred horse breeding and racing. He served as president of the American Jockey Club for about twenty years, even though Jews were barred from membership until many decades later. Belmont had a lavish Long Island estate, on which he housed several prize thoroughbreds. In the late 1880's, he moved his stables to Lexington, Kentucky, to take advantage of the more conducive climate and superior training facilities. His horses led the nation in earnings for the two years preceding his death, and one of his thoroughbreds may have been the first horse to be sold for $100,000 at auction.

Belmont went on to hold important positions in several racing clubs in New York and New Jersey, and the annual Belmont Stakes race was named for him. The inaugural Belmont Stakes took place in 1867 at Jerome Park, and the winner was a filly named Ruthless. With the Kentucky Derby and the Preakness Stakes, the Belmont Stakes eventually became part of the famed Triple Crown of horse racing. In the years since its inception, the race has been held at various racetracks in and around New York City, including Morris Park in the Bronx and Aqueduct in Queens.

In the early twentieth century, Belmont's son, August Belmont, Jr., and attorney William Collins Whitney built the Belmont Park racetrack in Nassau County, Long Island, New York. The track opened in 1905, and since then the Belmont Stakes has been held there each year in June, with the exception of a few years when it was staged at other race courses. Winners of the Belmont Stakes include champion thoroughbreds Man o' War (1920), Secretariat (1973), Whirlaway (1941), Seattle Slew (1977), and Citation (1948).

Since 1925, the course has been one-and-a-half miles in length, the longest of the three racetracks that are the sites of the Triple Crown. Until 1920, horse races at Belmont Park were run clockwise, as they are on English courses. The park can accommodate up to ninety thousand people, with seats available for thirty-three thousand; on occasion, more than eighty thousand people have attended races.

In 1955, the New York Racing Association purchased the track and renovated the course to make it more structurally sound. The rebuilt racetrack opened in 1968, after the facility had been closed for several years. In latter years, crowds generally thinned because of the popularity of off-track betting, which is legal in New York.

Belmont Park is open for racing from early May to the middle of July and in early September to late October. The course operates throughout the year as a training center for thoroughbreds.

---

came the party's national chairman and urged reconciliation with slaveholders before the onset of the Civil War. Although he did not support slavery, Belmont did not fight for its abolition. During the Civil War, despite his opposition to President Abraham Lincoln's policies, Belmont was convinced the Union would prevail and used his international connections to prevent European banking interests from financially supporting the Confederate government. He also provided funding to organize a German-American regiment from New York. In 1872, after twelve years, he stepped down from active leadership of the Democratic Party but continued his financial support of the organization.

Like many of his extremely wealthy Gilded Age contemporaries, Belmont enjoyed his place within society, but he was not considered to be among the notorious "robber barons," who appeared to value the accumulation of wealth above all else. Although apparently remaining nominally Jewish, Belmont was admitted to social and sporting venues ordinarily not open to those of his faith. He was, as a result, not well regarded by his fellow wealthy German Jews, perhaps because they believed he had somehow betrayed his religious heritage.

Belmont was proud of his American citizenship and was quoted as stating, "I prefer to leave to my children, instead of the gilded prospects of New York merchant princes, the more enviable title of American citizens." That said, he continued to spend prodigiously. His wine bills alone were said to exceed $20,000 in some months, an amount worth several hundred thousand dollars in twenty-first century money. He also continued to add to his fabled art collections, which were sold at auction after his death.

As Belmont aged his health began to deteriorate, and he suffered from what was then called dyspepsia, no doubt brought on by his high living. His private life had its share of tragedy. One of his daughters died young and a son committed suicide. It is ironic that his love of horses may have contributed to his own death. He caught cold, which turned into fatal pneumonia, while presiding at a New York horse show in late 1890. Upon his death, his son and namesake, August Belmont, Jr., assumed control of the banking empire and the family continued to exert a powerful presence through succeeding generations.

LEGACY

August Belmont not only accrued great wealth but also was a respected diplomat and sportsman. He was highly regarded for his relative honesty in conducting business and for his principled political views. However, his profligate ways were a subject of criticism, and he is said to have been the prototype of the somewhat shady entrepreneur Julius Beaufort in Edith Wharton's Pulitzer Prize-winning classic novel *The Age of Innocence* (1920).

Belmont's loyalties lay with the Democrats, unlike many his fabulously wealthy contemporaries who were aligned with the Republican Party. His leadership and fi-

nancial support undoubtedly strengthened the party during the long years of Republican ascendancy. Belmont did much to make horse racing a respectable activity in the United States, creating the Belmont Stakes, which is one of the most important events in the sport. His name was kept alive by the generations of distinguished August Belmonts who followed.

—Roy Liebman

FURTHER READING

Belmont, August. *Letters, Speeches, and Addresses of August Belmont: From The Hague, on the Causes and Conduct of the Civil War, on the Financial Policy of the United States, and Others*. Privately printed, 1890. Reprint. Whitefish, Mont.: Kessinger, 2007. A collection of Belmont's papers that was privately issued as a tribute following his death. His papers reflect his passionate concerns about the fate of the Union and record his received wisdom about national and international financial matters. This book expands his collection *A Few Letters and Speeches of the Late Civil War*, privately printed in 1870.

Black, David. *The King of Fifth Avenue: The Fortunes of August Belmont*. New York: Dial Press, 1981. A lengthy biography of almost nine hundred pages, concentrating on his diplomatic career and his activities during the Civil War.

Bowman, John S., ed. *Cambridge Dictionary of American Biography*. Cambridge, England: Cambridge University Press, 1995. A reference book containing an informative entry on Belmont.

Ingham, John N., ed. *Biographical Dictionary of American Business Leaders*. Westport, Conn.: Greenwood, 1983. A reference book with an entry on Belmont.

Katz, Irving. *August Belmont: A Political Biography, 1813-1890, Jewish-American Banker*. New York: Columbia University Press, 1968. A relatively brief biography that concentrates primarily on Belmont's political activities.

Stone, Richard. *Belmont Park: A Century of Champions*. Lexington, Ky.: Eclipse Press, 2005. Commemorates the hundredth anniversary of Belmont Park with portraits and essays on seventy championship thoroughbreds.

See also: Clarence Dillon; Anthony Joseph Drexel; Otto Kahn; Andrew Mellon; Richard B. Mellon; J. P. Morgan; First Baron Rothschild; Mayer Amschel Rothschild; Nathan Mayer Rothschild; James Stillman; Moses Taylor; William Collins Whitney.

JAMES GORDON BENNETT, JR.
American newspaper publisher

Bennett inherited his wealth and proprietorship of the New York Herald *from his father, James Gordon Bennett, Sr., but he became a leader in the journalism industry in his own right. His wealth benefited charity, and he also sponsored novel sporting events and world exploration.*

Born: May 10, 1841; New York, New York
Died: May 14, 1918; Beaulieu-sur-Mer, France
Sources of wealth: Inheritance; media; telegraph
Bequeathal of wealth: Relatives; charity

EARLY LIFE
James Gordon Bennett, Jr., was born in 1841 in New York City, the first of four children of James Gordon Bennett, Sr., and Henrietta Agnes Crean. Bennett spent much of his youth in France. After receiving his education from his mother and private tutors, Bennett attended École Polytechnique in Paris. He enjoyed playing polo and yachting, and in 1857 he joined the New York Yachting Club, eventually becoming its commodore. When he returned to New York on May 15, 1861, the nation was engaged in the Civil War. Bennett enlisted in the U.S. Revenue Marine, serving for a year as a third lieutenant on the *Henrietta*, a yacht donated by his father in support of the Union cause.

FIRST VENTURES
While still enjoying a lavish playboy lifestyle, Bennett interned with the *New York Herald*. He became the newspaper's managing editor in 1866, the same year he won the first transatlantic yacht race. In 1867, Bennett was made chief executive officer of the *Herald*, which had a daily circulation of ninety thousand and annual profits of $400,000. That same year, Bennett founded the New York *Evening Telegram*, a source of sensational news and a predecessor of tabloid journalism. Bennett had an aptitude for hiring exceptional writers and for making news, and he spared no expense in his quest for exclusive media coverage. He assigned reporter Henry Morton Stanley to cover several stories, including Stanley's discovery of David Livingstone, a physician and a missionary in Africa. Another of Bennett's reporters, Janurias MacGahan, covered the Franco-Prussian War, atrocities leading to the Russo-Turkish War, and attempts to find the Northwest Passage. Bennett's newspaper also provided extensive coverage of George A. Custer's massacre in 1876. In addition, Bennett helped finance expeditions to the Arctic and to the North Pole.

MATURE WEALTH
James Gordon Bennett, Sr., died in 1872, leaving proprietorship of the newspaper to his son. On January 1, 1877, Bennett committed a scandalous act that virtually barred him from high society and put him in an unfavorable limelight. He was engaged to marry Caroline May, and he urinated into the fireplace at her parent's home. The wedding was canceled, and soon thereafter, Frederick May, Caroline's brother, whipped Bennett and challenged him to a duel, in which neither man was injured. Bennett eventually moved to Paris, where he managed the *Herald* via cable.

Bennett was dissatisfied with the services provided by the existing telegraph cable monopoly, and he and businessman John William Mackay established the Commercial Cable Company. Their new firm effectively reduced the costs of sending international telegrams and ended single company domination. In 1887, Bennett launched a Paris edition of the *Herald*, which promoted good will between the United States and France but was not financially profitable. He similarly founded a London edition of the *Herald* in 1889, but it folded in 1891. By 1899, Bennett foresaw the advantages of wireless communication and paid Guglielmo Marconi $5,000 to demonstrate his radiotelegraph system's live reporting of the America's Cup Races.

Absentee management; competition from other publishers, including Joseph Pulitzer of the *New York World* and Adolph Simon Ochs of *The New York Times*; and extravagant spending weakened the *Herald* during the 1900's. However, Bennett's newspaper continued to maintain a reputation for good reporting throughout World War I. On September 10, 1914, Bennett married a widow, Baroness de Reuter, whose father, Paul Reuter, founded Reuters news agency. On May 14, 1918, Bennett suffered a brain hemorrhage and died of heart disease in Beaulieu-sur-Mer, France.

LEGACY
Covering breaking news, conducting worldwide interviews, and reporting shocking tales were Bennett's obsessions as a newspaper publisher, and he and the other publishers of his time changed the nature of American journalism. During his lifetime, he spent more than

$30 million financing research expeditions and sporting events and making charitable donations. Bennett bequeathed the majority of his estate to establish the James Gordon Bennett Memorial Home for journalists. However, there were not enough funds in his estate to fulfill all of the bequests specified in his will, and in 1918 his family sold both the *New York Herald* and the *Paris Herald*. Six years later, both newspapers were sold to the *New York Tribune*, and the two New York newspapers merged to become the *New York Herald Tribune*. The *Paris Herald* was renamed the *International Herald Tribune*, an English-language international newspaper which continues to be published in the twenty-first century under the ownership of The New York Times Company.

—*Cynthia J. W. Svoboda*

FURTHER READING

Hudson, Frederic. *Journalism in the United States, 1690 to 1872*. Reprint New York: Kessinger, 2005.

O'Connor, Richard. *The Scandalous Mr. Bennett*. Garden City, N.Y.: Doubleday, 1962.

Schroeder-Lein, Glenna R., and Richard Zuczek. *Andrew Johnson: A Biographical Companion*. Santa Barbara, Calif. ABC-CLIO, 2001.

Seitz, Don C. *The James Gordon Bennetts: Father and Son, Proprietors of the "New York Herald."* Indianapolis, Ind.: Bobbs-Merrill, 1928.

See also: Cyrus H. K. Curtis; Cyrus West Field; Jay Gould; John William Mackay; Samuel F. B. Morse; Joseph Pulitzer; Russell Sage.

SILVIO BERLUSCONI
Italian entrepreneur and politician

First elected in 1994, Berlusconi has served several terms as prime minister of Italy. He used his wealth and position as a media tycoon to propel himself into political prominence as the head of a center-right coalition. He later became one of the most powerful individuals in Italy, despite several scandals.

Born: September 29, 1936; Milan, Italy
Sources of wealth: Media; real estate
Bequeathal of wealth: Unknown

EARLY LIFE
Silvio Berlusconi (SIHL-vee-oh behr-lew-SKOH-nee) grew up in Milan, Italy, in a middle-class family, the oldest of three children of Luigi Berlusconi, a banker, and Rosa Bossi. Berlusconi helped to put himself through college as a bass player in a band and a nightclub singer on Mediterranean cruise ships. He graduated in 1961 with a law degree from the University of Milan. In 1965, he married Carla Elvira Dall'Oglio, his first wife. The couple had two children.

FIRST VENTURES
Berlusconi initially made his fortune in real estate in the 1960's. He lacked experience in construction, but he always possessed a remarkable talent for sales. By the 1970's, Berlusconi moved into television. Italian television in this era generally featured cultural and public service programming. Berlusconi added American shows, such as *Dynasty* and *Wheel of Fortune*, while developing such uniquely Italian programs as the world's first nude game show.

By the 1990's, Berlusconi's Fininvest holdings company included the three Italian national television networks; Montadori, Italy's largest book and magazine publisher; the nation's largest film production company; the country's largest department store chain; the most successful soccer team, Milan AC; the Cinema 5 chain of theaters; a major insurance and mutual fund company; and a daily newspaper, *Il Giornale*. His television networks commanded about 45 percent of Italy's viewing audience and about 60 percent of television advertising revenue. The Italian left, concerned about Berlusconi's power, spoke of passing antitrust legislation to break up his empire. In defense, Berlusconi moved into politics.

MATURE WEALTH
On January 26, 1994, Berlusconi embarked on his political career by addressing the Italian people on all three of his national television networks. Shown in the study of his eighteenth century villa behind a commanding desk, Berlusconi gave the impression of already being head of Italy. Within two months, he had created a new political party, Forza Italia (Forward Italy). In May, 1994, Berlusconi took office as prime minister. At the end of 1994, however, Berlusconi stepped down when some members of his center-right coalition left the government amid allegations that he had authorized the payment of bribes while still a private citizen in order to advance his

Silvio Berlusconi. (Bongarts/Getty Images)

business interests. He remained a major political figure and returned to the prime minister's office in 2001; he assumed his third term in office on May 8, 2008.

Forbes magazine named Berlusconi one of the world's richest people in 2005. It is an accolade that he continued to hold in 2010, despite some personal difficulties. Berlusconi had three children with second wife Veronica Lario, whom he married in 1990 after divorcing Dall'Oglio in 1985. Lario filed for divorce in 2009 after charging Berlusconi with romancing eighteen-year-old

Noemi Letizia. The episode became a major scandal in Italy, with Berlusconi claiming that his relationship with Letizia was merely paternal, though it did little to dent his enormous popularity among the Italians.

Legacy

Berlusconi has used his charisma and communications skills to create a culture built around the ideas of success, personal wealth, and material well-being. He is representative of changes in both Italy's economy and its culture. As Italy moved away from an industrial economy and began to enjoy a period of extraordinary prosperity, Berlusconi developed his fortune in television by emphasizing the values of affluence and materialism.

While Berlusconi remains alive, it is difficult to predict his legacy, but it is likely that he will be remembered for his optimism and sales ability. He is the most prominent Italian business leader of his generation. As a politician, he united Italy's conservative parties and formed an alliance with the center to push the left wing out of power. He dominated Italian politics at the end of the twentieth and the start of the twenty-first centuries.

—*Caryn E. Neumann*

Further Reading

Ginsborg, Paul. *Silvio Berlusconi: Television, Power, and Patrimony.* New York: Verso, 2004.

Shin, Michael E., and John A. Agnew. *Berlusconi's Italy: Mapping Contemporary Italian Politics.* Philadelphia: Temple University Press, 2008.

Stille, Alexander. *The Sack of Rome: How a Beautiful European Country with a Fabled History and a Storied Culture Was Taken over by a Man Named Silvio Berlusconi.* New York: Penguin Press, 2006.

See also: Walter Annenberg; Barbara Cox Anthony; Michael Bloomberg; Anne Cox Chambers; Katharine Graham; John H. Johnson; Robert L. Johnson; John Kluge; Rupert Murdoch; Samuel I. Newhouse; Kerry Packer; Ted Turner.

SAMUEL BERNARD
French banker and trader

Bernard's wealth enabled France to remain a strong military power and had a significant influence on the politics of Europe, as it financed Louis XIV's major wars. Bernard's life demonstrates how the bourgeoisie began its rise to political and economic power in France.

Born: October 29, 1651; Sancerre, France
Died: January 18, 1739; Paris, France
Also known as: Comte de Coubert
Sources of wealth: Banking; trade
Bequeathal of wealth: Children

EARLY LIFE

Samuel Bernard, comte de Coubert, was born in Sancerre, France, on October 29, 1651. He was the son of Jacques-Samuel Bernard, a successful painter. Although Bernard and his father were born in France, the Bernard family was of Dutch origin. The family professed the Protestant faith and was of the bourgeois class. The family initially lived in Sancerre, a Protestant stronghold, and then in Paris. Bernard would have received a standard bourgeois education enabling him to acquire a profession in business or trade.

FIRST VENTURES

Bernard began his professional career as a merchant of gold brocade and jewelry. However, he soon became involved in banking. At the time, many Protestants had fled predominantly Catholic France. Bernard received considerable assistance in starting his banking ventures from the Protestant refugees living abroad. In 1676, Bernard publicly renounced his Protestant faith in order to advance his career as a banker. However, it was always known that he maintained his Protestant beliefs, and he became known as the most successful of the Protestant bankers.

In 1685, King Louis XIV created the Compagnie de Guinée, a trading company engaged in the slave trade. Bernard was among the founding members chosen by Louis XIV. The company traded in gold and other merchandise, as well as slaves, and its business made a significant contribution to Bernard's wealth. From 1690 to 1691, his wealth was further increased by a policy of comte de Pontchatrain, France's minister of the marine, which permitted the sale of goods acquired through piracy.

MATURE WEALTH

By 1695, Bernard had gained a reputation as the wealthiest banker in Europe. While his wealth had continuously increased, the royal treasury of France had fallen into serious debt. Louis XIV needed funds to finance his military campaigns. Consequently, in 1697, Louis XIV, although not happy to turn to a Protestant banker, had his ministers obtain a loan of 11 million francs from Bernard to the royal treasury. In exchange, Bernard received a title of nobility. This ennoblement was granted on the condition that Bernard would not abandon his banking and commercial ventures so his money would always be available to the Crown.

In 1708, Louis XIV again found himself in need of money to finance his wars and turned again to the Protestant banker. This time, Louis's financial controller, Nicolas Desmarets, arranged a meeting of the king with Bernard at the gardens of Marly. Although Bernard was extremely wealthy and had been ennobled, the king felt it beneath his dignity to receive the banker in his palace. Bernard provided a loan of 19 million francs to fund the War of the Spanish Succession. When Louis XV succeeded his grandfather as king, Bernard continued to enjoy his favored position as royal financier. In 1719, Bernard purchased a château and lands in Seine-et-Marne, France. He rebuilt the château from 1724 to 1727 and built another mansion in Paris. Louis XV made Bernard the comte de Courbet in 1725 and five years later appointed him the counselor of state. In 1731, Bernard purchased additional land in Normandy.

At the time of his death on January 18, 1739, Bernard left an estate valued at 33 million francs. The title comte de Courbet was passed to his eldest son, Samuel-Jacques Bernard.

LEGACY

As a banker and trader, Samuel Bernard played a significant role in creating the institution of banking. He made important contributions to the French economy by financing both business ventures and government policies, and he influenced the operations of the trading companies. Although born neither a noble nor a Catholic, two attributes of the ruling class in seventeenth and eighteenth century France, Bernard was a powerful figure in the political and economic life of France and its court. His financial success helped change the strict class structure of Old Regime France and laid part of the groundwork for a social system in which success in business and wealth would become equivalent to inherited nobility.

—*Shawncey Webb*

FURTHER READING

Beik, William. *Louis XIV and Absolutism: A Brief Study with Documents*. Boston: Bedford/St. Martin's, 2000.

Jones, Colin. *The Great Nation: France from Louis XV to Napoleon*. London: Penguin, 2002.

Lewis, W. H. *The Splendid Century: Life in the France of Louis XIV*. Reprint. Prospect Heights, Ill.: Waveland Press, 1997.

See also: Nicolas Fouquet; John Law; Louis XIV.

BESS OF HARDWICK
English aristocrat and landowner

The daughter of a gentleman farmer, Bess of Hardwick rose to become the second-wealthiest woman in England. She built two of the greatest houses in the country and became the forebear of several aristocratic families.

Born: c. 1527; Derbyshire, England

Died: February 13, 1608; Hardwick Hall, Derbyshire, England

Also known as: Elizabeth Hardwick (birth name); Elizabeth Cavendish; Elizabeth St. Loe; Elizabeth Barlow; Elizabeth Talbot; Elizabeth Shrewsbury

Sources of wealth: Marriage; real estate

Bequeathal of wealth: Children; relatives

EARLY LIFE

Elizabeth Talbot, Countess of Shewsbury, better known as Bess of Hardwick, was born Elizabeth Hardwick around 1527. The Hardwicks were gentlemen farmers, who at the time of Bess's birth farmed 450 acres in Derbyshire, rented another one hundred acres in Lincolnshire, and leased Hardwick Hall, a country house. Bess's father, John Hardwick, died while she was still a baby. When Bess was two, her mother married Ralph Leche, which made the family's financial situation more secure, although they were not wealthy. Bess received the typical home education of a sixteenth century girl, learning to read and write, figure, and run a household.

At about age twelve, Bess was sent to the Zouche family at Codnor Castle in Derbyshire in order to finish her education. In 1543, she married Robert Barlow (or Barley), a boy two years younger than she, who died shortly after, leaving Bess with only a widow's share of one-third of the Barlow estates, a relatively small amount that was tied up in litigation for several years.

FIRST VENTURES

After the death of Barlow, Bess entered the service of Lady Frances Grey, a distant relative and niece to King

Henry VIII by his sister Princess Mary and Charles Brandon, duke of Suffolk. Here Bess began to move in the top tier of Tudor society, and it was probably at Grey's Bradgate estate that she developed the interest in decor and furnishings that later led her to build and decorate some of the greatest houses in England. During this time, Bess met Sir William Cavendish, treasurer of the king's chamber for King Edward VI, who was more than twice Bess's age when she married him on August 20, 1547.

Bess likely did not envision founding a dynasty when she married Cavendish, but he certainly represented financial security and social advancement, and their marriage seemed to be a happy one. Bess gained a title and was presented at court; she also learned to manage Cavendish's two houses and became stepmother to his three children. Bess quickly learned to supervise the household accounts, and Cavendish was probably responsible for teaching her the business sense that served her well throughout her life. The Cavendishes lived generously, gambling and entertaining as expected at court, but within their means, a prudent practice Bess continued throughout her life.

MATURE WEALTH

In December, 1550, the Cavendishes purchased Chatsworth, a fine estate with two manors and a number of houses and land in various towns, for the bargain price of £600, the first of many careful purchases of land in which Bess participated. Chatsworth became Bess's personal rebuilding and decorating project for the next decade.

Sir William Cavendish died on October 25, 1557, leaving Bess a widow for the second time. Bess had six children of her own by this time, and she was still responsible for Cavendish's two daughters. In 1559, Bess married again. Her third husband, Sir William St. Loe (variously spelled St. Lowe, Saintlowe, and Sentloe), was the captain of the guard and chief butler of England, serv-

HARDWICK HALL

Hardwick Hall, located on a hill between Chesterfield and Mansfield in the Derbyshire countryside of England, was the birthplace of Elizabeth Talbot, Countess of Shrewsbury, more commonly known as Bess of Hardwick. Bess bought the house in 1583 after it had been held in chancery under the jurisdiction of the High Court of Justice since the death of her brother James Hardwick in 1581. She purchased not only the house but also its lands for £9,500, a significant sum at this time.

Beginning in 1588, Bess had the Old Hall renovated, raising the building to four stories and more than doubling its size. In 1590, Bess ordered foundations dug for a new house at Hardwick designed by Robert Smythson, an architect who also designed Wollaton Hall, Burghley House, and Burton Agnes Hall. Smythson's style was a distinctly English interpretation of Renaissance architecture, and he made extensive use of glass, particularly at Hardwick.

Bess was able to move into the Old Hall in 1592, from which she could see the new house being built with local timber, sandstone, and limestone. Other materials came from Bess's lands, with the lead for the roof and the plumbing coming from mines at Barlow, the iron from Wingfield, alabaster from Tutbury, and black marble from Ashford in the Water. When Bess's stepson Gilbert Talbot, with whom she was on poor terms, proved to be the primary local supplier of glass, she brought in other glaziers to make her own glass.

The new Hardwick Hall was completed in 1599, although Bess moved in on October 4, 1597. Although it was smaller than the Old Hall, with only forty-six rooms compared to the Old Hall's fifty-five, and was not as finely plastered and decorated inside, Hardwick Hall was state-of-the-art architecture for its time. Large windows enhanced the delicate, symmetrical design, giving rise to the old rhyme "Hardwick Hall,/ More glass than wall."

Bess decorated Hardwick Hall luxuriously, with an extensive collection of fine furnishings and embroideries, many of the latter made by her own hand. Hardwick Hall served as the secondary residence to the dukes of Devonshire, Bess's descendants, until 1956, when the structure was donated to Her Majesty's Treasury. In the twenty-first century, Hardwick Hall is a National Trust site administered by English Heritage. It is open to the public and displays many of the original furnishings, a spectacular and historically valuable collection of late sixteenth and early seventeenth century embroideries, tapestries, and furniture.

the queen and a large annual income, Bess was an extremely eligible widow.

Her 1568 marriage to George Talbot, sixth earl of Shrewsbury, was preceded by a double marriage of four of their children: Mary Cavendish married Shrewsbury's eldest son, Gilbert, and Bess's heir Henry Cavendish married Lady Grace Talbot. The latter marriage would transfer ownership of Cavendish lands to the Shrewsbury family, and Shrewsbury's own marriage to Bess would give him control of both Cavendish and St. Loe lands during Bess's lifetime.

After three marriages, Bess was a careful woman. Before marrying Shrewsbury, she required a marriage jointure which stipulated that she would keep Chatsworth and some other properties during her lifetime and that the rents for the Shrewsbury manors of Handsworth, Bolsterstone, and Over Ewedon would be provided to her for life. As a result of her fourth marriage, Bess became one of the highest-ranking women at court in her position as the countess of Shrewsbury.

When Shrewsbury became the jailer of Mary, Queen of Scots, at the command of Queen Elizabeth I, he and Bess expected this to be a temporary duty that would gain them the favor of the queen. Instead, Mary's imprisonment was a fifteen-year burden on Shrewsbury that drained his coffers and strained his marriage with Bess. Bess preferred to spend time with her children and grandchildren rather than live in the uncomfortable conditions at Tutbury, where Mary was held prisoner. Bess also pursued her own financial ventures, in addition to encouraging Shrewsbury to purchase land and arranging advantageous marriages for their children.

Shortly after the birth of her first grandchild in 1571, Bess loaned her brother James Hardwick money to secure Hardwick Hall by obtaining a mortgage on the building. She leased James's coal and ore mines, from which she intended to profit after Shrewsbury's example, but it is unclear what she intended to do with Hardwick Hall. She was able to purchase the hall in 1583 after her brother's death two years earlier.

ing Queen Elizabeth I. St. Loe owned large estates in Gloucestershire and Somerset. Bess and St. Loe seem to have been in love, but St. Loe was also a practical choice for a woman seeking to secure a fortune for her descendants.

Bess's third marriage made her a wealthy woman. St. Loe died without a male heir in either 1564 or 1565, probably poisoned by his brother. He left his entire estate to Bess, to the displeasure of his brother and two adult daughters. As a lady of the bedchamber with the favor of

The Shrewsburys' marriage collapsed gradually but bitterly. It is possible that Shrewsbury suffered from dementia, but he may have become bitter and paranoid because of ill health and the trials of caring for Mary, Queen of Scots, for fifteen years. The separation of Shrewsbury and Bess was marked by constant legal wrangling and petitions to Queen Elizabeth I and her advisers. Bess was not allowed to live at Chatsworth, the home she had spent ten years rebuilding. However, the queen resolved a dispute about the money that Shrewsbury owed Bess by ruling in Bess's favor.

Shrewsbury died on November 18, 1590, and while his mistress stole many items of furnishing, plate, and other portable goods, Bess regained ownership of her lands. She still retained incomes from the Barlow, Cavendish, and St. Loe estates, as well as one-third of the income of the Shrewsbury estates, said to be £3,000 per year, a very large sum at this time. Among the properties she controlled were Bolsover Castle and its coal mines, as well as the lead mines, glassworks, and forge of Wingfield Manor. The Shrewsbury estate itself was drained of cash by Mary, Queen of Scots, and by the annual payments to Bess and Shrewsbury's children, so Bess was in a more stable financial situation than Shrewsbury's own heir, Gilbert Talbot.

As Chatsworth was owned by her eldest son, Henry Cavendish, who disappointed her, and Wingfield did not belong to her outright, Bess turned her attentions to Hardwick Hall, renovating the old building and commissioning a new hall. When Bess died on February 13, 1608, she had amassed a fortune worth thousands of pounds to bequeath to her children, a long way from the 40 marks of her original dowry.

LEGACY

In life, Bess of Hardwick was the second-wealthiest and most powerful woman in England, after Queen Elizabeth I. In death, she founded an aristocratic dynasty. Of the six children Bess had with Sir William Cavendish who survived to adulthood, their second son, William, was the forebear of the dukes of Devonshire, and their third son, Charles, was the forefather of the dukes of Newcastle and of Portland. Through her daughter Frances, Bess was the forebear of the earls of Manvers and the dukes of Kingston and of Rutland; through her daughter Mary, Bess was the ancestor of the earls of Pembroke and of Kent and the dukes of Norfolk. Bess's Chatsworth

manor became the seat of the dukes of Devonshire. In the twenty-first century, Hardwick Hall was considered to be one of the most important English country houses, an early example of the English interpretation of Renaissance architecture. A National Trust site, Hardwick Hall contains one of the largest collections of sixteenth and seventeenth century English embroideries and textiles, preserved for posterity by Bess's descendants.

—*Melissa A. Barton*

FURTHER READING

Devonshire, Deborah, and Simon Upton. *Chatsworth: The House*. London: Frances Lincoln, 2002. Cowritten by the duchess of Devonshire and illustrated with excellent photographs, this book covers the history, architecture, furnishings, and grounds of the first house Bess expanded and furnished, which later became the seat of the dukes of Devonshire.

Durant, David N. *Bess of Hardwick: Portrait of an Elizabethan Dynast*. London: Peter Owen, 1999. A classic biography of Bess. Durant's focus is largely on the building of Hardwick Hall, Bess's lasting material legacy. Includes black-and-white illustrations.

Durant, David N., and Philip Riden. *The Building of Hardwick Hall*. 2 vols. Chesterfield, England: Derbyshire Record Society, 1980-1984. Although the first volume is out of print and somewhat difficult to find, this is the definitive account of the building of Hardwick Hall, meticulously researched from numerous primary sources, many of which are reproduced in the books.

Levey, Santina M. *The Embroideries at Hardwick Hall: A Catalogue*. London: National Trust, 2007. A comprehensive, illustrated catalog of the sixteenth and early seventeenth century embroideries at Hardwick Hall, which offers a glimpse into wealthy Elizabethan life and tastes. Includes color photographs.

Lovell, Mary S. *Bess of Hardwick: Empire Builder*. New York: W. W. Norton, 2006. Lovell uses sixteenth century letters and account books to uncover details of Bess's life, making the case for Bess as a shrewd and remarkable but caring woman committed to providing for her descendants. Includes color plates.

See also: Deborah Cavendish; Georgiana Cavendish; Henry Cavendish; Francis Drake; Sir Thomas Gresham; Sir Horatio Palavicino; Sir John Spencer.

JEFF BEZOS
American entrepreneur, merchant, and computer scientist

After a brief but successful Wall Street career, Bezos followed his dream and founded Amazon.com. Guided by his vision and his commitment to customer service, Amazon became one of the most successful Internet retailers and made Bezos a billionaire before he was forty. He uses his wealth to promote learning by awarding scholarships via the Bezos Family Foundation.

Born: January 12, 1964; Albuquerque, New Mexico
Also known as: Jeffrey Preston Bezos
Sources of wealth: Computer industry; sale of products
Bequeathal of wealth: Spouse; children; scholarship

EARLY LIFE
Jeffrey Preston Bezos (JEHF-ree PRES-ton BAY-zohs) was born in Albuquerque, New Mexico. He was a gifted child and spent summers at his grandfather's ranch, where he herded cattle and repaired windmills. He tinkered with electronics and made a few small inventions when he was young. His father, Miguel, was an executive of the Exxon oil company, and Bezos had a privileged upbringing. He was an excellent student in high school and graduated as class valedictorian. He graduated summa cum laude from Princeton University, earning degrees in electrical engineering and computer science, and was a member of Phi Beta Kappa.

FIRST VENTURES
Bezos's first position out of college in 1986 was with a start-up company, Fitel. He left the company in 1988 to work at Bankers Trust, where he developed software for fund management. He honed his skills well enough that he became vice president before leaving in 1990 for D. E. Shaw & Company, a global investment and technology development firm. At Shaw, Bezos helped create a successful high-technology system for managing hedge funds. He eventually became the company's youngest senior vice president at the age of thirty. Bezos credits David Shaw, the company's founder, as an inspiration to him and acknowledges Shaw's influence in helping him become a good manager. Bezos left the company in 1994 to start his own business.

Bezos had been researching the burgeoning Internet and was amazed to discover that it was growing at a rate of more than 2,000 percent per year. He did his research and decided that the market for books would be one of the easiest to enter and would benefit the most from the technology of the Internet; the massive number of titles available could not be contained in a traditional brick-and-mortar bookstore. He also discovered that even the largest bookstore controlled only 12 percent of the market, so there seemed to be enough room for another big company, which is what he was planning on starting. He chose his location in Seattle, Washington, since it had a wealth of technically skilled people and was also located near a major book warehouse. He decided on the name Amazon for his company; the world's longest river by volume reflected the concept behind his business.

Jeff Bezos unveils Amazon.com's Kindle electronic book reader. (AFP/Getty Images)

MATURE WEALTH

Bezos hired four employees and opened his business in the garage of his house. His employees wrote the software for the company and Amazon.com sold its first book in July, 1995. He wanted to create a company that people thought of first when they needed to make a purchase. Although Bezos initially started with books, he wanted Amazon to become a retailer that could provide almost anything. Bezos built his company around two main principles: get big fast and end-to-end customer service. He initially sought to cater to customers by providing access to more titles than any other bookseller. When Amazon launched, its initial offering was more than 1 million titles; even the largest competitor could provide only 300,000 titles because of warehousing constraints. Bezos expanded the company's merchandise to more than three million titles by 1998. He also provided features on the Amazon.com Web site and services, such

as e-mails when a customer's favorite author released a new book and online book reviews. He discounted books by 10 to 30 percent off their normal purchase price. Amazon.com soon began to sell music compact discs and films in order to better serve its customers. Bezos even had a corporate policy enabling employees to implement features that would benefit the company without having to consult their bosses, known as the "Just Do It" program.

Bezos's eye toward customer service paid off and Amazon.com flourished. Within six weeks of the sale of its first book, Bezos moved himself and his employees into a two-thousand-square-foot space. Within six months, he had to move to a seventeen-thousand-square-foot building. In 1997, there were 614 people on Amazon's payroll, and Amazon.com was receiving 50,000 hits per day. Sales were a big part of what drove the growth. In 1995, annual sales were a little more than $500,000; 1996 sales figures hit nearly $16 million; and sales figures for 1997 climbed to $147 million. Bezos stuck to his "get big fast" philosophy, fueling Amazon's growth by reinvesting much of the money earned back into the company. At one point, Amazon's growth was 3,000 percent per year.

Amazon went public in 1997, with each share initially priced at $18. This price jumped to nearly $100 per share by the end of the following year. All seemed to be going well, but there were some trials that Amazon had to pass. The debt that Amazon had incurred was costing the company $125 million in interest each year. Even though the company had holdings estimated at around $8 billion by the end of 1999, Amazon had yet to turn a profit. The burst of the dot-com bubble saw Amazon's stock drop from its high of $92 per share to less than $15 per share in 2001. Wall Street did not have confidence in either the company or Bezos's business plan, which did not explain how Amazon was going to make a profit from marginal sales transactions. The company had also lost $90 million on roughly $1 billion in sales that year.

Another major bookseller, Barnes & Noble, had entered the online sales arena, and it was forecasted that Amazon would be unable to compete. Bezos stuck to his plan, however, claiming that Barnes & Noble would

THE BEZOS FAMILY FOUNDATION

Miguel and Jacklyn Bezos originally invested $300,000 in order to help their son, Jeff Bezos, start Amazon.com, and as a result they became wealthy. They had always seen the value of a good education. Jeff Bezos himself was an excellent student and was featured in the 1977 book *Turning on Bright Minds: A Parent Looks at Gifted Education.* Jeff continued to perform well in college, graduating with honors from Princeton University.

Bezos's parents established the Bezos Family Foundation to further the cause of education. The foundation is private and independent. Miguel and Jacklyn Bezos, along with their children and the children's spouses, serve as directors. According to its mission statement, the foundation strives to strengthen educational opportunities for everyone, regardless of economic circumstances, and to cultivate learning as a lifelong process that begins in early childhood.

The foundation created the prestigious Bezos Scholars Program in 2005. The program is hosted at the Aspen Institute and brings together twelve of the country's top public high school juniors at the Aspen Ideas Festival. Twelve educators are also invited to the program. All expenses are paid through a scholarship. The students meet world leaders, thinkers, and artists; past speakers have included President Bill Clinton, Senator Arlen Specter, and Secretary of State Colin Powell. The program is designed to foster leadership skills and to teach those who attend to pass along what they have learned.

In 2008, the Bezos Family Foundation Endowed Chair for Early Childhood Learning was established in order to support research and teaching in the critical area of early childhood education. The organization also aims to disseminate its research to a broad audience of educators, parents, caregivers, and the community at large so that the findings can be used to promote excellence in education.

not focus on logistics and customer service as his company did. Most of Amazon's customers stayed true to the company, with an estimated 70 percent of the firm's revenues being generated from return business.

Amazon implemented free shipping on orders of more than $25 as another customer service measure, and in 2003 the company saw its first profitable year. Bezos partly attributes this profit to the decision to implement free shipping. Amazon.com had forty-three million customers by the end of 2004. That year, a market researcher conducted a survey on customer satisfaction at the top twenty e-commerce sites and Amazon placed first. Amazon grew by acquiring other companies, such as the Internet Movie Database and Back to Basics, a toy retailer. It also forged relationships with other companies in order to expand its merchandise. For example, the company created relationships with retailers Toys R' Us and Circuit City in order to provide a wider selection of toys and electronics.

Through all of this, Bezos has profited well. His net worth was estimated at $12.3 billion in 2010 by *Forbes* magazine, placing him at twenty-eighth on the magazine's list of the United States' four hundred wealthiest citizens.

LEGACY
Bezos has blazed a trail for online businesses and proved that an e-commerce company can be both profitable and sustainable. Amazon.com. remains one of the largest-volume e-commerce sites. Bezos identifies customer satisfaction as one of the most important features of his company, and Amazon has grown because of his philosophy. Traditional bookstores have had to adapt and learn from Bezos's strategies in order to compete against the business that he originally launched out of his garage. Amazon's sales continue to grow, while his rivals struggle to compete.

In 2000, Bezos started another company called Blue Origin, hinting that it was developing technologies that could be used in space. Recognizing the importance of education, he also established the Bezos Family Foundation, which sponsors a scholars program for high school students.

—*James J. Heiney*

FURTHER READING
Leibovich, Mark. *The New Imperialists*. Upper Saddle River, N.J.: Prentice Hall, 2002. Stories about five modern entrepreneurs, including Bezos, and insights into their lives. The book also describes how they pushed their companies into positions of market dominance.

Marcus, James. *Amazonia*. New York: New Press, 2005. A view of the rise, plummet, and rise again of Amazon.com as seen through the eyes of an employee. Describes the thrill of making history and the devotion of Amazon's employees.

Ryan, Bernard. *Jeff Bezos: Business Executive and Founder of Amazon.com*. New York: Ferguson, 2005. A biography about Bezos that covers the period from his childhood to his Amazon.com days. Shows his take on how to become an Internet entrepreneur.

Spector, Robert. *Amazon.com: Get Big Fast*. New York: HarperBusiness, 2000. Tries to fill in the gaps that are commonly left in reports of Amazon's company history. Follows Bezos's career from his days on Wall Street through Amazon's rise.

Stone, Florence. *Business the Amazon.com Way: One Hundred Secrets of the World's Most Astonishing Web Business*. Oxford, England: Capstone, 1999. Covers Amazon.com's foray into the new territory of selling items beyond books, compact discs, and films. Provides insights into how Bezos created the successful company and his designs on the future.

See also: Paul Allen; Steven Ballmer; Sergey Brin; Mark Cuban; Michael Dell; Larry Ellison; Bill Gates; Steve Jobs; Gordon E. Moore; David Packard; H. Ross Perot.

ANDRIES BICKER
Dutch banker, merchant, and politician/statesman

Bicker was a member of a prominent family in Amsterdam, rising quickly through the city's political ranks and serving a number of terms as its mayor. Besides wielding political power, he added to his family's considerable wealth as a banker, landowner, merchant, and administrator of the Dutch East India Company.

Born: 1586; Amsterdam, Dutch Republic (now in the Netherlands)
Died: June 24, 1652; Amsterdam, Dutch Republic
Sources of wealth: Inheritance; trade; banking; real estate
Bequeathal of wealth: Unknown

EARLY LIFE

Andries Bicker (AHN-drees BIH-ker) was the son of Gerrit Bicker and Alyd Boelens. Christened on September 14, 1586, he grew up in one of the most powerful and distinguished families of Amsterdam. His grandfather Peter was a prominent grain merchant and brewer, and his father, besides carrying on these trades, held the position of town councillor and became a founding director of the Dutch East India Company (Vereenigde Oost-Indische Compagnie, or VOC). Andries's uncle Laurens Bicker was one of the first Dutch traders in West Africa, while his brothers Cornelis, Jacob, and Jan also became active traders in various parts of the world. He married Catharina Gansneb von Tengnagel, the daughter of another influential family, on February 22, 1615.

FIRST VENTURES

Bicker's adult years were characterized by steadily growing power and influence in a number of spheres of Amsterdam life. By 1614, he had become a city commissioner, dealing with such matters as small business and marriage contracts. In 1616, he entered the *vroedschap* (city council) of Amsterdam, and in 1622 he was chosen for the higher position of *schepen* (alderman) in the council, a position to which he was returned in 1623 and 1625. In 1624, Bicker served as a commissioner of the Amsterdamsche Wisselbank (Exchange Bank or Bank of Amsterdam), and he held a similar position with the Banken van Leening (Banks of Loans), the first of which had been established in Amsterdam in 1614.

MATURE WEALTH

It is virtually impossible to separate the story of Bicker's life from that of the Bicker family or from the tumultuous history of the city of Amsterdam and the country of which it was the most important component. Five years before Bicker's birth, the northern provinces of what had been known as the Low Countries had declared their independence from Spain as the Republic of the Seven United Netherlands, or Dutch Republic. The ensuing conflict, which pitted the Protestant Dutch against Catholic Spain, continued intermittently until 1648, when Spain recognized the republic's independence in the Peace of Munster. During the same period, the new country built a large merchant fleet and acquired a vast colonial empire, creating a golden age of prosperity and culture. It was against this backdrop that Bicker accumulated wealth, power, and prestige.

In 1627, after rising through the governing ranks of Amsterdam, Bicker began serving the first of what would eventually be nine terms as *burgomaster* (mayor) of Amsterdam. He was then only forty. He also served on the Board of Admiralty of Amsterdam from 1637 to 1639, and again from 1650 to 1652. He was a member of the Estates of Holland (the *staten*, or parliament of the province in which Amsterdam is located) from 1643 through 1645, and of the Estates-General (Staten-Generaal) of the Netherlands from 1646 through 1648. Besides these governmental positions, Bicker was a colonel in Amsterdam's *schutterij* (town guard) and a leader of the Arminians, or Remonstrants, a religious group criticized by other Protestant denominations as being too closely aligned with the state.

The four Bicker brothers so dominated the international trade of their day that they were commonly said to have divided the world among them. Andries Bicker himself dealt in the fur trade with the Grand Duchy of Moscow and in the spice trade with southern Asia. His father had been one of the VOC's founders in 1602, and his younger brother Jacob had become a director in 1610. Thanks to the manner in which representation on the governing board was allotted, Amsterdam was virtually guaranteed control of the large trading company, and when Jacob withdrew from its administration in 1641, it was only natural that Bicker himself become a director. It was a position he held until his death.

In 1646, Bicker and six other members of the extended Bicker family held positions in the government of Amsterdam, leading to the recognition of a seemingly all-powerful "Bicker League" that ran the city's affairs and determined its direction. The most famous Dutch

THE DUTCH EAST INDIA COMPANY

The Dutch East India Company (Vereenigde Oost-Indische Compagnie, or VOC) was established in 1602 by a number of Dutch traders, including Andries Bicker's father, Gerrit Bicker, as a joint-stock company holding a monopoly over Dutch trade with Asia. In addition, it undertook military operations to oust other European merchants and to dominate intraregional trade. Empowered to act as the legal representative of the Dutch Republic, it also came to exercise a significant degree of overall political control over most of the East Indies (Indonesian Archipelago) on behalf of the republic, and even minted its own coinage.

The Portuguese had been the first Europeans to reach India and the East Indies by sea, and they dominated the enormously profitable spice trade during the sixteenth century. However, they proved unequal to the naval might and commercial vitality of the Dutch. The VOC established its first trading post in the region at Banten on the island of Java in 1603. A fort and settlement at Batavia (now Jakarta, Indonesia) on the same island subsequently became the headquarters of the company's regional operations. In 1641, the year in which Andries Bicker became a director, the VOC drove the Portuguese from Malacca on the Malay Peninsula, and during the remainder of the century the Portuguese were almost entirely ousted from the region. The VOC set up other trading posts in Persia, India, Ceylon, China, and Japan, although it eventually abandoned these posts, along with those in Malaya.

The VOC was administered from the Dutch Republic by a board of delegates known as the Heeren XVII, or Seventeen Gentlemen. Eight of these delegates—a near majority—represented Amsterdam, while the remaining nine were drawn from five other Dutch ports. Potential shareholders could buy stock in the company, and, should they wish, sell the stock on the Amsterdam Stock Exchange, which had been established for that express purpose. Economic historians date the creation of the modern stock exchange, in which participants share profits and losses, to this arrangement, and many have viewed the VOC as the first modern corporation.

The VOC was the largest trading company in the world for the first century of its existence and returned large profits to its shareholders. However, in the early eighteenth century it went into a slow but eventually fatal decline—a condition due in large part to its failure to develop new crops and its increasingly corrupt and inefficient administration. The kingdom of the Netherlands took over its responsibilities in 1796, administering its remaining territories as the colony of the Dutch East Indies.

peace between Sweden and the Polish-Lithuanian Commonwealth. He also worked to establish a new series of trade agreements among the Baltic nations, and in 1643 he helped broker peace between Sweden and Denmark-Norway with the Second Treaty of Brömsebro.

Along with the other members of his family, Bicker was anxious to bring the Dutch conflict with Spain to a conclusion, and at one point he went so far as to finance, have built, and even pay for provisioning a naval fleet for Spain. When criticized for his seemingly unpatriotic actions, Bicker pointed out that if he had not done so, someone else would have provided the money and he would have lost the profit.

Bicker's overriding loyalty to his family and his city eventually brought him into open conflict with William II, prince of Orange, the *stadtholder* (governor) of several of the Dutch provinces, who hoped to strengthen the central government and his own position in wider European affairs at the expense of the provinces. Although the *schutterij* prevented William's troops from entering Amsterdam, fear of loss of trade led the city to sue for peace. Under the terms of the resulting treaty, Bicker and his brother Cornelis were removed from the *vroedschap*, and although they resumed some positions with the death of William in November, 1650, Bicker himself was by that time in failing health. He died on June 24, 1652.

LEGACY

During his life Bicker undertook a number of roles—political, commercial, social, military, and religious—likely to contribute to the survival and growth of his family's fortune. Thus during the 1640's, when the "Bicker League" was at its most influential and the VOC was expanding the vast territory in which it operated, he was arguably one of the wealthiest and most powerful men in the world.

Bicker and his wife had a number of children, and, as

poet of the time, Joost van den Vondel, celebrated the family and its patriarch by writing:

As far and wide as Bicker's flag o'ershadowed the vast ocean
And plied those waters with his mighty vessels richly laden
To tow the golden harvest of the world to Holland's
   bosom . . .

Bicker's prominence, his reputation for moderation, and his interest in ending conflicts that hindered trade led to several diplomatic ventures. He was involved in negotiating the 1635 Treaty of Stuhmsdorf, which established was customary at the time, Bicker strove to ensure that his offspring contracted strategic alliances of marriage, either with other branches of the Bicker family or with other, equally wealthy families. In one case he actually exercised his lawful power by refusing to allow his son Gerard to marry Alida Koninks because of her inferior fortune and status; the couple did not marry until several years after the patriarch's death.

—Grove Koger

FURTHER READING

Adams, Julia. *The Familial State: Ruling Families and Merchant Capitalism in Early Modern Europe.* Ithaca, N.Y.: Cornell University Press, 2005. Analysis of the role of the family in England, France, and the Dutch Republic during the seventeenth century, arguing that the "familial state" was the typical power structure throughout Europe at the time. Bibliography.

Israel, Jonathan I. *The Dutch Republic, Its Rise, Greatness, and Fall, 1477-1806.* Oxford, England: Clarendon Press, 1995. Comprehensive historical study of the republic during the period of its greatest importance. Includes references to the Bickers and the VOC. Illustrations, maps, and extensive bibliography.

Masselman, George. *The Cradle of Colonialism.* New Haven, Conn.: Yale University Press, 1963. History of the VOC in the context of the development of the Dutch Republic and the rivalry between the Dutch and other European powers in Southeast Asia. Illustrations, maps, and extensive bibliography.

Neal, Larry. "Venture Shares of the Dutch East India Company." In *The Origins of Value: The Financial Innovations That Created Modern Capital Markets,* edited by William N. Goetzmann and K. Geert Rouwenhorst. New York: Oxford University Press, 2005. Description of the financial innovations introduced by the VOC and analysis of why later institutions, such as the British East India Company, proved to be even more successful. Graphs and reproductions of early VOC documents.

Prak, Maarten Roy. *The Dutch Republic in the Seventeenth Century.* Cambridge, England: Cambridge University Press, 2005. Readable history of the country during the period in which Bicker and his family exercised greatest control and enjoyed greatest prestige. Illustrations and suggestions for further reading.

See also: Wilhelmina.

MOHAMMED BIN LADEN
Saudi Arabian construction magnate and investor

Mohammed bin Laden became a billionaire during the construction boom that resulted from the swift rise in Saudi Arabian oil wealth during the mid-twentieth century. One of his many sons, Osama Bin Laden, became notorious as a leader of al-Qaeda, the Islamic extremist group that was responsible for the September 11, 2001, attacks on the World Trade Center and the Pentagon.

Born: 1908; Rubat, Hadhramaut, Yemen
Died: September 3, 1967; ʾUsrān, Saudi Arabia
Also known as: Moḥammed bin ʿAwaḍ bin Lāden
Sources of wealth: Construction business; investments
Bequeathal of wealth: Relatives

EARLY LIFE

Moḥammed bin ʿAwaḍ bin Lāden, also known as Mohammed bin Laden (moh-HAH-mehd bihn LAH-dehn), was born into a poor family in the Hadhramaut region along the coast of Yemen around 1908. The exact date of

his birth is not known because celebration of birthdays was not a custom at the time and there was no central government to record births. He was the son of ʿAwaḍ bin Lāden and the eldest of his parents' three sons and three daughters. His father died when bin Laden was young, probably before he reached adolescence. Bin Laden needed to provide income for his family, but the Hadhramaut area offered few opportunities for employment. Bin Laden sailed to Africa probably shortly after 1920, taking a job as a store sweeper in Ethiopia. While there, he lost his right eye; according to differing accounts, he lost his eye either in an accident or when an older man threw a ring of keys at his face. Whatever the cause, bin Laden had a glass eye for the rest of his life.

Bin Laden returned home, but he later followed many other Yemeni youths who emigrated to Saudi Arabia. Around 1925, he traveled to the Red Sea port of Jidda, the gateway to the Islamic holy city of Mecca. Here he initially earned a living as a dockworker and a porter, carrying the bags of affluent pilgrims to Mecca. Initially, bin

---

THE SAUDI BINLADIN GROUP

Mohammed bin Laden, the patriarch of the bin Laden family, in 1931 founded the construction firm that would later be known as the Saudi Binladin (or Binladen) Group. Throughout the years, the company has built numerous buildings in Saudi Arabia, as well as in other Middle Eastern countries, generating billions of dollars for the firm and the bin Laden family.

After he assumed the throne in 1964, King Faisal of Saudi Arabia gave the bin Laden company a monopoly on national construction, a decision that increased the firm's assets to more than $5 billion (about $20 billion in 2010 dollars). Eventually, the bin Ladens held exclusive contracts for all mosque construction and restoration in Saudi Arabia, as well as in several other Islamic nations. This included a contract to restore the Al-Aqsa Mosque, among the most sacred Islamic sites in Jerusalem's Old City.

The bin Ladens also received contracts to build some of Saudi Arabia's major highways. Before the bin Laden company constructed these roads, many of the connections between Saudi cities had amounted to little more than footpaths. In addition, the firm obtained contracts in the $1 to $2 billion range for military bases, as well as a $1 billion contract for a royal palace in Mecca. Holy venues in Mecca, the world center of Islam, were renovated by the company for more than $4 billion.

Following Mohammed bin Laden's death in 1967, his eldest sons, headed by Salem bin Laden, renamed the company Binladen Brothers for Contracting and Industry. At its height, this company employed as many as forty thousand people in thirty-six countries. Like his father, Salem bin Laden died in an aircraft accident, when the private plane in which he was riding became ensnared in power lines near San Antonio, Texas, in 1988.

After 1990, the company became known as the Saudi Binladin Group, with that name registered by another of Mohammed's sons, Bakr bin Laden. The company maintains extensive interests in engineering, manufacturing, construction, and telecommunications, as well as in real estate development and urban planning. In the twenty-first century, the firm has constructed airports, apartment blocks, bridges, and tunnels, as well as highways.

The Saudi Binladin Group works throughout the Islamic world and is Egypt's largest foreign company. It received some funding from the United States, as well as other countries, in order to rebuild parts of central Beirut that had been ruined in Lebanon's civil war. The company maintains offices in London and Geneva, Switzerland, as well as throughout the Middle East in such major cities Cairo, Beirut, Amman, and Dubai. The firm also has developed business relationships with major multinational corporations, including Unilever, General Electric, Citicorp, and HSBC Bank. By 2009, the company's gross revenues exceeded $5 billion per year. According to some reports, the Binladin Group also owns major equity stakes in Microsoft Corporation, Boeing, and other major American companies.

Laden and his younger brother Abdullah slept in a ditch they had dug in the sand. Later, when he was a rich man, bin Laden hung the scarred leather bag he had used to haul pilgrims' personal effects in his office.

Bin Laden was about five feet eight inches tall, and he was known for his skill at organizing other people's work in a practical and efficient manner. He was a spirited practical joker and an avid dancer of traditional steps, some of which he performed while shooting pistols into the air. He was especially good at cultivating and retaining important friends long before he gained access to the inner circles of the Saudi royal family.

FIRST VENTURES

Within a few years, bin Laden no longer was a porter and had became known around Jidda for doing small-scale construction work, such as fixing arches and renovating the facades of old buildings. With the arrival of the Great Depression in the early 1930's, the economy of Jidda collapsed as the pilgrim trade declined. Bin Laden found himself on the road looking for work. He entered the oil business by taking a job as a bricklayer with the oil firm Aramco in Dhahran, Saudi Arabia. The oil revenue that was pouring into the coffers of the Saudi royal family soon would make bin Laden wealthy, as some of that income would finance his construction projects.

After holding several menial jobs, bin Laden shortly after 1930 made the acquaintance of Ibn Saʿūd, who would eventually become the first king of the modern Saudi state. The relationship between the two men enabled bin Laden to become wealthy by constructing buildings for the king. As the "royal builder," a status established by a royal edict in 1950, bin Laden and his family reputedly became the richest nonroyal family in Saudi Arabia. Bin Laden initially built homes for the royal family, learning about construction while on the job, and eventually took on larger projects.

Bin Laden accumulated his fortune through his acute

business sense and his ability to cultivate royal contacts, offering the monarchy quality work at a relatively low price. He initially became wealthy by constructing and restoring mosques in Saudi Arabia under contract to the royal family. In 1955, bin Laden's status was solidified when a royal decree named him a minister of state in Saudi Arabia. Bin Laden also became a legend in his hometown in Yemen, where he was an inspiration to the many thousands of Yemenis who had migrated to Saudi Arabia for employment.

MATURE WEALTH

After performing construction work on King Ibn Saʿūd's palace, bin Laden's firm was contracted to renovate buildings in the city of Mecca. His company built religious structures in other cities as the Saudi oil boom provided revenue for such work after World War II. The bin Ladens became confidants of the royal family, a relationship that involved a high degree of trust, shared secrets, and friendship. The relationship continued after bin Laden's death, with his children establishing ties with the children of the royal family. The elder bin Laden sons often attended the same schools as the children of the king, including the elite Victoria College in Alexandria, Egypt, and the children traveled in the same social circles. Victoria College was widely attended by students from elite families in the Arab nations, as well as by families of other notable people, such as the actor Omar Sharif. The bin Ladens were as close to Saudi royalty as anyone without shared blood.

In 1964, bin Laden's confidant Faisal became king of Saudi Arabia, and this further enhanced bin Laden's wealth by providing him with contracts for more massive construction projects. The kingdom had been mismanaged under King Saud, the son of King Ibn Saʿūd, and Saudi Arabia had a brush with insolvency despite its rising oil wealth. Bin Laden offered his business acumen, and a sizable sum of money, to improve the nation's economy.

After he amassed wealth in construction, bin Laden invested in oil and other ventures. He was killed when his company aircraft crashed near ʾUsrān, Saudi Arabia, on September 3, 1967.

LEGACY

Mohammed bin Laden lived simply even after he acquired wealth, and he continued to be a devout Muslim. Moreover, he demanded the same of his children, traits that the world would come to know in Osama, his most militant son. Because Mohammed died before the evolution of the more militant interpretations of Islam, it is

hard to know if he would have approved of Osama's jihad, which included the killing of almost three thousand people on September 11, 2001.

Mohammed bin Laden's fortune was passed on to his many sons, and his family continued operating his construction business. He was married twenty-two times and had at least fifty-four children. However, he retained a maximum of four wives at once, as allowed by Islamic law, divorcing former wives as he acquired new ones. A family history written by Carmen bin Laden indicates that Mohammed was flying to the site of his twenty-third wedding the day he was killed in the airplane crash. The direct descendants of Mohammed bin Laden probably number more than six hundred people. Osama Bin Laden was Mohammed's seventeenth child, born in 1957, and his only son with his tenth wife, the Syrian woman Hamida al-Attas.

Ties between the royal family and the bin Ladens occasionally have been tested as the result of radical Islamic activity. In the seizure of the Grand Mosque in Mecca, radicals used bin Laden construction trucks to smuggle weapons into the holy city. In 1990, the bin Laden family disowned Osama. Saudi Arabia later revoked Osama's passport and stripped him of citizenship because he had criticized the state for allowing United States troops onto Saudi soil following the 1991 Gulf War. Osama also is subject to an arrest warrant issued by the Saudi government on May 16, 1993.

—*Bruce E. Johansen*

FURTHER READING

Bin Ladin, Carmen. *Inside the Kingdom: My Life in Saudi Arabia.* New York: Warner Books, 2004. Carmen, former sister-in-law of Osama Bin Laden, married into the bin Laden family and later was divorced. She describes her experiences with the family, as well as her sorrow over the September 11, 2001, attacks.

Coll, Steve. *The Bin Ladens: An Arabian Family in the American Century.* Penguin Press, 2008. An extensive historical account of the bin Laden family from Mohammed's early years to about 2007, richly detailed and elegantly written.

Shadid, Anthony. *Legacy of the Prophet: Despots, Democrats, and the New Politics of Islam.* Boulder, Colo.: Westview Press, 2002. Provides context concerning social and political aspects of Islamic radicalism in the late twentieth and early twenty-first centuries.

Unger, Craig. *House of Bush, House of Saud.* New York: Scribner, 2004. Alleging business associations between the bin Laden family, George H. W. Bush, and George W. Bush, the book was used as a source in Michael Moore's documentary film *Fahrenheit 9/11*.

Wright, Robin. *Dreams and Shadows: The Future of the Middle East*. New York: Penguin Press, 2008. Wright, a reporter for several U.S. national publica-

tions, finds reason for optimism in this examination of Middle Eastern politics, in which the bin Laden family has played a pivotal role.

See also: Mohammed Hussein Ali Al Amoudi; Al-Waleed bin Talal.

GHANSHYAM DAS BIRLA
Indian industrialist, entrepreneur, politician/statesman, and philanthropist

Birla was one of the most influential businessmen of twentieth century India. He built his family's business into one of India's major manufacturing conglomerates, and he was intimately associated with the nationalist cause. Publisher, industrialist, educator, philanthropist, and an associate of Mahatma Gandhi, his unique contributions to the development of modern India made him a household name.

Born: April, 1894; Pilani, Rajasthan, India
Died: June 11, 1983; London, England
Also known as: Shri Ghanshyam Das Birla; G. D. Birla
Sources of wealth: Manufacturing; sale of products
Bequeathal of wealth: Children; educational institution

EARLY LIFE

Shri Ghanshyam Das "G. D." Birla (shree gahn-SHEHM dahs BIHR-la) was born in 1894 in Palani, Rajasthan, India, one of three sons of Baldev Das Birla (1863-1956), a wealthy Marwari trading caste member from Calcutta and the son of Shiv Naraayana Birla (1838-1910), a moneylender who founded the family business. Ghanshyam was tutored in Hindi and arithmetic and learned the Vaishnav religion from his family. As was the custom, at age eleven he married Durga Somani, who died in 1909 following the birth of their first son, Lakshmi Niwas "L. N." Birla (1909-1994).

As a teenager, Birla worked for his father, a Mumbai cotton dealer. There he learned accounting and English, a language not typically studied by Marwaris at this time. In 1910, Birla left for Kolkata to establish his own jute brokerage, under the tutelage of his father-in-law Mahadev Somani. He was betrothed to Mahadevi Kharva (d.1926), with whom he had three sons, Krishna Kumar, Basant Kumar, and Ganga Prasad. His first enterprise, G. M. Birla and Company, was registered in 1911.

FIRST VENTURES

Despite British dominance of cotton and jute mills and discriminatory practices, which included forbidding Indians the use of elevators in British factories, the Marwaris had established inroads into jute and cotton dealerships by the early twentieth century. Jute prices rose considerably during World War I. Birla became wealthy and established an export office in London. After the war he established a new company, Birla Brothers, which would become one of the most well-known Indian-owned companies of the colonial era, and he purchased a cotton mill. He overcame attempts by British producers to stymie his launch of a jute mill, a struggle that began to shape his nationalist politics, and he survived the difficult period of the 1920's rupee devaluation. By his thirtieth birthday, Birla had established successful cotton mills and trading companies, and he had become skilled at training fellow Marwaris as managers rather than relying on Europeans, thereby facilitating Marwari dominance of India's postindependence business community. He assisted in the formation of the nationalist Indian Chamber of Commerce and, soon thereafter, the influential Federation of Chambers of Commerce of India in 1927. He was a sponsor of the Free Press of India, the first national press agency, and briefly ran for local elected office. Birla's reputation as a successful entrepreneur and an important person within the Marwari community emboldened his interest in the nationalist cause.

MATURE WEALTH

In the early 1930's, Birla expanded into sugar and paper mills, complementing the family's smaller publishing, soap, insurance, and chemical businesses. The companies survived the Great Depression by aggressively competing with the weakening European oligopolies. In the 1930's, Birla became explicitly involved in the nationalist cause, primarily as a major contributor to the Indian

National Congress and as an associate of Mahatma Gandhi, a leader of the Indian independence movement who had met Birla in 1916. Birla accompanied Gandhi to the Round Table Conference in London in 1931 and 1932, where representatives of Great Britain and India discussed the future constitution of India. Birla and Gandhi grew close. Gandhi encouraged Birla and his peers to act as strong supporters of independence, and he supported the industrialists' viewpoint that economic development free from colonial dependence and control was a solution to India's poverty. Birla famously declined to accept a British knighthood, and in this era he established his role as a key link between the Indian worlds of business and politics, going on to become an influential adviser to many policy makers. He was also a generous provider of resources to the independence movement, a fact that irritated the British and caused concern among his brothers.

Birla became friends with many Indian National Congress leaders, including Vallabhbhai Jhaverbhai Patel (1875-1950). As an industrialist, Birla counseled compromise between the Indian National Congress and the British and cooperation between labor and capital. He opposed the socialist leanings of some in the Indian anticolonial movement, and he later had cool relations with the left-leaning Prime Minister Jawaharlal Nehru (1889-1964). Birla believed that the acquisition of knowledge was essential in building a modern India. Toward this end he became a lifelong supporter and advocate of educational institutions.

Birla's industries expanded during and after World War II, supplying essential manufactured goods as the country reached independence and the economy expanded. Prices of jute and other staples again spiked during the war, earning Birla the resources to expand in the postwar period. Transportation, industrial supplies, and agricultural goods dominated the companies' activities. While some of their growth came from the acquisition of European companies, the companies expanded in other ways. In 1942, Birla founded Hindustan Motors of Kolkata, and the company's Ambassador model, based on a British car design, dominated Indian roads for many years in the taxi service and government transport. The car company enjoyed a dominant market position until it began competing with other automakers in the 1980's. Another Birla firm of this era, the Textile

THE BIRLA INSTITUTE OF TECHNOLOGY AND SCIENCE

Ghanshyam Das Birla's contributions to the field of education stemmed from his perception that his own lack of formal schooling affected his life and from his intense desire to see India build a modern industrial capacity. He saw education as foundational, and he set up hundreds of rural schools. He brought the educator Maria Montessori to his home in Pilani in the 1940's so she could promote the benefits of public schools. A Montessori society was established in Pilani, and the Birla Public School was founded as a Montessori school in 1944.

Birla viewed the lack of an Indian-educated, professional sector as a particular disadvantage to the country's industrial and social development. In 1929, he established a high school in his hometown of Pilani, where he later founded a college focusing on science, business, and pharmacy studies. The college added programs in engineering and electronics in the 1940's and 1950's. Originally registered as a "society" under state registration guidelines, the school was granted university status by the government in 1964, and the various programs were joined into the Birla Institute of Technology and Science, commonly known as BITS. Birla was the institute's chairman.

In the 1960's, BITS became a premier engineering and business school. It received support from the Ford Foundation and entered into an alliance with the Massachusetts Institute of Technology, which transformed BITS into a university similar to those in the United States. The institute was the first in India to build a department of space engineering and rocketry; it also established the Small Industries Entrepreneurs' Park in order to promote effective practices and to aid in funding for business start-ups. The Birla Institute of Management Technology was founded in 1988. Under the chancellorship of Birla's son, Krishna Kumar Birla, institute campuses were established in Goa and Hyderabad, and in 1990 a branch opened in Dubai. Several internationally recognized research centers also were opened, including facilities focusing on robotics, software, and women's studies.

BITS is known for requiring its students to work on real-world projects, and it is prized for its extensive connections with industry. It has remained a privately funded school, renowned for its academic rigor, and it consistently ranks among the top universities in India.

Machinery Corporation (TEXMACO), profited from the dearth of equipment imported from England during the war. In short, with the decline of British influence in the Indian economy, Birla's enterprises reached a new level of dynamism.

After Indian independence and the partition of Pakistan from India, Birla's business empire grew to include tea, textiles, plastics, and the country's largest cement producer, and he eventually led one of India's largest industrial conglomerates. However, tragedy struck in 1947, when Gandhi was assassinated while visiting the Birla home in Delhi, abruptly ending the men's thirty-two-year friendship. Birla's nationalist credentials and his relationships with Patel and Nehru enabled the industrialist to mold commercial growth to India's development policies. One exception was Birla's desire to found a steel enterprise, which was frustrated in the 1950's by the government's decision to focus on publicly owned steel capacity. By the end of the 1950's, Birla controlled more than 150 companies. His wealth and commercial dominance upset many competitors and those on the Indian left, who accused him of monopolistic practices. That such growth occurred even though Birla's attempts to persuade Nehru to pursue economic liberalization failed is an indication of Birla's resourcefulness.

During the administration of Prime Minister Indira Gandhi, however, Birla's political connections decreased, and he faced increasing pressure from left-wing politicians to share his wealth and his industrial licensing privileges, which accounted for 20 percent of government licenses from 1957 to 1966. By the end of his career, Birla controlled two hundred companies, divided into autonomous entities and managed by family members and allies. Products included railway and other industrial equipment, aluminum (Hindalco), textiles, and agricultural goods, and the group owned foreign enterprises in Africa and Southeast Asia. By the time of his death in 1983, Birla's conglomerate was surpassed in size in India only by the Tata Group of industries. The Birla group's inheritors, in particular the Aditya Birla Group, which was run by Birla's grandson Aditya Birla (1944-1995), ensured that Birla's industrial heritage continued to thrive.

LEGACY

Birla combined his skills as an industrialist with the political dream of an independent India. He saw no distinction between his nationalism and his desire for his country to realize its industrial prowess. Through two world wars, an epic anticolonial battle, and struggles over India's economic liberalization, his life is a window into twentieth century India. He established many of India's modern industries, and he was instrumental in initiating its independence in technology and engineering education. His contributions to the transformation of India from a largely rural society, dominated by a strong colonial power, to a society of technology, industry, and education were seminal. His personal generosity, charitable nature, and meager lifestyle have rightly inspired numerous educational awards that bear his name.

—*Eric Schuster*

FURTHER READING

Birla, Ghanshyam Das. *In the Shadow of the Mahatma: A Personal Memoir.* Mumbai, India: Orient Longmans, 1953. Birla's essays on his friend and the project for independence bring to light how Gandhi's teachings influenced the industrialist's outlook.

Goswami, Omkar. "Then Came the Marwaris: Some Aspects of the Changes in the Pattern of Industrial Control in Eastern India." *Indian Economic and Social History Review* 22, no. 3 (September 1, 1985): 225-249. Detailed analysis of the influence of the Marwari caste on economic development in colonial and independent India.

Herdeck, Margaret, and Piramal Gita. *India's Industrialists.* Boulder, Colo.: Lynne Rienner, 1985. Includes a concise exposition and analysis of the Birla group's business evolution and how it influenced Birla and his brothers.

Jaju, Raina Nivasa. *G. D. Birla, a Biography.* Delhi, India: Vikas, 1985. Hagiographic but detailed retelling of the business and political life of Birla.

Kudaisya, Medha M. *The Life and Times of G. D. Birla.* New York: Oxford University Press, 2006. The only academic study of the magnate analyzes Birla's political, familial, and business evolution, with a deep background of political and social contexts.

Vinita. *Icons of Indian Industry.* Chennai, India: Sura Books, 2007. Detailed biographical overviews of Birla, J. R. D. Tata, and Ardeshir Godrej provide an interesting comparison of their histories and personalities.

See also: Mukesh Ambani; Jamsetji Tata.

JOHN INSLEY BLAIR
American railroad executive

Blair earned a fortune as president of sixteen railroads and board member of at least as many others. He used his vast resources to support causes dear to his heart, particularly the Presbyterian Church and various educational institutions, including the Blair Presbyterian Academy.

Born: August 22, 1802; Warren County, New Jersey
Died: December 2, 1899; Blairstown, New Jersey
Also known as: Plain John I
Source of wealth: Railroads
Bequeathal of wealth: Relatives; charity; educational institution; church

EARLY LIFE
John Insley Blair was the fourth of eleven children born to Scottish immigrants John and Rachel Insley Blair. Blair was a direct descendant of the patriot John Blair, Jr., who in 1720 came to New Jersey from Scotland and was one of the signers of the Declaration of Independence. The Blair family was close-knit, and Blair pursued many of his early business endeavors with a brother or other relative.

Blair's formal schooling was intermittent and ended at age eleven, when he reportedly told his mother, "I have seven brothers and three sisters. That's enough in the family to be educated. I am going to get rich." After that prophetic pronouncement, he went to work in a cousin's store to learn the retail trade. He proved to be a quick study and when the cousin left, Blair became the sole proprietor. In September, 1826, he married Nancy Ann Locke, with whom he had four children, Emma, Marcus, De Witt, and Aurelia.

FIRST VENTURES
Blair opened a general store in Butts Bridge, New Jersey, the community that in 1839 was renamed Blairstown in his honor. At age twenty-eight, he turned this first store into a chain of five. Along with his other business interests, he served as the town's postmaster for twenty-six years. His other business interests included, but were not limited to, wholesaling, flour mills, cotton mills, banking, and mining of both coal and iron. In some of these enterprises, he worked in partnership with one or more of his brothers or brothers-in-law.

Blair correctly guessed that the railroad would hold the key to America's dominance as an industrial nation during the nineteenth century. He also figured that the towns served by railroads would be the ones to prosper. A staunch Republican from the party's birth in 1854, he was a delegate at every nominating convention for the remainder of his life, and he felt especially honored to have participated in the nomination of Abraham Lincoln for president in 1860.

MATURE WEALTH
It was in the growing railroad industry that Blair found his true calling, and he made a name for himself among the other railroad industry giants of the times, including Jay Gould, James J. Hill, George Mortimer Pullman, and Edward H. Harriman, to name just a few. His first foray into the business was with the organization of the Delaware, Lackawanna & Western Railroad (DL&W) in 1852. He became president and remained a board member and major stockholder of the DL&W for the rest of his life. He served as president of other railroad companies, including the Sioux City and Pacific, Cayuga and Susquehanna, Chicago and Northwestern, Liggett's Gap, Sussex Valley, and Warren rail lines. In all, he became president of sixteen railroad companies, and he sat on the board of directors of at least that many more.

Blair recognized the railroads' opportunities resulting from the rapid expansion of the American West. His railroads, including his Sioux City branch of the Union Pacific Railroad, set the pace of this growth. With Congressman Oakes Ames, Blair won the charter for the United Pacific, and he personally oversaw the laying of the first one hundred miles of its track. Ames, as president of the Crédit Mobilier of America, a railroad construction company, was later charged, along with thirteen other members of Congress, with graft, corruption, and fraud. Blair was innocent of any wrongdoing. His sterling reputation for honesty and his strong code of personal ethics kept him from being damaged in the resulting scandal.

Towns sprouted up as soon as railroad tracks were laid. Blair laid out at least eighty new towns along these far-reaching tracks. His responsibilities required frequent travel, and when he was not conducting business from his home in New Jersey, he worked out of the office in his private railcar, an indulgence that was actually a necessity. He is believed to have owned more miles of rail than any other individual owner.

For Blair, retirement was not an option, and he continued working at a pace that men half his age would have had difficulty matching. He never slowed down until he

123

reached age eighty-five, when he decided to reduce his frequent travel from forty thousand to twenty thousand miles per year, though he still started work before daylight and put in a full day. His phenomenal drive stemmed from his genuine love of business in general and the railroad business in particular.

While most of his vast fortune came from his railroad lines, he also founded the Belvidere National Bank in Belvidere, New Jersey, and he continued to own stock in various mining companies. He ran for governor of New Jersey in 1868, but he lost the race to the Democratic candidate, the incumbent Theodore Randolph. He died at age ninety-seven in the house where he had lived most of his life, and in the town where he was widely respected and known as "Plain John I." Despite his great wealth, he lived simply and remained an unpretentious man. He found it ironic that someone with almost no education had been selected to serve as a trustee on Princeton University's board of directors.

Blair was a lifelong member of the Presbyterian Church, and he supported it with the same generosity he had shown various schools, including his beloved Blair Presbyterian Academy. At the time of his death in 1899, Blair's wealth was reported at more than $70 million.

LEGACY

A devout Presbyterian, Blair founded more than one hundred churches. Not coincidentally, they were all located in the Western towns in which he had laid out his railroads. His greatest legacy is the Blair Academy, initially called the Blair Presbyterian Academy. For fifty years, he was the school's principal benefactor. His gifts of land and cash funded the school's growth, making the academy the respected institution it remained into the twenty-first century.

Blair also gave generously to colleges, including Princeton University, Grinnell College, and Lafayette College. Princeton's Blair Hall was named for him, and

THE BLAIR ACADEMY

The Blair Presbyterian Academy was founded in 1848 by railroad magnate John Insley Blair, with help from the Presbyterian Church and some residents of Blairstown, New Jersey. Blair, a lifelong Presbyterian, understood the importance of education, even though he had personally eschewed it in favor of going out into the world to work. He wanted to ensure that the children of local farmers and townspeople would receive an education. Blair hoped his private preparatory school would provide instruction based upon the values of the Christian faith and that this schooling would prepare students to be future community leaders.

In 1860, Blair selected outstanding students for what he called Blair Academy's Secret Society, or the Elite 1848, with 1848 apparently referring to the year the school was established. Among other pursuits, the society actively assisted the Underground Railroad and worked to hold the Union together during the Civil War.

The school initially was open to both girls and boys, but it limited admissions to boys in 1915, eventually reinstating a coeducational admissions policy in 1970. By the twenty-first century, girls accounted for about half of its enrollment. The school, now known as the Blair Academy, expanded over the years until its campus contained forty-two buildings on 425 acres. Classes are provided for ninth- through twelfth-grade students who are either day or boarding students. Virtually all of Blair's graduates go on to college.

While academics take precedence over athletics, the school competes successfully in the Mid-Atlantic Prep League, and in 2010 three former students were playing in the National Basketball Association: Charlie Villanueva of the Detroit Pistons, Royal Ivey of the Philadelphia 76ers, and Luol Deng of the Chicago Bulls. Other alumni have held prominent places in government, business, literature, and the arts, including John Sebastian, the lead singer and guitarist for the Lovin' Spoonful band.

Blair Academy has, on average, an enrollment of 450 students. The school boasts of its faculty-student ratio of one teacher for seven students, with average class size limited to ten students. Among the special programs offered are honors courses, independent study, spring break community service trips, and study abroad. Upper grades adhere to a dress code, and attendance at religious services is required. Students and faculty are equally responsible for maintaining discipline. Financial aid to students in need exceeds $3 million annually.

Over the years, the academy has become more diverse, with students from nearly every state, as well as from twenty-three countries. It maintains the Judeo-Christian values of its founder and is still strongly tied to the Presbyterian Church, specifically the presbytery of Newton, New Jersey. Although its character has changed over the years, one thing has remained constant: an ongoing reputation for academic excellence. In 1992, the National Register of Historic Places officially recognized the historical and architectural significance of the campus's original buildings, which are designed in the Romanesque style.

he served on the university's board of directors. Having voluntarily ended his own schooling at age eleven, he felt intuitively that the days of self-made men would soon be a thing of the past, and success in the future would be unattainable without the foundation of a solid education.

After his death, his son De Witt Clinton Blair took over his father's business and philanthropic interests and continued supporting the causes Blair held dear, including making generous contributions to Blair Academy, funding new buildings as the school continued to grow in size and in reputation.

—Norma Lewis

FURTHER READING

Ambrose, Stephen. *Nothing Like It in the World: The Men Who Built the Transcontinental Railroad*. New York: Simon & Schuster Adult Publishing Group, 2001. An account of how two rail companies, the Union Pacific and the Central Pacific, accomplished the seemingly impossible engineering feat of connecting the country east to west by rail via the First Transcontinental Railroad in 1869. The Union Pacific is one of the sixteen railroads with which Blair was associated.

Blair, John Insley. *Papers*. Southern Methodist University. Blair's papers have been collected and preserved by the DeGolyer Library at Southern Methodist University and can be accessed online through Texas Archival Resources Online, http://lib.utexas.edu/taro/index.html. The collection covers the years 1831-1898 and is divided into three sections: correspondence (mostly business, and mostly having to do with his railroads); miscellaneous manuscripts and documents including newspaper clippings; and business documents.

Ward, James A. *Railroads and the Character of America, 1820-1887*. Knoxville: University of Tennessee Press, 1986. A detailed and well-researched presentation of the early railroad industry and the major role it played in the Western expansion of the United States and in the country as a whole.

See also: Jim Brady; William Andrews Clark; Jay Cooke; Charles Crocker; Daniel Drew; John W. Garrett; Jay Gould; Edward H. Harriman; James J. Hill; Mark Hopkins; Collis P. Huntington; Daniel Willis James; George Mortimer Pullman; Russell Sage; Leland Stanford; William Thaw; Cornelius Vanderbilt; William Henry Vanderbilt.

MICHAEL BLOOMBERG
American politician and media executive

Bloomberg parlayed a $10 million severance payment from Salomon Brothers investment bank into a multibillion-dollar fortune in less than two decades. As founder of Innovative Market Systems, he developed a method of installing messaging terminals in businesses that became the standard in the United States. He used the enormous profits from his business to become a noted philanthropist, and he was elected the mayor of New York City in 2001.

Born: February 14, 1942; Boston, Massachusetts
Also known as: Michael Rubens Bloomberg
Sources of wealth: Sale of products; media
Bequeathal of wealth: Charity

EARLY LIFE
Michael Rubens Bloomberg was born on February 14, 1942, at St. Elizabeth's Hospital in Boston, Massachusetts, the older of two children born to William Henry Bloomberg and Charlotte Rubens Bloomberg. His parents were the children of Russian Jewish immigrants. In 2009, his mother was more than one hundred years old and reportedly still in good health. Bloomberg and his family lived in the middle-class Boston neighborhood of Medford, where he finished high school in 1960. Bloomberg was an above-average student, receiving high marks.

After graduation, Bloomberg enrolled in Johns Hopkins University, from which he graduated in 1964 with a B.S. degree in electrical engineering. He then enrolled in the Harvard Business School, from which he graduated two years later with an M.B.A. degree. After graduating from Harvard, Bloomberg took a position with Salomon Brothers, a Wall Street investment bank, where he eventually rose to the position of head of equity trading and then of systems development. After a merger in 1981, Bloomberg was dismissed from Salomon Brothers and opened his own company. In 1975, he married Susan Brown Bloomberg. The couple had two daughters,

Emma, born in 1979, and Georgina, born in 1983, before they divorced in 1993.

FIRST VENTURES

Bloomberg received a very generous severance package of $10 million from Salomon Brothers, which he used to found his own company, Innovative Market Systems, in 1981.The company installed messaging terminals that supplied businesses with the latest news, real-time financial data, and stock quotes. The giant Merrill Lynch investment bank (now Bank of America Merrill Lynch) was Bloomberg's first customer. Merrill Lynch installed twenty-two terminals in its offices and ultimately invested $30 million in Bloomberg's enterprise. Bloomberg renamed his company Bloomberg L.P. in 1986, and by the next year the firm had installed more than five thousand of these "Bloomberg terminals." As these terminals proliferated, Bloomberg expanded into radio and other media. He founded a cable television network in 1994, went online with Bloomberg.com in 1995, and es-

tablished the Bloomberg Press publishing company in 1996.

He became a billionaire by 2000, by which time his name was synonymous with business information systems. In 2010, *Forbes* magazine listed him as number twenty-three on its list of world billionaires, with his net worth estimated at $18 billion.

MATURE WEALTH

Bloomberg eventually turned his attention from business to philanthropy and politics. In 2001, he gave up his position as chief executive officer of Bloomberg L.P. to run for mayor of New York City, seeking to replace incumbent Rudy Giuliani, who was ineligible for a third consecutive term. In order to run, Bloomberg, who had been a Democrat all his life, switched parties and became a Republican.

Bloomberg chose not to accept public campaign funds, and reportedly dedicated more than $73 million of his own money on the race, outspending his Democratic opponent by more than five to one. He urged voters to elect him by insisting that New York City's economy was suffering from the September 11, 2001, attacks on the World Trade Center and needed a mayor who had business experience. He represented himself as being in favor of abortion rights, the legalization of same-sex marriage, stricter gun control laws, and citizenship rights for undocumented aliens, and many saw his positions as a betrayal of Republican principles. Bloomberg won the election by a narrow margin despite what some critics called his "fuzziness" on several key issues. The election was the first time in the history of the city that two Republicans were elected mayor consecutively.

At Bloomberg's urging, New York City was the site of the 2004 Republican National Convention, where he soundly endorsed incumbent George W. Bush for a second term as president. Bloomberg was reelected mayor in 2005 by a 20 percent margin, the largest ever for a Republican mayor of New York City. By some estimates, he spent more than $74 million on his campaign. In 2007, amid further criticism that he was ignoring Republican values, Bloomberg formally left the Republican Party and declared himself an Independent.

During his first term as mayor, Bloomberg concentrated primarily on reforming public education. His statistically oriented, results-based approach has drawn considerable criticism from the teachers' union and praise from the public. He supported an increase in teachers' salaries, including incentives for superior teaching. He opposed social promotion, while supporting after-school

Michael Bloomberg. (Getty Images)

programs to help disadvantaged students. During his second term, Bloomberg concentrated on addressing the issues associated with poverty. He also made the human immunodeficiency virus (HIV), diabetes, and hypertension his top public health priorities. He extended a smoking ban to all commercial establishments in New York City and banned restaurants from serving foods with trans fats. He started a $7.5 billion affordable housing plan to aid half a million people who were living in or near poverty. He was also responsible for initiating Opportunity NYC, a program aimed at helping poor New York citizens break the poverty cycle.

Bloomberg also became deeply involved in environmental issues throughout his tenure as mayor. He is convinced that global warming is a reality and that large cities must address the problem of climate change if catastrophe is to be averted. In 2007, he initiated a plan, PlaNYC: A Greener, Greater New York, which calls for the reduction of carbon dioxide emissions through the use of cleaner, more efficient fuels and encourages greater use of public transportation. He hopes his plan will help prepare New York City for a projected population increase of more than one million people by 2030. Bloomberg accomplished all of these reforms while balancing New York City's budget, turning a $6 billion deficit into a $3 billion surplus. His critics point out that in order to accomplish this turnaround, Bloomberg cut public services and increased property taxes.

In 2008, Bloomberg reversed his longtime support for term limits, persuading the city council to change municipal law and enable him to seek a third term as mayor. This move angered many New Yorkers, some of whom voted for his opponent, William Thompson, Jr., in the 2009 mayoral election. This resentment was cited as one reason that Bloomberg won the race by a closer-than-expected margin. Bloomberg, the richest man in New York City, spent $102 million on his reelection, at that time the most expensive self-financed campaign in American history.

Supporters mounted a concerted effort to draft Bloomberg for a presidential run in 2008. Bloomberg seemed interested in running as an Independent candidate but ultimately decided against an attempt. He did not, however, rule out a run in 2012. His blend of fiscal conservatism, social liberalism, and business acumen would seem to make him a desirable candidate for many moderates in the United States.

In addition to his political activities, Bloomberg has been heavily involved in philanthropy since acquiring great wealth. In 2008, he and Bill Gates, cofounder of Microsoft Corporation, gave $500 million to help Third World countries control tobacco use, especially among minors. Bloomberg donated $300 million to his alma mater, Johns Hopkins University, where he chaired the board of trustees from 1996 to 2002. Some estimates put the total amount of money given or pledged by Bloomberg since 2001 at more than $1 billion.

THE JOHNS HOPKINS UNIVERSITY BLOOMBERG SCHOOL FOR PUBLIC HEALTH

John D. Rockefeller and William Howard Welch founded the Johns Hopkins School of Hygiene and Public Health in 1916, and over the years it became the model for schools of public health throughout the world. On April 20, 2001, university trustees renamed the school the Johns Hopkins University Bloomberg School for Public Health in honor of a $300 million gift provided by businessman Michael Bloomberg, who would later become mayor of New York City.

The institution is the largest school of public health in the world, employing 530 full-time and 620 part-time faculty and providing instruction to 2,030 students from eighty-four countries. The school boasts more than fifty research centers and institutes and ranks first in federal research support from the National Institutes of Health. In 2007, it placed first in *U.S. News and World Report*'s rankings of schools of public health.

Located across from the Johns Hopkins Hospital in East Baltimore, Maryland, the school offers master's degrees in public health, health science, health administration, and science, as well as three doctoral degrees. It also provides postdoctoral training and residency programs in preventive medicine and occupational medicine. The institution publishes *The Johns Hopkins Public Health Magazine*; *Journal of Health Care for the Poor and Underserved*; *Epidemiologic Review*; and *Progress in Community Health Partnerships: Research, Education, and Action*. The *American Journal of Epidemiology* is published by Oxford University Press on the school's behalf. Among the school's more notable alumni are Virginia Apgar, one of the pioneers in the field of neonatology; former Surgeon Generals Leroy Edgar Burney and Antonia Coello Novello; Donald A. Henderson, who was instrumental in the eradication of smallpox; Bernard Roizman, a virologist who is considered the world's leading expert on the herpes simplex virus; and Alfred Sommer, a professor emeritus at the school who has conducted research on the causes, consequences, and control of vitamin A deficiency.

LEGACY

Bloomberg's legacy is already well established. Between 2004 and 2007, he pledged more than $600 million to charity. He has been especially active in supporting efforts to combat tobacco use among adolescents worldwide. He has donated tens of millions of dollars to New York City recipients ranging from arts organizations to support efforts for people and families dealing with cancer. He has also endowed a professorship at Harvard University and supported Jewish religious organizations.

In addition to his philanthropic activities, Bloomberg's legacy includes his public service. As mayor of New York City, he has been a leading advocate of educational reform and improving the quality of life for all New Yorkers through crime prevention and public transportation improvements. He has received numerous awards for both public service and philanthropy.

—Paul Madden

FURTHER READING

Bloomberg, Michael. *Bloomberg by Bloomberg.* New York: Wiley, 2001. Ghost written autobiography concentrating primarily on Bloomberg's business career. Few details about his personal life, but devotes a considerable amount of space to his political views and his philanthropic efforts. Attempts to explain his changing political parties prior to running for mayor.

Purnick, Joyce. *Mike Bloomberg: Money, Power, Politics.* New York: PublicAffairs, 2009. A detailed biography of Bloomberg, concentrating on his political career. Portrays Bloomberg as a business and political genius, who has shifted his political positions to keep up with changing public attitudes, and as a philanthropist who has given much of his vast fortune to charities, particularly those concerned with education.

Rowland, Mary. *Best Practices for Financial Advisors.* New York: Bloomberg Press, 1997. A how-to book for financial advisers, with advice on ethical business practices approved by Bloomberg. Contains much wisdom derived from Bloomberg's own personal philosophy of business and investing.

Silverstein, Edward M. *Michael Bloomberg: A Biography.* New York: Heinemann Educational Books, 2009. A brief and very flattering biography of Bloomberg, written for a high school audience. Features a time line highlighting important events in Bloomberg's life, photographs, and a bibliography of print and electronic sources.

See also: Walter Annenberg; Barbara Cox Anthony; David and Frederick Barclay; Silvio Berlusconi; Anne Cox Chambers; Katharine Graham; John H. Johnson; Robert L. Johnson; John Kluge; Rupert Murdoch; Samuel I. Newhouse; Kerry Packer; John D. Rockefeller; Ted Turner.

SULTAN HASSANAL BOLKIAH
Bruneian ruler

Sultan Hassanal Bolkiah of Brunei is one of the richest rulers in the world primarily because of his nation's vast oil and natural gas reserves. The sultan and his family are known for building the world's largest palace, enjoying a lavish lifestyle, and providing the citizens of Brunei with generous benefits and tax credits.

Born: July 15, 1946; Brunei Town (now Bandar Seri Begawan), Brunei

Also known as: Haji Hassanal Bolkiah Mu'izzaddin Waddaulah; Sultan and Yang Di-Pertuan of Brunei Darussalam

Sources of wealth: Inheritance; oil; real estate

Bequeathal of wealth: Children

EARLY LIFE

Haji Hassanal Bolkiah Mu'izzaddin Waddaulah, better known as Sultan Hassanal Bolkiah (sool-TAHN HAH-sah-nahl bowl-KEE-eh), the twenty-ninth sultan of Brunei, was the eldest son of the late Sultan Omar Ali Saifuddien III and Raja Isteri Pengiran Anak Damit. Little information is available about Bolkiah's early years. The majority of his education was private and was obtained in Brunei, although he attended high school at Victoria Institution in Kuala Lumpur, Malaysia, where he joined the Cadet Corps. He later enrolled at the United Kingdom's elite Royal Military Academy Sandhurst, graduating in 1967. Since becoming sultan of Brunei, Bolkiah has been awarded honorary degrees from universities in Russia, Indonesia, the United Kingdom, Thai-

ISTANA NURUL IMAN

Istana Nurul Iman, Palace of the Light of Faith, is the world's largest palace. It is the official residence of Sultan Hassanal Bolkiah, the ruler of Brunei, and is located on the Brunei River south of the nation's capital, Bandar Seri Begawan. Philippine architect Leandro V. Locsin designed the structure and it was built by a Philippine company, Ayala International. Construction began in 1984 at an estimated cost of $1.4 billion.

Istana Nural Iman contains 788 rooms, 257 bathrooms, 5 swimming pools, an air-conditioned stable for 200 polo ponies, a 110-car garage, a banquet hall that accommodates 4,000 guests, and mosques for 1,500 worshipers. The residence also features 564 chandeliers, 44 stairwells, and 18 elevators. The exterior is decorated with Islamic and Malay motifs of pointed arches, latticework, arabesque and pierced screens, and intricate geometric designs, and the building is topped by twenty-two-carat golden domes and vaulted roofs. Stylized flower motifs are visible in the handwoven carpets throughout the palace and in the glass mosaics. The interior of the building was constructed from native hardwoods, Moroccan red onyx, and an estimated sixteen acres of marble. Istana Nurul Iman's waterfront location gives the palace the appearance of literally floating along the horizon.

In addition to being the residence for the royal family, Istana Nurul Iman is the seat of Brunei's government, housing the prime minister's office, a throne room large enough for two thousand occupants, and rooms for state functions and official audiences with Sultan Bolkiah. The structure measures almost 2.2 million square feet, making it the largest palace in the world, bigger than the Royal Palace in Madrid (almost 1.5 million square feet), Great Britain's Buckingham Palace (828,818 square feet), and France's Palace of Versailles (551,218 square feet). Istana Nurul Iman Palace is closed to the public, except for the annual Islamic celebration of Hari Raya Idulfitri (the festival at the end of the Muslim fasting month), when approximately 110,000 visitors are invited during a three-day period.

---

under martial law in 1962, the same year the nation's legislative council was dissolved. Bolkiah reconstituted the legislative council in 2004. Two years later, he changed Brunei's constitution to make him legally infallible. The sultan also holds the government positions of prime minister, minister of defense, and minister of finance.

Brunei's population numbers approximately 225,000 residents. Using some of his nation's oil and natural gas profits, which amount to billions of dollars each year, Bolkiah initiated projects aimed at improving the quality of Bruneians' lives. Education is free from preschool through college, and citizens receive free medical care. Home and auto loan interest rates are considered modest, there is no income tax, and generous pensions are provided. In 2008, the International Monetary Fund ranked Bruneians as having incomes averaging $50,117 annually—the fifth highest income in the world, behind Qatar, Luxembourg, Norway, and Singapore. Oil and natural gas reserves are expected to continue to bring wealth to Brunei well into the twenty-first century. In 1983, the sultan established the Brunei Investment Agency, which invests in foreign oil and natural gas reserves and has holdings in corporations, real estate, and currencies.

land, and Singapore. His father, Sultan Omar, bestowed the title of crown prince on Bolkiah in 1961. Sultan Omar abdicated in 1967, elevating Bolkiah to the position of sultan. By 2009, Bolkiah, who had been married three times, had two wives and was the father of twelve children.

FIRST VENTURES

Brunei's economic wealth is based on its extensive reserves of oil and natural gas. The country's royal family has ruled for more than five hundred years, providing national stability. From 1888 to 1984, Brunei was a British protectorate, and the sultanate was allowed to manage the nation's economic resources for domestic consumption. The Brunei constitution of 1959 gave the sultan full executive authority to run the country. Brunei was placed

MATURE WEALTH

In the early twenty-first century, Brunei was the fourth largest oil producer in Southeast Asia and the ninth largest exporter of natural gas in the world. Brunei Shell Petroleum, co-owned by the nation of Brunei and Royal Dutch Shell Corporation, is the country's major oil and natural gas production company. A division of this corporation liquefies the majority of the nation's natural gas and sells it to Japan. About 67 percent of Brunei's crude oil is consumed by Australia, Indonesia, and Korea, and Japan and China are also major purchasers. Mitsubishi, Royal Dutch Shell, and the Brunei government collectively invest in a number of international projects with natural gas revenue.

There is no clearly defined distinction between Brunei's revenues and those appropriated by the sultan and the royal family. The sultan has been annually listed by *Forbes* magazine as one of the richest men in the world. The sultanate's revenues permitted construction of the world's largest palace in Brunei's capital city, Bandar Seri Begawan. Bolkiah's wealth also enabled him to purchase the Dorchester Hotel in London and shopping centers and hotels in Singapore. He expanded the runway at Brunei International Airport, making it the longest runway in the world. In 1996, the Dorchester and a group of other luxury hotels, including properties in Beverly Hills, California, Paris, and Milan, Italy, became part of the newly created Dorchester Collection. Bolkiah's other business enterprises include the Nudhar Corporation, which owns an 18 percent stake in Patersons Securities, and the Bahagia Investment Corporation, a Malaysian company that invests in real estate.

In 2002, the Brunei government began developing the nation as an international financial center with an emphasis on Islamic banking. The country is also promoting ecotourism, building a cyberpark that will be used to develop an information technology industry, and is assisting small and medium-sized businesses. These enterprises aim to diversify Brunei's economy and make it less dependent on fluctuating oil and natural gas prices and on the nation's diminishing oil and gas reserves.

LEGACY

Much publicity about Bolkiah centers on speculation about his personal wealth and the purchases made by him and other members of the royal family. In 2007, *Forbes* ranked the sultan of Brunei as the world's richest man, with his wealth estimated at $22 billion, and the sultan spends his wealth extravagantly. Photographs of the royal family display members wearing expensive jewelry and carrying symbols of office covered in gold and precious stones.

The sultan is reputed to have amassed one of the largest automobile collections in the world, with between three and six thousand cars worth more than $4 billion. The collection focuses on the purchase of unique and unusual concept cars. *Guinness World Records* estimated that Bolkiah owns five hundred Rolls-Royces, including the last Rolls-Royce Phantom VI, made in 1992. The British newspaper *Daily Mirror* reported in 2007 that the sultan owned 551 Mercedes-Benzes, 367 Ferraris, 362

Bentleys, 185 BMWs, 177 Jaguars, 160 Porsches, 130 Rolls-Royces, and 20 Lamborghinis.

The sultan's private plane, a Boeing 747-400, cost an estimated $233 million, including $3 million in gold-plated furniture. Bolkiah also owns more than two hundred polo ponies transported on Royal Brunei Airlines, the national carrier that he created. In 1997, he purchased a red diamond weighing less than one carat for more than $800,000.

In the first decade of the twenty-first century, however, his wealth was believed to be compromised by his younger brother Prince Jefri Bolkiah, who used revenues from the Brunei Investment Agency to invest in business ventures that eventually failed. The sultan initially accused Prince Jefri of embezzling $15.4 billion from the authority, but the sultan later dropped these charges.

—*William A. Paquette*

FURTHER READING

Chalfont, Arthur Gwynne Jones. *By God's Will*. New York: Weidenfeld and Nicolson, 1989. The first major biography in English on the life of Sultan Hassanal Bolkiah, chronicling how he led the country to become independent from Great Britain.

Kershaw, Roger. *Monarchy in South East Asia: The Faces of Tradition in Transition*. London: Routledge, 2001. Examines the history and contemporary role of Southeast Asian monarchies in Cambodia, Thailand, Malaysia, Brunei, Indonesia, and Laos.

Majid, Harun Abdul. *Rebellion in Brunei: The 1962 Revolt, Imperialism, Confrontation, and Oil*. London: I. B. Tauris, 2007. Recounts how British intervention during the revolt prevented Brunei from coming under the influence of Chinese Communism.

Saunders, Graham E. *A History of Brunei*. London: Routledge Curzon, 2002. An excellent survey of Brunei history from its colonial era under a British protectorate to independence.

World Political Leaders Library. *Brunei: Sultan Haji Hassanal Bolkiah Muizzaddin Waddaulah*. Washington, D.C.: International Business, 2008. An English-language biography.

See also: Al-Waleed bin Talal; Elizabeth II.

ORLANDO BONSIGNORI
Italian banker and merchant

Bonsignori and his brother inherited from their father a thriving banking and wool trade concern. Under Bonsignori's direction, the firm expanded and adopted the name Gran Tavola. Numerous factors (agents) represented Gran Tavola from England to the Balkans, and the firm conducted business with the Papacy. At Bonsignori's death, Gran Tavola was unrivaled among Sienese firms, but its vulnerabilities would lead to its ultimate demise.

Born: c. 1210; place unknown
Died: c. 1273; place unknown
Sources of wealth: Banking; trade
Bequeathal of wealth: Unknown

EARLY LIFE

Orlando Bonsignori (Ohr-LAHN-doh Bohn-see-nyor-ee) was born in the early thirteenth century to Bonsignore di Bernardo, a small-time merchant in the city-state of Siena, whose name in its Latin genitive form became the family surname. Very little is known of the family's history or that of Bonsignori himself until he entered the family business on his own. Family records for much of this period no longer exist, and public records regarding members of the merchant class in Siena are scant, except regarding their participation in civic activities. The medieval *Cronaca senese* (chronicle of Siena) ascribes the founding of the Bonsignori *società* (company) to the year 1209, and it would have been around this time that Orlando was born. He most probably would have worked in the family business alongside his brother Bonifazio, accumulating connections, capital, and experience. One of the family's activities included a share in collecting the customs duty for salt entering Siena and Grosseto, and another was small-scale banking on behalf of the Papacy in Rome.

FIRST VENTURES

The earliest mention of Orlando Bonsignori appears in Siena's tax records for 1229. His very low civic tax liabilities then and in the 1230's indicate that he had yet to emerge among Siena's major business figures. His emergence as an important businessman remains shrouded, but it seems clear that he and his brother Bonifazio superseded their father and quickly entered the thirteenth century world of international finance. The keys to the brothers' success appear to be their family solidarity and papal banking connections. Along with several other merchants from Siena, the two brothers are mentioned in papal registers from 1235.

MATURE WEALTH

The Papacy had been a major financial player in Italy and throughout Western Europe. Beginning around 1233, the Piccolomini *società*, headed by Angeliero Solafico, served as the papal depository. These bankers loaned the popes cash to meet their immediate needs wherever these financiers and the Papacy shared business interests. The popes also received infusions of cash from local papal collectors, holding it for use locally or for transfer when needed. The greater the bankers' capitalization, the greater their use to the Papacy.

The Bonsignori brothers began working with the popes through the Bonsignori company under Pope Gregory IX. Bonifazio represented the family business, as well as the city of Siena, at the papal court, while Orlando remained in Siena, managing the efforts of partners and agents who operated in an ever-widening geographic circle. The brothers' business expanded under Pope Innocent IV, earning them special treatment, papal protection, and the court title *familiares nostri* (members of our household). The pope's support was a useful means for the Bonsignori brothers to pressure other debtors to repay their loans.

Pope Alexander IV was engaged in an active struggle with the Hohenstaufen heirs of Emperor Frederick II, and he made much greater demands on the Bonsignori bankers than his predecessors. With Bonifazio's death in 1255 and the restructuring of the firm, Orlando organized the Gran Tavola dei Bonsignori, or "great table of the Bonsignori." The word "table" is equivalent to the Italian *banca*, meaning bench, and was meant to indicate a much grander financial structure than the Bonsignori family had previously operated.

By this time, Bonsignori's firm had reached a high point in its fortunes as a merchant banking company, and it had done so in partnership with members of other entrepreneurial clans. By expanding his partners while maintaining control of the business, Bonsignori controlled a much larger capital base from which to make loans. The Gran Tavola was the largest banking operation in thirteenth century Siena and one of the greatest of its day throughout Europe. It remained in operation until it went bankrupt in 1298.

In 1260, Pope Alexander IV placed an interdict (a communal excommunication) on Siena, which sided with the Ghibellines, a political faction that supported the Hohenstaufen rulers of the Holy Roman Empire against the pope. At the time, Siena was battling the Guelphs, the pope's supporters in his conflict with the Hohenstaufen heirs, in Florence; Bonsignori, whose civic obligations included seven cavalrymen (*cavallata*), was serving in Siena's army. Pope Urban IV confirmed the interdiction against Siena in 1262, but he specifically exempted the Bonsignori family and their Gran Tavola. This papal action forbade observant Christians from repaying loans or debts held by other Sienese companies, which left the Bonsignori firm in the unique position of continuing to conduct business when other Sienese bankers could not.

However, papal banking was only one facet of Bonsignori's commercial activity. Although he generally acted as his company's principal, he usually represented a consortium of merchants or bankers, but since none of their commercial records survives it is impossible to know his investments and profits. In 1253, he gained partial control over the silver mines at Montieri near Volterra, and he probably participated in the cloth trade between central Italy and the annual fairs in Champagne, France. As a banker he served King Henry III of England at least sporadically from 1249; another of his customers was the abbot of Saint-Germain-des-Prés, France, whose

---

GRAN TAVOLA

After the death of his brother Bonifazio and with increased papal demands for money, Orlando Bonsignori restructured and expanded his Siena-based banking concern, founding the Gran Tavola dei Bonsignori in 1255. Bonsignori's hold over papal finances grew ever tighter during the 1260's, gaining the Gran Tavola a near monopoly on papal business transactions.

By 1260, the Sienese civil government and many of its citizens had developed strong Ghibelline political affiliations, supporting the Hohenstaufen Dynasty in its battle with the Papacy, which was supported by the Guelphs. Bonsignori sided with the Ghibellines, but he continued to conduct business with the Papacy, and the Papacy overlooked Siena's ties to the Ghibellines. In 1265, Bonsignori repaid this papal support by agreeing with Pope Clement IV to form a *società* (company), which included himself and twenty-six other merchants. This newly created business collected 200,000 lire for the support of Charles of Anjou's efforts to drive Manfred Hohenstaufen from Italy.

Bonsignori continued to control the Gran Tavola until his death around 1273, though with his absence from Siena from 1270 to 1273 the organization began to unravel. His son Fazio d'Orlando and nephew Niccolò di Bonifazio took over some of his functions, but nonfamily members gained control and the Gran Tavola entered a long period of decline. In the late 1280's and early 1290's, the Gran Tavola still played a major part in papal finance, but its role was dwindling, and the Bonsignori family's participation in the company was similarly fading. In 1289, a reorganization resulted in a *società* of five Bonsignoris and eighteen outsiders, with capital of 35,000 gold florins; the balance of power shifted even further away from Bonsignori control in 1292. Disagreements over leadership, decision making, and re-source allocation, as well as distrust, weakened the firm internally, and outsiders spread rumors that further crippled the company. Rising competition from Florentine bankers, lack of cooperation from the aggressive King Philip the Fair of France, dwindling papal support, and Sienese Guelphs' disaffection with the essentially Ghibelline firm undermined the Gran Tavola's effectiveness.

On August 9, 1298, most of the Gran Tavola's partners who were not Bonsignoris petitioned the Sienese government to protect their assets and delay the payments they owed to Siena. Their assets were scattered all over Europe, and additional time could help them meet their fiscal obligations. Panic set in and demands for restitution intensified. A blue-ribbon panel was formed to decide the Gran Tavola's fate, and the result was the termination of the firm's charter.

In 1302, Sienese officials began an investigation into members' assets, all of which, excluding their wives' dowries, were liquidated to pay creditors. In 1307, the Sienese effort was renewed; in 1308, the French king published his claims that the firm owed him 54,000 *livres tourneois* and jailed Sienese merchants in France as hostages. This led to a general undermining of Sienese fortunes and the collapse of several other Sienese companies, including the Malavolti, Squarcialupi, and Tolomei firms, during the following decade.

During the liquidation of the Gran Tavola, the Papacy claimed a loss of 80,000 florins, restitution of which it sought in 1345 at a time when Florentine banking firms, such as the Bardi and Peruzzi companies, were failing dramatically. A papal interdict placed on Siena resulted in negotiations and an agreement from remaining Bonsignori family members to pay 16,000 florins to the Papal Curia during a thirteen-year period, an obligation the family met.

---

association with Gran Tavola began in 1250. Good service resulted in success, and both laymen and ecclesiastics who needed cash transacted business with Bonsignori.

In dealing with the pope, Bonsignori could hold funds in deposit, exchange currencies (of which there were scores at the time), transfer funds from deposit to creditors, and make loans in a variety of currencies. Each of these transactions produced income for the Gran Tavola. However, the business experienced risk when its customers did not repay their loans. In the late 1260's, Bonsignori money simultaneously funded both Charles of Anjou, a Guelph supporter, and Henry of Castille, a Ghibelline backer. Bonsignori also invested in land, most of which was located in the vicinity of Sant'Angelo in Colle, Italy, and was worked by peasants through a form of sharecropping.

In 1270, Bonsignori lent money to help Charles of Anjou beat his imperial rival and secure Siena for the Guelphs. Bonsignori, who supported the Ghibellines, and his family fled Siena, overseeing a kind of government in exile in Cortona. This exile severely stressed the Gran Tavola, which continued to operate from Siena. Bonsignori died circa 1273, survived by his wife Imiglia and their seven children.

LEGACY

The Gran Tavola began to decline after Bonsignori's death. In his lifetime, however, his vision, organizational skills, and charisma enabled him to secure a place among Italian merchant bankers and eventually to dominate this occupation. He was able to separate his strongly held political beliefs from his professional activities, as evidenced by his financial support for the Guelphs despite his political support for the Ghibellines. He used his wealth to benefit Siena, providing aid to a local hospital, paying hefty taxes, offering thousands of dollars in loans, and helping the local economy by remaining solvent when the rest of Siena was under papal interdict.

—Joseph P. Byrne

FURTHER READING

English, Edward D. *Enterprise and Liability in Sienese Banking, 1230-1350.* Cambridge, Mass.: Harvard University Press, 1988. Elaboration of the author's doctoral dissertation with special attention to the Bonsignori family. The chapters "Papal Banking and Politics" and "The Bonsignori and European Banking" provide information on the period of Orlando Bonsignori's administration, while "The Failure of the Bonsignori" chronicles the fall of the Gran Tavola.

Housley, Norman. *The Papal Angevin Alliance and the Crusades Against Christian Lay Powers, 1264-1343.* New York: Oxford University Press, 1982. Outlines the major role played by the Gran Tavola in the early stages of the Papacy's support for the aspirations of Charles of Anjou against the Hohenstaufens, especially in the 1260's. Based largely on Pope Clement IV's letters.

Lunt, William E. *Papal Revenues in the Middle Ages.* 2 vols. New York: Octagon Books, 1965. Although dated, this remains a classic study of the fiscal roles played by the Bonsignori bankers and the Gran Tavola for the various popes, drawn from papal registers and other documents.

Waley, Daniel. *Siena and the Sienese in the Thirteenth Century.* New York: Cambridge University Press, 1991. General overview of the Sienese state and culture that depicts the city-state as typical of other places in medieval Italy. Bonsignori is discussed sporadically as an atypical member of society.

See also: Ridolfo de' Bardi; Agostino Chigi; Francesco Datini; Giovanni de' Medici; Lorenzo de' Medici; Jacopo de' Pazzi; Filippo di Peruzzi.

SCIPIONE BORGHESE
Italian cardinal and art patron

Borghese used his position as Pope Paul V's assistant cardinal and the pope's nephew to acquire the finest art and to restore some of the most exquisite monuments in Rome. The paintings, sculptures, and architecture he commissioned remain some of the best examples of Italian Renaissance art in the world.

Born: 1576; Rome (now in Italy)
Died: October 2, 1633; Rome
Also known as: Scipione Caffarelli (birth name)
Sources of wealth: Inheritance; real estate; church
Bequeathal of wealth: Relatives; artistic patronage; museum

EARLY LIFE
Scipione Borghese (shih-pee-OH-neh bohr-GAY-zeh) was born Scipione Caffarelli, the son of Marcantonio Caffarelli and Ortensia Borghese, sister of Pope Paul V. He attended Collegio Romano in Rome and the University of Perugia, taking degrees in philosophy and law. In 1605, his uncle, the pope, made him a cardinal and granted him permission to use the Borghese name and coat of arms. The young cardinal has been described as having a jovial personality; he was apparently much more outgoing and sociable than his rather stern uncle.

FIRST VENTURES
Borghese benefited immensely from his uncle's nepotism. He occupied many prominent positions in the Roman Catholic Church, including archbishop of Bologna, superintendent *negotiorum sanctae sedis*, prefect of the Tribunal of the Apostolic Signature of Grace, librarian of the Holy Roman Church, protector of Loreto, archpriest of the Lateran Basilica, and *camerlengo* (chamberlain) of the Sacred College of Cardinals. For each office, Borghese accrued revenues through salaries, papal taxes and fees, and gifts. His annual income in 1616 was about 160,000 scudi (a single scudo was equivalent to about 3.5 grams of gold).

He invested in valuable land around Rome, especially in the Alban Hills. In the first part of his career, Borghese commissioned several renovations of religious buildings. His restorations of the St. Andrew and St. Sylvia Chapels near San Gregorio Magno al Celio in Rome are early examples of the ecclesiastical works he sponsored.

MATURE WEALTH
Borghese used part of his wealth to make a name for himself as a preserver of Rome's glory. His religious archi-

tectural projects included the restoration of the San Sebastiano basilica and reconstruction of the San Crisogono church. His secular projects included the renovation and expansion of the Palazzo Borghese and the Villa Borghese. Borghese's gardens were beautiful—canopies of greenery with vineyards, wooded areas, and formal arrangements of flowers. These important projects, however, pale in comparison to Borghese's art collection.

Borghese collected antiquities as well as contemporary art. His collection included artworks by Caravaggio, Raphael, Perugino, Guido Reni, Peter Paul Rubens, and Titian. Borghese acquired a reputation for being ruthless in his efforts to acquire artworks. For example, a painting by Raphael disappeared from a church in Perugia and somehow ended up in Borghese's collection. In another instance, Borghese imprisoned the painter Domenichino for refusing to sell him a painting already promised to another cardinal. Borghese eventually got the painting he desired.

Borghese, however, recognized and supported artistic genius. His early patronage of the sculptor Gian Lorenzo Bernini launched that artist's stellar career. Just before Borghese's death, Bernini captured the rounded face of his patron in bronze twice. These busts were later displayed in the Galleria Borghese. Borghese continued to lavish his wealth on art, religious building restorations, and improvements to his magnificent villas until his death in Rome in 1633. He was buried in Santa Maria Maggiore.

LEGACY
In some ways, Scipione Borghese was a typical cardinal nephew of a Renaissance pope: a recipient of unearned wealth, who had to deal with the jumble of business, government, and politics that characterized life in the Papal States. Borghese stands out, however, because of the extraordinary art collection he left behind. After the death of his uncle Pope Paul V in 1621, Borghese moved to the Palazzo Borghese, where he relocated most of his paintings, creating the Galleria Terrena. His sculptures were housed at the Casino Borghese, a museum on the property of the Villa Borghese that was established for his statuary.

Seventeenth century Italian art flourished because of Borghese's largesse. He preserved precious religious architecture and antiquities. His unique style, which was evident in his homes and gardens, could be said to have helped launch an entirely new form of artistic expression—the Roman Baroque.

—*Janet M. Ball*

FURTHER READING
Magnuson, Torgil. *Rome in the Age of Bernini.* Vol. 1. Stockholm, Sweden: Almquist and Wiksell, 1982.

Morrissey, Jake. *The Genius in the Design: Bernini, Borromini, and the Rivalry That Transformed Rome.* New York: William Morrow, 2005.

Paul, Carole. *The Borghese Collections and the Display of Art in the Age of the Grand Tour.* Burlington, Vt.: Ashgate, 2008.

See also: Alexander VI; Lorenzo de' Medici.

JOHN BOUVIER
American investor, stockbroker, and socialite

One of the heirs to the Bouvier fortune, John Bouvier augmented his wealth with a seat on the New York Stock Exchange. Living in an apartment building in New York known for its wealthy residents and highlighting the city's social scene, "Black Jack" imparted his sense of style to his daughters, Jacqueline Kennedy Onassis and Lee Radziwill.

Born: May 19, 1891; East Hampton, New York
Died: August 3, 1957; New York, New York
Also known as: John Vernou Bouvier III; Black Jack Bouvier
Sources of wealth: Inheritance; financial services
Bequeathal of wealth: Children; dissipated

EARLY LIFE
The Bouvier fortune was established by Michel Bouvier, a French émigré who arrived in Philadelphia in 1815 following Napoleon I's defeat at Waterloo. Owning furniture factories, speculating in land and construction, and becoming rich from his interests in coal mines, Bouvier died in 1872 with a fortune equivalent to about $30 million in 2010. This fortune was multiplied several times by his son, Michel Charles Bouvier. John Vernou Bouvier (BOO-vyay-ay) III was Michel's great-grandson, born to John Vernou Bouvier, Jr., and his wife, Maud Frances (née Sergeant) Bouvier.

Young John was raised on the Bouvier country estate, Woodcraft, in Nutley, New Jersey. He had a younger brother, William, and three younger sisters, Edith and the twins Michelle and Maud. John attended the Morristown School and Philips Academy Exeter before enrolling at Yale University. Cole Porter was a classmate, and Bouvier and Porter sang together in the Yale Glee Club, becoming lifelong friends. Upon graduation, Bouvier became a stockbroker on Wall Street, where he earned the nickname "Black Jack" for his perpetual tan, debonair airs, and sense of derring-do. The handsome Bouvier was often noted for his resemblance to the actor Clark Gable. Bouvier served briefly in the army during World War I.

FIRST VENTURES
In 1922, Bouvier bought a seat on the New York Stock Exchange for $115,000 (equal to about $2 million in 2010), and he founded his own Wall Street firm. His firm was profitable and he became a man-about-town, touring New York City in a chauffeured Lincoln Zephyr motorcar. He was a highlight of New York high society, known for keeping a stable of racehorses, throwing lavish parties, and dating attractive women. He flew up and down the East Coast in a private jet to attend swanky events. On July 7, 1928, Bouvier married Janet Norton Lee. Their daughter, Jacqueline Lee, was born on July 28, 1929. With the stock market at an all-time high, Bouvier's profits from his brokerage firm approached $1 million a year. A second daughter, Caroline Lee, was born on March 3, 1933.

Bouvier was at first hardly affected by the stock market crash on Black Tuesday, October 29, 1929, because he had sold short about $100,000 worth of securities in order to profit if stock prices declined. In 1932, the Bouviers moved into an eighteen-room duplex apartment at 740 Park Avenue, in a building built and owned by Bouvier's wealthy father-in-law, James Lee. The imposing, nineteen-story, limestone-clad structure, located on Park Avenue between Seventy-first and Seventy-second Streets, was the most extravagant apartment building in New York City. All of the apartments were at least two floors tall and contained every modern convenience. In his apartment, Bouvier added gold plating to the bathrooms and wood paneling to the common rooms. A room of his apartment was converted into a small gym so he could maintain his trim physique.

In addition to their Manhattan apartment, John and Janet resided in the Bouvier family country estates, Lasata and Wildmoor, in exclusive East Hampton, New York, where they were waited upon by a small army of servants, nannies, maids, chauffeurs, and cooks. They dined in New York's finest restaurants, such as Longchamps and La Rue. Bouvier's horse stable continued to grow, and he introduced his daughters, known as Jackie and Lee, to the sport of horseback riding, taking them on jaunts through Central Park. Bouvier was a prominent member of New York's exclusive Maidstone, Yale, and Racquet Clubs, and he had a Stutz touring car custombuilt for his leisure. Jackie and Lee enjoyed a privileged lifestyle, traveling in Bouvier's four chauffeured limousines, attending society affairs, and being indulged by their father, who doted on them.

MATURE WEALTH

In 1933, Bouvier earned $2 million in the stock market (about $24 million in 2010). However, as the Great Depression ground on and the stock market continued to plunge, Bouvier lost this amount and much more. When his grandfather died in 1935, leaving an estate worth $1.65 million, Bouvier was distressed that his father, John Bouvier, Jr., inherited the bulk of the estate, while Bouvier himself received only a small bequest. By 1936, Bouvier's net worth had plummeted to $100,000. To support his lavish lifestyle, he had to borrow money from his father and father-in-law. However, his extravagance soon got the better of him. As a result of his womanizing, he and Janet separated in 1936. By 1939, the separation had become bitter, with John claiming that Janet abused their daughters by spanking them and Janet hiring a detective

John Bouvier walks alongside his daughter Jacqueline while she is riding horseback. (©Bettmann/CORBIS)

740 PARK AVENUE: THE WORLD'S RICHEST APARTMENT BUILDING

Apartment buildings are usually not associated with the very wealthy; in fact, these buildings originated as tenements for the poor. However, throughout the world there are some apartment buildings that are synonymous with wealth. For example, the Naseef building in Riyadh, Saudi Arabia, constructed by the wealthy merchant Omar Naseef in 1882, contained more than one hundred apartments and rooms for his extended family. For a century, the tree in front of the building was the only tree in Riyadh, which exemplifies the building's prestige and status. The Albert Hall Mansions, built in London in the 1880's, were the most fashionable British apartments for decades.

The Manhattan borough of New York City has long been the site of beautiful apartment buildings designed by some of the nation's leading architects. For example, the stately Dakota building is a National Historic Landmark. However, the apartment house at 740 Park Avenue, highlighted in a 2007 "biography of a building," has earned renown for being the "world's richest apartment building." Its residents are a microcosm of wealthy American society, and the building, like many dense living quarters, has been the site of friendships, jealousies, gossip, love affairs, and rivalries, all of which were magnified by the wealth of its inhabitants.

The 740 Park Avenue building, constructed just before the stock market crash of 1929, was designed to be the most luxurious dwelling on tree-lined Park Avenue. Nicknamed "Croesus's Sixty Acres," Park Avenue in the 1920's was the residence of the world's largest concentration of millionaires, and the street had an aggregate wealth of $3 billion. The building at 740 Park Avenue would become known to

some as "Plutocrats Palace." Its builder and owner, James Lee, was John Bouvier's father-in-law, and its architect was Rosario Candela, the city's leading apartment designer. The nineteen-story building was clad in expensive Indiana limestone.

The building is a cooperative, in which residents buy shares in their apartments. The building is actually a series of mansions, built vertically rather than horizontally. It contains thirty-one apartments, and each apartment is a duplex or triplex, with interior staircases, marble floors, fireplaces, servants' quarters, libraries, loggias, spacious rooms with twelve-foot ceilings, and ample sunlight.

John Bouvier and his family were among the first residents of the building. John D. Rockefeller, Jr., moved there in 1936. Other wealthy residents over the years included liquor company magnate Edgar Bronfman, Sr.; businessman Ronald Lauder; financier and investor Henry Kravis; Marshall Field III, a scion of the wealthy retailing family; investor Ronald Perelman and his former wife Faith Golding; bridal gown designer Vera Wang; Irene Guggenheim of the Guggenheim family; J. Watson Webb, a film editor and heir; heiress Flora Whiting; several Vanderbilts and Chryslers; Greek shipping tycoon Stavros Niarchos; Ecuadoran "Banana King" Luis Noboa and his wife Mercedes; and Steven J. Ross, former chief executive officer of Time Warner, and his former wife Courtney. Billionaire industrialist David H. Koch purchased an apartment for $17 million. In 2000, businessman Stephen A. Schwarzman paid $37 million for artist Saul Steinberg's thirty-four-room triplex. In 2008, Courtney Ross sold her apartment for $60 million.

---

to document John's extramarital affairs. On July 22, 1940, Janet was granted a divorce on the grounds of adultery.

Bouvier was again disappointed when his father died in 1948. John Bouvier, Jr., had inherited the bulk of the Bouvier fortune but had consumed it as the patriarch of the Bouvier dynasty, incurring huge expenses for his Manhattan, New Jersey, and Long Island estates and paying for his often extravagant children. Bouvier did inherit more than $100,000 from his father, as well as a release from the debts he owed the estate. However, he realized that his opportunity to acquire the kind of fortune that was being accumulated by another Catholic American investor—Joseph P. Kennedy, whom the Bouviers regarded with some disdain—had been lost.

For a man whose life had begun with great promise, Bouvier's latter years were marked by a certain pathos.

His considerable fortune was overshadowed by his even more considerable expenses. When his former wife Janet remarried into the wealthy Auchincloss family, Bouvier began vacationing in Cuba, forsaking his former Long Island haunts. He drank heavily; he was so intoxicated on the day in 1953 on which his daughter Jacqueline married Senator John F. Kennedy of Massachusetts that he failed to make it to the wedding ceremony, even though he had been scheduled to give his daughter away in marriage. However, upon returning to bachelor life, Black Jack maintained his sense of style. He was well known in New York society for his exquisitely tailored clothes, dressing glamorously in expensive, buttoned-down shirts from Brooks Brothers with club ties from F. R. Tripler & Co., polished black shoes, and suit jackets sporting silk handkerchiefs. In wintry weather, he donned double-breasted overcoats and black homburg hats. He dined in

New York's finest restaurants with his young paramours, and he haunted the Polo Bar of the Westbury Hotel, looking for new conquests. In 1955, he sold his seat on the New York Stock Exchange for $60,000, equal to about $700,000 in 2010. He died two years later.

LEGACY

The Bouviers were the first Catholic family of wealth and distinction to enter New York high society. The Bouvier fortune was considerable, but it did not survive John Bouvier, Jr., illustrating the famous American adage about the rise and fall of dynastic wealth going "from shirt sleeves to shirt sleeves in three generations." Neither John Bouvier III's inheritance nor his Wall Street profits were enough to sustain his magnificent lifestyle. Although he lacked the substance of great wealth, Bouvier certainly possessed an abundance of its accoutrements. Handsome and debonair, he illuminated high society in Manhattan and the Hamptons. He was known for his immaculate dress, insouciance, manly glamour, luxury apartments, horses, gambling, soirees, fine dining, and liquor. His romantic adventures were legendary.

By itself, all this would only make him a charming rake of little historical significance. However, by all accounts he passed on his style, charm, and charisma to his two daughters, Jackie and Lee. Lee married Prince Stanislas Radziwill of the Polish royal family. Jacqueline's husband became the forty-first president of the United States, tragically assassinated by Lee Harvey Oswald in 1963. As First Lady, Jacqueline was widely admired for her panache, style, and elegance, inherited from her father. Although John did not have much of the Bouvier fortune with which to enrich his daughters, his daughter Jacqueline was associated with several other historic fortunes—those of her stepfather Hugh D. Auchincloss, Jr., the Kennedy family, and her second husband, Greek shipping tycoon Aristotle Onassis.

—*Howard Bromberg*

FURTHER READING

Bouvier, Kathleen. *Black Jack Bouvier: The Life and Times of Jackie O's Father.* New York: Pinnacle Books, 1979. An intimate and admiring biography of Bouvier written by his niece by marriage. Captures his rakish charm and elegance.

Bradford, Sarah. *America's Queen: A Life of Jacqueline Kennedy Onassis.* New York: Viking, 2000. Well-researched biography, recounting Bouvier's glamorous style and amoral approach to marital fidelity, as well as Jacqueline Kennedy's admiration for her father.

Davis, John. *The Bouviers: From Waterloo to the Kennedys and Beyond.* Washington, D.C.: National Press Books, 1993. Written by another member of the extended Bouvier family, who has written books about other families of great wealth, such as the Guggenheims.

_____. *Jacqueline Bouvier: An Intimate Memoir.* New York: John Wiley and Sons, 1996. With inside knowledge of the Bouvier family, Davis, a cousin of Jacqueline Kennedy, describes how much she was influenced by her father, John Bouvier.

Gross, Michael. *740 Park Avenue: The Story of the World's Richest Apartment Building.* New York: Broadway Books, 2005. Social history of the apartment building constructed by John Bouvier's father-in-law, in which Bouvier and other wealthy New Yorkers resided.

Pottker, Jan. *Janet and Jackie: The Story of a Mother and Her Daughter, Jacqueline Kennedy Onassis.* New York: St. Martin's Press, 2001. Emphasizes the role of Janet Lee in the life of her daughter, Jacqueline Kennedy, with insightful comments on the marriage of Janet and John Bouvier.

Samuel, Larry. *Rich: The Rise and Fall of American Wealth Culture.* New York: Amacom, 2009. Entertaining sociology of the very wealthy. Describes Park Avenue in the 1920's as the premier residential street of New York's elite. Provides an extensive bibliography on America's wealthy class.

See also: Brooke Astor; Clarence Dillon; Doris Duke; Joseph P. Kennedy; Charles E. Merrill; Consuelo Vanderbilt.

ANTHONY N. BRADY
American investor, contractor, and utility magnate

Brady owned public utilities and street railway and other transportation systems, and he was a major investor. He was a primary stockholder, director, and president of more than fifty corporations, including American Tobacco, Brooklyn Rapid Transit, and Standard Oil.

Born: August 22, 1843; Lille, Norde, France
Died: July 22, 1913; London, England
Also known as: Anthony Nicholas Brady
Sources of wealth: Utilities; transportation systems; investments
Bequeathal of wealth: Relatives; charity

EARLY LIFE
Anthony Nicholas Brady was born in Lille, Norde, France, on August 22, 1843. He moved with his parents to Troy, New York, in 1857, and he received his elementary school education there. Brady expressed no inclination to pursue higher education, which his parents probably could not have afforded. Instead, he was attracted to business ventures, and at age fifteen he began working in the barbershop of the Delavan House Hotel in Albany, New York.

FIRST VENTURES
When he was nineteen, Brady started a tea store and opened branches in Troy, Albany, and New York City. These shops were one of the first examples of a chain store operation in America, although some called his enterprise a monopoly. Because Brady's profits from the tea stores were relatively small, he pursued other business ventures to generate additional income.

Brady became interested in construction in New York State, and he began contracting to build sewers, pavements, and other public improvements. He even purchased granite quarries to furnish materials for his contracts. He later was the Chicago contractor for the Manhattan Oil Company of Lima, Ohio. Brady also became interested in public utilities. He eventually took control of the Albany Gas Light Company, and with some investors he bought gas plants in Troy and Chicago.

MATURE WEALTH
As his income grew, Brady purchased traction (transportation) lines in Providence, Rhode Island. Eventually, he began focusing his business ventures on New York City,

which seemed the most promising area for his commercial activities. In 1887, he helped reorganize the Brooklyn Rapid Transit Company (later the Brooklyn Manhattan Transit Company), and he served as chairman of the company's board of directors for twenty-six years. In 1912, he was influential in expanding Brooklyn Rapid Transit to include both the Coney Island and Brooklyn lines, strengthening his control of the city's public transportation system. Brady also purchased street railways in Washington, D.C., and Philadelphia, and he extended his interests in public electric utilities, notably the New York Edison Company.

Brady was a major stockholder in some fifty corporations, including Standard Oil Company. He also was president of New York Gas and a director of Westinghouse Electric Company, American Tobacco Company, U. S. Rubber, United States Cast Iron Pipe and Foundry, two mining companies, Union Carbide and Carbon Corporation, Mohawk-Hudson Power Corporation, and dozens of power and light companies in New York State and in Japan.

LEGACY
Brady died in July, 1913, and left his $85 million estate to his family, including his sons James Cox Brady and Nicholas Frederic Brady, who managed their father's wealth. Nine months before his death, two of his seven children—Flora Brady Gavit and Mary Brady Tucker—and the wife of his son James died in a transit accident in Connecticut. As a result, Brady's estate created the Anthony N. Brady Memorial Medals. In 1914, the American Museum of Safety presented the first of these annual awards to the American electric street railway that made the greatest contributions to accident prevention and industrial hygiene. Brady's heirs also used money from his estate to found the Anthony Brady Memorial Laboratory at Yale University's school of medicine and a maternity hospital and infant care home in Albany, and they helped finance Walter P. Chrysler's automobile company.

—*Anita Price Davis*

FURTHER READING
McGovern, Charles F. *Sold American: Consumption and Citizenship, 1890-1945*. Chapel Hill: University of North Carolina Press, 2006.
Macmillan, Donald. *Smoke Wars: Anaconda Copper, Montana Air Pollution, and the Courts, 1890-1924*.

Helena, Mont.: Montana Historical Society Press, 2000.

Yanik, Anthony J. *Maxwell Motor and the Making of the Chrysler Corporation.* Detroit: Wayne State University Press, 2009.

See also: William Henry Aspinwall; Daniel Drew; James Buchanan Duke; Samuel Insull; John D. Rockefeller; Thomas Fortune Ryan; William Thaw; Peter A. B. Widener.

JIM BRADY
American investor and salesman

Brady, a Gilded Age salesman and investor, supported a lavish lifestyle, collected diamond jewelry, invested heavily and successfully in the New York Stock Exchange, started several businesses, and donated generously to medical institutions.

Born: August 12, 1856; New York, New York
Died: April 13, 1917; Atlantic City, New Jersey
Also known as: James Buchanan Brady; Diamond Jim Brady
Sources of wealth: Trade; investments
Bequeathal of wealth: Friends; medical institutions

EARLY LIFE
James Buchanan Brady grew up in Hell's Kitchen in New York City. His father was Daniel Brady, an Irish immigrant who owned Brady's Saloon; the family lived above the bar. When the saloon's profits dwindled after his father's death and his mother's remarriage, eleven-year-old Brady and his thirteen-year-old brother Daniel worked as bellboys at the luxurious St. James Hotel in an upper-class district of New York City.

John M. Touchey, an executive and later the general manager of the New York Central Railroad, took an interest in Brady and paid for his education. Brady continued to work as a bellboy while attending school. With Touchey's help, Brady secured a job in the baggage department at Grand Central Station. After only two years on the job, seventeen-year-old Brady became station agent while continuing his education.

FIRST VENTURES
When Brady was twenty-one, he became head clerk at New York Central Railroad and helped his brother Daniel secure a job with the railroad. Unbeknownst to Brady, Daniel began to steal from the railroad, and, as a result, both brothers lost their jobs. In 1879, Touchey once again helped Brady, asking Charles Moore to hire Brady as a salesperson for Moore's railroad supply company, Manning, Maxwell, and Moore.

At this time, Brady began exhibiting the penchant for luxurious living and lavish spending that would earn him the nickname Diamond Jim. He believed that personal appearance was important, and with the help of a friend

Jim Brady. (Archive Photos/Getty Images)

who was a tailor, he wore clothes that conveyed success. He also began collecting elegant jewelry, including some pieces with diamonds, to enhance his appearance. He frequented the most exclusive clubs and restaurants in the company of elegant young women, eating heartily but drinking only orange juice. His nights extended into the wee morning hours.

MATURE WEALTH

Brady eventually became the most successful salesman in America, and his work made Manning, Maxwell, and Moore a financial empire. In 1902, he began to establish some steel companies.

At the same time, Brady continued to lavish friends, associates, clients, and even newsboys with gifts, and he did not neglect himself. He became vastly overweight with his overindulgence in food and unhealthy living habits. Although he never married, Brady's extravagant social life included relationships with Edna McCauley and singer Lillian Russell. He and Russell remained best friends. Brady owned the first automobile in New York City. His treasures included thirty sets of jewelry worth $1 million, which would later be liquidated at his estate sale.

Brady's health declined with his excesses and long nights of celebration. When he had to seek medical help, his doctor admitted him to Johns Hopkins Hospital, predicting he had only one day to live. After the surgical removal of the largest gallstones ever extracted up to that time, Brady survived. In gratitude, he heaped gifts upon his caregivers and exorbitant donations upon the hospital.

However, Brady's health problems eventually forced him to change his occupation. He began investing heavily and successfully in the New York Stock Exchange. His investments vastly increased his wealth, which eventually exceeded $12 million.

Brady's health continued to decline, and he eventually suffered from angina pectoris, stomach ulcers, diabetes, and kidney problems. Instead of reentering a hospital, Brady spent his last months in the Shelbourne Hotel in Atlantic City, New Jersey. He died in Atlantic City on April 13, 1917.

LEGACY

Brady's extravagant living and spending epitomize the ostentatious displays of wealth that characterized the Gilded Age in late nineteenth century America. His rise from a poor boy in New York City to a successful millionaire exemplifies the upward mobility that was available to some businessmen in that era and is an important part of his legacy. Photographs of his jewelry collection, with its thirty complete sets of items, including matching belt buckles, tie clasps, cuff links, and bracelets, explain his nickname Diamond Jim. However, he also used his wealth philanthropically, endowing the James Buchanan Brady Urological Institute in 1912 and making contributions to the Cornell Medical Center. The congenial and free-spending Brady could be as generous to charities as he was to his friends and clients.

—Anita Price Davis

FURTHER READING

Fields, Armond. *Lillian Russell*. Jefferson, N.C.: McFarland, 2008.

Jeffers, H. Paul. *Diamond Jim Brady: Prince of the Gilded Age*. New York: J. Wiley and Sons, 2001.

Morrell, Parker. *Diamond Jim Brady: The Life and Times of James Buchanan Brady*. Reprint. Whitefish, Mont.: Kessinger, 2005.

See also: John Insley Blair; William Andrews Clark; Jay Cooke; Charles Crocker; Daniel Drew; John W. Garrett; Jay Gould; Edward H. Harriman; James J. Hill; Mark Hopkins; Collis P. Huntington; Daniel Willis James; George Mortimer Pullman; Leland Stanford; William Thaw; Cornelius Vanderbilt; William Henry Vanderbilt.

RICHARD BRANSON
British entrepreneur

In 2010, Branson was listed in Forbes *magazine as the 221st-richest person in the world, with an estimated net worth of $4 billion. A self-made man, Branson became a very successful entrepreneur through a wide variety of business ventures, including music sales, music production, air and rail transportation, banking, and soft drinks.*

Born: July 18, 1950; Shamley Green, Surrey, England
Also known as: Sir Richard Charles Nicholas Branson
Sources of wealth: Entertainment industry; banking; transportation systems
Bequeathal of wealth: Spouse; children; charity

EARLY LIFE
Richard Branson was born on July 18, 1950, in Shamley Green, Surrey, England. His father, Edward James Branson, was an attorney; his mother, Eve, was a former airline flight attendant who managed the household after marrying. Branson's parents were loving and supportive, and his mother was fond of setting challenging goals for him. Branson was educated in boarding schools, initially Scaitcliffe Preparatory in Windsor Great Park and subsequently Stowe in Buckinghamshire. He did not attend

Richard Branson. (Getty Images)

college. Branson suffers from dyslexia, a learning disorder that results in difficulty with reading and spelling, and he performed poorly in academics. However, he was popular in school because of his ability to converse effectively and connect with others.

FIRST VENTURES
Branson's first significant business venture occurred in 1967, when he and a childhood friend established *Student*, a periodical focused on the interests of secondary school and college students. *Student* was notable because it seemed to bring out the best in Branson's can-do nature. He secured interviews with many notable figures of the time, including John Lennon and Yoko Ono; convinced numerous large corporations to advertise in the periodical; and also managed to get arrested. The arrest was a result of his advertising venereal disease counseling and condom availability in *Student*. The police alleged that Branson violated two statutes, the 1889 Indecent Advertisements Act and the 1917 Venereal Disease Act. He was acquitted on the charge related to the Venereal Disease Act but was later convicted on the Indecent Advertisements Act charge and sentenced to pay a token fine equivalent to $14.

Branson's next significant business venture was the opening of a record store in London in 1969.

He expanded to mail-order record sales the following year and eventually opened additional stores, ultimately creating the huge Virgin megastore chain of music shops. This business venture also resulted in Branson's arrest after British customs officials charged him with selling nontaxed records, which he claimed to export. Branson settled out of court by paying the required customs duties and penalties.

MATURE WEALTH
Throughout the 1970's, Branson expanded his line of Virgin record shops, opening stores throughout the United Kingdom and ultimately throughout the world. The stores boasted extensive inventory and an informal atmosphere that appealed to young people. This formula proved successful and was the start of the Virgin empire.

In 1971, Branson bought a country manor in Chipton-on-Cherwell near Oxford, England, with the intention of converting the home into a recording studio. He felt there was a need for a more relaxed environment in which music artists could record. He also saw the potential for making a profit. Later that year, Mike and Sally Oldfield arrived at the manor to make a recording. Mike Oldfield's choice of the manor as a recording location was fortunate for Branson because Oldfield went on to record the multi-platinum Tubular Bells album at the manor. *Tubular Bells* earned a great deal of money for the new Virgin Records label that Branson launched in 1972. Over the years, income from sales of *Tubular Bells* would pull the Virgin Group, Ltd., back from the brink of bankruptcy and provide vital capital for the establishment of new business ventures.

Throughout the 1970's, Virgin Records struggled to stay solvent. Mike Oldfield was a consistent earner, but other artists did not prove as successful, and in 1980 the company lost $13.5 million. This financial picture changed drastically in 1982, when Virgin Records signed Boy George and Culture Club to the label. That year, the company earned a profit of $3 million, and in 1983 profits climbed to $16.5 million. The little Virgin label that other music publishers had derided was now a major force in the record industry.

Branson established Virgin Atlantic Airlines in 1984 with a single leased Boeing 747 jumbo jet. Virgin Atlantic initially had only one route, from New York's John F. Kennedy International Airport to London's Gatwick Airport. The maiden flight from Gatwick to Kennedy started with a bang, literally, when one of the jet's four large engines ingested birds on takeoff and had to be shut down. Not to be deterred, Branson continued to move forward, ultimately building Virgin Atlantic into a profitable and popular airline. Along the way, he had to endure a lengthy legal battle with British Airways. Branson accused British Airways of libel, and the Virgin Records label had to be sold in order to raise capital to keep the airline viable. The lawsuit against British Airways concluded with Branson and Virgin Atlantic settling for more than $900,000 in damages.

In 1986, Branson made the decision to publicly trade stock in the Virgin Group. A huge level of interest accompanied this initial public stock offering. Unfortunately, the stock did not appreciate as hoped. In addition,

THE VIRGIN EARTH CHALLENGE

On February 9, 2008, Richard Branson and Al Gore, the former U.S. vice president and Nobel Peace Prize winner, announced the Virgin Earth Challenge. The challenge offers a $25 million reward to the individual or entity that proposes a viable method of mitigating greenhouse gases from Earth's atmosphere.

Greenhouse gases are created by burning fossil fuels and are responsible for retention of solar heating and a resultant gradual warming of Earth's atmosphere. This warming phenomenon is causing climatic changes, including melting glaciers and polar ice caps, which result in rising ocean levels and significant alterations in weather patterns. The predominant greenhouse gas is carbon dioxide. Proponents of the global warming theory suggest that the greenhouse gas phenomenon will be cataclysmic for the Earth.

Specifically, the Virgin Earth Challenge seeks to encourage the development of a commercially viable new technology to remove anthropogenic greenhouse gases from the atmosphere in order to improve the stability of Earth's climate. It is estimated that more than two hundred billion metric tons of carbon dioxide have collected in the Earth's atmosphere over the last two hundred years, a 25 percent increase over pre-Industrial Revolution levels. The technology that will win the Virgin Earth Challenge must be capable of removing significant amounts—defined as one gigaton or more per year—of greenhouse gases from the environment for a period of not less than ten years. The results achieved by the technology must achieve "long-term" benefits, with the prize conditions suggesting a one-thousand-year time period.

Winners of the $25 million prize will receive an initial payment of $5 million when their greenhouse gas removal project is initiated, with the remaining $20 million to be paid at the successful completion of the ten-year project. Judges for the challenge include Branson, Gore, and four internationally recognized scientists and scholars. Branson and Gore are hopeful that the offer of $25 million will be sufficient to stimulate research resulting in a significant reduction in the rate of global warming.

Branson did not like the additional oversight and direction that the operation of a public company entailed. Consequently, in late 1987 all issued stock was bought back at the original purchase price and Virgin once again became a private company.

In 1991, Virgin Records signed Janet Jackson for a record $25 million single-album deal. The signing of an artist for a single record instead of several was unheard of and the music industry perceived this deal as extremely risky. However, Virgin Records continued to prosper and began looking to purchase another label, Thorn/EMI, in order to gain control of this firm's lucrative record rights inventory. Ironically, when Virgin Atlantic Airlines fell on hard economic times, it was Thorn/EMI that purchased the Virgin recording label for an astounding $1 billion. This huge infusion of cash allowed Virgin Atlantic Airlines to survive and gave Branson the financial wherewithal to continue expanding his empire.

The 1990's found Virgin expanding into a very diverse collection of business ventures, including Virgin Cola, a soft drink company; Virgin Money, a banking and investment company; Virgin America, an American-based airline; Virgin Mobile, a telecommunications company; Virgin Trains, a British rail provider; and Virgin Galactic, a space tourism company. Although all of the ventures are significant in some way, Virgin Trains and Virgin Galactic are probably the most intriguing. Virgin Trains is Branson's attempt to revitalize and modernize the British rail system. By 2009, Virgin was managing a significant portion of Britain's rail transportation, with the west of England served by a modern high-speed train system designed and implemented by the company. Virgin Galactic is Branson's attempt to beat big government at its own game—namely, spaceflight. In 2004, Branson's partners in Virgin Galactic, Paul Allen, cofounder of Microsoft Corporation, and aircraft designer Burt Rutan, won the Ansari X prize for conducting the first civilian launch of a reusable space vehicle twice within a two-week period. Allen and Rutan were awarded $10 million for their efforts. Rutan also designed a spacecraft in which Virgin Galactic planned to take clients on brief spaceflights. On December 7, 2009, SpaceShipTwo was rolled out in the Mohave Desert—the first public appearance of a commercial passenger spacecraft.

Branson has publicly stated that his goal is to continue to expand his enterprises whenever the Virgin Group has money. This formula has proven highly effective for the Virgin empire, which in 2009 employed more than fifty thousand people in a highly diverse collection of companies.

LEGACY

Richard Branson has made significant impacts on each of the industries into which he has ventured. From music to airlines and on to spaceflight, Branson has raised the bar of quality and competitiveness. Consumers have benefited greatly from Branson's Virgin Group by receiving higher quality and lower prices. His adventurous and exciting life are both fascinating and inspirational. Truly a self-made man, Branson triumphed over dyslexia to become one of the richest people in the world.

Like many ultrarich individuals, Branson has turned his efforts toward altruistic causes. He has used his money to build medical clinics in Africa and pledged $25 million to fund the Virgin Earth Challenge, an award designed to stimulate innovation in the mitigation of greenhouse gases in Earth's atmosphere. Branson was instrumental in bringing together a group of worldly intellectuals known as the Elders, including South African leaders Nelson Mandela and Desmond Tutu and Kofi Annan, the former secretary general of the United Nations. The Elders seek to objectively solve difficult global conflicts.

—*Alan S. Frazier*

FURTHER READING

Bower, Tom. *Branson*. London: HarperCollins UK, 2009. A much darker view of Branson than that spun by his many autobiographical books. Bower paints Branson as a rather devious and scheming entrepreneur who has violated various laws, including those concerning illicit drug use.

Branson, Richard. *Business Stripped Bare: Adventures of a Global Entrepreneur*. London: Virgin Books, 2008. Account of the Virgin Group, including information on Virgin America, Virgin Mobile, and Virgin Galactic.

_____. *Losing My Virginity: How I've Survived, Had Fun, and Made a Fortune Doing Business My Way*. New York: Three Rivers Press, 1999. Anecdote-laced account of the Virgin way of doing business.

_____. *Losing My Virginity: Richard Branson, the Autobiography*. London: Virgin Books, 2007. Candid and lively account of Branson's life from boyhood through entrepreneurship, closing with details on his offer of philanthropy, the Virgin Earth Challenge. Includes numerous photographs spanning Branson's life.

_____. *Screw It, Let's Do It: Fourteen Lessons on Making It to the Top While Having Fun and Staying Green*. London: Virgin Books, 2008. More lessons from the unconventional and incorrigible Branson. He distills his previous autobiographical works into a synopsis of fourteen important points.

Dearlove, Des. *Business the Richard Branson Way: Ten Secrets of the World's Greatest Brand Builder*. Chichester, England: Capstone, 2007. Basic overview of Branson's management style, with a cursory attempt at comparative analysis of Branson and other business leaders.

See also: Paul Allen; Mark Cuban; David Geffen; Robert L. Johnson; Sumner Redstone; Steven Spielberg.

THOMAS BRASSEY
British railroad and construction contractor

Brassey's wealth came from his large contracting business, which built railroads, docks, bridges, and ports. He took advantage of the rapid development of railroads in the mid-nineteenth century, bringing to their construction a high degree of business integrity and engineering skill.

Born: November 7, 1805; Buerton, Cheshire, England
Died: December 8, 1870; Hastings, Sussex, England
Sources of wealth: Construction business; railroads
Bequeathal of wealth: Children

EARLY LIFE

Thomas Brassey (BRAS-see) was the son of John Brassey, a long-established Cheshire farmer, living just south of Chester. Home-schooled at first, Thomas was then sent to a school in the city of Chester for four years. His father then apprenticed him to William Lawton, a land surveyor who was primarily employed by a Welsh landowner, Francis Price.

Brassey did so well that Lawton took him into partnership and in 1826 placed him in charge of a new business in Birkenhead, Cheshire. This little community was involved in the development of Liverpool as Great Britain's major port and was soon thriving. Brassey helped develop nearby brickworks and quarries. When Lawton died, Brassey took over the business and also became Price's land agent. In December, 1831, he married Maria Harrison, who encouraged him to move into railroad contracting.

FIRST VENTURES

Brassey's first venture into contracting was the building of a four-mile stretch of road leading to Birkenhead. Through this project, in 1834 he met George Stephenson, a leading railroad engineer, who persuaded Brassey to bid for the construction of the Dutton Viaduct on the Grand Junction Railway, one of the first long-distance railroads in Britain. Although unsuccessful in this bid, Brassey was awarded the contract for the Penkridge Viaduct on the same line in 1835.

After completing this project, he was asked to bid on additional contracts for the railway. He moved his family to Stafford and then to London in 1836 to facilitate these contracts. He worked with Stephenson and then with Stephenson's engineering pupil, Joseph Locke. Brassey also made successful bids for stretches of other early railroad lines in Cheshire, Yorkshire, and Scotland.

MATURE WEALTH

Meanwhile, other European countries were moving into railroad construction. Locke was appointed engineer on the new Rouen-Paris line, and in 1841 he invited Brassey to bid for it. Brassey worked with another British contractor, Sir William Mackenzie, on this rail line, thereby setting a precedent of being willing to work with other contractors. Between 1841 and 1844, Brassey and Mackenzie built 437 miles of French railways. In 1846, one of Brassey's viaducts at Barentin collapsed. Brassey rebuilt the viaduct at his own expense. The 1848 revolution in France forced Brassey to look elsewhere for work.

Great Britain was now in the midst of a railway mania, and work was readily available back home. By the time the mania subsided in the early 1850's, it was estimated that Brassey had been involved in the construction of more than one-third of all the railroads built during the decade, his largest undertaking being the Great Northern Railway, for which Brassey employed between five and six thousand laborers, or "navvies."

Between 1850 and 1870, Brassey took on multiple contracts throughout Europe, Canada, Argentina, India, and Australia. He later diversified into the construction of docks, sewerage systems, and ships. For these projects he set up his own building works just outside Birkenhead.

In 1867, failure of a railroad over Mont Cenis caused him much stress and a breakdown. Although he insisted on resuming his labors, his health could not withstand the pace, and he suffered a stroke in 1868. He died from a brain hemorrhage two years later, leaving some $20 million in assets and funds.

LEGACY

Thomas Brassey's outstanding legacy was the huge network of railroads he established all over the world. All of these railways were built to the highest standard. He had gained a reputation for total integrity, which extended to the welfare of his workers. He had superb business acumen, as well as an eye for selecting deserving men to whom he could delegate work. Many of his subordinates were able to earn their own fortunes.

However, none of his three sons followed him into the business, choosing instead to enter politics, in which they all became members of Parliament. His oldest son was made a baron and wrote a book on his father's business theory. In his biography of Brassey, Sir Arthur Helps praises Brassey for being the best type of self-made man that industrial Britain had produced.

—*David Barratt*

FURTHER READING
Haynes, Douglas. "The Life and Work of Thomas Brassey." *Cheshire History* 45 (2006): 57-66.
Helps, Sir Arthur. *The Life and Works of Mr Brassey.* 1872. Reprint. Stroud, England: Nonsuch Press, 2006.
Stacey, Tom. *Thomas Brassey: The Greatest Railway Builder in the World.* London: Stacey International, 2005.
Walker, Charles. *Thomas Brassey: Railway Builder.* London: Frederick Muller, 1969.

See also: Ninth Duke of Bedford; John Ellerman; Hugh Grosvenor; Thomas Holloway; Samuel Loyd; Moses Montefiore; William Weightman.

DONALD BREN
American real estate developer

Bren, the developer of the Irvine Ranch in Southern California and other properties, has given generously to educational causes, especially to the University of California system. In addition, he has contributed greatly to the arts in the Los Angeles area and donated to medical research and environmental projects.

Born: 1932; Los Angeles, California
Also known as: Donald Leroy Bren
Source of wealth: Real estate
Bequeathal of wealth: Educational institutions; medical research; artistic patronage

EARLY LIFE
Donald Leroy Bren is the older of two children born to Milton and Marion (née Newbert) Bren. His father was a real estate developer, best remembered for the development of Sunset Boulevard in Los Angeles, and a producer of motion pictures, including several of the *Topper* films. His mother was a friend of future First Lady Nancy Reagan. His parents divorced in 1947. Bren's father later married Claire Trevor, an Academy Award-winning actor. His mother married Earle Jorgensen, a steel tycoon who became a member of President Ronald Reagan's kitchen cabinet.

Bren attended public schools in Los Angeles. After graduating from high school in 1950, he attended the University of Washington in Seattle on a skiing scholarship. He graduated from college in 1954 with a degree in business administration and economics. In 1956, he tried out for the Olympic ski team but injured himself and failed to qualify. He then served a three-year tour of duty as a Marine Corps officer.

FIRST VENTURES
In 1958, equipped with a college degree, his father's real estate contacts, and $10,000 in borrowed money, he formed the Bren Company and built a house in Orange County, California, on speculation, thus launching a spectacular real estate career. He reinvested the profits from that first house and the others that followed. In 1963, he and two partners started the Mission Viejo Company, which planned and developed a community of eleven thousand acres that became the city of Mission Viejo, California, thus beginning his career as a developer of planned communities. Bren was president of the Mission Viejo Company from 1963 to 1967.

He sold his interest in the Mission Viejo property to one of his partners in 1969 for a substantial profit, and he then bought it back for a much lower price in 1972. He held the property for five years and then resold it to Philip Morris for a large profit. Bren promptly reinvested this profit, and he and a group of partners purchased the Irvine Company, which owned large tracts of land in Irvine, California, and the Irvine Ranch. Bren, the vice chairman of the company's board of directors, was also the largest single stockholder, owning 34.3 percent of the firm's shares. He became the majority shareholder by 1983, and in 1996 he bought all the outstanding shares and eventually became the company's sole owner.

MATURE WEALTH
The Irvine Company grew out of a ranch founded in 1864 by James Irvine, Llewellyn Bixby, and Benjamin and Thomas Flint. The property contains 185 square miles originating from three adjacent Mexican land grants. In 1894, James Irvine II incorporated the land as the Irvine Company. The Irvine Ranch is a separate entity of ninety-four thousand acres, of which the company retains forty-four thousand acres for development and the rest as a wilderness and recreational preserve. The ranch accounts for about one-fifth of Orange County, which is located south of Los Angeles.

THE DONALD BREN FOUNDATION

Real estate developer Donald Bren formed the foundation that bears his name in order to disperse the huge sums of money he planned to donate to charity, especially to education and to environmental projects and research. The Donald Bren Foundation has given more than $200 million to support education in California, primarily in Orange County. More than $100 million of that amount has gone to kindergarten through twelfth-grade education, including a $20 million donation that expands enrichment programs in art, music, and science; an $8.5 million gift to THINK Together, an after-school program in the Santa Ana Unified School District in Orange County and other areas of Southern California; and millions of dollars in donations for programs that reward outstanding teachers and provide scholarships for worthy high school seniors.

In addition, the foundation has contributed more than $100 million to colleges and universities in and outside the University of California system, especially the University of California at Irvine and the University of California at Santa Barbara. This money has primarily been used to create endowed professorships with the aim of attracting top-rated scholars to the University of California system, but the grants have also endowed chairs at the California Institute of Technology, Chapman University, and the Marine Corps University in Quantico, Virginia. Altogether, the Donald Bren Foundation has endowed fifty chairs. The foundation also gave $20 million to help establish a law school at the University of California at Irvine, and it has donated $20 million to that university's School of Information and Computer Sciences, which was renamed the Donald Bren School of Information and Computer Sciences in recognition of the gift.

In its environmental efforts, the foundation has set aside more than fifty thousand acres in Orange County formerly owned by the Irvine Ranch for wild lands, parks, and trails. The state of California designated these lands a California Natural Landmark and the U.S. Department of the Interior acknowledged them as a National Natural Landmark. The foundation also committed $50 million to support the Irvine Ranch Conservancy and its research programs that aim to promote the protection, enhancement, and public enjoyment of the Irvine Ranch's parks, trails, and wild lands. In 2000, the foundation gave $1.5 million to the San Joaquin Wildlife Sanctuary in Orange County.

In addition, the foundation has donated considerable funds to leading research institutions, such as the Burnham Institute for Medical Research. The Burnham Institute conducts research into cancer, neurosciences and aging, and infectious and inflammatory diseases. Other research projects supported by the Donald Bren Foundation include efforts to find cures for human diseases, to improve the overall quality of life, to discover computer science solutions to improve human lives and corporate operations, and to seek interdisciplinary approaches to solve environmental problems.

The company became prominent during the 1960's as a developer of suburban master-planned communities and continued to operate into the twenty-first century. The Irvine Company owns and manages office buildings throughout Southern California, and it also owns and operates several commercial properties, including the Irvine Spectrum Center, Fashion Island in Newport Beach, California, and The Market Place in Tustin, California.

One of the planned communities developed by the company is the city of Irvine, California, which was formally incorporated on December 28, 1971. By the beginning of 2009, Irvine's population was 212,793, and the community covered almost seventy square miles. Originally planned by architect William Pereira as a community of fifty thousand people surrounding a new University of California campus, the new city turned out to be considerably larger than originally foreseen. Planned communities like Irvine have adequate housing in a variety of price ranges, schools of all levels, places of employment, parks, libraries, communication and transportation facilities, shopping centers, and places of worship. Irvine's streets all have landscaping allowances, with power line rights-of-way serving as bicycle corridors. Parks and greenbelts link ecological preserves, and reclaimed water irrigates the greenery. Irvine and other planned communities are completely self-contained living environments that offer a higher quality of life to their residents than many other areas.

Through the enterprises of the Irvine Company, Bren amassed an enormous fortune. In 2008, *Forbes* magazine's list of the four hundred richest Americans ranked Bren as the wealthiest American real estate developer, estimating his net worth at more than $12 billion.

Bren no sooner accumulated great wealth than he began giving it away to charitable causes. In 2008, *BusinessWeek* magazine ranked Bren at number nine on its list of the fifty most generous philanthropists in the

United States. The magazine estimated that Bren had pledged more than $907 million since 2003 and had given away more than $1.3 billion during his lifetime, mostly to educational institutions. His contributions included the endowment of distinguished professorships and chairs at the University of California, California Institute of Technology, Chapman University, and Marine Corps University. He has also given substantial sums for public kindergarten through twelfth-grade school systems in Southern California, including an $8.5 million gift to THINK Together, an after-school program for at-risk children in Orange County and other areas of the state. In addition, Bren donated $20 million to Orange County schools in order to expand enrichment programs in music, art, and science.

Bren has received many awards and honors for his philanthropy. He was elected a fellow of the American Academy of Arts and Sciences and was awarded the University of California's Presidential Medal, which is the university's highest honor recognizing significant contributions to the university system and to higher education. Bren has also donated to the arts and has been heavily involved in environmental preservation. Some observers have noted that Bren's philanthropic endeavors are more pragmatic than altruistic and seek to improve Irvine by making the community a better place to live and a more desirable place to own property.

Bren also used some of his wealth to participate in politics. He was an early supporter of President George H. W. Bush and later of his son, President George W. Bush. Bren is a skiing buddy and financial supporter of California governor Arnold Schwarzenegger and a donor to Republican legislative candidates and the Republican National Convention. He also became involved in Senator John McCain's unsuccessful bid for the presidency in 2008.

LEGACY

Even though his life is far from over, Bren has already assured his legacy through his philanthropy. His donations to the University of California to endow professorships have attracted to the university campuses world-class scientists and scholars who have kept these schools in the forefront of the academic community. His financial support of kindergarten through twelfth-grade education in Orange County has already produced generations of well-educated citizens, prepared for careers in the workforce and for higher education. His gifts to the arts and to cultural and environmental projects have enhanced the quality of life for Southern California residents and secured the continued prosperity of the area. Most of all, his development of well-planned communities balancing workplaces, transportation, education, shopping, recreation, and places of worship has improved the quality of life of thousands of citizens. His motives for his philanthropy may have been selfish, but the results have benefited the entire community.

—*Paul Madden*

FURTHER READING

Arellano, Gustavo. *Orange County: A Personal History.* New York: Scribner, 2008. A Mexican American journalist gives a very different perspective of Orange County and Bren from that offered elsewhere. Arellano tells the story of his family's less-than-cordial welcome to Orange County and their trials and travails over more than six decades of dealing with Republicans, evangelical Christians, and wealthy Anglos, including Bren.

Callahan, Nathan. *Suburban Manners: An Irreverent View of the 1990's as Witnessed in the Politics, Wealth, and Culture of Orange County, California.* Los Angeles: Mainstreet Media Books, 2008. A journalist and radio talk show host pokes fun at the rich and famous of Orange County, devoting an entire chapter to Bren.

Francis, Stephen, ed. *Irvine Ranch.* Los Angeles: Visual Reference, 2004. Color photographs illustrate the planned community of Irvine Ranch and its attempts to balance business, education, work, everyday life, and recreation.

Oppenheimer, Rex. *Foundation of Integrity: A History of Irvine Ranch.* Los Angeles: Heritage Media, 2002. A short, popular history of Irvine Ranch from the earliest times to around 2002. Written in the style of a booster advertisement for the community of Irvine, California, the book extols the virtues of the city as a safe environment for business enterprise, higher education, family living, and top entertainment.

See also: Sheldon Adelson; Leona Helmsley; John D. MacArthur; Jay A. Pritzker; Donald Trump; Steve Wynn.

SERGEY BRIN
American computer scientist and high-tech magnate

Brin and Larry Page, created a global phenomenon—the Google search engine. Google not only is a company and brand name but also has become a verb meaning to access information on the Internet.

Born: August 21, 1973; Moscow, Soviet Union (now in Russia)
Also known as: Sergey Mikhailovich Brin
Source of wealth: Computer industry
Bequeathal of wealth: Spouse; children; charity

EARLY LIFE
Sergey Mikhailovich Brin, better known as Sergey Brin (SIHR-gay brihn), was born in Moscow, Soviet Union, on August 21, 1973, to Michael and Eugenia Brin. His parents, both brilliant individuals, wanted to work in the Soviet space program, but the Communist government unofficially barred Jewish people from the top professional positions, including working in university physics and astronomy departments. Michael taught mathematics at a university. In 1978, fed up with the pervasive anti-Semitism in the Soviet Union and the potential limited future for young Sergey, the Brins applied for an exit visa. Michael was fired from his job at the university for filing the exit visa, but the visa was approved in 1979, and the Brins fled to the United States, eventually settling in Maryland.

Sergey, now six years old, went to a Montessori school that would foster his creativity, while Michael became a mathematics professor at the University of Maryland, and Eugenia eventually was employed as a research scientist at the National Aeronautics and Space Administration (NASA). Sergey was a quiet child who quickly learned English and was interested in puzzles, maps, and mathematical games. He had a relatively normal middle-class upbringing, attending public high school and graduating in three years. He graduated near the top of his class at the University of Maryland three years later, majoring in mathematics and computer science. He won a National Science Foundation scholarship for graduate school and earned his master's degree at Stanford University in 1995. Brin chose Stanford for its beauty, prestige, and reputation for supporting high-tech entrepreneurs.

FIRST VENTURES
Brin met Larry Page, a University of Michigan graduate, at a Stanford University doctoral program orientation in

The founders of Google, Sergey Brin (above) and Larry Page at the company's headquarters in Mountain View, California, in early 2004. (AP/Wide World Photos)

1995. Both men were sons of high-powered intellectuals, had strong mathematics and computer science backgrounds, and were Jewish, opinionated, and cocksure. They bonded immediately, relishing intellectual combat.

As a university research project, Brin and Page began to devise a better way to search and harness information on the Internet. At this time, Yahoo!, Inc., and America Online provided the dominant Internet search engines, but these companies focused on offering moneymaking services, like e-mail, news, and weather reports. Brin and Page believed that Internet searching could be improved, and they decided to build their own company, eventually taking a leave from Stanford. Combining Brin's interest in data mining with Page's interest in information linking, they set out to make Internet searching more intuitive and relevant by ranking links between Web pages according to their relative importance. Building upon the academic concept of measuring topicality and value based on citations in research papers, the men devised a system of Web page links that enabled them to rank the importance and relevance of Web sites. They called their system the PageRank algorithm. This system was a major breakthrough in Internet search technology and was the basis for the company they decided to call Googol (later changed to Google), a mathematical term meaning the number one followed by one hundred zeros.

Brin and Page began gathering dozens of inexpensive computers in their dormitory room as their method of searching the Internet by relevance proved to be superior to any other search technique. The initial version of Google was part of the Stanford University Web site, but the computer servers needed to operate Google were in Brin and Page's dormitory room, and the two needed to expand. After soliciting funds from friends, family, and faculty members, the two obtained enough money to purchase additional servers and move their operation into a rented garage in nearby Menlo Park, California. While working in this garage, the garage owner's sister, Ann Wojcicki, became friendly with Brin, and the two later married.

Brin and Page began to introduce their company to executives of other Silicon Valley businesses and landed an audience with Sun Microsystems' cofounder and Silicon Valley investor Andy Bechtolsheim. Bechtolsheim liked what he saw and wrote a check for $100,000 to "Google, Inc." instead of to "Googol." Page and Brin spent two weeks filing the paperwork needed to form a company named "Google," while keeping the $100,000 check.

MATURE WEALTH

Google quickly drew a loyal following of users during the dot-com bubble in the late

---

GOOGLE.ORG: AN EXPERIMENT IN ACTIVE PHILANTHROPY

Sergey Brin and Larry Page, the billionaire founders of Google, have used their incredible intellect and extreme wealth for a number of philanthropic initiatives, including Google.org, a venture that uses Google's global information reach. The two men committed approximately $1.1 billion to Google.org based on their firm's stock price in 2004, the year that this charitable arm of their company was established.

After taking Google public in 2004, Brin and Page promised investors they would make a social impact on the world that would be greater than that made by Google itself. Google has pledged to donate 1 percent of the company's equity and profits to philanthropy. By early 2010, Google.org had provided more than $100 million in grants and investments to numerous recipients.

In early 2009, Larry Brilliant, the "chief philanthropy evangelist" of Google.org, stated that the charity would establish a stronger alliance with Google's engineers and technicians to take a more targeted approach to issues believed to be of the greatest global importance.

Google.org focuses on providing financial assistance in the broad global areas of clean energy, health, information access, and "special projects." Its clean energy initiatives include grants and investments to discover forms of renewable energy that are cheaper than coal, to reduce greenhouse emissions, and to accelerate the commercialization of plug-in vehicles. Global health initiatives include the prediction and prevention of global outbreaks of diseases, the identification of disease "hot spots," and the provision of a rapid response to emerging threats, such as infectious disease and climate risk. Information access projects, according to Google.org's Web site, seek to use Google's global information technology to "inform and empower," improve public services, and spur the growth of "small- and medium-sized enterprises." "Special projects" includes fundraising for global causes, such as support for global disease eradication efforts and for disaster response and recovery.

Brin and Page are personally involved in Google.org, demonstrating their belief in the necessity of ethical, principled, and peaceful global living. They believe that technology, science, and intelligence will solve the needs of the planet, and to that end, they have opened up their wallets as well as their hearts.

1990's and survived after the bubble burst in 2001. While many other high-tech companies failed, Google pressed on with unrivaled growth and soaring popularity. Brin and Page wanted their company to earn the respect of the Wall Street business community, so they hired seasoned software executive Eric Schmidt as the company's chief executive officer. Schmidt oversaw Google's daily operations, while copresidents Brin and Page continued to devise innovative technologies and services for the firm. Brin and Page joked that Schmidt was the adult influence in a company filled with youth and exuberance.

In the spring of 2004, Wall Street brokers and investors finally took notice of Google when the company filed the necessary paperwork for its initial public stock offering. There had been rumors that the privately held Google was a strong company, but when it released its staggeringly large revenue and profit figures, there was no doubt that the firm was financially successful. The small-text advertisements that Google included in its search results were especially profitable, generating enormous revenues.

Google's stock began to be publicly traded on August 16, 2004, with an unusually high price of $85 per share. This initial public offering raised $1.67 billion, making Google a $23 billion company and Brin and Page instant billionaires. Many Google employees also became millionaires. In 2008, Google's stock price exceeded $500 a share, one of the largest market capitalizations in history (market capitalization measures the size of a business in relation to the price of its stock and the number of shares held by investors). Google is also one of the most successful companies in corporate history, and its success has generated personal fortunes of more than $15 billion each for Brin and Page.

Although he is a young billionaire, Brin does not spend money as lavishly as many would expect. He continues to be heavily involved in the management and growth of Google, the maintenance and funding of the company's philanthropic arm, Google.org, and the Google Foundation, as well as other charities. He has come to embrace his Russian heritage as an active member of the American Business Association of Russian Professionals, an organization founded to support the Russian-speaking professional community in the United States. However, Brin has a few extravagances. He and Page jointly own a number of aircraft, including two Gulfstream 5 business jets, a Dornier-Alpha fighter jet, and a private Boeing 767 purchased in 2005. The purchase of the Boeing 767, which Brin has called the "party plane," occasioned one of the few times that he and Page

were criticized by the media. They have also been questioned about housing the Google fleet at NASA's Moffett Field in Santa Clara, near the "Googleplex" corporate offices. Brin's response to this criticism was that the jets needed to be at the NASA facility because they carry devices for specific atmospheric measurements to be conducted during flight. The explanation did little to quell the ire of their critics.

In 2007, Brin made a $5 million down payment to become a space tourist in 2011 as one of at least two passengers onboard the first private Soyuz flight to the International Space Station (ISS). The few previous space tourism flights have been for single passengers and have occurred during official missions to reprovision the ISS. Brin's private flight will not be an official mission but a true space ride, with one or two other passengers onboard. The estimated cost of this flight is at least $50 million.

LEGACY

Brin is a third-generation mathematician and a brilliant computer scientist. He and Page are pioneers in Internet search technology, in Web site advertising, and in building one of the most well-known and successful companies of the Internet Age. He is a relatively young billionaire, so his legacy continues to evolve.

Following the philanthropic lead of Bill Gates, cofounder of Microsoft, Brin has actively used his considerable wealth and influence to effect positive change throughout the world. With the creation of Google.org and the Google Foundation, and, to a lesser extent, his assistance of the Hebrew Immigrant Aid Society (HIAS), the organization that helped the Brin family flee the anti-Semitism of the Soviet Union, Brin has pledged to aggressively support causes that are important to him. His contributions to the Michael J. Fox Foundation for research into Parkinson's disease are notable because Brin's mother is afflicted with this disease, and Brin may have inherited the gene for this disorder.

—Jonathan E. Dinneen

FURTHER READING

Auletta, Ken. *Googled: The End of the World as We Know It*. New York: Penguin Press, 2009. Essentially tells the story of two Googles: the company itself, including its cofounders Brin and Page, and "google" as a metaphor for Internet's destruction of the "old media."

Girard, Bernard. *The Google Way: How One Company Is Revolutionizing Management as We Know It*. San

Francisco: No Starch Press, 2009. Focuses on Google's unconventional employee and management practices. Describes how job applicants are tested to determine their innovation and creativity and how Brin, Page, and Schmidt have created a working environment that elicits employees' best work through competition and an understanding of human nature.

Lowe, Janet. *Google Speaks: Secrets of the World's Greatest Billionaire Entrepreneurs, Sergey Brin and Larry Page.* Hoboken, N.J.: John Wiley & Sons, 2009. An inside look at the personal and business lives of the Google founders, their business practices, and their philosophies, written by a best-selling author.

Stross, Randall. *Planet Google: One Company's Audacious Plan to Organize Everything We Know.* New York: Simon & Schuster, 2008. A simple, well-written overview of Google and its business. The book explains how Brin and Page started Google while they were students at Stanford University and made it their mission to organize all of the world's information.

Vise, David. *The Google Story: Inside the Hottest Business, Media, and Technology Success of Our Time.* New York: Random House, 2005. A detailed account of Google cofounders Brin and Page, focusing on their backgrounds, their motivations, and their personal growth.

See also: Paul Allen; Steven Ballmer; Jeff Bezos; Mark Cuban; Michael Dell; Larry Ellison; Bill Gates; Steve Jobs; Gordon E. Moore; David Packard; H. Ross Perot.

EDGAR BRONFMAN, SR.
Canadian liquor company magnate

Bronfman and his brother inherited their father's liquor distillery, Seagram & Sons, and increased its business by expanding and diversifying the company's products and holdings. Bronfman next used his wealth and social position to advance Jewish philanthropies and causes throughout the world.

Born: June 20, 1929; Montreal, Quebec, Canada
Also known as: Edgar Miles Bronfman, Sr.; Edgar M. Bronfman
Sources of wealth: Inheritance; sale of products
Bequeathal of wealth: Children; charity

EARLY LIFE
Edgar Miles Bronfman (BRONF-mahn), Sr., was born in Montreal, Quebec, to Samuel and Saidye Bronfman on June 20, 1929. He was the third of four children and the older of two sons. Growing up in Montreal, Bronfman attended Trinity College School in Ontario, Canada. As a young man, he rebelled against his father by denying his Judaism, turning his back on his family's liquor distillery, and attending Williams College in the United States. However, he returned to Montreal to attend McGill University, from which he earned his bachelor's degree in history, with honors, in 1951. He reconciled with his father and began to work with him at Seagram & Sons immediately after his graduation.

FIRST VENTURES
Bronfman worked at Seagram in Montreal from 1951 to 1957. He initially was an accounts payable clerk, but he was always in his father's shadow. Although Samuel Bronfman seemed to be handing control of Seagram to the next generation, he remained an active and vocal owner, retaining full veto power. In 1957, Edgar Bronfman was given control and appointed president of the company's American subsidiary; his younger brother, Charles, assumed the presidency of the company's Canadian-based business. At this time, the American subsidiary of Seagram & Sons accounted for 81 percent of the company's business.

MATURE WEALTH
As president of the American subsidiary, Bronfman began restoring Seagram's prestige by resurrecting the defunct Calvert Reserve brand of whiskey, renaming it Calvert Extra. He went on a personal appearance tour and was featured in company advertisements to help market the new product. He expanded into marketing more diverse types of liquor, including vodka, gin, and wine. At the end of 1965, Bronfman had increased Seagram's international presence to 119 countries and the company's sales earnings exceeded $1 billion. Even though the years from 1961 to 1971 saw a 40 percent decrease in the worldwide market for whiskey, under

Bronfman's control Seagram actually increased its market by 9 percent. In 1975, four years after his father Samuel's death, Bronfman changed the name of the firm to Seagram Company Ltd.

Bronfman used the power and wealth he had acquired at Seagram to underwrite his first major venture into a nonliquor industry. In 1969, he became president of MGM (Metro-Goldwyn-Mayer) Studios after having bought $40 million of MGM stock. In one year under his creative control, MGM lost $25 million and Bronfman was forced to resign. This diversion into the film business cost Seagram $10 million.

After returning his attention to Seagram, Bronfman reorganized the company, naming his brother Charles president of the entire firm, with responsibility for both American and Canadian operations. By 1977, the company earned a profit of $84 million. Although Seagram's product line was doing well, not all of Bronfman's enterprises were as successful. In the 1980's, in an effort to diversify Seagram's holdings, he attempted three corporate takeovers. After his $2.3 billion sale of Texas Pacific, the oil company his father had bought for $50 million in 1963, Bronfman contacted St. Joseph Minerals with a buyout plan, but he was rejected.

Edgar Bronfman, Sr. (©CORBIS Entertainment)

His offer to take over Conoco Oil Co. also was refused, even though it was more than generous at $17 more per share than Conoco's market price. However, in the bidding process Seagram did acquire a 32 percent share in Conoco, which Seagram traded for a 24 percent share in E. I. du Pont de Nemours and Company. The relationship with du Pont proved to be very lucrative and stable, and it lasted until 1995, when the company was sold by Bronfman's son and heir. In 1981, Bronfman purchased Westmount Enterprises in order to market a new line of gourmet frozen foods, and he teamed with Coca-Cola to produce and distribute bottled mixed drinks and cocktails.

Bronfman was married five times to four different women, none of whom was Jewish. He had five children with his first wife and two with his third (and fourth) wife. He is one of the world's most important Jewish figures and has had an enormous impact on Jewish and Israeli affairs. His long commitment to Jewish causes is evident by his roles in various organizations. From 1979 until 2007 he was the president of World Jewish Congress, an organization dedicated to fighting anti-Semitism and promoting Jewishness. However, the organization also holds some controversial positions, such as supporting a two-state solution in Israel, promoting dialogue between Jews and moderate Muslims, and stopping the construction of new Israeli settlements in contested areas. Bronfman, who worked tirelessly with the organization and received much praise and recognition for his endeavors, left office in the midst of scandal over misuse of funds and his relationship with Israel Singer, the secretary general of the organization, whom Bronfman dismissed in 2007. Bronfman continues to be an outspoken supporter and critic of Israel and plays an important role as adviser to American policy makers on issues concerning Israel.

Bronfman's increasing interest in Jewish philanthropy and the Israeli-Arab peace process prompted him to turn over control of the Seagram company. When he announced his successor, he shocked the business world by naming his younger son, Edgar Bronfman, Jr. Everyone had expected that the college-educated Samuel Bronfman II would be made president instead of Edgar, Jr., who had forgone college in order to break into the entertainment business. Edgar, Jr.'s, disastrous initial foray into this business made him seem unsuitable as the head of a multibillion-dollar family business. Subsequently, this choice had dire effects on the Bronfman empire and fortune. Rifts in the family and the dissipation of the family's wealth have followed as a result of the younger Bronfman's business decisions. In his retirement, Edgar Bronfman, Sr., has been mute on the subject of his son's stewardship of the company and has turned his attention to writing books, Jewish causes, and other philanthropic enterprises.

LEGACY

Edgar Bronfman, Sr.'s, legacy is almost entirely tied to his connections with Jewish philanthropy. Believing that Jews must maintain a Jewish identity, he devotes much of his money and time to promoting Jewish and Israeli causes. While serving as the president of the World Jewish Congress, he was instrumental in publicizing Jewish concerns and fighting worldwide anti-Semitism. For example, under his presidency, this organization exposed Austrian president Kurt Waldheim's past participation in Nazi activities. Bronfman was also deeply involved in negotiations with the Swiss government concerning Jewish property that was illegally confiscated during World War II. In addition, Bronfman has helped thousands of Soviet Jews emigrate to the United States. As head of the World Jewish Restitution Organization, Bronfman fought for the return of stolen Jewish items confiscated during the war, not simply for financial restitution. He is the largest single sup-

---

BRONFMAN YOUTH FELLOWSHIPS IN ISRAEL

The Bronfman Youth Fellowships were established by Edgar Bronfman, Sr., in 1987 to create educational experiences that would enrich the lives of American and Canadian Jewish teenagers. Although not a religious Jew himself, Bronfman is a staunch supporter of Zionist and Jewish causes. The Bronfman Youth Fellowships embody his principles and beliefs. He wants to help educate a generation of Jewish leaders and influential citizens who are strongly committed to Israel and connected to their own Jewishness. He further hopes to encourage Jewish pluralism by bringing together teenagers from diverse backgrounds, from the ultraorthodox to the agnostic and atheist and from small communities and large cities. Through these fellowships, he seeks to create discussion among Jewish people with disparate voices, so that despite individual differences the Jewish community can attain a united vision of the importance of perpetuating its heritage.

Every year, twenty-six sixteen-year-old high school juniors are chosen to participate in the fellowship program. It is an intensive, five-week-long experience in Israel, during which students study the Torah, learn about Israel's ancient and modern history, meet with Israeli leaders and politicians, and experience Israeli culture throughout the country. The fellows are also required to attend study sessions in New York City both before and after the trip. As of 2009, there were more than five hundred fellows, half of whom went on to attend Ivy League colleges, fifteen of whom were Rhodes Scholars, and many others who received other scholarships and were beginning their professional lives as leaders in many fields, such as medicine, law, writing, and filmmaking.

The success of the Bronfman Youth Fellowships program led Bronfman to inaugurate an Israeli version of the program, Amitei-Bronfman, in 1998. Young people in this program study together in Israel and spend their senior year of high school attending schools in the United States. The highly successful program Birthright Israel, which annually sends thousands of Jewish college-aged students to Israel for free ten-day trips, is based on the Bronfman Youth Fellowships program and financially supported the Samuel Bronfman Foundation, which Edgar Bronfman, Sr., established in honor of his father. These trips are designed to allow many Jewish students from around the world to visit Israel for the first time, with the goal of infusing them with a sense of connectedness to this nation.

---

porter of Hillel, the international college-based Jewish organization. In his other philanthropic enterprises, he is a benefactor of McGill University, many museums and fine arts causes, and various other charities.

—Leslie Neilan

FURTHER READING

Bronfman, Edgar M. *Good Spirits: The Making of a Businessman.* Kirkwood, N.Y.: Putnam Adult, 1998. Bronfman's autobiography, in which he discusses the history and development of his family's businesses. He also includes information about his philanthropic endeavors and provides a final chapter of practical business advice for entrepreneurs and business professionals.

_____. *The Making of a Jew.* Kirkwood, N.Y.: Putnam Adult, 1996. This memoir traces Bronfman's early years as an atheist to his discovery of his deep-felt Jewishness and devotion to Zionism. He discusses his fight against anti-Semitism and his role in shaping Israeli and Jewish life in the twentieth century.

_____. *The Third Act: Reinventing Yourself After Retirement.* Kirkwood, N.Y.: Putnam Adult, 2002. A straightforward discussion of how to continue being productive after retirement. Bronfman draws on examples from his own life and the lives of others, discussing how to stay active and involved.

Bronfman, Edgar M., and Beth Zasloff. *Hope Not Fear: A Path to Jewish Renaissance.* New York: St. Martin's Press, 2008. Bronfman argues that modern Judaism has become a response to oppression rather than a joyous celebration of tradition and intellect. He advocates for open dialogue, intermarriage, and turning away from the Holocaust and toward the future.

Faith, Nicholas. *The Bronfmans: The Rise and Fall of the House of Seagram.* New York: Thomas Dunne Books, 2006. A biography of the Bronfman family, it covers the building of the Seagram empire under Samuel Bronfman and the resulting loss of billions of dollars in revenue by his heirs. It presents the loss as one of the largest ever suffered by a single family.

McQueen, Rod. *The Icarus Factor: The Rise and Fall of Edgar Bronfman, Jr.* Toronto: Doubleday Canada, 2004. Although this book focuses on the business life of Edgar Bronfman, Jr., it includes information about Bronfman, Sr.'s, decision to leave Seagram in the hands of his younger son and the effects this decision has had on the family's business and fortune.

See also: Emilio Bacardi; Samuel Bronfman; Ernest Gallo; Edward Cecil Guinness.

SAMUEL BRONFMAN
Canadian liquor company magnate

Bronfman entered the liquor distributing business at the beginning of Prohibition. By working around legal loopholes, he became the largest liquor distributor in North America and introduced aged whiskey to the Canadian and American markets. He devoted his adult life to philanthropy and Zionism.

Born: February 27, 1889; Soroki, Bessarabia, Russian Empire (now in Russia)
Died: July 10, 1971; Montreal, Quebec, Canada
Source of wealth: Sale of products
Bequeathal of wealth: Children; charity

EARLY LIFE
Samuel Bronfman (BRONF-mahn), whose last name means "liquor man" in Yiddish, was born into a wealthy Russian-Jewish family and was one of eight children. The family fled czarist Russia, fearing the anti-Jewish pogroms there, and settled in Canada in 1889. Despite their wealth in Russia, the Bronfmans lived in poverty during their first years in Canada. Samuel's father, Yechiel Bronfman, who had been a tobacco farmer in Russia, soon realized that farming was not going to be his occupation in Canada. He began a series of jobs, first as a laborer, then in a saw mill, and finally as a merchant selling firewood and whitefish. He eventually began trading horses, which led the family to open a small hotel. The railroad boom helped their hotel take off, and soon the family was running three Canadian hotels.

FIRST VENTURES
In 1903, Samuel Bronfman purchased his first hotel and began running the family business with his brother Harry. In 1916, Samuel purchased the Bonaventure Liquor Store Company in Montreal. When Canada enacted Prohibition in 1918, the hotel business began to fall off sharply. Bronfman realized that much of the profit at his hotels was actually coming from their bars, and he decided to go into the liquor business full time. Bronfman and his brothers—Harry, Abe, and Allan—began selling spirits throughout Canada at great profit because of their scarcity during Prohibition. In 1918, a Canadian law made the importation, manufacture, and transportation of all liquor illegal, unless it was used for medicinal purposes. In response, Bronfman purchased the contract for Dewar's whiskey from the Hudson's Bay Company and began marketing his whiskey as elixirs and tonics through drugstores.

In 1919, the United States adopted its own Prohibition law, the Volstead Act. Prohibition was taken more seriously in the United States than in Canada, where there was not much actual implementation of the antidrinking legislation. By 1924, all Canadian laws against adult consumption of liquor were repealed. The Bronfman brothers, however, had used the period of Prohibition to build up an efficient distribution system, and in 1924 they founded the Distillers Corporation of Montreal, which sold cheap whiskey. This company's infrastructure allowed Bronfman to supply American bootleggers with liquor from 1919 until 1933, the end of Prohibition in the United States.

MATURE WEALTH

Because of American Prohibition, Bronfman was able to purchase 300,000 gallons of alcohol in the United States in 1919 and bring it to Canada, where it was used to make 800,000 gallons of liquor. He distilled the product into whiskey, selling it at a 500 percent markup. In 1926, Bronfman sold a 50 percent share in Distillers Corporation to the Distillers Company, a group of British distillers that controlled most of the world's market for Scotch whiskey. This transaction gave Bronfman the sole right to distribute the Haig, Black & White, Dewar's, and Vat 69 brands in Canada. In 1928, Bronfman expanded his Distillers Corporation by purchasing Joseph E. Seagram & Sons, the largest liquor distillery in Canada. With Bronfman as vice president, the new company, Distillers Corporation-Seagram Limited, made $2.2 million in profits in 1928. However, American Prohibition was having a negative effect on sales, and by 1930, profits had declined. Bronfman purchased warehouses all along Canada's eastern border with the United States and founded Atlantic Import and Atlas Shipping, two companies that facilitated the shipping of liquor into the United States. Although it was illegal to receive liquor shipments in the United States, it was not illegal for a Canadian to sell liquor, and in 1934, when the Bronfman brothers were tried for bootlegging, their case was dismissed.

Anticipating the eventual repeal of the Volstead Act in the United States, Bronfman had stockpiled whiskey; this stock was the largest private supply of aged whiskey in North America. In 1933, Bronfman acquired 20 percent of Schenley, a producer of rye whiskey. When Bronfman asked the board of directors of the Scotland-based Distillers Company to increase the price of Scotch whiskey, the board refused. In response, the Bronfman brothers raised enough money to buy out the Distillers Company's holdings in Distillers Corporation-Seagrams Limited, and Samuel Bronfman became president of Joseph E. Seagram & Sons. He then purchased a distillery in Indiana, establishing the American branch of Seagram's business.

SAMUEL AND SAIDYE BRONFMAN FOUNDATION

Founded in 1952, the Samuel and Saidye Bronfman Foundation was established by Samuel Bronfman and his wife, in their names and the names of their four children, in order to allocate family money for charitable and philanthropic purposes. Samuel and Saidye Bronfman shared the belief that civilization depended on the development and support of community values, and they dedicated their foundation to the support of these values. The foundation provides venture capital to nonprofit organizations, as well as to deserving individuals, in order to foster cultural and civic projects, with consideration given to sustainable enterprises. The organization is one of Canada's largest private philanthropic funds distributing money from a single family.

Among its contributions, the foundation provided financial support for higher education in Canada, with donations to McGill University and the University of Saskatchewan, among other schools. In 1971, Samuel Bronfman funded the construction of the Bronfman Building at McGill University to house the newly established Desautels Faculty of Management.

The foundation also provided funds for many artistic enterprises, including construction of the Saidye Bronfman Centre for the Arts, a community theater, art gallery, and fine arts school in Montreal commonly known as "the Saidye." By 2009, the structure had been replaced by the new Segal Centre for the Performing Arts. The foundation also donated $1.5 million to the Canada Council for the Arts, and these funds were used to create a trust providing yearly awards to crafts artists.

Both Samuel and Saidye Bronfman were recognized for their commitment to philanthropy by the creation of the Samuel Bronfman Award, presented to a recipient who has excelled in humanitarian work, and the Saidye Bronfman Award, given to artists whose work exemplifies creativity and excellence in execution.

Samuel's son, Edgar Bronfman, Sr., established the Samuel Bronfman Foundation in honor of his father. This organization seeks to inspire a renaissance in Jewish life, to educate young people about Judaism, and to strengthen the Jewish community. The foundation is a major supporter of Hillel, the college-based group devoted to campus Jewish life, and Birthright Israel, which provides free trips to Israel for non-Israeli college-aged applicants.

Relations with Schenley were not always smooth, however, and when Bronfman learned that Schenley would not agree to age its rye whiskey, he ended his associations with this company. For years, the two companies vied for first place in worldwide whiskey sales, with Seagram emerging the victor in 1947. At about this time, Bronfman forced his brothers out of the business and took over company management, insisting that only his sons, Edgar and Charles, would ever inherit or work for Seagram.

Bronfman was committed to changing the face of the whiskey business. He wanted to distance his name from the 1922 murder of his brother-in-law, Paul Matoff, by American bootleggers and remove the perception that his product was cheap rotgut. He insisted that Seagram sell blended, aged whiskey and opened "blending libraries" in New York, Montreal, and Scotland, where scientific processes were used to ensure his products' consistency and quality. To further ensure the quality of his product, Bronfman revolutionized the marketing and distribution of whiskey by selling it when it was already aged and bottled. Until this time, whiskey was shipped in kegs, which allowed for variations in the quality of the final product. Bronfman wanted all of his customers to know exactly what they were purchasing and be able to count on the integrity of the Seagram name. This practice soon became the industry standard. In the 1930's, Bronfman established a large-scale advertising campaign extolling the virtues of moderate and social drinking.

Bronfman purchased Maryland Distillers, including its Calvert brand, in 1934, and in 1936 he opened a distillery in Kentucky. In 1939, he purchased the Chivas brand's distillery in Scotland and created Chivas Regal as a tribute to King George VI when the king and his wife visited Canada. In the 1940's Bronfman expanded his company's product line to include the development and distribution of other types of spirits and wine. He became partners with a German vintner to purchase the Paul Masson vineyards and winery in California. Seagram further expanded by purchasing distilleries in the West Indies that made rum, including the Captain Morgan brand, and the champagne companies that produced Mumm and Perrier-Jouet, among other brands. By 1965, Bronfman's combined worldwide liquor enterprises were operating in 119 countries at a yearly profit of $1 billion.

Bronfman also commissioned architect Ludwig Mies van der Rohe to design his American headquarters in New York, and Mies van der Rohe's Seagram Building, a skyscraper in midtown Manhattan, remains a New York City landmark. In addition, Bronfman purchased Texas Pacific Coal and Oil Company for $50 million; after his death, his heirs eventually sold this firm for $2.3 billion.

Samuel Bronfman died of prostate cancer in 1971. He had always wanted to feel accepted by society and never felt that he achieved this goal. However, his reputation in Canada and the world was so great that upon his death he finally achieved the recognition he desired, when, on the occasion of his funeral, Montreal's airport had to be closed to regular air traffic in order to accommodate the private jets of the dignitaries attending the service.

LEGACY

Samuel Bronfman's legacy is seen in many arenas, not simply the liquor business. His lifelong work was centered on philanthropy dedicated to fighting anti-Semitism and supporting cultural institutions. In 1951, he met with Shimon Peres, the future prime minister of Israel, to help procure weapons for Israel. Using his contacts in the Canadian government, Bronfman was able to purchase $2 million worth of guns at half price. When Peres could not pay, Bronfman threw a fund-raising dinner and obtained the money. From 1939 to 1962, Bronfman was president of the Canadian Jewish Congress. He also provided a good deal of support to McGill University in Montreal, despite its history of anti-Semitism. Perhaps his greatest legacy to the country of Canada was the creation of the Samuel and Saidye Bronfman Foundation, which is dedicated to providing private capital for artistic and other ventures. He was made Companion of the Order of Canada in 1967 and awarded the Chevalier de la Légion d'honneur by France in honor of his support of Zionism.

—*Leslie Neilan*

FURTHER READING

Faith, Nicholas. *The Bronfmans: The Rise and Fall of the House of Seagram.* New York: Thomas Dunne Books, 2006. A biography of the Bronfman family, it covers the building of the Seagram empire under Samuel Bronfman and the resulting loss of billions of dollars in revenue by his heirs. It presents the loss as one of the largest ever suffered by a single family.

Gordon, Grant, and Nigel Nicholson. *Family Wars: Classic Conflicts in Family Business and How to Deal with Them.* London: Kogan Page, 2008. The Bronfmans are featured as an example of family feuds and their effects on family-owned businesses.

Marrus, Michael R. *Samuel Bronfman: The Life and Times of Seagram's Mr. Sam.* Waltham, Mass.: Brandeis University Press, 1991. Chronicles Bronfman's life from his birth to the creation of the largest liquor business in the world. Provides a great deal of detail about Bronfman's businesses and deal making, while also fleshing out the details of his private life.

Newman, Peter C. *Bronfman Dynasty: The Rothschilds of the New World*. Toronto: McClelland & Stewart, 1978. Argues that Samuel Bronfman deserves recognition as one of the great entrepreneurs and philanthropists of the twentieth century.

Schneider, Stephen. *Iced: The Story of Organized Crime in Canada*. Mississauga, Ont.: John Wiley & Sons, 2009. History of organized crime in Canada, with material concerning the Bronfman family from their beginnings to their rise to prominence and their participation in bootlegging during Prohibition.

See also: Emilio Bacardi; Edgar Bronfman, Sr.; Ernest Gallo; Edward Cecil Guinness.

MOSES BROWN
American textile manufacturer, merchant, and abolitionist

Brown was born into a prominent commercial and seafaring family in colonial New England, and he was instrumental in establishing the textile industry there. The most significant of his charitable bequests were to Brown University and to a private preparatory school.

Born: September 23, 1738; Providence, Rhode Island
Died: September 6, 1836; Providence, Rhode Island
Sources of wealth: Manufacturing; trade
Bequeathal of wealth: Relatives; charity; educational institution.

EARLY LIFE

Moses Brown was a member of a business-oriented family that was involved in various commercial enterprises in and around Providence, Rhode Island. While Brown's formal schooling ended when he was about thirteen, he learned business and seafaring skills through his family's business. The Brown family was involved in the African slave trade, although this was never their primary business venture. In 1764, Moses and his brother John Brown organized a slaving voyage of the ship *Sally*, which ended disastrously, with more than half of the slaves dying. This experience turned Brown away from the slave trade, and he eventually became one of the first abolitionists in America.

FIRST VENTURES

Brown ended any direct involvement with the slave trade immediately after the voyage of the *Sally*. He continued to work in the family firm, formally known as Nicholas Brown and Company, until the early 1770's. In 1773, his wife Anna died, prompting a spiritual crisis that led Brown to embrace the Quaker faith. He withdrew from active business work and devoted himself to religion, charity, and social reform, especially the cause of abolition. He moved to an estate named Elmgrove outside Providence and directed farming operations there, raising Merino sheep and experimenting with a variety of crops and techniques of crop rotation. In November, 1773, he freed the six slaves that he personally owned, and he renounced any financial interest in other slaves that were owned in common by the family.

MATURE WEALTH

After the American Revolution, Brown worked to establish the textile industry in the United States. He joined with a son-in-law, William Almy, and another relative to form Almy & Brown in order to begin textile mill operations. In 1789, Brown hired Samuel Slater, an immigrant from Great Britain with knowledge of the cotton textile industry, to examine some cotton spinning equipment that Brown's workers could not get to work properly. Great Britain at this time would not export cotton milling equipment and forbade the export of even the drawings or plans for building such machinery. Slater, however, had smuggled out valuable "mental baggage" and knew how to rebuild Brown's equipment.

In December, 1790, Slater worked with Brown to open the first water-powered cotton textile mill in the United States at Pawtucket, Rhode Island. Three years later, Slater became a partner in Brown's firm. While the milling industry made Slater wealthy, Brown claimed that he never made money from it but had simply recouped his initial investments. By the time both Slater and Brown died in the 1830's, New England had become second only to Great Britain as a center of the cotton milling industry. Brown was also involved in the founding of a bank in Providence in 1791, and he served as an officer of the bank for several years. In the early 1800's, Brown once again retired from active business pursuits.

LEGACY

Although he never accumulated a truly massive fortune, Brown made gifts to numerous charities and reform groups throughout his lifetime. His most important legacies were the founding of Brown University and the Moses Brown School. While Brown University received support from many members of the Brown family, it was Moses who led the effort in 1770 to relocate the school, then called Rhode Island College, from Warren, Rhode Island, to Providence. In 1804, in honor of the generosity of Brown's nephew Nicholas Brown, the school took the name Brown University. In the twenty-first century, Brown University has faced considerable controversy over the fact that some of its original bequests were from

people involved in the slave trade. Moses Brown also led an effort and donated land to establish a Quaker boarding school in Providence in 1784. In 1909, the school took the name the Moses Brown School.

—*Mark S. Joy*

FURTHER READING

Jones, Augustus. *Moses Brown, His Life and Services: A Sketch*. 1892. Reprint. Whitefish, Mont.: Kessinger, 2009.
Rappleye, Charles. *Sons of Providence: The Brown Brothers, the Slave Trade, and the American Revolution*. New York: Simon & Schuster, 2006.

See also: Sir Richard Arkwright; Paul Cuffe; Nicholas Longworth; Francis Cabot Lowell; James Morrison; John Rylands; Samuel Slater.

WARREN BUFFETT
American investor and philanthropist

Buffett, an investor and philanthropist known worldwide as the Oracle of Omaha, parlayed investment savvy with his friends and family's capital into Berkshire Hathaway, Inc., which had the highest-priced stock in the history of the New York Stock Exchange. With an estimated net worth of $47 billion in 2010, Buffett became one of the richest people in the world during the late twentieth and early twenty-first centuries.

Born: August 30, 1930; Omaha, Nebraska
Also known as: Warren Edward Buffett; the Oracle of Omaha
Source of wealth: Investments
Bequeathal of wealth: Relatives; charity

EARLY LIFE

Warren Edward Buffett (BUHF-feht) was born on August 30, 1930, in Omaha, Nebraska, the son of Leila and Howard Buffett. Howard (1903-1964) was a Republican member of the House of Representatives, who earned his living trading stocks. He was elected to Congress in 1942, the first of four terms, representing eastern Nebraska as an ardent opponent of President Franklin D. Roosevelt. Howard earned some notoriety in Congress for returning a salary increase to the U.S. Treasury.

At age eleven, Warren Buffett purchased his first

stock through his father's firm, three shares of Cities Service (now CITCO) for $37. He sold the stock for $40, and, upon watching the stock's price reach $200, later remarked that he had learned an early lesson in what became his lifelong investment philosophy: find good value, buy, and hold. (Stock in Buffett's company, Berkshire Hathaway Inc., reached $140,000 a share in 2007, and $90,700 in 2009, and in accordance with his philosophy has never been split.) Buffett filed his first income tax return at age thirteen, deducting a bicycle, which he used to deliver newspapers, as a business expense. He graduated from Woodrow Wilson High School in Washington, D.C., in 1947, earned a B.S. degree at the University of Nebraska in 1950, and received an M.S. in economics from Columbia University in 1951.

FIRST VENTURES

In 1956, after working briefly for his father and for other investment firms, Buffett opened Buffett Associates, Ltd., his first investment partnership, with $100 from his own pocket and $105,000 from limited partners, all of them family and friends. Between 1956 and 1969, the value of Buffett's portfolio exploded as he earned an average of 30 percent a year, between three and four times the market average, while working from an office in his home.

The "Berkshire Hathaway" name initially belonged to

a declining textile firm in which Buffett's firm began buying stock in 1962. Seven years later, Buffett shed the firm's textile mills and made Berkshire Hathaway a holding company for his several partnerships. Early on, Buffett directed his investment acumen at insurance companies because their large cash reserves provided a ready source of investment capital. In January, 1979, Berkshire Hathaway's stock began trading at $775 a share, and by December it nearly doubled to $1,310. By that time, Buffett's net worth of $620 million put him among *Forbes* magazine's four hundred richest people for the first time.

Berkshire Hathaway invests heavily in name-brand companies, such as Coca-Cola, that are dominant in their industries, as well as in smaller businesses that are well managed and have niche markets that help them succeed. Once Berkshire Hathaway buys a company, existing management is usually allowed to run it. However, Buffett himself reserves the right to set the compensation of the chief executive officer.

MATURE WEALTH

Buffett's companies are known for their tight financial operations, and Moody's Investors Service often gives them AAA ratings, the highest possible credit ranking. Buffett often waits for stock prices to fall before investing in assets that he considers top-of-the-line. His success with this approach has spawned a cottage industry of Buffett watchers who emulate his methods. He is also known to withhold investments during periods of stock speculation and rising prices and to avoid buying stock in companies that lack discernable asset value. This approach prevented Berkshire Hathaway from losing money when the dot-com bubble burst in the early years of the twenty-first century.

Buffett taught his children the risks of uninformed gambling by buying them an antique slot machine and a stack of quarters, with the proviso that he would retain the machine's winnings. Soon, the quarters were back in his pocket. This is not to say that Buffett will not take risks. After two devastating Atlantic hurricane seasons in

Warren Buffett. (AP/Wide World Photos)

THE SUSAN THOMPSON BUFFETT FOUNDATION

The Susan Thompson Buffett Foundation, with an office in Omaha, Nebraska, manages Warren Buffett's charitable giving. It was named in honor of Warren's first wife after her death in 2004. The foundation initially gave away about $12 million annually from an asset base of about $500 million. Grants increased to about $150 million annually by 2009, as Buffett directed some of his $62 billion in assets to the foundation. Money from Susan's estate, reportedly about $2 billion, also was added to the foundation's asset base.

Buffett also is directing a large proportion of his fortune (about 85 percent, as of 2006) into charities operated by Bill Gates, cofounder of Microsoft Corporation, and his associates, principally the Bill and Melinda Gates Foundation. Buffett has said that the Gates Foundation would be better able to manage large amounts of money than his own foundation. Most of Buffett's wealth comes from his stock in Berkshire Hathaway, Inc., in which he holds about 40 percent of the shares.

Most of the Buffett foundation's awards are by internal nomination only, and they tend to focus on education, health care (notably family planning, including access to abortion), international relief efforts, arts, environment, and civil liberties. Individual grants have ranged from a few hundred dollars to several million. However, some money is given for educational purposes, entirely in Nebraska, for programs that are open to public application. The foundation, for example, provides scholarships covering tuition and fees up to $3,200 per semester, with an added textbook allowance of $400, for undergraduate students enrolled in public universities and colleges, including community colleges, in Nebraska. The foundation each year also recognizes teaching excellence in the Omaha public schools with fifteen awards of $10,000 each. Nominations for these awards are accepted from parents, former students, teachers other than the nominee, school administrators, and members of the general public.

2004 and 2005, he bought heavily into coastal insurance, figuring that an El Niño weather pattern would quell the storms in 2006. He was correct, and he earned millions of dollars for Berkshire Hathaway. Buffett has quipped that he spends a lot of time watching The Weather Channel.

On November 3, 2009, Buffett acquired Burlington Northern Santa Fe Corp., the United States' largest rail transporter of grain and coal, for a record $34 billion. "It's an all-in wager on the economic future of the United States," Buffett said in a statement about the deal. "I love these bets."

Buffett is well known in Omaha as a public citizen. He can occasionally be spotted on any given weekend ordering ice cream with Bill Gates, a cofounder of Microsoft Corporation, at an Omaha Dairy Queen, a chain that Berkshire Hathaway owns. He also may be spotted playing bridge with Gates or taking dozens of business and journalism students from the University of Nebraska at Omaha to lunch. On occasion, he visits Omaha schools to teach children to play the ukulele.

Berkshire Hathaway's annual meetings in early May are cultural events, drawing thousands of investors and filling the Qwest Center, Omaha's largest indoor arena. The annual meeting, timed to coincide with Buffett's often-humorous annual statement to stockholders, can draw fifteen thousand to twenty thousand people, providing a major boost to the local economy that observers have called "the Woodstock of Capitalism."

Buffett is famous not only for his investment acumen but also for his disregard of the ostentatious consumption made possible by great wealth. He is famously frugal, continuing to live in the same home in central Omaha that he bought in 1958 for $31,500. He also owned a larger house in Laguna Beach, California, that he sold in 2004. Having purchased a corporate jet in 1989 for almost $10 million, he named it "The Indefensible" because he earlier had criticized similar purchases by other companies.

Buffett is known as a genial and equitable employer, a longtime Democrat, and a sharp critic of unfair employment practices that take advantage of poorly paid people. He was an early supporter of Democratic presidential candidate Barack Obama. Buffett also has criticized low property tax rates in California, using a home he owned there until 2004 to compare tax rates on the California house with those on his home in Omaha. Buffett is also a self-described agnostic.

A persistent critic of executive overcompensation, Buffett draws an annual salary of $100,000 from Berkshire Hathaway. He believes that widespread debt will hurt the American economy and the country's currency in the long run, and he has been careful about investing in foreign companies.

Buffett is a critic of the market system and the monetary value that it places on certain kinds of work. He believes that the market system unfairly rewards some people, such as a heavyweight boxer who can knock out another fighter, or a Major League Baseball player with a high batting average, while a good teacher or nurse is underappreciated. The Susan Thompson Buffett Foundation sponsors an annual competition for the best teachers in Omaha schools, with monetary rewards.

Buffett and his wife Susan separated in 1977, although they remained married until Susan died in 2004. On his seventy-sixth birthday, Buffett married Astrid Menks, who had lived with him since he and Susan separated. Before Susan left Omaha for San Francisco to pursue a singing career, she had arranged for Astrid, a former housekeeper in the Buffett home, to meet Warren. The three were close friends; they attended social events together at times, and they sent cards to friends that were signed "Warren, Susie and Astrid."

LEGACY

Buffett believes that people whose talents are amply rewarded by the capitalist marketplace owe a debt to society. His charitable donations are a return to society for the market value of what he considers to be his own peculiar talent. Several times, Buffett has offered to auction off a meal with him for good causes. Many aspiring investors will pay hundreds of thousands of dollars for an hour or two of Buffett's time; one investor paid $620,000 for a lunch date. During September, 2006, Buffett auctioned his well-used Lincoln Town Car on the eBay Web site for $73,200, and he donated this money to Girls, Inc., a national organization that works to empower girls.

Both Buffett and Bill Gates have become major philanthropists. In June, 2006, Buffett pledged to give about three-quarters of his assets ($30.7 billion) to charity, with 85 percent going to the Bill and Melinda Gates Foundation—the largest donation in the history of corporate philanthropy.

Buffett has established relatively small foundations headed by each of his three children, Susie, Howard, and Peter. He opposes large-scale transfer of big estates within families, and he has vigorously opposed elimination of inheritance taxes on grounds that concentrating wealth is socially dysfunctional.

—*Bruce E. Johansen*

FURTHER READING

Buffett, Warren E. *The Essays of Warren Buffett: Lessons for Corporate America*. Selected, arranged, and introduced by Lawrence A. Cunningham. Rev. ed. New York: L. Cunningham, 2007. Buffett's investment thinking in his own words, often humorous and prescient, with historical perspective seasoned by decades of investing.

Hagstrom, Robert G. *The Warren Buffett Way: Investment Strategies of the World's Greatest Investor*. New York: John Wiley Sons, 1997. One of several books that outline Buffett's investment strategy and record, attempting to explain why he has been successful over the long term.

Kilpatrick, Andrew. *Of Permanent Value: The Story of Warren Buffett*. Birmingham, Ala.: AKPE, 1994. Covers Buffett's investments and record to the early 1990's, with an emphasis on his theories of "value investing" for the long term that have provided spectacular returns for his stockholders.

Lowenstein, Roger. *Buffett: The Making of an American Capitalist*. New York: Random House, 1995. A detailed biography of Buffet and his family to the mid-1990's, with emphasis on his midwestern roots, his early life in Omaha, and his views as a humanistic capitalist.

O'Loughlin, James. *The Real Warren Buffett: Managing Capital, Leading People*. London: Nicholas Brealey, 2004. Buffett's philosophy of human nature, investing for the long term, and how to provide leadership in corporate America during turbulent times.

Schroeder, Alice. *The Snowball: Warren Buffett and the Business of Life*. New York: Random House, 2008. An "authorized" biography that nevertheless strikes a candid tone about Buffett's personal and professional lives. The author spent hundreds of hours interviewing Buffett.

See also: Bernard Cornfeld; Bill Gates; Carl Icahn; Kirk Kerkorian; T. Boone Pickens; George Soros.

ANGELA BURDETT-COUTTS
British aristocrat and philanthropist

Burdett-Coutts may have been the wealthiest woman in nineteenth century Great Britain. She was a patron of writers, particularly Charles Dickens, with whom she pursued social reforms. Devoting her life to charitable work, she was admired throughout England.

Born: April 21, 1814; London, England
Died: December 30, 1906; London, England
Also known as: Angela Georgina Burdett-Coutts; Angela Georgina Burdett (birth name); First Baroness Burdett-Coutts
Source of wealth: Inheritance
Bequeathal of wealth: Spouse; charity

EARLY LIFE

Thomas Coutts, the grandfather of Angela Georgina Burdett-Coutts (buhr-DEHT-coots), was one of the most successful bankers in British history. While presiding over Thomas Coutts & Co. bank for sixty years, he accumulated a personal fortune of £900,000. His daughter Sophia married Sir Francis Burdett, and the couple had five children, of whom Angela was the youngest. Young Angela was raised in the finest aristocratic manner in an elegant London home and two historic country estates, Ramsbury Manor and Foremarke Hall. She traveled throughout Europe and learned several foreign languages.

In 1837, Angela inherited the bulk of her grandfather's fortune from his deceased wife, making her the richest heiress in England. She acquired half-ownership of Thomas Coutts & Co. bank, Thomas Coutts's houses, and his personal possessions, gold, and annuities. The newspapers estimated her inheritance at almost £2 million, with an annual income of £80,000. While this amount may have been exaggerated, there was no doubt that she had inherited an enormous amount of money; her wealth was equal to several billion dollars in 2010 U.S. currency. Although she was not the first woman to inherit a fortune in real property, no other English woman had ever controlled so much liquid wealth. According to the terms of her grandfather's will, she was required to add Coutts to her surname, which was hyphenated as Burdett-Coutts.

FIRST VENTURES

For a woman living in the Victorian era, Burdett-Coutts showed unusual independence, setting up her own mansion in London on the corner of Stratton and Piccadilly Streets. She loaned Queen Victoria a large sum of money to enable the queen to pay off her debts. Burdett-Coutts wore expensive clothes and exquisite diamonds that had been inherited from her family, including a tiara that had belonged to Marie-Antoinette. Her art collection contained paintings by Sir Joshua Reynolds and other English portraitists. She owned valuable china. Her library included first folios of the works of William Shakespeare and historic letters from Charles II and Georgiana Cavendish, duchess of Devonshire.

With her unencumbered fortune, Burdett-Coutts was sought after by suitors, but she was skeptical of their motives. She apparently was also ashamed of a skin condition. She was besieged by marriage proposals. Although she rejected each one, she was impressed by a young writer she met in 1838, Charles Dickens. She and Dickens would remain lifelong friends and correspondents. For eighteen years, she was harassed (or in modern terms, stalked) by a psychotic Irish barrister, Robert Dunn, who imagined he was courting her. In the 1840's, she became well acquainted with England's great hero, Arthur Wellesley, the duke of Wellington. Despite her interest, however, he never proposed marriage. Through the intervention of the great scientist Michael Faraday, she joined the Royal Institution of Great Britain 1847. She encouraged the mathematical genius Charles Babbage to publish his children's stories.

MATURE WEALTH

Burdett-Coutts devoted her wealth to philanthropic work, assisting hundreds of charities. She involved the young Dickens in her charitable works, and he roamed the slums of London looking for impoverished residents worthy of Burdett-Coutts's charity. He brought to her attention the wretched condition of the Field Lane Ragged School, which she then supported for many years. In 1847, Dickens encouraged her to take action to alleviate prostitution in London. With Dickens's guidance, she subsidized Urantia Cottage for needy women who might otherwise resort to prostitution. Urantia Cottage housed thirty women. She also followed Dickens's advice in building model apartments in Columbia Square in the 1860's. In 1864, she built Columbia Square Food Market to improve the food supply of the apartments' residents. She gave generously to the Church of England in her own country and throughout the world. She endowed bishoprics in Australia, Canada, and St. Helena. In Westminster, one of London's worst slums, she built a religious complex with a school, a vicarage, and a church. She also rebuilt St. Stephen's Technical Institute in Westminster.

Burdett-Coutts was eager to fund charities in the British colonies, especially the African colonies in Nigeria and what is now South Africa. In 1847, she became friends with the remarkable James Brooke, who had improbably become the raja of Sarawak, a kingdom near Borneo. She wanted to make Sarawak a protectorate of Great Britain; failing in that, she gave the raja large sums of money to help him govern his unruly subjects.

Burdett-Coutts tried to keep her charity work a secret but was unable to do so. In recognition of her philanthropy, she was made a baroness by Queen Victoria in 1871. Burdett-Coutts was the first woman to be raised to the peerage because of her own efforts, rather than those of a spouse.

On February 12, 1881, having rejected suitors for forty years, she married her secretary, William Lehman Ashmead-Bartlett, to the surprise of English society. Ashmead-Bartlett, who was twenty-nine years old (Burdett-Coutts was sixty-seven), took the surname Burdett-Coutts and was known as W. L. Burdett-Coutts.

Burdett-Coutts died on December 30, 1906, at the age of ninety-two. She was given the honor of a burial in Westminster Abbey. During her lifetime, it is estimated that she donated more than £3 million to charity.

LEGACY

For many reasons, Angela Burdett-Coutts was a remarkable woman. She was one of the wealthiest women in nineteenth century England. She pursued her own ideas of how she should use her wealth, rejecting conventional marriage. She formed friendships and close associations with three of England's most remarkable personalities, the duke of Wellington, the raja of Sarawak, and Charles Dickens. She subsidized writers like Dickens, but, more important, she recognized and supported Dickens's de-

---

LITERARY PATRONAGE AND WEALTH

Writers have been assisted by wealthy patrons since antiquity. The most famous classical patron was Gaius Maecenas, a wealthy Roman of the first century B.C.E., who supported Vergil and Horace, as well as other writers. Maecenas's support was of such significance that his name has become synonymous with patronage of literature and art. Maecenas provided more than financial assistance to writers. He also offered valuable advice. Both Vergil and Horace stated that Maecenas's critiques of their writing helped them with their work. Maecenas did not support the arts out of personal vanity, as did many later patrons, but as a civic duty and a means to improve Roman culture.

The Elizabethan writers Christopher Marlowe, Ben Jonson, and William Shakespeare all appear to have benefited from the patronage of the wealthy. Shakespeare dedicated his sonnets to the mysterious W. H., apparently an aristocratic patron. Sir Thomas Walsingham provided patronage to Elizabethan writers Marlowe, George Chapman, Thomas Nashe, and Thomas Watson. Patronage of writers was also common in eighteenth century England. However, unlike other writers of the Augustan Age, the satirist, novelist, and poet Jonathan Swift publicly denounced patronage and refused to accept assistance. In China, the wealthy salt merchants of Yangzhou sparked a literary renaissance in the eighteenth century by vying to be patrons. The Ma brothers, Ma Yueguan and Ma Yuelu, subsidized numerous poets and scholars. Another wealthy salt merchant, An Qi, gave the scholar Zhu Yizun a gift of 10,000 taels in order to write classical works of philosophy. In nineteenth century England, Angela Burdett-Coutts provided some financial support to her friend, writer Charles Dickens, a relationship that also involved their common work to alleviate poverty in London.

One of the most significant literary patrons was the nineteenth century American capitalist Henry Huttleston Rogers. Rogers helped John D. Rockefeller build the Standard Oil Company, from which Rogers made a great fortune, and he also amassed wealth from other oil, mining, banking, manufacturing, and railroad companies. At the end of the century, Rogers's fortune was estimated at more than $100 million, making him one of the twenty-five wealthiest Americans in history. Rogers was known to be ruthless in business, but he could be generous to authors, as exemplified by his relationship with writer Mark Twain. After some failed business ventures in the 1890's, Twain faced bankruptcy. Rogers quietly provided assistance to Twain, who credited Rogers with saving him from ruin. Rogers also paid for Helen Keller's education at Radcliffe College and provided her with a generous subsidy upon graduation. Keller subsequently dedicated her book, *The World I Live In* (1908), to Rogers. Rogers also furnished subsidies for the work of Booker T. Washington. Rogers did not want his donations to be publicized and his gifts have been described as "secret philanthropy."

sire to help the poor of London, an ambition that matched her own. More than anything else, she was a true philanthropist, devoting the majority of her life and fortune to a wide array of charitable works.

—Howard Bromberg

FURTHER READING

Gold, Barbara. *Literary Patronage in Greece and Rome.* Chapel Hill: University of North Carolina Press, 2009. A study of the social stratification, traditions, and wealth of Greece and Rome that led to a blossoming of literary patronage.

Griffin, Dustin. *Literary Patronage in England, 1650-1800.* Cambridge, England: Cambridge University Press, 1996. A study of patronage in English literature during the Augustan Age, with a chapter on Jonathan Swift's ambivalence toward aristocratic patrons.

Healey, Edna. *Lady Unknown: The Life of Angela Burdett-Coutts.* London: Sidgwick and Jackson, 1978. Recounts the life of Burdett-Coutts, pointing out parallels with Queen Victoria, who gained her inheritance—the throne of England—within months of Burdett-Coutts's inheritance of her grandfather's fortune.

Messent, Peter. *Mark Twain and Male Friendship: The Twichell, Howells, and Rogers Friendships.* New York: Oxford University Press, 2009. Includes an account of Twain's close relationship with the oil magnate Henry Huttleston Rogers, who helped subsidize his works.

Orton, Diana. *Made of Gold: A Biography of Angela Burdett-Coutts.* London: Hamish Hamilton, 1980. Focuses on Burdett-Coutts's position in Victorian society, with an emphasis on the impact of her wealth. Aims to correct mistakes in earlier biographies. Includes illustrations.

Patterson, Claire Burdett. *Angela Burdett-Coutts and the Victorians.* London: John Murray, 1953. Written by a great-niece of Burdett-Coutts. Tells the story of Burdett-Coutts's friendships with leading Victorians, such as the duke of Wellington, Charles Dickens, and the raja of Sarawak. With access to family papers, these stories are primarily told through correspondence between Burdett-Coutts and friends.

Slater, Michael. *Charles Dickens: A Life Defined by Writing.* New Haven, Conn.: Yale University Press, 2009. Emphasizes the tireless, multifaceted public life of Dickens, including Burdett-Coutts's influence on his politics, charitable endeavors, and writing.

See also: Nikolaus Esterházy; Phoebe Apperson Hearst; Gaius Maecenas; Laura Spelman Rockefeller; Jane Stanford; Eleanor Elkins Widener.

ADOLPHUS BUSCH
American brewer and industrialist

Busch built a beer-brewing empire that eventually became Anheuser-Busch Companies and later was acquired by Belgian brewer InBev.

Born: July 10, 1839; near Mainz, Hesse (now in Germany)

Died: October 10, 1913; near Langenschwalbach, Germany

Sources of wealth: Manufacturing; sale of products

Bequeathal of wealth: Children

EARLY LIFE

Adolphus Busch (ay-DOHL-fus buhsh) was born near Mainz, Hesse, on July 10, 1839, the youngest of twenty-one children. As a boy, he began working with his father, a wine merchant and brewing supplies dealer. He was educated in Mainz and Darmstadt and attended high school in Brussels. When he was seventeen, he went to work as a shipping clerk in a mercantile house in Cologne. Here he learned valuable business skills that would allow him to amass his great fortune.

FIRST VENTURES

When he became eighteen, Busch left Germany for the United States and set up his own supply store with his brother Ulrich. Two other Busch brothers had already left for America and had settled in St. Louis, Missouri, which was quickly becoming a virtual German colony. He married Lilly Anheuser, and his brother Ulrich married her sister Anna, in a double ceremony in 1861.

Busch went in to the brewing business in 1865 with his wife's father, Eberhard Anheuser, who already owned the struggling Bavarian Brewery Company. Together they created Budweiser, a lighter and sweeter variety of beer than others at the time. Busch worked hard to have his beer sold in taverns, even paying some owners

Adolphus Busch. (The Granger Collection, New York)

MATURE WEALTH

Busch was able to amass his wealth by keeping ownership of the company within the family When he first went to work for Anheuser, there were 480 shares of stock in the company—238 belonging to him, 2 shares to the brewmaster, and the remaining 240 shares split between Anheuser and his daughter Lilly. After Anheuser's death in 1879, Busch began buying up shares of the company from Anheuser's relatives, increasing his total shares from 238 to 267. He also created a vertically integrated corporation by owning companies that supplied the materials necessary to make his beer. He owned glass bottle plants, ice-making businesses, refrigerated railroad cars, and eventually the railroads themselves. Production increased by more than 200 percent by 1880, with a record production of more than 130,000 barrels of beer. He added workers and buildings at the brewery in St. Louis and employed guides to give tours of the facility to visitors. In the fifteen years since Busch went into business with Anheuser, he had taken a small local brewery and turned it into a national empire that was generating more than $2 million a year.

Busch's heirs continued his marketing legacy, with the most notable and longest-running campaign being the world-famous Budweiser Clydesdales, an iconic eight-horse hitch (team) that travels to more than one thousand events annually. The company also mass-markets its products through major sports sponsorships and partnerships, and since 1980 it has allied with Major League Baseball, the National Hockey League (NHL), National Basketball Association (NBA), twenty-eight National Football League (NFL) teams, Major League Lacrosse, the Professional Golfers' Association of America (PGA), the Ladies Professional Golf Association (LPGA), the U.S. Olympic team, the Olympic Games, and the Fédération Internationale de Football Association (FIFA) World Cup.

LEGACY

While he lived lavishly and never thought twice about spending money to close business deals and expand his enterprises, Busch still managed to amass more than $50 million by his death in 1913, at the age of seventy-four. His estate was the largest ever probated in the state of Missouri. Over the years, he had given generously to education and other charities, but his prime focus was cre-

to keep it on tap, although it tasted horrible. When the brewers finally created a good-tasting batch, the beer became a sought-after beverage. As Budweiser became popular, Busch gradually reduced the number of beers manufactured by the company in order to focus on the most profitable brands.

When Anheuser died in 1879, Busch took over as president of the company. Busch increased production and turned a small brewing company into a city-sized corporation housed in St. Louis. In the laboratories at Anheuser-Busch, scientists developed a new pasteurization technique that allowed beer to be shipped without refrigeration, which meant that beer could be transported from coast to coast without turning sour. Busch was also famous for his ingenious marketing and sales techniques. He focused on building a brand, and because of this, Budweiser beer remains one of the most recognizable products in the world.

ating an empire out of his small brewing city in St. Louis. In July, 2008, Anheuser-Busch made the decision to sell to Belgian brewer InBev for $75 a share. The acquisition of Anheuser-Busch by InBev, which had more than 120,000 employees in more than thirty countries around the world, created the world's largest brewing company. InBev agreed to reserve a spot on the board for the chief executive officer of Anheuser-Busch, August A. Busch IV, and kept the North American headquarters in St. Louis in order to retain the history of the iconic American brand. In 2009, the company was led by Busch IV, and the Busch family had a total fortune of more than $1.3 billion.

—R. Matthew Beverlin and Sara Schulte

FURTHER READING

Hernon, Peter, and Terry Ganey. *Under the Influence: The Unauthorized Story of the Anheuser-Busch Dynasty.* New York: Simon & Schuster, 1991.

Krebs, Roland, and Percy J. Orthwein. *Making Friends Is Our Business: One Hundred Years of Anheuser-Busch.* Chicago: Cuneo Press, 1953.

Ogle, Maureen. *Ambitious Brew: The Story of American Beer.* Boston: Harvest Books, 2007.

See also: Emilio Bacardi; Edgar Bronfman, Sr.; Samuel Bronfman; Ernest Gallo; Edward Cecil Guinness.

MANUEL CALVO
Spanish planter, merchant, and banker

Born in Spain, Calvo made a fortune in the shipping, sugar, and banking industries of nineteenth century Cuba, which he used to oppose Cuban independence and to support numerous charities.

Born: December 25, 1816; Portugalete, Spain
Died: 1904; Cadiz, Spain
Also known as: Manuel Calvo y Aguirre; Don Manuel Calvo
Sources of wealth: Agricultural products; shipping; banking; slave trade
Bequeathal of wealth: Charity

EARLY LIFE
Manuel Calvo y Aguirre (MAHN-yew-ehl CAHL-vo ee ah-GEER-ray) was born in Portugalete in the Basque region of Spain in 1816. His father Mathias was captain of a ship in the Cantabrian coast guard. Manuel studied seamanship and sailing with his father from the age of twelve to eighteen.

FIRST VENTURES
At eighteen, Calvo moved to Spain's prosperous colony of Cuba to seek his fortune. He worked as a clerk in Cuba's flourishing shipping industry. By nursing his savings through eight years of hard work, he was able to become a shipowner. With his profits he established a company, which by 1850 monopolized shipping from the Vuelta Abajo port district in Cuba to the Isle of Pines (now the Isla de la Juventud). His ships also transported slaves from Africa.

MATURE WEALTH
At the height of his success in shipping, Calvo had the sudden idea to create a sugar conglomerate. At the time, sugar was a leading industry in Cuba, but its production tended to be piecemeal. Calvo established a sugar plantation and mill of almost 120 square kilometers, which he named after his hometown. Calvo's Portugalete mills processed sugar through its entire production cycle, from extracting the sugar from sugarcane to packaging and exporting the finished product. He also processed alcohol from sugarcane. Calvo lived in an opulent mansion on his plantation. As a leading planter, Calvo was necessarily involved in the question of Cuban slavery, which did not end until 1886. In 1870, Calvo communicated his support for emancipating newborn slaves to Julían

de Zulueta, Cuba's largest and most notorious slaveholder.

Calvo spent summers in his hometown of Portugalete, and in 1872 he built an imposing neoclassical mansion on the new waterside promenade. He formed a business relationship with another wealthy Basque in Cuba, Antonio López y López, vice president of the Compañía Transatlántica and future marquis of Comillas. Along with other wealthy Catalonians, they started the successful Colonial Hispanic Bank in 1876. Calvo contributed one million pesetas for his shares of the bank enterprise.

With his wealth, Calvo was able to influence politics. He sent money in 1870 to help place Amadeo, the duke of Aosta, on the Spanish throne. Calvo was perhaps the leading aristocratic opponent of Cuban independence, claiming it was merely a pretense for United States' domination. He subsidized the expenses of the Spanish army in quelling Cuban revolts. The Colonial Hispanic Bank also extended a huge loan to the Spanish government in 1876 to pay for the exile of insurrectionist leaders. Apparently, Cuban nationalists burned down Calvo's sugar mills in retaliation. A widower, Calvo decided to emancipate all of his slaves and return permanently to his Spanish birthplace.

In Spain, Calvo provided for charitable works and supported educational institutions in Portugalete, contributing 30,000 pesetas to repair the tower of the Basilica of Holy Mary, destroyed in the civil war of 1874. He also sponsored charitable concerts to benefit soldiers wounded in the imperial wars in Cuba and the Philippines.

Calvo died in 1904. As he had no children, his will left his mansions in Cuba and Portugalete to local governments on the condition that both homes be renovated as hotels and cafeterias, with the revenue from these enterprises used to assist the indigent. His life is commemorated by a beautiful bronze pantheon in the Portugalete cemetery created by the well-known sculptor Josep Llimona i Bruguera (1864-1934). The steamship Manuel Calvo, in operation until 1959, also commemorated Calvo. The Manuel Calvo Foundation in Portugalete exists into the twenty-first century, continuing to promote civic projects and to assist disadvantaged members of society.

LEGACY
Basques from Spain formed a major element of Cuba's emerging capitalist class in the nineteenth century.

Calvo, by his wealth and political involvement, was a leader of this group. His fortune was made first in shipping and then multiplied in sugar and bank holdings. He funded military efforts to suppress Cuban independence, which were often brutal. Returning to his native Spain, however, he became a model of charity, funding projects throughout his hometown of Portugalete on behalf of the poor. The Manuel Calvo Foundation continued it philanthropic efforts in Portugalete in the twenty-first century.

—*Howard Bromberg*

FURTHER READING

Perez, Louis, Jr. *Cuba Between Empires: 1873-1902.* Pittsburgh, Pa.: University of Pittsburgh Press, 1998.

Thomas, Hugh. *Cuba: Or, The Pursuit of Freedom.* New York: Da Capo Press, 1998.

Weissman, Muriel. *Sugar Baron: Manuel Rionda and the Fortunes of Pre-Castro Cuba.* Gainesville: University Press of Florida, 2003.

See also: Miguel de Aldama; Emilio Bacardi; Antonio López y López; José Xifré.

SEBASTIÃO CAMARGO
Brazilian industrialist and conglomerate owner

Camargo led the second generation of Brazilian business leaders who built mammoth conglomerates with international profiles. The Camargo Corrêa Group benefited from consistent and massive government funding, international capital, and Camargo's business acumen.

Born: September 25, 1909; Jaú, São Paulo, Brazil
Died: August 26, 1994; São Paulo, São Paulo, Brazil
Also known as: Sebastião Ferraz de Camargo Penteado
Sources of wealth: Construction business; manufacturing; steel; metals refining
Bequeathal of wealth: Children; charity

EARLY LIFE
Sebastião Ferraz de Camargo Penteado, better known as Sebastião Camargo (seh-bash-tee-OWHN kah-MAR-goh), grew up on a plantation in the interior of the wealthy state of São Paulo, Brazil. His family was large and its fortune declined after his father died when Camargo was an adolescent. Supporting himself as a construction worker, Camargo acquired a cart and donkey and hauled debris and earth from construction sites. He profited from burgeoning road construction in the region.

FIRST VENTURES
Learning the techniques for construction site preparation, Camargo became a small-scale contractor. In partnership with a lawyer, Sylvio Brand Corrêa, he acquired sufficient capital to set up a modest company, the Camargo Corrêa Engineering and Building Co. Acquiring a tractor, he achieved a strategic advantage over his competitors. In the period after World War II, foreign investment in Brazil increased, stimulating a massive construction boom for new factories, housing, hydroelectric plants, and roads. A consuming magnet for this construction was the building of Brasília (1956-1960), Brazil's new capital, during the presidency of Juscelino Kubitschek. To win a portion of the contracts for this city's construction, Camargo resolved to impress authorities by assembling a fleet of tractors from all of his construction sites. He paraded them at the proposed site for Brasília, demonstrating that his company had sufficient resources for the massive urban undertaking.

MATURE WEALTH
The profits and publicity that Camargo Corrêio accrued pushed the company into the forefront of major Brazilian building operators. The firm now entered the period of mammoth construction projects under government auspices, with which it became synonymous. Company projects included the building of a hydroelectric dam on the Paraná River in the 1960's, which required construction of a satellite city for workers. The following decade, the company built an eight-mile-long bridge that spanned Guanabara Bay in Rio de Janeiro. The firm laid the multilane interstate highway between Rio de Janeiro and São Paulo through daunting mountainous terrain, and it forged through tropical rain forest to construct the Trans-Amazon Highway. Camargo's company also laid the gas line between Brazil and Bolivia and raised the colossal $15 billion Itaipú dam between Brazil and Paraguay, distributing electricity to the two countries.

Astute in pursuing horizontal and vertical integration of his businesses, Camargo cultivated relations with political leaders and competitors, minimizing risk. The businesses included steelmaking, aluminum, agriculture, and textile operations. In the 1990's, Camargo's personal wealth, valued at more than $1 billion, put him on *Forbes* magazine's list of billionaires. He and his wife had three daughters, and he included their husbands in the management of his companies. Because of his origins, Camargo retained certain rural habits, such as often appearing with a rustic pipe in his mouth. One of his nicknames was "China" because he had certain Asian facial features and an inscrutable business manner. He also had a passion for hunting, leading expeditions in Africa and Alaska.

LEGACY

Camargo quite literally constructed modern Brazil. He might be described as the "bricklayer of Brazil," except his companies used reinforced concrete. After the company's work building Brasília, Camargo Corrêa construction sites became omnipresent in Brazil, neighboring countries, and other parts of the world. Thereby,

Camargo's enterprises both contributed to and benefited from the rise of Brazil as a regional economic power. However, his dominance resulted more from government patronage than from market competition, and his extreme wealth reflected the chronic income chasm between rich and poor people in Brazil.

—*Edward A. Riedinger*

FURTHER READING

Dean, Warren. *The Industrialization of São Paulo, 1880-1945.* Austin: University of Texas Press, 1969.

Fausto, Boris. *A Concise History of Brazil.* Cambridge, England: Cambridge University Press, 2006.

Kohlhepp, Gerd. *Itaipú, Basic Geopolitical and Energy Situation: Socioeconomic and Ecological Consequences of the Itaipú Dam and Reservoir on the Rio Paraná (Brazil/Paraguay).* Braunschweig, Germany: F. Vieweg, 1987.

See also: Jorge Wolney Atalla; Francisco Matarazzo; José de Moraes.

ANDREW CARNEGIE
American industrialist, investor, and philanthropist

Carnegie rose from obscurity as a penniless immigrant to become an extraordinarily wealthy industrialist. He created a new form of social philanthropy that sought to improve people's lives through the establishment of museums, libraries, and concert halls.

Born: November 25, 1835; Dunfermline, Fife, Scotland
Died: August 11, 1919; Lenox, Massachusetts
Sources of wealth: Steel; investments
Bequeathal of wealth: Charity; educational institution

EARLY LIFE

Andrew Carnegie (AN-drew kahr-NAY-gee) was born in Dunfermline, Scotland, the son of William Carnegie and Margaret Morrison. When hard times fell upon Scotland in the mid-1800's, William, a weaver, decided that America offered a better life. Borrowing money, the family immigrated to Allegheny, Pennsylvania, in 1848, where, at the age of thirteen, Andrew started work as a bobbin boy in a cotton mill. The work was hard and not well paid, so in 1850, when Carnegie's uncle suggested he apply for work at the Ohio Telegraph Company, the

young man found a position as a telegraph messenger boy. This job provided Carnegie with free admission to plays and productions at a local theater, sparking his lifelong love of William Shakespeare. A local businessman, Colonel James Anderson, allowed Carnegie to borrow books freely from Anderson's four-hundred-volume library, a practice that convinced Carnegie of the value of lending libraries.

Carnegie continued to seek better employment, and his hard work and careful observation of the Ohio Telegraph Company's equipment enabled him to become a telegraph operator for the Pennsylvania Railroad. His boss at the railroad, Thomas A. Scott, took an interest in Carnegie, and the young man's subsequent rise in the company was swift, culminating in a position as superintendent of the railroad's division in Pittsburgh, Pennsylvania.

FIRST VENTURES

However, having a better-paying job did not satisfy Carnegie's desire for success. In 1855, guided by advice from Scott, Carnegie invested $500 in Adams Express. Carnegie later invested in the Pullman sleeping car division of the Pennsylvania Railroad Company. George Mortimer Pullman's invention of the sleeping car allowed businessmen to travel long distances in comfort, and one of Carnegie's earliest successes was his partnership with Pullman. Since Carnegie worked for the Pennsylvania Railroad's western division, he was positioned to benefit financially from improvements to Pullman's service. With America growing exponentially, railroad-related industries seemed to be a wise investment. The railroad became an even more vital service during the Civil War, when trains transported Union army munitions and troops.

Accumulating capital, Carnegie also invested money in ironworks and bridge-building companies, and his sound business sense enabled him to make money from these and other investments. For example, when he invested $40,000 in Storey Farm in Venango County, Pennsylvania, he garnered a profit of more than 100 percent; the oil wells and cash dividends from the property generated more than $1 million.

MATURE WEALTH

Carnegie left the railroad company in 1865 to concentrate on other business enterprises.

Because Pittsburgh was a mercantile and industrial center of the North during the Civil War, Carnegie sought to create a highly integrated, centralized plant for the manufacture of steel goods there. In 1875, he opened his first steel plant, the Edgar Thomson Steel Works, in Braddock, Pennsylvania. He carefully planned the 1883 purchase of the rival Homestead Steel Works, a company that included iron and coal fields in its list of assets. He maneuvered his company, renamed Carnegie Steel in 1892, into a position to become the largest producer not only of steel rails but also of pig iron and coke.

Carnegie created the Union Ironworks and the Keystone Bridge Works in Pittsburgh with the stated intent of replacing the city's wooden bridges with steel replacements. He helped build and owned stock in the Eads Bridge, a landmark steel structure crossing the Mississippi River in St. Louis, Missouri. The Eads project exemplified the new applications for which steel could be used. Carnegie solidified his growing fortune by employing the novel concept of buying into different industries related to the same product. He was interested not just in steel but also in the subsidiary processes of coke and pig iron manufacturing, coal mining, and oil refining. This vertical integration of services proved to be lucrative for Carnegie and his colleagues, even though working conditions for Carnegie's employees continued

Andrew Carnegie. (Library of Congress)

to be harsh and punitive. Carnegie's partner, Henry Clay Frick, had to quell a riot after a strike by workers at the Homestead steel mill escalated into a full-scale melee, resulting in the deaths not only of rioters but also of security workers.

By 1901, Carnegie was ready to change the focus of his life from the accumulation of wealth to its charitable distribution. J. P. Morgan, a prominent banker, assisted Carnegie in the preparations for what would become one of the largest buyouts in American history. Carnegie had spent years acquiring companies whose products were integral parts of the steel industry, so Morgan bought out not only Carnegie's businesses but also several other steel-related companies. By March 2, 1901, Morgan had conceptualized the founding of the United States Steel Corporation (better known as U.S. Steel), which was capitalized at $1.4 billion. Carnegie personally gained $225,639,000, which was paid to him in fifty-year gold bonds.

Carnegie had been involved in charitable projects for some time prior to the buyout. Two of the pleasures of his early life, books and theater, were areas in which he felt he could make a difference in the lives of working people. To this end, he had established lending libraries, funding more than three thousand of them by the end of his life.

Besides libraries, Carnegie believed that the proper funding of educational institutions, such as colleges, trade schools, and universities, was essential for the improvement of the public. In 1899, he donated £50,000 to establish the University of Birmingham in England. In 1901, he gave $2 million to the city of Pittsburgh to construct the Carnegie Institute of Technology (now part of Carnegie Mellon University) and donated $10 million through the Carnegie Trust for the Universities of Scotland to build institutes of higher learning in his native country.

Perhaps to counter a lifetime of resentment he faced from those who labored in his mills, Carnegie arranged for some of his fortune to be placed in pension funds, which former employees of the Homestead Steel Works could receive after retirement. Always a stalwart defender of the importance of education, Carnegie developed a pension fund for American college professors as an additional incentive for those who desired not only to pursue higher education but also to educate others. This retirement fund, later known as TIAA-CREF, continued to provide sizable benefits for its investors into the twenty-first century. Although Carnegie stipulated that religious schools had to become secular in order to receive his funding, his love of great music, both sacred and secular, led him to finance the building of seven thousand church organs. He participated in other artistic endeavors, including the building of New York City's Carnegie Hall and the Carnegie Museum of Art in Oakland, a suburb of Pittsburgh.

When Carnegie died on August 11, 1919, his solemn promise to disburse the bulk of his estate benefited many charities and made the once-despised tycoon a figure of philanthropy and conscience.

LEGACY

Carnegie was one of the greatest, and richest, captains of industry in nineteenth century America. He played a key role in developing American steel manufacturing, creating what would become a major national industry for many years to come. His business acumen and shrewd investments enabled him to rise from a poor immigrant to a powerful tycoon, typifying the success of other businessmen during America's Gilded Age.

He also set a new standard for charitable donations and public service. A desire to improve people's lives was a keynote of much of Carnegie's philanthropy. He built Carnegie Hall, for example, in order to stage productions that would lift the spirits of New Yorkers, just as Carnegie himself was heartened by the many plays he watched while working for the Ohio Telegraph Company. His early love of reading similarly led him to finance a network of public libraries. He performed an equally needed public service in 1884 by donating $50,000 to Bellevue Medical College in order to establish a new histological laboratory for the study of disease.

THE CARNEGIE FOUNDATION

An individual's decision to pursue a career in public education was one of the noblest pursuits Andrew Carnegie could envision. However, he recognized that teaching was a profession that lacked the respect it deserved and, for this reason, tended to pay poorly. Consequently, be believed that few people other than idealists and incompetents chose to teach in public schools, preferring the stable pay provided by private schools and universities, In 1905, Carnegie decided to rectify this problem by creating a foundation with the specific goal of improving, enriching, and dignifying the teaching profession. He lobbied for an act of Congress to enhance his foundation's influence, a goal that eventually was met.

The foundation continues to operate in the twenty-first century. It employs teachers, administrators, and researchers who devise the best means of applying universal educational standards in curricula of students and prospective teachers. Throughout its history, the foundation has made several notable achievements in the field of education. Perhaps its most important accomplishment was the establishment of Pell grants, which assist low- and middle-income students in financing their higher educations. The foundation created the Graduate Record Exam (GRE), a test that seeks to provide a standardized benchmark for the acceptance of college students into graduate programs of study. In 1910, the foundation published *The Flexner Report*, which advocated improved standards for American medical schools.

In the beginning of the twenty-first century, the foundation explored new uses for existing technology and the application of new technology in the classroom. By working with other organizations, like the Bill and Melinda Gates Foundation, a "wired" classroom using digital technology has ceased to be a dream for public schools and is being studied for broad implementation. The foundation has also increased its focus on improving basic skills classes for adult learners by providing additional funding for community colleges.

Carnegie had a particularly broad view of improving social welfare and was not shy about preaching his ideology to others. When he published his article "The Gospel of Wealth" in the June, 1889, issue of *North American Review*, he intended the article to be a guide for living a full life. He argued that too many wealthy individuals in history had sought fortune only to better their own lives. Instead, he declared, socially responsible individuals should spend only the first half of their lives in the pursuit of riches; the second half should be spent donating their wealth to worthy charities and institutions.

—*Julia M. Meyers*

FURTHER READING

Baker, James T. *Andrew Carnegie: Robber Baron as American Hero*. Belmont, Calif.: Wadsworth/Thomson, 2003. Various views on Carnegie's rise from poverty to riches and his many charitable endowments.

Carnegie, Andrew. *Autobiography of Andrew Carnegie*. New York: Houghton Mifflin, 1920. Also available in digital format by Tutis Digital Publishing (2009). From his birth as a poor boy in Scotland until his later years, entrepreneur and philanthropist Carnegie explains the forces that shaped him and his view of the obligations of the rich toward the country that sheltered him.

Morris, Charles R. *The Tycoons: How Andrew Carnegie, John D. Rockefeller, Jay Gould, and J. P. Morgan In-* vented the American Supereconomy. New York: Times Books, 2005. During a time of rampant growth and economic change, these four men reinvented what it meant to be an American businessman. Their business acumen and their competitiveness during the nineteenth century fostered the growth of consumerism and production that promoted the modern "middle-class" consumer.

Nasaw, David. *Andrew Carnegie*. New York: Penguin, 2006. A very complete biography of Carnegie.

Standiford, Les. *Meet You in Hell: Andrew Carnegie, Henry Clay Frick, and the Bitter Partnership That Transformed America*. New York: Crown, 2005. The title of this work is based on a true occurrence. At the end of his life, Carnegie asked to meet once again with his former friend, but now bitter enemy, Henry Clay Frick. Frick is said to have curtly informed Carnegie that he would meet him in Hell. This exchange exemplifies the best and the worst of these men and the Gilded Age in which they lived. Both men started out poor and rose to dominate the world of big industry, particularly the steel industry in Western Pennsylvania.

See also: Peter Cooper; Henry Clay Frick; Bill Gates; Alfred Krupp; Bertha Krupp; Andrew Mellon; J. P. Morgan; Henry Phipps; George Mortimer Pullman; Charles M. Schwab; Joséphine de Wendel.

ROBERT CARTER
American planter, merchant, and landowner

Carter was one of the wealthiest men in colonial America, amassing land throughout Virginia that allowed him to generate a fortune from the sale of tobacco and other products.

Born: c. 1663; Lancaster County, Virginia
Died: August 4, 1732; Lancaster County, Virginia
Also known as: King Carter
Sources of wealth: Real estate; trade; agricultural products; slaveholding
Bequeathal of wealth: Children; charity

EARLY LIFE

The younger son of well-to-do Virginia planter John Carter, Robert Carter spent his early years at Corotoman, the family farm on Virginia's Northern Neck. The house-hold included his parents (later a stepmother), elder brother John Carter II, and later John's wife, as well as dozens of servants and slaves. John Carter died in 1669, leaving Corotoman to Robert's elder brother, who became Robert's guardian. In 1672, Robert was sent to England for an education in the classics but also to learn the rudiments of the tobacco trade. Six years later, he returned to Virginia to take up life as a farmer and merchant.

FIRST VENTURES

In his will, Carter's father left him one thousand acres, land sufficient to allow him to live independently. After returning from England, however, he continued to live at Corotoman, and when he married Judith Armistead in 1688, he brought her to live there. Carter learned from his brother the intricacies of managing vast land holdings. In 1690, John Carter II died, and Robert inherited the six-thousand-acre estate.

MATURE WEALTH

Carter realized that tobacco depleted the land's nutrients rapidly and that the only way to provide financial security for himself and his family was to increase the size of his land holdings. For the next thirty years, he systematically sought opportunities to purchase other plantations and undeveloped land, both of which he used to produce goods that would generate significant profits when sold in the colonies or abroad. A shrewd businessman, he spent much of his time acquiring land on the Northern Neck and throughout Virginia, hiring overseers to run what quickly became a small empire of tobacco plantations. He was not always a favorite among the gentry, however; he may have acquired the sobriquet King Carter because he often behaved high-handedly in his dealings with others. He was frequently in court, where he brought suit against associates, friends, and even family members in an effort to preserve and expand his holdings for himself and his heirs. Carter sired eleven children—four with his first wife, who died in 1699, and seven more with second wife, Elizabeth Landon.

In colonial Virginia, wealth and land came with political responsibility, and Carter held office for most of his adult life. He served in the House of Burgesses, the colonists' elected assembly, and for a time was Speaker of the House. The king appointed him to the Governor's Council, on which he served a term as its president, and he was acting governor of colonial Virginia for a year. Carter was able to use these appointments to supplement his income from farming; at the time, government officials profited from their appointments to positions that allowed them to receive commissions or stipends for their work. Carter made the most of several appointments, especially as an agent for lands granted by the king to Thomas Fairfax, sixth Lord Fairfax of Cameron, in the region of Virginia where Carter lived. In this capacity, Carter was able to obtain large tracts of land in his sons' names, thereby increasing the family's holdings.

Carter died at Corotomon on August 4, 1732, and was buried in nearby Christ Church.

LEGACY

When he died, Carter was considered the richest man in Virginia. His estate included £10,000 and several plantations with more than 300,000 acres and 1,000 slaves. Always concerned for his children's welfare, he divided his property among them, ensuring that they had sufficient land and resources to keep them among the colony's most affluent and influential families. He made small bequests to a number of charities, but his most significant endowment was to Christ Church, the parish to which his family belonged. With his money, religious leaders were able to erect one of the finest churches in the colony.

—*Laurence W. Mazzeno*

FURTHER READING

Brown, Katharine. *Robert "King" Carter: Builder of Christ Church*. Staunton, Va.: Lot's Wife Publishing, 2001.

Dowdey, Clifford. *The Virginia Dynasties: The Emergence of "King" Carter and the Golden Age*. New York: Bonanza Books, 1969.

Hume, Ivor Noël. *Martin's Hundred*. Charlottesville: University Press of Virginia, 1991.

See also: Benjamin Franklin; John Hancock; William Penn; George Washington.

YACOUB CATTAUI
Egyptian banker, industrialist, and landowner

Cattaui prospered under the Egyptian governors in the nineteenth century, each of whom relied on Jewish families to create revenue for the country. Under the governors' favorable auspices, Cattaui was able to own banks and to set up and run other commercial interests.

Born: 1800; Cairo, Egypt
Died: 1883; Cairo, Egypt
Sources of wealth: Banking; trade; real estate
Bequeathal of wealth: Children; medical institution; educational institution

EARLY LIFE

Yacoub Cattaui (YAH-coob kat-TOW-ee) was the eldest son of Eliahou Khadar Cattaui, who settled in Cairo, Egypt, as part of an influx of immigrants who arrived in the country during the late eighteenth and early nineteenth centuries. The governor of Egypt, Muḥammad ʿAlī Pasha, invited foreigners to settle there so he could use their skills and knowledge in his attempt to modernize the country. As part of this modernization, Yacoub obtained many concessions from the government, including financial privileges and the right to operate flour mills in the vicinity of Cairo.

FIRST VENTURES

After the death of Muhammed Ali in 1849, the new governor, ʿAbbās I, appointed Cattaui director of the treasury, as well as lessee of certain government monopolies, such as the fisheries and customs. ʿAbbās's successor Saʿid used Cattaui as his private banker and appointed him *sarraf bashi* (chief banker), which made Cattaui responsible for all the other bankers employed by the government. Eventually, Cattaui became president of the Jewish community of Cairo.

Cattaui married Mazel Negrin and the couple had three children: Moise, Aslan, and Sembra. Cattaui later married Esther Morgana, and with her had five more children: Gamilla, Youssef, Renee, Ellie, and Elena. The Cattaui residence on Cherifein Street in Cairo was situated in the middle of a large garden overlooking what is now Talaat Harb Square. The street, Kasr al-Nil, was often called Rue Cattaui.

MATURE WEALTH

An important factor in the growth of the Cattaui family's wealth was the acceptance with which Jews were welcomed in Cairo during the eighteenth and nineteenth centuries. Visitors to Cairo in 1840 remarked that a population more respectful of all religious beliefs would be difficult to find. Eliahou Alghazi, Cattaui's brother-in-law, was instrumental in establishing schools for Jewish children in Cairo, and these institutions were the envy of some European visitors.

This welcoming attitude toward Jews, as well as the implementation of new types of banking, made it possible for the Cattaui family to reach high positions in the Egyptian government. Jews worked to set up various banks, including the National Bank of Egypt, the Egyptian Credit Foncier, and Banque Misr. These banks assisted in international trade, land development, the construction of industrial plants and infrastructure, and other forms of national expansion. An incident in 1880 points to the wealth of Cattaui and of his family. In that year, Crown Prince Rudolf of Austria visited Cairo, and Cattaui used the occasion to endow the construction of a hospital in Rudolf's name. By the time of his death in 1883, Cattaui, his in-laws, his sons Moise and Aslan, and their sons had established themselves as one of the wealthiest families in Cairo.

LEGACY

After Cattaui's death, his sons Aslan and Moise carried on the family banking and sugar refining industries in Cairo and in Alexandria. In 1905, the *Egyptian Gazette* reported that Moise's extensive real estate holdings included six thousand square meters of Nile River frontage in the fashionable Cairo district of Kasr al Dubara. Probably the most distinguished member of the family was Cattaui's oldest grandson and Aslan's son, Joseph Aslan Cattaui (1861-1942). Joseph obtained his degree in engineering in France in 1882, and he then spent time in Moravia, where he became familiar with all phases of the sugar refining industry. He returned to Egypt and became a technical and financial adviser, assisting in the construction of the Heluan Railway and the water supply system for the town of Tantah and in the reconstruction and expansion of a major Egyptian sugar refinery and the Wadi Kom-Ombo Company, a sugar firm.

—*Winifred Whelan*

FURTHER READING

Faur, José. "Sephardim in the Nineteenth Century: New Directions and Old Values." *Proceedings of the American Association for Jewish Research* 44 (1997): 29-52.

Grunwald, Kurt. "On Cairo's Lombard Street." *Tradition* 17, no.1 (1992): 8-22.

Raafat, Samir. "Dynasty: The House of Yacoub Cattaui." *Egyptian Mail*, April 2, 1994.

Targan, Hana. "The 'Gate of Heaven' (Sha'ar Hashama-yim) Synagogue in Cairo (1898-1905): On the Contextualization of Jewish Communal Architecture." *Journal of Jewish Identities*, 2, no.1 (2009): 31-54.

See also: David Sassoon.

DEBORAH CAVENDISH
British aristocrat and businesswoman

Cavendish worked with her husband and then her grandson to restore the family fortunes of the dukes of Devonshire, particularly putting Chatsworth House, the main family residence and one of Britain's stateliest homes, on a sound financial footing.

Born: March 31, 1920; Asthall Manor, Oxfordshire, England

Also known as: Deborah Vivien Freeman-Mitford Cavendish; Deborah Vivien Freeman-Mitford (birth name); Dowager Duchess of Devonshire

Sources of wealth: Inheritance; real estate; tourism

Bequeathal of wealth: Unknown

EARLY LIFE
Deborah Cavendish was born Deborah Vivien Freeman-Mitford, the youngest of six talented and extraordinary girls, who, with one brother, constituted the family of David Freeman-Mitford II, Baron Redesdale, and his wife Sydney. The girls were allowed considerable freedom in growing up in their country estate, encouraged to be beautiful and to marry young and well. Two of them, Nancy and Jessica, became writers. Another, Diana, after a scandal married Oswald Mosley, the British fascist leader, and spent three years in prison during World War II. By contrast, Jessica became a member of the American Communist Party. Deborah herself met Nazi leader Adolf Hitler in 1937.

Deborah became the family peacemaker in this divergence of political philosophies. More important, under the tutelage of a neighbor, society leader Nancy Lancaster, Deborah became known as the real beauty of the family, and in 1941 she married Andrew Cavendish, the younger son of the eleventh duke of Devonshire. The Cavendishes were an old, established, aristocratic family, dating back to the sixteenth century. They had been named the dukes of Devonshire in 1694 in exchange for supporting the Glorious Revolution (1688-1689), in which King James II was deposed and William III and Mary II become the new Protestant sovereigns.

At the time of his marriage to Deborah, Andrew Cavendish was serving in the Coldstream Guards. As he had no immediate prospects of inheriting his father's title, Cavendish took a job with the Macmillan publishing house, with which the Cavendishes had family connections. Harold Macmillan, later the British prime minister, was Cavendish's uncle.

FIRST VENTURES
However, during World War II, Cavendish's older brother was killed in action in Belgium in 1944, and although he was married to Kathleen Kennedy, the sister of future president John F. Kennedy, the couple had no children. This meant that Andrew, as heir, assumed the title marquis of Hartington, and Deborah became the marchioness. When his father died in 1950, Andrew became the eleventh duke of Devonshire, and Deborah was now the duchess.

The Cavendish family's primary estate was at Chatsworth House, in Derbyshire's Peak District, and was one of the most stately homes in the country. The Cavendishes owned other estates, including Lismore Castle in Ireland, Bolton Abbey in Yorkshire, a London residence in Mayfair, and a London club. The family also had developed the seaside resort of Eastbourne in the nineteenth century, and they still owned large parts of the town.

However, Chatsworth was in bad condition by World War II, when it was used as a girls' boarding school. After Andrew's father died, crippling death duties were imposed on the estate in the 1950's. For a while it looked as if the estate would go the way of many old homes in Great Britain, to be either sold or donated to the nation through the National Trust. Deborah, however, urged Andrew to retain the Chatsworth estate as a family home and to find ways to make it financially viable and to pay off the duties. In 1967, these duties were negotiated at the sum of £7 million and were paid off in twenty-four years. As part of the process, the Cavendishes were required to give the state a number of art treasures, including one of their three Rembrandts, and sell off part of the grounds.

CHATSWORTH HOUSE

The original Chatsworth House was a Tudor-style residence built in the sixteenth century by Sir William Cavendish while he was married to the redoubtable Bess of Hardwick. Cavendish had gained lands in East Anglia from Henry VIII while disposing of the monasteries the king had taken from the Catholic church. Bess, who came from Derbyshire, persuaded Cavendish to sell the East Anglia lands and buy property in the Derwent Valley of England's Peak District. After Cavendish's death, Bess married the earl of Shrewsbury and continued to develop the small manor house originally on site into a five-story mansion. The construction project eventually cost £80,000 and was a point of some contention between Bess and her husband. Mary, Queen of Scots, was briefly imprisoned at Chatsworth House.

The house remained in the family after Bess's death. In 1618, her son William Cavendish was named the first earl of Devonshire. After the Glorious Revolution (1688-1689), the old Tudor mansion was gradually replaced by a substantial new residence, built under the guidance of architect William Talman, and formal gardens were laid out. The first of the gardens' water features, fed by water from the surrounding moors, also were constructed at this time, to be expanded by successive landscape architects. In the eighteenth century, James Paine and Lancelot "Capability" Brown, leading landscape and garden designers, made the setting even more magnificent as the dukes of Devonshire became even more important. For example, between 1750 and 1790, William Cavendish, fourth duke of Devonshire, was prime minister for six months beginning in November, 1756, and five other family members held seats in Parliament. New paintings and furnishings also were acquired. A new wing was built in the nineteenth century, but it was demolished in 1919.

In 1826, William George Spencer Cavendish, sixth duke of Devonshire, appointed a twenty-three-year-old head gardener, Joseph Paxton, who designed an innovative conservatory and other landscape features; Paxton later designed the Crystal Palace, which housed the Great Exhibition of 1851 in London's Hyde Park. The sixth duke was primarily responsible for building the home's seventeen-thousand-book library.

The 36,000-acre Chatsworth estate features a 1,000-acre deer park and 105 acres of formal gardens, with many greenhouses and prize collections of camellias and crocuses. The grounds also contain numerous water features, including fountains, cascades, artificial valleys, ponds, and lakes. The residence itself has 175 rooms, 21 kitchens, 13 acres of roofs, more than 3,000 feet of passages, and 17 staircases. Chatsworth is also the location of a large farm shop, employing more than one hundred people, a restaurant, and a bookstore.

Deborah and her husband chose to restore Chatsworth's house and grounds and to open the estate to the public, charging visitors an entrance fee. The public would be able to view the contents of the house, including the family's art collection, which included paintings by Frans Hals, Sir Anthony van Dyck, and Rembrandt. Deborah saw other business opportunities for the property, such as growing farm produce to be sold at an estate shop; publishing booklets about the house, gardens, and artworks; and opening a restaurant. She later published cookbooks with recipes served at the estate's restaurant. These ventures resulted in the family's loss of privacy, the expense of restoration, and the hard work of operating the estate and its related businesses.

MATURE WEALTH

The Cavendishes set up a charitable trust fund in 1981, endowing it with the proceeds from the sale of a number of artworks, including one painting that was sold to the Getty Museum. These art sales, as well as the income derived from the public tours and other estate-related ventures, generated sufficient wealth to make the estate economically viable.

In all of these enterprises, Deborah provided the entrepreneurial drive and vision, and her sense of style kept the family tradition of elegance and nobility intact. A number of other country estates that did become self-sufficient, including some that became safari parks, lost this sense of style and tradition. However, Deborah's innate aristocracy retained Chatsworth as the "Palace of the Peak."

Her husband, Andrew, was involved in a number of other activities. In the early 1960's, he held several positions in the Conservative administration of his uncle, Prime Minister Harold Macmillan. Andrew also enjoyed horse racing, serving as steward of the Jockey Club from 1966 to 1969. Andrew preferred to live at Chatsworth, while Deborah spent time at their Mayfair house.

Deborah's activities also included buying modern art to replace the artworks she had sold, purchasing works by such artists as L. S. Lowry, Gwen John, and Lucien Freud. She copyrighted some of the wallpaper designs and other decorative features of Chatsworth and marketed them under the imprint of Chatsworth Design, and she also developed several hotels that the Cavendishes owned. She continued her writing, branching out from books about Chatsworth to works about her own life and times.

LEGACY

When Andrew died in May, 2004, the estate was inherited by his son Peregrine, who became the twelfth duke of Devonshire. Deborah went to live in an old refurbished vicarage on the Chatsworth estate. However, the new duke did not have the desire to operate Chatsworth, so the dowager duchess, as Deborah was now known, teamed up with one of her fifteen grandchildren, William, earl of Burlington, to continue the work of running Chatsworth as a financial enterprise.

Deborah Cavendish's legacy has been to maintain for both the Cavendish family and the British people a priceless family estate, fully restored to the vision of its previous owners and developers, accessible to the general public, and in a stunningly beautiful part of England. She has been able to retain the best characteristics of the British aristocratic tradition. In 1999, she was appointed Dame Commander of the Royal Victorian Order for her services to the queen's royal collection.

—*David Barratt*

FURTHER READING

Devonshire, Deborah. *Home to Roost: And Other Peckings.* London: John Murray, 2009. Memoirs and essays by the dowager duchess, covering most of her life. She writes in a deceptively simple style.

Devonshire, Deborah, and Simon Upton. *Chatsworth: The House.* London: Frances Lincoln, 2002. The most popular of the duchess's books about Chatsworth, she takes the reader on a historical tour of its buildings, furniture, and art treasures. This book replaces two earlier books she wrote about the house in 1982; other books cover the grounds and provide recipes.

Fermor, Patrick Leigh. *In Tearing Haste: Letters Between Deborah Devonshire and Patrick Leigh Fermor.* London: John Murray, 2008. These letters date to the beginning of the friendship in 1956 at Lismore Castle, and they encapsulate Deborah's lifestyle and world in an entertaining way.

Mosley, Charlotte, ed. *The Mitfords: Letters Between the Six Sisters.* London: The Fourth Estate, 2007. Reprints about 5 percent of the voluminous lifelong daily exchange of letters between Deborah and her sisters.

Pearson, John. *The Serpent and the Stag: The Story of the House of Cavendish, and the Dukes of Devonshire.* New York: Holt, Rinehart & Winston, 1983. The best full-length history of the Cavendish family, even though in need of some updating.

See also: Bess of Hardwick; Georgiana Cavendish; Henry Cavendish.

GEORGIANA CAVENDISH
British socialite

Cavendish's wealth enabled her to shine in late eighteenth and early nineteenth century England as a leader in fashion and politics. However, the expenses of maintaining her position and her love of gambling (a common vice among the eighteenth century aristocracy) meant that much of her life was lived in financial need.

Born: June 7, 1757; Wimbledon, Surrey, England
Died: March 30, 1806; London, England
Also known as: Georgiana Spencer (birth name); Duchess of Devonshire
Sources of wealth: Inheritance; marriage
Bequeathal of wealth: Dissipated

EARLY LIFE

Georgiana Spencer Cavendish was born in 1757 to John Spencer, first earl of Spencer, and his wife Margaret Georgiana Spencer. Georgiana enjoyed the benefits of the Spencers' wealth and social status, traveling extensively and gaining a social and cultural polish that would become a hallmark. She met her future husband, the very wealthy and socially prominent William Cavendish, fifth duke of devonshire, while traveling with her family in the Austrian Netherlands in 1772. The two determined to wed, despite concerns over their future compatibility and Georgiana's youth. They were married on June 7, 1774.

FIRST VENTURES

The young duchess quickly established herself in London society. A leader of fashion, she was responsible for the introduction of numerous styles of dress, including the ostrich-feather headdress. In 1783, Cavendish rejected her elaborate fashions of previous years in favor of a simple muslin dress, and she again set the tone for many London ladies.

In London, Cavendish acquired a vice that would haunt her life—gambling. She played very heavily and moved in a circle of fast-living aristocratic Londoners who congregated at the duke's London residence, Devonshire House. One heavy gambler who would have a great impact on Cavendish's subsequent career was the Whig politician Charles James Fox, a longtime friend and political ally. Cavendish campaigned vigorously, and controversially, for Fox's election to the House of Commons from the constituency of Westminster. During the energetic campaign of 1784, she was criticized for undue intimacy with working-class voters, including trading votes for kisses. Cavendish also became friends with the heir to the throne, Prince George, the future George IV.

MATURE WEALTH

Cavendish played a diminished political role after 1784, as the Whigs were out of power. Her private life was also unhappy, as her husband had established his mistress, Lady Elizabeth Foster, in the household. Foster had originally been Cavendish's friend and the relationship between the two women and the duke was complex. Foster used Cavendish's spiraling gambling debts in an unsuccessful maneuver to get the duke to legally separate from his wife. Cavendish was also discredited by the Whig Party's failure in the Regency Crisis of 1788, when the madness of King George III seemed to offer the opportunity for the Whigs' ally, Prince George, to come to power as regent for his father. Following George III's recovery, the Devonshires went into voluntary exile on the European continent.

In 1791, Cavendish became pregnant with the child of the young Whig politician Charles Grey, with whom she had been having an affair for about two years. The duke gave her the choice of divorce or separation, and Cavendish opted to live with her household in Naples, returning to England in 1793 after the birth of her child. During the next decade, Cavendish lost most of her sight because of an infection and lived a more socially retired life, eventually giving up gambling (although her large debts continued to cause great strain) and devoting much of her time to collecting minerals and improving the ducal houses.

After the resignation of the ministry led by Fox's old rival William Pitt the Younger in 1801, Cavendish returned to politics as Fox's ally, helping to promote a reconciliation between Fox and Prince George and attempting to keep the Whig Party together as a coherent body. The short-lived Ministry of All the Talents, a unity government formed in 1806, included Fox and was also viewed as a political triumph for Cavendish. She died of a liver disease shortly after the ministry's formation.

LEGACY

Cavendish demonstrated the ability of a wealthy woman to play a leading part in the cultural and political affairs of her time, despite the widespread criticism she received for behavior unbecoming to her gender.

—William E. Burns

FURTHER READING

Chapman, Caroline, and Jane Dormer. *Elizabeth and Georgiana: The Duke of Devonshire and His Two Duchesses*. Hoboken, N.J.: John Wiley, 2002.

Foreman, Amanda. *Georgiana, Duchess of Devonshire*. New York: Random House, 2000.

Masters, Brian. *Georgiana, Duchess of Devonshire*. London: Hamish Hamilton, 1981.

See also: Bess of Hardwick; Deborah Cavendish; Henry Cavendish.

HENRY CAVENDISH
British scientist

Cavendish used his inherited wealth to fund personal scientific experiments. He lived a thrifty existence and in solitude for most of his adult life, but he was a highly respected scientist of the eighteenth century.

Born: October 10, 1731; Nice, France
Died: February 24, 1810; London, England
Also known as: Honourable Henry Cavendish
Source of wealth: Inheritance
Bequeathal of wealth: Relatives

EARLY LIFE
Henry Cavendish was born in 1731 in Nice in the south of France, where his mother was convalescing in the mild climate. His parents came from British aristocracy, although their status was earned though service to the government. Cavendish was raised by his father and servants after his mother died in 1733. He received schooling from home until eleven and then attended a private school near London. He developed an early interest in science and at eighteen entered Cambridge University. Cavendish was extremely shy and uncomfortable around people, especially strangers and women.

FIRST VENTURES
Cavendish left Cambridge in 1753 before graduating and built a private laboratory in his family's London home. Although his father shared his son's interest in science, he was unhappy that his son did not follow a career more typical of nobility, such as political or public service. Consequently, he provided his son with only a modest allowance of £500 a year. It nevertheless enabled Cavendish to equip his laboratory with instruments for his early experiments.

In the 1780's, Cavendish inherited an enormous fortune from a first cousin, who admired his dedication to science. He moved to a mansion in the north of London and rented another home south of London in Clapham Common, where much of his important scientific work was conducted. When his father died in 1783, Cavendish inherited an additional fortune and was reputed to be the wealthiest scientist of his day.

MATURE WEALTH
Having unlimited funds, Cavendish was able to buy or construct the best scientific instruments of the period, which were essential for his accurate measurements in the areas of chemistry and physics. Cavendish studied the properties of gases and was a careful experimenter

and analyst. One of his most important discoveries was to show that water—long thought to be an element—was actually composed of two elements, hydrogen and oxygen. He also investigated electrical phenomena and developed an interest in gravitation.

Although he spent a considerable fortune on his scientific instruments and on renovating his homes to accommodate his research, Cavendish was remarkably frugal in all other aspects. He had no desire for fancy food or clothing, generally wearing suits from the previous century. Nor did he have any interest in the things his family valued, such as land acquisition, material wealth, politics, or marriage. Aside from money spent on his re-

Henry Cavendish. (Library of Congress)

search, his only extravagance was an extensive personal library. As he grew older, Cavendish became even more reclusive and eccentric. In order to avoid contact with his servants, he built a staircase at the back of his house for his personal use. Rarely did he leave the house, except once a week for professional meetings at the Royal Society. On these occasions, he would go to great lengths to avoid meeting people.

At Cavendish's death, he was reported to be the largest holder of bank stock in England. He left more than £1 million in his will, of which £700,000 went to his cousin Lord George Cavendish. The remainder was distributed to other family members.

LEGACY
Science historians regard Cavendish as a brilliant eighteenth century scientist. However, without access to a personal fortune, he would not have been such a productive researcher. Financial independence enabled Cavendish to work in isolation. Many scientists of the time worked in universities as teachers to support themselves, but because of his extreme shyness and other eccentrici-

ties it is unlikely Cavendish could have tolerated close contact with people had it been necessary for him to seek employment.

—*Nicholas C. Thomas*

FURTHER READING
Berry, A. J. *Henry Cavendish: His Life and Scientific Work*. London: Hutchinson, 1960.
Jungnickel, Christa, and Russell McCormmach. *Cavendish, the Experimental Life*. Lewisburg, Pa.: Bucknell University Press, 1999.
McCormmach, Russell. *Speculative Truth: Henry Cavendish, Natural Philosophy, and the Rise of Modern Theoretical Science*. New York: Oxford University Press, 2004.
Wilson, George. *The Life of the Honorable Henry Cavendish: Including Abstracts of His More Important Scientific Papers*. Reprint. Whitefish, Mont.: Kessinger, 2008.

See also: Bess of Hardwick; Deborah Cavendish; Georgiana Cavendish; James Smithson.

ANNE COX CHAMBERS
American publisher, media owner, and philanthropist

Chambers and her younger sister Barbara Cox Anthony tended and grew their father's media empire during the second half of the twentieth century and into the twenty-first century, with Chambers wielding considerable influence in newspaper, radio, television, and cable subscriber markets from her home base in Atlanta, Georgia.

Born: December 1, 1919; Dayton, Ohio
Also known as: Anne Cox (birth name)
Sources of wealth: Inheritance; media
Bequeathal of wealth: Children; charity; educational institution

EARLY LIFE
Anne Cox Chambers was born in 1919, the daughter of James M. Cox, a Dayton, Ohio, publisher who was then the governor of Ohio, and of Cox's second wife, Margaretta Parler Blair. Chambers was raised in a home where she learned how to expand and run a media empire, while also developing a lifelong allegiance to the Democratic Party. Her father, a high school dropout, had become a reporter, bought a Dayton newspaper, exerted his growing

influence to become a three-term governor of Ohio, and was the Democratic nominee for president of the United States in 1920, with Franklin D. Roosevelt as his vice presidential running mate.

FIRST VENTURES
Although Cox lost his bid for the presidency, he shrewdly expanded Cox Enterprises into the developing radio market in the 1930's and the new television market in the 1940's before his death in 1957. Chambers studied at Finch College in Manhattan, married Robert William Chambers in 1955, and had three children. After her brother Jim, Jr., died in 1974, Chambers, who then co-owned the family company with her younger sister Barbara Cox Anthony, had opportunities to help guide Cox Enterprises, and the corporation would eventually enter the cable and Internet markets. From her home in Atlanta, Georgia, Chambers chairs the board of Atlanta Newspapers, Inc., and has broken new ground for women by serving as a director of the Bank of the South (from 1977 to 1982), a director of Coca-Cola (1981-1991), and the first female member of the board of directors of the Atlanta Chamber of Commerce.

MATURE WEALTH

In 1988, Chambers ceded control of Cox Enterprises to her nephew James Cox Kennedy, while remaining actively involved as an adviser to the company. In the twenty-first century, Cox Enterprises, a multibillion-dollar media corporation, continued to be a significant force among the select group of major American communications businesses, owning many newspapers, radio and television stations, a large cable company, a used-car retailer, and an Internet company. Anthony, Chambers's last remaining sibling, died in 2007. The following year, Chambers was considered the fourth-richest woman in America, with assets totaling more than $13 billion. After the economic downturn in the closing months of President George W. Bush's administration, her assets were estimated to have dropped to around $9 billion, but this still ranked her in a tie for number forty-three on the *Forbes* magazine list of the world's richest people, and she remained the wealthiest person in Georgia.

LEGACY

Chambers has done much laudable philanthropic work in the arts, such as supporting museums, among them the High Museum of Art in Atlanta and the Whitney Museum of American Art and the Museum of Modern Art in New York City. However, her greatest legacy has been her unwavering support as a fund-raiser for the Democratic Party. She provided financial assistance to Barack Obama during his 2008 presidential campaign, and she has offered similar funding to other party candidates, most notably President Jimmy Carter. Carter, who came from Plains, Georgia, and had been governor of that state, appointed Chambers to be American ambassador to Belgium from 1977 through 1981. Chambers's philanthropy subsequently extended to the Carter Center, which Carter developed in 1982 as a policy institute affiliated with both the Carter Presidential Library and Emory University. Chambers also actively supports the Council of American Ambassadors and is a founding trustee of the Southern Center for International Studies, a nonprofit educational institute based in Atlanta.

—Scot M. Guenter

FURTHER READING

Chambers, John Whiteclay, II. "Jimmy Carter's Public Policy Ex-Presidency." *Political Science Quarterly* 113, no. 3 (Fall, 1998): 405-425.

Glover, Charles F. *Journey Through Our Years: The Story of Cox Enterprises, Inc.* Atlanta, Ga.: Longstreet Press, 1999.

Halpern, Diane F., and Fanny M. Cheung. *Women at the Top: Powerful Leaders Tell Us How to Combine Work and Family.* Malden, Mass.: Wiley-Blackwell, 2008.

Stone, Clarence N. *Regime Politics: Governing Atlanta, 1946-1988.* Lawrence: University Press of Kansas, 1989.

See also: Walter Annenberg; Barbara Cox Anthony; Lord Beaverbrook; Silvio Berlusconi; Michael Bloomberg; Katharine Graham; William Randolph Hearst; John H. Johnson; Robert L. Johnson; John Kluge; Rupert Murdoch; Samuel I. Newhouse; Kerry Packer; Ted Turner; Oprah Winfrey.

FATEH CHAND
Mughal banker and government official

An immensely wealthy and influential banker to the Bengali nawabs (provincial governors) and Mughal emperors, Fateh Chand was awarded the title of Jagat Seth, or "banker of the world."

Born: c. 1680; Bengal, India
Died: 1744; Bengal, India
Also known as: Jagat Seth; Baidnath; Banker of the World
Source of wealth: Banking
Bequeathal of wealth: Children; relatives

EARLY LIFE
Hiranand Shah, the grandfather of Fateh Chand (FAHT-eh chahnd), established a saltpeter trading and banking enterprise around 1652 in Patna, India. His son Manik Chand expanded the business into Murshidabad, the capital of the Bengal province of the Mughal Empire. When Manik Chand died in 1714, his nephew and adopted son, Fateh, succeeded to the business. Like many of the bankers and merchants of the Mughal Empire, Fateh Chand was a Jain.

FIRST VENTURES
Chand's moneylending enterprise was headquartered in Murshidabad in eastern India. Governed by a dynastic line of nawabs (provincial governors), Bengal was the wealthiest and most populous of the *subahs* (provinces) of the Mughal Empire. The Mughals had risen to power through conquest and plunder, but they had learned to govern their economy with order, taxes, and a stable currency. The basic coin of the realm was the silver rupee, which would be worth about $20 in 2010 currency.

Chand had banking branches in the cities of Dhaka, Patna, Delhi, and Murshidabad. He made loans, bought and sold gold and silver, repaid loans for merchants, and exchanged foreign currencies. Early in his career, he was made the treasurer general of Bengal. A major source of Chand's revenue was the interest that Bengali *zamindars* (landholders) would pay him on the loans they needed in order to pay taxes due the Mughal government. As Chand grew wealthier, he was also able to bankroll the European trading companies in East India. From 1718 to 1730, the British East India Company borrowed an average of almost 500,000 rupees a year from Chand. The French and Dutch East India Companies similarly borrowed great sums from him. Chand charged a standard interest rate of 12 percent annually. The schedule of ship-ping left European merchants chronically short of capital and they were forced to pay Chand's rates.

MATURE WEALTH
Chand's most profitable enterprise was his service as banker to the Mughal rulers. The Mughal Emperor Farrukh Siyar honored Chand with the title Jagat Seth (Banker of the World), which recognized the essential role that Chand's banking house played in the Mughal Empire. The title was passed down to Chand's heirs, although there is also evidence he had to pay the emperor 500,000 silver rupees for the privilege. The great British parliamentarian Edmund Burke called Chand the "Rothschild of India," and the British historian Robert Orme called Chand "the greatest money-changer and banker in the known world."

Chand was entrusted with the operation of the imperial mint at Murshidabad, a central government function and a major source of revenue for his family. It has been disputed whether Chand had exclusive use of the mint and the right to set rates of seigniorage, or government revenue from the manufacture of coins. European traders complained about Chand's control of the Bengali economy and the rapacious use he made of his minting privilege. Chand was the largest purchaser of silver bullion in the Mughal Empire, minting 5 million rupees worth of coins each year. There were other wealthy bankers in Bengal, such as Umichand, who left an estate of 4.2 million rupees. However, the wealth of Jaget Seth was staggering, estimated at around 70-140 million rupees, the equivalent of billions of dollars in 2010 currency.

The wealth of the house of Jagat Seth was so great that it played a role in dynastic changes. In 1727, Fateh Chand helped install Shuja-ud-Din Muhammad Khan as the nawab of Bengal. In 1740, Chand was instrumental in Alivardi Khan's deposition of Nawab Sarfaraz Khan. The house of Jagat Seth assisted the English victory at the Battle of Plassey in 1757, when a British East India Company force commanded by Robert Clive gained sovereignty over East India. After Chand's death, his heirs Mahtab Rai and Swaroopchand headed the house of Jagat Seth.

LEGACY
The greatest banker in the history of the Mughal Empire, Jagat Seth Fateh Chand served as the treasurer and minister of the Bengal province and as the chief moneylender to the European trading companies and the Mughal rul-

ers. Assisting the English accession of India, the house of Jagat Seth remained the bankers of the British East India Company until 1773. The descendants of Chand retained the title of Jagat Seth until 1912.

—Howard Bromberg

FURTHER READING
Chaudhury, Sushil. *From Prosperity to Decline: Eighteenth Century Bengal*. Delhi, India: Manohar, 1999.

Little, J. H. *The House of Jagat Seth*. Calcutta: Calcutta Historical Society, 1967.
McLane, John R. *Land and Local Kingship in Eighteenth-Century Bengal*. Cambridge, England: Cambridge University Press, 2002.

See also: Aurangzeb; Robert Clive; Abdul Ghafur; Shah Jahan; Virji Vora; Shantidas Zaveri.

DHANIN CHEARAVANONT
Thai agribusinessman, investor, and landowner

Chearavanont's business accomplishments and fortune benefited his family and helped Thailand secure a significant role in international markets. His financial insights affected the policies of foreign countries, especially China.

Born: January 28, 1939; Bangkok, Thailand
Also known as: Dhanin Chiaravanont
Sources of wealth: Agricultural products; trade; real estate
Bequeathal of wealth: Children; relatives; charity

EARLY LIFE
Dhanin Chearavanont (TA-nihn GEE-rah-wah-non) was born on January 28, 1939, in Bangkok, Thailand, the son of Chia Ek Chow and Kimkeea. His parents had emigrated from Shantou, Guangdong Province, in southern China to Siam (now Thailand) in 1919. Chearavanont's father and uncle brought vegetable seeds from their family's Chinese farm to Bangkok. By 1921, the brothers established the Chia Tai seed store. As a boy, Chearavanont helped his three older brothers package seeds for customers. He attended both Thai and Chinese schools. In 1956, Chearavanont studied at Hong Kong Commercial College. He later was a student at National Defence College in Bangkok. Chearavanont married his wife, Tawee Watanalikhi, in 1962. They have five children, sons Supakij, Narong, and Supachai and daughters Varnnee and Thipaporn.

FIRST VENTURES
In 1953, Chearavanont's family established a mill in order to manufacture livestock feed and renamed their business Charoen Pokphand (CP) Group. They later opened mills to produce feed for livestock throughout

Asia. CP also shipped eggs, ducks, chickens, and hogs to domestic and foreign markets. By 1964, Chearavanont directed CP's agribusiness endeavors.

Impressed with the contributions of scientific research to increasing meat yields, Chearavanont imported chickens bred to mature quickly from Arbor Acres Farm in Hartford, Connecticut. He also contacted nutrition experts to prepare feeds that would enhance the growth of chickens. In Thailand, Chearavanont contracted with farmers to raise chickens he provided them. He introduced his poultry husbandry methods to farmers in nearby Asian countries, increasing CP's profits. Chearavanont also implemented processing techniques enabling CP to earn income from every aspect of producing livestock through delivering meat to markets. He arranged for farmers to use specially prepared feeds to raise shrimp or fish from larvae or eggs. CP purchased harvested shrimp and fish, freezing and exporting yields.

MATURE WEALTH
Chearavanont strove to identify and pursue entrepreneurial opportunities before his competitors. He invested in land, stores, factories, and gas stations, securing alliances with 7-Eleven, Honda, and other corporations. Interested in developing businesses in China, by 1978 Chearavanont had registered CP in that country. Aware of emerging technologies, Chearavanont invested in petrochemicals and fiber optics in the 1980's, establishing Telecom Asia.

CP's livestock feed business continued to prosper, ranking first in Thailand and fifth globally. CP owned more than one hundred feed mills in Asia, Europe, and North America, with yields averaging fourteen million tons annually in the early 1990's.

CP's success worldwide contributed to Chearavanont's elite financial status. In September, 1992, *Fortune* magazine included Chearavanont on its list of world billionaires. In 1995, *Forbes* estimated Chearavanont's family's wealth at $5.5 billion, the richest in Thailand. CP generated annual revenues of $8 billion. Chearavanont and his brothers each owned 13 percent of CP.

During the 1997 Asian economic crisis, Chearavanont sold numerous CP properties and concentrated on agribusiness income sources. By 2002, CP had survived the crisis and continued to expand, despite the early twenty-first century avian flu epidemic threatening Chearavanont's poultry businesses. Chearavanont responded by quarantining CP facilities. Under Chearavanont's leadership, CP earned revenues totaling $13 billion in 2002.

In 2006, Chearavanont attained the rank of 317 on the *Forbes* list of the world's richest people; CP's sales totaled $14 billion that year. In September, 2009, *Forbes* ranked Chearavanont, who was worth $3 billion, the second-wealthiest person in Thailand.

LEGACY
Chearavanont's wealth impacted Asians by providing them an inexpensive source of sustenance with protein and nutrients. Many people had been unable to purchase meat until CP's affordable products were sold. These

foods became a regular component of many people's diets, strengthening bodies while reinforcing Asian economies. In an attempt to reduce rural poverty, Chearavanont promoted the payment of equitable prices to rice farmers for their crops instead of demanding low charges that benefited commercial companies like CP. He shared his wealth through donations to schools and charities, such as Synergos, which fights poverty. He also supported hospital and agricultural programs that were sponsored by Thailand's royalty.

—*Elizabeth D. Schafer*

FURTHER READING
Hiscock, Geoff. *Asia's New Wealth Club: Who's Really Who in Twenty-first Century Business, the Top 100 Billionaires in Asia*. Naperville, Ill.: Nicholas Brealey, 2000.
Tanzer, Andrew. "The Birdman of Bangkok." *Forbes* 149, no. 8 (April 13, 1992): 86-89.
Vorasarun, Chaniga. "The Price of Rice." *Forbes Global* 4, no. 15 (September 15, 2008): 40-41.

See also: Liu Yongxing; Seng Sae Khu; Thaksin Shinawatra.

IVAN BORISOVICH CHERKASSKY
Russian aristocrat and government official

Cherkassky was a nobleman who headed the Russian government for twenty years. He accumulated great personal wealth, particularly in the form of land, and became the richest man in Moscow. Cherkassky used his wealth and political capital to exert great influence on the government, supporting the rising power of the Romanov Dynasty.

Born: c. 1580; Russia
Died: April 4, 1642; Russia
Sources of wealth: Inheritance; real estate
Bequeathal of wealth: Relatives

EARLY LIFE
Prince Ivan Borisovich Cherkassky (EE-vahn boor-EE-soh-vihch chehr-KAHS-kee) was the only son of Boris Kanbulatovich Cherkassky and Marfa Nikitichna Romanova. His father was a Circassian prince who converted to Christianity and served the czar from around

1575 through 1576. Cherkassky's mother was the sister of Filaret, the patriarch of the Russian Orthodox Church who coruled Russia with his son Michael Romanov from 1619 to1633. Cherkassky had a sister, Irina Borisovna Cherkasskaya.

At this time, the boyars (princes) of Circassian origin were some of the most powerful figures in the Russian court, closely allied with the rising Romanovs. Cherkassky was born into a wealthy, politically active family. In 1599 and 1600, the regent Boris Godunov had Cherkassky and other Romanov supporters arrested. Cherkassky was exiled in 1601 but returned to Moscow the following year.

FIRST VENTURES
The Cherkassky boyars maintained close ties to families in their Circassian homeland and with each other, keeping their land and other wealth in the family. This practice helped make them the richest boyar clan in Russia.

While little direct information is available about how Ivan Borisovich Cherkassky built his personal fortune, his management of government money suggests a shrewd monetary sense. At some point between 1600 and 1610, Cherkassky became *kravchy*, an honorary position at court, but Czar Vasily Shuysky removed him from that position. Cherkassky married Evdokiya Vasilievna Morozova, sister of Boris Ivanovich Morozov, a prominent boyar and statesman. Cherkassky's wealth probably helped him survive the Time of Troubles (*Smutnoe Vremya*) between the end of the Rurik Dynasty in 1598 and the establishment of the Romanov Dynasty in 1613.

Cherkassky became a boyar in 1613, shortly after Michael Romanov became czar, but he did not rise to prominence at court until Filaret became coruler with Michael in 1619. Under the joint rule of Filaret and Michael, Cherkassky became head of the Musketeers Chancellery (1623-1642), the Apothecary Chancellery (1624-1642), the Foreign Mercenary Chancellery (1622-1642), and the Great Treasury (1622-1642).

MATURE WEALTH

By 1624, Cherkassky was already one of the most powerful men at court. He was trusted not only with Filaret's money and military but also with the czar's medical care. Observers from Sweden and Germany readily marked him as the head of government. The German traveler Adam Olearius noted not only Cherkassky's power but also his personal wealth, which included the hamlet of Pavlovo. Contemporaries knew that Cherkassky managed government affairs well, and this skill presumably extended to his personal properties.

Cherkassky's work in the Musketeers Chancellery illustrates both his military and fiscal strategy. Between 1619 and 1642, Cherkassky worked with Filaret to improve the *pomestie* system, which granted the use of parcels of land in exchange for military service. Rents from these lands went to the service member, but the ownership of the land remained with the czars. Under Cherkassky's leadership, servicemen were granted land, cash subsidies, and temporary tax immunities. These measures ensured that the Russian army remained strong without leading to financial problems, albeit at the expense of the peasants.

By 1635, Cherkassky dominated the chancelleries as well as the Boyar Duma, the advisory council of nobles, a position he retained until his death. Cherkassky's wealth, likely derived primarily from land revenues, continued to grow. He died on April 4, 1642, without children, leaving his estate to a cousin.

LEGACY

Cherkassky's cousin and heir, Iakov Kudenetovich Cherkassky, was a boyar and powerful figure at court. Iakov played a major role in the political rivalry of 1645-1650, supporting Nikita Romanov against Boris Ivanovich Morozov for leadership of Russia. Iakov came to replace Ivan Borisovich Cherkassky in the Russian court as the wealthiest and most politically prominent member of a wealthy and powerful family. Without their accumulation and management of wealth, it is doubtful that the Cherkassky boyars would have achieved such political preeminence and influence on Russian history.

—*Melissa A. Barton*

FURTHER READING

Bushkovitch, Paul. "Princes Cherkasskii or Circassian Murzas: The Kabardians in the Russian Boyar Elite, 1560-1700." *Cahiers du monde russe* 45, nos. 1/2 (2004): 9-30.

Davies, Brian. *Warfare, State, and Society on the Black Sea Steppe, 1500-1700*. New York: Routledge, 2007.

Shubin, Daniel H. *Tsars and Imposters: Russia's Time of Troubles*. New York: Algora, 2009.

See also: Aleksandr Danilovich Menshikov; Nikita Romanov; Grigory Stroganov; Felix Yusupov.

AGOSTINO CHIGI
Italian banker and merchant

Chigi was one of the wealthiest bankers and merchants in late fifteenth and early sixteenth century Europe. Active primarily in Rome as the banker to the pope, he was also an important patron of the arts. His art patronage is epitomized by the Villa Farnesina, the residence he built in Rome.

Born: c. 1465; Siena (now in Italy)
Died: 1520; Papal States (now in Rome, Italy)
Also known as: Il Magnifico
Sources of wealth: Banking; trade
Bequeathal of wealth: Spouse; children; artistic patronage

EARLY LIFE
Agostino Chigi (ahg-oh-STEE-noh KEE-jee) was born around 1465, and according to the baptismal rolls of Battistero di San Giovanni in Siena, he was baptized at this cathedral on November 29, 1466. Chigi was born into a wealthy Sienese family of merchants. His parents were Mariano Chigi (1439-1504) and Caterina Baldi. Mariano was well known in Siena and held important political and financial positions, including that of Sienese ambassador to the Holy See. Like his son Agostino, Mariano was a patron of the arts, and he commissioned the painter Perugino, the artist Raphael's teacher, to create a major altarpiece. In addition to receiving a basic education in letters as appropriate to his social standing, Agostino learned the banking and financing business, first at his father's offices in Siena and Viterbo and in 1487 in Rome at Ambrogio Spannocchi's firm, which performed accounting services for the Holy See.

FIRST VENTURES
Perhaps as early as 1487, the Chigis, father and son, together with Stefano Ghinucci, opened a banking business in Rome. This newly established financial firm, which was managed by Agostino, flourished in the 1490's. The firm's dealings covered the full business spectrum, from trade in grain, wine, and livestock to currency exchange and tax accounting. The company's most important loan before the end of the fifteenth century was finalized in December, 1499, when Agostino convinced his partners to lend 3,000 ducats to Cesare Borgia, son of Pope Alexander VI, when Borgia was overseeing military campaigns in northern Italy for his father. Agostino had started financing Borgia's operations in 1498.

Since the 1490's, Agostino had achieved considerable

distinction on his own. In 1492, he was named director of the papal salt marshes (salt was an important commodity in the premodern world), of the customs operations of the Papal States, and of the taxes imposed by the Holy See. These appointments were crucial for Chigi's development as a businessman and financier. He became inextricably involved with the financial affairs of the pope, and he also developed an extensive network of international connections, which eventually supported the opening of more than one hundred offices of his firm in Italy and branches from London to the Levant. While primarily devoted to doing business with the pope, Chigi also lent considerable sums to Charles VIII, the king of France, who occupied Rome in 1496; to the Medici family (4,000 ducats); and to the *condottiere* (mercenary soldier) Guidobaldo da Montefeltro in 1497 (111,173 ducats).

MATURE WEALTH
The foundation of Chigi's mature wealth was the concession he received from the pope in December, 1500, to manage the alum mines at Tolfa, leasing them for 34,000 ducats per year. Until then, the alum mineral, a crucial ingredient in dyeing processes in which it serves as the binding agent between the cloth and the dye, was imported in Europe from the Ottoman Empire. In just a few years, during which he also bought all the smaller alum mines in Italy, Chigi gained dominance of the alum market, achieving a virtual monopoly on this commodity in Europe—a monopoly that was made official in Flanders in 1508 for a payment of 85,000 ducats. Chigi extended his sales of alum throughout the East, all the way to China. In addition to improving alum extraction techniques, he assembled a commercial fleet of about one hundred ships to distribute the mineral, harboring the fleet at Porto Ercole in Tuscany, a city-port that he rented from the Republic of Siena for 8,000 ducats. The alum business was particularly lucrative: In 1520, Chigi's net profits from the mineral reached 300,000 ducats.

In 1502, Chigi founded his own financial firm, the Banco Chigi, in partnership with his father and a friend, Francesco Tommasi. The original capital committed to the venture was 8,000 ducats, with 3,250 each from Chigi and his father and 1,500 from Tommasi, and the partners agreed to split their profits and risks according to these proportions. Combining his living and office spaces, Chigi rented the large house that had been occupied by his father's business since 1476. Thanks to

VILLA FARNESINA

Agostino Chigi, the wealthiest financier of Renaissance Europe and an influential banker to several popes, had a villa built as his palace immediately outside the city walls of Rome. The home acquired the name Villa Farnesina in 1573, when the property was purchased by the Farnese family.

Villa Farnesina is the quintessential Italian Renaissance urban villa, with its decoration emulating similar homes built in this period. In building this residence, Chigi was inspired by Florentine palaces, and he viewed the construction of other Italian villas. At the end of the fifteenth century, Chigi also witnessed the creation of important private buildings with complex decorations in Siena and Rome, including the Belvedere of Pope Innocent VIII, the Palazzo della Cancelleria, and the Borgia Apartment in the Vatican. Chigi was impressed by the frescoes painted on the walls of the Sistine Chapel, which were completed by renowned painters called to Rome by Pope Sixtus IV.

The architectural design of Chigi's villa was completed by Baldassarre Peruzzi, who began working on the project in 1505. Chigi moved into the villa in the summer of 1511, the year in which Raphael began to paint the now-famous fresco decorations on its walls and ceilings, which were completed in 1512. The iconography of these frescoes is complex, and scholars remain uncertain about many of the paintings' details. However, it is clear that in *The Triumph of Galatea*, which embellishes the loggia on the main floor of the building, the primary theme of the fresco is Chigi's own horoscope, while the frescoes in the Sala del Fregio allude to the death of Chigi's first wife and his marriage to his second. While Raphael is surely the most famous artist who worked on the building, Chigi invited other leading painters to contribute to his villa's decorations, including Peruzzi, Sebastiano del Piombo, and Il Sodoma. Three artists who studied and worked with Raphael—Giovanni da Udine, Giovan Francesco Penni, and Giulio Romano—helped the master painter complete the decorations on the Loggia of Amore and Psiche.

his shrewdness, Banco Chigi prospered even after a Genoese clergyman became Pope Julius II in 1502. Even though Julius gave his business to Genoese firms, Chigi had lent him considerable sums through which he secured his election to the Papacy, and these loans guaranteed Chigi's business with the Holy See.

Chigi remained close to Julius as the pope's trusted friend, banker, financier, political adviser, ambassador, and patron of the arts. He followed the pope in two military campaigns in 1506 and 1510, and it is said that Chigi instigated the second one in order to protect his alum business from the Ferrarese family's interference. Julius excommunicated Chigi's adversaries, and he also entrusted Chigi to handle the financial arrangements that would ally the Venetian Republic with the Holy League against France in the War of the League of Cambrai in

1511. The friendship between the pope and his banker is epitomized by the fact that Julius officially adopted Chigi into the pope's family in 1511. Among the many privileges granted through this adoption, a special benefit was the integration of the oak leaves, the symbol of the coat of arms of Julius's family, the della Rovere, into Chigi's coat of arms.

Perhaps inspired by the patronage policies of Popes Sixtus IV, Alexander VI, and Julius II, Chigi understood that the success of any urban leader is closely tied to his public image. Accordingly, he used his wealth to fashion his public persona in a variety of ways, from holding extravagant parties and memorable processions in Rome to being the supportive patron of celebrated artists and the donor of major public projects. This policy is instantiated early in Chigi's career by his donation to build a new church in Tolfa. In Rome, Chigi's participation in three projects conceived during Julius's term as pope stand out: Chigi provided the funds to build and decorate two prominent chapels, one in Santa Maria della Pace and a second one, his funerary chapel, in Santa Maria del Popolo. He had the pope's favorite painter, Raphael, decorate these churches with frescoes. Chigi also hired Raphael to complete the complex decorative program of his urban palace, Villa Farnesina.

In 1513, Julius was succeeded by Pope Leo X, a Florentine cleric. Chigi managed to remain a primary financial personality in the new pope's administration by lending Leo considerable sums during the papal conclave, at which Leo was elected pope.

Three noteworthy events in Chigi's personal life took place in the early sixteenth century: In 1508, his first wife, Margherita Saracini, died, leaving him childless. His proposal to marry Margherita Gonzaga, the natural daughter of the duke of Mantua, through a gift of 10,000 ducats (Chigi's inheritance at the time was valued in excess of 400,000 ducats) proved unsuccessful. In 1512, Chigi married Francesca Ordeaschi and they had three sons.

In his 1519 will, he left his estate to his sons, none of whom was of age and one of whom had yet to be born.

Chigi died peacefully in his sleep at home after a busy workday in 1520.

LEGACY

Of Chigi's three sons, only Lorenzo survived into adulthood. Unfortunately, because of his son's poor business sense and the many lawsuits arising from his estate, Chigi's wealth was basically dissipated by the time Lorenzo died in September, 1573. Surely, as the more than five thousand attendees to his funeral suggest, Chigi's impact on the people and culture of Rome was considerable, his wealth and his business having touched the lives of many. Chigi's patronage had a lasting influence on the visual arts, which was particularly evident in his support of Raphael.

—Renzo Baldasso

FURTHER READING

Frommel, Christoph Luitpold, ed. *La Villa Farnesina a Roma = The Villa Farnesina in Rome*. 2 vols. Modena, Italy: Panini, 2003. Definitive publication on Villa Farnesina, detailing its building, decoration program, and history through the centuries. The second volume is particularly useful for the splendid illustrations documenting in detail the entire building.

Gilbert, Felix. *The Pope, His Banker, and Venice*. Cambridge, Mass.: Harvard University Press, 1980. Readable account detailing the friendship between Pope Julius II and Chigi in matters of international politics and art patronage. This study is particularly valuable for its contextualization of the interaction between these two figures.

Quinlan-McGrath, Mary. "The Astrological Vault of the Villa Farnesina: Agostino Chigi's Rising Sign." *Journal of the Warburg and Courtauld Institutes* 47 (1984): 91-105. In-depth article detailing the last parts of the astrological fresco program at Villa Farnesina, demonstrating that the paintings represent Chigi's own life horoscope and confirming that they reference his birth date.

Rowland, Ingrid D., ed. *The Correspondence of Agostino Chigi (1466-1520) in Cod. Chigi R.V.c: An Annotated Edition*. Vatican City: Biblioteca Apostolica Vaticana, 2001. Presents the original and English translations of Chigi's mercantile correspondence. The content of the letters reveals his human nature, documents his business dealings, and presents his acumen as a patron of the arts.

_____. "Render unto Caesar the Things Which Are Caesar's: Humanism and the Arts in the Patronage of Agostino Chigi." *Renaissance Quarterly* 39 (Winter, 1986): 673-730. This lengthy and important article describes Chigi's politics of patronage of the visual arts—particularly his commissions to Raphael in his chapel in Santa Maria della Pace, his mortuary chapel in Santa Maria del Popolo, and at the Villa Farnesina—detailing his attempt to devise a myth for his persona.

See also: Alexander VI; Giovanni de' Medici; Lorenzo de' Medici; Jacopo de' Pazzi; Filippo Strozzi.

WALTER P. CHRYSLER
American automobile magnate

Chrysler became wealthy almost as a by-product of his lifelong passion for automobile design. His earnings allowed him to take great personal risks in advancing automotive technology, which materially influenced the development of transportation in the United States and ultimately the world.

Born: April 2, 1875; Wamego, Kansas
Died: August 18, 1940; Great Neck, New York
Also known as: Walter Percy Chrysler
Sources of wealth: Manufacturing; sale of products; real estate
Bequeathal of wealth: Children

EARLY LIFE

Walter Percy Chrysler (KRIS-lehr) was born in Kansas when that state was just emerging from its days as a frontier outpost. The son of a railroad worker, Chrysler chose to forgo attending college to become a machinist's apprentice with the railroads. In 1901, he married Della Forker, a childhood friend; they eventually had four children. Chrysler rose quickly in the railroad industry, becoming in succession a foreman, supervisor of works, and eventually, at age thirty-three, superintendent of locomotive maintenance for the Chicago & Great Western Railway. A dispute with the company's president led him to move to the American Locomotive Company in Pittsburgh. In 1912, he was in charge of manufacturing, earning a handsome annual salary of $8,000, when he was recruited to become manager of works for the Buick Motor Company in Flint, Michigan. Always a lover of automobiles, Chrysler accepted the offer and began his meteoric rise to prominence in America's new growth industry, personal transportation.

FIRST VENTURES

Executives at Buick and its parent company, General Motors (GM), soon recognized Chrysler's ability to cut costs and improve manufacturing processes. He became general manager and president of Buick in 1916 and executive vice president of GM in late 1918. His compensation rose exponentially, until he was earning $500,000 in annual salary and stock options. Eventually, however, he and William Crapo Durant, the president of GM, had a falling out over issues involving strategic management philosophy. Chrysler walked away from his job at Buick in 1919 and cashed in his stock, netting a profit of $10 million.

Walter P. Chrysler. (Hulton Archive/Getty Images)

MATURE WEALTH

Chrysler was not out of work long. Late in 1919, he agreed to take what was deemed a temporary job, serving as the de facto chief operating officer of Willys Motors at an annual salary of $1 million. He moved his family to New York, where he bought an estate on Long Island in 1923. Over two years he revamped operations at Willys, significantly reducing the company's debt. At the same time he was assisting Willys, Chrysler signed on to help the struggling Maxwell Motor Company improve its fortunes. Maxwell and its affiliate, Chalmers Motors, had fallen on hard times and incurred substantial debt.

At Maxwell, Chrysler worked under terms similar to those at Willys. He sought to streamline manufacturing procedures and restore public confidence in brands that had once been popular until rumors of shoddy production cut into sales. To assist him in identifying and correcting deficiencies with the Willys and Maxwell models, Chrysler hired a trio of young engineers: Fred Zeder, Owen Skelton, and Carl Breer. These men solved many technical problems plaguing Willys and Maxwell autos. They also were entrusted by Chrysler to help create the first car to bear his name, the Chrysler Six, the development of which was financed in part with Chrysler's own money. The Chrysler Six was introduced in 1924 as part of Maxwell Motors' annual offerings.

A year later, Maxwell Motors was reorganized as the Chrysler Corporation, with Walter P. Chrysler as its president. Over the next five years, Chrysler made several daring moves to position his company as a direct competitor to the giants of the industry, GM and the Ford Motor Company. The boldest of these initiatives was made in 1928, when Chrysler acquired Dodge Brothers Motor Car Company and introduced a new automobile, the Plymouth. Purchasing Dodge Brothers, a company larger at the time than Chrysler Corporation, allowed Chrysler to develop a product line similar to that offered by GM, with cars available at various price ranges to appeal to different segments of the market. Most important among these brands was the Plymouth, introduced as a direct competitor to Ford and Chevrolet. Even though the stock market crash of 1929 and the ensuing depression affected Chrysler Corporation, by 1933 the company was once again healthy and outselling many of its rivals. By the middle of the decade, Chrysler Corporation had overtaken Ford to become the number-two auto manufacturer in America. However, the introduction of the Airflow line of cars in 1934 proved a modest disaster, as the public never warmed to their radical style, and the line had to be discontinued in 1937.

GREAT WEALTH AND THE AUTOMOBILE

During the first four decades of the twentieth century, the American automobile industry went on a roller-coaster ride that produced immense wealth for some and great losses for others. The nascent industry looked to many like a place to make their fortunes. Hence, in 1908, there were 253 auto manufacturers in the United States alone. Over time, innovations in technology, skillful pricing policies, and the development of brand loyalty, combined with significant fluctuations in the nation's economy, led to a drastic reduction in the number of manufacturers. By the beginning of World War II, there were only the "Big Three"—General Motors, Chrysler, and Ford—and half a dozen smaller firms. Henry J. Kaiser and other investors, who were successful in other businesses, lost considerable sums in their ventures into the auto industry. On the other hand, a few people who put money into the major companies made out handsomely. For example, before they began manufacturing automobiles under their own name, parts makers John F. Dodge and his brother Horace Dodge realized a $32 million return from a $10,000 investment in the Ford Motor Company.

Alfred P. Sloan, who took over General Motors from William Crapo Durant in 1923, became a multimillionaire over the course of his career. To avoid paying excessive estate taxes, he began contributing to a number of educational and medical institutions, and he established and endowed the Alfred P. Sloan Foundation with gifts of more than $300 million. Walter P. Chrysler earned tens of millions of dollars, much of which he invested in real estate or put back into the automobile business, as he supported innovative technologies that helped shape the future of the industry. His $8.8 million estate reflects only part of the wealth that he accumulated over his lifetime. Henry Ford may have benefited the most from his involvement in the auto industry. Reports during the 1920's estimated his personal fortune at more than $1 billion, and shortly before his death he established the Ford Foundation with a bequest exceeding $500 million, instantly making it the largest charitable organization in America.

Even among those who were successful in the automotive industry, the men who had risked much did not always keep the wealth they accumulated. For example, Durant had already become a millionaire from auto manufacturing when he founded General Motors in 1908, but he ended up losing virtually everything he had earned in the recession of 1919. Only a bailout by his company's board of directors, which gave him a $3 million stipend to leave the firm, allowed him to start over. In the next decade, he built another fortune at Durant Motors, but he lost everything again in the stock market crash of 1929. He lived the last twenty-five years of his life on a modest pension arranged by Sloan, the man who replaced him at General Motors, and gifts from Chrysler, who had worked for him briefly at General Motors.

While automobiles remained Chrysler's passion, he branched out into other ventures that he saw as either complementary to his principal business interests or worthy of his attention for other reasons. In 1930, he completed construction of the Chrysler Building in New York City, which became the company's principal office complex. Under his direction, the company began manufacturing marine engines, and its partnership with Chris-Craft, a boat manufacturer, proved profitable. Less successful, however, were his efforts in commercial air conditioning and railroad trucking.

Chrysler's success in the automobile industry rested on several key principles. First, he was keen on improving production efficiencies so his cars could be sold at greater profit margins than those of his competitors. Second, he was firmly committed to innovation in engineering and to the delivery of high-quality products. As a result, his cars generally offered buyers more options and more advanced technology than competitors' vehicles for the same cost. Unlike Henry Ford, Chrysler was able to hire highly competent lieutenants and give them the freedom to operate their division free from constant micromanagement. Finally, he was a risk taker who staked his own fortunes on the success of his company, as demonstrated by the structure of his contracts at Chrysler Corporation. In his tenure there, he never received a salary much above $200,000; instead, he augmented his base wage with profit-sharing and stock options. While these benefits provided little income in the lean years of the Depression, in 1928 his share of company profits was approximately $2.5 million.

Chrysler retired as the company's president in 1935, turning over operations to his hand-picked successor, K. T. Keller. Nevertheless, he remained active in the company that bore his name. Notably, in 1937 he helped negotiate an important labor agreement with the United Auto Workers. Shortly after completing these union negotiations, however, Chrysler suffered a stroke. In 1938, his wife Della died suddenly. Chrysler lingered two more years before he died on August 18, 1940.

Chrysler Building, Midtown Manhattan, New York, 1932. (Library of Congress)

LEGACY

Shortly after his death, Walter P. Chrysler's estate was valued at $8,854,761. This sum seems rather modest when compared to the fortunes of Henry Ford or Alfred P. Sloan, the president and chief executive officer of GM, but in 1940, the country was just emerging from the decade-long Depression, and the value of stocks, real estate, and commodities, such as art works, had still not recovered their full value. With the exception of a few small benefices, the bulk of Chrysler's estate was divided equally among his four children.

The corporation Chrysler established continued throughout the twentieth century as one of America's "Big Three" automakers, although serious problems brought it to the brink of bankruptcy more than once. It survived for a time on its own, and in 1998 it merged for a brief period with the German firm Daimler-Benz before being acquired by a private equity group in 2007. Attempts to return to profitability after the recession of 2008 centered on a recommitment to the principles that

Walter P. Chrysler espoused as important above all others: innovation and quality.

—Laurence W. Mazzeno

FURTHER READING

Chrysler, Walter P., and Boyden Sparkes. *Life of an American Workman*. New York: Dodd, Mead, 1950. Chrysler's autobiography, initially serialized in 1937 in *The Saturday Evening Post*, in which he offers a firsthand account of his rise to prominence in the automotive industry and stresses what he considers the keys to his success.

Curcio, Vincent. *Chrysler: The Life and Times of an Automotive Genius*. New York: Oxford University Press, 2000. Comprehensive biography providing details about Chrysler's personal life and his career as an executive in both the railroad and automotive industries.

Davis, Donald F. *Conspicuous Production: Automobiles and Elites in Detroit, 1899-1933*. Philadelphia: Temple University Press, 1988. Surveys the growth of the automotive industry, describing the business environment in which Chrysler rose to prominence and made his personal fortune.

Hyde, Charles K. *Riding the Roller Coaster: A History of the Chrysler Corporation.* Detroit: Wayne State University Press, 2003. Offers background on the corporation; outlines Chrysler's efforts to make his firm a competitor with General Motors and Ford. Provides details about the company's experiences in the six decades after Chrysler died.

Weiss, H. Eugene. *Chrysler, Ford, Durant, and Sloan: Founding Giants of the American Automotive Industry.* Jefferson, N.C.: McFarland, 2003. Sketches the careers of the four men most influential in shaping the

modern American automotive industry; pays special attention to new materials about Chrysler's life and business philosophy.

Yanik, Anthony J. *Maxwell Motor and the Making of the Chrysler Corporation.* Detroit: Wayne State University Press, 2009. Traces the history of the company Chrysler acquired and transformed into the Chrysler Corporation. Describes his efforts to reshape the firm in accordance with his own philosophy of automotive design and sales.

See also: Chung Ju Yung; John F. Dodge; Harvey Firestone; Henry Ford; Soichiro Honda; Alfred P. Sloan.

CHUNG JU YUNG
South Korean entrepreneur, industrialist, and mechanical engineer

Chung founded Hyundai Group, a conglomerate that became the largest business entity in Korea. Concentrating on construction, ship and car manufacture, and technology, Chung's businesses became important employers and helped to build modern infrastructure on the Korean Peninsula. Chung's success in rapidly acquiring foreign technologies was instrumental in shaping the economy of twentieth century South Korea.

Born: November 25, 1915; Tongchon Kangwon, Korea (now in North Korea)
Died: March 21, 2001; Seoul, South Korea
Sources of wealth: Manufacturing; sale of products; construction business
Bequeathal of wealth: Children; relatives

EARLY LIFE
Chung Ju Yung (chung jew yeong) spent his early years working, along with his five younger brothers, on his father's small farm in Asan, on the east coast of Korea near what later became the demilitarized zone. Despite hard work, the family remained poor and often did not have enough to eat. Chung received only an elementary education. Hoping to earn more money to support his family, he repeatedly left Asan without his father's permission. First, he worked for a short time as a construction laborer, and later he studied accounting in Seoul. After each of these attempts to improve his circumstances, he returned to the family farm. Finally, Chung left for Seoul again, this time finding work in construction and

other jobs. Taking a job as a delivery man for a small rice company, he impressed the owner and customers with his dedication to performing every task exactly to specification.

FIRST VENTURES
When the owner of the rice shop decided to sell, Chung had saved sufficient funds to become owner. He ran his Kyungil Rice Store successfully until a government regulation forced him to close in 1939. Shortly thereafter, Chung purchased a car repair shop, financing this acquisition without collateral through a business contact whose trust he had won. Chung's Ado Service Garage prospered until 1943, when it was nationalized by the Japanese. Chung lost most of his investment.

Following the departure of the Japanese at the end of World War II, Chung returned to Seoul and bought another car repair shop. He called his business Hyundai ("modern") Auto Service. Chung noticed that the wealthiest customers in Korea were the United States Army agents. Since most of the American contracts were for construction, Chung used profits from Hyundai Auto Service to found Hyundai Civil Works Company. Starting as a subcontractor, Chung learned every aspect of the business. His trademark was finishing every project on time and on budget, even if Hyundai lost money. Chung believed that he had to build capital in trust, as well as in assets. His strategy paid off; in 1950, with the start of the Korean War, Chung won the trust of the United States Army by successfully completing construction contracts in a challenging wartime environment. Hyundai Construction, the cornerstone of Chung's wealth, was now a respected company.

MATURE WEALTH

Hyundai Construction built its reputation during the reconstruction following the Korean War (1950-1953). Hyundai's first major contract was to rebuild a bridge on the Nakdong River in 1955. In 1957, Hyundai was hired to build five new bridges over the Han River. Chung aggressively bid on projects in which his company had little experience, compensating by hiring quick learners. Even though Hyundai had never built a highway, it won a contract to build the Pattani-Narathiawat Highway in Thailand. Next, Chung lobbied Korean President Park Chung Hee to build a highway from Seoul to Pusan. Hyundai constructed 40 percent of the Kyungbu Expressway, completed in 1970. Enjoying the confidence of Korea's president, Chung was now in charge of Korea's most powerful construction company.

Chung founded Hyundai Motor Company in 1967, and in 1976 the company built Korea's first export car, the Pony. As the car company grew, Chung continued to diversify his holdings. Hyundai Heavy Industries launched two major ships in 1974. By the mid-1980's, Hyundai was Korea's largest company, holding interests in high-technology firms, as well as in construction. Chung was now one of the wealthiest men in the world.

LEGACY

In 1997, the Asian financial crisis forced Hyundai Group to restructure. Chung and his brothers sold much of the company's interests in auto manufacture and concentrated on heavy industry, especially shipbuilding. Hyundai Group continued to prosper. Chung worked until his death in 2001. He left control of the company to one of his eight sons, Chung Mong Hun.

Chung can be said to be the one man who built the South Korea of the late twentieth and early twenty-first centuries. From arrival at Inchon to a drive between any two major cities in South Korea on the Kyungbu Expressway, no one can visit this country without seeing the results of Chung Ju Yung's vision.

—Wells S. Hansen

FURTHER READING

Amsden, Alice Hoffenberg. *Asia's Next Giant: South Korea and Late Industrialization.* London: Oxford University Press, 1989.

Kirk, Donald. *Korean Dynasty: Hyundai and Chung Ju Yung.* New York: M. E. Sharpe, 1994.

Steers, Richard M. *Made in Korea: Chung Ju Yung and the Rise of Hyundai.* New York: Routledge, 1999.

See also: Giovanni Agnelli; Walter P. Chrysler; John F. Dodge; Henry Ford; Soichiro Honda; Alfred P. Sloan.

EDWARD C. CLARK
American lawyer, industrialist, and real estate investor

Clark, drawing on his background in patent law, helped settle significant patent litigation for Isaac Merrit Singer's sewing machine. As president of the Singer Manufacturing Company, Clark pioneered purchasing and marketing strategies that revolutionized the burgeoning domestic appliance industry. He then used his considerable wealth to develop real estate in both Manhattan and the Catskills region of upstate New York, notably in Cooperstown.

Born: December 19, 1811; Athens, Greene County, New York

Died: October 14, 1882; Cooperstown, New York

Also known as: Edward Cabot Clark; Edward S. Clark

Sources of wealth: Law practice; manufacturing; real estate

Bequeathal of wealth: Children

EARLY LIFE

Edward Cabot Clark was born in 1811 in Athens in the foothills of the Catskill Mountains in south central New York. His father was a potter. Clark, a sickly child, attended a private academy in Athens and at twelve was enrolled in Lenox Academy, a public preparatory school, in Lenox, Massachusetts. Homesick soon after arriving, Clark simply departed Lenox and returned home on foot, a trip of almost thirty miles. His father promptly returned him to school. Over time, Clark developed a love of learning through an ambitious self-designed reading program that drew on the resources of the academy's library.

At fifteen, Clark was admitted to Williams College and graduated in 1830. Deciding on law, he entered the firm of Ambrose Jordan in Hudson, New York, and in 1833 he was admitted to the bar. In 1835, he married Jordan's oldest daughter, Caroline, and two years later became a partner in her father's firm, which in 1838 set up a lucrative practice in New York City.

FIRST VENTURES

Over the next decade, Clark established a considerable reputation in the contentious field of patent litigation. The firm prospered (Clark's father-in-law served as the state's attorney general). Clark maintained an unassuming social profile (he was a Sunday school teacher), preferring to dedicate his considerable talents to his work and to his devoted wife and their only child, Alfred. Among the clients Jordan & Clark accepted was Isaac Merrit Singer, an eccentric inventor and part-time actor from Boston. In the early 1840's, Singer had invented a revolutionary machine for carving wood and metal into signs, although the sole prototype had been destroyed in a boiler explosion. Litigation involving that design had originally brought Singer to Clark's firm. Around 1850, Singer had tinkered with the existing model of a sewing machine. The machine design had proven stubbornly unworkable. In just eleven days, Singer made three key changes in the design: He redesigned the shuttle to make it go in a straight up-and-down line rather than in a circle; he redesigned a straight rather than a curved needle; and he used a spinning-wheel-style foot pedal rather than a hand crank to move the apparatus. The redesign worked.

Because the redesign depended on elements of other sewing machine prototypes, notably those of Elias Howe, Singer was sued for patent infringement. When Howe subsequently won the suit and tried to bar Singer from selling the so-called Singer machine, Singer appealed to Clark. Recognizing the potential profit from such a machine, Clark resigned from the law firm and became Singer's partner in 1851.

MATURE WEALTH

In 1856, in a groundbreaking settlement devised in part by Clark, all the pending litigants in a variety of patent infringement lawsuits involving the sewing machine agreed to pool their patents into a single corporation, the Sewing Machine Combination, proceed with production, and divide the revenues. As part of the agreement, I. M. Singer & Co., with Clark as half owner, began to mass-produce sewing machines, and by 1860 Singer led the market, with seventy-four factories producing more than 111,000 machines annually.

Although recognized for his brilliant legal maneuverings against a flurry of potentially crippling patent lawsuits Clark also directed the company with remarkable success. Even as Singer's flamboyant lifestyle and high-profile philandering created controversy (he was a bigamist, with more than a dozen children with four or five women), Clark quietly dedicated himself to the company, relocating its principal facilities to New York City, overseeing expansion into foreign markets, and spearheading an aggressive marketing campaign designed to offset conservative, middle-class resistance to a labor-saving machine designed to give women free time. In addition, Clark devised the "hire purchase plan," the first institutionalized payment program. The cost of a new sewing machine represented a $125 investment at a time when the average domestic income was a little more than $500 a year. To alleviate concern, owners could put $5 down and pay as little as $3 a month until the machine was paid off. The results of this plan were phenomenal.

When Clark's patience with attending to the scandals (and the resulting lawsuits) associated with Singer reached an end in 1863, Clark reorganized the company's management, and with brilliant legal maneuvering he bought out Singer, who retired to southern England, but not before inserting a codicil in the settlement forbidding Clark from running the company until after Singer's death. Thus for more than a dozen years, Clark was the de facto president of the company, making most of its marketing and business decisions and overseeing its rise to international success, including opening plant facilities in Europe, Indochina, and South America. Upon Singer's death in 1875, Clark served seven years as the chief executive officer of a company he had been running for close to fifteen years.

His family fortune now estimated at $25 million, Clark began investing in Manhattan real estate projects, notably funding the controversial Dakota apartment building in 1880, a vast and intricate apartment complex for the rich, its scale inspired by Clark's love of the majesty of the American Plains. The building is located in the upper West Side of Manhattan, so far removed from the urban center of New York City that pundits, deriding the construction as Clark's Folly, suggested that Clark should build it out in the Dakota Territory. Each of the structure's sixty-five lavish apartments (some had more than twenty rooms) was individually designed—no two were alike. With its prominent gables and its Renaissance-style balconies and staircases, the complex quickly became an architectural showpiece.

Clark retired from active leadership of the sewing machine company in 1882, although the Clark family maintained controlling interest in the firm and would run it much like a family business for more than seventy years. Clark retired to the beautiful Glimmerglass region of

---

NATIONAL BASEBALL HALL OF FAME

Whether redefining the domestic life of American culture through the marketing of the first practical sewing machine; spearheading the revitalization of picturesque Cooperstown, New York, into a vacation destination affordable for the middle class; redrawing the urban landscape of Manhattan; or funding philanthropic causes in support of the arts and immigrant rights, the heirs of Edward C. Clark viewed his fortune as a vast resource integral to the development of the American way of life. It is perhaps no surprise, then, that the Clark family fortune would become entwined with the Great American Pastime.

In 1908, a blue-ribbon committee commissioned by organized baseball determined that the first baseball game in America had been played under the guidance of Abner Doubleday in the fields near Cooperstown in 1839. In 1935, Ford Christopher Frick, the commissioner of baseball, announced ambitious plans for the approaching centennial of the game that would include a hall of fame commemorating the game's best players.

Stephen C. Clark, Sr., Edward's grandson, who ran the resort hotel his family had built in Cooperstown, was gifted with the same marketing savvy his grandfather had possessed. He saw the potential tourist appeal for the museum in Cooperstown, which was reeling in the depths of the Depression. In 1937, Clark, in fact, had purchased a weatherbeaten ball supposedly used during that first game (it had cost him $5) and displayed it in downtown Cooperstown, along with other memorabilia from the early days of base-

ball. That the 1908 commission's findings would eventually be exposed as unreliable did nothing to hinder the enthusiasm with which Clark, using the commission's conclusions, approached the challenge of selling Frick on the idea of putting the museum in the pastoral village setting of Cooperstown rather than the more obvious urban environs of New York or Boston. Frick was won over. Clark deeded a generous acreage of land for the museum and even financed the $40,000 conversion of a dilapidated school gymnasium into the museum facility.

The museum was dedicated on June 12, 1939, with much fanfare; a country weary of a decade-long economic catastrophe embraced the facility, honoring what had become the national pastime. Clark would serve as the museum's president until his death in 1960. The Clark family continued to maintain a presence on the facility's board of directors into the twenty-first century.

By then, the National Baseball Hall of Fame and Museum was the most visited museum of its kind in the world, attracting more than 350,000 visitors annually. In addition to the hall of fame, the museum and its annex (significantly expanded to more than 60,000 square feet) houses more than 165,000 items relating to the game. Its library and research facility catalog more than a half million books, radio recordings, photographs, transcripts, and television broadcasts, all available to the public. Its mission—to preserve history, honor excellence, and connect generations—has made Cooperstown the shrine of America's pastime.

Lake Otsego near Cooperstown, New York, where his wife's family had long ago settled and where the Clark family summered. Although he maintained estates in Paris and Rome, it was the area around Cooperstown that he loved. Much of the Cooperstown area had been decimated by a massive fire in 1862. It was largely the financial resources and the business acumen of Clark that brought the town back to prosperity, restoring its hospital and university, as well as financing numerous other civic projects, including an art museum.

At the time of his death in 1882, Clark left the majority interest in the Singer company, as well as his real estate investments, to his son Alfred. Alfred lacked Clark's business acumen, but, something of an artist (he studied to be a concert pianist), he shared his father's passion for architecture, building concert halls and music schools. Alfred, however, was known primarily for funding struggling artists, setting up generous salaries for life for painters and musicians he deemed worthy, beginning a

tradition of philanthropy that the family would continue, notably in undertaking a public campaign to build affordable housing for New York City's burgeoning immigrant population shortly before World War I.

LEGACY
The wealth of Edward C. Clark came largely from his facile business acumen. In an era when the well-being and time management of housewives were marginalized and their ability to run any type of machinery dismissed, Clark created a marketing plan designed to bring efficiency and ease within the financial reach of even the poorest households, reflecting his own modest beginnings. Against the wastrel Singer, Clark was a model of unassuming industry, a classic Gilded Age businessman and a conservative family man who never considered wealth as a license for profligate living.

Most important, Clark, despite being one of the dominant figures in the industrial age, never abandoned his love of the land. A product of the Catskills foothills and raised with a profound appreciation for the scale and organization of nature, he married into a family with a long-standing interest in the wilderness made part of the American imagination by author James Fenimore Cooper. Clark invested most heavily in real estate, which he saw as the responsible and wise stewardship of the land.

—*Joseph Dewey*

FURTHER READING

Bissell, D. C. *The First Conglomerate: 145 Years of the Singer Sewing Machine*. Brunswick, Maine: Audenreed Press, 1999. Indispensable account of the business plan for the corporation founded by Clark. Includes extensive data about Clark's business innovations and marketing plans.

Brandon, Ruth. *Singer and the Sewing Machine: A Capitalist Romance*. Oxford, England: Oxford/Kodansho, 1996. Highly readable account of the eccentric lifestyle and engineering genius of Isaac Merrit Singer and the era of inventions and patent wars. Includes a detailed description of Clark's role in litigation and the subsequent contentious relationship of Clark and Singer.

Calder, Lendol. *Financing the American Dream: A Cultural History of Consumer Credit*. Princeton, N.J.: Princeton University Press, 1999. Helpful look at the context of Clark's innovative hire-purchase plan, describing how it was a manifestation of the boom-bust capitalism cycles of the Gilded Age.

Reisler, Jim. *A Great Day in Cooperstown: The Improbable Birth of Baseball's Hall of Fame*. New York: Da Capo Press, 2007. Engaging account of the dubious claims of Cooperstown, New York, as the home of baseball, including the Clark family's role in bringing the museum to Cooperstown and in managing the facility. Effective description of Cooperstown's history. Illustrated.

Weber, Nicholas Fox. *The Clarks of Cooperstown*. New York: Knopf, 2007. Indispensable, highly readable, thorough history of five generations of the Clark family, with a detailed account of its numerous philanthropic endeavors. Focuses primarily on the family's long-standing support of the contemporary art scene. Handsomely illustrated.

See also: Samuel Colt; John Deere; Anthony Joseph Drexel; James Buchanan Duke; Alfred I. du Pont; Cyrus Hall McCormick; Isaac Merrit Singer; William Collins Whitney.

WILLIAM ANDREWS CLARK
American copper mining and railroad magnate and politician

In building a financial empire in the West during more than thirty years of ruthless business negotiations involving mining, banking, and the railroad, Clark epitomized the aggressive capitalist spirit and unabashed greed of the Gilded Age. Clark, who saw wealth as entitlement to political power, admitted that he bribed Montana lawmakers so he could obtain a seat in the U.S. Senate.

Born: January 8, 1839; Connellsville, Pennsylvania
Died: March 2, 1925; New York, New York
Sources of wealth: Mining; railroads
Bequeathal of wealth: Children; museum

EARLY LIFE
William Andrews Clark was born in a log cabin in the coal fields of southwestern Pennsylvania on the outskirts of Pittsburgh. Little is known of his childhood; as his influence grew and his wealth accumulated, he worked to keep his early years from public scrutiny. His parents were first-generation Scottish and Irish immigrants,

who, hoping for a better life, homesteaded west to Iowa in 1856, when Clark was seventeen. With little taste for farming, Clark, a bright student, considered a career in teaching.

After completing studies at Iowa Wesleyan College, a small Methodist institution, Clark taught school in Missouri and became interested in law. During his time in Missouri, Clark came to believe deeply in the importance of states rights and of controlling the power of a centralized, federal government. Consequently, he enlisted in the Confederate army at the outbreak of the Civil War, but he either deserted or was discharged in 1862.

FIRST VENTURES
Restless and eager to make his mark, Clark headed west to take advantage of the area's mining boom. After briefly mining quartz in Colorado, in 1863 he arrived in Bannack, then the capital of the Montana Territory. He had modest success, earning an estimated $1,500 from his gold discoveries in the area's rivers. He made his ini-

tial fortune by developing supply lines to Salt Lake City, and later to St. Louis, in order to outfit mining camps with equipment and food. He then used the capital from this venture to invest in banks that owned the land rights to mining stakes in the vast Montana Territory, and, in turn, he took over the rights to this land when the mining companies went bust. Over the next decade, Clark, gifted with uncanny business savvy and driven by an uncomplicated love of accumulating wealth, expanded into numerous mining operations, as well as newspapers, smelting plants, banks, lumbering and ranching interests, utilities, and railroads.

By the early 1870's, when Montana's gold rush appeared to be over, the territory was electrified by news of a massive copper strike. Given the reach of Clark's holdings and his interest in smelting, the copper strike proved his long-anticipated financial bonanza. By the mid-1880's, Clark and Marcus Daly, who had made a fortune in silver and headed a mining conglomerate, the Anaconda Copper Mining Company, became the dominant financiers (and chief rivals) of the cooper-rich Montana Territory.

MATURE WEALTH

To Clark, it was natural—even inevitable—that wealth brought political power. Using the influence of his newspapers, Clark emerged during the 1880's as a powerful and charismatic voice for Montana statehood. He chaired two conventions, in 1884 and 1889, where participants worked to draft a state constitution. For Clark, however, politics was always an extension of his own interests. He worked most diligently to secure restrictions on the

---

THE WILLIAM ANDREWS CLARK MEMORIAL LIBRARY

Although William Andrews Clark spent his life focused on accumulating wealth, wielding political clout, and managing scores of industries, his son had far different ambitions. William Andrews Clark, Jr., was born into privilege. By the time he was born in Butte, Montana, in 1877, his father was already among the wealthiest men in the West. Despite living in the relative cultural backwater of the American frontier, young Clark developed a love of music, learning to play the violin, and of poetry and fiction.

With his father's blessing, Clark began living part of each year in the temperate climate of Southern California. It was an exciting place for a young man with unlimited wealth. He acquired prime acreage in Los Angeles and built a lavish showplace mansion. He sought to foster the arts in the young community, single-handedly financing in 1919 what would become the Los Angeles Philharmonic and providing a generous endowment to ensure the orchestra's operations.

It was his book collection, however, that became the focus of his cultural activities. During more than two decades, Clark assembled a wide-ranging collection of first editions, rare books, autographed letters, and original manuscripts of the British writers he loved, including William Shakespeare, John Milton, Geoffrey Chaucer, and later works by Charles Dickens and the Romantics, including William Blake and Lord Byron. Originally pursuing acquisitions that intrigued him, Clark eventually concentrated on two areas: seventeenth century British literature and the works of the Irish playwright Oscar Wilde. His interest in seventeenth century England included collections of music and operas, particularly those composed by George Frideric Handel and Henry Purcell, as well as groundbreaking works of scientific investigation from the likes of Sir Isaac Newton and astronomer Edmond Halley. Clark's fascination with Wilde led him to collect not only manuscripts and letters but also a rich trove of photographs and production notes from several of Wilde's plays, as well as artifacts from Wilde's contemporaries, including William Butler Yeats and John Millington Synge.

In 1924, Clark arranged to construct a library on the prime acreage he had originally purchased. He hired Robert D. Farquar, a Southern California architect schooled in classic European design, who would later help plan the Pentagon outside Washington, D.C. When the library opened in 1926, its lavish French Revival exterior, its magnificent foyer and other ornate interior details, and its beautifully appointed gardens made it a prominent cultural showplace. Even before its opening, Clark had decided that upon his death the library and its priceless collection would be donated in the memory of his father to the newly opened University of California at Los Angeles (UCLA). Long after Clark's death in 1934, that bequeathal remained the most generous in UCLA's history.

In the twenty-first centry, the Clark Library, one of UCLA's twelve libraries, anchors the university's prestigious Center for Seventeenth and Eighteenth Century Studies. The center administers numerous scholarships, fellowships, and endowed professorships; hosts international colloquiums; and sponsors an award-winning series of academic publications. Within the library's spacious study rooms, academics and other patrons pursue original research in the collection of more than 100,000 rare books and almost 25,000 original manuscripts.

amount of money that the federal government could tax mining interests. A fiery orator, Clark sought election as the territorial representative to Congress in 1888, only to lose to a virtual unknown, raising suspicions that Daly had tampered with ballots.

After Montana was admitted to the union in 1889, Clark, a Democrat, ran unsuccessfully in both 1889 and 1893 for a seat in the U.S. Senate. At this time, state legislators chose senators, and when Clark ran again in 1899, the Democratic-controlled Montana legislature selected him, only to have the selection immediately challenged when evidence of Clark's massive bribery came to light. Characteristically, Clark admitted that he had paid hundreds of thousands of dollars in bribes, but he argued that influence peddling was an inevitable part of a democratic system. By the time Clark arrived in Washington, D.C., the Senate had already voted to unseat him. He then attempted a backhanded maneuver to return by relinquishing his Senate seat and, after waiting for the governor to be out of state, having the lieutenant governor, a crony of his, appoint him to fill his own vacated seat, only to have the governor nullify the appointment when he returned. Clark was finally elected on his own in 1901, although accusations of fraud were raised involving the powerful miners' bloc. Clark served a single term in the Senate, distinguished only by his fierce fight against federal government protection of the mineral-rich Western lands.

While in office, Clark still worked to extend his business interests, developing new railroad lines to connect the burgeoning populations in Nevada, Arizona, and California with Salt Lake City, as well as speed transportation of his copper ore. Along with the help of his younger brother, a banker, Clark saw the potential for Western development. In contentious rivalry with other financiers, notably Edward H. Harriman of the Union Pacific Railroad, Clark purchased thousands of acres of ranch land and water rights critical to a transportation system and created a line, the San Pedro, Los Angeles & Salt Lake Railroad, which not only placed him among the wealthiest men in America but also helped guarantee the economic development of the Southwest. Clark is credited with establishing what would become Las Vegas, now the seat of a Nevada county that bears his name. Perhaps Clark's most lasting legacy is Clarkdale, Arizona, founded in 1912 as the site for his vast smelting operations. Clark helped design the town, laying out streets and investing in a cutting-edge communications network of telephones and telegraphs, electricity, medical facilities, and sewer systems, making Clarkdale a prototype of a planned community.

Rich beyond measure, after the end of his Senate term in 1907 Clark left the West entirely and moved to a spacious mansion with more than one hundred rooms on fashionable Fifth Avenue in New York City, where over the next fifteen years he spent lavishly to outfit the house. He also invested in more than seven hundred pieces of European art, ranging from ceramics and tapestries from antiquity to canvases by the Old Masters and French Impressionists. Upon his death in 1925, at the age of eighty-six, his entire collection was bequeathed to the Corcoran Gallery in Washington, D.C., along with a sufficient contribution to construct a wing to house the artworks.

At his death, Clark's fortune was estimated at $200 million. After his wife's death in 1893, Clark financed the career of an aspiring starlet, whose unexpected pregnancy the year Clark was elected to the Senate compelled him to marry her. Although his will bequeathed $2 million to her, the bulk of the estate was distributed among the children of his first wife. The children variously sold the assets and diversified their inheritance. After the demolition of Clark's ostentatious Manhattan home in 1928, little remained of his fortune.

LEGACY

Clark had the keen eye of a consummate capitalist entrepreneur. As a first-generation Westerner, he was positioned to take advantage of a frontier culture, with its virtually limitless resources ripe for exploitation and little in the way of regulation to disturb the steady aggrandizement of personal wealth. However, his vast wealth left little imprint. For all his political endeavors, he is remembered in the twenty-first century as a cautionary tale of corruption, specifically for the fiasco of his attempt to get appointed to the Senate after he had resigned. His fortune was made largely from his manipulation of two industries—mining and the railroad. By the time of his death, his mining enterprises were exhausted and the railroad had lost its central economic position. Because he saw wealth only in personal terms—endorsing no charity, endowing no university, and supporting no public cause—his legacy extended little beyond his death.

—Joseph Dewey

FURTHER READING

Glasscock, Carl B. *The War of the Copper Kings.* 1935. Reprint. Powell, Wyo.: Western History, 2002. Landmark account of the era in which Clark made his fortune. Vivid and highly readable. Includes a detailed account of Clark's feud with Anaconda.

Howard, Joseph Kinsey. *Montana: High, Wide. and Handsome.* Lincoln: University of Nebraska Press,

2003. Important account of Montana's history that includes a helpful summary of Clark's economic and political impact.

Land, Barbara, and Myrick Land. *A Short History of Las Vegas*. 2d ed. Reno: University of Nevada Press, 2004. One of the few histories of Las Vegas to include its first decade and the visionary work of Clark and his railroad.

Malone, Michael P., and William L. Lang. *The Battle for Butte: Mining and Politics on the Northern Frontier, 1864-1906*. Seattle: University of Washington Press, 2006. Fascinating account of Clark's era. Argues that the economic wealth of first-generation mineral entrepreneurs was essential to the West's political spirit of independence and pride.

Starr, Kevin. *Inventing the Dream: California Through the Progressive Era*. New York: Oxford University Press, 1986. Part of a highly respected multivolume history of California. Chronicles the whirlwind development of Southern California and the impact of Clark's railroad interests and his son's cultural philanthropy.

See also: Charles Crocker; Marcus Daly; James G. Fair; James Clair Flood; John W. Garrett; Jay Gould; Edward H. Harriman; George Hearst; F. Augustus Heinze; James J. Hill; Mark Hopkins; Collis P. Huntington; John William Mackay; William S. O'Brien; Leland Stanford; William Thaw; Cornelius Vanderbilt; William Henry Vanderbilt.

CLEOPATRA VII
Egyptian monarch

Cleopatra was the last Hellenistic monarch to rule Egypt, the wealthiest area of the ancient Mediterranean world. The potential of Egypt's vast natural resources and wealth drew the attention of Julius Caesar and Marc Antony, each of whom viewed an alliance with Cleopatra as a means to enhance his own wealth and power.

Born: 69 B.C.E.; Alexandria, Egypt
Died: August 3, 30 B.C.E.; Alexandria, Egypt
Also known as: Cleopatra VII Thea Philopator; Cleopatra Philopator
Sources of wealth: Inheritance; agricultural products; trade
Bequeathal of wealth: Confiscated

EARLY LIFE
Cleopatra (klee-oh-PA-trah) VII Thea Philopator was born to Ptolemy XII Auletes, a descendant of Ptolemy Soter, the Macedonian general who assumed rule over Egypt following the death of Alexander the Great. In keeping with ancient Egyptian custom, the members of the ruling Ptolemaic Dynasty promoted themselves as divine, and the young Cleopatra was raised in lavish splendor befitting her status as a goddess. She received an excellent education, learned nine languages, and is said to be the only Ptolemaic ruler to learn the native Egyptian language. As she matured, Cleopatra used her divine status, her fine education and strong linguistic skills, and her limitless and sometimes ruthless ambition

to establish herself as sole ruler of Egypt, thereby controlling the resources of the richest area in the ancient Mediterranean.

FIRST VENTURES
Cleopatra knew well the importance of controlling and manipulating Egypt's vast wealth.

For millennia the Nile River's annual flooding had left rich soil in which crops flourished. Egypt's agricultural abundance provided grain for a significant portion of the peoples of the Mediterranean, earning Egypt the distinction of being the breadbasket of the ancient world. Egypt also had many natural resources, such as flax for oil and linen, stone for construction, papyrus for making paper, salt for preserving foods, and semiprecious stones, such as malachite, carnelian, and amethyst. Egypt's most prized natural resource was gold, which was highly sought after for coinage and jewelry. With its well-developed trade system, Egypt exchanged its produce, goods, and natural resources with far distant lands, thereby increasing the standard of living in all areas, including Egypt itself.

MATURE WEALTH
Chief among the importers of Egypt's resources was Rome, which by the time of Cleopatra controlled all of the Mediterranean, except Egypt itself. Cleopatra was keenly aware of the tenuous position that Egypt held in regard to Rome; Rome's powerful military machine was capable of conquering Egypt at any time. Cleopatra

The court of Cleopatra VII. (F. R. Niglutsch)

knew it was essential that she maintain Egypt's economic security by continuing trade with Rome, while at the same time preserving Egypt's independence and her own personal power.

When Julius Caesar arrived in Alexandria in 48 B.C.E., the twenty-one-year-old Cleopatra charmed the fifty-two-year-old Caesar with her linguistic skills, intelligence, and lavish display of power. Their close political and personal relationship staved off Roman aggression and benefited the economic status of both Egypt and Rome. When Caesar was assassinated in 44 B.C.E., Egypt's position vis-à-vis Rome was again placed in jeopardy.

In 42 B.C.E., Cleopatra secured another close political and personal alliance, this time with Marc Antony, one of the individuals who came to power in Rome following Caesar's death. Again, Cleopatra used her political expertise and personal charms to win over this powerful Roman leader, thereby holding off a potential Roman military attack on Egypt, and, at the same time, temporarily securing the economic status of Egypt.

Back in Rome, the grandnephew and heir of Julius Caesar, Octavian (the future Emperor Augustus), feared that Antony would use Cleopatra's wealth and power to secure his own dominance over Rome. In 31 B.C.E., Octavian and his forces set sail and met the combined forces of Cleopatra and Antony at the Battle of Actium, where Octavian's forces were victorious. The defeated Cleopatra and Antony retreated to Alexandria, where, a year later, they committed suicide rather than be subject to Octavian.

LEGACY

Cleopatra had used her control over Egypt's wealth in her attempts to stave off Roman aggression and domination. In the end, Rome's determination and military power proved too strong, even against Cleopatra and the wealthiest Mediterranean nation of its time. Upon Cleopatra's death, Rome annexed Egypt and Egypt became Rome's richest province. Throughout its remaining history, Rome used Egypt's agricultural produce, natural resources, and great wealth to sustain its peoples, to extend its boundaries, and to create the largest empire the world had ever known.

—*Sonia Sorrell*

FURTHER READING
Burstein, Stanley Mayer. *The Reign of Cleopatra*. Norman: University of Oklahoma Press, 2007.

Chauveau, Michel. *Cleopatra: Beyond the Myth*. Translated by David Lorton. Ithaca, N.Y.: Cornell University Press, 2002.
Tyldesley, Joyce. *Cleopatra: Last Queen of Egypt*. New York: Basic Books, 2008.

See also: Amenhotep III.

ROBERT CLIVE
British merchant and military leader

Clive's military success in India laid the foundations for the British Empire's eventual control of that country. Clive became rich as a result of his Indian service, and as news of his wealth spread, the British government became increasingly interested in India, and businessmen and other individuals dreamed of earning a fortune there.

Born: September 29, 1725; Stychei, Shropshire, England
Died: November 22, 1774; London, England
Also known as: First Baron Clive of Plassey; Clive of India
Sources of wealth: Trade; government; conquest
Bequeathal of wealth: Spouse; children

EARLY LIFE
Robert Clive (kliv), son of a minor landowner and lawyer, attended school in Shropshire and in London at Merchant Taylors' School, but he was not a good student. He was a prankster and a troublemaker. He was tall, moody, and sensitive, as well as a daredevil with a fierce temper who loved fighting. He was also, importantly, a lucky person who had numerous close brushes with death throughout his life but survived them all. Clive also suffered from bouts of depression. His father was able to arrange a clerkship for him in the British East India Company (founded in 1600), and in 1743 Clive sailed to India to serve as a writer (clerk) at the British settlement at Fort St. George in Madras (now Chennai).

FIRST VENTURES
At Madras, Clive began to read widely, but he was bored. He reportedly tried to commit sui-

cide, but his gun failed to fire. Two years later, his fortune changed as a result of the British-French rivalry in India. The French attacked Madras in 1746 and captured it. Clive escaped to another British settlement, Fort St. David, where he volunteered for the military and was appointed to the rank of ensign. In 1749, now a lieutenant and an untrained but born soldier, Clive was highly praised for his successful attack on Tanjore. When hostilities ended, the French returned Madras to the British,

Robert Clive. (Library of Congress)

and Clive was appointed steward of Fort St. George, receiving a commission on every supply for the facility. His stewardship made him a very wealthy man.

Clive attained fame when he attacked Arcot in 1751, captured the city, and withstood a siege of fifty-three days. This battle began a series of military victories in south India against the French and their Indian allies. Clive returned to England in 1753, a national hero with a seventeen-year-old wife and a considerable fortune.

MATURE WEALTH

Clive went back to India in 1756 to become deputy governor of Fort St. David. However, Fort William, the British fort at Calcutta, was captured by Sirāj al-Dawlā, the nawab of Bengal. Sirāj al-Dawlā held 146 British men, women, and children in the fort's guardroom, dubbed the Black Hole of Calcutta. According to some reports, 123 of the captives suffocated during their time in this confined space. The British, determined to obtain revenge and retribution, appointed Clive commander of the punitive force. Clive recaptured Calcutta on January 2, 1757, and took the city of Chandanagar in March. At the Battle of Plassey, on June 23, 1757, Clive defeated Sirāj al-Dawlā, and this victory led to Clive's fame as the founder of the British Empire's control of India.

Following the battle, Clive established the British as the dominant power in Bengal, the richest province in India. He led his ally Mir Ja'far to the capital city of Murshidabad, where Mir Ja'far was appointed the nawab of Bengal. Clive received £234,000 and the title of *mansabdar* (officeholder), and he was entitled to a rent of £30,000. Overnight, Clive had become one of the richest men in Great Britain. Returning to England in 1760, he purchased two hundred shares of the British East India Company at £500 each and several houses and then

returned to Bengal in 1765 to serve as governor for two years. On August 12, 1765, Clive was personally given the grant by the Mughal emperor to collect the revenue of Bengal, Bihar, and Orissa, which, in practice meant he was the government in those areas. This led to the creation of "British India," and the British would expand in all directions to create their empire.

Clive eventually returned to England. Ill, he committed suicide at his London home in 1774 in one of his bouts of depression and was buried in an unknown grave.

LEGACY

The wealth that Clive generated in India led the British government to become increasingly interested in this part of the world. The government determined that the British East India Company should hold on to Bengal and its vast wealth, the French should be removed from India, and, if necessary, the British should take over India to safeguard their investments there.

Great Britain eventually created the second British Empire by expanding upon the territory that Clive had captured.

—Roger D. Long

FURTHER READING

Bayly, C. A. *Indian Society and the Making of the British Empire.* Cambridge, England: Cambridge University Press, 1988.

Harvey, Robert. *Clive: The Life and Death of a British Emperor.* New York: St. Martin's Press, 2000.

Marshall, P. J. *Bengal: The British Bridgehead, Eastern India, 1740-1828.* Cambridge, England: Cambridge University Press, 1987.

See also: Fateh Chand; Samuel Fludyer.

JACQUES COEUR
French merchant, statesman, and financier

Coeur, a fifteenth century merchant, trader, and financier, amassed the greatest fortune ever made by an individual Frenchman. His innovations and business methods had lasting effects on medieval commerce and trade. As a wealthy entrepreneur, he created trade routes in France and opened up French trade with the Levant.

Born: c. 1395; Bourges, France
Died: November 25, 1456; possibly Chios, Greece
Sources of wealth: Trade; inheritance
Bequeathal of wealth: Relatives; confiscated

EARLY LIFE

Jacques Coeur (jahk kur) was born in Bourges, France, around 1395. He was the son of Pierre Coeur and Dame Bacquelier, the widow of a butcher. Pierre was a furrier of modest fortune; his marriage advanced him in the society of Bourges, since the Butchers' Corporation was one of the more powerful trade guilds in the city. Jacques's brother Nicolas became archbishop of Luçon, and his sister married Jean Bochetel, secretary to the king. Jacques was educated at the École de la Sainte-Chapelle in Bourges but did not attend university. From an early age, he intended to be a merchant like his father.

In 1418 or 1420, Coeur married Macée de Léodepart, the daughter of the provost of Bourges and former valet of the duc de Berry. The marriage placed Coeur in the top tier of Bourges society. He and his wife had five children of whom there is a record. Two of the children, Jean and Henri, entered the Church, with Jean becoming archbishop of Bourges and Henri appointed canon of la Sainte Chapelle. Another son, Geoffroy, entered the king's service as a functionary; Ravand joined his father in business; and Coeur's only daughter, Perrette, married Jacquelin Trousseau, the viconte de Bourges.

FIRST VENTURES

Soon after his marriage and with the aid of his mother-in-law, who had been previously married to a banker, Coeur became a manager of one of the twelve exchange houses of Bourges. In 1429, he founded a coinage business with two associates. He was accused of falsifying the quality of his coins and faced imprisonment. However, King Charles VII granted him a pardon.

In 1432, Coeur made his first trip to the Levant with a group of merchants from Montpellier. There is consider-able disagreement among scholars of the Middle Ages as to the purpose of his travels. The trip could have been a spiritual pilgrimage, a diplomatic mission for the duc de Bourgogne, an investigative expedition to scrutinize the Muslims in preparation for a Crusade, or a voyage to establish trade with the Levant. Although Coeur did eventually establish a highly profitable trading business with Levantine merchants, he did so twelve years later; it is not very probable that trade was the purpose of the 1432 trip. However, he did return to France with knowledge he would use to build his vast trading empire.

MATURE WEALTH

Once back in France, Coeur established a trading company and exchange at Montpellier. He quickly built a reputation as an astute financier and trader. He became involved in the silk industry at Florence, where he had a silk-manufacturing facility. He joined the Arte della Seta, the silk makers' guild. In 1436, Charles VII summoned him to Paris and bestowed the office of *argentier* (master of the mint) on him. Coeur served in this office from 1436 to 1451, having complete control of the ordinances governing the coinage of France. In 1438, Charles VII made Coeur the court banker and a member of the king's council. Coeur also became the collector of the salt tax.

Holding these offices placed Coeur in a most advantageous situation for expanding his business activities and increasing his wealth. He was in contact with all members of the royal court and all of the foreign countries with which France dealt politically and commercially. Consequently, he was able to acquire goods from all regions of France and from many other countries. He became involved in the salt market in the Loire and Rhone Valleys and in the wheat market in Aquitaine, and he imported wool from Scotland. He also began to import spices, cloth, and other products from the Levant. He established a trade circuit which commercially linked the French cities of Paris, Rouen, Montpellier, Lyons, Avignon, and Limoges.

In 1444, he outfitted his first ship for trading with the Levant. By 1449, he had a fleet of seven trading ships and had established trading houses and exchanges in major towns in France, including Paris, Montpellier, Marseille, Lyons, and Tours. His trade with the Levant increased his wealth through the sale of merchandise, but, more important, it enabled him to make enormous profits from the differences in the currencies of France and other countries. By 1449, Coeur possessed a fortune whose worth no other individual Frenchman would ever match. He established himself as the creditor of Charles VII and the members of the royal court.

Evidence of his wealth was visible throughout France as he purchased and built private houses and chapels in his native Bourges, in Lyons, and elsewhere. Coeur owned property throughout France. In 1443, he began construction of his *grande maison* (great house) at Bourges. The building was extraordinary for its time both in size and in elaborateness of decoration.

In addition to his involvement in trade and finance, Coeur played a very important role in the affairs of state both in France and abroad. In 1444, Charles VII sent him to the Languedoc as one of the commissioners charged with overseeing the newly established parliament there. In 1448, he visited Pope Nicholas V at the Vatican. While there, Coeur succeeded in bringing about an agreement between Nicholas V and Amadeus VIII (Antipope Felix X), which ended the papal schism.

Coeur's relationship with Charles VII provided many of the avenues that enabled him to attain his great wealth, but it also brought about his downfall. Coeur was favored by both the king and his mistress Agnès Sorel, who was the first of the royal mistresses to exert significant political influence. In 1441, the king granted letters of patent to the Coeur family, which gave it status as nobility. The king placed Coeur in a most influential position in his government. Coeur in return provided assistance, primarily in terms of money, to the king. However, he also assisted the king and his mistress in more private ways. Coeur's son-in-law Jacquelin Trousseau owned the Château Bois-Sir-Aimé near Bourges, where Charles VII and Sorel wished to spend their summers. The residence was in very poor condition, and Coeur paid to have it renovated for the king and Sorel. Coeur was among Sorel's favorites, and he served as her confidant. Given her influence over Charles VII, it is very possible that Coeur owed much to her for the favors he received from the king.

Whatever the case may have been, Sorel's death in 1450 brought about Coeur's downfall. With the death of Sorel, Coeur lost his protection at court, and Charles VII lost the

one person who was able to dispel his depression. It was rumored that Sorel had been poisoned, and soon accusations against Coeur as the murderer reached the king. Scholars have clearly established Coeur's innocence and emphasized the extreme jealousy and animosity of the courtiers toward Coeur, an ennobled bourgeois and extremely wealthy upstart to whom most of the courtiers owed large sums of money. Another factor which probably influenced Charles VII was his intense hatred of his son Louis. While Coeur remained loyal to the king, he also had an amiable relationship with Louis.

On July 31, 1450, Coeur was arrested at the Château de Taillebourg. He was charged with treason to the king, poisoning Sorel, practicing alchemy, and financial wrongdoing. He was imprisoned at Poitiers, tortured, forced to admit guilt, and brought to trial with the king's prosecutor Jean Dauvet presiding. Coeur's sentence to

JACQUES COEUR PALACE

Jacques Coeur began construction of his great house in 1443. He always referred to it as his *grande maison*, a term used in his time to designate an extremely large and richly decorated private house. The house was not called the Jacques Coeur Palace until the Bourges tribunal occupied it in 1820.

Coeur hired the very best builders and workmen to build his house. Colin Le Picard, the king's master builder, was in charge of construction. The firms, workshops, and crews Coeur employed had built the palace of Jean, duc de Berry, and this residence was located near the house where Coeur had lived as a child. Coeur's *grande maison* was elaborately decorated with a profusion of sculptures and carvings of his emblem of hearts and shells, in combination with the fleur-de-lis emblem of the king. Coeur was a very loyal subject of Charles VII, priding himself on his relationship with the king, and he had a large statue of Charles VII on horseback placed inside the entry to his new home.

It took eight years to complete the palace. Coeur himself never lived in the house on a permanent basis, although he did host dinners and celebrations there. His arrest and incarceration at almost the exact moment of its completion prevented him from enjoying this elaborate residence, which was the symbol of his success and wealth. The house, along with all of his other holdings, was confiscated by the government. The palace was returned to the family on August 5, 1457, but was sold for the first time by one of Coeur's grandsons on October 7, 1507. From that time, the palace had several different owners, including Jean-Baptiste Colbert (1619-1683), an influential member of Louis XIV's government, and the magistrates of Bourges. In 1923, the French government purchased the palace and declared it a historic monument. In the twenty-first century, the palace is a national monument open to the public.

death was proclaimed on May 23, 1453, and read to him on June 3. Due to the intervention of Pope Nicholas V, the sentence was reduced to imprisonment until such time as Coeur would manage to pay a fine of 550,000 livres. On October 27, 1454, Coeur escaped from Poitiers, and with the help of his family and others he managed to reach Rome, where he found protection with Nicholas V. In 1456, he left Rome on an expedition supposedly to fight the infidels. Coeur died on November 25, 1456, possibly at Chios, Greece.

LEGACY

Jacques Coeur was an outstanding businessman and entrepreneur. His activities as a trader and financier created a trade network within France and also opened up new markets in other European countries and in the Levant. His system of setting up separate companies for his various business ventures was revolutionary for his time. By hiring managers and agents to represent him in exchanges and stores in towns throughout France, he developed a multilevel business organization, which was in a sense a precursor of the modern structure of business. In addition, his enormous wealth sustained France and enabled Charles VII to finance the troops necessary to halt the English conquest. Coeur's *grande maison*, which he had built in Bourges at the height of his success as an entrepreneur, is one of the most beautiful and impressive structures in France. As he amassed his fortune, his influence had an important impact on France, and by consequence the world, in the areas of international trade and business entrepreneurship.

—*Shawncey Webb*

FURTHER READING

Bishop, Morris. *The Middle Ages*. New York: American Heritage, 2001. Good introductory text about the Middle Ages. Treats towns and trade, the role of the bourgeoisie, and how merchants, such as Coeur, changed the economic base from land to money.

Hunt, Edwin, and James Murray. *A History of Business in Medieval Europe*. New York: Cambridge University Press, 1999. Discusses the development of guilds and corporations, and how business changed in the fifteenth century. Includes a list of further readings.

Lopez, Robert S. *The Commercial Revolution of the Middle Ages*. New York: Columbia University Press, 2001. In-depth presentation of daily activities of merchants and traders, including marketplaces, contracts, loans, agents, factors, and means of exchange.

Potter, David, and William Doyle, eds. *France in the Later Middle Ages, 1200-1500*. New York: Oxford University Press, 2003. Covers French politics and society, including the Hundred Years' War, the nobility, and the king and his officials, with special attention to the financial officers and the king's revenues.

Reyerson, Kathryn L. *Jacques Coeur: Entrepreneur and King's Bursar*. New York: Longman, 2004. One of the few biographies of Coeur in English. Well researched and current. Recounts Coeur's career in a historical context.

See also: Louis XIV.

JOHN COLET
British philanthropist, theologian, and scholar

Colet's inherited wealth was primarily significant for the philanthropic manner in which he spent it, which set an important precedent in an era when such benevolence was by no means common. The principal object of his spending was St. Paul's School, a pioneering institution that became a model for many others.

Born: c. 1466; London, England
Died: September 16, 1519; Sheen, Surrey, England
Source of wealth: Inheritance
Bequeathal of wealth: Educational institution

EARLY LIFE

John Colet (KAHL-et) was the son of Sir Henry Colet of Wendover, who was a leading member of the Worshipful Company of Mercers, the most powerful of the liveried companies of the city of London at the time. The guild had been established to represent general merchants, but its core membership consisted of dealers in textiles, whose business underwent a boom in the late fifteenth century as fine clothing and linen became increasingly important as a means of displaying status and wealth. Sir Henry was knighted by King Henry VII in 1486 in recognition of his support at the crucial battle of Bosworth Field, in which King Richard III was overthrown. He served two terms as the lord mayor of London in 1486 and 1495.

Sir Henry's wife, the former Christian Knyvet, bore him a great many children, although the exact number is not known. The scholar Desiderius Erasmus, who knew and greatly admired "Dame Christian," as well as her son John Colet, recorded the number as twenty-two—eleven boys and eleven girls—but there is no documentary confirmation of that figure. The great majority, at any rate, died in infancy, leaving only two sons, Richard and John, to grow to adulthood.

John Colet's early education included a spell at Saint Antholin's Hospital, but few other documentary details of his youth survive until he went into the Church, which was then a recognized career path for the younger sons of respectable folk. At that time, his older brother Richard was expected to take over Sir Henry's business interests and was regarded as the businessman's heir.

In 1485, Colet became a rector at Dennington in Suffolk, whose living was in the gift of his mother's family, and from 1490 to 1494 he was rector at Thurning in Huntingdonshire, that living being in his father's gift. He traveled on the Continent thereafter, probably as much as a tourist as a scholar, but when he met the celebrated humanist Erasmus for the first time in 1495 he apparently had a change of heart. The subsequent correspondence and friendship of the two scholars extended for more than twenty years. Erasmus evidently made a deep impression on Colet, seemingly galvanizing a religious commitment that had formerly been little more than a useful source of income and transforming it into a genuine vocation.

FIRST VENTURES

Colet was ordained as a deacon in 1497 and as a priest in 1498. He was already canon of York by then, and in 1499 he acquired the parish of Stepney, which was then the richest in England. He was said by later commentators to have studied at both Oxford and Cambridge Universities, graduating from Magdalen College, Oxford, in 1501, and obtaining his doctorate in 1504, but again, contemporary documentary evidence is lacking. There is, however, no possible doubt as to the quality of his intellect

John Colet. (Hulton Archive/Getty Images)

ST. PAUL'S SCHOOL

John Colet founded St. Paul's School in 1509, building the institution on a plot of land north of St. Paul's Cathedral in London. Colet endowed the school with estates that initially provided an income of £112 a year (the sum escalated considerably over time) and appointed the Worshipful Company of Mercers as school trustees. He hired the famous grammarian William Lilye to serve as the first high master at an annual salary of 13 shillings, twice that of the headmaster of Eton College, a British boarding school for boys. St. Paul's was subsequently designated as one of the nine original public schools by the Public Schools Act of 1868, the title referring to the fact that it was supposedly open to anyone.

Initially the school provided accommodation for 153 pupils, that number being determined because of its association with the account in the Gospels of "the miraculous draught of fishes" secured by Peter at Christ's behest. Colet had in mind, of course, Christ's assertion that he would make Peter a "fisher of men," and the school was Colet's instrument for carrying forward that work. Education was provided in "literature and etiquette." The former included the Greek and Latin literature made available within Christendom in association with the Renaissance, whose Aristotelian and Platonic components embraced philosophy and protoscience, as well as the Scriptures and commentary thereon. Etiquette instruction embraced codes of behavior hopefully intended to make civil society more polite, constructive, and, in the most general sense, humanistic. Tuition was free, but the pupils had to pay for their own wax candles—a not inconsiderable expense.

The educational philosophy of St. Paul's School retained the stamp of Colet's ideas for many years after his death, in part because he collaborated with Lilye and other teachers on the perennially reprinted basic textbook that eventually became known, somewhat misleadingly, as the *Eton Latin Grammar.* St. Paul's School survived into the twenty-first century, although it had long since been relocated from the heart of the city of London to a much larger site in the suburb of Barnes.

considerable. Colet's preaching at St. Paul's gave humanist ideas their most significant platform in England, and his sermons on Paul's Epistles, which attempted to overturn then-conventional scholastic interpretations, became highly controversial. His ideas interacted with those of Thomas More and other important English theologians of the day. However, Colet published very little. Although printing was firmly established in England during his lifetime by his father's fellow Mercer William Caxton, Colet regarded printing more as an asset for education than as a means of preserving his own ideas. For this reason, what survived of his writings was a belated patchwork of oddments, and he left less of an impression behind him than some of his less able contemporaries. His enthusiasm for reform led, perhaps inevitably, to charges of heresy being lodged against him by more conservative clergymen, but he was stoutly defended by William Warham, the archbishop of Canterbury, and was never in any real difficulty.

MATURE WEALTH

Colet does not seem to have obtained control of his father's fortune when he reestablished St. Paul's School, but when he did begin managing his inheritance he set about employing it in the cause dearest to his heart. There had been a school attached to St. Paul's Cathedral in London since 1103, but it had been used in its early days entirely as a means of training the clergy, and by the early sixteenth century it had fallen into disuse as that role had been taken on by the universities. The school that Colet had in mind was a very different institution, whose primary purpose would be the education of laymen, with a view to extending learning and culture beyond the bounds of the Church establishment, eventually to embrace the whole of civil society—or, at least, its upper strata.

Colet made no attempt to achieve any further promotion within the Church hierarchy, although he became a close ally of the ambitious Thomas Wolsey and did not relax in his reformist agitation while he was part of Wolsey's clique. Colet was chosen to preach the sermon when Wolsey was appointed a cardinal in 1515. Wolsey was influential in having Colet appointed to the privy council of King Henry VIII, who had come to the throne

and education, even if the latter was slightly belated and mostly autodidactic. What is certain is that his prospects underwent a drastic change when his brother Richard died in 1503, leaving Colet and Dame Christian as Sir Henry's joint heirs when the latter died in 1505. Dame Christian, who came from a mercantile family herself, apparently continued to manage the family's business interests and remained a force to be reckoned with in the Company of Mercers, although, as a woman, she was ineligible for membership therein. There was never any question of Colet leaving the Church, and his mother seems to have supported his vocation wholeheartedly.

In 1505, Colet was appointed dean of St. Paul's Cathedral, and his influence within the Church then became in 1509. Henry thought sufficiently highly of Colet to appoint him as his chaplain for a while, but Colet was a pacifist who steadfastly opposed Henry's French campaigns, and that conscientious opposition eventually proved too much for the king to bear.

Colet began to suffer repeated attacks of what was generally known as "the sweating sickness," or dropsy, in 1517, although the severe attrition the illness inflicted on his physical strength did not bring him to the brink of death until the summer of 1519. Always unostentatious in his dress and frugal in his habits, Colet dutifully made provision in his will for a small grave in the grounds of St. Paul's and a modest commemorative stone. However, his mother, who survived him by four years, was still influential in the Company of Mercers, and the guild eventually paid for the establishment of a much more lavish tomb, which survived the Great Fire of London in 1666 but had to be moved thereafter.

LEGACY

Colet's material legacy was, in essence, St. Paul's School and everything it stood for. As a reformer within the Church, he was controversial in his lifetime, and his reputation thereafter was subject to the winds of change associated with the Reformation, which altered direction several times in sixteenth century England. As a pioneer in the educational field, however, his contribution was unchallengeable, and the fact that he spent his money on the values he extolled in his sermons earned him a great deal of well-deserved respect.

—*Brian Stableford*

FURTHER READING

Arnold, Jonathan. *Dean John Colet of St. Paul's: Humanism and Reform in Early Tudor England.* New York: I. B. Tauris, 2007. The shortage of hard information about Colet's life did not prevent publication of a series of biographies, most of them derived from *The Life of Dr. John Colet . . .* (1724) by Samuel Knight. Arnold's biography conscientiously places the information in the context of modern historical research and understanding.

Chatterjee, Kalyan Kumar. *In Praise of Learning: John Colet and Literary Humanism in Education.* New Delhi, India: Affiliated East-West Press, 1974. An account of Colet's ideas, achievement, and influence in the field of education, with particular reference to the precedents set by St. Paul's School.

Jayne, Sears. *John Colet and Marsilio Ficino.* Westport, Conn.: Greenwood Press, 1980. A work in a similar vein to that of Miles (below), which narrows the field of focus somewhat in attempting a more precise account of the European influences that helped to shape Colet's thought.

Lupton, J. H. *A Life of John Colet, Dean of St, Paul's and Founder of St, Paul's School.* London: G. Bell and Sons, 1887. One of the most useful biographies, by virtue of the fact that it appends a significant selection of English translations of Colet's own writings, which were composed in Latin and are usually reprinted in that language.

Miles, Leland. *John Colet and the Platonic Tradition.* London: Allen and Unwin, 1962. A detailed account of Colet's theological position, which attempts to set it in the context of the new and resurgent ideas associated with the Renaissance, especially those of the English Platonists, who became increasingly influential in English education during the sixteenth century.

See also: Walter de Merton.

SAMUEL COLT
American inventor and industrialist

Colt's arms manufacturing enterprise earned a fortune, which he and his widow ultimately used for philanthropic and artistic purposes.

Born: July 19, 1814; Hartford, Connecticut
Died: January 10, 1862; Hartford, Connecticut
Also known as: Colonel Colt
Sources of wealth: Patents; manufacturing; sale of products
Bequeathal of wealth: Spouse; charity; artistic patronage

EARLY LIFE
Samuel Colt was born in Hartford, Connecticut, the son of Christopher and Sarah Colt. His father was a farmer and would-be silk manufacturer, and his family was financially comfortable. Colt did not do well in school, mostly because he attended more closely to books on scientific and technical subjects than to the regular curricular materials. He became fascinated by guns, gunpowder, electricity, and laughing gas. Some of his youthful experiments with electrically fired gunpowder mines were both spectacular and dangerous. In 1832, at age eighteen, he went to sea. On his first voyage he developed the idea of a repeating firearm with a revolving cylinder. The crucial parts were whittled out of wood; these pieces are displayed at the Colt Firearms Collection at the Museum of Connecticut History in Hartford.

FIRST VENTURES
On his return to the United States, Colt persuaded his father to support the development of his invention. Early experiments failed, as Colt tried to deal with the problem of multiple-chamber explosions. He also had trouble making the parts of his revolvers from good quality steel. At one point he was forced to support himself by giving public laughing gas demonstrations, using the name Doctor S. Coult.

In 1835, after further work, Colt, who had by then obtained two patents on his revolver, set up a factory in Paterson, New Jersey. This enterprise failed, but Colt's revolver had not gone unnoticed, and a large order from the Texas Rangers in 1847 enabled him to reestablish his business in Hartford. The business was so successful that he was able to retire his entire debt by 1849. His income enabled him to build a huge factory, as well as a large manor house that he called Armsmear. His success was more the result of his industrial techniques than of his patents. Because of his extensive development of jigs and other manufacturing fixtures to make interchangeable parts, he was able to use semiskilled workers rather than craftsmen to produce his firearms.

MATURE WEALTH
Colt's employee policies were extremely enlightened by the standards of his time. A significant portion of the company's income was used to provide employee housing, a ten-hour workday, a one-hour lunch break, and rudimentary medical facilities. Even after these expenditures, his arms business was extremely profitable. He traveled extensively; many of his guns were sold to foreign governments, as well as to the United States Army. His company also made thousands of sales to private customers. Colt's income was enormous; when he died in 1862, his estate was valued at $15 million.

Some of Colt's money was used to finance civic projects, including a band, community hall, and other facili-

Samuel Colt. (Library of Congress)

ties. He and his wife, Elizabeth Jarvis Colt, had become patrons of the arts as soon as his company had become profitable. From the outset, their mansion, Armsmear, was intended to be as much museum as private dwelling. It had both public and private rooms, which were richly decorated with commissioned furniture, statuary, Sèvres-style porcelain vases, and paintings. A picture gallery was built, to which the public was given access. A horticultural conservatory also was constructed and was subsequently relocated and rebuilt several times by Elizabeth after Samuel's death. There was, of course, a large arms museum associated with Colt's factory.

Colt was only forty-seven years old when he died, and the bulk of his fortune was managed by his widow, Elizabeth. She continued to support the arts, develop Armsmear, and contribute to Hartford's civic culture until her death in 1905. None of the couple's children survived her death.

LEGACY

Colt Manufacturing Company, LLC, the successor to Colt's Patent Firearms Manufacturing Company, continues to survive into the twenty-first century, not quite as grand as it had been during the nineteenth century but still producing profits for its owners. Some of the furnishings and art collected at Armsmear, as well as the large collection of firearms, are under the protection of the Wadsworth Atheneum, the oldest public art museum in the United States. Armsmear itself was converted into a home for Episcopalian women under the terms of Elizabeth Colt's will. Half of the acreage on which Armsmear stood was given to the city of Hartford and is now Colt Park.

Samuel Colt's life and career—and that of his wife—are worth studying for two reasons. One was his gifted development of techniques for mass production and his advanced notions of sound employee relations. The second, and perhaps the more important, was the Colts' dedication of their fortune to public causes, particularly to the fine arts.

—Robert Jacobs

FURTHER READING

Hosley, William N. *Colt: The Making of an American Legend*. Amherst: University of Massachusetts Press, 1996.

Keating, Bern. *The Flamboyant Mr. Colt and His Deadly Six-Shooter*. Garden City, NY: Doubleday & Company, 1978.

Rywell, Martin. *Samuel Colt: A Man and an Epoch*. Harriman, Tenn.: Pioneer Press, 1952

See also: Alfred I. du Pont; Irénée du Pont; Alfred Krupp; Bertha Krupp; Alfred Nobel; Basil Zaharoff.

JAY COOKE
American investment banker

Cooke has been called "the financier of the Civil War." He led the effort to sell government bonds to pay for the Union war effort. After the Civil War, Cooke became a major backer of the Northern Pacific Railway, until that line's bankruptcy caused the failure of his banking firm.

Born: August 10, 1821; Erie County (now Sandusky), Ohio
Died: February 18, 1905; Ogontz, Pennsylvania
Source of wealth: Banking
Bequeathal of wealth: Relatives; charity

EARLY LIFE

Jay Cooke was one of the first children born in a small frontier settlement that eventually became Sandusky, Ohio. His family was prominent in business and politics in Ohio. His father, Eleutheros Cooke, was a lawyer, railroad investor, and real estate speculator, and he served as a member of the Whig Party in the House of Representatives from 1831 to 1833. Cooke began working as a clerk in a local store when he was fourteen years old. In 1836, he went to work in a firm involved with the fur trade in St. Louis, Missouri. When that firm failed during the Panic of 1837, Cooke moved to Philadelphia. He had saved about $200, and he went into business with other members of his family in the shipping and transportation industries. He worked as a ticket agent for a canal packet boat line and for various railroads.

FIRST VENTURES

Cooke's entry into the world of banking, where he would make his major mark, was in 1839, when he went to work for the banking house of E. W. Clark and Company, the largest private banking firm in the nation at that time. Clark and Company was heavily involved in railroad promotion and in raising money for new railroad lines being built throughout the eastern United States. While the firm was already large and prosperous when Cooke came to work there, the greatest growth of the company was in the 1840's and 1850's. When the Second Bank of the United States was dismantled as a result of President Andrew Jackson's "Bank War," private firms, such as Clark and Company, became more powerful. The firm also was a major marketer of U.S. Treasury bonds during the Mexican War of 1846-1848. Within a few years, Cooke was promoted to junior partner in the firm. He became known as an expert in valuing the currency issued by various private banks throughout the country and at spotting counterfeit currency. After the Panic of 1857, Cooke left Clark and Company. Over the next few years, he was involved in railroad investments and in the unification of several Pennsylvania canal companies into a single firm. The major source of Cooke's wealth was his banking firm, Jay Cooke and Company, which he opened in Philadelphia on January 1, 1861.

MATURE WEALTH

Cooke's brother Henry was a good friend of Salmon P. Chase, the former governor of Ohio who became President Abraham Lincoln's first secretary of the Treasury. Chase offered Cooke the position of assistant secretary of the Treasury, but Cooke declined. Later, Chase gave Cooke a contract to sell war bonds for the government during the Civil War. Cooke made such an impressive record selling bonds that in March, 1862, Lincoln suggested that Cooke be made supervisor of all government bond sales.

Cooke is sometimes credited with the invention of the modern war bond drive. He sought to sell bonds to the small investor instead of focusing on the wealthy people who usually made such investments. Cooke believed that patriotic sentiment would lead many middle-class people to make small investments. He sold bonds in denominations as small as $50 and offered credit arrangements for purchasers. At one point, Cooke had more than twenty-five hundred agents selling bonds for him. A large-scale advertising campaign disseminated information about the war bond drive

to prospective purchasers. Eventually, other banking firms began to criticize Cooke's virtual monopoly on the marketing of government bonds, and Chase stopped using Cooke as the government's agent. Later, however, when the sale of bonds was declining, Lincoln encouraged William Pitt Fessenden, who had replaced Chase as secretary of the Treasury, to turn again to Cooke. Over the course of the Civil War, the bonds Cooke sold and the bank loans he arranged raised more than $3 billion for the Union war effort.

Cooke had a substantial fortune before the Civil War, but he became much wealthier over the course of the war. The commissions he made for selling government bonds were relatively small—only one quarter of 1 percent—

Jay Cooke and Company's bank during the Panic of 1873. Cooke's bank had invested heavily in the Northern Pacific Railroad. The railroad's bankruptcy resulted in the failure of Cooke's bank and the demise of his personal fortune. (Library of Congress)

and he paid the salaries of his staff and the advertising costs out of these commissions. However, his knowledge of how the government would use the money he raised and where purchases would be made allowed him to make extensive investments in firms that were doing business with the government. Such use of insider knowledge was not illegal at the time. By 1870, Jay Cooke and Company had three hundred people working in offices in Philadelphia, Washington, D.C., New York City, and London. By the early 1870's, Cooke's fortune was probably in the range of $7 million to $10 million. With profits from his Civil War bond sales commissions, Cooke built a fifty-three-room, seventy-five-thousand-square-foot mansion on a two-hundred-acre estate in Elkins Park, just north of Philadelphia. He named this home Ogontz for a Wyandot Indian chief whom he had known and admired as a young man. He also purchased Gibraltar Island in Put-in-Bay on Lake Erie, where he built a more modest fifteen-room mansion, which he often favored because of the great fishing in Lake Erie.

When Lincoln was assassinated, Cooke realized that this shocking news might panic investors, who would scramble to sell their government bonds. He sent orders to his agents to buy all government bonds that were offered for sale in order to stem any massive sell-off. He told Fessenden that he would "fully maintain the credit of the nation in this crisis." Lincoln died on Saturday, April 15, 1865. On the following Monday, Cooke walked down Wall Street, buying up government bonds with his own funds; by Wednesday, the bond sell-off was over.

After the Civil War, Cooke became involved in the financing of the Northern Pacific Railway, which was to be built from Duluth, Minnesota, to the Puget Sound region in the Washington Territory. Cooke undertook to sell bonds for the railroad, but the early management of the line was inefficient, and cost overruns were excessive. When the Northern Pacific declared bankruptcy in 1873, Cooke's banking firm also failed, and he lost his personal fortune. In later years, he managed to pay off his debts and acquire a second fortune through various business endeavors, including a gold mine in Utah in which both

THE OGONTZ SCHOOL FOR YOUNG LADIES

When the bankruptcy of the Northern Pacific Railway in 1873 caused the failure of Jay Cooke and Company and eventually led to Cooke's personal bankruptcy, he was forced to sell one of his beloved homes, Ogontz, which was located in Elkins Park, Pennsylvania. Cooke had built this lavish mansion in 1863. A few years after his bankruptcy, Cooke had made a second, albeit smaller fortune through various business ventures, and he repurchased Ogontz. Eventually, he decided he could not maintain both this home and his Gibraltar estate, located on an island in Put-in-Bay on Lake Erie. Cooke arranged for the Ogontz mansion and the surrounding estate to be leased by the Chestnut Street Female Seminary, a finishing school for the daughters of elite families, which had been founded in Philadelphia in 1850. This school moved to Ogontz and was renamed the Ogontz School for Young Ladies. The school leased the Ogontz estate for $15,000 per year and was located there for thirty-four years. The student body was generally from some of the wealthiest families in the United States and averaged around one hundred students per year.

One of the most prominent figures associated with the Ogontz School was Abby Sutherland, a graduate of Radcliffe College who came to Ogontz in 1902. She eventually served as headmistress and president of the school, and in 1912 she purchased the facility from its original owners. Joseph Widener, who owned land next to the Ogontz estate, desired to buy the land from Cooke's heirs, and Cooke's family arranged for Widener to purchase the property. Shortly after buying the Ogontz estate, the Widener family tore down Cooke's original mansion and built another home on the property.

When the Ogontz estate was sold, Sutherland relocated the school to larger facilities in 1916, although the name Ogontz School for Young Ladies was maintained at the new location in the Rydal Park area of Abington, Pennsylvania. Amelia Earhart, who later became a famous aviator, was a student in the first class at this new campus. In 1950, Sutherland decided to close the Ogontz School and made a gift of the Abington campus to the Pennsylvania State University system. By the twenty-first century, this was the site of Penn State Abington.

Cooke and Jay Gould were investors. After leasing his former Ogontz mansion to a girls' school, Cooke built a smaller home nearby and also named it Ogontz. He died there in 1905 after slowly declining health.

LEGACY

Cooke was one of the first major investment bankers in the United States. Later firms would grow much larger than his, but in many ways, Cooke pioneered the sale of investments to small-scale buyers. He focused on the sale of government war bonds, but later investment bankers would use similar techniques in marketing private stocks and bonds to a broad market of clients. Cooke deserves much credit for helping the federal government tap the wealth of the northern states to finance the Civil War.

While Cooke did accumulate an impressive personal fortune, his career illustrates the volatile nature of the world of high finance. Although he lost his first fortune in the bankruptcy of the Northern Pacific Railway, that line eventually became a major regional railroad, justifying his earlier confidence in its potential.

—*Mark S. Joy*

FURTHER READING

Gordon, John Steele. *Hamilton's Blessing: The Extraordinary Life and Times of Our National Debt*. New York: Penguin Books, 1997. An excellent, highly readable study of the significance of the national debt in American history. Has considerable coverage on Cooke's sale of war bonds to finance the Civil War.

Hammond, Bray. *Sovereignty and an Empty Purse: Banks and Politics in the Civil War*. Princeton, N.J.: Princeton University Press, 1970. One of the standard studies of banking policy in the United States during the Civil War. Deals extensively with Cooke's efforts to sell war bonds for the federal government.

Josephson, Matthew. *The Robber Barons: The Great American Capitalists, 1861-1901*. New York: Harcourt Brace Jovanovich, 1934. Reprint. San Diego: Harcourt Brace Jovanovich, 1961. Josephson's book was the first major study of the robber barons. Although Cooke was not seen as one of the more infamous robber barons, he was considered part of this group.

Lubetkin, John M. *Jay Cooke's Gamble: The Northern Pacific Railroad, the Sioux, and the Panic of 1873*. Norman: University of Oklahoma Press, 2006. Deals extensively with Cooke, covering his involvement with the Northern Pacific Railway, which led to the failure of his banking firm and his personal bankruptcy.

Oberholtzer, Ellis Paxson. *Jay Cooke: Financier of the Civil War*. 2 vols. Philadelphia: George W. Jacobs, 1907. A highly favorable and detailed study of Cooke's life, focusing on his early years and the Civil War, with less coverage of his later life.

See also: George F. Baker; John Insley Blair; William Andrews Clark; Daniel Drew; Anthony Joseph Drexel; Stephen Girard; Hetty Green; Andrew Mellon; Richard B. Mellon; George Peabody; Russell Sage.

PETER COOPER
American industrialist, inventor, and philanthropist

Cooper employed his inventing genius and commercial acumen to establish one of the great industrial fortunes of the early United States. With foresight, he used his wealth for civic and philanthropic ventures, notably founding Cooper Union College of New York City.

Born: February 12, 1791; New York, New York
Died: April 4, 1883; New York, New York
Sources of wealth: Patents; manufacturing; real estate; investments; steel
Bequeathal of wealth: Children; educational institution

EARLY LIFE

Peter Cooper was born in 1791 in New York City, the fifth of nine children of John and Margaret Cooper. When Cooper was a boy, his father moved the family to Peekskill, New York, where John took up a dozen livelihoods as a farmer, shopkeeper, shoemaker, hatmaker, furrier, beekeeper, builder, brewer, and brick maker, among other occupations. The engines of Cooper's future success—mechanical innovation and a shrewd business sense—can be traced to his father's enterprises. However, while John barely made a living for his family, Cooper's ventures would flourish wildly. Although Cooper received little schooling, he tinkered endlessly, his boyhood inventions including a double-wheel washing machine. At seventeen he became an apprentice to a New York City carriage maker.

FIRST VENTURES

Cooper's talent for combining mechanical skill with industrial enterprise brought him successive fortunes. Finishing his apprenticeship, he engaged in various ventures. He manufactured a cloth-shearing machine. He opened a furniture shop and a grocery. He bought property and rented out apartments. He patented numerous inventions, including improvements to the construction of steam boilers, marble tabletops, and salt makers. In 1827, Cooper purchased a struggling glue factory with the proceeds from his enterprises. Experimenting with various ingredients, he patented high-quality glues that

Peter Cooper's steam-driven locomotive Tom Thumb races against a horse in August, 1830. Cooper also invented an instant table gelatin that was the forerunner of Jell-O. (Hulton Archive/Getty Images)

could compete with the costly European imports. Capturing the import market, Cooper was soon earning a spectacular income of $100,000 a year.

Cooper added to the factory's success by devising an inexpensive brand of isinglass—a transparent gelatin used in foods—and by inventing and marketing the first instant table gelatin, the forerunner of the fabulously successful product Jell-O.

In 1828, Cooper began speculating in real estate, buying three thousand acres in Maryland near the newly incorporated Baltimore and Ohio Railroad. When the railroad made slow progress, Cooper built a makeshift prototype steam locomotive out of industrial materials on hand—the famous Tom Thumb. After a demonstration drive of Tom Thumb, which showed the potential of railroad steam engines on America's rough terrain, Cooper was able to sell his land at many times the purchase price, acquiring his second fortune. Maintaining meticu-

lous accounts of the growth of his wealth his entire life, Cooper estimated his fortune in 1833 at $123,459, the rough equivalent of $70 million in 2010.

MATURE WEALTH

By 1846, Cooper had accumulated a fortune of $385,500. In 1837, he built an iron foundry in New York, moving it to Trenton, New Jersey, in 1845 to accommodate its rapid expansion and twenty-five thousand employees. Improving every facet of the iron-making process, Cooper became an innovator in an industry that would make several of America's greatest fortunes: iron- and steelmaking. In 1853, his company pioneered the production of iron rails and lightweight structural iron beams necessary for building New York City skyscrapers. In the 1870's, the company pioneered the open-hearth method of steel production, a process whereby metal is efficiently converted into steel by burning out the impurities in a hearth (basin) heated by a furnace. Out of his profits, Cooper helped finance the laying of the first successful transatlantic cable in 1866.

In 1856, Cooper's real estate and stock holdings were worth more than $1.1 million. His wealth had grown almost tenfold in two decades, and he had become one of the United States' wealthiest industrialists. Cooper, his wife Sarah, and their children lived in a mansion in fashionable Gramercy Park in Manhattan.

Cooper increasingly turned his attention to philanthropic and civic matters. With his belief in scientific progress, democracy, and the benefits of public education, he conceived of endowing a college that would offer a free education to all qualified students, as well as night classes for workers and auditoriums for civic discourse and debate. He purchased a city block at Seventh Street between Third and Fourth Avenues, near the Astor Li-

brary and Astor Place Opera House. In 1858, an imposing brownstone building was completed at the site at a cost to Cooper of $630,000. In 1859, the Cooper Union for the Advancement of Science and Art opened to students and laborers alike, regardless of sex, religion, or race. With free tuition and night classes, it was an instant success and a prototype for future American universities. Cooper Union also had a dramatic effect on the political world, when on February 27, 1860, Abraham Lincoln advanced his nomination for president with his brilliant "Cooper Union" address.

While continuing to oversee both his growing industries and Cooper Union, Cooper devoted much of the last quarter of his life to civic activities. Drawing upon a lifetime as a self-made industrialist and ardent democrat, he formed a theory of finance and government, eventually published in his collected works, *Ideas for a Science of*

THE COOPER UNION FOR THE ADVANCEMENT OF SCIENCE AND ART

In the Cooper Union for the Advancement of Science and Art, Peter Cooper founded one of the most innovative educational enterprises in American history. Aware of his own educational shortcomings, Cooper wanted his college to be free to all admitted students. An ardent and practical democrat, he also wanted his school to play a role in the nation's political life and industrial success.

It would be difficult to say that he was not successful. Even before the school opened, the nine-hundred-seat Great Hall of Cooper Union established itself as one of the nation's most important sites for political speech. In February, 1860, the candidate for the Republican nomination for president, Abraham Lincoln, delivered one of his most famous speeches on slavery, which helped propel him to the presidency. Over the next 150 years, the Great Hall auditorium would witness speeches in favor of workers' rights and women's suffrage, as well as the first meetings of the National Association for the Advancement of Colored People (NAACP) and the American Red Cross. Presidential candidates and presidents alike—Ulysses S. Grant, Grover Cleveland, William Howard Taft, Theodore Roosevelt, Woodrow Wilson, Bill Clinton, and Barack Obama—followed Lincoln's example in giving memorable speeches in the Great Hall.

As an educational institution, Cooper Union has been equally successful. Its early years provided wide access to education and established Cooper Union as a model for future American universities. The school was coeducational, making no distinction among races or religions, and free to the children of the working class. Cooper Union offered

night classes for laborers and a Female School of Design. Reflecting its founder's practical successes, the school emphasized education that was forward-looking, scientific, and technological, including courses in architecture, electrical engineering, telegraphy, photography, stenography, and oratory. It offered a free library to the public and meeting spaces for artists and inventors. The success of Cooper Union helped inspire Matthew Vassar to found Vassar College for Women in 1861, Ezra Cornell to found Cornell University in 1865, and Andrew Carnegie to launch his various educational institutions.

Throughout its history, Cooper Union continued to provide a top-notch, free education to thousands of students, including inventor Thomas Edison, designer Milton Glaser, "Batman" creator Bob Kane, sculptor Augustus Saint-Gaudens, and Supreme Court Justice Felix Frankfurter. By the twenty-first century, it was organized into three schools—the School of Art, the Irwin S. Chanin School of Architecture, and the Albert Nerken School of Engineering—and it had become one of the most selective colleges in the country, admitting a mere 8 percent of applicants. Located near its original brownstone building in New York's East Village (at Cooper Square and Astor Place), it remains a vital institution in the city's life. Cooper Union celebrated its 150th anniversary on February 12, 2009. Relying on the endowment begun by Peter Cooper, which by that anniversary had surpassed the $600 million mark, Cooper Union continues to offer a full-tuition scholarship to every admitted student.

Good Government (1883). Cooper's proposals rested on a theory of currency, which he believed had to be placed at the service of labor and the business cycle rather than affixed to a rigid standard of gold. In 1876, Cooper ran for president on the Independent Party, better known as the Greenback Party. His platform relied on "financial reform and industrial emancipation," but its heart was the replacement of gold-backed currency by legal-tender dollars, or greenbacks, backed by the credit of the U.S. Treasury. His ticket received fewer than 100,000 votes nationwide, but the twentieth century would see the United States adopt a flexible, fiat currency that resembled Cooper's ideas.

Sarah Cooper died in 1869, and Cooper died in 1883. Their son Peter assumed much of the management of the ironworks. Their daughter Amelia married Abraham Hewitt, who was wealthy in his own right and would serve as mayor of New York City from 1887 to 1888. In Cooper's lifetime, he had endowed Cooper Union with some $1,550,000. In his will, he bequeathed the college an additional $155,350. He also left trusts of $250,000 for the benefit of his children and $350,000 for the benefit of his grandchildren, with the remainder of the trust eventually to be transferred to Cooper Union.

LEGACY

Peter Cooper's riches were the result of his many talents. He was a brilliant inventor who enriched the world with gelatin, industrial glues, and a prototype steam locomotive, among other inventions. He turned his best ideas into successive fortunes, demonstrating acumen both as a manufacturer and as an iron and steel industrialist—the most successful in nineteenth century New York. He remained unpretentious and practical. His greenback advocacy was not that of the wealthy eastern establishment, but, Cooper believed, of the common man looking for entrepreneurial opportunity free of debt and a slavish mercantilism. Most of all, in establishing Cooper Union, he showed that for a man of great wealth to be esteemed in American history, he had to be as imaginative and fruitful in bestowing his fortune as he had been in acquiring it.

—*Howard Bromberg*

FURTHER READING

Beckert, Sven. *The Monied Metropolis: New York City and the Consolidation of the American Bourgeoisie, 1850-1896*. New York: Cambridge University Press, 2003. This scholarly study of the wealthiest residents of early New York City highlights Cooper as New York's richest industrialist. With extensive maps and graphs showing the distribution and incomes of New York's richest.

Gordon, John Steele. *The Business of America*. New York: Walker, 2001. One of the leading historians of American business highlights America's most innovative businesspersons. Portrays Cooper as the first great philanthropist of American industrial fortunes.

Hedjuk, John. *Education of an Architect—A Point of View: The Cooper Union School of Art and Architecture, 1964-1971*. New York: Random House, 2000. An influential book by the chairman of the Cooper Union department of architecture, documenting the innovative projects of its students. Includes drawings, photographs, models, and manifestos.

Holzer, Harold. *Lincoln at Cooper Union: The Speech That Made Abraham Lincoln President*. New York: Simon & Schuster, 2004. A recounting of Lincoln's famous Cooper Union address of 1860, in which the future president decried expansion of slavery into the federal territories. Holzer makes a case for this speech as pivotal to Lincoln's gaining the presidency.

Lienhard, John. *How Invention Begins: Echoes of Old Voices in the Rise of New Machines*. New York: Oxford University Press, 2006. An account of mechanical inventions in Western culture. Chapter 13 recounts Cooper's contributions to technology and education. Includes excellent illustrations.

Nevins, Allen. *Abram S. Hewitt, with Some Account of Peter Cooper*. New York: Harper Brothers, 1935. Reprint. New York: Octagon Books, 1967. The fullest account of Cooper's life (and that of his son-in-law and business partner) by a prominent historian. Includes an appendix recording the growth of Cooper's fortune according to his books.

Raymond, Rossiter W. *Peter Cooper*. 1901. Reprint. Freeport, N.Y.: Books for Libraries Press, 1972. This reprint of the one-hundred-page volume in the Riverside biographical series presents a nearly contemporaneous view of Cooper.

See also: Andrew Carnegie; Samuel Colt; George Eastman; Thomas Edison; Harvey Firestone; Edwin Herbert Land; Samuel F. B. Morse; Isaac Merrit Singer; George Westinghouse.

FIRST EARL OF CORK
British aristocrat, landowner, and investor

The first earl of Cork assembled an enormous estate in the southern Irish province of Munster during the late sixteenth and early seventeenth centuries under the English government's official plantation scheme. Using his position within the Irish administration, many of Boyle's gains were illicit and exemplified the rapaciousness of English colonization in Ireland.

Born: October 13, 1566; Canterbury, Kent, England
Died: September 15, 1643; Youghal, County Cork, Ireland
Also known as: Richard Boyle (birth name); Richard Boyle Cork
Sources of wealth: Government; real estate; trade
Bequeathal of wealth: Children; relatives

EARLY LIFE
The first earl of Cork was born Richard Boyle in 1566, the second son of Kentish landowner Roger Boyle and his wife Joan (née Naylor) Boyle. Beginning in 1583, Boyle attended Corpus Christi College at Cambridge University and then worked at Middle Temple, London, as a clerk to complete his legal training. At Middle Temple, Boyle gained the confidence of a family friend, Sir Edward Waterhouse, chancellor of the Irish exchequer. Waterhouse was also a chief proponent of settling the Irish province of Munster with English landowners in response to the Desmond Rebellions against English rule (1569-1573, 1579-1583). Through Waterhouse, and with reportedly forged documents, Boyle first traveled to Ireland in 1588, gaining a position as deputy escheator under the patronage of Geoffrey Fenton. In this official position, Boyle was responsible for the valuation, distribution, and sale of recently confiscated Irish estates in Munster. The Tudor policy of confiscating lands owned by Irish lords in rebellion against the Crown and using these lands as plantations for English settlers arose at the same time that Boyle entered government service.

FIRST VENTURES
As deputy escheator Boyle dealt with a specific area of confiscation policy known as "concealed lands" that was then under review by the English administration in Dublin. Although plans for the Munster plantations had evolved before Boyle's arrival in Ireland, the complex systems of landholding and legal title among the Irish and the assessment of land values delayed settlement ventures. The primary impediments to settlement were issues about how much land the Irish lords actually owned, under what terms, and its exact worth. Litigation brought by Irish landowners against confiscation clogged the Dublin courts through the 1580's and 1590's. In sifting through the claims, valuations, and boundaries of the approximately 300,000 acres considered to be forfeited to the Crown, Boyle became very familiar with the most productive and fertile regions of Munster. Without hesitation he claimed some of the best lands for himself, and he handed out other claims to friends and associates—for a charge—through the early 1590's. These initial and illegal land claims, though not without numerous investigations of corruption later, secured Boyle's future wealth and enabled him to develop his properties and buy out other English claimants in Munster.

MATURE WEALTH
To further secure his property, Boyle married Joan Apsley in November, 1595. Boyle's father-in-law, William Apsley, held title to lands near Limerick, of which his daughter was coheir. By the time of his marriage, however, the plantation system in Munster and its administrators were under investigation by the English authorities. Boyle was among those accused of corruption and abuse of power. Boyle was arrested and imprisoned briefly in 1596, but he was released through his growing network of patrons and associates. No charges were brought against him. Disgraced, and with his wife Joan recently deceased after giving birth to a stillborn child, he returned to London and worked for Sir George Carew, the newly appointed lord president of Munster. On Boyle's return to Ireland in 1600 with Carew, he secretly received notice that Sir Walter Ralegh's lands in Munster were up for sale. Taking advantage of the fact that Ralegh needed cash rapidly, Boyle paid £1,500 for some forty-two thousand acres that included County Waterford and most of County Cork, with the majority of the down payment coming from the dowry in Boyle's second marriage, to Catherine Fenton, daughter of his first patron in Ireland. Boyle's second marriage provided him not only with a dowry for a down payment on Ralegh's estate but also with future heirs—seven sons and eight daughters. With this legal purchase of Ralegh's Irish estate, Boyle consolidated his holdings into a small empire across southern Ireland that was valued at some £30,000 per year. For his assistance to Carew, Boyle was knighted on his wedding day in July, 1603.

After his marriage, Boyle placed all his energy into cultivating new patrons and political relationships as added insurance against future claims against his lands and titles. To further secure his claims, Boyle made contacts within the new Stuart Dynasty. In 1605, Boyle was given complete title and control of all his property by King James I.

Boyle used the labor of experienced English and other European settlers in Ireland to develop fisheries along rivers and the country's southern coast, to mine iron, and to create iron foundries. On his newly enclosed estates, cattle rearing; glassmaking; brewing; the production of cheese, cloth, wool, and leather; and his orchards and horse and deer farms enhanced his efforts to turn Munster into a highly profitable and industrious little England. In order to facilitate trade and to export the produce of his estates, Boyle developed the port town of Youghal in County Cork. Southern Ireland's increasing trade connections with English and other Atlantic port cities, such as Bristol and Bordeaux, France, and the area's growing role in supplying food for ships bound for the English colonies in America, all served to expand Boyle's fortune. Boyle succeeded in attracting some four thousand English settlers, many of them skilled tradesmen, to his expansive holdings. By 1641, nearly a third of the estimated twenty-two thousand English-born persons residing in Munster lived on Boyle's property. In addition, he developed several towns, including Bandon, Mallow, and his personal estate lands at Lismore in County Cork, to facilitate local markets and industry. During the 1630's, Boyle spent about £30,000 to purchase English estates in Dorsetshire.

Boyle also invested his time and wealth in political appointments in Ireland and England. He was elected to the Irish parliament and then to the Irish privy council in 1613. These appointments provided him with fruitful contacts among the new Anglo-Irish planter class and with members of the English aristocracy, notably the

ENGLISH PLANTATIONS IN IRELAND

The English plantations in Munster in the late sixteenth century and in Ulster in the early seventeenth century paralleled the settlement of Virginia and later the Massachusetts Bay Colony, as the British historically considered Ireland a template for other colonization ventures. The plantation system had evolved from several attempts by the English crown, beginning in the twelfth century, to control and pacify Ireland. In the sixteenth century, the granting of noble titles to Irish lords and official recognition of their lands, a policy known as surrender and regrant, produced neither peace nor security in Ireland.

During the Desmond Rebellions against English rule (1569-1573, 1579-1583), English authorities decided on a harsher course of action: the complete forfeit and confiscation of the estates of Irish landlords who participated in the rebellions. In the context of England's ongoing war with Spain, Ireland was viewed as a backdoor to England. Catholic Spain delivered funding and soldiers for Catholic Irish lords battling their English adversaries in 1579, 1595, and 1601. From this broader European perspective, English officials viewed the new Irish plantation policy as both politically sound and financially expedient. The immense bureaucracy that emerged to administer these plantations afforded individuals the chance to profit rapidly in land deals, investment schemes, or graft, and one of the most noted opportunists was Richard Boyle, the future first earl of Cork.

Queen Elizabeth I and her administration began granting lands in Munster to English settlers in 1585. These settlers, also known as undertakers, were often English military veterans in Ireland; poet Edmund Spenser and future American colonizer Sir Walter Ralegh both were rewarded with claims in Munster. The undertakers were limited to holding twelve thousand acres, and they paid no Crown rent for three years and no customs duties. The undertakers were to colonize their newly acquired lands with English-born settler-farmers who would double as a militia. By 1598, some four thousand English had settled in Munster, well short of the projected twelve thousand. The final goal of these plantations was a civilizing mission to assimilate the native Irish into English culture, society, and the Protestant religion.

The reality of the Munster and Ulster plantations was quite different from the theoretical policy. In both places, substantial numbers of Irish tenants remained on the undertakers' properties. However, the development of towns, roads, and ports and the exploitation of natural resources, such as timber, coal, iron ore, and fishing, completely changed the Irish landscape within a generation. The plantation system did succeed in producing immense profits for a small number of landholders, including Boyle, in introducing small-scale industry into Ireland, and in increasing trade contacts for Irish agricultural products with England, Europe, and the Americas. However, the final goal of the plantation system—anglicizing the Gaelic-speaking Catholic Irish population—met with very limited success and fed Irish resentment against English rule into the twentieth century.

first duke of Buckingham, a favorite at the royal court. Boyle's goal was twofold: He sought to secure his holdings in Munster through political friendships and to find suitable spouses for his eleven surviving children. Boyle earned a new patent on his Munster estate in 1614, and he then purchased two noble titles for himself—Lord Boyle in 1616 and earl of Cork in 1620—for the estimated cost of £4,500. He also procured the title viscount of Dungarvan for his heir. Boyle allocated portions of his growing fortune for public and private loans to the English government, and these loans to the cash-strapped Stuart regime halted further court action against his landholdings. By 1629, Boyle also held the posts of Lord Justice of Ireland and Lord Treasurer, and he was promoted to the English privy council in 1640.

In the last decade of his life, Boyle confronted the greatest challenges to his estates, first from Thomas Wentworth, Lord Deputy of Ireland, and then from the native Irish during the Irish Rebellion beginning in 1641. Boyle's heir Sir Lewis "the Valiant" Boyle was killed in military action in 1642. During his later years, Boyle composed a defensive and providential autobiography, *True Remembrances* (1623), on his rise to power in Ireland. On his death in 1643, Boyle's son Roger, Lord Broghill, assumed control of the estate.

LEGACY

The most visible part of Boyle's legacy was the economic development of Munster and the creation of a permanent area of English settlement in Ireland. Although much of this achievement rested on Boyle's exploitation of his political connections and the native Irish population, Munster was the most commercially and agriculturally developed region in Ireland through the eighteenth century. Much of Boyle's energy and funding went toward his children's education and their suitable aristocratic marriages. Boyle's heirs would influence English and Irish politics, as well as British arts and sciences. His daughters Catherine, Lady Ranelagh, and Mary, the countess of Warwick, were both noted intellectuals, as was their youngest brother, Robert Boyle, a scientist and founding member of the Royal Society during the Restoration period. Boyle's second son, Richard, the second earl of Cork, was made an English peer. Several of

Boyle's daughters married into aristocratic English families in Ireland, providing ancestral ties to Munster properties and Irish politics; the descendants of these marriages dominated the Irish parliament into the eighteenth century. Among the other beneficiaries of Boyle's career were his brother John Boyle and three male cousins, all of whom he assisted in gaining appointments in the established Church of Ireland in the 1620's.

Boyle was a patriarch who kept a tight hold over his properties, his children, and his growing network of inlaws. Although he has been rightly described as a "buccaneer," he was a caring father and husband. The funerary memorial to his second wife Catherine at St. Patrick's Cathedral in Dublin, and his letters to his children, indicate a compassionate man and contradict what his numerous detractors wrote about him during his lifetime.

—*Tyler T. Crogg*

FURTHER READING

Canny, Nicholas. *Making Ireland British, 1580-1650.* Oxford, England: Oxford University Press, 2001. An analysis of English colonial visions for Ireland focusing on Edmund Spenser.

_____. *The Upstart Earl: A Study of the Social and Mental World of Richard Boyle, First Earl of Cork, 1566-1643.* Cambridge, England: Cambridge University Press, 1982. An attempt to discover Boyle's mind-set and private life via personal letters.

Connolly, S. J. *Contested Island: Ireland, 1460-1630.* Oxford, England: Oxford University Press, 2008. Excellent general background for the sometimes haphazard English plantation process in Ireland.

MacCarthy-Morrogh, Michael. *The Munster Plantation: English Migration to Southern Ireland, 1583-1641.* Oxford, England: Clarendon Press, 1986. Very good analysis of the politics, economics, and demographics of English settlements in southern Ireland.

Townshed, Dorothea. *The Life and Letters of the Great Earl of Cork.* New York: Dutton, 1904. Edited collection of Boyle's letters and his book *True Remembrances.*

See also: Bess of Hardwick; Francis Drake; Sir Thomas Gresham; Sir Horatio Palavicino; Sir John Spencer.

FEDERICO CORNARO
Italian merchant, landowner, and aristocrat

Cultivating sugarcane in Cyprus and processing and selling sugar from his commercial base in Venice, Cornaro became rich as the world's first sugar magnate.

Born: c. 1335; Venice (now in Italy)
Died: 1382; Venice
Sources of wealth: Agricultural products; trade
Bequeathal of wealth: Spouse; children

EARLY LIFE
Federico Cornaro (feh-deh-REE-koh kohr-NAH-roh) was born to Nicolò Cornaro in early fourteenth century Venice. The Republic of Venice was emerging as the leading commercial port of the Italian city-states; it would soon boast the wealthiest and most dynamic economy of early Renaissance Europe. The Cornaro family was one of the patrician families of Venice, tracing its roots to the famous Cornelli family of classical Rome.

FIRST VENTURES
In the late Middle Ages, sugar had become one of the most desired commodities in Europe. Cornaro and his brothers Fantino and Marco entered the sugar trade, establishing commercial contracts with the kingdom of Cyprus, the leading producer of sugar in the Mediterranean. Venice had long had commercial contacts with Cyprus. Around 1360, Cornaro acquired a century-old palace in St. Luke's square on Venice's Grand Canal, in which he hosted the future Albert III, Duke of Austria, during Albert's visit to Venice in September, 1361.

In December, 1361, King Peter I of Cyprus came to Venice to seek aid against the advancing Turks. At the request of Pope Innocent VI, King Peter stayed in the Cornaro palace. In 1365, Cornaro provided the large sum of 60,000 gold ducats to King Peter. In exchange, Cornaro received the Piscopia peninsula on the island of Cyprus as a tax-free fiefdom. Cornaro was also knighted with the Cyprus Order of the Sword and allowed to install the Cypriot royal lion in the Cornaro coat of arms.

MATURE WEALTH
With a brother stationed in Cyprus and another in Venice, Cornaro was able to take full advantage of his sugar concession. Employing their Venetian wealth, the Cornaro brothers reorganized the sugar industry of Cyprus. They imported a skilled workforce, built new sugar mills, irri-

gated the sugarcane fields, and improved industrial techniques for processing the sugarcane with immense sixteen-hundred-pound copper kettle boilers. As a result, they were able to manufacture a superior and less expensive sugar product for the tables of Europe. In addition to his sugar monopoly, Cornaro was later granted monopolies in Cyprus's salt and cotton in partial repayment of his loan to King Peter, allowing him to dictate prices in all three commodities.

In 1379, the Venice tax assessments recorded Cornaro's wealth at 150,000 ducats. He was the wealthiest Venetian citizen, and given the commercial prosperity of Venice, he may well have been the wealthiest European merchant of the fourteenth century. Cornaro solidified his status by seeing that his son Pietro married into the Cypriot royal family. Cornaro also assumed several diplomatic posts in Venice. In 1381, he donated a portion of his fortune to support Venice in its wars against Genoa.

Cornaro died in 1382, leaving his vast estate to his wife Bianca and his sons Pietro and Giovanni. In his will, Cornaro requested that he be buried in the Basilica of Sancta Maria Gloriosa dei Frari. His son Giovanni complied with his wishes, building the Cornaro-Piscopa Chapel with a magnificent statuary monument to his father.

LEGACY
In the late medieval period, the great merchants of Europe were no longer the itinerant peddlers of earlier centuries but were ship owners and traders operating on routes that connected the great cities of Europe. Federico Cornaro was one of the most successful of these early entrepreneurs. With his brothers, he centralized the processing of sugar, producing the raw sugar on Cyprus, refining it in Venice, and selling it on European trading ships. Receiving a fiefdom on the Piscopia peninsula of Cyprus, Cornaro is considered the progenitor of the distinguished Piscopia branch of the Cornaro family. Among his famous descendants are Cardinal Patriarch Federico Cornaro (1579-1653), who served as the patriarch doge of Venice, and Elena Cornaro Piscopia (1646-1684), the first woman in history to be awarded a doctorate of philosophy degree. The Cornaro-Piscopia Palace, later named the Loredan Palace, was described by the renowned English architectural critic John Ruskin as one of the "loveliest" in Venice, with a "grace almost unri-

valed." This building has been incorporated into the Venetian government municipal center.

—*Howard Bromberg*

FURTHER READING
Cornaro, Luigi. *A Short History of the Cornaro Family.* Whitefish, Mont.: Kessinger, 2005.

Guernsey, Jane. *The Lady Cornaro: Pride and Prodigy of Venice.* New York: College Avenue Press, 1999.
Lane, Frederic. *Venice, a Maritime Republic.* Baltimore: Johns Hopkins University Press, 1973.

See also: Miguel de Aldama; Ridolfo de' Bardi; Manuel Calvo; Francesco Datini; Claus Spreckels.

BERNARD CORNFELD
American financier

Cornfeld established Investors Overseas Services (IOS), the largest mutual-fund sales organization outside the United States. However, his improper management of the company and battles with the Internal Revenue Service led to his imprisonment and the loss of much of his wealth.

Born: August 17, 1927; Istanbul, Turkey
Died: February 27, 1995; London, England
Also known as: Benno Cornfeld (birth name); Bernie Cornfeld
Sources of wealth: Financial services; investments
Bequeathal of wealth: Children

EARLY LIFE
Bernard Cornfeld was born in Turkey, and his parents immigrated to the United States when he was three years old. The family eventually settled in Brooklyn, New York, where Cornfeld attended public schools and graduated from Abraham Lincoln High School. After graduation, Cornfeld served two years in the U.S. Maritime Service. In 1947, he was successfully treated for stuttering, a problem he had had since childhood. He enrolled at Brooklyn College, where he majored in psychology and graduated in 1950.

FIRST VENTURES
Afer graduation, Cornfeld took odd jobs. He drove a taxicab for a while, and in 1954 he spent nine months in Philadelphia working as a youth counselor for B'nai B'rith. Cornfeld's next job was selling mutual funds for Investors Planning Corporation in Philadelphia. He recommended that the company expand overseas, but after company officials declined his advice, Cornfeld left the firm and sailed for France, where he explored opportunities to sell mutual funds abroad. As a result of this trip, Cornfeld created his own mutual-fund sales organization, Investors Overseas Services (IOS), in 1955. Three years later, he moved his company from Paris to Geneva,

Switzerland, and in 1960 he registered IOS in Panama. In 1965, Cornfeld purchased Investors Planning Corporation, for which he had once worked. Many of his business operations were beyond the surveillance of any country and outside the reach of many regulators.

MATURE WEALTH
Cornfeld's company, IOS, became the largest mutual-fund sales organization outside of the United States and channeled hundreds of millions of dollars into American mutual funds. IOS expanded to include an insurance company, real estate interests, and offshore investment funds.

However, the Securities and Exchange Commission (SEC) investigated IOS and accused Cornfeld of breaking American laws governing mutual funds. He and the commission settled out of court in 1967. Cornfeld agreed to cease his operations in the United States and to limit his investments in American mutual funds.

Before IOS's implosion in 1970, when its stock dropped from $18 to $2 per share, Cornfeld's personal wealth was about $100 million, and the company had an estimated value of $2.5 billion. The board of directors of IOS forced Cornfeld from the company. Robert Vesco, the new head of IOS, embezzled $224 million from the company and fled to the Caribbean. Vesco later served thirteen years in a Cuban prison for producing and marketing a "miracle" cancer drug without the government's knowledge.

In the early 1970's, a group of about three hundred IOS employees informed Swiss authorities that Cornfeld and company cofounders had pocketed part of the proceeds of a stock issue raised by employees in 1969. As a result, Swiss prosecutors in 1973 charged Cornfeld with fraud, and he was arrested while on a visit to Geneva. He served eleven months in a Swiss jail before being freed on a bail surety of $600,000. Cornfeld always maintained he was innocent of the charges, blaming the fraud

Bernard Cornfeld. (Hulton Archive/Getty Images)

on other IOS executives. His trial eventually took place in 1979 and lasted three weeks, with the judge finally acquitting him.

Cornfeld spent the rest of his life fighting the U.S.Internal Revenue Service (IRS) after the agency accused him of improprieties regarding his tax payments. In 1976, a California court convicted Cornfeld of employing an illegal device to make long-distance telephone calls without charges. Creditors seized his Beverly Hills estate. In 1990, *Forbes* magazine reported that Cornfeld still owed the IRS $15 million.

From his Swiss castle, Cornfeld began planning a comeback and continued speculating on various international business operations. In 1994, he suffered a stroke shortly before Christmas and did not recover. His friends helped pay his medical expenses after he died on February 27, 1995.

LEGACY

Cornfeld helped popularize mutual funds as an investment option. His mutual-funds sales company, Investors Overseas Services, was worth $2.5 billion before its 1970 collapse. He created the first mutual funds to offer check-writing privileges and the first offshore funds that invested in American mutual funds. His improper business practices, however, eventually eclipsed his accomplishments, destroying both his business and his reputation.

—Anita Price Davis

FURTHER READING

Cantor, Bert. *The Bernie Cornfeld Story.* New York: L. Stuart, 1970.

Colbert, David. *Eyewitness to Wall Street: Four Hundred Years of Dreamers, Schemers, Busts, and Booms.* New York: Broadway Books, 2001.

Henriques, Diana B. "Bernard Cornfeld, 67, Dies: Led Flamboyant Mutual Fund." *The New York Times*, March 2, 1995, p. 10

Raw, Charles, Bruce Page, and Godfrey Hodgson. *Do You Sincerely Want to Be Rich?* New York: Broadway Books, 2005.

See also: Carl Icahn; Charles E. Merrill; T. Boone Pickens; Charles R. Schwab; George Soros.

JAMES CRAGGS
British landowner and politician

Craggs amassed a fortune through his financial ability and connections with leading British politicians and generals. His career demonstrates the corruption of early eighteenth century British politics.

Born: baptized June 10, 1657; Wolsingham, Durham, England
Died: March 16, 1721; London, England
Also known as: James Craggs the Elder
Sources of wealth: Government; investments
Bequeathal of wealth: Children; government

EARLY LIFE
James Craggs was born in 1657, the son of Anthony Craggs and his wife Anne. Young Craggs attended a free grammar school in Bishop Auckland. When the family was forced to sell its property, Craggs was thrown back on his own resources. After he had become wealthy and powerful, Craggs's many enemies mocked his early poverty and charged that he had been a footman.

Arriving in London in 1680, Craggs served several noblemen. In 1684, he married Elizabeth Richards, the daughter of a corn merchant, who may have been a domestic servant to Sarah Churchill, who later became the duchess of Marlborough. Whether the connection was through Elizabeth or not, Craggs made his fortune through his ties with Sarah and her husband, John Churchill, who later became the first duke of Marlborough.

FIRST VENTURES
Craggs laid the foundation for his immense fortune when he was private secretary to John Churchill. Craggs speculated in contracts to supply clothing to the British army, then fighting the Wars of the League of Augsburg (1689-1697). He was briefly held in the Tower of London for failure to supply the Parliamentary commissioners of public accounts with information regarding alleged improprieties in his administration of the clothing contracts. He also took a large bribe from Sir Thomas Cooke, the head of the British East India Company. The company was then engaged in a desperate struggle to maintain its monopoly over English trade with India, and Craggs was influential enough to be a valuable asset to the firm. Craggs maintained his connection with the British East India Company into the eighteenth century, serving as a director and negotiating the merger of the old and new companies.

MATURE WEALTH
Like his patron Marlborough, Craggs benefited from the War of the Spanish Succession (1701-1714). He served as secretary to the master-general of the ordnance and the clerk of the deliveries of the ordnance. Craggs was also elected to the House of Commons, where, like his patron Marlborough, he eventually allied with the Whig Party ministers. In addition to looking after his own and Marlborough's interests, Craggs worked to advance the political and diplomatic career of his only surviving son, also named James Craggs (1686-1721). In 1709, Craggs had his portrait painted by Sir Godfrey Kneller, the favorite portraitist of the Whig elite.

When the Whigs were replaced by the Tories, Craggs continued to function as an intermediary between Marlborough and the new ministry. However, as relations between Marlborough and the Tory cabinet deteriorated, Craggs also became politically marginalized, losing his parliamentary seat in 1713. Craggs continued his political alliance with the Whigs, particularly Marlborough's son-in-law Charles Spencer, third earl of Sunderland. When Queen Anne died in 1714 and was succeeded by George I, the Whigs came back into power, and so did Craggs. Craggs received the lucrative position of joint postmaster-general in 1715.

Both Craggs and his son were deeply involved in the activities of the South Sea Company, a firm established to help manage Great Britain's national debt after the War of the Spanish Succession. Occupying a position between the business and governmental worlds, the elder Craggs was a leader in the scheme to convert government debt into South Sea stock and in efforts to bail out the company when its stock began to fall in late 1720. An inquiry revealed that he and Sunderland had received large bribes of stock, for which they had not paid. Adding to Craggs's troubles was the death of his son on February 16, 1721, which had a devastating impact on him. Craggs himself died a month later; his death was widely rumored to be a suicide. His estate was fined £68,920 as compensation for his role in the South Sea "bubble."

LEGACY
At his death, Craggs's estate was valued at £1.5 million. His heirs were his three daughters, Margaret, Elizabeth

and Anne, all married to members of Parliament. However, his and his son's complicity in the South Sea bubble left the family's name in disgrace.

—*William E. Burns*

FURTHER READING

Balen, Malcolm. *The King, the Crook, and the Gambler: The True Story of the South Sea Bubble and the Greatest Financial Scandal in History*. New York: Fourth Estate, 2004.

Field, Ophelia. *The Favourite: Sarah, Duchess of Marlborough*. London: Hodder & Stoughton, 2002.

Snyder, Henry L., ed. *The Marlborough-Godolphin Correspondence*. Oxford, England: Clarendon Press, 1975.

Tomlinson, H. C. *Guns and Government: The Ordnance Office Under the Later Stuarts*. London: Royal Historical Society, 1979.

See also: Sir John Banks; Stephen Fox; Thomas Guy; First Duke of Marlborough; William Pulteney.

MARCUS LICINIUS CRASSUS
Roman politician, landowner, and military leader

Crassus, one of the wealthiest men in ancient Rome, acquired a vast fortune to further his political career. In doing so, he became one of the most powerful and influential figures of the late Roman Republic, along with Julius Caesar, Pompey the Great, and Cicero.

Born: c. 115 B.C.E.; place unknown

Died: 53 B.C.E.; near Carrhae (now Harran, Turkey)

Sources of wealth: Real estate; slaveholding; conquest; investments

Bequeathal of wealth: Spouse; children

EARLY LIFE

Marcus Licinius Crassus (MAR-kuhs li-SIHN-ee-us KRAS-suh), though born into an illustrious Roman family (the Licinii clan), was raised in modest surroundings compared with his patrician contemporaries. His father, Publius Licinius Crassus, a celebrated politician and general in his own right, endeavored to instill the tenets of moderation and temperance in his offspring, most likely because of economic necessity, as well as principle. The young Crassus lived with his father, his mother (Vinuleia), and two married brothers in a single dwelling, quite small in comparison with the houses of other Roman nobility. As the son of a Roman senator, Crassus received an education typical for a young man of his background, one firmly grounded in the rhetorical arts, history, and philosophy. Tragedy struck the Licinii household in 87 B.C.E., when both Crassus's father and an older brother were killed as a result of General Gaius Marius's rise to power. The vicissitudes of a Roman civil war left Crassus both physically vulnerable and financially limited. Forced to flee Rome to the confines of Spain, Crassus, with only 300 talents to his name (a sum roughly equivalent to $4.2 million), joined the forces of Lucius Cornelius Sulla, the political rival of Marius.

FIRST VENTURES

The years spent fighting Marius under Sulla's tutelage from 83 to 81 B.C.E. proved revelatory to Crassus, who later remarked that one could not be considered truly wealthy unless one could support an army out of one's personal income. However, Crassus's political ambitions were advanced not by military success but through the acquisition of enormous wealth. After the forces of Marius had been routed, Sulla and Crassus marched on Rome and enjoyed the fruits of plunder, which sprouted from the property of their defeated rivals. Crassus took advantage of any opportunity to enrich himself. In Spain he had pillaged the city of Malaca, and later in Italy he appropriated for himself the spoils from the captured Umbrian city of Tuder.

It was not, however, the treasure from broken cities but the proceeds from real estate sales which became the foundation of Crassus's growing fortune. Crassus had accumulated large amounts of land, buying at low cost the confiscated property owned by Sulla's political foes and selling it at a premium. This kind of questionable profiteering was a practice common to Sulla himself and his followers, but Crassus's avarice was further demonstrated by his blatant manipulation of the proscription lists, which contained the names of those whose property was to be confiscated. Crassus's association with Sulla ended only when he added a man's name to the proscription lists—without Sulla's authorization—for the sole purpose of obtaining the man's property.

MATURE WEALTH

Crassus used his rapidly increasing fortune to fund his political career, and in the year 70 B.C.E. he was rewarded for his efforts with his first consulship. Much of his wealth came from the sale of valuable real estate in the city of Rome itself. It would be a mistake to say that Crassus was a land developer per se, for he tended to avoid building on the property he purchased. He often said that people who liked to build houses needed no enemies, since they would far too easily ruin themselves. During the years of the late Roman Republic, newly enrolled senators needed houses in Rome rather than estates in the country to maintain their recently acquired status and to have a place to live while the senate was in session. In pursuit of suitable land for the homes of his senatorial clientele, Crassus was utterly relentless. For example, during the year 73 B.C.E. he spent so much time hovering around a Vestal virgin named Licinia in order to pressure her to sell him her lucrative suburban villa that he was accused of impropriety. In the end, Crassus was cleared of any wrongdoing and acquired Licinia's estate. Property in poorer sections of Rome did not escape Crassus's roving eye. He often bought for next to nothing houses damaged or destroyed by fires. Some hostile accounts suggest that the fires' origins may be traced to Crassus himself, as he or his agents often materialized to make an offer just as the fires started. Dealing in real estate was extremely profitable, demonstrated by the fact that Crassus sold a house in Rome to his sometime rival Cicero for the tidy sum of 3.5 million sesterces, or $17.5 million in twenty-first century American currency.

When Crassus became consul in 70 B.C.E., he could afford public displays of his wealth. Although records are not clear as to the total amount of Crassus's fortune at the time, he was able to dedicate 10 percent of this wealth to the Temple of Hercules, to host a public banquet with ten thousand tables, and to provide enough grain to feed every citizen in Rome for three months. Considering that population estimates for Rome number a little less than one million inhabitants for this time period, Crassus's expenditure was considerable.

SLAVERY AND WEALTH IN ANCIENT ROME

Slavery existed in Roman society from its beginnings. References to the institution can be found in the earliest inscription, dated to the eighth century B.C.E. However, Rome became more dependent on slave-based labor beginning in the second century B.C.E. as a result of its wars of expansion against the Greeks, Carthaginians, and Macedonians. Large numbers of slaves from captured cities, as well as prisoners from defeated armies, flowed into Rome and other parts of Italy. Studies estimate the slave population in Italy by the end of the first century at around two million.

Roman elites used slaves in many occupations. Slaves toiled as unskilled laborers on the large plantations (*latifundiae*) of Sicily or in Spanish silver mines. Skilled slaves worked as household servants, administrators, and entertainers. Educated Greek slaves were used as tutors. During the first century, wealthy Roman aristocrats used slaves primarily as labor on their country estates, but they also flaunted their status by owning retinues of slaves to attend to their needs in the city. The prices of slaves depended on their skill and education. For example, Cato the Censor, a Roman aristocrat noted for his parsimony, never paid more than 1,500 drachmas for an agricultural slave (roughly $60), while a highly educated Greek grammarian could fetch up to 700,00 sesterces ($3.5 million).

The large number of slaves in Roman society created the potential for large-scale rebellions. Rome experienced a number of slave wars, including two in Sicily (135-132 B.C.E. and 104-100 B.C.E.), as well as the famous slave war of Spartacus (73-71 B.C.E.), put down by Marcus Licinius Crassus, a leading Roman politician.

An important difference between ancient Roman slavery and New World slavery in the modern period is that servitude in Rome was not race-based. In addition, Roman slaves could purchase their own freedom, as well as be freed by their masters. It was customary for manumission clauses to be included in wills. Nevertheless, slaves enjoyed little legal protection and were completely subject to the whims of their owners.

In addition to assets derived from the sale of land, Crassus possessed a diverse portfolio, which included numerous silver mines, alleged holdings in tax collection companies, and, of course, many slaves. Crassus stated that it was a master's responsibility to care for this valuable "human capital" which was vital for the running of estates. Ancient sources maintain that Crassus owned a small army of highly skilled slaves whose training and education their master personally supervised. Crassus used slaves with masonry, woodworking, and architectural skills in his real estate ventures. Slaves who were trained as administrators, clerks, and readers were also employed by Crassus or hired out for their services.

Crassus's financial investments were all calculated primarily with an eye to his political advancement. These investments enabled him to extend his political aspirations far beyond the consulship, as shown by his election to the position of censor in 65 B.C.E. He won a second consulship in 55 B.C.E. Throughout his career, Crassus used his wealth to establish political networks and build alliances that made him one of the Roman Republic's leading political figures. He commonly granted interest-free loans to friends and associates in exchange for favors, engendering obligations that could be used to advance his own ambitions. In 62 B.C.E., for instance, Crassus stood as guarantor of Julius Caesar's debts to the sum of 820 talents (roughly $11.5 million), allowing Caesar to further his political career as praetor of Spain. In doing so, Crassus paved the way for an alliance (the first so-called triumvirate) with Caesar, in which he, Caesar, and Pompey would monopolize political power in Rome from 60 to 53 B.C.E.

In the end, Crassus's ambition proved to be his undoing. Attempting to follow in the footsteps of Alexander the Great, Crassus led and funded a military expedition against the Parthians, Rome's eastern enemy. He and one of his sons died in battle in 53 B.C.E. near the city of Carrahe. Neither his personal estate, which at the time of his death was worth 7,100 talents ($99.5 million), nor the 10,000 talents ($140 million) he had earlier taken from the Temple of Jerusalem could save him from a Parthian's blade.

LEGACY

The ancient sources have not been kind to Crassus. His wealth has become proverbial, and the man himself is portrayed as an example of unbridled avarice. A particularly resonant example is that of the Parthians pouring molten gold down the throat of the decapitated head of Crassus to mock his greed. Yet upon reflection, Crassus's career differed little from those of his contemporaries, such as Julius Caesar or Pompey, who both plundered their way to the top of Roman politics. Even Crassus's wealth, although considerable, was less than that of Pompey or Sulla. What made Crassus different from men such as Pompey, Sulla, or Caesar was the fact that money, and not military command, was the key to his acquisition of political power.

Despite the unsavory origins of his wealth, Crassus conscientiously employed his financial resources as a servant of the Roman people. Moreover, Crassus did not engage in conspicuous consumption or lavish entertainments. True to his upbringing, he always lived modestly, and his dinners were distinguished by the quality of his guests rather than of his table. Crassus maintained that success in life lay not only in the careful management of money but also in the equally astute management of people.

—*Byron J. Nakamura*

FURTHER READING

Cicero. *Selected Letters*. Translated by P. G. Walsh. Oxford, England: Oxford University Press, 2008. Cicero, a contemporary and sometime political opponent of Crassus, provides incidental but insightful details on Crassus and the political machinations of the last days of the Roman Republic.

Gruen, Erich. *The Last Generation of the Roman Republic*. Berkeley: University of California Press, 1995. A masterful account of the politics during the last days of the Roman Republic. With fulsome notes and bibliography, this is the foundational work on the subject.

Marshall, B. A. *Crassus: A Political Biography*. Amsterdam: A.M. Hakkert, 1976. A thorough treatment of Crassus, which deemphasizes the presumed animosity between Crassus and Pompey.

Plutarch. *Fall of the Roman Republic: Six Lives*. Translated by Rex Warner. Reprint. Harmondsworth, England: Penguin, 1981. An important primary source on Crassus's life written during the second century C.E.

Sampson, Gareth. *The Defeat of Rome in the East: Crassus, the Parthians, and the Disastrous Battle of Carrhae, 53 B.C.* Barnsley, England: Pen & Sword Military, 2008. A vivid account focusing on Crassus's campaign against the Parthians.

Ward, Alan. *Marcus Crassus and the Late Roman Republic*. Columbia: University of Missouri Press, 1977. A well-researched biography of Crassus, which attempts to rehabilitate his position in his alliance with Pompey and Julius Caesar.

See also: Claudius Aesopus; Gaius Maecenas; Roscius.

RICHARD CRAWSHAY
British ironmaster and industrialist

For three decades in the eighteenth and nineteenth centuries, Crawshay ran one of the world's largest ironworks, turning out cannons vital to the British war effort and metallic products instrumental to the cultural changes in the Industrial Revolution. The business earned enormous sums for Crawshay and his descendants until the early twentieth century.

Born: 1739; Normanton, Wakefield, England
Died: June 27, 1810; Cardiff, Wales
Sources of wealth: Manufacturing; sale of products
Bequeathal of wealth: Children; relatives

EARLY LIFE
Born near Leeds, England, Richard Crawshay (CRAW-shay) was the son of a Yorkshire farmer. At the age of sixteen, Crawshay left home for London, where he apprenticed at Bicklewith's, a bar iron warehouse, selling flatirons. Upon Bicklewith's retirement in 1763, Crawshay took over the profitable enterprise as sole proprietor. That same year, he married Mary Bourne and would eventually father four children: William, Anne, Elizabeth, and Charlotte. Within a decade, his company was specializing in products that provided a low-cost alternative to expensive Swedish and Russian iron. Now a leading purveyor of iron, Crawshay had grown wealthy, and he began looking for new enterprises in which to invest.

FIRST VENTURES
Beginning in the early 1770's, Crawshay continued to expand his iron company. In 1775, he went into business with British-born former tobacco merchant Anthony Bacon, who had founded the Cyfarthfa Ironworks at Merthyr Tydfil, Wales. Employing a process that transformed inferior pig iron into strong bar iron, Bacon won government contracts to produce ordnance—primarily cannons and cannonballs—for the British military. The highly lucrative cannon-making venture continued until 1782, when Bacon became a member of Parliament and was prohibited by law from securing government contracts. Upon Bacon's death in 1786, Crawshay, assisted by his son William, took over management of the Cyfarthfa Ironworks, in partnership with London merchant William Stevens and former Cyfarthfa forge manager James Cockshutt.

MATURE WEALTH
At Cyfarthfa, Crawshay enhanced and improved the ironworks. He installed a reverberatory furnace necessary for the newly invented process of puddling, which removed impurities from pig iron. He added a rolling mill to shape the molten metal into girders for buildings and bridges, rails for fledgling railways, and weapons of war. Such improvements fueled the Industrial Revolution of the late eighteenth and early nineteenth centuries, made Cyfarthfa Ironworks into one of Great Britain's largest industries, and allowed Crawshay to become one of the nation's wealthiest men.

Crawshay continued to build his business over the next two decades by adding furnaces and rolling mills. To facilitate the transport of his company's iron products, he strongly supported the Glamorgan Canal, which opened in 1794 and sped the delivery of iron to Cardiff, the capital and chief port of Wales. Throughout his lifetime, Crawshay continuously expanded Cyfarthfa, and by 1810 the facility boasted six blast furnaces, employed more than one thousand workers, and produced in excess of twenty thousand tons of iron, becoming one of the world's largest producers.

At his death in 1810, Crawshay left an estate valued at £1.5 million (more than £100 million in 2010). Three-eighths of his estate was willed to his son William; the remainder was bequeathed to a son-in-law, Benjamin Hall, and to a nephew, Joseph Bailey, both of whom had long been involved in iron production at Cyfarthfa.

LEGACY
Although Richard Crawshay had hoped his son William would follow him into the iron-making business, William confined himself to acting as agent for the ironworks' products from a London office. William's fortune of some £50 million was left to his five children. His son William II managed Cyfarthfa after his grandfather Richard's death, greatly expanding the business, and he built Cyfarthfa Castle at a cost of more than £2 million. At his death, he divided his vast holdings among his three sons, with the youngest, Robert, acquiring Cyfarthfa Ironworks and Cyfarthfa Castle.

Robert Crawshay converted Cyfarthfa to steel production. Following his death in 1879, Robert's sons continued the business until the company was sold in 1902. The former Cyfarthfa Ironworks produced materials during World War I and ceased operations in 1919. By the twenty-first century, Cyfarthfa Castle was a school. The building is one of few reminders of the enormous wealth once generated from the long-closed ironworks in the economically depressed community of Merthyr Tydfil, once one of Wales's largest towns.

—*Jack Ewing*

FURTHER READING

Crawshay, Richard. *Letterbook of Richard Crawshay, 1788-1797.* Cwmbran, Wales: South Wales Record Society, 1993.

Ince, Laurence. *The South Wales Iron Industry, 1750-1885.* Cardiff, Wales: Merton Priory Press, 1993.

Wallace, Anthony F. C. *The Social Context of Innovation: Bureaucrats, Families, and Heroes in the Early Industrial Revolution, as Foreseen in Bacon's "New Atlantis."* Lincoln: University of Nebraska Press, 2003.

See also: Sir Richard Arkwright; Peter Cooper; Henry Phipps; Joséphine de Wendel.

ENRIQUE CREEL
Mexican landowner, businessman, and politician

Creel combined outstanding business acumen, a fortuitous union of powerful and wealthy families, and excellent timing to build a political and financial empire in Chihuahua, Mexico, that flourished during the long tenure of Mexican president and virtual dictator Porfirio Díaz.

Born: August 30, 1854; Chihuahua, Chihuahua, Mexico

Died: August 18, 1931; Mexico City, Mexico

Also known as: Enrique Clay Creel Cuilty; Henry Clay Creel (birth name)

Sources of wealth: Trade; mining; manufacturing; railroads; real estate

Bequeathal of wealth: Children; relatives; government

EARLY LIFE

Enrique Clay Creel Cuilty, better known as Enrique Creel (ehn-REE-kay kreel), was the eldest of seven children born to American Reuben Waggener Creel, who served as an interpreter in the Mexican War (1846-1848). Reuben had stayed in Mexico following the war, become a successful merchant, grown wealthy after marrying into the prominent Irish-Mexican family of his wife, Paz Cuilty, and served as an American consul in Chihuahua in the early 1860's. Enrique grew up in luxurious circumstances, was privately tutored, and took several educational jaunts abroad before joining his father's business at age fourteen.

FIRST VENTURES

While in his teens, Creel became head of the family upon his father's death in 1873. Like his father, he married well. Creel wed Angela Terrazas, the daughter of Don Luis Terrazas, an influential politician, landowner, and

rancher. Intelligent and ambitious, Creel emulated his father-in-law. Together, Creel and Terrazas created an oligarchy that ruled Chihuahua, Mexico's largest—and during this era, most strategic—state, bordering New Mexico and Texas. The two men collectively controlled almost nine million acres of land (Creel owned almost two million acres of the total), on which they operated haciendas and ranches that supported hundreds of thousands of cattle, sheep, and horses.

In 1878, after Porfirio Díaz became the president of Mexico, Creel followed Terrazas's example by entering local politics. Creel used his wealth to build a fortune, founding banks and telephone companies and erecting textile mills and granaries. In 1887, he established and served as president of Chihuahua's first Chamber of Commerce, which facilitated trade with foreigners who flocked to Mexico to take advantage of investment opportunities.

MATURE WEALTH

Creel continued to expand his holdings. He became an executive in a national dynamite and explosives concern, engaged in mining, and built thousands of miles of railroad track to transport raw materials to and from the United States, boosting the Mexican economy in the process. By the turn of the century, he held many important corporate positions, including president of the Monetary Commission, the Central American Railway, the Bankers Association, the Casino of Chihuahua, the state telephone company, and the Mining Bank. In 1904, Creel followed his father-in-law into office as governor of Chihuahua, serving until 1906 and again from 1907 to 1910. Between 1910 and 1911, he was President Díaz's secretary of foreign relations and acted as interpreter when

Díaz and U.S. President William Howard Taft met in Mexico.

When Pancho Villa led the Mexican Revolution that overthrew Díaz, Creel went into exile in the United States in 1913. Much of his land and many of his holdings—particularly his banks and mines—were confiscated. After Álvaro Obregón was elected Mexican president in 1920, Creel returned to Chihuahua and rebuilt his empire. In addition to serving as business adviser to Obregón, Creel recovered his banking and railroad concerns and recouped more than one million acres of land. By the time of his death at age seventy-six in 1931, Creel was able to leave a sizable estate for his children, Alberto, Juan, and Adela.

LEGACY

Although his heirs lost a considerable amount of land during the agrarian reforms of the 1930's, the Creel family, through its descendants, continued to wield influence in Mexico. The tradition of marrying into power, used to advantage by the Creel and Terrazas families, was maintained before and after Creel's death. Creel's daughter, Adela, married former Chihuahua governor Joaquín

Cortazar. Other prominent figures related to Creel by marriage have included Chihuahua Governor Silvestre Terrazas, industrialist and politician Alberto Terrazas Cuilty, businessman Juan Terrazas Cuilty, the minister of the interior and politician Santiago Creel Miranda, and Intermex Industrial Parks executive Jaime Creel Sisniega. Some physical assets of Creel's empire remained into the twenty-first century, including the Chihuahua-Pacific Railroad and the town of Creel, a tourist destination at Copper Canyon in the Sierra Madre Mountains.

—Jack Ewing

FURTHER READING

McLynn, Frank. *Villa and Zapata: A History of the Mexican Revolution*. New York: Basic Books, 2002.

Maurer, Noel. *The Power and the Money: The Mexican Financial System, 1876-1932*. Palo Alto, Calif.: Stanford University Press, 2002.

Wasserman, Mark. *Persistent Oligarchs: Elites and Politics in Chihuahua, Mexico, 1910-1940*. Durham, N.C.: Duke University Press, 1993.

See also: Raúl Baillères; Carlos Slim.

CHARLES CROCKER
American railroad magnate, financier, and real estate developer

Crocker's wealth was derived primarily from his investment in Central Pacific Railroad's construction of a portion of the first transcontinental railroad, which was completed in 1869. In later years, he became a major financier and real estate developer in California.

Born: September 16, 1822; Troy, New York
Died: August 14, 1888; Monterey, California
Sources of wealth: Railroads; real estate
Bequeathal of wealth: Spouse; children

EARLY LIFE

Charles Crocker was born to a middle-class farm family in upstate New York. When he was fourteen, his family moved to a farm in Marshall County, Indiana. Crocker had little formal education because he dropped out of school to help support his family. He worked as a farm laborer, in a sawmill, and in an iron forge. He later said that his experiences in supervising work crews in these early jobs were a key to his success in the construction of the Central Pacific Railroad.

Charles Crocker. (Archive Photos/Getty Images)

Construction workers for the Central Pacific Railroad stand on flatcars near Promontory Point in 1868, a year before the transcontinental railroad was completed. The opening of this railroad generated millions of dollars for the "big four" owners of the Central Pacific—Charles Crocker, Mark Hopkins, Collis P. Huntington, and Leland Stanford. (Library of Congress)

FIRST VENTURES

In 1845, Crocker established his own iron forge, but he sold this firm in 1849 and went to California to mine for gold. After two years of mining with little success, Crocker went into business selling supplies to miners. By 1854, he had become one of the wealthiest men in Sacramento, where he became acquainted with the other men who would form the leadership of the Central Pacific Railroad—Leland Stanford, Collis P. Huntington, and Mark Hopkins. In 1861, these men, who came to be known as the Big Four, invested $24,000 to establish the Central Pacific Railroad. The following year, Congress passed the Pacific Railroad Act, which chartered the new Union Pacific Railroad to build the eastern end of a new transcontinental railroad. The Central Pacific was given the contract to build the western end of this line.

MATURE WEALTH

It was railroading that made Crocker truly wealthy, and he later invested that wealth in a variety of other business ventures. The directors of the Central Pacific Railroad contracted with a separate firm that Crocker had formed to do the actual construction of the rail line. What many people did not know at the time was that many of the directors of the railroad were also investors in this construction company, so they were essentially paying themselves for building their own railroad.

After the transcontinental railroad was completed in 1869, Crocker remained affiliated with the Central Pacific but also began investing in other ventures, especially in California real estate. He was a prominent backer of some of the large-scale irrigation projects that turned the San Joaquin Valley into a major agricultural center. In 1871, Crocker became president of the Southern Pacific Railroad, and in 1884 he oversaw the merger of the Central Pacific Railroad and the Southern Pacific, creating one of the largest western rail lines. Crocker also became a major regional financier.

Crocker built a magnificent mansion in the Nob Hill section of San Francisco and had a second home in New York City. He was badly injured in a carriage accident in New York City in 1886, and he never fully recovered. He died in 1888 at a new resort hotel that the Southern Pacific Railroad had built at his urging in Monterey, California.

LEGACY

Crocker's legacy was a mixed one. He left a tremendous fortune to his family, estimated at $20 to $40 million, and his wealth contributed to the rapid development of the economy of California in the late 1800's. However, there were many charges of fraud concerning how he acquired this wealth, and the Southern Pacific Railroad, which its opponents dubbed the Octopus, was accused of monopolistic practices. Unlike many industrialists who made philanthropic gifts out of a sense of either gratitude or duty, or at least to forestall public criticism of their great wealth, Crocker gave virtually nothing to charity either during his life or in bequests after his death. His career contributed significantly to the creation of the "robber baron" image of American businessmen.

—*Mark S. Joy*

FURTHER READING

Ambrose, Stephen E. *Nothing Like It in the World: The Men Who Built the Transcontinental Railroad, 1863-1869.* New York: Simon & Schuster, 2000.

Josephson, Matthew. *The Robber Barons: The Great American Capitalists, 1861-1901.* New York: Harcourt Brace Jovanovich, 1934. Reprint. San Diego: Harcourt Brace Jovanovich, 1961.

Lewis, Oscar. *The Big Four: The Story of Huntington, Stanford, Hopkins, and Crocker.* New York: Alfred A. Knopf, 1938.

See also: John Insley Blair; Jim Brady; William Andrews Clark; Jay Cooke; Daniel Drew; Henry M. Flagler; John W. Garrett; Jay Gould; Edward H. Harriman; James J. Hill; Mark Hopkins; Collis P. Huntington; Daniel Willis James; George Mortimer Pullman; Russell Sage; Leland Stanford; William Thaw; Cornelius Vanderbilt; William Henry Vanderbilt.

CROESUS
Lydian king and conqueror

Croesus inherited the empire of Lydia from his father Alyattes and expanded it to include the entire area between the Aegean Sea and the Halys River, thus acquiring legendary wealth. He used his fortune to aggrandize his status and to adorn Sardis, his capital. A military defeat to Cyrus the Great of Persia cost him his kingdom, his wealth, and his freedom.

Born: c. 595 B.C.E.; Lydia, Asia Minor (now in Turkey)

Died: c. 546 B.C.E.; Sardis, Asia Minor (now in Turkey)

Also known as: Croisos; Kroisos

Sources of wealth: Inheritance; conquest

Bequeathal of wealth: Dissipated

EARLY LIFE

Croesus (KREE-suhs) was born in the twenty-third year of the reign of his father Alyattes, who had conquered and destroyed Smyrna and continued a war begun by his father Sadyattes against the Greek port city of Miletus. During the war, Alyattes caused the Temple of Athena to burn down. When Alyattes became ill and did not recover, he inquired of the Delphic Oracle, which declared that he would not recover until the temple was rebuilt. In response, Alyattes was more generous than required, for he built two temples to Athena and was rewarded not only with the restoration of his health but also with the longest reign of any member of his dynasty, fifty-eight years. No doubt Croesus learned from his father's experience to respect the oracle and to live in accordance with its dictates.

FIRST VENTURES

Although Alyattes preferred Croesus, his son by his Carian wife, to his other son Pantaleon, his son by a Greek wife, there was a faction that supported Pantaleon. When Alyattes allowed Croesus to succeed him as king, Croesus killed Pantaleon by drawing him across a carding comb, destroying his half brother with more cruelty than necessary to secure his position against conspiracy.

Croesus assumed power as king of Lydia at the age of thirty-five and immediately attacked Ephesus, a Greek city on the Aegean coast. After attacking Ephesus, Croesus made war on every Ionian and Aeolian state, alleging, as the ancient historian Herodotus explains, "some motives of responsibility upon some, others upon others, greater charges upon those when he could find them, trifling ones upon others." After subduing all the

Greeks of Asia, Croesus imposed tribute on them, and this tribute elevated him to the status of the superrich. The other source of his massive fortune was the natural wealth of Lydia, where the river Pactolus was filled with golden sands and lush, fertile valleys were conducive to agriculture.

Croesus at first planned to continue his acquisition of wealth by conquering the Greeks who lived on the islands of the Aegean, but he was persuaded of the impracticality of Lydia becoming a naval power. Instead, he conquered virtually all the peoples who lived west of the Halys River and annexed them to Lydia. At this point, Croesus and Lydia were at the height of their wealth.

MATURE WEALTH

One indication of Croesus's great wealth was the change he instituted in Lydian coinage, the world's oldest, traditionally attributed to earlier members of the Mermnadae, Croesus's dynasty. Before Croesus, Lydian coins were made of electrum, a mixture of gold and silver found in nature in the ratio of one part silver to four parts gold. Croesus, perhaps to flaunt the wealth of his land, minted coins of pure gold. There were two kinds of Lydian coins, known as Croeseids, one weighing a little less than four-tenths of an ounce meant for trade inside Asia, and another weighing about one-half of an ounce for trade with the Ionian Greeks.

It was probably during this time that some artifacts, like those of the Karun Treasure, were purchased or commissioned by Croesus. That he was a patron of the arts is attested to by Herodotus, who reports of a silver bowl made by the noted craftsman Rhoikos, a colossal cauldron that could hold 2,700 gallons made by the Spartans, and columns for the Temple of Artemis in Ephesus, later known as the Croesus Temple in homage to its benefactor.

The most famous account of Croesus's wealth comes in the story of the visit by the Athenian statesman Solon to Croesus's kingdom. Solon is received cordially, and on the third or fourth day of his visit, Croesus instructs

---

THE KARUN TREASURE

The Karun Treasure, also known as the Lydian Hoard and the Croesus Treasure, consists of about 450 artifacts discovered in the small village of Gure, about fifteen miles from Uşak in western Turkey, where the items are displayed at the Uşak Archaeological Museum. The objects were found by farmers in the mid-1960's in three tumuli, or ancient burial mounds. Many of the objects were sold to the Metropolitan Museum of Art in New York City in violation of both Turkey's laws on antiquities and UNESCO's (United Nations Educational, Scientific, and Cultural Organization) Convention on the Means of Prohibiting and Preventing the Illicit Import, Export, and Transfer of Ownership of Cultural Property. When the Metropolitan Museum put these items on display, the artifacts came to the attention of Turkish officials, who pursued all legal avenues to have them returned to Turkey. In 1993, the museum returned the items.

Among the most notable objects are a gold brooch in the shape of a horse with wings and a sea monster's tail (called a hippocampus), from which dangle three tassels, each ending in an ornate pomegranate; a silver water jug with a handle in the form of a human figure that arches backward; acorn-shaped pendants on a gold necklace; bracelets with intricately carved lion heads; and ornate silver bowls. Many of the objects are like no others in the world.

No doubt the names "Karun Treasure" and "Croesus Treasure" are used because of the renowned fame of King Croesus, for "Karun" is the name of a rich Persian who has been called the Persian Croesus. Similar names also appear in the Bible in the figure of Korah in Exodus and in the Qur'ān in the figure of Kuran. Both are individuals who, like Croesus, were exceedingly wealthy, exhibited incredible arrogance, and ended badly. For presumptuously leading a rebellion against Moses, Korah is punished by being swallowed up by the earth (Exodus 16.33), and Kuran, for his arrogant devotion to things of this world, is also swallowed up by the earth. In Turkey, there were rumors of divinely sent miseries afflicting the peasants who had sold the Karun treasures to smugglers.

It is extremely unlikely that the objects of the Karun Treasure were actually in Croesus's treasure-houses, for the tumulus mounds in which they were buried date from the seventh century B.C.E., while Croesus lived a century later. Still, as artistic styles were slow to change, the artifacts are probably very much like those that Solon would have seen when he toured the treasure-houses of Sardis.

---

his servants to give Solon a tour of the treasuries (note the plural), where Solon sees the great objects and evidence of Croesus's prosperity. After Solon has seen the treasures, there ensues one of the most celebrated conversations of antiquity. Croesus asks Solon,

> Guest-friend from Athens, much talk of your wisdom has come to us, and of your wandering for the purpose of seeking wisdom and of seeing the world. Now the desire has come to ask whether someone, of all you have seen, is the most prosperous.

Herodotus attributes to Croesus the wish to hear that he is the most prosperous of all people. Solon, however, replies that Tellus of Athens, a man of moderate means, is the most prosperous. Solon then declares that not Croesus but two Argive athletes, Cleobis and Bito, are the second most prosperous. The conversation ends with Solon's discourse on the nature of true happiness, which does not depend on wealth and on the precarious nature of worldly prosperity.

Herodotus attributes the eventual fall of Croesus in part to the king's delusion about his own happiness, although this particular misconception is a symbol of Croesus's more general delusion about being able to control events. Croesus believed that because of his wealth he was in control of his destiny. One way for ancients to be in control was to know the future, and they could learn the future by making direct inquiries to the oracle at Delphi. As king of Lydia, Croesus feared the growing power of Persia, which was becoming dominant under its dynamic king Cyrus the Great. Croesus sent to Delphi to ask what would happen if he attacked Persia. The oracle replied with its famous ambiguity, "You will destroy a great empire." Confident that he would destroy Persia, Croesus invaded this country, but he was defeated by the more resourceful Cyrus. The kingdom of Croesus was absorbed by Persia, and Croesus was to be executed by being burned alive. While on the pyre and as the flames were beginning to spread, Croesus remembered Solon's warning about the precarious nature of Fortune, and, the story goes, as if to show that Fortune can turn in positive as well as negative directions, the god Apollo sent a rainstorm that doused the fire, proving to Cyrus that Croesus was beloved of the gods.

Croesus spent the rest of his life as a slave in the Persian court, advising Cyrus and his psychopathic son Cambyses. As adviser, Croesus showed that he had learned wisdom from his suffering, though this knowledge was not always appreciated by the madman Cambyses. Croesus is said by the poet Bacchylides to have been transported to the mythical Hyperboreans by Apollo. The less romantic Herodotus reports Croesus's service as adviser to the Persian monarchs, but he lets Croesus simply disappear, without any mention of his death. In this way, Herodotus is perhaps contrasting Croesus with Tellus of Athens, a man of moderate wealth who died a glorious death fighting for Athens and was rewarded with a state funeral at public expense.

LEGACY

Few persons have been so spectacularly conspicuous for a quality that their names exemplify that characteristic. Just as calling someone an "Einstein" signifies that the individual is extraordinarily intelligent, or calling someone a "Hitler" or a "Stalin" means that the individual is ruthlessly evil, so calling someone a "Croesus" suggests that the person either has great wealth ("to be as rich as Croesus") or has suffered a complete reversal of fortune. Starting as the ruler of a prosperous empire, Croesus became overconfident, and in his overconfidence he overreached, both in his kingship and in his family, and lost everything, living out his days in increasing obscurity until dying a death that passed without note. Like Priam, king of wealthy Troy, Croesus became a symbol of Fortune's power to destroy.

—*James A. Arieti*

FURTHER READING

Asheri, David, Alan Lloyd, and Aldo Corcella. *A Commentary on Herodotus Books I-IV*. Oxford, England: Oxford University Press, 2007. A thorough commentary on the writings of Herodotus, who chronicled Croesus's life. Takes into account the relevant scholarship from antiquity on.

Herodotus. *The Landmark Herodotus: The Histories*. Edited by Robert B. Strassler, translated by Andrea L. Purvis. New York: Pantheon Books, 2007. The main source of information about Croesus, who serves as the embodiment of Herodotus's principle that human happiness does not last long. For Herodotus, Croesus's life is the measure by which he judges the lives of all other historical figures.

Ramage, Andrew, and Paul Craddock. *King Croesus' Gold: Excavations at Sardis and the History of Gold Refining*. Cambridge, Mass.: Archaeological Exploration of Sardis, Harvard University Art Museums, in association with the British Museum Press, 2000. Describes how a team of archaeologists from Harvard and Cornell Universities unearthed a refinery in Sardis where gold and silver were purified during Croesus's reign.

Waxman, Sharon. *Loot: The Battle over the Stolen Treasures of the Ancient World*. Henry Holt, 2008. An absorbing journalistic account of the history and controversy involving the Karun Treasure and Turkey's struggle to have it restored.

See also: Hipponicus II; Marduk-nāsir-apli; Midas.

MARK CUBAN
American entrepreneur, investor, and basketball team owner

Unlike sports team owners who remain quietly on the sidelines (or in plush skyboxes), Mark Cuban is publicly and vocally identified with the Dallas Mavericks basketball franchise. During the games, Cuban sits courtside, often yells at officials or players on the opposing team, and in the eyes of fans and commentators is clearly connected with the Mavericks.

Born: July 31, 1958; Pittsburgh, Pennsylvania
Sources of wealth: Computer industry; media; sports franchise; investments; entertainment industry
Bequeathal of wealth: Charity

EARLY LIFE
Mark Cuban was born into a relatively poor family. He started his first job when he was young and worked his way through college by performing a series of odd jobs. He attended the University of Pittsburgh for a year and then transferred to Indiana University, graduating in 1981. After college he moved to Dallas, Texas, where he first took a job as a bartender. He then worked for a short time as a salesman for a computer software company. He was fired from this job, which led him to found his own company, MicroSolutions.

FIRST VENTURES
At MicroSolutions, Cuban provided software and other computer services to companies. He admittedly knew very little about software, but both at the software company and at MicroSolutions Cuban taught himself the business after making the sale. In essence, he would tell people that he could provide services that he had no experience delivering. He then would quickly read computer manuals cover to cover so he would be able to offer the services he promised. MicroSolutions grew slowly, with only a few employees during the first few years, but it did manage to grow. One of its most important large clients was Perot Systems, a company founded by H. Ross Perot several years before Perot's first presidential campaign in 1992. Cuban's efforts were fairly successful, even though MicroSolutions never grew into a major software company. In 1990, Cuban sold the company to CompuServe, an Internet services firm. Cuban made about $2 million on the deal, which allowed him to enjoy financial freedom for a time.

MATURE WEALTH
In Cuban's next large venture, he funded a friend's effort to broadcast college games over the Internet. This enterprise began on a very small scale, but it eventually grew, and less than four years after its creation the company, now called Broadcast.com, employed three hundred people. In 1999, at the height of the dot-com boom, Broadcast.com was sold to Yahoo!, Inc., and Cuban received billions of dollars worth of Yahoo! stock. Cuban and his partner Todd Wagner became rich, but they also shared the wealth with many of the employees who initially came to work for the company, and some sources estimate that hundreds of these employees became millionaires.

Cuban decided to diversify his portfolio, which is why he fared better than many others who made their wealth in technology and saw their fortunes decline when the dot-com bubble burst. Cuban made a number

Mark Cuban. (AP/Wide World Photos)

THE FALLEN PATRIOT FUND

The Fallen Patriot Fund of the Mark Cuban Foundation helps families of military personnel who were killed or seriously wounded while fighting in the Iraq War. The patriot fund was established in 2003 at the behest of Mark Cuban, and the Mark Cuban Foundation provided much of its initial funding. Cuban matched the first $1 million in donations, and additional financing was provided by the Bank of America, which matched its employees' donations of $25 to $5,000. Since its inception, many film screenings and other fund-raisers have generated money for the fund, and some musicians have donated proceeds from their songs. As of 2009, the fund had disbursed a little more than $4 million.

The focus of the fund is to provide relief from immediate financial distress for the spouses and children of military personnel who were killed or seriously injured in battle. Many of the grants have been for $10,000, and each award is tailored to the needs of a family. Mark's brother, Brian Cuban, is involved with the fund and also manages the Mark Cuban Foundation. Mark plays an active role in the organization, and he has appeared at a number of its award ceremonies. The fund does not express an opinion on the Iraq War, and it has received favorable publicity and donations from both supporters and opponents of the conflict.

of high-profile purchases, including buying the Dallas Mavericks basketball team from H. Ross Perot, Jr., the son of one of Cuban's major clients at MicroSolutions.

Cuban has been very public about his ownership of the Mavericks. While many National Baketball Association (NBA) franchise owners sit in luxury boxes, Cuban always sits courtside, where he freely expresses his feelings about the referees and rival teams. He has been fined more than $1 million for his behavior; these fines were paid to the NBA and are believed to be a record for a team owner. He matched these fines with donations to a variety of groups, including organizations involved in cancer research and the treatment of enzyme disorders. He also donated more than $1 million to relief efforts after the terrorist attacks on September 11, 2001.

Cuban has upgraded the Mavericks' facilities in order to attract potential free agents and to generally improve the team. During the 2009 NBA playoffs, Cuban gained notoriety for getting into a shouting match with an opposing team's player. Despite his often over-the-top behavior at games, Cuban's ownership has benefited the Mavericks. He took a team that seldom made and rarely won the NBA championship playoffs before his acquisition, and he helped make it a team that frequently competed in the playoffs and advanced to the finals in 2006, losing the championship to the Miami Heat in six games.

Besides the Mavericks, Cuban has also been involved

in a variety of technological ventures. He is a significant investor in 2929 Entertainment, a company that aims to control all aspects of a film's production. One of the films produced by the company was *What Just Happened* (2008), directed by Barry Levinson and starring actor Robert De Niro. The firm also owns art theaters and produces television shows. Cuban is also an owner of Magnolia Pictures, a film production company best known for producing *Redacted* (2007), which presented a fictionalized account of the rape and murder of a young Iraqi girl in 2006. *Redacted* generated controversy, and the company had to delete images in the film that might have resulted in lawsuits.

Cuban co-owns HDNet, one of the first companies to provide high-definition satellite television to subscribers. HDNet was founded in 2003, several years before most viewers were familiar with high-definition television. In 2007, Cuban founded HDNet Fights, a company that airs and promotes mixed martial arts and other combat sports on his network. He has said he would like to present mixed martial arts events "in a manner more in line with other professional sports."

Cuban has tried to purchase other enterprises. A longtime Chicago Cubs fan, he made an unsuccessful bid to buy the baseball team when it was up for sale in 2007. He also has expressed interest in buying either the Pittsburgh Penguins hockey team or the Pittsburgh Pirates baseball franchise, having ties to these teams because he grew up in Pittsburgh. In 2010, he bid $598 million to purchase the Texas Rangers, a Major League Baseball team, during the team's bankruptcy auction, but his bid was denied and the team was purchased by an investment group led by Hall of Fame pitcher Nolan Ryan. There also has been speculation that Cuban is trying to start a new football league.

In 2008, the Securities and Exchange Commission (SEC) filed a civil suit against Cuban, claiming he had used confidential information to make a profit. The suit alleged that he had privileged information about Mamma.com, Inc., an Internet search engine company in which he had invested, and that he used this information to sell his stock at a profit. Cuban claimed he had not violated any laws. On July 17, 2009, a federal judge dismissed the lawsuit, ruling that the SEC could not hold

Cuban liable for insider trading because the agency did not allege that Cuban had agreed not to trade based on confidential information he received about the company.

LEGACY

In many ways, Cuban is rewriting the role of American sports franchise owner and entrepreneur. Most owners stay out of the headlines and away from their teams. Cuban does neither. He is a very public fan and advocate for his team and is sometimes so noticeable that he distracts from the games themselves. Cuban, however, is generally entertaining and always serves as a topic of conversation. Whether an owner like Cuban is good for a team has yet to be determined, but he definitely has altered public perception of an owner's role.

Cuban is also part of an emerging generation of highly visible, superrich Americans who have no qualms about publicly expressing their beliefs. He seeks attention for his comments and publicity campaigns, not for the conspicuous consumption for which wealthy people previously sought notice. However, like wealthy people in previous generations, he has used some of his wealth in philanthropic endeavors.

—Scott A. Merriman

FURTHER READING

Berenson, Alex. *The Number: How the Drive for Quarterly Earnings Corrupted Wall Street and Corporate America*. New York, Random House, 2004. This book, with a foreword by Cuban, discusses corporate fraud in the 1990's and why the Securities and Exchange Commission did not catch more of the perpetrators.

Ericksen, Gregory K. *Net Entrepreneurs Only: Ten Entrepreneurs Tell the Stories of Their Success*. New York: John Wiley, 2000. Contains interviews with ten successful people who founded Internet businesses, including Cuban and the founder of Priceline.com. These people won Ernst and Young's Entrepreneur of the Year awards.

Leonard, Devlin. "Mark Cuban May Be a Billionaire, but What He Really Needs Is Respect." *Fortune* 156, no. 8 (October 15, 2007): 172. Profile of Cuban, discussing his business career, his $57 billion sale of Broadcast.com to Yahoo!, and his film and professional sports enterprises.

Livingston, Jessica. *Founders at Work: Stories of Startups' Early Days*. Berkeley, Calif.: Apress, 2008. Tells the story of several successful startups, including Apple, Inc., and Flikr photo-sharing, and discusses why they were successful. Interviews the founders of these companies.

See also: Paul Allen; Steven Ballmer; Jeff Bezos; Sergey Brin; Michael Dell; Larry Ellison; Bill Gates; Steve Jobs; Gordon E. Moore; David Packard; H. Ross Perot; George Steinbrenner; Ted Turner.

PAUL CUFFE
American merchant, shipbuilder, farmer, and moneylender

The wealthiest African American in the early United States, Cuffe was a merchant, landowner, shipbuilder, store owner, miller, farmer, and moneylender. He used his fortune in a humanitarian effort to transport freed slaves to West Africa, with mixed results.

Born: Janaury 17, 1759; Cuttyhunk Island, Massachusetts
Died: September 7, 1817; Westport, Massachusetts
Also known as: Paul Slocum (birth name); Paul Cuffee
Sources of wealth: Shipbuilding; trade; moneylending; real estate
Bequeathal of wealth: Spouse; children; relatives; educational institution; charity

EARLY LIFE

Kofi, the father of Paul Cuffe (KOO-fee), was born in Ghana, Africa, and was sold into slavery in 1728 to a prominent Quaker family in Massachusetts. Through hard work, Kofi was able to earn his independence by the 1740's. Paul Cuffe's mother, Ruth Moses, was a Native American of the venerable Wampanoag tribe, who had shared a Thanksgiving dinner with the Pilgrims. Kofi, who was known as Cofee Slocum when he was a freedman, married Ruth in 1746 and moved to Cuttyhunk, an offshore Massachusetts island. They had ten children, including Paul Cuffe, who was born in 1759.

When he was fourteen, Paul shipped aboard a New England whaler. On his voyages he learned arithmetic and navigation. The Revolutionary War broke out a few years later, restricting the New England maritime trade, but Cuffe profited as an intrepid blockade runner. On February 25, 1783, Cuffe married Alice Pequit, also of the Wampanoag tribe; they would have seven children. Cuffe was described by his contemporaries as a man of quiet dignity, pious, and unselfish. Although rightly recognized in history for his achievements as an African American, it is important to remember that Cuffe was equally of Native American heritage.

FIRST VENTURES

With his profits from his trading voyages, Cuffe expanded his fleet. Forming a shipbuilding and purchase partnership with his brother-in-law Michael Wainer, Cuffe acquired a twelve-ton schooner. Soon he added a twenty-ton schooner. From 1787 to 1795, Cuffe sold some of his smaller boats to obtain larger ships, including a twenty-five-ton whaling schooner, the *Sunfish*; a forty-two-ton schooner, *Mary*; and the sixty-nine-ton, sixty-two-foot square-sterned schooner, the *Ranger*. Besides whaling and cod fishing, Cuffe traded timber, livestock, food, corn, apples, cotton, and flour. His fleet of boats traveled up and down the east coast from Newfoundland to the Caribbean. A single trip to Maryland in the winter of 1795-1796 netted him a profit of more than $1,000. In February, 1797, he purchased a 140-acre farm on the Westport River in Massachusetts for $3,500. By 1800, his holdings had expanded to two hundred acres. He bought a gristmill and a windmill in order to refine the foodstuffs he shipped. His total assets were worth about $10,000, equivalent to several hundred thousand dollars in 2010.

MATURE WEALTH

By the beginning of the nineteenth century, Cuffe was the wealthiest person of color in the United States. With revenue from his farming, shipbuilding, and trading businesses he was able to donate his time and money to civic-minded enterprises. He was a remarkably farsighted man. Believing in education, he used his own funds to construct and operate a school on his land in order to educate his children and other children residing in the town of Westport, Massachusetts. This institution was one of the first integrated schools in the United States. A Quaker, Cuffe donated $600 in 1813 for the construction of a substantial Friends meetinghouse in Westport. He lobbied the Massachusetts courts in order to obtain voting rights for taxpaying African Americans.

One of Cuffe's most significant ventures was his effort to create overseas colonies for freed American slaves. Given the difficult circumstances facing former slaves in the United States, including possible reenslavement under the fugitive slave laws, many progressive Americans supported the idea of repatriation of freed blacks to Africa. Cuffe's travels convinced him that America's former slaves could prosper in West Africa and he joined efforts to arrange for immigration to Sierra Leone. In 1811, he formed the Friendly Society of Sierra Leone to improve conditions for newly arrived blacks. He traveled to Great Britain to meet with the leaders of the African Institution. In 1812, he met with President James Madison to discuss African colonization. In December, 1815, with the end of the War of 1812, Cuffe spent $4,000 to enable nine families to settle in Sierra Leone, but he had difficulty raising the funds needed to continue with his emigration plans. In 1817, he began collaborating with the newly formed American Colonization Society.

Although increasingly busy with his humanitarian ventures, Cuffe did not entirely neglect his businesses. He had a wharf and warehouse constructed on his river property. From 1802 to 1803, the *Ranger* alone made seventeen commercial landings, netting Cuffe $5,000. In 1802, he built a 162-ton brig, the *Hero*, for his fleet. In 1806, he built a ninety-one foot, 268-ton, double-decked, three-masted ship, the *Alpha*. Cuffe captained the *Alpha* on trips to the South, to England, and to Russia. He opened a store in New Bedford, Massachusetts, to sell the merchandise his ships imported from Europe and the Caribbean. In 1807, he obtained a 109-ton brig, the *Traveler*, and two years later, the *Hero*, refitted and reregistered as a bark, brought Cuffe $1,700 in profits. In 1815, he sold the *Alpha* for $6,550. With his large ships he was able to sail more frequently to the West Indies, Europe, and Africa, transporting cotton, plaster, wood, pitch, oil, clothing, livestock, salt, hardware, spices, and passengers. He built up his landholdings by acquiring two additional farms and several salt marshes, with an eye toward opening a salt mine. He loaned money to his neighbors. However, his dream of yearly passenger trips to Sierra Leone in order to establish and serve a thriving colony of former slaves did not come to fruition.

LEGACY

In an era when most blacks in the United States were slaves or were poor freedmen, and when most Native Americans lived in poverty, Paul Cuffe was able to amass a large fortune in a number of businesses that were dominated by white men. His accumulation of wealth was a remarkable achievement, as were his humanitarian ef-

MINORITIES AND WEALTH

The story of minorities—ethnic, racial, and religious—and the creation of wealth is one of the more remarkable in economic history. It is a story of both obstacle and opportunity, of frustration and achievement, of discrimination and success. Minorities have faced persecution, but they have also been able to seize opportunities for economic advancement. Ethnic and religious minorities form tight-knit groups. Kinship ties lead naturally to networks of suppliers, traders, and agents. Many rulers were satisfied to see their minority populations engaged in trade and business, especially as these populations' vulnerable status allowed for heavy taxation, and even occasional confiscation.

In medieval Europe, Christians were forbidden from lending money at interest, as a form of usury. Jews, however, were allowed to become usurers, and some Jews made a profit by lending money to non-Jews. For example, as Venice became a great economic power in the fifteenth century, its Jewish population, although confined to a ghetto, served a valuable economic function as moneylenders to Venetian merchants. In the eighteenth and nineteenth centuries, the Rothschilds were able to build their great fortunes while barely out of the ghetto.

The religious minorities of India—the Jains, Parsees, and Ismāʿīlī Muslims—have long been active in commerce. The Jains, who are reluctant to harm living things in husbandry and agriculture, took naturally to commerce. The Mughal emperors, themselves foreign rulers of India's vast Hindu population, encouraged ethnic and religious minorities to continue their commercial ventures. Great fortunes were made by traders, who in turn paid large amounts of taxes to the Mughals.

Armenians were successful merchants worldwide, as were the Christian Coptic businessmen in Muslim Egypt, the Raskolniki Christian minority in Russia, and the Protestant Huguenots in Catholic France. In China, the Hakka minority has earned great wealth in commerce. The Chinese,

dispersed from their homeland, have succeeded in business everywhere; their success in Indonesia helped spark a massacre in 1956 that resulted in the deaths of hundreds of thousands of Chinese immigrants. Successful Indian businessmen were expelled from Uganda by Idi Amin in 1972.

The Spanish New World empire depended on Genoese bankers. The Latin American nations succeeding to the Spanish empire have seen the success of many minorities, none more so than the Lebanese, with billionaires such as Luis Noboa and Carlos Slim. In various countries, Pakistanis, Koreans, and West Indians, to name just a sample of ethnic minorities, have achieved the great commercial success denied them in their homelands. The list of minorities who have overcome great odds is endless, proving that any ethnic group can show its entrepreneurial drive under the right conditions.

Societies differ in their treatment of women and wealth. However, in a world where legal title to property was often limited to men, the rise of wealthy women is equally remarkable. The Bible and Qurʾān speak with wonder of the wealth of the Queen of Sheba. Jane Stanford, Laura Spelman Rockefeller, and Joan Kroc are counted among America's greatest philanthropists.

Minorities continue to confront obstacles to success. A minority population is subject to discrimination, isolation, purges, expropriation, and massacre. The African continent was ravaged by slavery. When African Americans were eventually freed from slavery in the United States, they then encountered racist Jim Crow laws, segregation, and sharecropping. These conditions make the achievements of Paul Cuffe, an African American and Native American who lived in the late eighteenth and early nineteenth centuries, all the more remarkable. He not only attained a sizable fortune but also spent his wealth on farsighted ventures in education, religion, and emigration.

forts to transport freed slaves to West Africa and his support of other charities. Cuffe faced many obstacles, but he knew how to seize opportunity, and in so doing he became a very wealthy man.

When Cuffe died in 1817, his estate was valued by the Bristol County probate court at a little more than $20,000, including $4,119 in real estate and $14,023 in personal property. The record of his various property holdings ran to eight handwritten pages. His will left most of his personal goods and income to his wife, with a large portion of his estate to be equally shared among his

children. He also left generous amounts of money to his grandchildren, siblings, and cousins, and to the Westport Society of Friends.

—*Howard Bromberg*

FURTHER READING

Braudel, Fernand. *The Wheels of Commerce.* Vol. 2 in *Civilization and Capitalism: Fifteenth-Eighteenth Century.* Translated by Sian Reynolds. Berkeley: University of California Press, 1992. Monumental economic history of the modern world through the eighteenth century, with a section on the pivotal role of minorities in the economic life of many nations.

Diamond, Arthur. *Paul Cuffe*. New York: Chelsea House, 1989. Biography for young adult readers in the Black Americans of Achievement series.

Harris, Sheldon. *Paul Cuffe: Black America and the African Return*. New York: Simon & Schuster, 1972. Emphasizes Cuffe's prominence as a "man of color," with excerpts from his voluminous journals and letters.

Muller, Jerry. *Capitalism and the Jews*. Princeton, N.J.: Princeton University Press, 2010. Examines perhaps the most successful of all minorities in generating wealth: the Jews. The four chapters cover the financial history of the Jewish people in relation to themes of usury, capitalism, communism, and nationalism, respectively.

Salvador, George. *Paul Cuffe, the Black Yankee, 1759-1817*. New Bedford, Mass.: Reynolds-DeWalt, 1969. Short biography focusing on Cuffe's success as a New England merchant and trader.

Thomas, Lamont. *Paul Cuffe: Black Entrepreneur and Pan African*. Urbana: University of Illinois Press, 1988. Originally published in 1986 under the title *Rise to Be a People: A Biography of Paul Cuffe*, this well-documented biography relies on newly uncovered archives to fill out the remarkable story of Cuffe's efforts at creating an African sanctuary for freed American slaves.

Wiggins, Rosalind. *Captain Paul Cuffe's Logs and Letters, 1808-1817: A Black Quaker's "Voice From Within the Veil."* Washington, D.C.: Howard University Press, 1996. With a perceptive introduction on Cuffe's place in the African diaspora, tells the story of his mature years through a selection of his letters and ship log entries from the last decade of his life.

See also: John Jacob Astor; Moses Brown; Elias Hasket Derby; Benjamin Franklin; Stephen Girard; John Hancock; Francis Cabot Lowell; Robert Morris; Samuel Slater; Stephen Van Rensselaer III; George Washington.

HUGH ROY CULLEN
American oil magnate

Cullen embodied the daring spirit of the first generation of Texas oil wildcatters. His calculated gambles to find unsuspected oil reserves made him one of the richest industrialists of the 1920's. Cullen distributed more than 90 percent of his wealth to a range of charitable projects in his native state.

Born: July 3, 1881; Denton County, Texas
Died: July 4, 1957; Houston, Texas
Source of wealth: Oil
Bequeathal of wealth: Children; educational institution; artistic patronage

EARLY LIFE
Hugh Roy Cullen was born on a farm in Denton County, Texas, just south of the Oklahoma border, the grandson of a prominent politician in the early years of Texas statehood. His father died soon after Cullen was born, and his mother moved the family to San Antonio, then little more than a cattle ranching frontier town. Money was tight, and Cullen completed only the fifth grade before he started working, initially bagging candy for $3 a week. Mindful of the importance of education in the development of character, Cullen maintained a strict regimen of self-imposed studies. However, he was restless. At seventeen, he set out on his own and moved south to Schulenburg, Texas, to pursue the opportunities of cotton brokering, initially as a general office worker but quickly moving into cotton trading, maintaining a significant market in both Texas and Oklahoma.

FIRST VENTURES
In 1903, Cullen married Lillie Cranz, the daughter of a wealthy rancher. They quickly had five children, a son and four daughters. Although successful as a cotton broker with a well-earned reputation for hard work and integrity, Cullen wanted roots for his family. He moved his family to Houston in 1911 to pursue interests in real estate. Houston, incorporated only twenty years earlier, offered boom opportunities for land investment, and for more than five years Cullen worked the real estate market with tenacity and diligence, establishing himself as a force in Houston's burgeoning economy. While handling transactions involving vast tracts of open country around the Houston area, Cullen was introduced to the oil business that was just beginning to take off. At this time, southeast Texas was in the first flush of the so-called Gusher Age, in which this area of the state (and Okla-

homa) would become, in a ten short years, the center of the world's richest and most lucrative oil deposits. It was an exciting time for those willing to take the risks of drilling. Little was known about the extent of the oil reserves, and companies would often go bankrupt and individual fortunes would be lost before drillers hit significant deposits. With typical daring, Cullen quickly earned a reputation as a wildcatter, willing to finance drilling in fields either outside the range of already marked deposits, and therefore considered a much higher risk, or in fields already abandoned as unpromising.

MATURE WEALTH

With remarkable luck, Cullen struck large deposits in quick succession in Pierce Junction, Blue Ridge, and Rabb's Ridge, among other areas. His strategy was simple: When confronted with evidence that the drilling was futile and a field was dry, he instructed his men to drill deeper. With the high-risk devil-may-care attitude that typified the first-generation Texas wildcatters, Cullen pursued gushers. He loved prospecting and was uninterested in maintaining whatever oil deposits he might find, preferring to sell them off quickly and putting that money into new ventures. His strategy worked. In 1932, he established the Quintana Petroleum Company to manage his considerable properties and extensive drilling operations. Along with his son, Cullen was a hands-on chief executive officer, visiting oil fields and often taking part in the construction of the giant derricks. He would tell reporters how much he loved to hear a gusher when it would first come in.

By the early 1930's, with the United States in a deep economic depression, Cullen, along with oil tycoons Clint Murchison, Sr., Sid W. Richardson, and H. L. Hunt, became the core of an ultraweathy social class new to Texas, who had at their command millions of dollars and who flaunted their wealth in ostentatious mansions, world travel, art collections, and all the other manifestations of a wealth beyond measure. Cullen alone of the so-called Big Four maintained a relatively modest lifestyle, although he did have a taste for expensive clothing and built a palatial estate outside Houston. Instead, Cullen began to return his considerable wealth to the Houston community he loved, giving sizable donations, notably to hospitals and schools.

In 1937, the newly opened University of Houston sent Cullen a standard fund-raising brochure that touted the new school's mission to make college education accessible to Houston's working class. The idea appealed to Cullen, and thus began his nearly twenty-five-year com-

Hugh Roy Cullen. (Time & Life Pictures/Getty Images)

mitment to the university. Initially, although land had been donated for the campus, there was no money to construct buildings. Immediately, Cullen donated $350,000, sufficient to construct a liberal arts building, named the Roy Gustav Cullen Memorial Building for Cullen's son, who had died in an oil rig accident two years earlier. Cullen never wavered in his support of the university. He eventually dontated more than $20 million, including a most eccentric $2 million contribution in 1954, when the Houston football team defeated rival Baylor University. In recognition, Cullen served for twelve years as the chair of the university's board of regents.

In addition to his support of the university, Cullen in 1948 donated oil properties worth in excess of $160 million to establish the Cullen Foundation, which funded worthwhile projects in the Houston area. After World War II, Cullen provided considerable financing for the arts as Houston struggled to diminish its reputation as a cultural backwater. Cullen funded the city's symphony, and the Cullen Foundation later provided a world-class sculpture garden for the city's Museum of Fine Arts, named for the Cullens, and a state-of-the-art theater, the Worthham.

Although his oil drilling and his largesse became legendary in Texas, Cullen also maintained a presence on the national stage, largely through his support of conservative political causes. Initially a Democrat, reflecting his working-class background, Cullen was associated with the states-rights movement and its deep discontent with the reach of President Franklin D. Roosevelt's New Deal initiatives during the late 1930's. When discontented Southern Democrats broke with the party over the nomination of Harry S. Truman in 1948, Cullen, feisty and plainspoken, was a staunch financial backer of the Dixiecrats. When Truman won, Cullen became a supporter of Dwight D. Eisenhower, a Republican, and he ultimately contributed money to Joseph McCarthy, an ultraconservative U.S. senator. Cullen decried Communism and its threat to the capitalist system, which, in his view, rewarded hard work and commitment. In the last years of his life, Cullen also associated himself with controversial views and was a vociferous opponent of civil rights and welfare.

However, his charity work defined him in his native state. When he died in 1957, although he took generous care of his family and left an estate valued at between $250 and $300 million, it was estimated that he had given away nearly 95 percent of his accumulated wealth.

LEGACY

Hugh Roy Cullen was never entirely comfortable with the millions of dollars he accumulated. In his view, nature had put the oil in the ground; he had just found it. He knew that in the oil business, luck played a major role in a person's success or failure, and he attributed his success primarily to his remarkably good fortune. It was this sort of down-to-earth sensibility that endeared Cullen to Tex-

---

THE CULLEN FOUNDATION

In the years immediately after World War II, still smarting from his futile efforts to displace the hold of the liberalism of the late Franklin D. Roosevelt on the national Democratic Party, Hugh Roy Cullen turned his attention to Houston, Texas. There, with the advice and support of his wife, he decided to set up a massive charity foundation that would be patterned on another philanthropic institution established with oil money, New York City's Rockefeller Foundation. However, his organization would be different from the Rockefeller Foundation. Cullen directed that the mission of his foundation would be to serve the nonprofit organizations in Texas only, preferably the Houston area specifically.

It was this sort of insular logic that kept the Cullen Foundation, endowed in late 1948 with more than $160 million worth of productive oil properties in south Texas, from attracting wide national attention, even though it was among the five richest philanthropic institutions in the country. Cullen determined his foundation would focus on Texas because he wanted to return to the state what its rich earth had given him. The trustees of his foundation were his three daughters, and the Cullen family maintained an active interest in the foundation's operations into the twenty-first century.

Initially, given Cullen's lifelong interest in supporting university education, much of the foundation's funds were directed to the University of Houston, long a pet project of Cullen. However, the foundation also maintained an interest in funding medical research, and it contributed millions of dollars to the Texas Medical Center and the College of Med-

icine at Baylor University, among other facilities. The foundation also supported endeavors in the arts, notably the Houston Symphony and the Houston Museum of Fine Arts. In addition, the foundation donated significant amounts of money to public service organizations, such as the Boy Scouts, the Young Men's Christian Association (YMCA), a variety of inner-city athletic programs designed to address Houston's growing problems of delinquency and juvenile crime, adult literacy programs, and vocational training programs.

Unlike most foundations, the Cullen Foundation accepts and reviews grant applications throughout the year instead of during specified times. Grants are awarded nearly continuously according to need, which conforms to Cullen's own fiercely pragmatic sense of putting money to work. Over the years, the foundation has made donations ranging from a few thousand to several million dollars.

In 1970, the foundation diversified, creating three separate branches, one devoted to education, another to health care and medical research, and the third to the performing arts. Although the original oil properties upon which the foundation's wealth rested have long since been depleted, the wise management of investments has ensured that the foundation, and its mission, have survived more than fifty years of boom and bust cycles in the Texas oil business. As of 2009, the foundation had dispersed more than $400 million. In 2005, accounting records placed the market value of the Cullen Foundation at $180 million, making it among the most stable philanthropic foundations in the country.

ans. Cullen, like the other Texas oil barons of his era, had no desire to become a national celebrity. Aware that he lacked the refinement of higher education and culture, Cullen propagated an image of himself as street-smart, direct, and honest. Not surprisingly, he saw his fortune largely as a chance to give back to his community. This civic spirit of practical philanthropy is, in the end, Cullen's most sustained legacy.

—*Joseph Dewey*

FURTHER READING

Burrough, Bryan. *The Big Rich: The Rise and Fall of the Greatest Texas Oil Fortunes.* New York: Penguin Press, 2009. Highly readable account of fifty years of Texas's Big Four, who went from scrappy wildcatters to flamboyant millionaires and were ultimately victims of their own business miscalculations, overspeculations, and world oil market fluctuations.

Kilman, Ed, and Theo Wright. *Hugh Roy Cullen: A Story of American Opportunity.* Reprint. White Fish, Mont.: Kessinger, 2007. Reprint of a sympathetic biography that emphasizes Cullen's oil successes and lauds his subsequent philanthropic enterprises as a model of capitalism at a time of national economic catsatrophe.

Olien, Roger M., and Diana Davids Hinton. *Wildcatters: Texas Independent Oilmen.* College Station: Texas A&M University Press, 2007. Anecdotal account of Cullen's generation of oil tycoons, with particular emphasis on the impact that Texas oil had on the world economy and energy technology.

Olien, Roger M., and Diana Davids Olien. *Oil in Texas: The Gusher Age, 1895-1945.* Austin: University of Texas Press, 2002. Historic account of sweeping economic changes in Texas during the first fifty years after oil was discovered. Particularly vivid description of Texas before the oil boom and the world and culture that produced the wildcatters.

Rundell, Walter. *Early Texas Oil: A Photographic History, 1866-1936.* College Station: Texas A&M University Press, 1997. Vivid history of Cullen's era, amply illustrated with helpful maps and photographs of the wildcatters' claims. Includes vivid accounts of the dangers and risks of wildcatting.

See also: Edward L. Doheny; J. Paul Getty; Calouste Gulbenkian; Armand Hammer; H. L. Hunt; Clint Murchison, Sr.; Joseph Pew; Sid W. Richardson; John D. Rockefeller; William Rockefeller; Harry F. Sinclair.

CYRUS H. K. CURTIS
American magazine and newspaper publisher

Curtis capitalized on Americans' interest in periodicals in the late nineteenth and early twentieth centuries, making the Curtis Publishing Company an influential multimillion-dollar operation. He is best known for his hugely successful magazines, The Ladies' Home Journal *and* The Saturday Evening Post.

Born: June 18, 1850; Portland, Maine
Died: June 7, 1933; Wyncote, Pennsylvania
Also known as: Cyrus Hermann Kotzschmar Curtis
Source of wealth: Media
Bequeathal of wealth: Children; educational institution; medical institution; museum

EARLY LIFE

Cyrus Hermann Kotzschmar Curtis was born in 1850 in Portland, Maine, the son of Cyrus Libby Curtis and Salome Ann Cummings Curtis. His family was of average means. Curtis's artistic father named him after a Bos-

ton musician, Hermann Kotzschmar. When twelve-year-old Curtis needed money to buy fireworks to celebrate the Fourth of July, he turned to his mother for assistance. Although she gave him some change, she suggested he earn additional money to buy the fireworks. Later, Curtis met a friend trying to sell his last three copies of the *Courier* newspaper on the street. Curtis offered him three cents for all of the copies and then resold them for three cents each. With his nine cents, he bought his own copies of the *Courier* and sold these for a total of eighteen cents. To make more money, he looked for customers with no access to the newspaper and marketed the publication to them. This event marked the beginning of his publishing career.

FIRST VENTURES

Young Curtis developed a reputation for his industrious behavior and was contacted by the *Courier*'s rival, the *Portland Press*. The *Press*'s business manager offered

---

THE SATURDAY EVENING POST

The *Saturday Evening Post* has been published for almost three hundred years, and the publication's longevity can be attributed to the insight and dedication of several visionaries, including publisher Cyrus H. K. Curtis. Curtis was especially interested in the historical roots of the periodical, which was called the *Pennsylvania Gazette* when Benjamin Franklin founded it in 1728.

Curtis believed that men would read business articles related to their work if these pieces were written and presented accurately. When he discussed this idea with peers, he received a negative response, with his critics arguing that there was no market for a men's business magazine. Their comments did not discourage Curtis. To test his idea, he bought *The Saturday Evening Post* for $1,000 when its owner died in 1897. At this time, the magazine was a struggling weekly with only four pages. Employees at the Curtis Publishing Company fondly called the publication "the singed cat."

Curtis hired George Horace Lorimer as the editor and pressed forward with his dream. During the next five years, he spent more than $1 million in advertising costs to build circulation for the *Post*. More than forty automobile manufacturers bought full- or double-page ads in 1914, making the *Post* a national showcase for the growth of industrial businesses in the early twentieth century. The magazine published high-quality business articles and editorials, boosting its circulation to one million readers. By the 1930's, circulation had climbed to almost three million, the largest magazine circulation in the world, and the publication earned $47 million in advertising revenue.

Editor Lorimer deviated from the normal magazine content to place creative artwork on the magazine's cover. Americans soon recognized *Post* covers with Norman Rockwell paintings of family and rural life and looked forward to each issue. Rockwell, a twenty-two-year-old unknown in 1922, painted 319 covers during a fifty-year career with the *Post*, which ended in December, 1963. Inside the magazine, readers found articles and fiction by such famous writers as Sinclair Lewis and F. Scott Fitzgerald.

In 1969, *The Saturday Evening Post* was bought by a new owner who moved the editorial content toward articles about health, medicine, and disease prevention. In 2009, *The Saturday Evening Post* continued to be published six times a year by The Saturday Evening Post Society and had a subscriber base of 350,000.

---

him a steady income of $2 per week to cover an early-morning newspaper route. Curtis accepted, rising at four o'clock each morning for four years, delivering his newspapers, and getting to school by nine o'clock. Later, a manager at the *Portland Argus* offered him more money, and Curtis went to work for the *Argus*. However, the young entrepreneur began to dream of owning a newspaper and working for himself. In partnership with a friend, fifteen-year-old Curtis wrote and published *Young American*, a newspaper for boys, in 1863. The printing costs left the partnership in debt, and Curtis's parents dissolved the business.

Curtis bought a small handpress for $2.50 in order to print his own newspaper. When a businessman queried Curtis about the cost of advertising in his newspaper, Curtis found a new source of revenue to support his efforts. He began accepting other printing jobs in order to garner additional income. However, on July, 4, 1866, Portland was devastated by a fire that reached Curtis's home. His publishing business was lost as his family escaped with their lives and only a few of their belongings. With the family in financial crisis, Curtis left school at age sixteen to work and never attended college. He became an errand boy for a dry goods store and was later promoted to salesman.

MATURE WEALTH

Curtis moved to Boston, where he earned $2 per week more than he had received from his job in Portland. Soon he was offered an additional 25 percent commission by an advertising agency, and he sold advertisements to make extra money during his lunchtime. After a year, he struck out on his own, developing a partnership to publish the *People's Ledger* in 1872. He eventually bought his partner's interest in this publication for $600. With limited capital to invest in the *People's Ledger*, Curtis was blessed with a benefactor, W. C. Allan. Later, Curtis moved his newspaper to Philadelphia, where his printing costs were reduced by $1,500 a year. Curtis was now a hardworking, optimistic, twenty-six-year-old newspaper publisher.

Curtis eventually sold the *People's Ledger*. The owners of the *Philadelphia Press*, a newspaper with a circulation of thirty-five thousand, asked Curtis to become its manager for $15 per week and a 25 percent commission on the advertising he sold. Although he performed well, Curtis wanted to start his own publication, *Tribune and Farmer*. One specialty column in this publication, "Women and Home," gained such popularity that Curtis decided to make it a separate supplement and sold it by subscription for fifty cents per year. His wife, Louisa Knapp Curtis, who was the author of the column, edited the new supplement, called *The La-*

dies' *Home Journal and Practical Housekeeper.* The first issue of the publication appeared in 1883; three years later, the last three words were deleted from the title.

Curtis gave up his partnership in *Tribune and Farmer* to devote all of his time to *The Ladies' Home Journal.* The magazine prospered, and its circulation grew to 100,000 readers. Curtis secured the services of well-known writers, such as Louisa May Alcott. When he raised the subscription price from fifty cents to $1 per year, he lost some subscribers but improved his overall financial position. In 1889, Edward W. Bok became the editor, and the magazine had a circulation of 500,000. In 1904, *The Ladies' Home Journal* was the first magazine to have a circulation of more than one million.

In June, 1891, Curtis formed a stock company, the Curtis Publishing Company. The firm's board of directors agreed to buy 4,950 shares of stock with a value of $100 per share, generating capital of almost $500,000. Curtis was president of the board and held a controlling interest in the newly formed company. The Curtis Company of New Jersey was founded in 1900 and assumed the older company's business. In 1907, Curtis Publishing Company had capital of $2.5 million, which increased to $5 million in 1910. In 1929, advertising revenues for the company rose to $73 million, dropping to $67 million during the Great Depression in 1930.

Curtis became interested in *The Saturday Evening Post,* a weekly periodical that had been founded by Benjamin Franklin in 1728. However, by the late nineteenth century the periodical was poorly edited and teetered on the brink of financial demise. Intrigued by its heritage, Curtis paid $1,000 to purchase *The Saturday Evening Post* in 1897. He made the magazine a success. In 1933, *Time* magazine reported that the *Post* had a circulation of 2.9 million. With his creative spirit and sound business approach, Curtis lived to see the *Post* generate more than $22.5 million in revenue in 1932 and $47 million in 1933. In the same years, *The Ladies' Home Journal*'s advertising revenue was about $8.1 million and $15 million, respectively.

Curtis used his wealth to purchase the finer things of life. In 1922, *The New York Times* ran a story about a George Romney painting that Curtis had bought, which was valued between $60,000 and $70,000. In an interview, Curtis said his wife was the art collector, not he. He did speak fondly of his yacht, the *Lyndonia,* where he spent half of his time. The yacht, listed in his wife's name, cost $450,000.

Curtis suffered a heart attack in the summer of 1932 while he was on his yacht and was admitted to a hospital in Philadelphia. He remained in poor health until he died on June 7, 1933.

LEGACY

Cyrus H. K. Curtis has been called one of the richest men in history. Adjusted to 2008 inflation rates, he was worth an estimated $43.2 billion. He was a generous man, donating to various causes, including the Franklin Institute ($2 million) and the University of Pennsylvania ($1 million). Curtis Island, for which he donated the land and the building that became the Camden Yacht Club, is where Curtis spent many summers. After his death, his daughter Mary Louise Curtis Bok established the Curtis Arboretum in Wyncote, Pennsylvania, to honor her father, who enjoyed nature. Curtis donated his Kotzschmar Memorial Organ to Portland, Maine, and Bok would later donate the Curtis Memorial Organ to Christ Church in her father's memory.

A world-renowned publisher in his time, Curtis represents the American dream of a person from humble roots with few advantages who works hard to achieve his or her goals. With little formal education, Curtis used his ingenuity and business acumen to invest and secure his goal of building a publishing business. He was known as a man of integrity who refused to allow poor industry practices or unscrupulous marketing schemes to taint his business. He understood the importance of target advertising to finance his publications. He was perhaps the first publisher to develop a research department in order to study the relationship of his subscribers and print media to advertising. Curtis believed in hiring competent editors and managers and then supported their work. He was a kind and approachable man, who used his wealth to move his business forward and to support worthwhile projects.

—Marylane Wade Koch

FURTHER READING

Bok, Edward W. *A Man From Maine.* New York: Charles Scribner's Sons, 1923. Bok, the son-in-law and a former editor for Curtis, provides a candid insight into Curtis's life from childhood until after his death in 1933.

Curtis Publishing Company Records. Philadelphia: Historical Society of Pennsylvania, 2009. The Web site located at http://www.hsp.org/files/findingaid 3115curtispublishing.pdf includes an abstract with key information on Cyrus Curtis and records about the Curtis Publishing Company from 1891 to 1968.

Fuller, Walter D. *The Life and Times of Cyrus H. K.*

Curtis. New York: The Newcomen Society of England, American Branch, 1948. Provides insights from a former president of Curtis Publishing Company into key aspects of Cyrus Curtis's life and business.

Krabbendam, Hans. *The Model Man: A Life of Edward William Bok, 1863-1930*. Atlanta, Ga.: Rodopi, 2001. Describes the life of Bok, a Dutch-American who was editor of *The Ladies' Home Journal* and married Curtis's only daughter.

Time. "The Press: After Curtis." July 17, 1933. Summary review of Curtis's life and business written a month after his death that includes key points about his business in the early 1930's.

Walker, Nancy A. *Shaping Our Mothers' World: American Women's Magazines*. Jackson: University of Mississippi Press, 2000. Walker, a Vanderbilt University professor, explores how magazines, including Curtis's *The Ladies' Home Journal*, affected the image of women and helped define their role in the post-World War II era.

See also: James Gordon Bennett, Jr.; William Randolph Hearst; Joseph Pulitzer.

MARCUS DALY
American copper mining magnate

A poor Irish immigrant, Daly learned about mining firsthand and used his experience to develop the incredibly productive Anaconda copper mine in the Montana Territory. The mine made him wealthy, and the diversified industries associated with the enterprise attracted sufficient population to achieve Montana's statehood.

Born: December 5, 1841; Derrylea, County Cavan, Ireland
Died: November 12, 1900; New York, New York
Source of wealth: Mining
Bequeathal of wealth: Spouse; charity; medical institution

EARLY LIFE
Marcus Daly was the youngest child born into a large family of poor tenant farmers in rural Ireland. He received a rudimentary education at home from his mother. At the age of fifteen, soon after the devastating famine of 1845, he left Ireland for the United States. Arriving in New York City, he worked for five years at a number of menial jobs until he could save up enough money to travel west to California, where a married sister lived.

FIRST VENTURES
In California, Daly labored in a gold mine and rose to foreman. He used his newfound mining skills to obtain a similar position at the Comstock Lode silver mine in Virginia City, Nevada, and remained there from 1862 to 1868. Daly subsequently managed silver mines in Ophir, Utah, for the Walker brothers, a banking and mining family. At Ophir, Daly met and married Margaret Price "Maggie" Evans in 1872; they would have three daughters and a son. In 1874, Daly became an American citizen.

Late in the 1870's, Daly went to the Montana Territory to investigate other Walker mining interests. He stayed there, invested in a silver claim, and soon sold the mine for a large profit. In 1881, with financial assistance from San Francisco backers, including George Hearst (William Randolph Hearst's father), Daly bought another silver mine known as the Anaconda. The mine's true value proved to be a huge vein of copper, essential to the new industries of telegraphy and electricity.

MATURE WEALTH
To support the copper mine, Daly built the town of Anaconda, complete with facilities for water and power. He erected the world's largest smelter in Butte, Montana. He also built a railroad between the two towns to transport ore, and he bought up timberlands to provide fuel for the smelter. By 1890, the year after Montana became the forty-first state, Daly's copper mines were producing $17 million in annual revenues.

Daly had by now grown wealthy, and he diversified. He planted fruit orchards, founded banks, began ranching, and started breeding racehorses. His horse *Scottish Chieftain* won the Belmont Stakes in 1897. Daly also established the *Anaconda Standard* newspaper, which he used as a platform to thwart the political ambitions of rival copper magnate William Andrews Clark. He constructed Riverside, a magnificent twenty-four-thousand-square-foot mansion, near the town of Hamilton, which he also developed.

Marcus Daly. (The Granger Collection, New York)

In the mid-1890's, the Anaconda Copper Mining Company was incorporated, with Daly as president. In 1895, a Rothschild syndicate briefly entered into partnership with the company before the Standard Oil Company purchased the mine in 1899. Daly, plagued by diabetes and a heart weakened by years of hard labor, died in New York City at the age of fifty-eight on November 12, 1900. After Daly died, his wife honored his request to destroy his personal records and correspondence, depriving the world of knowledge about a man who rose from rags to riches.

LEGACY

Although the Anaconda mine and smelter that Daly founded changed ownership and expanded several times after his death, these enterprises operated continuously for nearly a century, providing employment for thousands of workers before the smelter closed in 1980. In the twenty-first century, the freestanding, 585-foot-high smelter smokestack was all that remained of the facility. The towns Daly established to support his various enterprises, Hamilton and Anaconda, continued to thrive. Although the *Anaconda Standard* shut down in 1931,

the Daly Mansion and the Margaret Daly Memorial Gardens and Arboretum remained popular tourist attractions. Daly's widow, Margaret, endowed the Marcus Daly Memorial Hospital in 1929, and she used her late husband's wealth to assist numerous charitable causes, including the Boy Scouts and area churches, until her death in 1941.

—Jack Ewing

FURTHER READING

Glasscock, Carl B. *The War of the Copper Kings*. 1935. Reprint. Helena, Mont.: Riverbend, 2002.

Hyde, Charles K. *Copper for America: The United States Copper Industry from Colonial Times to the 1990's*. Tucson: University of Arizona Press, 1998.

Malone, Michael P. *The Battle for Butte: Mining and Politics on the Northern Frontier, 1864-1906*. Seattle: University of Washington Press, 2006.

See also: William Andrews Clark; James G. Fair; James Clair Flood; Meyer Guggenheim; George Hearst; F. Augustus Heinze; Moritz Hochschild; John William Mackay; William S. O'Brien; Charles Rasp.

ALIKO DANGOTE
Nigerian industrialist and merchant

Dangote, one of the most successful businessmen in West Africa, is said to be worth more than $3 billion. In 2008, Forbes *magazine ranked him as one of the wealthiest black African citizens. Only two people of African descent—Saudi businessman Mohammed Hussein Ali Al Amoudi and African American businesswoman Oprah Winfrey—were wealthier.*

Born: April 10, 1957; Kano, Nigeria
Also known as: Alhaji Aliko Dangote
Sources of wealth: Trade; manufacturing
Bequeathal of wealth: Unknown

EARLY LIFE

Alhaji Aliko Dangote (ahl-HAH-zhee ah-LEE-koh dahn-GOH-tay) was born on April 10, 1957, in Kano, Nigeria. His father, Mohammed Dangote, was a successful businessman and politician, and his mother, Hajiya Mariya Sanusi Dantata, was related to the kola nut trader Alhassan Dantata, who died in 1955 as the wealthiest man in Nigeria. As was customary, Dangote was taken from his parents at six months of age and sent to live with

his grandfather Sanusi Dantata, a wealthy and successful trader. Dangote was educated at local schools, where he made pocket money selling candy to his classmates. For a time he attended Al-Azhar University in Cairo, Egypt.

FIRST VENTURES

Dangote was influenced by his family to go into business. He worked for a time for his grandfather, and in 1977 he borrowed money from Dantata to set himself up as a commodities trader, importing cement and other building materials. At first he worked out of his hometown of Kano, a large city in the north of Nigeria known for its groundnut pyramids. As he gradually expanded his business and his influence, he relocated to the then-capital city of Lagos, where he began importing cars and the massive amounts of cement needed for Nigeria's economic expansion. In 1981, he formed the corporation that later became the Dangote Group.

MATURE WEALTH

Dangote owns and is chairman and chief executive officer of the Dangote Group, a multinational firm spread across West Africa. The company is, at its core, a commodities trader, dealing in oil, gas, and food commodities, as well as shipping, and it also has interests in banking, vehicle leasing, and real estate. The group controls more than 60 percent of Nigeria's trade in sugar—an essential ingredient in the manufacture of beer and soft drinks. The firm also has industrial interests, including Obajana Cement, Africa's largest manufacturing plant for cement; a flour mill; salt-processing facilities; textiles; and the publicly traded Dangote Sugar Refinery, with Dangote himself as major stockholder. With control of these basic commodities, and with the rapid influx of cash when he took the Dangote Sugar Refinery public, he has made a fortune.

Dangote has used this wealth to establish himself as a key player in Nigerian politics, contributing millions of dollars to election campaigns and to private charities controlled by important politicians. There have long been suspicions that these contributions have functioned as bribes, guaranteeing Dangote favorable treatment, but no formal charges have been brought against him. There has also been criticism that while Dangote has profited, most of his workers continue to live in poverty. However, Dangote is often praised for investing his money in West Africa, rather than abroad.

LEGACY

Within Nigeria and neighboring West African nations, Aliko Dangote is a household name. He is Nigeria's largest employer, as well as the man behind the Dangote sugar and Dangote flour in every home and the Dangote freight trucks on every road. As a successful businessman, he is an inspiration to younger Nigerians, who hope to be equally wealthy. Outside West Africa, Dangote is known as one of the world's richest Africans, a full participant in the global economy and an example that the wealth generated by this economy can be available to people everywhere.

—*Cynthia A. Bily*

FURTHER READING

Fick, David S., ed. *Entrepreneurship in Africa: A Study of Successes.* Santa Barbara, Calif.: Greenwood Press, 2002.

Forrest, Tom G. *The Advance of African Capital: The Growth of Nigerian Private Enterprise.* Charlottesville: University of Virginia Press, 1994.

Mahajan, Vijay. *Africa Rising: How Nine Hundred Million African Consumers Offer More than You Think.* Philadelphia: Wharton School, 2008.

See also: Mohammed Hussein Ali Al Amoudi.

FRANCESCO DATINI
Italian banker and merchant

Datini rose from modest origins to amass one of the largest fortunes in early fourteenth century Italy, almost all of which he bequeathed to a charitable foundation which existed into the twenty-first century. Of even greater significance is the enormous archive of documents relating to his personal and business life that also survives in Prato, Italy.

Born: c. 1335; Prato, Tuscany (now in Italy)
Died: August 16, 1410; Prato, Tuscany
Also known as: Francesco di Marco da Prato Datini
Sources of wealth: Banking; trade
Bequeathal of wealth: Spouse; charity

EARLY LIFE

Francesco di Marco da Prato Datini, better known as Francesco Datini (frahn-CHEHS-co DAH-tee-nee), the son of a Prato innkeeper, was born around 1335. Little is known of him until 1348, when the Black Death struck Italy and all of Europe. Datini was left an orphan as the

disease killed his mother, two brothers, a sister, and finally his father. His life was haunted by multiple recurrences of the plague, and his experience as an orphan informed his wishes for the distribution of his wealth after his death. Datini's father left his two remaining sons a small inheritance of 50 florins each, along with a house and a bit of farmland.

FIRST VENTURES

Datini, already an apprentice merchant at the time of his father's death, relocated in the company of other Italians to Avignon, France. This town was the home in exile of the popes during the so-called Avignon Papacy (1305-1378), and the papal court was a major center of the luxury trade. Using his meager resources, Datini engaged in the trading of numerous commodities, including armor, religious items, and especially cloth, for which Prato was a center of production. A document suggests that a relative sent Datini an amount of fine cloth, which he sold for a handsome profit. Continuing to buy low and sell high,

---

THE DATINI ARCHIVES

The legacy of Francesco Datini is twofold: He created a charitable foundation with a bequest of some 70,000 florins that in the twenty-first century continued to perform good works in Prato. Arguably, however, the greater legacy lies in the documents Datini left behind. They constitute the largest surviving collection of business papers of an individual in Europe before the nineteenth century.

In his will, Datini asked that all of his papers be preserved, and it seems that his executors obeyed. The knowledge of these documents' existence was lost in the sixteenth century, however, and they remained undiscovered until renovations were undertaken at Datini's home about 1860. When workmen broke through a wall into an unused stairwell, they discovered the contracts, letters, and account books stored in canvas bags.

The archives consist of more than 500 account books, 300 deeds of partnership, 400 insurance policies, and more than 150,000 letters. It is to the survival of these documents that Datini owes his fame. He left behind more business documents than were left by all other Florentine businessmen during his lifetime. He had branch businesses and partnerships around the Mediterranean in Avignon, Valencia, Barcelona, and Majorca, as well as in the Italian cities of Prato, Florence, Pisa, and Genoa, and he corresponded with his agents in these cities weekly or even daily. This correspondence has been partially published, although most of these publications are in Italian. From them, scholars have learned in exquisite detail the commercial activities of at least one early Renaissance entrepreneur.

While the large number of documents is unusual, it appears that Datini's business practices were similar to those of other, smaller Prato businessmen. Contracts, accounting systems, instruments of credit, and dispute resolution practices were essential to both local and international business. His personal letters—Datini wrote almost daily to his wife and almost as often to his friend, Ser Lapo Mazzei—provide a wealth of information for social and family historians. All these documents are the basis of his biographies, especially Iris Origo's book *The Merchant of Prato: Francesco di Marco Datini, 1335-1410* (1986).

The Datini Archives are housed in the home Datini built in Prato and make up the bulk of the Archivio di Stato di Prato. Since the mid-twentieth century, the Casa Datini has been the site of an annual conference on economic history, the Istituto Internazionale di Storia Economica "Francesco Datini."

Datini remained in Avignon for more than thirty years. In 1376, when he was about forty years old, he married sixteen-year-old Margherita Bandini, a Florentine noblewoman in exile. The age difference between the two was typical of marriages in Italian merchant households. They had no children together, though Datini sired at least two illegitimate children. When the papal court returned to Italy in 1378, Datini soon followed. He returned to Prato and set up business in nearby Florence in 1382, leaving partners and agents to manage his affairs at his offices in Avignon.

MATURE WEALTH

By the time he returned to Prato, Datini was wealthy but not exceptionally so. He continued his practice of patient accumulation and reinvestment of many small profits. Over time, he became the wealthiest man in Prato and one of the richest in all of Tuscany.

His developing business interests can be seen by the guilds he joined. As he invested in the manufacture, import, export, and sale of textiles, he became a member of the cloth guild in 1383. As he sought the higher profits available through the sale of silks and other luxury items, he joined the silk merchants' guild in 1388. As he gradually moved from managing credit between his far-flung branches to handling credit for others, he joined the bankers' guild in 1399. This last membership was short-lived and ended in 1403. In the last years of his life, Datini may have lost his zeal for accumulating more wealth, and his close friends and religious advisers warned him of the sin of usury. He always denied making dishonest gains; however, he left a large sum of money for his executors to distribute to unnamed beneficiaries, perhaps to atone for usurious loans.

Business practices in early Renaissance Italy were the most sophisticated in Europe, and Datini's methods of conducting business were quite advanced. He formed frequent partnerships, both for the production and sale of local goods and for the creation of overseas branches. He and his partners joined forces for a set period of time,

he slowly built his resources into significant wealth. Profits in the luxury trade were high, significantly greater than profits from investment in either land or manufacturing.

By the 1360's, Datini owned a shop in Avignon, supplied armor to mercenaries fighting on all sides of the numerous wars, and engaged in maritime insurance and money changing (banking). He had increased his original investment to almost 10,000 florins in less than twenty years.

each contributing some share of capital, assuming that share of risk, and reaping the same share of profits. An office in Pisa was replaced by one in Genoa in 1392, and in the next year, Datini had offices throughout Spain. He also maintained his ties with Avignon. To conduct business over such distances, he corresponded with each of his agents weekly and required the same of them. He also made use of letters of exchange and letters of credit, and a complex double-entry bookkeeping system kept his accounts straight. As major partner, he insured his own shipments from losses at sea, and he gradually invested excess capital in providing the same insurance for the shipments of other merchants.

Business enterprise was an honored profession at the time, but it was also risky. Many businessmen went bankrupt. Their only protection came from diversification and wide geographical distribution. However, with greater risk came higher profits. Biographer Iris Origo calculated that Datini's profit from the manufacture of local wool was perhaps 7 to 10 percent, while for some silk and luxury goods profit could be as high as 30 percent. Profit from banking and loans was between 15 and 20 percent.

The documentation of Datini's personal account books and letters provides an unusually detailed knowledge of his life. While he was frugal about many things, especially day-to-day expenditures, he lived well and in some areas even extravagantly. Inventories of his property showed that he, his wife, and his adopted (illegitimate) daughter had many clothes, and these clothes were of rich materials compared to the attire of the family's contemporaries. Similarly, Datini ate well and took pride in serving distinguished guests lavish and unusual banquets. To his family, he could be alternately stingy or generous and it pleased him to give lavish gifts to his social betters.

The major extravagance of his mature years was his grand house, or palazzo. He had begun accumulating the necessary land for this residence even before he permanently returned to Prato in 1382, and construction began around 1390. The complex of buildings included the house, his commercial offices, stables, and outbuildings, all set within a garden stocked with exotic animals. The house was a typical arrangement of rooms around an open courtyard on two floors, plus an attic. Datini hired some of the best-known painters of Florence to decorate the interior walls with images. Documents about contracts, bills, and disputes still exist, as do some of the paintings themselves. By 1399, Datini estimated that he had spent 6,000 florins on the house and its furnishings, or about 10 percent of his total wealth at the time.

LEGACY

In Datini's life, two things were important: faith and trade. His ledgers always began with some variation of the phrase, "In the name of God and of profit." The conflict between God and profit, plus his experiences with the plague and human frailty, meant that for much of his life he was anxious about his fortunes in this life and in the next. In his will, Datini made provision for both his surviving wife and his illegitimate daughter and her offspring. From the remainder of his estate, he gave a significant gift to establish a foundling hospital, the Ospidale degli Innocenti (hospital of the innocents), in Florence. In addition, he bestowed the vast majority of his wealth, including his house, personal property, and lands, to endow a charitable organization to be administered outside the usual church structures. This foundation (or *ceppo* in Italian) was to help orphans and unwanted children.

In his will. Datini also asked that all of his papers be preserved. These papers are the basis for the detailed knowledge of his business practices and personal life, and they have become known as the Datini Archives of Prato.

—Jean Owens Schaefer

FURTHER READING

Byrne, Joseph P. *The Black Death*. Westport, Conn.: Greenwood Press, 2004. Chapters 4 and 7 describe the effect of and responses to the plague, as well as providing a brief biography of Datini and a translation of his father's will. Includes an annotated bibliography.

Dunlop, Anne. *Painted Palaces: The Rise of Secular Art in Early Renaissance Italy*. University Park: Pennsylvania State University Press, 2009. Chapter 1 discusses both the surviving paintings in Datini's house in Prato and the documents relative to its construction and decoration. Illustrated.

Goldthwaite, Richard A. *Wealth and the Demand for Art in Italy, 1300-1600*. Baltimore: The Johns Hopkins University Press, 1993. This authority on wealth and its uses in the Renaissance mentions Datini throughout the text. The introduction and discussion of the economic background (pages 1-68) are important for understanding the structure of wealth and its accumulation.

Marshall, Richard K. *The Local Merchants of Prato: Small Entrepreneurs in the Late Medieval Economy*. Baltimore: The Johns Hopkins University Press, 1999. While dealing only incidentally with Datini,

Marshall provides the local context for Datini's success. Includes a detailed discussion of business practices of the times. Extensive notes and bibliography.

Origo, Iris. *The Merchant of Prato: Francesco di Marco Datini, 1335-1410.* Boston: Nonpareil Books, 1986. While somewhat dated, this is still the basic biography in English. Based on the rich archives in Prato, this work employs not only the business ledgers and account books but also the letters between Datini and his wife for a full view of his activities. Extensive notes.

See also: Ridolfo de' Bardi; Orlando Bonsignori; Agostino Chigi; Giovanni de' Medici; Lorenzo de' Medici; Jacopo de' Pazzi; Filippo di Peruzzi; Filippo Strozzi.

ARTHUR VINING DAVIS
American aluminum magnate and real estate developer

Davis's vast wealth resulted from his involvement in the evolution of the Aluminum Company of America (Alcoa), of which he was chief executive officer for more than fifty years. He developed markets for aluminum products in both household and industrial uses. In later life, he became an important property developer in Florida and other locations.

Born: May 30, 1867; Sharon, Massachusetts
Died: November 17, 1962; Miami, Florida
Sources of wealth: Metals refining; real estate
Bequeathal of wealth: Relatives; friends; charity

EARLY LIFE
Arthur Vining Davis was the son of a Congregational minister, Perley B. Davis, and his wife, Mary Francis. Davis attended Roxbury Latin School in Boston and graduated from Amherst College in 1888. Through a family friend and parishioner, Alfred Hunt, Davis took a job in Pittsburgh in 1888. He earned $14 a week as one of the first five employees of the newly formed Pittsburgh Reduction Company (PRC), which used an innovative electrolytic process to refine aluminum.

FIRST VENTURES
PRC was built around an invention of Charles Martin Hall, who in 1886 patented a process for producing inexpensive aluminum. In 1887 this metal was selling for $8 a pound. Hall, with hands-on assistance from Davis, produced PRC's aluminum, a process that required constant expert attention. Both men initially worked twelve-hour days (or nights). They were able to refine about fifty pounds of aluminum a day. The company cut the price to $2 a pound, but still found few buyers.

Nevertheless, PRC's operations were sufficiently successful that it was able to take on more employees, enabling Hall and Davis to pursue more creative activities. By September, 1889, the firm was producing 475 pounds of aluminum per day and was enlarging its production facilities. The firm's fortunes further improved in 1890, when the banking firm of two brothers, Andrew Mellon and Richard B. Mellon, agreed to provide credit. By then, Davis was in charge of internal operations. During the 1890's, Davis's efforts focused on improving the production processes and reducing costs, and he spent much time close to the production line. Davis and other company officials sometimes borrowed money in their own names to cover payrolls.

Davis's effectiveness as a manager led PRC's stockholders to grant him 104 shares of stock in March, 1890. The stock was not traded publicly, but the Mellons valued it at $60 per share. Thus Davis was nominally worth more than $60,000. Another ten thousand shares of company stock were outstanding. Davis was appointed assistant general manager of PRC in 1893. By 1897, PRC was producing eight thousand pounds of aluminum a day. When Hunt died in 1899, Davis became the dominant manager of the firm. In 1910, he was formally designated as president of the company.

In 1896, Davis married Florence Holmes. After her death in 1908, he married Elizabeth Weiman, who died in 1933. Both marriages were childless.

MATURE WEALTH
In its early years, PRC recognized the crucial importance of patent protection, and it was the target of a patent infringement suit initiated in 1897. In 1903, PRC reached an accommodation with the Electric Smelting and Refining Company, enabling each firm to use the other's patented processes. From its beginning, PRC vigorously expanded its production capacity. By the end of 1892, the price of aluminum had fallen below $1 a pound, and output more than doubled in one year, reaching 138,000 pounds in 1893. Facilities were developed at diverse locations where electric power was cheaply available. In

1893, PRC became the first major customer for electric power from the new Niagara Falls hydroelectric complex. The firm built a facility at Shawinigan Falls, Canada, in 1901.

Expanding production was futile unless the market for aluminum could expand. Davis and his associates experimented with the manufacture of products made from aluminum, converting their oldest plants from refining to fabrication. The plant at New Kensington, Pennsylvania, was equipped with a forge, tube mills, rolling mills, and a significant casting operation. Davis supervised the process by which aluminum was rolled out in sheets to manufacture products like aluminum tea kettles. Quality control considerations led the company to enter the cookware business in 1895, producing under the Wearever brand. A wholly owned subsidiary, the Aluminum Cooking Utensil Company, developed door-to-door sales by college students, an activity that was thriving as late as 1938.

By 1898, PRC employed 260 workers. Davis's aggressive pursuit of new markets was demonstrated the following year, when he contracted to provide aluminum cable conductors to a utility company in San Francisco, even though PRC was not set up to make these products. Davis hastily arranged for PRC to install a rod mill and other wire and cable machinery at its plants, and soon the company had become a well-established manufacturer of aluminum wire for electrical uses. PRC also responded aggressively to the opportunities provided by the rapid growth of automobile production after 1900. In addition, the firm acquired bauxite deposits in Arkansas and began processing alumina, a white granular material properly called aluminum oxide, in East St. Louis, Illinois.

PRC's output of basic aluminum pig escalated rapidly, from 216,000 pounds in 1893 to one million pounds in 1896 and five million in 1900. By 1909, the firm had four thousand employees. The company had become profitable by 1893, but almost all of the profit was plowed back into the firm during the 1890's. Significant cash dividends began to be distributed in 1899. In 1907, PRC changed its name to the Aluminum Company of America; by 1910, the firm was commonly referred to by its acronym,

Alcoa. Davis's wealth increased alongside the growth and profitability of the company.

Charles Martin Hall died in 1914, leaving two hundred shares of Alcoa stock to Davis. Hall's estate was estimated at $30 million, and most of it went to educational institutions. Davis was designated as one of the two trustees who administered the bequests. Although Davis's wealth at this time probably did not match Hall's, Davis was certainly a millionaire by then.

During its first half century, PRC/Alcoa effectively held a monopoly on aluminum refining. After its basic patents expired in 1909, Alcoa was targeted for antitrust prosecution in 1912. Davis was undoubtedly one of the architects of his firm's nonconfrontational response. The company accepted a consent decree in June, 1912, agreeing to discontinue some practices of which it had been accused, without admitting guilt.

Following America's entry into World War I in 1917, Davis played a central role in negotiations for sales of aluminum to the government. In April, 1917, Alcoa sold two million pounds to the government for 27.5 cents a pound, although the market price was around 60 cents. In September, Davis negotiated a price of 38 cents, but he agreed to refund any excess over costs as determined by the Federal Trade Commission. Most of these sales were ultimately settled for 32 cents. Alcoa's accommodating stance was rewarded, as the company was given wide latitude in determining customer priorities in times of shortage. The war gave strong impetus to the develop-

Arthur Vining Davis. (Getty Images)

ment of aircraft, with aluminum playing a large part in both fuselage construction and engine design.

Davis was involved in many aspects of Alcoa's international expansion after the war. He negotiated with tobacco tycoon James Buchanan Duke to acquire in 1925 Duke's project for hydroelectric development in Canada. This acquisition led to the installation of extensive production facilities at the new town of Arvida in Quebec, with the name "Arvida" derived from the first two letters of Davis's first, middle, and last names. Davis took an intense personal interest in the town, making sure it developed recreational, religious, educational, and medical facilities.

Despite his involvement in the development of this new Canadian town, Davis was the principal influence that led Alcoa to back away from multinational operation. In June, 1928, Alcoa transferred control of thirty-four companies to the newly created Aluminum Limited of Canada. Stock in the new company was distributed pro rata to existing Alcoa shareholders, including Davis. His younger brother Edward became head of the new firm. In 1929, Alcoa's organizational structure was changed, and Davis became chairman of the board, but without reduction in authority.

In 1925, Davis was involved in a scheme to sell off part of the Alcoa stock held by the Hall trust (the estate of Charles Martin Hall, of which Davis was a trustee) to a syndicate, of which Davis was a member. The trust beneficiaries supported the scheme, which enabled them to sell stock that paid very low dividends and receive the proceeds in cash. As a result of these sales, Davis was able to buy 61,000 shares on very advantageous terms. However, when the stock rose in value, the trust beneficiaries complained that they had been swindled. Davis was pressured into relinquishing the bulk of his newly acquired stock, valued at $3 million.

In April, 1937, Alcoa was indicted for antitrust violations, initiating one of the longest cases on record. In the summer of 1938, Davis was the principal witness for his company's defense. He was on the stand for six weeks, and his testimony extended to more than two thousand pages in the trial transcript. In July, 1942, the district

---

ARTHUR VINING DAVIS FOUNDATIONS

In 1952, Arthur Vining Davis established and endowed a foundation under a living trust. He was one of the foundation's original trustees, along with his brother, a nephew, and his stepson-in-law. Two other foundations, known as No. 2 and No. 3, began operating in 1965, and their structures were modeled on foundation No. 1. The first foundation operated for forty-two years before it merged with No. 2 in 2001, reducing the number of foundations to two.

According to the Web site for these foundations, Davis had "great confidence" in the founding trustees, and he instructed them to use the foundations' earnings "for programs that would, in their best judgment, strengthen our nation's future." However, he specified that the organizations' donations should be made only within "the United States and its possessions."

At the end of 2007, foundations No. 2 and No. 3 had total assets of $256 million. These organizations provide grants to institutions whose activities fall into five areas: private higher education, secondary education, graduate theological education, health care, and public television. The foundations seek to strengthen four-year liberal arts colleges that stress good teaching and where a majority of students major in humanities, science, and mathematics. They also favor schools that serve disadvantaged populations and support innovative professional development programs aimed at high school teachers. The foundations' health care emphasis is on encouraging caring attitudes, and they have provided funding for the Public Broadcasting System (PBS).

In 2007, the foundations awarded $11.8 million in grants. These grants included a donation of $350,000 to a Los Angeles television station for a documentary on Joseph Stalin and his relations with the Allies, $200,000 to Berea College for renovation of residential buildings, $200,000 to Duke University Medical Center for integrative self-care for physicians, $200,000 to Mills College for construction of a natural science facility, $200,000 to the Princeton Theological Seminary for library special collections, and $200,000 to Swarthmore College for endowment of an Arabic program.

---

court dismissed all the government's charges. In his decision, the judge remarked on "the great number of witnesses . . . competitors as well as customers of Alcoa, who have completely exculpated Alcoa from blame and have praised its fairness as well as its helpfulness to the aluminum industry. . . . Such conduct of those witnesses, nearly all of whom were entirely independent, is in great part a tribute to Mr. Arthur V. Davis." The judge also described Davis as the man "who, chiefly and primarily, has built up and made Alcoa what it is today." The federal government appealed to overturn the judge's decision, and the case continued to be heard in appellate and district courts. Finally, in 1950, a district court judge ruled against the divestiture of Alcoa.

During World War II, aluminum was once again a strategic war material, especially for the construction of aircraft. Alcoa expanded production capacity to a vast degree, building twenty-two plants that were temporarily owned and operated by the federal government. Aluminum output climbed to seven times its prewar level. Davis spent much time in Washington, D.C., coordinating aluminum sales with the government. He received a Presidential Certificate of Merit for his wartime achievements. After the war, the disposal of the government's aluminum plants was a critical element in creating new competitors and settling the antitrust case without overt penalty to Alcoa. Davis was instrumental in providing royalty-free patent access for the new competitors.

Davis largely withdrew from direct management of Alcoa by the end of the 1940's and retired from the company in 1957. He moved to Florida and became a major real estate investor. His holdings included significant properties in the city of Miami, and he had other property interests in the Bahamas and Cuba.

LEGACY

Davis was a stocky man with a bulldog appearance and personality. He was notoriously egocentric and bullying. His wealth developed as he shaped Alcoa into a remarkably successful firm that provided valuable products and good jobs. Davis was able to identify and motivate talented employees to achieve technological progress and efficiency. By 1935, Alcoa was the nation's twenty-seventh largest industrial corporation. Despite the appearance of monopoly, neither its profits nor its pricing reflected monopoly behavior. Alcoa was remarkably diplomatic in its dealings with customers, competitors, and the government.

Davis left an estate of about $400 million, much of it deriving from his real estate activities through his Arvida Corporation, a Florida real estate development company. He was reportedly the fifth-richest man in America. About $300 million of his estate was distributed to his foundations.

—Paul B. Trescott

FURTHER READING

Carr, Charles C. *Alcoa: An American Enterprise.* New York: Rinehart, 1952. Carr was a longtime director of public relations for Alcoa, but his book is solid narrative, not mere puffery.

Graham, Margaret B. W., and Bettye H. Pruitt. *R and D for Industry: A Century of Technical Innovation at Alcoa.* Cambridge, England: Cambridge University Press, 1990. Stresses Davis's involvement in the firm's steady attention to improving technology.

Jacobs, David G., ed. *The Foundation Directory.* 31st ed. New York: Foundation Center, 2009. The Davis foundations are described at pages 477-478.

McGoun, William E. *Southeast Florida Pioneers: The Palm and Treasure Coasts.* Sarasota, Fla.: Pineapple Press, 1998. Chapter 27 examines Davis's real estate activities.

Smith, George David. *From Monopoly to Competition: The Transformations of Alcoa, 1888-1986.* New York: Cambridge University Press, 1988. Demonstrates Davis's skill in managing a monopoly without his company looking like one.

See also: James Buchanan Duke; Charles Engelhard, Jr.; Meyer Guggenheim; Solomon R. Guggenheim; Andrew Mellon; Richard B. Mellon; Simón Iturri Patiño.

JOHN DEERE
American entrepreneur, industrialist, and merchant

Deere employed blacksmith skills, product insight, and marketing instinct to create an international business. He designed a steel plow that was the founding product for his company, the basis for one of the oldest existing businesses in the United States, and the source of his wealth.

Born: February 7, 1804; Rutland, Vermont
Died: May 17, 1886; Moline, Illinois
Sources of wealth: Patents; manufacturing; sale of products
Bequeathal of wealth: Children

EARLY LIFE
John Deere was born in 1804 in Rutland, Vermont, the youngest of five children of William Rinold Deere and Sarah (née Yates) Deere. A year after John's birth, William, a tailor, moved the family to Middlebury, Vermont. In 1808, William embarked on a trip to England but did not return. Since the family's income was modest, Deere received a basic education at the local school, and at the age of seventeen he was apprenticed as a blacksmith to Captain Benjamin Lawrence. In exchange for four years of service to Lawrence beginning in 1821, Deere earned his room and board, clothing, a modest income, and the essential skills necessary to be a good craftsman. Afterward, Deere honed his skills as a journeyman, working for several other blacksmiths, before opening his own shop.

FIRST VENTURES
Deere continuously sharpened his skills and soon earned a reputation as a fine craftsman. After marrying Demarius Lamb in 1827 and starting a family, Deere borrowed funds to buy land and build his own smithy. On two separate occasions fire destroyed the shop, leaving Deere in debt at a time when Vermont was suffering from an economic depression. Because of bleak local circumstances, Deere chose to venture west to seek his fortune. In 1836, he temporarily left his family behind and followed several other Vermont natives to Grand Detour, Illinois. In this new community, Deere quickly found high demand for his blacksmith skills. Within two days of his arrival, Deere's forge was in operation.

MATURE WEALTH
Soon after arriving in Illinois, Deere learned that wooden and iron plows stuck in the rich midwestern soil, making the task of cultivation a difficult one for farmers. Deere experimented, at first using an old abandoned sawmill blade, and he concluded that highly polished steel and a newly shaped moldboard would improve tilling. In 1838, in partnership with Major Leonard Andrus, Deere built and sold three steel plows. Over the next few years, Deere's business continued to grow; by 1846 his company was manufacturing one thousand plows annually.

As the need for raw materials and improved transportation services increased, Deere decided to relocate his business seventy-five miles southwest, along the Mississippi River in Moline, Illinois. Leaving his old partner behind, he took on new associates Robert N. Tate and John M. Gould. This affiliation allowed Deere to concentrate on sales and marketing. The associa-

John Deere. (©Bettmann/CORBIS)

FIG. 2.—Hand plow.

A wood engraving of John Deere's steel plow. Deere's invention was the founding product for his company and the source of his wealth. (The Granger Collection, New York)

tion lasted until 1852. In the following year, Deere's son Charles entered the company as its bookkeeper.

By 1857, Deere's company was producing ten thousand plows annually but was also suffering from cash flow problems. The firm was in jeopardy during the Panic of 1857, but reorganization gave Charles management control. With John as the president and Charles overseeing daily operations, the company avoided bankruptcy. In 1863, John's son-in-law Stephen H. Velie joined the company, and Deere helped organize the First National Bank of Moline. Demarius Deere died in 1865, and John married her sister Lucinda in 1867.

After operating for thirty-one years as a partnership or single proprietorship, the business in 1868 incorporated under the name John Deere & Company. Deere became the second mayor of Moline in 1873. Thirteen years later, Deere died in Moline at the age of eighty-two.

LEGACY

While John Deere was not the first person to manufacture plows from steel, his determination, perceptiveness, energy, and ingenuity resulted in a product that made his name synonymous with the steel plow industry. He de-

signed and sold a workable plow for homesteaders who were transforming American prairie lands into productive farmlands. By designing reliable agricultural equipment, modernizing production, and using innovative marketing, Deere established an industrial empire.

—*Cynthia J. W. Svoboda*

FURTHER READING

Broehl, Wayne G., Jr. *John Deere's Company: A History of Deere & Company and Its Times*. New York: Doubleday, 1984.

Dahlstrom, Neil, and Jeremy Dahlstrom. *The John Deere Story: A Biography of Plowmakers John and Charles Deere*. DeKalb: Northern Illinois University Press, 2005.

Magee, David. *The John Deere Way: Performance That Endures*. Hoboken, N.J.: Wiley, 2005.

See also: Peter Cooper; George Eastman; Thomas Edison; Cyrus Hall McCormick; Samuel F. B. Morse; George Mortimer Pullman; Isaac Merrit Singer; George Westinghouse.

MICHAEL DELL
American entrepreneur, computer engineer, and industrialist

Dell is one of the wealthiest technology magnates in the United States. He proved that a direct-order system for selling computers could work and could also be very profitable. He and his wife have established a foundation that seeks to end world poverty and to improve urban education.

Born: February 23, 1965; Houston, Texas
Also known as: Michael Saul Dell
Sources of wealth: Computer industry; sale of products
Bequeathal of wealth: Charity

EARLY LIFE
Michael Saul Dell was born in 1965 in Houston, Texas. He attended school there and was an average student. He was successful in other endeavors, making more than $10,000 by selling the *Houston Post* newspaper. He also gained experience with computers and began thinking about the computer business.

Michael Dell. (AP/Wide World Photos)

Dell attended the University of Texas at Austin, and while in college he started his own computer firm, PC's Limited, in 1984. His company soon proved successful. Dell obtained additional capital from family members and dropped out of school to devote himself to his business. Although he did not graduate from the University of Texas at Austin, he later donated more than $50 million to the school. In 1989, Dell married Susan Lieberman, who had worked in commercial real estate and owned a fashion boutique. The couple had four children and made their home in Austin.

FIRST VENTURES
In 1987, PC's Limited changed its name to Dell Computer Corporation, and since 2003 the company has been called Dell, Inc. In its early years, the company initiated a number of innovations. Rather than simply selling personal computers, the company let customers adapt its products to meet their needs. The firm also sold and advertised its products directly to the public instead of in retail stores or other venues, and its advertisements listed product prices. These practices enabled the firm to turn a profit and to generate millions of dollars worth of revenue.

MATURE WEALTH
Michael Dell continued his practice of advertising prices and selling directly to the public. He also managed to convince the public to buy his computers without testing them first. Conventional wisdom at the time was that people would want to try out a personal computer before purchasing it. Dell, however, gambled that his products' reduced prices and custom-ordered features would outweigh customers' desire for a trial run. He was right, and his business boomed. In addition to selling to individuals, the company garnered lucrative contracts with major businesses and the government.

Dell Computer Corporation grew rapidly from 1987 through the early 1990's, expanding its customer service and technical support departments to keep up with customers' demands. However, in 1993 and 1994 the company had a series of setbacks. The company's rapid hiring failed to keep pace with its sluggish revenue growth. The firm also miscalculated market demand for its laptop computers and other products. As a result, the corporation lost money for the first time in 1993. Michael Dell hired some experienced managers and introduced new products. He also stopped selling his computers in retail stores and refocused his marketing efforts on direct sales, eventually enabling customers to order products via the telephone or the Internet.

After 1995, the company grew quickly; by 1998, it proclaimed itself to be the largest desktop-computer seller in the world and one of the largest overall computer sales companies. The next step was to move into the peripheral market, including the market for printers and servers. Dell Computer sought to become a one-stop shop, where customers could purchase all computer-related products and accessories, and where these products would be compatible. Company sales suffered after the terrorist attacks on September 11, 2001, and Dell had to lay off thousands of employees. The company, however, continued to gain market share. However, by the mid-2000's, other computer companies had caught up with Dell. Starting in 2002, the corporation tried selling its products at retail kiosks and opened a store, but these efforts failed. Dell was more successful in its partnerships with Wal-Mart Corporation, Sam's Club, Best Buy, and other retailers who sold its products.

Michael Dell remained chief executive officer of the company until 2004, when he stepped down and became chairman of the board; he reassumed the position of chief executive officer in 2007. At this time, Dell, Inc., sought to expand into developing markets, including those in Brazil and Russia.

Michael Dell's personal worth significantly declined as a result of the economic recession that began in 2008. It is estimated that his wealth decreased about 25 percent between 2001 and 2009, but he still was worth about $12 billion. He was number 37 on *Forbes* magazine's 2010 billionaires list, with an estimated net worth of $13.5 billion. Dell has been involved in philanthropic efforts. He and has wife established the Michael and Susan Dell Foundation, which seeks to improve education and childhood health and to eliminate urban poverty.

LEGACY

Michael Dell was one of the pioneers of the personal computer industry, developing techniques for manufacturing and marketing these products. In the early 2000's, his company was the most profitable computer manufac-

---

THE MICHAEL AND SUSAN DELL FOUNDATION

In 1999, Michael Dell and his wife Susan established a foundation that, in the words of its Web site, supports "children's causes as a way to make an even greater difference in a measurable way, particularly for those children living in urban poverty." The foundation focuses on three areas—urban education, childhood health, and the economic stability of families—and has provided assistance in the United States, Africa, and India.

About one-third of the foundation's grants are allocated to education. The organization has identified areas in the United States where large school districts are underperforming and seeks to improve education through the use of technology and by providing scholarships to encourage children to attend college. In addition, the foundation addresses literacy issues in areas outside the United States.

The organization also seeks to improve childhood health, particularly in India, where there are no health care services in many urban slums. Among its services, the foundation provides meningitis vaccinations and supports clean water initiatives. In the United States, the organization is addressing childhood obesity, which some medical experts claim is epidemic and has increased the incidence of type 2 diabetes in children. Michael and Susan Dell's work on behalf of health care is evident at the University of Texas at Austin, where the couple have financed construction of three medical facilities: Dell Children's Medical Center, Dell Pediatric Research Institute, and the Michael and Susan Dell Center for Advancement of Healthy Living. In the area of family economic stability, the foundation has provided small loans for families and is developing measures to determine whether these loans are effective.

---

turer in the world. Although it eventually was eclipsed by other companies, Dell, Inc., remained one of the largest computer manufacturers. The company successfully employed both the direct-marketing concept, selling its products directly to end users instead of offering computers in retail stores, and the customization of computers to customers' specification. Through his foundation, Dell has sought to improve the lives of children, and he has also made generous donations to the University of Texas at Austin.

—Scott A. Merriman

FURTHER READING

Dell, Michael, and Catherine Freeman. *Direct from Dell: Strategies That Revolutionized an Industry.* New York: Harper Business, 1999. This book was written at the height of Dell's early fame, just after his company became the largest computer seller. Includes an index and a time line.

Hazeldine, Simon, Chris J. Norton, and Michael Dell.

Bare Knuckle Customer Service: How to Deliver a Knockout Customer Experience and Hammer the Competition. New York: Lean Marketing Press, 2008. Includes a foreword by Dell and information about how to organize a successful customer service program. One of the authors worked with the customer service department at Dell, Inc. Offers several real-world examples, including a chapter on one very effective customer service effort.

Holzner, Steven. *How Dell Does It*. New York: McGraw-Hill, 2005. Informative exploration of why Dell was successful and how that success can be copied.

Iaquinto, Anthony, and Stephen Spinelli, Jr. *Never Bet the Farm: How Entrepreneurs Take Risks, Make Deci-sions, and How You Can, Too*. Hoboken, N.J.: Jossey-Bass, 2006. Discusses several principles for running a business. Includes a list of university centers that provide help to entrepreneurs and a selected bibliography.

Payton, Robert L., and Michael P. Moody. *Understanding Philanthropy: Its Meaning and Mission*. Bloomington: Indiana University Press, 2008. Discusses the meaning and methods of philanthropy. Includes a bibliography and source notes for the text.

See also: Paul Allen; Steven Ballmer; Jeff Bezos; Sergey Brin; Mark Cuban; Larry Ellison; Bill Gates; Steve Jobs; Gordon E. Moore; David Packard; H. Ross Perot.

ELIAS HASKET DERBY
American merchant

Derby contributed to the growth of commerce and prosperity in Salem, Massachusetts, while amassing the largest fortune in the United States in the eighteenth century. The privateers of Salem, many of them financed and owned by Derby, contributed significantly to the sea defense of the colonies during the American Revolution. After the war, duties imposed on imports from the east Indian trade provided revenue for a stable federal government.

Born: August 16, 1739; Salem, Massachusetts
Died: September 8, 1799; Salem, Massachusetts
Also known as: America's First Millionaire
Sources of wealth: Trade; shipping; privateering
Bequeathal of wealth: Children

EARLY LIFE
Elias Hasket Derby was born on August 16, 1739, in Salem, Massachusetts, the son of Richard Derby, Sr., a Salem sea captain and shipowner. Derby's two brothers became sea captains, while he was trained as a merchant in his father's counting house. At the age of fifteen, having studied naval architecture and maritime trade, he was already keeping his father's accounts. Richard Derby, Sr., retired by 1760, sending his ships out under other captains, including his sons Richard, Jr., and John, and entrusting Derby with control of the land operations of the family business.

In 1762, Derby married Elizabeth Crowninshield. The couple moved into a brick Georgian-style house that Richard, Sr., built for them. Their home was the earliest brick house in Salem and one of the finest surviving examples of Georgian architecture. From the windows of this house, where his seven children were born, Derby could look out on the Derby Wharf and supervise the loading and unloading of his ships.

FIRST VENTURES
Shipping was an enterprising and profitable industry in coastal New England in the mid-eighteenth century. Able captains and shipowners were also traders, buying goods in one port to sell at a profit in another. The Derby ships carried New England products, such as lumber and fish, to the West Indies, where they would take on cargoes of molasses, sugar, and coffee, then sail on to Spain, Gibraltar, and Portugal for luxury goods, such as wine, furniture and, fine textiles. Shipping was a risky business. During the late colonial era, hostilities between the British and French interfered with the trade upon which Salem depended. French privateers in the West Indies captured many Salem vessels, including numerous Derby ships, selling the ships and their cargo and ransoming their crews. In 1760, Derby, his father, and his brother Richard Derby, Jr., were among the signers of a petition to the colonial governor requesting a convoy for protection of the commercial fleet.

Finding the British government's tariffs and restrictions on colonial trade oppressive, the Derbys were among those who supported the movement for independence from Great Britain. Derby and Richard, Jr., were members of the Salem regiment when hostilities broke out in 1775. Captain John Derby, sailing in a fast Derby ship, was the first to carry the news of the Battle of Lexington to London and to return to the colonies with the British response.

MATURE WEALTH

When war was declared, Derby was ready. His first privateer, the *Sturdy Beggar*, set sail in 1776, capturing several British merchant ships, selling their cargoes, and ransoming their crews. The Salem merchant fleet turned to privateering against the British in earnest. By 1778, privateering had become one of Salem's principal industries, with larger and faster ships being built and armed specifically for the purpose of capturing British ships. The privateers were commissioned by the Provincial Congress to interfere with British commercial and naval operations, but the profits went to the shipowners. Derby underwrote more privateering ventures than any other individual in the American colonies. He was lucky; he lost only one ship during the revolution. He was also an innovator, bringing shipbuilders to Salem to construct the strongest and fastest ships. Privateering during the American Revolution offered employment for Salem's men, provided scarce goods to the colonies, and contributed a considerable part to the American war at sea. Privateering during the revolution also made Derby a wealthy man.

When the war ended in 1783, Derby looked east for new markets, new ports, and new uses for his strong, fast ships. The traditional West Indian ports, controlled by the British, were now closed to the Americans. However, the Indian Ocean was now open to American vessels since they were no longer restricted by the British East India Company's commercial monopoly. Derby was a leader in reinventing American commerce. In 1784, he sent the first American ship to St. Petersburg. Yankee ships began to venture farther east from bases in Cape Town and Mauritius, buying and selling cargoes of tea, spices, silks, and porcelain. By 1785, when he sent his first ship to China, Derby was already the wealthiest merchant in Salem. The ship *Grand Turk* had been built for him as a privateer in 1781; in 1785, it was one of the first American vessels to arrive in Canton.

In 1787, Derby launched his family in the India trade. A Derby ship was the first to fly the American flag in Cal-

---

> ## THE DERBY SUMMER HOUSE
>
> The Derby Summer House was designed for Elias Hasket Derby in 1793 by Samuel McIntire, the most prominent wood-carver, house builder, and cabinetmaker in Salem, Massachusetts. McIntire constructed the house on Derby's farm in Danvers (now part of Peabody), Massachusetts, during the summer of 1794.
>
> The lovely Summer House is a rare and important example of American Federal architecture. It is a two-story structure located in the center of a formally landscaped garden. The lower story is entered by an arched entrance, which was originally open and designed for shelter from the rain. The room above was designed for tea or a light afternoon meal. This peaceful and serene room, with its coved ceiling, paneled wainscoting, built-in cupboards for tea implements, and ornamental Chinese figures, is a cool and lovely place with a view of the beautifully landscaped gardens below.
>
> The Summer House, with its Palladian character and exquisitely carved details, epitomizes the American Federal style of architecture as practiced by McIntire. The roof is dominated by two figures, known as the Reaper and the Milkmaid, which were carved by the Skillin Brothers of Boston. The urns on the roof, the festoons over the windows, and the columns were carved by McIntire himself.
>
> In 1901, Ellen Peabody Endicott, the wife of William Crowninshield Endicott, Sr., bought the Summer House and had it moved to her summer house and farm, Glen Magna, located four miles away in Danvers. The Summer House remained there in the twenty-first century, sited in gardens designed by Frederick Law Olmsted and George Heussler. The Endicott family owned Glen Magna until 1958, when Louise Thoron Endicott, the wife of William Crowninshield Endicott, Jr., willed it to the Danvers Historical Society. The Derby Summer House has been listed on the National Register of Historic Places since 1968. The Glen Magna house and gardens are a popular spot for weddings and other functions, and the gardens and Summer House can be visited and enjoyed by the public.

---

cutta harbor, and Derby ships were the first to carry cargoes of cotton from Bombay to China. Derby was the first Salem merchant to employ a supercargo (business agent) on his ships. He sent his son Elias Hasket Derby, Jr., known as Hasket, on the *Grand Turk*. Hasket spent three years on the island of Mauritius, selling the ship's cargo of American products and then selling the *Grand Turk* itself, buying two more ships with the proceeds. Hasket ultimately returned to Salem with goods from India that were sold at an enormous profit at his father's store on Derby Wharf.

Derby ships never took part in the slave trade, and Derby was considered a benevolent employer. He was reputed to provide fresh vegetables to his seamen, a provision that was unusual in his day. He also took care of the families of his employees who died or were disabled in his service.

In the postrevolutionary period, some of Derby's wealth was spent on commissioning and building a number of Salem's important Federal-style houses. In 1780, Derby and his wife Elizabeth had commissioned Salem carpenter Samuel McIntire to build them a larger house next door to their brick Georgian house on the waterfront. With Derby patronage, McIntire would become a significant New England wood-carver and architect. The Derbys never occupied the new house. Elizabeth Derby was an ambitious woman who desired a house in a newer, more fashionable neighborhood, away from the noises and odors of the commercial waterfront. An uptown mansion was purchased and restored with many McIntire details. At the same time, a grand mansion house was planned. Initially designed by Boston architect Charles Bulfinch, the final design was executed by McIntire. The ornate Derby Mansion was completed in 1799. Derby and Elizabeth occupied it for only a few months, as first Elizabeth and then Derby died in 1799. At the time of his death, Derby's fortune was worth more than $1 million, earning him the title of America's First Millionaire.

LEGACY

Elias Hasket Derby's legacy was his contribution to the development of an American style of architecture. His patronage gave Samuel McIntire the opportunity to design some of America's most significant eighteenth century buildings. Derby also provided patronage to landscape gardener George Heussler, whom Derby hired in 1790. Heussler worked on both of Derby's town residences and his farm, and he was responsible for a new style of beautifully landscaped gardens at the homes of the wealthy in Essex County, Massachusetts.

Derby died within a few months of moving into his grand mansion, and his eldest son, Elias Hasket Derby, Jr., inherited Derby's farm and mansion. Derby's son lived in the mansion for a decade before putting it up for sale and moving to Charlestown. The trade embargo and the War of 1812 had damaged Salem's economy, and no buyer was found for the large and elaborate residence. In 1815, the mansion was torn down and the land given to the town for a permanent market, which eventually became Derby Square.

—Susan Butterworth

FURTHER READING

Bean, Susan S. *Yankee India: American Commercial and Cultural Encounters with India in the Age of Sail, 1784-1860*. Salem, Mass.: Peabody Essex Museum, 2001. The book's first section, "Pioneering the India Trade," discusses Derby's role in the east India trade. Explains the nature of privateering and the Salem trade in the decades before and after the American Revolution, which are essential to understanding the source of Derby's wealth.

Derby, Elias Hasket. *Memoir of Elias Hasket Derby, Merchant of Salem, Massachusetts*. 1857. Reprint. Salem, Mass.: The New England & Virginia Company, 2002. A reprint of an article that originally appeared in the February, 1857, issue of *Hunt's Merchant's Magazine and Commercial Review*. This unsigned biographical work makes use of letters and primary sources to reconstruct Derby's genealogy, early life, role in pre- and post-Revolutionary War trade, privateering, and legacy.

Howard, Hugh. *Dr. Kimball and Mr. Jefferson: Rediscovering the Founding Fathers of American Architecture*. New York: Bloomsbury USA, 2006. This study of Fiske Kimball, historian and museum director who pioneered research into early American architecture, includes a chapter "Meanwhile in Massachusetts," with information on the Derby family and the Derby Mansion in Salem. Clear and concise.

Kimball, Fiske. *The Elias Hasket Derby Mansion in Salem*. Salem, Mass.: Essex Institute, 1924. A twenty-page monograph followed by reproductions of the original plans and drawings of the mansion. A thorough study of primary documents, including letters, invoices, and drawings.

_____. *Mr. Samuel McIntire, Carver: The Architect of Salem*. Portland, Maine: Southworth-Anthoensen Press, published for the Essex Institute of Salem, Mass., 1940. Reprint. Gloucester, Mass.: P. Smith, 1966. Kimball's research into original drawings and documents is the basis for this still important source. Contains much information on the Derby houses and numerous photographs and drawings.

Lahikainen, Dean T. *Samuel McIntire: Carving an American Style*. Lebanon, N.H.: University Press of New England, 2007. Relies on Kimball's 1940 volume on McIntire for much of its information. Includes an updated bibliography and format, as well as beautiful color plates and discussion of the Derby houses and furnishings.

See also: Moses Brown; Paul Cuffe; Benjamin Franklin; Stephen Girard; John Hancock; Robert Morris; Samuel Slater; Israel Thorndike; Stephen Van Rensselaer III; George Washington.

CHARLES HENRY DE SOYSA
Sri Lankan landowner, agriculturist, and merchant

De Soysa, a native of Ceylon born to privilege, distinguished himself during the height of British colonial rule by his efficient development of thousands of acres of fertile farmland, as well as the use of his wealth to fund hundreds of public projects of benefit to his country.

Born: March 3, 1836; Muratuwa, Ceylon (now in Sri Lanka)
Died: September 29, 1890; Muratuwa, Ceylon
Also known as: Sir Charles Henry de Soysa
Sources of wealth: Inheritance; real estate; agricultural products
Bequeathal of wealth: Children; charity; medical institution

EARLY LIFE
By the time Sir Charles Henry de Soysa (dah SOY-sah) was born in 1836, his father, Jeronis, was among the wealthiest traders in southwest coastal Ceylon (now Sri Lanka). By cooperating with the British colonial government, Jeronis de Soysa prospered, trading in commodities, such as coffee, cinnamon, and coconut. During the nation's economic downturns, he enhanced his wealth by purchasing thousands of acres of relatively cheap but fertile farmland.

An only child (his sister died in infancy), young Charles grew up mindful that this financial empire would be his inheritance. However, in ways that would foreshadow his later life, the young boy respected the reach and magnitude of his father's financial resources, as well as his father's willingness to dedicate large sums of money to the public good, building roads, irrigation systems, schools, and hospitals in the impoverished towns that serviced his plantations.

FIRST VENTURES
At eighteen, de Soysa was among the first class accepted at St. Thomas College in nearby Mutwal. Poor health would compel de Soysa to return to his family estate, and he would complete his general education with tutors. However, his father provided him an invaluable education in entrepreneurship and estate management by arranging for de Soysa to receive additional training from internationally renowned tutors with backgrounds in business and finance.

In 1862, when de Soysa was twenty-six, his father died suddenly. De Soysa was prepared for this death, and he quietly assumed control of his father's multimillion-dollar commodities empire. In 1863, de Soysa married the only daughter of another wealthy Ceylonese planter. The combined wealth of both families gave the young couple a celebrity and influence that were enjoyed by few Ceylonese. However, even as he moved his young bride into a lavish mansion on more than 130 acres on the outskirts of Moratuwa, and even as his family grew to fourteen children, de Soysa had little interest in cultivating an ostentatious lifestyle. One of his few indulgences was the purchase of ornamental birds, like peacocks, and he also enjoyed watching the movements of a herd of his own elephants. Out of respect for his father, he was dedicated to expanding the resources his father had left him in order to pay tribute to the man who had shaped de Soysa's moral vision of wealth as a means to achieve significant public good.

MATURE WEALTH
With relatively minor investments in cinnamon, citronella, and coconuts, de Soysa recognized the danger of relying too heavily on Ceylon's fickle coffee crop, as his father had done. De Soysa controlled thousands of acres of coffee plantations, enough to survive the crop's numerous cycles of failure. During a cataclysmic coffee bust in the 1880's, when the crop was destroyed by a fast-spreading leaf disease, de Soysa's enterprises were among the few to prosper. However, he looked to expand his agricultural concerns into more stable crops, notably tea, that were amenable to Ceylon's growing season. Within a decade, his tea was among the most popular products in the British Empire, valued for its light color and sweetness.

A savvy and visionary manager, de Soysa reorganized his father's farming estates, reducing staff, expanding benefits for workers, and emphasizing efficient crop storage to lessen the likelihood of spoilage and rot. He expanded his range of agricultural interests by importing cattle from Australia and India; the cows were used for their milk, and the bulls were used to transport produce among de Soysa's more than sixty estates, with a total of nearly twenty-five thousand acres. He purchased tracts of prime land with the hope of future development and invested in mining operations.

His interest in improving the efficiency of his agricultural operations never waned. Indeed, he gave the colonial government a considerable amount of money and nearly one hundred acres near Kanatte in order to set up an experimental model farm, on which agricultural research promoted technological advances in irrigation systems and crop rotation practices. Not everything he tried succeeded, including a catastrophic attempt to raise cotton, but de Soysa became renowned for his entrepreneurial spirit, his support of agricultural research, and his dedication to expanding the cash crop base of his island country.

However, what made de Soysa a legendary figure among the people of Ceylon was his unparalleled interest in philanthropic enterprises. Despite being the richest Ceylonese of any era, de Soysa was known for mingling among working-class people, talking and laughing with the poorest. He made charitable contributions without the expectation of recognition; for de Soysa, wealth was a means to an end, not an end in itself. Modest, self-effacing, and humble, he sought simply to help as many

of the needy as he could. From the moment he controlled his family's holdings, he directed that a significant part of his inheritance would be distributed to local communities. Although most of his donations financed public works projects, such as hospitals, schools, road systems, and railroad tracks, he always welcomed individual petitioners who came to his home in search of financial assistance. De Soysa's biography recounts his encounters with people seeking funds and his acts of charity, which were marked by fabulous signs of divine pleasure.

In connection with the much publicized state visit of the Prince and Princess of Wales to Ceylon in 1875, de Soysa financed the construction of and provided funding for the staff and faculty for two preparatory schools in Moratuwa that were named in honor of the visiting royalty when the schools opened in 1876. He constructed clinics to serve the country's poorest inland territories. At the height of the coffee crisis, de Soysa awarded an

DE SOYSA HOSPITAL FOR WOMEN

As a generous philanthropist concerned with the welfare of the indigent and passionately committed to public causes for which there were clear and evident solutions, Ceylonese entrepreneur Charles Henry de Soysa took up the plight of poor women, who in the mid-nineteenth century often faced the difficult trials of childbirth without hospital care. Although the medical system, which received the patronage of British colonial officials, provided substantial health care for most Ceylonese, the nation's poorest people did not benefit. Indeed, in the late 1870's, when de Soysa, himself the father of fourteen children, was first made aware of the dimensions of the problem, Ceylon's underclass had one of the highest infant and maternal mortality rates in Asia.

Typical of his legendary magnanimity, de Soysa committed all the funds necessary to begin construction of what would be only the second lying-in hospital in Asia, a facility designed to provide medical care during the final stages of pregnancy and after childbirth. With de Soysa's backing, property was secured in Moratuwa, the home base of de Soysa's economic empire, and on December 13, 1879, the De Soysa Lying-in Home was opened. The facility had twenty-two beds and supervised fifty-two births during its first year of operation. The hospital continued to receive financial assistance during de Soysa's lifetime and after his death in 1890.

The hospital succeeded in its mission, not only providing cutting-edge care without charge to the poor but also serving as a teaching hospital, where midwives and nurses were trained to assist in childbirths. Within fifteen years, the number of deliveries at the facility had risen to more than five hundred annually. During the early twentieth century, the hospital broke new ground in Ceylonese medicine, conducting the nation's first successful cesarean section in 1905, opening the country's first fully equipped operating theater in 1907, and accepting the first class of students trained in obstetrics and gynecology in 1915. By the 1920's, the facility was assisting in more than two thousand births annually and had branched into providing preventative care for a variety of early infant illnesses.

In 1940, a new administrative office building was added to the facility, which was then renamed the De Soysa Hospital for Women. In conjunction with the newly opened University of Colombo, the hospital took the lead in training a new generation of physicians and nurses in maternal and infant care. After Sri Lanka's independence, the facility pioneered the introduction of family planning and education about safe sex practices. Beginning in the 1980's, the hospital expanded its services to treat medical disorders in pregnant women that threatened the health of their babies. The facility opened its first intensive care unit in the early 1990's. De Soysa Hospital for Women has been recognized by UNICEF (United Nations International Children's Emergency Fund) for its exemplary dedication to the welfare of children, its first-rate training program, and its mission to provide Sri Lanka with top-notch maternity care.

acre of prime farmland to each of one hundred families devastated by the economic collapse. An Anglican, de Soysa nevertheless paid for the construction of Buddhist temples, recognizing the central position that this religion held for the Ceylonese people. He donated vast sums to build and staff new hospitals, both in Ceylon and in London, including several facilities devoted to the treatment of children's diseases.

On August 2, 1890, de Soysa was bitten by a rabid street dog and on September 29, he died from complications of the attack. He was only fifty-four years old. His death was an occasion of unprecedented national mourning. His funeral, held two days after his death, was said to be the largest single public gathering in Asia in the entire nineteenth century. His estate was later set at more than a million rupees, excluding his numerous property holdings. It remains the largest individual estate in Sri Lankan history.

LEGACY

The achievement of de Soysa, whose accumulated wealth matched or exceeded most Victorian-era magnates, never secured international attention, largely because he did not seek such celebrity. His legacy is his unselfish devotion to his country. At a time when Ceylon, as a British colonial outpost, was uncertain of its own cultural identity, de Soysa emerged as his tiny island's most powerful figure. His interest in developing new technologies for addressing agricultural production problems and his visionary sense of opening Ceylon's economic markets to a wider variety of crops make de Soysa one of the most important Sri Lankans of any era. However, his legendary acts of munificence and his genuine compassion for the problems facing Sri Lanka's poorest classes have secured for him a place of profound respect and near-worship in his home nation, undiminished more than a century after his death.

—*Joseph Dewey*

FURTHER READING

Duncan, James S. *In the Shadows of the Tropics: Climate, Race, and Biopower in Nineteenth Century Ceylon*. Surrey, England: Ashgate, 2007. Study of the revolution in the coffee plantation system in Ceylon during the mid-nineteenth century. Explains Sri Lanka's role as a British possession and discusses the coffee crisis of the 1880's.

Peebles, Patrick. *The History of Sri Lanka*. Westport, Conn.: Greenwood Press, 2006. Important and accessible study of the long history of the nation, with chapters devoted to the economic success in the nineteenth century, which, as argued here, was largely the legacy of de Soysa and his estates system.

_____. *Social Change in Nineteenth Century Ceylon*. Colombia, Mo.: South Asia Books, 1995. Far-reaching examination of de Soysa's era that includes discussions of the economic evolution and the religious, social, and cultural conditions. Discusses de Soysa's philanthropy and its place in the emergence of Ceylon as an independent nation.

Pendergrast, Mark. *Uncommon Grounds: The History of Coffee and How It Transformed Our World*. New York: Basic Books, 2000. A sweeping look at more than four centuries of coffee production. Focuses on the twentieth century but positions Sri Lanka's defining cash crop of de Soysa's era within a historical context to understand the importance of the crop to British interests.

Wenzlhuemer, Roland. *From Coffee to Tea Cultivation in Ceylon, 1880-1900: An Economic and Social History*. Boston: Brill, 2008. Landmark account of the rise of de Soysa's financial empire, specifically his decision to branch out into tea production, and its impact on the development of Ceylon.

See also: Ninth Duke of Bedford; John Deere; Cyrus Hall McCormick.

CLARENCE DILLON
American investment banker and wine connoisseur

In the era immediately following World War I, a period associated with reckless speculation and extravagant spending among the wealthy, Dillon maintained a quiet, bold, gentlemanly pragmatism that enabled him to broker some of the decade's most significant financial transactions. These deals made his investment bank—Dillon, Read, and Company—among the most influential institutions of its era.

Born: September 27, 1882; San Antonio, Texas
Died: April 14, 1979; Far Hills, New Jersey
Also known as: Clarence Lapowski (birth name)
Source of wealth: Banking
Bequeathal of wealth: Children; relatives

EARLY LIFE

Samuel Lapowski, a penniless Polish Jew who had immigrated to the United States in the 1870's, arrived in San Antonio, Texas, in 1878. The town was already shaking free of its cattle culture provincialism. Railroad service enabled the city to become a destination for immigrants searching for opportunities that were disappearing in the industrial Northeast. Lapowski opened a clothing business. He married, and in 1882 his only child, Clarence, was born.

Lapowski, who wanted his son to realize the fullest promise of their adopted country, saw education as the foundation of that success. The family became naturalized citizens in 1891 and Lapowski changed his family's name to Dillon, an Americanized version of his French mother's maiden name. The clothing business thrived and the family relocated to Abilene, Texas. Samuel arranged for Clarence to attend the prestigious Worcester Academy in Massachusetts, a preparatory school considered a feeder campus for Harvard University.

FIRST VENTURES

His years at Harvard gave Clarence Dillon his first taste of the sophisticated world of the wealthy. He loved the patrician lifestyle and was given the nickname Baron. When he completed his education at Harvard in 1905, he was the only graduate to own a car. Dillon married Anne McEldin Douglass in 1908. Shortly before his marriage, he had been injured in Milwaukee, when, as he was waiting at a railroad station, an express train rode through at full speed at the same time that a Saint Bernard was crossing the tracks. The train hit the large dog, throwing

its body at the crowd at the platform and injuring Dillon's skull, which put him in a coma for a week. The couple took an extended two-year tour of Europe after the wedding, primarily in Switzerland and in southern France, where Dillon came to love the picturesque vineyard country. When Dillon returned, at the recommendation of a Harvard classmate he joined the prestigious brokerage firm of William A. Read & Company, which was among the oldest Wall Street operations, dating back to 1832. Over the next eight years, Dillon demonstrated a remarkably facile mind for banking, quickly rising to partner and then to the presidency of operations. The firm's name was changed to Dillon, Read & Company in 1920.

MATURE WEALTH

At a time when many bankers and stockbrokers encouraged clients to speculate and pursue high-risk investment strategies in order to make quick fortunes, Dillon was strikingly different. His style was quiet, low-risk, low-key, and conservative. He practiced relationship banking, depending on his expanding network of contacts to influence decisions regarding the direction of bank projects. Dillon buttressed his investment decisions with research, creating a business strategy for his company. His firm's reputation grew, and Dillon, Read was asked to direct the banking operations for Germany's payment of its massive war reparations as part of the armistice that ended World War I.

During the 1920's, Dillon established himself among the foremost financial giants of his era, known for visionary projects, often bold and daring, that he executed with a methodical passion for details. Dillon, Read would buy corporations with outstanding debts, then bring in new management teams to operate these firms, in turn generating huge profits for Dillon, Read.

Dillon's reputation largely rested on his involvement in two headline-making financial deals. Goodyear Tire and Rubber Company, which had made its fortune in bicycle tires, had attempted to expand into the new and potentially lucrative automobile market, but with disastrous mismanagement the company became overextended, verged on bankruptcy, and eventually went into receivership. In 1921, Dillon replaced Goodyear's management team and without court assistance brokered a settlement that satisfied the company's bankers, creditors, stockholders, and employees. Drawing on his network of Ivy

League associates, Dillon raised more than $100 million for the struggling company. Within five years Goodyear was the largest rubber company in the world. In 1925, Dillion outbid the legendary J. P. Morgan to purchase Dodge Brothers Motor Car Company, which was struggling with mismanagement after the deaths of its original founders. Dillon paid $146 million for the automobile firm, then the largest cash transaction in the history of American business. Despite heroic efforts to redirect the company's operations, within three years Dillon arranged the sale of Dodge to the Chrysler Corporation.

During his twenty years directing operations for Dillon, Read, Dillon set a style of quiet negotiations and conservative investment policy. Although not particularly dazzling, this style guaranteed long-term fiscal stability for the firm and a reputation for reliability and success. Indeed, in the financially strapped 1930's, New York City hired the firm to underwrite construction of the Triborough Bridge. In addition, Dillon, himself a connoisseur of European living, directed the expansion of banking operations overseas. By World War II, Dillon, Read was one of the most influential investment banks in the world and Dillon among the richest men in America.

During his half-century tenure at the firm, Dillon maintained an affluent lifestyle that he believed wealth should bring. In negotiations, he was courtly, gentlemanly, and patient. His lifestyle was sophisticated, cultured, always tasteful, and the very embodiment, despite his Jewish heritage, of an East Coast white Anglo-Saxon Protestant. His family was never rocked by scandal, his international banking operations were never investigated, and his reputation was never tarnished with gaudy excesses typical of first-generation wealth. At the sumptuous twelve-thousand-acre estate he built in Far Hills, New Jersey, called Dunwalke, Dillon pursued his passion for elegant living. His interests ranged from breeding prize cattle to garden design. He was an amateur ornithologist and photographer. He loved to hunt and ride horses. However, his primary passion was wine, nurtured

CHÂTEAU HAUT-BRION

The lush vineyards of Bordeaux in southwestern France produce some of the world's most exquisite—and expensive—red and white wines. The soil, a thin composite of gravel, limestone, and sand resting atop a clay subsoil, is good for little except raising grapes, and the region's reputation has defined not only fine wine for centuries but also the sophisticated and cultivated lifestyle of the aristocratic wealthy who are its enthusiastic aficionados. Within the Bordeaux region, the Château Haut-Brion is located a mile from Bordeaux and has long been considered a unique operation. It is the only vineyard estate not located in the Médoc region to have received the "first growth" rating—the highest ranking accorded French vineyards. Château Haut-Brion's reputation for wine production has been chronicled during more than four centuries in which it has provided gold medal wines to Europe's wealthy and powerful.

Clarence Dillon, whose profound love for the French culture came as much from his grandmother's family as it did his own experiences in France, appreciated the finer expressions of wealth, notably the love of fine wines. In 1934, Bordeaux, along with the rest of Europe, was reeling from the global economic recession. Times were hard, and the château had fallen into disrepair after a succession of lackluster vineyard directors who were unwilling and financially unable to revive the moribund business. Dillon, who at the time was spending half of each year in his investment firm's Paris offices, toured the vineyard countryside in Bordeaux looking for an investment potential among a handful of châteaux that were in economic straits similar to Haut-Brion's and were up for sale. However, he fell under the spell of Haut-Brion, and he later told interviewers that its wine was his favorite of the Bordeaux clarets. The spacious estate grounds, with more than 125 acres, provided Dillon ample room to indulge his other passion—horse riding.

Dillon, however, was hardly a dilettante. He was able to accomplish for Château Haut-Brion what he had done for any number of faltering companies in the United States. He restructured the vineyard's management team, bringing in experts not only in winemaking but also in the economics of running a global corporation, and he spent millions in modernizing the physical plant, which did not even have electricity. Dillon's financial resources and his business acumen quickly improved the economic condition of the vineyard, and within a decade it was once again a world-class operation.

The Dillon family maintained direct involvement in vineyard operations into the twenty-first century. The château has purchased several rival vineyards and has diversified into a number of premium, award-winning, vintage lines, several bearing Dillon's name. The company continues to use cutting-edge technology to maximize efficiency, including a computer network to tap global distribution possibilities.

by his love of the French countryside. (Dillon, Read maintained a corporate office in Paris where Dillon lived six months of the year.) In 1935, after visiting Bordeaux, he purchased one of its most storied vineyards, the Château Haut-Brion.

Dillon eased into a gentle retirement from the firm he had established as a world-class operation. His only son, C. Douglas Dillon, would begin to manage Dillon, Read's operations in the late 1940's in a smooth transition of authority. Dillon gradually became less involved in the operations of his vineyard, entrusting its management to a nephew, and he enjoyed a lengthy and satisfying retirement, living until the age of ninety-six. Although he would live to see his firm marginalized by the deregulation and speculation of the 1960's and 1970's, he died before Dillon, Read was acquired and then divested by the Bechtel Group in the mid-1980's.

LEGACY

One generation removed from the Jewish ghettos of Eastern Europe, Clarence Dillon became the leading American investment banker during both the prosperity of the 1920's and the economic anxieties of the Depression, his wealth estimated at between $150 and $200 million. He embodied the temperament and lifestyle of Old World wealth, taste, and sophistication. As a financier, Dillon thrived on the advice and counsel of his Ivy League contacts. Under Dillon's stewardship, Dillon, Read avoided bold and risky speculations, earning a reputation as a cautious, conservative, and solid firm that relied on the relatively narrow circle of Dillon's network of associates, a practice necessarily abandoned in the increasingly computerized global investment field after World War II.

—*Joseph Dewey*

FURTHER READING

Brook, Stephen. *The Complete Bordeaux: The Wines, the Châteaux, the People.* London: Mitchell Beazely, 2004. Clear and accessible overview of the highly complicated world of winemaking. Chronicles Dillon's rescue of Châteaux Haut-Brion.

Fleuriet, Michel. *Investment Banking Explained: An Insider's Guide to the Industry.* New York: McGraw-Hill, 2008. Any understanding of Dillon's considerable achievement depends on understanding the complicated (and often intricate) world of high finance and investments. This is a readable explanation, detailed and rigorously explained, geared for a general audience.

Parrish, Michael E. *Anxious Decades: America in Prosperity and Depression, 1920-1941.* New York: Norton, 1994. Puts Dillon's considerable financial success in an appropriate context as that of a banker able to thrive in both economic booms and busts.

Perez, Robert C. *Clarence Dillon: A Wall Street Engima.* Lanham, Md.: Madison Books, 1995. Fascinating account of Dillon's life that focuses on his complicated relationship with his own Jewish heritage as he became the embodiment of white Anglo-Saxon Protestant culture.

Sobel, Robert. *The Life and Times of Dillon, Read.* New York: Dutton, 1991. Argues that the firm's conservative style, taking its cue from Dillon's own style, contributed both to its incredible success and to its eventual marginalization as investment banking radically changed in the 1970's and 1980's.

See also: George F. Baker; John Bouvier; John F. Dodge; Anthony Joseph Drexel; Otto Kahn; Joseph P. Kennedy; Charles E. Merrill; J. P. Morgan.

WALT DISNEY
American artist and entrepreneur

Disney was only an average artist, but he was a great storyteller and showman who established one of the major media and entertainment corporations of the twentieth and twenty-first centuries.

Born: December 5, 1901; Chicago, Illinois
Died: December 15, 1966; Burbank, California
Also known as: Walter Elias Disney; Retlaw Elias Yensid
Sources of wealth: Entertainment industry; media; real estate
Bequeathal of wealth: Children; educational institution; charity

EARLY LIFE
Walt Disney, the son of Elias and Flora Call Disney, was born in Chicago in 1901. While growing up, Disney and his family lived in Chicago, on a farm in Missouri, and in Kansas City. He drew cartoons for his high school newspaper, and his formal training in art came from classes at the Kansas City and Chicago art institutes. Disney tried to join the U.S. Navy during World War I but was rejected because he was underage. He dropped out of high school in 1918 to join the American Red Cross and was sent to France to drive an ambulance.

He returned to the United States in 1919, settling in Kansas City to begin a career as a commercial artist. After reading a book on animation, he decided to go into the animated cartoon business and made a deal with a local movie theater chain to show his earliest cartoons.

FIRST VENTURES
Disney's "Laugh-O-Grams" became so popular in the Kansas City area that he was able to expand his studio and hire additional animators. However, he was an inexperienced businessman, and his first studio eventually went bankrupt. Disney moved to Los Angeles in 1923 with only a suitcase and $40. He tried to get a job with one of the film studios, but after no one hired him he set up his own. He started his studio in a garage and later moved into a building on Hyperion Avenue in the Silver Lake district of Los Angeles. The studio remained there until 1939, when Disney opened a larger facility in Burbank.

His cartoon series Alice Comedies (1924-1927), based on Lewis Carroll's book *Alice's Adventures in Wonderland* (1865), was moderately successful, and in 1927, Universal Pictures contracted with him for a new series. These cartoons, featuring Oswald the Rabbit, were so successful that Disney expanded his studio and hired more animators. In February, 1928, Disney was prepared to renew his contract, but Charlie Mintz, his distributor, wanted to reduce Disney's fee for each cartoon. Disney also discovered that Universal, not Disney, owned the rights to Oswald, and that Mintz believed he could make the cartoons without Disney by hiring away most of Disney's staff. Disney walked away from the deal and from that time on became aggressively vigilant about protecting his intellectual properties.

MATURE WEALTH
To replace Oswald, Disney based a new character on a mouse he had adopted as a pet while living in Kansas City. The character's name was originally Mortimer but was later changed to Mickey Mouse by Disney's wife Lillian, who did not like the name Mortimer. Disney failed to find a distributor for the first two cartoons star-

Walt Disney. (Library of Congress)

WALT DISNEY WORLD

In 1959, Walt Disney began looking for land for a second theme park to build on the success of Disneyland, located in Anaheim, California. Marketing surveys showed that only 2 percent of Disneyland's visitors came from east of the Mississippi River, where 75 percent of the United States' population then lived. Disney also disliked the businesses that had grown up around Disneyland and wanted control of a much larger area of land for his next major enterprise.

Disney flew over the site southwest of Orlando, Florida, where Walt Disney World eventually was built on November 22, 1963, the day President John F. Kennedy was assassinated. However, the site was not his first choice. He had previously flown over and applied to the Sanford, Florida, city council to allow him to build a theme park near this city, but his application was declined because the council members did not want the crime they believed would accompany tourism.

One of the advantages of the Orlando site was the well-developed network of roads in the area. Three interstate highways and the Florida Turnpike connected Orlando with the rest of Florida, the East Coast, and areas north and west of the state. McCoy Air Force Base (later renamed the Orlando International Airport) was located east of the site.

Disney died in 1966. Construction of the theme park began the following year, and Walt Disney World opened on October 1, 1971, consisting of the Magic Kingdom theme park and two hotels, the Contemporary and the Polynesian. Disney World later added three theme parks: Epcot (in 1982), Disney's Hollywood Studios (1989), and Disney's Animal Kingdom (1998). By 2009, Disney World was the most visited and largest recreational resort in the world, and contained two water parks, Typhoon Lagoon (1989) and Blizzard Beach (1995); thirty-two hotels; five golf courses; a bus service; a monorail train system; and numerous shopping, dining, and entertainment facilities, including Walt Disney World Village Marketplace (1975) and Pleasure Island (1989). The recreation complex employed sixty-six thousand people with an annual payroll of $1.2 billion, making it the largest single-site employer in the United States. At its peak, the resort owned roughly thirty thousand acres, which is about the size of San Francisco, or about twice the size of Manhattan Island. Portions of the original property were sold off, including the land later occupied by Celebration, Florida, a town built by the Disney corporation.

solo in 1939. Merchandising deals, especially the famous Mickey Mouse watch, generated additional cash for Disney.

Disney began a series of musical shorts called Silly Symphonies in 1929 with *The Skeleton Dance*. *Flowers and Trees* (1932) was the first cartoon filmed in Technicolor, and it was so successful that Disney, who had an exclusive five-year license for the Technicolor process, switched all his cartoons from black and white to color. Disney released his most commercially successful cartoon short of all time, *The Three Little Pigs*, in 1933, and it included the hit song "Who's Afraid of the Big Bad Wolf?"

Disney began developing a full-length feature animated film in 1934, and in February, 1938, released *Snow White and the Seven Dwarfs*, the year's most commercially successful motion picture. *Pinocchio* and *Fantasia* were released in 1940 and *Bambi* in 1942, but they were financial disappointments because World War II had closed off the European market. Only the relatively inexpensive *Dumbo* (1941) made a profit during its initial release. However, *Snow White* was released for a second time in 1944, and Disney learned that animated features could become cash cows by rereleasing them every seven years to a new audience of children.

After the United States entered World War II in 1941, Disney concentrated on making training and instructional films for the military; war propaganda shorts, such as *Der Fuehrer's Face* (1942); and the feature *Victory Through Air Power* (1943), which combined animation and live action. The Disney studios also created inexpensive package films that contained collections of cartoon shorts. These included *Saludos Amigos* (1942), its sequel *The Three Caballeros* (1945), *Fun and Fancy Free* (1947), and *The Adventures of Ichabod and Mr. Toad* (1949).

After World War II ended in 1945, Disney returned to work on full-length animated features. Both *Alice in Wonderland* (1951) and *Peter Pan* (1953), which were begun before the war, were finished and released. *Cinderella* (1950) became Disney's most commercially successful film since *Snow White*. During this period, Disney further developed the concept of feature-length

ring Mickey, *Plane Crazy* and *The Gallopin' Gaucho*, which were both silent films. The third Mickey Mouse cartoon, *Steamboat Willie*, added sound in 1928. *Steamboat Willie* was an instant success, and all future Disney cartoons were released with sound tracks. Goofy the dog and Donald Duck were originally supporting characters in the Mickey Mouse cartoons, but they eventually surpassed Mickey in popularity and began starring in their own cartoons in 1937; Mickey's dog Pluto similarly went films that combined live action and animation, such as *Song of the South* (1946) and *So Dear to My Heart* (1949). He revived the concept more than a decade later when he made *Mary Poppins*, based on the books by P. L. Travers. *Mary Poppins* was released in 1964 and became the most successful Disney film of the decade. It was also the most technically advanced film to that point in its combination of animation and live action.

While Disney's two daughters were growing up, he and his wife had difficulty finding places to take them on weekends. He got the idea for a children's theme park after visiting Children's Fairyland in Oakland, California, in the late 1940's. This idea eventually developed into a concept for a larger park that became Disneyland, which opened on July 17, 1955, and was immediately successful. Visitors from around the world came to Anaheim, California, to visit Disneyland, enjoying its attractions, such as the Peter Pan ride, which were based on Disney films. Around the same time, Disney expanded into live-action films that would not include animation. *Treasure Island* (1950) was his studio's first live-action feature, and subsequent films, such as *20,000 Leagues Under the Sea* (1954) and *The Shaggy Dog* (1959), did well at the box office.

Disney broke into television with the special show *One Hour in Wonderland*, which aired in 1950. He hosted a weekly anthology series titled *Disneyland*. He leveraged his film library by showing cartoon shorts and excerpts from animated features on his television program. After 1955, the show became known as *Walt Disney Presents;* when it converted from black and white to color in 1961, Disney changed its name to *Walt Disney's Wonderful World of Color. The Mickey Mouse Club*, a syndicated daily variety show which occasionally showed cartoons from Disney's library, debuted on television in 1955.

In his later years, Disney spent significant amounts of his own money on developing the California Institute of the Arts (CalArts), which was formed in 1961 from the merger of the Los Angeles Conservatory of Music and the Chouinard Art Institute. When Disney died in 1966, one-fourth of his estate went to CalArts. He also donated thirty-eight acres of land that he owned in Valencia, California, for the school to construct a campus.

LEGACY

Walt Disney helped create the twentieth century entertainment industry. He and his studio elevated the art of animation, raising the standards of animated films and using this medium, which initially focused on short sub-

jects, to produce full-length features. His studio also produced successful live-action films and innovative television programs. Disneyland and its successor theme parks offered the public new attractions where families could spend their leisure time.

The Walt Disney Company of the twenty-first century owns theme parks in California, Florida, France, and Japan; vacation resorts; water parks; hotels; cruise ships; motion-picture and television studios, such as Pixar; Internet sites; record labels; publishing houses; cable television networks, such as ESPN and Soapnet; and the American Broadcasting Corporation (ABC). On August 31, 2009, the company announced it had paid about $1.4 billion to acquire Marvel Entertainment, a comic book and action hero company. The firm also licenses Disney characters to toy, watch, clothing, and other manufacturers.

—Thomas R. Feller

FURTHER READING

Barrier, Michael. *Hollywood Cartoons: American Animation in Its Golden Age.* Oxford, England: Oxford University Press, 1999. A history of American animated cartoons up to the 1960's.

Broggie, Michael. *Walt Disney's Railroad Story.* Virginia Beach, Va.: Donning, 2005. Biography of Disney focusing on his love of railroads.

Disney, Walt. *Walt Disney: Conversations.* Edited by Kathy Merlock Jackson. Jackson: University Press of Mississippi, 2006. Collection of interviews with Disney dating from 1929 to 1966.

Gabler, Neal. *Walt Disney: The Triumph of American Imagination.* New York: Random House, 2006. Meticulously researched biography written by the first writer granted complete access to the Disney archives.

Mosley, Leonard. *Disney's World: A Biography.* Chelsea, Mich.: Scarborough House, 2002. Biography of Disney written by a film scholar.

Peri, Don. *Working with Walt: Interviews with Disney Artists.* Jackson: University Press of Mississippi, 2008. Collection of interviews with people who worked directly with Disney.

Schickel, Richard, and Ivan R. Dee. *The Disney Version: The Life, Times, Art, and Commerce of Walt Disney.* Chicago: Ivan R. Dee, 1997. Chronicles Disney's life and work, questioning his achievements and shortcomings.

Sherman, Robert B., and Richard M. Sherman. *Walt's Time: From Before to Beyond.* Santa Clarita, Calif.:

Camphor Tree, 1998. Memoir by the brothers who wrote songs and musical scores for *Mary Poppins*, other Disney features, and shows and rides at Disneyland and Disney World.

Watts, Steven. *The Magic Kingdom: Walt Disney and the American Way of Life.* Columbia: University of Mis-

souri Press, 2001. Documents Disney's role in the creation of American consumer culture.

See also: Richard Branson; Mark Cuban; David Geffen; Robert L. Johnson; Rupert Murdoch; Sumner Redstone; Steven Spielberg.

JOHN F. DODGE
American automaker, industrialist, and entrepreneur

Dodge was the business mind behind Dodge Brothers, using his financial acumen to implement his younger brother's patents and engineering ideas. The brothers' automobile company became known for manufacturing high-quality motor vehicles.

Born: October 25, 1864; Niles, Michigan
Died: January 14, 1920; New York, New York
Also known as: John Francis Dodge
Sources of wealth: Manufacturing; sale of products; investments
Bequeathal of wealth: Spouse; children; educational institution

EARLY LIFE
John Francis Dodge was born in 1864, and his brother and eventual business partner was born four years later. Throughout their lives the brothers were inseparable. They spent their early days in Niles, a town in a poor county of southwest Michigan. Their father, Daniel Rugg Dodge, ran a foundry and machine shop, where he built and maintained engines for riverboats traveling on the St. Joseph River. In the years immediately following the Civil War, riverboats were commonly used to transport goods. As the transportation revolution took hold, automobiles replaced horses and buggies, and railways replaced riverboats as the links between major cities. Both John and Horace learned their father's trade, but John possessed better managerial skills than his brother.

FIRST VENTURES
The family struggled and moved several times before settling in Detroit, Michigan. There, the brothers worked for a boilermaker and later for a typography company. Through his tinkering, Horace devised a sealed ballbearing device for bicycles that kept out dirt, and he patented his invention. John convinced Horace to use their savings to start their own bicycle business, which struggled to remain open. Rather than suffer with a failing company, the brothers sold it to a Canadian firm. Under

the terms of the sale, the brothers continued to make bicycles using Horace's patent, for which they would receive royalties. When the Canadian firm failed and reneged on its promised royalties, John arranged to cancel his claims against the company in exchange for first pick of the machinery left at its plant.

With this machinery, the brothers again went into business, founding the Dodge Brothers Machine Shop in 1902. They manufactured stoves and boilers and contracted with automaker Ransom Olds to build transmissions for his single-cylinder Oldsmobile. In 1903, the Dodge brothers entered into a contract to supply Henry Ford, who was starting his own automobile company, with most of the parts needed to build Ford's Model T. The Dodges provided the chassis for this vehicle, while Ford added the body, wheels, and tires.

MATURE WEALTH
The contract with Ford earned the brothers millions of dollars. According to the contract, Dodge Brothers would be the exclusive supplier of automotive parts for the new Ford Motor Company; if Ford's company went bankrupt, the Dodges would receive all of Ford's assets. Henry Ford was short on cash, so the brothers agreed to provide automobile parts in exchange for $10,000 worth of shares, or 10 percent of Ford Motor's stock. Once the first Model T sold, the Dodge-Ford contract was solid. Ford Motor made half of all the automobiles manufactured worldwide, and Dodge Brothers produced two-thirds of the parts for these vehicles. The brothers profited twice in their business dealings with Ford: first in making and selling him parts, and second in receiving dividends from their stock in his company. John Dodge also served as vice president of Ford Motor Company for several years.

In 1907, John married his third wife, Matilda Rausch. His first wife, Ivy, died in 1901 from tuberculosis, and he was married for only four years to his second wife. Matilda became his secretary after she graduated from

Gorsline Business College in 1902. They had three children.

Demand for Ford cars, and therefore for automotive parts, was growing. By 1910, Dodge Brothers needed to build a new plant. The brothers chose Hamtramck, a Polish community bordering the city of Detroit. By then, the brothers had been supplying Ford with parts for nearly a decade. Horace made many suggestions for improving Ford's vehicle, but Ford would not listen. However, the Dodges continued to supply the parts and earn stock dividends as Ford's company thrived.

When Ford Motor's Highland Park plant was nearly completed, however, John realized that Ford would no longer need the brothers' auto parts. John decided that Horace's ideas could make the automobile easier to drive, especially for women. John resigned as vice president of Ford Motor, and the brothers retooled their Hamtramck plant in order to make their own vehicles.

Using their stock profits from Ford Motors, they financed the Dodge Brothers Motor Car Company, established in 1913. The brothers had such a solid reputation within the automobile industry that they received applications from twenty thousand people for Dodge dealerships before their company was even ready to produce vehicles. The first car rolled out of the Dodge Main plant in Hamtramck on November 14, 1914. It had an electric starter so women did not have to crank-start the car, a sliding-gear transmission, and rear-wheel brakes. Within three years, Dodge Brothers Motor Car Company became the fourth largest American auto manufacturer.

MEADOW BROOK HALL

Meadow Brook Hall in Rochester Hills, Michigan, is often called America's castle. It is the fourth largest house museum in the United States, known for its grand scale, architectural detail, and fine craftsmanship. Construction began on the manor house in 1926 and was completed in 1929 at a cost of nearly $4 million.

Five years after John F. Dodge's death, his widow Matilda decided to transform the family's country home at Meadow Brook Farm into an estate. The family had been visiting the fifteen-hundred-acre farm since John purchased it in 1908. When Matilda and Anna, John's sister-in-law, sold Dodge Brothers Motor Car Company for $147 million, Matilda decided to reside at Meadow Brook.

While honeymooning with her second husband, lumber broker Alfred G. Wilson, in 1925, Matilda was inspired by castles and manor homes in England. As a result, Meadow Brook Hall was designed in a Tudor Revival style. The 88,000-square-foot mansion has 110 rooms and houses Matilda's vast collections of art and furnishings.

Although it was influenced by the style of sixteenth through eighteenth century English manor homes, Meadow Brook Hall was made from American materials that were commonly used during the Arts and Crafts Movement, a style of architecture that was popular in the final years of the nineteenth and early years of the twentieth centuries. Meadow Brook Hall is constructed of wood timber, brick, and sandstone; clay shingle tiles add to the charm of thirty-nine brick chimneys to create a unique roof line. Carved plaster ceilings and stained-glass window insets accent elaborately detailed wood and stone carvings featured throughout the interior. All of the hardware and ceramic art tiles are handmade.

Every modern amenity available in the 1920's was incorporated into the design, including central heating, two elevators, four kitchens, and a full-size home theater. A few rooms were designed and decorated in specific architectural revival styles. For example, the eighteenth century neoclassical style was selected for the dining room and Matilda's study; one of the bedrooms was designed in American Colonial style; and Matilda's room and another bedroom included French rococo elements. The mansion's beautiful decorations, complete with statues and artwork from various historical periods and styles, represent the lavish lifestyle of American industrialists of the early twentieth century.

To celebrate the end of construction, Matilda and Alfred G. Wilson hosted a housewarming party attended by 850 guests on November 19, 1929. It was only three weeks after the stock market crash that ushered in the Great Depression. Matilda eventually moved to Sunset Terrace, which was built as a retirement home on Meadow Brook Farm, and resided there until Wilson died in 1962. She then returned to Meadow Brook Hall, where she lived until her death in 1967.

In 1957, the Wilsons donated all of Meadow Brook Farm, including the mansion, to establish what would later become Oakland University. Meadow Brook Hall opened to the public in 1971 and remained a popular attraction into the twenty-first century. The facility hosts around ninety events a year and is visited by about 100,000 people annually. The site also houses an outdoor concert pavilion and Meadow Brook Theatre. Both the hall and the grounds are important as significant works of architecture, as well as a tribute to the Dodge family.

During World War I, Dodge Brothers made ambulances and other vehicles for the war effort, along with the delicate recoil firing mechanisms for French cannons that were vital to the Allied artillery. The brothers built and equipped a new factory in Hamtramck solely for the precision manufacturing of these recoil devices.

Meanwhile, Henry Ford was angry that stock profits from his company were funding his competition and stopped paying the brothers dividends. John Dodge responded by filing suit against Ford, who eventually was forced to pay $9 million in back dividends. In 1919, the brothers sold their remaining Ford Motor stock to Ford's company for $25 million.

In less than two decades, Dodge Brothers amassed $200 million, the equivalent of $1.5 billion in 2010. The brothers celebrated their prosperity by purchasing yachts (the largest was longer than two hundred feet) and building mansions. John bought Meadow Brook Farm, a fifteen-hundred-acre property in Rochester Hills, Michigan, and the farm became the family's country getaway. John gave his wife a check for $1 million as a Christmas gift in 1919; Horace bought his wife a pearl necklace once owned by Catherine the Great and valued at $850,000.

In 1920, while at the International Automobile Show in New York City, Horace caught the flu. A worldwide flu pandemic that had begun in 1918 had not abated, and soon John was also sick. John died in January, 1920, and Horace died later that year. Their widows kept the automobile company until 1925, when they sold it for $146 million.

LEGACY

John and Horace Dodge were among the pioneers of the American automotive industry. They achieved success through vision and an unflagging dedication to their work. The Dodge name became synonymous with quality vehicles. John was the mastermind behind the business transactions of the brothers' various enterprises, and his shrewd dealings early in their career enabled them to amass enough wealth to finance the formation of their own foray into automobile manufacture. Implementing improvements to make the automobile more convenient and enjoyable rapidly launched the Dodges into the ranks of the top four companies in the automotive industry. The Dodge brand continued after their deaths, eventually becoming part of Chrysler Group, LLC.

John Dodge's fortune is a symbol of the American dream, a rags-to-riches story of entrepreneurial success. In 1957, John's widow and her second husband donated Meadow Brook Farm, which included Meadow Brook Hall and their collections of art and furnishings, and $2 million to Michigan State University for the creation of a new university in Oakland County. The site eventually became Oakland University.

—Lisa A. Wroble

FURTHER READING

Berger, Michael L. *The Automobile in American History and Culture: A Reference Guide.* Westport, Conn.: Greenwood Press, 2001. Focuses on biographies of auto pioneers and histories of car companies to assess the impact of the automobile on American culture.

Hyde, Charles K. *The Dodge Brothers: The Men, the Motor Car, and the Legacy.* Detroit: Wayne State University Press, 2005. A scholarly study of both the men and their company. Chronicles their beginnings in a poor county of Michigan and the skills they learned as machinists that led to their rapid rise in the burgeoning auto industry.

McPherson, Thomas A. *The Dodge Story.* Osceola, Wis.: MBI, 1992. Focuses primarily on the Dodge brothers' company but also provides information on the brothers' early lives and backgrounds. Describes the rapid success of the Dodge touring car, which prompted innovative new models. Includes many photographs of Dodge vehicles.

Pitrone, Jean Maddern. *Tangled Web: Legacy of Auto Pioneer John F. Dodge.* Hamtramck, Mich.: Avenue, 1989. Biography of the man who was the financial mastermind behind Dodge Brothers, describing how John F. Dodge built the company through innovation, shrewd business deals, and luck.

Pitrone, Jean Maddern, and Joan Potter Elwart. *The Dodges: The Auto Family Fortune and Misfortune.* South Bend, Ind: Icarus Press, 1981. Chronicles the innovative Dodge brothers as they created their fortune and describes the result of that fortune after their untimely deaths when they were in their fifties.

See also: Walter P. Chrysler; Chung Ju Yung; Harvey Firestone; Henry Ford; Soichiro Honda; Alfred P. Sloan.

EDWARD L. DOHENY
American oil magnate

Doheny's discovery of oil in Los Angeles was the foundation of the oil boom in Southern California, and thus he played a considerable part in the economic development of the region. He was also instrumental in establishing the oil industry in Mexico.

Born: August 10, 1856; Fond du Lac, Wisconsin
Died: September 8, 1935; Los Angeles, California
Also known as: Edward Laurence Doheny
Source of wealth: Oil
Bequeathal of wealth: Spouse; charity

EARLY LIFE
Edward Laurence Doheny (doh-HEE-nee) was born in Fond du Lac, Wisconsin, in 1856, the son of Irish immigrant Patrick Doheny and1 Eleanor Quigley Doheny, originally from Newfoundland, Canada. A bright student, Edward left high school at fifteen, and his father's death not long thereafter obliged him to find work. After about two years with the U.S. Geological Survey in Kansas, he set out to prospect for gold and silver in the Southwest, an enterprise that yielded him little gain after almost fifteen years of effort. His prospecting partner, Charles Canfield, found considerable success on his own, both in prospecting and in real estate.

FIRST VENTURES
In 1883, Doheny married his first wife, Carrie Wilkins, and during his prospecting years he met Albert B. Fall, who was to play a major role in his future life. Doheny, Carrie, and their young daughter came to Los Angeles in 1890 or 1891, and after studying law he was admitted to the bar. However, his legal practice was as unsuccessful as his previous venture, and he apparently was almost penniless by the time he reached his mid-thirties.

The story of Doheny's subsequent rise to wealth has somewhat of the aura of a tall tale. In 1892, reduced to doing odd jobs, he supposedly spied a cart with its wheels coated in a certain type of tar or pitch (called "brea" by the Spanish-speaking Angelenos). When he discovered the source of this tar, near what would later be Los Angeles's Dodger Stadium, he and former partner Canfield leased the land. In 1893, with the use of a tool made from the sharpened trunk of a eucalyptus tree, Doheny and Canfield excavated the land until oil was found, and the well they built began producing some forty barrels a day. It was the first major oil discovery in Los Angeles.

MATURE WEALTH
Despite his previous failures, Doheny proved to be a shrewd businessman. He and Canfield discovered oil at several other sites and began selling it to local businesses. An oil boom ensued that was rife with wild speculation; an estimated twenty-three hundred wells were dug in the city within five years. The partners also persuaded railroad companies to switch their locomotive fuel from coal to oil, and other industries followed suit.

In about 1900, Doheny formed the Pan American Petroleum and Transport Company, a subsidiary of his Mexican Petroleum Company, which he established in order to look for oil in Mexico and which eventually controlled more than 1.5 million acres of Mexican land. Ma-

Edward L. Doheny, left, and his attorney Frank Hogan arrive at the Capitol in 1924 to attend a Senate committee investigation regarding the Teapot Dome scandal. (AP/ Wide World Photos)

jor oil companies previously had come to Mexico primarily to distribute oil, but Doheny's firm was one of the first to produce oil on a large scale there. Although the company was one of the largest in Mexico, it remained susceptible to the vagaries of Mexican politics and revolution. At one point, Doheny had a private army of more than six thousand men to protect his interests, and he was said to have urged the United States government to invade the country in order to stabilize the Mexican government. Thus, he became a classic imperialist. He used the oil that he could not sell to the railroads or was unsuitable for fuel to pave roads in Mexico. Doheny's fortune grew with the needs of the burgeoning American automobile industry, and he also expanded his operations to South America and Great Britain. In the second decade of the twentieth century Mexico became a net exporter of oil. It is said that during his lifetime, Doheny discovered more oil than any other person in the world.

Now the possessor of a vast fortune estimated to be $150 million, one of the largest in America, Doheny contributed many millions of dollars to Catholic causes, including the construction of churches. He wed his second wife, a telephone operator, in 1900 after his first wife committed suicide. His second wife was also named Carrie (née Betzold), but she was generally known by her middle name, Estelle. The couple lived in the fabled mansion in Los Angeles that Doheny purchased a year after their marriage.

Doheny became involved in Democratic Party politics, losing a bid for nomination as vice president on the party's ticket in 1920. A few years later, his life began a downward spiral as he became embroiled in a scandal involving his longtime friend Fall, now the secretary of interior in President Warren G. Harding's administration. In 1924, a U.S. Senate investigation uncovered evidence of a $100,000 payment from Doheny to Fall in order to obtain a no-bid contract for the U.S. Navy's oil reserves in the Elk Hills of California. Another oil magnate, Harry F. Sinclair, had similarly paid

THE DOHENY AND GREYSTONE MANSIONS

The 22-room, 10,500-square-foot French château-like home that oil magnate Edward L. Doheny and second wife Estelle purchased in 1901 was originally built from 1899 to 1900 for the Oliver Posey family. The Dohenys purchased it fully furnished for $125,000. The residence was designed by the architects Theodore Eisen and Sumner Hunt and incorporated elements of the Gothic, English Tudor, and California Mission styles. One of its more spectacular features was the fabulous Pompeian Room, which contains art-glass panels, a mosaic floor with marble imported from southern Europe and Africa, Tuscan marble columns, and a dome constructed of more than twenty-eight hundred pieces of gold favrile glass from the Long Island factory of Louis Comfort Tiffany. Doheny Mansion also contained a bowling alley and a shooting gallery. The home is located on Chester Place, a small exclusive street of impressive mansions developed by Doheny near downtown Los Angeles in the West Adams district. Eventually, to discourage casual visitors, Doheny bought all the other houses and gated the street for greater privacy.

The Dohenys lived in the mansion until Edward died in 1935, and Estelle continued in residence thereafter, occupying the home for more than fifty years. She had not liked the house when they moved in and over the years made many renovations, apart from the extensive repairs that were required after the mansion was damaged in the 1933 earthquake. The home was willed to the Catholic Church in 1958 following Estelle's death and since the 1960's has been part of the campus of Mount St. Mary's College, founded in 1925.

Greystone Mansion was the hilltop home of Edward L. "Ned" Doheny, Jr., his wife, Lucy, and their five children. However, three months after moving into the residence, Ned was found murdered there in February, 1929. Greystone Mansion has fifty-five rooms in forty-six thousand square feet, including a recreational wing with a projection room, a bowling alley, and a billiards room. The residence was originally on a site of four hundred acres, took two years to build, and cost some $4 million, equal to about $43 million in 2010 currency. The English Tudor-style mansion was designed by architect Gordon Kaufmann and in its time was compared to Hearst Castle, the fabled estate of William Randolph Hearst. Unoccupied as a private home for many years, by the twenty-first century it was owned by the city of Beverly Hills and had been the setting of scenes in numerous films, including *Spiderman*, and television programs, as well as being the venue for indoor and outdoor concerts. It has also been suggested that Greystone was the prototype for the mysterious mansion in Raymond Chandler's novel *The Big Sleep* (1939).

Fall for the oil concession at the Teapot Dome fields in Wyoming. As a result of what was termed the Teapot Dome Scandal, Doheny and the other two men were forever to be associated with a corrupt Harding administration. Although Doheny claimed he had not bribed Fall but had given him an interest-free unsecured loan, he, Sinclair, and Fall were indicted on bribery and conspiracy charges. Following a trial, Fall was convicted of accepting a bribe and sentenced to one year in prison, but, illogically, Doheny was found innocent of offering the bribe. Despite his acquittal, all of Doheny's government leases were canceled, and he did not finally emerge from under a legal cloud until 1930.

He had by that time retreated from public life and suffered another blow when Edward L. "Ned" Doheny, Jr., his son and namesake, was found murdered in February, 1929, at Greystone, Ned's Beverly Hills mansion. It was the house his father had built for Ned as a gift, and Ned had taken possession just a few months before his death. The thirty-five-year-old Ned, who was the father of five, was shot by Hugh Plunkett, his friend and secretary, who then committed suicide. Although speculation ran rife, the motive for the slaying was never conclusively proven.

Doheny became a near-recluse after his son's death, spending most of his time in his estate. He died of old age in 1935 and was buried in a tomb made of Carrara marble, a gift from Pope Pius XI in gratitude for the millions of dollars that Doheny had donated to the Catholic Church.

LEGACY

At the time of his death, Edward L. Doheny appeared to be a broken man and much of his good work had been forgotten in the wake of scandal. His wife, a convert to Catholicism who had been named a papal countess by the Church, later endowed the Carrie Estelle Doheny Eye Foundation, a research laboratory and eye bank. She also bought a mansion of thirty rooms that she donated to the Sisters of St. Joseph of Carondelet. It is said that immediately upon her husband's death, Mrs. Doheny had all of her husband's private papers burned, thus presenting substantial difficulties for future biographers.

Doheny almost single-handedly established the oil industry in Southern California and was a significant factor in the economic growth of California and Mexico. He played a large role in persuading major industries to convert from coal to oil, thus vastly enlarging the potential market for oil.

His name lives on in some significant places. Because he was instrumental in developing the city of Beverly Hills, one of its major thoroughfares, Doheny Drive, is named for him. Doheny State Beach is also named in his honor, as are libraries at the University of Southern California and St. John's Seminary. He is said to be the prototype for the character of the ruthless oilman in Upton Sinclair's book *Oil! A Novel* (1927), which was the basis for the 2007 film *There Will Be Blood*.

—*Roy Liebman*

FURTHER READING

Ansell, Martin. *Oil Baron of the Southwest: Edward L. Doheny and the Development of the Oil Industry in California and Mexico.* Columbus: Ohio State University Press, 1998. An attempt to rehabilitate Doheny's image by presenting a sympathetic account of his success as an entrepreneur. Claims Doheny should have credit for being one of the pioneer builders of the West.

Bonino, Mary Ann. *The Doheny Mansion: The Story of a Home.* Los Angeles: Edizioni Casa Animata, 2008. A lavishly illustrated history of the Doheny mansion in downtown Los Angeles.

Davis, Margaret L. *Dark Side of Fortune: Triumph and Scandal in the Life of Oil Tycoon Edward L. Doheny.* Berkeley: University of California Press, 1998. A well-balanced if largely sympathetic biography of Doheny. The author had access to a newly discovered collection of Doheny correspondence.

Dictionary of American Biography. New York: American Council of Learned Societies, 1944-1958. This noted reference book contains an article about Doheny.

La Botz, Dan. *Edward L. Doheny: Petroleum, Power, and Politics in the United States and Mexico.* New York: Praeger, 1991. This first full-length biography of Doheny takes a left-wing approach in presenting him as a ruthless man who hid behind an image of the benevolent philanthropist. Relies heavily on secondary sources and U.S. Department of State archives.

Phillips, Charles, and Alan Axelrod, eds. *Encyclopedia of the American West.* Woodbridge, Conn.: Macmillan Reference USA, 1996. A reference book that features an article about Doheny.

Weber, Francis J. *Southern California's First Family: The Dohenys of Los Angeles.* Fullerton, Calif.: Lorson's Books and Prints, 1993. Focuses mainly on the Dohenys' art collections and library.

See also: Henry M. Flagler; J. Paul Getty; Calouste Gulbenkian; Armand Hammer; H. L. Hunt; Clint Murchison, Sr.; Joseph Pew; Sid W. Richardson; John D. Rockefeller; William Rockefeller; Harry F. Sinclair.

CAPTAIN ROBERT DOLLAR
American lumberman and shipping company executive

Dollar, who still ranks as one of Scotland's fifty wealthiest men, successfully built lumber and shipping industries and generously supported many charitable organizations in Scotland, the United States, and other countries.

Born: March 20, 1844; Falkirk, Scotland
Died: May 16, 1932; San Rafael, California
Also known as: The Grand Old Man of the Pacific
Sources of wealth: Lumber; shipping
Bequeathal of wealth: Relatives; charity

EARLY LIFE

Captain Robert Dollar was born in 1844 in Falkirk, Scotland, the first son of William and Mary (née Melville) Dollar. When Robert was nine years old, his mother died and his grieving father turned to alcohol for comfort. Three years later, Dollar left school to work a lathe in a machine shop for sixty cents a week. In that same year, his father married their servant girl, Mary Easton. Dollar's second job was in a lumber-shipping company. In 1857-1858, the Dollar family migrated to Canada.

After working in a barrel stave factory, Dollar obtained a position at a lumber camp north of Ottawa. He and his brother used their $26 monthly earnings to buy their parents a farm. To advance his career, Dollar taught himself basic writing and math skills and learned French from the loggers. When he was twenty-one years old, Dollar became manager of the logging camp.

FIRST VENTURES

In 1872, Dollar and a partner bought their own lumber camp. This venture was ill fated, as the price of logs fell, leaving the partners with a $5,000 debt. Undeterred, Dollar worked his debt off in three years. During this time, he married Margaret Proudfoot and settled in Bracebridge, Ontario, where he established a Masonic lodge and donated lumber to the Presbyterian Church. The couple eventually had four children: Alexander Melville, Robert Stanley, Mary Grace, and John Harold.

While living in Bracebridge, Dollar formed a partnership with Henry H. Cook and ventured into the export business, transporting wood to England. In 1882, he used his earnings to buy land in Michigan for $1.25 per acre and to set up a sawmill in what became known as Dollarville. By 1884, Dollar had earned enough money to visit his birthplace in Falkirk, where he donated funds to the city's first library.

MATURE WEALTH

Dollar became a naturalized American citizen in 1888 and moved his family and business operations to California. He added redwood forests and new sawmills to his rapidly growing enterprise. Dollar's lumber business was now a leader in the industry, and he needed a more effective method of transporting lumber along the Pacific coast. He purchased a steamship, *The Newsbo*, which quickly proved its worth, and he then acquired additional ships. He incorporated the Dollar Steamship Co. in 1901-1902 and extended his trade to China and Japan. Frequent voyages and personal appearances in China gained him respect with the Chinese government.

Over the next twenty-five years, Dollar expanded his international shipping business and added a new line of government passenger ships, as well as worldwide cargo and passenger services. He also purchased additional land in Canada and built a timber mill town in British Columbia called Dollarton. Dollar, the lumber giant of the West, had also become the leading American shipowner—the "Grand Old Man of the Pacific." Dollar founded a successful business model that amassed millions of dollars. His propensity for hard work and his business acumen made him a leader in two different industries. His sons joined his businesses, too. On March 19, 1928, one day before his eighty-fourth birthday, Dollar was featured as the cover story in *Time* magazine, and during the next year additional articles about him appeared in *The Saturday Evening Post*.

Dollar died of bronchial pneumonia in 1932. Thousands of friends attended his funeral.

LEGACY

Captain Robert Dollar's wealth was the result of his determination and faith. His Scottish Presbyterian values, resourcefulness, and perseverance made a formerly penniless man into an affluent businessman worth $40 million. This self-educated man also became director of several banks. During his lifetime, Dollar donated to charities in the United States, the Philippines, Scotland, and China. His donations helped support orphanages, a seminary, a library, churches, schools, and the Young Men's Christian Association (YMCA) in China. His home in San Rafael, California, is the site of the Falkirk Museum.

—Cynthia J. W. Svoboda

FURTHER READING
Dollar, Robert. *Memoirs of Robert Dollar*. San Francisco: W. S. Van Cott, 1918.
Forbes, B. C. *Men Who Are Making the West*. Reprint. Whitefish, Mont.: Kessinger, 2003.
Roland, Alex, W. Jeffrey Bolster, and Alexander Keys-sar. *The Way of the Ship: America's Maritime History Reenvisioned, 1600-2000*. Hoboken, N.J.: John Wiley and Sons, 2008.

See also: John Ellerman; James J. Hill; Cornelius Vanderbilt; Frederick Weyerhaeuser.

FRANCIS DRAKE
English privateer and navigator

Drake obtained his vast wealth as a commissioned privateer for Queen Elizabeth I of England during the 1570's. By capturing and pillaging Spanish ships and colonies, Drake inspired other Englishmen to become privateers.

Born: c. 1540; Crowndale, near Tavistock, Devonshire, England
Died: January 28, 1596; at sea, off the coast of Porto Bello, Panama
Also known as: Sir Francis Drake, Sr.; El Draque
Sources of wealth: Conquest; privateering
Bequeathal of wealth: Unknown

EARLY LIFE
Sir Francis Drake, Sr., was born in Crowndale, near Tavistock, England, around the year 1540. He was the oldest child of Edmund Drake, a yeoman farmer, and Mary Mylwaye. His father was forced to flee Tavistock because of religious persecution for his Protestant beliefs. The family settled in Kent and lived in the hull of a ship. Shortly after the birth of the family's twelfth child, Drake's mother died. His father, who was unable to care for all twelve children, encouraged them to find work at sea when they reached their teen years. Drake apprenticed with a sea captain involved in coastal trade, and when the captain died, Drake inherited his ship.

FIRST VENTURES
Drake sold the ship and relocated to Plymouth, where he worked for his relative John Hawkins on one of Hawkins's ships. In 1566, Drake embarked on a slave-trade voyage in the Spanish Caribbean colonies. The following year, as the captain of one of six ships, he sailed to Africa and the Caribbean colonies on an illicit slave-trade mission for Hawkins. Between 1570 and 1571, Drake embarked on two additional exploratory trips, and in 1572, he returned to the Caribbean on a pillaging expedition.

MATURE WEALTH
In 1577, Queen Elizabeth I commissioned Drake to sail on a secret expedition to the Pacific coast of South America in order to explore and pillage Spanish fleets and colonies. Drake left Plymouth aboard the *Pelican* on December 13, 1577, with a fleet of four additional ships. He added the Spanish ship *Mary* to his fleet after capturing it near the African coast. Because of harsh weather, the death of many of his crew members, and damage to his fleet, by 1578 Drake had only one ship left, which he re-

Francis Drake. (Library of Congress)

named the *Golden Hinde*. He reached the Straits of Magellan on August 20, 1578. Along the way, he continued to amass a fortune by attacking and stealing from Spanish ships and colonies.

On March 1, 1579, Drake captured the Spanish ship the *Nuestra Señora de la Concepción*, and he stole a massive amount of gold, silver, and jewels. Afterward, he sailed toward North America and landed in a small bay in northern California that was named in his honor. Drake named the land the country of New Albion and claimed the area for Elizabeth I. He finished his circumnavigation of the globe by traveling across the Pacific Ocean to the Cape of Good Hope in South Africa. Drake arrived home in 1580, now a very wealthy and famous sea captain. On April 1, 1581, Queen Elizabeth knighted Drake on the deck of the *Golden Hinde*.

Although Drake was now a very rich man, he continued to sail on missions for Queen Elizabeth. In 1585, the queen hired Drake and equipped him with a fleet of more than twenty ships to raid Spanish colonies and ships in the New World. During the yearlong voyage, Drake captured Santiago, Santo Domingo, and St. Augustine in Florida. In 1587, he set sail a third time for Queen Elizabeth with a mission to stop the shipping of supplies in and out of the ports of Spain and Portugal. In 1588, he commanded the English fleet that defeated the Spanish Armada and made Great Britain the world's greatest sea power. Drake returned to England and semiretired. On January 28, 1596, while leading an expedition to Panama, Drake died of dysentery while onboard his ship.

LEGACY

Drake's sailing skills and bravery brought him great wealth and also earned him the respect of his country. His successes at sea helped Great Britain establish naval supremacy and inspired others to become privateers. Drake also was the first Englishman to circumnavigate the globe.

—Bernadette Zbicki Heiney

FURTHER READING

Bawlf, R. Samuel. *The Secret Voyage of Sir Francis Drake, 1577-1580*. New York: Walker, 2003.

Kelsey, Harry. *Sir Francis Drake: The Queen's Pirate*. New Haven, Conn.: Yale University Press, 1998.

Whitfield, Peter. *Sir Francis Drake*. New York: New York University Press, 2004.

See also: Samuel Bellamy; Elias Hasket Derby; John Hawkwood; Israel Thorndike.

DANIEL DREW
American investor

Drew was one of the great nineteenth century robber barons. He was involved in insider trading and manipulating stock prices; he also engaged in predatory pricing to maintain monopoly power for his firms. Although he died impoverished, when he was wealthy he contributed money to establish the Drew Theological Seminary, which became Drew University.

Born: July 29, 1797; Carmel, New York
Died: September 18, 1879; New York, New York
Sources of wealth: Railroads; investments; transportation systems
Bequeathal of wealth: Educational institution

EARLY LIFE

Daniel Drew was born on a farm in Carmel, New York, in 1797. He grew up poor and virtually illiterate, as did most children of small farmers at that time. During the War of 1812, President James Madison began to draft men into the military; those who did not want to fight were offering $100 to people who would take their place. Regarding this as easy money, Drew became an army substitute. He served three months but saw no combat.

After the war, Drew used his $100 to buy cattle, herd them to New York City, and sell them to city butchers. During one drive he gave his cattle large quantities of salt before they entered Manhattan and let them drink all the water they wanted, thereby increasing their weight. Since he was paid based on the weight of his herd, Drew earned extra money through this scheme. Continually employing this ruse, Drew drove cattle into Manhattan from Ohio, Kentucky, and Illinois and became very wealthy.

FIRST VENTURES

This money let Drew purchase the Bull's Head Tavern, a popular watering hole for drovers. The tavern had a thick safe, and guests gave Drew their money for safekeeping. By taking some of this money and investing it, Drew became a banker and a speculator. His small fortune soon became a large fortune.

While on the lookout for good investment opportunities, Drew became aware of Cornelius Vanderbilt. Vanderbilt was part of the Hudson River Association, which ran boats up and down the Hudson River between Manhattan and Albany, New York. Vanderbilt had argued with his partners, and he bought two boats and ran them in competition with association vessels. As a result, the association lost a lot of money, and it eventually had to buy out Vanderbilt.

Drew replicated Vanderbilt's business methods. He started a competing boat line and squeezed the Hudson River Association until it bought him out. Then he started another line under someone else's name, which was also bought out. The association was so weakened by its continual purchase of rival companies that it eventually sold its business to Drew.

As the owner of the sole means of transportation along the Hudson River, Drew pushed up the price on all river trips. When competition would arise, Drew would reduce his prices. Sometimes he would charge nothing, or even pay people to take his boats, knowing that he had the resources to outlast his rivals. When his competition went out of business, Drew would then charge exorbitant rates and accumulate reserves to fight off the next firm seeking to enter the market.

MATURE WEALTH

During the 1840's, Drew became interested in stock trading. He opened a brokerage business in 1844 that specialized in transportation stock, and he began buying stock in the railroads that were starting to operate in the eastern United States. Drew quickly learned that it was easier to make money trading stock shares than running a business.

He also discovered how easy it was to make money manipulating stock prices. One of his famous schemes was dubbed "the handkerchief trick." Meeting with investors, Drew would pull out his handkerchief to mop his brow. A slip of paper with a large buy order would fall to the floor; Drew would pretend not to notice. When Drew left the meeting, other investors would grab the paper and buy the listed stock. Drew, however, had purchased the touted stock before the meeting. When the other investors bought the stock, driving up its price, Drew sold out at a large profit.

Drew focused most of his attention on the Erie Railroad, then the largest rail network in the world. He acquired competitors of Erie, as well as all the steamboat

lines between Manhattan and upstate New York. At the time, trains could not go directly into Manhattan; they stopped just outside, transferring people and goods onto steamships to complete the trip. By monopolizing transport links in and out of Manhattan, Drew was able to squeeze the Erie Railroad. He offered its main competitor, the New York Central Railroad, better rates on his steamboats into Manhattan. This created financial problems for Erie, and company officials were forced to put Drew on Erie's board of directors and make him company treasurer. These positions enabled Drew to make money from his inside knowledge about the railroad. Before favorable information was announced, he bought Erie stock and profited when the stock price rose. Before bad information was announced, Drew would sell Erie's stock short and buy it back at a lower price after the bad news became public.

Not satisfied gaining money from normal price changes, Drew sought to manipulate the price of Erie stock. When he wanted prices to rise, he would spread positive rumors. When he wanted prices to go down because he had sold short, he would circulate rumors that the railroad was in financial difficulty, or he would have someone obtain a court injunction to prohibit Erie from paying dividends.

With his growing fortune, Drew bought a lot on Seventeenth Street in Manhattan, facing Union Square, and built a four-story mansion, a barn, a cow shed, and a horse stable. Drew, however, had even greater ambitions. He sought to acquire the Erie Railroad and become even wealthier. When Erie decided to extend its rail line by connecting New Jersey and Manhattan, Drew created difficulties for the project. He circulated rumors on Wall Street that there were logistical problems building the tunnel underneath the Hudson River and financial problems at Erie. He also sought to tie up the New York State legislature, which had to approve the construction project. As a result of these actions, capital for the project became scarce, which enabled Drew to come to the rescue. He lent Erie the money it needed, taking the railroad line as security for the loan.

Vanderbilt, wary of Drew from previous dealings with him, wanted to keep Drew from controlling the railroad company. Vanderbilt started buying Erie stock in order to control the railroad himself. Drew, however, got the Erie board of directors to approve a $10 million offering of new stock and bonds in order to replace the railroad's iron rails with steel rails and build a third rail allowing narrow-gauge trains to run on Erie lines. Vanderbilt got an injunction from a Manhattan judge prohibiting Erie from issuing any more stock. In response, Drew and his colleagues Jay Gould and James Fisk got a judge from Binghamton, New York, to order Erie to issue more stock. The three men began printing new shares of Erie stock and selling them to Vanderbilt. When it became clear that they could keep printing and selling new shares, the price of Erie stock tumbled.

Vanderbilt lost a small fortune of $7 million, but he obtained a contempt of court order against Drew, Gould, and Fisk and warrants issued for their arrest. Fearing they would be arrested, the three fled to New Jersey. Safe from the legal arm of New York, they attacked Vanderbilt's rail lines. They reduced Erie's rates for the trip between Buffalo and Manhattan in order to compete with Vanderbilt's New York Central Railroad. They also announced a plan to start a boat line that would charge only fifty cents for a trip between these two cities in order to draw customers away from Vanderbilt's Hudson Railroad. The Drew-Vanderbilt battle eventually ended when Vanderbilt agreed to let Drew keep his money, and Drew agreed to relinquish control of the Erie Railroad.

Nonetheless, Drew sought to make one more killing on Erie stock. Drew, Gould, and Fisk deposited $14 million into various banks. They then sold short in Erie stock and withdrew their $14 million from the banks. The banks, however, had already lent out the money. The bankers were forced to call in their loans, while individuals had to sell their Erie stock in order to repay their bank loans. Stock prices tumbled. Gould, Fisk, and Drew made a fortune, but the economic impact was devastating; people blamed the three for the economic mess. Fearing for his life, Drew decided to abandon the scheme and put money back into Manhattan banks.

In the early 1870's, Drew was one of the wealthiest living Americans. However, his fortunes reversed when the 1873 stock market panic resulted in the demise of several brokerage firms in which he was a partner. Drew had to mortgage his home and take as much property as possible out of his name. In 1887, he lost more money after Gould brought him into a plan to increase Erie stock prices; Gould, however, was really arranging to lower prices. Eventually, Drew was forced to declare bankruptcy.

DREW UNIVERSITY

Drew University is located in Madison, New Jersey, about thirty miles west of Manhattan, on a wooded 186-acre campus nicknamed "the university in the forest." In the nineteenth century, the site housed the antebellum estate of businessman Daniel Drew, who donated the estate and $250,000 to establish the Drew Theological Seminary. The first students attended classes at the seminary in 1867. The College of Missions was added in 1920, offering a course of study for women. In 1928, Arthur and Leonard Baldwin donated $1.5 million to help build an undergraduate liberal arts college, and these educational institutions eventually became known as Drew University.

By 2009, the university was providing a range of undergraduate and graduate programs and emphasizing interdisciplinary courses of study. The Caspersen School for Graduate Studies, which opened in 1955, offers masters of arts degrees and doctoral programs in teaching, poetry, arts and letters, and medical humanities; the Theological School provides masters and doctoral degrees in theological studies and prepares students to enter the ministry. About twenty-five hundred students are enrolled at Drew, the majority of them undergraduates, and most of the students live on campus. The annual tuition, more than $35,000 a year, makes Drew one of the most expensive colleges in the United States.

Drew University employs about 155 full-time faculty members. The archives of the United Methodist Church are housed on the campus, and the library has a large number of documents related to author Willa Cather. During the summer, Drew University is home to the New Jersey Shakespeare Festival.

LEGACY

Daniel Drew was one of the great American robber barons. His methods for earning money were certainly illegal by twenty-first century standards. He engaged in predatory pricing, manipulated stock prices for his own gain, and traded stock based on insider information. In the nineteenth century, however, such activities were normal and usually thought to be smart business practices.

Drew's legacy, however, was not entirely negative. Having had many religious experiences throughout his life and professing to be a devout believer, in the 1860's he donated a large sum of money to establish the Drew Theological Seminary in Madison, New Jersey. The school eventually grew to become Drew University, one of the nation's top liberal arts colleges.

—Steven Pressman

FURTHER READING

Browder, Clifford. *The Money Game in Old New York: Daniel Drew and His Times.* Lexington: University

Press of Kentucky, 1986. A scholarly account of the financial manipulations in which Drew engaged during his lifetime.

Josephson, Matthew. *The Robber Barons: The Great American Capitalists, 1861-1901*. New York: Harcourt Brace Jovanovich, 1934. Reprint. San Diego: Harcourt Brace Jovanovich, 1961. The classic work on the nineteenth century robber baron era in the United States. Contains a detailed history of the lives and schemes of Drew, Gould, Fisk, and Vanderbilt.

Minnigerod, Meade. *Certain Rich Men*. New York: G. P. Putnam's Sons, 1927. A biographical and journalistic account of the lives of seven wealthy Americans, including Drew.

White, Bouck. *The Book of Daniel Drew*. New York: George H. Doran, 1910. Although somewhat speculative and fictional in parts, this work remains the standard biography of Drew.

See also: John Insley Blair; Jim Brady; Jay Cooke; Henry M. Flagler; John W. Garrett; Jay Gould; Hetty Green; Edward H. Harriman; James J. Hill; Mark Hopkins; Collis P. Huntington; Daniel Willis James; George Mortimer Pullman; Russell Sage; Leland Stanford; Cornelius Vanderbilt.

ANTHONY JOSEPH DREXEL
American banker and landowner

Drawing on substantial wealth derived from his successes in banking and real estate ventures, Drexel became a major philanthropist, founding the Drexel Institute of Science and Technology (now known as Drexel University) in 1891. He also established a network of brokerage houses and financial institutions with offices in New York, San Francisco, London, and Paris.

Born: September 13, 1826; Philadelphia, Pennsylvania
Died: June 30, 1893; Carlsbad, Bohemia (now Karlovy Vary, Czech Republic)
Sources of wealth: Inheritance; banking; real estate
Bequeathal of wealth: Relatives; charity; educational institution

EARLY LIFE
A member of a prominent Philadelphia family deeply involved in banking, brokerage, and finance, Anthony Joseph Drexel (DREHK-suhl) got an early start in his family's enterprises. At the age of thirteen, he took his first job at the banking institution founded in 1836 by Francis Martin Drexel, his Austrian-born father. Possessed of a singular aptitude for banking and finance, young Drexel was a fast learner and an enthusiastic and imaginative businessman. When he was twenty-one, he became a partner in his father's financial firm, Drexel and Company, the corporation that would soon become Drexel Burnham Lambert, one of the most distinguished financial houses in the United States.

FIRST VENTURES
Five years after the death of his father in 1863, Drexel, growing restless and eager to expand, left his father's firm to establish a new banking corporation, Drexel, Harjes and Company, which he founded with his partners, John H. Harjes and Eugene Winthrop, in 1868. This company, based in Paris, had a broad international reach. Drexel had greatly increased his fortune during the post-Civil War building boom, for much of which Drexel's company arranged financing. Investment banker Jay Cooke provided considerable sums for the Union cause during the Civil War, and most of this funding derived from the patronage of Drexel's corporations.

MATURE WEALTH
Drexel obtained the funding for George Child to purchase the *Philadelphia Public Ledger*, the first newspaper in the United States to be both politically independent and highly successful. Drexel became a partner with Child in the newspaper. When Drexel's former office boy, Henry Codman Potter, became a bishop in the Episcopal Church, Drexel worked with him to bring about the construction of the largest church in the United States, the Cathedral of Saint John the Divine in New York City. Much of the funding for constructing the cathedral was obtained through Drexel's efforts. When his niece, Katharine Drexel, began to establish an innovative network of schools throughout the United States for African Americans and Native Americans, something almost unimaginable in the last half of the nineteenth century, Drexel

not only arranged much of the financing for this enterprise but also made substantial personal contributions to these schools. Katharine, founder of the Sisters of the Blessed Sacrament, devoted her life to working with minorities, and in recognition of this work she was beatified, achieving sainthood in the Roman Catholic Church in October, 2000.

Drexel had a unique skill in arranging the issuance of government bonds as they were being prepared for marketing. This was a profitable undertaking and helped to establish Drexel as a trustworthy financier who could be depended upon to deal efficiently and honestly with complex financial matters. He also excelled in helping the rapidly expanding American railway system to garner the extensive financing it required. Meanwhile, Drexel was much involved in providing the American mining industry with the needed financial resources for its expansion. Ever devoted to Philadelphia, Drexel bought considerable real estate in the city and its environs, becoming one of the largest property holders in the area.

Despite his prominence in banking circles, Drexel was an intensely private person. He declined to be interviewed and did not keep a diary or a journal. Although he was often encouraged to enter the political arena, he always refused. He destroyed most of his personal papers. Most important, however, he was a highly moral person about whom there was never any breath of scandal, financial or sexual.

So socially withdrawn was Drexel that when Drexel Institute held its opening ceremonies on December 17, 1891, an event attended by an estimated two thousand people, Drexel declined to attend, explaining that he was still in mourning for his wife, Ellen, who had died three months earlier. The opening of the institution was marked by the attendance of such notables as Andrew Carnegie, Thomas Edison, J. P. Morgan, Vice President Levi P. Morton, three members of President Benjamin Harrison's cabinet, U.S. senator Chauncey Depew, and dozens of other luminaries. The establishment of Drexel Institute was as much Ellen's idea as it was her hus-

DREXEL UNIVERSITY

The charitable contribution for which Anthony Joseph Drexel is most remembered is his founding of a unique institution of higher learning, the Drexel Institute of Art, Science, and Industry, renamed Drexel Institute of Technology in 1936 and Drexel University in 1970. During the 1880's, Drexel had been toying with the notion of creating an educational institution. He had made substantial contributions to the network of schools established by his niece, Katharine Drexel. These schools, affiliated with the Roman Catholic Church, were created to serve the educational needs of African Americans and Native Americans.

Drexel realized the obstacles faced by members of racial minorities and by women wishing to gain educations. By the end of the 1880's, he began to conceive the idea of establishing an institution of higher learning in Philadelphia that would serve the needs of a broad range of students, most of them from the Philadelphia area. Admission would be open to all students, regardless of race, gender, religious affiliation, or social class—a stipulation unheard of in contemporary private institutions of higher learning. Drexel's idea germinated quickly, and in 1891 construction began on this private institution that was to meet the educational needs of people of limited means, many of whom had little access to higher education. Drexel spent almost $1 million to construct the buildings in which the institution would be housed and an additional $2 million to staff and equip the university.

Drexel was a practical man. He realized that his university would attract the greatest number of students if it differed from existing private schools of higher learning. To this end, Drexel Institute initiated cooperative programs in which students took time off from their classes to work, for remuneration, in fields related to their studies. The institution also offered a broad selection of night courses, thereby enabling students with full-time jobs to pursue their education while maintaining the jobs needed to support themselves. Generous scholarships were also available to those in need.

Drexel also built his institution within walking distance of a nearby railway station and near several tramlines, enabling students to have accessible transportation to the campus from anywhere in the area. Drexel Institute was largely a commuter's college. Its working-class student body was diverse in backgrounds and ages. Students typically earned their undergraduate degrees in five or six years, compared with four years at most other private colleges.

Drexel University has consistently been at the forefront of many innovative educational programs. Since 2000, it has had the largest medical school in the United States. The medical school, located on two separate campuses, was created by merging two existing institutions—the Hahnemann Medical School and the Women's Medical College of Pennsylvania—with Drexel University.

band's. The last public event that she hosted in her suburban Lansdowne home, Runnymeade, was a reception for people who had been instrumental in establishing the school.

Although Drexel had derived a great deal of his educational philosophy from his niece, Katharine, he had definite ideas regarding education. He had the good sense, however, to realize that conditions change and the institutions that serve people best are those that remain flexible. He did not, therefore, impose his ideas on Drexel Institute.

Drexel's greatest gift was his ability to help people discover their own deep-seated potential and flourish as a result of such discoveries. Prominent among those he influenced in this way were Morgan, Cooke, Child, and his niece, Katharine, who was close to her uncle. Morgan was an underachiever. He lacked self-confidence and seemed to be headed nowhere until, at the urging of his father, Junius Spencer Morgan, Drexel became involved in the young man's life. However, Drexel did not receive full credit for affecting Morgan's life, largely because all of the papers relating to Drexel were destroyed on his orders, whereas the Morgan papers have been preserved.

J. P. Morgan and Company, which became one of the world's most celebrated banking establishments, was actually founded by Drexel, not by Morgan. Drexel and Morgan became partners in 1871 with the founding of Drexel, Morgan and Company. This new partnership was based in New York City, but it served as an agent for Europeans investing in the United States. When Drexel, Morgan was established, Drexel Harjes, now in business for three years, became the French affiliate for the banking corporation that would eventually be called J. P. Morgan and Company and was later known as J. P. Morgan Chase.

The Drexel-Morgan partnership was very strong and had a vast impact upon the growth of industry in the United States. Drexel, Morgan and Company and J. P. Morgan and Company were responsible for the financing that led to the establishment of three corporate giants, General Electric Company, International Harvester Corporation, and United States Steel Corporation (better known as U.S. Steel), to say nothing of many smaller companies. United States Steel, which Morgan took over from Carnegie, became the world's first billion-dollar corporation.

LEGACY

Drexel died in 1893. Upon his death, it was revealed that he had left Drexel Institute $1 million and much of his valuable art collection. He also provided every clerk at Drexel and Company with $100 for every year of service. He had established three trusts for family members. His estate was valued at between $25 and $35 million, the largest on record in Pennsylvania at that time.

Besides his corporate contributions, Drexel's legacy was firmly established with his founding of the Drexel Institute of Technology. This institution embodied an educational and social philosophy that was unique at the end of the nineteenth century, a philosophy completely compatible with the democratic ideals of the United States.

—R. Baird Shuman

FURTHER READING

Gallman, J. Matthew. *Mastering Wartime: A Social History of Philadelphia During the Civil War.* Philadelphia: University of Pennsylvania Press, 2000. This reprint of Gallman's 1990 study has valuable information on how Drexel helped to finance the Union cause.

Geisst, Charles R. *Wall Street: A History.* New York: Oxford University Press, 1997. Provides valuable insights into Drexel's role in making Wall Street the financial center of the United States.

Papadakis, Constantine. *Drexel University: A University with a Difference—the Unique Vision of Anthony J. Drexel.* New York: The Newcomen Society of the United States, 2001. A brief, lucid overview of Drexel University written by its president.

Rottenberg, Dan. *The Man Who Made Wall Street: Anthony J. Drexel and the Rise of Modern Finance.* Philadelphia: University of Pennsylvania Press, 2001. A comprehensive assessment of Drexel and his contributions to finance and to American education.

Strouse, Jean. *Morgan: American Financier.* New York: Random House, 1999. An extensive study of the rise of J. P. Morgan and of his financial relationship to Drexel, who helped to subdue some of Morgan's excesses.

See also: George F. Baker; Andrew Carnegie; Jay Cooke; Daniel Drew; Thomas Edison; Jay Gould; Hetty Green; J. P. Morgan; George Peabody; Russell Sage; Jacob Schiff; James Stillman.

DORIS DUKE
American socialite, philanthropist, and investor

Duke was a generous philanthropist during her lifetime. Her will endowed the Doris Duke Charitable Foundation, which provides grants for medical research, wildlife preservation, child abuse prevention, and the performing arts. Her foundation also supports three estates that are educational or recreational centers open to the public.

Born: November 22, 1912; New York, New York
Died: October 28, 1993; Beverly Hills, California
Sources of wealth: Inheritance; real estate
Bequeathal of wealth: Charity

EARLY LIFE
Doris Duke was born in New York City on November 22, 1912. She was the only child of American tobacco and energy tycoon James Buchanan Duke and his second wife, Nanaline Holt Inman, a southern aristocrat and widow of William Patterson Inman. At her birth, Duke was called the world's richest baby. She had a loving relationship with her father, who treated her as an adult. She had personal servants, including a chauffeur, bodyguards, maids, nurses, and private tutors. Duke led a sheltered life without close friends of her own age. She developed a love for gospel singing on a trip to Harlem in New York City with her father. On his deathbed, Duke's father told her to trust no one. He died on October 10, 1925, before her thirteenth birthday, leaving her $100 million ($1.25 billion in 2008).

FIRST VENTURES
Duke's father left only a small trust fund to his wife, so the mother-daughter relationship was strained. When her mother began selling family assets, the fourteen-year-old Duke sued her mother in order to stop her. After her father's death, Duke read bags of mail that he had hidden from her. Death threats and demands for money made Duke realize there were people who hated her for her wealth. For the rest of her life, she would value privacy and security. However, the media was fascinated with the lives of the rich and relentlessly pursued Duke.

When the stock market crashed in 1929 and many of Duke's affluent friends lost their fortunes, she helped them financially, often secretly. Duke anonymously purchased organs for thousands of small churches in the United States. At the age of twenty-one, Duke used money from a trust fund to establish her first foundation, Independent Aid, later called the Doris Duke Charitable Foundation. This foundation was established to perform primarily anonymous philanthropy throughout Duke's life.

MATURE WEALTH
In February, 1935, Duke married thirty-eight-year-old Jimmy Cromwell, a playboy with political ambitions. His family had lost much of its fortune, so he needed Duke's financial support. She gave him a monthly allowance of $10,000 (the equivalent of $125,000 in 2008). Their honeymoon was a two-year trip around the world, during which Duke developed a passion for Southeast Asian and Islamic culture. She purchased priceless art treasures. Their last stop was Honolulu, Hawaii, where Duke built a winter home, Shangri La, in 1937.

Shangri La became Duke's private retreat, where she could escape unwanted publicity. She built it to house her collection of Islamic art and to create a unique blend of Islamic and Hawaiian architecture and landscape. For more than fifty

Doris Duke in her car. (NY Daily News via Getty Images)

THE DORIS DUKE CHARITABLE FOUNDATION

Doris Duke was famous for her vast wealth and often scandalous life, but she was also a generous philanthropist, dancer, musician, art collector, and environmentalist. On October 28, 1993, Doris Duke died at the age of eighty. She wanted the bulk of her $1.2 billion estate to be donated to charity for the improvement of humanity. After years of bitter litigation and numerous claims to her fortune, her estate was finally settled. The Doris Duke Charitable Foundation (DDCF) was created in 1996 to improve the quality of people's lives. In keeping with Duke's wishes, DDCF set up grant programs in four areas: performing arts, environmental conservation, medical research, and child abuse prevention.

Her will also called for three operating foundations to be funded by the DDCF in order to manage and preserve three properties. The Duke Farms Foundation manages the twenty-seven-hundred-acre Duke Farms in Hillsborough, New Jersey. Duke's father, tobacco and energy tycoon James Buchanan Duke, had developed this family estate as a public park for the enjoyment of nature, and Doris, a lifelong conservationist, had designed greenhouse gardens reflecting diverse areas of the world. The Doris Duke Foundation for Islamic Art preserves Shangri La, Duke's palace in Honolulu, Hawaii. The Newport Restoration Foundation manages historic houses in Newport, Rhode Island, and Rough Point, her summer home in Newport. All properties are educational or recreational resources open to the public.

The first grants were awarded in 1997. From 1997 through 2008, DDCF approved 947 grants totaling more than $648 million to nonprofit organizations in the United States. In 2008, grants totaled almost $66 million.

In its first decade, the foundation's endowment nearly doubled to $2 billion. However, with fluctuations in portfolio returns and economic downturns, the foundation's financial assets totaled about $1.4 billion as of December 31, 2008. On March 18, 2009, a letter from DDCF's president Edward P. Henry addressed how declining assets and uncertain economic conditions would affect the foundation's future work. He stated that in 2009, internal operating costs would be reduced by 20 to 25 percent, total grant spending would be reduced by 25 percent, and special initiatives in climate change and African health would progress at half the previously planned budget.

In April, 2009, DDCF awarded $3.6 million in grants to four organizations to help states safeguard nature in an era of climate change. The recipients were the Association of Fish and Wildlife Agencies, Defenders of Wildlife, National Wildlife Federation, and the Theodore Roosevelt Conservation Partnership. In May, 2009, the foundation awarded a $2 million grant to the Environmental Defense Fund's Center for Conservation Incentives to enable the center to provide private landowners with incentives to conserve farms, forests, ranches, and other natural areas critical for the nation's wildlife.

---

years, Duke purchased or commissioned pieces for the collection of about thirty-five hundred artifacts. The five-acre Shangri La overlooks the Pacific Ocean and Diamond Head and showcases a seventy-five-foot saltwater pool and exotic gardens.

Cromwell became the U.S. ambassador to Canada in 1939, and the couple was often separated. Convinced that Cromwell was a fortune hunter, Duke was unhappy and had scandalous affairs. In 1940, she gave birth to a premature baby girl, Arden, who lived only one day. Her doctors told Duke she would not be able to have more children. For the rest of her life, Duke grieved for Arden. Cromwell and Duke divorced in 1943.

In 1945, Duke became a foreign correspondent for the International News Service. After World War II, she was a writer for *Harper's Bazaar* in Paris, where she met Porfirio Rubirosa, a Dominican diplomat, race car driver, and polo player. They married in September, 1947. He was a notorious playboy, and Duke allegedly had paid

$1 million to his previous wife Danielle Darrieux to divorce him. Rubirosa and Duke divorced in 1948.

During her lifetime, Duke made wise investments in real estate. She owned five homes, managed by a permanent staff of more than two hundred people. Her properties included Shangri La, the twenty-seven-hundred-acre Duke Farms in New Jersey, a Beverly Hills mansion, a Park Avenue penthouse, and Rough Point, her summer home in Newport, Rhode Island.

In 1988, at the age of seventy-five, Duke legally adopted thirty-five-year-old Charlene "Chandi" Heffner, whom Duke believed was the reincarnation of her deceased daughter, Arden. Heffner's friend Bernard Lafferty became Duke's butler, and James Burns, Heffner's boyfriend, became Duke's bodyguard. In 1990 in Hawaii, Duke became mysteriously sick and was knocked unconscious during a fall. Lafferty agreed with Duke that Heffner and Burns were plotting against her. Lafferty and Duke moved to her Beverly Hills mansion. In 1991,

Duke ended her relationship with Heffner, who filed a breach-of-contract lawsuit.

During her last years, Duke was a recluse, mistrustful of friends and relatives. It was rumored that Lafferty isolated and controlled her. At his suggestion, she had a series of operations. In 1992, she fell and broke her hip days after getting cosmetic surgery. During recuperation, she took antidepressants, painkillers, and tranquilizers.

In April, 1993, Duke signed her final will, which named Lafferty as the executor of her estate. She also stated that she regretted the adoption of Heffner, who should not be allowed to inherit from Duke's estate or the two trust funds set up by Duke's father.

After a knee operation in July, 1993, she suffered a stroke, was hospitalized, and was put on feeding and breathing tubes. After returning home in September, 1993, she was an invalid and had to be heavily sedated with high doses of morphine. Duke died on October 28, 1993, and was cremated within twenty-four hours. Her ashes were scattered into the Pacific Ocean. Duke left most of her $1.2 billion estate to charity.

Probate lasted nearly three years. The litigation involved numerous claimants and complex issues. Duke's nurse, Tammy Payette, asserted that Lafferty had hastened Duke's death with high doses of morphine in order to keep Duke from changing her will. As Lafferty's health deteriorated, he agreed to resign as executor of Duke's estate for a cash settlement. Heffner sued the trustees and eventually settled for $65 million. Probate ended in 1996 with the establishment of the Doris Duke Charitable Foundation. Estate and legal fees had already reached $10 million by 1997.

Legacy

During her lifetime, Duke was an extremely generous and often anonymous philanthropist. She left most of her $1.2 billion estate to create one of the world's most richly endowed foundations. The Doris Duke Charitable Foundation was established in 1996 to improve the quality of people's lives by awarding grants and preserving Duke's historic estates as educational, environmental, and cultural resources.

Her controversial life, wealth, and mysterious death entered popular culture, including the film and television industries. In 1999, CBS (Columbia Broadcasting System) presented the four-part miniseries *Too Rich: The Secret Life of Doris Duke*, starring Lauren Bacall as Duke and Richard Chamberlain as Lafferty. In 2008, HBO (Home Box Office) broadcast *Bernard and Doris*, a semifictional drama starring Susan Sarandon as Duke and Ralph Fiennes as Lafferty, which received numerous Screen Actors Guild, Emmy, and Golden Globe awards.

—Alice Myers

FURTHER READING

Duke, Pony, and Jason Thomas. *Too Rich: The Family Secrets of Doris Duke*. New York: HarperCollins, 1996. A candid, inside portrait written by Duke's cousin and godson. Includes illustrations and index.

Levy, Shawn. *The Last Playboy: The High Life of Porfirio Rubirosa*. New York: Harper Paperbacks, 2006. Entertaining and revealing biography which includes the intriguing story of Duke's relationship with Rubirosa, her second husband. Contains illustrations, bibliography, and index.

Littlefield, Sharon. *Doris Duke's Shangri La*. Honolulu: Honolulu Academy of Arts, 2002. Showcases the architectural grandeur of Duke's Hawaiian refuge and its extensive Islamic art collection. Includes illustrations and bibliography.

Mansfield, Stephanie. *The Richest Girl in the World: The Extravagant Life and Fast Times of Doris Duke*. New York: Pinnacle Books, 1999. Entertaining biography which includes details of her many friendships with the rich and famous. Contains illustrations, bibliography, and index.

Schwarz, Ted. *Trust No One: The Glamorous Life and Bizarre Death of Doris Duke*. New York: St. Martin's Press, 1997. Written with Tom Rybak, a member of Duke's personal staff, this biography explores her mysterious death and how she followed her father's advice to trust no one. Includes illustrations, bibliography, and index.

Tingley, Nancy. *Doris Duke: The Southeast Asian Art Collection*. New York: The Foundation for Southeast Asian Art and Culture, 2003. A scholarly documentation of the collection, with beautiful color photographs throughout the book. Includes bibliography and index.

Valentine, Tom, and Patrick Mahn. *Daddy's Duchess*. Secaucus, N.J.: Lyle Stuart, 1997. This unauthorized biography written by two former employees is a controversial chronicle of Duke's life. Includes illustrations and index.

See also: Eighteenth Duchess of Alba; Brooke Astor; Vincent Astor; James Buchanan Duke; Barbara Hutton; Joan Kroc; Marjorie Merriweather Post; Consuelo Vanderbilt; Gloria Vanderbilt.

JAMES BUCHANAN DUKE
American tobacco and hydroelectric industrialist

Duke emerged as a typical rags-to-riches success in the cigarette and hydroelectric power businesses in the post-Civil War South. His trust fund, the Duke Endowment, has greatly contributed to the welfare of the Carolinas in the areas of health care, child care, religion, and higher education.

Born: December 23, 1856; Durham, North Carolina
Died: October 10, 1925; New York, New York
Also known as: Buck Duke
Sources of wealth: Manufacturing; sale of products; utilities
Bequeathal of wealth: Children; relatives; educational institution; charity

EARLY LIFE
James Buchanan "Buck" Duke was born in 1856 in Durham, North Carolina, the youngest son of Washington Duke and his second wife, Artelia Roney Duke. He received some schooling at local academies and attended New Garden School in Greensboro, North Carolina (now Guilford College), and the Eastman Business College in Poughkeepsie, New York. Duke, however, spent more time working on his father's farm and later in the family's tobacco product business than pursuing his education.

FIRST VENTURES
When Washington Duke returned from military service after the Civil War, he found that his farm had been ravaged by Union troops, but a load of tobacco stored in a shed somehow escaped confiscation. At that time tobacco was so scarce that Washington's load of tobacco sold quickly, and he switched from farming to tobacco production. He was the first person to plant tobacco in Durham, in 1858, and he founded William Duke and Sons Company in 1865 to process tobacco. By 1872, the Duke family sold 125,000 pounds of tobacco annually.

James Duke and his brother Benjamin Duke took over the company in the 1880's. Having difficulty competing with another well-established tobacco firm, Blackwell and Co., they decided to switch from tobacco production to cigarette manufacture, since cigarettes were then a new product. To compete with the four companies that produced 80 percent of cigarettes for the market, James Duke acquired a license to install two machines invented by James Albert Bonsack, which would roll his company's cigarettes, enabling him to produce cigarettes more quickly and efficiently than his competitors. Three years later, he moved his company to New Jersey to take advantage of the state's corporation laws and to exploit the markets in the northern and western United States.

MATURE WEALTH
By 1890, Duke's company provided 40 percent of the cigarettes marketed in the United States. Using the Bonsack machines, the company could produce more cigarettes than all its competitors combined. In addition, Duke merged with his four competitors, forming the American Tobacco Company, and then gradually obtained control of the American cigarette business. His next step was to enter the international market in order to compete with British companies. Duke reached an agreement with the British companies that enabled him to control the American market, while the British firms would dominate the market in British territories; Duke and the British firms also established the British-American Tobacco Company in order to cooperate in the sale of tobacco to the rest of the world. As a result of this agreement, by the beginning of the twentieth century Duke controlled 90 percent of the American and half of the international tobacco markets.

In 1906, the U.S. Supreme Court found Duke's company guilty of violating the Sherman Antitrust Act and ordered the corporation to divide into three separate companies: Liggett and Myers, the P. Lorillard Company, and the American Tobacco Company. According to the Court, Duke's business used illegal secret agreements and false public promotions to monopolize the market. In 1911, the Court again divided the American Tobacco Company into smaller companies. Duke now controlled only three companies, but with a capitalization of more than $500 million his power within the tobacco business remained strong. Around this time, Duke also sold his company's shares in the British-American Tobacco Company.

Another source of Duke's wealth was his hydroelectric business. He founded the Southern Power Company (now known as Duke Power) in 1905 to provide electricity to the Duke family's textile factory, which opened in 1892 and was managed by his brother Benjamin. Southern Power gradually became the sole electric supplier to cotton mills and other industrial companies, as well as to

---

DUKE UNIVERSITY

Trinity College, a Methodist-related school, was established in Randolph County, North Carolina, in 1838. Businessman Washington Duke helped the school relocate to Durham, North Carolina, in 1892. His son James Buchanan Duke helped build a new university near the school, providing $21 million from the Duke Endowment for construction. At the insistence of William Preston Few, the president of Trinity College, James Duke agreed to name the new school Duke University, with "Duke" referring to both Washington and James Duke.

Duke's original campus (now called East Campus) was rebuilt with Georgian-style buildings at a cost of $4.8 million, with construction beginning in 1925 and ending in 1927. The university's building committee expended more than $16 million for the Gothic-style buildings in the West Campus, the site of Duke Chapel, and for the purchase of more than five acres of land. The 210-foot chapel was the most expensive building on campus, built at a cost of $2.3 million, with construction completed in 1935. In 2008, the Duke Endowment provided $50 million to enable the Duke Medical Center to construct a building for medical education and to develop a state-of-the-art inpatient facility for pediatric patients.

In 1972, Trinity College merged with the Woman's College to become Trinity College of Arts and Sciences, the undergraduate liberal arts college of Duke University. Many of Duke University's goals are identical with the educational goals of the Duke Endowment. For example, in order to attract talented faculty, the university provides endowment funds for faculty chairs. In past decades, it has had the sixth highest number of Fulbright, Rhodes, Truman, and Goldwater scholarship recipients in the nation. Duke recruits top students from around the country, accepting about 20 percent of applicants, 96 percent of whom rank in the top 10 percent of their high school classes. The school has adopted a need-blind admissions policy, which accepts students based on their academic performance and potential without considering applicants' financial status or ability to pay for a college education. After a student is admitted, the university then commits to providing 100 percent of his or her financial need for all four years of undergraduate education.

In 2004, Duke University's research expenditures topped $490 million, and funding since then has increased 14.5 percent. In 2007, Duke launched a $30 million program called Duke Engage to provide students with community service opportunities. The school has also developed a joint medical program with the National University of Singapore.

investments in textile mills and corporations that produced cotton and wool.

Duke owned homes and estates in Charlotte, North Carolina; Somerville, New Jersey; New York City; and Newport, Rhode Island. These homes and estates were large and housed Duke's sculpture collections. The Charlotte mansion, for example, had forty-five rooms and twelve baths. With more than twenty-seven hundred acres of woods, lakes, and fields, Duke Farms in Hillsborough remained the largest private landholding in New Jersey into the twenty-first century. Duke acquired control of the Raritan Water Power Company partly as a means of supplying water to a chain of lakes, fountains, and streams on this estate.

The Duke family was well known in North and South Carolina for their generous philanthropy. Washington Duke helped relocate Trinity College from Trinity to Durham in 1892, and he gave the school a $100,000 endowment in 1896. James Duke's first gift to the school was a library building and $10,000 for books. On December 11, 1924, he established the Duke Endowment, a $40 million trust fund with designated beneficiaries in the Carolinas. His indenture of trust specified four educational institutions as beneficiaries: Trinity College (now Duke University); Furman University in Greenville, South Carolina; Johnson C. Smith University in Charlotte; and Davidson College in Davidson, North Carolina. Other beneficiaries included nonprofit hospitals and child-care institutions in the Carolinas, Methodist churches, and retired Methodist preachers in North Carolina. On his death, Duke left about half of his estate, or $67 million, to the trust fund, increasing the Duke Endowment to $107 million.

Duke became ill with pneumonia and died in New York City on October 10, 1925. Like his father and brother, he was buried in the Memorial Chapel on the campus of Duke University. The remainder of his estate, or the equivalent of about $1 billion, went to twelve-year-old Doris Duke, his only child from his second marriage, to Nanaline Holt Inman. As a result, Doris became the richest girl in the world, while her mother received only a small trust fund. In addition, Duke allocated $2 million to other relatives, including the children of his father's brothers and sisters.

cities and towns in the Piedmont region of North and South Carolina. From 1907 to 1925, the company built eleven power plants. In 1915, Duke purchased hydroelectric power resources on the Saguenay River in Quebec, Canada. He also increased his wealth with extensive

LEGACY

James Buchanan Duke exemplified the American entrepreneurs, who, despite a lack of education, could rise from rags to riches through confidence and business acumen. While he was certainly an inspiring person in the business world, he was more important for the societal contributions made by his Duke Endowment. His practice of financial stewardship was inspired by his Methodist faith and his father, who was also a generous benefactor.

By the twenty-first century, the Duke Endowment, based in Charlotte, North Carolina, was one of the largest charitable foundations in the United States, valued at more than $2.7 billion. The endowment supported child care, health care, the Methodist Church, and higher education in the Carolinas. Its goal in promoting education was to educate people of principle and promise whose future contributions would benefit society. Funding from the Duke Endowment has allowed select colleges and universities to construct landmark facilities, attract talented faculty, recruit top students, improve affordability, support research, encourage innovation, and pioneer new roles for other universities and communities.

—Anh Tran

FURTHER READING

Bryan, John Morrill, and Robert C. Lautman. *Duke University: An Architectural Tour.* New York: Princeton Architectural Press, 2000. Provides an insider's look at the historic and interesting gardens and buildings on the university campus. Includes color photographs.

Durden, Robert F. *Bold Entrepreneur: A Life of James Buchanan Duke.* Durham, N.C.: Carolina Academic Press, 2003. Portrays Duke as a business genius, an avid horticulturist, and a man who invested in a plan for perpetual philanthropy in the Carolinas.

_____. *Lasting Legacy to the Carolinas: The Duke Endowment, 1924-1994.* Durham, N.C.: Duke University Press, 1998. Describes the creation of the Duke Endowment, its relationship with Duke Power Company, its impact on philanthropy, and how it was affected by tax reform laws.

Porter, Patrick G. "Origins of the American Tobacco Company." *The Business Review* 43 (1969): 59-76. Discusses Duke's innovations in the American tobacco industry. Considers his career and the early history of the American Tobacco Company as case studies in the history of business advertising and the birth of big business in the United States.

Sobel, Robert. *The Entrepreneurs: Explorations Within the American Business Tradition.* New York: Beard Books, 2000. Explores the lives and careers of nine representative innovators in business during the last two hundred years, with chapter 5 devoted to Duke.

See also: Arthur Vining Davis; Doris Duke; Thomas Fortune Ryan; Peter A. B. Widener.

ALFRED I. DU PONT
American industrialist and real estate developer

Du Pont used the wealth he acquired in his family's gunpowder works to develop the Florida panhandle. After his death, he bequeathed funds to provide care for chronically ill children in Delaware, eventually becoming the nation's largest single benefactor for children's health care.

Born: May 12, 1864; Brandywine Valley region, Delaware
Died: April 28, 1935; Jacksonville, Florida
Also known as: Alfred Irénée du Pont
Sources of wealth: Inheritance; patents; manufacturing; sale of products; investments; real estate
Bequeathal of wealth: Spouse; children; charity

EARLY LIFE

Alfred Irénée du Pont (dew pont) was born on May 12, 1864, the eldest of five children. His grandfather, Eleuthère Irénée du Pont (1771-1834), founded the family gunpowder business in the Brandywine Valley region of Delaware, and the business flourished because it obtained lucrative government contracts during the War of 1812. Alfred's father, Eleuthère Irénée du Pont II (1829-1877), was a senior partner in the family business. Because of his leadership and the large contracts obtained during the Crimean War and the Civil War, the business thrived. The du Ponts controlled much of Delaware politics, and by 1872 they were able to drive most of their rivals out of business, thus gaining a monopoly. Alfred frequently visited the gunpowder works with his father.

Life dramatically changed for Alfred at an early age. He began to lose his hearing after a boyhood swimming incident. When he was thirteen, his mother and father died within a month of each other. The five du Pont children were sent to boarding schools. Alfred attended the prestigious Andover Academy and then the Massachusetts Institute of Technology (MIT), where he joined his cousin, T. Coleman du Pont. Alfred was on the Andover Academy boxing team, played the violin, and had a talent for musical composition and for understanding the intricacies involved in the operation of machinery. At MIT, he studied chemistry, mathematics, and German, which at the time was a necessary language for understanding chemistry.

FIRST VENTURES

In 1884, upon completing his sophomore year, du Pont went to work in the family business. Within five years he had worked his way up from an entry-level common laborer at the Hagley Gunpowder Mills to the position of yard supervisor. By then, his loss of hearing was nearly complete and people had to communicate with him in writing. Nevertheless, du Pont quickly gained a reputation as a gunpowder expert, inventing new machinery to improve the efficiency and safety of the gunpowder manufacturing process. During his life, du Pont registered

Alfred I. du Pont. (The Granger Collection, New York)

more than two hundred patents, most of which were related to gunpowder production. Within five years he was made a junior partner at the firm, along with his cousins, Coleman and Pierre, and the company was renamed E. I. du Pont de Nemours and Company.

In 1889, du Pont negotiated a license for "smokeless" gunpowder from a Belgian firm. The company made large profits from European sales and from government contracts during the Spanish-American War of 1898. By the end of the war, du Pont gunpowder was the first choice of the American armed forces. With the death of Edward du Pont in 1902, the other three senior partners considered selling the company to a rival firm. However, Alfred and his two cousins convinced the senior partners to turn the company over to the three younger men in exchange for promissory notes and shares of stock. As a result, Coleman became president, Pierre became treasurer and executive vice president, and Alfred served as vice president for operations and was also in charge of gunpowder production. Unfortunately, Alfred's hearing impairment was compounded by an additional physical problem, when in 1904, he lost an eye in a hunting accident.

MATURE WEALTH

As the older generation of du Pont managers made way for the new, the very nature of the family business was dramatically transformed. The three cousins, all MIT graduates, strongly believed that the company should diversify and pioneer innovative products, such as new types of paints, dyes, and plastics. Alfred supported research to create these products. The company had to decide if it would conduct research in departmental or general laboratories. Alfred argued that the company could do both, and he was able to get his way. However, Alfred's cousins generally considered him to be entirely too conservative in his business decisions and embarrassingly radical in his personal life. While Alfred was the undisputed "czar" of gunpowder operations, it was Coleman who was the master of the increasingly complex organizational structure and Pierre who was the financial wizard of the corporation as it became heavily involved in new technologies.

Increasingly, Albert's views ran contrary to those of his cousin Pierre. Alfred's personal life was also a divisive factor in his deteriorating relationship with his two cousins. Alfred divorced his first wife, the mother of his four children, in 1906, and the following year he married Alicia Bradford, a second cousin whose former husband worked for the company. To add to family concern, Alfred built his new wife a forty-seven-thousand-square-foot mansion in Wilmington, Delaware, housed on three hundred acres and designed in eighteenth century château style by renowned architects. The estate was named Nemours after the ancestral French town from which the du Ponts originated. For a leading national family in turn-of-the-century America, Alfred's personal life was embarrassing, if not scandalous.

The outbreak of World War I in 1914 caused a tremendous acceleration of gunpowder shipments, particularly to England and France, and increased prosperity for the three cousins. However, another war was brewing. In 1915, Alfred's two cousins decided to sell a large block of stock to company officers and directors. The company was clearly headed toward becoming a public corporation instead of a family-owned business. Alfred protested, and he then sued Pierre and Coleman. When the case was decided against Alfred in 1917, he resigned from the corporation and maintained life-long enmity toward Coleman and Pierre.

Deciding to use his fortune to pave his own way in the financial world, du Pont established an investment firm, Nemours Trading Corporation, and an import-export operation in New York. He also invested in banks. Ultimately, he acquired a 60 percent interest in Delaware Trust Company.

In January, 1920, du Pont's wife Alicia died of a heart attack. One year later, he married Jessie Ball, a descendant of George Washington's mother, and moved to Florida. Jesse was a high school teacher and thirty-six years old when she married the nearly deaf fifty-seven-year-old du Pont. They began life together by building an elegant mansion in Jacksonville, Florida, and investing in south Florida real estate. Aiding his investment strategies was Jesse's brother, Edward Ball, who involved du Pont in the purchase of tens of thousands of acres in the Florida panhandle, including most of the city of Port St. Joe, the Apalachicola Northern Railroad, the St. Joseph Telephone & Telegraph Company, and several banks. In 1927, du Pont created the Gulf Coast Highways Association as a lobbying agency to obtain government funds for highway construction in the panhandle. However, the

THE NEMOURS FOUNDATION

When Alfred I. du Pont died in 1935, he left an estate valued at $40 million and a will setting up a charitable foundation to provide health care services to children. Exactly why he chose this as the focus of his philanthropy remains a mystery, since there is no record of his involvement with chronically ill children during his lifetime. The foundation was to be named after his French ancestral home, Nemours, and was to devote its attention to the needs of children in du Pont's native state of Delaware.

Originally the foundation operated the Alfred I. du Pont Hospital for Children in Wilmington, Delaware, founded in 1940 to provide health care for crippled children. The hospital maintained this focus for the next four decades and then expanded to offer health care services to the elderly.

The death of Alfred's third wife, Jesse Ball du Pont, in 1971 greatly increased funding for the Nemours Foundation. In addition, Alfred du Pont's brother-in-law, Edward Ball, expanded the foundation after his death in 1981, when he left much of his vast estate for the care of children in Jacksonville, Florida. The bequest resulted in construction of the Nemours Children's Hospital in Jacksonville and the creation of dozens of pediatric clinics in Delaware, Florida, New Jersey, and Pennsylvania. Ball's bequest also led to significant funding for medical research aimed at discovering new means of treating diseases affecting children. In 2004, the foundation founded Nemours Health and Prevention Services, which takes a holistic approach to children's health and is focusing its initial efforts on a childhood obesity program in Delaware and an early dyslexia detection program in Jacksonville

The Nemours Foundation also maintains the popular *Kid's Health* Web site, which provides information about children's mental and physical health spanning the period from birth to adulthood. The three-hundred-acre Nemours Mansion and Gardens in Wilmington, Delaware, is also operated by the foundation. The forty-two-thousand-square-foot mansion, located on the grounds of the Alfred I. du Pont Hospital for Children, was built in Louis XIV château style and is furnished with antiques and many works of art. It is open for public tours, which conclude with a visit to the chauffeurs' garage, where the family's antique cars are on display. The Nemours Mansion and Gardens completed a $39 million restoration in 2008.

In 2009, the trust founded by Alfred I. du Pont was valued at $4.6 billion. Since 1940, 3 percent of the trust's funds have been distributed annually for health care, earning Alfred I. du Pont the distinction of being the nation's largest single benefactor for children's health care.

onset of the Great Depression forestalled most of these ambitious development plans. In 1929, du Pont helped save the Florida National Bank by giving the bank $15 million of his own funds to maintain its solvency.

Du Pont died in Jacksonville, Florida, in 1935, at the age of seventy. His wife Jessie continued his philanthropic interests until her death in 1970, while her brother, Edward Ball, managed du Pont's investments. By the time of Ball's death in 1981, du Pont's $40 million trust had increased to more than $2 billion.

LEGACY

Alfred I. du Pont's expertise in gunpowder production and his role in helping to save the du Pont corporation from dissolution resulted in the growth of one of America's major and most enduring businesses. Although personal choices caused him to be regarded as the "du Pont family rebel," his life accomplishments earned him a place in history as an important member of an illustrious American family. The construction of two elegant mansions, one in Delaware and one in Florida, indicates that he did not stray too far from the lifestyle of opulent American families.

　　Du Pont's later entrepreneurial role in trying to stimulate economic growth in the Florida panhandle earned him recognition from the Florida Department of State in 2000, when he was named one of the "great Floridians." However, his greatest legacy is as a philanthropist. By establishing the Nemours Foundation, du Pont contributed his considerable financial resources to benefit the health of children.

—Irwin Halfond

FURTHER READING

Chandler, Alfred D., and Stephen Salsbury. *Pierre S. Du Pont and the Making of the Modern Corporation.* Knoxville, Ill.: Beard Books, 2001. A biography of Alfred du Pont's cousin, containing much information about his relationship with Alfred.

Gaines, Francis P. *Edward Ball and the Alfred I. Du Pont Tradition.* 1959. Reprint. Whitefish, Mont.: Kessinger, 2006. A study of the role of Alfred du Pont's brother-in-law in completing Alfred's life's work.

Kinnane, Adrian. *Du Pont: From the Banks of the Brandywine to Miracles of Science.* Baltimore: Johns Hopkins University Press, 2002. A scholarly history, spanning two centuries, of the development of one of America's most enduring and influential corporations.

Wall, Joseph Frazier. *Alfred I. Du Pont: The Man and His Family.* New York: Oxford University Press, 1990. A lengthy and fascinating study of du Pont's personality and career.

Winkler, John K. *The Du Pont Dynasty.* 1935. Reprint. Whitefish, Mont.: Kessinger, 2005. Colorfully written, though at the expense of historical accuracy.

See also: Henry Francis du Pont; Irénée du Pont; Alfred Nobel; James Smithson; William Weightman.

HENRY FRANCIS DU PONT
American art collector, horticulturist, and philanthropist

Du Pont amassed the world's most extensive collection of American antique furniture, furnishings, and decorative arts. He housed the objects in Winterthur, his Delaware mansion, where he used the estate and the collection to create the Winterthur Museum and its extensive gardens for the enjoyment and education of the public.

Born: May 27, 1880; Winterthur, Delaware
Died: April 10, 1969; Winterthur, Delaware
Sources of wealth: Inheritance; real estate
Bequeathal of wealth: Children; museum; educational institution

EARLY LIFE

Henry Francis du Pont (dew pont) was born into one of the wealthiest and most prominent families in the United States. His autocratic father, Henry Algernon du Pont, valedictorian of his class at the U.S. Military Academy at West Point and later a U.S. senator from Delaware, was disappointed in Henry Francis (better known as Harry), a shy boy who loved flowers and collecting birds' eggs and stamps. The only surviving son of seven children, Harry was very close to his mother, Mary Pauline Foster du Pont.

　　At age thirteen, the young du Pont was sent to board at the Groton School in Massachusetts. Never a good student, he graduated last in his class. Du Pont went on to Harvard University, where he studied planting procedures, the cultivation of shrubs and trees, and greenhouse maintenance at the Bussey Institution, Harvard's college of practical agriculture and horticulture. He graduated in 1903.

FIRST VENTURES

For the first time in 1901 and then almost every summer until the outbreak of World War I, du Pont traveled to Europe with his father to visit the great gardens, nurseries, and exhibitions of the times. He was particularly impressed with the design and color of English formal gardens.

After his father's election to the U.S. Senate in 1906, du Pont relocated to Washington, D.C., to serve on the senator's staff. However, a nervous condition that caused his fidgeting, poor handwriting, and mumbled speech made him unable to perform his job. His heart was at his family's Delaware mansion, Winterthur, where he had already planted daffodils in the estate's March Bank. It was not long before Senator du Pont realized that he should cede management of the estate's grounds and gardens to his son.

Du Pont worked assiduously at developing the two-thousand-acre farm. He raised a prizewinning herd of Holstein-Friesian cattle (the familiar black and white dairy cows), and he engaged landscape architect Marian Cruger Coffin to help him integrate planned gardens with the natural environment. By the early 1920's, the Winterthur estate had become almost a village unto itself. The approximately 250 inhabitants worked at the dairy farm and managed the estate's turkeys, chickens, Dorset sheep, hogs, purebred Percherons and other horses, guinea hens, Muscovy ducks and mallards, wheat fields, vegetable and flower gardens, greenhouses, a sawmill, tennis courts, a golf course, a railroad station, and a post office.

In 1916, du Pont married Ruth Wales, a New York neighbor of future president Franklin D. Roosevelt. The couple had two daughters, Pauline Louise and Ruth Ellen.

MATURE WEALTH

On tax returns and travel documents, du Pont listed his occupation as "farmer," but in 1923 a visit to friends J. Watson and Electra Webb in Vermont stimulated the career that would win him world-class recognition. Electra Webb collected American antiques, and a huge cupboard and its Staffordshire dishes caught du Pont's appreciative eye. For the next thirty years he sought out and acquired examples of historic American craftsmanship. (Both the cupboard and the Staffordshire dinnerware are displayed at the Winterthur Museum.) He became known as a discriminating connoisseur who always acted as his own agent, personally inspecting, judging, and negotiating every purchase.

When he inherited the Winterthur estate and another $50 million in 1927, du Pont conceived the idea of housing a great collection in a great mansion, and he expanded his father's house. Between 1929 and 1931, construction progressed on a $4.3 million, 150-foot-long addition that doubled the size of the main house at Winterthur. More than one hundred stonecutters and masons worked on the project, and much of the stone was quarried on the estate's property. Other, smaller expansions and renovations were contracted between 1931 and 1951.

As he worked at filling his 175 rooms with themed collections, du Pont could not help but compare his acquisitions to those of the new American Wing at the Metropolitan Museum of Art in New York City. In 1949, as befits a member of a hugely competitive family, he hired Joseph Downs, curator of the American Wing, to be the full-time photographer and cataloger of his holdings. He also employed Charles Montgomery, a Harvard graduate and antiques collector, to establish a professional staff to manage Winterthur as a museum.

Before Winterthur could be opened to the public, however, the du Ponts needed a place to live. Du Pont initiated construction of a new home to be called The Cottage a few hundred yards from the mansion. Hardly a "cottage" by any standards, the multistory stone building was designed in the Regency style by architect Thomas Waterman. The house had 21,345 square feet of living space.

In his report to classmates at his fiftieth Harvard reunion, du Pont wrote, "I have not wandered very far afield." Indeed, he spent his entire eighty-eight years deeply attached to Winterthur. After opening the museum in 1951, he devoted most of his time to his gardens. One of his greatest pleasures was walking among his plantings. He also loved the sunlit meadows, the paths through the woods, and the peaceful quiet of perhaps the finest country estate in America.

In 1961, du Pont was asked by First Lady Jacqueline Kennedy to chair the committee overseeing the renovation of the White House. Using his extensive contacts and his expertise, du Pont was able to obtain many donations of fine art and antique furniture. He frequently disagreed, however, with the consulting interior designer, Stéphane Boudin.

Henry Francis du Pont died in 1969, a month before his eighty-ninth birthday, and is buried in the Du Pont de Nemours Cemetery in Wilmington, Delaware.

LEGACY

The rare and exquisite objects of du Pont's Winterthur collection are a magnificent gift to the American people, a gift that chronicles the evolution of the nation's aesthetic development and its lifestyle preferences. Perhaps

THE WINTERTHUR MUSEUM

The Winterthur Museum in the Brandywine Valley of Delaware holds the world's foremost collection of antique American decorative arts and furniture. Its sixty acres of themed and color-balanced gardens and its nine-story mansion, with historically accurate and insightful displays of Americana, were the life work of Henry Francis du Pont. The buildings and the 983 acres upon which they stand had been home to five generations of the du Pont family. In 1951, du Pont gifted them to the Winterthur Museum Corporation for the enjoyment of the public and the preservation and appreciation of historic American lifestyles.

The Winterthur permanent collection comprises approximately eighty-nine thousand objects that were created or used in America between 1640 and 1840. The holdings include furniture, glass, textiles, quilts, embroidery, jewelry, silver, pewter, ironworks, ceramics, clocks, sculpture, paintings, and other works of art on paper. Tankards by Paul Revere; furniture by Newport, Rhode Island, cabinetmakers; paintings by Gilbert Stuart and Benjamin West; and a sixty-six-piece dinner set once owned by George Washington are among the notable items.

More than 200,000 visitors annually tour Winterthur. The 175 rooms in the mansion are organized either thematically or chronologically. Because Henry Francis du Pont insisted that no fences, ropes, or other control devices be allowed to mar a guest's enjoyment of the collection, most rooms are open to the public only on guided tours for small groups. An advance appointment is required.

During the 1990's, more than fifty-three thousand square feet of public space was built adjacent to the main museum building. Called the Galleries and the Visitors Center, these facilities feature self-guided tours through a permanent exhibition of eight hundred household objects. Items on display range from tea services to toys, from long rifles to musical instruments, from necklaces to tankards, and from chairs to armoires. The Galleries also provide space for rotating exhibits, such as the American quilts collection of 2008.

The Winterthur Library and Research Center (almost seventy thousand square feet) includes more than eighty-seven thousand volumes and approximately half a million manuscripts and images, most of which are relevant to American decorative arts, material culture, and architecture. The building also houses extensive conservation, research, and education facilities, including the Winterthur Program in Early American Culture and the Winterthur/ University of Delaware Art Conservation Program.

Outdoors, the paths through the garden areas are open to the public. By choosing and placing plantings with consideration to seasonal blooming and color, du Pont created an ever-changing but permanent landscape of beauty. Among the named gardens are the Azalea Woods, the March Walk, the Sundial Garden, the Pinetum, the Lookout, the Quarry, and the Goldfish Pond and Waterfalls. Winterthur's rhododendrons are famous worldwide. There is also an Enchanted Woods area for children.

The name "Winterthur" comes from a town in Switzerland that was the ancestral home of James Antoine Bidermann, husband of Evelina Gabrielle du Pont. Bidermann designed the first residence on the estate and began building in 1837. The property remained in the du Pont family until the creation of the Winterthur Museum.

---

equally important, however, is the estate itself. By observing the mansion and other buildings and the breathtaking gardens, visitors can learn what it meant to be an incredibly wealthy person living in the United States during the first half of the twentieth century. In addition to the pleasures and treasures of Winterthur, du Pont contributed to the development of courses of study in American culture and art conservation at Winterthur and at the University of Delaware. The Society of Winterthur Fellows, established in 1951, continues to function in support of du Pont's ideas and goals.

Despite his passions for art, collecting antiques, horticulture, and breeding livestock, du Pont also took an active part in the management of both E. I. du Pont de Nemours and Company and General Motors. In everything he did, he reached for excellence or perfection. His life exemplifies the American ideals of leadership, generosity, public service, and outstanding planning and management.

—Carolyn Janik

FURTHER READING

Cooper, Wendy A., et al. *American Vision: Henry Francis du Pont's Winterthur Museum.* Washington, D.C.: National Gallery of Art, 2002. Both the history of the museum and its holdings are the focus of this volume. Includes color photographs.

Karp, Walter. "Henry Francis du Pont and the Invention of Winterthur." *American Heritage* 34, no. 3 (April/ May, 1983). This very readable article tells how the character and personality of Henry Francis du Pont affected the creation of the Winterthur Museum. It can be accessed without charge at http://www.american heritage.com.

Lidz, Maggie. *Life at Winterthur: A du Pont Family Album*. Winterthur, Del.: Henry Francis du Pont Winterthur Museum, 2001. Recounts du Pont's family life in a brief text and black and white photographs.

Lord, Ruth. *Henry F. du Pont and Winterthur: A Daughter's Portrait*. New Haven, Conn.: Yale University Press, 1999. This intimate and tasteful book records the heritage of the du Pont family and a daughter's search for the real person that was her father. Includes index, black and white photographs, family trees, and references.

Winkler, John K. *The Dupont Dynasty*. Reprint. Whitefish, Mont.: Kessinger, 2005. Follows the du Pont family from the time they left France in 1802 to becoming gunpowder manufacturers for the U.S. military through the development of DuPont, one of the world's largest chemical companies.

See also: Ninth Duke of Bedford; Alfred I. du Pont; Irénée du Pont; Henry Clay Frick; Isabella Stewart Gardner; J. Paul Getty; Armand Hammer; Collis P. Huntington; Nicholas Longworth; Andrew Mellon; Abby Aldrich Rockefeller.

IRÉNÉE DU PONT
American chemical engineer and industrialist

Du Pont helped build his family's company from a gunpowder producer to one of the nation's major chemical manufacturers. His wealth was passed on to immediate family members, with a fraction of it allocated to build an elegant mansion in Cuba.

Born: December 21, 1876; Brandywine Valley, Delaware
Died: December 12, 1963; Wilmington, Delaware
Sources of wealth: Inheritance; manufacturing; sale of products
Bequeathal of wealth: Children; relatives

EARLY LIFE
Irénée du Pont (IHR-eh-nay dew pont) was born in 1876, the seventh of eleven children. His great-grandfather, Eleuthère Irénée du Pont (1771-1834), founded the family gunpowder business at Brandywine Valley, Delaware. The company initially flourished when it obtained lucrative government contracts during the War of 1812, and its business became even more profitable during the Crimean War (1854-1856) and Civil War (1861-1865). Irénée's father, Lammot du Pont (1831-1884), was a partner in the family corporation, and his mother, Mary Belin du Pont, came from a family that had headed the du Pont company's accounting department.

Irénée spent his first five years at the family mansion, Nemours. The residence was owned by the du Pont company, as were all the nearby homes of his uncles, cousins, and important but unrelated company managers. In the winter of 1881, Lammot moved his large family to West Philadelphia in order to head a plant designed for the production of a new explosive, nitroglycerin. On March 29, 1884, the seven-year-old Irénée learned that his father and five others had been killed instantly in an explosion at the nitroglycerin plant. Although fatherless, the family was financially secure. Male leadership of the family fell to Irénée's older brother, Pierre, who maintained a close and lifelong relationship with Irénée and their younger brother Lammot.

Irénée studied at Andover and then followed Pierre in attending the Massachusetts Institute of Technology (MIT). He joined the Phi Beta Epsilon fraternity. Ultimately, he gained recognition as one of the first of the du Pont brothers to contribute more than $400,000 to the fraternity. Irénée graduated in 1897 with a bachelor's degree in chemical engineering and went on to earn a master's degree the following year. Upon graduation, he was hired by Pierre's former MIT roommate and close friend, William H. Fenn, to work for Fenn's construction company in Wilmington, Delaware. Irénée married in 1900 and raised a family consisting of five girls and one boy. By the time of his death in 1963, he had thirty-five grandchildren and five great-grandchildren.

FIRST VENTURES
In 1902, du Pont carried out Fenn Construction's expansion of the E. I. du Pont de Nemours and Company headquarters in the Equitable Trust Company Building in Wilmington, designing an additional two stories for the

XANADU

In 1927, Irénée du Pont decided to search for the ideal place to build a retirement retreat. He found his location in Varadero, Cuba, in the form of 1,328 acres of tropical splendor, with five miles of pristine beaches backed by the San Bernardino crags. Here he built his mansion, Xanadu, on a cliff fifteen yards from the ocean. Xanadu was designed by the architects Evelio Govantes and Felix Cabarrocas and constructed by the Frederick Sneard Corporation. The residence was completed on December 30, 1930, at a cost of $1.3 million.

This four-story mansion contained eleven bedrooms with adjoining baths, three large terraces, and seven balconies. Each room had an ocean view. The floors were made of Cuban, Italian, and Spanish marble, and precious woods were used for the ceilings, staircase rails, and columns. In front of the house was a private dock. In 1932, Irénée installed the largest privately owned organ in Latin America in Xanadu's basement, and the organ piped music to different sections of the mansion. The elegance of Xanadu was matched by its beautiful location and lush landscape. The property featured gardens with tropical plants and coconut and other fruit trees. Parrots and cockatoos were transported to the gardens in abundance to make the gardens appear even more exotic.

Irénée spent several months a year at Xanadu, usually escaping the cold Delaware winters after New Year's Day. Important corporate guests were often invited to Xanadu and were awed by the manmade and natural beauty. Varadero, Cuba, attracted many other notable people, both famous and infamous. Cuban leader Fulgencio Batista y Zaldívar and mobster Al Capone built mansions there, and the area was a site of resort hotels and casinos frequented by film stars and an assortment of gangsters. After Fidel Castro wrested control of Cuba from Batista in 1959, Castro eventually confiscated Xanadu and nationalized the mansion and the property on which it was located.

Irénée last visited Xanadu in March, 1957. He died on December 12, 1963, the same day that his former mansion opened as the restaurant Las Americas, with Soviet cosmonaut Valentina Tereshkova among the diners. In 1999, Xanadu housed the Varadero Golf Club, which was the site of the European Tour Grand Final in 1999 and 2000. By 2009, the golf club had been remodeled by the Cuban government and converted to a clubhouse with six rooms for rent, a restaurant on the first floor, and a wine cellar in the basement.

manager, and he and Lammot were considered the brightest of the new generation of du Pont leadership.

In 1907, the federal government filed an antitrust suit against the du Pont company, alleging restraint of trade in the explosives industry. A federal court ruled against the firm in 1911, and a year later du Pont agreed to divest itself of enough assets to create two competing gunpowder and dynamite manufacturers. As a result of this litigation, Irénée maintained a lifelong hatred of "big government." During the Great Depression, he became an outspoken critic of President Franklin D. Roosevelt's policies, which involved the government in the nation's economic recovery. There has been speculation that in 1933 Irénée may have participated in a plot by prominent businessmen to remove Roosevelt from office.

As a chemical engineer, Irénée was always excited about the possibilities of new products. In 1908, he became fascinated by a new way to use guncotton to make nitrocellulose-based artificial leather. The du Pont company expanded its manufacture of this product in 1910 by acquiring the Fabrikoid Company, the largest maker of artificial leather.

In 1914, as World War I loomed on the horizon, an entirely new executive committee was appointed at du Pont, with Irénée as chairman. Coleman's interests turned to other business matters, and Pierre was responsible for the firm's day-to-day operations. Meanwhile, a decision to issue common stock and create a bonus plan for corporate management split the family, as Pierre du Pont fought Alfred I. du Pont in a major court battle.

structure. Within a year he was recruited by his first cousin T. Coleman du Pont, the president of the family firm, who wanted Irénée to head the company's engineering division. Irénée was also put in charge of appraising gunpowder operations. In 1904, Pierre appointed Irénée to the company's board of directors. Pierre's rise in the company meant increasing responsibilities for his brothers Irénée and Lammot. They had Pierre's complete confidence, and in turn he received their unqualified loyalty. Irénée soon became assistant general

World War I was of major significance to the du Pont company. The war created an enormous demand for explosives that necessitated a rapid expansion of the firm's production. By 1916, World War I had generated such huge profits for du Pont that the company was able to give all of its shareholders a 100 percent return on dividends. Following America's entry into the war in April, 1917, Pierre sent Irénée to Washington, D.C., to negotiate a fair price for du Pont company gunpowder with the War Industry Board.

MATURE WEALTH

In 1915, Pierre, who owned stock in General Motors (GM), was elected chairman and a director of the automobile company. After World War I, du Pont's directors invested $25 million in GM, and GM became a major customer for du Pont's new durable quick-drying lacquer paint, marketed under the name Viscolac and later refined under the names Duco and DuLux. In 1920, Pierre became president of GM, and Irénée succeeded him as president of the du Pont company.

During his term as company president, Irénée reorganized the management structure at du Pont, allowing daily management decisions to be made by individual departments, each with its own production, sales, and research departments, as well as general managers who were answerable to the firm's executive committee. Under this decentralized management structure, the du Pont company earned a fortune by manufacturing durable paint for cars, cellophane, and a host of other products. The firm's management structure soon became a model for many other large corporations. Irénée also made department managers responsible for worker safety, which became an aspect of daily operating procedures.

On March 15, 1926, Irénée was succeeded by his brother Lammot as president of du Pont, and Irénée was elected chairman of the board of directors. One year later, he decided to enter into semiretirement and sought a location to build a sumptuous estate. He found such a site on the white sand beaches of Varadero, Cuba, where he built a mansion named Xanadu, after the legendary palace of the Mongol ruler Kublai Khan. Xanadu was completed in late December, 1930. Irénée spent several months each year at Xanadu and remained on the du Pont board of directors until his full retirement in 1958. At this time, his personal wealth, tabulated by *Fortune* magazine, was between $200 and $400 million, making him one of the two richest members of the du Pont family and one of the twenty richest Americans. At the time of his retirement, the du Pont Corporation employed ninety thousand workers in seventy-four plants worldwide.

LEGACY

Irénée du Pont, along with his bothers Pierre and Lammot, played a major role in the growth of E. I. du Pont de Nemours & Company, transforming the corporation from a large gunpowder producer to one of the world's largest chemical manufacturing conglomerates. Irénée helped steer DuPont (as it is commonly known) into diversified production and instituted a decentralized management system that became a worldwide model for large corporations. In doing so, he became one of the twenty wealthiest Americans, enjoying his semiretirement in a mansion on a luxurious 1,328-acre estate. However, his possible involvement in a corporate conspiracy to overthrow the presidency of Franklin D. Roosevelt and his alleged strong positive feelings for the antisocialist policies of Adolf Hitler have relegated this corporate giant to historical obscurity.

—Irwin Halfond

FURTHER READING

Archer, Jules. *The Plot to Seize the White House*. New York: Hawthorne Books, 1973. A controversial study based on testimony drawn from hearings of the House Committee on Un-American Activities.

Chandler, Alfred D., and Stephen Salsbury. *Pierre S. Du Pont and the Making of the Modern Corporation*. Knoxville, Ill.: Beard Books, 2001. A biography of Pierre, containing much information about his relationship with his brother Irénée.

Kinnane, Adrian. *DuPont: From the Banks of the Brandywine to Miracles of Science*. Baltimore: Johns Hopkins University Press, 2002. A scholarly history, spanning two centuries, of the development of one of America's most enduring and influential corporations.

Wall, Joseph Frazier. *Alfred I. Du Pont: The Man and His Family*. New York: Oxford University Press, 1990. A lengthy and fascinating study of the personality and career of this entrepreneur and philanthropist.

Winkler, John K. *The Du Pont Dynasty*. 1935. Reprint. Whitefish, Mont.: Kessinger, 2005. History of the du Pont family. Colorfully written, though at the expense of historical accuracy.

See also: Alfred I. du Pont; Henry Francis du Pont; Alfred Nobel; James Smithson; William Weightman.

GEORGE EASTMAN
American inventor, industrialist, and philanthropist

Eastman was the inventor of roll film, the founder of the Eastman Kodak Company, and the popularizer of photography as a hobby and leisure activity. He used his wealth, amassed as head of a premier American business, to support educational institutions and medical advances by donating large sums of money to colleges, universities, and hospitals.

Born: July 12, 1854; Waterville, New York
Died: March 14, 1932; Rochester, New York
Sources of wealth: Patents; manufacturing; sale of products
Bequeathal of wealth: Educational institution; charity

EARLY LIFE
George Eastman was born July 12, 1854, in an upstate New York village about twenty miles from Utica. His father, George Washington Eastman, died in 1862, leaving the family in such dire financial straits that when young Eastman reached his teens, he had to drop out of high school to support his mother, Maria Kilbourn Eastman, and his sister. He worked as a messenger and office boy for insurance agencies, eventually progressing to better-paying positions as policy filer and occasional policy writer. He studied accounting at night in order to get a better paying job. By 1874, he was working as a junior clerk at a savings bank in Rochester, New York.

At the age of twenty-four, Eastman was solvent and planned a vacation to Santo Domingo, where he intended to invest in property. Advised by a friend to take photographs of the properties in which he was interested, Eastman purchased photographic equipment and was immediately fascinated by photography. He did not get to Santo Domingo, but he continued to develop his interest in photography.

FIRST VENTURES
At that time, photography was such a complicated process and the equipment was so cumbersome that Eastman decided to make photography more user-friendly. He began studying about photography and experimenting with formulas resulting in a high-quality emulsion and a machine that produced dry photographic plates, which were less difficult to use than the wet plates employed by photographers. It took him three years of experimentation, but by 1880 he had a patent for his machine and had set up a small company in Rochester, where he manufactured the dry plates that photographers soon preferred.

He soon realized that while his dry plates made taking pictures easier for professional photographers, professionals were about the only people who could use the huge, complicated cameras. He began looking for a way to make photography more accessible to amateurs. As he saw it, three things were needed: The photographic plate must be made of a lighter-weight, less breakable material than the conventional glass; the camera must be smaller and lighter, so it would not require a tripod; and the photographic image needed a simpler developing process. All photographs taken the conventional way had to be processed within minutes of exposure, which required photographers to transport all the necessary chemicals and equipment to their photo shoots in order to immediately develop their images.

When Eastman finally developed roll film and a small

George Eastman. (Smithsonian Institution)

handheld camera that addressed the first two concerns, he conceived the idea of having the users simply mail the roll of exposed film to his company for developing. He advertised that his business, which he named the Kodak Company, would enable the people who used his cameras and film to merely "press the button; we do the rest." By 1897, the name "Kodak" was known worldwide. Amateur photographers embraced the easy-to-use camera and film. When in 1889, Eastman worked with Thomas Edison to develop a strong, flexible roll film for use in Edison's motion-picture camera, the kinetograph, Eastman's company began to grow into the Kodak empire and Eastman became one of the wealthiest men of his time.

MATURE WEALTH

Through dynamic advertising and sound business practices, Eastman made Kodak a prosperous company. He was one of the first businessmen to provide dividends to his employees in a form of profit sharing. He also established disability benefit plans, retirement annuities, and life insurance for his workforce. He believed these policies engendered worker goodwill and loyalty to the company, which, in turn, helped ensure high productivity and increased profits.

Although his first Kodak camera cost $25 in 1888, Eastman developed the one-dollar Brownie camera, which anyone could afford and use easily. He soon had Americans of all kinds buying his cameras and film. The profits of his company were enormous.

Perhaps because Eastman never married or had children, he was an extremely generous donor to various charities. A firm believer in the value of good dental care, perhaps because both he and his mother had suffered from tooth problems, he established a dental clinic and a dental program for children in Rochester. He sent donations abroad to England, France, and other countries to establish dental clinics in large cities. He was responsible for creating a school of dentistry at the University of Rochester. The fact that his mother suffered from a debilitating disease that confined her to a wheelchair, and an older sister contracted and died from polio at a young age, no doubt encouraged his support of hospitals and other health-related institutions.

Eastman was especially interested in educational institutions. His father in 1854 established and began operating a business school, Eastman's Commercial College.

A British advertisement for Kodak's Brownie camera, which sold for five shillings, equivalent to about $1.25 in U.S. currency. This camera and George Eastman's other innovations made photography accessible to the general public. (Hulton Archive/Getty Images)

However, when his father died in 1861, his father's partner took over control and management of the school, and the Eastmans had no further connection to it. Eastman, a high school dropout, understood the value of education and sought to help several institutions. He gave magnanimous donations of as much as $54 million to the University of Rochester. He also gave more than $25 million, anonymously, to the Massachusetts Institute of Technology because he was impressed by the caliber of its graduates, several of whom he hired for his company. His parents had been raised by abolitionist parents involved with the Underground Railroad. With such a background,

Eastman donated $2 million each to the predominantly African American colleges Tuskegee Institute and Hampton Institute.

His inclination toward philanthropy started early in his life. At a time when he was still working for others and his salary was only $60 a week, he gave $50 to a small school, Mechanics Institute of Rochester, that went on to become the Rochester Institute of Technology, a school with more than ten thousand students by the twenty-first century.

Eastman was a community-conscious booster of Rochester. He wanted to improve the quality of people's lives and provide opportunities for them to enjoy natural beauty and beautiful music well played. With that in mind, he channeled some of his money to the support of a

city symphony orchestra. To ensure that there would always be well-trained musicians to play beautiful music, he established a school of music at the University of Rochester, where students could study and train to become expert musicians. He also supported the public parks, where everyone could enjoy the pleasures of nature.

Eastman retired from daily management of the Kodak Company in 1925 at the age of seventy-one, becoming chairman of the board. He spent much of his retirement in philanthropic pursuits that placed him in the same league as the better-known philanthropists of the time, such as Andrew Carnegie and John D. Rockefeller. Eastman also traveled to Europe, where he avidly toured art galleries. He bought many paintings, acquiring one of the best private collections in the country. He went on safari in Kenya and Uganda and bagged a white rhinoceros and an elephant.

By 1930, he had developed a degenerative spinal cord disease that caused him intense pain. When he began having trouble standing and walking after always being an active person, he became depressed. His mother's final years were spent in a wheelchair, and he had no desire to suffer the same unhappy fate. He proceeded to put his affairs in order by reviewing his will and making changes. He invited some friends to his home to witness the will changes and to say what they did not realize at the time would be their last good-byes. After they left, he went to his room, took an automatic pistol, and committed suicide with a shot to the heart. He was seventy-seven years old.

LEGACY

By developing and producing an easy-to-use camera and handy film, George Eastman enabled amateur photographers to capture their memories in realistic pictures. His innovative roll film also made possible the development of motion-picture entertainment. These inventions brought him great wealth, which he used for the betterment of his own and other communities.

Eastman said that people with wealth either could hold on to it to leave for oth-

---

EASTMAN SCHOOL OF MUSIC

George Eastman always loved music and thought music appreciation could be cultivated if music was made accessible to the community. Hiring musicians, he said, was easy, but it was "impossible to buy" the appreciation of music. He believed that if more people enjoyed music, more people would support community efforts to make music resources, like symphony orchestras, available. Because he felt supporting such aesthetically enriching opportunities for a community was worthwhile, he established the Eastman School of Music and a concert hall within it.

The Eastman School of Music is located at the University of Rochester in Rochester, New York. Eastman established the school in 1921 for the purpose of providing, for those who wished to become musicians, a musical education in an environment most conducive to their attaining excellence and professionalism.

The school's first director was Norwegian pianist Alfred Klingenberg, who was succeeded in 1924 by American composer Howard Hanson. During Hanson's four decades as director, the school made great strides in its development to become a reputedly fine school. By 2008, it was listed in the Kaplan/*Newsweek* college guide as the "hottest school for music" in the United States. Other national rankings place it first in music education, composition, and piano performance; second in instrumental performance, conducting, jazz, and piano/organ/keyboard; and fourth in opera/vocal performance.

The school offers bachelor of music degrees in performance, music education, composition, musical arts, theory, and jazz and contemporary music; master of arts and master of music degrees in ethnomusicology, music theory, and pedagogy; and doctoral degrees in composition, music education, musicology, and theory. In 2009, it had more than ninety-five teachers and an enrollment of about five hundred undergraduates and four hundred graduate students. About 25 percent of these students were from foreign countries. The Eastman Community Music School had about one thousand students ranging in age from preschoolers to people in the eighties.

ers to deal with after they died, or could "get into action and have fun" while still alive, "adapting" their wealth to the "human needs" they saw around them. He said he chose to "get into the action."

Eastman gave away more than $100 million to educational institutions, medical facilities, and cultural organizations. He founded the Community Chest, later the United Way, to help support his city of Rochester. He pioneered the first profit-sharing program for employees in America. He promoted music appreciation with his support of the Eastman School of Music and the Rochester Symphony Orchestra. He endowed learning with his gifts to colleges and universities, and he promoted better health with the many dental clinics he helped establish. A modest and unassuming man, he nonetheless left a mark of distinction on the business world and many other aspects of American society.

—Jane L. Ball

FURTHER READING

Ackerman, Carl W. *George Eastman.* New York: Houghton Mifflin, 1930. Reprint. Clifton, N.J.: A. M. Kelley, 1973. A biography based on Eastman's files and voluminous correspondence, with insights into the Kodak Company and Eastman's era.

Brayer, Elizabeth. *George Eastman: A Biography.* Rochester, N.Y.: University of Rochester Press, 2006. A candid biography of Eastman, with detailed explora-tion of his business acumen, infrequent failures, and considerable successes.

Grimm, Robert T., ed. *Notable American Philanthropists: Biographies of Giving and Volunteering.* Westport, Conn.: Greenwood Press, 2002. Profiles seventy-nine individuals and families, George Eastman among them, who made major contributions to the world and American society. Lists their most important gifts and good deeds and explores the philosophies, motivations, and justifications for their philanthropy.

Tedlow, Richard S. *Giants of Enterprise: Seven Business Innovators and the Empires They Built.* New York: Harper Business, 2001. With chapters on other tycoons like Henry Ford and Andrew Carnegie, chapter 2 discusses how Eastman's invention of the Kodak camera built an enduring corporate empire and created a mass market.

West, Nancy M. *Kodak and the Lens of Nostalgia.* Charlottesville: University of Virginia Press, 2000. Biographical details about Eastman, as well as discussion of the history and evolution of Kodak's advertising strategies. Reproduces many actual advertisements, some in color.

See also: Andrew Carnegie; Samuel Colt; Peter Cooper; Thomas Edison; Edwin Herbert Land; Samuel F. B. Morse; George Mortimer Pullman; John D. Rockefeller III; Isaac Merrit Singer.

THOMAS EDISON
American inventor and entrepreneur

Edison's wealth accumulated from investors' ongoing support, corporate stocks, and the sales of his inventions. Although often impoverished, he eventually gained personal fortune and prosperity through obsessive work habits that resulted in new advances in technology. His inventions revolutionized industry, communications, and business.

Born: February 11, 1847; Milan, Ohio
Died: October 18, 1931; West Orange, New Jersey
Also known as: Thomas Alva Edison; The Wizard of Menlo Park; The Napoleon of Invention
Sources of wealth: Patents; sale of products; investments
Bequeathal of wealth: Spouse; children; scholarship

EARLY LIFE
Thomas Alva Edison was the seventh and last child of Canadian emigrants Samuel and Nancy Edison. The family was forced to flee Canada and move to Ohio because Samuel supported a failed revolt against the Canadian government. Young Edison developed a keen interest in learning and discovery due to his parents' scholarly influence. Nancy, a teacher, home-schooled Edison and encouraged his use of the local library, where he was reputed to have read every book in the collection. Of early interest to him were Sir Isaac Newton's theories of physics. By age fourteen, he was already an entrepreneur, earning more than $10 a day selling snacks at a railroad station and publishing his own newspaper, *The Weekly Herald.*

In his early twenties, Edison was a freelance inventor while working for the Western Union Telegraph Company in Boston and New York. Ambitious and hardworking, he forged a path that would eventually bring him fame, notoriety, and fortune.

FIRST VENTURES

While employed with Western Union, Edison acquired his first patent, for a machine to automatically record the votes of legislative bodies. Financially, the machine was unsuccessful because politicians preferred the roll-call vote, which gave them an opportunity to state their opinions. Edison vowed never again to invent something that would not sell.

Destitute, Edison borrowed $35 to travel to New York. He repaired a malfunctioning stock ticker machine in an office and was hired there for $300 a month. After Edison sold his redesigned Edison Universal Stock Printer in 1874 for $40,000 (more than $800,000 in 2010), he constructed a laboratory in Newark, New Jersey, to manufacture the machines. In 1876, he moved to his new

Thomas Edison in his laboratory. (Library of Congress)

Edison Laboratory in Menlo Park, where he and five thousand employees would work on more than forty inventions. Edison became known as the Wizard of Menlo Park.

MATURE WEALTH

Edison took risks, remained optimistic, and was persistent. For him, failure was not permanent but only represented a first unsuccessful attempt. His genius was valued enough at the time to attract willing contributors to fund his projects. In 1875, the Atlantic and Pacific Telegraph Company provided Edison with $13,500, and Western Union supplied another $5,000, so he could continue his work on automatic telegraphy. The gift funded his laboratory in Menlo Park, an enterprising venture requiring considerable backing.

In Menlo Park, Edison invented the carbon-resistance telephone transmitter (1876) and the phonograph (1877). Now regarded as an eminent inventor, he received $10,000 from five investors to establish the Edison Speaking Phonograph Company for further development of the phonograph. In 1879, Edison burned a carbonized sewing thread filament for more than thirteen hours and developed the Edison dynamo, which provided a constant electric current. Edison found wealth and fame with the success of the incandescent lamp when it became commercially viable. In 1878, one share of stock in his Edison Electric Light Company was worth $3,500. A staff physicist, who was hired at $12 a week, sold five shares in the company for $5,000 each.

In 1882, the first commercial central power station using incandescent lamps provided lighting for one square mile of New York City, initiating the electric age. Transportation and industrial markets began to rely heavily on the use of electricity, and night lighting evolved into a twenty-four-hour service. The newly formed Edison General Electric Company merged with other manufacturing companies. Although the company bore his name, Edison was just a partner. J. P. Morgan, members of the Vanderbilt family, and other investors provided the necessary capital. Edison received stock valued at $3.5 million. Eventually, Edison General merged with Thompson-Houston in 1892 and was renamed General Electric Company. General Electric supported Edison with an annual grant of $85,000, far less than the $250,000 he expected. Years later, he learned that his stake in the company was worth about $4 million.

In 1882 and 1883, Edison contracted for power stations in Brockton, Massachusetts, and Sunbury, Pennsylvania. He secured a patent for the "Edison effect," which effectively regulated the flow of electric current. This revolutionary discovery became the foundation for the manufacture of diodes, radios, televisions, and computer transistors.

In 1887, Edison constructed the first and largest research and development center in West Orange, New Jersey. His newest project was the kinetoscope, the predecessor to a motion-picture camera. The kinetoscope was a crude machine that enabled viewers to see magnified and backlit film moving past a small opening. As with the phonograph, Edison failed to realize the entertainment potential of the kinetoscope to the general public. However, his distributor formulated a successful publicity plan which required Edison to lend his name to the new Vitascope, an early film projector, but to otherwise remain in the background. The first film screening using a Vitascope was held in Los Angeles and attracted twenty thousand viewers, with another ten thousand who showed up but were not admitted. The new industry of film production was born.

The 1890's was a profitable time for Edison because he established a phonograph and phonograph recording business, capitalizing on the home entertainment market. Coin-in-the-slot phonographs occupied railway stations, arcades, and phonograph parlors throughout the United States; a San Francisco distributor of these products claimed $4,000 in revenue within six months. Edison's additional inventions included the fluoroscope (an X ray fluorescent screen) and concrete molds for precast buildings. From 1900 until 1910, Edison's primary and formidable challenge was the development of a storage battery that was suitable for electric vehicles. However, by the time work was completed on the alkaline battery, vehicles had switched to gasoline power. Developing the battery appeared to be a losing proposition, but Edison's patience paid off. Soon, railway cars, signals, ships, and even miners' lamps were using the alkaline battery. Edison's investment compounded, and the alkaline battery proved to be his most lucrative product. In 1911, Edison formed Thomas A. Edison, Inc., which controlled most of his enterprises, including phonographs, records, motion-picture equipment, and batteries.

THE EDISON MEDAL

In 1904, a trust fund was established in honor of Thomas Edison to award a gold medal each year to an individual with meritorious accomplishments in the fields of electrical science, electrical engineering, or electrical arts. Nomination criteria for this award include patents, leadership and contributions in an individual's field of endeavor, honors awarded, duration of dominance, and originality. Such prestigious recognition is a testament to Edison, who demonstrated these criteria throughout his lifetime.

Edison secured 1,368 patents between the ages of fourteen and eighty-four, about one patent every two weeks. His patents pertained to numerous inventions in the fields of communications, entertainment, medicine, and various industries. He gained and lost fortunes in some of his endeavors, but he had the unique ability to withstand severe monetary losses and recover quickly. He died a millionaire because he held to the principle of inventing something only if there was a need for it and people would buy it. Edison was cantankerous, disagreeable, and overly competitive. However, he was also an organizer, a visionary, meticulous to detail, and an excellent business promoter. To raise financial backing he made sure his inventions were featured on the front pages of newspapers and often arranged impressive demonstrations. Edison was adept at managing his fame. He capitalized on his reputation as the world's greatest inventor, which rewarded him financially.

The Edison Medal reflects contributions to society by distinguished and notable individuals. The first award, consisting of a gold medal, a small gold replica, a certificate, and an honorarium, was presented in 1909 by the Institute of Electrical and Electronics Engineers (IEEE). Among past honorees are George Westinghouse, Alexander Graham Bell, and Nikola Tesla. Other awards have been presented for research in microwave and radar remote sensing technology, programmable read-only memory, and broadband optical fiber communications. The medal serves as a symbol for men and women who have turned ideas into reality for the benefit of humankind.

By age sixty-four, Edison had ceased to work long hours and was entrusting associates to operate his business ventures. Emphasis was placed on improving existing products rather than inventing new ones. With World War I approaching, Edison was appointed to the Naval Consulting Board for scientific work with submarines and related naval operations. Friends Henry Ford and Harvey Firestone urged Edison to discover an alternate source for rubber automobile tires, but this final project was not completed. In his eighties, he spent more time in his Glenmont, New Jersey, home in declining health. He lingered near death for about two weeks with kidney failure before succumbing on October 18, 1931. Out of respect, President Herbert Hoover asked communities across the country to extinguish all electric lights at ten o'clock in the evening, eastern time, on the day of Edison's funeral.

LEGACY

For Edison, money had value only if it was used to benefit others. Since Edison was not independently wealthy, he relied on associates to support his endeavors. Accordingly, his financial situation ranged from bankruptcy to prosperity depending on the success of his business ventures related to the design and marketing of his inventions. His partnerships with others, however, allowed him to continue his work toward new discoveries and to achieve recognition as "the Napoleon of invention."

Edison's wealth provided the creation of the world's first industrial research laboratory that encouraged staff teamwork and strengthened mass production at unprecedented levels. He invented better communication devices, introduced home entertainment through phonographs and motion-picture cameras, and improved countless industrial commodities.

—Douglas D. Skinner

FURTHER READING

Baldwin, Neil. *Edison: Inventing the Century.* New York: Hyperion Books, 1996. Portrait of Edison, a complex and visionary genius who transformed the modern age. Contains much information on his family life, highlighting his two wives and children.

Essig, Mark. *Edison and the Electric Chair: A Story of Light and Death.* New York: Walker, 2003. In-depth study of a side of Edison not generally known: His invention of the lightbulb led to his involvement in the development of the electric chair. Contains photographs and other illustrations.

Jonnes, Jill. *Empires of Light: Edison, Tesla, Westinghouse, and the Race to Electrify the World.* New York: Random House, 2003. Narrative of the interaction of three giants of the electric age and their philosophies and battles with each other. Describes the effects of legal and corporate interests in the electric industry. Includes sixteen pages of photographs.

Pretzer, William S. *Working at Inventing: Thomas A. Edison and the Menlo Park Experience.* Baltimore: Johns Hopkins University Press, 2002. Focuses on Edison's Menlo Park laboratory from 1876 to 1882, when his work centered on communications, the phonograph, and the lightbulb. Contains maps and illustrations.

Stross, Randall. *The Wizard of Menlo Park.* New York: Crown, 2007. A well-researched book by a university business professor. Provides a summation of Edison's life, his contributions to society, his career, his associates, and his family. Contains eight pages of photographs.

Wehrwein, Michele Albion. *The Florida Life of Thomas Edison.* Gainesville: University Press of Florida, 2008. Introspective account of Edison's home life in Ft. Myers, among the flora and fauna. Details his daily research and recreation habits and his impact on the community.

See also: Samuel Colt; Peter Cooper; George Eastman; Harvey Firestone; Henry Ford; Samuel Insull; Edwin Herbert Land; J. P. Morgan; Samuel F. B. Morse; Isaac Merrit Singer; Cornelius Vanderbilt; George Westinghouse.

ELEANOR OF AQUITAINE
French royalty and landowner

Eleanor's wealth was based on the vast properties she owned in France. She received income from Aquitaine and Poitou as well as from other properties owned while she was queen of France and later of England.

Born: c. 1122; Bordeaux or castle of Belin, southern France

Died: April 1, 1204; the Abbey of Fontevrault, Anjou, France

Also known as: Eleanor of Guyenne

Sources of wealth: Inheritance; marriage; real estate

Bequeathal of wealth: Children; church

EARLY LIFE

Eleanor of Aquitaine (EL-eh-nor uhv AK-wuh-tayn) was one of three children born to William X of Poitier, and Aquitaine and Aenor of Chatellerault. She was named after her mother, who died when Eleanor was eight; Eleanor's name "alia-Aenor" means "the other Aenor." There is some disagreement among scholars as to when and where Eleanor was born. She was the older daughter, and when her brother died, under the laws of the land, Eleanor became heir to her family's estate. There is no argument as to the wealth she inherited. The county of Poitou and the duchy of Aquitaine covered a vast area of what is now southwest France. Aquitaine, whose name means "land of waters" in Latin, is so named because of the number of rivers there. Its temperate climate promoted agriculture, and the domain was fertile, producing grain, fruit, and wine. The export trade in wine and salt contributed to the wealth of the duchy.

Growing up, Eleanor became used to luxuries and was fascinated by the troubadour culture adopted in aristocratic circles. Her grandfather William IX wrote what is considered the first troubadour poetry, celebrating love and the beauty of women. The court of the dukes' of Aquitaine was frequented by poets and musicians and was the center of western European culture. Unlike other noblewomen, Eleanor was taught to read and write in her native tongue, *langue d'oc*, the language of southern France, and given instruction in Latin. When her father died in 1137, she became countess of Poitou and duchess of Aquitaine; she was barely fifteen and the richest heiress in Europe. Before her father died, he had appointed the French king, Louis VI, also known as Louis the Fat, as her guardian. To avoid other suitors, Louis, whose territory was much smaller than Eleanor's, promptly betrothed her to his son.

FIRST VENTURES
Eleanor's father had died on Good Friday, April 9, during an Easter pilgrimage, and King Louis, who was not well, pushed for a quick marriage. His son Louis had been destined for the Church, but he became heir to the French crown when his older brother died. Young Louis was sixteen, and he and Eleanor married on July 25, 1137, in the cathedral of Saint André in Bordeaux. As a well-bred young woman, Eleanor had no choice in her bridegroom. Before the summer's end, Louis VI had died. Eleanor's husband, now Louis VII, ascended to the throne and Eleanor became queen of France. She relocated to Paris and exerted her influence, bringing music and verse from the south into the court. She learned Parisian French and showed a capacity for Aristotelian logic, highly popular with the university students of Paris. She failed at her principal occupation—to provide an heir. However, in 1145 she gave birth to a daughter, Marie.

When Pope Eugenius III asked the king to go on a Crusade to the Holy Land, the king readily assented, and Eleanor insisted on participating. They left France in June, 1147. Eleanor was enchanted with the bright clothes and the exotic nature of Byzantine culture in Constantinople, and at Antioch the king and queen were hosted by Eleanor's uncle Raymond. Again speaking the language of her childhood and surrounded by luxury, El-

Eleanor of Aquitaine. (The Granger Collection, New York)

eanor refused to leave for Jerusalem and had to be dragged from her uncle's palace. This event was the climax to a failing marriage. There was a brief reconciliation, and in 1150 Eleanor gave birth to a second daughter, but the marriage was over. Her failure to provide a male heir and Eleanor's efforts to secure an annulment due to consanguinity within the fourth degree of kinship resulted in an annulment on March 21, 1152. Her lands were returned to her.

MATURE WEALTH
On May 18, 1152, less than two months after her divorce, Eleanor married her second husband, and this time the bridegroom was her chosen mate. She married Henry Plantagenet, duke of Normandy and count of Anjou. Although both Henry and Eleanor were technically vassals of the king of France and should have sought his permission to marry, they did not, realizing that the king would have forbidden their union. As the result of their marriage, Eleanor was now the duchess of Aquitaine and Normandy and the countess of Poitou and Anjou; Henry

acquired by marriage almost half of what is now France. Although Henry was eleven years younger than Eleanor, the marriage suited both.

In 1154, with the death of King Stephen, Henry became King Henry II of England, and Eleanor was again a queen. Her list of titles was impressive: queen of England; lady of Ireland; duchess of Normandy, Aquitaine, and Gascogne; and countess of Poitou, Saintonge, Angoumois, Limousin, Auvergen, Bordeaux, Agen, Anjou, Maine, and Touraine. Henry also endowed her with numerous manors, consequently increasing her already substantial wealth. As queen, Eleanor was actively involved in political life and traveled extensively in England and France. She acted as regent in England when Henry was abroad and continued to act as feudal lord in

Poitou and Aquitaine. She also provided Henry with heirs. They had eight children—five sons and three daughters.

As her children grew, Eleanor's marriage to Henry weakened. In 1168, when Henry returned full control of Aquitaine to Eleanor, she relocated to Poitiers and established a court where she had grown up. Her court extended beyond governing into a center of culture and the arts. Enabled by her wealth, Eleanor served as a patron of the arts. Poets gathered, and the concept of courtly love flourished, as did conspiracy.

When Henry divided his continental possessions among his sons, providing them with titles but not true power, trouble began. In 1173, Eleanor, aided by her former husband King Louis VII, stood behind her sons when they rebelled against Henry. Henry defeated his challengers, pardoned his sons, and removed Eleanor from France. He considered divorcing her, but he chose not to because he did not want to lose her lands in Aquitaine and Poitou. Henry tried to make Eleanor become a nun; she refused. Consequently, Eleanor was virtually held prisoner in Salisbury Castle for fifteen years. For a woman whose wealth enabled her to travel freely, who was accustomed to having political power, and who was used to the luxuries of fine clothes, foods, and wines and of interesting and stimulating visitors, the period of imprisonment was difficult. Her financial resources were cut off, and her lifestyle was described as "Spartan."

When Henry II died, the heir to the English throne, Richard I, immediately freed his mother. Eleanor again became regent of England when Richard went on a Crusade, and it was Eleanor who worked to raise the ransom of 100,000 marks of silver when Richard was imprisoned. When Richard was returned, she retired to the abbey at Fontevrault but continued to be involved in ruling her lands. After Richard died, Eleanor again became politically active, working to have her last son John accepted and crowned king of England. King John rewarded her support by proclaiming she was to retain Poitou and Aquitaine for the rest of her life and be "lady" over all his possessions. Over

THE PALACE OF JUSTICE IN POITIERS

The Palais du Justice, or Palace of Justice, was originally the ducal palace for the dukes of Aquitaine. Located in Poitiers, the capital of Poitou, France, it was the second palace on the site. The first palace was built during the ninth century at the highest spot in town, above a Roman wall. During Merovingian times, the structure served as the seat of justice. After the first palace was completely destroyed by a fire in 1018, a new palace was built by the dukes of Aquitaine. In 1104, William IX, Duke of Aquitaine, added a tower on the town side, known as *tour Maubergeonne*. It was named for his mistress Amauberge ("the dangerous"), whom he installed there. Amauberge was the grandmother of Eleanor of Aquitaine, and Eleanor spent her childhood in the palace.

Between 1191 and 1204, Eleanor refurbished the structure, creating sumptuous domestic spaces and constructing a dining hall, the *Salle des pas perdus*. This "hall of lost footsteps," so named because of its vastness, measured fifty meters in length and seventeen meters in width. Eleanor created a proper setting for a queen. The palace was full of music, poetry, chivalric behavior, and expensively dressed aristocrats who drank fine wines and ate exquisite food.

The palace was also where Eleanor, with her daughter Marie, countess of Champagne, presided over the Courts of Love. A young knight would petition the court, which consisted of Eleanor, Marie, and other high-born women, about an aspect of his behavior toward his lady, and the court of women would decide his fate. The second book of Andreas Capellanus's *Liber de arte honeste amandi et reprbatione inhonesti amantis* (1184-1186; book of the art of loving nobly and the reprobation of dishonorable love) was based on one of Eleanor's rulings.

Over the years there were changes to the palace. Eleanor's great hall was remodeled; the original beamed ceiling was covered, and the walls were painted. Jean, duc de Berry (1340-1416), rebuilt part of the palace that had been destroyed by a fire. Over the years, various reconstruction projects were carried out, and Eleanor's court of love eventually became a court of law.

the years, Eleanor had provided financial support to the abbey at Fontevrault. It was here that her husband Henry and son Richard were buried. Eleanor spent her last days at the abbey. There is some speculation that she took the veil and became a nun, but this has never been substantiated. Eleanor died in April, 1204, and was buried beside Henry.

Legacy

Eleanor of Aquitaine's lands were inherited by her sole surviving son, John. They would eventually be lost, as was the rest of the Angevin Empire to France in a war that would last one hundred years. Eleanor left a legacy in her contribution to and fostering of the literature of the times, specifically her involvement in the Courts of Love. Her principal legacy was her sons and daughters and their offspring, who reigned on the thrones of Europe

—Marcia B. Dinneen

Further Reading

Boyd, Douglas. *Eleanor, April Queen of Aquitaine*. Stroud, England: Sutton, 2004. A readable yet scholarly account of Eleanor as a "modern woman" for her time. Includes maps and illustrations.

Kelly, Amy. *Eleanor of Aquitaine and the Four Kings.*

Cambridge, Mass.: Harvard University Press, 1950. The classic book on Eleanor and her times. Includes notes, a bibliography, and a map of France.

Meade, Marion. *Eleanor of Aquitaine, a Biography*. New York: Hawthorn Books, 1977. A readable biography that occasionally veers into fiction. Includes scholarly notes, a bibliography, and a map of the Angevin Empire.

Owen, D. D. R. *Eleanor of Aquitaine*. Cambridge, Mass.: Blackwell, 1993. Includes information about Eleanor's life, as well as the legends about her. Contains a detailed chronology.

Swabey, Ffiona. *Eleanor of Aquitaine, Courtly Love, and the Troubadours*. Westport, Conn.: Greenwood Press, 2004. Includes material on Eleanor's life and family, as well as information about her other legacy—the promotion and support of the concept and lifestyle of courtly love.

Weir, Alison. *Eleanor of Aquitaine, a Life*. New York: Ballantine Books, 1999. A thorough, readable examination of Eleanor's life and times. Includes an extensive bibliography of primary and secondary sources, as well as genealogical tables.

See also: Aaron of Lincoln; Godric of Finchale.

Elizabeth II
British monarch

The wealth of Queen Elizabeth II of Great Britain, the best-known monarch of the twenty-first century, has been estimated at $420 million, although the extent of her fortune has never been publicly documented.

Born: April 21, 1926; London, England
Also known as: Elizabeth Alexandra Mary (birth name); Princess Elizabeth; Lilibet; Elizabeth Windsor; Elizabeth Alexandra Mary Mountbatten-Windsor
Sources of wealth: Inheritance; real estate; government
Bequeathal of wealth: Unknown

Early Life

Elizabeth II was born into the royal British Windsor family in 1926. Her father, the duke of York, was second in line to the British throne. However, the abdication of King Edward VIII propelled the duke into the monarchy as King George VI in 1936. From 1940 until 1945, Elizabeth lived at Windsor Castle, and she served a stint in the army during World War II. The British royal family lived

modestly in a time of great deprivation, both during and after the war.

Shortly after the war, Elizabeth was reunited with and subsequently married a distant cousin, Philip Mountbatten, who was then living off his navy pay. He was named the duke of Edinburgh and allocated an annual allowance from the civil list, the funds that the government of Great Britain provides for numerous members of the royal family. Elizabeth and Philip married in November, 1947, and they moved into a small palace in London. The young couple soon had two children, Charles and Anne. In February, 1952, George VI died, and Elizabeth ascended the throne with Prince Philip as her consort.

First Ventures

On her accession, Queen Elizabeth II received two different forms of wealth. The first was in the form of possessions that were attached to the monarchy, and this wealth was placed in a trust. Elizabeth could not dispose of these possessions, which consisted of a number of the

Elizabeth II at the opening session of Parliament in 2010. (AP/Wide World Photos)

royal palaces, other real estate, treasure, and collections of art and jewelry, including the crown jewels, kept at the Tower of London. The best known of the palaces are Buckingham Palace, Windsor Castle, and Holyrood House in Edinburgh, Scotland.

The second form of wealth, inherited from her father, was private and at her own disposal. This inheritance included several buildings, notably Balmoral Castle and its estates in Scotland and Sandringham House and estate in Norfolk, England. She also was bequeathed artworks and various treasures. In addition, Elizabeth obtained a large annual sum from the civil list in order to supplement the income derived from the duchy of Lancaster, her hereditary property.

MATURE WEALTH

Over time, both sources of Elizabeth's wealth grew through a natural increase in value and the many gifts the queen received regularly. The queen was also given the best financial advice concerning investments, which were limited primarily to blue chip bonds and stocks, and the value of these investments has increased considerably during the many years of her reign. She has been renowned as a careful money manager, with her one indulgence being the development of her stables. She has hired the best horse trainers, and her horses have always performed well.

After a serious fire at Windsor Castle spurred a national debate about who should bear the costs of restoration, the queen agreed to pay income tax beginning in 1992. At the same time, she began assuming some of the payments to her children that had been included in the civil list, with the exception of funds for her son Charles, Prince of Wales, and for some of the minor royalty.

The queen's finances are kept secret, so the amount of even her private wealth remains a subject of conjecture. In 2001, *Forbes* magazine judged her private wealth to be about $420 million, which was much lower than most previous estimates. This figure consisted of her private property, valued at $150 million; her art, jewelry, furniture, and horses, with a value of about $110 million; and the remainder obtained through investments.

LEGACY

Queen Elizabeth II has been able to move the British monarchy into the twenty-first century as a significant and honored institution. Part of this respect derives from the conservative display of her wealth, which she exhibits just enough to maintain her dignity as head of state, while refraining from the public extravagance that would invite criticism. The secrecy of her finances and lack of accountability for her wealth have invited ongoing criticism, but every indication is that her fortune is well managed.

—David Barratt

FURTHER READING

Graham, Tim. *Jubilee: A Celebration of Fifty Years of the Reign of Her Majesty, Queen Elizabeth II*. London: Cassell, 2002

Lacey, Robert. *Royal: Her Majesty Queen Elizabeth II*. New York: Time Warner, 2002

Pimlott, Ben. *The Queen: Elizabeth II and the Monarchy*. New York.: HarperCollins, 2001.

See also: David and Frederick Barclay; Sultan Hassanal Bolkiah; Deborah Cavendish; Gerald Grosvenor; Anita Roddick; J. K. Rowling; David Sainsbury; Wilhelmina.

JOHN ELLERMAN
British shipping magnate, businessman, and investor

Ellerman quietly forged a vast corporate empire from his careful acquisitions of a variety of ailing enterprises, notably shipbuilding firms and newspapers, and in the process accumulated the largest personal fortune in British business history.

Born: May 15, 1862; Hull, Yorkshire, England
Died: July 16, 1933; London, England
Also known as: Sir John Reeves Ellerman, first
  baronet
Sources of wealth: Shipping; real estate;
  investments
Bequeathal of wealth: Spouse; children

EARLY LIFE
Although he would become by most records the wealthiest British citizen in history, Sir John Reeves Ellerman, first baronet, unlike other Victorian magnates who thrived as celebrities, was fiercely protective of his private life. Thus, little is known of his early years. He was born in the village of Kingston upon Hull in northeast England. His father, a first-generation German immigrant who worked as a corn merchant with modest interests in commodities shipping, provided a quiet middle-class upbringing. His father died when Ellerman was nine. Ellerman attended but did not graduate from King Edward VI School, a prestigious preparatory school in the heart of Birmingham. As an adolescent, he resisted what he perceived as the arbitrary authority of teachers and maintained a close relationship with his mother. These difficulties stemmed from his embrace of nonconformity, his determination to go his own way.

FIRST VENTURES
Ellerman began to live on his own when he was fourteen. He moved to Birmingham and was licensed as a chartered accountant, which was unusual in an era when such work was frequently performed by bankers and secretaries. He relocated to London, where, by the age of twenty-four, he was directing his own accounting firm. He worked diligently to establish his company's reputation as one of London's most trusted accountancy firms. Most important, his work gave him access to financial records of distressed companies. With a savvy business acumen, Ellerman arranged to purchase the most promising of these floundering firms, drawing for the most part on his own capital but networking throughout London's most affluent circles for investors. He then restructured the firms' operations to give them, as well as himself, new opportunities for profit.

In 1892, upon the death of millionaire Liverpool shipbuilder Frederick Richards Leyland, Ellerman made his boldest move. As the head of a consortium of investors, he purchased the massive Leyland Line, with its fleet of twenty-two cargo and passenger ships. At the time, Ellerman had little background in shipping, but the opportunity presented by this company, which was experiencing a power vacuum after Leyland's death, was promising. Over the next decade, Ellerman became engaged in the management of the shipping line and he doubled the size of its fleet. Ellerman's shipping operations supplied critical naval carriers for ammunition and troops that helped ensure a British victory in the Second Boer War (1899-1902).

MATURE WEALTH
In 1901, American financier J. P. Morgan purchased the Leyland Line from Ellerman, although Ellerman continued directing operations and maintained direct ownership of half of the ships. Ellerman recognized the financial potential in shipping, which was the most efficient way to move goods, and during a time of relative peace the potential for international trading was clear. He used his considerable assets to purchase small shipping lines, forming the London, Liverpool and Ocean Shipping Company. Ellerman acquired smaller shipping lines until he eventually changed the name of his company to Ellerman Lines in 1903; the shipping firm would continue to expand. Ellerman became known for his relentless appetite for acquisition, notably his purchase in 1916 of more than sixty ships belonging to Thomas Wilson Sons, at the time among the largest private shipping firms in the British Empire.

Eventually, Ellerman branched out into other business ventures. At the height of his financial operations just before World War I, he controlled more than seventy breweries and twenty mines, and he had controlling interest in a number of major newspapers, notably *The Times*, *Daily Mail*, and the *Financial Times*. In addition, he bought up numerous lots of prime real estate in the heart of London with an eye toward development. His wealth was estimated at close to £70 million, or roughly $300 million, and as his fortune accumulated, he wielded an increasing influence in worldwide trade.

THE JOHN ELLERMAN FOUNDATION

The son of Sir John Reeves Ellerman, first Baronet, did not share his father's considerable business acumen, nor was he interested in the operations of his father's vast financial empire. Although Sir John Reeves Ellerman, second Baronet, passed the bar exam, the junior Ellerman was far more interested in zoology than in law. He pursued this interest, and by the time of his father's death in 1933, he had become a world-recognized authority on small rodents. Ellerman conducted his research on rodents in places as far away as South Africa and Asia. He was equally devoted to the arts, particularly music, the theater, and light opera.

Upon inheriting the majority of his father's estate, however, Ellerman assumed the responsibility for its management by turning a significant portion of it over to charitable institutions that assisted a wide range of causes, including veterans' homes, hospitals for the blind, educational institutions in London's poorest neighborhoods, and commissions that funded promising artists. By the mid-1950's, when his own poor health compelled him into a kind of semiretirement in the balmy climate of South Africa, the junior Ellerman had become known as one of London's foremost philanthropists.

In 1973, shortly before his death, Ellerman restructured his majority interest in Ellerman Lines, taking 79 percent of his shares and establishing two trusts chartered to make grant money available for any registered charity in the United Kingdom. Like his father, Ellerman was uninterested in publicity, and he strongly vetoed the idea of naming the trusts after his family, instructing the trust funds to be known as the Moorgate Fund and the New Moorgate Fund.

During the next two decades, these funds would become among the most sought-after grant providers in the United Kingdom, providing sums ranging from £10,000 to £100,000 in areas that included, but were not limited to, health and disability charities, social welfare bureaus, arts councils, and conservation and environmental enterprises. Unlike other large foundations, the Moorgate funds welcomed unsolicited applications from any service or charitable organization. Despite the enormous financial resources of the funds and their ambitious mission, they required only that an applying charity strive to make a real difference in its community, with special interest in those enterprises that sought practical ways to help the poor and disadvantaged.

In 1992, the two funds merged to become the John Ellerman Foundation, named for both father and son. Although the Ellerman Lines, which were the source of the family's fortune, had declined as the global market moved away from shipping in the 1970's and 1980's, the foundation itself remained financially healthy into the twenty-first century. By 2009, the foundation had distributed, on average, more than £5 million a year to between 160 and 200 separate charities.

Ellerman never pursued celebrity, nor did he seek to promote himself, his family, or his operations for public acknowledgment. When he was made a baronet in 1905 in recognition of his contributions to the Boer War effort, he actually turned down a far more prestigious peerage. He never lived in an ostentatious estate, never hosted sumptuous gatherings, never traveled, and never used his wealth to accumulate possessions or indulge expensive tastes. He and his family lived a simple, private life in Mayfair, an exclusive area in west London. His guarded sense of privacy had much to do with protecting his family from public scrutiny. He maintained what in the Victorian era was an unconventional relationship by living for nearly two decades with Hannah Glover, whom he had not married and with whom he had a daughter, born in 1894, and a son, born in 1910. In an effort to make clear the line of inheritance to his son, Ellerman in 1911 established his relationship with Glover as legal by taking advantage of an obscure Scottish law, applicable throughout the United Kingdom, that said a man and

woman living together for twenty-one days were married.

Ellerman maintained hands-on direction of his expanding empire, although he moved its headquarters from London to Liverpool and later opened an operations office in Glasgow, Scotland. By the outbreak of World War I, Ellerman Lines controlled critical trading routes throughout the Mediterranean Sea, as well as important new lines to the American markets and to Asia and Africa. During World War I, Ellerman again provided naval support for the British government, with his fleets of more than one hundred ships assisting the Royal Navy by providing troop ships and ammunition carriers. His own trading enterprises declined, compromised by the security risks of wartime.

However, after the war, Ellerman, although nearing sixty, committed himself to rebuilding the Ellerman Lines. He negotiated with the defeated German government to purchase its decommissioned ships, and within five years of the 1918 armistice Ellerman was again in command of one of the most successful shipping conglomerates in the world. In 1921, Ellerman was named to the Order of the Companions of Honour, an exclusive recognition bestowed by the monarchy in order to commend civilian contributions to the welfare of the British Empire.

Although the global economic catastrophe of the 1930's took its toll on his empire, when Ellerman died in 1933 he was regarded as the wealthiest individual in British history, with the exception of the nation's monarch. Yet few people in Great Britain knew him, and the newspapers, even those he owned, scrambled to find a photograph to accompany his obituary. Ellerman's estate was assessed at a £38 million, or roughly $140 million, excluding his considerable liquid assets, and was more than three times the size of what had previously been the nation's largest estate. Although he provided for both his wife and his daughter, who was by then an accomplished novelist, two-thirds of his estate was left to his son.

LEGACY

Despite his considerable wealth, John Ellerman sought neither power nor recognition. With the confident, careful logic of a trained accountant, Ellerman constructed a business empire, an example of the methodical accumulation of wealth based not on daring but rather on study and professional care. During five decades, Ellerman came to define a new kind of entrepreneurship. He embodied two characteristics that would later be considered antithetical: He was both a corporate raider and a white knight. Opportunistic and with an insatiable appetite for acquiring floundering businesses, Ellerman would pounce on promising companies that were either too small or too deeply in crisis to resist him, and he would then, with managerial savvy and a knack for efficiency, make these firms profitable, while using these profits to finance newer, wider acquisitions.

—Joseph Dewey

FURTHER READING

Fremont-Barnes, Gregory. *The Boer War, 1899-1902.* Oxford, England: Osprey, 2003. Provides a basic understanding of the war that first brought the Ellerman Lines its national reputation. Includes accounts of the service provided by Ellerman's ships and its importance to the war effort.

Halsey, A. H. *Twentieth-Century British Social Trends.* New York: Palgrave Macmillan, 2000. Includes a helpful discussion of the economic impact of Ellerman and his shipping empire within a broader context of pre-World War I Great Britain.

Kirkaldy, Adam Willis. *British Shipping: Its History, Organisation, and Importance.* Boston: Adamant Media, 2004. Indispensable account of the pivotal role of Ellerman and his shipping interests. Includes a measure of the range of Ellerman's empire and traces its decline in the years following World War II.

Morris, Charles R. *The Tycoons: How Andrew Carnegie, John D. Rockefeller, Jay Gould, and J. P. Morgan Invented the American Supereconomy.* New York: Times Books, 2005. Because Ellerman was the only British plutocrat on a par with American giants of the Gilded Age, this book provides a sense of Ellerman's era. Includes a fascinating account of Morgan's business dealings with the reclusive Ellerman.

Taylor, James Arnold. *Ellermans: A Wealth of Shipping.* London: Wilton House Gentry, 1976. Still the only reliable account of the family and its achievements by a company insider and family confidant. Skirts the eccentricities of the family's personal lives and maintains its focus on the business dealings and public activities.

See also: David and Frederick Barclay; Captain Robert Dollar; James J. Hill; Stavros Niarchos; Aristotle Onassis.

LARRY ELLISON
American computer magnate

Ellison's brilliance and aggressiveness created Oracle Corporation, one of the most successful and powerful technology companies, and made him a multibillionaire. Known as a brutally tough businessman, he also has contributed to numerous charities and founded the Ellison Medical Foundation.

Born: August 17, 1944; Bronx, New York
Also known as: Lawrence Joseph Ellison
Sources of wealth: Computer industry; sale of products
Bequeathal of wealth: Children; charity; medical institution

EARLY LIFE

Lawrence Ellison was born in the Bronx borough of New York City on August 17, 1944, to a nineteen-year-old single mother named Florence and an unknown father.

Young Larry contracted a severe case of pneumonia, prompting Florence to send the nine-month-old child to live with her aunt and uncle, Lillian Spillman Ellison and Louis Ellison, in Chicago. The Ellisons, Russian-Jewish immigrants, welcomed Larry into their family and adopted him. Louis was very demanding of Larry, and when Larry learned that the Ellisons had adopted him, he became more independent and tough-minded.

Ellison excelled at math and science, aspiring to be a doctor. He attended the University of Illinois at Urbana-Champaign for two years, quitting when his adoptive mother succumbed to cancer. He later attended the University of Chicago for a semester but never graduated.

FIRST VENTURES

Ellison moved to California's Silicon Valley in 1966, and during the next eight years he worked at various technol-

Larry Ellison delivers the keynote address at the Oracle Open World Conference. (AP/Wide World Photos)

THE ELLISON MEDICAL FOUNDATION

Billionaire Larry Ellison, a founder and the chief executive officer of the Oracle Corporation, founded the Ellison Medical Foundation in 1998, teaming up with his friend scientist Joshua Lederberg to fund research in the biological processes of aging. These studies include examining illnesses like Parkinson's disease, Alzheimer's disease, and cancer. Ellison is the sole financier of the foundation, having contributed hundreds of millions of dollars to the organization.

Ellison, a science and health buff, was attending a weekend seminar on the Human Genome Project at Stanford University in 1992 and was mesmerized by Lederberg's eloquence and intelligence. Lederberg, the former president of Rockefeller University in New York City, was a cowinner of the Nobel Prize in Physiology or Medicine in 1958. The scientist won over Ellison immediately, and Ellision invited Lederberg to lunch, thus beginning a friendship based on each man's deep love of science and desire to learn more.

Ellison accumulated massive wealth throughout the 1990's but had no set philanthropic goals. He decided, with Lederberg's help and vision, to fund a medical foundation to support top scientists in their research without the documentation and effort needed to obtain government grants. Ellison, who lost his adoptive mother to cancer and has a brother-in-law with Parkinson's disease, has always been consumed with maintaining a healthy lifestyle. For this reason, he established the Ellison Medical Foundation to conduct research in the basic biological sciences relevant to understanding the human life span and age-related diseases and disabilities.

The Ellison Medical Foundation partnered with the American Federation for Aging Research (AFAR), creating the Ellison/AFAR Postdoctoral Fellows in Aging Research Program. The program is designed to encourage and further the careers of promising postdoctoral fellows in the biological and biomedical sciences and to establish these fellows in the field of aging research.

During the 2003 America's Cup race, Ellison was asked to explain the differences between his passions for business, sailing, and the progress made by his foundation. Ellison said that molecular biology held more appeal than racing sailboats because the biology "race" and the people in it were more interesting and the prize was larger.

Lederberg died in 2008 at age eighty-two. He was awarded the Presidential Medal of Freedom, the highest civilian award in the United States, in 1996. The Ellison Medical Foundation continues to pursue the mission that Lederberg envisioned.

---

ogy jobs. While working at Ampex, a small technology firm, Ellison teamed with Robert Miner and Edward Oates to write a database program for the Central Intelligence Agency (CIA). The three partners named the program Oracle.

Ellison left Ampex for Precision Instruments (later named Omex), which, like Ampex, was in the business of converting microfilm to videotape. Omex was looking for contractors to program their mass storage system, so Ellison, then vice president of the company, formed Software Development Laboratories in 1977 with his friends Miner and Oates. They won the $400,000 contract at a third of the price of the next lowest bid; Ellison put up just $2,000 to fund the business.

Ellison hoped to build and market his own product and was inspired by a series of International Business Machines (IBM) white papers that detailed System R, the prototype database that IBM was building. System R was a relational database management system, and the white papers outlined the specifications and structured query language needed to organize and access the system's data. Ellison scrapped his database model and used the IBM white papers as the blueprint for his new and improved Oracle database.

Software Development Laboratories changed its name to Relational Software, Inc. (RSI), in 1979. Ellison owned 60 percent of RSI, with Miner and Oates each owning 20 percent. Ellison traveled relentlessly in the following years, successfully marketing his company and its Oracle database. He became a millionaire, acquiring cars and boats. RSI was later renamed the Oracle Corporation after the firm's flagship program.

MATURE WEALTH

Oracle beat IBM to the market for relational database management systems by more than two years, creating a product that could be used across a broad range of computer hardware and software systems. Oracle became profitable by 1982 with $2.5 million in earnings, and it then doubled its profit in 1983 when it expanded to Denmark.

As the use of computers increased in the early to mid-1980's, businesses scrambled to manage data, and Oracle fought and outsold its competitors. Company revenues in 1985 climbed to $23 million, and the following year sales doubled to $55.4 million, with Ellison's stake in the company now worth $90 million. Oracle went public in 1986, one day before another technology firm, Microsoft Corporation, also became a public company. While Microsoft became a hit with its Windows software, which was sold primarily to individuals, Oracle sold its products to companies and governments. The stage was set for a competition between the two companies and their two soon-to-be-billionaire founders: Microsoft's Bill Gates and Oracle's Ellison.

Oracle ended the 1980's as the top company name in database management systems, attaining the largest number of end users in the world, top-level customers, and a reputation as a technology innovator. Oracle became a member of Standard & Poor's 500 and was one of the largest and most powerful software companies in the world. Ellison accumulated hundreds of millions of dollars during the 1980's.

Oracle's unstoppable growth was halted in early 1990, however, when its aggressive expansion plans revealed flat earnings because of an accounting error, and the value of the company's stock dropped precipitously. Problems were exacerbated in April, 1990, when a dozen shareholders brought suit against the company for allegedly making false and misleading earnings forecasts. The lawsuit led to an internal audit and management restructuring, with Ellison taking on the additional role of chairman of the board, along with his positions as president and chief executive officer. The once-praised company and its founder were criticized when Oracle reported its first quarterly loss in mid-1990, and the company scrambled to avert a possible bankruptcy. Ellison came under fire for his company's combative sales and marketing practices and his lavish lifestyle. Oracle's stock lost more than $2.7 billion in market value in six months and, consequently, Ellison's net worth, mostly tied to his company's stock, took a big hit.

Oracle acknowledged that it had grown too rapidly, restated 1990 earnings, and shed more than 10 percent of its employees. During 1991, the company regrouped and rebuilt, attaining sales of $1 billion. Oracle added $1 billion to its revenues annually from 1992 to 1998, and Ellison, now a multibillionaire, continued to burnish his playboy image by buying exotic cars, yachts, and private jets, including two fighter jets. He also spent ten years building an estimated $200 million, twenty-three-acre estate in Woodside, California, designed in a style based on Japanese medieval architecture.

Ellison has always been a calculated risk taker in business and in his personal life, with several children from several marriges. His thirst for adventure has led him all over the world, where he has flown, sailed, explored, climbed mountains, and lived a life few others could rival. He is a licensed instrument-rated pilot and an accomplished sailor. He had a life-changing experience during the harrowing Sydney to Hobart Yacht Race in 1998, when a strong storm ravaged the racing fleet, costing six sailors their lives. His yacht, the eighty-foot *Sayonara*, and his crew were relatively unscathed in the storm, and he won the race. However, Ellison swore he would no longer compete in sailing competitions. Still, he remained involved in the sport, becoming the second largest investor in BMW Oracle Racing, a team that is a perennial challenger in the America's Cup race. Ellison's love of the ocean extends beyond sailing to high-end yachting. He and entertainment executive David Geffen co-own one of the largest private yachts in the world, the *Rising Sun*, a 452-foot superyacht launched in 2004.

LEGACY

Larry Ellison is a pioneer in the software industry. He has had a tremendous impact on global business information management, and he has also created a personal fortune rivaled by few others. His inventions and business practices will be studied for generations, and his tens of billions of dollars and eccentric lifestyle will probably be criticized equally long. At one point in 2000, Ellison was the richest person in the world, briefly surpassing rival Bill Gates, when Ellison's net worth reportedly exceeded $60 billion.

—Jonathan E. Dinneen

FURTHER READING

Southwick, Karen. *Everyone Else Must Fail: The Unvarnished Truth About Oracle and Larry Ellison*. New York: Crown, 2003. An unauthorized portrait of Ellison as an evil genius, outlining his innovation and brilliance but also his ruthlessness. Southwick, a technology writer, recognizes Ellison's assets, but unlike many other Ellison biographers, she also underscores his harsh and controversial business tactics.

Stone, Florence. *The Oracle of Oracle: The Story of Volatile CEO Larry Ellison and the Strategies Behind His Company's Phenomenal Success*. New York: AMACOM, 2002. A quick view of the history of Oracle and a review of the core business strategies Ellison instilled in the company, with excellent examples.

Symonds, Matthew. *Softwar: An Intimate Portrait of Larry Ellison and Oracle*. New York: Simon &

Schuster, 2003. An inside look at the personal life and career of Ellison by an experienced business writer and commentator. The book contains commentary by Ellison.

Wilson, Mike. *The Difference Between God and Larry Ellison*. New York: HarperCollins, 1997. A behind-the-scenes look at how Ellison started Oracle and turned it into a global leader. The author, an investiga-tive reporter, had access to Ellison, to his current and former employees, and to many others, resulting in a detailed portrayal of Ellison.

See also: Paul Allen; Steven Ballmer; Jeff Bezos; Sergey Brin; Mark Cuban; Michael Dell; Bill Gates; David Geffen; Steve Jobs; Gordon E. Moore; David Packard; H. Ross Perot.

CHARLES ENGELHARD, JR.
American industrialist and racehorse owner

Engelhard built the largest precious metals refining company in the world, with major operations in the United States and South Africa. He and his wife Jane lived lavishly on several estates, racing an army of thoroughbred horses and making donations to the American Wing of the Metropolitan Museum of Art.

Born: February 15, 1917; New Jersey
Died: March 2, 1971; Boca Grande, Florida
Also known as: Charles William Engelhard, Jr.;
   The Platinum King
Sources of wealth: Metals refining; horse breeding
Bequeathal of wealth: Spouse; children; charity

EARLY LIFE
Charles William Engelhard (EHN-gehl-hahrd), Jr., was born to wealth, which he greatly increased. His father, Charles Engelhard, established the Hanovia Chemical and Manufacturing firm in 1902, which processed gold and other precious metals, such as platinum and silver. Charles, Sr., and his wife lived in a mountain estate they called Craigmore, located in New Jersey. In 1940, they established the Charles Engelhard Foundation for charity. Charles, Jr., was their only child. Charles, Jr., was raised in a strict atmosphere that prepared him to inherit his father's business. He graduated from Princeton University. In World War II, he was a bomber pilot with the U.S. Air Force. After the war, he went to work in his father's firm. In 1947, he married a widow, Jane Reiss, who also came from a wealthy family. She was born Marie Annette Jane Reiss in 1917 in Shanghai, the daughter of Hugo Reiss, who ran a successful worldwide import-export company. In June, 1939, Jane married Fritz Mannheimer, the leading banker in Europe, who had built an art collection worth tens of millions of dollars. Several months after the wedding, Mannheimer died in mysterious circumstances. During their marriage, Charles and Jane raised five daughters: Annette, from Jane's first marriage to Mannheimer, and the couple's own children, Susan, Sophie, Sally, and Charlene. In 1949, the couple bought a 172-acre estate in New Jersey, called Cragwood.

By the time of his death in 1950, Charles Engelhard, Sr., had expanded his firm to become the world's largest refiner and fabricator of gold, silver, and platinum, as well as the world's largest precious metals smelter. He left his $20 million estate to Charles, Jr.

FIRST VENTURES
Charles, Jr., expanded the family business many times during the following decades. He raised revenue through his astute use of technology, applying important innova-tions to the precious metals refining industry. In 1948, Engelhard opened a branch in South Africa in order to sell art objects and jewelry made of gold. During the next thirteen years, Engelhard became an industrial giant in South Africa. His success in refining and selling plati-num earned him the nickname the "Platinum King." His gold, silver, and platinum bars became world-famous and were a widely accepted form of precious metals cur-rency. In South Africa, he also traded uranium, dia-monds, and timberland.

In 1958, Engelhard amalgamated his holdings into Engelhard Industries, which had $200 million in annual sales. In addition to metals refining, Engelhard Indus-tries sold ceramic products, jewelry, pharmaceuticals, medical and dental equipment, automotive and aircraft parts, and equipment for the nuclear, petroleum, and plastics industries. In 1959, Engelhard's precious metals operations alone netted $3.7 million, and his net worth was estimated at $100 million. In 1961, he began selling shares of his company to the public, retaining a 43 percent ownership; the company's revenues that year were $1.43 billion. Within a few years, revenues had climbed to $10 billion. Engelhard Industries conducted business in fifty countries. It is widely believed that author Ian Fleming based the villainous character of Auric Goldfinger in his James Bond novel *Goldfinger* (1959) on Charles Engelhard, Jr. As one of the largest foreign operators in South Africa, Engelhard came under criticism because of that nation's policy of apartheid. He sold his South African operations shortly before his death in 1971.

MATURE WEALTH

Charles and Jane Engelhard employed their wealth ambitiously and strategically. They were large-scale contributors to the Democratic Party and friends with Lyndon B. Johnson, the party leader who later became president and for whom the Engelhards often hosted gatherings at their estate. Charles entered politics in 1955 when he ran for the New Jersey State senate. He was narrowly defeated by another multimillionaire, editor Malcolm Forbes. In 1961, Jane was appointed to the White House Redecoration Committee.

The Engelhards lived amid luxurious surroundings. Charles and Jane owned homes in New Jersey, Quebec, Florida, Maine, Paris, and Johannesburg, South Africa.

WEALTH AND GOLD

Nothing symbolizes wealth as much as gold. From the beginning of civilization, gold has been desired, hoarded, fought over, shaped into exquisite jewelry and decorations, and, most important, considered the ultimate currency and source of wealth. Gold is a metal with the symbol Au on the periodic table of the elements. This precious metal is treasured because of its unique qualities. Gold is lustrous and brilliant to behold, and it does not tarnish with use or wear. It is impervious to almost any other element, and it is thus almost indestructible. Gold is rare. It also is soft and malleable, and it can be molded into almost any conceivable shape, however fine.

The legendary status of gold dates back to antiquity. In Greek mythology, Perseus sought the Golden Fleece. King Midas of Phrygia was famed for his "golden touch." King Croesus of Lydia minted gold coins, which were a part of his vast wealth. The ancient Romans extracted large amounts of gold from the Las Medulas mine in Spain. Even Aesop's goose laid golden eggs.

The medieval Mali Empire was built on huge quantities of gold, to the amazement of the world. At the same time, alchemists sought to turn base metals into gold; they did not succeed, but they did contribute to the development of chemistry. In later years, the Spanish conquistadors demanded the gold of the Aztec emperor Montezuma II and the Inca emperor Atahualpa. Other conquistadors brought themselves to destruction searching for El Dorado, the lost city of gold. In the nineteenth century, Aga Khan I, imam of the Ismāʻīlī Muslims, was weighed against a pile of gold bullion, donated by his followers to match his weight.

Archaeological finds became famous when they uncovered objects made of gold. When archaeologist Howard Carter discovered the mummy of Pharaoh Tutankhamen, the ancient Egyptian leader was entombed in a solid gold casket weighing 296 pounds, and he was wearing a solid gold funerary mask weighing 24 pounds. The Karun Treasure, a collection of ancient Lydian objects from the seventh century B.C.E., included golden birds and horses.

Throughout history, treasure hunters searched for Valverde's gold, rumored to be the remainder of Atahualpa's gold, hidden from the Spanish; the buried gold treasure of seventeenth century pirate William Kidd; gold from the treasure ship *Republic*, lost when it sank in 1865; and the gold stolen by the Nazis. Once gold is found, hoards of miners rush in to seize it. The gold rushes in California in 1849, Australia in 1851, South Africa in 1886, and the Klondike in 1897 have become legendary for having attracted hundreds of gold seekers eager to strike it rich.

The most beautiful and valuable coins in history have been made of gold: the aureus and solidus of ancient Rome, the Venetian ducat, the Byzantine bezant, the Islamic dinar, the British sovereign, the South African Krugerrand, and the American "double eagle" twenty-dollar gold piece, designed by sculptor Augustus Saint-Gaudens. The Chinese emperor Xianzong is credited with the first use of paper money in the ninth century, but paper money was backed by gold. For example, the U.S. dollar was supported by gold reserves in Fort Knox, Tennessee, and other locations. In the twentieth century, both Great Britain and the United States went off the gold standard, as did most of the world's nations, as a result of the Bretton Woods Agreement of 1944. Economist John Maynard Keynes labeled the gold standard a "barbarous relic." However, time has yet to tell whether fiat currency—money declared legal tender—can remain useful if it is not backed by gold.

Their chief residence was Cragwood, a Germanic turreted castle on an estate in New Jersey. This estate boasted a menagerie of animals, including lions, parrots, peacocks, and prize golden retrievers. Charles paid $1 million to create a salmon river for his personal fishing. The couple also owned apartments in Rome, New York City, and London. When they traveled, they were waited upon by a team of secretaries, drivers, butlers, valets, and chefs. The Engelhards owned three jets and a helicopter. They accumulated a multimillion-dollar art collection, which included works by Edgar Degas, Pierre-Auguste Renoir, Édouard Manet, and Paul Cézanne.

The Engelhards were an important couple in New York society. Jane was an elegant woman, who was perennially included on lists of the ten best-dressed women. Charles became passionate about horse racing, spending more than $15 million for 240 thoroughbred racehorses. Engelhard was one of the most successful racehorse owners, and his horses scored 213 victories in nine years. He owned stables in North Carolina, England, and South Africa. His best-known horse, Nijinsky II, is considered one of the greatest horses in thoroughbred history. Nijinsky II won the English Derby several times and was a British Triple Crown champion. At the end of Nijinky II's racing career, Engelhard sold the horse to a stud farm for $5.4 million.

Along with their lavish lifestyle, the Engelhards were generous philanthropists. Jane was a devout Catholic and contributed to Catholic causes. She also donated valuable antiques to the White House's collections, including an eighteenth century Neapolitan crèche. The Engelhards gave $500,000 to Boys Town of America and $1.25 million to Rutgers University, and they provided funds to construct a library at Harvard University's Kennedy School of Government. (The library does not bear the Engelhard name because of controversy about Charles's involvement in South Africa during the years when apartheid was the government's official policy.) The Engelhards also made large donations to development projects in South Africa.

Because of his lavish lifestyle, Charles gained weight, and this increase may be an explanation for his sudden heart attack, and death, at the age of fifty-four. He left a fortune of $250 million. Jane continued to run the Charles Engelhard Foundation, which in 2003 had assets of approximately $100 million. She gave $10 million to the American Wing of the Metropolitan Museum of Art in New York City. The wing's Charles Engelhard Court is one of the highlights of the museum, and it contains a reflecting pool, nineteenth and twentieth century American sculptures, and elegant plants. Jane died on February 2, 2004.

LEGACY

Charles Engelhard, Jr., gained his fortune from his worldwide metals refining and smelting operations, and he spent much of his wealth on lavish living and horse racing. His wife, Jane, who had an equally remarkable personal history, was a driving force in the Engelhard operations, especially in the couple's charitable donations. The Charles Engelhard Foundation financed various environmental and substance abuse programs. Jane also provided funding to build the Charles Engelhard Court at the Metropolitan Museum of Art. This court underwent a major renovation from 2007 to 2009.

—*Howard Bromberg*

FURTHER READING

Barrett, Ward. "World Bullion Flows, 1450-1800." In *The Rise of Merchant Empires: Long Distance Trade in the Early Modern World, 1350-1750*, edited by James Tracy. Cambridge, England: Cambridge University Press, 1993. Analyzes the flow of gold and silver bullion in trade between Europe, Asia, and the Americas in order to assess world economics.

Bernstein, Peter. *The Power of Gold: The History of an Obsession*. New York: John Wiley and Sons, 2000. Intriguing account of the power of gold in human imagination and history.

Braudel, Fernand. *The Wheels of Commerce*. Vol. 2 in *Civilization and Capitalism: Fifteenth-Eighteenth Century*. Translated by Sian Reynolds. Berkeley: University of California Press, 1992. Monumental economic history of the modern world through the eighteenth century, with an insightful section on gold and silver in world markets.

Gross, Michael. *Rogue's Gallery: The Secret History of the Moguls and the Money That Made the Metropolitan Museum*. New York: Broadway Books, 2009. An account of the rich persons and their gifts that have made the Metropolitan Museum of Art the wealthiest museum in the world, with an estimated value as high as $400 billion. Chapter 6 is devoted to the Engelhards and their donations.

Reich, Cary. *Financier—The Biography of Andre Meyer: A Story of Money, Power, and the Reshaping of American Business*. New York: Quill, 1983. Biography of a leading financier who was a close friend and associate of Jane Engelhard.

Ryan, Pat. "The Walking Conglomerate." *Sports Illus-*

trated, April 28, 1969, 64-74. An account of Engelhard's wealth and his devotion to horse racing, which his fortune made possible.

Schleicher, William, and Susan Winter. *Somerset Hills: The Landed Gentry*. Dover, N.H.: Arcadia, 1997. A collection of historic photographs, including the

Engelhards' Cragwood estate, overlooking Ravine Lake in New Jersey.

See also: Arthur Vining Davis; Meyer Guggenheim; Solomon R. Guggenheim; Moritz Hochschild; Andrónico Luksic; Simón Iturri Patiño.

BÉATRICE EPHRUSSI DE ROTHSCHILD
French aristocrat, heiress, and socialite

Ephrussi de Rothschild used her wealth to indulge her passions for travel and art. She amassed a vast art collection during her travels, which she left to the French Academy of Fine Arts, along with her estate in Saint-Jean-Cap-Ferrat, France, for the creation of a public museum.

Born: September 14, 1864; Paris, France
Died: April 7, 1934; Davos, Switzerland
Also known as: Charlotte Béatrice Ephrussi de Rothschild; Charlotte Béatrice de Rothschild (birth name)
Sources of wealth: Inheritance; marriage
Bequeathal of wealth: Museum

EARLY LIFE
Charlotte Béatrice Ephrussi de Rothschild (shahr-LUHT bay-ah-TREES eh-frew-SEE deh ROTH-child) was born in Paris, France, in 1864, a member of the French branch of the Rothschild banking family. She was the second daughter of Mayer Alphonse James Rothschild, who headed the French Rothschilds; his wife, Leonora de Rothschild, was a British Rothschild and his first cousin once removed. Béatrice and siblings Bettina Caroline de Rothschild and Édouard Alphonse James de Rothschild were raised at the family mansion at 2 rue Saint-Florentin in Paris and at the Château de Ferrières, a historic nineteenth century château located east of Paris. Her father was an avid art collector, and Béatrice came to share his passion for works of art.

FIRST VENTURES
Through her family's business interests in the Baku area of present-day Azerbaijan, Béatrice became acquainted with Maurice Ephrussi, a Russian-born French banker, art collector, and racehorse breeder who was fifteen years her senior. She and Ephrussi were married in Paris in 1883. They established residences in Paris, the Reux

municipality in the Basse-Normandie region of France, and Monte Carlo, Monaco. The couple would have no children.

Ephrussi de Rothschild traveled extensively, befriending art dealers and experts and building a collection of paintings, sculptures, antique furniture, porcelain, and objets d'art. In 1902 she commissioned the Rothschild Fabergé egg, one of the few made for anyone outside the Russian imperial family, which she gave as an engagement present to her brother's future wife, Germaine Alice Halphen.

MATURE WEALTH
When her father died in 1905, Ephrussi de Rothschild inherited a substantial portion of his immense fortune. She purchased about seventeen acres of French Riviera land on the Saint-Jean-Cap-Ferrat peninsula, where, between 1905 and 1912, she oversaw the painstaking construction of a fanciful Italianate villa with elaborate gardens and stunning views of the Mediterranean Sea. She named her retreat Île-de-France after a favorite cruise ship, and she reproduced the sense of being aboard a ship at sea by designing the main garden to resemble the deck of an ocean liner, complete with gardeners dressed as sailors.

Ephrussi de Rothschild filled her villa with her extensive collections, and she kept a small menagerie of exotic animals in her gardens. She acquired eighteenth century furniture that had belonged to France's Queen Marie-Antoinette, and she had a Temple of Love erected in her garden that was a replica of the one near the queen's Petit Trianon château at Versailles.

Despite the attention she lavished on its creation, Ephrussi de Rothschild only occasionally stayed at the Île-de-France. After her husband's death in 1916, she left Saint-Jean-Cap-Ferrat behind, residing instead at the couple's Monte Carlo villa. Near the end of her life, she lived in Davos, Switzerland, where in 1934 she died of tuberculosis at the age of sixty-nine. In her will she bequeathed her art collections and her estate at Saint-Jean-Cap-Ferrat to the Academy of Fine Arts of the Institute of France, with instructions that these donations be used to create a museum with the ambiance of a private home.

LEGACY

Béatrice Ephrussi de Rothschild is remembered as the hugely wealthy, somewhat eccentric Rothschild who built and inhabited Île-de-France, now better known as the Villa Ephrussi de Rothschild. Thanks to her bequest to the French Academy of Fine Arts, her seaside retreat has become a Saint-Jean-Cap-Ferrat landmark enjoyed by more than 150,000 visitors a year. It is the French Riviera's only great Belle Époque estate of its kind that has been opened to the public. As such, it provides a window onto a vanished era, when European aristocracy and the wealthiest international elite dominated the resort towns of the French Riviera. Her villa and collections also af-

ford the visitor insights into the life and lifestyle of the art-loving Ephrussi de Rothschild herself.

—Karen N. Kähler

FURTHER READING

Académie des Beaux-Arts, Institut de France. *Villa and Gardens Ephrussi de Rothschild*. Paris: Culture-spaces, 2009.

Christie's. *Russian Works of Art, Including the Rothschild Fabergé Egg*. London: Author, 2007.

Rothschild, Miriam, Lionel de Rothschild, and Kate Garton. *The Rothschild Gardens: A Family's Tribute to Nature*. New York: Abbeville Press, 2004.

See also: Cornelia Martin; Abby Aldrich Rockefeller; First Baron Rothschild; James Mayer Rothschild; Mayer Amschel Rothschild; Nathan Mayer Rothschild; Consuelo Vanderbilt.

CHARLES ERGEN
American telecommunications magnate

Ergen and two partners pooled their resources and began their business by selling full-size satellite television dishes in rural Colorado. This joint venture, eventually called EchoStar Corporation, and another company, Dish Network, became giants in the telecommunications industry, and Ergen became a billionaire.

Born: March 1, 1953; Oak Ridge, Tennessee
Also known as: Charles William Ergen
Sources of wealth: Media; telecommunications; investments
Bequeathal of wealth: Charity

EARLY LIFE

Charles William "Charlie" Ergen (EHR-gehn), the fourth of five children of William K. and Viola S. Ergen, was born in 1953 in Oak Ridge, Tennessee. When he was four years old, Ergen and his father, a nuclear physicist, witnessed the Soviet satellite Sputnik 1 in orbit. Ergen attended the local public schools and graduated from Oak Ridge High School in 1971. That same year his father died, and Ergen had to work his way through college. He graduated from the University of Tennessee in 1975 and the Babcock Graduate School of Management at Wake Forest University in 1976. After receiving certification

as a public accountant, Ergen worked as an auditor for a textile company and then as a financial analyst for PepsiCo's Frito-Lay division. In 1978, Ergen quit his job and became a professional gambler, but he and his partner James "Jim" DeFranco got into trouble in Las Vegas after being charged with counting cards at the blackjack tables.

FIRST VENTURES

In 1980, Ergen, DeFranco, and Candy McAdams, who would later marry Ergen, began marketing television satellite dishes from the back of their truck. They spent $60,000 to start their company, initially called Echo-Sphere, because the satellite dish was shaped like a sphere, and later renamed the EchoStar Corporation. The business profited by selling satellite dishes in rural areas of Colorado, Utah, and Wyoming.

With hard-nosed tactics, a gambling nature, and a quick intelligence, Ergen worked mercilessly to advance his business. His strategies included avoiding competition by maintaining low prices, staying attuned to legislative proceedings that affected the media and telecommunications industries, and eagerly providing lawmakers with evidence in support of reforms and improvements that would benefit his company. Ergen demonstrated technological knowledge in the telecommunications business and insisted upon providing his customers with cutting-edge services. By 1987, Ergen had concluded that the future of his business depended upon extending his enterprise beyond merely selling equipment and hardware. In order to have more control of the delivery of television programs, Ergen opted to have EchoStar invest in direct satellite broadcasting.

MATURE WEALTH

In the early 1990's, Ergen expanded his business to include small-dish satellite services, and he founded Dish Network as the broadcasting services division of his business. Having obtained a direct broadcasting satellite license from the Federal Communications Commission, Ergen's company could now provide national broadcasting services. In the mid-1990's, EchoStar launched the first of several satellites, began selling its stock publicly, and created a Dish Network infomercial with Ergen as the host of Charlie Chat. During the late 1990's, Dish Network became the first company to broadcast local television channels via satellite.

Throughout the 1990's and early twenty-first century, Ergen's business flourished. Millions of people subscribed to Dish Network, and he became one of the richest men in America. By 2002, EchoStar employed fifteen thousand people and was worth $10 billion. In 2007, he was the wealthiest Colorado resident and the twenty-seventh-richest person in the United States, but the zealous Ergen wanted more. He ruthlessly pursued merger deals with other companies, including Rupert Murdoch's News Corporation. This merger failed, but Ergen managed to gain News Corporation's satellite assets.

Ergen worked to provide discount prices while offering customers the latest technologies. These tactics garnered 13.7 million subscribers. However, inadequate marketing campaigns, litigation, high-definition television, and cable television competition during a period of economic downturn caused Ergen to lose more than $2.2 billion in 2008.

LEGACY

In the process of building EchoStar and Dish Network, Ergen became a wealthy telecommunications tycoon. His philanthropy has included political contributions to both major political parties and donations to the Colorado Mountain Club and Children's Hospital in Colorado.

—Cynthia J. W. Svoboda

FURTHER READING

Anderson, Jenny, and Steven Brull. "EchoStar Spins into Orbit." *Investor: International Edition* 27, no. 3 (March, 2002): 68-79.

Cohen, Adam. "Satellite Shutdown." *Time*, August 20, 2001, p. 64.

Heary, Donald F. *Cutthroat Teammates: Achieving Effective Teamwork Among Professionals*. Homewood, Ill.: Dow Jones-Irwin, 1989.

See also: Barbara Cox Anthony; Silvio Berlusconi; Michael Bloomberg; Anne Cox Chambers; Robert L. Johnson; John Kluge; Rupert Murdoch; Thaksin Shinawatra; Carlos Slim; Ted Turner; Oprah Winfrey.

PABLO ESCOBAR
Colombian drug trafficker

Escobar rose to power during a time of great violence in Columbia's history. His ruthlessness enabled him to control the world's most powerful—and lucrative—cocaine cartel. Escobar used some of his ill-gotten wealth to benefit the poor.

Born: January 12, 1949; Medellín, Colombia
Died: December 2, 1993; Medellín, Colombia
Also known as: Pablo Emilio Escobar Gaviria;
    El Doctor; El Patron
Sources of wealth: Narcotics trafficking; real estate
Bequeathal of wealth: Spouse; children; government

EARLY LIFE
Pablo Emilio Escobar Gaviria (PAH-bloh ee-MEEL-ee-oh EHS-koh-bahr gah-VEER-ee-ah) was born in 1949 in Medellín, Colombia, the son of Abel de Jesus Escobar and Helmilda Gaviria. His family would have been considered middle class. He grew up in Envigado, a suburb of Medellín, during a period referred to locally as "the violence," a time of great bloodshed and ineffective law enforcement. Escobar was involved in criminal activities in high school. He eventually dropped out.

FIRST VENTURES
Escobar moved up to stealing automobiles and selling them for parts. However, he found he could make more money by bribing officials to provide new titles for the cars and then reselling the vehicles. By 1976, Escobar moved into the world of drug smuggling. He was arrested shortly after his marriage to Maria Victoria Henao Vellejo after he was caught smuggling thirty-nine kilograms of cocaine. He then showed the cunning and ruthlessness that would become his trademark. After rejecting a bribe, the judge on the case recused himself as the result of a ploy by Escobar. The officers who arrested Escobar were murdered. When Escobar finally decided to move into cocaine distribution, he simply murdered the local drug kingpin, Fabio Restrepo, and took over his business.

MATURE WEALTH
Escobar organized the other cocaine smugglers into a cartel. He made sure the laboratories which processed the cocaine were hidden in the rainforests. He organized the drug cartel like a corporation and personally supervised every stage of the drug-dealing process. He adopted a philosophy of *plata o plomo* (silver or lead) as a way of dealing with his enemies. People who did not take his bribes were killed with no remorse.

As his empire grew, he started to purchase airplanes and managed to get two airlines under the Medellín cartel's control. He supervised a network of drug distribution points throughout North America. The profits of the cartel were comparable to those of the largest multinational corporation. Drug traffickers in Medellín and surrounding areas were giving Escobar between 20 and 35 percent of their profits. He invested in real estate in the United States and had numerous estates in Colombia, one of which boasted a private zoo and twenty artificial lakes. *Forbes* magazine estimated his wealth to be close to $25 billion in 1989, which ranked him as the seventh-richest man in the world. He controlled roughly 80 percent of global cocaine distribution.

Pablo Escobar. (AP/Wide World Photos)

Despite his criminal background, Escobar gave freely to the poor and was seen as a Colombian Robin Hood. He built low-cost housing and lighted sports arenas for the public. He funded the construction of many churches. He was so popular that he was even elected to the Colombian congress.

However, the violence he created eventually caught up with him. In 1993, aided by a local organization of people who had been affected by Escobar's activities, the U.S. Drug Enforcement Administration and Colombian police tracked him down after an arduous search. He was killed in Medellín during a gunfight.

LEGACY

The Colombian government seized many of Escobar's properties and either gave them to the poor or used them for government purposes. Escobar's activities were one of the reasons President Ronald Reagan initiated his war on drugs. The depth of the corruption caused by Escobar's wealth and his influence were far-reaching and took years to ferret out.

Escobar continued to be held in high esteem by some, particularly the poor, because of his public works. His wife inherited some of Escobar's vast wealth and was later jailed for money laundering. His daughter inherited the remains of Escobar's estate after a long legal battle.

—James J. Heiney

FURTHER READING

Bowden, Mark. *Killing Pablo: The Hunt for the World's Greatest Outlaw*. New York: Atlantic Monthly Press, 2001.

Escobar Gaviria, Roberto, and David Fisher. *The Accountant's Story: Inside the Violent World of the Medellín Cartel*. New York: Grand Central, 2009.

Mollison, James, and Rainbow Nelson. *The Memory of Pablo Escobar*. London: Chris Boot, 2007.

See also: William Jardine; John Palmer; David Sassoon; Wu Bingjian.

NIKOLAUS ESTERHÁZY
Hungarian aristocrat, military leader, and art patron

Esterházy was born into wealth as a member of the house of Esterházy, a noble family with a considerable fortune. His thirty-year financial commitment to support the eminent composer Joseph Haydn established his reputation as a significant patron of the arts.

Born: December 18, 1714; Galanta, Kingdom of Hungary (now in Slovakia)
Died: September 28, 1790; Vienna, Austria
Also known as: Nikolaus Joseph Esterházy
Sources of wealth: Inheritance; real estate
Bequeathal of wealth: Children; employees; charity

EARLY LIFE

Nikolaus Joseph Esterházy (EHS-ter-hah-zee) was the son of Prince Joseph Simon Antal (1688-1721). Esterházy's ancestors, Count Nikolaus Esterházy (1583-1645) and his son Prince Paul Esterházy (1635-1713), acquired the family's fortune through marriage, by acquiring land from the Protestants during the Counter-Reformation, and from the conquest of the Turks. Because of their loyalties to the Habsburg Dynasty and the Roman Catholic Church, the Esterházy family accumu-

lated enormous wealth and became the largest landowners in the Habsburg Empire.

Nikolaus Joseph Esterházy was educated by the Jesuits, a religious order of priests and scholastic students known for its commitment to education. Esterházy's exposure to music and philanthropy at an early age influenced his later decision to become a patron of the arts. In 1737, he married Maria Elisabeth, the daughter of the count of the Holy Roman Empire.

FIRST VENTURES

Esterházy distinguished himself in an Austrian military career. As commander of an infantry brigade at Kolín in 1757, he successfully led his men to victory and was rewarded with an appointment as captain of Empress Maria Theresa's Hungarian bodyguard. He also received the coveted Order of the Golden Fleece. Following the death of his older brother Prince Paul Anton in 1762, Esterházy assumed the title of prince.

MATURE WEALTH

Schloss Esterházy, a grand palace in Eisenstadt, Austria, served as the primary residence for the Esterházy family.

In 1762, Esterházy began construction of the Esterhaza Palace in Fertőtó, Hungary, that became known as the Hungarian Versailles because of its unrivaled splendor. A benefactor to his employees, Esterházy distributed his wealth among them by paying pensions to the elderly and supplementing the incomes of widows. He also donated funds to hospitals in Eisenstadt and Fertőtó and supplied medicine.

Esterházy retained the services of composer Joseph Haydn, who had been hired by Esterházy's brother Paul Anton. For thirty years, Haydn repaid his new employer by transforming Esterházy's orchestra into one of the finest in Europe and by composing symphonies, operas, orchestral and chamber works, and music for a puppet theater. Esterházy revered Haydn, often rewarding him with gold ducats and twice restoring the composer's burned home.

In addition to being a supreme patron of the arts, Esterházy was renowned for his jewels and extravagant clothing. The Esterházy jewels included rubies, topazes, pearls, and emeralds. His hussar's cap was adorned with approximately five thousand diamonds that simulated plumes. His sword and sheath sported jewels, as did a belt of pearls and diamonds. All the armor worn by male family members was decorated with precious jewels.

When his wife Princess Maria Elisabeth died in February, 1790, Esterházy became despondent. Haydn's music failed to restore the prince's spirit and Esterházy died seven months later.

LEGACY

A nobleman and aristocrat who possessed enormous wealth as a member of the house of Esterházy, Nikolaus Esterházy could have lived a secluded and pampered life without regard to the plight of others. Instead, he assumed the role of benefactor to one of the most prestigious and prolific composers of the time—Joseph Haydn. In the history of music, there are few composers who have benefited from such generous financial support and creative encouragement as Esterházy provided Haydn. Haydn composed 106 symphonies, almost all of which were completed at Esterhaza Palace, in addition to his many other works. Because of his steadfast devotion to Haydn, Esterházy is rightfully considered to be a monumental figure in eighteenth century music.

—*Douglas D. Skinner*

FURTHER READING

Geiringer, Karl, and Irene Geiringer. *Haydn: A Creative Life in Music*. Berkeley: University of California Press, 1982.

Jones, David Wyn. *Oxford Composer Companions: Haydn*. New York: Oxford University Press, 2002.

Saide, Stanley, and John Tyrrell. *The New Grove Dictionary of Music and Musicians*. 29 vols. New York: Oxford University Press, 2003.

See also: Angela Burdett-Coutts; Archduke Friedrich of Austria; Gaius Maecenas; Lorenzo de' Medici.

JAMES G. FAIR
American mining magnate, real estate speculator, investor, and politician

Fair and his three colleagues made a fortune mining the rich deposits of silver on the Comstock Lode. However, some observers claimed that his great wealth ruined his character, earning him the nickname Slippery Jimmy.

Born: December 3, 1821; Clogher, County Tyrone, Ireland
Died: December 28, 1894; San Francisco, California
Also known as: James Graham Fair; Slippery Jimmy
Sources of wealth: Mining; real estate; investments
Bequeathal of wealth: Children; relatives; charity

EARLY LIFE
Born into a peasant family in a small village near Belfast, James Graham Fair immigrated with his family to the United States in 1843. He grew up on a farm in Illinois, receiving what education he obtained in the public schools. He moved to Chicago in his mid-teens, where he received training in business.

At nineteen he set out for the California gold fields, where he prospected for gold in the Feather River region. He apparently learned much about gold mining in California. People who knew him at the time described him as very mechanically inclined and hardworking, with a sharp business mind. He married Theresa Rooney, the daughter of an Irish saloon owner, in 1861. Rooney was Catholic and Fair was a Protestant, which caused tension in their marriage, as the couple disagreed about the faith in which to raise their children. Fair eventually moved to Nevada, where he operated a mill on the Washoe River and became superintendent of several mines in the region of Virginia City.

FIRST VENTURES
In 1867, Fair became the superintendent of the Hale and Norcross Mine in Virginia City, one of the largest and most prosperous enterprises in the area. At that time he and three other Irishmen—James Clair Flood, John William Mackay, and William S. O'Brien—formed a company popularly known as the Bonanza firm and began to acquire shares in the silver mines on the Comstock Lode. Fair's partners were Irish Catholics, while he was a Protestant, and this would be a future source of conflict between them.

Between 1867 and 1873, the Bonanza firm made large fortunes for the four partners. In 1873, Fair was instrumental in the discovery of the so-called big bonanza, one of the largest silver strikes ever found. From 1873 to 1882, the big bonanza produced more than $105 million worth of silver ore (almost $2.5 billion in 2010). After 1882, the production of the Comstock rapidly declined, although ore continued to be extracted from the mines until the 1940's.

MATURE WEALTH
Fair later claimed most of the success of the Comstock operation derived from his own efforts, and most of its failures from the mistakes of his partners. Fair's claims are not without a basis in fact. His mechanical aptitude and flair for organization were instrumental in the successes of the Bonanza firm. A tireless worker, Fair spent most of his time belowground in the mines during the years of greatest productivity.

The Bonanza partners greatly augmented their earnings from the mines by collateral enterprises. They organized three major companies: the Pacific Mill and Mining Company, which owned and operated the mills that processed the ore; the Pacific Wood, Lumber and Flume Company, which supplied the millions of dollars worth of timber needed by the mines; and the Virginia & Gold Hill Water Company, which supplied water to the mines. These subsidiary enterprises made the four principal owners of the Bonanza firm many millions of dollars.

Fair invested much of the profits he made from the Comstock discoveries in San Francisco real estate; Nevada Bank; the South Pacific Coast Railroad, which ran down the east side of San Francisco Bay; and manufacturing. His real estate holdings prospered, making him another fortune. The Nevada Bank for a time became the largest bank in the United States during the height of the silver boom. The South Pacific Coast Railroad became one of the most profitable lines in California. All of these ventures together made Fair one of the wealthiest men in the United States.

According to some observers, the acquisition of great wealth ruined Fair's character, making him selfish, avaricious, and duplicitous and earning him the sobriquet "Slippery Jimmy." Those who knew him at this time said he took pride in being more clever and trickier than other men. Although Fair had the reputation of "knowing the value of a dollar," he did indulge himself and his family

THE COMSTOCK LODE

The Comstock Lode was the first great silver discovery in the United States and one of the greatest mineral discoveries in the history of the world. Mormons on their way to the California gold fields made the initial discovery of minerals in northern Nevada during the spring of 1850. These earliest discoverers continued on to California in search of richer pickings, and they were followed by others on their way to the California fields during the next few years. By 1853, around two hundred men were actively mining the area.

In 1857, two brothers from Pennsylvania, Ethan and Hosea Grosh, discovered the mine that was later called the Comstock Lode. The Grosh brothers died of injuries sustained while crossing the Sierra Mountains, and Henry T. P. Comstock claimed their cabin and lands. Several other prospectors also filed claims on area mines. All of these early discoverers of the Comstock Lode's wealth eventually died in poverty.

When news of the gold and silver discoveries spread, a stampede of prospectors ensued. More than seventeen thousand fortune-seekers rushed to Nevada between 1859 and 1865. The usual claim-jumping and litigation resulted. During those years, an estimated $50 million worth of ore (more than $250 million in 2010 dollars) was extracted from the area, while about $10 million was spent on law suits. Beginning in 1865, men later called the "bank crowd" began acquiring mine shares and mills in the area of Virginia City, Nevada. They built the Virginia and Truckee Railroad in order to link the mines with other areas, and the railroad drastically reduced transportation costs. The bank crowd also took over or started land, water, and freighting companies.

Four Irishmen—James G. Fair, James Clair Flood, John William Mackay, and William S. O'Brien—formed a partnership popularly known as the Bonanza firm in 1867. In 1873, the Bonanza firm, led by Fair, made the largest single silver discovery in history, the "big bonanza." Between 1873 and 1882, the partners' mineral strike produced more than $105 million worth of silver ore (almost $2.5 billion in 2010 dollars).

During its most productive years, the Comstock Lode produced approximately $305 million worth of ore (around $75 billion in 2010 dollars), which financed much of the industrial expansion of the United States during the latter part of the nineteenth century. The technological innovations made while exploiting the Comstock had ramifications far beyond the mining industry. For example, A. S. Hallidie's development of a flat-woven, wire rope used to haul ore from deep underground was later adapted for use in San Francisco's cable cars. However, the development of the Comstock Lode also resulted in the deforestation of many surrounding mountain ranges and had other negative environmental consequences for the Western United States.

wealth won him election to the U.S. Senate. He served an undistinguished six years, focusing on silver issues at a time when other senators were moving to demonetize silver. Fair's one speech in the Senate was delivered during discussions about the Chinese Exclusion Act of 1882; he fulfilled his campaign promise to uphold white supremacy. Fair's wife divorced him in 1882 on the grounds of habitual adultery. He did not stand for re-election to the Senate in 1886 and returned to San Francisco, where he took up residence in two rooms on the third floor of the Lick House, which he had bought in the early 1880's.

Back in San Francisco, Fair concentrated on his real estate and banking investments and his railroad enterprises. In 1888, the usually parsimonious Fair paid Hubert Howe Bancroft $15,000 to write a short, very flattering biography of him. Fair lived a solitary life, making no close friends. In 1890, when his daughter married the scion of another wealthy family, she did not invite Fair to her wedding. Nevertheless, he gave the couple a wedding present of $1 million, or so he told a San Francisco newspaper.

Fair continued to be interested in mining ventures, buying holdings in Wyoming, Idaho, Arizona, Georgia, and abroad. By 1893, he owned sixty acres of San Francisco's most fashionable areas. He bought office buildings, rooming houses, warehouses, small hotels, and other income-producing properties, all of which he allowed to run down, claiming that San Francisco real estate taxes were so high that they precluded him from making any improvements to his holdings. By the time of his death in 1894, his income from rents averaged almost $250,000 a month (more than $10 million in 2010 dollars).

Fair died alone and friendless, with only his physician and his nurse at his bedside. The coroner's report listed his cause of death as heart failure. Fair's obituary in the San Francisco *Chronicle* said he did not have an intimate friend in the world, and the *Examiner* published a scathing account of his life and character and his unhappy relations with his wife and children.

in the luxury of a world tour. By ocean liner and railway, they visited most of the famous tourist areas of the world in 1880.

After Fair returned to the United States in 1881, his

LEGACY

Fair's will left small sums to his sister and two brothers and smaller amounts to his nurse and two office workers. Three orphan asylums (Catholic, Protestant, and Hebrew) received $125,000. The bulk of his estate was left in trust for his three surviving children. Another will came to light, this one handwritten and leaving his estate directly to his children without the trust. The ensuing litigation by his children and by a host of people claiming to be his wives, his daughters-in-law, his illegitimate children, and various other relatives reduced his estate by an estimated $2 million in legal fees.

His business efforts did advance the industrialization of the United States, but Fair himself made no efforts to benefit humanity in any direct way. None of his descendants who were the beneficiaries of his wealth made any meaningful contributions to society. As far as can be told, Fair's great accumulation of wealth—approximately $45 million, or more than $1 billion in 2010 dollars—benefited only the creature comforts of him and his family.

—Paul Madden

FURTHER READING

Drabelle, Dennis. *Mile-High Fever: Silver Mines, Boom Towns, and High Living on the Comstock Lode.* New York: St. Martin's Press, 2009. A lively account of the politics, intrigue, treachery, and outright criminality in Nevada and California in the late nineteenth century, the era in which Fair made his fortune on the Comstock Lode.

James, Ronald M. *The Roar and the Silence: A History of Virginia City and the Comstock Lode.* Reno: University of Nevada Press, 1998. Account of the early years of Virginia City and the surrounding area. Contains references to Fair and the other exploiters of the Comstock Lode.

Lewis, Oscar. *Silver Kings: The Lives and Times of Mackay, Fair, Flood, and O'Brien.* Reno: University of Nevada Press, 1986. Brief biographical accounts of the lives and careers of the four men most responsible for the discovery and exploitation of the Comstock Lode. Paints an unflattering picture of Fair, describing him as devious, conniving, and well deserving of the nickname Slippery Jimmy.

Peterson, Richard H. *The Bonanza Kings: The Social Origins and Business Behavior of Western Mining Entrepreneurs, 1870-1900.* Lincoln: University of Nebraska Press, 1977. Biographical accounts of the lives of Fair and many other men who made fortunes in Western mining during the late nineteenth century. Presents Fair as an unscrupulous and greedy individual who took unfair advantage of others.

Smith, Grant H., and Joseph V. Tingley. *The History of the Comstock Lode, 1850-1997.* Reno: Nevada Bureau of Mines and Geology, 1998. A comprehensive account of the discovery and exploitation of the mineral resources of the Comstock Lode. Contains many references to Fair, including a brief biographical sketch.

See also: William Andrews Clark; Marcus Daly; James Clair Flood; Meyer Guggenheim; George Hearst; F. Augustus Heinze; John William Mackay; William S. O'Brien.

SIR JOHN FASTOLF
English military leader and landowner

Sir John Fastolf was one of the first English knights to make a fortune as a professional soldier and convert it into income-producing investments, thus reflecting crucial changes in the gradual transformation of the feudal system of English social organization into a protocapitalist society.

Born: c. 1378; Caister, Norfolk, England
Died: November 5, 1459; Caister, Norfolk, England
Sources of wealth: Conquest; real estate
Bequeathal of wealth: Friends

EARLY LIFE

Little is known about the early life of Sir John Fastolf (FAW-stolf) except that he was the son of a Norfolk gentleman, John Fastolf of Caister. Sir John might have served as a squire to Thomas Mowbray, duke of Norfolk, before entering upon a military career. He served in Ireland in 1405-1406 under the duke of Clarence, the younger brother of the future King Henry V, and Fastolf seems to have remained with Clarence for about ten years.

Fastolf's financial fortunes received their first significant boost when he married on January 13, 1409, presumably for money. His wife Millicent was the daughter of Robert, Lord Tiptoft, but she had recently augmented her own fortune considerably upon the death of her first husband, Stephen Scrope of Castle Combe in Wiltshire. In consequence, Fastolf came into possession of lands that brought in a handsome annual income of £240.

FIRST VENTURES

Fastolf obtained a new opportunity to enhance his fortunes when Henry V began campaigning vigorously in France, with the intention of recovering England's lost possessions there. Fastolf was never an intimate of the king, although he did fight with him at the Battle of Agincourt in October, 1415. His first French campaign appears to have been with Clarence in Aquitaine in 1412-1413, when he was rewarded with the appointment of deputy constable in Bordeaux. He was also captain of Soubise and Veyres in 1413-1414.

Fastolf did not stay with Henry's army after Agincourt but returned to Harfleur with the duke of Exeter. He fought at Valmont while it was besieged by the French, and he was present at the sieges of Caen and Rouen with both Clarence and Exeter. Fastolf became captain of Harfleur and Fécamp, and he was granted four lordships in the vicinity of Caux in 1419. As well as obtaining the title to various holdings of captured land, Fastolf was able to augment his purse with ransoms demanded for influential captives seized in battle. Although there is no reason to doubt the honesty of his patriotism, he was essentially a professional soldier, who expected to make capital out of his endeavors, and he did so on a scale that made him one of the most successful mercenaries of all time.

When Henry V died in 1421, having returned to France to assist Clarence after the latter's defeat at Baugé, Henry's son was a mere infant. One of Henry's brothers, John, duke of Bedford, became regent. Bedford immediately formed a new military organization to continue the French campaign, with Fastolf and other experienced professionals at its core. Fastolf was a member of the regent's council from 1422 until Bedford's death in 1435, and he remained one of Bedford's most trusted military commanders.

MATURE WEALTH

Bedford rewarded Fastolf with additional captaincies, and Fastolf distinguished himself during Bedford's victory at Verneuil in August, 1422. Fastolf boasted that he ransomed the prisoners he took in that battle for 20,000 marks, but he only managed to collect part of the sum. He was made a Knight of the Garter in 1426, and his military

triumphs in France continued apace. He took part in an assault on Maine in 1427, and he was appointed governor of Le Mans after capturing it. He also took the title of baron from one of several fiefs he was granted in the area. Fastolf began sending considerable sums of money back to England, which were used to add more land to his holdings, mostly around Caister in Norfolk.

In February, 1429, while transporting provisions to English troops besieging Paris, Fastolf was attacked at Rouvray and won what came to be known as the Battle of the Herrings after using barrels loaded with fish as a stockade. In June of that year, however, he took part in an attack on Beaugency with John Talbot, earl of Shrewsbury, which went badly. During the retreat, the English forces were overwhelmed at Patay and the rearguard was massacred; only the vanguard, led by Fastolf, escaped. Although the French historian Jehan de Waurin put the blame squarely on Shrewsbury's recklessness, Shrewsbury accused Fastolf of cowardice. Fastolf was eventually vindicated and continued to enjoy Bedford's full confidence, but the accusation tainted Fastolf's reputation in England.

When Bedford died in 1435, the English campaign in France suffered a dire blow, from which it never recovered. Fastolf did everything possible to retain his French lands and the income they provided. He retained a full-time attorney at the Court of Paris, Jean de Paris, to press his claims for land, ransoms, and jurisdictions, but the tide had turned and his holdings there were steadily worn away by a process of attrition. The fact that he was one of Bedford's executors kept Fastolf very busy for the next three years, and he was unable to defend his French claims as forcefully as he might have wished. He eventually decided to return to England permanently. He bought the Boar's Head tavern in Southwark, along with a town house, as well as expanding and improving his lands in Norfolk.

Fastolf appears to have spent nearly £14,000 buying property in England and an additional £9,500 improving it. In 1445, his English holdings brought him an annual income of £1,061; his remaining French lands still brought him £401, a fraction of their worth ten years before. He invested and spent on a lavish scale, but his background and former alliances made him suspect in a new political climate, as the Wars of the Roses became increasingly bitter, and he became the target of determined enmities. In 1452, he paid for the construction of Caister Castle, which was intended to serve as his country seat. It was one of the first English castles to be built out of brick, although it was otherwise orthodox—which

SHAKESPEARE'S FALSTAFF

According to all of the evidence, Sir John Fastolf was an expert military commander and an efficient businessman, austere in his habits, and not at all given to hypocrisy. Was it not for the unjust and self-serving accusation of cowardice of John Talbot, first earl of Shrewsbury, and the duke of Suffolk's avaricious persecution, Fastolf might have enjoyed a long-lasting reputation that was not only unsullied but heroic. Writings survive that describe Fastolf as cruel and ruthless, and perhaps he was in and after battle, but he does not seem to have been a violent man when not engaged in military service. However, the fact that a lingering taint still clung to his reputation long after his death was undoubtedly partly responsible for the fact that William Shakespeare, under pressure from a descendant of Sir John Oldcastle, changed a character's name from Oldcastle to Sir John Falstaff between the first and second drafts of *Henry V* (pr. 1598-1599; pb. 1600).

Oldcastle really had been a friend of "Prince Hal" (Henry V) during the king's younger and wilder days. Oldcastle might possibly have encouraged Henry in the sowing of his youthful wild oats, but Oldcastle was probably not the self-indulgent, cowardly, mendacious, and hypocritical character that Shakespeare described, and who was, in essence, depicted as being the exact opposite of everything that Henry V eventually became. Oldcastle would not have been the first actual individual that Shakespeare had comprehensively trashed in the interests of dramatic effect; Richard III came off worst of all in that respect. However, the fact that Oldcastle had a surviving descendant who might take umbrage as far as violence forced the playwright to improvise.

Falstaff was a fictitious name, but its origin was clear enough, especially given the fact that Fastolf was known to have owned the Boar's Head tavern in Southwark. Because of Falstaff's depiction in Shakespeare's play, Fastolf's posthumous reputation was blackened far more deeply than the earl of Shrewsbury or the duke of Suffolk could ever have imagined possible. Things might have been different if Fastolf had managed to found a college in Caister to serve as his memorial. However, in the absence of such a monument, the image of Falstaff—which took on a strange life of its own, evolving far beyond Shakespeare's original intention—superimposed itself so completely on Fastolf's identity as to almost efface the memory and reputation of the real man, at least until the twentieth century rehabilitation.

John Paston. Paston's care in preserving his family's correspondence enabled future historians to know much about Fastolf and about much else that happened in Norfolk in the fifteenth century, although the original bound volumes of "the Paston letters" were dispersed and lost, and the authenticity of later printed editions became somewhat controversial.

Fastolf's great ambition during the last ten years of his life appears to have been the founding of a college at Caister, but his political and financial troubles prevented him from doing so, and with that end in mind he made Paston the executor of his will. Paston was still engaged in economic warfare with the duke of Suffolk, however, and Fastolf's death in 1459 only made the task of defending Fastolf's holdings more difficult. It was not until 1470 that a small parcel was eventually handed over to Magdalen College, Oxford University, by which time the Caister project had been conclusively abandoned, and the rest of Fastolf's fortune had been eroded by the expenses of its defense.

LEGACY

Because his attempt to found a college came to nothing, and most of the money he left for that purpose was dissipated by Paston, Fastolf's principal material legacy was Caister Castle. The castle eventually fell into ruins, along with most of the other relics of the twilight of English feudalism. In the twenty-first century, what remained of the building, augmented with subsequent additions, was a private museum, home to the largest collection of motor vehicles in Great Britain. The difficulties that the humbly born Fastolf experienced in hanging on to his wealth, under harassment from the traditional aristocracy, reflect the awkwardness of the English transition from feudalism to protocapitalism. Fastolf also left a very peculiar "legacy" of another sort, thanks to the adaptation of his name by William Shakespeare for one of the playwright's most memorable but least worthy characters, and that, too, might be a reflection of aristocratic antipathy to the new breed of upwardly mobile moneymakers.

—Brian Stableford

is to say, quandrangular in shape, with towers at the corners and equipped with a moat.

The construction of Caister Castle was obstructed by troubles that had begun in 1447, when the duke of Suffolk launched a long campaign attempting to seize various lands in Norfolk and dispossess the owners, including Fastolf. Suffolk eventually went so far as to lay a charge of treason against Fastolf, although Fastolf does not appear to have been politically active. While defending himself against this continual harassment, Fastolf formed a strong alliance with a neighboring landowner,

FURTHER READING

Armstrong, C. A. J. "Sir John Fastolf and the Law of Arms." In *War, Literature, and Politics in the Late Middle Ages*, edited by C. T. Allmand. Liverpool, England: Liverpool University Press, 1976. A succinct analysis of the significance of Fastolf's career, also reprinted in Allmand's *England, France, and Burgundy in the Fifteenth Century* (1983).

Davis, Norman, Richard Beadle, and Colin Richmond, eds. *The Paston Letters and Papers of the Fifteenth Century*. Oxford, England: Oxford University Press, 2004-2006. The definitive edition of one of the crucial documents of the period, which provides a wealth of information about the society of the day and its upheavals, including details of Fastolf's later life and the struggle to execute his will.

Duthie, David Wallace. *The Case of Sir John Fastolf and Other Historical Studies*. London: Smith, Elder, 1907. The title essay began the twentieth century reappraisal of Fastolf's career, pointing out its signifi-cance as a reflection of the social changes of its era and laying the groundwork for more detailed academic studies and Robert Nye's literary account.

McFarlane, K. B. "The Investment of Sir John Fastolf's Profits of War." *Transactions of the Royal Historical Society*, Series 7 (1957): 91-116. Attempts to reconstruct the money trail of Fastolf's eventually ill-fated financial endeavors.

Nye, Robert. *Falstaff, Being the Acta Domini Johannis Fastolfe: Or, Life and Valiant Deeds of Sir John Faustoff*. New York: Arcade, 2001. A new edition of a novel first published in London in 1976. Although it is a work of fiction, its wittily scrupulous analysis of the complexities of Fastolf's life and its perverse Shakespearean echo makes a useful supplement to such academic sources as Armstrong and McFarlane.

See also: John Hawkwood; John of Gaunt; William Sevenock.

MOHAMED AL-FAYED
Egyptian investor and businessman

Fayed, an Egyptian-born businessman, emerged victorious after a long battle for control of Harrods department store. His son Dodi al-Fayed died with Diana, Princess of Wales, in an automobile crash in Paris in 1997.

Born: January 27, 1929; Bakos, Alexandria, Egypt
Sources of wealth: Retailing; investments; real estate
Bequeathal of wealth: Unknown

EARLY LIFE
Mohamed al-Fayed (moh-HAH-mehd al-FI-ehd) was born in 1929 in Alexandria, Egypt, which at that time was under British administration. Fayed claims he comes from an old, wealthy, and distinguished family, but critics argue otherwise. His father was an elementary schoolteacher. Fayed's earliest business endeavors were selling soft drinks to his friends and selling sewing machines door-to-door.

FIRST VENTURES
After World War II, Fayed and his two younger brothers founded Genavco (General Navigation Company), a shipping firm that ran ferries on the Mediterranean and Red Seas. When Egyptian leader Gamal Abdel Nasser nationalized much of the nation's economy, Genavco re-

Mohamed al-Fayed holds a bottle of Imperial Majesty, the most expensive commercially available perfume ever sold, which cost more than $198,000. (AP/Wide World Photos)

Harrods department store at Christmas, 2000. (Getty Images)

located in Genoa, Italy. Fayed's first marriage was to a sister of Adnan Khashoggi, a notorious international arms dealer, whom some critics credit for Fayed's initial business successes. The Fayeds had one son, Dodi, before the couple's marriage ended in divorce.

MATURE WEALTH

In the 1960's, Fayed became a principal adviser to Rāshid ibn Saʿīd Āl Maktūm, the ruler of the emirate of Dubai. Not a modest man, Fayed claims that he was primarily responsible for the emirate's emergence as a major financial center. He encouraged British investment in the territory, and he also invested in construction and shipping operations, the latter through his company International Marine Services (IMS).

Fayed apparently also became an adviser to Sultan Hassanal Bolkiah of Brunei, one of the world's richest men. It was later rumored that Fayed illegally acquired $1 billion from the sultan's various business accounts. With his British contacts, relocating to London in 1974 was an obvious move for Fayed. There he added "al-" to his name, with its allusions to the elite, and some in the

British press consequently referred to him as the "phony pharaoh." Generally, however, the British political and social establishment accepted Fayed's claims that he was a legitimate businessman.

In London, Fayed invested in Lonrho, Plc., which was heavily involved in the African mineral industry. Lonrho was headed by R.W. "Tiny" Rowland, a flamboyant businessman who was committed to diversifying Lonrho's investments and sought to gain control of the House of Fraser, which included Harrods, the world-famous London department store. In 1984, Fayed bought 30 percent of the House of Fraser's shares, and in a bitter contest he succeeded in acquiring the remaining shares the following year by outbidding Rowland. The dispute continued for years, during which Fayed and Rowland suborned politicians and resorted to inflammatory claims about each other in the media. Fayed was arrested, accused of bribing Conservative members of Parliament and cabinet officials. He later unsuccessfully sued for false arrest. The conflict was finally resolved in favor of Fayed in 1992, and he subsequently removed from Harrods' food halls a shark's head on which the word "Tiny" was written.

Fayed became executive chairman of Harrods in 1989, and he claims that he spent £400 million to refurbish and upgrade the iconic store. The House of Fraser went public in 1994, selling its shares on the London Stock Exchange, but Fayed retained Harrods as his personal property.

Some of his other acquisitions include L'Hôtel Ritz in Paris, the villa of the duke and duchess of Windsor, and Britain's Fulham football (soccer) club.

LEGACY

Fayed had four children with his second wife, a Finnish woman. His entire business career has been controversial, particularly as recounted in the British media, which has accused him of being a serial liar and a thief. After the death of his son Dodi and Princess Diana, Fayed accused the British royal family of murdering the two in order to prevent Diana from marrying Dodi and converting

to Islam. In 2008, an official investigation dismissed his allegations, ruling that the deaths were accidental. Because of his notoriety, neither Conservative nor Labour governments have been willing to grant him British citizenship.

—Eugene Larson

FURTHER READING

Bower, Tom. *Fayed: The Unauthorized Biography.* New ed. London: Pan Books, 2003.

Gregory, Martyn. "The Diana Inquests Are Stranded on Planet Fayed." *The Spectator*, June 30, 2007.

Orth, Maureen. "Holy War at Harrods." *Vanity Fair* 58 (September, 1995); 70.

See also: Mohammed Hussein Ali Al Amoudi; Al-Waleed bin Talal; Mohammed bin Laden; Sultan Hassanal Bolkiah.

CYRUS WEST FIELD
American paper merchant and transatlantic telegraph cable builder

Field built a profitable paper business in New York in the 1840's and 1850's. He then gained international renown as the organizer and driving force in the effort to lay an underwater telegraph cable connecting Europe and North America.

Born: November 30, 1819; Stockbridge, Massachusetts
Died: July 12, 1892; New York, New York
Also known as: Cyrus W. Field
Sources of wealth: Trade; telegraph
Bequeathal of wealth: Dissipated

EARLY LIFE

Cyrus West Field was born in Stockbridge, Massachusetts, in 1819. His father was a stern, influential Congregational minister. All of Field's brothers who survived to middle age achieved notable success in occupations ranging from writing to serving as a justice of the U.S. Supreme Court and president of the Massachusetts Senate. At age fifteen, Field moved to New York City to begin an apprenticeship in the city's leading dry goods store, where he quickly rose to become a senior clerk. At age eighteen, he returned to western Massachusetts, working for his brother as bookkeeper, general assistant, and then sales representative at a paper mill.

FIRST VENTURES

At age twenty, Field married and became the junior partner in Root & Company, a wholesale paper dealer in New York City. Within six months, Root went bankrupt, but Field settled the debts of his former employer at thirty cents on the dollar and reorganized the firm under his own name. The company purchased supplies for papermakers and marketed their products. Field used his knowledge of the industry, close ties with Massachusetts papermakers (especially Crane & Company), and rising demand for paper to build an immensely successful business. Putting in exceptionally long hours and rarely delegating work, Field became the "uncontested dean" of New York paper merchants, amassing a net worth of almost $250,000 ($7.2 million in 2010 currency) by 1852. At this point, although it was not legally required, he paid off his company's old debts at their face value plus 7 percent interest, turned business duties over to a junior partner, and took a lengthy trip to South America with noted landscape painter Frederick Church.

MATURE WEALTH

Semiretirement did not suit the energetic Field. In 1854, Field's brother Matthew introduced him to Frederick Gisborne, whose Newfoundland Electric Telegraph Company owned rights to run a telegraph line to the eastern-

Cyrus West Field holds a section of his transatlantic cable. (The Granger Collection, New York)

most point in North America. Gisborne was a fugitive from fraud charges because his company had run out of funds to pay its workers after making little progress stringing a telegraph line through the rugged Canadian region. Field seized on the idea of buying out the company and using it as a springboard to lay a cable across the Atlantic connecting Europe and North America from Newfoundland to Ireland. He contacted Samuel F. B. Morse, inventor of the telegraph, to assess the project's plausibility and Matthew Fontaine Maury, head of the U.S. Naval Observatory, who explained that the ocean floor in this region of the Atlantic was ideal for a cable. Next, Field turned to wealthy New York City residents for funding, convincing Peter Cooper, Moses Taylor, Marshall Roberts, Chandler White, and others of the plan's merits.

Field then bought Gisborne's company, negotiated a new charter with the Newfoundland government, and recommenced construction of the original line. As ex-

penses mounted, he traveled to England to find additional investors. An attempt to lay the Atlantic cable in 1857 failed after the line snapped, sending half a million dollars worth of material to the ocean floor. Success in laying the cable in 1858 brought transatlantic jubilation, and Field was hailed as the Columbus of America. Unfortunately, sending signals through the cable proved difficult and it went completely dead within a month. Skeptics claimed the cable never actually delivered any messages and alleged that Field was engaged in a hoax enabling him to make a substantial profit while preventing the company's charter from expiring. While these charges were rebutted, some historians maintain that Field's claims of successfully sending news over the wire were fraudulent.

Although Field was determined to see the project's successful completion, an official inquiry into the causes of the cable's failure and the outbreak of the Civil War caused delays. As the war ended, Field obtained use of the *Great Eastern*, the world's largest steamship, arranged new funding, and obtained a more advanced cable. Again, in 1865, the cable snapped in mid-ocean. Unbowed, Field arranged a fourth attempt in 1866 that succeeded, as did the recovery of the 1865 cable from the ocean floor. With two cables in operation and a monopoly on transatlantic service, the Anglo-American Telegraph Company began earning substantial profits.

Field remained busy for the next twenty years, investing in a range of businesses, including ownership of substantial telegraph holdings and a New York daily newspaper, the *Mail and Express*, and management of the Manhattan Railway, an elevated commuter line whose fortunes he turned around. His wealth reached about $6 million ($140 million in 2010 currency). He played a significant role in politics and may have inadvertently helped swing the 1884 presidential election when he arranged a gala dinner at Delmonico's restaurant for the Republican candidate, James G. Blaine, and many of his wealthy supporters. The opposition press depicted Blaine as a friend of the privileged and Grover Cleveland eked out a win in New York and the electoral college.

Inexplicably, in 1887 Field began speculating in the stock market, touting the Manhattan Railway in his newspaper and borrowing money to buy company shares on a thin margin, as his purchases pushed its price up. When the price began to fall, he was overextended and lost virtually his entire fortune within a few days. The press portrayed the collapse as a vile plot by Field's friend and associate Jay Gould, but a fairer reading shows that this was not the case. Field sank into illness and depression, abetted by a series of family losses and the collapse of his son's brokerage firm amid evidence of substantial fraud.

LEGACY

As Field's assets evaporated, his primary legacy is the example of his relentless energy, vision, enthusiasm, and organizational talent in successfully laying the transatlantic cable. His name will forever be linked with that major breakthrough in long-distance communications.

—Robert Whaples

FURTHER READING

Blondheim, Menahem. *News over the Wires: The Telegraph and the Flow of Public Information in America, 1844-1897*. Cambridge, Mass.: Harvard University Press, 1994. This monograph does a superb job of putting the era's telegraph and commercial news business in context and suggests that news transmissions over the first Atlantic cable were a hoax.

Carter, Samuel, III. *Cyrus Field: Man of Two Worlds*. New York: Putnam, 1968. This is the most comprehensive work on Field's life and career. However, the book lacks documentation and the author is uncritical of Field.

Klein, Maury. *The Life and Legend of Jay Gould*. Baltimore: Johns Hopkins University Press, 1997. This work is very critical of the traditional account of Field's demise.

See also: James Gordon Bennett, Jr.; Jay Gould; John William Mackay; Samuel F. B. Morse; Russell Sage.

MARSHALL FIELD
American retailer

Field introduced an innovative approach to the dry goods industry by transforming the need to purchase everyday items into a pleasant shopping experience. The introduction of exotic foreign imports, consistent pricing, and an inviting store environment became the hallmark of Marshall Field and Company. This approach not only made Field's personal fortune but also revolutionized the mercantile industry.

Born: August 18, 1834; near Conway, Massachusetts
Died: January 16, 1906; New York, New York
Sources of wealth: Retailing; real estate
Bequeathal of wealth: Children; charity

EARLY LIFE

Marshall Field was born in 1834 on a farm near Conway, Massachusetts, the son of John Field IV and Fidelia Nash. The Fields were direct descendants of the Puritans who arrived in Massachusetts in the seventeenth century. Field's family valued education, and he received his early schooling at the local public school and later at a nearby academy. At the age of seventeen, he moved to Pittsfield, Massachusetts, where he took a position in a dry goods store. Ironically, Mr. Davis, his first employer, felt that because of his shyness, Field would not have a future in merchandising. Despite his boss's opinion, Field learned a great deal from this job.

Marshall Field. (Library of Congress)

FIRST VENTURES

Field left Pittsfield after a year and headed west to make his fortune. He arrived in Chicago in 1856 and lived with his brother. He obtained employment as a clerk at Cooley, Wadsworth & Company, one of Chicago's largest dry goods firms. In 1863, he married Nannie Douglas Scott, and they had two children, Marshall Field, Jr., and Ethel Field. From 1856 to 1865, Field, with his frugal lifestyle and hard work ethic, was able to save more than $30,000, enough to buy into a business partnership.

MATURE WEALTH

Within four years after becoming a clerk at Cooley, Wadsworth & Company, Field advanced to the position of junior partner. In 1864, John V. Farwell, senior partner of Cooley, Farwell, & Company, offered both Field and the company bookkeeper, Levi Leiter, the opportunity to become partners in the firm. They readily accepted his offer and the firm became Farwell, Field & Company. Shortly thereafter, the new partners heard that Potter Palmer, one of Chicago's leading businessmen, was looking to dispose of several of his commercial interests. Instantly, Field and Leiter saw an opportunity to become Palmer's business partners. The three men began negotiating in late 1864 and reached an agreement in January, 1865. As part of their agreement, they created a new dry goods store, Field, Palmer, Leiter & Company. The new company proved to be so successful that Field and Leiter were able to pay Palmer back in full within two years. In 1867, Palmer withdrew from the partnership in order to

Elevator girls at Marshall Field's department store in Chicago in 1947. (Time & Life Pictures/Getty Images)

THE FIELD MUSEUM OF NATURAL HISTORY

The Field Museum of Natural History was called the Columbian Museum of Natural History when it was founded in Chicago in 1893. It was housed in the Fine Arts Building, one of the structures built for the 1893 World's Columbian Exposition, which was held in Jackson Park. The museum's concept originated from a concern that the various biological and anthropological exhibits featured at the exposition would be lost to posterity. Citizens and business leaders came up with the idea of creating a permanent museum to exhibit these scientifically valuable specimens and to create educational displays for public enjoyment. Reluctant at first to become involved in such a project, merchant Marshall Field was finally persuaded in 1893 by fellow millionaire Edward D. Ayer to contribute $1 million toward the establishment of such a museum. Field subsequently made a bequest in his will of $8 million to ensure the museum's continued existence.

In 1905, the museum's name was changed to the Field Museum of Natural History in honor of its principal benefactor. The museum quickly grew in both scope and size as it began acquiring additional specimens through donations and collection expeditions throughout the world. In 1921, the museum moved a few miles south from its Jackson Park location to Grant Park, where it remained into the twenty-first century.

The museum is one of the most important natural science museums in the world. It has four major departments—botany, zoology, anthropology, and geology—which house more than twenty-four million specimens. The institution promotes collections-based research and offers scientists from around the world the opportunity to access its collections. Its exhibition halls offer the public a wide variety of exhibits ranging from insects to Egyptian mummies. The museum is perhaps most famous for Sue, the nearly complete skeleton of a *Tyrannosaurus rex.*

Another source of pride is the museum's Pritzker Laboratory for Molecular Systematics and Evolution. The laboratory's mission is to collect and analyze genetic data. The museum also houses the Robert A. Pritzker Center for Meteoritics and Polar Studies, which combines the traditional study of meteorites with biological research about polar regions. The center preserves meteorite collections belonging to the Field Museum and other institutions and conducts research expeditions to the Arctic and Antarctica.

concentrate on his real estate holdings, and the store became Field, Leiter & Company.

Field, Leiter & Company prospered until its six-story building, located at State and Washington Streets, was destroyed in the great Chicago fire of October, 1871. Field and Leiter acted quickly and saved a considerable amount of their merchandise. Within weeks of the fire, they were able to open a temporary store, and six months later, they moved into an unburned building, providing merchandise to Chicago residents as the city began to rebuild. Benefiting from Chicago's revitalization and construction boom, Field, Leiter & Company was back in business on State Street by October, 1873. Another fire destroyed the store in 1877, and once again, Field and Leiter moved quickly, opening a nearby temporary store within a month of the fire. This store would occupy this site until 1879, when the business moved into a new structure built on the site of their original shop. The partnership of Field and Leiter lasted until 1881, when Field and his junior partners bought out Leiter's interest in the business. Now Field was in complete control of his new firm—Marshall Field & Company.

Over the next twenty-five years, Marshall Field & Company expanded its business to such an extent that it became the largest wholesale and retail dry goods enterprise in the world, with annual sales of more than $60 million. Later expansion would include branches in New York, France, Germany, Great Britain, Japan, and Switzerland. The success of Marshall Field & Company was based on its combination of retail and wholesale merchandising. In conjunction with his prominent retail store on State Street, Field also operated a nearby wholesale facility that sold merchandise in bulk to smaller businesses across the country. The wholesale store made huge profits for the company because its Chicago location enabled it to provide merchandise for the growing markets in the Midwest and West. Never content with his success, Field was always looking for ways to lower costs and increase profits. One of his ideas was to manufacture his own merchandise in factories located in Australia, China, Germany, Italy, and Spain, an approach that eventually would become standard practice for many other businesses.

In Chicago, Field's State Street store remained the premier destination for quality shopping. It provided customers with such innovative services as an interior design department, personal shopping assistants, an easy return policy, home delivery, and a bargain basement. In later years, this store would feature The Walnut Room, a high-quality restaurant, and would gain renown for its festive appearance and holiday decorations. In addition to his merchandising, Field made a fortune in real estate. He was a leading advocate for the development of downtown Chicago, and at the time of his death, it was estimated that more than half of his $125 million wealth was invested in land. Field died of pneumonia in New York City on January 16, 1906.

LEGACY

Initially, philanthropy was not one of Marshall Field's principal interests. At times he could be very generous, and at other times his actions could be somewhat inhumane. On one hand, Field was the stereotypically tyrannical nineteenth century capitalist. He was notorious for paying his workers the lowest possible wages and he hated labor unions. He opposed clemency for the defendants in the May, 1886, Haymarket Riot in Chicago, and he was a strong advocate for the use of the federal soldiers to break up the 1894 Pullman railroad strike.

On the other hand, he gave millions of dollars to support education and cultural development. As his fortune grew, and at the urging of other wealthy Chicago businessmen and civic leaders, Field eventually became a noted philanthropist. Among his philanthropic projects were a charter membership in the Art Institute of Chicago, the donation of ten acres of prime land for the establishment of the University of Chicago, and, in 1893, a $1 million contribution to the founding of the Columbian Museum of Natural History, which later became Chicago's Field Museum of Natural History. In addition, his will contained an $8 million bequest to the museum to ensure its future existence. Field's philanthropic legacy continues into the twenty-first century through his descendants, who remain faithful supporters of Chicago's educational and cultural activities.

—*Paul P. Sipiera*

FURTHER READING

Alexander, Edward P. *Museums in Motion: An Introduction to the History and Functions of Museums.* Walnut Creek, Calif.: AltaMira Press, 1996. Provides the reader with an insider's look into the museum industry and how it has evolved over time. It serves as a good background reference to gain an understanding of what constitutes a museum.

Madsen, Axel. *The Marshall Fields: The Evolution of an American Dynasty.* Hoboken, N.J.: John Wiley and Sons, 2002. Provides excellent insight into the lives of the Field family from its founder to the present, illustrating the contrast between the family's financial success and personal failure.

Marden, Orison. *How They Succeeded: Life Stories of Successful Men Told by Themselves.* 1901. Reprint. Whitefish, Mont.: Kessinger, 2005. Includes interviews with prominent people to gain insight into their personal success stories.

Tebbell, John. *The Marshall Fields: A Study of Wealth.* New York: E. P. Dutton, 1947. Reviews the history of one of Chicago's most prominent families from its patriarch, Marshall Field, through the post-World War II era.

Wendt, Lloyd, and Herman Kogan. *Give the Lady What She Wants! The Story of Marshall Field and Company.* Chicago: Rand McNally, 1952. An oft-quoted source of information about Marshall Field and the founding of Marshall Field & Company.

See also: Julius Rosenwald; Alexander Turney Stewart; Nathan Straus; John Wanamaker; F. W. Woolworth.

HARVEY FIRESTONE
American inventor and industrialist

Firestone's rubber tire innovations and business savvy made him one of the wealthiest tire entrepreneurs in the United States during the advent of the automobile industry.

Born: December 20, 1868; Columbiana, Ohio
Died: February 7, 1938; Miami Beach, Florida
Also known as: Harvey Samuel Firestone
Sources of wealth: Patents; sale of products; real estate
Bequeathal of wealth: Children

EARLY LIFE

Harvey Samuel Firestone was born in 1868 on his family farm in Columbiana, Ohio. He was the second child of Benjamin Firestone and A. Catherine Flickinger. Firestone graduated from Columbiana High School and then completed a business college course in Cleveland, Ohio. In 1895, he married Idabelle Smith, a composer and songwriter from Jackson, Michigan. The couple had five sons and one daughter.

FIRST VENTURES

After completing his business course, Firestone took a job with his uncle's business, the Columbus Buggy Company. By 1892, he had become the district manager in charge of Michigan sales. However, in 1896 the buggy company went bankrupt.

That same year, with financial support from a friend, Firestone moved his family to Chicago, where he opened a rubber wheels company. In 1899, he sold the company and earned a profit of almost $42,000. Firestone continued to be interested in the tire business and how it would be affected by the emerging automobile industry. By the beginning of the twentieth century, he had acquired a patent for a process of attaching rubber tires to wheels.

MATURE WEALTH

In 1900, Firestone relocated his family to Akron, Ohio, where many of the country's tire manufacturers were based. With $10,000 and his tire patent, Firestone and a group of investors opened the Firestone Tire & Rubber Company on August 3, 1900. At the company's inception, Firestone owned 50 percent of the corporation. During the first few years in business, the company sold tires manufactured by other firms and did not make much of a profit. In 1903, Firestone not only began to manufacture his own tires but also started to make a specially designed pneumatic tire for automobiles. In 1906, Henry Ford ordered two thousand sets of tires from Firestone. In 1907, Firestone's growing company sold 105,000 tires at a profit of $538,177. That same year, Firestone began marketing a tire with dismountable rim that allowed both the wheel and the tire to be removed together. This innovation eventually became known as the spare tire.

By 1913, Firestone's tire sales had exceeded $15 million, and he was ranked as one of the Big Five in the tire industry, alongside Goodyear Tire and Rubber Company, B. F. Goodrich, U.S. Rubber, and Fisk Rubber. In 1923, Firestone introduced the balloon tire, which eventually became the standard for most American automobiles. In 1924, he and Ford worked together to break Great Britain's monopoly on the world's rubber supply.

Harvey Firestone. (Hulton Archive/Getty Images)

In 1926, they purchased a million acres of land in Liberia and developed a plantation that provided them with an independent source of rubber.

In 1928, Firestone opened his first "one stop service center" that provided customers with numerous automobile-related services, including gasoline, oil changes, brake services, and tires. In 1932, Firestone stepped down as company president, while his five sons continued to take active roles in the business. By 1937, the company was supplying more than a quarter of all automobile tires in the United States and had capital in excess of $108 million. Firestone died of a coronary thrombosis at his winter home in Miami Beach, Florida, on February 7, 1938.

LEGACY
Harvey Samuel Firestone's interest in rubber tires and their use on automobiles made his family-owned tire manufacturing business a leader in the tire industry. Many of his innovations became standards for the automobile industry, including the creation of his company's own rubber supply and the conception of the modern garage, where numerous automobile services could be offered to customers at one location. Firestone's business ingenuity and his tire inventions earned him the distinction of being one of America's wealthiest industrialists.

—Bernadette Zbicki Heiney

FURTHER READING
Dickson, Paul, and William Hickman. *Firestone: A Legend, a Century, a Celebration.* New York: Forbes, 2000.

Firestone, Harvey Samuel, Jr. *Man on the Move: The Story of Transportation.* New York: Putnam, 1967.

Lief, Alfred. *The Firestone Story: A History of the Firestone Tire & Rubber Company.* New York: Whittlesey House, 1951.

See also: Walter P. Chrysler; John F. Dodge; Henry Ford; André Michelin; Alfred P. Sloan.

HENRY M. FLAGLER
American entrepreneur, industrialist, and philanthropist

Flagler used a fortune acquired in the oil industry to build railroads and luxury hotels in Florida, thus establishing that state as a prime destination for tourists and enabling his heirs to pursue numerous philanthropic endeavors.

Born: January 2, 1830; Hopewell, New York
Died: May 20, 1913; West Palm Beach, Florida
Also known as: Henry Morrison Flagler
Sources of wealth: Oil; railroads; real estate; tourism
Bequeathal of wealth: Spouse; children; charity

EARLY LIFE
Henry Morrison Flagler was born into the family of a Presbyterian minister in Hopewell, New York. His father, the Reverend Isaac Flagler, married Elizabeth Caldwell Morrison Harkness after the death of her first husband, providing a family connection that would give young Flagler his start in business. Flagler left school after the eighth grade and moved to Bellevue, Ohio, where he worked in his cousin's grain business, L. G. Harkness and Company, for $5 a month plus room and board. By the time he left this company in 1849, Flagler had demonstrated his worth as a salesman, increasing his salary to $400 a month. In 1852, he joined another family business, D. M. Harkness and Company, and soon married Mary Harkness. Their first child, Jennie Louise, was born on March 18, 1855, and their second child, Carrie (who would die at the age of three), on June 18, 1858. On December 2, 1870, Mary gave birth to Henry's only son, Harry Harkness Flagler, who would later become an important philanthropist in his own right.

FIRST VENTURES
Flagler's entry into the salt business failed with the declining price for salt that followed the Civil War. His small fortune eliminated, Flagler returned to another Harkness family businesses, where he met John D. Rockefeller, who was working at that time for a firm that sold grain and other produce on commission. When Rockefeller left the grain business to enter the emerging petroleum industry, he approached Flagler for a loan to support his new venture. Stephen Vanderburgh Harkness agreed to become a silent partner in Rockefeller's company only if Rockefeller gave Flagler a position as partner. In 1870, the chemist Samuel Andrews joined with Rockefeller, Harkness, and Flagler to create the company that would soon be known as Standard Oil.

Within two years, Standard Oil had purchased or merged with all other oil companies in Cleveland and embarked on a plan to become a major national industry. The company's headquarters was relocated to New York, and by 1879, Standard Oil had captured 90 percent of the American oil market. By producing only the amount of oil needed to maintain a consistently high price, the original partners in the company all became extremely wealthy. Flagler and his wife purchased a spacious home on Fifth Avenue, but because of Mary's poor health the couple also spent part of each year in Florida on the advice of Mary's doctor. Through their winters in the Jacksonville area, Flagler became convinced that the region had potential for development and began formulating plans that would eventually introduce him to yet another source of wealth.

MATURE WEALTH

Flagler's wife Mary died on May 18, 1881, the year before the Standard Oil Trust was formed. This trust pioneered a new concept in business: Rather than functioning as the property of any individual owner, Standard Oil would be owned in common by a group of stockholders, with major decisions rendered by a board of trustees. Instead of receiving profits directly from the company's operations, Rockefeller, Flagler, and the other partners received their incomes from trust certificates, which became more valuable as the business continued to expand. On June 5, 1883, Flagler married Ida Alice Shourds, who had cared for Mary in her final illness. Because of Flagler's familiarity with Florida, the couple honeymooned in St. Augustine, which Flagler found distressingly lacking in convenient hotel accommodations.

With the trust now in charge of Standard Oil's day-to-day operations, Flagler began building a hotel worthy of St. Augustine's history and charm. Named the Hotel Ponce de Leon, Flagler's 540-room resort started the trend of making Florida a tourist destination for America's elite. Realizing that a major hotel would prosper only if it were easy to reach, Flagler purchased and extended local railroad lines, eventually forming the Florida East Coast Railway. The almost instantaneous success of the Ponce de Leon after it opened in 1888 caused Flagler to continue expanding his tourist empire. He proceeded south to Daytona with the Hotel Ormond in 1890 and extended his railroad to West Palm Beach in 1894, which he initially believed would be the southernmost point to which tourists would travel. Flagler's Royal Poinciana Hotel on the shores of Lake Worth

Henry M. Flagler. (©Bettmann/CORBIS)

boasted 1,150 rooms, and in 1896, he opened the Palm Beach Inn on a pristine stretch of Atlantic coastline.

In addition to the Ponce de Leon, Flagler operated two other hotels in St. Augustine: the Alcazar, which later became the Lightner Museum, and the Cordova, which had been built by Franklin Smith in 1888 and originally named the Casa Monica (the name it was given once again following its 1997 restoration). Flagler's hotels were innovative for their features and luxurious appointments. At one time, the Cordova had the largest indoor heated pool anywhere; the Alcazar was one of the earliest examples of poured concrete construction in the United States; and the Royal Poinciana Hotel once boasted that it was the largest wooden structure in the world. Flagler's guests would frequently arrive at his hotels in private railcars, attended by a sizable household staff and equipped with numerous trunks of clothing. Guests would often change their clothing for each meal and wear the latest fashions for the numerous parties, balls, and social gatherings held in the hotels and at nearby estates.

Flagler's hotels originally remained open only from

mid-December through late February, since Florida summers proved too hot for the elite clientele from Philadelphia, Boston, and New York. However, when cold winters hampered business in 1894 and 1895, Flagler decided to extend his railroad south to Biscayne Bay Country, a site that avoided the frigid conditions farther north. Julia Tuttle, a local citrus grower, offered Flagler a substantial land grant in order to develop the area, and by 1896 Flagler had provided the infrastructure necessary for a city to thrive. When it was proposed that the new town be called Flagler, the industrialist demurred, preferring the name Miami after the tribe of Indians that had given their name to a local river. It was thus in the new city of Miami that Flagler opened his Royal Palm Hotel in 1897.

For several years, Ida Alice's mental health grew increasingly unstable, and in 1901 Flagler took advantage of a new law that allowed him to divorce her on the grounds of insanity. On August 24 of the same year,

Flagler married Mary Lily Kenan, the sister of the philanthropist William Rand Kenan, Jr. As a wedding present, Flagler built Mary Lily a lavish estate, which she named Whitehall, not far from the Palm Beach Inn, later renamed The Breakers in honor of the waves that continually lapped its sandy beaches. Flagler then spent seven years extending his railroad to Key West. He and his wife also became central figures in the Palm Beach social scene and helped inaugurate what became known as the season, an annual period when the wealthy would migrate from the north to Flagler's luxurious hotels along the eastern coast of Florida. In 1913, Flagler suffered a severe fall at Whitehall and died on May 20. He was buried in St. Augustine in a plot that he shares with his first wife and his eldest child, Jennie Louise.

LEGACY

Henry Morrison Flagler's influence on Florida was substantial. He helped transform what had been a largely un-

Alcazar Hotel, St. Augustine, Florida, in 1889. Henry M. Flagler built three hotels in this city in order to promote tourism in the area. (©Bettmann/CORBIS)

FLAGLER MUSEUM, WHITEHALL

Created as a wedding present for Henry M. Flagler's third wife, Whitehall is today regarded as a leading example of Gilded Age architecture. When construction of the palatial Palm Beach, Florida, residence was completed in 1902, the *New York Herald* described Whitehall as "more wonderful than any palace in Europe, grander and more magnificent than any other private dwelling in the world."

Flagler entrusted the project to the architects John Carrère and Thomas Hastings, whose first major commission had been Flagler's in St. Augustine and who later went on to design the New York Public Library. Carrère and Hastings's design featured an entry hall where guests would be met by a marble image of the emperor Augustus (based on the marble statue *Augustus of the Prima Porta*, now in the Vatican), an ornate clock by the cabinetmaker François Linke, and a full-length portrait of Flagler by Raimundo de Madrazo y Garreta. Overhead, the domed ceiling was adorned with a massive painting depicting the Oracle of Delphi surrounded by a number of mythological and allegorical figures. This juxtaposition of styles from various periods reflected the tendency of Gilded Age patrons to combine symbols of luxury irrespective of their divergent styles. Elegant spaces for formal and casual dining, individually designed guest bedrooms, more than twenty bathrooms, and central heating suggest the house's primary role in receiving and entertaining Flagler's friends. Whitehall's technological features included telephones and electric lighting, making the mansion highly advanced for its time.

The sixty-thousand-square-foot primary structure consisted of fifty-five rooms centering on an open courtyard in imitation of Italian villas, and the residence was filled with marble and gilded surfaces. To the right of the courtyard on the first floor were a drawing room, dining room, and breakfast room; to the left were a library, music room, and billiard room. On the second floor the bedrooms were named for their decor, such as the Yellow Roses Room, the Silver Maple Room, and the Heliotrope Room.

After the death of Flagler's widow in 1917, Whitehall became the property of her niece, Louise Clisby Wise Lewis, who later sold the property to investors. The new owners transformed the property into a hotel, and once Palm Beach became a popular tourist destination they built a three-hundred-room hotel annex at the back of the building. This additional structure was demolished in 1963, and the mansion was restored to its original state, becoming the Flagler Museum. The building is listed on the National Register of Historic Places. In 2005, a pavilion in the style of a grand railway station of the Gilded Age was added to the grounds, in part to house Flagler's private railroad car.

inhabited region into a major tourist destination, established a standard for luxury in the hotel industry that would be imitated by many successors, and helped create the city of Miami. Flagler's wealth also became the basis for numerous philanthropic enterprises through the efforts of his third wife and his son. The William R. Kenan, Jr., Charitable Trust, named for the brother of Mary Lily Kenan Flagler, became a major benefactor of the University of North Carolina at Chapel Hill and has funded numerous other educational and cultural endeavors at such institutions as Florida Atlantic University, Sweet Briar College, Princeton University, and the Smithsonian Institution. In 1968, another of Flagler's heirs, Lawrence Lewis, Jr., founded Flagler College, using the former Hotel Ponce de Leon as its central building. The fortune developed by Henry Morrison Flagler through his enterprises in oil, railroads, and the hotel industry thus continues to benefit the educational and cultural activities throughout the region that Flagler once called home.

—*Jeffrey L. Buller*

FURTHER READING

Akin, Edward N. *Flagler, Rockefeller Partner and Florida Baron.* Gainesville: University Press of Florida, 1991. Probably the best scholarly account of Flagler's life available. Thoroughly footnoted with extensive and detailed information.

Braden, Susan R. *The Architecture of Leisure: The Florida Resort Hotels of Henry Flagler and Henry Plant.* Gainesville: University Press of Florida, 2002. An exhaustively researched account of Flagler's role in the resort hotel industry in Florida. Places each of Flagler's hotels in its historical, architectural, and cultural context.

Chandler, David Leon. *Henry Flagler: The Astonishing Life and Times of the Visionary Robber Baron Who Founded Florida.* New York: Macmillan, 1986. A general overview of Flagler's life that is highly readable, presenting a good introduction to the age of such figures as John D. Rockefeller, Cornelius Vanderbilt, and Flagler.

Graham, Thomas. *Flagler's St Augustine Hotels: The*

Ponce De Leon, the Alcazar, and the Casa Monica. Sarasota, Fla.: Pineapple Press, 2002. A brief but engaging overview of Flagler's three great hotels in northeast Florida, written by a professor of history at Flagler College.

Standiford, Les. *Last Train to Paradise: Henry Flagler and the Spectacular Rise and Fall of the Railroad That Crossed an Ocean.* New York: Crown, 2002. A popularized account of Flagler's last great endeavor—

the plan to extend his Florida East Coast Railway to Key West.

See also: John Insley Blair; Jay Cooke; Charles Crocker; Edward L. Doheny; John W. Garrett; Edward H. Harriman; James J. Hill; Mark Hopkins; Collis P. Huntington; George Mortimer Pullman; John D. Rockefeller; John D. Rockefeller III; Harry F. Sinclair; Leland Stanford; Cornelius Vanderbilt.

JAMES CLAIR FLOOD
American silver mining magnate

Flood, one of the silver kings, became rich through his investment in Nevada's famed Comstock Lode. Typical of wealthy people in the Gilded Age, Flood engaged in spectacular consumption, becoming one of the leading citizens of San Francisco during the city's maturation in the 1870's.

Born: October 25, 1826; Staten Island, New York

Died: February 21, 1889; Heidelberg, Germany

Sources of wealth: Mining; investments

Bequeathal of wealth: Spouse; children

EARLY LIFE

James Clair Flood, the son of poor Irish immigrants, attended New York City public schools for a few years before becoming apprenticed to a carriage maker. In 1849, he joined the rush to California's gold mines by taking the route that sailed around Cape Horn. Flood did not aim to make his fortune by mining gold but instead hoped to sell custom-built carriages to the rich miners. He soon discovered, however, that there was no demand for his carriages. Flood worked for a few months as a carpenter before trying his luck with placer mining in the Yuba River. He had more success than most and returned to San Francisco with $3,000 in gold dust. Flood used the money to buy a farm in Illinois but did not care for farming. He married in 1853 and decided to engage in another enterprise.

FIRST VENTURES

Flood returned to San Francisco in 1854, where he repaired wagons. He went bankrupt in the recession of the 1850's, as did his neighbor, William S. O'Brien. Flood formed a partnership with O'Brien that would continue for the rest of their lives. Having concluded that men drank in good times as well as in bad, they opened a saloon, the Auction Lunch, in 1857.

Flood picked up tips from the stockbrokers who visited his saloon. Flood then studied the stock market, and

James Clair Flood. (The Granger Collection, New York)

he and O'Brien made a considerable fortune through speculation by 1868. The two owners sold the Auction Lunch and went into business as full-time stockbrokers. In this capacity, they met two speculators from Virginia City, Nevada, James G. Fair and John William Mackay, who were trying to take over a Comstock Lode silver mine. The four men formed a partnership that would turn them into silver kings. By 1872, Flood had an estimated income in excess of $500,000 a month.

MATURE WEALTH

Flood celebrated his wealth by buying the most expensive carriage on the market, as well as the handsomest team of horses. He traded his modest house for one that had been owned by John Selby, the former mayor of San Francisco. The Selby house, named Fair Oaks, became the first in a series of mansions that Flood would own. As he continually traded up and spent millions of dollars on each renovation, the silver king captured the attention of San Franciscans. Linden Towers, one of the Flood mansions, long stood as one of Northern California's foremost examples of Baroque architecture. The Floods frequently held dinners, and almost every distinguished visitor to San Francisco stopped at the Flood mansion. Visitors to Linden Towers saw a drawing room finished in carved walnut with walls of embossed velvet, a music room in rosewood and satinwood, and a dining room paneled in English mahogany with ceiling frescoes by an Italian artist. They admired a sixty-foot fountain and an artificial lake stocked with game fishes, as well as a private racetrack.

Flood, who had joined his three silver partners in opening the Bank of Nevada in 1875, believed that wealth brought philanthropic obligations. He sent Christmas checks to San Francisco's orphan asylums and old people's homes. However, he refused to dole out "unearned" cash because he believed these gifts would destroy the recipients' initiative and self-respect. After years of poor health, Flood died of Bright's disease in 1889.

LEGACY

Flood's legacy is that of many rich men in America's Gilded Age. He came rather quickly to incredible wealth and spent his money almost as quickly as it came in. To maintain his wealth, Flood periodically manipulated silver stocks and disrupted the economy of the Northern California coast. Contemporary critics blamed him for impoverishing thousands. Flood's life shows the best and the worst of the excesses of his era.

—*Caryn E. Neumann*

FURTHER READING

Lewis, Oscar. *Silver Kings: The Lives and Times of Mackay, Fair, Flood, and O'Brien, Lords of the Nevada Comstock Lode.* Reno: University of Nevada Press, 1986.

Makley, Michael J. *John Mackay: Silver King in the Gilded Age.* Reno: University of Nevada Press, 2009.

See also: William Andrews Clark; Marcus Daly; James G. Fair; Meyer Guggenheim; George Hearst; F. Augustus Heinze; John William Mackay; William S. O'Brien.

SAMUEL FLUDYER
English textile merchant

Fludyer dominated the West Country woolen-cloth trade in the mid-eighteenth century. He used his wealth to climb the social and political ladder of eighteenth century England.

Born: 1704 or 1705; London, England
Died: January 18 or 21, 1768; London, England
Also known as: Sir Samuel Fludyer, first baronet
Source of wealth: Trade
Bequeathal of wealth: Children

EARLY LIFE
Sir Samuel Fludyer (FLUHD-yehr), first baronet, was born in 1704 or 1705 to the London clothier Samuel Fludyer and his wife, Elizabeth de Monsallier. As was the custom, young Samuel was trained in his family's business and did not receive a formal education. In addition to learning the wool textile trade in London, he accompanied the pack trains that moved merchandise between the London merchants and the cloth production areas of the West Country—predominantly the counties of Wiltshire and Gloucestershire. Since he did not come from the upper class, it is not surprising that his early life is poorly documented.

FIRST VENTURES
At an unknown date, Fludyer entered an independent cloth-trading partnership with his brother Thomas. The two brothers are listed as "warehousemen" or wholesalers in London directories of the time, but they also received woolen cloth on consignment from manufacturers in their positions as Blackwell Hall factors. (Blackwell Hall was the site of the Woolcloth Exchange.) The brothers sold cloth far beyond London, exporting their trade to other locations in Great Britain and to Britain's colonies in America. As the papers of their business do not survive, many aspects of its day-to-day operations are unknown. Fludyer seems to have been the more important of the two brothers. By 1750, the brothers' credit and economies of scale were so well established that Fludyer's notes circulated as currency in the wool country, and the brothers had become the dominant force in the British wool trade. At the same time Fludyer married Jane Clerke.

MATURE WEALTH
Such was Fludyer's power as a purchaser that he began to exert control over production, assigning manufacturers to produce specific kinds of cloth at specified prices in a manner unprecedented in the wool trade. He also began to contract directly with dyers rather than sell white cloth which customers would arrange to have dyed. By 1760, he had branched out from his original base in the West Country to Yorkshire, another key area of woolen production. Fludyer also ventured into other areas of business, bidding with several others for a concession for the coal mines at Cape Breton, which Britain had won in the Seven Years' War.

Fludyer's wealth led to political power and influence. He was elected a director of the Bank of England, the central financial institution of the British Empire, in 1753, and he served as the bank's deputy governor from 1766 to 1768. He was also a London alderman, and in 1761-1762 he served as the city's lord mayor, the highest position for members of the city's business elite. In 1754, Fludyer was elected a member of the House of Commons, representing the Wiltshire borough of Chippenham, a major cloth center. Fludyer would promise to supply Chippenham manufacturers with wool and buy their cloth on favorable terms in order to secure their votes. He then used his position in Parliament to support his highly profitable work as a government contractor during the Seven Years' War.

Fludyer moved into England's social, economic, and political elite. His second wife, whom he married on September 2, 1758, was Carolina Brudenell, a niece of the earl of Cardigan. In 1755, Fludyer was knighted, and in 1759 he was made a baronet with a seat at Lee in Kent County. He was reportedly worth £900,000 when he died in 1768.

LEGACY
Fludyer's career demonstrated the opportunities for businessmen to advance themselves socially and economically in eighteenth century England. Although Fludyer was not associated with technological advances in cloth manufacture, the enormous scale and centralization of his enterprises helped set the stage for the massive transformations of the textile industry that would take place during the Industrial Revolution. However, as was common during the eighteenth century, his descendants lived as landed gentry rather than carrying on his cloth business.

—*William E. Burns*

FURTHER READING

Michinton, Walter E., ed. *Industrial South Wales, 1750-1914: Essays in Welsh Economic History.* Reprint. London: Taylor and Francis, 2006.

Price, Jacob M. *Capital and Credit in British Overseas Trade: The View from the Chesapeake, 1700-1776.* Cambridge, Mass.: Harvard University Press, 1980.

Smail, John. *Merchants, Markets, and Manufacture: The English Wool Textile Industry in the Eighteenth Century.* New York: St. Martin's Press, 1999.

Truxes, Thomas M. *Irish-American Trade, 1660-1783.* New York: Cambridge University Press, 2004.

See also: Sir Richard Arkwright; Moses Brown; Francis Cabot Lowell; John Rylands; Samuel Slater.

HENRY FORD
American industrialist, inventor, and entrepreneur

Ford established an automotive manufacturing firm that became one of America's most successful businesses in the first half of the twentieth century and was the largest privately held company in the country. During his lifetime, Ford amassed a personal fortune that made him one of America's first billionaires.

Born: July 30, 1863; Springwells Township (near Dearborn), Michigan
Died: April 7, 1947; Dearborn, Michigan
Sources of wealth: Manufacturing; sale of products
Bequeathal of wealth: Relatives; charity

EARLY LIFE

Henry Ford was born in 1863 on a farm outside Dearborn, Michigan. Although his formal education was limited, his keen interest in mechanical devices, especially engines, led him at age sixteen to leave home for Detroit, where he obtained an apprenticeship in a factory. Returning to Dearborn a few years later, he worked on farm machinery and ran a lumber business, spending his leisure hours experimenting with the construction of a horseless carriage. In 1891, he married Clara Bryant; two years later she gave birth to their only child, Edsel. Ford returned to Detroit in 1891 to work for the Edison Illuminating Company, rising quickly to become chief engineer of a power substation. His real passion, however, lay in developing a motorized vehicle, a feat he accomplished in 1896 when he successfully tested his Quadricycle on Detroit streets.

FIRST VENTURES

Almost immediately after Ford completed his first prototype vehicle, he began seeking financing to establish an automobile manufacturing firm. Several prominent Detroit businessmen underwrote the formation of Ford's Detroit Automobile Company, which began operating in 1899 but closed down eighteen months later. Undaunted, Ford began building and racing high-performance vehicles, using his success to persuade a new group of investors to create the Henry Ford Company. Unfortunately, that enterprise failed as well, chiefly because Ford was unable to develop a reliable vehicle that could be mass-produced inexpensively. For the next two years, he continued experimenting with chassis and engine design, and in August, 1903, twelve men, including Ford and Andrew Malcomson as principal shareholders, launched the Ford Motor Company. Ford did not invest his own money; instead, he was named general manager at an annual salary of $3,000.

MATURE WEALTH

The Ford Motor Company was an immediate success, largely because Ford's Model A vehicle appealed to the American public. It was easy to operate and inexpensive, especially when compared to other companies' models. During the next four years, Ford and his team developed additional models, several of which were also well received by buyers. Shrewdly, Ford also created the Ford Manufacturing Company to produce and supply parts for his automobile firm, keeping those profits for himself. In 1906, Ford bought out Malcomson, giving Ford a majority of stock in the Ford Motor Company. He then had virtually free rein to direct the company's future.

Within less than a decade, what was a respectably successful firm among dozens of American automobile manufacturing operations became the dominant company in the industry. Ford's meteoric rise began in 1907 with the introduction of the Model T. Ford's vision was to make a car that most working-class Americans could afford. Over the next two decades, Ford would consistently increase production and reduce the price of this automobile, taking advantage of the Model T's popularity to build a national network of dealerships. Ford was able to produce the Model T efficiently and profitably by developing the moving assembly line, allowing workers to remain at their work stations while partially assembled cars came to them for further work. At the same time, he established a number of innovative labor practices to recruit and retain workers in his assembly plants. The company expanded rapidly to meet demand, constructing a major facility at Highland Park in 1910 and another one at River Rouge in 1915-1919. Between 1907 and 1927, fifteen million Model T's were manufactured.

The profitability of Ford's operation skyrocketed. Company profits in 1909 were approximately $2 million. By 1914, that figure exceeded $16 million; in 1915, the company declared a $60 million dividend. In 1918, some shareholders began to question Ford's decision to reinvest most of the profits from the company into plant expansion. After a lengthy lawsuit and behind-the-scenes negotiations, Ford managed to buy out all the other shareholders. For the next forty years, all Ford

Henry Ford. (Library of Congress)

stock was held by the Ford family. By 1929, the company was showing an annual profit of $90 million, and it earned a $40 million profit the next year despite the onset of the Great Depression.

Although precise figures on the value of Ford's holdings were never available, most business analysts agreed that by 1927 his net worth exceeded $1 billion. During this same period he became a popular national figure; at one point, there was even a movement to draft him as a presidential candidate. Admiration for him waned somewhat during World War I, however, when he lobbied to keep the United States out of the conflict, although he did eventually agree to manufacture vehicles for the government. At about this time, he began a series of vicious attacks on Jews, promoting his anti-Semitic ideology in the Dearborn *Independent*, a newspaper he owned for nearly a decade. Ford reached the nadir of his popularity in 1938, when he agreed to accept an award from Adolf Hitler's government.

Although Ford made his son Edsel president of Ford Motor Company in 1919, he continued to direct the corporation's ventures while taking on a number of other projects in which he had special interest. Ford always wanted to control all aspects of automobile manufacturing, so over time he acquired steel mills, lumber and mining operations, a rubber plantation, and various transportation assets. He also began Fordson Tractor in 1910, and at one time or another was engaged in agricultural research, wireless communications, hydroelectric power generation, and housing development. Eventually, Ford's business operations extended to Canada, Mexico, South America, and across Europe. Closer to home, Ford built the Henry Ford Hospital in Detroit from his own funds in 1915, and he supported several educational institutions that aided immigrants and underprivileged children. After World War I, he began collecting antiques and other objects of Americana; to display these artifacts, he created the Edison Institute and Greenfield Village in Dearborn.

Ford was always a hands-on manager, a technique that served his company well in its early years but began to be a liability during the 1920's. By 1923, the Model T, which had captured 40 percent of the automobile market, began to lose market share. Ford had to be prodded to drop this line and produce more modern vehicles in response to competition, especially from General Motors' Chevrolet division. During the 1930's, Ford became something of an absentee director, frequently relying for advice on his close associate Harry Bennett, a former security guard whose high-handed methods of dealing

FORD FOUNDATION

Prompted by a change in tax laws that would have deprived his family of a significant portion of his wealth upon his death, Henry Ford established the Ford Foundation in 1936, and he changed his will so the foundation would receive a substantial share of Ford Motor Company stock when he died. Upon Ford's death in 1947, the foundation obtained stock valued at more than $500 million, making it one of the largest philanthropic organizations in America. Ford's grandson Henry Ford II became chair of a board that included a number of nationally respected business and educational leaders as trustees.

Initially, the foundation supported causes in which the Ford family had a special interest, but after World War II its scope began to widen. Its headquarters was moved to Pasadena, California, and the board began implementing a strategy geared toward social activism, supporting causes such as civil rights and urban planning. In the mid-1950's, the foundation moved its headquarters to New York City. Eventually, the foundation became independent of the Ford family, although Henry Ford II remained a trustee until 1976. From 1966 to 1979, the foundation was led by McGeorge Bundy, a former adviser to President John F. Kennedy, whose strong stance on a number of social issues prompted Ford dealers around the country to complain that the foundation's activities were hurting sales of Ford products.

During the 1950's and 1960's, the foundation's assets grew to more than $3 billion, but a recession and zealous spending dropped its value to $1.5 billion by the mid-1970's. Subsequently, however, the foundation recovered its financial health and continued to support charitable causes worldwide. Foundation funds brought economic reforms to developing nations around the world, improved the lives of the poor, and supported environmental initiatives worldwide. At the same time, sound investments and a growing economy allowed the foundation to improve its finances, so that in 2008 its assets exceeded $11 billion.

agerial assistance from a team of former Army officers who had helped direct logistics for America's expeditions in Europe and Asia during World War II. By the time Henry Ford died in 1947, the company seemed to be returning to prosperity.

LEGACY

Throughout his life, Henry Ford kept information about his personal wealth guarded from the public, but estimates place his net worth at the time of his death at a figure exceeding $1 billion, including his homes, investments in various businesses, and a personal bank account worth $26.5 million. To protect this vast fortune from the large inheritance tax that would have been imposed under laws passed in 1933, Ford added a codicil to his will in 1936, dividing up Ford Motor Company stock into two types: Class A stock, 95 percent of the company's total assets, would be transferred to the Ford Foundation at Ford's death; this stock would not provide foundation directors any voting rights within the Ford Motor Company. The remaining 5 percent of stock, designated Class B, was to be held by family members, who would retain the right to direct company operations. In less than a decade after Ford died, however, Henry Ford II and other Ford Motor Company executives decided to convert the company to a publicly owned corporation, although the family retained control of the firm's operations for many more years.

—*Laurence W. Mazzeno*

with both union organizers and other Ford executives caused great turmoil within the organization. By the outbreak of World War II, the company was losing money on automobile production; however, $6.5 billion in government contracts kept the company afloat during the war when auto production was halted. Ford Motor Company made a major contribution to the war effort by producing jeeps, tanks, trucks, and the B-24 Liberator bomber.

Unfortunately, Ford never provided his company with a strong succession plan. When his son Edsel died unexpectedly in 1943, Ford was required to reassume the presidency of Ford Motor Company. Two years later, prompted by his wife and other family members, he agreed to turn over operations to his twenty-five-year-old grandson. Henry Ford II immediately fired Bennett and restored some order to the company, obtaining man-

FURTHER READING

Brinkley, Douglas. *Wheels for the World: Henry Ford, His Company, and a Century of Progress, 1903-2003.* New York: Viking, 2003. Comprehensive history of Henry Ford and the company he created. Details Ford's efforts to make his company the premier automobile manufacturer in the world, and examines the fate of the firm in the half century after his death.

Bryan, Ford R. *Beyond the Model T: The Other Ventures of Henry Ford.* Rev. ed. Detroit: Wayne State University Press, 1997. Describes Ford's involvement in a number of business, educational, and civic ventures outside the automobile industry.

Collier, Peter, and David Horowitz. *The Fords: An American Epic*. New York: Summit Books, 1987. Chronicles Ford's rise to prominence in the automobile industry and assesses the impact of his legacy on succeeding generations of his family.

Gelderman, Carol W. *Henry Ford: The Wayward Capitalist*. New York: Dial Press, 1981. Biography aimed at exposing the many sides of Ford's personality. Offers an explanation for his success as an industrialist.

Lacy, Robert. *Ford: The Men and the Machine*. Boston: Little, Brown, 1986. Examines Ford's efforts to build his automotive empire and subsequent attempts by family members to keep the company profitable and innovative.

Watts, Steven. *The People's Tycoon: Henry Ford and the American Century*. New York: Knopf, 2005. Scholarly study focusing on Ford's popularity with the American public.

See also: Giovanni Agnelli; Walter P. Chrysler; Chung Ju Yung; John F. Dodge; Thomas Edison; Harvey Firestone; Soichiro Honda; André Michelin; Alfred P. Sloan.

NICOLAS FOUQUET
French aristocrat and government official

Fouquet used his wealth to replenish the royal treasury and sustain the French monarchy. His wealth provided the financial support for seventeenth century artists, writers, musicians, and other talented individuals. He created Vaus-le-Vicomte, the model for Versailles, giving France two magnificent châteaux.

Born: 1615; Paris, France
Died: March 23, 1680; Pignerol, France
Also known as: Nicolas Foucquet
Sources of wealth: Inheritance; marriage; banking
Bequeathal of wealth: Spouse; artistic patronage

EARLY LIFE
Nicolas Fouquet (nee-koh-lah few-KAY) was born in 1615 in Paris, France. He was a member of an affluent family belonging to the *noblesse de la robe* (court nobility). His grandfather had been a merchant in Nantes; his father François had risen in rank to be an adviser to Cardinal de Richelieu, prime minister during the reign of Louis XIII. Nicolas was educated by the Jesuits and entered the legal profession at a very young age. In 1628, he was admitted as a lawyer to the parliament of Paris.

FIRST VENTURES
In 1636, Fouquet purchased the post of *maître des requêtes*, a court office. In 1641, Fouquet's wealth was already such that he purchased the village of Maincy and the château Vaux-le-Vicomte, located not far from Paris. At the time, the château was small and unpretentious, but Fouquet would later make it the most elaborate home in France.

As a *maître des requêtes*, he belonged to the group of court officers from whom the *intendants* were chosen.

Intendants were court officials whose duties were to oversee the provincial governments' financial, policing, and judicial activities. Fouquet was first appointed as an *intendant* in 1642 by Prime Minister Jules Mazarin. He held various intendancies from 1642 to 1650. The Wars of the Fronde, the rebellion of a certain faction of the nobility against Mazarin and the young King Louis XIV, broke out in 1648. It lasted until 1653; during this time, Mazarin had to leave Paris and Fouquet not only remained loyal to him but also ensured the safety of his property.

MATURE WEALTH
In 1650, Fouquet obtained the prestigious and powerful office of *procureur général* (attorney-general) to the Parliament of Paris. The following year, he married Marie de Castille, who also belonged to a wealthy family of the *noblesse de la robe*. The marriage made him the owner of Belle Asize, his wife's estate, and added considerably to his wealth. With the end of the Fronde in 1653, Mazarin returned to Paris. In return for his loyalty and because of his ability, Mazarin appointed Fouquet *surintendant de finance* (finance minister). The combination of the offices of *procureur général* and *surintendant de finance* made Fouquet the most powerful man in France, since he controlled the king's finances and also the judicial court's activity.

The royal treasury had been virtually depleted in 1648; the private investors who had loaned money to the king had not received a profit on their investment and were unwilling to invest more. As prime minister, Mazarin was in desperate need of money to finance the administration, the war with Spain, and the costs

THE VICOMTE OF BRAGELONNE

Nicolas Fouquet appears as one of the characters in *Le Vicomte de Bragelonne* (1848-1850; *The Vicomte of Bragelonne*, 1857), the third volume of Alexandre Dumas *père*'s three-volume historical romance about d'Artagnan and the king's musketeers. Dumas's novel is set in the 1660's, the time during which Louis XIV was establishing himself as an absolute monarch. It was also during these years that the king arrested and imprisoned Fouquet. The main characters of the novel are d'Artagnan and his three comrades, the musketeers Athos, Porthos, and Aramis. Dumas mixes fact and fiction in his tale. Among a tangle of plots, including efforts to restore the English throne to Charles II, an attempt to place Louis's brother Philippe upon the French throne, and the love affair of Louis and Louise de la Vallière, Dumas weaves into the story the account of Fouquet's downfall at the hands of Louis and his adviser Jean-Baptiste Colbert.

Dumas also involves Fouquet in the intrigue that places Philippe on the throne of France. Aramis is the main conspirator in the plot and kidnaps Louis so that Philippe can become king. Hoping to obtain help from Fouquet, Aramis tells him that he has kidnapped Louis and imprisoned him in the Bastille and that Philippe is now king. Contrary to what Aramis had expected, Fouquet immediately liberates Louis, an action which just happens to take place on the evening of the party Fouquet has thrown for Louis at Vaux-le-Vicomte. Colbert has convinced Louis that Fouquet has stolen money from the royal treasury to build Fouquet's great château and to finance the elaborate party. With no regard for the fact that Fouquet rescued him, Louis has him arrested and imprisoned.

The characterization of Fouquet in the novel reflects his ambition and enormous financial success, as it depicts the party at Vaux-le-Vicomte and both Colbert and Louis's envy of Fouquet. It also reflects Fouquet's almost naïve loyalty to King Louis XIV.

In 1657, Fouquet had begun to renovate Vaux-le-Vicomte. As a member of the *noblesse de la robe*, he had to deal with the fact that his nobility was not inherited. The *noblesse de l'épée* (inherited or old nobility) refused to accept the *noblese de la robe* as their equals; in their opinion, the *noblese de la robe* were and would always be upstart bourgeois who had purchased their titles. Consequently, appearances were very important to Fouquet. He needed to parade his wealth in order to show the old nobility that he lived in the same or in a better manner than they did. Added to this desire, Fouquet actually had an appreciation for beauty and artistic quality. He was very generous in his support of artists and writers, and by 1657 he was extraordinarily rich.

Thus when he began the renovation of Vaux-le-Vicomte, he obtained the services of the very best architect of the time, Louis Le Vau; the very best painter and decorator, Charles Le Brun; and the most talented landscape gardener, André Le Nôtre. The renovations took four years and were not completed until 1661. Once the magnificent château and grounds were finished, the house and other buildings occupied almost one hundred acres of land, with highly elaborated gardens that extended for more than a mile. Vaux-le-Vicomte was the most beautiful and luxurious château in France.

As *surintendant de finance*, Fouquet had performed his duties well. He had replenished the royal treasury and provided funds for the royal administration and for the wars and extravagances of the court. He fully expected Louis XIV to name him prime minister upon the death of Mazarin, who was in failing health. However, Fouquet was to be disappointed in this ambition. Mazarin's private secretary Jean-Baptiste Colbert also had ambitions to become the king's foremost adviser and administrator. Louis XIV, who had been terrified by the Fronde, feared the power of the nobility; for Fouquet to become prime minister was not an eventuality that either the king or the nobles favored. Louis XIV decided to rule personally without a prime minister. As Mazarin's death approached, Colbert began to indicate to the king that Fouquet was not to be trusted.

of entertainment and maintenance for the court. Thus, Fouquet's duty as *surintendant de finance* was to raise a large sum of money quickly. Since Fouquet was in charge of both raising the money and prosecuting any financial misconduct, he had a wide-open field in which to generate funds. Fouquet was loyal to Mazarin and the king, but he was also interested in increasing his own wealth. He employed two methods to enlarge his personal fortune. Fouquet negotiated loans using his own property as security. What he was actually doing was borrowing the money himself and then loaning it to the royal administration. He also obtained other loans directly on the security of the state. His techniques were legal and allowed him to make considerable profits. Fouquet was stricken seriously ill in 1658. Unable to perform his duties and raise money by negotiating loans, he sold Belle Asize to provide the funds necessary for the army.

Although some of his friends tried to caution him in regard to Colbert and the king, Fouquet did not perceive any danger. When the king expressed a desire to visit Vaux-le-Vicomte, Fouquet, who was proud of his château and eager to show it to the king and the nobles, immediately set about arranging a festive party for the king and the court. On August 17, 1661, Fouquet welcomed the king and his entourage to Vaux-le-Vicomte, where he entertained them with a tour of his gardens, a dinner, a ballet-comedy by Molière with music by Jean-Baptise Lully, and an abundance of fireworks. Fouquet entertained six thousand guests at a cost of 120,000 livres. This was the high point of Fouquet's career; he was the richest man in France, and as *procureur général* and *surintendant de finance*, the most powerful.

The magnificence of the château and its gardens and the elaborate festivities only served to intensify Louis XIV's extreme jealousy and hatred of Fouquet. Everything Fouquet possessed and offered totally eclipsed what the king owned. Louis XIV took his council of ministers to Nantes for a meeting. He had already persuaded Fouquet to relinquish his office of *procureur général*. In Nantes on September 5, 1661, Fouquet was arrested by his friend Charles de Batz de Castlemore, known as d'Artagnan, captain of the king's musketeers. The king called for a special court session and had Fouquet tried on charges of theft from the royal treasury. The trial lasted for three years and finally produced a verdict of guilty and a sentence of banishment. Louis XIV commuted the sentence to life imprisonment. Fouquet was sent to the citadel at Pignerol and his wife was exiled. The Crown sequestered all of Fouquet's wealth. Nicolas Fouquet died in prison on March 23, 1680. Vaux-le-Vicomte was eventually returned to Fouquet's wife.

LEGACY

Nicolas Fouquet is the most successful example of an ambitious bourgeois who rose in seventeenth century French society. He not only acquired great wealth through his financial expertise but also recognized and appreciated excellence in the work of creative individuals and employed his wealth to assist them. While Fouquet was ostentatious and took pleasure in exhibiting his wealth, he also helped establish standards of good taste, even in excess. His château Vaux-le-Vicomte and its gardens stand as a model of beauty in architecture and landscape gardening. Although Fouquet attained both enormous wealth and power, he always remained loyal to the French crown.

—*Shawncey Webb*

FURTHER READING

Beik, William. *Louis XIV and Absolutism: A Brief Study with Documents*. Boston: Bedford/St. Martin's, 2000. Good discussion of the Fronde, Mazarin, and Colbert and how Louis XIV interacted with the court, the church, and the provinces.

Drazin, Charles. *The Man Who Outshone the Sun King: A Life of Gleaming Opulence and Wretched Reversal in the Reign of Louis XIV*. Philadelphia: Da Capo Press, 2008. Detailed portrayal of Fouquet's life from his early school days to his rise to prominence to his years spent in prison. Good historical context and accounts of events of the time. Very readable.

Goldstein, Claire. *Vaux and Versailles: The Appropriations, Erasures, and Accidents That Made Modern France*. Philadelphia: University of Pennsylvania Press, 2007. Good for understanding what Vaux and Fouquet meant to French national style. Gives an account of how much Louis XIV took from Vaux in terms of objects, artists, writers, and concepts to create Versailles.

Lewis, W. H. *The Splendid Century: Life in the France of Louis XIV*. 1953. Reprint. Prospect Heights, Ill.: Waveland Press, 1997. One of the best presentations of Louis XIV's France. Includes chapters on every aspect of life: court, army, church, towns, commoners, education, and letters.

Soll, Jacob. *The Information Master: Jean-Baptiste Colbert's Secret State Intelligence System*. Ann Arbor: University of Michigan Press, 2009. Good presentation of Colbert and his rise to power. Describes how he used a network of information to establish and increase royal authority.

See also: Samuel Bernard; John Law; Louis XIV.

STEPHEN FOX
British government official, financier, and politician

Fox rose from obscurity to become one of the wealthiest men of his day. His financial savvy enabled the Restoration government of Charles II to function and survive, and Fox continued throughout his life to provide his economic acumen to the British court.

Born: March 27, 1627; Farley, Wiltshire, England
Died: October 28, 1716; Chiswick, England
Also known as: Sir Stephen Fox
Sources of wealth: Government; moneylending; real estate
Bequeathal of wealth: Spouse; children

EARLY LIFE
Stephen Fox was the son of William Fox and Margaret Pavy Fox, one of ten children in the Fox household, most of whom lived to maturity. The concept of family loyalty that Fox developed while growing up in relative poverty remained a strong influence on him throughout his life. He was educated under the auspices of his mother's uncle at Salisbury Cathedral choir school. Although he had no university education, he is believed to have received a gentleman's upbringing, to which was added a sound education in bookkeeping and financial management. He joined his brother John at court and remained there as his brother's helper for two years, informally taking over his brother's office as closet keeper in the chapel at St. James's. From this position, Fox became a page to Lady Stafford, then the countess of Sutherland; the earl of Leicester; and finally Henry, Lord Percy, a favorite of Queen Henrietta Maria, the wife of King Charles I.

FIRST VENTURES
When he was nineteen, Fox became gentleman of the horse to Percy, who was in exile on the Continent. In this position, Fox for the first time publicly demonstrated the money management that would mark the foundation of his wealth. Fox used his time abroad to study foreign languages. When King Charles II joined the exiled queen in France, Fox became associated with his court and traveled with Charles. Fox did not go to Scotland with Charles, but remained in Holland, where he gained a reputation as an accountant who controlled every detail of expenditure. Returning to England, Fox went to work for the earl of Devonshire, helping the earl handle his estate receipts. When the exiled Charles II asked Fox to resume his services in 1653, Fox left Devonshire and returned to France to serve in an impoverished British court, financed by an irregularly paid pension from the French monarch. This movement from certain employment to an uncertain venture marked Fox as a man willing to take risks—either because he remained loyal to the monarchy or because he envisioned a day when Charles's loyal followers would reap the benefits of their support during the king's exile.

MATURE WEALTH
The Restoration of Charles to the British throne brought Fox the opportunities he had anticipated, although not always speedily. Fox earned significant notice because he was the first to tell Charles II of the death of Oliver Cromwell, who had ruled Great Britain during the king's exile. Back in England, Fox expected to obtain a high office as reward for his faithful services to Charles, but like many others he had to accept a lower office and wait until court protocol and the deaths of older officers would allow him to rise. Although Fox apparently wanted the position of cofferer, controlling the money of the royal household, he was offered junior offices, first as the chief clerk comptroller and then as the second clerk of the Green Cloth—stepping stones to senior offices in the royal household. These offices provided small salaries but lucrative perquisites and allowances. Many who held these offices also accepted gratuities; Fox refused these as ungentlemanly and advised his own protégés to avoid them. Fox was also granted an estate for his loyal services.

Fox's career ascendancy and personal fortune began with his position as an informal financial agent, raising and dispensing "secret service"—the term for money that went directly to the royal household instead of being disbursed by the Exchequer (government treasury). Most of these funds were not actually "secret," and they allowed the royal family to have more flexibility in its expenditures than the Exchequer system afforded.

Fox subsequently received the position of paymaster of the king's guards, which led to his ever-greater participation in the financial transactions of the realm. As the officer who paid the king's armed forces, Fox had to engage in considerable planning, for money was not readily available, and a delay in payment might lead to a breakdown in the guards' morale, or even mutiny. Fox demonstrated his ability as paymaster, and as a result received additional responsibilities with regard to funding what was becoming a royal standing army. Fox developed "the

Undertaking" to ensure prompt payment. Using this system, he borrowed substantial sums of money to pay the army, in return receiving interest on these loans until the army's pay was issued by the government, at which point Fox received a small portion of the soldiers' pay. Fox was able to raise money on the scale necessary to finance the king's army because of his personal pledge to stand behind his loans and his reputation for financial probity. Throughout his financial career, although he did make private loans to individuals, much of his wealth came from arranging loans to the government, or, increasingly, directly loaning the government money from his rapidly growing fortune. Fox eventually rose to other positions in the government, culminating in his becoming First Lord of the Treasury, although, to his chagrin, the position of cofferer eluded him. He was able to buy or obtain many positions for members of his extended family. He also served in Parliament.

One of Fox's most enduring legacies was his involvement in founding the Royal Hospital Chelsea, one of many charitable institutions he established or influenced. Fox started acquiring land during the middle part of his career, probably with a view to establishing his sons in estates when they came to a marriageable age. Fox outlived many of his children, however, and apparently at one time despaired of leaving a son to carry on his name. At this point, he made plans to provide for the children and grandchildren of his daughters, at least one of whom he had supported throughout her marriage until her death. Fox's marriage to Christiana Hope, however, provided him with a male heir to inherit the bulk of his estate.

His favorite house, built at Chiswick, was to be his country home. He made the house comfortable with expansive gardens and beautiful furnishings. He retired to Chiswick, where he spent the last years of his life, and there he died in 1716, having become one of the richest men of his time.

THE ROYAL HOSPITAL CHELSEA

The legacy of Stephen Fox is nowhere greater than at the Royal Hospital Chelsea. Although the idea of establishing the Royal Hospital is sometimes attributed to Charles II's mistress Nell Gwyn, the facility was undoubtedly conceived by Charles II, who was well aware of the Hôtel Royal des Invalides founded by Louis XIV in France. The plight of military men who had served Charles and his father was readily apparent throughout the kingdom, as most of the soldiers who were no longer able to serve were released without adequate pensions. These men often were reduced to begging as a means of support, or they remained in the military beyond their ability to perform their duties, thus weakening the armed forces.

Although Charles had the inspiration to build the hospital and proposed its founding in 1681, government money was not readily available. At this point Charles turned to Fox, on whom he had relied in other financial matters, and Fox came up with a means of financing the project. Money was regularly deducted from the army's pay, and Fox allocated some of these funds to the hospital. Charles contributed some of the money that Fox held in "secret service" accounts to the project; these accounts contained funds that were directly disbursed to the royal household instead of being dispensed by the Exchequer (government treasury). Additional funding was raised through donations and by charging fees on military officers' commissions. Fox offered to buy the site on which the hospital would be built. This land was once held by the Crown and was subsequently given to the Royal Society, which had not constructed a building on the property. Fox also loaned money without interest, perhaps as much as £6,000 pounds, for the project.

Charles II set the first foundation stone in February, 1682, and he continued to support the hospital until his death in 1685. Fox guided the project in its initial years, overseeing its building plans, operation, and staffing, as well as providing financial support, and the project was completed under the guidance of the earl of Ranelagh. By the time the hospital admitted the first pensioners in 1692, the military had implemented a pension system. Since more retired military men wanted to live at the facility than could be accommodated, hospital residents were required to surrender their pensions; these residents were called "in-pensioners," while nonresidents were termed "out-pensioners."

The hospital was designed by architect Christopher Wren, and his buildings remained on the site into the twenty-first century. By that time, the hospital site also housed the National Army Museum, and the Chelsea Flower Show had been held on the property every year since 1913. In 2010, the facilities were being renovated and redesigned to meet the needs of twenty-first century in-pensioners.

LEGACY

Stephen Fox was a prudent and honest financier who provided faithful and reliable service, often at risk to his own fortune. He helped establish a more sophisticated financial system for the British government, serving that government during periods of tremendous challenge, including the Restoration and the Glorious Revolution (1688-1689). He used his fortune to help others gain wealth, both by investing money for others and by helping others—including members of his family—embark upon careers in the government. Although he lived well, he was a model of fiscal responsibility both at home and in his government, keeping tight and honest accounts throughout his life.

—*Susan Jones*

FURTHER READING

Barnard, T. C. *The Dukes of Ormonde, 1610-1745.* Woodbridge, England: Boydell and Brewer, 2000. Chronicles the political careers of the first and second dukes of Ormonde and their relations with Fox.

Clay, Christopher. *Public Finance and Private Wealth: The Career of Sir Stephen Fox, 1627-1716.* Oxford, England: Clarendon Press, 1978. Detailed review of Fox's career and life.

Dean, Charles Graham Troughton. *The Royal Hospital Chelsea.* London: Hutchinson, 1950. Comprehensive history of the hospital.

Eyre, Richard. *A Sermon Preach'd at the Funeral of the Honourable Sir Stephen Fox Knight, November 7, 1716, at Farly in Wilts.* London: Printed by H. Clark for Jonah Bowyer. 1716. Provides significant contemporary insights.

Hutton, Ronald. *Charles the Second: King of England, Scotland, and Ireland.* Oxford, England: Clarendon Press, 1989. Describes Fox's influence on financial affairs.

Jeffrey, Sally. "The Flower of All the Private Gentlemen's Palaces in England: Sir Stephen Fox's 'Extraordinarily Fine' Garden at Chiswick." *Garden History* 32, no. 1 (Spring, 2004): 1-19. Explores Fox's use of wealth to develop a fine house and gardens.

Millar, Oliver. "Artists and Craftsmen in the Service of Sir Stephen Fox and His Family." *Burlington Magazine* 137, no. 1109 (August, 1995): 518-528. Review of Fox's contributions as a sometime patron of the arts.

Miller, John. *After the Civil Wars: English Politics and Government in the Reign of Charles II.* New York: Longman, 2000. Reviews the historical background of Charles II's reign, including information about politics and finances relevant to Fox.

Pittis, William. *Memoirs of the Life of Sir Stephen Fox, Kt., from His First Entrance upon the Stage of Action, Under Lord Piercy, till His Decease . . . to Which Is Added a Succinct Account of His Will and Testament. . . .* London: Printed for John Sackfield. 1717. Contemporary biography of Fox.

See also: Sir John Banks; James Craggs; Thomas Guy; First Duke of Marlborough; William Penn; William Pulteney.

BENJAMIN FRANKLIN
American inventor, author, publisher, politician, and statesman

Franklin described many ways for achieving financial success in his most famous work, Poor Richard's Almanack, *but he mostly identified wealth as the end result of some individual's hard work and thrift. Such aphorisms as "a penny saved is a penny earned" have become so common that few recognize it as a misquote of a popular saying written by Franklin.*

Born: January 17, 1706; Boston, Massachusetts
Died: April 17, 1790; Philadelphia, Pennsylvania
Also known as: Poor Richard; Richard Saunders; Timothy Turnstone; Mrs. Silence Dogood; Harry Meanwell; Alice Addertongue
Sources of wealth: Media; writing
Bequeathal of wealth: Children; educational institution; charity; cities of Boston and Philadelphia

EARLY LIFE

Benjamin Franklin was born to Josiah Franklin and Abiah Folger on January 17, 1706, the youngest of ten sons and the fifteenth of seventeen children. Josiah was a tallow chandler (soap and candle maker), but he wanted his youngest son to become a minister and somehow managed to send Benjamin to Boston Latin School for two years before the family's educational funds ran out. This brief schooling nevertheless instilled in Benjamin a love of reading and writing, which, for a time, seemed to suit him for an apprenticeship at his brother James's newspaper, the *New England Courant.* By 1721, however, Franklin was taking more interest in the content of the newspaper than in its production and wanted to contribute his own thoughts to the newspaper's columns. Refused permission to submit a letter for publication,

Benjamin Franklin. (Library of Congress)

Franklin instead adopted the persona of Mrs. Silence Dogood, a wealthy widow, and attached this pseudonym to writings he submitted to the newspaper. Given Franklin's natural bent for literature and language, Mrs. Dogood turned out to be a popular correspondent for *Courant* readers. However, when James found out that Mrs. Dogood was, in reality, his fifteen-year-old brother, he was furious and administered a beating that, quite literally, sent Franklin packing.

FIRST VENTURES

Abandoning his apprenticeship, Franklin escaped to Philadelphia with, he often remarked, only enough money in his pockets to buy a few loaves of bread. Franklin relished the change of scene, however. He already knew the printer's trade from his years in his brother's shop, so while he earned his keep working in a printing house, he endeavored to find out if there was sufficient interest in the literary circles of Philadelphia to support another newspaper. An encounter with Pennsylvania governor Sir William Keith encouraged Franklin in his pursuit, but after having traveled to London and seen the cost of presses, ink, and paper, Franklin discovered that

Keith had no interest in actually paying for any of the newspaper's expenses. He worked for a time as a typesetter in the Smithfield suburb of London, but he grew despondent and returned to Philadelphia in 1726 under the sponsorship of Thomas Denham, who hired Franklin to be the bookkeeper and clerk in his trade business.

Perhaps because he was temporarily stymied in his desire to run his own publishing company, Franklin founded the Junto, a group of tradesmen and artisans like himself who were interested in reading the great works of literature and discussing the political and social issues of the day. Franklin's impulse to write was stirred by the regular exposure to like minds. Given that books were expensive, the Junto pooled its resources first to jointly store their own books and then to buy books of interest to the group. Always one to provide structure to any system that seemed ill-defined, Franklin wrote out a charter to form the Library Company of Philadelphia and hired Louis Timothee, the first true librarian in America, to look after the expanding collection. A new building, constructed in 1791, formalized the arrangement, which, having no competition for its services, proved to be surprisingly profitable as a subscription library.

MATURE WEALTH

Loyal to his friend Denham, Franklin was not able to realize his dream of publishing his own newspaper until after the tradesman's death. In 1730, having learned firsthand that he could not count on the nebulous promises of the typical patron, Franklin established the *Pennsylvania Gazette* by himself from his earnings. This newspaper was Franklin's first real success. Just as he had hoped, sales of *Poor Richard's Almanack* (1732-1757) were brisk. The almanac included not only the typical meteorological data available in other farmers' almanacs but also Franklin's brand of folk wisdom, sprinkled liberally with his humorous asides. He consistently sold around ten thousand copies of this work each year it was published, which more than adequately supported Franklin's new common-law wife, Deborah Read, and their children. He even felt comfortably settled enough to provide a home and education for his illegitimate son, William.

The 1740's and 1750's were prosperous times for Franklin. Because of the success of the *Gazette*, he was able to sell newspaper franchises in cities outside Philadelphia. Once financially established, Franklin was free to pursue his many other interests. He was fond of inventing practical items, like bifocals, swim fins, the lightning rod, and the Franklin stove. Partly because he had no need for additional income and partly because of his Puritan upbringing, Franklin never chose to patent his most potentially lucrative inventions. He seemed to consider the free availability of his ideas as being essential for the betterment of society. In a similarly public vein, much of Franklin's later life, concerned with politics and public affairs, became the stage on which his earlier idealism was put into action.

In June, 1749, Franklin became a justice of the peace in Philadelphia, and on August 10, 1753, he was appointed to be joint deputy postmaster general and immediately started instituting postal reforms. By 1757, Franklin had been sent to London by the members of the Pennsylvania Legislature to act as a colonial agent and demand that the Penn family, the colony's titular proprietors, stop interfering in Pennsylvania's internal affairs. Because of this appointment, Franklin's former tolerance of British corruption became strained. In the beginning, although Franklin had suffered many personal disappointments in London, he had Loyalist sympathies of his own. England, in comparison to the more rustic American colonies, was a nexus for culture and literature. He might have even considered living there permanently were it not for the fact that his wife intensely feared travel by ship and would not leave home. These feelings notwithstanding, the colonies' virulent hatred of the Stamp Act of 1765 shocked Franklin and made him reconsider his assumed loyalties.

The Hutchinson affair finally caused Franklin to support America's break from Great Britain. Having been selected by the monarchy to govern Massachusetts, Thomas Hutchinson not only ignored the desire of his constituency to demand Parliamentary representation; he also secretly sent letters to the king requesting the removal of the colonists few "British" freedoms. Franklin had remained in London after his intercession for the Pennsylvania colony failed, acting as a representative for Georgia, New Jersey, and Massachusetts. While in London, he managed to obtain several of Hutchinson's letters and was incensed by their lack of integrity. He subsequently made sure that the letters were brought to America and shown to politically powerful and influential colonists. The English foreign ministry publicly condemned Franklin for stealing the letters.

Back in Philadelphia, Franklin was elected to the Second Continental Congress, working with Thomas Jefferson and the other Framers to draft the Declaration of Independence. In 1776, having signed the politically explosive document, Franklin accepted a post as ambassador to France and the court of Louis XVI.

After a popular term of service in France in support of the newly independent American government, Franklin returned home one last time to Philadelphia, where he died on April 17, 1790, at the age of eighty-four. At his funeral, more than twenty thousand mourners paid their final respects to Franklin, who had left much of his fortune to his daughter Sally Franklin and her husband Richard Bache in recognition of her tender care of him in his old age.

LEGACY

Franklin believed that because he owed his wealth and talents to the beneficence of an appreciative public, he needed to actively improve people's lives. For this reason, he refused to patent inventions he believed would benefit society, and he declined to accept a salary for the

---

BENJAMIN FRANKLIN INSTITUTE OF TECHNOLOGY

In 1785, French mathematician Charles-Joseph Mathon de la Cour wrote an essay mocking Benjamin Franklin's wildly popular *Poor Richard's Almanack* called "Fortunate Richard." A parody of American optimism, Mathon de la Cour's Richard donates £1,000 to his hometown, Boston, and the same amount to his adopted home, Philadelphia—a sum of about $4,400. The single caveat for this donation is that it must remain untouched in a trust for five hundred years; both interest and principal could not be disbursed until the end of the specified period.

Although intended as a joke, Franklin was amused and intrigued by Mathon de la Cour's idea. He did, in fact, establish separate trusts for Boston and Philadelphia, each containing the sum of £1,000 and each with the similar restriction that the money be allowed to earn interest for two hundred years before final disbursement. By 1990, the Philadelphia trust contained a sum of more than $2 million, while the Boston trust yielded almost $5 million. In gratitude for such a fortuitously foresighted gift, the city of Boston used Franklin's accumulated donation to establish a school that would be named the Franklin Technical Institute. The institute opened in 1908, and it remained in operation into the twenty-first century, renamed the Benjamin Franklin Institute of Technology. The institute has always been a trade school that focuses on providing a solid, practical education for its attendees.

Philadelphia also used Franklin's delayed donation for public edification. The city appropriated its trust funds to establish the Franklin Institute, a museum that in the twenty-first century presents exhibits about science and technology.

work he performed in some of his political appointments. Similarly, in his will he stipulated that some of his fortune should go to the creation or improvement of educational institutions. Unlike many of the other Founding Fathers, Franklin never sought the presidency. He had an impartial view of American politics and society that allowed him to remain a member of the common folk, even when he was an elder statesman.

—*Julia M. Meyers*

FURTHER READING

Franklin, Benjamin. *The Compleated Autobiography.* Compiled and edited by Mark Skousen. Washington, D.C.: Regnery, 2006. An edition of Franklin's own account of his life.

Houston, Alan. *Benjamin Franklin and the Politics of Improvement.* New Haven, Conn.: Yale University Press, 2008. Looks at Franklin's philosophy and his contributions to commerce, the citizen militia, immigration, and population. Franklin desired to improve himself, and he thought society would benefit if each person tried to do the same.

Lemay, J. A. Leo. *The Life of Benjamin Franklin.* Philadelphia: University of Pennsylvania Press, 2006. The first of seven books on various aspects of Franklin's

writings, this volume focuses on Franklin's works until the age of twenty-four. In addition to his writings, Lemay details the colonial politics and the difficult religious relations in the colonies during Franklin's lifetime.

McCormick, Blaine. *Ben Franklin—America's Original Entrepreneur: Franklin's Autobiography Adapted for Modern Times.* Irvine, Calif.: Entrepreneur Press, 2005. One of the most fascinating accounts of Franklin's business ability and how it is applicable to those starting a twenty-first century business.

Pangle, Lorriane Smith. *The Political Philosophy of Benjamin Franklin.* Baltimore: Johns Hopkins University Press, 2007. Written by a professor at the University of Texas at Austin, this book reflects her interest in Franklin's ideas about how economic conditions affect liberty, especially how citizens view their work and the value of their contributions to their country. Presents many of Franklin's views on Christianity, God, and eternal life.

See also: Moses Brown; Paul Cuffe; Elias Hasket Derby; John Hancock; Robert Morris; William Penn; George Washington.

HENRY CLAY FRICK
American industrialist, entrepreneur, and art patron

Frick embodied the American Gilded Age robber baron in the means he employed to amass his fortune. This image, however, contrasts with the primary use of his wealth, which was collecting art and providing for the museum that displays his collection.

Born: December 19, 1849; West Overton, Pennsylvania
Died: December 2, 1919; New York, New York
Sources of wealth: Steel; investments
Bequeathal of wealth: Children; museum; educational institution; charity

EARLY LIFE

Henry Clay Frick was born in 1849 in West Overton, Westmoreland County, Pennsylvania, where he was also raised. The second of six children of Elizabeth Overholt and John Frick, Frick was named in honor of Henry Clay, the U.S. senator from Kentucky and the leader of the Whig Party. Described as a frail child, Frick was prone to

bouts of "inflammatory rheumatism," which left him in a weakened state for extended periods of time.

While considered an average student, Frick excelled in mathematics. For a brief period in 1866, he attended Otterbein College in Westerville, Ohio. His interest, though, was in obtaining the knowledge that would help him attain his childhood dream of being a millionaire before he died. He was inspired by his grandfather, Abraham Overholt, who owned a distillery and was one of the richest men in Westmoreland County.

FIRST VENTURES

While Frick's grandfather was a wealthy man, his immediate family was not. The opportunities available to Frick paid rather modestly, but he was a hard worker, which caught the eye of his grandfather, who offered him a better paying job as a bookkeeper in the distillery. It was not long, however, before his grandfather died, and Frick was once again looking for a job.

He found a new one with a cousin, Abraham Tintsman, who owned coal fields southeast of Pittsburgh, Pennsylvania, and was in the business of producing coke, which is made by baking coal to remove impurities and is used in the production of steel. Only a marginally profitable business at the time, Frick got in on the ground floor of the growing steel industry in the Pittsburgh area. Initially borrowing from his family, who had inherited money from his grandfather, Frick became a partner in Tintsman's business in 1871. Frick's determination and business acumen expanded the business and his share of it.

The recession of 1873 devastated the steel industry, and, in turn, the coke business. However, through his vigilance in keeping costs low and his ties to lenders, such as Thomas Mellon, Frick was able to expand his business during these difficult times and emerge from them with about 25 percent of the nation's coke-producing capacity and much of the best coal. By his thirtieth birthday in 1879, Frick had attained his childhood dream and was worth $1 million.

MATURE WEALTH

With the expansion of the steel industry in the Pittsburgh area, Frick's coke business continued to grow. Given coke's importance in the production of steel, it seemed natural that the two industries would forge closer ties. Frick's largest buyer was Andrew Carnegie's growing steel empire. In 1882, Frick and Carnegie joined forces, with Frick acquiring an interest in Carnegie's small coke business and Carnegie acquiring an interest in Frick's company. Closer ties between the two companies proved to be very profitable for both but trying for each.

In Carnegie, Frick gained a partner with funds to allow the further expansion of his coke business; with Frick, Carnegie gained a talented businessman with the ability to cut costs and enlarge his steel business. The union of these two self-made men, though, was not always harmonious. In 1887, workers in the coke industry went on strike. Siding with his fellow coke producers, Frick would not give in to their demands. The disruption in coke production idled steel production, which prompted Carnegie, with his now controlling share in Frick's company, to settle with the workers. In response, Frick choose to resign rather than give in to Carnegie's demand for a settlement.

When the strike was finally settled, and the other coke producers conceded to provide a lower wage than the salary Carnegie had agreed to pay, Carnegie found that Frick had been right and wanted to get him back. By early 1889, Frick not only was back running the coke

business but also was the chairman of the steel business, which came with a larger share of ownership. With Frick now firmly in control of the management of both businesses, he continued to apply his aggressive strategy of containing costs and buying out competitors when opportunities arose.

As the demand for steel for railroads and construction expanded, Frick's strategy for growth and integration of the various parts of the business proved to be very profitable. By 1891, Carnegie Steel was producing more than 20 percent of the steel in the United States. Growing profits did not lessen Frick's resolve to cut costs when possible. His determination was demonstrated in 1892, when workers went on strike at the Homestead steel mill. Unwilling to continue negotiations with the union representing the striking workers once his offer was rejected, Frick brought in employees of the Pinkerton National Detective Agency to regain control of the mill. When the detectives were confronted by the armed striking workers, the battle that ensued resulted in the deaths of ten people, with another sixty wounded. Ultimately victorious in crushing the union, Frick helped tip the balance in the struggle between labor and management in favor of management.

The growth in profits did not lessen the on-again, off-again tension between Frick and Carnegie. With Frick resigning as chairman of Carnegie Steel in 1894 and Charles M. Schwab in charge and adding to the profitability of the company, the relationship between Frick and Carnegie continued to deteriorate. Following an unsuccessful attempt by a group that included Frick to buy Carnegie's share of the business, and continued tensions between Frick's coke company and Carnegie's steel company over the price of coke, Carnegie in 1900 attempted to use a provision of the partners' agreement to force Frick to sell his shares of the business at book value, only a fraction of the market value. Frick triumphed in the fight that followed, and all the partners profited when J. P. Morgan bought Carnegie Steel and integrated it into the newly formed United States Steel Corporation (better known as U.S. Steel) in 1901.

Frick's share of the new company amounted to $61.4 million, of which about half represented his share of Carnegie Steel and the remainder his share of the coke company. This amount was significantly more than the $1.5 million that Carnegie offered for Frick's shares in the steel company when he had tried to force him to sell.

In the years before his death, Frick sold off nearly all of his shares in U.S. Steel to buy interests in railroads, which he referred to as the "Rembrandts of investment."

FRICK COLLECTION, NEW YORK CITY

Inspired by the Wallace Collection in London, which Henry Clay Frick first visited with Andrew Mellon in 1880, and by Isabella Stewart Gardner's activities at Fenway Court in Boston, the Frick Collection is the lasting legacy of Frick's passion for collecting art. Frick bequeathed 131 paintings and numerous drawings, prints, and decorative objects to establish a public gallery after his death. Housed in the collector's New York City mansion on Fifth Avenue at Seventieth Street, the museum showcases Frick's excellent taste in fine art and his personal preferences in acquiring works. Frick's move to New York in 1905 was, in part, a result of his desire to move his growing art collection out of Pittsburgh, with its soot-filled air.

Frick first began to collect art in the early 1880's, purchasing a clock designed by Louis Comfort Tiffany and a landscape painting by local artist George Hetzel for his Pittsburgh apartment. Like most of America's captains of industry during the Gilded Age, as his wealth increased, his tastes turned mainly to the Old Masters, with a focus on Italian, French, English, Spanish, Flemish, and Dutch art of the sixteenth through eighteenth centuries. He began to acquire such works beginning in the mid-1890's, purchasing paintings primarily from established dealers, Roland Knoedler and Joseph Duveen in New York.

Like many of his era, he sought and followed the advice of famed connoisseur Bernard Berenson. However, unlike some of his peers, who collected art only as a symbol of their cultural "arrival" or as an investment, Frick approached his hobby with a deep personal interest, asking to have works sent to his mansion "on approval" so he could live with them and see how he liked them prior to finalizing a purchase. Many of the works in his collection served as visual reminders of important events, places, or people in Frick's life, such as his daughter Martha, who died at a young age, which had a profound impact on him.

Among the highlights of the collection are Diego Velázquez's painting of Philip IV of Spain; works by Giovanni Bellini, El Greco, Agnolo Bronzino, Rembrandt, Jan Vermeer, and Sir Joshua Reynolds; and a room from Grasse, France, decorated by French rococo-style painter Jean-Honoré Fragonard with a series of panels depicting *The Progress of Love*, which once belonged to J. P. Morgan. The latter purchase was especially fitting, as Fragonard's work is also among the highlights of the Wallace Collection. However, Frick also exhibited more progressive taste in art, purchasing works by Édouard Manet and Edgar Degas and amassing a notable collection of works by American expatriate James McNeill Whistler.

In addition to the legacy of his own collection, Frick also influenced his younger friend from Pittsburgh, Andrew Mellon, to collect art, personally introducing him to the dealer Joseph Duveen in Manhattan. Mellon's collection is today the centerpiece of the National Gallery of Art in Washington, D.C., and reveals the same excellent taste and eye for quality exhibited by his mentor.

By 1906, Frick was the largest private owner of railroad stocks in the world.

At the time of his death in 1919, Frick's estate was estimated to be worth nearly $150 million, with financial assets valued at $77.5 million and his art collection at $50 million. His New York City home and $15 million were destined to become the Frick Collection, the museum that in the twenty-first century continued to house a substantial part of his art collection. In addition, about one-sixth of his estate went to family members, with his daughter Helen Clay Frick the major beneficiary. The remainder of his estate was distributed to Princeton University, Harvard University, the Massachusetts Institute of Technology, a number of hospitals in the New York City and Pittsburgh areas, and various other public philanthropies.

LEGACY

The name of Henry Clay Frick is associated with the means he used to acquire his wealth and the institution he endowed to display it. In his legal but ruthless dealings with labor and competitors, Frick's business life helped define the term "robber baron." In the final year of his life, he played a role in the defeat of the League of Nations, which he felt would subordinate the United States to the will of lesser countries. The Frick Collection stands as his most enduring legacy, displaying the passion he had for art and his desire to share it with the public.

—Randall Hannum

FURTHER READING

Harvey, George. *Henry Clay Frick: The Man*. New York: Scribner's, 1928. A flattering portrayal of Frick's life, this book was written by one of his friends at the request of Frick's family.

Sanger, Martha Frick Symington. *Henry Clay Frick: An Intimate Portrait*. New York: Abbeville Press, 1998. Written by one of Frick's great-granddaughters, this book links Frick's collection of art with events in his public and private lives.

Schreiner, Samuel A. *Henry Clay Frick: The Gospel of Greed.* New York: St. Martin's Press, 1995. This is the first book-length biography written after Helen Clay Frick's death. Her vigilance in protecting Frick's legacy and papers is thought to have dissuaded researchers during her lifetime.

Standiford, Les. *Meet You in Hell: Andrew Carnegie, Henry Clay Frick, and the Bitter Partnership That Transformed America.* New York: Crown Publishers, 2005. Offers an interesting look at the relationship between Carnegie and Frick and how this relationship shaped the foundation of the U.S. steel industry.

Warren, Kenneth. *Triumphant Capitalism: Henry Clay Frick and the Industrial Transformation of America.* Pittsburgh, Pa.: University of Pittsburgh Press, 1996. Presents a scholarly look at Frick's role in shaping the steel industry, as revealed through his business correspondence.

See also: Andrew Carnegie; Isabella Stewart Gardner; Alfred Krupp; Andrew Mellon; J. P. Morgan; Henry Phipps; Charles M. Schwab; Joséphine de Wendel.

ARCHDUKE FRIEDRICH OF AUSTRIA
Austrian aristocrat and military leader

A member of the house of Habsburg, Archduke Friedrich was reputed to be the wealthiest Habsburg from a junior line of the dynasty. His wealth derived from land, investments, palaces, and an extensive art collection.

Born: June 4, 1856; Brno, Moravia (now in the Czech Republic)
Died: December 30, 1936; Ungarisch-Altenburg (now Mosonmagyaróvár), Hungary
Also known as: Archduke Friedrich of Austria; Duke of Teschen
Sources of wealth: Inheritance; real estate; investments
Bequeathal of wealth: Children; confiscated

EARLY LIFE
Archduke Friedrich (FREE-drihk) of Austria, duke of Teschen, was born at the Castle Gross-Seelowitz in the Moravian kingdom of the Austrian Empire. Friedrich was the eldest son of Archduke Karl Ferdinand and Archduchess Elizabeth Franziska of the Teschen line of Habsburgs descended from Karl, the first duke of Teschen, a younger son of Holy Roman Emperor Leopold II. Friedrichs' mother was the daughter of Archduke Ferdinand of the Habsburgs' Italian Modena line. His only sister, Maria Christina, married King Alfonso XII of Spain and was the mother of Alfonso XIII. His younger brothers were Eugen, a military officer and the leader of the Teutonic Knights, and Charles Stephan, a naval officer and landholder in Austrian-ruled Poland.

FIRST VENTURES
Archduke Friedrich was educated by private tutors and pursued a career in Austria's imperial army. He married Princess Isabella of Croÿ, who was from an aristocratic Belgian family, on October 8, 1878. The couple had eight daughters and one son. The death of Friedrich's uncle, Albrecht, duke of Teschen, in 1895 gave Friedrich and his brothers vast estates throughout the Austro-

Archduke Friedrich of Austria. (Hulton Archive/Getty Images)

Hungarian Empire. As the eldest son, Friedrich inherited extensive landholdings at Ungarisch-Altenburg (now Mosonmagyaróvár), Hungary; Belleje and Saybusch (now Żywiec), Poland; Seelowitz (now Židlochovice) and Frýdek-Místek, now in the Czech Republic; and Pressburg (now Bratislava), now in Slovakia, making him one of the largest landowners in the Austro-Hungarian Empire. Friedrich was given his uncle's Vienna residence, the Albertina Palace, with its extensive art collection. Their dynastic status and financial wealth positioned Friedrich and Isabella to pursue advantageous marital alliances for their children.

MATURE WEALTH

With six marriageable daughters (two died in infancy), Archduchess Isabella hoped to marry her eldest daughter, Maria Christina, to Archduke Francis Ferdinand, the nephew and heir to Emperor Francis Joseph I of Austria. The plan backfired when Francis Ferdinand married Isabella's lady-in-waiting, Countess Sophie Chotek, in 1900. None of Isabella's daughters achieved a major dynastic alliance. The family's political ambitions were directed toward the future of their only son, Archduke Albrecht.

The assassination of Francis Ferdinand and Sophie in 1914 resulted in the outbreak of World War I and led Emperor Francis Joseph I to appoint Friedrich the supreme commander of the Austro-Hungarian army. Friedrich was promoted to the rank of general field marshal on December 8, 1914. Friedrich's appointments were viewed as ceremonial, with the actual control of the battlefield in the hands of Franz Conrad von Hötzendorf, chief of staff of the Austro-Hungarian army. Emperor Karl I took over as supreme commander in February, 1917.

LEGACY

The collapse of the Austro-Hungarian Empire in November, 1918, led to the empire's dissolution into the kingdom of Hungary and the republics of Poland, Czech-oslovakia, and Austria, as well as the confiscation of much of Archduke Friedrich's wealth. Austria seized the Albertina Palace and its art collection, eventually permitting Friedrich to remove the palace's furnishings. In 1921, an American syndicate gained control of Friedrich's confiscated property, which had an estimated worth of $200 million. The syndicate argued that this property was private, not state property associated with the former imperial family. It remains unclear how much Friedrich ultimately received from the syndicate's transaction. In 1929, Czechoslovakia reached an undisclosed financial settlement with Friedrich over confiscated land; Hungary permitted the archduke to retain control over his lands there. The furnishings of the Albertina Palace were removed to Friedrich's estate at Mosonmagyaróvár.

Since Hungary was a kingdom without a designated king, Friedrich and Isabella used their financial resources to promote their son Albrecht for the throne. Their plans dissolved when Albrecht made a nondynastic marriage in 1930. Isabella died in 1931 and Friedrich in 1936. His funeral testified to his once influential and financially powerful position, with the largest assemblage of international royalty attending an event in Hungary since World War I. What remained of his Teschen estates was divided among his surviving children, with Albrecht receiving the largest share.

—*William A. Paquette*

FURTHER READING

Brook-Shepherd, Gordon. *The Last Empress*. New York: HarperCollins, 1991.

_____. *The Last Habsburg*. New York: Weybright and Talley, 1968.

Snyder, Timothy. *The Red Prince*. New York: Basic Books, 2008.

See also: Nikolaus Esterházy.

JAKOB FUGGER
German banker and merchant

Fugger created the most famous and wealthy family merchant enterprise in Europe in the early sixteenth century. Through his banking system, he established a close financial relationship with the Habsburg rulers, who allowed him to gain a monopoly on the copper and silver trades. His money helped elect German emperors and archbishops and allowed him to establish an Augsburg settlement for the working poor.

Born: March 6, 1459; Augsburg, Bavaria (now in Germany)
Died: December 30, 1525; Augsburg, Bavaria
Also known as: Jakob the Rich; Jakob Fugger II; Jacob Fugger
Sources of wealth: Banking; trade
Bequeathal of wealth: Relatives; charity

EARLY LIFE
Jakob Fugger (YAHK-ob FUHG-ehr) was born on March 6, 1459, in the free imperial city of Augsburg, Germany. He was the seventh and youngest son of Jakob Fugger the Elder and Barbara Basinger and the grandson of Hans Fugger, a weaver. Hans moved to Augsburg in 1367 and nine years later became a weaver guild master and subsequently a merchant. His two sons, Andreas and Jakob the Elder, carried on the family trade and worked together for almost two decades. After they separated in 1454, Andreas's son eventually went bankrupt, while Jakob the Elder founded a prosperous family textiles business. After Jakob the Elder's death in 1469, his ten-year-old son Jakob prepared for an ecclesiastical career, and he later took his first orders in a Franconian monastery. After all but two of his brothers died, Jakob was recalled from the monastery to join the family business in 1478.

FIRST VENTURES
Textile trade and production was the key to Augsburg's wealth in the fifteenth century. Locally produced linen was combined with cotton imported from Venice to produce a mixture called *Barchent*. After the death of Jakob the Elder, who was the seventh-richest man in Augsburg, his oldest son Ulrich and his widow continued the family business. In 1478, the surviving sons Ulrich and Georg introduced Jakob the Younger to the family business and sent him to be apprenticed in Venice and Rome. In 1479, Jakob returned to Augsburg and was put

in charge of the firm's Italian trade, and during the next two years he traveled to the various branches of the firm. Most important for the future development of the Fugger fortune, by the mid-1480's he was urging the firm to take part in the iron, silver, and copper mining trade in Salzburg and Tyrol (a region in the Alps that is now part of Austria and Italy).

MATURE WEALTH
Trade in woven goods, silks, and velvets continued to be important to the Fugger business, but far more valuable for the massive expansion of the firm's wealth was its involvement in credit and mining operations. While Jakob's older brothers proposed some of the firm's credit transactions with Rome and the Habsburgs, the successful and astonishingly profitable trade in copper and silver resulted from Jakob's initiatives. He was the driving force behind the Fugger exploitation of the copper and silver production in central and Eastern Europe. Until the 1550's, when the Spanish American mines produced significant amounts of silver, Tyrol and Hungary had the largest silver and copper mining production facilities in Europe.

Banking and mining were closely interwoven, since the Fuggers obtained mining interests and general support from rulers in exchange for loaning these nobles money. The Fuggers had had mining interests in Salzburg since 1480, but Jakob in 1485 was instrumental in directing the firm into the precious metal trade in Tyrol. On December 5, 1485, the Fuggers entered into a business arrangement with Count Sigmund of Tyrol, who was deeply in debt because of his war with Venice. The Fuggers quickly gained control of most of the silver trade in Tyrol. Jakob, who was considered the representative of the firm in Tyrol, played a crucial role in protecting the firm's metal interests in the region after Count Sigmund was forced to give up his throne on March 16, 1490. A secret Fugger financial arrangement with Sigmund's successor as ruler of Tyrol, the Habsburg emperor Maximilian I, protected the firm's interest in the region.

Between 1487 and 1497, the Fuggers earned more than 400,000 gold gulden from the silver trade in Tyrol. In 1522, Jakob expanded his silver and copper trade in the region by obtaining and directly exploiting mining properties. The symbiotic relationship between the Fuggers and the Habsburg rulers was crucial for the welfare of the Fugger firm over the next four decades and it was

THE FUGGEREI ENCLAVE

Jakob Fugger established three foundations—two for religious institutions and the third, the Fuggerei, for the working poor. The Catholic religious foundations—a chapel in St. Anna Monastery and a sermon fund for St. Moritz Church in Augsburg—were lost to the Protestants, but the housing project, the Fuggerei, survived the Protestant Reformation in Augsburg and continued the memory of the Fuggers.

On February 26, 1516, Jakob purchased property from a widow on the outskirts of Augsburg. At the same time, he made a contract with the city council which mentioned the housing foundation. He (and his heirs) agreed to pay taxes for the settlement area, but he was given tax relief on the structures he built and improved in that space. In an additional stipulation, the housing project was never to be under the control of the church.

Between 1517 and 1523, fifty-two single-story row houses were constructed. Forty-three houses were duplexes, with one family living downstairs and another upstairs. Each family had a living space of forty-five square meters. With one exception, all had backyard gardens where residents could keep small animals.

In 1521, Jakob issued a document establishing rules for the settlement. The housing project was designed for citizens of Augsburg who were pious Catholics and poor workers or artisans. The residents could not be welfare recipients. Each family was obligated to pay one gulden rent a year, which was equal to the monthly salary of a day laborer. The tenants signed a written commitment to pray daily for Jakob and his family; unlike residents of medieval poor houses, Jakob's tenants prayed in the privacy of their homes. A caretaker, whose residence was the gatehouse of the settlement, was hired to maintain the buildings. The settlement was administered by two male members of the Fugger family and two men selected from outside the family. In a subsequent testament in 1525, Jakob obligated his nephews to maintain the homes.

In 1531, Alexander Berner first referred to the settlement as "the Fuggerei." The settlement had a wider range of residents than traditional housing for the poor, which accommodated only old men or widows. Moreover, it provided more than the traditional one room by offering three rooms to a family, and each family had its own entrance. Most of the inhabitants were artisans or day laborers with families. Jakob's motive for establishing the Fuggerei was both religious and social. The project aimed to help hard workers and their families who were "house poor."

On February 25, 1944, Allied bombers destroyed half of the original homes and damaged the rest. In 1946, reconstruction began with the support of the original foundation capital, and during the next five years much of the facility was rebuilt and modernized, eventually becoming an old-age settlement limited to married couples and widows.

The housing complex continues to operate into the twenty-first century. Residents must be Catholic, at least fifty-five years old, and have lived in Augsburg for twenty years, and they are required to pray. The original Latin inscription at the entrance of the Fuggerei continues to pay homage to Jakob and his brothers, Ulrich and Georg.

---

fundamental to the Habsburgs' European political ambitions. In 1519, Jakob bribed the German electors to ensure the election of the Habsburg ruler Charles I of Spain as Charles V, Holy Roman Emperor.

Jakob's business ventures in Hungary proved to be even more profitable than those in Tyrol. Exploiting the rich copper mines in Slovakia (then part of Hungary) required both technical knowledge and vast investments. Jakob established a relationship with a Hungarian mining specialist, Johann Thurzo, who had leased several mines near Neusohl, Hungary (now in Slovakia) and was able to extract water from the mines. In 1495, Jakob organized a Fugger-Thurzo consortium to mine and trade the Hungarian copper and silver. To cement the business arrangement, Thurzo's son and daughter married members of the Fugger family. The mined copper was later sold as sheets and plates, while the silver went to the Hungarian mint, Venice, Nuremberg, and Leipzig. The Hungarian operations were immensely profitable, earning a total of 1.5 million gold gulden. When the Imperial Diet of Germany attempted to charge the Fuggers with illegal monopoly practices, the Habsburg rulers Maximilian I and Charles V protected the family firm. On May 13, 1523, Charles V issued a mandate from Toledo, Spain, declaring that the concentrated wholesale trade in ores was not a monopoly.

In 1494, Ulrich, Georg, and Jakob pooled their capital and formed a family trading partnership, granting equal rights to all of the brothers. In honor of the oldest brother, the firm was named Ulrich Fugger and Brothers of Augsburg. In 1502, when the contract was renewed, Jakob emerged as the clear leader of the partnership. After the death of his last surviving brother in 1510, Jakob on December 30, 1512, negotiated a contract with his nephews and renamed the firm Jakob Fugger and Brothers' Sons.

In addition to his metal trade, Jakob continued to profit from the transfer of church funds from Germany to Rome. Jakob also obtained financial interests in Spain from Charles V. Between 1511 and 1527, the income of the Fugger family firm increased by 927 percent. Jakob used some of his wealth to acquire vast landholdings, and in 1511 and 1514 he was granted titles of nobility from the Habsburg emperor. His marriage to Sybille Artzt in 1498 lasted for almost three decades but the couple did not have any children. Suffering from a growth below the navel and realizing that little time was left, Jakob wrote his last will on December 22, 1525, naming his nephew Anton as his successor as the head of the Fugger family firm. Jakob died on December 30, 1525, remaining true to the Catholic faith in an increasingly Protestant Augsburg.

LEGACY

In 1460, the Medici Bank of Florence was the most influential business organization in Europe. One century later, the Fugger firm had replaced the Medici as Europe's largest firm. These capitalists of the Renaissance played a key role in the economic expansion of Europe in the fifteenth and sixteen centuries. However, after the death of Anton Fugger, the Fugger commercial fortune declined and eventually vanished when the bankrupt Habsburgs defaulted on their loans. The Fuggers became titled landlords.

The prosperity of central Europe during Jakob's lifetime was undermined by the religious conflict between Catholics and Protestants. Jakob inadvertently contributed to this conflict by financing the election of Albrecht von Brandenburg as archbishop of Mainz. In order to recoup Jakob's investment, the pope increased the sale of indulgences and allowed the Fuggers to collect half of this income, a decision that unleashed the fury of Martin Luther and his followers. After Jakob's death, Augsburg became a Protestant city.

—Johnpeter Horst Grill

FURTHER READING

Crossen, Cynthia. *The Rich and How They Got That Way: How the Wealthiest People of All Times from Genghis Khan to Bill Gates Made Their Fortunes.* New York: Crown Business, 2000. The author, an editor at *The Wall Street Journal,* devotes one of her ten chapters to "Money Begets Money: Jacob Fugger." Bibliography.

Hanson, Michele Zelinsky. *Religious Identity in an Early Reformation Community: Augsburg, 1517-1555.* Boston: Brill, 2008. Important for understanding the Protestant impact on Jakob Fugger's two religious charities. Bibliography, index.

Koenigsberger, H. G., and G. T. Mosse. *Europe in the Sixteenth* Century. New York: Holt, Rinehart, and Winston, 1969. Scholarly chapter on "Economic and Social Life" examines the business and social activities of European merchants, with numerous references to Jakob Fugger. Bibliography and index.

Matthews, George T., ed. *The Fugger Newsletter.* New York: Capricorn, 1970. Correspondence from Fugger's agents providing information on family business activities and European affairs between 1568 and 1604. Scholarly introduction by Matthews.

Smith, Pamela H., and Paula Findlen, eds. *Merchants and Marvels: Commerce, Science and Art in Early Modern Europe.* New York: Routledge, 2002. Includes a scholarly chapter by Mark A. Meadows on Hans Jakob Fugger, the nephew of Anton Fugger, who collected exotica during the sixteenth century. Illustrated, notes, index.

Strieder, Jacob. *Jacob Fugger the Rich: Merchant and Banker of Augsburg, 1459-1525.* 1931. Reprint. [Hamden, Conn.]: Archon Books, 1966. Still the best short introduction to Jakob Fugger's life available in English. Bibliography, index, and appendix.

See also: Agostino Chigi; Francesco Datini; Lorenzo de' Medici; Jacopo de' Pazzi; Filippo Strozzi; Bartholomeus Welser.

ERNEST GALLO
American vintner

The son of Italian immigrants, Gallo was the driving force and business genius behind the wine company that he founded with his brother Julio. From the cheap Thunderbird to wine coolers to expensive imports, the E. & J. Gallo Winery shaped wine tastes in contemporary America.

Born: March 18, 1909; Jackson, California
Died: March 6, 2007; Modesto, California
Sources of wealth: Manufacturing; sale of products
Bequeathal of wealth: Children; medical research

EARLY LIFE
Ernest Gallo (EHR-nehst GAL-loh) was born in 1909 in Jackson, California, the first of three sons of Italian immigrants Giuseppe "Joe" Gallo and Assunta "Susie" Biano Gallo, whose parents ran a family winery. After a five-year separation provoked by Joe's violence, Susie and Joe reconciled and the family moved to Oakland, where Joe ran a small wine company, a retail liquor business, a saloon, and a hotel. When Prohibition neared, Joe sold his businesses and bought vineyard property in Antioch, California, anticipating that raising and selling wine grapes would remain a legal activity. Ernest and his younger brother Julio were forced to work from sunrise to after dark in the vineyards, attending public schools in the middle of the day. During Prohibition, Joe became involved in various bootlegging schemes with his brother, Michelo (Mike), a flamboyant hustler who served several prison sentences.

In 1925, after purchasing forty acres in Modesto, California, that would become the enduring home base of the Gallo family, Joe went into the grape shipping business. Ernest accompanied his father and the wine shipments to the Chicago exchange. The teenager immediately plunged into selling and demonstrated his abilities as a shrewd businessman. He returned to high school, graduated with honors, and enrolled in agricultural courses at Modesto Junior College. In 1927, Ernest went to Chicago alone, delighted with his new responsibilities and independence, for his father still bullied him at home.

FIRST VENTURES
In 1929, Joe built underground tanks to save his harvest, essentially starting a winery, which was illegal. He shipped wine under the legal "juice" label. Ernest wanted to partner with his father but was rejected. Another source of tension was Joe's treatment of his youngest son. Born in 1919, Joe, Jr., was his father's favorite and suffered none of the abuse leveled at the two older boys.

In 1930, Ernest announced his plans to enter the wine business after Prohibition was repealed and to marry Amelia Franzia, the daughter of a wealthy winery owner. The couple spent their honeymoon at the 1931 grape market in Chicago. Anticipating the December, 1933, repeal of Prohibition, Ernest filed an application to open a bonded wine storeroom, but the petition was denied because he did not own a bonded winery. That same month, Joe and Sallie were found dead of gunshot wounds at the run-down home in Fresno to which they had moved suddenly and secretly months before. Officially the deaths were recorded as murder-suicide, but there was speculation then and later that the Gallos had been ordered killed by the syndicate. The older brothers became guardians of young Joe, Jr., and Ernest imposed a code of silence on the family regarding the shocking deaths.

Twenty-four-year-old Ernest was granted permission to continue his father's business. He and his brother Julio formed a partnership, the E. & J. Gallo Winery, excluding Joe, Jr. During an interview with an inspector from the Bureau of Alcohol, Tobacco, and Firearms, Ernest claimed he did not know Mike Gallo, an uncle who was serving a prison sentence for bootlegging, later amending his statements to say that Mike "had been removed from us as a relative." With a craving for respectability and a knack for revisionist history, Ernest moved forward with his grandiose plans to build Gallo into the largest winery in the state and then the nation.

By 1935, the Gallo winery was producing an annual yield of 350,000 gallons. Ernest sometimes traveled five months at a time, working grueling hours and expecting others to do likewise. In the winter of 1936, he was hospitalized for exhaustion; his six-month hospital stay became one of many Gallo secrets. After his convalescence, Ernest returned with his typical vigor, adding a distillery, expanding production to a full array of sweet, fortified wines and table wines, and purchasing a distribution company in New Orleans, making it the first Gallo-controlled distributor. The entrepreneur was determined to learn how to build, market, and sell a brand. He spent the winter of 1940-1941 interviewing businessmen; from these contacts Ernest devised an intensive and carefully structured sales program that broke new ground in marketing strategies. In March, 1942, Ernest applied for the first trademark Gallo name and claimed it had been used continuously by his family since 1909. Company restructuring papers filed in 1944 listed the winery's capital stock at $500,000, with the home and vineyards valued at $760,000. A division of labor had been set, with Ernest in charge of sales and marketing and Julio supervising the vineyards, the laboratory, and wine production. Their oft-repeated boasts that Julio would "make all the wine you can sell" and Ernest would "sell all the wine you can make" made the arrangement public.

MATURE WEALTH

After World War II, the brothers developed lighter wines sold with aluminum screw-tops to ensure consistent taste. In the 1950's and 1960's, the Gallos used a huge blending vat to create a uniform blend, making the wine's vintage irrelevant. By the early 1950's, the Gallo

winery was America's largest winemaking facility. A light, mellow, red table wine called Vino Paisano di Gallo, sold in a rounded jug bottle, was Gallo's signature product. A bottling plant built in Modesto added to the company's vertical integration pattern.

A micromanager, Ernest demanded full loyalty from his employees, and all middle management reported directly to him. The "three Rs" of Gallo salesmanship, described by one writer as "rigorousness, relentlessness, and ruthlessness," summarized Ernest's approach. In the summer of 1957, Gallo introduced a flavored, fortified wine called Thunderbird that sold for sixty cents a quart. It became an instant hit, especially in poor, urban neighborhoods, and its success pushed production levels to thirty-two million gallons that year. Several years later, Gallo developed Ripple, another low-end product popular with college students.

Although hugely profitable, these street wines undercut Ernest's desire to be seen as a respectable, discerning

Wine storage tanks at the Gallo Winery in Modesto, California, in 1972. (©Bettmann/CORBIS)

THE ERNEST GALLO CLINIC AND RESEARCH CENTER

In 1980, Ernest Gallo, cofounder and co-owner of the E. & J. Gallo Winery, provided a $3 million endowment to establish the Ernest Gallo Clinic and Research Center at the University of California, San Francisco. The facility was founded to investigate the effects of alcohol on the brain and to conduct research in other aspects of neuroscience. The founding director of the clinic and center, physician Ivan Diamond, developed a cellular and molecular biology research program to study the fundamental mechanisms of alcohol. In the late 1990's, after carefully scrutinizing the facility's program, California lawmakers made a major financial allocation to the center. These funds enabled the center to expand its staff and facilities. In 1999, the center moved to a newly built space in Emeryville, California.

The second director, Raymond White, joined the center in 2002. White, an expert in human genetic mapping, and his colleagues in the human genetics laboratory developed large sets of genetic data from which they could identify key components of susceptibility to alcoholism. Under White's leadership, the center's mission to translate scientific discoveries into clinical applications had been strengthened.

By 2009, the center had grown to employ a staff of more than 155 in its Emeryville location. Facilities included major laboratories in cell biology, biochemistry, molecular biology, pharmacology, neurophysiology, behavioral pharmacology, and physiology, as well as in invertebrate, mouse, and human genetics. The center had expanded beyond its initial research in alcoholism to study the effects of substance abuse. In addition to its research mission, the center's goal is to play an important part in the development of new and more effective therapies to treat the serious national health problems of alcoholism and substance abuse.

---

vintner. He launched a "Beautiful Wines" campaign, featuring Gallo's first champagne, Eden Roc, in 1966, as well as "Gallo's Gourmet Trio": Hearty Burgundy, Chablis Blanc, and Pink Chablis. Delighted to be featured with his brother on the cover of *Time* in 1972, Ernest was dismayed by the story's emphasis on Gallo's "pop wine." In an effort to change the company's image, Ernest also began hiring executives with master's degrees in business administration and experience in consumer sales.

The 1970's began with enormous expansion and a stream of successful new products. However, the company suffered from the national boycott against Gallo wine that César Chávez, leader of the United Farm Workers, began in 1973 because of Gallo's support of the International Brotherhood of Teamsters. In February,

1974, 100,000 people marched on the Gallo "temple" in Modesto to protest the company's policies. Chávez finally terminated the boycott in 1978. During this same period the winery was investigated by the Federal Trade Commission (FTC) for alleged intrusion into distributors' business and alleged illegal practices by its sales force. The FTC ordered monthly inspections of Gallo records in order to monitor company activities. Sales leveled during the tumultuous 1970's, but by 1981 Gallo led nationally in wine sales, shipping 131 million gallons.

Ernest increased his involvement in politics. During 1989 and 1990, the Gallo family contributed more to federal candidates ($294,110) than any other American family. While his sons attended Norte Dame and Stanford Universities, Ernest gave large gifts to each school. He also provided a $3 million endowment to establish a clinic and research center in his name at the University of California at San Francisco.

In 1983, Ernest and Julio's younger brother, rancher Joe Gallo, Jr., launched Joseph Gallo Cheese Company. After a series of unresolved negotiations regarding the use of the Gallo name on these cheese products, Ernest and Julio filed a complaint against Joe and his son Mark, who was co-owner of the company. Joe and Mark countersued to obtain one-third of the winery's ownership, which was valued at more than $200 million. Litigation continued for several years until a final injunction enjoined Joe and Mark from using the Gallo name as a trademark. The brothers remained estranged for the rest of their lives.

In the early 1990's, the winery expanded its vineyard properties, which would eventually encompass ten thousand acres, and continued its pattern of buying grapes from independent growers. New Gallo vintage-dated varietals and premium wines were introduced, increasing the Gallo share of the premium market. The company ranked number one in sales, with an estimated 4.3 million cases sold in 1991, but the majority of Gallo profit continued to come from street wines. In the next decade the company shifted its emphasis, importing wine and also exporting millions of cases of wine to scores of countries each year.

In 2006, *Forbes* magazine estimated Ernest's net worth at $1.2 billion. The next year Ernest died at his home in Modesto, just days before his ninety-eighth birthday.

LEGACY

Along with his brother Julio, Ernest Gallo created a wine empire during seven decades. Known for his somber dedication to work and his often ruthless practices, Ernest was a skilled entrepreneur and a master of marketing strategies. However, this single-minded ambition resulted in bitter litigation against his youngest brother and tore the family apart.

— Carolyn Anderson

FURTHER READING

Conaway, James. *Napa: The Story of an American Eden.* 2d ed. Boston: Houghton Mifflin, 2002. Provides good background on the history of California wineries.

Hawkes, Ellen. *Blood and Wine: The Unauthorized Story of the Gallo Wine Empire.* New York: Simon & Schuster, 1993. A detailed family biography with fifty-three pages of endnotes, as well as photographs. Sympathetic to Joe, Jr.'s, side in the litigation with his older brothers.

Henderson, Bruce, with Ernest Gallo and Julio Gallo. *Ernest & Julio: Our Story.* New York: Times Books, 1994. A rags-to-riches story, substantially embellished, mostly told by Ernest.

Time. "American Wine: There's Gold in Them Thar Grapes." November 27, 1972. Cover story on the success of the Gallo winery. Claims that six Gallo brands accounted for 90 percent of the sixty million gallons of "pop wine" sold in 1971.

Tucille, James. *Gallo Be Thy Name: The Inside Story of How One Family Rose to Dominate the U.S. Wine Market.* Beverly Hills, Calif.: Phoenix Books, 2009. Written by an American business authority, this social history pictures Ernest as a thug and a genius. Considers the parents' death a mob hit.

See also: Emilio Bacardi; Edgar Bronfman, Sr.; Samuel Bronfman; Adolphus Busch; Clarence Dillon; Edward Cecil Guinness.

ISABELLA STEWART GARDNER
American art patron

Gardner was a fashionable figure in Boston society and a patron of the arts. She befriended famous writers and artists and was the subject of a celebrated portrait by John Singer Sargent. In 1903, five years after her husband's death, she used his wealth to open her world-renowned museum.

Born: April 14, 1840; New York, New York
Died: July 17, 1924; Boston, Massachusetts
Also known as: Isabella Stewart (birth name);
   Mrs. Jack; Donna Isabella; Isabella of Boston
Source of wealth: Inheritance
Bequeathal of wealth: Museum

EARLY LIFE

Isabella Stewart Gardner was born in 1840 in New York City. Her father, David Stewart, made his fortune in the Irish linen trade and in mining investments, and her mother, Adelia Smith, came from a successful farming family. Educated in private schools, Gardner developed an interest in art at a young age and even then dreamed of creating some sort of house for her art. She spent part of her early life in Paris, where she met Julia Gardner, the sister of her future husband, John ("Jack") Lowell Gardner, who would be quite willing to place his fortune at her disposal in acquiring the art that quickly became the focus of her life.

The friendship with Julia led directly to Isabella's marriage to Jack, whom she met at a family gathering in Paris. The couple settled in his hometown of Boston. Depressed after the early death of her son, Gardner traveled widely in the United States, Europe, Asia, and the Middle East. However, Venice, a meeting ground for many expatriate American artists, became her favorite place. Her love of antiques and Italian art by the Old Masters and her admiration for the intimate palazzi of the city all contributed to her decision to establish her own highly personal museum at her residence, Fenway Court, and to make that site a place where the public could appreciate art masterpieces.

FIRST VENTURES

Unlike many other wealthy men and women of her generation, Gardner did not merely collect art. She also sponsored and lavishly entertained artists, buying their work and making a public spectacle of how she used her wealth. She was treated like American royalty and given nicknames, such as Donna Isabella and Isabella of Boston. Indeed, she claimed (without much foundation) to be a descendant of the Stuart royal family of England and Scotland.

Gardner and her husband began buying art in the 1880's. Although Gardner would eventually be known for her collection of famous paintings, she initially spent her fortune on tapestries, sculpture, antiques, stained glass, mantelpieces, silver, ceramics, doors, photographs, and manuscripts—all kinds of items that resulted in the rebuilding on American soil of a European style of life and architecture. In this way, Gardner became the forerunner of other great American art collectors like William Randolph Hearst, whose "castle" not only contained great works of art but also was constructed along the lines of classical European architecture.

MATURE WEALTH

In 1891, Gardner's father died, and she inherited a fortune of $2.1 million (estimated to be worth as much as $40 million in 2010). Although it was already clear to Gardner that she wanted to create a very personal and intimate home and museum that would showcase her art, she had to consider carefully how her scheme could compete with the collections of other wealthy art patrons, especially Henry Clay Frick, Andrew Mellon, and J. P. Morgan. These men possessed fortunes that were easily thirty times as large as hers.

Just as worrisome were the art brokers, who often bilked their clients by selling them fake masterpieces. Indeed, Gardner and her husband had been so victimized in 1888. Not until Gardner began dealing in 1894 with Bernard Berenson, an art collector himself and considered a world authority on Italian Renaissance art, did Gardner begin in earnest to acquire a collection of great works that would eventually take their place in her museum. With Berenson's guidance, Gardner began to acquire the work of Rembrandt, Titian, Édouard Manet, and other Renaissance and modern masters—in all nearly seventy pieces that would attract worldwide attention and praise.

When Jack Gardner died in 1898, Isabella acquired another fortune that accelerated her plans to open her own museum. She did not, however, simply want a grandiose building to house her art. On the contrary, she wanted a structure built on an intimate scale, so that anyone visiting the museum would think of it as a home of art, which indeed it was, since Fenway Court, the name of Gardner's residence, was indeed her domicile, as well as the site of her art collection.

In the first years of the Isabella Stewart Gardner Museum's existence, it functioned as a rather exclusive site open less than one month a year on days when the public was invited to visit the collection. It was important to Gardner that the display of her wealth and art reflect her own personal sense of beauty and place. In the first two decades of the twentieth century, she established the location for each work of art, a location that was never to be changed, a tribute to the way Gardner used her wealth to shape her sense of beauty and culture.

A case in point is the Dutch room, featuring the work of Rembrandt and his disciples, which became the site of pilgrimage for art lovers. She cunningly had the room placed at the top of a staircase and gave it a Dutch guildhall look, with well-worn ceramic floor tiles, carved wood paneling, silk green-gold fabrics, and late sixteenth cen-

Isabella Stewart Gardner. (Library of Congress)

tury tapestries. Here, paintings by Albrecht Dürer, Hans Holbein the Younger, Sir Anthony van Dyck, and Peter Paul Rubens could be viewed in a setting that resembled the world in which they were created. It was this room that became the main target of a robbery that occurred on March, 1990, when thieves disguised as policemen stole paintings and other artwork estimated to be worth $600 million. Gone were the Gardners' most precious possessions: works by Rembrandt, Jan Vermeer, and other world-famous artists. As of 2010, the case had never been solved, even though there was an outstanding reward of $5 million for information leading to the recovery of the paintings.

These works and many of the others that were not stolen have appreciated in value—so much so that their true worth in monetary terms is almost incalculable. During her lifetime, Gardner might pay $100,000—then a seemingly extravagant sum—for a single painting that would decades later be appraised for millions of dollars.

In 1919, Gardner suffered the first of a series of strokes that would ultimately end her life on July 17, 1924. Aware that she would need to create the financial means to perpetuate her art collection and her museum, she established a $1 million endowment. In the first decades after her death, this endowment, carefully managed, was sufficient to the purposes Gardner had in mind. By the 1960's, however, the Gardner Museum began to suffer from the restrictions placed upon it in her will. Neither the art nor its placement could be significantly altered or sold; for this reason, the Gardner, unlike other museums dealing with a fluctuating economy and art market, as well as the vagaries of fundraising for public institutions, had strained its ability to preserve its collection. The museum also could not acquire art that did not fit into Gardner's range of interests. Similarly, the shrinking endowment resulted in the lax and inadequate security system that made the museum vulnerable to the most spectacular art robbery of the twentieth century.

LEGACY

In spite of the restrictions that Gardner placed on her museum and the 1990 robbery, the Gardner Museum remained one of the great treasure houses of world art. Under astute leadership, temporary exhibits of contemporary art have enhanced the institution's broad appeal to the public. Because the basic physical structure can-

ISABELLA STEWART GARDNER MUSEUM

Isabella Stewart Gardner designed her home and museum to evoke Venetian architecture, in particular the Grand Canal's Palazzo Barbaro. However, instead of attempting to duplicate a Venetian street, in which her building would be approached through a series of arches and columns, she employed the arches and columns motif in an inner courtyard filled with foliage and flowers.

The success of this building has much to do with Gardner's hands-on design. Although she employed an architect, she visited the construction site daily, supervising and, when necessary, even arguing with workmen about various details. She thought nothing of demolishing her own plans when they proved visually unappealing. As a result, her guiding hand created one of the most romantic places in Boston, suffused with the fragrance of jasmine trees and orchids.

Gardner took an entire year to situate her artwork into her new museum-home, making sure that the vases, tables, and other furniture and furnishings were an exact and exquisite match for the paintings, sculpture, and textiles she wanted to display. As many art critics have noted, the building and its art become a kind of performance that is entirely the product of a woman who enjoyed her role as a public figure and benefactor.

Gardner was not shy about showing off her wealth and the world she could create with it. Unlike many accomplished, wealthy persons, she did not elude the press or publicity. She wanted her name, acquisitions, and wealth to meld together in the public mind. Owning and enjoying art, in her view, was one of the great pleasures of the world that the public ought to embrace. She used her fortune for many other charities, and through her museum she established programs for the public that associated her great fortune with the improvement of her community and world.

not be changed, the museum has maintained a historic character that remains an attraction in its own right. Gardner's wish to make the museum seem like a home has been perpetuated by displaying paintings without labels or attributions and with the kind of dim lighting associated with a home rather than with a public building. Thus the proximity to great art that Gardner sought to foster has been honored. In March, 2009, a controversial decision by a Massachusetts court allowed the museum to go ahead with plans for a new building—a clear deviation from Isabella Stewart Gardner's will. Museum officials planned to devote much of the new space to temporary exhibitions and amenities designed to appeal to contemporary museum visitors.

—Carl Rollyson

FURTHER READING

Boser, Ulrich. *The Gardner Heist: The True Story of the World's Largest Unsolved Art Theft*. New York: Collins, 2009. Although Boser focuses on a thorough investigation of suspects and the detectives who seek to solve the Gardner case, his book also contains a sharp portrait of Isabella Stewart Gardner, her world, and her museum.

Goldfarb, Hilliard T. *The Isabella Stewart Gardner Museum: A Companion Guide and History*. New Haven, Conn.: Yale University Press, 1995. A beautifully illustrated and authoritative work.

Shand-Tucci, Douglass. *The Art of Scandal: The Life and Times of Isabella Stewart Gardner*. New York: HarperCollins, 1997. Calls Gardner a pioneering multiculturalist because of her friendships with Jews, homosexuals, and others considered scandalous by Victorian society. As the title suggests, this biography is written in a florid, romantic style.

Tharp, Louise Hall. *Mrs. Jack: A Biography of Isabella Stewart Gardner*. Boston: Isabella Stuart Gardner Museum, 2003. This new edition of a book first published in 1965 is the official biography, comprehensive and authoritative, by a biographer of Boston's important families.

Vigderman, Patricia. *The Memory Palace of Isabella Stewart Gardner*. Louisville, Ky.: Sarabande Books, 2007. Besides providing a detailed tour of the museum, Vigderman describes the important women in Isabella Stewart Gardner's life, including the wives of art connoisseur Bernard Berenson, historian Henry Adams, and Asian expert Ernest Fenellosa.

See also: Henry Clay Frick; J. Paul Getty; Peggy Guggenheim; Solomon R. Guggenheim; Armand Hammer; Andrew Mellon.

JOHN W. GARRETT
American railroad and shipping executive

Garrett, president of the Baltimore and Ohio Railroad during its most prosperous period, transformed it into a profitable company and established Baltimore as a thriving seaport. He also contributed to the founding of Johns Hopkins University and the university's medical school.

Born: July 31, 1820; Baltimore, Maryland
Died: September 26, 1884; Deer Park, Garrett County, Maryland
Also known as: John Work Garrett
Source of wealth: Railroads
Bequeathal of wealth: Children; charity

EARLY LIFE

John Work Garrett was born in Baltimore, Maryland, in 1820. He and his brother Henry eventually became partners with their Irish immigrant father, Robert Garrett, in a mercantile and shipping business, which eventually evolved into banking. John Garrett had an affinity for business, and at nineteen he left college to work with his family. The Garretts were visionary and entrepreneurial, and they expanded their business, acquiring hotels and warehouses, building a steamship that traveled between Baltimore and San Francisco, and developing Balti-

more's port so American goods could be exported to Europe and South America and merchandise could be imported from aboard.

FIRST VENTURES

Garrett's interest in shipping prompted him to become an active stockholder in the Baltimore and Ohio Railroad (B&O). His desire to ensure a positive return for stockholders motivated him to speak out at directors' meetings, asserting his ideas about the railroad's financial operations. His speeches impressed another large stockholder, Johns Hopkins, who nominated Garrett for the presidency of B&O. After being elected to this position, Garrett immediately instituted economic practices that earned the stockholders large dividends, and he promised this would be his consistent goal. Garrett's attention to detail and his many business connections enabled him to fulfill his promise. He maintained the rails in good condition, added train cars, and took advantage of business possibilities which benefited B&O and increased his personal fortune.

MATURE WEALTH

For Garrett, opportunities to strengthen both B&O and his fortune abounded. At the beginning of the Civil War, he realized his business could prosper by its support of the Union. He made the B&O an instrumental force in the war by using the railroad to move troops. He kept workers busy repairing the right-of-way, which was often a target of Confederate attacks. After the war, he purchased old warships, some of which he refitted in order to transport rail materials from Liverpool to Baltimore and to carry grain and coal to Europe. Some of the other warships were adapted for use as passenger ships that brought immigrants to Baltimore. Many of these immigrants were subsequently employed at the B&O. Garrett also invested in coal mines in Cumberland, Maryland, and in the construction of dry docks and grain silos in order to export grain and coal from the Locust Point area of Baltimore. Garrett consistently provided B&O stockholders with better than average dividends.

The most influential man in Maryland, Garrett shaped much of public life in Baltimore. He brought together two of Baltimore's wealthiest men—Hopkins, who was looking for future investments, and George Peabody, a former Baltimore resident who founded the city's Peabody Institute. At Garrett's suggestion, Peabody persuaded Hopkins to appoint a board of trustees, with Garrett as one of its members, in order to establish a university and medical school. The result was the founding of Johns Hopkins University and Johns Hopkins Medical School and Hospital.

Garrett died in September, 1884, at the age of sixty-four, exhausted and bereaved by the death of his beloved wife ten months earlier.

LEGACY

Garrett created a thriving railroad and seaport in Baltimore. He demonstrated how to make money, wield influence, and use his wealth philanthropically. He served on the boards of various charitable organizations, brought the Young Men's Christian Association (YMCA) to Baltimore, and organized the Economic Relief Association of the Baltimore and Ohio Railroad. He facilitated the founding of Johns Hopkins University and its medical school through his influence and his successful railroad, which greatly contributed to the fortune of university namesake Johns Hopkins.

Garrett left his fortune to his children. His daughter Mary Elizabeth raised funds for Johns Hopkins University School of Medicine, providing much of her own fortune to the institution with the stipulation that it admit women. Garrett's grandson bequeathed one of Garrett's magnificent estates, the Evergreen House, to Johns Hopkins University.

—Bernadette Flynn Low

FURTHER READING

Fee, Elizabeth. "Evergreen House and the Garrett Family: A Railroad Fortune." In *The Baltimore Book: New Views of Local History*, edited by Elizabeth Fee, Linda Shopes, and Linda Zeidman. Philadelphia: Temple University Press, 1991.

Johnson, Larry E. "The Baltimore & Ohio Railroad Survived Numerous Hardships of War in Its Service to the Union." *America's Civil War* 19, no. 1 (March, 2006): 14-16.

Sander, Kathleen Waters. *Mary Elizabeth Garrett: Society and Philanthropy in the Gilded Age*. Baltimore: The Johns Hopkins University Press, 2008.

See also: John Insley Blair; Jim Brady; Jay Cooke; Charles Crocker; Jay Gould; Edward H. Harriman; James J. Hill; Johns Hopkins; Mark Hopkins; Collis P. Huntington; Daniel Willis James; George Peabody; George Mortimer Pullman; Russell Sage; Leland Stanford; William Thaw; William Henry Vanderbilt.

BILL GATES
American businessman and philanthropist

Gates, cofounder of Microsoft Corporation, earned his vast wealth through his pioneering work in the personal computer industry. In the twenty-first century, he and his wife Melinda pledged to direct their personal and corporate funds toward ending poverty and disease in Third World countries.

Born: October 28, 1955; Seattle, Washington
Also known as: William Henry Gates III
Sources of wealth: Inheritance; computer industry
Bequeathal of wealth: Spouse; charity

EARLY LIFE

William Henry "Bill" Gates III was the second of three children born to William H. Gates, Sr., an attorney, and Mary Maxwell Gates, a board member of First Interstate Banc System. As the only son of upper-middle-class parents, he was expected (and encouraged) to become a lawyer like his father. He was sent to Lakeside School, an expensive preparatory school, where he was first exposed to computers in the form of an ASR-33 teletype terminal and some time on the General Electric server. His early attempts at computer programing produced a number of simple programs, including a tic-tac-toe game, and impressed school officials. In 1971, Gates's early manifestation of talent encouraged the Lakeside administration to hire him to write programs for the school's computers, using a programing language that would automate the lengthy process of class assignments. He graduated in 1973, scored 1590 out of 1600 on the Scholastic Aptitude Test (SAT), and decided to continue studying computers at Harvard University.

FIRST VENTURES

At Harvard, Gates continued to exhibit the talent that would enable him to succeed in the developing computer industry. In 1975, Micro Instrumentation and Telemetry Systems (MITS) developed a new microcomputer, the Altair 8800, and Gates, along with partner Paul Allen, saw this as an opportunity to start their own company, Microsoft Corporation. Microsoft pro-

vided the Altair with a suitable operating system called Altair BASIC (Beginner's All-Purpose Symbolic Instruction Code). The company subsequently developed MS-DOS (Microsoft Disk Operating System), which Gates eventually sold to International Business Machines (IBM) for a one-time fee of $50,000.

Altair BASIC and MS-DOS were not, in themselves, particularly profitable to Gates. He was more determined to stalwartly retain the copyrights to these systems in complete disregard for programming conventions of the time, which leaned toward the open-source approach, allowing wide accessibility to a software's source code. Gates cleverly retained all rights to his software in order that he could market MS-DOS not only for use on IBM's personal computers but also for the many IBM imitators that subsequently flooded the market. Gates foresaw an untapped demand for personal computers that even the computer manufacturers themselves had missed, and it was this remarkable foresight and protectiveness over his product that would guarantee him massive returns for his minuscule outlays. Given Gates's immediate success, it is not surprising that when he decided to leave Harvard to

Bill Gates testifies in 2010 before a Senate Foreign Relations Committee hearing on global health. (AP/Wide World Photos)

focus on running Microsoft, his parents gave him their full blessing to pursue his dreams.

MATURE WEALTH

Microsoft went through an extensive restructuring and reincorporation in 1981 with the intention of buttressing the solid sales of MS-DOS, as well as creating a new and more visually oriented version of the system that would appeal to consumers who were not computer programmers and were unhappy with the technical feel of computers. Microsoft and IBM initially created a new operating system, OS/2, but Microsoft eventually dropped out of this project and IBM obtained the exclusive license to this system. OS/2 failed to significantly improve sales of personal computers. On November 20, 1985, Microsoft successfully launched its newly developed Windows OS for retail sale. The new operating system enjoyed immediate and explosive success. After ten years in business, Microsoft made an initial public stock offering in 1986. Eventually, the stock's price would skyrocket, making four of the company's employees billionaires and twelve thousand other employees millionaires. Gates also continued to form inroads into other technological products, like Corbis, a digital imaging company, which he established in 1989.

As he became accustomed to the heady experience of managing such a highly and immediately lucrative business, Gates in 1994 decided to pursue more personal goals. He married Melinda French on January 1 and assisted her in the formation of the influential Bill and Melinda Gates Foundation. With the subsequent birth of three children—two girls and a boy—the couple purchased a sixty-six-thousand-square-foot home in Medina, Washington, and outfitted it appropriately. The $125 million house overlooks Lake Washington, has a sixty-foot swimming pool, and boasts an extensive library intended to house such treasures as Leonardo da Vinci's *Codex Leicester* (one of Leonardo's scientific journals written between 1490 and 1519), bought at auction for $30.8 million. Despite the trappings of wealth implied by its twenty-five-hundred-foot gym and its one-thousand-foot dining room, the home has been described

---

BILL AND MELINDA GATES FOUNDATION

As Bill Gates rose from relative obscurity to extreme wealth, a great deal of social pressure was placed on him to turn his attention to the needs of others. Agreeing that he should be more socially responsible, Gates studied the lives of famous philanthropists like John D. Rockefeller and Andrew Carnegie to decide how his wealth could be invested for its maximum social impact. Discussions with his fiancé, Melinda French, whom he married in 1994, convinced him to sell some of his personal Microsoft Corporation stock and found the William H. Gates Foundation. Although the foundation provided computer equipment to schools serving disadvantaged students throughout the United States, Gates was dissatisfied with the organization's inability to address more deeply rooted global problems. In 2000, his wife persuaded him to combine three family trusts into a larger and more comprehensive entity—the Bill and Melinda Gates Foundation—which would seek global rather than national change in the lives of the impoverished.

The Bill and Melinda Gates Foundation is the largest "transparent" global charity; every dollar donated is openly accounted for, and the foundation's methods are open to the scrutiny of its benefactors. The organization has chosen as its particular project the eventual eradication of malaria, and the foundation is one of the largest purchasers of vaccines for preventable diseases in the Third World. Warren Buffett, a longtime friend and chief executive officer of Berkshire Hathaway, Inc., was so impressed with Gates and his wife's enthusiasm and candor that in 2006 he donated $44 billion to charity, the majority of it earmarked to be released in installments of $1.5 billion per year, to the couple's foundation. By 2007, Bill and Melinda Gates had donated almost $28 billion, making them the second most generous philanthropists in the country.

---

as a welcoming retreat for its family from the notoriously draining aspects of public life. For a man listed in *Forbes* magazine as the wealthiest American from 1995 to 2007, and again in 2009, Gates has resisted the more tawdry temptations of a billionaire's life. He values his privacy and avoids the limelight, having felt the scorn of the media in 1998, when Microsoft was on trial for alleged antitrust violations and Gates was labeled as arrogant and evasive under questioning.

The federal government's antitrust litigation focused on many legal issues regarding Microsoft's allegedly noncompetitive practices. Gates had resolved to remain the exclusive marketer of his company's software. He knew he could not maintain complete and perpetual control over the many aspects of the computer industry, but he was surprised when he failed to anticipate a new demand for user-friendly "gateways" to computer servers and the various communications between servers known as the Internet superhighway. A competing company had launched its entry program, Netscape, to a pleased and appreciative market. Gates responded by making agreements with computer manufacturers to offer his proprietary Internet software, Internet Explorer, to consumers as part of a hardware and software package deal. The creators of Netscape, and others in the computer industry, complained that Gates was monopolizing the available hardware vendors by requiring exclusive contracts—a predatory way of ensuring his product's sales. Judicial review confirmed that Microsoft was maintaining a monopoly and needed to be divided into smaller companies. The federal government filed suit against Microsoft, alleging that Gates's anticompetitive practices enabled him to monopolize the market for computer operating systems.

While division into two companies would not greatly harm Gates, he did not want Microsoft to be split. Fortunately for Gates, in 2001 President George W. Bush offered Microsoft a settlement that would prevent the forced division that Gates's opponents desired. Bush accepted Gates's proposal to step down as chief executive officer of Microsoft and instead become an adviser, assisting the company in its software production. This agreement reduced Gates's workload, providing him more time to focus on philanthropic work.

LEGACY

Gates has said that when he dies, he does not intend for his children to inherit anything more than the relatively small sum of $10 million each, The vast majority of his fortune will be dispersed to a variety of charities performing a wide range of activities, including improving computer facilities in public schools and purchasing and distributing vaccines for use in Third World countries. He prefers that his legacy be a world less ravaged by disease than the provision of funds that could tempt his children to become profligate spendthrifts, interested only in the pursuit of pleasure. Gates has also pledged to work with other charities in order to address public needs that cross traditional boundaries between these organizations. For example, investor Warren Buffett so admired the compassion of Gates and his wife that Buffett also pledged to distribute the bulk of his $44 billion estate toward charitable goals after his death.

—*Julia M. Meyers*

FURTHER READING

Bank, David. *Breaking Windows: How Bill Gates Fumbled the Future of Microsoft.* New York: Free Press, 2001. Describes Microsoft's internal disputes between those who wanted to keep the company dominant by aggressively marketing its operating system, Windows, and those who championed a more open standard that allowed customers to choose among systems.

Dearlove, Des. *Business the Bill Gates Way: Ten Secrets of the World's Richest Business Leader.* New York: Amacom, 1999. Chronicles Gates's life from his college dropout days to his position as the world's richest man.

Manes, Stephen, and Paul Andrews. *Gates: How Microsoft's Mogul Reinvented an Industry—and Made Himself the Richest Man in America.* Beaverton, Oreg.: Touchstone, 2002. Not only includes biographical material about Gates but also recounts his twenty turbulent years in the computer industry.

Raatma, Lucia. *Bill Gates: Computer Programmer and Entrepreneur.* Chicago: Ferguson, 2000. Focuses on Gates's early education and training.

Rivlin, Gary. *The Plot to Get Bill Gates: An Irreverent Investigation of the World's Richest Man—and the People Who Hate Him.* New York: Three Rivers, 2000. Uses Herman Melville's novel *Moby Dick: Or, The Whale* (1851) to describe rivals of Gates and Microsoft.

Slater, Robert. *Microsoft Rebooted: How Bill Gates and Steve Ballmer Reinvented Their Company.* New York: Portfolio, 2004. Describes the government's antitrust trial, Microsoft's loss of employees following the burst of the dot-com bubble, losses during other economic downturns, and the company's attempts to reinvent itself.

See also: Paul Allen; Steven Ballmer; Jeff Bezos; Sergey Brin; Warren Buffett; Andrew Carnegie; Mark Cuban; Michael Dell; Larry Ellison; Steve Jobs; Gordon E. Moore; David Packard; H. Ross Perot; John D. Rockefeller III.

Just Right

American Edition

Jeremy Harmer
& Carol Lethaby

Student's Book

HEINLE
CENGAGE Learning™

Australia • Brazil • Japan • Korea • Mexico • Singapore • Spain • United Kingdom • United States

HEINLE
CENGAGE Learning™

Just Right: Upper Intermediate, Student's Book, American Edition
Jeremy Harmer, Carol Lethaby

ISBN-13: 978-0-462-00023-7

ISBN-10: 0-462-00023-0

Heinle
20 Channel Center Street
Boston, MA 02210
USA

Cengage Learning is a leading provider of customized learning solutions with office locations around the globe, including Singapore, the United Kingdom, Australia, Mexico, Brazil, and Japan. Locate your local office at **www.cengage.com/global**

Cengage Learning products are represented in Canada by Nelson Education, Ltd.

Visit Heinle online at **elt.heinle.com**

Visit our corporate website at **www.cengage.com**

Text acknowledgements
p.8 Dream or Nightmare, based upon articles by Dan Kennedy and Mark Meltzer; p.13 Google search engine, reproduced kindly by Google; p.28-9 How could we get it so wrong based upon an article by Jonathan Glancey, ©The Guardian; p.43-44 Based upon an article by Tim Adams; p.44 Based upon an article by Ed Douglas, © Ed Douglas; p.50 The Anger Page, based upon various articles; p.52 How to Teach Writing, Jeremy Harmer © Jeremy Harmer; p.66 Based upon article by John Gibb and various others; p.73 Article 1 by Sarah Wilkin, ©Adhoc Publishing; p.73 Article 2 based upon an article Max Luscher; p.73 Article 3 by Victoria Moore, ©The Independent on Sunday 6.05.01; p.73 Article 4 based upon article from, The Observer; p.81 Article 1 granted by kind permission of the Vegan Action Group; p.81 Article 2 granted by kind permission of the Greenpeace Organisation; p.81 Article 3 granted by kind permission of Dr Mercola; p.81 Article 4 based upon an article by Monsanto; p.84 Longman Dictionary of Contemporary English 4, ©Pearson Education; p.87 Statistical Table based upon information from The Vegan Research Panel; p.87 Pie chart based upon information from Balwynhs School, Australia; p.93 Based upon an article by Brian Bates, ©Brian Bates; p.101-2 Notes by Elenor Coppola published by Simon and Schuster, © Faber and Faber; p.108 Adrian Mole The Wilderness Years by Sue Townsend, © Sue Townsend 1993. Permission granted by Curtis Brown Group Ltd; p.115 Based upon a story by Edward De Bono; p.125 About a boy by Nick Hornby, ©Penguin Group USA; p.126 Paula by Isabel Allende, ©HarperCollins; p.126 The Green Mile, by Stephen King, ©Stephen King; p.127 White Teeth by Zadie Smith (Hamish Hamilton, 2000, ©Zadie Smith, 2000; p.139 Based upon an article by L.D. Meagher; p.140 Based upon an article by Lisa Margonelli; p.145 Midsummer, Tobago from Sea Grapes by Derek Walcott, published by Jonathan Cape. Used by permission of the Randon House Group Limited; p.145 Like Beacon by Grace Nichols, ©Grace Nichols. Permission granted by Curtis Brown Group Ltd; p.145 Handbag by Ruth Fainlight, ©Ruth Fainlight; p.151 Small Boy by Norman MacCraig, ©Birlinn;

Audio acknowledgements
p.5 Little House on the Prairie, by Laura Ingells Wilder, reproduced by kind permission of HarperCollins Children's Books (USA); p.16 Stormy Weather, lyrics by Ted Koehler & Harold Arlen reproduced kindly by Fred Ahlert Music. Performed by Billie Holliday reproduced kindly by Universal Music; p.22 White Teeth by Zadie Smith, reproduced kindly by AP Watt on behalf of Zadie Smith; p.26 Midsummer, Tobago from Sea Grapes by Derek Walcott, published by Jonathan Cape. Used by permission of the Randon House Group Limited; p.26 Like Beacon by Grace Nichols, ©Grace Nichols. Permission granted by Curtis Brown Group Ltd; p.26-7 Handbag by Ruth Fainlight, ©Ruth Fainlight; p.27-8 Interview between Jan Blake & Presenter, ©Jan Blake; p.29 Small Boy by Norman MacCraig, ©Birlinn; Beanfields (Live) by Penguin Café Orchestra, reproduced kindly by Penguin Café Orchestra and Virgin Music; Debussy: String Quartet 3rd Movement, reproduced kindly by EMI Music.

Photo acknowledgements
p.6 1 ©Inmagine/Alamy, 2 ©Toshihide Gotoh/Dex Image/Alamy, 3 ©Royalty Free/Corbis, 4 ©Russell Underwood/Corbis, 5 ©Rob Gage/Photo Network/Alamy; p.11 ©Dynamic graphics Group/IT Stock Free/Alamy; p.17 tl ©Arkansas Democrat-Gazette, tr ©Rene Burri/Magnum Photos, bl ©Associated Press, AP, br ©Corbis; p.24 a ©Luca I. Tettoni/Corbis, b ©Jeremy Harmer, c ©Hulton-Deutsch Collection/CORBIS, d ©Jeremy Harmer; p.29 Main ©Royalty Free/Corbis, Insert ©Royalty Free/Corbis; p.35 l ©Ingram Publishing/Alamy, r ©Royalty Free/Corbis; p.36 ©Paul Joynson Hicks/Jon Arnold Images/Alamy; p.39 a ©Scott Hortop/Alamy, b ©Alan MacWeeney/Corbis, c ©Brand X Pictures/Alamy, d ©Buzz Pictures, e ©Royalty Free/Corbis, Danny ©Royalty Free/Corbis, Carmen ©Ron Chapple/Thinkstock/Alamy, Jack ©Royalty Free/Corbis, Marcus ©Royalty Free/Corbis, Ellie ©Bob Thomas/Alamy; p.40 a ©Royalty Free/Corbis, b ©ROB & SAS/Corbis, c ©Don Mason/Corbis, d ©Ron Chapple/Thinkstock/Alamy; p. 43 ©Tom Jenkins, p.44 tr ©UNKNOWN, bl ©PA Photos/EPA; p. 47 ©John Lawrence Photography/Alamy, Insert ©NANO CALVO/VWPICS/Visual&Written SL/Alamy.com; p. 50 ©Anthony Redpath/Corbis; p.52 Brandon Cole Marine Photography/Alamy; p.58 t Comstock Images/Alamy, c Bananastock/Alamy, b Comstock Images/Alamy; p.69 l ©Royalty Free/Corbis, ct ©Joe Sohm/Alamy, cb ©Michael Saul/Brand X Pictures/Alamy, r ©Michael Saul/Brand X Pictures/Alamy; p.71 ©Tate Gallery; p.84 a ©Shout/Alamy, b ©Owen Franken/Corbis, c ©Owen Franken/Corbis, d ©Steve McDonough/Corbis, e ©Royalty Free/Corbis, Chris ©Image 100/Alamy, Jed ©ImageState/Royalty Free/Alamy, Julia ©Image100Alamy, Martin ©Cameron/Corbis, Naomi ©Royalty Free/Corbis; p.92 Gandalf ©New Line/Everett (EVT)/Rex Features, Bridget ©Corbis Sygma, Amelie ©Steve Sands/New York Newswire/Corbis, Rocky ©Everett Collection/Rex Features, a ©Big Cheese Photo LLC/Alamy, b ©Royalty Free/Corbis; p.93 tl ©Gregory Pace/Corbis, tr ©Gregory Pace/Corbis, bl ©CinemaPhoto/Corbis, br ©Photo Japan/Alamy; p.101 ©SIPA Press/Rex Features; p.105 ©Royalty Free/Corbis; p.106 ©CSU Archv/Everett (EVT)/Rex Features; p.111 l ©Reuters/Corbis, c ©Eyebyte/Alamy, r ©London Weekend Television (LWT/KMK)/Rex Features; p.114 a ©Neal Preston/Corbis, b ©Rufus F. Folkks/Corbis, c ©Corbis; p.115 d ©Bettmann/Corbis, e ©Reuters/Corbis, f ©Reuters/Corbis, g ©Reuters/Corbis, h ©Manuel Blondeau/Corbis, l ©Mitchell Gerber/Corbis; p.118 ©Jean Pierre Amet/Corbis; p.120 t ©Kevin Lock/ZUMA/Corbis, b ©Reuters/Corbis; p.123 l-r ©John-Marshall Mantel/Corbis, ©D. Herrick/DMI (DMW)/Rex Features, ©MC Pherson Colin/Corbis Sygma, ©Reuters/Corbis, ©Roger Ressmeyer/Corbis, ©Rune Hellestad/Corbis, ©Matt Baron/BEI(BEI)/Rex Features, ©AP Photo/Eric Risberg NO; p.124 ©Sam Barcroft (SFT)/Rex Features; p.135 ©Roger Vaughan Picture Library; p.136 ©Bettmann/Corbis, ©Bettmann/Corbis; p.138 ©Gianni Dagli Orti/Corbis; p.145 t © Brooks Kraft/Corbis, c ©Paul Taylor, b ©David Sillitoe; p.147 ©Jan Blake, used with kind permission; p.152 tl ©Tim Clark used with kind permission, tr ©The artist/Courtesy the artist and Jay Jopling; b ©PA Photos; p.156 ©Buddy Mays/Corbis

Printed in China
6 7 8 15 14 13

Contents

Skills

Language

UNIT 1
Winning, hoping, giving

→ question forms
→ money words and sayings
→ expressing sympathy

Vocabulary: money words and sayings

1 a **Look at the following sayings. What do you think they mean?**

b **Answer these questions in groups.**

- What is your attitude to money? Which proverbs do you agree or disagree with? Why?
- Do you have any similar sayings in your language?

> Money can't buy you love.
> Money makes the world go around.
> Money is the root of all evil.
> Money doesn't grow on trees, you know!
> A fool and his money are soon parted.

2 **Read each of the statements a–e. Match each one with a picture of the person who said it (1–5).**

a "Listen to me, son. I had a lot of credit cards, and I took out loans to pay my debts. Now I'm bankrupt. Money has ruined my life. Don't let the same thing happen to you."

b "I've just been collecting my winnings. That's $7,000! Fantastic!"

c "I've saved a lot of money and I've invested in successful companies, that kind of thing. So I guess you could say I was pretty well off."

d "Money? It just slips through my fingers. I'm permanently broke! But hey, who cares. I'm happy!"

e "Since I lost my job, I find it really hard to make ends meet. At the end of each month I'm broke!"

Explain the meaning of the words and phrases in blue.

3 **Role-play** Student A takes on the personality of one of the speakers (a–e) from Activity 2, but doesn't tell the other students which one.

The other students interview Student A about any subject except money. The students have to guess who Student A is.

Example: STUDENT B: Do you have a big house?

STUDENT A: A big house? I have three big houses!
(Student A is role-playing the rich woman.)

4 The verbs in the box can all be used with money (e.g. *to borrow money*). Copy and complete the table with as many verbs from the box as possible. Use a dictionary if necessary.

blow	borrow	donate	earn	gamble
get	give	invest	lend	lose	make
pay	put	save	spend	take	win

What a wise person does	earn, ...
What a foolish person does	
What a kind person does	

Compare your table with a partner's. Are there any words which you can't put in the table? Which ones can fit into more than one category?

5 Read the following phrases. Look up the meanings of any words you do not know.

a .... a little money every month

b .... a couple of dollars from a friend

c .... a pay raise to the employees

d .... about $80 a week on clothes

e .... away all my savings

f .... $50 to cancer research

g .... money into a new music company

h .... money on an expensive new camera

i .... money out of a cash dispenser

j .... my debts

k .... my savings in a new company

l .... $10 to my brother

m .... $30 a week

n .... $2,000 on the last race

Complete the phrases with verbs from Activity 4. Sometimes more than one verb is possible.

Example: a save / spend / invest a little money every month (There are other possibilities.)

6 Tell the class about someone real or imaginary, using as much language as you can from Activities 4 and 5.

Example: I knew this man who gambled all his money away on horseracing. He never invested any money, never paid his debts and was always broke. And then one day he won a lot of money, put all his money into a friend's company, and now he's a millionaire!

7 Money in phrases Using a dictionary or some other source, find definitions for the following phrases.

a not for love nor money

b a waste of money

c let's see the color of your money

d to be a little short of money

e to be rolling in money

f to give somebody a run for their money

g to have money to burn

h to marry into money

i to put your money where your mouth is

j to throw money at something

Student A gives the definition, Student B gives the phrase.

Example: STUDENT A: A spoken way of saying "I want to know that you can pay for this!"

STUDENT B: "Let's see the color of your money!" (c)

Reading: lottery dreams

8 Discussion Answer these questions with a partner.

a Have you ever bought a lottery ticket?

b Have you, or anyone you know, ever won anything?

c If you won a lot of money, would you do any of these things?
- go crazy and buy lots of expensive things
- buy gifts for your family
- give up work
- move to a more expensive neighborhood
- invest your money carefully
- donate money to good causes
What else might you do?

9 Read the article *Dream or Nightmare?*, on page 8, quickly. Where do sentences *a–f* fit in the article? The first one is done for you.

a Lynette Nichols was a bookkeeper before she won about $17 million in the lottery. 2

b So why does a sudden win cause so many problems?

c Brett Peterson was just 19 and working as a busboy in a small restaurant in California.

d So, do you still want to win the lottery?

e On top of this, big winners are not prepared for the new expectations that people now have of them.

f John and Sandy from Ohio won about $12 million and almost immediately the letters and phone calls started.

DREAM OR NIGHTMARE?

Have you always dreamed of winning the lottery? Everyone does, don't they?

After reading Janet Bloom's article, you might change your mind.

For many, a big win in the lottery is their dream and so they buy tickets every week hoping for "a dream come true." When they win, they think, they will be able to stop doing their boring job and live a life of luxury. But if their numbers really do come up, that dream often becomes a nightmare.

(1) .... When he found out he was going to receive a $2 million payout in the lottery, he immediately gave up work, lent money to all his friends, whether or not they would be able to pay it back, and went out on a wild spending spree. Within months he had huge credit card debts and no money left to pay them. A year later, he had taken a job as a sales clerk to try to make ends meet.

(2) .... Did it bring her happiness? Not exactly. She and her husband immediately started fighting over money. She couldn't believe that he was wasting it on electronic toys for himself, while he objected to her buying expensive cars for her family. They ended up in court in a trial that cost them both hundreds of thousands of dollars and, of course, they're now divorced.

(3) .... Everyone, from crazy inventors to people needing help putting their kids through college, wanted a donation from them. Their own kids lost all their friends when they moved to a more expensive neighborhood and they spent way too much time and energy worrying about their own safety. And to make matters worse, they both lost their jobs as accountants.

(4) .... Well, it seems that a large win can put enormous stress on people who are not prepared for it. The majority of people who win are people who did not have a lot of money before. They tend to come from blue-collar backgrounds and have been used to working full time and living "paycheck to paycheck." When they get this unexpected windfall, they don't know how to cope. Very often they stop working and they move. But these are probably the two worst things

they can do. Who lives in wealthy neighborhoods? Wealthy people of course—people who are used to having and spending money. Moving to these areas alienates lottery winners from their familiar world and friends. From one day to the next, they lose the structure that the working day offers and they no longer have the support system of neighbors who come from similar backgrounds around them. They find themselves surrounded by strangers from a different world with different life experiences, and on top of that, they have plenty of free time on their hands.

(5) .... Their friends expect them to be generous and pay for everything and they receive requests from strangers asking them to donate money to a particular cause. Very often, lottery winners do not have much experience in investing money wisely and end up making disastrous financial decisions, which quickly eat up their winnings. Many past lottery winners have commented on how easy it is to spend a lot of money very quickly once they started to believe, on a daily basis, that "money is no object."

(6) .... If you do win, the best advice is probably to get yourself some good, independent financial advice and, more importantly, to be aware that becoming rich overnight could radically change your life—and not necessarily for the better.

We want to hear from YOU. How do you handle money? What would you do if you won the lottery? Would you save or spend? Write and let us know.

10 Fact check Read the article again. Copy and complete the table with information about Brett, Lynette, and John and Sandy. The first one is done for you.

	Brett	Lynette	John and Sandy
Job(s)	a *busboy* b	f	j
How much did they win?	c	g	k
Main problems	d e	h i	l m n

11 Match the two parts of the sentence according to what you read in *Dream or Nightmare?*

a People who win money unexpectedly
b They can feel separated from
c They receive letters and phone calls from
d They don't know how to

1 ... invest money well.
2 ... people who want money.
3 ... are not usually prepared for it.
4 ... their family and friends.

Do you agree with these statements? Look for evidence from the text and give reasons for your answers.

Example: a *Yes, it's true. In the text, there are examples of people who spend their new money unwisely, or who start arguing because they don't know how to handle it.*

12 Varieties of English The text is written in U.S. English. Look at these words and expressions from British English. What U.S. English word or expression is used in the text to mean the same thing?

British English	U.S. English
a a wealthy area	
b neighbours	
c working-class backgrounds	
d pay-packet to pay-packet	
e supporting their children while they are at university	

13 Vocabulary Explain the meaning of the following words as they appear in the text.

a objected to (paragraph 2)
b windfall (paragraph 4)
c alienates (paragraph 4)
d wisely (paragraph 5)
e disastrous (paragraph 5)
f eat up (paragraph 5)
g overnight (paragraph 6)

Language in chunks

14 Look at how these phrases are used in the text and then use them in the sentences which follow. You may have to change them to make them fit.

a dream come true   to end up (doing something)
(to have) time on one's hands
to make matters worse   money is no object
way too much (of something)

a That girl is never at school and when she has .... she gets into trouble.
b They spent all their money and .... they then borrowed money to buy a car.
c The cost of the project doesn't matter at all. ....

d We didn't know what to buy with the money we won and we .... depositing it all in a bank account that pays high interest.
e Kevin had .... money as a kid— his parents gave him everything he wanted— and now he doesn't know how to manage his own financial affairs.
f Getting this new job was .... for me. I really enjoy it, the hours are great and the salary is good.

15 Write questions using the phrases in Activity 14. Interview a classmate and tell the other students what they said.

16 Noticing language There are seven questions in the text. Are they all the same kind? What is the difference between them?

17 Discussion Answer these questions in groups.

a Do you think it would change your life if you won a lot of money? Why? Why not?

b What things in your life would you change? Why?

c What things would you keep the same? Why?

Grammar: question forms

18 Find questions that have the same grammatical form as the four examples below (the verb tense is not important). Copy and complete the table.

a Did you spend all the money you won?

b Do you like gambling?

c Does she spend a lot of money on computer equipment?

d How many people came?

e How often does someone win?

f I'm on time, aren't I?

g Is it going to rain tomorrow?

h It's not very likely, is it?

i She's been here before, hasn't she?

j That's never going to happen, is it?

k What took three hours?

l What did you do when you found out you'd won?

m Which team won?

n Who called you on the phone?

o Why did they buy such an expensive car?

p You can't retire from work yet, can you?

Question type 1 (yes / no)	*Did they win the lottery?*
Question type 2 (question tag)	*They won the lottery, didn't they?*
Question type 3 (open-ended question)	*What did they win?*
Question type 4 (question about the subject / agent)	*Who won the lottery?*

Look at **1A** in the **Mini-grammar**. Do you want to change any of your answers?

19 Write down the names of two people and two places that are important to you. Give the names to a partner. Your partner asks questions about the names, using each of the four question types from Activity 18 at least once.

Examples: STUDENT A: *Who's Pieter?*

STUDENT B: *He's the man who taught me to play the guitar.*

STUDENT A: *Did you find it easy?*

STUDENT B: *Not at first. But when I joined a group I learned fast.*

STUDENT A: *How did you get along with the people in the group?*

STUDENT B: *Quite well, most of the time.*

STUDENT A: *Did you have some disagreements?*

STUDENT B: *One or two!*

20 Spoken questions Read questions *a–i* below and then listen to the conversations on Track 1. Say which of the following functions (*1–6*) B's questions correspond to.

1 "asking" to try and get someone to agree with us

2 asking because we don't know the answer

3 asking to confirm what we think we know

4 asking to make sure we heard correctly (or because we want to question what we heard)

5 asking to make sure we heard the question correctly (or because we want to "question" the question)

6 exclamations

a A: I love this restaurant.
  B: Me too. Isn't this food great?
  6 – exclamations

b A: I lost the money.
  B: You lost the money? Oh no.

c Aren't you the person who called last night?

d We're never going to win the lottery, are we?

e A: I bet $1,000 on a horserace.
  B: You did what?

f We're not going bankrupt, are we?

g A: Why are you so unhappy?
  B: Why am I so unhappy? I just am.

h A: I'm writing a book.
  B: You're writing a book, are you?

i A: There were 200 people at the party.
  B: There were how many?

Look at **1B** in the **Mini-grammar**. Do you want to change any of your answers? What different question forms are used for each function (*1–6*)?

21 Conversations Have conversations which start with the following statements. Use question functions 4 and 5. Use as many different question types as possible. Use **1B in the Mini-grammar** to help you.

a I never want to see you again! *You never want to see me again? Why not?—Because of what you said.* etc.
b I'm late for work!
c It's going to be a busy day at the office tomorrow.
d She gave all her winnings to an animal shelter.
e She invested $20,000 in the stock market.
f We won $500!
g They finished dinner at 2:00 in the morning.
h They invited 14 people for dinner.
i We waited for six hours.
j Why are you investing all your money?
k Why don't you like buying lottery tickets?

22 In groups Each student chooses one of the following topics. Use the questions to make notes so that you can tell the others about it.

a
A day when you or someone you know won something

What did you / they win? What did you do after? How did you feel?

b
A party you went to

How did you get there? How many people were there? What kind of people were they? What happened? How did you get home?

c
A sporting event you saw or played in

What happened? Who was playing? What were the most memorable moments? Who did what?

d
An extraordinary trip you went on

Where were you going? What happened? Why extraordinary? What did you do?

Tell your story. The other students interrupt you as often as possible using question functions *1–6* from Activity 20.

Functional language: expressing sympathy

23 Read the statements in the box. How many can you use for each situation (*a–h*)?

I'm so sorry to hear that.   *a*
I'm really sorry about that.   *a*
That's such a shame.   *a*
That's so sad.   *a*
What a pity.
It's a real shame that things didn't work out for you.
It's a pity that you're not feeling well.
That's a shame.   *a*

a Your friend has lost her cat.
b Your friend lost all the money from her investments.
c Your friend loses her job after 10 years.
d Your son studied hard, but failed his math test.
e The weather is not good and your partner wanted to go away for the weekend.
f A guy you know didn't get the job he wanted.
g Your friend's daughter didn't win the prize she was expecting to win.
h Your daughter is not feeling well and doesn't think she will be able to play in a game.

24 Copy and complete the table. Listen to Track 2. Match the conversations *1–8* to the statements and the situations *a–h* from Activity 23.

Conversation	Statement	Situation
1	I'm so sorry to hear that.	c
2		
3		
4		
5		
6		
7		
8		

25 Copy and complete this table with different ways of expressing sympathy.

Using a clause	Using an exclamation
a I'm (so) ......*sorry*........ that you are having financial difficulties.	e What a ....!
b It's (such) a .... that you didn't talk to someone before it happened.	f What a ....!
c It's a (real) .... that your family is not supporting you.	g That's (such) a ....!
d It's (really) .... that you will have to sell your house.	h That's a (real) ....!
	i That's a (real) ....!
	j That's (so / really) ....!
	k I'm (so) ....!

What is the effect of using *so* / *such* / *real* / *really*?

Pronunciation: stress

26 Listen to Track 3 and underline the stressed syllables in the sentences. Then circle the word that is stressed most of all.

Example: That's such a shame!

a I'm so sorry that you lost your job!
b It's so sad that he lost all the money.
c It's such a shame that they had to leave that beautiful house.
d It's such a pity that you didn't save the money.
e That's such bad luck!

27 Now practice saying the sentences with the same use of stress.

28 Pair work React to these situations. Use *so* and *such* with appropriate stress.

a Your sister lost her billfold and all her money on the first day of her vacation.
b Two of your friends lost a lot of money at a Las Vegas casino.
c The house of a family in your neighborhood caught fire and burned down last week.
d A colleague of yours lost her job at the office two weeks ago.

29 In pairs Imagine you are in these situations (*a–e*) and take turns reacting to them using the expressions in the box in Activity 23. You can invent the details.

a You didn't pass your English test after you studied hard.
b You had an argument with one of your friends about what to do over the weekend.
c You have a terrible cold and you don't feel like doing anything.
d You have had a terrible day. Everything that could go wrong has gone wrong.
e You lost a lot of money.

Example: STUDENT A: Guess what? I didn't pass my English test. I worked really hard for it.

STUDENT B: What a shame. What are you going to do?

30 Think of two disappointments in your life or the life of someone you know. Tell your partner about them.

Example: STUDENT A: I was disappointed when I didn't pass my driving test.

STUDENT B: Oh, that's a shame. What happened?

Speaking: making a decision

31 In groups Rewrite the following sentence so that it reflects the group's opinions.

People shouldn't give money to charities.

32 Choose one of the following five charities and read the information about it.

Web Images Groups News Froogle **more »**
Charities
Google Search I'm Feeling Lucky
Advanced Search
Preferences
Language Tools

a **Adopt a minefield** (www.landmines.org) raises awareness and funds to clear landmines and help survivors of landmines around the world.

b **Médecins Sans Frontières** (www.msf.org) provides emergency medical assistance in over 80 countries where healthcare is insufficient or non-existent.

c **WaterAid** (www.wateraid.org.uk) provides clean water and sanitation for the millions of people who have no access to this vital resource.

d **Stop Global AIDS** (www.stopglobalaids.org) raises money to fight the disease with prevention measures, care for victims, providing affordable medication and influencing political opinion.

e **The WWF** (www.panda.org) helps to conserve the world's biological diversity, ensure renewable natural resources, and promotes good consumption policies.

In your own words, and without looking back at the book, explain what the charity you have selected does, and say why it might be a good idea.

Listening: money advice

35 Why might people at different ages visit a financial advisor? Would you visit a financial adviser? Why?

36 Listen to Track 4. Choose the best answer.

Don wants to:

a ... learn how to invest money.
b ... talk about how to pay his debts.
c ... find out how to make more money.
d ... manage his money better.

37 Listen to Track 5. Copy and complete Suzanne Moore's notes about Don.

33 In groups You have some money that you wish to donate to a charity. Choose one of the charities in Activity 32. Compare your choice with another group.

Speaking and writing: ellipsis

In writing, we generally make complete questions and sentences. In informal speech, however, we often leave out all but the most important words.

Examples: "Nice day!" instead of "Isn't it a nice day?" or "It's a nice day, isn't it?" "Coffee?" instead of "Would you like a coffee?" "Raining." instead of "It's raining."

34 What might be the full (written) form for A's utterances in the following exchanges?

a A: Surprised?
  B: Yes, just a bit.
b A: Difficult exam?
  B: No, not too bad.
c A: Cookie?
  B: No thanks. I've just eaten.
d A: Nice car.
  B: Thanks. Glad you like it.
e A: Going to rain.
  B: Yes, I think you're right.
f A: Drink?
  B: Yes, let's.
g A: Starting a new job tomorrow.
  B: You're doing what?
h A: Hot!
  B: Yes it is.

Can you think why / where the conversations took place?

Suzanne Moore – *Independent Financial Advice*	
Spends now	**Ways to save**
Spends (a) $............ per week on food.	Shop at (b) ....
Goes to (c) .... four times a week.	Go (d) .... a week.
Spends (e) .... on rent.	Maybe find somewhere cheaper.
Buys (f) .... a week.	Only buy one.
Goes to the movies once a week.	Go (g) ....
Eats in the (h)	Make a sandwich at home.

38 Listen to Tracks 4 and 5 again. Complete these sentences with the words you hear.

a I'm not a big .... , but I just can't seem to make ends meet.
b I'm an English lit. .... so I have a lot of work.
c Hmmm—that's a .... , isn't it?
d You're going to have to make a ....
e ... whatever you spend your money on—your ....
f And then on the other side, you write down what you could change and .... on to save money.
g How much money do you spend on .... per week?
h It .... from one week to the next, but I'd guess about $100.
i They often have good prices and ....
j ... and try to share the expenses with your ....

What do these words and expressions mean?

39 Answer these questions in groups.

a Do you think the financial adviser gave Don good advice? Explain your answer.
b What things do you typically spend your money on?
c Are you good at budgeting? Why or why not?
d How do you save money?

Writing: mind maps

40 Mind maps can be used to help you to brainstorm and organize your ideas before you start a piece of writing.

Look at this mind map. Which one do you think is the central theme, *a*, *b* or *c*?

a winning the lottery
b seeing a financial adviser
c investing for the future

Compare your answer with a partner and give reasons for your choice.

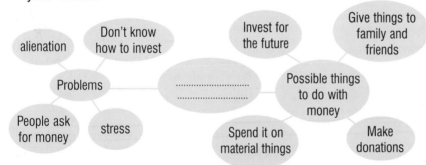

41 Copy and complete the mind map below with your own ideas and associations. Then show your mind map to a partner and explain it. How similar is your partner's map?

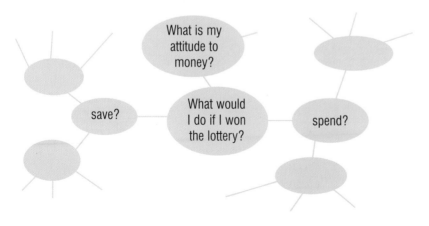

42 Writing Look at the end of the article from page 8 below.

> We want to hear from YOU. How do you handle money? What would you do if you won the lottery? Would you save or spend? Write and let us know.

Write a short letter in answer to these questions in the article.

Divide your writing into three paragraphs and use your mind map to help you.

Paragraph 1: my attitude to money.

Paragraph 2: why I would spend some money and what I would spend it on.

Paragraph 3: why I would save some money and how I would save it.

43 Compare your letter with other students. Have you written similar things? What are the main differences?

Review: grammar and functional language

44 Imagine you were going to interview this woman who has just won the lottery. What questions would you ask her?

Example: *How much did you win?*

45 Read this interview with the woman. Based on her responses, what are the interviewer's questions? You can look at Activities 18–22 for help.

INTERVIEWER: So, (a) *how do you feel*?
MAUREEN: I feel great. This is the most amazing feeling.
INTERVIEWER: So, tell us your story. (b) ....?
MAUREEN: No, this is the first time I've ever bought a ticket.
INTERVIEWER: (c) ....?
MAUREEN: Well, things were not going too well in my life. I lost my job, first.
INTERVIEWER: I'm sorry to hear that. (d) ....?
MAUREEN: Then one of my children was sick and needed a lot of care.
INTERVIEWER: That's very sad. I'm so sorry. (e) ....?
MAUREEN: Well, I had to borrow a lot of money and use credit cards and I just found it so difficult to make ends meet.
INTERVIEWER: That's such a shame. (f) ....?
MAUREEN: Well, yes. My friend, Emma—she was great, but she was short of money herself, so she couldn't really help me there.
INTERVIEWER: So, you live in Los Angeles, (g) ....?
(h) ....?
MAUREEN: In the candy store. I was in there buying some chocolate and something made me buy a ticket for the first time in my life.
INTERVIEWER: And (i) ....?
MAUREEN: Well, we were watching television and they were reading out the winning numbers and I took a look at my ticket and I saw that I had those numbers.
INTERVIEWER: (j) ....?
MAUREEN: Well, I called Emma right away.
INTERVIEWER: (k) ....?
MAUREEN: She came around and we had to call to claim the prize.
INTERVIEWER: (l) ....? Was it you or Emma?
MAUREEN: She had to do it. I was shaking all over.
INTERVIEWER: So, (m) ....?
MAUREEN: Well, the first thing is to get proper care for my little boy and then I want to pay off all my debts and start working again.
INTERVIEWER: You're not going to work, (n) ....?
MAUREEN: Oh, yes. I want to set a good example for my kids. I plan to go back to school and study to be a nurse. That's my dream.

Was there anything in Maureen's story that surprised you?

46 Look at these situations. In pairs, imagine the conversation between the people in the pictures. Look at Activities 23–25 for help.

Example:
STUDENT A: *I failed my math test, mom.*
STUDENT B: *That's such a shame, Charlie, but did you study for it?*

47 In pairs Think of a famous person that you both know. Imagine you are going to interview her / him. Write down at least ten different questions you would like to ask.

Role-play the interview.

Example:
STUDENT A: *Mr. Mandela, how long did you spend in prison?*
STUDENT B: *27 years.*

Review: vocabulary

Word List

bankrupt   broke   credit card
disastrous   loan   objected to
overnight   to alienate
to blow   to borrow   to donate
to earn   to eat up   to gamble
to get   to give   to invest (in)
to lend   to lose   to make
to pay   to put   to save
to spend   to take   to win
windfall   winnings   wisely

Word Plus

a dream come true
"A fool and his money are soon
   parted." *
a waste of money
let's see the color of your
   money
"Money can't buy you love."
"Money doesn't grow on trees,
   you know!"
money is no object
"Money is the root of all evil."
"Money makes the world go
   around."
not for love nor money
to be a little short of money
to be rolling in money
to end up (doing something)
to find it hard to make ends
   meet
to give somebody a run for their
   money
to have money to burn
(to have) time on one's hands
to make matters worse
to marry into money
to put your money where your
   mouth is
to throw money at something
way too much (of something)

*Phrases in quotation marks are
conversational phrases.

48 Answer these questions about the Word List and Word Plus.

a Which is your favorite new expression and why?
b Which is the expression that you think is the most useful?
c Choose five words that you can associate and explain why you
   chose those five words.

Example: "blow", "waste", "spend", "throw", "lose": these are
all words about spending money.

● ● ● Pronunciation

49 Copy and complete the table with as many words as you can from
the Word List and Word Plus.

/ʌ/ – m**o**ney	/æ/ – g**a**mble	/e/ – g**e**t

Check your answers by listening to Track 6.

Add more words of your own to the list.

50 Listen to these sentences on Track 7. What do you notice about
the stress of the word *object*?

Money is no object for my brother.
I object to people who waste money on gambling.

Practice saying these sentences with the correct pronunciation
of *object*.

a That's a very strange object.
b Did she object to the bank charges?
c When he said he was going to gamble with our money,
   I objected.
d Those objects over there are very rare and precious.

Find other pairs of words like 'object and ob'ject.

51 Tell one story about someone you know using as many of the
expressions in the Word List and Word Plus as you can. See who
can use most expressions.

Example: My friend, Rick, finds it hard to make ends meet.
He spends all the money he earns and then he uses
his credit cards. I always tell him that money doesn't
grow on trees, but he throws his money at ridiculous
things and does not invest wisely ...

UNIT 2
Photographs

→ *used to* and *would*
→ photography
→ asking for help

Speaking: choosing a photograph

1 Find out the following information about your partner.

   a Do you have a camera? If so, what kind is it?
   b What do you take photographs of?
   c Do you "photograph well"? (Do you like yourself in photographs?)

2 **In groups** You are going to judge the finalists in a photography competition on the theme of "the most powerful black and white images of the 20th century." Agree on at least five criteria you will use to make your judgment.

Examples: • the picture is interesting
               • the picture tells us something about the person (or people)

3 Use your criteria to choose a winner from the following photographs.

4 Choose one of the photographs and try to answer the following questions.

   a When was the picture taken?
   b Where was the picture taken?
   c What is the relationship between the people?
   d How do they feel?
   e What happened before the picture was taken?
   f What happened after the picture was taken?
   g How important are photographs like these? Why?

Reading: more than a moment

5 Read the text in Activity 6 quickly; don't study it in any detail. Which of the four pictures (a–d) in Activity 3 is being talked about in the text?

6 Read the following sentences and then decide where they should go in the text. There is one sentence too many.

a And because of this black children were finally admitted to whites-only schools.
b The first test case of this ruling occurred in Little Rock, Arkansas, in 1957 when nine black students tried to attend classes at the Central High School. **1**
c Finally, at the ceremony 40 years later, she and her victim met face to face.
d He called for greater understanding between races, a call which echoes down the years in the wake of misunderstandings between different peoples and religions of the world.
e The photographs Counts took that day were soon published all over America and the world.
f William Counts had been a student at the Central High School himself.
g And so there was.

MORE THAN A MOMENT

Some photographs, like the one taken by photographer William Counts outside the Central High School in Little Rock, Arkansas (U.S.A.) all those years ago, are so powerful that they help to change the course of history.

In 1954 the Supreme Court of the United States of America decided that segregated education (previously accepted as "separate but equal") was unconstitutional.

1 b But racism was a fact of life in those days, and many white Americans were bitterly opposed to multiracial schooling. The governor of the state of Arkansas, Orval Faubus, sent soldiers of the National Guard to the high school to stop black children from attending classes there, and to "maintain order."

2 f Now 26 years old, he arrived at the scene with his camera after only a few days as a photographer with the *Arkansas Democrat* newspaper. Nobody paid him too much attention because he was a local man. As a result he was not attacked by the angry crowds as many photographers from out of town were that day, and he was able to take his famous picture.

Counts had recognized immediately that the moment the black students tried to get to the school there would be trouble. **3 g** Elizabeth Eckford, the first of the nine, was turned back by the soldiers, and Counts, running backwards in front of her, started taking his pictures. And that was how the world saw a picture of a 15-year-old white girl, Hazel Bryan, shouting abuse at the black student. "The crowd were right in her ear," Counts recalled many years later, "they were yelling their hate, but she [Eckford] never lost her composure, she just remained so dignified, so determined in what she was doing."

4 e They caused outrage. Dwight Eisenhower, the president of the United States, saying how moved he was by pictures of the "disgraceful occurrences," took control of the National Guard and ordered federal troops to escort the "Little Rock Nine" to school despite the objections of the Arkansas governor. Desegregated education had begun.

Forty years later, the nine black students were awarded the Congressional Medal of Honor by American president Bill Clinton in a ceremony at the Central High School. In his speech, he said, "Like so many Americans, I can never fully repay my debt to these nine people. For with their innocence, they purchased more freedom for me, too, and for all white people." But he was far from optimistic about the future of race relations: "Today, children of every race walk through the same door, but then they often walk down different halls," he said. "Not only in this school, but across America, they sit in different classrooms, they eat at different tables. They even sit in different parts of the bleachers at a football game. Far too many communities are all white, all black, all Latino, all Asian. Indeed, too many Americans of all races have actually begun to give up on the idea of integration and the search for common ground."
5 d

And what of Hazel Bryan Massery, the girl with her face screwed up in anger and hatred? Five years after the photograph was taken she called up Elizabeth Eckford to apologize. "I am deeply ashamed of the photograph," she said later, "I was an immature 15-year-old. That's the way things were. I grew up in a segregated society and I thought that's the way it was and that's the way it should be."

6 c "I wanted to end my identification as the poster child for the hate generation, trapped in the image captured in that photograph. I know my life was more than a moment." And William Counts was there to take a new photograph of another moment—of reconciliation.

7 **Discussion** What is your reaction to Hazel Bryan's actions as a 15-year-old and as a 55-year-old?

8 **Fact check** Who were the following people, what did they do, and when did they do it?

Name	a Who?	b What?	c When?
Hazel Bryan	– white student at Little Rock's Central High School	– shouted at a black student – apologized – reconciled with the black student	– 1957 – 1962 – 1997
William Counts			
Bill Clinton			
Dwight Eisenhower			
Orval Faubus			
Elizabeth Eckford			

9 Which words from the text in Activity 6 tell you that the following statements are true? Underline them.

a Education was not integrated in 1953.
b Separate education for black and white children was not in agreement with the laws of the country.
c A white girl was rude to Elizabeth Eckford.
d The crowd were making a lot of noise.
e Elizabeth Eckford behaved in a way that should have made people respect her.
f People were very upset by the photograph.
g The governor of Arkansas did not agree with the president's actions.
h The "Little Rock Nine" did not have much experience of life.
i Hazel Bryan looked very angry in the photograph.
j Hazel Bryan was not very grown up.

Language in chunks

10 Match the phrases in italics from the text (*a–g*, on the left) with their explanations (*1–7*, on the right).

a *a fact of life*
b *bitterly opposed to*
c *I can never fully repay my debt to*
d *in the wake of*
e *she never lost her composure*
f *there would be trouble*
g *to change the course of history*

1 after (and as a result of) an event
2 make things different for ever
3 something that is or was always true
4 in strong disagreement with
5 something bad was going to happen
6 stopped looking calm
7 give someone what we think we owe them

11 Use the words in parentheses to rewrite the following sentences so that they mean more or less the same. Use the phrases in italics from Activity 10.

a She didn't seem to be upset when the police arrested her. (composure)
b Everybody gets colds and flu from time to time. (fact)
c Nothing was ever the same after the Industrial Revolution. (course)
d It is impossible to thank you enough. (debt)
e I am totally against your plan. (bitterly)
f They built new flood defenses after the terrible storm. (wake)
g When he saw the people in the stadium, he knew things were going to go wrong. (trouble)

12 Noticing language Find at least one more example of the following verb tenses in the text.

- past simple of the verb *to be* (example: *racism was a fact of life*)
- past simple with other verbs (example: *the Supreme Court decided*)
- passive sentence (example: *he was not attacked*)
- past continuous (example: *they were yelling*)
- past perfect (example: *William Counts had been a student*)

13 Discussion Bill Clinton said, "I can never repay my debt to these people." Can you think of two other people in history who we should be grateful to? Compare your choices with other students.

Functional language: asking for help

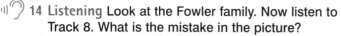

14 Listening Look at the Fowler family. Now listen to Track 8. What is the mistake in the picture?

15 Complete the following requests with *stand over there* or *standing over there*.

a Can you .... ?
b Could you .... ?
c Do you think you could .... ?
d I'd like you to ....
e I wonder if you would mind .... ?
f Would you mind .... ?
g You couldn't .... , could you?

Which of the requests a–g are more formal / polite than the others?

16 In groups Take turns to decide where the other members of your group should stand or sit for a photograph. Now get them into the right positions.

Example: STUDENT A: Where do you want us to go?

STUDENT B: Well, I'd like Tom to sit down here.

STUDENT C: OK.

STUDENT B: And Mary, could you ...

17 Use words from two or three of the boxes to ask for a favor. Consult a dictionary if necessary.

do give help lend	me	a favor a hand out

Example: Could you help me out?

18 a Copy and complete the table with expressions from the box.

> Certainly.   I can't really.   I'd rather not.
> I'm afraid I ...   No problem.
> Of course I could / would.   OK.   Sorry, but ...
> Sure.   That depends on what it is.   Well ...
> Why should I?   Yes, of course.

1 Agreeing to a request
Certainly.

2 Could be either "yes" or "no"

3 Saying "no" to a request

b How many ways can you say "yes" to the following request?

Would you mind giving me a hand?

●●● Pronunciation: intonation clues

19 Read the conversations and listen to the people on Track 9 saying "no." Should the first speaker ask them again? Why? Why not?

a SPEAKER A: Would you answer the door?
SPEAKER B: I can't really.

b SPEAKER A: Could you lend me some money?
SPEAKER B: I'd rather not.

c SPEAKER A: Can you help me tidy this room?
SPEAKER B: Sorry, but I have a lot to do.

d SPEAKER A: Would you collect my prints when you're in town?
SPEAKER B: Why should I?

e SPEAKER A: You couldn't help me paint this wall, could you?
SPEAKER B: I'm afraid I can't.

20 Have the conversations in pairs. Student A makes the request and Student B says "no", choosing an intonation. Should A continue the conversation or not? Does Student B agree?

●●

21 Say "no" to the following requests using the word given, and adding an excuse.

a Could you help me with my homework? (really)

I can't really. I have to wash my hair!

b You couldn't give me a lift downtown, could you? (rather)
c Can you help me tidy the darkroom? (afraid)
d Do you think you could lend me your camera? (sorry)
e Would you mind giving me a hand with this painting? (why)
f I wonder if you'd mind giving me a hand with this photographic equipment. (really)
g Could you lend me a hand with my shopping? (afraid)
h You couldn't help me deliver these letters, could you? (sorry)
i Do you think you could give me a hand with the dishes? (rather)

Are the replies polite, neutral or quite strong?

22 Conversation writing In pairs, choose one of the following situations.

a You are on vacation with a friend. You ask a stranger to take a photograph of you both.
b A number of friends have turned up unexpectedly. You want your friend to help you to cook them a meal.
c You are moving into a new office. You ask someone you do not know very well to help you unpack boxes of files and books.
d There's a storm outside. You want your friend to give you a lift to college in their car.

Write your conversation and act it out for the class.

Vocabulary: photography (compound nouns)

●●●●●●●●●●●●●●●●●●●●●●●●●●●●●●●●●

23 Look at the pictures and answer the questions.

Which camera:
a ... has a *flash*?
b ... has a *viewfinder*?
c ... has a *zoom lens*?
d ... is a *digital camera*?
e ... is a *throwaway camera*?

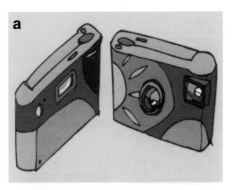

a

b

24 Match the words with the best definitions.

photo
photograph
snap

a a picture not taken by a professional, but taken quickly and informally, often of a place you visit
b a picture taken with a camera
c an informal word for a picture, especially of you, your friends, your family or places you have visited

25 Look at the diagrams. Match the pictures with the following phrases.

- put the memory card in the camera
- upload the pictures to a computer
- take pictures
- view pictures on the screen
- buy a memory card
- burn a CD with the pictures
- send the CD to a friend

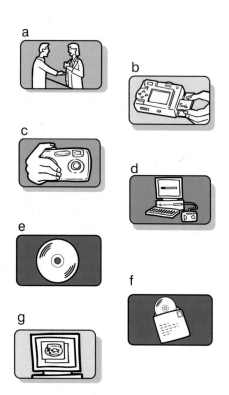

a

b

c

d

e

f

g

26 Writing Describe a photo which you like and which was taken by you or someone you know. What kind of picture is it? What kind of camera was it taken with? What was the procedure (traditional or digital)?

27 Compound nouns Use the clues (a–h) to make compound nouns.

What is a / an:

a ... booth where you get a photo for a passport?

   1 *a photo booth*

b ... man who works with a camera?

c ... photograph taken at a wedding?

d ... photograph taken for a passport?

e ... opportunity (for a politician or film star, etc.) to have their photo taken?

f ... room which is dark (for developing films)?

g ... frame to put a photo in?

h ... recorder for video?

What do the following mean?

- photogenic
- photo finish

28 a Match the nouns in box 1 on the left with the appropriate nouns in box 2 on the right. Some words from box 2 may be used more than once.

1	alarm	mother
	birthday	newspaper
	contact	race
	credit	shopping
	greenhouse	steering
	heart	washing
	human	windshield

2	article	machine
	attack	relations
	bag	rights
	card	tongue
	clock	wheel
	effect	wiper
	lens	

b Test your partner, using the words from boxes 1 and 2.

Example: STUDENT A: *What do you call a clock with an alarm?*

STUDENT B: *An alarm clock.*

c Copy and complete the description of compound nouns with further examples from Activities 27 and 28a.

> Some compound nouns are one-word only (examples: *tablespoon, homework, ...*). Some are two separate words (examples: *town hall, living room, ...*) and some are joined by a hyphen (examples: *decision-making, ice-skating, ...*). There are no rules for this. If in doubt, use two words without a hyphen, but check in your dictionary.

29 In pairs Choose one of the following and tell your partner about it.

- a photo album belonging to you or someone in your family
- a photograph album you'd like to have or make
- pictures in frames in the place where you live
- the best photographs you've seen (in a book, in newspapers, etc.)
- the last roll of film you took
- the last time you got a passport
- wedding pictures you know or would like to see

Grammar: the past (tenses and habits)

30 Read the sentences. What is the correct sequence of events? (*a* is first.)

a I was driving home when it happened. 1
b I didn't mind what they had done. 12
c I had been to a party with my friends. 3 4
d I had only drunk orange juice at the party. 4 5
e I was listening to the radio in my car. 2
f I was relieved that nothing terrible had happened. 11
g My brake light was not working and so they followed me. 7
h The police stopped me two miles from home. 3
i Then they drove away. 10
j They had seen me two minutes before. 6
k They made me breathe into a Breathalyzer. 8
l They warned me about my brake light. 9
m They were only doing their job. 13

Look at **2A–2D** in the **Mini-grammar**. Do you want to change your answer?

31 Without looking at Activity 30, tell the story in your own words.

32 **Work it out** Look at the examples and answer the questions which follow.

Examples: He used to play tennis when he was younger.
I used to live in a house but now I live in an apartment.
We would go to the beach every July when we were young.
~~I would have a red bicycle when I was a boy.~~

a How do we describe habits in the past?
b When we describe past states with verbs like *be, believe, have, live, think*, etc., can we use *used to*, or *would* or both?

Check your answers by looking at **2B–2C** in the **Mini-grammar**.

33 Replace the verbs and phrases in blue with phrases using *used to* or *would*. Remember that sometimes *would* is not possible.

Example: They used to live in a small wooden cabin.

Things have changed since my great-grandparents' day. They were poor blue-collar people. They lived in a small wooden cabin with no bathroom and an outdoor toilet. It was quite a hard existence and people got sick all the time.

Every morning my grandfather walked three miles to work. He worked eight hours a day in a steel factory. He complained about the noise all the time but no one really listened. Everybody complained about the noise. While he was at work my grandmother looked after the children and used what little money she had to try and clothe and feed them. Often she didn't have enough money for the food she needed and so she took in laundry from rich families to earn some extra money.

When I think of those two people I don't know how they did it. Life was a real struggle for them.

34 Compare your lives (and the way you travel) with your grandparents' or great-grandparents' lives when they were your age.

Example: My grandfather used to live on a farm in the country, but I live in an apartment in the city.

Word Choice: *remember*, *remind* and *forget*

35 Look at the Word Choice notes for *remember*, *remind* and *forget* on page 56 in the booklet. Complete the following sentences with the most likely verb. You may have to change the tense.

  a Did you ... to turn off the light?
  b I'll never ... the first time I saw Mount Fuji.
  c I ... to mail the letter and so I missed the entry date for the competition.
  d I ... getting home late, but I've completely ... what we talked about all night.
  e ... me to call him when I get home.
  f Don't ... to take your notes to the lecture.
  g I ... her taking the photograph, but I can't ... why we were in London.
  h If you ... I'll never forgive you!
  i If you don't ... him he'll ... to do it, I guarantee you.

36 Complete the sentences with *didn't*, *use*, *used* or *wouldn't*.

  a I didn't .... to take photographs when I was younger, but I do now.
  b Didn't you .... to be a professional photographer?
  c We'd meet in the evening, ... we?
  d You used to play baseball, ... you?
  e I am not .... to living in an apartment. It's strange.

  • How do we usually make negative sentences and questions with *used to*?
  • How do we make tag questions for *used to* and *would*?
  • Which sentence is about present habits?

  Check your answers by looking at **2E–2F in the Mini-grammar**.

37 Interview How much can you remember about life at your elementary school? Interview a partner and find out:

  • ... how they got to school.
  • ... what they did there.
  • ... what happened at different times of the day.
  • ... if they had any special friends and what they did together.
  • ... if they had any teachers with special habits.
  • ... anything else they remember especially well.

Example: I think I used to walk to school with my father. Sometimes, when it was raining, he took me in the car, but mostly, yes, we just walked.

Listening: what our photographs remind us of

38 Listen to Track 10. Match the photographs with the speakers. The speakers are in the right order.

  Peter   Jane   Kate   Betty

How old do you think the speakers are? Why?

39 Fact check Who:

  a ... learnt to ski when he was young?
  b ... once had a box camera?
  c ... has a mother who teaches?
  d ... has lived in various different countries?
  e ... visited Bolivia?
  f ... went to a place that looked better than pictures of it do?
  g ... didn't enjoy school in Johannesburg very much?
  h ... used to go for long walks?
  i ... had a vacation by the sea every summer?
  j ... has a sister who went to Chile?
  k ... acted like a tourist guide?

40 History and places Listen to Track 10 again. What do the speakers say about:

a ... Peru, the Spaniards, Cuzco and Machu Picchu?
b ... The Grand Palace in Bangkok?

41 Words and phrases Listen to Track 10 again or look at the Audioscript. Match the words and phrases in italics in the first column with their equivalent meanings in the second column.

a *diplomat* 10
b *fabulous*
c *I'd so like* to go back
d *it dates back to* the 18th century
e *it's not a patch on the real thing*
f *kind of like* tourist guides
g *primitive*
h *scenery*
i *slopes*
j Thailand was *really cool*
k the dog *passed away*
l *trail*

1 a path, usually in the wilderness
2 as if we were
3 died
4 enjoyable
5 I would very much like
6 it happened / was built in
7 it is not as good or impressive as the thing itself
8 really fantastic
9 sides of mountains that people ski down
10 someone who works for their government, but in an embassy in a different country
11 the countryside (mountains, rivers, etc.) that you see before you
12 very old-fashioned, unsophisticated

42 In pairs Discuss one of the following topics.

a Tell your partner about a photograph from your past that you really love. Perhaps it's a photograph of you, or one that you took. Better still, bring it to class.
b Jane says, "There are places like that, aren't there? You know, no matter how often you've seen photographs, it's just not a patch on the real thing." Do you agree with her? Have you ever been to a place like that?

Tell the class what you heard from your partner.

Writing: headlines (précis)

43 Look at the following newspaper headlines and answer the questions.

a What is the story behind the headlines, do you think?
b What, typically, is left out in newspaper headlines? What verb?

Shake-up in car-parking charges

Family "owe lives" to smoke alarm

Little Rock photographer dies at 70

Photo booth murder suspect arrested

Queen's horse in photo finish win

44 Summary writing Read the following story. How many headlines can you write which summarize the story using some of the words in blue? (You may have to change some of the words, e.g. from verbs to nouns, etc.)

A mother of three escaped injury when the car she was driving plunged into a river. She had been driving home after dropping her children off at school. She was rescued by a passing bike rider who dived into the river and pulled her from the car. "I owe that man my life," said Mrs. Martha Galvan. "He's a hero, but his identity is a mystery. He ran off after he had rescued me so I don't know who he is."

Example: River plunge mother escapes injury.

45 Read the following stories and note the words you may want to use in headlines which will summarize them.

pick up

When James Knight, a college student, went to collect his photographs at Walgreens 24-hour developing center on Thursday, he got the shock of his life. Two of the photographs showed his girlfriend standing in a street in Chicago. But behind her were two robbers running out of a bank. "I didn't notice them at the time," Knight said, "but when I showed them to the police they were very excited." The police have since made two arrests.

The Swedish singer Carla was making no comment yesterday after an incident at Mexico City Airport in which she hit out at a press photographer, breaking his nose. The attack took place as the singer was arriving from Sweden for a countrywide tour. Witnesses said that Carla posed for the waiting photographers with her 6-year-old daughter who is accompanying her, but when one photographer, American Brad Puttnam, kept taking photographs of the mother and daughter, the singer lashed out. Puttnam is threatening to sue. The singer's publicity aide says that Carla regrets the incident and just wants to be left alone.

Write as many headlines as you can for the stories. Get as much information in the headlines as possible. Compare the headlines. Which are the most successful?

Review: grammar and functional language

46 Favorite things Try to remember what it was like when you were a child. What were your three favorite activities or experiences? Look at Activities 32–33 for help.

a at home
b during vacations
c over the weekend

47 Match the following requests (*1–6*) with the correct answers (*a–f*). Look at Activities 14–22 for help.

1 Do me a favor and make me some coffee.
2 Do you think you could help me with the dishes?
3 I wonder if you'd be good enough to help me.
4 Would you mind getting me a roll of film when you go to town?
5 Would you mind giving me a hand with this table?
6 You couldn't help me with these boxes, could you?

a   *I wonder if you'd be good enough to help me. (3)*

   – It depends on what you want. I can carry your suitcases if that's your problem.

b   ....

   – Not at all. Where do you want it to go?

c   ....

   – Of course I wouldn't. What kind does your camera take?

d   ....

   – Of course. Where do you want them to go?

e   ....

   – Sorry. I'd love to, but I have to go. Brad's waiting for me.

f   ....

   – Why should I? I'm working just as hard as you.

Review: vocabulary

Word List

alarm clock   birthday card
cameraman   contact lens
copies   credit card
darkroom   digital camera
diplomat   disposable camera
enlargements   fabulous
film   flash   greenhouse effect
heart attack   human rights
mother tongue
newspaper article
passport photograph
photo booth   photo finish
photogenic   photo frame
photo opportunity   primitive
race relations   really cool
scenery   shopping bag   slope
snap   steering wheel
to develop   to pass away
trail   VCR   viewfinder
washing machine
wedding photograph
windshield wiper   zoom lens

Word Plus

a fact of life
bitterly opposed to
in the wake of
to be kind of like
to be not a patch on the real
   thing
to change the course of history
to date back to
to know there will be trouble
to never be able to repay a
   debt to
to never lose your composure

48 Which five words from the Word List would be the best / most useful ones for you if you were:

a ... a backpacker?
b ... a politician?
c ... a housewife or househusband?
d ... an actor?

Give reasons for your answers.

Example: *a a credit card—I wouldn't have to carry cash with me.*

● ● ● Pronunciation

49 Copy and complete the table with as many individual words as you can from the Word List.

/θ/ – thin	/ð/ – the	/f/ – five	/v/ – very

Check your table by listening to Track 11. Then add more words to your table and answer the questions.

a Which parts of the mouth do we use to make the sounds?
b What is the difference between /θ/ and /ð/? What is the difference between /f/ and /v/?

50 **Sound chains in teams** How many words from the Word List or Word Plus can you say in 60 seconds? Student A says a word, Student B has to say a new word which has at least one sound from Student A's word. Student C has to say a new word with at least one sound from Student B's word. Student D's word must have a sound from Student C's word.

Example: STUDENT A: *copies*
STUDENT B: *cool (/k/ from "copies")*
STUDENT C: *develop (/l/ from "cool")*
STUDENT D: *primitive (/p/ from "develop")*

51 **Newspaper headlines** Use as many words from the Word List as possible to write imaginary headlines. You will have to use other words too.

Example: *Zoom lens snaps credit card cameraman*

Invent a story to go with the headline.

Example: *Someone with a zoom lens who was taking a picture of a street caught (on film) a cameraman, John Smith, taking money from a credit card machine.*

52 Take one of the phrases from Word Plus and think of a situation to use it in. Tell your partner about it. Start with a sentence using the phrase. Your partner has to guess the situation.

Example: STUDENT A: *I am bitterly opposed to all those digital cameras. The quality isn't as good as film and now everybody thinks they can do a job that it has taken me 50 years to learn. So if you want to work here, you'd better be prepared to use some of the old ways.*
STUDENT B: *Maybe you are a photographer giving a young apprentice a job.*

UNIT 3
Wolf

→ adverbs and adverbial phrases
→ metaphor (animals)
→ warnings and threats

Reading: wolves

1 **Metaphor and idiom** Complete the sentences with a word or phrase from the box. Consult a dictionary if necessary.

> crying wolf   keep the wolf from the door
> lone wolf   wolf   wolf in sheep's clothing
> wolf (down) your food   wolf whistle

a A man who actively pursues different women used to be called a ....

b A person who seems pleasant but is actually nasty is sometimes called a ....

c If you earn just enough money to survive, you ....

d If people call for help when they don't really need it, we say they are ....

e Someone (usually male) who likes to live or work alone used to be called a ....

f When some men see an attractive woman, they make a loud sound called a ....

g When you eat too quickly, we can say that you ....

2 Answer the following questions.

a What impression of wolves is given by the sayings in Activity 1?

b Do you have any "wolf" sayings in your language?

c How would you describe the same ideas in your language?

3 One of the following mini-paragraphs represents the view of the writer, Peter Hedley, about wolves. Which do you think it is?

a Wolves are savage predators who attack human beings. They hunt on their own and abandon their young at an early age.

b Wolves are hated by most humans, but in reality they are sociable animals who love singing, playing and dancing.

c In stories wolves are always portrayed as dangerous and bad (as devils and werewolves) because of the way they behave in the wild.

d Wolves are beautiful beasts, but they make a terrible noise when there is a full moon.

Now read the text. Were you right?

How could we get it so wrong?

Recent controversies over the reintroduction of wolves to parts of the United States and Scotland yet again focus on one of nature's most misunderstood beasts.
Peter Hedley **takes up the story.**

Once upon a time, much of the world was populated by wolves. They ranged all over the United States and Canada, Siberia, and much of mainland Europe, as well as Great Britain, and if humans hadn't come along, they would still be there in great numbers. But man did come along, farmed the land, objected to the wolves killing their livestock, and so gradually drove them out of the homes that had once been theirs.

Wolves are not victims in our language and our literature, however. In fairy tales, they are seen as evil and dangerous, always ready to eat people. Remember the time when Little Red Riding Hood thinks that a wolf is her grandmother? "What big teeth you've got, grandmother!" she says, and the wolf, disguised as her grandmother, growls back sadistically, "all the better to eat you with, my dear!" In Prokofiev's musical fable *Peter and the Wolf*, the old grandfather speaks for us all at the end when he says, "Ah, but if Peter hadn't caught the wolf, what then?!"

In medieval times, the devil was often portrayed as a wolf, and the concept of a werewolf—the man who turns into a savage monster on the night of the full moon—is still a popular figure in both books and movies.

If you really want to see how English-speaking humans think of the wolf, just look at the language! "A wolf in sheep's clothing" is not a pleasant person and a "wolf-whistle" is not a pleasant sound!

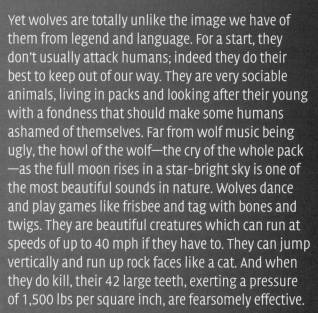

Yet wolves are totally unlike the image we have of them from legend and language. For a start, they don't usually attack humans; indeed they do their best to keep out of our way. They are very sociable animals, living in packs and looking after their young with a fondness that should make some humans ashamed of themselves. Far from wolf music being ugly, the howl of the wolf—the cry of the whole pack —as the full moon rises in a star-bright sky is one of the most beautiful sounds in nature. Wolves dance and play games like frisbee and tag with bones and twigs. They are beautiful creatures which can run at speeds of up to 40 mph if they have to. They can jump vertically and run up rock faces like a cat. And when they do kill, their 42 large teeth, exerting a pressure of 1,500 lbs per square inch, are fearsomely effective.

But the fact remains that we love the lion, the king of the jungle, another killer that spends much of its time asleep and often practices infanticide, while we demonize the wolf, one of the most beautiful animals in the world. Only occasionally do writers treat them nicely; for example, a she-wolf is supposed to have suckled the twins Remus and Romulus, who went on to found the city of Rome. If only the boys had stayed with her, perhaps they would have learned to love and respect each other. But instead they went back to the human world, Romulus killed his brother and Rome was founded in rivers of blood.

And so, while man kills animals in their millions, often just for the fun of it, the wolf on the mountain, out in the wilderness, running over the Siberian wastes, represents a state of natural grace that we do not know and can never obtain, even though we dream of it in our hearts. Perhaps that's why, in the end, we hate the wolf so much—for having something we can never get our hands on.

4 **In pairs** Discuss the following questions.

- What, if anything, surprised you in the text?
- Why do we hate wolves, according to Peter Hedley? Do you agree with him?

5 **Fact check** Who or what:

a ... was the reason farmers didn't like wolves?
b ... is Little Red Riding Hood?
c ... is *Peter and the Wolf*?
d ... was the image of a wolf used for many years ago?
e ... do wolves use instead of frisbees?
f ... sometimes kills their own or their mate's young?
g ... killed his brother?

6 **Vocabulary** Explain the meaning of the following words as they appear in the text.

a ranged (paragraph 1)
b victim (paragraph 2)
c fairy tale (paragraph 2)
d sadistically (paragraph 2)
e portrayed (paragraph 3)
f legend (paragraph 5)
g sociable (paragraph 5)
h demonize (paragraph 6)
i Siberian wastes (paragraph 7)

Language in chunks

7 Look at how these phrases are used in the text and then use them in the sentences which follow. You may have to change them a little to make them fit.

> ashamed of (themselves)   for a start   in the end   just for the fun of it
>
> to do (their) best   to get (your) hands on   to keep out of (our) way

a Don't come anywhere near me. Just ....
b I didn't come yesterday because .... , after a long day, I just didn't have the energy.
c I don't mind if I pass or fail. I just want to ....
d I've always wanted to own one of Picasso's paintings. I'd love to .... one.
e Bungee jumping isn't good for me or useful or anything. I do it ....
f Why do I want to leave my job? Well, ... , I'm not enjoying it any more.
   But there are many other reasons too.
g Why did you cheat on your exam? You should be ....

8 Choose two of the phrases and write sentences in which you use them as naturally as possible.

9 **Noticing language** Label the following words and phrases from the text according to which of the questions in the box they answer.

> How?   How often?   When?   Where?

a once upon a time (paragraph 1)   *When?*
b all over the United States (paragraph 1)
c out of (their) homes (paragraph 1)
d sadistically (paragraph 2)
e in medieval times (paragraph 3)
f vertically (paragraph 5)
g only occasionally (paragraph 6)
h nicely (paragraph 6)

Are the eight words / phrases *adverbial* (= they describe verbs) or *adjectival* (= they describe nouns)?

10 **In pairs** Copy the table and add one more question of your own. Interview your partner and complete the table with his or her answers.

Questions	Answers
a What is your favorite wild animal?	
b What is your favorite domestic animal?	
c What animal would you most like to be? Why?	
d What animal would you most like to study / photograph / know more about? Why?	
e ...	

Tell the class what your partner said.

Vocabulary: animal metaphors

11 In groups Look at the picture. Describe one of the animals, saying what they do, where they live, etc. The other students have to guess which animal it is.

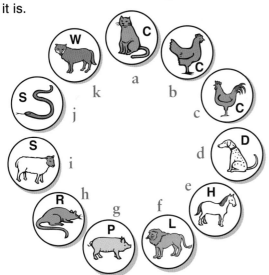

12 Find creatures from Activity 11 which make the following noises (one animal makes two of the noises).

| bark | bleat | cluck | crow | growl | grunt |
| hiss | howl | neigh | purr | roar | squeal |

13 Listen to Track 12 and choose one of the verbs (in the past tense) for each blank.

a "Turn that music down," he ....
b "Get out of my house," he ....
c "I'm not really sure I want to do this," he
....
d "Why should I care?" he.......................... .
e "Don't expect to get away with this," she
....
f "That was so lovely," she ....
g "I've just been given a fantastic grade for my composition," she ....

14 Language research Find out what you would expect or understand if:

a ... someone had a sheepish grin.
b ... someone was being really catty.
c ... someone had a pony tail.
d ... someone was really cocky.
e ... something was dog-eared.
f ... something was really fishy.
g ... someone was rather mousy.
h ... someone's room was a real pigsty.
i ... someone was really ratty.
j ... someone's new invention turned out to be a real turkey.

15 Animal idioms Complete the following sentences with an animal idiom from the box.

fishing for compliments
from the horse's mouth
going to the dogs
hold your horses
in the doghouse
kill two birds with one stone
let the cat out of the bag
making a real pig of
smell a rat
the lion's share

a .... ! We haven't decided whether to go to the movies yet and you're halfway out the door.
b He contributed most of the money for the costs of the concert so he gets .... of the profits.
c I know the story's true because I heard it .... I mean he's the one who's most involved.
d Let's .... We can go to the supermarket and fill up with gas right next door.
e I can't help it. I .... There's something wrong with his plan.
f She's really angry with me because I left the freezer door open. I'm really ....
g He's really .... He just doesn't seem to care about himself anymore. He spends all his time wasting money at parties.
h Sheila's "surprise" party isn't a surprise any more. Someone ....
i Stop .... You know we all think you are a terrific cook, so you don't need to get us to tell you all the time.
j Stop eating so much, Michael. You're .... yourself.

In pairs Choose any three of the animal idioms and use them in sentences. Explain who is saying them, in what situation and why.

16 Test items Write five sentences with blank spaces, to be completed with words or phrases from Activities 12–15.

Example: *I'm really hungry. I'm going to make a real .... of myself.*

Give your sentences to other students. Can they complete them successfully?

Grammar: adverbs

17 Adverbs and adjectives Read the following story. Are the words which follow the letters *a–t* adjectives (describing nouns) or adverbs (describing verbs)?

I was in a hurry. I was going to meet my girlfriend at 6 o'clock (**a**) sharp. I'd had a (**b**) late meeting and so I got to the bus stop (**c**) late and missed my bus. I decided to walk home the short way.

In most big cities you can see people sleeping (**d**) outside, and my route took me past a very (**e**) rough area where there were lots of dangerous-looking people. I had chosen (**f**) wrong. My fault.

Someone started shouting at me. I looked around. A man with an (**g**) extremely (**h**) ugly face was shouting at me, and many of his friends were getting up. The situation was turning (**i**) ugly. One of the men put his foot out and I fell (**j**) flat on my face. I was in (**k**) deadly danger.

At that moment a car roared round the corner and stopped (**l**) short. My grandmother (who had never driven in her life) called out my name. I'm a (**m**) cowardly kind of guy, so I jumped up and got into her car. We roared away. She drove (**n**) fast. She was driving a (**o**) fast car.

"I haven't seen much of you (**p**) lately," she said. I said nothing. I wasn't feeling too good.

"Can I talk (**q**) freely?" she said, and when I agreed she went on, "you've learned your lesson the (**r**) hard way. Don't go to that area again." At that moment, we reached the crossroads and she hit the brakes (**s**) hard, and turned to tell me off a bit more. But I could (**t**) hardly hear her.

Her voice was disappearing into the distance ... Then I woke up. It had all been a terrible dream.

Find examples from the text for each of the following explanations.

1 Some adjectives look just like adverbs (e.g. ...) and some adverbs look just like adjectives (e.g. ...). You can tell which is which by seeing whether they are describing a noun or a verb.
2 Some words can be both adjectives and adverbs (e.g. ...).
3 Some adverbs can have more than one form (e.g. ...).

18 Word formation Read 3A in the Mini-grammar and make the adjectives in the box into *-ly* adverbs.

basic   calm   chronic   clear   definite   extreme
fantastic   funny   futuristic   happy   possible
sadistic   terrible   tidy   vertical

19 Adverbs of manner In pairs, choose a verb from the verb box and two adverbs from the adverb box to make two-line exchanges.

VERB BOX	ADVERB BOX	
argue	fast	quiet
criticize	intelligent	rude
drive	loud	slow
eat	messy	soft
run	nasty	stupid
speak	nice	tidy
talk	noisy	untidy
write	polite	

Example: STUDENT A: *Please don't argue so loudly.*
STUDENT B: *All right, I'm sorry. I'll talk quietly, OK?*

20 Adverbs and adverbial phrases Copy and complete the table with the adverbs and adverbial phrases in the box.

a lot   angrily   at 6 o'clock   before   certainly
clearly   daily   eventually   every evening
finally   from time to time   hardly ever
in a friendly way   in my room   in the park
never   next week   noisily   now and then
often   on April 30th   out of the window
probably   soon   twice a year   upstairs
very well   with great patience

Type of adverb	Examples
Manner *how is / was it done?*	
Place *where is / was it done?*	
Time *when is / was it done?*	
Indefinite frequency *how often, more or less, is / was it done?*	
Definite frequency *how often is / was it done?*	
Certainty *How sure are you?*	

Look at 3B in the Mini-grammar. Think of two more adverbs or adverbials for each category.

21 Word order Are the following sentences correct, wrong or borderline (= not wrong, but not very natural)?

a Always I try to watch wildlife movies on television.   *wrong*

b I go only a few times a year to the movies.

c I haven't seen often television programs about wolves.

d I might possibly have seen that movie—I can't remember.

e I saw on January the 23rd my first wolf in the wild.

f I will have almost certainly finished reading this wildlife book before I see you.

g Never trust a lone wolf!

h She talked enthusiastically in the living room this evening.

i She went this evening enthusiastically to the party.

j The program will probably start at about 6 o'clock.

k They did quietly not go home.

l Through the window she could see the wolves.

Now look at 3C in the Mini-grammar. Do you want to change your opinion about any of the sentences? Can you correct or improve the sentences that are wrong or borderline?

Example: *a I always try to watch wildlife movies on television.*

22 Tell your partner about the following things.

• a hobby (e.g. playing the guitar)
• a regular activity (e.g. studying, working)
• something you may or may not do next week (e.g. going to stay with your brother)

Use as many adverbs or adverbials as possible from the box in Activity 20.

Example: *I play the guitar every evening in my room. I don't play it very well.*

23 Expand the following sentences using as many adverbs or adverbials as possible.

a She got home.
b She heard a noise.
c She went to investigate.

How does the story end, do you think?

Functional language: warnings and threats

24 Where might you hear or see the following?

a Come any closer and I'll shoot!
b Danger—Keep away from skin and eyes.
c I wouldn't go in there if I was you ...
d Never talk to me like that again, do you understand!
e Warning—Smoking can cause heart attacks.

25 Listen to Track 13 and the way the people speak. Are the sentences warnings or threats?

a Do that again and I'll get really angry.   *threat*
b Don't ever take my things without asking again, do you understand?
c Don't move! There's a wolf behind you.
d I would think very carefully before I said another word.
e I wouldn't go swimming there if I was you.
f I'm warning you not to drive that fast again.
g If you talk like that, you'll be in serious trouble.
h Never talk to me like that again.
i Speak to me nicely or I'll cry.
j Watch out! There's a bear behind you.

26 Which kind of warnings or threats are the sentences in Activity 25?
Match the letters *a–j* with the descriptions *1–6* in the table below.

Example: *a   2*

Description	Examples
1 Warnings with exclamations (imperatives, affirmative and negative)	*Be careful! Look out! Don't move!*
2 Threats with the imperative	*Say / Do that again and ... Stop that, or ...*
3 Threats with negative imperatives	*Never do that again!*
4 Threats with If + will sentences	*If you don't finish your homework on time, you'll have to leave the class.*
5 Threats / Warnings with If + would sentences	*I wouldn't go in there if I was you.*
6 Threats with the present continuous	*I'm telling you ...*

Pronunciation: main stress

27 Where would you put the main stress in the following sentences? Underline the syllable.

a Don't ever criticize me in public again!
b Look out!
c I would think very carefully before I tried that again.
d I'm warning you. Don't do it.

e Never do that again.
f Stop. Right now.
g Watch out! Behind you!

Listen to Track 14. Did the speakers agree with you?

28 Say the sentences in the same way as the speakers.

29 What would you say in the following situations?

a A friend is about to dive into a swimming pool.
You know the water is very cold.

I wouldn't go in there if I was you.

b A wolf has just attacked one of your animals. You talk to it as if it was human.

c An American friend has threatened to tell your best friends something bad you said about them.

d Someone has just said something nasty to you and you don't want them to do it again.

e Someone is about to step on a banana skin.

f You are a traffic cop. You have decided not to give someone a parking ticket, but ...

g You are furious with someone who has just borrowed your laptop computer without asking you.

h You are teaching someone to drive and they've just scared you half to death. Now they've turned off the engine.

i Your boss is about to pick up a very hot plate.

j Your American cousin (who you don't like very much) has just spilt coffee all over the book you're reading.

30 a Choose one of the pictures and write a short scene to accompany it in which one character warns or threatens the other, and their reply.

b Rewrite your conversation like a movie script and add adverbial directions saying how the characters should speak and move. Look at the box in Activity 20 for ideas.

Example: **1**

Lecturer (with great patience): Don't ever hand in work late again, do you understand?

Listening: a story

))) 31 **Listen to Track 15 and say which of these three books the extract comes from.**

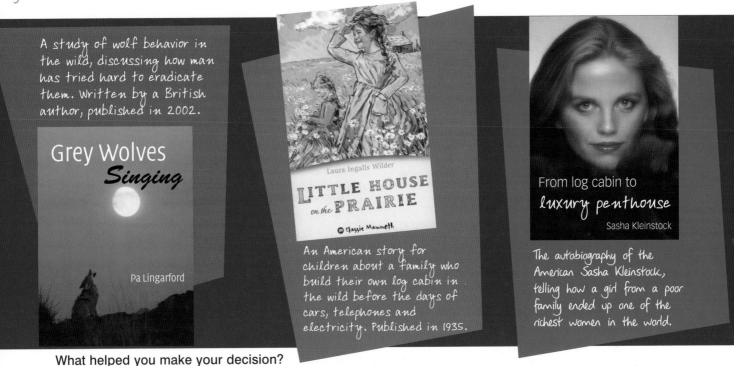

A study of wolf behavior in the wild, discussing how man has tried hard to eradicate them. Written by a British author, published in 2002.

Grey Wolves
Singing

Pa Lingarford

Laura Ingalls Wilder

LITTLE HOUSE *on the* **PRAIRIE**

📖 Classic Mammoth

An American story for children about a family who build their own log cabin in the wild before the days of cars, telephones and electricity. Published in 1935.

From log cabin to
luxury penthouse

Sasha Kleinstock

The autobiography of the American Sasha Kleinstock, telling how a girl from a poor family ended up one of the richest women in the world.

What helped you make your decision?

))) 32 **Listen to Track 16 and then answer these questions.**

a What woke the girl up?
b What did she see?
c What did she hear?
d Who protected her?
e What stopped the girl being frightened?

33 **Think of three things (or events) in your childhood which were similar to the girl's experiences and three things (or events) which were different.**

Example: Once, when I was 10, I went out and
I saw ...
But we didn't live ...

34 **Work it out Answer the questions a–d.**

a What is a quilt and how many are mentioned in the extract?
b Who or what is Jack?
c Why does the writer talk about window holes instead of windows?
d Who is Mary?

Word Choice: *hear* and *listen (to)*

35 **Look at the Word Choice notes for *hear*, *listen*, and *listen to* on page 56 in the booklet.**

Complete the spaces in these lines with a form of *hear*, *listen* or *listen to*.

a I can .... a noise coming from those woods, but I don't know what it is.
b There's no point in talking to me, I'm not ....
c When he's alone, he likes .... his old jazz CDs.
d I looked over at Ruth. She was .... intently with a look of complete concentration.
e There's no point in talking to me. With all this noise, I can't .... a thing.
f Laura could .... the wolves' breathing all round the house.
g I'm prepared to .... your point of view, but I don't expect to agree with it.
h Be quiet! I'm trying to .... their conversation.
i Go on! I'm ....

36 Listen again to Track 16 and complete the following extracts from the story with between one and five words.

   a Jack .... his teeth.

   b She wanted to go to Pa, but .... bother him now.

   c He stood his gun against the wall and .... to the window hole.

   d Laura lifted her toes into a crack in the wall and she .... on the window slab, and she looked and ....

   e When they saw Pa and Laura looking out, the middle of the circle .... way.

   f Go to sleep. Jack and I will ....

   g She lay and listened to the breathing of the wolves .... the log wall.

37 What was your favorite story when you were a child? Tell your partner about it.

Speaking: comparing pictures

38 Differences and similarities Student B, turn to Activity Bank 1 on page 156. Student A, look at the picture on this page. Find five similarities and differences between your picture and Student B's.

39 Discussion Ask your partner the following questions.

   a Ivory sales (from elephant tusks) have been declared illegal, yet poachers still kill elephants secretly so they can sell ivory. What is the correct punishment for ivory poachers, do you think?

   b Elephants are used for work in some countries. Do you agree with this?

   c Elephants are shown in circuses around the world. How do you feel about this?

   d Recently an elephant charged into a crowd at a circus and killed a spectator. What should happen to that elephant?

   e Some elephants are kept in zoos. Do you agree with this? Why? Why not?

Do you agree with your partner?

Writing: linking words and phrases

40 a Read the question and the student composition which answered it. Is the student generally in favor of zoos or not?

Write a composition discussing the following statement.

Nobody should enjoy going to zoos which keep animals in cages.

I'd like to start this composition by saying that I have enjoyed going to zoos and looking at animals in the past. It's always very exciting to look at creatures you have never seen before. But many people say that zoos are not pleasant places and the animals are in cages and don't have their freedom. And if you deny animals their freedom and keep them in enclosed spaces, they become ill and psychologically disturbed.

But people who support zoos say that the animals are well looked after and fed, something that does not always happen to them in the wild. And zoos have started many breeding programs to save endangered species. So many animals that might have become extinct are now still alive.

If I had thought about it when I first went to see a zoo, I would have been unhappy about animals in cages, and I now think that is wrong. But some of the wildlife parks in various countries in the world give animals both security and freedom. So those are the ones I approve of.

So I think that zoos are often cruel places. Proper wildlife parks are a better way for man to preserve species while, at the same time, giving us all a chance to see animals in a natural habitat. But I am sure many families will still take their young children to visit zoos.

---

   b In formal writing, we use more sophisticated words than *and*, *but* and *so*. Replace the words in blue in the student's composition with the following words and phrases. Use each one once only.

> as a result   and furthermore   however
> in conclusion   therefore,   in contrast   moreover
> not only that, but   nevertheless
> on the other hand
>
> Notes:
> * *However* is always followed by a comma. When it occurs in the middle of a sentence, it has a comma before it too.
> * *Moreover* generally occurs at the beginning of a sentence or a clause (e.g. after a semicolon). In the middle of sentences, it usually occurs with *and* and has commas before and after it (*... and, moreover, ...*).

Now check your answers with the text in Activity Bank 2 on page 156.

41 Read the following composition question.

Zoos are absolutely vital for the protection of various animal species.

Make notes in English for and against the opinion given.

42 Plan your own composition (three or four paragraphs).

Paragraph 1: introduce the topic. (*I'd like to start by ...*)
Paragraph 2: set out arguments / give reasons.
Paragraph 3: set out more arguments / give more reasons.
Paragraph 4: draw your own conclusion. (*In conclusion therefore ...*)

43 Write your composition, using some or all of the linkers from Activity 40b.

Review: grammar and functional language

44 Write sentences using some of the following words as either adjectives or adverbs.

Read your sentences to your partner. Can they say whether it is an adverb or an adjective? Look at Activity 17 for help.

fast	hard	late	loud	pretty	rough
slow	tight	ugly	well	wrong	

Example: STUDENT A: That was pretty funny!
STUDENT B: Is "pretty" an adjective?
STUDENT A: No.

45 Make sentences about yourself using the verbs below. Add adverbs or adverbial phrases of manner, place, time, definite / indefinite frequency and certainty. Look at Activity 20 for ideas.

Things I do:
- eat
- feel nervous
- feel regret
- feel tired
- like reading books
- sing
- sleep
- stay silent
- study
- talk to animals
- watch people

Example: I frequently eat noisily in restaurants at about 7 o'clock!

46 What are the people saying? What words can go in the speech bubble in each case? Add a threat or a warning. Look at Activities 24–30 for help.

Review: vocabulary

Word List

catty cocky dog-eared
dogged fairy tale fishy
mousy pigsty pony tail
portrayed range ratty
real turkey sadistically
sheepish grin (Siberian) wastes
sociable to bark to bleat
to cluck to crow
to demonize to growl
to grunt to hiss to howl
to neigh to purr to roar
to squeal victim wolf

Word Plus

ashamed of themselves
for a start
from the horse's mouth
in the doghouse
in the end
just for the fun of it
lone wolf
the lion's share
to cry wolf
to do their best
to fish for compliments
to get (your) hands on
to go to the dogs
to hold your horses
to keep out of our way
to keep the wolf from the door
to kill two birds with one stone
to let the cat out of the bag
to make a real pig of
to smell a rat
to wolf (down) your food
wolf in sheep's clothing
wolf whistle

47 What are your two (a) favorite and (b) least favourite animals? Are there any words or phrases in the Word List or Word Plus that can be used with your animals? Can you find any more words or phrases about your animals in your dictionary?

Pronunciation

48 List words (including compound nouns and adjectives) of two syllables or more in the Word List and complete the following tasks.

a Which is the stressed syllable?
b What is the vowel sound in the stressed syllable? Underline it.
c Can you find other words with the same stressed vowel sound?

Example: f_i_shy—v_i_ctim

Listen to the words on Track 17 and check your answer.

49 Say the words of the following phrases as separate words. Then say them as phrases. How does the pronunciation of the individual words change, if at all?

a ashamed of themselves
b for a start
c from the horse's mouth
d in the end
e just for the fun of it

Listen to Track 18 and repeat the phrases like the speakers.

50 **In pairs** Choose one of the animal metaphors from the Word Plus box. Without looking at a dictionary, write your own definition for the expression, and then include the phrase in two example sentences.

Example: from the horse's mouth—from the person who knows most about the subject

I heard the story in the cafeteria, but then I asked my boss, because I wanted to hear it from the horse's mouth.

51 **Game** List the animals from the picture in Activity 11. Team A says the name of an animal. Team B gets one point for a word associated with the animal, and two points for any metaphorical phrase that includes the animal.

Example: TEAM A: cat

TEAM B: purr (= 1 point)

Don't be so catty! (= 2 points)

UNIT 4
Just for fun

→ present perfect continuous
→ hobbies and activities
→ asking for clarification / buying "thinking time"

bird watching

Listening: things people do for fun

fisherman   *sky diving*

1   What are the people doing? Would you like to do it yourself? Why? Why not?

binoculars

 a

 b

 c

 d

e

2   Look at the people. Which of the activities from Activity 1 do you think they do just for fun?

*Caving
Spelunking*

Danny   *fishing @ angling*   Carmen   *spelunking* b d c   Jack   *train spot* f e   Marcus   *golf* g h   Ellie   *sky diving* j i

Listen to Track 19. Were you correct?

3   Listen again. Who says ... ?

   a It gives you time to think.
   b I've begged her to stop.
   c And that's the truth.
   d I've never had any trouble.
   e I'll take your word for it.   *I don't want to try*
   f The only downside is that it can be pretty cold. *almost*
   g I'm not addicted to it or anything.
   h You can't be serious.
   i It's not for everybody.
   j People call us nerds.

4   Which of the phrases in Activity 3 mean ... ?

   a I've asked as strongly as possible. *I've begged.*
   b I could easily stop doing it.
   c I believe you, but I don't want to try it.
   d Only some people enjoy it.
   e very boring people who are interested in silly little details (slang)
   f the one disadvantage
   g That's a ridiculous suggestion.

5   In pairs Student A asks Student B about the five people in Activity 2. How many questions can A think of, and how many answers can B give?

   Example: STUDENT A: *How does Danny spend his spare time?*

   STUDENT B: *He goes fishing. He's an angler.*

Vocabulary: hobbies and activities

6 What do we call someone who ...

a ... arranges flowers?
flower arranger

b ... plays golf?

c ... climbs mountains?

d ... climbs rocks?

e ... collects stamps?

f ... dives through the sky?

g ... fishes?

h ... explores caves?

i ... keeps bees?

j ... makes models?

k ... skis on water?

l ... spots (watches) trains?

m ... dives (swims under water) with a scuba tank?

n ... uses a skateboard?

o ... uses a snowboard?

p ... walks up and down hills?

q ... watches birds?

7 a Look at the names you've found in Activity 6: which are compound words and which are words with different forms? (e.g. verb + -er = noun)

Example: *compound words:*
    flower arranger
    verbs + "-er": skier

b What do we call the activity?

Example: *flower arranging*

8 **Language research** Using a dictionary or any other source, find out what activities you might use the following objects with.

a album   *stamp collecting*

b binoculars

c gloves

d glue

e goggles

f helmet

g magnifying glass

h mask

i money

j net

k notebook

l oxygen tank

m rod

n skis

o flashlight

p vase

q wetsuit

9 Where would you put the phrases on the following line?

hate | ————————————————— | love

a I am addicted to

b I really like

c I am crazy about

d I am not crazy about

e I am not really into

f I am not very interested in

g I don't really care about

h I am obsessed by

i I am really into

j I do not enjoy

k I do not like

l I get a kick out of

m I really enjoy

n ... doesn't do much for me

o ... turns me on

p ... doesn't really turn me on

10 Say how you feel about the activities mentioned in the unit so far.

Example: *I'm really addicted to water-skiing, but skiing on snow doesn't do much for me.*

11 **In groups** Write questions for the people in the pictures. Ask about their hobby, their lives, their daily routines, their likes and dislikes, etc.

A student chooses one of the four characters. The other students in the group have to interview the student as if he / she was that character. The student should answer any question in the way he / she thinks the character would.

Example: c

STUDENTS: *Aren't you frightened of bees?*

BEE-KEEPER: *Not really. But I have to be careful.*

STUDENTS: *What do you do when you are not with your bees?*

BEE-KEEPER: *Umm, well I like scuba diving!*

Speaking: making a presentation

12 Preparation Complete the following tasks.

a Choose a hobby or an activity that you would like to talk about, either because you do it just for fun or because you would like to do it.

b Make notes in answer to the following questions.

Why do you want to talk about it?

What is special about it?

Have you ever done it and what was it like?

OR Would you like to do it and why?

What kind of person does this activity?

When and where is the best place or time to do it?

Who is the best person to do it with?

What would you say to encourage other people to do it?

What does it feel like?

What else would you like to say about it?

c Use your notes to plan your talk. You can follow this outline plan.

what you're going to talk about and why
↓
what it is
• what it's like
• how you do it, etc.
↓
conclusions

13 Giving a presentation in groups

Stage 1
STUDENT A: give your presentation.
STUDENT B: you are a kind critic. Write down any examples of good English that you hear.
STUDENT C: you are a harsh critic. Write down any mistakes you hear.
STUDENTS D, E, etc: write down questions you want to ask when Student A has finished.

Stage 2
In groups, Students D, E, etc. ask their questions and Student A answers them.

Stage 3
Students B and C give their kind critic / harsh critic reports.
The group discusses the reports.

Grammar: present perfect continuous (and simple)

14 What's the problem with each of the following sentences?

a I have lived in New York since a long time.

b I haven't seen him yesterday.

c I've just only realized who you are.

d I've tried never rock climbing and I don't think I want to.

e I have tried a couple of times cliff diving but it frightened me so I'm not going to do it again.

f I have watched freediving on television last night and it was very boring.

g I have forgotten already the name of the world cliff diving champion.

Look at 4A–4D in the Mini-grammar. Do you want to change your answers?

15 In which one of the following situations is the present perfect simple (*has done* / *have done*) NOT used?

a when we want to talk about a recent past action with present consequences

b when we want to talk about a completed / finished action in the past (and we don't want to make any connection with the present)

c when we want to talk about an action which started in the past and is still continuing

d when we want to talk about general experiences that have affected us in our lives

16 Choose the simple (*has done*) or continuous (*has been doing*) form of the present perfect for the following sentences.

a Bruce (skydive) <u>has been skydiving</u> for three years and he wants to keep doing it.

b He (make) .... 60 jumps in competitions so far this year.

c For the last four months, he (see) .... a girl he met in Greece. She's a nurse in a hospital emergency room.

d He (ask)............................... her to marry him and she (agree) ....

e He (buy) .... a beautiful ring for her. She loves it.

f His fiancée (never jump) .... because she doesn't like heights.

g She (go) .... to Bruce's skydiving competitions for the last few months.

h She (not enjoy) .... a single one of them.

i He (promise) .... to give up his hobby, but she won't believe him until he does.

j He (watch) .... her at work twice, but he's not going to do it again.

k He (never be able) .... to stand the sight of blood!

Look at 4A–4F in the Mini-grammar. Do you want to change your answers?

17 Use **4A–4F in the Mini-grammar** to decide whether the following sentences are correct or wrong.

a I've been taking tennis lessons for a few weeks now.

b I've been having six tennis lessons so far.

c This is only the second time I've been seeing a cliff diving competition.

d I've been understanding most of his lectures.

e She's been visiting her grandmother on Sundays for the last year and a half.

f He's gone to English classes for the last two months.

g This mountain has been being here since the dawn of time.

h She's been climbing mountains since she was a child.

i I've been dreaming about skydiving.

j How many dreams about skydiving have you been having?

18 Conversations Match the conversations to the pictures.

1 A: How have you been keeping?
  B: Not too bad, but I don't get out much.

2 A: What have you been doing with yourself since we last met?
  B: Oh well, I went skiing a couple of weeks ago.

3 A: Where have you been hiding recently?
  B: What? Oh, er, nowhere. I've just been working quite hard, that's all.

Choose one of the pictures *a–c* and continue the conversation. How many examples of the present perfect continuous can you include in the conversation? (Use questions like the ones in the box below.)

> Have you been getting enough sleep?
> Have you been skiing since you got back?
> Have you been seeing anyone special?
> How have you been keeping up with your work?
> How have you been getting on with your colleagues / fellow inmates?

a

b

c

Reading: looking danger in the face

19 Copy the table. Choose <u>one</u> of the three texts, read it and complete the appropriate column of your table about that person.

	Text 1	Text 2	Text 3
a Name of main character	Dustin Webster		Leo Houlding
b Name of person in the photograph (if different)			—
c Date and place of birth of main character		1974	
d What the main character does		free Diving	Climbing
e What is special about what he does			Slacklining
f How the main character started			
g Achievements (if listed)			Barcelona
h Any other interesting information			

20 Talk to students who read the other two texts and complete your table based on what they tell you.

Example: Text 1

STUDENT A: What's the main character's name?

STUDENT B: Dustin Webster.

1

American-born Dustin Webster has loved high diving ever since his parents took him to see high divers at an amusement park in San Diego when he was 11. He went backstage to ask the divers how they did it and six years later he joined their team. He has been high diving ever since.

The kind of diving Dustin does is called cliff diving, and it's not like the diving you see in the Olympics. For a start the distance from the board to the water (about 25 yards) is much greater than that. And secondly, cliff divers like Dustin do triple and quadruple somersaults on the way down. This makes cliff diving highly skilled and extremely dangerous. Many of them suffer injury and, on occasions, death if they land in the water on their stomachs or their backs. "From 25 yards up, you fall a bit like a grand piano," Dustin says cheerfully. They have been known to break their legs if they land on a fish or a piece of seaweed.

When you watch cliff divers, you get a real sense of how absolutely terrifying it is. They stand on the edge of the board and look down, far far down, and then they launch themselves twisting into the air. No matter how many times you do it, Dustin and his colleagues say, you never lose the fear just before you jump.

So how come Colombian Orlando Duque, who has just beaten Dustin to become the latest cliff diving champion, looked so still and God-like as he stood above a saltwater lake in Greece, arms outstretched, his long black hair falling down his back, protected by nothing except a small pair of red swimming trunks? That day, back in July, he looked more like the statue of Christ in Rio de Janeiro than a frail human being. And then he was gone, falling through the air, doing his famous back loop with four twists, incredibly graceful and frighteningly vulnerable. And it worked. When that day's competition was over, Duque had won the prize.

When world champion Francisco "Pipin" Ferreras went to Baja California in 1996 to try and break the world freediving record, he did not realize that he would meet the young woman who would soon become his wife. But that is what happened, for she had been doing a university thesis on freediving and he was the one person she wanted to talk to about it. Audrey Mestre, the woman doing the thesis, was born in France on August 11, 1974. Her grandfather and her mother were both spearfishers and, as a result, Audrey had been diving since she was a child. She won her first swimming race when she was two and a half years old and began scuba diving when she was 13.

In 1990 she moved (with her family) to Mexico, and it was there that she started freediving—diving with no breathing apparatus, something that people who fish with spears have been doing for as long as there have been people living by the sea. But modern freedivers try to break world records all the time to see who can go deepest, and for how long, without any oxygen at all.

Pipin Ferreras is a world champion and pretty soon his new girlfriend (Audrey, soon to be his wife) was joining him in his record attempts. In 1997 she did a free dive of 80 yards and in 1998 she dived to 115 yards with her husband. Things really took off in May 2000, however, when, off the coast of the Canary Islands, she broke the female freediving world record by reaching a depth of 125 yards and coming back in two minutes and three seconds. Only one year later, she reached 130 yards.

But freediving is a dangerous sport. On October 12, 2002, Audrey was in the Dominican Republic attempting to beat a record set by U.K. freediver Tanya Streeter. This time she went too far, there was an accident, and she died.

When carpenter Mark Houlding took his seven-year-old son Leo climbing up a 10,000 ft. mountain in Morocco a few years ago, he probably didn't realize what he had started. But ever since then, Mark's little boy has been climbing higher and higher, and doing more and more dangerous things just for the fun of it.

People first started to hear of Leo Houlding when one day at the age of 16, he walked up to a highly dangerous cliff face in Wales and chose to climb it "on sight" instead of planning it and doing a practice climb with ropes like most experienced climbers do. At one point he became stuck for more than half an hour, but he closed his eyes and felt for good holds with his hands. Then he lost his grip and thought "this is it!" but he kept going and made it to the top.

With his crazy courage, youthful good looks, and disrespectful attitude, Houlding is not popular with everyone in the careful world of climbing—the activity which is still his first love. But that has not stopped him trying other sports too. For example, he only tried snowboarding a few times before he took himself down one of the most dangerous mountain runs in Switzerland.

His special party trick, however, is called "slack-lining," which is like tightrope walking except that the rope is much looser and, as a result, much more difficult to walk on—and therefore much more dangerous. He does this everywhere, on fences or even on rope barriers hundreds of feet above nothing.

"I don't want to die," Leo says nonchalantly, "but I'm not particularly afraid of it. I just want to make enough money as a climber so I can keep doing it. And for the last three years I've been traveling all over the world doing exactly that." And it's true: he's climbed in Chile, India, Thailand, Switzerland and Britain to name just a few of the countries he gets to. Recently, for example, he's been climbing in and around Barcelona in Spain. And how did he spend his spare time when he was there? Looking down at the city from the very top of some of the biggest construction cranes in the world.

21 In pairs Discuss the following questions.

a Which of the three activities in texts 1–3 would you most or least like to do? Why?

b Choose one of the three characters in the texts. What would you most like to ask them?

22 Vocabulary Look at these sentences from the texts. What parts of speech are the words in blue? What words or phrases can replace the words in blue without changing the meaning too much?

a Then they launch themselves twisting into the air.

verb – "then they throw themselves"

b They have been known to break their legs if they land ... on a piece of seaweed.

c He looked more like the statue ... than a frail human being.

d And then he was gone ... incredibly graceful and frighteningly vulnerable.

e She had been doing a university thesis on freediving.

f She ... began scuba diving when she was 13.

g Freediving [means] diving with no breathing apparatus.

h With his crazy courage ... and disrespectful attitude, Houlding is not popular with everyone.

i "I don't want to die," Leo says nonchalantly.

Language in chunks

23 Match the phrases in italics from the text (a–g) with their meanings (1–7).

a *break world records*
b *amusement park*
c *lost his grip*

d things *really took off*
e *this is it*
f *to name but a few*

g *went backstage*

1 a small number of a much larger list
2 started to become really successful
3 visited the area where the performers were relaxing / getting changed
4 I am going to fall / die
5 become the best a number of times
6 a place to ride on large machines and play games for prizes
7 couldn't hold on to something

24 In pairs Ask your partner the following questions.

a What world record would you most like to break?
b What is your favorite amusement park ride?
c Have you ever lost your grip—either in actual fact or metaphorically?
d Has there ever been a time in your life when things really took off for you?
e Has there ever been a moment in your life when you thought 'this is it'?
f What people do you most admire (answer using the phrase *to name but a few*)?
g Have you ever been backstage in a theater / concert hall? Describe it.

25 Noticing language How many examples of the present perfect continuous form can you find in the texts?

26 Memory Choose one of the people in the texts and write five comprehension questions about that person.

Close your book. Ask someone your questions. Try and answer someone else's questions. How good is your memory?

Functional language: asking for clarification / buying "thinking time"

27 Listening Read the conversation. What is it the woman doesn't want to do? Find a suitable word for the gap.

WOMAN: I've been looking for you everywhere.
MAN: Excuse me?
WOMAN: I've been trying to find you but I couldn't see you anywhere.
MAN: Well now you have found me! I haven't been hiding or anything. I've been around. Actually I've been ...
WOMAN: Look, it's not that I'm not interested or anything, but I need to talk about the ... umm ... about the _____ tonight.
MAN: Yeah?
WOMAN: Yes. I'm not sure if I really want to go.
MAN: Why not?
WOMAN: Well because I'm not really in the what-do-you-call-it? ...

MAN: Mood?

WOMAN: Yes, that's it, I'm not in the mood.

MAN: Uh-huh?

WOMAN: And anyway there'll be lots of people from the office, and I see enough of them during the day. Do you know what I mean? I just don't want …

MAN: Well yes, but they all really want you to go and there'll be lots of other people too. Anyway, I want to go.

Listen to Track 20. Were you correct?

28 Copy and complete the table with the expressions in blue from the conversation in Activity 27.

If you:	Words and phrases
… can't think what something is called:	a
… want time to think because you don't know what to say next or because you don't want to say what you are going to have to say:	b
… want to check that someone understands or agrees with what you are saying:	c
… want to ask someone to repeat something that they have just said because you didn't hear or understand it:	d
… want to show that you're listening to what someone is saying and you want them to go on (two examples):	e
… want to say something / interrupt when someone else is talking:	f
… want to change the topic of the exchange or go back to an earlier subject:	g

29 Add the following to the table in Activity 28. (Some words and phrases can be used more than once.)

1 Could you repeat the question / that?
2 Er …
3 I didn't quite catch that.
4 Mmm.
5 Pardon me?
6 Right.
7 Sorry to interrupt, but …
8 Well …
9 what's-her-name / what's-his-name
10 thingamajig
11 Yes.
12 You know …

30 What words or phrases from Activities 27–29 could you use in the following conversation? Choose a word or phrase for each letter (a–f).

A: Have you seen my dark glasses anywhere?
B: (a) ....
A: I can't find my glasses. Have you seen them?
B: Weren't you using them earlier on?
A: Well yes, (b) .... I was but I can't remember where I put them.
B: Honestly, you are hopeless. Sometimes I don't know what to do with you.
A: (c) ....
B: It's true. You're always forgetting things. Losing things. I mean only yesterday you couldn't find …
A: (d) .... I do need to find my glasses.
B: It's really irritating, always having to look for things that you've lost. It gets me all irritated. (e) ....
A: Yes.
B: And that's not a good thing.
A: (f) .... It's not that serious, honestly.
B: Hey, wait a minute. Aren't those your glasses there?
A: Oh yes. Great. I'll be going then. Goodbye.
B: Bye.

●●● Pronunciation: intonation

31 Listen to Track 21. Is the man just showing that he is listening or does he want the woman to repeat what she has said—or say more? Write a period (.) or a question mark (?) after each of his words.

a Yeah	**e** Right
b Excuse me	**f** Excuse me
c Uh-huh	**g** Uh-huh
d Yeah	**h** Right

Did the man's voice go up or down in each case?

32 In pairs Student A reads the statements and Student B responds with one-word answers (*yeah*, *right*, *m'mmm*, *uh-huh*, etc.). Is Student B just listening or do they want Student A to say more or repeat?

Example: *a*

STUDENT A: You know I've been reading that book about skydiving.

STUDENT B: M'mmm?

STUDENT A: You want me to repeat!

a You know I've been reading that book about skydiving.
b I've been looking for you everywhere.
c I've always wanted to see that singer live.
d I had a really fantastic time at Morag's party.
e I've just finished reading Sarah's new book.
f That movie was really shocking.
g It was a beautiful day yesterday.
h I didn't enjoy that class.

Writing: email interview

33 Read the email interview with Emma Sanchez Moore and answer the questions.

a Would you like to meet her? Why? Why not?
b Are there any words you do not understand? Check them with a partner.
If you still don't know what they mean, use your dictionary.

The email interview

Twenty-three-year-old Emma Sanchez Moore is a paraski champion. Paraskiing, whether on snow or on water, uses a small parachute to pull the skier along. Emma lives in Detroit with her family, but she spends a lot of her time paraskiing off beaches all over the world, especially in Mexico, her parents' native land. Both her brothers have won titles as barefoot skiers, but Emma still prefers the parachute.

What is your most vivid childhood memory?
When my Dad took me water-skiing for the first time in Acapulco. We were in Mexico for a vacation with my grandparents. All I was told was "shut up and hold on!"
Which living person would you most like to go on a fantasy date with?
Enrique Iglesias—because he has the best voice, he's good-looking, and he's like me, he lives in two cultures.
What three words best describe you?
Fit, funny, beautiful (only joking about the last one!).
What is your idea of perfect happiness?
Calm water and early morning sunshine, just before the skiing starts.
What is your greatest fear?
That I'll break something and not be able to ski anymore.
Who or what is the greatest love of your life?
My family, especially my two brothers Ryan and Oliver.
What is your greatest regret?
That I didn't work harder at school.
How do you relax?
I go clubbing with my friends.
How would you like to be remembered?
As someone who loved life.
What is the most important lesson life has taught you?
If something's worth doing, it's worth doing well.

Speaking and writing:
speaking-like and
writing-like

34 Are the following phrases, sentences, and questions more writing-like or speaking-like? How do you know?

a Fantastic, aren't they?
b I think they are fantastic.
c See you later.
d I was like "fine" and he was like "OK."
e I said that it was fine and he replied that it was OK.
f I'm not going to put up with it any more.
g I'm not going to tolerate it any more.
h You're not from around here, are you?
i Do you come from this neighborhood?
j You're a skydiver?
k Check out the new cafeteria! Awesome!
l It is worth investigating the new cafeteria.

Include two speaking-like phrases in a short conversation.

35 Answer the questions from the interview in Activity 33 about you. Compare your answers with a partner.

Example: *My most vivid childhood memory is …*

36 In pairs Think of ten more questions you could send for an email interview. (E.g. What makes them sad / happy, things they like / don't like, friendships, tastes in music, hopes for the future, etc.)

37 Send your questions to your classmates, or email your interview questions to a friend.

Review: grammar and functional language

38 Match the questions in the first list (*a–j*) with the list below (*1–10*). Look at Activities 14–18 for help.

a Have you been reading my private diary?
b Have you been studying as hard as you ought to?
c Have you been taking money from my billfold? → *wallet*
d How have you been getting along with your new roommate?
e What have you been eating since you last came to see me?
f Who have you been seeing recently?
g Why have they been following us for the last hour?
h Why have you been missing lessons recently?
i You look exhausted. What have you been doing?
j You've been falling asleep in class. Why is that?

1 Absolutely fine. She's really good company. *d*
2 I don't know. Perhaps they think we'll lead them to the money. *g*
3 I've been practicing for the diving competition. *h*
4 I've been working nights at the local hospital. *j*
5 No one special. Just a friend. Honestly. *f*
6 No, honestly I haven't. It just fell open when I picked it up. *c*
7 No, of course I haven't. But I'd like a bit more allowance → *money* every week. *a*
8 Not really. I keep getting distracted. *b* *to less*
9 The same as before. I haven't managed to ⌐cut down on⌐ chocolate, I'm afraid. I just can't do it. *e*
10 Working out at the gym. I really gave myself a hard time. *i*

Who asks the questions, do you think? Who answers them? What's the situation?

Example: *a It could be brothers and sisters, or a teenager and a parent.*

39 Think of activities for each of the following categories.

a something you haven't been doing recently (but should have been doing)
b something you've always done
c something you've been doing for the last few weeks
d something you've done a few times (but would like to do more often)
e something you've done, but wouldn't like to do again
f something you've never done

In pairs Tell your partner about the activities. Does your partner have similar things to say?

40 Rewrite the following conversation, trying to ask for clarification and "buy time." Include as many expressions from Activities 27–30 as you can.

A: I've been thinking of taking up water-skiing.
B: Have you?
A: Yes. It looks quite exciting.
B: Do you think you're strong enough?
A: Yes, of course, why not?
B: Well, you're not exactly fit, are you?
A: I'm not sure that's true. I walk to work every day, and I walk backwards and forwards to the water cooler in the office at least three …

Review: vocabulary

Word List

album   angling   apparatus
beekeeper   binoculars
bird watcher   disrespectful
flower arranger   frail
flashlight   gloves   glue
goggles   golfer   helmet
hillwalker   magnifying glass
mask   money
mountain climber   net
nonchalantly   notebook
oxygen tank   rock climber
rod   scuba diver
skateboarder   skis   skydiver
snowboarder   spelunker
stamp collector
thesis   to launch yourself
torch   trainspotter   vase
vulnerable   water-skier
wetsuit

Word Plus

"It doesn't do much for me." *
"it turns me on"
things really took off
"This is it."
to be addicted to
to be crazy about
to be not crazy about
to be not very interested in
to be obsessed by
to be really into
to break a world record
to get a kick out of
to go backstage
to give [something] a try
to lose your grip
"to name but a few"
to really enjoy
to really like

*Phrases in quotation marks are
conversational phrases.

41 Choose three of the occupations from the Word List that you would like to try. What three objects would be the most important for each of the occupations? Can you find the objects in the Word List?

Compare your answers with a partner.

Pronunciation

42 Listen to Track 22. How many sounds are there in the following words?

Example: glue: three (/g/, /l/ and /u:/)

a angling
b binoculars
c goggles
d notebook
e skateboarder
f thesis
g trainspotter

43 Find all the words in the Word List with three or more syllables (including compound nouns). Which is the stressed syllable in each case? Which words are always stressed on the first syllable?

Example: 'beekeeper

Check your answers by listening to Track 23.

44 **Instant role-play** Choose two of the hobbies / activities. Two people, one for each hobby / activity, meet and have a conversation. Decide where they meet and what the topic of the conversation is. Role-play the conversation as quickly as possible.

45 **In pairs** Design a questionnaire to find out how people feel about either different sports or different hobbies. In your questionnaire, make sure you have a way of writing down how interested people are, using phrases from Word Plus.

Example:

How would you describe your interest in pop music?	Addicted to it	Crazy about it	Really like it	Interested in it	Not interested in it

Use your questionnaire to ask other students about their interests.

Example: How would you describe your interest in pop music? Are you addicted to it? Crazy about it? ...

UNIT 5

Getting angry

→ the third conditional
→ being angry
→ wishes and regrets

Reading: what's anger all about?

1 Discussion How would you answer the following questions?

- What is anger?
- Why do people get angry?
- What's wrong with anger?
- What should you do if you start getting angry?

Now read the web page. Are the opinions there the same as yours?

THE ANGER PAGE

What is anger?

Anger has many sources. Often it is an emotion which is <u>secondary to some other emotion</u> that you are feeling—like fear, guilt, or relief. So the parent who shouts at her child who gets home late is using anger as a way of displacing fear. Sometimes it is the result of a sense of great unfairness—such as when someone is wrongly accused of a crime, or finds that their partner has not been telling them the truth, or feels a passionate sense of social injustice.

But anger may have other causes too. We know that animals can be made more aggressive if the limbic parts of their brains are stimulated; thus overstimulation of the limbic (emotional) center of the brain may override the neocortex (the reasoning part).

Changes in hormone levels seem to cause anger too, and inheritance plays a part as does our upbringing. The more we are raised in anger, the more anger we are likely to feel later in our lives.

Is anger bad for you?

Most researchers think that chronic anger leads to an increased risk of heart attack, but studies show that suppressing anger is bad for you too. Women who constantly suppress their anger, for example, show a higher mortality rate than those that don't. When partners suppress their anger, one study suggests, this is more damaging to the woman's health than the man's. So it seems that while frequent anger is bad for you (heart attacks, high blood pressure, suppression of the immune system), the suppression of anger is worse.

Some commentators suggest that using anger consciously is a good thing, provided it is not too extreme or out of control, but others are convinced that anger could be one of the main factors controlling our emotional and physical health.

Dealing with anger

Almost everyone agrees that dealing with anger is important so that we don't let it control us or make us say or do things we would later regret. We should be aware of our angry thoughts and try to challenge them. Perhaps when someone cuts us off at a traffic light, we should worry about why they drive that way rather than get furious. We should try and relax, take a deep breath, and decide whether we really want to go over the top! That way we can be angry only when we want to be.

<u>Are there anger types?</u>   <u>Differences between men and women</u>   <u>Controlling anger</u>

Home | About Us | Subjects A – Z | Contact Us | Behavior modification classes | Search

2 **Meaning check** Find words and phrases in *The Anger Page* which tell you that the following statements are true. The first one is underlined for you.

a Anger is often a reaction to some other feeling.

b We often shout to get rid of other feelings.

c Anger may be the result of some particular brain activity.

d Family background may affect how angry we are.

e We think anger is bad for us.

f Controlling anger may be harmful.

g We should try to be in charge of our own anger.

h We should pause before we get angry.

3 **Follow the links** Work in groups of three.

STUDENT A: follow the first link (Are there anger types?) by looking at Activity Bank 3 on page 157.

STUDENT B: follow the second link (Differences between men and women) by looking at Activity Bank 8 on page 159.

STUDENT C: follow the third link (Controlling anger) by looking at Activity Bank 15 on page 163.

4 **In groups of three** Students A, B and C, discuss the links you have followed. What did they say? Do you agree with what you read there?

5 **Comprehension check** Complete the following tasks based on what you found out in Activity 4 (do not look back at the text).

In your own words,

a ... describe different anger personality types.

b ... explain how or if anger affects men and women differently.

c ... give advice on how to deal with anger.

Language in chunks

6 Complete the sentences with these phrases from the text in Activity 1 and the Activity Bank. You may have to change the phrases a little.

build up over (a long) time (see Activity Bank 3)   cut somebody off
feel trapped (see Activity Bank 3)   go over the top
on the surface (see Activity Bank 15)   out of control
shades of gray (see Activity Bank 3)   take a deep breath
use your imagination (see Activity Bank 15)

a When we want people to think a bit more creatively, we often say
"........................".

b If something ...., it means it increases very gradually.

c If you ...., it is as if you are in a prison and can't get out.

d If someone is ...., it means it will be difficult to quiet them down or restrain them.

e If someone ...., it means that they behave in an exaggerated way which is not appropriate to the situation.

f If somebody ...., it means they drive right in front of you, often quite fast, and take your position.

g When you ...., you fill your lungs with air once—and perhaps it gives you time to think.

h Some people can look calm ...., but actually, inside, they're feeling very angry.

i If you see things in ...., it means you do not think they are completely simple.

7 **Conversation writing** Use at least three of the phrases in a conversation between two friends who are having (or have just had) an argument.

8 **In pairs** Copy and complete the table with ideas about what you can do when / if you meet someone who is angry.

Useful things to do when someone is angry	Things that are NOT useful to do when someone is angry
tell them to calm down	

Compare your table with another pair.

Grammar: the third conditional

9 Look at the following sentences. Which describes events:

a ... that are real?
b ... that may happen?
c ... that are hypothetical because they probably won't happen?

1 If you got angry with me, I'd get very upset.
2 If you get angry with me, I'll be very upset.
3 If you get angry all the time, people tend to get upset with you.

Look at **5A–5D in the Mini-grammar**. Do you want to change your answers?

10 Answer the following questions.

• What do you do if people get angry with you?
• What will you do the next time your friend gets angry with you?
• What would you do if your friend got angry with you?

Write three similar *What ... if ...* questions for real, possible, and hypothetical situations. Ask your partner.

11 Read the story and complete the tasks which follow it.

How Jesse got his arm back

Eight-year-old Jesse Arbogast was playing in the sea late one evening in July 2001 when a seven-foot bull shark attacked him and tore off his arm. Jesse's uncle leaped into the sea and dragged the boy to shore. Jesse's aunt gave the boy mouth-to-mouth resuscitation because he had stopped breathing. They called the emergency services and a helicopter flew Jesse to hospital. It was much quicker than a trip by road.

Jesse's uncle, Vance Flosenzier, ran back into the sea and found the shark that had attacked his nephew. He picked it up and threw it on to the beach. A ranger shot the fish, the shark's jaws relaxed, and they were able to open them and reach down into its stomach and pull out the boy's arm.

At the hospital a plastic surgeon, Dr. Ian Rogers, spent 11 hours reattaching Jesse's arm. "It was a complicated operation," he said, "but we were lucky. If they hadn't recovered the arm in time, we wouldn't have been able to do the operation at all."

According to local park ranger Jack Tomosvic, shark attacks are not that common. "Jesse was just unlucky," he says, "evening is the shark's feeding time. And Jesse wasn't in a lifeguard area. This would never have happened if he had been in a designated swimming area."

When reporters asked Jesse's uncle how he had had the courage to fight a shark, he replied, "I was angry and you do some strange things when you're angry."
This is a true story.

a **In pairs** Ask and answer as many questions as you can about the story using *who* and *what*.

Example: STUDENT A: Who went swimming?
STUDENT B: Jesse.

b Look at the two *if* sentences spoken by Dr. Rogers and Jack Tomosvic.

• Do they describe real or hypothetical situations in the past?
• How would you explain the grammar of the sentences to another student using these elements?

| if | have + past participle | would | not |

Compare your description with **5E in the Mini-grammar**.

c Make as many similar *if* sentences about the story of Jesse Arbogast as you can.

Examples: If Jesse hadn't played in the sea, the shark wouldn't have attacked him.
Jesse would have died if his aunt hadn't given him mouth-to-mouth resuscitation.

12 A game of consequences Ask what people did yesterday—and then keep asking about what would have happened if they hadn't done it!

Example: STUDENT A: What did you do yesterday?

STUDENT B: I got up at about 7 o'clock.

STUDENT A: What would have happened if you hadn't got up?

STUDENT B: I would have missed the bus.

STUDENT A: What would have happened if you had missed the bus?

STUDENT B: I would have gotten to work late.

STUDENT A: What would have happened if you had gotten to work late?

STUDENT B: etc.

13 Study 5E in the Mini-grammar again. Now read the story. Who can make the most *if* sentences using different modals and different tenses in consequence clauses?

Jane passed all her exams and so she got into college. It was there that she was introduced to Dave. He had just broken up with his girlfriend and was feeling sorry for himself, and so he was pleased to meet someone new. In the end they realized they were in love and so they got married.

Dave was studying law and was all set to be a lawyer, but when Jane was accepted on a postgraduate course in Montreal they moved to Canada. Without that they would probably still be in the U.S.A. Dave got a job as an actor on a radio program, and now he is a well-known TV and radio personality. Jane works as a librarian. They have two children who are, of course, Canadian citizens.

They were thinking of returning to the U.S.A. next year, but Dave has just been given the main announcer's job on Channel 5, so it looks like they're going to stay.

Vocabulary: being angry

14 Look at the picture. Who:

a ... doesn't like someone?

b ... wants someone to be relaxed?

c ... finds someone's behavior difficult to put up with?

d ... is / was surprised?

e ... describes the way someone is at the moment?

f ... got very angry?

15 Language research Use a dictionary to find out which of the words in the box mean (a) *angry*, (b) *fed up with*, (c) *to drive somebody crazy*, (d) *to get very angry*, (e) *to relax*, (f) *sulky*?

annoyed	to keep your cool
bad-tempered	to keep your head
furious	to lose it
grouchy	to lose your cool
grumpy	to lose your
irritable	temper
moody	to make somebody
sick and tired of	cross / angry
to calm down	
to get on	
somebody's	
nerves	

What expressions do the speakers (a–f) use?

16 Write four questions using language from Activities 14 and 15.

Examples: *When was the last time you lost your cool?*

When was the last time somebody got on your nerves?

Ask other people in the class.

Rules
- Answers may be true or false.
- Answers must not offend anyone else in the class.

18 Complete the following sentences.

a He got so fed up .... his brother that he lost his temper .... him.

b I wish she hadn't been in such a bad mood .... me.

c If I hadn't been so angry .... the situation I wouldn't have said what I did.

d He was sick and tired .... the way she talked to him.

e When he told her his news, she completely lost her temper .... him.

f I am annoyed .... her constant rudeness. She will have to leave my class.

g I'm sorry I got angry .... you.

h He was absolutely furious .... the decision we had taken.

i He got angry .... her, but she didn't notice.

17 Grammar What words follow the words and phrases from Activities 14 and 15? Copy the table and tick the appropriate boxes.

		about (something)	*at* (something / somebody)	*by* (something / somebody)	*of*	*with* (something / somebody)
to be / to get	angry	✓	✓			✓
	annoyed					
	fed up					
	furious					
	in a bad mood					
	mad					
	sick and tired					
to lose (your) temper						

Word choice: *argument, fight* and *quarrel*

19 Look at the Word Choice notes for *argument, fight, quarrel,* and *row* on page 57 in the booklet.

20 Fill in the blanks in the sentences with *argument, figh* or *quarrel.* You cannot use the same word in two consecutive sentences.

a Last night, Mr. Leung and his boss had a big .... You could hear it from miles away!

b Normally, Mr. Leung doesn't have .... with people. He's a very peaceful guy.

c His sister, however, often picks a .... with people who annoy her.

d She had a .... with someone across the street who was rude about her dog.

e Mr. Leung got cross with her and they had a real ....

f But .... like that between brother and sister are rare.

g They do sometimes have silly .... about things like food and furniture.

Which three words can also be verbs? Which word has to change to be a verb?

21 Speaking Answer the questions about yourself. Then ask your partner. Do you have the same answers?

- What time would you like to get up in the morning?
- How do you usually feel in the morning?
- What's your "low" time during the day?
- What's the best time of the day for you?
- What things make you annoyed or irritated during the day?
- What time do you usually go to bed?

Who are "morning" people (people who like to get up early and leap straight into action) in the class? Who are "night" people (who like to stay up very late and really come alive later on)?

Speaking: investigation role-play

22 The interview Read the situation for a role-play.

Last night, a car was stolen at 6:00PM from outside 23 Scholars' Lane. It was a red Jaguar, license-plate number NY XRX 634. The suspect is charged with the crime. If charged and found guilty, he may go to prison because he has been in trouble with the police before.

Two police officers are questioning the suspect in the interview room. Because the suspect is just under 18 years old, his parent is also present. And there is the suspect's lawyer there too.

In groups of five Choose one of the following roles: suspect, police officer 1, police officer 2, lawyer or suspect's parent.

SUSPECT: look at Activity Bank 4 on page 157.
POLICE OFFICER 1: look at Activity Bank 5 on page 158.
POLICE OFFICER 2: look at Activity Bank 9 on page 160.
LAWYER: look at Activity Bank 16 on page 164.
SUSPECT'S PARENT: look at Activity Bank 17 on page 164.

23 This is the start of the interview.

POLICE OFFICER 1: *All right everybody, I am turning on the tape recorder.*
This is an interview with [name of suspect]. My name is [name of police officer 1] and with me in the room is Police Officer [name of police officer 2], the suspect's lawyer [name of lawyer] and [name of parent], the suspect's parent. It is [time] on [day + date].
Now then, [name of suspect], let's start, shall we? Where were you last night?

The police officers have ten minutes to come to a conclusion about the guilt or innocence of the suspect.

Listening: keeping calm

24 How do you stop yourself from getting angry? Think of at least three ways.

Listen to Track 24. Are any of the ways that Dr. Kepa Khan suggests similar to yours?

25 Copy and complete the table (in note form) with Dr. Khan's anger management techniques.

Type of technique	Examples / What it means
a Relaxation	
b Cognitive restructuring	
c Silly humor	

26 In your own words, explain why Dr. Kepa Khan gets angry and say what he does to control himself.

27 Listen to Track 24 again. Read the following tape extracts. Note the missing words and whether Jay Reno (R) or Dr. Khan (K) said them.

a What's the ...._point of_.... this "anger management"? R

b Umm, yes, well I .... , but anyway, the point of anger management ...

c You can't .... the causes of these feelings, you see, but with luck ...

d Well no, ... , it's not that simple.

e If you .... , it often helps.

f A lot .... that's going to do.

g .... boring.

h ... you understand why you're irritated but that .... isn't going to help.

i You're ....! Tell me you're ....

j I don't think so. It's all .... , isn't it.

k ... that would .... wouldn't it!

28 Based on what Dr. Khan says, use these verbs to give advice about ways of managing anger.

visualize
breathe
repeat
picture
change

Example: You can visualize a relaxing experience.

Functional language: wishes and regrets

29 Look at the pictures. Guess what the people are thinking.

30 Wishes and regrets Based on the words of the four speakers, can you explain how we say that:

a ... we want something to change now or in the future?

b ... we regret something that happened / didn't happen?

c ... we regret something that we did or didn't do?

d ... it's a pity that a situation isn't different?

Listen to Track 25. Were you correct?

31 Use the following prompts to make sentences with *I wish* or *if only*.

What a pity that:

a ... I ever met you! I wish I'd never met you!

b ... I can't afford a new car.

c ... I can't understand the Welsh language.

d ... I don't like classical music like my friend does.

e ... I left my address book at home.

f ... I am in the doghouse.

g ... I went to their party.

h ... my parents keep asking me when I'm going to get a real job.

i ... people keep swimming in unguarded areas.

j ... people won't stop criticizing wolves.

k ... she keeps letting the cat out of the bag.

l ... she told me what she thought of me.

m ... the government won't do something about environmental pollution.

32 Choose one of the pictures (*a–e*). Write sentences about what the character (or shark) wishes about now and about the past.

Example: picture a

I wish I hadn't hit that policeman.

I wish I was at home.

33 Listen to Track 26. Which of the two words do you hear?

a	cash	catch
b	<u>fuschia</u>	future
c	mashing	matching
d	share	chair
e	sheep	cheap
f	shin	chin
g	shoes	choose
h	washing	watching
i	wish	which

34 Which of the two sounds corresponds to the following spellings?

a *ch* in a few words, but not normally at the beginning unless they are foreign words (*machine, champagne*)
b *ch* in a lot of words (*chin, rich*)
c *sh* (*shop, wish, fashion*)
d *ture*, but not at the beginning of a word (*picture, future*)
e *tch* (*watch, kitchen*)
f *s* in some words (*sure, insurance*)
g *ci* + vowel at the end of many words (*musician, delicious*)
h *ti* + vowel at the end of many words (*education, intonation*)

Can you give more examples for each spelling?

Writing: designing leaflets

35 **In pairs** Look at the leaflet for *Aroma* on the next page and complete the tasks.

a Describe *Aroma*, and what it does, to your partner in your own words.
b Do any of the three courses interest you:

... a lot?
... a little?
... not much?
... not at all because they're all silly?

36 Look at the design for the leaflet.

a Do you think it is effective?
b What is the purpose of the front cover? Would you design a cover like that?
c Do you like the use of color headings and "bullet" points? Are they easy to read and notice?
d How important are the photographs on the back?
e How would you design a leaflet differently?

Aroma staff:

Sally Grace NAL, director

Justin Knocker

Helena Kollect

Contact Aroma at:
The Aroma Center
316 West 58th Street, New York, NY 10016
Tel: 212-968-4533
Email: enquiries@arofengcol.com
Website: www.arofengcol.com

AROMA
AROMA
AROMA
AROMA
AT
A

Using nature's gift to keep you calm

Courses in

AROMATHERAPY
- How different smells affect our mood
- Designing aroma zones
- Judging the best aromas on the market

FENG SHUI*
- The theory of Feng Shui explained
- Putting Feng Shui into practice at home
- Putting Feng Shui into practice at work

RELAXING COLOR
- How color affects our mood
- Color combinations
- Designing rooms with color in mind

*Feng Shui is the ancient Chinese science which tells people the best place to put furniture in a room or house for maximum comfort and success.

---

37 Choose one of the following and then copy and complete the table about it.

- an anger management center (Use the Audioscript for Track 24 for information about anger management)
- a center offering classes in different kinds of music (pop, rock, classical, techno, house, etc.)
- a new gym offering a variety of services
- a new cafeteria at school, college, or work
- something else you would like to do if you had the money

38 Write the words for your leaflet based on your decisions in Activity 37.

Questions / Topics to be decided	Notes / Decisions
What kind of a place is it?	
The name of the place (think up something interesting)	
What services the place offers (and brief explanations of what these services are)	
Names of the staff	
An address, phone number, website, etc.	

39 Design your leaflet on a piece of 8½ x 11 paper which will be folded in half, as in the following diagram.

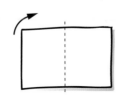  

Review: grammar

40 Find pictures which answer the following questions about Zenta's bad luck / good luck story.

a What happened when Zenta turned off the alarm?
b Why did it take her a long time to get to work?
c What happened when she arrived at work very late?
d What happened when she told him that he was behaving badly?
e What did she do when she was fired?
f What happened when she met the lawyer?
g What happened when she fell in love with the lawyer?

41 Zenta's day—and her life—could have turned out differently. Make *if* sentences about how things might not have been the same. Look at Activities 9–13 for help.

Example: If she hadn't turned off the alarm, she might not have gone back to sleep.

42 Complete the following conversations. Say what the situation is in each case. Use your imagination.

a A: If only I'd brought my camera.
B: Why?
A: ....

b A: I wish I was just slightly taller.
B: What on earth for?
A: ....

c A: I wish I hadn't called in sick at work today.
B: Why? You <u>were</u> sick, weren't you?
A: Yes, but ....

d A: If only I'd listened a little more carefully!
B: Why, what difference would that have made?
A: ....

e A: I wish I'd watched that TV program last night.
B: Really? Why that one especially?
A: ....

f A: If only you'd given me some warning!
B: What difference would that have made?
A: ....

Review: vocabulary

annoyed
bad-tempered
furious
grouchy
grumpy
irritable
moody
sulky
to picture
to visualize

"Take it easy!" *
"Use your imagination."
in a bad mood
on the surface
out of control
shades of gray
to be caught off balance
to be really fed up
to be sick and tired of
to build up over (a long) time
to calm down
to cut somebody off
to feel trapped
to get on somebody's nerves
to go over the top
to keep your cool
to keep your head
to lose it / your cool / your
 temper
to make somebody angry
to take a deep breath

*Phrases in quotation marks are
conversational phrases.

43 Where would you put words from the Word List and Word Plus on the following line?

not angry | --- | very angry

44 Listen to the speakers on Track 27. How would you describe their mood using words from the Word List?

a I don't agree with you.   *grumpy*
b Will you stop doing that?
c I don't want to go to the party.
d Why should I tidy my room?
e If I hear one more word from you, you'll be in real trouble.
f You are not going to get away with this.
g Oh why did you have to do that?
h No! No! No! No!

Apart from the words themselves, what tells you how they feel?

● ● ● Pronunciation

45 Write sentences using phrases from Word Plus. Say them aloud. Mark the stressed syllables and say where the main stress / stresses go.

Example:  On the 'surface, things seemed O'K, but ...

46 **The last time** Choose a phrase from Word Plus and tell your partner about the last time you or somebody was in that situation. Use as many words and phrases from the Word List and Word Plus as possible.

Example: I was really fed up last Monday, and this is why ...

UNIT 6
Looking forward

→ future perfect and continuous
→ seeing and believing
→ speculating

Vocabulary: seeing and believing (multiple meanings in words and phrases)

1 **Meanings** Look at these groups of sentences. Are the meanings of *see* and *believe* (in blue below) exactly the same for each sentence in a group?

a 1 Looking up, he thought he saw something flash across the night sky.
  2 He could see that she was unhappy, although he didn't know why.
  3 Let's see if this works, shall we?
  4 Did you see the game on television last night?

b 1 Now that you've explained it, I can see where I went wrong.
  2 Now that I am a parent, I see things differently.
  3 I can't see her being happy in that job, can you?
  4 It's the same old story. I've seen it all before.

c 1 I'll be seeing her tomorrow.
  2 I saw Jane yesterday. She was waiting for a bus.
  3 He's seeing a patient at the moment.
  4 They've been seeing a lot of each other recently.

d 1 You shouldn't believe everything you read in the papers.
  2 Police believe that the attacker was male and about 30 years old.
  3 It's hard to believe that the pyramids were constructed without any modern machinery.
  4 Some people believe in reincarnation (having more than one life).

2 Choose three of the sentences in Activity 1 to match the pictures a–c.

3 a **In pairs** Choose one of the groups (*a–d*) in Activity 1 and find a different way of saying each sentence in the group using different words.

 b Using a dictionary or any other source, what other words can you think of which have a number of different but related meanings?

4 **Belief and disbelief** Where do items *a–k* fit on this line?

complete | --- | complete
disbelief   belief

  a I accept what you say.
  b I don't believe you.
  c I think that's ludicrous. / That's totally out of the question.
  d I'll give you the benefit of the doubt.
  e I'll take it at face value.
  f I'm rather cynical about your claims. / I'm not so sure about this.
  g I'll take your word for it.
  h I'm going to take that with a grain of salt.
  i I'm fairly skeptical about all this.
  j I'll take it on trust.
  k I doubt what you are saying.

How many phrases with *give* or *take* can you find in the list?

5 **In groups** Look at the following beliefs and predictions.

- By the year 2050, we'll be able to fly on our own.
- People with blue eyes are more intelligent than people with green eyes.
- Learning English is easy if you speak a European language as a first language.
- There is a world something like our Earth somewhere in the solar system.
- Eating meat is bad for you.

Add two more (reasonable or crazy) of your own.

6 **In pairs** Student A offers a prediction. Student B uses one of the words or phrases from Activity 4 to comment on it.

Example: STUDENT A: *By the year 2050, we'll be able to fly on our own.*
STUDENT B: *I'm going to take that prediction with a grain of salt.*

7 **Word in phrases** Read the explanations of the phrases *in italics*. Complete the sentences with *believe* or *see*.

Sentence	Meaning
a ....*Believe*.... *it or not*, they have agreed to get married.	I know it sounds ridiculous, but ...
b I *don't* .... *a word* of it!	It's just not possible.
c I just don't .... *eye to eye* with her.	She and I don't agree.
d It's difficult to .... *the point of* the movie.	I don't understand why the movie was made.
e Justice must be done, and must be .... *to be done*.	It must be clear that justice is taking place.
f Let's .... *how it goes*, shall we?	We'll try it and deal with any problems if and when they happen.
g *If you* .... *that, you'll* .... *anything*.	You can't possibly think that this is true.
h .... *you later*.	Goodbye.
i .... *from this distance*, the events of 1973 are difficult to understand.	When we consider something a long time after the event, ...
j *She* .... *herself* as the leader of the group.	She thought of herself as ...
k The movies? *I don't* .... *why not*.	Yes, I agree with the idea.
l You're saying he's changed the way he behaves? *I'll* .... *that when I see it*.	I really don't think it is true unless I see it with my own eyes.
m He'll .... *off* the opposition easily.	He will win easily.
n When they saw the spaceship, they could *scarcely* .... *their eyes*.	They were very surprised.
o You want your car fixed? *I'll* .... *what I can do*.	I will do my best.

Speaking and writing: spoken vs written phrases

8 Look at the phrases with *believe*, *see*, *take* and *give* in Activities 4 and 7 and answer the following questions.

  a Is each phrase formal or informal?
  b Which of the phrases are you more likely to hear in conversation rather than read in print?
  c Which of the phrases sound more like written phrases?

9 Take any two of the phrases you chose in Activity 8 and write a short conversation which includes both of them.

Listening: the paranormal

10 **In pairs** The words on the right are all examples of "paranormal" beliefs. Discuss the meaning of the words with a partner.

Which ones are connected with talking about the future?
Do you know any other ways of knowing what is in the future?

> astrology ESP faith healing
> fortune-telling ghosts magic
> palmistry tarot cards telepathy UFOs

11 Look at the items in Activity 10. Give them a score from 1 (= "I believe in this") to 3 (= "I don't believe in this").

Compare your answers in groups and explain your answers. Are you a "believer" in the paranormal or a "skeptic"?

12 Now listen to Track 28. Who is the "believer"? Who is the "skeptic"? Why?

13 Listen to Track 28 again and match the beginnings of the sentences in the first column with the ends of the sentences in the second column.

a The man thinks that 6	1 ... without mystery life is very boring.
b Dr Hyman became a skeptic when	2 ... is too cynical.
c The man believes that if	3 ... he deliberately read someone's palm badly and they said it was accurate.
d The woman thinks that the man	4 ... the woman.
e When the woman calls the man "Mr. Clever," she is	5 ... we hear things often enough, we start to believe them.
f The woman thinks that	6 ... there is a rational explanation for everything. *a*
g The man likes	7 ... making fun of him in a friendly way.

Who do you agree with? The man or the woman?

14 Listen to Track 28 again and complete this summary of the conversation.

Two people are eating (**a**) ......*pizza*...... in a (**b**) .... They seem to have a friendly relationship. They start talking about the (**c**) .... and the man surprises the woman by (**d**) .... that he doesn't believe in any paranormal phenomena. His cynicism (**e**) .... when he heard an American professor talking about an (**f**) .... from his youth. Against the protests of the woman, the man suggests that he (**g**) .... write a zodiac description of her without (**h**) .... anything about astrology. He believes that there is always a (**i**) .... explanation for everything, but that people start to (**j**) .... things if they see or hear them often enough. The woman thinks that it is a pity that the man is so (**k**) .... since it makes his life less (**l**) .... The man admits that there is only one mystery he doesn't have the (**m**) .... to.

Do you think the woman will give the man some of her pizza?

15 Meaning check What does the man say about:

a ... crystal balls?
b ... tea leaves?
c ... "Your horoscope" in the newspaper?
d ... people who have lived "past lives"?
e ... people who see flying saucers?
f ... people's responses to suggestion?

16 Complete these utterances from Track 28 with one word for each gap.

a So you .... that stuff now?
b Oh come on, you're not saying all that is .... ?
c .... doing so far?
d There isn't any mystery ....
e How do you figure .... ?
f You wouldn't believe it, ... ?
g Well if there isn't any mystery in life, ... ?
h Well now, that ....

17 Group writing Read the man's pretend horoscope from the recording for Track 28.

You are a person who longs to be happy but sometimes you're sad. You like to shine in conversation but sometimes it's difficult for you. You sometimes don't get the love you think you need, but next week you should concentrate all your efforts on someone near to you.

Write your own short general star sign description like the man did. Show it to other students in the class. How well does it describe them?

Functional language: speculating

18 Listen to Track 29. Two friends are discussing a soccer game. Complete their conversation with the word or words that you hear.

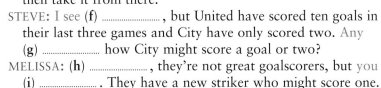

4 - 4 - 2

STEVE: What (**a**) _do you think about_ the big game on Saturday?

MELISSA: Well, it's (**b**) .... really. United have great forward players and City have a great defense.

STEVE: (**c**) .... , but United haven't lost a game for three months. What are (**d**) .... of City winning?

MELISSA: As (**e**) .... see, City need to sit back and wait for United to make a mistake and then take it from there.

STEVE: I see (**f**) .... , but United have scored ten goals in their last three games and City have only scored two. Any (**g**) .... how City might score a goal or two?

MELISSA: (**h**) .... , they're not great goalscorers, but you (**i**) .... They have a new striker who might score one.

STEVE: What (**j**) .... the score will be?

MELISSA: I (**k**) .... , but if (**l**) .... , City will surprise a lot of people.

STEVE: I'm (**m**) .... , but if they do, I'll take you out to lunch.

MELISSA: All right. You're on.

19 Now copy the table and write the phrases in blue that you completed in Activity 18 in the correct column.

Asking for speculation	Speculating	Accepting / Rejecting speculation
What do you think about ...		

20 Now write these expressions under the appropriate heading from Activity 19.

a Do you think ... ?
b Not a chance!
c If you ask me, ...
d It's hard to say for sure, but ...
e You may be right there.
f You must be joking!
g What do you reckon?
h Do you suppose ... ?
i I reckon ...
j I wouldn't be surprised if ...
k Do you have any idea about ... ?
l Is there any chance that ... ?
m Do you really think so?

21 In pairs Speculate about the following things in the future.

Example: a

STUDENT A: Do you think people will drive electric cars in the future?

STUDENT B: I wouldn't be surprised if that happened. People are already driving hybrid gas / electric cars.

STUDENT A: I'm not convinced. I think …

a Will people drive electric cars?
b Will people live on the moon?
c Will computers do all the work?
d Will people learn everything using computers?
e Will there be no television?
f Will there be a cure for all major illnesses?
g Will new illnesses appear?
h Will human beings be able to live forever?
i Will people be able to travel in time?
j Will there be human clones?

22 In pairs Work with a partner and use at least three of the expressions you noted in Activities 19 and 20 to have conversations about these topics.

a your future
b the weather
c an important sports event
d your next English test

Speaking: interview and role-play

23 In groups Find out who:

- … has been to a fortune-teller.
- … has never been but would like to go to a fortune-teller.
- … believes that fortune-tellers can say meaningful things about the future.
- … would like to be a fortune-teller.

24 In groups Complete the following tasks.

a Think of six questions you could ask a fortune-teller.
  Make sure you have the right words to ask an English-speaking fortune-teller.
b Think of six predictions that fortune-tellers are likely to make.

25 Role-play Divide the class into fortune-tellers and customers.

a Each fortune-teller must decide what method they want to use (palm-reading, crystal ball, tea leaves, etc.).
b Each customer must decide what questions they want to ask.

Customers visit as many fortune-tellers as they can. Who is the best fortune-teller?

Reading: what kind of future?

26 Make two predictions about the future under these headings, which are similar to the example.

Humankind and medicine	Humankind and the universe
By 2030, the common cold will have been cured.	

Now read the text *Wings, Babies and the Pollution of Planets* on page 66. Are your predictions included in it?

27 Read the text again and match the titles *a–h* to the paragraphs *1–8*.

a Making it a place where we can live   7
b Operations at a distance
c Finding a new place to live
d Right *and* wrong about the future
e His predictions are based on fact
f Grow your own new body parts?
g Less than 100 years away
h A top doctor makes predictions

Wings, Babies, and the Pollution of Planets

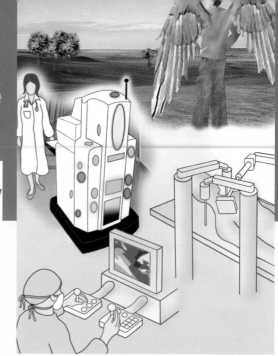

Predicting the future has always been a risky business, but recent claims are almost literally unbelievable. Or are they?

Back in 1949, the scientist Johan von Neumann made a statement which was both extraordinarily wrong and profoundly correct. "It would appear," he wrote, "that we have reached the limits of what it is possible to achieve with computer technology, although I should be careful with such statements, as they tend to sound pretty silly in five years." How true! Looking into the future has always been a dangerous occupation.

William Futrell isn't afraid to make predictions, however. As one of America's top plastic surgeons, he foresees a time when people will be flying around using their own wings, men will be having babies, and when we lose a leg in an accident the hospital will just grow a new one for us—using our own DNA.

You can't dismiss Futrell's predictions as pure fantasy, not given the fact that he is one of the leading authorities in his field. He has trained at least 20 professors and directors of U.S. medical institutions. "What's changed," he says, "is that we're mapping the human genome, the code for all life. And we can now extract stem cells for this kind of reconstructive work from a person's adipose tissue" (that's fat, to you and me).

When people dismiss Futrell's ideas as fanciful, he points out how far we've come. At the hospital where he works, robots take X-rays and other medical supplies to and from the wards; in Florida, in 2001, a doctor operated on a patient by remote control for the first time. Using computers and the Internet, he removed the gall bladder of a woman in France, 3,500 miles away. These things were once unimaginable.

And now, perhaps, we'll be able to grow wings and replace any body parts which become old or damaged. "Believe me," Futrell says, "wings are not a long way off." And he means it.

But even if we learn how to cure our bodies and end up living for ever, there isn't anything we can do about the fact that one day, as the sun gets hotter, this Earth will be an uncomfortable place to live. According to astronomical engineer Robert Zubrin, the Earth will become extinct "unless we bring Earth life out with us into the universe." And the only place to go is Mars—it has water, carbon dioxide and nitrogen. But at the moment it is too cold and dry for human habitation. We'd die within seconds of stepping onto its surface. So we'll just have to do something about it.

"The first step to making Mars habitable is to warm it up," says NASA scientist Chris McKay. His plan is to drop off a pollution-making machine that will scoot around the surface of the planet spewing out greenhouse gasses, thus shortcutting the slow process of evolution. The next step is oxygen—and what better oxygen-makers do we have than trees?!

McKay predicts that we'll be living on Mars some time in the next 80 years. "By that time," he says, "the planet will have its algae and bacteria, and we'll have planted forests of trees. It'll be just right for human habitation." The only problem is that we won't all fit. Mars is only a tenth the size of Earth.

28 Fact check Answer these questions based on the text.

a Why was von Neumann both right and wrong?

b What are the two developments that mean we could now potentially grow a new limb?

c What was so unusual about the gall bladder operation in 2001?

d Why would humans die on Mars?

e How could Mars be made habitable for humans?

f How soon could we live on Mars, according to McKay?

29 Find these words in the text and explain their meaning.

a foresees (paragraph 2)

b leading (paragraph 3)

c mapping (paragraph 3)

d reconstructive (paragraph 3)

e fanciful (paragraph 4)

f extinct (paragraph 6)

g shortcutting (paragraph 7)

Language in chunks

30 Look at how these phrases are used in the text and then use them in the sentences which follow. You may have to change them to make them fit.

> to tend to   to dismiss something as   a long way off
> to warm something up   to scoot around   to spew out   by that time

a I don't think we'll be living on the moon in the near future— I think that's still ....

b We need to .... these vegetables in the microwave before we can eat them.

c Mars might be habitable by the year 2100, but .... most of us won't be alive anymore.

d I can't believe you .... that idea .... foolish. I think it's a great idea.

e My mother just bought a new bicycle so that she can .... town to do her shopping.

f Most people .... think that doctors have to be present to perform an operation, but that's not necessarily true.

g The old car was .... clouds of smoke when I saw it at the side of the highway.

31 Noticing language Here are five predictions from the text. How many different kinds of the *will* future are used? What do they mean?

a People will be flying around using their own wings.

b Men will be having babies.

c The Earth will become extinct.

d We'll be living on Mars.

e By this time we'll have planted forests of trees.

32 Which of the predictions do you think will come true and which do you think are not going to happen?

33 Discussion Talk about these questions in groups.

Would you like to:
• ... live on Mars?
• ... have wings?
• ... have a remote operation?
• ... see men having babies?

Grammar: future perfect and future continuous

34 Read the following sentences. Which describe (1) something that (we guess) is happening now, (2) plans for the future which are fixed and decided, (3) something that is going to be completed in the future and (4) something that will be in progress at a particular moment in the future?

a By this time tomorrow, we'll have finished all our exams. 3

b Don't bother to go to his house. He'll have gone to work by now.

c Don't go over to their house now. They'll be having dinner.

d I'll be leaving on Friday. I have my ticket.

e I'll have been working in this bank for 20 years in January.

f The garage says they'll have fixed the car by 6.

g This time next week, we'll be flying to Paris.

h Will you be coming to our party?

Look at 6A–6D in the Mini-grammar. Do you want to change your answers?

35 Invent answers for the following questions using the future continuous or the future perfect. **Use 6A–6D in the Mini-grammar to help you.**

a Do you know where Peter is at the moment?
b How long have you been studying English?
c Do you have anything planned for the weekend?
d Do you think they're having a good time on vacation?
e Are you an optimist or a pessimist about the future of the world?
f What are your hopes for the next ten years?

36 What, if any, is the difference between the following pairs of sentences? Can you think of a context for each one?

a 1 Will you stay the night at our place?
  2 Will you be staying the night at our place?

b 1 When will you finish that letter?
  2 When will you have finished the letter?

c 1 How long will you have worked at this school by the end of the year?
  2 How long will you have been working at this school by the end of the year?

d 1 They'll be putting the baby to bed at about 7:00PM
  2 Let's not arrive just yet. They'll be putting the baby to bed.

e 1 We will have completed our research by October.
  2 We'll be completing our research in October.

37 Complete these conversations with an appropriate form of the future. If more than one answer is possible, explain why.

a HOTEL GUEST: I'm calling to tell you that we (**1.** arrive) .... late. We (**2.** be) .... there by 10.00p.m.
RECEPTIONIST: Well, I (**3.** go) .... home by then, but I (**4.** leave) .... a note for the person on duty.

b JANE: Wow! I can hardly believe it—we (**5.** come) .... to this restaurant for 14 years in August.
DAVID: Is it that long? The food's great so I guess we (**6.** eat) .... here for the next 14 years, too.

c MAUD: (**7.** stay) .... you .... in tonight, dear? I think I (**8.** go) ....over to Judy's house for a couple of hours.
HENRY: Yes, I (**9.** work) .... all night. I have a report to finish. But I think it's too early to go over. They (**10.** not have) .... dinner and they (**11.** not put) .... the children to bed.

Pronunciation: strong and weak forms in contracted sentences

38 Listen to these sentences on Track 30. Underline the stressed words and notice the pronunciation of *have*.

a I'll have been working here for five years.
b By next March we'll have been married for three years.
c Do you think they'll have finished by now?
d I'm sure she'll have arrived home by now.
e Soon we'll have been living in this town for 15 years.
f Yes, I think they'll have put the kids to bed by now.

Practise saying the sentences with the same stress and the same pronunciation of *have*.

39 In pairs Ask and answer these questions. Ask at least two more questions after each answer.

Example: a
  A: What will you be doing at this time next year?
  B: I'll have finished college and I'll be working.
  A: Where will you be working?
  B: ...

a What will you be doing at this time next year?
b How long will you have worked at your present job by the end of the year?
c Where will you be going on your next vacation?
d How long will you have been studying English by the end of this course?
e What will you be doing in five years' time?
f Name two things you will have finished by the end of this month.

Writing: planning compositions

40 What will life be like in the year 2050? Look at this student's notes on different aspects of the future. Use her notes to write her introductory paragraph about a day in her life in 2050.

Home
- living on Mars
- people—live forever
- scientists—discover a way for people to live forever

Technology
- a robot—bring me coffee and breakfast in bed
- talk to friends on Earth / moon on X-ray communicator

Food
- food—dehydrated / in pills
- nothing will grow on Mars

Compare your paragraph with a partner's and then look at Activity Bank 18 on page 164.

41 Make notes about your own ideas about life in the year 2050 under the following headings.

Compare your ideas in groups.

- technology
- work
- transportation
- entertainment
- science and medicine
- school
- clothing
- problems

42 Use your ideas to write about a day in your life in the year 2050. Include the following information.

- general life circumstances
- getting up in the morning
- your daily routine
- the end of the day

Discussion Read each other's texts and decide which one you think is most likely to be a true picture of life in the year 2050.

Review: grammar and functional language

43 Put this conversation in order.

a You must be joking! Everyone listens to CDs.
b Thanks, but do you know what I heard the other day?
c Yes, but there'll be new technology by then.
d No. What?
e Wow! You have a great collection of CDs.   1
f And CDs will become like vinyl records are now—antiques!
g They believe that by the year 2010, CDs won't be used much.
h Well yes, I suppose that's possible.

44 Read these predictions from Ray Kurzweil, an inventor, entrepreneur and futurist. Complete them, using a form for talking about the future. Look at Activities 34–37 for help.

a In the year 2009, the majority of text (create—*passive*) .... by speech recognition.
b By the year 2020, computers (exceed) .... the memory capacity of the human brain and we (be able) .... to buy these computers for $1000.
c In the year 2020, we (have) .... relationships with automated personalities and we (use) .... computers as teachers and companions.
d In the year 2029, information (feed) .... from computers straight into the human brain along direct neural connections. By that year, computers (read) .... all the world's literature.
e The difference between humans and computers (become) .... unclear by 2029 and when machines tell us they are conscious, we (believe) .... them.
f In the year 2049, we (eat) .... food that has been created by molecular engineering and there (be) .... no need for agriculture.
g By the year 2099, computers and humans (join) .... completely.

45 **In pairs** Which of these predictions do you think will come true and which ones do you think will not come true? Ask for speculation, speculate and accept and reject speculation about these predictions.

Review: vocabulary

*Phrases in quotation marks are
conversational phrases.

46 Look at the phrases in Word Plus. Which do you think are the most useful? Choose five that you can learn as chunks of language and use regularly.

 Pronunciation

47 **Word stress** Underline the stressed syllable in these words.

a extinct
b fanciful
c ludicrous
d skeptical
e reconstructive
f shortcutting

Now listen to Track 31 and check your answers.

48 Listen to these phrases on Track 32 and mark which syllables have the main stress.

a pinch of salt
b face value
c benefit of the doubt
d eye to eye
e take it on trust

49 Listen to these sentences on Track 33 and note the syllables that are stressed.

a That's totally out of the question.
b I could scarcely believe my eyes.
c I don't see why not.
d I'll see what I can do.
e Let's see how it goes.
f See you later.

50 Look back over the unit and use the words and phrases to talk about the future predictions that were made in the unit.

Example: STUDENT A: People living on Mars? I think it's totally out of the question.

STUDENT B: Really? I see it being possible in the future. When the machinery is better.

UNIT 7

Out of the blue

→ *needs doing | have something done*
→ colors
→ taking something to be fixed

Vocabulary: colors

1 **In pairs** Look at *Nataraja* by the British artist Bridget Riley. You have one minute.

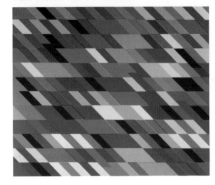

  a Now cover the picture with your hand. How many colors were in it? Make a list. (If you have any problem with the names of colors, look at Activity Bank 10 on page 160.)

  b Look at the picture again. Did you remember all the colors?

  c Do you like the painting? Why? Why not?

  d Which room of your house would you put the painting in? Why?

2 **Language research** Using a dictionary or another source, join the following adjectives, used to describe colors, with a color.

> brilliant dark faded bright
> pale dull light muddy

Which of your phrases describes (a) a strong color, (b) a color that is not strong, or (c) a color that could be either strong or weak?

3 Describe things (objects, landscapes ...) you know or have seen, using as many words from Activity 2 as you can.

4 Match the following color descriptions with the people's clothes.

> beige coffee-colored cream golden brown
> khaki lime-green mustard scarlet

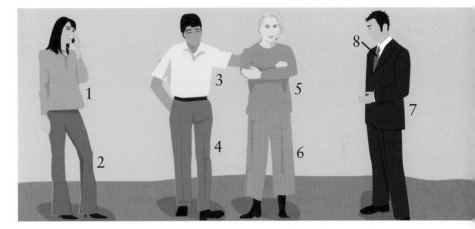

5 **In pairs** Ask your partner to describe the color of some or all of the following.

- their bicycle, motorcycle, or car
- a room in their house, and the things in it
- their favorite article of clothing
- the stationery they carry with them to class
- their bag or briefcase

6 Color meaning

  a What color do people from your culture associate with the following emotions or events?

- anger
- cold
- cowardice
- death
- embarrassment
- fear
- jealousy
- purity
- sadness / depression

  b Do you see colors in the same way?

  Do other cultures associate colors in the same way?

  c In your community:

- ... what color do women traditionally get married in?
- ... what color do people traditionally wear at funerals?
- ... are there any other colors for special occasions?

7 Metaphor Choose the correct color for each blank (a–o).

black   blue   green   red   white   yellow

After an evening of painting the town (a) _red_ (when we'd had a wonderful time going from club to club celebrating), I went around to my friend Matilda's house. The night was as (b) _____ as ink, but I could see that the lights were on. Just as I got to the door, I heard the sound of raised voices and then the door opened and Henry (one of Matilda's colleagues) ran out of the house. In the light I could see that he was as (c) _____ as a sheet. "Henry," I called when I caught up with him, "what's the matter?" And he told me his story.

That morning, he had spoken to Matilda and they had realized that they were in love. I was (d) _____ with envy. Matilda was absolutely beautiful. But that evening, while I was in town with the others, her father had come in just as they were kissing on the sofa. Matilda went bright (e) _____ with embarrassment, and Henry jumped to his feet.

Matilda's father just saw (f) _____ . He started shouting. "That's it," he yelled, "I've caught you (g) _____-handed!" and then pulled a pistol from his pocket. That's when Henry ran. "You're (h) _____!" the older man shouted after him. "Just a horrible little coward. Go away and never come back!"

By now the poor man was shivering, (i) _____ with cold. I gave him my coat. "The thing is," he said unhappily, "what am I going to do now?"

Henry walked around in a (j) _____ mood for days because he thought he would never be able to see Matilda again. But then, out of the (k) _____ , he got a call from her. It was a complete surprise. "I'm sorry about my father," she said, "he's really not as (l) _____ as he is painted. Everyone says he's cruel, but he isn't really. I know he screamed (m) _____ murder at you, and I did try to talk to him about it. At first he just wouldn't listen to me. 'You can go on till you're (n) _____ in the face,' he said, and I was about to give up when my mother persuaded him to let us see each other again. So now he's given us the (o) _____ light. Do you want to come over this evening?"

"Will your father be at home?" Henry asked.

8 Complete the color metaphors and then match them with their meanings.

a to be blue with ... _cold_
b to be in a black ...
c to be not as black as ...
d out of the ...
e to be ...
f to be as black ...
g to be as white ...
h to be green with ...
i to catch someone ...
j to give someone the ...
k to go (bright) ...
l to go on until you are ...
m to paint ...
n to scream / yell ...
o to see ...

1   to be better than people say
2   to be very dark
3   to be very gloomy
4   to be very jealous
5   to behave as if you are very afraid
6   to blush
7   to continue for some time without having any effect
8   to go out and behave exuberantly
9   to look very frightened
10 to look / feel very cold
11 to allow someone to do something
12 to shout very loudly for some time
13 to suddenly get very angry
14 to surprise someone in the middle of doing something wrong
15 with no warning

9 Storytelling Take one of the color metaphors and use it as the title of a story about your life. Make notes about your story.

Use your notes to tell your story to the class. Include other color metaphors too, if you can.

Reading: color effect

10 Read the following sentences. They each summarize one of the paragraphs in the text *The pink police station*. What do you think each paragraph will say?

a Choose an appropriate color for whatever you're doing
b Choosing room colors is important
c Color and the nervous system
d Color preferences reveal personality
e Good color choices match eye color

Read the text. Match the summaries with the correct paragraphs.

THE PINK POLICE STATION

If color is energy, is blue right for the dining room?

1 Now here's a theory: You and I are energy. We are color. When we're feeling fed up and run-down, this may mean that we have too much or too little color in us. Each of us is inadvertently attracted to one color more than others, and the reason for this is that colors have energy in them, and that is what draws us to them. Every color affects our cell structures, sending very fine chemical vibrations on to our nervous system, which via the pituitary gland directs our body. For instance, blue light makes our cells expand but red light makes them contract. Each color in the spectrum, in other words, has its own special effect on us and as we absorb its energy it travels via the nervous system to the part of the body that needs it. And so, as people look for alternatives to mainstream conventional medicine which they think is unsatisfactory, and seek new ways of making themselves well, they—we—have turned to color therapy as a new way of chilling out, a way of restoring our individual states of optimum well-being and restoring an appropriate physical and mental balance.

2 You think that sounds too extreme? Well, according to the Swiss psychologist Max Luscher, color and personality are so closely linked that he developed a test to reveal character traits by the sequence in which a subject chooses colors. The test is now used by psychologists and governments across the world—and a version of it even appears on the Internet for anyone to use.

3 Top color therapist Angela Wright agrees that color elicits a strong psychological response—which is why the appearance of rooms in a house is so vital to its inhabitants' well-being. "The biggest mistake interior designers make is not to take into account the personality of the client whose home they are decorating and the activity associated with a particular room," she says. For instance, if you painted your dining room blue, then, says Wright, "you'd have very boring dinner parties because that color is calming. As a result, everyone would be on their best behavior." One police force in southern Britain was so convinced by theories of color that they painted their cells pink— a nurturing, romantic color—to try and stop their temporary guests feeling aggressive.

4 According to fashion expert "Annie," a columnist for Britain's *Observer* newspaper, certain colors suit people better than others, and so care should be taken when selecting clothes. There's nothing new about that of course. People with good dress sense have always worried about what to wear, and colors go in and out of fashion. But Annie goes further than this. She suggests that the best colors are those that complement or reflect the wearer's eye color. If you have hazel eyes, for example, certain shades of green are just right. However, in what seems like a contradictory point of view, she is adamant that people should be allowed to wear whatever colors they feel good about, even if they are not appropriate: "I know people who don't really suit red, for example," she wrote in a recent column, "yet derive enormous pleasure from wearing it, and who has the right to tell them otherwise?" Well no one has the right, but perhaps it would be kind!

5 So there it is. Color counts, and it's important for all of us. If the kitchen needs repainting, or if you're thinking of having the living room done; if you feel like having your hair dyed or you just want to go out and spend money on clothes, work out what color suits your personality and your looks best: learn which ones will affect your nervous system and how they will do this. Take color seriously and it will improve your life—and make you feel good about it too.

11 Discussion Talk about the following questions.

- How do colors affect you psychologically?
- Would you be interested in taking the computer version of Max Luscher's color test?
- Do you agree that a room's color affects what happens there?
- How do you personally choose the color of your clothes?
- Will you take the advice in the last paragraph?

12 Fact check Read the text on page 73 again and choose the best answer.

a The energy of a particular color:
  1 ... makes us feel fed up.
  2 ... attracts us to the color.
  3 ... always expands our cells.

b People are attracted to color therapy because:
  1 ... they are disillusioned with their lives.
  2 ... they've lost confidence in normal doctors.
  3 ... their doctors say color is good for them.

c Max Luscher's test:
  1 ... is now only used by psychologists in Switzerland.
  2 ... reveals the sequence in which governments use the Internet.
  3 ... is designed to show what kind of a person you are.

d Interior designers make mistakes because they:
  1 ... don't consider what kind of people they are designing for.
  2 ... understand why they should paint dining rooms blue.
  3 ... are convinced by the theory that pink calms people down.

e The best colors for clothes:
  1 ... are hazel and green if your eyes are blue.
  2 ... go with the color of the wearer's eyes.
  3 ... are shades of red that the wearer likes.

13 Vocabulary Which of the words in blue in the text on page 73 means the following?

a get
b gets something from someone
c look good with
d looking after, caring for
e ordinary
f relaxing completely
g small shaking movements
h the opposite of *expand*
i very sure
j without meaning to

Language in chunks

14 What do the following phrases from the text *The pink police station* **mean?**

a has its own special effect on us (paragraph 1)
b seek new ways of (paragraph 1)
c elicits a strong psychological response (paragraph 3)
d on their best behavior (paragraph 3)
e has the right to (paragraph 4)

15 Rewrite the following sentences using the phrases in blue.

a I don't like brilliant sunshine. *has a bad effect*
b Interior designers want to combine colors. *seeking new ways of*
c The color red seems to make bulls react. *elicits a strong psychological response*
d When their grandmother comes to dinner, the children are always good. *on their best behavior*
e No one can order me about. I'm a free agent. *has the right to*

Speaking: making joint decisions

16 Look at the picture of the student recreation room and the items that can go in it.

In small groups You are going to live in a student dorm and this is the recreation room (living room, TV room, etc.) that you share. Decide on the following.

a You can have any six of the items from the list. Which will you choose? ("Four chairs" or "two armchairs" count as one item.)

b What colors will you choose for:
  • ... the rug?
  • ... the drapes?
  • ... the walls?
  • ... the ceiling?

Explain the reasons for your decisions.

Example: I think we should have a brown rug, because the coffee stains won't show.

17 Compare your decisions with other groups.

Listening: the new house

18 Listen to the conversation on Track 34 and answer the questions.

a Where are the speakers flying from?
b Where are they flying to?
c What's the weather going to be like on the journey?
d What do you know about Carol? Mark?
e How does Carol feel about getting home? Why?

19 Listen to Track 34 again. Copy and complete the table about the problems that Carol and her husband have with their house.

What part of the house?	What's the problem?	Who's going to fix it?
a		
b		
c		
d		
e		

20 Listen to Track 35. Answer the following questions.

a What colors are mentioned in the conversations between Bob and Carol? What are they for?
b Where is Bob when he calls the first time?
c What does Bob want Carol to decide about the first time he calls?
d Where is Bob when he calls for the second time?
e What does Bob want Carol to decide the second time he calls?
f What do you think Carol feels about returning home? Why?

Language in chunks

21 Look at the following sentences from Tracks 34 and 35 and complete the tasks.

a I'm not looking forward to getting home.
b We can't afford any more.
c I need you to make a decision.
d It depends on what light beige looks like.
e Looks like we're in for a bumpy ride.
f I'm glad we're out of it.
g For Heaven's sake, what is it this time?
h I haven't the slightest idea.

• Who says the sentences in the conversation?
• Explain what the phrases in blue mean as if you were explaining them to someone in a lower-level class.
• **In pairs** Use the sentences in two- or three-line exchanges.

Grammar: *needs doing; have something done*

22 Look at the pictures and say what needs to be done / what needs doing using the following verbs (you can use some of the verbs more than once).

change   clean   cut   fix   iron   paint   repair   replace   respray

a — hair, shirt, pants, shoes

b — bumper, windshield, tire, door

c — roof, door, gate, grass

Example: a *The man's hair needs to be cut.*

Look at **7A–B in the Mini-grammar**. Do you want to change your answers?

Word Choice: *fix, repair,* and *service*

23 Look at the Word Choice notes for *fix*, *repair*, and *service* on page 57 in the booklet.

24 Note down the appropriate form of *fix*, *mend*, *repair*, or *service* needed to complete these sentences.

  a The washing machine needs ... . It works, but it hasn't been looked at for two years.

  b You want me to ... your car buddy? I think I could do it sometime this afternoon.

  c In conclusion, I think we need to ... the damage to the building as soon as possible.

  d She's ... her dress at the moment. It got ripped when she climbed over the fence.

  e Your car should be ... every 10,000 miles.

  f When do you think the highway department will ... that hole in the road?

  g Why do you want to change things? You know that old saying, "If it ain't broke, don't ... it."

  h I wouldn't bother to have the radio ... . I'd just buy a new one. It's cheaper.

  i I'm taking my shoes to that store on the corner. They need ... .

25 Read what Bruno is saying and complete the tasks which follow.

> I'm going to fix my shirt. Then I'm going to get my hair cut and dyed blond. Then I'm going to have my car serviced. And then I'm going to the theater because we're having our new production designed by the famous artist Patricia Langley, and I have to meet her.

  a Which task is Bruno going to do himself? Which tasks is someone else going to do?

  b When do we include the name of the person who is going to do the task?

  c Where do we put adjectives which give details about the task?

  d What order do the following elements go in? Copy the diagram and complete it.

  (optional) adjective   by somebody   done   have   something

  ☐ + ☐ + ☐ + ☐

Look at **7C–D in the Mini-grammar**. Do you want to change your answers?

26 Look at the people and say what they are going to have done.

Example: **a** *Ruth's going to have her dresses cleaned.*

a Ruth
b Alistair
c John
d Carol
e Mike
NEW TIRES FITTED HERE

27 Read **7D in the Mini-grammar** and then complete the sentences which follow with whichever is most appropriate, *get* or *have*.

a ... *Get* your teeth fixed—or they'll get worse.
b He didn't ... the tree cut down in time. It fell into the neighbor's yard.
c He ... his car resprayed a bright yellow. Now he wishes he hadn't bothered.
d I ... my leg operated on—that's why I can't play basketball at the moment.
e I think you should ... your brakes looked at. That bicycle is not safe.
f I'm going to ... my picture taken for a passport photograph.
g I'm going to ... this shirt dyed green. I think it'll go well with my suit.
h I'm never going to ... the heater repaired—I've called the company at least 20 times.
i If you don't ... your thesis checked by your supervisor soon, you'll never be able to finish it.
j She ... her hair dyed pink yesterday.

28 Say what you would like to have done to some or all of the following.

- your house
- your hair
- your car
- your clothes
- your bicycle
- something else

Example: *I'd like to have the brakes on my bicycle fixed.*

29 Match the two columns to make sentences about Caroline's nightmare day.

a She got her cellphone
b She got her parents' car
c She had her bag
d She had her coat
e She had her dinner
f She had her hat
g She had her picture

1 ... blown off in the wind.
2 ... confiscated by the history teacher.
3 ... eaten by the dog.
4 ... ripped by a passing bike rider.
5 ... stolen on the way to school.
6 ... taken before she was ready.
7 ... towed away by the police.

- Are the sentences describing something that Caroline organized or bad experiences that happened to her?
- Is the *have* construction the same as Activities 22–28? Are the meanings the same or different?
- Have any of these things (or something similar) ever happened to you? Tell your partner about it.

Functional language: taking something to be fixed

30 Listening Listen to Track 36. Which is the correct picture?

a
b
c

31 Listen to Track 36 again and answer the questions.

   a What two problems is the car owner worried about?

   b Who's going to look at the car?

   c When will the car be ready, according to Mr. Bolton?

32 Complete these sentences and questions from the conversation (one word per blank).

   a MR. BOLTON: Back .... a .... , Charlie.

   b CLIENT: Well, there's .... coming from the ....

   c CLIENT: Whenever I .... into fourth gear, it .... a .... click.

   d MR. BOLTON: Can you .... it .... us?

   e CLIENT: When can I .... ?

   f CLIENT: But you will .... it .... ?

   g MR. BOLTON: I'll try and .... it .... by 4 o'clock.

   h MR. BOLTON: How does .... ?

   i CLIENT: I'll come .... 4:00 then.

33 Do sentences *a–r* below belong in the first or the second column?

What the customer might say

What the service provider might say
a, ...

   a Can you leave it overnight?

   b Could you take a look at the windshield wipers?

   c I can't get it to play CDs.

   d I think I've got a flat tire.

   e I was wondering if you could fix my bike.

   f I'll get it looked at.

   g I'll have that taken care of.

   h I've brought my car to be serviced.

   i It doesn't seem to want to play tapes.

   j The brakes don't seem to be working.

   k The radio doesn't work.

   l There seems to be a noise coming from the engine.

   m We don't seem to have a record of that.

   n What seems to be the problem?

   o What's the name?

   p When do you need it by?

   q When I turn it on, nothing happens.

   r Whenever I try and record onto a minidisk, it just doesn't work.

Pronunciation /s/, /z/ and /tʃ/

34 Look at the following words from the conversation on Track 36. Divide them into three columns, depending on the pronunciation of the letters in blue.

change   Charlie   checked   course
depends   noise   outside   perhaps
promises   said   suppose   switch   us

Check your answers by listening to Track 37.

35 Choose one of the three sounds. Who can think of the most words with the sound in 60 seconds?

36 Vocabulary Choose one of the following objects from the list.

- car
- bicycle
- stereo
- cellphone
- watch
- printer
- laptop computer

In pairs Write about things that often / sometimes go wrong with these items.

37 Using language from Activities 32 and 33, make conversations in which Student A takes one of the items from Activity 36 to be fixed.

Writing: instructions

38 Discussion When you buy a new item of technology (cellphone, microwave oven, computer, digital watch, etc.):

- ... how easy is it to make it work?
- ... how easy is it to read the instructions that are given? Why?

39 Look at the pictures on page 79 and find an instruction that matches them.

Setting up your Sony notebook

1 *Unpacking your Sony notebook*
Unpack your Sony notebook and check the complete contents of the box. The letters A to H correspond to the letters on the cover flap image.

A) Main Unit	E) Rechargable battery pack
B) AC adapter	F) Sony Documentation pack
C) Power cord	G) Phone cable
D) Product Recovery CD-ROMS	H) Phone plug (country-specific)

2 *Inserting the battery pack*
Before inserting the battery pack, please turn off your computer. Move the lock lever on the bottom of the computer to the UNLOCK

position. Align the grooves on the side of the battery with the tabs on the back of the computer, and slide the battery toward the computer until it clicks into place. Slide the lock lever into the LOCK position to secure the battery on the computer.
The battery pack supplied with your computer is not fully charged at the time of purchase.

3 *Attaching the power cord*
You may use either AC power or a battery pack as a power source. Plug the AC adapter cable into the DC connector of the computer. Plug the prongs into the AC outlet.

4 *Opening the notebook*
Lift the cover in the direction of the arrow.

5 *Starting the notebook*
Press the power button on the computer to turn on the power. The power indicator turns on.

For detailed information, refer to the printed documentation or take a look at the **VAIO Info Center** installed in your hard disk drive.

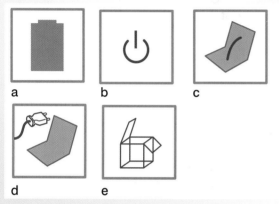

40 **Without looking back at the instructions above, can you recreate any of them, using the words and phrases in the boxes (and other words like auxiliary verbs, prepositions, etc.)?**

Verbs check insert lift plug press
turn off unpack

Nouns AC adapter cable battery pack
computer contents of the box cover
DC In connector notebook power button

Now look back at the instructions. Were you right?

41 **Choose one of the following tasks and complete tasks *a–c*.**

* recording a message on your telephone answering machine
* using a washing machine
* sending an email
* using a carwash
* something else that you choose

a Make a list of the words you need in your language and then find English equivalents.
b Make a list of the things that need to be done and put them in order.
c Write instructions.

Review: grammar and functional language

42 **Complete the conversation with one word for each space.**

A: Good morning, sir. What can I (**a**) ....*do*.... for you?
B: Well, it's this watch of mine. It (**b**) .... seem to be working.
A: It probably (**c**) .... cleaning, sir.
B: Yes, I expect it (**d**) ....
A: Well, sir, can I take a look?
B: Yes, of (**e**) ....
A: Hmm, now let's take a look. (**f**) ....
B: Interesting? Why?
A: How long have you had this (**g**) .... , sir?
B: About 62 years. Exactly 62 years, actually.
A: Fantastic. It's a real museum piece. But you (**h**) .... have brought it to me earlier, sir, if you don't mind me saying.
B: No, no, not at all. I was (**i**) .... to (**j**) .... it fixed about 20 years ago, I think, but then I (**k**) .... about it.
A: Forgot about it?
B: Yes, but I can't (**l**) .... why.
A: Ah, I see. But anyway it needs (**m**) ...., as I said, and I need to do a bit of (**n**) .... on the cogs and gears of the mechanism. Can you leave it with me for a (**o**) .... days?
B: Umm, well I ...
A: When do you (**p**) .... it back?
B: By Thursday next week at the (**q**) ....
A: That won't be a (**r**) .... , sir.
B: Good. Right then, now I'm going to have my hair (**s**) .... and then I'm going to the tailors – I'm (**t**) .... (**u**) to .... a new suit made for me, you see.
A: That sounds enjoyable.
B: Oh I don't know. But I'm (**v**) .... a new girlfriend out to dinner next week so I need to look sharp, don't you think?
A: I suppose so, sir, yes.

Review: vocabulary

Word List

adamant	khaki
beige	light (+ color)
bright (+ color)	lime-green
brilliant (+ color)	muddy (+ color)
chilling out	mustard
coffee-colored	nurturing
conventional	pale (+ color)
cream	scarlet
dark (+ color)	to complement
dull (+ color)	to contract
faded (+ color)	to derive
golden brown	vibrations
inadvertently	

Word Plus

"for Heaven's sake" *
"I haven't the slightest idea."
as black as he is painted
as black as ink
as white as a sheet
blue with cold
can't afford
green with envy
in a black mood
it depends on what X is like
"out of the blue"
to be in for a bumpy ride
to be on your best behavior
to be out of it
"to be yellow"
to catch someone red-handed
to elicit a strong psychological
  response
to give someone the green light
to go bright red
to go on until you are blue in
  the face
to have its own special effect
  on somebody
to have the right to
to look forward to
to make a decision
"paint the town red"
"to scream blue murder"
"to see red"
to seek out new ways of doing
  something

*Phrases in quotation marks are
conversational phrases.

43 Find words or phrases in the Word List and Word Plus that make you feel warm, lukewarm (= neither hot nor cold) or cold. Explain why you feel like this about the words and phrases.

Example: *For me, "beige" is a cold color.*

Pronunciation

44 Copy and complete the table with as many words as you can from the Word List and Word Plus.

/eɪ/ – paid	/aɪ/ – fight

Check your answers by listening to Track 38.

Add more words of your own to the list.

45 Look at the phrases in Word Plus. How many words (apart from *to*) can you find with the schwa sound /ə/?

Example: *as black as he's painted*

a What kind of word or syllable is the schwa used for?
b Which syllables are stressed in the phrases you have chosen?

Check your answers by listening to Track 39.

46 Fish bowl Write the phrases from Word Plus on separate pieces of paper. Put the pieces of paper in a bowl.

In pairs, have conversations about one of the following topics.

- traveling by airplane
- favorite colors
- favorite songs or paintings
- favorite possession

The pairs must keep the conversation going.

At certain points, the student who is speaking takes a piece of paper from the bowl. They have to use the phrase on the piece of paper immediately as they continue the conversation.

UNIT 8
Food for thought

→ using articles
→ idioms (food and drink)
→ making a complaint

Reading: what we eat

1 In groups Look at these different pictures of food and discuss the questions below.

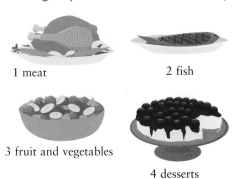

1 meat

2 fish

3 fruit and vegetables

4 desserts

5 fast food

6 vegetarian food

Which of these foods:

a ... are good for you?
b ... are bad for you?
c ... have you eaten?
d ... would you like to eat?
e ... would you not like to eat?
f ... are "comfort food"?

2 Read the short extracts (*1–4*) from different Web sites and match the extract to the website (*a–d*) it came from.

a www.mercola.com
the website of a medical doctor who specializes in nutrition and natural remedies

b www.monsantoafrica.com
a company which produces genetically-modified crops

c www.greenpeace.org
an organization in favor of protecting the environment

d www.vegan.org
a website dedicated to the arguments and health of people who don't use or eat animals

1 What is a vegan? A vegan (pronounced VEE-gun) is someone who avoids using or consuming animal products. While vegetarians avoid flesh foods, vegans also avoid dairy products and eggs, as well as fur, leather, wool, feathers, and cosmetics or chemical products tested on animals.

Why vegan? Veganism, the natural extension of vegetarianism, is an integral component of a cruelty-free lifestyle. Living vegan provides numerous benefits to animals' lives, to the environment and to our own health—through a healthy diet and lifestyle.

The consumption of animal fats and proteins has been linked to heart disease, colon and lung cancer, osteoporosis, diabetes, kidney disease, hypertension, obesity, and a number of other debilitating conditions. Cows' milk contains ideal amounts of fat and protein for young calves, but far too much for humans. And eggs are higher in cholesterol than any other food, making them a leading contributor to cardiovascular disease. The American Dietetic Association reports that vegetarian / vegan diets are associated with reduced risks for all of these conditions.

2 Genetic engineering of food is a risky process. Current understanding of genetics is extremely limited and scientists do not know the long-term effects of releasing these unpredictable foods into our environment and our diets. Yet, GE ingredients are freely entering our food without sufficient regulations and without the consent and knowledge of the consumer.

Although transnational companies and their political supporters want us to believe that this food is safe and thoroughly tested, growing awareness of the dangers from GE food has started a global wave of rejection by consumers, farmers and food companies in many of the world's largest food markets. Due to consumer pressure, supermarkets have taken GE food from their shelves, global food companies have removed GE ingredients from their products and leading pig and poultry producers have promised not to feed animals with GE feed.

3 Along with the saturated fat and cholesterol scares of the past several decades has come the notion that vegetarianism is a healthier dietary option for people. It seems as if every health expert and government health agency is urging people to eat fewer animal products and consume more vegetables, grains, fruits, and legumes. Along with this advice have come assertions and studies supposedly proving that vegetarianism is healthier for people and that meat consumption causes sickness and death. Several medical authorities, however, have questioned these data, but their objections have been largely ignored.

Many of the vegetarian claims cannot be substantiated and some are simply false and dangerous. There are benefits to vegetarian diets for certain health conditions and some people function better on less fat and protein, but, as a practitioner who has dealt with several former vegans (total vegetarians), I know full well the dangerous effects of a diet devoid of healthful animal products.

b

change

4 What has come to be called "biotechnology" and the genetic manipulation of agricultural products is nothing new.

Indeed, it may be one of the oldest human activities. For thousands of years, from the time human communities began to settle in one place, cultivate crops, and farm the land, humans have manipulated the genetic nature of the crops and animals they raise. Crops have been bred to improve yields, → *How much* enhance taste, and extend the growing season. *make it longer*

make it better

Each of the 15 major crop plants, which provide 90 percent of the globe's food and energy intake, has been extensively manipulated and modified over the millennia by countless generations of farmers intent on producing crops in the most effective and efficient ways possible.

Today, biotechnology holds out promise for consumers seeking quality, safety and taste in their food choices; for farmers seeking new methods to improve their productivity and profitability; and for governments and non-governmental public advocates seeking to stave off global hunger, assure environmental quality, preserve biodiversity, and promote health and food safety.

3 **Fact check** Who believes these things: vegans, Greenpeace, Dr. Mercola, or Monsanto?

a Humans need to eat some animal products.   Dr. Mercola
b Humans do not have to eat meat.   Vegans
c Genetically-modified food is bad for us. greenpeace
d Genetic engineering could feed the world. Monsanto
e Vegetarian diets can be more healthy than meat-based ones. vegans
f Genetic engineering is not a new thing. Monsanto
g We do not know what the effects of GM food on humans are. greenpeace

4 Match the words from the extracts *1–4* with their synonym or definition (*1–11*).

a numerous (extract 1)   4
b risky (extract 2)   5
c consent (extract 2)   8
d urging (extract 3)   6
e objections (extract 3)   9
f substantiated (extract 3)   3
g cultivate (extract 4)   1
h yields (extract 4)   7
i enhance (extract 4)   11
j millennia (extract 4)   2
k advocates (extract 4)   10

1 grow
2 thousands of years
3 proved
4 many, lots of
5 dangerous
6 trying to persuade, strongly advising
7 productivity, harvests
8 permission, agreement
9 expressions of disapproval
10 supporters
11 improve

Language in chunks

5 Complete the phrases *a–g* with as many of the words and phrases below as you can.

a   *a f*   *a f*   *a f*
condition   illness   sickness   disease   wave of rejection
hunger *d* terrorism *d* protest   destroying   winning *e* emotion
producing *e* protein   fat   animal products   vitamins *f*
dying earlier *e* poverty *f* living longer *e*

a a debilitating ... *disease   to aviod*   d stave off ...   f devoid of ...
b associated with ...   e intent on ...   g linked to ...
c global ... *poverty*   *to try hard*

6 Use one of the expressions you made in Activity 5 to complete these sentences as in the example.

a The United Nations got together to try to do something about the number of poor people in the world in a conference on ... *global poverty.*
b He ate a diet which was ... , because he knew of the dangers of fat to his health. *devoid of fat*
c Exercising every day has been ... . Experts say this can add five more years to your life. *associated with living longer*
d She was in a wheelchair, because of ... that she had had for 20 years. *a debilitating condition*
e The baseball player was ... . This was his last chance before he retired from the game. *intent on winning*
f She ate a chocolate bar to ... , since she would not be eating dinner for at least another two hours. *stave off hunger.*
g Obesity has often been ... , probably because of all the illnesses that it can cause. *associated with illness*

7 Make other sentences using the expressions.

8 Noticing language Look at these sentences from the four texts in Activity 2 and notice which nouns have a definite article, an indefinite article or no article.

a The consumption of animal fats and proteins has been linked to heart disease.

b Genetic engineering of food is a risky process.

c I know full well the dangerous effects of a diet devoid of animal products.

d The genetic manipulation of agricultural products is nothing new.

Find at least one more example from the texts of the use of the definite article, the indefinite article and no article before a noun.

9 In groups Answer these questions.

• What foods do you eat that are good for you?
• What foods do you eat that are bad for you?
• Do you approve of GM foods?
• What do you think about vegetarianism and veganism?
• How can we solve the problem of world hunger?

Vocabulary: food and drink (idioms)

10 Copy this nutritional pyramid and complete it with as many examples as you can think of.

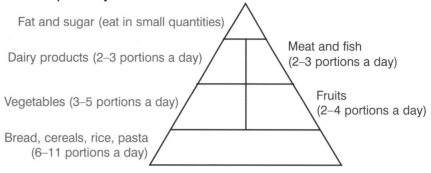

Fat and sugar (eat in small quantities)

Dairy products (2–3 portions a day)

Meat and fish (2–3 portions a day)

Vegetables (3–5 portions a day)

Fruits (2–4 portions a day)

Bread, cereals, rice, pasta (6–11 portions a day)

Compare your list with a partner.

11 Discussion Talk about the following questions.

a What does the pyramid suggest about the kind of foods we should eat?

b Does your average weekly food consumption look like this pyramid?

c How important is what you eat to you?

12 Food idioms Using a dictionary or any other source, complete the following idioms (in blue) by using words from the box. You will need to use some of the words more than once. You might have to change their form.

apple bacon beans bread cake cucumber egg
fruit cake hot cakes milk mustard pancake pie tea

a "You want me to put up a picture? That's easy. It's a piece of ... *cake* ."

b I don't like him much, but I'm still nice to him—I know which side my ... is buttered.

c "Don't think about the past because you can't change it. There's no point in crying over spilt ... ."

d I don't think we should give her the job. She's not good enough. She just can't cut the ... .

e I told a joke and absolutely nobody laughed. The joke fell as flat as a ... .

f "If this plan goes wrong, you should have another one ready: Don't put all your ... in one basket."

g Mrs. Allen's son is her favorite person. In fact he's the ... of her eye.

h My brother's crazy. He's as nutty as a ... .

i My friend helped me out of a really awkward and dangerous situation. He saved my ... .

j Since her husband lost his job, Susan is the one who brings home the ... .

k Playing the piano? That's easy. In fact it's as easy as ... !

l She told me to do it, she encouraged me, even though I didn't want to. She ... me on.

m Some people like gardening, but I don't. It's just not my cup of ... .

n This new kitchen gadget is fantastic. It's the best thing since sliced ... .

o This year, the new iPods have been a fantastic success in the stores. They've been selling like ... .

unit eight 83

p When she confronted him in front of all those people, his expression didn't change at all. He just stood there as cool as a ... .

q It was supposed to be a secret, but she couldn't help spilling the ... to her best friend.

r "If you don't do your homework, you can't go to the concert. You can't have your ... and eat it too!"

13 Look at the idioms in Activity 12. Are any of them similar to idioms in your language? If not, how can you say these things idiomatically?

Speaking and writing: when words are used

Some words are much more common in spoken English than in written English—or vice versa.

14 Look at the dictionary entries below. Are the words used more in spoken or in written English, according to the dictionary makers? How do you know in each case?

fan·cy¹ /ˈfænsi/ *adj.* comparative **fancier**, superlative **fanciest** **1** expensive and fashionable: *a fancy hotel*

THESAURUS
expensive, pricey, posh
→ see Thesaurus box at EXPENSIVE

2 unusual and complicated or having a lot of decorations: *I'd just like plain brown shoes, nothing fancy.* **3** [only before noun] fancy food is of a very high quality

fancy² *n.* [singular] old-fashioned a feeling that you like something or som~~~~: *Grant's taken a fancy to you.*

fe·ver /ˈfivər/ *n.* **1** [C,U] an illness in which you have a very high temperature: *Andy has a fever and won't be coming into work today.* | *She's running a fever* (=has a fever). **2** [U] a situation in which people feel very excited or anxious: *Baseball fans are gripped by World Series fever.* | *When the TV crews arrived, the demonstration reached fever pitch* (=an extreme level of excitement or anxiety). —**fevered** *adj.* → HAY FEVER, SPRING FEVER

fright·ened [S2] /ˈfraɪtnd/ *adj* feeling afraid ⊟ **scared**: *Don't be frightened. We're not going to hur~ you.* | [+of] *I was frightened of being left by myself i~ the house.* | *Her father had an awful temper and she wa~*

the frequency range of the human ear
fre·quent¹ [W3] /ˈfrikwənt/ *adj* happening or doing something often; ⊟ **infrequent**: **more/less frequen~** *Her headaches are becoming less frequent.* | *Train~ rushed past at frequent intervals.* | *She was a frequen~ visitor to the house.*
fre·quent² /frɪˈkwɛnt $ ˈfrikwənt, ˈfrikwənt/ *v* [T~ formal to go to a ~articular ~lac~~

Where can you see speaking-like language being used in writing in the modern world?

15 Look at your own dictionary. Find three words that are used more in spoken English than in written English, and three that are used more in written English than in spoken English.

Listening: where people like to eat

16 Look at these pictures. Which of these places would you like to eat at and why?

17 Which of these people would prefer to eat at the restaurants *a–e* in Activity 16, do you think?

Chris

Jed

Martin

Julia

Naomi

🔊 Listen to Track 40 and see if you were correct.

18 Listen again Who:

a ... thinks there are many factors to finding the perfect restaurant?

b ... doesn't like eating in expensive restaurants?

c ... thinks the people who serve at the restaurant are well mannered?

d ... is well known in the restaurant where he goes?

e ... thinks that the experience of eating is as important as the food?

19 Make a table to show what each speaker says about (a) food, (b) service, (c) atmosphere, and (d) price.

Compare your notes with a partner.

20 Imagine you are going to open a restaurant. Make notes about its food, design / theme, and the price of food there.

Compare in groups. Decide who would have the best restaurant.

Functional language: making a complaint

21 Put the conversation in a restaurant in order. Start with line i.

a The beans are undercooked too.

b Well, first of all, it's cold and the fish has a strange taste.

c Yes, ma'am?

d Certainly.

e What seems to be the problem, ma'am?

f I'm sorry, but there's something wrong with my meal.

g Yes, please. Could I see the menu?

h Would you like to order something else?

i Excuse me.   1

j I'm sorry about that. I'll take it back to the kitchen.

Now listen to Track 41 and check your answer.

22 Read the following sentences which were heard in a restaurant. Put them into three groups.

Starting to make a complaint	a, ...
Reasons for the complaint	
Ways of dealing with a complaint	

a I'm sorry but, ...

b This fish tastes awful.

c I don't want to complain, but ...

d I'm very sorry. I'll take it back to the kitchen.

e This chicken is not what I asked for.

f Would you like to speak to the manager?

g I don't like this hamburger.

h I hate to complain, but ...

i I'm not happy with this salad.

j Would you like to order something else?

k I have a complaint to make.

l This chocolate cake looks stale.

m There doesn't seem to be anything wrong with it.

n I'm afraid there's something wrong here.

o I'm afraid there's nothing I can do about it.

p This salad is gritty.

q Excuse me, but I'd like to speak to the person in charge.

r This meat smells burnt.

23 In pairs Which adjectives in the box could you use to complain about foods a–h below?

> undercooked   tough
> overcooked   burnt   stale
> greasy   raw   salty   awful
> spicy   cold   bland   gritty

a soup   *bland, ...*

b salad

c chocolate cake

d steak

e fish

f hamburger

g doughnut

h chicken

24 Role-play Imagine you are the customer in each of these situations (a–c). Make a complaint in person or on the telephone to your partner, who is the service provider.

a You have been waiting to be served at a table in a restaurant for 30 minutes.

b You take some food back to the supermarket where you bought it because there is something wrong with it.

c You are overcharged at a restaurant for two sodas and two bottles of water that you did not order.

Speaking: restaurant jokes

25 There are a lot of jokes about restaurants. Do you have jokes like the one on the right in your culture?

26 **In pairs** Student A, turn to Activity Bank 6 on page 158. Student B, turn to Activity Bank 11 on page 160.

27 **In pairs** Can you explain the jokes? Which is the funniest joke? Compare with other groups. Do you know any funnier restaurant jokes? What's your favorite simple joke in your language? Can you translate it into English?

Grammar: using articles

28 **In pairs** Look at these sentences and say why the definite article *the* is used or is not used before the nouns in blue.

  a Breakfast is an important meal. The breakfast I had today consisted of cereal and toast.
  b I find that I think a lot about food.
  c She told him it was a ripe mango. The mango was soft to the touch and a deep orange color.
  d I love to cook vegetables.
  e People are often happy to eat out in restaurants.
  f You must read the cookbook that he wrote.
  g We didn't see the restaurant that you recommended.
  h Animal fat is very important in some diets.

Look at 8C in the Mini-grammar. Do you want to change any of your answers?

29 Complete this paragraph using *the* or no article. Use **8C–D in the Mini-grammar** to help you. Compare with your partner.

When you ask some people what their hobby is, they will often say (**a**) "............... food." There is no doubt that what to eat occupies a lot of (**b**) .... day for a lot of people. Nowadays, it's very hard to know if you are eating (**c**) .... healthy food. On (**d**) .... TV and in (**e**) .... newspapers and magazines, we read about different diets which are supposed to help (**f**) .... people to stay healthy. The problem is that (**g**) .... experts often contradict each other, so it's hard to know what to believe. Yesterday, I saw a show that said that we should only eat (**h**) .... raw foods, like (**i**) .... fruits and (**j**) .... vegetables. Then I watched a show where (**k**) .... presenter said that we should eat a diet free of (**l**) .... carbohydrates.

30 Look at these sentences and identify whether they use the definite article (the), the indefinite article (a, an), or no article before the noun in blue. Use **8A–8D in the Mini-grammar** to help you.

  a Jackie has taken up the violin.
  b Do you want an apple? The apples are from the market, you know.
  c That's the craziest thing I've ever heard!
  d She really loves popcorn.
  e I'm sure I left a chocolate bar in the fridge.
  f The cherries are 90 cents a pound.
  g This lecture is about the potato and when it first arrived in Europe.
  h We love making curries. You must come over for one some time.
  i She looked at the chicken that the butcher was showing her.
  j She eats very well—her mother is a nutritionist.
  k The sun rises in the East and sets in the West.
  l Goulash is a dish which was first made by the Hungarians.

31 Choose the best option (definite article, indefinite article, no article) to complete this paragraph. Use **8A–8D in the Mini-grammar** to help you.

I've been (**a**) the / **a** vegan for about five years now. I was (**b**) the / a vegan for two years before that, but most of (**c**) the / - vegetarians I've ever met end up becoming (**d**) the / - vegans or going back to eating (**e**) the / - meat. The reason I stopped eating (**f**) the / - meat was that I didn't like how (**g**) the / - people keep and kill (**h**) the / - animals. It's not that I'm (**i**) the / an animal lover, but I have (**j**) a / - lot of respect for (**k**) the / - living things on this planet. I was (**l**) a / - student at the time and now I'm (**m**) an / - engineer and I have never regretted (**n**) the / a choice I made all those years ago.

32 Which of the following names do you know? Which need the definite article? Copy them out correctly.

Acapulco *no article*   Kremlin
Angkor Watt   Madagascar
Bermuda Triangle   Mississippi River
Buckingham Palace   Mount Vesuvius
Colorado   province of Buenos Aires
Eiffel Tower   Narita Airport
Grand Canyon   pyramid of Cheops
Golden Tower   state of Sonora
Harvard University   Statue of Liberty
Hilton Hotel   Taj Mahal
Iguaçu Falls   Temple of Heavenly Peace,
Krackow   Kyoto

Check you have understood by looking at **8C in the Mini-grammar.**

Pronunciation: weak and strong *the*

33 Listen to these sentences on Track 42. How is *the* said?

a This is the best restaurant in the city.
b This is the restaurant to be seen in in this city.
c Could I have the Atlantic salmon please?
d Do you have the ..., the crabs that are in season?
e We went down to the self-service buffet.
f Would you like to help yourself to the ice cream?

When do we use the two different pronunciations? Practice saying the sentences.

Writing: describing graphs and tables

34 Read the report about this table and identify these three parts of the report.

a conclusions which are based on the table
b description of what the table represents
c description of the information in the table

Table 1: *1,203 people in the U.K. were asked about genetically engineered foods.*

1	If you knew which food had GM ingredients and you could choose, which of these is your opinion?	
	I would never eat GE food.	42%
	I would prefer not to eat GE food.	51%
	I don't mind whether or not I eat GE food.	7%
	I would prefer to eat GE food.	0%
	I would always eat GE food.	0%

Report on Table 1
Part 1
This table shows the results of a survey carried out in the U.K. 1,203 people were asked whether they would eat food which contained GM ingredients.
Part 2
The results show that 42% of the people asked would never eat GM food if they knew that it had GM ingredients, while about half (51%) said that they would prefer not to eat GM food. 7% of the people surveyed said that they don't mind whether or not they eat GM food and no one said that they would prefer to eat GM food or would always eat GM food.
Part 3
This seems to show that people in the U.K. do not like GM food and do not want to eat it if they have a choice.

35 Now look at Table 2. Write a report on what the table shows, using the plan below.

Table 2: *Two hundred people were asked the following question "In your opinion, are the dangers of genetic modification of plants more important than the possible advantages?"*

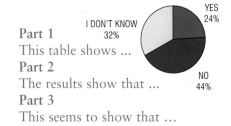

Part 1
This table shows ...
Part 2
The results show that ...
Part 3
This seems to show that ...

36 Choose a question to conduct a survey of your own. Use one of the questions from this section or a different question connected with food.

Example: Do you eat foods that are bad for you?
never / sometimes / often

Make a table of the results like Table 1 or Table 2. Then write a short report of the results.

37 **In pairs** Check that your reports have the three parts that are needed and that they can be clearly understood by people who read them.

Review: grammar and functional language

38 Complete this conversation with the definite article (*the*), the indefinite article (*a / an*) or no article. Look at Activities 29–34 for help.

CUSTOMER: Excuse me, but I'd like to speak to (**a**) ....the... manager of this store.

SALES CLERK: I'm afraid (**b**) .... manager is not here at the moment. Can I help you?

CUSTOMER: I want to make (**c**) .... complaint. I bought (**d**) .... box of (**e**) .... chocolates here last week and I tried one of (**f**) .... chocolates and it tasted stale.

SALES CLERK: I'm afraid I can't do anything since we don't make (**g**) .... chocolates, we only sell them. It's not our responsibility to replace (**h**) .... goods that we sell in (**i**) .... good faith.

CUSTOMER: So, what can I do?

SALES CLERK: You'll need to contact (**j**) .... manufacturers of (**k**) .... chocolates. They can refund your money or replace (**l**) .... chocolates.

CUSTOMER: How can I contact (**m**) .... manufacturers?

SALES CLERK: They are based in (**n**) .... United Kingdom, but you can find (**o**) .... address in (**p**) .... U.S.A., in (**q**) .... Ohio, on (**r**) .... side of (**s**) .... box.

CUSTOMER: Thanks for your help.

39 Match the complaint on the left with the response on the right.

a I'm sorry, but this steak is not what I asked for. *3*

b I hate to complain, but this salad seems rather gritty.

c Excuse me, but I'd like to speak to someone in charge about this meal.

d This apple pie looks very stale.

e I have a complaint to make. This chicken is undercooked.

f Excuse me, but this chocolate mousse tastes awful.

g I don't want to complain, but these potatoes are burnt.

h I'm sorry to complain, but I don't think this fish is fresh.

1 Oh. Yes, it does smell a little strange. Would you like to order a different dessert?

2 What seems to be wrong with it? Desserts are our chef's specialty.

3 I'm very sorry about that. I'll bring you what you ordered immediately.

4 I'll take it back to the kitchen. Would you like it cooked more or would you prefer something else?

5 I'm afraid there's nothing I can do about that. All our lettuce is triple-washed.

6 I'm very sorry about that. Would you like to order a different vegetable?

7 That's impossible. It was caught today.

8 Certainly. I'll get the manager for you.

40 **In pairs** Look at this picture and imagine the conversation between this guest and the hotel manager, who has given the man the last available room in the hotel and wants the guest to stay at the hotel. Hotel rooms are hard to find in the city. Look at Activities 21–25 for help.

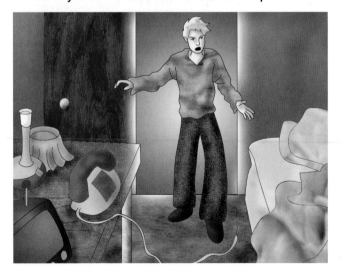

Example: STUDENT A: I'd like to make a complaint about my room.

STUDENT B: How can I help you, sir / ma'am?

STUDENT A: The room is very dark and there is no bulb in the lamp.

STUDENT B: I'll send someone up to fix that immediately, sir / ma'am.

STUDENT A: Another thing is ...

Review: vocabulary

Word List

advocate	risky
awful	salty
bland	spicy
burnt	stale
consent	substantiated
greasy	to cultivate
gritty	to enhance
millennium	tough
numerous	undercooked
objection	urging
overcooked	yield
raw	

Word Plus

"(She) just can't cut the mustard." *

a debilitating illness / condition

"a piece of cake"

"as cool as a cucumber"

"as flat as a pancake"

"as nutty as a fruit cake"

associated with living longer

devoid of emotion

global protest

intent on winning

"It's not my cup of tea."

linked to poverty

"the apple of (her) eye"

"the best thing since sliced bread"

"to be selling like hot cakes"

"to cry over spilt milk"

"to have your cake and eat it"

"to know which side your bread is buttered"

"to put all your eggs in one basket"

"to spill the beans"

to stave off disease

*Phrases in quotation marks are conversational phrases.

41 Look at the Word Plus list and answer the questions *a–d*.

   a Which is your favorite food expression and why?

   b Can you name something that is not your "cup of tea"?

   c Who is the "apple of your eye"?

   d Can you name something that is "a piece of cake" for you?

Pronunciation

42 Copy the table and put all the words in the Word List into the correct column according to the number of syllables they have.

One syllable	Two syllables	Three syllables	Four syllables	Five syllables
bland				

Now underline the stressed syllable in each word. Listen to Track 43 and check your answers.

43 In teams One team chooses Task A. The other team chooses Task B.

Task A: How many new words can you make from the letters of only the word *substantiated*? See who can make the most words.

Example: *ant, bus*

Task B: How many words can you make from the sounds of only the word *substantiated*?

Example: /ʃi/ —she

       /eɪt/ —eight

Who has the most words after three minutes?

44 In pairs Talk about a time when:

   a ... you or someone you know "put all your eggs in one basket." Was it a good thing or a bad thing? What happened?

   b ... you or someone you know "spilled the beans." What happened? Did someone get into trouble? Did it help someone?

UNIT 9

First impressions

→ adjectives
→ physical description (connotation)
→ taking ourselves to be fixed

Listening: *Café Talk*

1 **In pairs** Discuss the following with your partner.

  a When you meet a new person, what do you look at first?

- their hair
- ⊙ their face (eyes, mouth, etc.)
- their build
- what they are wearing

  b Which of the following will make you feel most positive about somebody?

- ⊙ They are <u>well groomed</u>. *جيّد الهندام*
- They are <u>well dressed</u>.
- They have a good physique.
- They look interesting.
- They look like you.

Compare the answers with the rest of the class.

2 Look at this artist's impression from the program *Café Talk*. Listen to Track 44 and answer the questions that follow.

slouched down

The *Café Talk* cast. From left to right, Sally (Laura McHearty), Greenslade (Richard Whiles), Mitch (Andy Varshun), and Seb (Jason Cutting).

  a Who does Sally like best, do you think: Greenslade, Mitch, or Seb?
  b Who sympathizes with Greenslade's opinions: Mitch, Sally, or Seb?
  c Who is Raj Persaud?

3 Read the following summaries. Listen to Track 44 again. Say which one is correct.

for example

  a Greenslade has read an article which says that people like and are attracted to people they feel comfortable with, e.g. their friends and families. This is because they look at themselves in the mirror and love their pets. Sometimes they look like their pets too and go on to marry older men or women.

  b Greenslade has read an article which says that people like and are attracted to people that look like their pets, e.g. their friends and families. This is because they see photographs of themselves and their pets. But some of them marry older people because they are very rich and have a lot of mirrors.

  c Greenslade has read an article which says that people like and are attracted to people they feel comfortable with, e.g. their friends and families. This is because their face is the one they usually see in the mirror and in pictures. They are also used to their family's faces. All of this affects the choice of husband or wife, for example.

4 Who (Greenslade, Mitch, Sally, or Seb) says each of these things?

  a Their minds, of course. *Mich*
  b What are you talking about? *Mich*
  c Where do you get this stuff? *Seb*
  d Leave him alone, guys. *Sally*
  e It makes sense. *Greenslade*
  f This is just like so boring. *Seb*
  g Think about it. *Greenslads*
  h What is it with you, Mitch? *Sally*
  i You talk a lot of nonsense. *Mich*
  j OK, that's enough. *Sally*
  k That's my business. *Sally*

Explain why they use these phrases in each case.

●●● Pronunciation: attitude

5 Listen to Track 45. What exactly do the phrases mean, and what attitude are the speakers conveying?

a Yeah, right.
b No really, Sally ...
c I read, Seb, OK?
d Says who?
e God!
f Well, sorry.
g You said.
h Pity.
i You do.

How could you tell what the speakers' attitudes were?

6 Say the phrases in exactly the same way as the speakers, using the same stress and intonation.

7 **Acting out** Read through the Audioscript for Track 44.

a Think about which words are stressed in each line.
b Think of how the phrases from Activities 4 and 5 are said on the recording.
c In groups, practice the conversation—or part of the conversation.
d Act out the conversation—or part of the conversation—for the class.

Vocabulary: physical description (connotation)

8 Copy and complete the table with the adjectives. Some may go in more than one column. Consult a dictionary if necessary.

appealing bright curly dark deep-set fine generous kind large long mean pointed protruding receding shiny small snub soft square straight strong thick thinning turned up wavy weak wide wiry

Chin	Eyes	Hair	Mouth	Nose
	appealing			

What does someone's hair look like if they have:

a ... a crew cut?
b ... a bald spot?
c ... highlights?
d ... a perm?
e ... extensions?

9 Describe the following people using words from Activity 8.

Example: The person in Picture "a" has a long nose, a wide, generous mouth and a strong chin.

10 Connotation Which of the following words have a positive meaning, which are neutral and which have negative overtones? Consult a dictionary if necessary.

a **thin:** emaciated⁻ lean⁺ puny⁻ skinny⁺ slender⁺ slight⁺ slim⁺ underweight

b **not thin:** chubby flabby muscular obese overweight⁺ plump pudgy stout voluptuous⁺ *women* well built

c **looks and appearance:** messy attractive beautiful cute elegant good-looking gorgeous handsome hideous plain pretty scruffy smart ugly well dressed

11 Intensifying and qualifying expressions Copy and complete the table with the phrases in blue.

a little overweight   a little plump   absolutely gorgeous
extremely beautiful   fantastically muscular   incredibly ugly
kind of bald   kind of skinny   rather attractive   rather ugly
somewhat

Phrases designed to make things not quite so strong

Phrases designed to emphasize an extreme quality

Make more combinations of phrase + description like the ones in the blue box above.

12 Describe the following characters in (a) a more positive and (b) a more negative way.

Gandalf

Amélie

Rocky

Bridget

Example: a Amélie is kind of slender.
b Amélie is rather skinny.

13 Describe someone (not in the class) who the other students should know. Can they guess who you are talking about?

Reading: hair

14 Read the two descriptions and match them with the photographs.

Emma is 26 years old. After school, she trained to be a hairdresser and worked for some time in a beauty salon. She retrained some years ago as a secretary and is now an executive secretary in a large law firm.

Stephanie is 27 years old. She has a degree in English literature from the University of Warwick (U.K.). She has worked for a bank and is now the human resources (personnel) manager for a large educational publisher.

a

b

Compare your choice with the class. How many people matched Photograph *a* with Emma and how many with Stephanie? What are the reasons for your choice?

15 Do you agree with the following statements?

a There are more natural blonds than dyed blond women in the world.
b Everyone thinks blonds are more attractive than, say, brunettes.
c It is an advantage for women to be blond.

Read the text on page 93. Does the article have the same opinion as you?

THE NEW BLOND BOMBSHELL

Do blonds have more fun? Women certainly assume so, for while only one in six is a natural blond, almost half of all women lighten their hair in some way or another.

Peroxide was discovered in 1818. Two centuries on, most blonds get a little help from the bottle. Last year they spent over $100 million on hair dye—and that doesn't include what they pay at a beauty salon to help to emulate blond role models such as Britney Spears, Sharon Stone, and Gwyneth Paltrow.

In fact many of these golden-haired icons are not natural blonds either. Even Marilyn Monroe started out as a freckle-faced brunette with medium skin tone. She wore pale make-up and dyed her hair platinum. So what is the mystery magnet that draws women to becoming blond? It must be strong, because even today across all races—not just white westerners—when people are asked to rate others for "attractiveness," they usually opt for those with lighter hair and skin. You only have to check out the TV commercials around the world to see how important the image of the blond has become.

Until recently, being blond or brunette was reckoned to be merely a matter of fashion. But something much deeper is driving our reactions to hair color. In fact, it turns out, being blond, whether natural or "fake," may not do women any good at all.

All blonds, but are they *real* blonds?

---

16 In groups of three Why do you think being blond may be a disadvantage for some women? To find out:

STUDENT A: turn to Activity Bank 7 on page 158.
STUDENT B: turn to Activity Bank 12 on page 161.
STUDENT C: turn to Activity Bank 19 on page 164.

17 In groups of three Copy and complete the table in note form with opinions from the texts. Don't look back at the texts.

Advantages of being a blond woman	Disadvantages of being a blond woman
Reasons:	Reasons:

18 Vocabulary Complete the sentences with the following work-related words. You can find the words in the texts and the writing section of this unit.

| applicant | appointed | résumé |
| equally qualified | PA | reject | salary |

a If you apply for a job, you are a job ....
b When you apply for a job, you generally send information about yourself, called a ....
c Two people who have studied the same thing are ....
d If the interviewers don't give you the job, they .... you.
e If you are the successful candidate for the job, you are ....
f The amount of money you get paid per month is called your ....
g The manager's chief aide is his/her personal assistant (often a higher-status job than a secretary). This is often shortened to ....

Language in chunks

19 Read the extracts from the texts on page 93 and in the Activity Bank. Replace the phrases in blue with words or phrases which mean almost the same.

    a Most blonds get a little help from bottles of hair dye.

    b While being blond may boost your social life, it can also damage your career prospects. (page 158)

    c It seems hardly credible that such changeable features as hair color could so influence recruitment decisions. (page 158)

    d The picture for me didn't play a major part. (page 161)

    e I made a studious attempt to ignore the appearance of the applicants. (page 161)

    f Under close questioning, they revealed that the ... stereotype had ... affected their judgment. (page 161)

20 Choose one of the blue phrases from Activity 19 and use it in an anecdote or a story.

21 Noticing language Look at all the texts (*The new blond bombshell* and Activity Bank) and find as many examples as you can of adjectives where two words are joined together.

Example: *golden-haired*

Grammar: adjectives and adjective order

22 Look at these sentences and answer the questions *a–c*.

- He had always wanted to be a tall, muscular, attractive man.
- She was tall, slim, and incredibly beautiful.
- He was wearing a yellow and green tie.
- She had always wanted to work in one of those tall concrete and glass buildings.
- Her boss was a silly old man.
- For the first two weeks, they got along very well.
- The last ten minutes of the interview went terribly slowly for the nervous, unprepared, blond woman.
- I want you to be quiet for the next three minutes. That's all.

    a When do we use *and* between adjectives and when don't we use *and*?

    b When do we use commas between adjectives and when don't we use commas?

    c When we use *first*, *next* and *last* with numbers, what's the correct order?

Look at **9A in the Mini-grammar**. Do you want to change your answers?

23 Rewrite the following incorrect sentences.

    a He had dark and thinning hair.

    b They are coming to stay for the two next days.

    c He looked handsome, elegant, rich. *

    d He behaved like a silly, young and fool.

    e She painted a happy voluptuous successful woman.

*In literary use, it is possible to miss out *and* when more than one adjective is used after a verb.

24 Two-word adjectives Read the text and complete the tasks which follow.

He was a well-off, good-looking, two-faced, red-haired TV presenter with a time-consuming job who married a world-famous, self-centered, big-headed singer after they had met in an air-conditioned duty-free shop at the airport.

At first things went well. It looked as if it would be a long-standing relationship. He was easygoing and she said she was warmhearted. They bought a big house in a built-up area and installed bullet-proof windows. She stopped singing and took a part-time job. She had to wear a shocking-pink uniform and so she quit. When he asked her why, she said she only wore handmade clothes, not badly designed coats. It was the first of many all-out arguments.

    a Describe the two people in your own words. Would you like to meet them? Why? Why not?

    b How many different two-word adjectives can you find in the text? How many different kinds are there? Use **9B in the Mini-grammar** to help you.

25 Make new adjectives by joining adjectives in the left-hand column with the words in the right-hand column. Say what they could describe.

absent	gray	
auburn	high	
bad	long	haired
brown	narrow	minded
curly	red	price
cut	short	sighted
dark	straight	skinned
fair	well	tempered
good	white	
near	hard	

Example: *absent-minded—an absent-minded professor*

Word Choice: *seem, appear* and *look*

26 Look at the Word Choice notes for *seem, appear* and *look* on page 58 in the booklet.

27 Complete the sentences with the appropriate forms of *seem, appear* or *look*.

a The president ...*appeared*... to be happy with the arrangement, Mr. Ambassador.
b She .... to have had her hair dyed blond.
c She .... fantastic!
d Your reaction .... to be kind of exaggerated, don't you think?
e They .... as if they are enjoying themselves.
f Ladies and gentlemen, the patient .... to be sleeping, but actually she is fully conscious.
g I should be careful. He .... as if he's pretty angry.
h What .... to be the problem?
i I .... to have made a mistake. I apologize, sir.

28 Adjective order Read the following phrases and complete the task which follows.

a a large knitted square Mexican blanket
b a big new seat
c a big-hearted curly-haired Spanish hunting dog
d a black German car
e a rectangular pink tablecloth
f big appealing bright-blue eyes
g gorgeous blond hair

Copy the diagram and complete it by putting the following adjective types in the correct order, based on the phrases *a–g*.

- color or origin
- opinion / judgment or size
- origin or material
- material or purpose
- shape / description or color
- size or shape / description

	+		+		+		+		+		+	noun

Are you right? Check you have understood with **9B–9C** in the Mini-grammar.

29 In pairs Ask your partner to list ten things he or she has in his / her room. Ask for descriptions and write the adjectives your hear. Give the adjectives and the nouns to another pair. Can they put them in the right order?

Example: STUDENT A: *Describe your guitar.*

STUDENT B: *It's an old Spanish guitar. My uncle gave it to me when he stopped playing.*

guitar
Spanish
old

Functional language: taking ourselves to be fixed

30 Listen to Track 46 and choose the correct picture.

Now listen to Track 47. Were you correct?

31 Listen to Track 47 again and answer the following questions.

  a When was Mr. Anderson last here?
  b What is he offered, and what does he get?
  c What does he think of his appearance?
  d What does he want to happen to his appearance?

32 Look at how we can keep appointments to "have ourselves fixed."

KEEPING AN APPOINTMENT TO HAVE OURSELVES FIXED

  a We can say why we have come like this:
  I have an appointment with Doctor Smith at 10 o'clock.

  b The receptionist or professional might tell us what to do like this:
  Would you like to ⎫ ⎧ *take a seat?*
  If you'll just ⎬ ⎨ *go through?*
  If you'd like to ⎭ ⎩ *come into my office?*

  c The professional can ask us what we want like this:
  How can I help you?
  What can I do for you?
  What brings you here?
  Why have you come to see me?

  d We can explain what we want like this:
  I'd like a haircut, please.
  I was thinking of having my nose straightened.
  I was wondering if you could ⎰ *do anything about ...*
  ⎱ *give me advice about ...*
  I have a toothache.

  e The professional can make suggestions like this:
  I recommend having some off the top and keeping the hair just above the ears.
  I would suggest that you take a few days off work.
  I think you'd better take some aspirin.
  I'm going to give you a prescription for some ...
  I think we could do something about your nose, yes.

Make new sentences by replacing the blue words with words of your own.

Example: I would suggest bangs, ma'am.
　　　　 I was thinking of having my hair really short.

33 Choose one of the following places.

  a the beauty salon or the barber's
  b the dentist's
  c the doctor's

Think of why you are going there. You can look at Activity Bank 13 on page 161 for words that you might want to use.

34 **Role-play** Students who have chosen the same place in Activity 33 go to their appointment at the hairdresser's, dentist's, or doctor's and wait their turn. Other students are receptionists, hairdressers, dentists, or doctors.

Writing: résumé

35 Look quickly at the following document. What is it for?

RÉSUMÉ

Name:	Neil Todd
Date of birth:	10/30/83
Address:	26 Kingston Drive
	Evanston, IL 26125

Schools / Colleges attended:

2001 – 2003	Parkridge Junior College
1997 – 2001	Oak Park High School
1995 – 1997	Oak Park Junior High School
1988 – 1995	Oak Park Elementary School

Employment record (including vacation jobs):

2002 November – present:
> part-time work at GAP clothing store

2002 March – September:
> Saturday work at Wal Mart

2001 July and August:
> part-time work at McDonald's

Hobbies and interests:
> I like listening to music and going out to clubs.
> I play the guitar. I enjoy basketball and played
> on the team at Oak Park.

Anything else you wish to say to support your application:
> My experience at the GAP means I know a lot about
> stores, so I would be just right for the job at the
> Speedo Sports Store.
>
> I am trying to get a job for six months so that I can
> then travel around Europe for a while.

References:

Mary Fischer	Paul Pritchard
Manager	Principal
GAP	Partridge Junior College
23 Main Street	34 Park Street
Evanston, IL 26124	Evanston, IL 26125

36 **In pairs** Compare people's résumés.

STUDENT B: look at the résumés for Bill Thomas in Activity Bank 14 on page 162.

STUDENT A: find out as many similarities as you can between Neil Todd and Student B's Bill Thomas.

Example: When was Bill Thomas born? (one similarity)

37 Answer the following questions.

a What jobs are Neil and Bill applying for?

b What are the main headings that people put on their résumés? Which one does Bill include which Neil leaves out? Why?

c What order do the dates go in?

d How important is it to put down some hobbies / interests, do you think?

38 Using the same headings as Neil and Bill's résumés, write:

- ... your own résumé.
OR
- ... the résumé of a fictional person you have dreamed up.

Make sure you include:

- ... at least two jobs (even if they were / are only temporary or part-time).
- ... something about your interests.

Speaking: the interview

39 a Which of the following topics are appropriate for a job interview?

1 why the applicant wants the job
2 whether the applicant has a girlfriend / boyfriend or is married
3 how the applicant got on in their last job
4 what the applicant's favorite color is
5 what the applicant does in their spare time
6 why the applicant thinks that he or she is right for this job
7 what time the applicant has dinner

b How would you ask the questions you have selected as appropriate?

Are there any other questions you would like to ask?

40 In groups Choose one of the following advertisements.

Train big cats in Las Vegas!

Appear in world-famous circus performances!

Big cats are lions, tigers, cheetahs, etc.

(No experience necessary: We supply on-the-job experience-based training.)

• Fabulous pay
• Fabulous conditions
• An exciting star-studded life

The successful candidate will be:

• energetic
• decisive
• ready for anything
• fit and healthy
• good-humored
• ambitious

Don't wait! Apply now

Have you ever wanted to write for a popular magazine?

Well now's your chance!

We are looking for someone to write a weekly column in our magazine on any topic they want.

• Excellent pay
• You become well known
• You have influence and people everywhere read your opinions. It's a fantastic opportunity

We provide:
• training
• editorial help
• entertainment allowance (you get a sum of money to spend on going out)

You provide:
• ideas
• imagination
• opinion
• enthusiasm

Volunteers wanted for new TV show

Supreme Challenge ™ will take 15 ordinary members of the public and put them in difficult physical circumstances (on mountains, in the jungle, at sea, etc.).

The winner gets $5m!!!

We are looking for volunteers who are:

brave • cheerful • fit • sociable • good in a crowd • competitive

a Give yourself a new name and a fictional résumé which would be appropriate for the job. Write down the main points.

b Think of the qualities and experiences that would make the interviewers like you.

c Think of the questions the interviewers are going to ask you and make a note of some good answers.

41 In groups Two or more students are interviewers. Two or more students are the applicants.

APPLICANTS: give the interviewers your name.
INTERVIEWERS: welcome the applicants and make them feel comfortable.

Role-play the interviews. Everyone votes on who should get the job (you cannot vote for yourself).

Example:

INTERVIEWER: Good morning, Miss Clarkson, do please take a seat.

APPLICANT: Thank you.

INTERVIEWER: I hope you didn't have any trouble finding us.

APPLICANT: No, it was easy, thank you ...

Review: grammar and functional language

42 Describe the following pictures using as many adjectives as you can in your sentence without making the sentence ridiculous. Pay attention to the order of the adjectives. Look at Activities 22–25 and 28 for help.

Example: a

This is an old, brown, Spanish ...

Made in Thailand

What Sweden does best!

43 How many questions? Describe an object using some adjectives, but don't say what it is, and don't use adjectives that are too obvious. The other students ask questions. You can answer only "yes" or "no." How many questions do they need to find the answer?

Example: STUDENT A: It's an expensive silver-colored flat Japanese thing.

STUDENT B: Is it a personal organizer?

STUDENT A: No, it isn't.

STUDENT C: Is it a minidisk player?

STUDENT A: No, it isn't that.

STUDENT D: Is it a computer?

STUDENT A: Yes, but ...

STUDENT B: Is it a laptop computer?

STUDENT A: Yes.

44 Complete this conversation with appropriate words (one for each space). Look at Activity 32 for help.

RECEPTIONIST: Good afternoon, sir, how can I (**a**) ....*help*.... you?

FARNABY: I'd like to (**b**) .... the doctor.

RECEPTIONIST: Do you have an (**c**) .... ?

FARNABY: Well no, but I just thought ...

RECEPTIONIST: Well you're in (**d**) .... I think we can fit you in.

FARNABY: Oh good. Thank you.

RECEPTIONIST: Can I take your (**e**) .... ?

FARNABY: Certainly. It's Farnaby, Giles Farnaby.

RECEPTIONIST: All right, Mr. Farnaby, if you'd just (**f**) .... to take a seat. Oh no, wait a minute, that won't be necessary. You can go (**g**) .... right now.

FARNABY: Thank you.

DOCTOR: Come in, Mr. Farnaby. Now (**h**) .... can I help you?

FARNABY: I just (**i**) .... to get something off my chest.

DOCTOR: Your chest?

FARNABY: Yes, (**j**) .... see, because ...

DOCTOR: If you'd just (**k**) .... to take off your shirt.

FARNABY: (**l**) .... ?

DOCTOR: Your shirt. Take off your shirt and (**m**) .... up on the bed. Then I can (**n**) .... you.

FARNABY: But I don't (**o**) .... to be examined.

DOCTOR: Why not? Your chest. You said (**p**) .... about your chest.

FARNABY: I said I wanted to get something off my (**q**) .... , you know ... tell you about something that's worrying me. Like getting the weight of this secret off my chest. You are a psychiatrist, (**r**) .... you?

DOCTOR: Oh I (**s**) ....

FARNABY: What?

DOCTOR: You want my brother, Angus McGloughlin. Crazy as anything. He's (**t**) .... door. I'm sorry the receptionist didn't tell you.

Review: vocabulary

appealing	pointed
applicant	pretty
appointed	protruding
attractive	pudgy
bald spot	puny
beautiful	receding
bright	résumé
chubby	salary
crew cut	scruffy
curly	shiny
cute	skinny
dark	slender
deep-set	slight
elegant	slim
emaciated	small
extensions	smart
fine	snub
flabby	soft
generous	square
good-looking	stout
gorgeous	straight
handsome	strong
hideous	thick
highlights	thinning
kind	to reject
large	turned up
lean	ugly
long	underweight
mean	untidy
muscular	voluptuous
obese	wavy
overweight	weak
PA	well built
perm	well dressed
plain	wide
plump	

equally qualified
to damage your career prospects
to get a little help from
to make a studious attempt
to play a major part
to seem hardly credible
under close questioning

45 If you could only keep five words from the Word List, what would they be? Why? If you had to throw away five words from the Word List, which would they be? Why?

Example: I'd like to keep "beautiful" because I like beautiful things.

⬤ ⬤ ⬤ Pronunciation

46 Copy and complete the table with as many individual words as you can from the Word List and Word Plus. (Note: one of the sounds does not appear in the lists.)

/ʃ/ – ship	/ʒ/ – pleasure	/tʃ/ – church	/dʒ/ – judge

Check your answers by listening to Track 48. Can you add more words to your table?

47 Which word doesn't belong in its group?

a attractive extensions protruding underweight voluptuous

b appealing deep-set lean receding square

c bright shiny slight thick untidy

Check your answers by listening to Track 49.

48 Casting directors In pairs, think of a story you both know well—a movie you have seen recently, for example, or your favorite TV show, or your favorite book. Imagine that you have been given money to make a new version of the story.

- Make a list of the main characters in the story.
- For each character, say what they should look like and what kind of character they should have.

Show your lists to other pairs. Has any one chosen the same story as you?

UNIT 10
Heavy weather

Reading: *The Storm*

H.W   Read

1 Predicting The words in the box come from the text you are about to read. What do you think the text is going to be about (look at the title of this section too)?

> boxes of pasta   candlelight
> carpet   editors
> espresso machine   floating
> flower beds   frogs   reel of film
> roads   shadows   water

Read the text on pages 101–102. Were you right?

2 Read the text again and put the following events in the correct order. Number 1 is done for you.

a Eleanor went downstairs. **12**
b Eleanor's sons and another man played cards. **9**
c Francis thought pasta was the answer. **6**
d Francis arrived home. **5**
e Francis pushed the car. **4**
f Francis put some music on. **8**
g It stopped raining. **10**
h Larry and Dean collected boxes of pasta. **3**
i People from the office came back to the house because they hadn't been able to get home. **2**
j Sofia caught some frogs. **7**
k The music started again. **11**
l Water began to get into the house. **1**

Note: *Cannes* is a place in France where they hold an annual film festival. *La Bohème* is an opera.

Eleanor Coppola is the wife of the film director Francis Ford Coppola, and mother of Sofia Coppola who is also a movie director. Many years ago, Eleanor went with Francis and their children Sofia, Roman and Giancarlo (Gio) to the Philippines where Francis was making one of his most famous films, *Apocalypse Now*. Eleanor wrote a diary of those days called *Notes*. The following extract describes an evening at the house they were renting.

The Storm

The storm got more exciting. Water started coming in the rooms downstairs. In some places the carpet looked like it was floating because there was a layer of water between it and the floor. The kids thought it looked like a water bed and were jumping on it. Pretty soon, the water was about six inches deep and it started out the bedroom door into the other rooms. Several people arrived from the office because the roads were so flooded they couldn't get home. It had taken them two hours just to get to our house. We were all in the kitchen opening bottles of Italian wine when someone realized that the boxes of pasta were sitting downstairs in the water. Larry and Dean took off their shoes and waded across the room, and started carrying the cartons upstairs. Francis finally arrived. He had been stuck at some flooded intersection for the past hour and a half. He had gotten out to push the car and was completely soaked. The editors had been at the house all day, preparing a reel of film for a screening at Cannes. They decided it was hopeless to try to make it home. So we began counting how many there were for dinner. There were 14, and the little half-eaten roast left over from lunch was about enough for four. Francis decided to make pasta.

Sofia put on her raincoat and was running around in the backyard. One section was under water and the frogs that usually hop around on the lawn there were all swimming. Sofia was chasing them and actually catching one now and then. The dirt from the flower beds was streaming into the swimming pool. Francis turned on *La Bohème* full volume. Marc, Roman, and Gio were playing a noisy game of poker. The thunder and rain were so loud we were all shouting at each other. Finally, we did have a terrific dinner. ▶▶

As we got to the dessert the electricity went off. We had bananas flambé by candlelight. After dinner, Francis and I were sitting on the couch looking toward the table. There were three candles and a group of people at each end of the long oval table. Francis was talking about how fabulous our eyes are that they can compensate for the low level of light and see perfectly clearly. You could never shoot in that amount of light. It was really beautiful. Francis was marveling at how the people at the table were so perfectly staged. Now and then, someone would get up and go to the kitchen, crossing behind or in front of the light. Each person was so perfectly placed, leaning a little forward or a little back, catching the light, making shadows on the wall behind and silhouettes in front. He said you could never get it as good if you staged it. After a while we went to bed. I guess the rain stopped for a bit and everybody decided to try to go home. They started out, they got to the main road and had to turn back.

The electricity came on at about four in the morning, and *La Bohème* started up, loud. The espresso machine began steaming, all the lights went on, and I went downstairs to shut things off. People were sleeping all over the place.

3 Did Eleanor enjoy the evening? How do you know?

Tell your partner about a meal with your family or friends that you have really enjoyed.

4 Vocabulary Match these definitions to the words in blue in the text on pages 101–102.

a a loud noise in the sky   thunder
b a piece of meat that has been cooked in an oven
c a place where roads cross each other
d arranged as if in a theater performance
e covered with water
f flowing quickly and in large amounts
g very wet
h walked slowly through water
i wonderful

5 Fact check Why:

a ... were the kids jumping on the carpet?
b ... did people arrive from the office?
c ... did Larry and Dean take off their shoes?
d ... was Francis very wet?
e ... did they cook pasta?
f ... was the swimming pool dirty?
g ... was everyone shouting at each other?
h ... did they eat by candlelight?
i ... are eyes better than cameras?
j ... did Eleanor get up in the middle of the night?

Language in chunks

6 Find the following phrases in the text *The Storm*.

a two examples of *looked like*
b a phrase which means *to succeed in getting back home*
c to turn on something full volume
d a phrase which means *from time to time*
e an activity that took place by candlelight
f something that can compensate for something

7 Use the phrases in blue and the two phrases you've found in sentences of your own. You may need to adapt them.

8 Varieties of English What words or grammar tell you that the following sentences are written in American English rather than British English?

a It started out the bedroom door into the other rooms.
b Someone realized that the boxes of pasta were sitting downstairs.
c He had gotten out to push the car.
d Sofia ... was running around in the backyard.
e I guess the rain stopped for a bit.

9 Noticing grammar Read the text again and find verbs written in the past. How many different types of past tense can you find?

10 Speaking Without looking at the book, tell the story of Eleanor's evening in your own words.

Speaking: consensus-reaching and role-play

11 Dinner party First, select the guests.

a Individually, write down the names of two people, living or dead, real or fictional, who you would most like to invite for dinner.

b In groups of five, compare your lists and agree on a final list of five guests (five of the original suggestions will have to be eliminated).

12 Now, organize the dinner itself.

a Agree on a seating plan and decide what you will serve the guests.

b Copy and complete the table.

> **Good topics for discussion**
> the weather, ...

> **Topics we should try to avoid**
> the war, ...

13 Role-play Join together with another group and either role-play their guests or ask them to role-play your guests for part of your dinner party.

Grammar: narrative (past simple, pastperfect simple, past continuous, pastperfect continuous)

14 a Match the words and phrases in the box with the days of the week.

> arguing with her colleagues   attending a long meeting
> partying till late the night before   driving too fast
> visiting her parents   watching sports on TV
> working out in the gym

MONDAY
physically exhausted

TUESDAY
mentally exhausted

WEDNESDAY
upset

THURSDAY
well fed

FRIDAY
stopped by the police

SATURDAY
relaxed

SUNDAY
headache

MARTHA'S WEEK

b With a partner, make up questions and answers about Martha's week. Use **10B** and **10D** in the **Mini-grammar** to help you.

Example: STUDENT A: Why was Martha exhausted on Monday evening?

STUDENT B: Because she had been working out in the gym.

15 Choose the best alternative in blue in the following story.

As he (**a**) walked / had walked out of the building where he worked, Simon was exhausted. He (**b**) worked / was working / had worked / had been working since 7:00 in the morning and he (**c**) was only finishing / had only finished / had only been finishing a few minutes before. Before (**d**) he had gotten / had been getting / got into the car, he (**e**) called / was calling his wife on his cell phone and (**f**) asked / was asking her if he should get anything on the way home. She said she (**g**) went / was going / had gone to the supermarket that morning before she (**h**) drove / was driving to the TV studio to be interviewed about her new book. He asked her about the interview. She said that she (**i**) talked / was talking / had talked / had been talking about her book when a studio light fell from the ceiling and (**j**) nearly killed / was nearly killing / had nearly been killing her. "I (**k**) was / had been really frightened," she said, "but I (**l**) continued / was continuing with the interview and gradually I (**m**) felt / was feeling OK. Still, it's great to be home. And no, we don't need anything."

Twenty minutes later, Simon had his own lucky escape. He (**n**) drove / was driving / had been driving along the beltway when he (**o**) was noticing / noticed something strange about the truck in front of him. Two minutes later, a large wooden plank (**p**) fell off / was falling off / had fallen off the back of the truck. Luckily, however, Simon (**q**) braked / was braking / had braked a few minutes before when he (**r**) saw / was seeing / had seen / had been seeing a movement on the truck and so the plank (**s**) was just missing / had just missed / just missed him.

The next morning, Simon (**t**) woke up / was waking up suddenly. He (**u**) had / was having / had had / had been having a terrible nightmare. It was all about studio lights and wooden planks. He (**v**) looked / was looking / had looked / had been looking over at his wife. She (**w**) was / was being / had been still asleep. He realized how lucky he (**x**) was / had been.

Look at 10A–10D in the Mini-grammar. Do you want to change your answers?

16 Join the sentences together using all the verbs. Look at 10E in the Mini-grammar to help you.

a Mary woke up. Mary got out of bed. Mary looked out of the window. Mary saw the tiger.
   Mary woke up, got out of bed, looked out of the window, and saw the tiger.

b Sally was sitting at her desk. Sally was talking on the telephone. Sally was drawing pictures on her notepad.

c They had been there all day. They had been studying the pictures. They had been deciding what to do with them.

d He took the ball from a player on the opposing team. He ran past a defender. He shot the ball into the back of the net.

e She was writing a letter. She was listening to music. She was eating a cookie. She was drinking a cup of coffee.

f They had been at the dinner table for an hour. They had been laughing. They had been enjoying each other's company. They had been talking about their vacation.

17 Look at the following pictures. Say what is happening in each one.

18 In groups Complete the following tasks.

a Think of a story which links all of the pictures *a–d* from Activity 17. You may have to change the order of events. Use as many simple and continuous tenses as you can.

b Compare your story with the other groups. Have they interpreted the pictures in the same way?

Vocabulary: weather words

19 Language research Copy the table. Complete the *Least severe / Most severe* column with words and phrases from the box.

> blazing sun   blizzard   breeze   downpour   gale   heavy shower
> heavy snowfall   light breeze   light shower   light snowfall
> strong breeze   strong sunshine   strong wind   sunshine
> torrential rain

	Least severe <-------------> Most severe	Associated verbs
rain	*light shower, heavy shower, ...*	
snow		
sun		
wind		

Put the following verbs in the right-hand column of your table.

> blow   drizzle   fall   howl   pour
> roar   scorch   settle   shine   whistle

20 Choose the correct verb for each gap.

a A light snow ....*fell*..... in the night.
b The rain was .... down the neck of my raincoat.
c A strong wind was .... from the southwest.
d The hurricane was nearly upon us. The wind was .... in my ears and I could hear nothing.
e It was .... Light rain fell continuously from a very dark sky.
f The wind was ....through the holes in the roof.
g The sun was .... through the afternoon clouds.
h The snow began to .... on the ground after two hours of heavy snowfall.
i She could see the blazing sun .... the earth and small cracks began to open.
j The wind was ....like a wolf as the storm began.

21 Read the following description of weather in Tikan (Guatemala). What is *thunder*? What is *lightning*?

The weather is completely predictable. In the summer—that's from January to May or June—we have bright sunshine every day. The only thing that stops that is the occasional cyclone. Then in the winter we have a rainy season—that's sunny mornings and then torrential rain (even thunder and lightning) in the afternoon, from two until six or seven.

a How different is this weather from the weather where you live?
b What is your favorite kind of weather? What is your least favorite kind of weather?

22 a Metaphor How many words or phrases based on weather can you find in the text? What do they mean?

Mary had a very sunny disposition and she was extremely generous. She constantly showered all her friends with presents. But when she appeared in the crowded room dressed in the latest clothes she had designed, people started to giggle and soon gales of laughter were echoing around the room. Pretty soon she was blazing with anger. "You have no right to laugh at me!" she thundered, and she stormed out of the room.

At first, everyone there was thunderstruck—shocked and silent. But then someone started to clap, very slowly, and then they all joined in, faster and faster until the ballroom was full of thunderous applause—though exactly what they were applauding was not quite clear.

The incident caused a storm of protest in the fashion world, but Mary's designs were a huge success.

b What's the worst weather you've ever been in? Write two sentences about it using words from Activities 19–22a. Read your sentences to the class.

Listing: *Stormy Weather*

23 **Read the mini web biography and answer the questions which follow.**

Billie Holiday (called "Lady Day" by her admirer and colleague, saxophone player Lester Young) was one of the most famous jazz singers of the 20th century. Although she had a small voice—she could not sing either very high or very low—her "behind-the-beat" phrasing, where she hung back from singing strictly in time, has been copied by many singers ever since. But what makes her special is the emotional intensity of her singing. When we listen to her performance she really seems to be living the words that she is singing.

Billie Holiday was born in Baltimore, Maryland in 1915 and started singing in clubs in Harlem, New York, when she was only 16 years old. Her finest period was between 1935 and 1942 when she made many recordings, often with Lester Young playing saxophone, including her most famous song, *Strange Fruit*, about a black victim of a lynching. She toured with the best jazz orchestras of the time, including the famous Count Basie orchestra.

Billie Holiday died aged 44 in New York in 1959.

Who:

a ... called Billie Holiday "Lady Day"?
b ... didn't have a very big voice?
c ... copied Billie's singing style?
d ... started a career at a very young age?
e ... seems to live the words of the songs?
f ... often played saxophone in Billie's recordings?
g ... had his own orchestra?
h ... was the subject of the song *Strange Fruit*?

24 **Listen to Track 50. Answer the following questions.**

a What is Monica Marcello's job?
b What kind of jazz does she like?
c Why does she like jazz?
d What's special about Billie Holiday, in Monica's opinion?
e Who was Harold Arlen?
f What's the song about?

25 **In pairs** Discuss the song. **Did you enjoy it? Have you heard it before? Are you tempted to buy it?**

Tell the class about your discussions.

26 **Complete the song lyrics with one word for each space. Some lines are repeated.**

Don't know why there's no (**a**) .... up in the (**b**) ....
Stormy weather
Since my (**c**) .... and I ain't (**d**) .... ,
Keeps rainin' all the time.

Life is bare, (**e**) .... and mis'ry (**f**) ....
Stormy weather
Just can't get my poor self (**g**) .... ,
I'm (**h**) .... all the time, the time
So weary all the time.

When he went (**i**) .... the blues walked in and (**j**) .... me
If he stays (**k**) .... old rockin' chair will get me.

All I do is (**l**) .... the lord above will let me (**m**) .... in the (**n**) .... once more.

Can't go on, ev'ry thing I had is (**o**) ....
Stormy weather
Since my (**p**) .... and I ain't (**q**) .... ,
Keeps rainin' all the time
Keeps rainin' all the time.

Check your answers with the Audioscript for Track 50.

27 **Vocabulary** What do you understand by the words and expressions in blue from the radio program and the song lyrics?

a not everyone's taste
b as a kid
c It just sort of started then.
d She doesn't even have much of a range.
e the way she puts over a lyric
f It gets to me every time.
g the blues walked in and met me
h old rockin' chair will get me

28 Look at the extracts from the studio conversation and the lyrics for *Stormy Weather* and answer the questions which follow.

Any favorite kind of jazz?
Not everyone's taste.
Don't know why ...
Keeps rainin' all the time
Gloom and mis'ry all the time

Just can't get my poor self together
Old rockin' chair will get me
Can't go on
Ev'rything I had ...

   a Find examples where sentences have been shortened so that certain words such as pronouns and verbs have been omitted. Why does this happen in conversation and in song lyrics?
   b Find examples where an apostrophe (') is used. What are the reasons for the apostrophe?

29 Look quickly at the Audioscript for Tracks 1–50. What kind of shortening can you find?

30 In pairs Role-play a radio program in which the host asks you questions about the following.

- your life
- your favorite sports, hobbies, etc.
- your favorite songs and why you like them so much.

Functional language: conversational gambits

31 Complete the dialogue with one of the following phrases.

- I don't want to interrupt, but
- On another topic altogether,
- Wait a minute, I'd just like to say ...
- Yes, and what's more ...
- Yes, and one shouldn't forget

MARION: I really worry about global warming, you know. We're having a lot more storms these days.
KURT: Yes ...
KARL: **(a)** .... you can't rely on the weather at all these days.
KURT: But ...
MARION: **(b)** .... that this has all happened only in the last 60 or 70 years.
KURT: But I think ...
MARION: **(c)** ...., have you seen the latest opinion poll?
KURT: **(d)** ....
WAITER: Excuse me, **(e)** .... do any of you own a Volkswagen Passat?
MARION: Yes, why?
KURT: But!.....

Now listen to Track 51 to check your answers.

32 Copy and complete the table with the following phrases.

(Yes, and) on top of that ①
(Yes, and) what's more ④
(Yes, but) looking at it from another angle / viewpoint ②
And as if that wasn't enough ①
And that's not all ①
By the way, speaking of ... ④
Could I just ask a question / say something? ①
Excuse me ④
Furthermore
Hey hold on / hang on a minute ④
I don't want to interrupt, but ③
If I could just get a word in edgewise ③
If I might just make a point / come in here ②
In addition ①
Incidentally, on the subject of ... ③
Moreover
Moving swiftly on
On another matter / topic altogether
One shouldn't forget
Wait a minute
We should remember
Yes, but on the other hand
Yes, but there again

①	Reinforcing what's being said	
②	Balancing what's being said	
③	Changing the subject	
④	Interrupting	

Which of the phrases are likely to be (a) more formal, (b) neutral, or (c) less formal?

33 **In groups** Write "reinforcement", "balancing", "changing the subject," or "interrupting" on many separate pieces of paper. Put the pieces of paper in a pile, face down, in the middle of the group. Individually, write sentences giving your opinion on some or all of the following topics.

- the weather
- restaurants
- keeping a diary
- people with blond hair
- the kind of food we eat
- the paranormal (fortune-telling, etc.)
- a topic of your choice

A student in the group says their sentence. Another student picks up one of the pieces of paper and reinforces, balances, etc., depending on what's written there.

Example: STUDENT A: *I think the weather's getting worse.*

STUDENT B: *picks up a piece of paper with "reinforcement" on it*

Yes, I agree, and it's making planning very difficult.

●● Pronunciation: intonation

34 Listen to the conversations *a–h* on Track 52. Is the man going to do what the woman asks or not? How do you know?

Example: a *Yes.*

He sounds ...

35 Reply to the people on Track 52 using the same intonation and tone of voice as the man did in activity 34. Then you'll hear if you were right.

a Well ...
b I'd rather not ...
c That depends on what it is.
d Why should I?
e I'd rather not.
f Well, I would really ...
g Why should I?
h I'd rather not.

Now listen to Track 53. Did the speakers reply in the same way as you?

Writing: diaries

36 Discuss the following questions with a partner.

a What different reasons are there for people to write diaries?
b What do people put in their diaries?
c Have you ever written a diary?
d Whose diary (anyone living or dead) would you most like to read?

37 Read these diary entries. Which of the following (*a–d*) describes them best, do you think (answer at the bottom of page 109)?

The diary entries are written by:
a ... a bicycle thief who lives in Oxford.
b ... a fictional character (who wants to be a writer), and the diary entries are meant to be funny.
c ... a Polish tourist, who is on vacation and goes sightseeing.
d ... a male model with a fear of dogs, who wants to find work in Oxford.

Monday April 15th
I was ten minutes late for work this morning. The exhaust pipe fell off the bus. Mr. Brown was entirely unsympathetic. He said, "You should get yourself a bicycle, Mole." I pointed out that I have had three bicycles stolen in 18 months. I can no longer afford to supply the criminals of Oxford with ecologically sound transport. Brown snapped, "Then *walk*, Mole. Get up earlier and *walk*."

Friday May 24th
A house on my way to work has acquired an American pit bull terrier. On the surface, it seems to be a friendly dog. All it does is stand and grin through the fence. But in future I will take a different route to work. I cannot risk facial disfigurement. I would like the photograph on the back of my book to show my face as it is today, not terribly scarred. I know plastic surgeons can work miracles, but from now on I am taking no chances.

Saturday May 25th
Oxford is full of sightseers riding on the top deck of the tourist buses and walking along the streets looking upward. It is extremely annoying to us residents to be asked the way by foreigners every five minutes. Perhaps it is petty of me, but I quite enjoy sending them in the wrong direction.

38 Choose one of the dates and answer the questions about it.

Monday April 15th

a Who is Mr. Brown?

b What is the diary writer's last name?

c Why doesn't the writer use a bicycle?

d Is the writer's comment about Oxford criminals serious, sarcastic, or funny?

Friday May 24th

a Why has the diary writer changed his route from his house to his work?

b What is the animal like?

c What does the writer fear?

d What is the connection between the following: disfigurement, scar, plastic surgery?

Saturday May 25th

a Where does the diary writer live?

b What do the tourists do?

c What does the writer enjoy doing?

d Do you sympathize with his criticisms of foreigners?

39 Diary writing Complete one of the following tasks.

a List four things you did yesterday and write them as a diary entry.

b Write a diary entry for yesterday in which you put four things that you would really like to have happened, but which did not actually happen.

c Choose a famous character (living or dead). Write a diary entry which they might have written.

The diary entries are from Adrian Mole: the Wilderness Years *by Sue Townsend, the humorous diary of a fictional character who always has bad luck and has peculiar opinions about everything (and who dreams of being a famous writer).*

Review: grammar and functional language

40 Read the English teacher's story and underline all the past tense verbs. How many different kinds are there? Can you find examples of sentences and clauses with one subject but more than one verb? You can look at Activities 14–18 for help.

A student once told me this story. He said he was walking along a street in Moscow thinking about nothing in particular and smoking a cigarette. It was the middle of winter. There was snow underfoot and on the rooftops above him there were huge blocks of ice. That's what he said anyway, and I had no reason to disbelieve him.

Anyway, this student's problem was that he was a heavy smoker. He had tried to give up many times and each time, he said, giving up had not been hard, but it had been impossible to prevent himself from starting again. So right there, on the sidewalk of a Moscow street with tall buildings all around him, he finished his cigarette and that would have been that, except that he instantly thought that he would like to have another one. So he took off his gloves, reached into his jacket pocket, got a pack of Marlboros and pulled out a cigarette. Next, as you would expect, he reached for the lighter he had bought himself the day before and then, right there in the street, in the cold, he stopped to light his cigarette, and another man who had been walking just behind him passed him as he went on along the sidewalk.

At that moment, a large block of ice detached itself from a roof above them and came crashing down into the street. It hit the man who had just passed my student, killing him instantly. If my student hadn't stopped to light a cigarette ... "Which just goes to show," he said to the other students in my class as he told his story, "that smoking is good for you." He swore that it was a true story and that he hadn't made it up.

Cover the story with your hand and re-tell it from memory.

41 In pairs Student A chooses one of the situations *a–f* and asks for help.

Student B answers and uses stress and intonation to mean the opposite of what is said. Look at Activities 34–35 for help.

Example: a

STUDENT A: *Could you help me to move a table in the yard?*

STUDENT B *(sounding doubtful)*: *Sure.*

You would like someone to:

a ... help you to move a table in the yard.

b ... help you push your car which has just broken down.

c ... talk to someone you know to find out what they really think of you.

d ... give you some advice about how to succeed in your work or your studies.

e ... mail a letter for you when they go to the store.

f ... take a package for a friend or family member in their suitcase on their flight to the place where your friend or family member lives.

Review: vocabulary

Word List

blazing sun	sunshine
blizzard	thunder
breeze	thunderstruck
downpour	to blow
equivalent	to drizzle
fabulous	to fall
flooded	to howl
gale	to pour
heavy shower	to roar
heavy snowfall	to roast
intersection	to scorch
light breeze	to settle
light shower	to shine
light snowfall	to stream (into)
soaked	to thunder
staged	to whistle
strong breeze	torrential rain
strong sunshine	waded
strong wind	

Word Plus

a storm of protest
a sunny disposition
by candlelight
gales of laughter
it crossed (my) mind
now and then
thunderous applause
to blaze with anger
to compensate for something
to know for sure
to look like
to make it home
to shower people with
   presents / gifts
to storm out of
to turn something on full
   volume

42 Choose your favorite kind of weather from the Word List. Why do you like that weather? What do you do in weather like that? Choose your least favorite kind of weather. Why don't you like that weather? What do you do in weather like that?

What is your favorite phrase from Word Plus? Tell the other students about your words and phrases.

●●● Pronunciation

43 Put words from the Word List in groups depending on the vowel sound of their stressed syllable. Each word in a group must share the same sound. Do not include *fabulous* or *strong*.

Example: The words "blizzard", "drizzle", "equivalent", "wind", and "whistle" all include the vowel sound /ɪ/ as part of their stressed syllable.

Listen to the speakers on Track 54. Have you made the same groups?

44 Find words in the Word List and Word Plus which have the following sound clusters.

a	b	c	d	e
/bl/	/br/	/dr/	/z/	/fl/
blazing, ...				
f	**g**	**h**	**i**	
/kr/	/kʃ/	/str/	/pr/	

Check your answers by listening to Track 55. Which do you find difficult to pronounce?

45 **In groups** Using phrases from the two lists, tell a story about being in a particular weather situation. Don't say what the weather was like when you tell your story. The other students have to guess.

Example: STUDENT A: Well, he had quite a sunny disposition, but that night, when we were watching television, the lights went out and we ended up having to rely on candlelight. He blazed with anger for some reason.

STUDENT B: It was a storm?

STUDENT A: Yes.

STUDENT C: With thunder and lightning? ...

UNIT 11

Famous for 15 minutes?

→ phrasal verbs
→ fame and notoriety
→ checking and confirming

Reading: reality TV

1 Complete these descriptions of TV shows with a word or phrase from the box.

> eliminated   deal with   reveal   criticized   humiliated   betraying

8 pm American Idol
See ten young singers sing and be
(**a**) … and encouraged by a group of
professional judges. Then we get to
vote and one person will be (**b**) …
from the show. Who will be the last
singer left?

9 pm Survivor
First episode of a new series. Sixteen
people are put on a remote island and
have to (**c**) … the difficulties of living
on an island. One by one, they vote
each other off the island, often (**d**) …
their friends, until one person is left.
The one person left wins one million
dollars.

11 pm Blind Date
Anything can happen on Blind Date.
Watch two strangers go on a date with
each other. Who will (**e**) … a lot of
personal details about themselves?
Who will be (**f**) …?

2 **In groups** If you were planning a reality TV show like the ones above,

    a … what area of life would you choose (e.g. the army, school teaching,
       nursing, hairdressing)?
    b … what would the "contestants" have to do?
    c … how would you choose the winner?

3 Read the text on page 112 quickly. Copy and complete the table with the four types
of reality TV show mentioned. Give one example of each one.

	a	b	c	d
Type of show	shows that go into someone's home			
Example				

Look at the TV shows in Activity 1. Which type are they all? Write them in your table too.

Why on Earth Do They Do It?

In 1968 Andy Warhol said, "In the future, everybody will be world-famous for 15 minutes." He was referring to the commercialization of all aspects of our lives. With the growth of reality TV, his prediction seems to be coming true.

Reality TV shows are becoming more and more popular in Britain, the U.S.A. and other parts of the world. You may not understand why, but the ratings for these shows are high and they are relatively cheap to produce since the makers of the shows don't have to pay actors—they often star ordinary people eager for fame and who will jump at any chance to achieve it. We'll tell you why later, but first, let's look at the different types of show that come under the heading of "reality TV."

Firstly, there are shows that go into someone's home and life and follow them around—*The Osbournes* is a typical example. The people on these shows are often famous and unusual in some way. This isn't always the case, of course, and sometimes the cameras may follow an ordinary doctor around or look at an everyday family as they deal with their problems. We get to look at other people's lives and compare them with our own.

Next, there are reality shows manufactured for TV, where the producers of the show put people into some kind of unusual situation and see how they react. In *Joe Millionaire*, 20 women were flown to a castle in France where they had the chance to meet Evan Marriott, who they were told was a multimillionaire. In fact, Evan was a construction worker. In *The Real World*, seven young strangers are put together in a house for four months and cameras follow them around; the audience gets to observe how they get along with each other as they gradually open up about who they are. By now, we're all familiar with shows like this.

Then, what about those reality shows about real life where the people who come on seem to have no limits about revealing all—about their private lives and anyone else's! *The Jerry Springer Show* is famous for its controversial subject matter and guests on the show often get into physical fights with each other. Then, there are real-life courtroom TV shows such as *Judge Judy* where people dispute a legal claim before millions of viewers. It seems that people on these shows will give very intimate details away and have no qualms about betraying their friends and family. Where do they find these people?

Last but not least, my own personal favorite, dating shows like *Elimidate* or *Blind Date*. On *Elimidate*, one person (either male or female) goes out on a date with four people of the opposite sex and one by one eliminates them until they finally choose the one person they would like to go on a "real" date with. People criticize and humiliate each other (and themselves in the process) to "win the competition."

So, can someone tell me why these shows are so popular? Why do we love to see people doing desperate things for their "15 minutes of fame"? Is it that we see ourselves in these ordinary people? Or is it the opposite? Do we like to be reassured that we are normal and it's everyone else that's crazy? And anyway, do the people on these shows really act like this when the cameras are not following them around?

Well, maybe they're not crazy, nor are they even trying to act naturally. Do you remember the days when people appeared on TV because they were famous? Well, times have changed and now appearing on TV is a good way to *become* famous. Many people are using their appearances on a reality TV show as a step into show business, hoping that their careers will take off once they have been seen by millions of people. Think about it— do you know any "celebrities" who started their career on a reality TV show? People who appear on reality TV are hoping for a bit more than the 15 minutes promised by Andy Warhol!

See you next week.

4 Fact check Read Julie Marsfield's article again. *True* or *False*?

a Andy Warhol's quotation is about reality TV.
b Huge numbers of people watch reality TV.
c Reality TV shows are usually expensive to make.
d Ordinary people often want to be on reality TV.
e Producers sometimes lie to people who go on the shows.
f People never talk about their personal lives.
g People on dating shows are always nice to each other.
h Most people probably act "unnaturally" on reality shows.
i After appearing on a reality TV show, some people become famous.

5 Explain the meaning of the following words as they appear in the text.

a commercialization (paragraph 1)
b ratings (paragraph 2)
c star (paragraph 2)
d eager (paragraph 2)
e manufactured (paragraph 4)
f controversial (paragraph 5)
g desperate (paragraph 7)
h appearances (paragraph 8)

Language in chunks

6 Look at how these phrases are used in the text and then use them in the sentences which follow. You may have to change them a little to make them fit.

with the growth of   jump at the chance   to reveal all   no limits as to
no qualms about   one by one   to be reassured

a I don't want .... My private life should be private.
b He .... of being on the show. At last he was going to be famous.
c She has .... going by herself. She loves traveling alone.
d Do you have .... what you will do for money? How could you take that job?
e Jake's parents were worried about leaving him, but they .... by the fact that Lois was an experienced babysitter.
f .... the sales of DVD players, there are fewer VCRs being sold.
g They went into the room .... and sat down at their desks.

Use the phrases in sentences of your own.

7 Noticing language Find the following verbs in the text.

get along with   give away   look at   take off

What do the verbs mean? Can you find other multi-word verbs in the text?

How are multi-word, or "phrasal" verbs, different from other verbs in the text?

8 Discussion Copy and complete the table about yourself.

	Agree	Disagree
I would never appear on a reality TV show.		
I would like to be famous.		
People should not become famous just because they have been on TV; they should have done something important first.		
If you want to be famous, you should be prepared to sacrifice your privacy.		

Check your answers with a partner and ask them at least two questions about each one of their answers.

Example: STUDENT A: I would never appear on a reality TV show.
STUDENT B: Why not?
STUDENT A: I'm a private person and I don't want everyone to know my business and ...

Tell the class what your partner said.

Vocabulary: fame and notoriety

9 Related words Look at the words associated with fame.

celebrity	eminence	fame	infamy	legend
notoriety	renown	star	stardom	superstar

Which of them can you make into (a) adjectives and (b) verbs? What changes (if anything) in each case?

10 Complete the following sentences with words (nouns or adjectives) from either Activity 9 or the box below.

well known	eye	name	VIP	headlines

a Shortly after winning American Idol, she *achieved* .... by spending all her winnings at expensive stores all over New York.

b You don't have to do anything much to be a .... You just have to be seen in the right places at the right time.

c Everyone knows this actress. She's a *household* ....

d *At the height of his* .... , he was known by almost everyone in the world.

e The problem about being famous is that you are always *in the public* ....

f He's having a fantastic career right now. You see him everywhere and *his* .... *is on everybody's lips.*

g As a result of her arrest, her name really *hit the* ....

h She made her .... as a gossip columnist on a national newspaper.

i To be a real .... , you have to be a movie star, famous fashion designer, or world leader. Or something else. But anyone can be quite .... in their own country just by being on television.

j To be *world-* .... , you need to be on every TV station on the planet!

11 Connotation Look at these sentences. Which of the words and expressions are <u>neutral</u> ways to talk about fame and which imply being famous in a <u>negative</u> way?

a He became *world-famous* after a number one hit single in 2003.

b They *achieved notoriety* for robbing five banks in a year.

c Stephen Hawking is an *eminent* scientist, known for his work on black holes.

d She's a *celebrated* author, who has had several bestsellers.

e Tonight the *renowned* journalist, Greg Pallast, will be appearing and presenting his new book.

f The *legendary* guitarist, Jimi Hendrix, died at a very young age. His music is still played widely.

g Tonight we welcome a pianist *of great renown*, Judy Marston.

h The *well-known* actress has appeared in three movies this year.

i She is known as an *infamous* liar and cheater in the world of sports.

j He rose to a position of *eminence* among followers of that faith.

k The singer *rose to stardom* in the 1980s, selling millions of records that were played everywhere.

12 How many people do you know about in the following categories?

a ... a classical musician?   c ... an athlete?

b ... a pop star?   d ... an army general?

Describe the people you have chosen using words from Activities 9–11.

13 Look at these pictures of people who are or were famous in the 20th and 21st centuries.

- Which ones do you know about?
- Why are they or why were they famous?
- What is your opinion of them?

a "If people don't get ... , it's a nice feeling."   *Bono, U2*

b "Heartthrobs are ... ." *Brad Pitt*

c "It has its ... and it has its ... ."

Marilyn Monroe

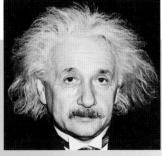

d "The world needs … and it's better they be harmless men like me than … like Hitler."
Albert Einstein

e "I cannot drink, smoke, or go to the karaoke. I must present a good … ." *Jackie Chan*

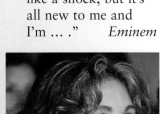

f "I'm always trying to escape from the … of expectation."
Shakira

g "It doesn't exactly feel like a shock, but it's all new to me and I'm … ." *Eminem*

i "I don't think I realized that the cost of fame is that it's … on every moment of your life."
Julia Roberts

h "I won't let all the money and glory … ."
Ronaldo

14 Complete what the characters in Activity 13 once said about fame, using one of the following words or expressions for each gap.

> a dime a dozen   compensations   drawbacks
> go to my head   heroes   image   in your face
> open season   pressure   taking it as it comes
> villains

Grammar: phrasal verbs

15 Phrasal verbs – Types 1 and 2 Match the verbs in italics in sentences *a–h* with their meaning below (*1–8*).

a The plane *took off* from Paris at half past three.
b A beautiful old building was *pulled down* to make room for the new freeway.
c He was *turned down* for the job of manager, but at least they gave him a raise.
d For two days the water heater was not working properly, and then it *blew up*.
e My plans didn't *work out*, so I've decided to leave the city and live in the country.
f I believed in you, but you *let me down*.
g She *put off* solving the problem until later.
h The couple had a lot of problems so they decided to *break up*.

1 demolish
2 disappoint
3 explode
4 leave the ground
5 postpone
6 refuse
7 separate
8 succeed

Read **11A–11C in the Mini-grammar** and say whether the verbs in italics are Type 1 or Type 2.

16 Read the story and match the phrasal verbs (in blue in the text) to the meanings *1–8* at the top of page 116.

This is a story told by Edward de Bono, the famous professor.

A movie producer owes his old business partner a lot of money over a movie project that failed. One day, the man comes by to collect his money. He has worked out a plan to get his money and he also wants to ruin the producer. He tells the producer that he will place a white stone and a black stone in a bag. The producer agrees that if his daughter chooses the white stone from the bag the debt will be canceled, but if she picks the black stone out, the man will get his house and land. The daughter sees that the man puts two black stones in the bag to trick the producer. The producer has brought his daughter up to be a fast thinker, so she does not speak up at this moment. Instead, she takes a stone from the bag and immediately drops it on the ground where there are many other stones—both black and white. The stone gets lost. She then points out that the stone that is left in the bag must be the opposite color of the one she chose. The man cannot admit that he was taking the producer in, so he has to agree to write off the debt.

a	come by	....	1	cancel
b	work out	....	2	devise, invent
c	pick out	....	3	explain, show
d	bring up	....	4	fool, deceive
e	speak up	....	5	raise, educate
f	point out	....	6	say something
g	take in	....	7	choose
h	write off	....	8	arrive

Are they Type 1 or Type 2 verbs?

Cover and practice telling the story from page 115 to your partner. Each time you use a phrasal verb, your partner writes down a synonym. Your partner now tells the story, replacing the synonyms with the original phrasal verbs.

17 Complete these sentences with one of the phrasal verbs from Activity 16 in the correct form.

a Sometimes my friend *comes by* to help me with my homework.
b I want you to help me .... a new textbook .... for my math class.
c Her parents .... her .... to be very independent.
d To get what you want, you have to .... You can't stay silent.
e She had no money. She needed to .... a way to make more money.
f The magician .... the little children .... They didn't realize it was a trick.
g The car was so badly damaged that they decided to .... it .... , claim the insurance, and get a new one.
h The teacher .... that there was a mistake in the book.

18 Phrasal verbs – Types 3 and 4 Copy and complete the table with words from the sentences below. Use 11D and 11E in the Mini-grammar to help you.

Type 3	
Type 4	

a If you want to be famous, you have to *put up with* losing your privacy.
b He was *looking for* his glasses and found them on the sofa.
c She had *fallen for* him the moment she saw him and they married within a year.
d Charlie Sheen and his brother Emilio Estevez *take after* their father, Martin Sheen. They are also actors.
e Stars often don't have time to *look after* their children themselves. They need someone to help them.
f Are you *looking forward to* the next Julia Roberts movie? I can't wait.

19 Match the verbs in italics in Activity 18 with their meanings.

a	put up with	1	search, try to find
b	look for	2	fall in love with
c	fall for	3	want something to happen soon
d	take after		
e	look after	4	tolerate
f	look forward to	5	resemble, look like
		6	care for

20 Read each conversation. Choose the correct form of one of the verbs in the box to fill the gaps.

check up on   come across   get along with
look down on   look into   pay back   run into

Jane and Don
JANE: You'll never guess who I (a) *ran into* this morning?
DON: Who?
JANE: Martha Westley, my old school friend. I (b) .... her so well when we were teenagers. Well, at the beginning anyway.
DON: And now?
JANE: I don't know. She really seemed to be (c) .... me, you know, disrespecting me.
DON: Why is she doing that?
JANE: I think she's (d) .... me .... because I stopped being her friend when we were about 14.

Harry and the detective
HARRY: I need someone to (e) .... my lawyer. I think he's stealing my mother's money.
DETECTIVE: I'll (f) .... it right away, sir. What makes you think he's stealing from her?
HARRY: I was helping my mother manage her accounts and I (g) .... some checks to him that my mother says she didn't sign.
DETECTIVE: OK, sir. I'll start right away.

21 Complete these sentences about yourself.

a At work / school, I'm not prepared to put up with ....
b I'm looking forward to ....
c In my family, people say I take after ....

Compare answers with a partner and explain what you've written.

22 Team game Using a dictionary, find as many phrasal verbs as you can. Write down their definitions.

a Team A reads the definitions to Team B.
b Team B gets one point if they say the correct phrasal verb and one point if they make a sentence using the phrasal verb correctly.
c Now Team B reads a definition to Team A.

Functional language: checking and confirming

23 Listen to Track 56. Complete the conversation with words or phrases that you hear there.

JOHNNY: OK. Let's do that one again.
CARRIE: When's the gig? Friday, (**a**) .... ?   **2**
JOHNNY: No, I keep telling you, it's on Thursday.
CARRIE: Oh, that's right. (**b**) .... we only have ten days?
JOHNNY: That's right. We really have to practice hard.
DAVE: And it starts at 7:00, (**c**) .... ?
JOHNNY: No, it starts at 8:00.
DAVE: Oh yeah. I remember now.
KATIE: And we're playing for an hour, (**d**) .... ?
JOHNNY: No, we're playing for 30 minutes.

KATIE: And we're doing ten songs, (**e**) .... ?
JOHNNY: No. We're doing six songs. I've told you all this three times.
DAVE: So, (**f**) .... make us famous?
JOHNNY: Listen. Rock bands are a dime a dozen. Fame takes hard work.
CARRIE: He's right. Come on, guys—let's take it from the top.

24 Read the information below and decide whether the words and phrases you chose for the conversation in Activity 23 are examples of:

1 a tag question (e.g. *It's at 7, isn't it?*)
2 a checking question to get confirmation (e.g. *She's a great actress wouldn't you say?*)
3 a question to find out information (e.g. *Do you mean we have to leave early?*)

25 Using the descriptions from Activity 24, say whether these sentences are examples of question types *1, 2* or *3*.

a They're famous, huh?   **2**
b They have a lot of fans, don't they?
c She's a good actress, wouldn't you say?
d Does the show start at 7:00?
e He never practices, does he?
f He's great, don't you think?
g Do you mean to say that we have to be there at 6:00?
h It's at 7:00, isn't it?
i Does that mean we have to practice tomorrow?
j They're celebrities, aren't they?
k It's on Friday, right?

26 Use checking questions to ask your partner their views about the following things.

a Reading about famous people is fun.
b Jennifer Lopez is a great singer.
c Tom Cruise was good in his last movie.
d Pele was the greatest soccer player of all time.
e Jackie Chan grew up in Hong Kong.
f Neither Mexico nor the U.S.A. have ever won the World Cup.
g The new semester begins in September.
h You need to get 80% to pass this English test.
i All famous people are talented.

Example: STUDENT A: *Reading about famous people is fun, don't you think?*
STUDENT B: *Sure. They have extraordinary lives, don't they?*

27 In pairs Look at Activity Bank 21 on page 165.

a Student A, ask B checking questions without looking back at the Activity Bank.
b Now change round. Student A can look at Activity Bank 21. Student B cannot, and so asks checking questions.

Example: STUDENT A: *The flight's at 8 o'clock, right?*
STUDENT B: *No, it's at 6 o'clock.*
STUDENT A: *Does that mean you have to be at the airport at 4 o'clock?*

28 Listen to these sentences on Track 57. Draw the arrow ↗ or ↘ according to the intonation you hear.

    a That was a great game, wasn't it?
    b You're coming to the party, aren't you?
    c Brad Pitt lives here, doesn't he?
    d She hasn't made a record in two years, has she?
    e They were on TV last night, weren't they?
    f You hadn't asked her about going on a trip, had you?
    g They didn't want to eat in that restaurant, did they?

Are the speakers asking because they want confirmation of something they know or because they probably don't know the answer?

29 Say the sentences using the same intonation as the speakers on Track 57.

30 Complete the sentences with the appropriate tag question and practise using the appropriate intonation.

    a The flight is at 2 o'clock, ... ?   – That's right.
    b He isn't coming, ... ?   – No, he isn't.
    c They live here, ... ?   – Uh-huh.
    d John and Maria don't like concerts, ... ?   – No.
    e You've been to Paris, ... ?   – Yes, I have.
    f They haven't eaten their dinner, ... ?   – No, they haven't.

Now listen to Track 58 and check your answers.

Listening: Diana's story

31 Look at the picture of Diana. Guess as you much as you can about who she is, where she's from, what she does, etc.

32 Read the following questions about Diana.

    a Where is Diana from?
    b What happened when she was 13?
    c How did she try to get accommodations when she went to Mumbai (then called Bombay)?
    d What time was it on Diana's watch when she knocked on the lady's door?
    e Why do you think the lady said "Come inside"?
    f What lesson does Diana draw from this experience in her life?

Now listen to Track 59. Answer the questions.

33 Diana went on to become quite famous. She won something. What do you think she won?

Listen to Track 60. Were you right?

34 Copy the table and make notes as you listen to Track 60 again.

What Diana was afraid of and why
The number of people watching the second competition
How she felt when she won her second big competition
What she did with the thing she won
What happened immediately after she won

35 **Vocabulary** Answer the questions about the words and phrases in blue. They are words and phrases that Diana uses.

a What is something you find daunting?

b What does it mean if we say that our hair is standing on end? Does Diana use the same expression? Why?

c If you give something your all, do you make a lot of effort or a little?

d If to trip means to fall over because something got in the way of your foot, what does trip over your words mean?

e When your mind goes blank, is it easy to decide what to say?

f If you feel euphoria, are you fantastically happy or terribly sad?

g Is a regular person an important person (like a movie star), or are they ordinary, like everyone else?

h What does a chaperone do?

i What is a cockpit and who usually sits there?

36 Listen to Tracks 59 and 60 again and follow the interview in the Audioscript. Then close your books and, in your own words, tell the story of one of the following events.

a the evening Diana found accommodations in Mumbai

b the time Diana won her big competition

37 **Discussion** In groups, give your opinions about these questions.

a What do you think about contests like the one Diana took part in?

b Would you like to meet someone who has won what Diana did? What would you say to them?

Speaking: decision-making (making a star)

38 **In pairs** Read this information about these singers and groups. Their musical / dancing ability has been rated from ***** (excellent) to * (bad).

Which ones would you listen to and why?

Name: The Brainstormers
Ages: 18–25
Image: rebellious, non-conformist
Musical ability: *****
Dancing ability: **
Type of music: rock

Name: Caitlin Curbey
Age: 22
Image: lively, sweet
Musical ability: ***
Dancing ability: *****
Type of music: pop music

Name: Ben Lomax
Age: 34
Image: deep, spiritual
Musical ability: *****
Type of music: intelligent ballads

Name: Star
Ages: 16
Image: clean, sweet
Musical ability: *****
Dancing ability: **
Type of music: pop

Name: LoneMan
Age: 23
Image: tough
Musical ability: ****
Dancing ability: ***
Type of music: rap / hip-hop

Name: Crystal
Ages: 28–30
Image: country, simple girls
Musical ability: *****
Type of music: country

39 **Group work** Imagine you are record producers. You can give a recording contract to one of these six acts. Decide who you are going to give the recording contract to and why.

Points to consider:
• age (of artist and listeners / buyers)
• market (what is "hot" at the moment)
• musical ability
• things you would like to change

Compare your decision with other groups. Give reasons for your decision.

Writing: researching for writing

40 Where do you usually get information when you need to write? Put *often* (o), *sometimes* (s), *rarely* (r), or *never* (n) in the brackets.

the Internet	[ ]	textbooks	[ ]
the library	[ ]	asking other people	[ ]
encyclopedias	[ ]	magazines	[ ]
a dictionary	[ ]	talking to an expert	[ ]
a grammar book	[ ]	other sources	[ ]

Compare with a partner. Which resource is the most valuable for you? Which one is the least useful?

41 Read this biography of Jackie Chan.

Jackie Chan was born in Hong Kong in 1954. His real name is Chan Kong Sang. His parents were very poor —his father worked as a cook and his mother worked as a housekeeper in the French Embassy. Jackie hated school and left after elementary school.

When he was 7, Jackie's parents enrolled him in the China Drama Academy and he often performed in public. Jackie Chan learned how to perform stunts at the academy, which he left when he was 17 to take up a career as a professional stuntman, appearing in Bruce Lee movies. Jackie's early career as an actor was not very successful and it was not until he added comedy to his action movies that he became very popular. Jackie Chan broke into Hollywood in the 1990s and is the biggest Hollywood movie star from Hong Kong. Today, Jackie Chan is famous all over the world with such movies as *Rush Hour 1*, *2* and *3*, and *Around the World in 80 Days*.

Write information from the text in note form about the following:

a [ ] date of birth
b [ ] his early career
c [ ] how famous he is
d [ ] what he learned in his studies (after school)
e [ ] what he thought of school
f [ ] what his position is today
g [ ] what made him famous
h [ ] where he studied after school
i [1] where he was born
j [ ] where he went to school
k [ ] who his parents were

In what order is the information presented in the text? Write 1–11 in the brackets. Why are things in this order?

Word Choice: *at the moment, at present, at this moment in time, at this time, currently, these days, today*

42 Look at the Word Choice notes on page 58 in the booklet.

43 Complete the sentences with *at the moment, at present, at this moment in time, at this time, currently, these days, today*. You can often use more than one phrase.

a .... I'm not practicing as much as I used to.
b .... we—that is the government—are looking at new ways of funding the movie industry.
c .... she is one of the most famous people on the planet.
d He's directing a film in Vietnam ....
e "................... I would like to turn to foreign policy," said the American President.
f They're .... unavailable.
g .... we are at a crossroads for mankind.
h .... I have nothing to add to my previous statement.
i .... I'm not planning any new movies or other project.

44 Now match the information about Shakira (Shakira Mebarak Ripoll) with the headings *a–k* in Activity 41.

- February 2, 1977
- started writing songs at 8 years old; signed a recording contract in 1990
- famous worldwide; best-selling records in English, Spanish and Portuguese
- developed her own style of music, combining her Latin and Arab influences with modern rock music
- Barranquilla, Colombia
- Colombian mother, Lebanese father

Now write a short biography of Shakira using the same information sequence as that in the text about Jackie Chan in Activity 41.

45 **In groups** Who is your favorite celebrity? What do you know about them already?
Discuss your celebrity with your group.

a Find out as much as you can about your celebrity using any or all of the resources mentioned in Activity 40.
b Write a short biography of your celebrity.

Review: grammar and functional language

46 Use the correct form of the phrasal verbs in the box to complete the sentences *a–h*. Look at Activities 15–20 to help you.

> turn down   pick out   put up with   fall for   break up
> look forward to   take after   look for   bring up

a If you want to be famous, you have to .... losing your privacy.

b Sometimes people go on reality shows .... fame.

c Movie stars often .... people because of their physical appearance and their relationships don't last long. They can .... within a year or two of meeting.

d People often .... their parents if they're in show business and become actors or musicians too.

e The children of famous people are often .... by other people because their parents are so busy and consequently the children don't have a normal childhood.

f If you're an actor, you have to accept that you will sometimes be .... for roles that you want. You have to be tough and accept rejection.

g People who are .... the latest record from their favorite singer will pay a lot of money to get it.

h Famous actors are very special and talented because they have been .... from the crowd and they stand out in some way.

Do you think these statements are true? Discuss them in groups and give examples of people you know.

47 What are the drawbacks and compensations of being famous? Copy and complete the table.

Drawbacks
Compensations

Now check your answers with a partner. Ask questions to check. You can look at Activities 23–27 to help you.

Example: STUDENT A: *Losing your privacy is a drawback, don't you think?*

STUDENT B: *Yes, but having a lot of money is a compensation, isn't it?*

Review: vocabulary

blow up	pick out
break up	point out
bring up	pull down
check up on	put off
come across	put up with
come by	run into
fall for	speak up
get along with	take after
let somebody	take in
down	take off
look after	turn somebody
look down on	down
look for	work out
look forward to	write off
look into	
pay back	

48 If you were famous, which of the words in the Word List and Word Plus on page 121 would you like people to use about you? Imagine you are appearing on a TV show and write how you would like to be introduced. In groups, practice introducing each other using the introduction that you wrote.

Example: "Tonight on the show, we have the guitarist who has hit the headlines and has become a legend in the music world. Ladies and gentlemen, please welcome ... (person's name)."

● ● ● Pronunciation

49 a Copy and complete the table with as many words as you can from the Word List and Word Plus 1 and 2.

/ʊ/ – pull	/yu/ – dispute

Add more words of your own to the list.

b **Nonsense stress game** Say the phrases from Word Plus 1 on page 121 using the nonsense syllable *der*, but get the stress right. Can the other students guess which phrase (or phrases) it can be?

Example: STUDENT A: *der DER der DER*

STUDENT B: *Your mind goes blank!*

● ●

50 Find a word from the Word List and Word Plus 1 and 2 to complete this dialogue.

MATT: Did you see *American Idol* last night?

CARMEN: Yes, I love that show. Those singers! I don't know how they (**a**) ....put..up..with..... the pressure.

MATT: Yeah, they're good, but good singers are (**b**) .... It's hard to get noticed. They have to have something special to sing in front of millions of people.

CARMEN: Yes, there's one singer who has a really cool (**c**) .... He always looks good and wears the latest clothes and has the latest haircut. He seems really calm and relaxed, he's just a (**d**) ....

MATT: Did you watch *Blind Date* after *American Idol*? That's always funny. Last night this one girl just (**e**) .... the guy all the time—she told him everything that was wrong with him. I felt so sorry for him. She was really (**f**) .... , she just wouldn't leave him alone. The guy didn't (**g**) .... at all—he hardly said a word about himself.

CARMEN: No, I don't watch that show. I hate the way they're always (**h**) .... the trust of the other person. They talk about really personal stuff that should be a secret between the couple. I watched *The Osbournes*, though. That show fascinates me. They will (**i**) .... any secret they have. There's nothing we don't know about them.

MATT: Yes, I think fame (**j**) .... They think they're so important and interesting. I'm not a fan of that show. I was watching *Survivor* on another channel to see who would be (**k**) .... this week. You never know, there are always unexpected things that happen on that show. Wow! Listen to us, we watch too much TV, don't we?

UNIT 12
Writing and writers

→ relative clauses
→ writing, books, and authors
→ agreeing and disagreeing

Vocabulary: writing, books, and authors

1 **In pairs** Read about these authors and complete the texts with the words in the box.

| background | plot | characters | prize-winning | prolific | adapted | best-selling | acclaimed | twists |

Stephen King has written more than 30 books since 1971, proof that he is a (**a**) .... author. His work deals mostly with horror and the supernatural.

John Grisham is a lawyer from Mississippi, who has penned more than 15 (**b**) .... novels, which have sold millions around the world. He's famous for (**c**) .... in his stories that leave the reader guessing until the last page.

Zadie Smith writes about the richness and diversity of multicultural, multi ethnic Britain in her (**d**) .... first book *White Teeth*, which won the Whitbread Award for a First Novel. She was born in London in 1975.

Amy Tan, born to Chinese parents, grew up in California. She writes about the problems of combining her Chinese (**e**) .... with her American reality and lifestyle.

Alice Walker is a highly (**f**) .... and respected author whose novels deal with the rights of women and African-Americans.

Nick Hornby is a London-based author who describes simply, intelligently, and hilariously everyday (**g**) .... and their lives.

Danielle Steel has authored around 60 books; most are romance novels. Over 20 of her books have been (**h**) .... for TV movies.

Isabel Allende is a Chilean writer who is known as a great storyteller—she has a gift for finding a good (**i**) .... and making it interesting.

2 Find as many similarities as you can between the writers. Put them into different groups.
Some writers may go in more than one group (e.g. Stephen King is American, a man, a thriller writer, etc.).

List the writers in order of preference. Who would you like to read? Compare your list with a partner.

3 Read this text about writing a book and getting it published, and discuss these questions.

    a Would you like to write a book? Why? Why not?
    b What kind of book would you write if you were a writer?

Becoming an author is no easy option when it comes to making a career move. First, there is the actual process of penning your first book. Whether you're interested in factual writing or fiction, be it an autobiography, a novel, a travel book, or even poetry, it will involve doing research of some kind before and as you write. Once you have the basic outline written and notes made (and that involves coming up with a good plot or story and devising all its twists and turns), you'll need to work on a draft of your first version. All this may take you longer than you think, especially if you have a full-time job at the same time.

Let's say you do have a completed manuscript: If you're a first-time writer, there follows the process of trying to find a publisher. You may have to read a few rejection letters and even consider self-publishing. If your work is to be published, next comes the whole editing process which may totally change your original work, but a good editor will help you to improve your descriptions and characters as well as the language used for the narrative and the overall structure of the work. Are you interested?

4 **Word building** Find as many words as you can from Activities 1–3 that can fit into this map of words associated with writing. Add more words to the word map.

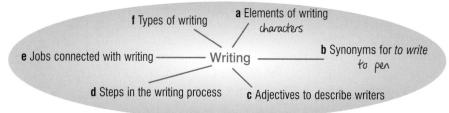

- **f** Types of writing
- **a** Elements of writing — *characters*
- **e** Jobs connected with writing — **Writing**
- **b** Synonyms for *to write* — *to pen*
- **d** Steps in the writing process
- **c** Adjectives to describe writers

5 **Same word, different grammar** Look at these sentences and notice how the words are used.

- He published the results of his *research* on Shakespeare. (noun)
- She knew she would need to *research* the topic further before starting her book. (verb)

Complete the following sentences with verbs made from nouns which are used in Activity 3.

    a The latest computer program was .... by a young teenager from Cambridge, England.
    b The written portrait of the president was .... by a close aide in the president's office.
    c When she came to our office, she .... her plans for the new company.
    d My advice is to .... your letter, show it your friends and then edit it before you send it. Otherwise you might regret it.
    e He .... the piece of paper in his hands so that in the end it was a crumpled mess.
    f There is no doubt that some people are .... to bring down the government.

Note: The words in (a) and (b) are only used as verbs in formal settings.

6 Using a dictionary, find words that can be both nouns and verbs. Do they have the same or different meanings?

    a Write sentences using the words as either nouns or verbs. Who can write the most correct sentences in the time?
    b Read your sentences to another pair. Tell them the word. They have to say whether it is a noun or a verb.

Reading: the blurb

7 How do you choose what to read? Which of these apply to you?

    a My friends suggest ideas.
    b I look at headlines or captions.
    c I look at the pictures.
    d I flick through the book or magazine.
    e I read the blurb (the short piece of information) on the back of a book.
    f My teacher assigns a book, newspaper article, or magazine for a class.
    g I read book reviews.
    h I belong to a book club.
    i I have a subscription to a newspaper / magazine.

Discuss the results with the whole class.

8 Look at the back cover from an extremely popular book. How is this "blurb" constructed? What is being written about in the sections *a–d*? (page 125)

Hugh Grant and Nicholas Hoult in *About a Boy*

From the acclaimed author of *High Fidelity* and *Fever Pitch* comes a great new novel about being a boy and becoming a man.

ABOUT A BOY

Will is 36 and doesn't want children. He's selfish and self-centered and doesn't mind admitting it. Will thinks of himself as an island like Ibiza and he just wants to be left alone in his world without any responsibilities from the mainland. Thanks to his dad writing a song which is known all over the world, he has a great income and will never need to work a day in his life and he leads a life he loves. The last thing on his mind is settling down or getting married or doing anything as uncool as having a family. He just wants to live blissfully by himself in his cool apartment in London, where he has massive speakers and an awe-inspiring music collection. Is that too much to ask?

Marcus is 12 and he knows he's weird. He has a strange habit of singing for no reason—sometimes in the middle of a math class. This, unfortunately, makes him a figure of fun to the whole school. Marcus blames it all on his mother, who makes him listen to Joni Mitchell instead of Nirvana and read books instead of playing on his Gameboy. He loves his mom, but she is kind of different from everyone else's mom. She won't let him eat fast food or drink soda and she wears strange clothes—and makes Marcus wear them too.

Then Marcus meets Will and he recognizes from a mile off that Will is cool. Marcus needs someone who knows what kind of running shoes he should wear and who Kurt Cobain is. And Marcus's mother needs a husband. It all seems so perfect to Marcus ...

NICK HORNBY was born in 1957 and studied at Cambridge University. He is a former teacher and now lives and works in North London. He is the author of several novels and is also the pop music critic for the *New Yorker* magazine.

"In his third novel, Hornby delivers another guaranteed bestseller—brilliant!"
Books Today Magazine

"Hornby is one of the funniest contemporary writers ... Will is a character every man struggling to face up to his responsibilities will relate to."
The Sunday Review

9 **Fact Check** Who:

a ... wrote a very famous song?
b ... wears unusual clothes?
c ... doesn't want to have children?
d ... tends to sing out loud?
e ... makes her son do things that are not cool?
f ... writes about pop music for a famous magazine?
g ... has a very large collection of music?
h ... wants someone to help him to be more cool?

10 **In groups** Does this sound like your kind of book? Why? Why not?

11 **Vocabulary** Find these words in the text and explain what they mean.

a mainland
b uncool
c blissfully
d massive
e running shoes
f former
g delivers
h guaranteed
i struggling

Language in chunks

12 **Match these expressions from the text with a definition (*1–7*).**

a to not mind admitting something
b to settle down
c awe-inspiring
d figure of fun
e from a mile off
f to face up to
g to relate to

1 to accept
2 to start living a stable, secure life
3 to be proud of, to not be ashamed of
4 easily, without difficulty
5 someone that people laugh at
6 to identify with, to understand
7 amazing, incredible

13 **Now use the expressions in Activity 12 in the sentences below. You may have to change them a little to make them fit.**

a My daughter liked to go to parties all the time, but now she has .... and is married with two children.
b He finally had .... the fact that he was 30 years old and needed to get a job and earn some money.

c Janet could tell .... that this man did not want to have any responsibilities.

d She was sick of being a .... Why did no one take her seriously?

e The view from the top of the mountain was .... It was absolutely beautiful.

f She found the characters in the novel very difficult to .... as they lived in a different country and in a different time.

g It was his 50th birthday and he .... He knew he looked good for his age and he had made a great life for himself.

14 **Noticing language** Look at these relative clauses from the blurb of *About a Boy*.

... a song which is known all over the world ... (section b, paragraph 1)
... his cool apartment in London, where he has massive speakers ... (section b, paragraph 1)
... his mother, who makes him listen to Joni Mitchell ... (section b, paragraph 2)

Why are the three different relative pronouns (in blue) used?

Find other examples of relative clauses in the text. Identify exactly what or who the relative pronoun refers to.

15 Choose *Paula* (on the left) or *The Green Mile*. Read the blurb about "your" book, but do not read the other blurb.

With *Paula*, Allende has written a powerful autobiography whose acceptation of the magical and spiritual worlds will remind readers of her first book, *The House of the Spirits*.

Paula is a vivid memoir that captures the reader like a suspense novel. When the daughter of Isabel Allende, Paula, falls into a coma, the author begins telling the story of her family for her unconscious daughter. In the development of the story, there appear before us bizarre ancestors, we hear both delightful and bitter childhood memories, incredible anecdotes from her young years, the most intimate secrets passed along in whispers. In the background, Chile is ever present as we read about the turbulent history of the nation and her family's years of exile.

"Beautiful and moving ... it has everything and everything is marvelous."
Los Angeles Times Book Review

"Fascinating ... in a rich, impeccable prose, she shares with us her most intimate sentiments."
Washington Post Book World

Born in Peru, Isabel Allende was raised in Chile. She worked as a journalist for many years and only began writing fiction in 1981.

Now, for the first time, all six exciting parts of *The Green Mile* come together in one volume to let you enjoy Stephen King's gripping masterpiece.

At Cold Mountain Penitentiary, along the lonely stretch of cells known as the Green Mile, killers like the psychopathic "Billy the Kid" Wharton and Eduard Delacroix await execution. Here guards as decent as Paul Edgecombe and as sadistic as Percy Wetmore watch over them. But good or evil, innocent or guilty, none have ever seen anything like the new prisoner, John Coffey. Is Coffey a devil in human form? Or is he a far, far different kind of being?

The truth emerges in shock waves in a way that will truly blow your mind.

"King surpasses our expectations, leaves us spellbound and hungry for the next twist of plot."   Boston Globe

"King's best in years ... A prison novel that's as haunting and touching as it is just plain haunted."
Entertainment Weekly

STEPHEN KING, the world's best-selling novelist, lives with his wife in Bangor, Maine.

a **In pairs** With a partner who read the same blurb as you, close your book and prepare an oral summary in your own words of the plot, the author and what people think of the book.

b **In groups** Work with another pair who read the blurb of the other book. Listen to their oral summary and then write your version of their blurb.

c Compare your written summary with the actual blurb of the book. What are the similarities and differences?

Listening: books and movies

16 Discussion List books that have been made into movies. If you have seen a movie of a book that you know (e.g. one of the Harry Potter stories), say which you prefer (book or film) and why.

17 Read this plot description from the novel *White Teeth* by Zadie Smith and answer the questions *a–h*.

Archie (Archibald) Jones, a British man, and Samad Iqbal, originally from Bangladesh, have been friends since they were soldiers together in the British Army in World War II. They both live and work in London where Archie is married to a Jamaican woman named Clara with whom he has one nine year-old daughter, Irie, while Samad is married to Alsana and has twin boys, Millat and Magid, who are also nine. Samad, who works as a waiter, has decided that Britain in 1984 is an unhealthy place to bring up his sons and is planning to send Magid to his family in Bangladesh in order to offer him a better education and upbringing. He has not told anyone except Archie about his plan; Magid does not know that his father is going to send him away. Archie has agreed to drive Samad and the child to the airport so that Magid can be put on the plane at 3:00AM

Who:

a ... served in the British Army?
b ... is married to Archie?
c ... is Irie?
d ... is Samad married to?
e ... are Millat and Magid?
f ... has family in Bangladesh?
g ... is going to go and live in Bangladesh?
h ... is going to drive to the airport?

18 Read the following scenes from a film treatment of *White Teeth*. What, in your opinion, is the relationship between Millat and Magid? Between Archie and Samad?

SCENE 25
Outside an Indian restaurant, Archie Jones is dressed in a long coat and is standing in front of his car. Samad Iqbal leaves the restaurant and approaches Archie, with his hand out to shake Archie's hand.

SAMAD
I won't forget this, Archibald.

ARCHIE
That's what friends are for, Sam, but I have to tell you something. I had to bring Millat and Irie too.

SAMAD
Why did you bring them?

ARCHIE
They all woke up when I went to get Magid.

SCENE 26
Interior of Archie's car. The three children are in the back seat, asleep, and wake up as the adults get in.

MILLAT
Hey Daddy! Where are we going, Daddy? To a secret disco party?

MAGID
Are we really? Where are we going?

IRIE
I want to go home. *(starts to cry)*

SCENE 27
Close-up on Samad's face. There are tears coming down his face. He looks straight ahead as he speaks.

SAMAD
We're going on a trip to an airport. To Heathrow.

IRIE, MILLAT, MAGID
Wow! Really?

SAMAD
And then Magid is going on a trip with Auntie Zinat.

SCENE 28
We see the three children in the back seat again.

MILLAT
Will he come back?

MAGID
Is it far? Will I be back in time for school on Monday? Only I have got to see what happens with my science experiment in photosynthesis—I put one plant in the cupboard and one plant in the sunlight and I have to see what happened.

MILLAT
Shut up about your stupid plants!

MAGID
Will I be back for school, Daddy?

SCENE 29
Close-up of Samad's face again as he struggles to answer his son.

SAMAD
You'll be in a school on Monday, Magid, I promise.

19 In groups For each scene explain where the camera has to be positioned.

20 Listen to the same incident from the original book on Track 61. Find:

a ... one scene that has been completely changed by the scriptwriter.

b ... some dialogue that has been changed by the scriptwriter.

c ... some dialogue that has been added by the scriptwriter.

d ... some dialogue that has been omitted by the scriptwriter.

Which version do you prefer? Why? Would you like to read the book? Would you like to see a TV or film adaptation of this book?

21 Fact check Listen to Track 61 again and say whether the following statements are true or false.

a The three children are warm.

b The twins are excited to see their father.

c Samad hugs his son tightly.

d Millat doesn't want Magid to come back.

e Samad wants to remember this car ride.

f Archie is worried that they will not get to the airport on time.

g Magid will be able to see his science experiment on Monday.

22 Pairs and groups Read the text of Track 61 in the Audioscript. Find words you don't completely understand.

a Compare your list with a partner. Agree on the five words you would most like to know the meaning of.

b Compare your list with another pair. Agree on a new list of three words.

c Look for the words in a dictionary.

d Tell the class what your words were and what they mean. Did any of the other pairs choose the same words?

Speaking: telling a story

23 Look at the pictures of Mary, her children Jake and Rachael and her husband.

a Put the pictures in order to tell a story.

b Think about how you would tell the story to a friend. You can make notes, but don't write the whole story down.

24 Pairwork Compare your versions of the story. Prepare a new version of the story that you are both happy with. Close your book and practice telling your story without looking at the pictures or your notes.

25 Tell your story to the whole class. Whose story is best?

Grammar: relative clauses

26 Read the sentences. Identify the relative clauses. Which are the relative pronouns / adverbs?

   a The meal that we ate at that restaurant was delicious.

     that we ate at that restaurant

   b The place where we went on vacation was very hot.

   c I didn't like the water that I drank from the kitchen sink.

   d Are you talking about the woman who lives next door?

   e He's the man whose children were at the gym.

   f I remember a time when I was very tired and couldn't sleep.

Look at 12A and 12B in the Mini-grammar. Do you want to change your answers?

27 Say whether the relative pronouns in Activity 26 are subjects or objects of the verb in the relative clause. Use **12A–12C in the Mini-grammar** to help you.

Example: *a that = object*

28 Combine these two ideas using relative clauses. Leave out the relative pronoun or adverb if possible.

   a The child was at the party and he was asleep.

     The child who was at the party was asleep.

   b I made this pie and it has a lot of calories.

     The pie ...

   c My mother grew up in a city and the prime minister was born in the city.

     My mother ...

   d There used to be no computers. My aunt remembers this time.

     My aunt ...

   e They are the parents of that child. They are very athletic.

     That is the child ...

   f Did you see that place? I used to live there.

     Did you see the place ... ?

29 Complete these definitions in your own words. Remember to use relative clauses.

   a A city is a place where ...

   b A great restaurant is a place ...

   c A healthy person is someone ...

   d A great party is one ...

   e A good book is one ...

   f A library is a place ...

   g The U.S. is a country ...

   h The weekend is a time ...

Compare and explain your answers to a partner. Do you have similar or different definitions?

30 Read these sentences and answer the questions below.

   a I walked her to her room, which was downstairs, and told her to get some more rest.

   b The bedroom which was downstairs was the coldest of all the bedrooms.

Look at the relative clauses in blue. Which one:

- ... is essential to the meaning of the sentence? (defining relative clause)
- ... provides extra information and could be omitted? (nondefining relative clause)

Look at 12A–12C in the Mini-grammar to help you.

31 Complete these relative clauses with appropriate pronouns.

   a The house .... I lived as a child was very big.

   b This is the man .... told me he saw a ghost.

   c Her dog, ... lay in the corner, looked at me the whole time.

   d My grandmother, ... is 92, is having a birthday party next week.

Are they defining or nondefining relative clauses?

● ● ● Pronunciation: what commas sound like

32 Listen to Track 62. Which sentence (*a* or *b*) does the speaker use? How do you know?

> **a** My sister, who lives in Sydney, never complains about the heat.
>
> **b** My sister who lives in Sydney never complains about the heat.

What is the difference in meaning between the sentences?

33 Now listen to Track 63. Put commas where necessary.

> **a** The house where I grew up is supposed to be haunted.
>
> **b** The houses where many people still live are over 200 years old.
>
> **c** His children who sometimes played by the river said they heard noises.
>
> **d** Her daughter who plays the piano once saw a ghost.
>
> **e** People who say they have seen a ghost often just imagined it.
>
> **f** Professor Macpherson who is an investigator of strange phenomena has never actually seen a ghost.
>
> **g** The ghost in our house which most of us have seen only appears about twice a year.

Are the relative clauses defining or nondefining?

34 Say the sentences like the speakers on Track 63.

● ●

35 Connect the sentences in this paragraph using defining and nondefining relative clauses.

Example: *My family, which is unusually large for a modern family, is very international.*

My family is very international. It is an unusually large family for a modern family. One of my brothers is an architect. He lives in Brazil. One of my sisters lives in Argentina. She is a singer. My parents are French. They live in Mexico. My aunts and uncles have houses all over Europe. They move around a lot. My grandparents are both in their nineties. They live in France. I once saw a ghost in our house. It is in Paris.

36 Write a paragraph about your family, using defining and nondefining relative clauses. Read the paragraph you wrote with the appropriate pauses and intonation.

Functional language: agreeing and disagreeing

● ●

37 Listen to Track 64. Match these four books with a summary (*a–h*). There is only one correct summary per book.

> - *Reaching the Top*
> - *Where the Flowers Grow*
> - *Watching Time Go By*
> - *Crying Over Spilt Milk*

> **a** succeeding in the business world
> **b** a biography of a famous person
> **c** a children's novel
> **d** a novel about human relationships
> **e** how to be a better gardener
> **f** a true story about climbing a mountain
> **g** using humor to improve your life
> **h** a book about movie stars

38 Listen to Track 64 again. Who liked which book? Copy and complete the table with ticks (✓) if they liked the book or crosses (✗) if they didn't.

	Reaching the Top	Where the Flowers Grow
Rachel	a	b
Garry	c	d
Marsha	e	f
Chris	g	h

	Watching Time Go By	Crying Over Spilt Milk
Rachel	i	j
Garry	k	l
Marsha	m	n
Chris	o	p

39 Match the start of phrases *a–i* with the appropriate endings *1–9*.

> **a** I agree up to a
> **b** Absolutely,
> **c** I couldn't
> **d** I couldn't agree
> **e** I see what
> **f** I'm with Marsha
> **g** I'm going to have
> **h** Nonsense! I have to
> **i** Well, I disagree with both

> **1** point with Rachel on this one.
> **2** agree more with Marsha.
> **3** disagree with Garry here.
> **4** less with Garry.
> **5** Marsha and Chris.
> **6** on this one.
> **7** to disagree with everyone here …
> **8** you're all saying, but …
> **9** Chris!

40 Listen to Track 64 again. Which of your phrases go in the gaps a–i?

HOST: Marsha Macdonald?

a MARSHA: .... For me it was a marvelous book, truly amazing. I loved it.

HOST: Chris Rogers?

b CHRIS: .... it's just not my kind of book, but it's quite good at what it tries to do, I suppose.

HOST: Marsha?

c MARSHA: .... I think this book is very interesting.

d RACHEL: It's such a clever and novel idea, using a garden growing as a symbol for a relationship and its development. .... I think this is a beautiful piece of fiction.

e CHRIS: ....—a particularly dull account of an interesting life.

f RACHEL: ....

HOST: Garry?

g GARRY: .... There were a few new insights into Monroe's life.

h RACHEL: ....! A very funny book ...

i MARSHA: ....and say that I found it very childish in dealing with very serious topics. Not my kind of book.

Are the expressions you have used for gaps a–i demonstrating strong agreement (*SA*), strong disagreement (*SD*), mild agreement (*MA*) or mild disagreement (*MD*)?

Example: a *SD*

41 Now decide whether the expressions a–v indicate strong or mild agreement, strong or mild disagreement.

a But don't you think that ...   *MD*
b Exactly!
c Fair enough, but on the other hand, ...
d I agree to a certain extent, but ...
e I couldn't agree more.
f I guess so.
g I know that's true.
h I suppose so.
i I'm afraid I just can't agree ...
j I'm not so sure.
k I'm sorry, I can't accept that.
l Nonsense!
m That's exactly what I think.
n That's not true.
o That's so right / You're so right.
p Yes, and on top of that ...
q Yes, but there's something else.
r Yes, I think that's right.
s You must be joking!
t You're surely not suggesting that ...
u You're telling me!
v I take your point, but what about ... ?

Now replace the expressions in Activity 40 with different expressions from Activity 41 so that the meaning stays the same.

Example: a MARSHA: *I'm afraid I just can't agree with Garry.*

42 **The agreement / disagreement chain** Write three sentences giving your opinion about one of the following topics.

a the money paid to actors / professional athletes
b whether reading novels is a good thing or a bad thing
c what you think of the fashion industry
d the effect of television violence on young viewers

Read your sentences to the class. Another student agrees or disagrees with what you said and gives their opinion. A third student agrees or disagrees, then adds an opinion. Now it's the turn of a fourth student … No student can use agreement / disagreement language that has been used already.

Example: STUDENT A: *I think baseball players are paid too much money.*

STUDENT B: *You're so right. They earn more in one game than most people earn in a year.*

STUDENT C: *Nonsense. That's a myth. And anyway, they give a lot of pleasure so why ...*

43 **Group role-play** Make a list of movies, books, or TV shows that you have all seen or read. Make notes about your opinions of each one.

Role-play a TV or radio show like the one on Track 64. One of you is the host and the other four are critics / guests. Give your opinions about the movie, show or book. Use expressions from Activities 40 and 41 to agree and disagree with each other. You can discuss the following topics.

- acting
- characters
- descriptions
- dialogue
- filming / scenery
- plot
- special effects

Writing: book reports

44 Read the first parts of these two book reports and decide whether you would like to read the book or not and why.

Gandhi: A Life by Yogesh Chadha is a book about the life of Mahatma Gandhi. It starts off with information about his life, such as where he came from and how he became a lawyer and then goes on to tell the incredible story of how this unusual man became one of the most influential men of the 20th century.

Carrie is a book by Stephen King about a young high school girl who has dangerous "special" powers. At school everyone thinks she is weird, so she decides to use her powers to get revenge.

What other information would you like to have seen to help you decide?

45 Look at these questions that you can use to help you to write a book report.

Are there any other questions that you think are important?

What's the name of the book?
Who's the author?
Where and when does the story take place?
Who are the main characters?
What are the main events? / What is the plot of the book?
Would you recommend this book to someone else? Why or why not?

Copy and complete the table with information about the last book that you read. Add your own questions to the table and answer them too.

46 Writing Use the answers to the questions to write a report on the book. Share your report with a partner.

Review: grammar and functional language

47 Punctuate the following sentences with periods, commas, question marks and capital letters where necessary. You can look at Activities 26–35 to help you.

a have you ever read the book i gave you

b have you seen the movie michael moore made about the american president

c i just can't relate to people who don't like turkish food

d i read my favorite book which was given to me by my sister-in-law in just one day

e in 1961 when i wasn't even born things were so different

f my aunt who just had her 90th birthday remembers a time when there were hardly any cars on the road

g she often travels to mexico where she once lived to see her friends

h the manuscript which can be seen at the british museum from january 2nd until april 30th is valued at about £350,000.

i when did you first meet mr graham whose house is up for sale

j when i was at school writing compositions which is easy for some people was very difficult for me

k written by a first-time author this book which has already sold one million copies is to be made into a movie

48 Write definitions for the following, using relative clauses.

a A good movie is ...
b A terrible restaurant is ...
c Good friends are ...
d A typical movie for young people is ...
e A good place to take someone in this town is ...
f The best thing to read when you're on vacation is ...

49 Read the conversation and then agree or disagree, using the words given in appropriate phrases.

HEATHER: I think baseball players are paid far too much money.

MAUREEN: (a. agree: *right*) *You're so right* . They earn more money in one game than most people earn in a year.

JED: (b. disagree: *true*) .... And anyway their careers are very short.

RUTH: (c. agree: *with Jed*) .... Baseball players deserve everything they get.

MAUREEN: (d. disagree: *joking*) .... Just because they can hit a ball they become millionaires.

RUTH: (**e.** agree: *point*) .... , but what about the pleasure they give to everyone?

MAUREEN: (**f.** disagree: *sorry / accept*) .... There are lots of people who don't like baseball at all.

JED: Well they're crazy then!

MAUREEN: (**g.** disagree: *suggest*) .... people who don't like baseball are crazy, are you?

JED: Yes.

MAUREEN: (**h.** disagree: *disagree*) .... That's like saying that all people who like classical music are snobs.

JED: (**i.** agree: *more*) ....

Review: vocabulary

50 Could you be a writer? Use five words from the Word List and Word Plus to describe the kind of writer you would like to be. Explain your words to your partner.

Example: I'd like to write an autobiography. I think I've had an interesting life and that's the easiest thing to write about.

● ● ● Pronunciation

51 a Find all the words in the Word List with more than two syllables. Ignore the word *to* in the infinitives (e.g. *(to) deliver*). Put the words in groups depending on which syllable is stressed.

Check your answers by listening to Track 65.

b Find all the words in the Word List and Word Plus that have the sound /f/ and which are followed by a vowel sound. What vowel sounds follow /f/? Which four words have the same sound?

Check your answers by listening to Track 66.

52 Just a minute Work in groups. You have one minute to talk about one of the words from the Word List without pausing, or repeating nouns or verbs, or going off the topic. If you pause or repeat a noun or verb or change the subject, the other members of the group can challenge you and *they* continue to speak on the topic. The winner is the person who is still talking at the end of one minute. One person keeps time and stops the clock every time there is a challenge.

Example: STUDENT A: "Awe-inspiring" is a very interesting word that can be used to describe a lot of things. There are people who do great things, like ...

STUDENT B: Stop the clock. You repeated "things." Start the clock. I know a person who is awe-inspiring—this is my sister. I am amazed at the way she ...

UNIT 13
Crime and punishment

→ the passive voice
→ crime and criminals
→ making deductions

Listening: crime doesn't pay

1 Look at these pictures of true crimes that went wrong. Can you guess what happened?

2 Now listen to Track 67 to check your answers and match one story to each picture.

3 Listen to Track 67 again and fill in the table with the information you hear.

	a What went wrong?	b What was stolen?
Story 1		
Story 2		
Story 3		
Story 4		
Story 5		

4 What do these words from the news reports mean?

a armored car
b getaway
c escape route
d handpicked
e without a hitch
f convicted
g sentenced
h appeal
i prosecuted
j shoplifting
k attempted
l in the course of
m shifted

5 **In pairs** Find a crime story in the newspaper, or one that you know about. Write the news item for it for an English-language news station.

Join with two other pairs and write a three-story news bulletin. Practice reading it.
Make recordings.

Vocabulary: crime and criminals

6 Word formation Copy and complete this table with the names of crimes and criminals, and with crime verbs.

Crime	Criminal	Crime verb
a murder		
b	assassin	
c		to hack into a computer
d		to rob
e mugging		
f		to burgle
g	thief	
h pickpocketing		
i shoplifting		
j		to commit arson
k embezzlement		
l	kidnapper	
m		to evade taxes

Think of other crimes and add these to the table. Compare in groups.

7 Write your own definitions of the crimes.

Now test your partner.

Example: STUDENT A: *to assassinate*
STUDENT B: *That means to kill a famous person, usually a political figure or leader.*

8 Dictionary work Use your dictionary to find the correct preposition to complete these verb forms.

a to admit .... something
b to convict / be convicted .... something
c to charge / be charged .... something
d to confess .... something
e to sentence someone / be sentenced .... something
f to arrest someone / be arrested .... something
g to suspect someone / be suspected .... something
h to find someone guilty / be found guilty .... something
i to be wanted .... something

9 Now read about these notorious criminals on this page and page 136 and complete the texts with the appropriate verb or preposition.

Jack the Ripper
Jack the Ripper lived in England in the 19th century. From August to November 1888, he killed at least seven women and the police could not catch him. He even sent letters to the police, (a) .... the murders and taunting the police. The Ripper was never caught so he was never (b) .... any crime and the killings stopped as suddenly as they had started.

Al Capone

Born in Naples, Italy, but brought up in New York City, Al Capone (1899–1947) was a notorious gangster who moved to Chicago and became connected with organized crime there. He was (c) .... being involved in killings, but he was never arrested (d) .... murder. He was eventually (e) .... with not paying money that he owed to the government in 1931, he was found (f) .... the crime and was (g) .... 11 years in jail. He was set free in 1939 because of illness.

Bonnie and Clyde

Bonnie Parker (1911–1934) and Clyde Barrow (1909–1934) were infamous criminals who robbed banks and stores and were (h) .... their crimes in Texas, Oklahoma, New Mexico, and Missouri between 1932 and 1934. Known for their love affair, they were always in the newspapers. Although they admitted (i) .... their crimes, they were never convicted (j) .... what they did, but were finally shot by the police while they were robbing a store. They were considered heroes by many and some people thought they did not deserve to die.

Compare your answers in groups. What were the crimes that they committed?

10 What other famous criminals from real life or the movies do you know? What were their crimes? What made them famous? Do you know what happened to them?

Speaking: Is crime ever justified? (discussion and role-play)

11 **In pairs** Read the three situations and decide how you would describe the crime in each case.

a Michael Trent was an unemployed construction worker. His wife was very sick and she needed an expensive medicine. He could not afford to buy her the medicine, so he broke into a drugstore at night and took the drugs that he needed.

b Maria (15) was from a poor family. At school they laughed at her because of her clothes. She stole from a department store to look nicer.

c Richard Moore needed good grades to get to college. He worked hard all the way through school, but a series of minor illnesses affected his grades in the final semester. His sister, Judy, was a computer expert and knew how to break into databases so she broke into the school database and got the answers to the exams.

12 **In groups** Read the situations again. What should the punishment be for each person?

13 **Role-play** Work in groups of five. Choose one of the stories (a–c) above and role-play the trial of the crime. Choose one of the following characters and read about your role in the Activity Bank.

Story a	Story b	Story c
Defendant	Defendant	Defendant
Michael Trent	Maria Metcalf	Judy Moore
Witness	Witness	Witness
Mrs. Trent	Maria's best friend	Richard Moore
Judge	Judge	Judge
Prosecuting attorney	Prosecuting attorney	Prosecuting attorney
Defense attorney	Defense attorney	Defense attorney

DEFENDANT: look at Activity Bank 20 on page 165.

WITNESS: look at Activity Bank 24 on page 167.

JUDGE: look at Activity Bank 22 on page 166.

PROSECUTING ATTORNEY: look at Activity Bank 23 on page 166.

DEFENSE ATTORNEY: look at Activity Bank 25 on page 167.

Conduct the trial using the information and instructions that you found in the Activity Bank.

Functional language: making deductions

14 Listen to Track 68 and complete this audioscript with the words that you hear.

PHIL: Hey Mom! There's a man going into our neighbor's house.

MOM: It (**a**) .... their son, Jack. He's watching their place while his parents are away on vacation.

PHIL: It (**b**) .... their son. The man's too old. He's about 45.

MOM: Well, it (**c**) .... Jack's brother. He sometimes comes to stay.

PHIL: I'm sure it's not Jack's brother! He's looking around very suspiciously. (**d**) .... he's a burglar.

MOM: You and your imagination, Phil. It's probably a friend.

PHIL: I don't think so, Mom. I've never seen him before.

MOM: Well, we don't know all their friends. He (**e**) .... to feed the cat while they're away.

PHIL: He's (**f**) .... feeding the cat, Mom. He's climbing in the window.

MOM: What? Are you sure? Let me see.

PHIL: Look—over there.

MOM: You're right – there's (**g**) .... something going on. No doubt about it. Let's call the police.

PHIL: OK, Mom.

15 Each of these sentences (*a–n*) can be followed by one of the sentences *1–14* in the table. Choose the correct one in each case.

a Jake's mother is older than that woman. 12
b The diamonds were found in his house.
c Hannah's been working all day.
d I think I recognize that man.
e I think it was an accident.
f That woman put something in her pocket.
g It's impossible—he's not that smart.

h Stephen has darker hair, I believe.
i I feel very tired and my throat hurts.
j He's been in jail three times for robbery.
k I think my mother was there, but I'm not sure.
l I hear noises outside.
m She was found innocent.
n There's a tall man outside with dark hair.

Possibility (when you are not quite sure if something is true)	Certainty (when you are sure that something is true)	Certainty (when you are sure that something is *not* true)
A Present	**C Present**	**E Present**
1 It **might** be a cold. 2 She **could** be shoplifting. 3 **Maybe** it's a friend from school. 4 **I don't think** that's him. 5 There **may** be someone walking around.	8 She **must** be tired. 9 He's **definitely** a criminal. 10 **That'll be** my son.	12 That **can't** be her. 13 She's **definitely not** a criminal.
B Past	**D Past**	**F Past**
6 He **might not have taken** the pen deliberately. 7 She **may have seen** the crime.	11 He **must have stolen** them.	14 He **couldn't have planned** the robbery.

Which box (*A–F*) would you choose for phrases *a–g* from Activity 14?

16 Which box (*A–F*) in Activity 15 on page 137 would you place the following sentences in?

   a *I don't know about you, but I think* he's a thief.

   b *If you ask me, he probably* took the radio by accident.

   c *I don't imagine that* it was someone who worked there who stole the money.

   d *For all I know*, he might have come in when I was out and stolen my keys.

17 Make appropriate deductions about these situations. How many different possibilities can you come up with? What makes you sure or not sure?

a

b

c

d

e

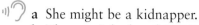

Pronunciation: sentence stress in deductions

18 Listen to Track 69 and mark (') the stressed syllables.

   a She might be a kidnapper.
   b They can't be burglars.
   c He could be an assassin.
   d He may have come to deliver the newspaper.
   e They must be going on vacation.

Now practice saying the sentences with the same use of stress.

19 Look at these sentences and mark the stressed syllables.

   a She must be visiting her sister.
   b They might have stolen the flowers.
   c He might be a kidnapper.
   d There may be a pickpocket.

Listen to Track 70 and check your answers.

20 In groups What do you know about this painting? Make notes of everything you know.

When you have finished, check Activity Bank 26 on page 167 and note any information that you have not already noted.

21 Did you know that the painting was once stolen? Read the story of the theft of the painting.

The theft of the Mona Lisa

On Monday, August 21, 1911, the Mona Lisa was stolen from the wall of the Louvre museum in Paris. No one noticed that it was stolen until the following day when Louis Béroud, a painter, went to see it. He saw it was missing and asked where it was. The painting was missing for two years before the case was solved.

22 In groups These are the different theories about who stole the Mona Lisa. Discuss the theories and discuss who you think stole the painting and why.

Theories

"The painting was accidentally destroyed so the museum is inventing the theft."
Jules Bernard, owner of an art gallery

"Some German art collectors think of themselves as our cultural rivals. They are jealous of France and they want to make the French collectors feel bad so they have stolen the picture."
Gaston Bologne, politician

"The Italians are still angry that the painting left Italy and they want it returned to Italy."
Jacques Durand, historian

"The employees in the Louvre want to show how bad security is."
Berthe Maupassant, ex-employee of the Louvre

"France has many problems. The theft of the painting will give people something else to think about."
Sabine Clouthier, homemaker

Look at the true story in Activity Bank 27 on page 168. Were you surprised?

23 In groups Do you know any stories of mysterious events which have never been properly explained? Tell the other students.

Reading: When is a crime not a crime?

24 In groups What would you do if you suddenly found something very valuable like a billfold in the street which had a lot of money in it? Would you keep it? Would you try to return it? Would you tell anyone?

25 Read *either* "Finders Keepers" *or* "Man 1, Bank 0". Is your story happy or sad?

Finders Keepers?

Joey Coyle wasn't doing too well. He was a dockworker by trade, but he had been unemployed for some time. He had a drug problem too and nothing went right for him. And even when it did, poor Joey managed to make a mess of it.

And then, on February 26 1981, Joey, aged 28, spotted a yellow box on the side of a road in Philadelphia. He looked around but there was nobody who might be the owner of such a box. He thought about it for a moment and then decided to pick it up and take it home. He figured it would make a good toolbox.

Before taking the box home, he opened it. He expected it to be empty. But it wasn't. Instead he found two bags inside with the words "Reserve Bank" printed on them. With his pulse quickening, he pulled the bags open and found himself looking at over a million dollars in $100 bills. Joey stared and stared and then quickly put the bags into his car and drove away.

A few minutes later, an armored money truck came roaring up to the place where the yellow box had been. The guards inside had realized that they had dropped the box out of the truck and had come back to look for it. But of course it wasn't there and they were left wondering how to explain to their company that they had misplaced a million dollars in cash.

Joey made a mess of his windfall as you might expect. One moment he was experiencing the euphoria of being rich beyond his wildest dreams and the next, he was experiencing a bad case of paranoia about being discovered and having "his" money taken away from him. He told everyone he met about his good luck and then swore them to secrecy. He had no idea what to do with the money, but his girlfriend put him in touch with gangster friends of hers who offered to help him invest his money and make it grow. In his confusion, Joey trusted them and within only a short time the money had gone.

Joey had lost all the money he had found, but that didn't mean he wasn't guilty of committing a crime. In the state of Pennsylvania, you are committing an offense if you do not try to return things with a value of more than $250. The police finally caught up with him and Joey was arrested and thrown in jail, but he was released when a jury found him not guilty because, they thought, he had become temporarily insane upon finding the money.

Sometime later, Joey's story was made into a Hollywood movie called *Money for Nothing*, starring John Cusack. Perhaps the unemployed dockworker's luck was about to change. But it was too late for Joey Coyle. He died before the movie was released.

Man 1, Bank 0

In 1995 Patrick Combs was living in San Francisco and trying desperately to make ends meet. He had just written a guide for college students called *Major in Success* and he was using the book to launch what he hoped would be a successful career as a motivational speaker, helping people to make the most of their talents and abilities. And no one needed his advice more than Patrick himself. Money had always been tight in Patrick's family and, at 28, he thought it was always going to be like that for him.

But you never know your luck! One day he found some junk mail that had been delivered to his mailbox. He was going to throw it away, but instead he decided to give it a quick look before getting rid of it. He found himself looking at a letter promising that if he sent money to a certain company, he would soon be receiving huge checks which would make him rich. And to prove it, the company had put a specimen check in with their letter—just to show their clients what riches would look like.

Patrick looked at the fake check despondently. It was a depressing reminder of how broke he was. But then he saw an opportunity for some fun. After all, he had nothing to lose. He thought it would be a funny joke to deposit the check in his account. He would give bank employees a laugh when they discovered that "some idiot" had tried to cash a junk mail check. So he giggled as he wrote in the amount of the deposit, $95,093.35, on the deposit slip. "I didn't think I was sticking money into the bank," he says. He didn't even bother to endorse the back by signing it as you are supposed to do.

After ten days, much to his shock, he found that the check had been cleared and the money had been credited to his account. (As he later learned, the check met the nine criteria of a valid check—and even the words "nonnegotiable" printed on the front did not negate it.) The junk mail company had succeeded in making the check look real—far too real. And to make matters worse for the bank, they had missed their own legal deadline to notify him that the check had bounced as a "noncash" item. With "money" in his account, Patrick became obsessed. He couldn't think of anything else. "It was an addiction," he says, "for two months I obsessed on whether I should take the money or give the money back." After researching his own legal position long and hard, he discovered that he was not legally responsible for returning the money—he had committed no crime.

But in the end, Patrick decided to do the "right" thing. He returned the money to the bank but only after he had insisted (and the bank had agreed) that the bank would write him a letter confirming that they had made a mistake in cashing the check. Patrick had by this time become a celebrity and he used the story to catapult his career as a motivational speaker. Today his money worries are over.

26 **Fact check** On your own, answer these questions about the story that you read.

  a When and where did the story take place?
  b What was the name, age, and occupation of the person in the story?
  c How much money did he get?
  d How did he get it?
  e Was he guilty of any crime?
  f What happened to the money?
  g What happened to the person in the story in the end?

27 Now find someone who read the other story. Use the *Fact check* questions in Activity 26 to find out everything about their story.

Find similarities and differences between the stories.

28 **Vocabulary** Match these meanings with the words in yellow from the two texts.

  a in short supply
  b accepted, recognized as valid
  c sign and make official
  d looked intensely at something
  e lost
  f the feeling that people are against you
  g laughed happily
  h promote very quickly
  i driving fast and noisily

29 **Noticing language** Look at this example of a passive sentence and answer the questions.

A lot of the money was given away by the charity.

  a Who or what is the agent (i.e. the person or thing who did the action – the "doer")?
  b Who or what is the object of the action (i.e. the person or thing that the action was "done to")?

Look back at the stories in Activity 25 and find other examples of passive sentences. Decide who or what the "doer" and the "done to" are in each case.

Language in chunks

30 Combine the words from the two circles to make phrases from the two stories. Three phrases start with *to make*.

a beyond his
b he had nothing
c his luck was
d nothing went
e to make
f to put someone
g to swear someone
h with his pulse

1 a mess of something
2 about to change
3 in touch with somebody
4 quickening
5 right for him
6 the most of something
7 to lose
8 to secrecy
9 wildest dreams
10 matters worse

31 Now use the phrases (or parts of the phrases) in the following sentences. You may have to change tenses, adjectives (e.g. *his*) or pronouns (e.g. *he* or *him*).

a .... Jennifer realized that she might have found the treasure she had been searching for since last week.
b After he had won the competition, he found that he was rich ....
c After he left his job, he found that .... anymore and so he decided to go back home.
d After years of poverty, and even though he didn't yet know it, George's ....
e He .... He said he would tell the world when he was ready, but until then he didn't want anyone to know.
f One of the things I've enjoyed most is .... friends they haven't seen for years.
g People who .... of every opportunity are usually more successful than those who don't.
h She admitted that she had .... her exam paper. She was sure she'd failed.
i She burned the toast and .... she spilled milk all over the kitchen floor.
j She thought she might as well try to escape from prison. After all she had ....

Now use at least four of the phrases in sentences of your own.

32 In groups Answer these questions.

a Who do you feel more sympathy for? Joey or Patrick? Why?
b What would you have done if you had been Joey?
c If you had been Patrick, what would you have done?

Grammar: the passive voice

33 Why is the passive voice used in these sentences? Read the possible reasons (1–4) below and match each sentence (a–i) with the best reason. Use **13B in the Mini-grammar** to help you.

a My car was stolen yesterday.   **1**
b When I got home, I found that the window had been broken. **1**
c The prisoners are taken to their cells at 11:00 PM and the lights are put out at 11:30.
d The experiment was conducted under controlled conditions.
e People are often arrested at soccer matches.
f You will be fined if you park your car in this zone.
g His case is being reviewed at the moment. *law*
h Oil was put into the jar and water was added.
i The garbage was being collected when I pulled the car into the driveway.

1 We do not know the person who did the action.
2 The identity of the person doing the action is obvious.
3 The action is what is important as part of a process, not who does it.
4 We are writing in formal language, such as for academic reports.

34 Complete these passive voice sentences using the correct tense of the verb in parentheses. Use **13A and 13B in the Mini-grammar** to help you.

a The results (take) *were taken* from the survey and then we wrote a report.
b The mail (deliver) *is delivered* at about 11:00 AM every day.
c When I arrived, the TV (move) *was been moved* to the living room. Everyone was helping because it was heavy.
d My PC (fix) *is being fixed* at the moment. I'm going to get it from the store tomorrow.
e The suspect (question) *has been questioned* and we are now ready to charge him.
f When I arrived home, I was surprised to find my house (break into) *had been broken into*
g Do you think the criminal (arrest) *has been arrested* by now?
h That package should (deliver) *have been delivered* by now.
i Later today, the defendant (sentence) *will be sentenced*

Should + have

35 Read this police report. How could you rewrite the sentences with verbs in blue in the passive (to make it more formal)? You may have to change the construction of the sentences the verbs occur in. Use **13A–13E** in the Mini-grammar to help you.

The suspect was followed ···

We *followed* the suspect along Parker Street and waited as he paid the taxi driver. He *entered* the Wishbone Club and we *saw* him talking to two *···two··· a baby were seen him talking* suspicious-looking young men, who were *holding* a baby. Someone came and *took* *The baby was taken and then ···* the baby away and then they left the young men to talk by themselves. At 2:00 PM, the two young men left the club and I *saw* them getting into *they were seen getting into* a black car. There was a tall man with *The car was being driven by a tall···* glasses who was *driving* the car. We *followed* the black car and it stopped *The black car was followed and it ····.* outside the City Bank. Then we *noticed* that the two men were wearing *masks were being worn by the two men* masks. The two men *entered* the bank and at this point we *called* the officers who were waiting in the bank *were called* and they *sounded* the alarm. We ran into the bank and *arrested* the two men and *put* handcuffs on them. Then we put them in the car and we *took* them to the police station. They *appeared* in court last week and the judge *sentenced* them to six months in jail for attempted bank robbery.

36 Now complete this report about a "reactions to crime" survey by writing the verb in parentheses in the correct form.

Over 500 people (**a.** interview) *were interviewed* in the survey conducted by the Society for the Prevention of Crime. It (**b.** find) *was found* that most people do keep their doors locked, but in rural areas many doors (**c.** keep) *are kept* open. It (**d.** hope) *is hoped* that by making crime prevention a priority, more alarms (**e.** install) *will been installed* in houses. The full report on the survey (**f.** publish) *will been published* this month in *Crime Prevention* magazine.

Prevent

37 A puzzle Put the paragraphs in order to tell a story.

a But then, just after he had walked past a house, he heard the sound of raised voices, and then the sound of someone shouting out, "Don't shoot me, John! Don't shoot!" This was the kind of thing that he was trained for so he turned back, but before he could get to the house he heard a gunshot. ③

b Without a second's thought, the policeman arrested the priest and charged him with murder. ⑤

c One summer evening, many years ago, a policeman was walking through the village where he had just been sent. He was looking forward to getting to know the various people who lived there. So far he knew none of their names. ①

d He realized something terrible had happened so he ran into the house. In the living room, he found himself face to face with a lawyer, a priest and an engineer. They were all standing over a dead body. ④

e He was whistling happily as he walked along. He could hear a car in the distance, and somewhere, someone was listening to the 6 o'clock news on the radio. ②

In pairs Did the policeman arrest the right person? How do you know? Retell the story as a news item. How many active and passive verbs do you need?

Writing: peer review

38 Copy and check the table to show if you agree with what other students say.

	Agree	Disagree
I like to work by myself. I can find what I need in the dictionary.		
My classmates know things that I don't know and I know things that they don't know.		
Sometimes I learn wrong things from my classmates.		
My classmates sometimes show me mistakes in my writing that I didn't see.		

Compare your answers in groups.

39 Read this letter written by Juan Manuel, a student, and correct the mistakes in it. The parts which have the mistakes are highlighted in blue.

The Crime Page

Do you know of any famous or unusual crimes? We'd love to hear about them. Send the facts to famouscrimes@thisweek.com. If we publish your story, we'll send you a year's free subscription to our magazine.

Dear Editor,

I want ~~to~~ tell you about a famous crime. This crime ~~was~~ happen~~ed~~ in my hometown of Guadalajara five years ago. A little boy was kidnap~~ped~~. People ~~was~~ were sure it was the family driver who ~~did take~~ had taken the boy and the father ~~get~~ had gotten mad and fired the driver. But the mother of the boy knew he couldn't ~~had~~ have done it. She trusted the driver. Then, su~~d~~denly, the father disappeared. Nobody knew where he ~~did go~~ had gone. The police looked for ~~the~~ man and they found him at the airport. He was trying ~~to~~ leave the country with the boy. The police gave the boy back to his mother and the father went to ~~the~~ jail.

Juan Manuel Alvarez

Compare your work with a partner to see if you made the same corrections.

40 Read Juan Manuel's writing again. Copy and complete this form about it.

Name of writer: Juan Manuel Alvarez	
Checked by:	
a Is the writing interesting?	Yes / Not sure / No, not really
b Does the writing contain enough information?	Yes / Not sure / No, not really
c I think the writing could be improved by: • •	

41 Write about one of the following topics (after making notes individually or in groups).

- a famous crime
- a crime that went wrong
- an imaginary crime
- your favorite crime film or story

Swap papers with a partner. Use the questions from Activity 40 to comment on your partner's writing.

Review

42 Read the following newspaper crime report. Put the verb in parentheses into the correct form of the active voice or passive voice. You can look at Activities 33–36 for help.

At Westchester County Court today, a notorious local car thief (**a.** sentence) *was sentenced* to a year in jail. Police officer Banks told the court that he (**b.** receive) *was received* a phone call on May 14 this year saying that a car (**c.** steal) *had been stolen*. About two hours later, the officer (**d.** alert) *was alerted* that the car (**e.** find) *had been found*. The car (**f.** immediately—claim) *was immediately claimed* by the owner and the police officer (**g.** accompany) *accompanied* Kevin Bryant, the owner, to pick up the car. On arriving, it (**h.** discover) *was discovered* that the radio (**i.** steal) *had been stolen* and the seats (**j.** vandalize) *had been vandalized*. Before the car (**k.** abandon) *was abandoned*, the thief (**l.** drive) *had been driving* it for about two hours. The fingerprints of the thief (**m.** find) *were found* all over the steering wheel and the thief (**n.** identify) *was identified* quickly _____ as Martin Merton, who (**o.** know) *was known* to the police. Mr. Merton (**p.** arrest) *was arrested* and the radio (**q.** find) *was found* in his possession. At the trial today, he (**r.** plead) *pleaded* guilty to auto theft and the judge (**s.** sentence) *sentenced* him to 12 months in prison. Merton (**t.** not expect) *was not expected* to appeal the sentence.

43 Imagine you are a reporter. Read these notes about a trial that you observed and write the report for the newspaper.

Roger Bartlett and Simone Rogers (19 years old)

72-year-old lady—Mrs. Edna Brooks

Feb 28 last year—Bartlett and Rogers broke into her home (she was asleep)

stole some money and her TV set and DVD player

one of Mrs. Brooks' grandchildren (Tom Brooks) studies with Bartlett and Rogers and heard them talking about the robbery in the cafeteria

Tom called the police—they went to Bartlett's house and found the stolen goods

judge ordered the young people (who seemed very sorry) to pay a fine and to do community service

Review: vocabulary

Word List

appeal	roaring
armored car	shoplifting
arson	thief
assassin	tight
attempted	to burgle
(crime)	to catapult
cleared	to endorse
embezzlement	to giggle
escape route	to hack (into a
euphoria	computer)
getaway	to mug
handpicked	to prosecute
kidnapper	to rob
murder	to shift
paranoia	to stare
pickpocket	

Word Plus

beyond his wildest dreams
(his) luck was about to change
in the course of
nothing went right for (him)
to admit to something
to arrest someone / be arrested
  for something
to be wanted for something
to charge / be charged with
  something
to confess to something
to convict / be convicted of
  something
to evade taxes
to find someone guilty /
  be found guilty of something
to have nothing to lose
to make a mess of something
to make matters worse
to make the most of something
to put someone in touch with
  somebody
to sentence someone /
  be sentenced to something
to suspect someone /
  be suspected of something
to swear someone to secrecy
with his pulse quickening
without a hitch

44 In pairs Find five words or expressions that you like or you think are really useful. Explain why you like the words or think they are useful to your partner.

Example: STUDENT A: I think "without a hitch" is a useful expression, because it's a way to describe something that went well without always saying "it was no problem." For example, if someone says to me, "How was the meeting at work today?," I can say "it went without a hitch."

●●● Pronunciation

45 Listen to Track 71 and find the words in the Word List. How many letters are "silent"? Which letters can't you hear in the speakers' voices?

Are these letters always silent? Listen to Track 72 and hear two different speakers say the same words.

46 Find two words from the Word List and two words from Word Plus that you like the sound of best (don't worry about the meaning). Compare your words with other students. Have you chosen the same ones?

47 What's the word? Choose a word or expression from the Word List or Word Plus. Make a definition which does not include the word or expression itself. Read your definition or explanation to your partner, who must try to guess what the word or expression is. You can ask questions and explain the expression more, but don't use the word itself.

Example: STUDENT A: This expression means "you do a thing badly."
STUDENT B: You mean like you play basketball badly?
STUDENT A: No, like the one time you make a mistake and do something badly.
STUDENT B: Is it "to make a mess of something"?
STUDENT A: Yes, that's right.

144 unit thirteen

UNIT 14
Stories from the heart

→ direct and indirect speech
→ poetic effect
→ expressing likes and dislikes

Reading: stories in poems

1 **In groups** How do you feel about poetry? Find two things that everybody enjoys reading or writing *more* than poetry and two things that everybody enjoys reading or writing *less* than poetry.

2 Look at the three titles of poems. *Don't* look at the poems on the right yet. What words would you expect to see / hear in each poem?

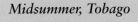

Midsummer, Tobago

Derek Walcott

Like a Beacon

Grace Nichols

Handbag

Ruth Fainlight

3 Listen to the poems being read on Track 73. Do you hear any of your words?

Now uncover the poems on the right and read them.

Midsummer, Tobago
Broad sun-stoned beaches.

White heat.
A green river.

A bridge,
scorched yellow palms

from the summer-sleeping house
drowsing through August.

Days I have held,
days I have lost,

days that outgrow, like daughters,
my harbouring arms.

Derek Walcott

Like a Beacon
In London
every now and then
I get this craving
for my mother's food
I leave art galleries
in search of plantains
saltfish / sweet potatoes

I need this touch of home
swinging my bag
like a beacon
against the cold

Grace Nichols

Handbag
My mother's old leather handbag,
crowded with letters she carried
all through the war. The smell
of my mother's handbag: mints
and lipstick and Coty powder.
The look of those letters, softened
and worn at the edges, opened,
read, and refolded so often.
Letters from my father. Odour
of leather and powder, which ever
since then has meant womanliness,
and love, and anguish, and war.

Ruth Fainlight

4 **In groups** Find at least two similarities and two differences between the three poems on page 145. What are they about? What feelings are the writers expressing?

5 Choose one of the boxes and ask another student to answer the questions you find there about the poems on page145.

Midsummer, Tobago	*Like a Beacon*	*Handbag*
a Explain the meaning of the following words and expressions. 1 broad 2 scorched 3 summer-sleeping house 4 drowsing 5 outgrow 6 harbouring **b** Explain how to get to the house from the beach, what the days are like and how Derek Walcott uses (and develops) the idea of "days I have held …"	**a** Explain the meaning of the following words and expressions. 1 craving 2 plantains 3 touch of home 4 swinging 5 beacon **b** Explain what it is the poet misses and how she compensates for this feeling.	**a** Explain the meaning of the following words and phrases. 1 crowded with letters 2 lipstick 3 powder 4 softened and worn at the edges 5 odour 6 womanliness 7 anguish **b** Explain what was in the handbag, who wrote the letters and what happened to them. Explain, in your own words, what the handbag makes the writer think of.

Now change pairs and answer questions about a different poem.

Change pairs again and ask or answer questions about the third poem.

6 Without looking back at the poems, tell their stories in your own words.

Vocabulary: poetic effect

7 Look at the evidence from the poems on page 145 and answer the questions.

The evidence	Broad sun-stoned beaches. White heat. A green river. scorched yellow palms the summer-sleeping house My mother's old leather handbag, crowded with letters The look of those letters, softened and worn at the edges
The questions	a Which "sentences" do not have verbs? What is the effect of this? b Which sentences or phrases have more than one adjective before the noun? c Which adjectives are formed by joining words together? What is the effect of this? d What grammar form is used <u>after</u> the nouns to describe them?

Style note: Poets have the freedom to make the kind of compound adjectives (like *sun-stoned* and *summer-sleeping*) which we don't often use in speaking—until they become widely used and accepted.

8 Use the words in italics to make compound adjectives.

a A book with used pages like the *ears of old dogs* is a ....*dog-eared*.... book.

b A flower that *smells foul* is a ....*foul-smelling*.... flower.

c A boy with *brown hair* is a .... boy.

d A man who has *fair skin* is a .... man.

e A person who *loves fun* is a .... person.

f A pop star who *looks good* is a .... pop star.

g A rose that *smells sweet* is a .... rose.

h A suit that is *made* (al)*ready* is a .... suit.

i A woman who is "*built well*" (e.g. who has a big strong body) is a .... woman.

j An egg that has been *boiled* but is still *soft* is a .... egg.

k An egg that has been *boiled* until it is *hard* is a .... egg.

l An experience which *blows* your *mind* is a .... experience.

9 Use past participles to describe the nouns in blue.

a Someone picked a rose and gave it as a sign of love.

a rose, picked and given as a sign of love

b A criminal hatched (= made) a plan.

c The neighbors' noise finally drove the woman crazy.

d Someone fired a shot in anger.

e Someone wrote a letter in anger.

f Jealousy destroyed the actor's career.

g Someone painted a picture in a fit of creativity.

10 Poetic effect is often created by putting adjectives and nouns together in unexpected ways. Sometimes the words contradict each other; sometimes, together, they create a striking effect.

Examples: *white heat; unkind love; black summer*

What strong and / or contradictory images can you make by putting adjectives and nouns together? (You can use the words in the boxes or come up with your own ideas.)

Adjectives
black   blue   blunt   cold   dangerous
desperate   difficult   easy   empty
full   happy   hot   kind   red   sad
selfish   sharp   white

Nouns
affection   animal   beach   despair
ghost   hatred   house   letter
love   noise   summer   victory

11 Writing Choose one of the topics in the box below.

a favorite place   a good friend   home
the contents of someone's pockets

a Write down as many words as you can think of related to the topic.

b Write at least one phrase or sentence for each of the following categories (you can use your own phrases or phrases from Activities 8–10).

• a compound adjective followed by a noun, e.g. *sun-stoned beaches, summer-sleeping house*

• a noun followed by past participles, e.g. *a handbag, crowded with letters; letters, softened and worn at the edges*

• strong / contradictory images formed by an adjective and a noun, e.g. *white heat, hateful love*

c Use your examples to write your own poem on the topic of your choice.

Listening: storyteller

12 Look at this picture. Where do you think this woman is from? What do you think she does?

Listen to Track 74. Were you right?

13 Listen to Track 74 again. In your own words, say what Jan thinks stories are for. Do you agree?

14 Read through the following questions and then say what you think Jan will say in Track 75.

a What did Jan do at the age of 19?
b Why did she go to a group called *Common Law*?
c What three things did she have to do for her audition?
d What story did she tell?
e Where did she get the song and game from?
f How did she learn it?
g What happened when she told it?

Listen to Track 75. Were you right? Answer the questions.

15 Listen to Track 76 and answer these questions.

Who or what:
a ... is *The Spitz*?
b ... has a reputation for being late?
c ... plays the drums?
d ... said he was tired and had to lie down?
e ... explained the stories five minutes before the show?
f ... was on the edge of creativity?
g ... weren't very enthusiastic at first?
h ... spoke to the audience to encourage them?
i ... had a fantastic experience?

Tell the story of Jan and Crispin's evening in your own words.

Language in chunks

16 Look at the Audioscript for Tracks 74–76 and find Jan's phrases (a–i). What do the phrases in italics mean? What was she talking about in each case?

a *a tried and tested theory*
b *Does that make sense?*
c something ... *I can't put my finger on*
d the opportunity *to delve deep* into your own consciousness
e I couldn't learn the whole story *word for word*
f from that moment *I haven't looked back*
g I kind of *went through the sequence of events*
h we were *on the edge of* our creativity
i I'm slightly *off kilter*

17 Translate the phrases into your language so that they mean the same as they do in the context that Jan used them.

18 Noticing language Look at these phrases from Tracks 74–76 which contain direct and indirect speech. Find examples of things people actually said (direct speech) and of people reporting what other people said (indirect speech).

a I said oh oh where can you earn some decent money then and she said oh as a storyteller so I said what's that and she said oh I'm a storyteller I think you'd be really good, I think you should come along to *Common Law* and you should audition.
b ... and he was like Oh God my brain and the traffic's awful and just let me lie here for five minutes, and I said we're on in five minutes and he said er yeah just give me five minutes ...
c I asked the audience to join in and sing it and they weren't giving us themselves and I said to them look you know, he was late, he was late ...

19 Storytelling When Jan told the story of *Why cat and dog are no longer friends*, she "read that and read it and read it and read it and read it," before she told her story. Choose one of the following topics and then make notes about it. Think of ways to make it as exciting or funny as possible. Then write out a version as correctly as you can. Read it and read it and read it.

Without looking back at what you have written, tell your story to a neighbor. Now tell it to another neighbor, practice it and then tell it to the whole class.

Topics:
- my most embarrassing moment
- my favorite story from a book, TV or the movies
- my most memorable injury
- why I was late
- any other story from your life

Grammar: direct and indirect speech

20 How would you report the following if (a) you were there and you were telling someone about it on your cell phone, (b) if it happened yesterday and (c) if it happened yesterday and you wanted to give it maximum dramatic effect (especially if you were writing about it)? Use **14A–14C in the Mini-grammar** to help you.

she had heard

she had been going

Jane — "I'm going to read my latest poem."

Carlos — "Would you like me to tell you a story?"

Renée — "I've heard their stories so many times before."

Danni — "I was going to paint a new picture, but I haven't got any ideas."

Example: Jane

(a) She says she's going to read her latest poem.

(b) She said she was going to read her latest poem.

(c) "I'm going to read my latest poem," Jane said.

21 Match the verb in the left-hand column with what was actually said in the right-hand column.

Paul — "This picture is telling us a story."

that picture was telling us a story

insist	m	a	"Let's go to the gallery."
accept	g	b	"If I were you, I'd stay at home."
apologize	h	c	"You just press the power button and put in a CD, then press play."
deny	e	d	"Come here right now!"
refuse	f	e	"I did not steal the painting."
compliment	L	f	"No, I won't do your homework."
suggest	a	g	"Sure. I'll come to the movies with you."
forgive	n	h	"I'm so sorry for losing your pen."
complain	K	i	"It must have been George who broke the window."
advise	b	j	"I'm the best artist in the world."
order	d	k	"This painting is much too expensive."
boast	J	l	"Your sculpture is beautiful."
agree	o	m	"You must come with me. You'll really enjoy it."
explain	C	n	"Forget about spilling the paint. It really doesn't matter."
blame	i	o	"You're absolutely right. That's a great poem."

Now report what was said. Use *he* or *she*.

Example: m He insisted that I went with him. He said I'd really enjoy it.

Look at 14E in the Mini-grammar. Do you want to change your answers?

22 In pairs Look at this picture of people at an art exhibition opening. What did the people say? Use **14B–14F in the Mini-grammar** to help you.

a I hate coming to art exhibition openings. They're so boring.

b You're right. They're so tedious.

c Why don't we go and get a drink?

d This artist lived in Paris for five years.

e Was he trying a new technique when he did this?

f Don't bother coming to this – it's awful.

g I've told you before, Charlie, don't touch the paintings!

h This looks like a child painted it.

i I love the use of color in your work.

j I'm experimenting with unconventional art.

Example: The artist explained that he was experimenting with unconventional art. The young woman told the artist that ...

● ● ● Pronunciation: strong and weak forms (*was* and *were*)

23 Listen to Track 77 and read the sentences *a–h*. Copy the sentences and questions. Circle *was* or *were* if it is unstressed and underline it if it is stressed.

a Were Pedro and Amanda at home yesterday?—Yes, they <u>were.</u>
b Where (were) you when I called?
c They said they were going to the gallery.
d He told me he was doing a new piece for the exhibition.
e Was Marlene at the exhibition?—Yes, she was.
f She asked me if we were taking any art classes.
g They were at the gallery. I saw them there.
h I told her that I was taking a sculpture class.

Read the sentences using the same stress as the speakers on Track 77.

24 Change these sentences to indirect speech and say them using the correct pronunciation of *was* / *were*.

a "I'm learning to paint," said Fumiko.
b Brian said, "We're going to the Picasso exhibition!"
c Maria asked, "Are you enjoying the museum tour?"
d Wilton and Gaby said, "We're very tired."

25 Which sentence in each pair is an example of informal speech? Which is more like formal writing / grammar?

a 1 He's like "that's cool" and I'm like "well yeah!"
2 He said that it was cool and I replied that it was.

b 1 So she goes "that's ridiculous" and then goes red in the face.
2 She said that it was ridiculous and then she went red in the face.

c 1 A man asked me where I was going and I asked him why he wanted to know.
2 So this guy he asks me where I'm going and I'm like "why do you want to know?"

d 1 He was about to lose control and so I suggested that he calmed down and he thanked me.
2 So he's like about to completely lose it and I'm like "calm down, OK" and he's like "thanks, I needed that."

e 1 We say "hello" and they go "what are you guys doing here?" and we go "well you invited us didn't you?"
2 We said "hello" and they asked us what we were doing there. We said that they'd asked us.

26 Are these notes referring to *be like*, to *go*, or both?

a used for reporting conversations
b informal and used when talking
c used mainly in British English
d an informal phrase, used especially in American English
e can describe a situation too
f can describe an action too

Speaking: reading aloud

27 Choose the poem (*Small Boy*) or the story extract from *Space Station 5* and complete the tasks which follow them.

Small Boy

He picked up a pebble
and threw it in the sea

And another and another
He couldn't stop

He wasn't trying to fill the sea
He wasn't trying to empty the beach

He was just throwing away
nothing else but

Like a kitten playing
he was practising for the future

when there'll be so many things
he'll want to throw away

if only his fingers will unclench
and let them go

Norman MacCaig

a Copy the poem.
b Listen to Track 78 and write in the commas and full stops in the poem, depending on how the speaker reads it.
c Check your version in the Audioscript.
d Listen to Track 78 again and read along with the speaker.
e Practice reading the poem.
f Read it to other students in the class who have worked on Track 79.

From *Space Station 5*

They had been up here for five years Five years for five people cut off from Earth since World War IV True the Moonshuttle came every six months with a supply of food but it was pilotless They had not been able to make contact with Moonbase for two years Cathy said it was weird

You say that three times a day Rosie answered

Well it's true It's weird and I don't think I can stand it much longer

Oh for Jupiter's sake shut up Go and play eight-dimensional death-chess and leave me alone You drive me crazy!

You shouldn't have spoken to me like that Cathy said quietly and left the cabin The door hissed behind her

a Copy the extract.
b Listen to Track 79 and write in commas, period points and inverted commas, depending on how the speaker reads it.
c Check your version in the Audioscript.
d Listen to Track 79 again and read along with the speaker.
e Practice reading the extract.
f Read it to other students in the class who have worked on Track 78.

Functional language: expressing likes and dislikes

28 Look at the picture. Listen to Track 80 and write the words that you hear in the spaces.

A: Look at that sculpture!
B: What do you think of it?
A: I don't like it (**a**) .... It (**b**) ....
B: Oh really? I (**c**) .... it very much.
A: I was talking to my friend. She said she (**d**) .... either.
B: Did she really? That's too bad.
A: Who's the artist?
B: It's Philip Martin.
A: Oh that explains it. I (**e**) .... his work. I find it too abstract. His sculptures aren't very convincing.
B: You really think so? I (**f**) .... his work a lot.
A: Well, we all have our different tastes, but all my friends tonight said his piece was (**g**) .... !
B: Did they?
A: Yes, they did. Anyway, nice to meet you. What's your name?
B: Ummm. Philip Martin. Nice to meet you too.

29 Expressing likes and dislikes Say whether the following words and phrases are (a) positive comments, (b) opinions that have changed over time, or (c) negative comments.

Dali is *the best*.
I've *grown to like* Yoko Ono's work.
I *adore* surrealist paintings.
I *can't stand* (looking at) watercolors.
I *don't have anything against* modern art.
I *don't mind* sculpture.
I *loathe* modern art.
I'm *crazy about* Picasso.
I *really like* modern art.
I've really *gone off* Michaelangelo.
I've *taken a liking* to the old masters.
Impressionism *doesn't do much for me*.
There's *nothing worse than* bad art.
You *can't beat* Van Gogh.
I'm *warming to* Frida Kahlo's painting.

a Which words are strongest in meaning?
b Which words suggest that something is taking or has taken quite a long time?
c Can you replace the words in red with words which have a similar meaning?
d Add more words to the categories (*a*, *b* and *c*) if you can.

30 Look at these three works of art and describe what you like and dislike about them. Imagine you are (a) talking to the artist, then (b) talking to a friend.

Example: STUDENT A: I like Anish Kapoor's sculpture very much. You can't beat simple elegant shapes.

STUDENT B: Oh really? I can't stand abstract sculptures.

31 In groups Answer these questions.

a Do you think it is good to always give your true opinion? Explain your answer.
b Have you ever said that you liked or didn't like something and then regretted it? Are you prepared to tell your partner about it?

32 Questionnaires Choose one of the following four topics and make a list of things you know about it. Make a questionnaire about what people like and don't like. Go around the class asking the other students about their likes and dislikes.

Topics:
• art • music • food • sport

Turning the world inside out
Anish Kapoor

Mother and child divided
Damien Hirst

My bed
Tracey Emin

Writing: movies and music

33 Listen to the two pieces of music on Track 81. As you listen, write down what scene from a movie they might come from.

34 In pairs Look at these opening scenes from two different movies. What music would you expect to hear as you watched them?

Film A:

SCENE 1

Exterior. Night. Ten years ago. A small side street in a city. Pools of light from street lights. We see a figure walk through one of the light pools toward us. He or she (it is difficult to tell) has a hat pulled down over the side of their face. The camera follows the figure as he or she walks past us.

SCENE 2

Interior. The same night. A smoky café. Crowded. People sit at tables, talking furtively. They're all waiting for something perhaps. Edgy. The camera pans over the tables until it gets to the door. Which opens. Silhouetted in the street lamp from outside stands the figure we saw in Scene 1.

Film B:

SCENE 1

Exterior. Bright sunlight. Aerial shot. We see blue sky and then the camera pans down to glittering surf and a long tropical beach. White sand stretching for miles. Palm trees. The camera continues along the beach and we become aware of a figure running towards us, a man, dressed in shorts and a T-shirt. No shoes. As the camera passes him, we see his face. He is clearly running as fast as he can.

SCENE 2

Exterior. We are behind the runner. We can hear his heavy breathing. He looks over his shoulder back towards the camera as if he is expecting to see something. As he does so, he seems to trip and pitches forward into the sand.

What kind of movies do you think the scenes come from? What will happen next?

35 In the scenes in Activity 34, what do you understand by the following words or phrases?

    a exterior
    b pools of light
    c figure
    d interior
    e pans
    f aerial shot
    g glittering surf
    h heavy breathing
    i pitches forward

Some of the "sentences" in the descriptions do not have verbs. Why is that? Is it acceptable here? When would it not be acceptable?

36 Choose one of the following movie categories.

| adventure | comedy |
| historical | horror | romance |

Imagine the first scene of your movie. Say:

a … where the scene takes place.
b … when the scene takes place (present day or historical, time of day, etc.).
c … who is in the scene or comes into it.
d … what the mood is.

37 Write the scene description in the same way as the examples in Activity 34. Say what music you would use in the background.

Review: grammar and functional language

38 Rewrite the following story using direct speech (the speakers' actual words). You can look at Activities 20–22 for help.

How they met

The artist and the gallery owner

At an exhibition of her paintings, a local newspaper reporter was just complimenting the artist, Tina Ferranti, on her use of color when a young man (Graeme Wright) walked up to one of her self-portraits with a large bucket full of black paint. The reporter saw him and ordered him to put the bucket down, but the young man refused. The reporter advised him to do what he was told and when the man boasted that he wasn't afraid of anyone, the reporter insisted that he put down the bucket because otherwise the police would be called.

Reluctantly, the young man agreed and he tried to deny that he had intended to damage the painting. When Tina Ferranti suggested that people didn't usually approach paintings carrying buckets of black paint, Graeme Wright finally admitted that he had been intending to destroy one of her paintings because he wanted to get publicity for his own art show at a little gallery further down the street. Ms. Ferranti forgave him and accepted his invitation to the show at his gallery.

Example: REPORTER: I really like your use of color.

39 Complete the blanks in the following sentences with as many words or phrases as possible. You can look at Activities 28–32 for help.

a I .... the sound of the cello. It's my favorite instrument.
b I .... the music they play in shopping malls. It really gets on my nerves.
c I'm .... Paul Auster's novels. I just love them.
d I ....the stories in this book. I didn't like them at first, but now—well I'm an enthusiast.
e I've .... Eminem. He was OK for a while, but not any more.
f Classical music .... I prefer something with a bit more beat.
g There's .... people who forget the punchline of a joke.
h I've .... poetry. I used to think I couldn't understand it, but I've suddenly realized how good some of it is.

Are any of these opinions similar to your own?

40 Conversation writing In pairs complete the following tasks.

a Fill in the blanks to create your own scene

A/an (*choose a profession*) .... meets a/an (*choose another profession*) .... at (*choose a location*) .... and they talk about (*choose a topic*) ....

b Write the conversation, using phrases from Activities 28–32.
c Act out your conversation for the class.
d Choose two of the conversations. How would the class report them?

Review: vocabulary

Word List

aerial shot	interior
anguish	lipstick
beacon	mind-blowing
broad	odor
brown-haired	plantain
craving	pools (of light)
crowded with	powder
dog-eared	ready-made
drowsing	scorched
edge	soft-boiled
exterior	softened
fair-haired	surf
figure	sweet-smelling
foul-smelling	swinging
fun-loving	to outgrow
glittering	to pan
good-looking	well built
harboring	womanliness
hard-boiled	worn

Word Plus

a tried and tested theory
heavy breathing
"I can't put my finger on" *
off kilter
on the edge of something
to delve deep into your own
   consciousness
to go through a sequence of
   events
to learn something word for
   word
to make sense (of something)
to not look back
to pitch forward
touch of home

*Conversational phrases.

41 Word auction Decide which words you want to "buy." Make a list. Don't tell anyone else.

You have $500. Bid against other students for words you really want. How many words can you buy (no one may bid more than $200 for any one word)?

●●● Pronunciation

42 Make a list of words from the Word List and Word Plus which you find difficult to pronounce. Compare your list with a partner.

a How many words are the same in both lists?
b What is difficult about the words you have selected: sounds or stress?
c What's the best way of improving your pronunciation of the "difficult" words?

43 The diphthong challenge Copy the table and find words in the Word List for all the sounds (except the ones in yellow).

Check your answers by listening to Track 82.

/eɪ/ – say	/aɪ/ – sigh	/ɔɪ/ – joy	/oʊ/ – boat	/aʊ/ – cow

/ɪr/– here	/ɛr/ – bear	/yʊ/ – pure	/uə/ – steward

Who can add the most words to all the parts of the table in the shortest possible time?

And, in the end…

44 Now that you have finished *Just Right Upper Intermediate*, copy and complete the table about your progress.

	How I have improved since I started *Just Right Upper Intermediate*	Things that still cause me difficulty	What I intend to do in the future to improve
Vocabulary			
Grammar			
Pronunciation			
Listening			
Speaking			
Reading			
Writing			

Activity Bank

1 [Unit 3]

Find five similarities and five differences between your picture and your partner's—but without looking at your partner's picture.

Now turn back to Activity 38 on page 36.

2 [Unit 3]

I'd like to start this composition by saying that I have enjoyed going to zoos and looking at animals in the past. It's always very exciting to look at creatures you have never seen before. <u>However,</u> many people say that zoos are not pleasant places <u>and furthermore</u> the animals are in cages and don't have their freedom. <u>Moreover,</u> if you deny animals their freedom and keep them in enclosed spaces they become ill and psychologically disturbed.

   <u>On the other hand,</u> people who support zoos say that the animals are well looked after and fed, something that does not always happen to them in the wild. <u>Not only that, but </u>zoos have started many breeding programs to save endangered species. <u>Therefore,</u> many animals that might have become extinct are now still alive.

   If I had thought about it when I first went to see a zoo, I would have been unhappy about animals in cages, and I now think that is wrong. <u>In contrast,</u> some of the wildlife parks in various countries in the world give animals both security and freedom. <u>As a result,</u> those are the ones I approve of.

   <u>In conclusion,</u> I think that zoos are often cruel places. Proper wildlife parks are a better way for man to preserve species while, at the same time, giving us all a chance to see animals in a natural habitat. <u>Nevertheless,</u> I am sure many families will still take their young children to visit zoos.

3 [Unit 5]

a Read the extract.

Are there anger types?

Psychologists have suggested a number of different personality types to explain why some people get angrier than others.

- *Absolutist thinkers* have a set of expectations and values which they require other people and events to conform to. They see the world in black and white, with no shades of gray, and if others don't give way to their demands, they become angry.
- *Ambitious anger* is the result of a personality that is driven, wants success and achievement very badly, and gets furious with anyone who gets in their way. Such people are ruthless and fixated, and anger is one of their weapons either consciously or subconsciously.

How angry are you? Personality questionnaire
Anger management – a growing trend

- *Chronically angry* people have a deep-seated problem but cannot respond to the source of their unhappiness so they take their anger out on others. This kind of anger might be the result of a bad marriage or the death of a parent. "The problem builds up over a long time, the person feels trapped and takes every opportunity to get at a weaker person."
- *Situationally aggressive* people, in contrast, get angry when they get stressed by a particular situation and can't cope with it. When that situation goes away, so does their anger.

b Copy and complete the chart, using your own words.

Type	Description of type

c What's your reaction to the information here? Do you agree with it?

Now turn back to Activity 3 on page 51.

4 [Unit 5]

Suspect
- You are seventeen-and-a-half years old.
- You did steal the car, of course, but you don't think the police have any proof since you set the car on fire when you had finished having a good time with it.
- You want to know where the police got their information. When they ask you what you were doing last night, you'll say you were with a friend.
- You enjoy having fun by being disrespectful to the police. You get angry when the lawyer tries to stop you from doing this.

Now turn back to Activity 23 on page 55.

5 [Unit 5]

Police officer 1
- You and your police colleague are in charge of the interview. You decide who says what and when.
- The suspect was seen taking the car by two other criminals, Ben and Joey, but you can't tell the suspect this, because that would put Ben and Joey in danger. So the only thing you can do is keep asking the suspect different questions about what he or she was doing last night in the hope that he or she will get confused and in the end confess.
- You have had enough of kids taking cars for fun. It makes you really mad. Anyway, you want to get home. Unfortunately, you lose your temper rather quickly. You get especially irritated when your partner tells you to calm down.

Now turn back to Activity 23 on page 55.

Now turn back to Activity 23 on page 55.

6 [Unit 8]

Read your first lines. Can B give you answers which are funny?

First lines of jokes
a Waiter! There's a fly in my soup!
b What's this fly doing in my soup?
c Hey watch out! Your thumb's in my soup!
d Do you serve crabs here?
e This egg is bad!
f Waiter! Where's my honey?
g Did you hear about the new restaurant on the moon?

Listen to B's first lines. Can you give answers which are funny?

Second lines of jokes
1 That must be the tea. The coffee tastes like glue.
2 Don't worry sir, it won't shrink.
3 No, sir, I always walk this way.
4 No, sir, that's a cockroach. The fly is on your steak.
5 Accidentally! I moved the lettuce and there it was.
6 About three or four inches, if you're lucky.
7 That's your sausage, sir.

7 [Unit 9]

Make sure you know the answers to the following questions about your text.

a What two disadvantages did Diana Kayle find for blond job applicants?
b What might be the connection between blond hair, youth and the bias against blond women?

Recent research conducted by, among others, Diana Kayle at California State University reveals—amazingly—that while being blond may boost your social life, it can also damage your career prospects. Blond females are rejected for jobs more often than equally qualified brunettes. And where blonds and brunettes are given similar jobs, the darker-haired applicants are awarded higher salaries. It seems hardly credible that such changeable features as hair color could so influence recruitment decisions, but the research findings are unequivocal.

So what lies behind this remarkable bias? One theory is that blond hair gives the appearance of youth. This is because people have lighter hair and skin when they are children than when they get older. So blond people are treated (unconsciously—we are not aware we are doing it) as if they were less intelligent, more naïve, more vulnerable, less mature, and less capable.

Find answers to the following questions from either Student B or Student C.

a   What was Brian Bates' experiment and what did it show?
b   What do men think of blonds?

Now turn back to Activity 17 on page 93.

8 [Unit 5]

a   Read the extract.

Differences Between Men and Women

Studies have long shown differences between the way men and women react, how they use anger and how anger affects them. However, this may be changing as society changes.

We do know that by the age of three, boys show three times as much aggressive behavior as girls do and that high levels of testosterone (the male hormone) have been linked with increased anger patterns. So it does seem that men, in general, are "angrier" than women.

Anger is also more acceptable in men than in women. Those women who show anger are often thought of as mad, bad, crazy and emotional. Studies suggest that many women in such situations suppress their anger or channel it in other ways such as eating disorders, for example. It is now thought that suppressing anger is extremely bad for people, especially women.

However, in the eyes of many researchers, the difference between the sexes may not be nearly as significant as changes in society which have led to an erosion of social skills in both men and women. In the modern world, we spend more time on the Internet or looking at the TV and not enough time talking to each other. We expect everything to happen quickly and as a result, we become frustrated very easily.

Women against anger
Shouting in the age of IT
Psychology Today

b   Copy and complete the chart with notes in your own words.

Topic	Your notes
Anger in men and women	
The acceptability of anger	
The modern world	

c   Do you agree with what you have read?

Now turn back to Activity 4 on page 51.

9 [Unit 5]

Police officer 2

- You and your police colleague are in charge of the interview. You decide who says what and when.

- The suspect was seen taking the car by two other criminals, Ben and Joey, but you can't tell the suspect this, because that would put Ben and Joey in danger. So the only thing you can do is keep asking the suspect different questions about what he or she was doing last night in the hope that he or she will get confused and in the end confess.

- You like your partner but you get really worried when he / she starts getting angry since this doesn't help in a police interview situation, so you try and calm your partner down. The only thing that makes you angry is when a suspect's mother or father tries to say that their child is not really to blame.

Now turn back to Activity 23 on page 55.

10 [Unit 7]

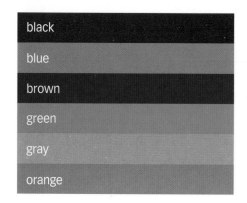
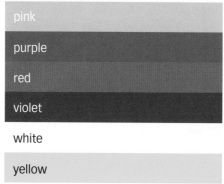

black	pink
blue	purple
brown	red
green	violet
gray	white
orange	yellow

11 [Unit 8]

Read your first lines. Can A give you answers which are funny?

First lines of jokes

a   Waiter! There's a fly in my soup!
b   Do you have frogs' legs?
c   Waiter! There's a worm on my plate.
d   How did you find your steak, sir?
e   Waiter! Your tie is in my soup.
f   This coffee tastes like soap!
g   How long will my sausages be?

Listen to A's first lines. Can you give answers which are funny?

Second lines of jokes

1   Thanks for your concern, sir, but it's not that hot.
2   We serve *anyone* here, sir.
3   Don't blame me, sir. I only laid the table.
4   Yes—great food but no atmosphere.
5   She left last week, sir.
6   It looks like it's swimming, sir.
7   Don't worry, the spider on the bread will get it.

12 [Unit 9]

Make sure you know the answers to the following questions about your text.

a What were the business students given and what was different about the job applicants?
b What different treatment was given to blond and brunette applicants?
c Why did the business students make the decisions they did?

Brian Bates did an experiment for a BBC television program. Business students were given résumés for six job applicants. There were photographs attached. Some of the candidates had brown hair, the others were blond.

When they were asked whether the photos had affected their choices, the business students were convinced that hair color had not influenced them. "The picture for me didn't play a major part," said one. "I made a studious attempt to ignore the appearance of the applicants," said another. "I focused primarily on the résumé," insisted a third.

But the result revealed a different story. While they had appointed the blonds and the brunettes almost equally to the job, they had awarded the brunettes a higher salary.

Under close questioning, they revealed that the blond stereotype had indeed affected their judgment. "The woman with blond hair is more of a wannabe—I would think she is probably an experienced secretary or something," confessed one. "She looks like a PA rather than a middle manager," said another. "The brunette does look more like one would imagine a middle manager would look."

Find answers to the following questions from either Student A or Student C.

a What were the results of Diana Kayle's research?
b What, if any, are the differences between blue- and brown-eyed children, and what does this suggest?

Now turn back to Activity 17 on page 93.

13 [Unit 9]

Wordbank for Activity 34

a Things you might complain to the doctor about:

aches	earache, headache, neck ache, stomachache (tummy ache), toothache
swollen ...	ankle, arm, ear, elbow, finger, foot, head, heel, knee, leg, neck, nose, shoulder, stomach, throat, thumb, toe, wrist
sore ... a pain in my ...	ankle, arm, back, big toe, collarbone, ear, elbow, eye, hand, heel, index finger, knee, leg, little finger, nose, stomach, throat, thumb, toes, tooth, wrist

b **What you might hear at the dentist's:**
Because you have a *cavity*, you might need a *filling*.

c **Things you might ask for at the hairdresser's:**

(blond) highlights
a (center) parting
bangs
a trim
quite long / short at the front / back
to have your hair layered

Find out as many similarities as you can between Bill Thomas and Student A's Neil Todd.

Example: When was Neil Todd born? (one similarity)

Name: Bill Thomas
Date of birth: 10/23/75
Address: 15 Park Drive, Evanston, IL 26123

Schools / Colleges attended:	
	1996 – 1997 Columbia University
	1992 – 1996 University of Illinois
	1988 – 1992 Oak Park High School
	1986 – 1988 Oak Park Junior High School
	1980 – 1986 Oak Park Elementary School

Qualifications:

M.A. in Journalism
B.A. Liberal Arts (History Major)

Employment record (including vacation jobs):

2001 – present:	reporter for the *Daily Tribune* newspaper
1997 – 2001:	working for the *Evanston Daily News*
1994 – 1997 (Christmas vacation):	working for the Post Office sorting Christmas mail
2001 July and August:	part-time working at McDonald's

Hobbies and interests:

I'm a big baseball fan (I'm a New York Yankees fan).
I play tennis and I enjoy taking photographs.

Anything else you wish to say to support your application:

I feel that my experience equips me perfectly for the job of Features Editor at the *Times* newspaper. The work I have done for the *Daily Tribune* (see enclosed documents) is exactly the kind that your advertisement is aiming for.
Colleagues at the *Daily Tribune* will tell you that I get along well with people and enjoy the atmosphere of a busy working newspaper.

References:

James Brown	Martha Galton
Editor	Editor
Daily Tribune	Evanston Daily News
6 Canal Street	29 Beacher Lane
New York, NY 10012	Evanston, IL 26125

Now turn back to Activity 36 on page 97.

a   Read the extract.

Controlling anger

Here are some ways of dealing with anger.

Change what you expect. If you don't expect too much, you won't be too disappointed. If you are more flexible about what you want and need, you are less likely to become angry when the situation doesn't match up to your expectations.

Empathize with the other person—try and understand his or her position. Why are they behaving like that? How would you feel if you were in their shoes? Can you sympathize with their reasons for being angry? Once you see things from their perspective, your anger may be replaced by concern.

Learn how to be assertive rather than aggressive. Being able to state a point of view or hold down an argument is different from shouting at someone.

Monitor your thoughts for traces of cynicism and general discontent. Then, when they come along, you're ready for them and you can minimize their effects.

Stop the clock. When you get angry, take a deep breath and stop the thoughts that are making you that way. Think of something pleasant instead, something you like and enjoy. Your anger will gradually lessen.

Surround yourself with positive people. The more people around you show that they are calm and happier, the calmer and happier you become too.

Use your imagination, not your voice. Imagine doing something terrible to the person who is annoying you and channel all your anger into your imagination. That way, you are free to act calmly and rationally on the surface.

Anger control classes   How anger changed my life   Never angry again

b   Copy and complete the chart with notes, using your own words.

Technique	How to do it
1	
2	
3	
4	
5	
6	
7	

c   Do you think these methods of controlling anger are useful?

Now turn back to Activity 4 on page 51.

16 [Unit 5]

Lawyer
- It is your job to represent the interests of the suspect.
- You try to stop the police from asking difficult questions—and you try to stop the suspect saying too much.

Now turn back to Activity 23 on page 55.

17 [Unit 5]

Suspect's parent
- You think your child is a good person and that if he or she has got into any trouble, it isn't his / her fault. It was difficult for the suspect when the other parent was sent to prison.
- If you think the police are being unfair to your child, you should tell them so—and make sure they realize it isn't really your child's fault.

Now turn back to Activity 23 on page 55.

18 [Unit 6]

In the year 2050, I'll be living on Mars. Even though I'll be 70 years old, I'll still be young, because scientists will have found a way for us to live forever. I'll get up when my robot comes to wake me and bring me coffee in bed and my breakfast. My breakfast will be just some pills. All food on Mars will be dehydrated, because nothing will grow there. I'll "think up" (dial) my friends on Earth and on the moon on my TPP (telepathy-phone) and we'll talk while I get ready for work.

19 [Unit 9]

Make sure you know the answers to the following questions about your text.

a What is the attitude of men to blond and brunette women? Are they right?
b What is the difference between blue-eyed and brown-eyed children, according to Jerome Kagan?
c What "common biological package" might exist, according to Jerome Kagan?

Men tend to rate blonds as more feminine but less intelligent than brunettes. Studies in Ireland confirmed that men rated blond females as of significantly lower intelligence than brunettes and in America, job applicants were rated as less capable and assigned a lower salary than brunettes. In other words, blonds are seen as attractive but dumb.

Tests show, of course, that there is no difference in intelligence between blond and brunette people. But there may be some character differences: American psychologist Jerome Kagan has investigated differences in temperament between blue- and brown-eyed infants and young children. He has discovered that children with blue eyes are far more likely to be shy and inhibited than dark-eyed children. Brown-eyed children are naturally bolder. He speculates that the genes for blond hair, blue eyes and shyness may be a common biological package.

Find answers to the following questions from either Student A or Student B.

a What is the connection between blond hair and youth—and what has this got to do with perceptions of intelligence?
b How did the blond stereotype affect the judgment of the business students in Brian Bates' experiment?

Now turn back to Activity 17 on page 93.

20 [Unit 13]

Defendants

You need to prepare a good reason for why you committed the crime. You need to justify why you did it. Try to make the judge understand why you did it.

a Michael Trent

Last Friday, your wife was in a lot of pain and you could not bear to see her like that, so you broke into the drugstore to take the drug, because you could not afford to buy it. No one was hurt when you stole the medicine and you did not carry a gun.

b Maria Metcalf

You are a very quiet girl, but you want to do well at school so that you can become a doctor in the future—you would like to work with young children who are sick. You are very sorry for what you did, but you felt very bad at school when the other students made fun of you for not having new things.

c Judy Moore

You hated to see your brother do badly at school when you knew that it was because he had been sick. You decided to help him by getting the exam answers just once until he had time to catch up with his classmates. You are very sorry for what you did.

The defendants' language box

> guilty / not guilty
>
> I would like to explain why …
>
> Although I was wrong to … , I did it because …

Play your part in the trial using the information and instructions that you find here.

21 [Unit 11]

Students A and B, try to memorize all the information on the posters, tickets and schedule.

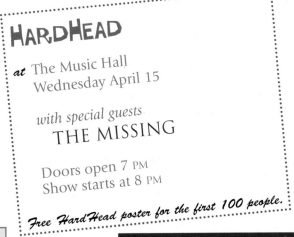

Meet the author
RUDOLPH MASTERS

at Diesel Bookstore
Thursday 7:30 PM

Rudolph Masters will be speaking about his latest book, *Time and Again*, and will be signing copies bought at the bookstore.

Arrive early to make sure you get a seat.

HARDHEAD

at The Music Hall
Wednesday April 15

with special guests
THE MISSING

Doors open 7 PM
Show starts at 8 PM

Free HardHead poster for the first 100 people.

Sunday March 5
Dep. San Francisco 18:00
Arr. Guadalajara 23:35
Meal served.
Be at the airport TWO hours before your flight.

World Cup Qualifier
Japan vs. Korea
AT: Seoul Stadium
KICK-OFF: 2:30 PM
Gates open 1 PM
No bottles or cameras allowed at the game.

a Student A, return to Activity 27 on page 117. Student B, answer A's questions.
b Now change around. Student A can look at this page. B returns to Activity 27 on page 117.

22 [Unit 13]

Judge

You must listen carefully to what the defendant, the witness and the attorneys say. At the end, you can ask questions until you decide if the defendant is guilty or innocent and what the punishment should be.

Questions to ask the defendant:
- Do you admit to the crime?
- Do you understand that what you did was wrong?
- Are you sorry for what you did?

The judge's language box

> Do you plead guilty or not guilty?
>
> I find you guilty / not guilty.
>
> I sentence you to X months / years in prison.

Conduct the trial using the information and instructions that you find here.

23 [Unit 13]

Prosecuting attorney

You must interview the defendant and the witness and try to get the defendant to admit to the crime. You want to show how bad the crime was.

Questions to ask:
- Where were you on the night / day of the crime?
- What exactly happened?
- Why did you do it?

The prosecuting attorney's language box

> I put it to you that you ... (= accusing someone)
>
> Do you really expect the court to believe that ... ?

Play your part in the trial using the information and instructions that you find here.

24 [Unit 13]

Witnesses

a **Mrs. Trent**
You have been very sick and you understand and appreciate why your husband did what he did, even though you don't agree with what he did.

b **Maria's best friend**
You feel sorry for Maria and want to protect her, so you must try to justify why she stole. She is a good student and a good friend. She helps you with your homework when you have problems.

c **Richard Moore**
You know your sister did it for you and you feel bad, but you don't want to be prosecuted yourself. You have to try to defend yourself and defend your sister.

Play your part in the trial using the information and instructions that you find here.

25 [Unit 13]

Defense attorney

You have to try to defend the actions of the defendant, by asking questions about the circumstances of the crime, so that the judge will understand and not give long sentences.

Questions to ask the defendant:
• Why did you commit the crime?
• Can you explain the circumstances very carefully?

Questions to ask the witness:
• Is the defendant a good person?
• Can you explain her / his behavior?

The defense attorney's language box

> In mitigation, I would like to explain that my client …
> (*In mitigation* is a legal term to say that a crime is less serious because the guilty person was not responsible or had reasons for doing what he or she did.)

Play your part in the trial using the information and instructions that you find here.

26 [Unit 13]

The Mona Lisa, or *La Gioconda* as it is also called, is probably the most famous painting in the world. It was painted between 1503 and 1505 by Leonardo da Vinci, the famous Italian painter. It was probably sold to François I of France shortly before Leonardo died, when he was living in France. In 1800, Napoleon had the painting hanging in his bedroom, but it was placed in the Louvre museum in 1804.

The Mona Lisa was stolen by Vincenzo Perugia, an Italian. He had worked at the Louvre in 1908 so the guards knew him. He had walked into the museum and noticed that the guard was not there, so he had stolen the picture by taking it from its frame and walking out with it hidden inside his painter's smock. He wanted the painting returned to Italy, because he felt it belonged in Italy.